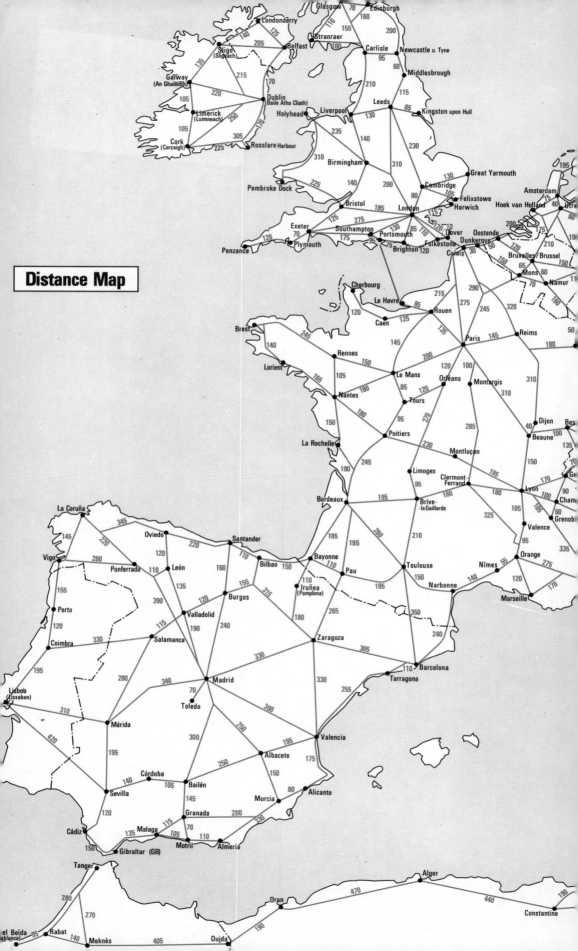

Distance Map

Note on Spellings
Note sur l'Orthographe
Bemerkungen zur Schreibweise
Note riguardando l'Ortografia
Notas sobre Ortografía

Spellings of place names in this atlas are in accordance with the national language. Alphabetical listings will therefore need to be used with care. Eg: Wien (Vienna); København (Copenhagen).

Countries are listed in alphabetical order by international distinguishing signs (see section 3, page 1).

Dans cet atlas, les lieux sont épelés selon la langue du pays. Donc la liste alphabétique devra être lue attentivement. Ex: Wien (Vienne); København (Copenhague).

Les pays sont classés par ordre alphabétique selon des signs distinctifs internationaux (voir section 3, page 1).

In diesem Atlas hält sich die Schreibweise der Ortsnamen an die jewellige Landensprache. Das alphabetische Verzeichnis bedarf deshalb besonderer Aufmerksamkeit bei dessen Gebrauch. Beispiel: København (Kopenhagen).

Die Länder sind in alphabetischer Reihenfolge gemäss den internationalen Landeskennzeichen aufgeführt. (Siehe Teil 3, Seite 1).

In questo atlante, i nomi delle località sono elencati conformemente all'ortografia della lingua del paese. Perciò, l'elenco deve essere usato con massima cura. Esempio: Wien (Vienna); København (Cobenhaghen).

I paesi sono elencati in ordine alfabetico secondo i segnali distintivi internazionali (vedi sezione 3, pagina 1).

La ortografía de los nombres propios de los lugares citados en este atlas está de acuerdo con el lengua nacional. Por lo tanto, la lista alfabética deberá ser usada con cuidado. Ejemplo: Wien (Viena); København (Copenhage).

Los países son listados en orden alfabético, según los signos distintivos internacionales (ver sección 3, página 1).

The dialling codes for London telephone numbers will change in May 1990. New codes are given in brackets.

Les préfixes pour les numéros de téléphone de Londres vont changer en mai 1990. Les nouveaux préfixes sont entre parenthèses.

Die Vorwahl für die Telefonnummern in London wird in Mai 1990 geändert. Die neuen Nummern sind in Klammer angegeben.

Il prefisso per i numeri telefonici di Londra sarà cambiato in Maggio 1990. I numeri nuovi sono indicati in parentesi.

Los códigos telefónicos de Londres cambrarán en mayo de 1990. Los nuevos códigos son dados entre paréntesis.

The information included in this atlas is necessarily only an outline. Further details regarding driving in Europe may be found in the RAC Continental Motoring Guide, or contact the tourist office of the country concerned.

Par nécessité, les renseignements contenus dans cet atlas ne sont qu'un guide. Des renseignements supplémentaires concernant la conduite en Europe peuvent être obtenus du Guide automobile européen de la RAC ou en prenant contact auprès du bureau de tourisme du pays concerné.

Die Informationen in diesem Atlas können aus verständlichen Gründen nicht ins Detail gehen. Ausführlichere Auskünfte betreffend Lenken in Europa können dem RAC Verkehrsführer des Kontinents entnommen werden, oder kontaktieren Sie das Fremdenverkehrsbüro des betroffenen Landes.

Le informazioni date in questo atlante sono evidentemente soltanto dei lineamenti. Ulteriori dettagli riguardando la guida in Europa possono essere trovati nella Guida Automobilistica Continentale del RAC, oppure contattate l'ufficio turismo del paese rispettivo.

La información incluída en este atlas es solo a nivel general. Mayores detalles con respecto a la conducción de automóviles en Europa puede ser encontrada en la RAC — Guía de Automovilismo Continental o contactando la oficina de turismo del país requerido.

First published 1990 by William Curtis Limited, 83 Clerkenwell Road, London EC1R 5AR.

© 1990 RAC/William Curtis Limited
Cartography © Recta Foldex
Highway Code Signs © Crown copyright
International Road Signs: The Royal Automobile Club — taken from information supplied by the OTA.
Editor: Patricia Hayne
Designer: Geoff Hayes
Cover design: Kelly Flynn

Printed in Germany

British Library Cataloguing in Publication data
RAC Atlas Europe
1. Europe. Maps, atlases
I. Royal Automobile Club
912.4

ISBN 1-871967-22-8
ISBN 1-871967-21-X pbk

MOTORING ATLAS ROUTIER
EUROPE

Contents

Distance map
International road signs · II
Tourist and motoring information · V
RAC information · XVI

Section 1: Road Maps
Legend 1:1,000,000 · 1
Legend 1:2,750,000 · 2
Key to maps · 3
Road maps · 4

Section 2: City Approach Maps
Legend · 2
Key to maps · 3
City approach maps · 4

Section 3: Index of Place Names
International distinguishing signs · 1
Index of place names · 2

Table des Matières

Carte des distances
Signalisation routière internationale · II
Renseignements touristiques et de l'automobilisme · V
Information RAC · XVI

Section 1: Cartes Routières
Légende 1:1,000,000 · 1
Légende 1:2,750,000 · 2
Tableau d'assemblage · 3
Cartes routières · 4

Section 2: Plans de Villes Synoptiques
Légende · 2
Index des cartes · 3
Plans de villes synoptiques · 4

Section 3: Localités Citées
Signaux de distinction internationaux · 1
Localités citées · 2

Inhaltsverzeichnis

Entfernungskarte
Internationale Verkehrszeichen · II
Touristik und Automobilinformationen · V
RAC Informationen · XVI

Teil 1: Strassenkarten
Zeichenerklärung 1:1,000,000 · 1
Zeichenerklärung 1:2,750,000 · 2
Bauanleitung · 3
Strassenkarten · 4

Teil 2: Stadtübersichtspläne
Zeichenerklärung · 2
Index · 3
Stadtübersichtspläne · 4

Teil 3: Ortsverzeichnis
Internationale Unterscheidungszeichen · 1
Ortsverzeichnis · 2

Indice

Carta delle distanze
Segnaletica stradale internazionale · II
Informazioni turistiche e stradali · V
Informazioni RAC · XVI

Sezione 1: Carte Stradali
Leggenda 1:1,000,000 · 1
Leggenda 1:2,750,000 · 2
Indice delle carte · 3
Carte stradali · 4

Sezione 2: Piante di Città Sinottiche
Leggenda · 2
Indice delle piante · 3
Piante di città sinottiche · 4

Sezione 3: Località Citate
Segnali distintivi internazionali · 1
Località citate · 2

Contenido

Mapa de distancias
Señales internacionales de carretera · II
Información turística y de tráfico · V
Información RAC · XVI

Sección 1: Mapas de Carreteras
Signos convencionales 1:1,000,000 · 1
Signos convencionales 1:2,750,000 · 2
Clave de mapas · 3
Mapas de carreteras · 4

Sección 2: Planos de Ciudades Sinópticos
Signos convencionales · 2
Indice de planos · 3
Planos de ciudades sinópticos · 4

Sección 3: Localidades Citadas
Señales internacionales distintivas · 1
Localidades citadas · 2

II

International Road Signs
Signalisation Routière Internationals
Internationale Verkehrszeichen
Segnaletica Internazionale
Señales Internacionales de Carreteras

Most road signs found in Europe are standard. The following may be unfamiliar:

La plus grande partie des panneaux de signalisation en Europe sont standardisés. Les suivants peuvent s'avérer peu courant:

Die meisten Verkehrszeichen in Europa entsprechen der Norm. Die folgenden könnten jedoch unbekannt sein:

La maggior parte dei segnali trovati in Europa corrisponde allo standard. Tuttavia, quelli seguenti potrebbero essere sconosciuti:

La mayoría de las señales encontradas en Europa son estándar. Las siguientes pueden ser desconocidas:

Signs indicating priority and junctions
Panneaux indiquant la priorité et les jonctions
Zeichen für vortrittsbestimmungen und Kreuzungen
Segnaletica di precedenza ed agli inorco
Señales indicando prioridad y cruces

Priority road
Rue ayant la priorité
Vorfahrtstrasse
Strada con diritto di precedenza
Vía prioritaria

End of priority
Fin de la priorité
Ende der Vorfahrtstrasse
Termine della precedenza
Fin de prioridad

Give way
Cédez le passage
Vorfahrt gewähren!
Dara la precedenza
Ceda el paso

Intersection (priority rule applies)
Croisement (les règles de priorité sont appliquées)
Kreuzung (Vortrittregel gilt)
Incrocio (regola della precedenza)
Intersección (regla de prioridad aplicada)

Intersection with tramway
Croisement avec un tram
Kreuzung mit Strassenbahn
Incrocio con tranvia
Intersección con rieles de tranvía

Approach to level crossing
Accès à un passage à niveau
Bahnübergang naht
Passaggio a livelli in vicinanza
Aproximación a paso a nivel

Non-standard signs which may be found in individual countries
Panneaux de signalisation non-standardisés qui se trouvent dans certains pays
Verkehrszeichen, die in den verschiedenen Ländern angetroffen werden, und nicht der europäischen Norm entsprechen
Segnali non-standardizzati che si trovano in paesi individuali
Las señales diferentes al estándar encontradas en particulares países

Diversion
Déviation
Umleitung
Deviazione
Desviación

Trams turning at yellow or red
Trams tournant au jaune ou au rouge
Einbiegende Strassenbahn wenn Ampel auf gelb oder rot
Tram gira a semafero giallo o rosso
Vueltas de tranvías en amarillo o rojo

Federal road with priority
Route fédérale avec priorité
Bundesstrasse mit Vorfahrt
Strada statale con precedenza
Carretera federal con prioridad

Federal road without priority
Route fédérale sans priorité
Bundesstrasse ohne Vorfahrt
Strada statale senza precedenza
Carretera federal sin prioridad

Lorries with trailers prohibited
Interdit aux camions à remorque
Verbot für LKWs mit Anhänger
Divieto di transito agli autocarri con remorchio
Camiones con remolque son prohibidos

Vehicles carrying dangerous goods prohibited
Interdit aux voitures transportant des matières dangereuses
Verbot für Kraftwagen mit gefährlicher Ladung
Divieto di transito ai veicoli con carico pericoloso
Vehículos transportando mercancías peligrosas son prohibidos

Buses only
Réservé aux autobus
Ausschliesslich für Busse
Corsia riservato agli autobus
Solo buses

Turn right or left
Tourner à droite ou à gauche
Rechts oder links abbiegen
Girare a sinistra o a destra
Voltee a la derecha o a la izquierda

U-turns permitted
Demi-tours permis
Wenden gestattet
Permesso di inversione di marcia a U
Vuelta en U permitida

Private cars only
Réservé aux voitures particulières
Nur für Privatfahrzeuge
Riservata agli autoveicoli privati
Solo carros privados

Lane prohibited to lorries
Voie interdite aux camions
Fahrbahn für LKWs verboten
Corsia proibita agli autocarri
Carril prohibido para camiones

Tunnel (use headlights)
Tunnel (allumer les phares)
Tunnel (Scheinwerfer benützen)
Tunnel (usate i fari)
Túnel (uso de luces principales)

Heavy coaches prohibited
Interdit aux cars chargés
Verbot fur schwere Busse
Divieto di transito ai pullman pesanti
Automóviles pesados están prohibidos

Motorway
Autoroute
Autobahn
Autostrada
Autopista

Throughroute
Semi-autoroute
Schnellverkehrsstrasse
Strada riservata agli autoveicoli
Semi-autopista

e way to postal vehicles
it de passage aux voitures des Postes
tfahrzeuge haben Vorfahrt
e la precedenza ai veicoli lenti
da el paso a vehículos de correos

Slow lane
Voie de droite
Fahrspur für langsame Fahrzeuge
Corsia riservata ai veicoli lenti
Carril reservado para vehículos lentos

Passing place for lorries
Bande de dépassement pour camions
Ueberholstrecke für LKWs
Posto da sorpasso per autocarri
Lugar de paso para camiones

Level crossing (flashing red light)
Passage à niveau (feu rouge clignotant)
Bahnübergang (blinkendes Rotlicht)
Passaggio a livello (luce rossa
  lampeggiante)
Paso a nivel (intermitente luz roja)

vel crossing (alternately flashing lights)
ssage à niveau (feux clignotants
ternants)
hnübergang (abwechselnd blinkende
chter)
ssaggio a livello (luci lampeggianti
ternativamente)
so a nivel (luces intermitentes)

 D

 Umleitung

Diversion
Déviation
Umleitung
Deviazione
Desviación

Street lights not on all night
Eclairage public nocturne intermittant
Strasse nicht die ganze Nacht uber
  beleuchtet
Strada non illuminata durante tutta la notte
Las luces de la calle no están encendidas
  durante toda la noche

Tram or bus stop
Arrêt du tram ou d'autobus
Strassenbahn- oder Bushaltestelle
Fermata tram o bus
Paradero de tranvías o buses

ersion for motorway traffic
viation pour trafic d'autoroute
leitung für den Autobahnverkehr
viazione per il traffico autostradale
sviación para tráfico en la autopista

 DDR

70-110
km

Recommended speed range
Vitesses conseillées
Richtgeschwindigkeit
Velocità raccomandata
Rango de velocidad recomendado

Sudden fog patches
Bouchons de brume soudaine
Unerwartete Nebelbänke
Banchi di nebbia improvvisi
Repentino sitio nebuloso

Slow lane
Voie de droite
Fahrspur für langsame Fahrzeuge
Corsia riservata ai veicoli lenti
Carril reservado para vehículos lentos

K

htseeing
urisme
henswürdigkeit
go turistico
tas turísticas

Compulsory slow lane
Voie de droite obligatoire
Obligatorische Fahrspur für langsame
  Fahrzeuge
Corsia obbligatoria per veicoli lenti
Carril obligatorio para vehículos lentos

Recommended speed limit on bend
Vitesse conseillée aux tournants
Richtgeschwindigkeit in der Kurve
Velocità raccomandata in curva
Velocidad recomendada en curvas

Traffic merges
Intersection
Einmündender Verkehr
Confluenza di traffico
Uniones de tráfico

E
P

70

commended maximum speed
esse maximum conseillée
pfohlene Höchstgeschwindigkeit
ocità massima raccomandata
xima velocidad recomendada

Take care
Attention!
Vorsicht!
Fate attenzione
Tenga cuidado

300

Turning permitted
Virage autorisé
Abbiegen gestattet
Permesso di inversione
Vuelta permitida

No entry
Entrée interdite
Verbotene Einfahrt
Divieto di accesso
Entrada proibida

mpulsory lane for motorcycles
e obligatoire pour motocyclistes
ligatorische Fahrspur für Motorräder
rsia obbligatoria ai motociclisti
rril obligatorio para motocicletas

Compulsory lane for lorries
Voie obligatoire pour camions
Obligatorische Fahrspur für LKWs
Corsia obbligatoria agli autocarri
Carril obligatorio para camiones

F

 SERREZ A DROITE

Keep well over to the right
Serrez à droite
Halten Sie sich ganz auf der rechten
  Strassenseite
Tenetevi alla destra
Manténgase sobre el lado derecho

Bus lane
Voie réservée aux transports en commun
Fahrspur für Busse
Corsia riservata agli autobus
Carril para buses

B

 M 23

torway   Start of motorway
toroute   Début d'autoroute
tobahn   Beginn der Autobahn
tostrada   Inizio dell'autostrada
topista   Inicio de Autopista

End of motorway
Fin d'autoroute
Ende der Autobahn
Fine dell'autostrada
Fin de Autopista

Diversion
Déviation
Umleitung
Deviazione
Desviación

Use both lanes
Utiliser les deux voies
Beide Fahrspuren benutzen
Disporsi su due file
Uso de ambos carriles

No overtaking by vehicles with trailers
Dépassement interdit aux voitures à
remorque
Ueberholverbot für Fahrzeuge mit
Anghänger
Divieto di sorpasso per autoveicoli con
rimorchio
Vehículos con remolque no deben
adelantar otros vehículos

Roads merge, black lane has priority
Intersection, la voie noire a la priorité
Strassenmündung: schwarze Fahrspur hat
Vorfahrt
Fusione di strade, corsia nera ha la
precedenza
Unión de carreteras, el carril negro tiene
prioridad

Passing place
Bande de dépassement
Ueberholstrecke
Posto da sorpasso
Lugar para adelantar

Route for heavy vehicles
Route réservée aux poids lourds
Route fur den Schwerverkehr
Percorso per veicoli pesanti
Ruta para vehículos pesados

Slow lane
Voie de droite
Fahrzeuge reserviert
Corsi riservata ai veicoli lenti
Carril reservado para vehículos lentos

No entry for pedestrians
Entrée interdite aux piétons
Durchgangsverbot für Fussgänger
Divieto di transito ai pedoni
Prohibida la entrada de peatones

Passing place
Bande de dépassement
Ueberholstrecke
Posto di sorpasso
Lugar para adelantar

End of B road
Fin de route B
Ende der B Strasse
Termine della strada B
Fin de carretera B

Crossing for cyclists
Passage pour cyclistes
Uebergang für Radfahrer
Passaggio per ciclisti
Cruce para ciclistas

Slow lane
Voie de droite
Fahrspur für langsame Fahrzeuge
Corsia riservata ai veicoli lenti
Carril reservado para vehículos lentos

Lane reserved for buses from 0700 to
1900 hrs
Voie réservée aux autobus de 0700 à 1900
heures
Fahrspur von 0700 bis 1900 Uhr für Busse
reserviert
Corsia riservata agli autobus dass ore
0700 alle 1900
Carril reservado para buses entre las
7:00 am y las 7:00 pm

Motorcycle track
Piste motocyclable
Spur für Motorräder
Corsia riservata ai motocicli
Vía para motocicletas

Give way to buses on mountain road
Droit de passage aux autobus sur route de
montagne
Vorfahrt an Busse auf Bergstrassen
Dara la precedenza ai veicoli postali su
strade da montagna
Ceda el paso a buses en terreno
montañoso

Cycle track
Piste cyclable
Fahrrad-Spur
Carregiata riservata ai ciclisti
Vía para bicicletas

Compulsory route for vehicles with
dangerous loads
Route obligatoire pour voitures
transportant
des matières dangereuses
Obligatorische Route für Fahrzeuge mit
gefährlicher Ladung
Percorso obbligatorio per veicoli con
carico pericoloso
Ruta obligatoria para vehículos con carga
peligrosa

Snow tyres or chains compulsory in 1
174km
Pneus cloutés ou chaînes obligatoire
174km
Winterreifen oder Schneeketten
obligatorisch auf 174km
Gomme da neve o catene obbligatori
174km
Ruedas especiales para terreno neva
cadenas son obligatorias en 174km

Motor vehicles only
Réservé aux voitures automobiles
Nur für Motorfahrzeuge
Corsi riservata a veicoli
Solo automóviles

Sightseeing
Tourisme
Sehenswürdigkeit
Luogo turistico
Visitas turísticas

End of built-up area
Fin d'agglomération
Ortsende
Fine dell'area edificata
Fin de área urbana

Maximum length of vehicle
Longueur maximum du véhicule
Maximale Länge von Fahrzeugen
Lunghezza massima del veicolo
Longitud máxima del vehículo

Tourist and motoring information
Renseignements touristiques et de l'automobile
Touristik und Automobilinformationen
Informazioni turistiche e stradali
Información turística y de tráfico

Breakdowns

If you break down on a motorway or other major route call for assistance using the roadside emergency telephones.

If you have taken out RAC Eurocover Motoring Assistance, or RAC Eurocover Premier Protection, consult your Assistance Document in the case of breakdown. Both RAC members and non-members can take out RAC Eurocover at the RAC Calais Port Office or the RAC European Control Centre. RAC members and non-member UK nationals who are not covered by RAC Eurocover can ring the RAC European Control Centre at Calais ☎ 21 96 35 30 for advice on the availability of rescue services.

Pannes

Si vous tombez en panne sur une autoroute ou autre route nationale, appelez pour demander de l'assistance en utilisant les téléphones d'urgence qui se trouvent en bord de route.

Pour plus d'information sur les services de secours, contactez le Centre de Contrôle Européen du RAC à Calais ☎ 21 96 35 30.

Pannen

Im Falle einer Panne auf einer Autobahn oder anderen Hauptverkehrsstrasse benützen Sie eines der Notruftelefone am Strassenrand, um Hilfe anzufordern.

Für weitere Auskünfte über die Verfügbarkeit von Rettungsdiensten wenden Sie sich an das Europäische Kontrollzentrum des RAC in Calais ☎ 21 96 35 30.

Guasti

Se avete un guasto alla vostra vettura sull'autostrada o su un altra strada principale, usate i telefoni di emergenza al margine della strada per chimare assistenza.

Per ulteriori informazioni sulla disponibilità di servizi di soccorso, rivolgetevi al Centro di Controllo Europeo del RAC a Calais ☎ 21 96 35 30.

Averías

En caso de sufrirse una avería en una autopista o carretera principal, solicite asistencia utilizando el teléfono de emergencia existente al borde de la vía.

Para más consejos relativos a averías y a la disponibilidad de los servicios de auxilio, comuníquese con el Centro Europeo del RAC en Calais ☎ 21 96 35 30.

Children in Cars

It is generally inadvisable to travel with children in the front seat of a vehicle unless it is equipped with a specially designed restraint. The following countries do not permit children under a certain age (in brackets) to travel in front seats:

Les Enfants en Voiture

Il est généralement déconseillé de voyager avec les enfants assis à l'avant de la voiture à moins qu'elle ne soit équipée d'un harnais spécialement conçu dans ce but. Les pays suivants ne permettent pas aux enfants en dessous d'un certain âge (entre parenthèses) de voyager à l'avant:

Kinder in Autos

Es ist im Allgemeinen nicht empfehlenswert, mit Kindern auf den Vordersitzen eines Wagens zu reisen, sofern das Fahrzeug nicht mit einer speziellen Ausrüstung versehen ist. Die folgenden Länder gestatten es nicht, Kinder unter einem bestimmten Alter (in Klammern) auf den Vordersitzen reisen zu lassen:

Bambini in Automobile

In genere è consigliabile fare viaggare bambini nei sedili anteriori a meno che il veicolo non sia attrezzato con un equipaggiamento apposito. Nei paesi seguenti i bambini sotto una certa età (in parentesi) non sono permessi di viaggare sui sedili anteriori:

Niños Viajando en Automoviles

En general no es aconsejable viajar con niños en las sillas delanteras de un vehículo, a menos que se usen sillas de protección especialmente diseñadas para ellos. Los siguientes países no permiten que niños menores de cierta edad (entre paréntesis) viajen en las sillas delanteras:

A (12)	**D** (12)*	**NL** (12)*
B (12)*	**DDR** (7)	**P** (12)*
BG (10)	**F** (10)	**PL** (10)
CH (12)	**GB** (1)*	**RO** (12)
CS (12)	**IRL** (12)	**YU** (12)

* unless fitted with child restraint
* à moins qu'elle ne soit équipée d'un harnais pour enfant.
* sofern nich mit einem Kindersitz versehen
* a meno che il veicolo non sia attrezzato di un seggiolino per bambini
* a menos que se cuente con sillas de protección especiales para niños

Priority

1 If in doubt, and in the absence of road signs, priority should be given to vehicles coming from the right, when driving on the right-hand side of the road.

2 Priority should generally be given to emergency vehicles emitting warning signals.

3 Priority should be given to trams in the following countries: A, B, BG, CH, CS, DDR, E, H, NL, S, SF, YU. Buses take priority in CH, D, H.

4 Ascending vehicles have priority on hills.

5 Pedestrians on zebra crossings have priority in BG, GB, NL.

6 Extreme care should be taken at roundabouts. In some countries (B, F, RO) traffic entering a roundabout may have priority over traffic already on the roundabout.

Priorité

1 En cas de doute, et en l'absence de panneaux de signalisation, les voitures venant de droite ont la priorité lorsque la conduite est à droite.

2 En général les voitures de secours émettant des signaux d'alarme ont la priorité.

3 Les trams ont la priorité dans les pays suivants: A, B, BG, CH, CS, DDR, E, H, NL, S, SF, YU. Les autobus ont la priorité en CH, D, H.

4 Les voitures ascendantes ont la priorité dans les montées.

5 Les piétons traversant les passages cloutés ont la priorité on BG, GB, NL.

6 Faire trés attention dans les carrefours à sens giratoire. Dans certains pays, (B, F, RO), les voitures abordant un carrefour à sens giratoire peuvent avoir la priorité sur les voitures déjà engagées dans le carrefour à sens giratoire.

Vorfahrtsregeln

1 Im Zweifelsfall, und wenn Verkehrszeichen fehlen, sollte dem von rechts kommenden Fahrzeug die Vorfahrt gewährt werden, sofern auf der rechten Strassenseite gefahren wird.

2 Die Vorfahrt soll immer Notfall-Fahrzeugen gewährt werden, die Warnzeichen von sich geben.

3 Die Vorfahrt soll in folgenden Ländern den Strassenbahnen gewährt werden: A, B, BG, CH, CS, DDR, E, H, NL, S, SF, YU. Busse haben Vorfahrt in CH, D, H.

4 Bergaufwärts fahrende Fahrzeuge haben auf Bergstrassen Vorfahrt.

5 Fussgänger auf Zebrastreifen haben Vortritt in BG, GB, NL.

6 Aeusserste Vorsicht gilt beim Kreisverkehr. In einigen Ländern (B, F, RO) hat der einmündende Verkehr Vorfahrt vor dem sich bereits auf dem Kreisverkehr befindenden Verkehr.

Precedenza

1 In dubbio ed in assenza di segnali stradali la precedenza viene data ai veicoli che vengono dalla destra, quando si guida sul lato destro della strada.

2 In genere, la precedenza viene data ai veicoli di emergenza che emettono segnali di allarme.

3 La precedenza e data ai tram nei paesi seguenti: A, B,BG, CH, CS, DDR, E, H, NL, S, SF, YU. I bus hanno la precedenza in CH, D, H.

4 Veicoli ascendenti hanno la precedenza in montagna.

5 Pedoni su passaggi pedoni zebrati hanno la precedenza in BG, GB, NL.

6 Massima prudenza viene data alle rotatorie. In qualche paese (B, F, RO) il traffico che entra nella rotatoria puo avere la precedenza sul traffico che si trova già sulla rotatoria.

Prioridades

1 En caso de duda y de falta de señalización en la vía, la prioridad debe ser dada a aquellos vehículos que vienen por la derecha, cuando la conducción se realiza sobre el lado derecho de la vía.

2 La prioridad debe generalmento ser otorgada a vehículos de emergencia, los ouales emiten señales de aviso.

3 La prioridad debe ser otorgada a los tranvías en los siguientes países: A, B, BG, CH, CS, DDR, E, H, NL, S, SF, YU. Los buses tienen prioridad en CH, D, H.

4 Vehículos ascendiendo terreno montañoso tienen prioridad.

5 Personas oruzando el paso para peatones tienen prioridad en BG, GB, NL.

6 Gran cuidado debe tenerse en las glorietas. En algunos países (B, F, RO) el tráfico entrando a una glorieta puede tener prioridad sobre el tráfico que circula alrededor de ella.

Time differences

Most European countries conform to the same time pattern. The following differences occur, however:

  One hour behind, except for a four-week period in October when European Summer Time has ended, but British Summer Time has not. During this period, the time is the same.

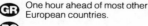 One hour ahead of most other European countries.

Décalages horaires

La plupart des pays européens sont à la même heure. Cependant les différences suivantes se présentent:

 Une heure de retard, à l'exception d'une période de quatre semaines en octobre, quand l'heure d'été européenne est terminée et l'heure d'été britannique continue. Pendant cette période, l'heure est la même.

 Une heure d'avance sur la plupart des autres pays européens.

Zeitunterschiede

Die meisten europäischen Länder halten sich an das selbe Zeitschema. Abweichungen gelten in den folgenden Fällen:

 Eine Stunde im Rückstand, mit Ausnahme einer vierwöchigen Zeitspanne im Oktober, wenn die europäische Sommerzeit zu Ende ist, die Britische Sommerzeit jedoch noch anhält. Während dieser Periode besteht kein Zeitunterschied.

 Sind den meisten anderen europäischen Ländern um eine Stunde voraus.

Differenze di orario

La più parte dei paesi europei seguono lo stesso tempo medio. Tuttavia, si presentano le differenze seguenti:

 Un ora indietro, con l'eccezzione di un periodo di quatro settimane nel mese di ottobre, quando il tempo estivo europeo è terminato, il tempo inglese no. Durante questo periodo l'ora è la stessa.

   Un ora in anticipo in rispetto alla maggior parte dei paesi europei.

Diferencias de tiempo

La mayoría de los países europeos se ajustan al mismo patrón de tiempo. Sin embargo, ocurren las siguientes diferencias:

Tienen una hora de atraso, excepto en un período de 4 semanas en octubre cuando el tiempo de verano europeo ha finalizado pero el del verano británico continua vigente. Por ello, durante esas semanas el tiempo es el mismo de la mayoría de países europeos.

   Tienen una hora de adelanto con respecto a la mayoría de países europeos.

Minimum Driving Age
Age Minimum de Conduite
Mindest — Fahralter
Età Minima per Guidare
Edad Minima Permitida para Conduci

Foreign drivers with a full driving licence may drive a temporarily imported vehicle under the age of 18.

Les conducteurs étrangers de moins de 18 ans titulaires d'un permis de conduire peuvent conduire temporairement une voiture importée.

Ausländische Lenker mit vollem Fahrausweis können ein vorübergehend eingeführtes Fahrzeug auch im Alter von weniger als 18 Jahren fahren.

Guidatori che hanno la patente di guida possono guidare una vettura importata temporaneamente pur di non avere compiato i 18 anni.

Conductores extranjeros menores de 18 años y con un permiso de conducir detallado pueden manejar un vehículo importado temporalmente.

Metric Conversion Table
Table de Conversion Métrique
Metrische Umrechnungstabelle
Tavola di Conversione Metrica
Tabla de Conversión al Sistema Métric

1 centimetre	0.39 inch
1 metre	1.1 yards
1 kilometre	0.62 mile
8 kilometres	5 miles
1 kilogram	2.2 pounds
1 litre	1.76 pints
10 litres	2.2 gallons
1 inch	2.54 centimetres
1 foot	30.5 centimetres
1 yard	0.91 metre
1 mile	1.6 kilometres
5 miles	8 kilometres
1 pound	0.45 kilogram
1 pint	0.57 litre
1 gallon	4.54 litres

Speed Limits (kilometres/h)
Limites de Vitesse (kilomètres/h)
Geschwindigkeitsbeschränkungen (km/Std.)
Limiti di Velocità (km/h)
Limites de Velocidad (kilómetros/hora)

	Built-up areas / Agglomérations / Innerorts / Agglomerazioni / Areas urbanas	Motorways / Autoroutes / Autobahnen / Autostrade / Autopistas	Motorways (minimum speed) / Autoroutes (vitesses minimum) / Autobahnen (Mindestgeschwindigkeit) / Autostrade (velocità minima) / Autopistas (mínima velocidad)	Dual carriageways / Routes jumelées / Schnellverkehrs-strasse / Strada a doppia carreggiata / Carreteras de doble calzada	Other roads / Autres routes / Andere Strassen / Altre strade / Otras carreteras
A	50	130	-	-	100
B	60	120	-	-	90
BG	60	120	-	-	80
CH	50	120	-	-	80
CS	60	110	-	-	90
CY	48 (30mph)	-	-	-	80-96 (50-60mph)
D	50	130+	-	-	100-130
DDR	50	100	50	-	80
DK	50	100	-	-	80
E	60	120	-	-	90-100
F	60	130	80*	110	90
GB	48 (30mph)	112 (70mph)	-	112 (70mph)	96 (60mph)
GR	50	100	-	-	80
H	60	120	-	100	80
I	50	110-130	-	-	90
IRL	48 (30mph)	112 (70mph)	-	112 (70mph)	96 (60mph)
L	60	120	-	-	90
N	50	80-90	-	-	80-90
NL	50	100-120	70	-	80
P	60	120	40	-	90
PL	60	110	40	-	90
RO	60	70-90	-	-	70-90
S	50	110†	-	-	70-110
SF	50	120	-	-	60-100
SU	60	-	-	-	110
TR	50	90	-	-	90
YU	60	120	-	-	80-100

Note: Further restrictions apply in many countries on vehicles with trailers and to novice drivers, or according to engine capacity, or on wet roads.

NB: D'autres restrictions relatives aux voitures à remorque, aux nouveaux conducteurs ou à la capacité du moteur, ou aux surfaces humides, sont en vigueur dans de nombreux pays.

Bemerkungen: Weitere Beschränkungen gelten in vielen Ländern für Fahrzeuge mit Anhänger und für Anfänger, oder entsprechend der Leistung des Motors, oder auf nassen Fahrbahnen.

Nota: Ulteriori restrizioni devono essere tenute in conto in tanti paesi per veicoli con rimorchio e guidatori alle prime, o secondo la capacità del motore, o sopra strade bagnate.

Nota: En muchos países se aplican mayores restricciones sobre vehículos con remolque y conductores novatos o según sea la capacidad del motor, o en las carreteras mojadas.

* *outside lane/sur la voie de gauche/auf der äussersten Fahrbahn/nella corsia esterna/en carril exterior*
+ *recommended/conseillée/empfehlenswert/raccommandata/recomendada*
† *90 in summer/90 en été/90 im Sommer/90 in estate/90 in verano*

Lights

Headlamp beams should be adjusted to the right for all European countries except the United Kingdom (GB) and Republic of Ireland (IRL), Malta (M), and Cyprus (CY), where vehicles drive on the **left-hand side of the road**.

In general when driving in Europe use dipped headlights at night and at all other times of reduced visibility. Sidelights may be permissible in built-up areas. The following specific rules apply:

Feux

Les phares doivent être règlés vers la droite dans tous les pays d'Europe à l'exception de la Grande-Bretagne (GB) de la République d'Irlande (IRL), Malte et Chypres (CY), où les voitures **roulent gauche**.

En général, quand vous conduisez en Europe, utilisez les phares codes la nuit à tous autres moments lorsque la visibili peuvent être est réduite. Les feux de position permis dans les agglomération Les règles spécifiques suivantes sont e vigueur:

A	Dipped headlights in built-up areas.	Phares codes dans les agglomérations.
B	Use dipped headlights from dusk to dawn.	Utiliser les phares codes de l'aube au crépuscule.
BG	Use dipped headlights in poorly lit towns.	Utiliser les phares codes dans les villes mal éclairées.
CH	Dipped headlights compulsory in tunnels; use sidelights for parking in poor visibility.	Phares codes obligatoires dans les tunnels; utiliser les feux de position pour stationnement en cas de visibilité réduit
CY	Lights should be used from ½ hour after sunset to ½ hour before sunrise.	Les phares doivent être allumés d'une heure après le coucher du soleil à une heure avant le levé du soleil.
D	Don't drive with sidelights.	Ne pas conduire avec les feux de positi
E	Use only sidelights in towns.	N'utiliser que les feux de position en vill
F	No full beam in towns. Parking lights compulsory. Conversion to yellow beam advisable.	Pleins phares interdits en ville. Feux de stationnement obligatoires. Conversion phares jaunes conseillée.
GBZ	Dipped headlights compulsory at night.	Phares codes obligatoires la nuit.
GR	No full beam in towns.	Pleins phares interdits en ville.
H	Dipped headlights compulsory in towns.	Phares codes obligatoires dans les ville
I	No full beam in towns.	Pleins phares interdits en ville.
N	Use dipped headlights at all times.	Utiliser les phares codes de jour et de n
NL	No full beam in towns.	Pleins phares interdits en ville.
P	No full beam in built-up areas.	Pleins phares interdits dans les agglomérations.
RO	No full beam where roads are lit.	Pleins phares interdits sur les routes éclairées.
S	Use dipped headlights at all times.	Utiliser les phares codes de jour et de nu
SF	Use dipped headlights at all times.	Utiliser les phares codes de jour et de nu
TR	Use dipped headlights after sunset in built-up areas.	Utiliser les phares codes après le couch du soleil dans les agglomérations.
YU	Use sidelights for parking in poor visibility.	Utiliser les feux de position pour le stationnement en cas de visibilité réduite

Petrol Coupons and Petrol

The following countries issue petrol coupons (for which payment is often required in a convertible currency) for foreign travellers:

Bons d'Essence et Essence

Les pays suivants délivrent des bons d'essence (pour laquelle le paiement est souvent exigé en devises convertibles) aux voyageurs étrangers:

BG	Compulsory. Available at border posts and inside Bulgaria.	Obligatoires. En vente aux postes frontaliers et en Bulgarie.
CS	Compulsory. Tuzex coupons available at frontier, Tuzex shops and Czech tourist offices or banks.	Obligatoires. Bons Tusex en vente à la frontière, dans les magasins Tusex et dar les bureaux de tourisme tchèques ou dar les banques.
DDR	Reduced price coupons available from main frontier posts. Non-refundable.	Bons à prix réduits en vente aux postes frontaliers principaux. Non-remboursables.
H	IBUSZ vouchers (optional for petrol; compulsory for diesel) available from exchange offices and travel agents. Non-refundable.	Bons d'essence IBUSZ (facultatifs); obligatoires pour le diesel. En vente dans les bureaux de changes et agences de voyages. Non-remboursables.
I	Concessionary coupons available from the RAC.	Bons de ristourne en vente auprès du RAC.

Scheinwerfer	Fari	Luces
Die Scheinwerfer müssen für die meisten europäischen Länder auf den Rechtsverkehr eingestellt werden, mit Ausnahme des Vereinigten Königreiches (GB), Irland (IRL), Malta (M), und Zypern (CY), wo die Fahrzeuge auf der **linken Strassenseite** fahren.	I fari devo essere aggiustati a la guida destra per tutti i paesi europei con l'eccezzione del Regno Unito (GB), la repubblicha irlandese (IRL), Malta (M), e Cipro (CY), dove i veicoli sono guidati sul **lato sinistro della strada**.	El haz de luz de los faros debe ser ajustado a la derecha para todos los países Europeos excepto el Reino Unido (GB), la república de Irlanda (IRL), Malta (M) y Chipro (CY), donde los vehículos transitan por el **lado izquierdo de la vía**.
Im allgemeinen fährt man in Europa nachts und immer bei beschränkter Sichtweite mit Abblendlicht. Standlicht könnte innerorts gestattet sein. Die folgenden bestimmten Regeln gelten:	In genere, quando guidate in Europe, usate i fari anabbaglianti di notte e quando la visibilità e ridotta. La luce d'ingombro essere permessa in aree urbane. Si applicano le regole specifiche seguenti:	En general, al manejar en Europa utilice las luces medias en la noche y siempre que la visibilidad se reduzca. Las luces laterales pueden ser utilizadas en áreas urbanas. Las siguientes específicas reglas se aplican:
Abblendlicht innerorts.	Fari anabbaglianti in aree edificate.	Luces medias en áreas urbanas.
Abblendlicht von Abend- bis zur Morgendämmerung.	Fari anabbaglianti dal crepuscolo all'alba.	Utilice luces medias desde el crepúsculo hasta el amanecer.
Abblendlicht in schwach beleuchteten Ortschaften.	Fari anabbaglianti in città mal illuminate.	Utilice luces medias en ciudades mal iluminadas.
Abblendlicht obligatorisch in Tunnels. Standlicht soll bei schlechten Sichtverhältnissen beim Parken verwendet werden.	Fari anabbaglianti obbligatori nei tunnel. Usate la luce d'ingombro per parcheggiare quando la visibilità e ridotta.	Las luces medias son obligatorias en túneles. Utilice luces laterales para pstacionar en sitios con mala visibilidad.
Scheinwerfer sollen ab ½ Std. nach Sonnenuntergang bis ½ Std. vor Sonnenaufgang benützt werden.	Fari devono essere accesi mezz'ora dopo il tramonto fino a mezz'ora prima dell'alba.	Las luces deben ser utilizadas desde la ½ hora posterior a la puesta del sol y hasta la ½ hora previa a la salida del sol.
Fahren mit Standlicht verboten.	Non viaggate con la luce d'ingombro.	No maneje con luces laterales.
Nur Standlicht wird in den Städten benützt.	Usate solamente la luce d'ingombro nelle città.	Utilice solo luces laterales en las ciudades.
Kein Fernlicht in Ortschaften. Parklichter obligatorisch. Umstellung auf gelben Lichtstrahl empfehlenswert.	Sono proibiti i fari abbaglianti in città. Luci di posizione obbligatorie. Conversione in raggi gialli raccomandata.	No utilice rayo de luz pleno en ciudades. Luces de estacionamiento obligatorias. Es aconsejable la conversión a rayos de luz amarillos.
Abblendlicht nachts obligatorisch.	Fari anabbaglianti obbligatori di notte.	Luces medias son obligatorias en la noche.
Kein Fernlicht in Ortschaften.	Sono proibiti i fari abbaglianti nelle città.	No utilice rayo de luz pleno en las ciudades.
Abblendlicht obligatorisch in Ortschaften.	Fari anabbaglianti obbligatori in città.	Las luces medias son obligatorias en las ciudades.
Kein Fernlicht in Ortschaften.	Sono vietati i fari abbaglianti in città.	No utilice rayo de luz pleno en las ciudades.
Immer mit eingeschaltetem Abblendlicht fahren.	Guidare sempre con i fari anabbaglianti accesi.	Utilice luces medias todo el tiempo.
Kein Fernlicht in Ortschaften.	Sono vietati i fari abbaglianti in città.	No utilice rayo de luz pleno en las ciudades.
Kein Fernlicht innerorts.	Sono vietati i fari abbaglianti in aree edificate.	No utilice rayo de luz pleno en las áreas urbanas.
Kein Fernlicht, wo Strassen beleuchtet sind.	Sono vietati i fari abbaglianti dove le strade sono illuminate.	No utilice rayo de luz pleno donde las vías están iluminadas.
Immer mit Abblendlicht fahren.	Guidare sempre con i fari anabbaglianti accesi.	Utilice luces medias todo el tiempo.
Immer mit Abblendlicht fahren.	Guidare sempre con i fari anabbaglianti accesi.	Utilice luces medias todo el tiempo.
Abblendlicht nach Sonnenuntergang, innerorts.	Guidare con i fari anabbaglianti accesi dopo il tramonto in aree edificate.	Utilice luces medias despúes de la puesta del sol en las áreas urbanas.
Standlicht beim Parken bei schlechten Sichtverhältnissen.	Parcheggiare con la luce d'ingombro accesa quando la visibilità e ridotta.	Utilice luces laterales para estacionar en sitios con mala visibilidad.

Benzin-Bons und Benzin	Buoni di Benzina e Benzina	Cupones para Gasolina y Gasolina
Die folgenden Länder geben Benzin-Bons (welche oft in konvertibler Währung bezahlt werden müssen) für ausländische Reisende heraus:	I paesi seguenti emettono buoni di benzina (per i quali pagamento e spesso richiesto in valuta convertibile) per viaggiatori stranieri:	Los siguientes países emiten cupones de gasolina (para los cualos el pago es frecuentemente requerido en moneda convertible) para viajeros extranjeros:
Obligatorisch. Erhältlich an Grenzübergangen und in Bulgarien.	Obbligatori. Disponibili alla frontiera e in Bulgaria.	Obligatorio. Disponible en los puestos fronterizos y dentro de Bulgaria.
Obligatorisch. Tuzex-Bons sind an der Grenze und in Tuzex-Shops erhältlich, sowie bei Fremdenverkehrsbüros und in Banken.	Obbligatori. Buoni Tuzex disponibili alla frontiera, in negozi Tuzex e presso gli uffici di turismo cecoslovacchi o banche.	Obligatorio. Cupones Tuzex disponibles en la frontera, tiendas Tuzex, oficinas de turismo Cgech o bancos.
Coupons zu reduziertem Preis sind an den wichtigsten Grenzübergangen erhältlich. Können nicht zurückerstattet werden.	Buoni a prezzo ridotto disponibili ai posti di frontiera più importanti. Non rimborsabili.	Cupones con precio reducido disponibles desde los principales puestos fronterizos. No reembolsables.
IBUSZ-Gutscheine (auf Wunsch für Benzin, obligatorisch für Diesel) sind in Wechselstuben und Reisebüros erhältlich. Können nicht zurückerstattet werden.	Buoni IBUSZ (facoltativi per benzina, obbligatori per diesel) disponibili da uffici cambio e agenzie di viaggio.Non rimborsabili.	Vales IBUSZ (opcionales para gasolina, obligatorios para diesel). Disponibles en oficinas de cambio y agentes de viaje. No reembolsables.
Konzessions-Gutscheine beim RAC erhältlich.	Buoni di concessionarie disponibili dal RAC.	Cupones privilegiados disponibles desde la RAC.

PL	Compulsory. Available at frontier posts, or Polish Tourist Office (Orbis) in Poland. Refundable.	Obligatoires. En vente aux postes frontaliers ou au Bureau polonais du Tourisme (Orbis) en Pologne. Remboursables.
RO	Compulsory. Available at frontier, tourist offices and some hotels.	Obligatoires. En vente à la frontière, dans les offices de tourisme et dans certains hôtels.
SU	Talon vouchers available at frontier, Intourist offices and hotels.	Bons à talon en vente à la frontière, aux bureaux Intourist et dans les hôtels.
YU	Concessionary coupons available at frontier. Refundable.	Bons de ristourne en vente à la frontière. Remboursables.
CS CY GR I	Do not import fuel in cans.	Ne pas importer des bidons d'essence.

	Seatbelts	**Ceintures de Sécurité**
A	👤*	👤*
B BG CS	👤	👤
CY	Strongly recommended.	Fortement conseillé.
D	👤*	👤*
DDR F	👤	👤
DK	Compulsory for drivers and front seat passengers over the age of 15, if fitted.	Port obligatoire pour les conducteurs et passagers avant âgés de plus de 15 ans la voiture en est équipée.
E	Compulsory outside built-up areas for drivers and front seat passengers, if fitted.	Port obligatoire en dehors des agglomérations urbaines pour les conducteurs et passagers avant si la voiture en est équipée.
GB	Compulsory for drivers and front seat passengers, and children under 14 in rear seats, if fitted.	Port obligatoire pour les conducteurs, passagers avant et pour les enfants à l'arrière de moins de 14 ans, si la voiture en est équipée.
GBZ	Recommended.	Conseillé.
GR H	👤	👤
I	👤 Children aged 4-10 must wear special restraints.	👤 Les enfants de 4-10 ans doivent porte harnais spéciaux.
IRL L N NL	👤	👤
P	Compulsory outside built-up areas for drivers and front seat passengers, if fitted.	Port obligatoire en dehors des agglomérations urbaines pour les conducteurs et passagers avant si la voiture en est équipée.
PL	👤	👤
RO	Recommended.	Conseillé.
S	👤* Children aged 7 and under should sit in a special child restraint, or on a seat which allows the use of normal seatbelts.	👤* Les enfants en dessous de 7 ans doivent porter un harnais spécialement conçu pour les enfants ou un siège qui permet l'usage normal des ceintures de sécurité.
SF	👤	👤
SU	👤 Seatbelts must be fitted.	👤 Les ceintures doivent être installées.
TR YU	👤*	👤*
👤	*Seatbelts must be worn by drivers and front seat passengers, if fitted.*	*Les ceintures de sécurité doivent être portées par les conducteurs et passagers avant si la voiture en est équipée.*
👤*	*Seatbelts must be worn in all seats, if fitted.*	*Les ceintures de sécurité doivent être portées par tous les passagers si la voitu en est équipée.*

Obligatorisch. Erhältlich an Grenzübergangen, dem polnischen Fremdenverkehrsbüro (ORBIS) in Polen. Rückerstattbar.	Obbligatori. Disponibili alla frontiera, o presso l'ufficio di turismo Polacco (ORBIS) in Polonia. Rifondibili	Obligatorio. Disponible en los puestos fronterizos o las oficinas culturales turístlcas (Orbis) en Polonia.
Obligatorisch. Erhältlich an Grenzübergangen, bei Fremdenverkehrsbüros und in einigen Hotels.	Obbligatori. Disponibili alla frontiera, uffici di turismo e presso qualche hotel.	Obligatorio. Disponible en la frontera, oficinas de turismo y algunos hoteles.
Talon-Gutscheine erhältlich an der Grenze, bei Intourist-Büros und Hotels.	Tallone di buoni disponibile alla frontiera, uffici Intourist e qualche hotel.	Vales Talon disponibles en la frontera, oficinas de turismo y hoteles.
Konzessionscoupons an der Grenze erhältlich. Zurückerstattbar.	Buoni di concessionarie disponibili alla frontiera. Rifondibili.	Cupones privilegiados disponibles en la frontera. Reembolsables.
Treibstoff-Behälter dürfen nicht eingeführt werden.	Bidoni di carburante non possono essere importati.	No se debe importar combustible dentro de latas.

Sicherheitsgurte / **Cinture de Sicurezza** / **Cinturones de Seguridad**

Sehr empfehlenswert.	Vivamente raccomandate.	Altamente recomendados.
Tragepflicht für Lenker und vorne sitzende Passagiere im Alter von mehr als 15 Jahren, sofern Gurte eingebaut.	Obbligatorie per guidatori e passeggeri di eta superiore a 15 anni che occupano i sedili anteriori, se montate.	Obligatorios para conductores y pasajeros de las sillas delanteras mayores de 15 años, siempre que sean provistos.
Tragepflicht ausserorts für Lenker und vorne sitzende Passagiere, sofern Gurte eingebaut.	Obbligatorie fuori di aree edificate per guidatori e passeggeri che occupano i sedili anteriori, se montate.	Obligatorios fuera de las áreas urbanas para conductores y pasajeros de las sillas delanteras, siempre que sean provistos.
Tragepflicht für Lenker und vorne sitzende Passagiere, sowie für Kinder im Alter von weniger als 14 Jahren auf den Rücksitzen, sofern Gurte eingebaut.	Obbligatorie per guidatori e passeggeri che occupano i sedili anteriori, e per bambini di meno di 14 anni che occupano i sedili posteriori, se montate.	Obligatorios para conductores y pasajeros de las sillas delanteras y para niños menores de 14 años en las sillas traseras, siempre que sean provistos.
Empfehlenswert.	Raccomandate.	Recomendados.
Kinder im Alter von vier bis zehn Jahren müssen spezielle Kindergurte tragen.	Bambini del età di 4 a 10 anni devono portare delle cinture apposite.	Niños entre los 4 y 10 años de edad deben viajar en sillas especialmente diseñadas para ellos.
Tragepflicht ausserorts für Lenker und vorne sitzende Passagiere, sofern Gurte eingebaut.	Obbligatorie fuori di aree edificate per guidatori e passeggeri che occupano i sedili anteriori, se montate.	Obligatorios fuera de las áreas urbanas para conductores y pasajeros de las sillas delanteras, siempre que sean provistos.
Empfehlenswert.	Raccomandate.	Recomendados.
Kinder im Alter von sieben oder weniger Jahren sollten in einem Kindersitz oder einem Sltz, der das Tragen von normalen Sicherheitsgurten erlaubt, mitgeführt werden.	Bambini del età di sette o meno anni dovrebbero essere seduti in seggiolini speciali o in un sedile che permette l'uso normale delle cinture.	Niños hasta los 7 años deben sentarse en una silla de protección especial o en la silla del carro usando los cinturones de seguridad normales.
Gurte müssen eingebaut sein.	Cinture devono essere montate.	Los cinturones de seguridad deben ser provistos.

Sicherheitsgurte müssen von Lenkern und vorne sitzenden Passagieren getragen werden, sofern eingebaut.

Sicherheitsgurte müssen auf allen Sitzen getragen werden, sofern eingebaut.

Cinture di sicurezza devano essere portate da guidatori e passeggeri che occupano i sedili anteriori, se montate.

Cinture di sicurezza devono essere portate in tutti i sedili, se montate.

Cinturones de seguridad deben ser utilizados por conductores y pasajeros de las sillas delanteras, siempre que sean provistos.
Cinturones de seguridad deben ser utilizados en todas las sillas, siempre que sean provistos.

Emergency Telephone Numbers
Numéros de Téléphone de Secours
Notruf-Nummern
Numeri Telefonici di Emergenza
Números Telefónicos de Emergencia

	Police / Police / Polizei / Polizia / Policía	Ambulance / Ambulance / Krankenwagen / Pronto soccorso / Ambulancia	Fire / Pompiers / Feuerwehr / Vigili del fuoco / Bomberos
A	133*	144*	122*
AND	17	18	18
B	101	100	100
BG	878011	150	160
CH	117	118	114
CS	158	155	150
D	110	110	112
DDR	110	115	112
DK	000	000	000
E	091 (Madrid/Barcelona)+	092	2323232
F	17	17	18
GB	999	999	999
GBZ	190	199	199
GR	100 large cities / grandes villes / grossstädte / grandi città / grandes ciudades; 109 Athens suburbs+ / banlieues Athènes + / pororte von Athen + / periferia di Athene + / suburbios de Athenas +	166 Athens+	199 Athens +
H	07	04	05
I	113	113	113
IRL	999	999	999
L	012	012	012
N	66900 Oslo+	201090/Oslo+ 112200	429900 Oslo+
NL	Refer to local directory / Consulter l'annuaire de la région / Im örtlichen Telefonbuch nachschlagen / Consultate l'elenco telefonico locale / Consulte la guía telefónica local	Refer to local directory / Consulter l'annuaire de la région / Im örtlichen Telefonbuch nachschlagen / Consultate l'elenco telefonico locale / Consulte la guía telefónica local	Refer to local directory / Consulter l'annuaire de la région / Im örtlichen Telefonbuch nachschlage / Consultate l'elenco telefonico locale / Consulte la guía telefónica local
P	115	115	115
PL	997	998	999
RO	055	081	061
S	90000	90000	90000
SF	000 Helsinki+	000 Helsinki+	000 Helsinki+
TR	1666666	1444998	—
YU	92	94	92

+ elsewhere refer to local telephone directory
  ailleurs consulter l'annuaire local
  anderswo schlagen Sie im örtlichen Telefonbuch nach
  altrove consùltate l'elenco telefonico locale
  en otra parte, consulte la guía telefónica local

* add local prefix
  ajouter le préfixe local
  fügen Sie die örtliche Vorwahl hinzu
  aggiungere il prefisso locale
  agregue el prefijo local

Essential Documents

When driving in Europe, it is essential to have with you a full driving licence, a current insurance certificate, the vehicle registration document (and a letter of authority if the vehicle is not registered in your name). In addition, you are strongly advised to take a green card (compulsory in E, GR, P, TR, YU).

An international driving permit is a legal requirement of some countries (including E, H, SU) and advisable for many others, especially if you intend hiring a car.

Drivers to Spain are advised to take a bail bond.

Visitors to Portugal require a special form of authority if the vehicle is not registered in your name.

For further requirements, contact the RAC or the relevant tourist office (see inside back cover), particularly if you are visiting non-EEC countries.

Documents Importants

Quand vous conduisez en Europe, un permis de conduire, un certificat d'assurance valable, les documents d'immatriculation de la voiture (et une lettre d'autorisation si la voiture n'est pas immatriculée en votre nom) sont essentiels. De plus, il est fortement conseillé de prendre avec soi une carte verte (obligatoire en E, GR, P, TR, YU).

Un permis de conduire international est obligatoire dans certains pays (y compris E, H, SU) et conseillé dans certains autres pays, surtout en cas de location de voiture.

En Espagne, on conseille aux conducteurs de prendre un cautionnement.

Au Portugal, les touristes doivent avoir une lettre d'autorisation spéciale si la voiture n'est pas immatriculée en leur nom.

Pour plus de renseignements, contactez le RAC ou l'office de tourisme approprié (cf. verso de la couverture à la fin du livre) surtout si vous vous rendez dans un pays non membre de la CEE.

Erforderliche Dokumente

Wenn man in Europa ein Auto fährt, muss man die folgenden Dokumente bei sich haben: gültiger Führerschein, Versicherungsausweis, Fahrzeugausweis sowie ein Ermächtigungsschreiben falls das Fahrzeug auf einen anderen Namen registriert ist). Ferner ist es sehr empfehlenswert, eine grüne Versicherungskarte bei sich zu haben obligatorisch in E, GR, P, TR, YU).

Ein internationaler Führerschein ist in einigen Ländern (einschliesslich E, H, SU) gesetzlich vorgeschrieben und für viele andere Länder empfehlenswert, besonders wenn man beabsichtigt, ein Auto zu mieten.

Autofahrern, die nach Spanien reisen wird empfohlen, eine Verpflichtungserklärung zur Stellung einer Kaution mitzunehmen,

Besucher von Portugal benötigen ein spezielles behördliches Formular, wenn das Fahrzeug nicht auf den eigenen Namen registriert ist.

Auskunft über weitere Vorschriften erhalten sie beim RAC oder beim zuständigen Fremdenverkehrsbüro (siene hintere innere Umschagseite), insbesondere wenn Sie Länder ausserhalb der EG besuchen.

Documenti Indispensabili

Guidatori che viaggiano in Europa devono portare con sé una patente valida, un certificato d'assicurazione, il libretto d'immatricolazione (e una lettera d'autorizzazione, se la vettura non è registrata sui nome proprio). Inottre, è raccomandabile di portare una carta verde (obbligatoria in E, GR, P, TR, YU).

Una patente di guida internazionale è richiesta dalla legge in certi paesi (compresi E, H, SU) ed è raccomandata per motti attri paesi, in particolare se desiderate noleggiare un 'automobile.

Si consiglia ai conducenti diretti per la Spagna di portare con sé una cauzione.

Viaggiatori per il Portogallo devono essere in grado di presentare un documento apposito d'autorizzazione se la vettura guidata non è registrata sui nome proprio.

Per ulteriori informazioni su requisiti, rivolgetevi al RAC oppure all'ufficio di turismo relativo (vedi pagina interna della copertina di retro), specialmente se visitate paesi fuori della CEE.

Documentos Imprescindibles

Cuando conduzca en Europea, es imprescindible tener con usted un permiso de conducir detallado, un certificado de seguros corriente, el documento de registro del vehículo (y una carta de autorización en caso de que el vehículo no este registrado a su nombre). Adicionalmente, es muy recomendable tomar una tarjeta verde, la cual es obligatoria en E, GR, P, TR, YU.

Un permiso de conducir internacional es un requisito legal en algunos países (incluyendo E, H, SU) y recomendable para muchos otros, especialmente si usted intenta alquilar un automóvil.

En España se recomienda tomar una fianza.

Los visitantes a Portugal requieren un especial formulario de autorización, cuando el vehículo no esta registrado a su nombre.

Para mayores requisitos, contacte a la RAC o la pertinente oficina de turismo (ver contraportada interior), particularmente si usted esta visitando un país no perteneciente a la Comunidad Económica Europea.

Drinking and Driving

Penalties all over Europe are high for drinking and driving. The RAC advises drivers not to drink at all.

Alcool au Volant

De fortes contraventions sont infligées dans toute l'Europe aux buveurs qui conduisent. Le RAC conseille aux conducteurs de s'abstenir totalement de boire.

Trunkenheit am Steuer

Trunkenheit am Steuer wird in ganz Europa mit schweren Bussen bestraft. Der RAC empfiehlt Fahrzeuglenkern, ganz auf alkoholische Getränke zu verzichten.

Bevande Alcoliche e la Guida

Le multe per coloro che bevono e guidano sono forti in tutta l'Europa. Il RAC consiglia ai guidatori di rinunciare a bere delle bevande alcoliche affatto.

Bebiendo y Manejando

Las multas para sancionar el delito de conducir bebido son muy atlas en todo Europa. La RAC recomienda a los conductores no tomar bebidad alcohólicas.

International Registration Plates

Any vehicle being driven outside the country of registration should display an international distinguishing sign on the rear (see Section 3, page 1).

Plaques d'Immatriculation Internationales

Tout voiture conduite en dehors du pays d'immatriculation doit indiquer un signe international distinct à l'arrière (cf. section 3, page 1).

Internationale Fahrzeug-Kennzeichen

Jegliche Fahrzeuge, die ausserhalb des Landes, in welchem sie registriert sind, gefahren werden, sollten am Heck das internationale Landeskennzeichen tragen. (Teil 3, seite 1).

Numero di Targa Internazionale

Qualsiasi veicolo guidato al estero deve portare il simbolo del paese di provenienza al retro. (Vedi sezione 3, pagina 1).

Placas de Registro Internacional

Cualquier vehículo viajando fuera del pais de registro debe tener una señal internacional distintiva en su parte trasera. (Ver sección 3, página 1).

Signalling

Audible warnings are not permitted in built-up areas in many countries, especially at night. Check with the RAC or the appropriate tourist office for specific details.

Signaux

Dans de nombreux pays, les avertisseurs sonores ne sont pas permis dans les agglomérations, surtout la nuit. Vérifier auprès du RAC ou de l'office de tourisme approprié les renseignements spécifiques.

Signalisierung

Akustische Warnzeichen sind in manchen Ländern innerorts, besonders nachts, nicht gestattet. Erkundigen Sie sich beim RAC oder dem zuständigen Fremdenverkehrsbüro für ausführliche Details.

Segnalazione

In tanti paesi, non e permesso dare dei segnali acustici in aree edificate. Riferitevi al RAC o al ufficio di turismo appropriato per dettagli specifici.

Señalizando

Avisos audibles no son permitidos en las áreas urbanas en muchos países, especialmente en la noche. Consulte con la RAC o la apropiada oficina de turismo para detalles específicos.

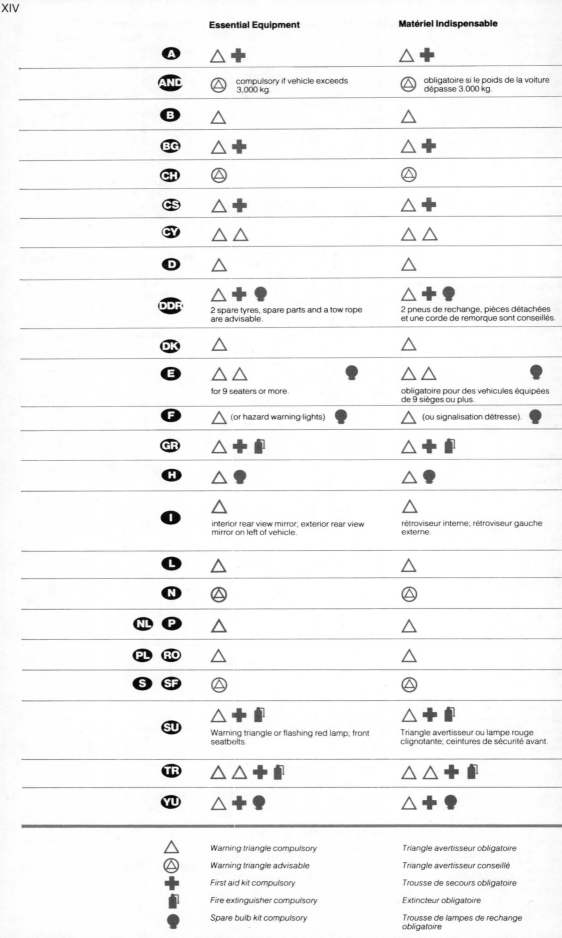

	Essential Equipment	Matériel Indispensable
A	△ ✚	△ ✚
AND	⊿ compulsory if vehicle exceeds 3,000 kg.	⊿ obligatoire si le poids de la voiture dépasse 3.000 kg.
B	△	△
BG	△ ✚	△ ✚
CH	⊿	⊿
CS	△ ✚	△ ✚
CY	△ △	△ △
D	△	△
DDR	△ ✚ 💡 2 spare tyres, spare parts and a tow rope are advisable.	△ ✚ 💡 2 pneus de rechange, pièces détachées et une corde de remorque sont conseillés.
DK	△	△
E	△ △ 💡 for 9 seaters or more.	△ △ 💡 obligatoire pour des vehicules équipées de 9 sièges ou plus.
F	△ (or hazard warning lights) 💡	△ (ou signalisation détresse). 💡
GR	△ ✚ 🧯	△ ✚ 🧯
H	△ 💡	△ 💡
I	△ interior rear view mirror; exterior rear view mirror on left of vehicle.	△ rétroviseur interne; rétroviseur gauche externe.
L	△	△
N	⊿	⊿
NL P	△	△
PL RO	△	△
S SF	⊿	⊿
SU	△ ✚ 🧯 Warning triangle or flashing red lamp; front seatbelts.	△ ✚ 🧯 Triangle avertisseur ou lampe rouge clignotante; ceintures de sécurité avant.
TR	△ △ ✚ 🧯	△ △ ✚ 🧯
YU	△ ✚ 💡	△ ✚ 💡

△	*Warning triangle compulsory*	*Triangle avertisseur obligatoire*
⊿	*Warning triangle advisable*	*Triangle avertisseur conseillé*
✚	*First aid kit compulsory*	*Trousse de secours obligatoire*
🧯	*Fire extinguisher compulsory*	*Extincteur obligatoire*
💡	*Spare bulb kit compulsory*	*Trousse de lampes de rechange obligatoire*

Erforderliche Ausweise	Attrezzatura Indispensabile	Equipo Esencial
obligatorisch wenn Fahrzeug Gewicht von 3000kg übersteigt.	obbligatorio per veicoli di un peso supperiore a 3000 kg.	obligatorio si el vehículo excede los 3000 kilogramos.
zwei Ersatzreifen, Ersatzteile und Schlepptau empfehlenswert.	due gomme di scorta, pezzi da ricambio e una traina sono consigliabili.	2 llantas de repuesto, piezas de repuesto y cuerda de remolque son aconsejables.
erforderlich für Fahrzeuge mit neun oder mehr Sitzplätzen.	obbligatori per veicoli a nove o più posti.	requerido para los vehículos de 9 sillas o más.
(oder Warnlichter).	(o fanale di segnalazione).	(o luces de advertencia).
innerer Rückspiegel, äusserer Rückspiegel auf der linken Seite des Fahrzeuges.	specchietto retrovisorio interiore e esteriore allla sinistra del veicolo.	espejo interior para visión trasera, espejo exterior para visión trasera, colocado al lado izquierdo del vehículo.
Warndreieck oder blinkendes Rotlicht, Sicherheitsgurte für die Vordersitze.	Triangolo o lampada rossa lampeggiante, cinture di sicurezza anteriori.	Triángulo de advertencia o lámpara roja intermitente, cinturones de seguridad frontales.

Warndreieck obligatorisch	Triangolo obbligatorio	Triángulo de advertencia obligatorio
Warndreieck empfehlenswert	Triangolo consigliabile	Triángulo de advertencia aconsejable
Erste Hilfe-Set obligatorisch	Cassetta di pronto soccorso obbligatoria	Equipo de primeros auxilios obligatorio
Feuerlöscher obligatorisch	Estintore obbligatorio	Extinguidor de incendios obligatorio
Ersatz-Glühbirnen obligatorisch	Lampadine di ricambio obbligatorio	Equipo de bombillas de repuesto obligatorio

RAC Travel Services

RAC European Service

The RAC can help to make your travels in Europe as safe, sure and enjoyable as can be. You don't need to be a member — anyone can make use of the services we offer. When you plan to take your car abroad we can provide expert advice, book your ferry crossings and motorail journey, provide maps, atlases, guide books and touring accessories; we can even supply International Driving Permits.

Emergency help

The RAC have a Europe-wide emergency service called RAC Eurocover Motoring Assistance. This is designed to help you out of trouble if you're unlucky enough to have a breakdown, accident or other mishap on your travels. The benefits include roadside assistance wherever you may be, a spare parts despatch service, hotel expenses or cost of onward travel by train or self-drive hire car, and we'll even provide a chauffeur if your only driver is ill.

For your personal protection we can also provide insurance cover at competitive rates against injury, medical expenses, loss of baggage and money, and other risks.

RAC Premier Protection is an even more comprehensive emergency service. This allows you to claim up to £3000 for various forms of motoring assistance to get you to your destination or to return home. You can choose the benefits that best suit you within this overall limit — hotel expenses, self-drive hire car, rail or air fares, and the cost of bringing a stranded vehicle home are just some of the options.

In addition you and your passengers are insured for all the risks covered by RAC Eurocover Personal Protection. This ultimate all-in-one service is personally managed through the RAC European Control Centre in Calais and is set in motion by a single telephone call on a direct line ☎ 05 29 01 12.

If you are only planning a stay of up to five days across the Channel — within a 200 mile radius of any Channel port — the RAC can still offer you peace of mind with our Short Break Get-You-Home service. For only a few pounds you can insure against the risk of being stranded if you have a breakdown, accident or the only driver becomes ill and cannot drive. In such cases you, your passengers and the vehicle will be repatriated.

Full details of these services are given in the current RAC European Service Brochure available from RAC offices, or from RAC Croydon ☎ 01 (081) 686 2525.

Motoring Holidays

Each year the RAC offers a programme of individual motoring holidays in France with a choice of recommended hotels, self-catering apartments or campsites with leisure facilities for all the family. We have also put together some touring holidays in regions that have a great deal to offer the independent traveller — Alsace, Burgundy, Provence and the Côte d'Azur, Perigord, the Loire Valley, Languedoc and the Pyrenees. Each holiday includes the hotel base, maps and a gazetteer of places to visit.

RAC Routes

For a small charge the RAC can also provide you with a route itinerary tailor-made to your requirements. Contact the RAC Routes Department, at RAC Croydon ☎ 01 (081) 686 2525, at least three weeks before you travel, giving details of the places you plan to visit, and we will supply you with an RAC Route Pack. This gives details of your route (scenic, motorway, non motorway — as requested), maps of the countries you are visiting, town plans and toll and ferry information as appropriate.

RAC Publications

If you are looking for a hotel or a campsite on the Continent then consult the RAC Continental Hotel Guide or the RAC Camping and Caravanning Guide — Europe. Both publications are fully revised every year and carry information on establishment size, facilities, prices and locations. They are just two of an extensive range of guides, maps and atlases available from the RAC. We have a series of maps covering Europe; regional maps of France; a French road atlas; a Continental Motoring Guide giving all the essential information for driving on the Continent; a series of Travel Guides with full colour illustrations introducing the traditions, culture and places to visit in each country or region. Plus a full range of publications covering Great Britain from the most comprehensive Hotel Guide available, detailing 6000 establishments, to large scale motoring atlases and regional maps.

Motoring Accessories

The RAC can supply all the motoring accessories that are compulsory when travelling in many European countries and advisable in all. For example the RAC advance warning triangle, which is made out of highly reflective material, with four stabilizing legs, and folds away for easy storage in its own protective case. Also compulsory in many countries is a set of emergency bulbs. The RAC can supply a pack of either halogen or asymmetric type bulbs, each containing replacement bulbs for headlamps, brake lights, side and tail lights, rear fog lights, indicators, reversing and number plate lights, plus two fuses.

Essential for Continental driving is some means of adjusting your headlamp beams. The RAC can suppy Beam Benders — universal headlamp converters which fit most vehicles. The benders don't block out part of the headlamp beam, but re-direct it at the correct angle. They are self-adhesive and no trimming or cutting is required and as they are only 1mm thick they do not impede headlamp wash/wipe systems. Also available are the easy-to-fit 'headlamp beam converters' which you cut to size from self-adhesive plastic.

For driving in France it is advisable to have yellow headlights and this can be achieved by using either headlamp yellow lacquer or headlamp yellow film. Both are easy to apply and remove.

A handy motorist's first aid kit containing a selection of useful wound dressings, bandages and plasters, scissors, latex gloves, antiseptic swabs and safety pins packaged in a sturdy plastic carrying case can be obtained from the RAC.

Compulsory in many countries and strongly advised in all cases is a car fire extinguisher. We offer a product extensively tested by RAC engineers.

For peace of mind carry your spare fuel in a safety fuel can containing 'explosafe', a unique wire mesh system which limits fuel surge and prevents explosions — version available for leaded and unleaded petrol.

The RAC blind spot mirror is an invaluable aid to the driver. It is a small convex mirror easily fitted to all types of exterior mirror, which increases the driver's viewing angle from approximately 13° to 62°.

We can also provide accessories designed to help you have a more comfortable journey such as the De-luxe travel pillow, which supports the head and neck and a similar Junior travel pillow for your children. The Pentland back rest, specially designed by a physiotherapist and approved by the medical profession, encourages a correct seating posture and helps prevent disorders of the back from developing.

For the reluctant sailor Seaband anti-travel-sickness wristbands are the answer — based on the ancient Chinese science of acupressure they counter nausea by applying pressure to a special area on your wrist.

If you are looking for space to carry those last minute extras try the RAC travel bag, a sturdy dark blue bag with carrying handle and a shoulder strap — or for food and drink a cool bag, an easy to clean, insulated bag with 22 litre carrying capacity, which folds flat for storage.

This is just a selection from the wide range of motoring accessories available from the RAC. For full details contact your nearest RAC office, or ring the RAC Publications Department ☎ 01 (081) 686 2525.

1

Road Maps

Cartes Routières

Strassenkarten

Carte Stradali

Mapas de Carreteras

Legend   Légende   Zeichenerklärung   Leggenda   Signos Convencionales
1 : 1,000,000

| 0 | 10 | 20 | 30 | 40 | 50 | 60 | 70 | 80 | 90 | 100 km |
| 0 | | 10 | | 20 | | 30 | | 40 | | 50 | | 60 miles |

Motorway with junctions
Autoroute à chaussées séparées avec accès
Autobahn mit Anschlussen
Autostrada con spartitràffico e stazioni di uscita
Autopista con cruces de carreteras

Motorway under construction
Autoroute à chaussées séparées en construction
Autobahn im Bau
Autostrada con spartitràffico in costruzione
Autopista en construcción

Projected motorway
Autoroute à chaussées séparées en projet
Projektierte Autobahn
Autostrada con spartitràffico in progetto
Autopista proyectada

Major throughroute with junctions
Autoroute sans chaussées séparées avec accès
Autostrasse mit Anschlussen
Autostrada senza spartitràffico con stazioni di uscita
Carretera de tránsito principal con cruces de carreteras

Major throughroute under construction
Autoroute sans chaussées séparées en construction
Autostrasse im Bau
Autostrada senza spartitràffico in costruzione
Carretera de tránsito principal en construcción

Projected throughroute
Autoroute sans chaussées séparées en projet
Projektierte Autostrasse
Autostrada senza spartitràffico in progetto
Carretera de tránsito proyectada

Road of motorway standard
Route conçue comme autoroute
Strasse mit autobahnähnlichem Ausbau
Strada con caratteristiche autostradali
Carretera que confluye a autopista

Road of motorway standard under construction
Route conçue comme autoroute en construction
Strasse mit autobahnähnlichem Ausbau im Bau
Strada con caratteristiche autostradali in costruzione
Carretera que confluye a autopista en construcción

International throughroute
Route de transit internationale
Internationale Fernstrasse
Strada di transito internazionale
Carretera de tránsito internacional

Regional throughroute
Route de transit régionale
Regionale Fernstrasse
Strada di transito regionale
Carretera de tránsito regional

Main connecting road
Route de communication principale
Hauptverbindungsstrasse
Strada di comunicazione principale
Carretera de conexión principal

Connecting road
Route de communication
Verbindungsstrasse
Strada di comunicazione
Carretera de conexión

Private road*
Route privée*
Privatstrasse*
Strada privata*
Carretera privada*

Footpath, mule-track
Sentier, chemin muletier
Fussweg, Saumpfad
Sentiero, strada mulattiera
Sendero, senda de mulas

Unmetalled road or road in bad condition
Route sans revêtement ou en mauvais état
Strasse ohne Belag oder in schlechtem Zustand
Strada senza rivestimento o in cattiva condizione
Carretera sin revestimiento
   o carretera en malas condiciones

Road unsuitable for caravans*
Route non recommandée aux caravans*
Strasse föllig ungeeignet für Wohnwagen*
Strada non raccommandabile per rulotte*
Carretera inapropiada para caravanas*

24%
Road with steep gradient (more than 15%)
Route à forte montée (plus de 15%)
Strasse mit starker Steigung (uber 15%)
Strada con forte salita (oltre il 15%)
Carretera con pendiente empinada (más de 15%)

Road with traffic restrictions
Route à trafic limité
Strasse mit verkehrsbeschränkung
Strada con limitazione di tràffico
Carretera con limitaciones para el tráfico

Toll road
Route à péage
Strasse mit Gebuhr
Strada a pedaggio
Carretera con peaje

Scenic route
Parcours pittoresque
Malerische Wegstrecke
Percorso pittoresco
Ruta pintoresca

4   6
15 5
Motorway distances in kilometres
Distances sur l'autoroute en kilometres
Autobahndistanzen in Kilometern
Distanze in chilometri sull'autostrada
Distancias en kilómetros en la autopista

7   5
3 15 6
Distances in kilometres
Distances en kilomètres
Distanzen in Kilometern
Distanze in chilometri
Distancias en kilómetros

7 E4 A11
Road numbering
Numérotage des routes
Strassennumerierung
Numerazione delle strade
Numeración de las carreteras

/F
Car ferry
Bac pour automobiles
Autofähre
Linea di navigazione
Transbordador para automóviles

Shipping route
Ligne maritime
Schiffslinie
Linea di navigazione
Linea de navegación

(X -IV)
Months of closure (roads, ferries, shipping routes)
Mois de clôture (routes, bacs, lignes maritimes)
Sperrmonate (Strassen, Fähren, Schiffe)
Mesi di chiusura (strade, traghetti, linee di
   navigazione)
Meses de clausura (carreteras, transbordadores,
   rutas de embarque)

Railway loading station for cars
Embarquement des voitures sur chemin de fer
Autoverlad auf Eisenbahn
Trasporto automobili per ferrovia
Estación de ferrocarril para transporte de automóviles

Railway; rack railway
Chemin de fer; chemin de fer à crémallère
Eisenbahn; Zahnradbahn
Ferrovia; ferrovia a cremagliera
Ferrocarril; ferrocarril de Cremallera

+++++++++++++
Cable railway, cable car, chair-lift
Funiculaire, téléférique, télésiège
Draht- und Luftseilbahn, Sesselbahn
Funicolare, teleferica, seggiovia
Funicular, teleférico, telesilla

★
Skilift*
Téléski*
Skilift*
Sciovia*
Telesilla*

⊕
Airport
Aéroport
Flughafen
Aeroporto
Aeropuerto

✈
Airfield
Aérodrome
Flugplatz
Campo d'aviazione
Campo de aviación

State frontier
Frontière d'état
Landesgrenze
Confine di stato
Frontera entre Estados

Regional boundary
Frontière régionale
Regionalgrenze
Confine regionale
Límite regional

Nature reserve
Réserve naturelle
Naturschutzgebiet
Parco nazionale
Reserva natural

Restricted area
Zone interdite
Sperrzone
Zona proibita
Area restringida

Distance point
Point de distance
Distanzpunkt
Punto di distanza
Punto de distancia

Locality of more than 100,000 inhabitants
Ville de plus de   100,000 habitants
Ort mit uber   100,000 Einwohner
Località con più di   100,000 abitanti
Localidad de más de   100,000 habitantes

Locality of   50,000–100,000 inhabitants
Ville de   50,000–100,000 habitants
Ort von   50,000–100,000 Einwohner
Località da   50,000–100,000 abitanti
Localidad de   50,000–100,000 habitantes

Locality of   10,000– 50,000 inhabitants
Ville de   10,000– 50,000 habitants
Ort von   10,000– 50,000 Einwohner
Località da   10,000– 50,000 abitanti
Localidad de   10,000– 50,000 habitantes

Locality of less than 10,000 inhabitants
Ville de moins de   10,000 habitants
Ort unter   10,000 Einwohner
Località fino a   10,000 abitanti
Localidad de menos de 10,000 habitantes

Hamlet, isolated house
Hameau, maison isolée
Weiler, alleinstehendes Haus
Borgo, casa isolata
Aldea, casa aislada

Place of interest
Localité remarquable
Sehenswerter Ört
Località interessante
Lugar de interés

Limburg

Summer holiday resort
Station de villegiature estivale
Sommerferienort
Località di villeggiatura
Centro de turismo para vacaciones de verano

Hörnum

Winter sports resort
Station de sports d'hiver
Wintersportplatz
Località di sport invernali
Centro de turismo para deportes de invierno

Bernau

Holiday resort throughout the year
Station de vacances pendant toute l'année
Ferienort während des ganzen Jahres
Località di vacanze durante tutto l'anno
Centro de turismo para vacaciones durante
   todo el año

Bad Ems

Spa
Station thermale
Heilbad
Stazione termale
Baños térmicos

♀
Cathedral, church, chapel
Cathédrale, église, chapelle
Kathedrale, Kirche, Kapelle
Cattedrale, chiesa, cappella
Catedral, iglesia, capilla

♀
Pilgrimage church, monastery
Eglise de pèlerinage, couvent
Wallfahrtskirche, Kloster
Santuario, convento
Santuario, monasterio

☿
Mosque
Mosquée
Moschee
Moschea
Mezquita

+
Parochial village*
Village paroissial*
Kirchdorf*
Villaggio parrocchiale*
Aldea parroquial*

♂
Castle
Château
Schloss, Burg
Castello
Castillo

▬
Palace, mansion
Palais, villa
Palast, Villa
Palazzo, villa
Palacio, mansión

⊓
Prehistoric monument
Monument de culture préhistorique
Vorgeschichtliches Kulturdenkmal
Monumento di civiltà preistorica
Monumento prehistórico

1 : 1,000,000

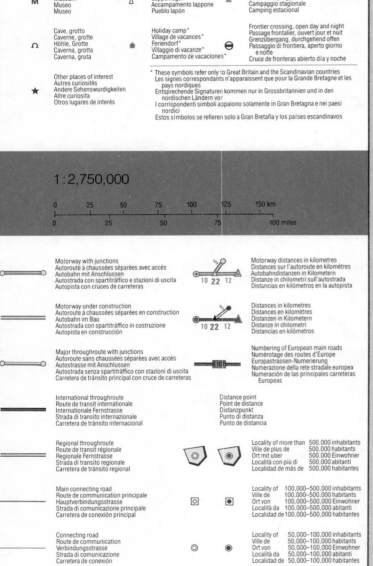

Ancient monument
Monument antique
Antikes Baudenkmal
Antichità
Monumento antiguo

Mediaeval ruin
Ruine du moyen age
Mittelalter Ruine
Rovine medioevo
Ruina medieval

Monument; Tower
Monument; Tour
Denkmal; Turm
Monumento; Torre
Monumento; Torre

Museum
Musée
Museum
Museo
Museo

Cave, grotto
Caverne, grotte
Höhle, Grotte
Caverna, grotta
Caverna, gruta

Other places of interest
Autres curiosités
Andere Sehenswurdigkeiten
Altre curiosita
Otros lugares de interés

Viewpoint
Point de vue
Aussichtspunkt
Punto panoramico
Punto panorámico

Lighthouse
Phare
Leuchtturm
Faro
Faro

Windmill
Moulin à vent
Windmühle
Mulino a vento
Molino de viento

Lapp settlement
Camp de lappons
Lappenlager
Accampamento lappone
Pueblo lapón

Holiday camp*
Village de vacances*
Feriendorf*
Villaggio di vacanze*
Campamento de vacaciones*

Isolated hotel; Motel
Hôtel isolé; Môtel
Alleinstehendes Hotel; Motel
Albergo isolato; Motel
Hotel aislado, motel

Beach
Plage
Strandbad
Spiaggia
Playa

Campsite open throughout the year
Camping permanent
Ganzjähriger Campingplatz
Campeggio aperto tutto l'anno
Camping abierto durante todo el año

Seasonal campsite
Camping saisonnier
Saisoncampingplatz
Campeggio stagionale
Camping estacional

Frontier crossing, open day and night
Passage frontalier, ouvert jour et nuit
Grenzübergang, durchgehend offen
Passaggio di frontiera, aperto giorno e notte
Cruce de fronteras abierto día y noche

* These symbols refer only to Great Britain and the Scandinavian countries
Les signes correspondants n'apparaissent que pour la Grande Bretagne et les pays nordiques
Entsprechende Signaturen kommen nur in Grossbritannien und in den nordischen Ländern vor
I corrispondenti simboli appaiono solamente in Gran Bretagna e nei paesi nordici
Estos símbolos se refieren solo a Gran Bretaña y los países escandinavos

1 : 2,750,000

0	25	50	75	100	125	150 km
0		25	50		75	100 miles

Motorway with junctions
Autoroute à chaussées séparées avec accès
Autobahn mit Anschlussen
Autostrada con spartitràffico e stazioni di uscita
Autopista con cruces de carreteras

Motorway distances in kilometres
Distances sur l'autoroute en kilomètres
Autobahndistanzen in Kilometern
Distanze in chilometri sull'autostrada
Distancias en kilómetros en la autopista

10 22 12

Motorway under construction
Autoroute à chaussées séparées en construction
Autobahn im Bau
Autostrada con spartitràffico in costruzione
Autopista en construcción

Distances in kilometres
Distances en kilomètres
Distanzen in Kilometern
Distanze in chilometri
Distancias en kilómetros

10 22 12

Major throughroute with junctions
Autoroute sans chaussées séparées avec accès
Autostrasse mit Anschlussen
Autostrada senza spartitràffico con stazioni di uscita
Carretera de tránsito principal con cruce de carreteras

E 107

Numbering of European main roads
Numérotage des routes d'Europe
Europastrassen-Numerierung
Numerazione della rete stradale europea
Numeración de las principales carreteras Europeas

International throughroute
Route de transit internationale
Internationale Fernstrasse
Strada di transito internazionale
Carretera de tránsito internacional

Distance point
Point de distance
Distanzpunkt
Punto di distanza
Punto de distancia

Regional throughroute
Route de transit régionale
Regionale Fernstrasse
Strada di transito regionale
Carretera de tránsito regional

Locality of more than 500,000 inhabitants
Ville de plus de 500,000 habitants
Ort mit uber 500,000 Einwohner
Località con più di 500,000 abitanti
Localidad de más de 500,000 habitantes

Main connecting road
Route de communication principale
Hauptverbindungsstrasse
Strada di comunicazione principale
Carretera de conexión principal

Locality of 100,000–500,000 inhabitants
Ville de 100,000–500,000 habitants
Ort von 100,000–500,000 Einwohner
Località da 100,000–500,000 abitanti
Localidad de 100,000–500,000 habitantes

Connecting road
Route de communication
Verbindungsstrasse
Strada di comunicazione
Carretera de conexión

Locality of 50,000–100,000 inhabitants
Ville de 50,000–100,000 habitants
Ort von 50,000–100,000 Einwohner
Località da 50,000–100,000 abitanti
Localidad de 50,000–100,000 habitantes

Railway
Chemin de fer
Eisenbahn
Ferrovia
Ferrocarril

Locality of 10,000–50,000 inhabitants
Ville de 10,000–50,000 habitants
Ort von 10,000–50,000 Einwohner
Località da 10,000–50,000 abitanti
Localidad de 10,000–50,000 habitantes

Car ferry
Bac pour automobiles
Autofähre
Linea di navigazione
Transbordador de automóviles

Locality of less than 10,000 inhabitants
Ville de moins de 10,000 habitants
Ort unter 10,000 Einwohner
Località fino a 10,000 abitanti
Localidad de menos de 10,000 habitantes

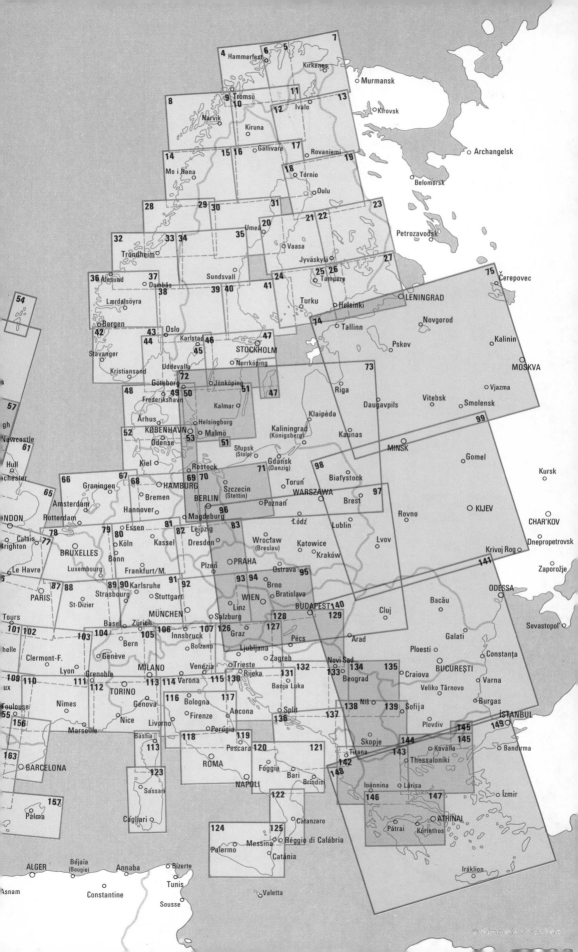

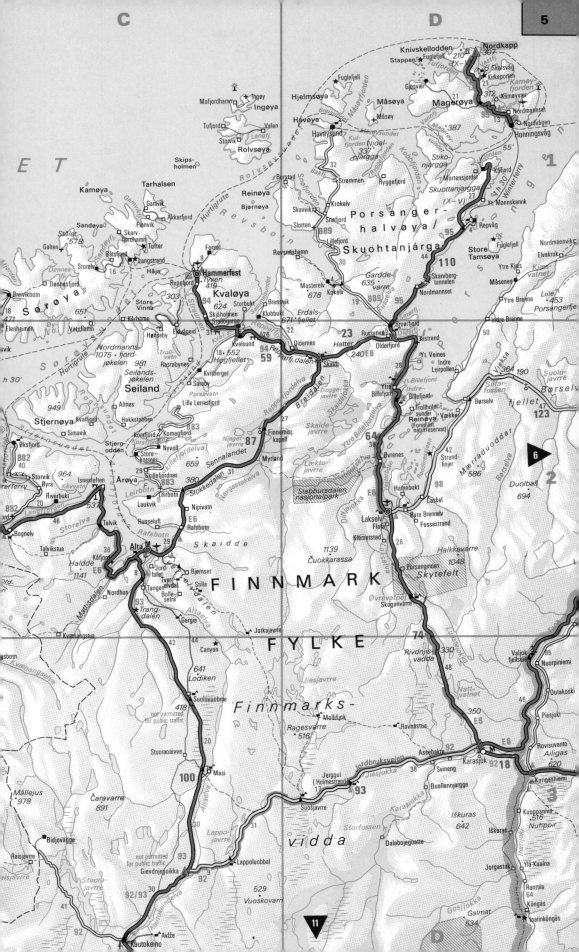

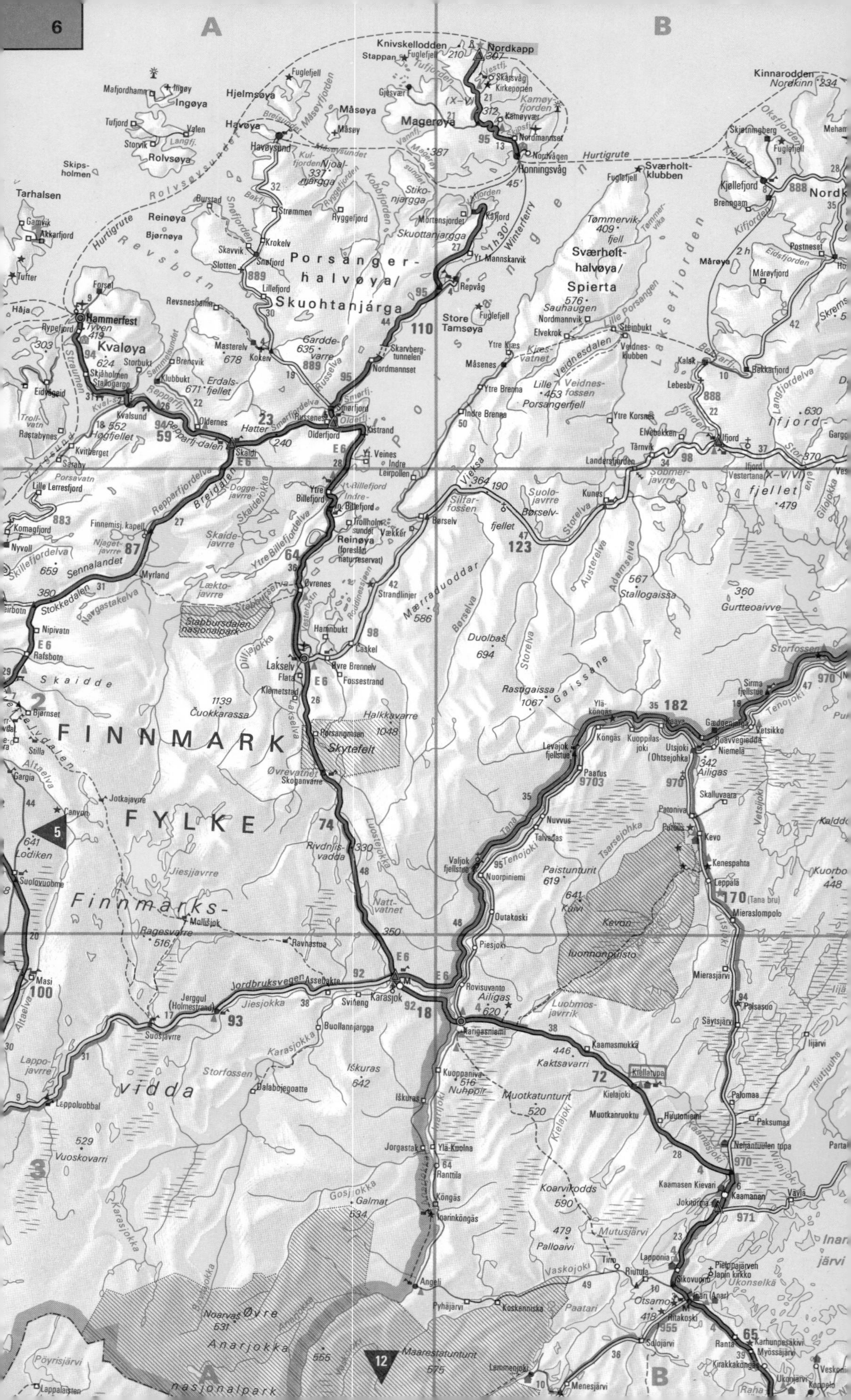
A
B
Knivskjellodden
Nordkapp
307
Stappan
Fuglefjell
Skarsvåg
Kirkeporten
Gjesvær
Magerøya
Kamøyvær
Nordmannset
Nordvågen
Honningsvåg
Hurtigrute
Måsøya
Måsøy
Hjelmsøya
Havøya
Havøysund
Mafjordhamn
Ingøy
Ingøya
Tufjord
Valen
Storvik
Rolvsøya
Skipsholmen
Tarhalsen
Gamvik
Akkarfjord
Tufter
Rolvsøysund
Reinøya
Bjørnøya
Burstad
Revsbotn
Strømmen
Ryggefjord
Krokelv
Skavvik
Snøfjord
Slotten
Lillefjord
Porsangerhalvøya/
Skuohtanjárga
Mortensjordet
Kåfjord
Yt. Mannskarvik
Repvåg
Store Tamsøya
Fuglefjell
Hammerfest
Tyven
419
Kvaløya
Forsøl
Håja
Rypefjord
Revsneshamn
Masterelv
678
Kokelv
Gardde-várre
635
Skarvbergtunnelen
Nordmannset
Smørfjord
Russenes
Olderfjord
Kistrand
Brensvik
Storbukt
Skjåholmen
Stallogargo
Klubbukt
Erdalsfjellet
671
Kvalsund
Oldernes
Eidvågeid
Høgfjellet
552
Hatter
Repparfjorddalen
240
Skaidi
E6
Rastabynes
Kvitberget
Saraby
Lille Lerresfjord
Breidalen
Repparfjordelva
Yt. Veines
Indre Leirpollen
Ytre Billefjord
In. Billefjord
Trollholmsund
Vækker
Reinøya (foreslått naturreservat)
Finnemisj. kapell
Komagfjord
Nyvoll
Skillefjordelva
659
Sennalandet
Myrland
Læktojavrre
Stabbursdalen nasjonalpark
Stokkedalen
380
Nipivatn
Rafsbotn
Skaidde
Øvrenes
Strandlinjer
Hamnbukt
Caskel
Lakselv
Flata
Øvre Brennelv
Fossestrand
Klemetstad
1139
Čuokkarassa
Halkkavarre
1048
Porsangmoen
Skytefelt
FINNMARK
FYLKE
Øvrevatnet
Skoganvarre
Bjørnset
Stilla
Gargia
Altaelva
Jotkajavrre
Canyon
641
Lodiken
Suolovuobme
Jiesjavrre
Finnmarksvidda
Mollišjok
Rivdnjisvadda
330
Nattvatnet
Ragesvarre
516
Ravnastua
350
Masi
Jordbruksvegen
Assebakte
Karasjok
Sirheng
Jerggul (Holmestrand)
Jiesjokka
Suosjavrre
Buollannjargga
Lappojavrre
Storfossen
Dalabojegoatte
Iškuras
642
Karasjokka
Leppoluobbal
529
Vuoskovarri
Gosjokka
Galmat
634
Noarvas
Øvre Anarjokka nasjonalpark
531
555
Maarestatunturi
575
Pöyrisjärvi
Lappalaisten
Angeli
Pyhäjärvi
Koskenniska
Paatari
Vaskojoki
Menesjärvi
Lemmenjoki
Solojärvi
Hitakoski
Otsamo
418
Inari (Anar)
Sikovuono
Pielpajärven
Riutula
Lapponia
Mutusjärvi
Palloaivi
479
Koarvikodds
590
Jorgastak
Ylä-Kuolna
Ranttila
Köngäs
Inarinköngäs
Kuoppaniva
516
Nuhppir
Muotkatunturit
520
Kielajoki
Muotkanruoktu
Kaamasmukka
446
Kaktsavarri
Kiellatupa
Karigasniemi
Rovisuvanto
Ailigas
620
Luobmosjavrrik
Piesjoki
Outakoski
Nuorpiniemi
Valjok fjellstue
Tenojoki
Paistunturit
619
Kuivi
641
Kevon luonnonpuisto
Nuvvus
Talvadas
Paatus
Levajok fjellstue
Köngäs
Yläköngäs
Kuoppilasjoki
Utsjoki (Ohtsejohka)
Ailigas
342
Skalluvaara
Patoniva
Kevo
Kenespahta
Leppälä
Tana bru
Mieraslompolo
Mierasjärvi
Palsasuo
Säytsjärvi
Iijärvi
Palomaa
Paksumaa
Neljäntuulen tupa
Nuorgam
Kaamasen Kievari
Kaamanen
Jokitörmä
Väylä
Inarijärvi
Ukonselkä
Karhunpesäkivi
Myössäjärvi
Ranta
Kirakkaköngäs
Ukonjärvi
Veskoniemi
Kaamasjoki
Utsjoki
Tana
Gædgenjarga
Roavvegiedde
Niemelä
Vetsikko
Sirma fjellstue
Tenojoki
970
Storfossen
Rastigaissa
1067
Gaissane
Duolbaš
694
Mærraduoddar
586
Børselva
Stallogaissa
567
Gurtteoaivve
360
Adamselva
Austerelva
Storelva
Børselv
Silfarfossen
Suolojavrre
Børselvfjellet
Kunes
Sommerjavrre
Landersfjorden
Tårnvik
Elvebakken
Ifjord
Ifjordfjellet
479
Vestertana
Storelva
Gilojokka
Ytre Korsnes
Lille Porsangerfjell
453
Veidnesfossen
Veidnesdalen
Veidnesklubben
Kjæsvatnet
Ytre Kjæs
Måsenes
Ytre Brenna
Indre Brenna
Elvekrok
Steinbukt
Nordmannvik
Sauhaugen
576
Lille Porsangen
Laksefjorden
Sværholthalvøya/
Spierta
Tømmervikfjell
409
Sværholtklubben
Fuglefjell
Porsangen
Kinnarodden
Nordkinn
234
Skjøtningberg
Fuglefjell
Kjøllefjord
Brenngam
Nordkinn
Kifjorden
Postneset
Mårøya
Mårøyfjord
Eidsfjorden
Bekkarfjord
Kalak
Lebesby
Langfjordelva
Ifjordfjellet
630
Stabbursnes
Lakselva
Luostejokka
Kautokeino
Vetsijoki
Kalddo
Kuorbo
448
Tsiutiuuha

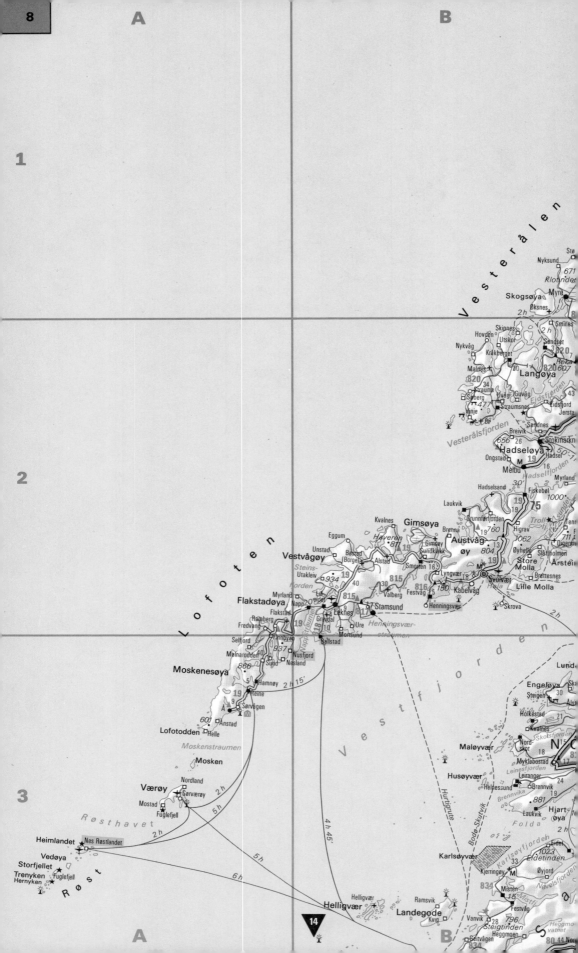

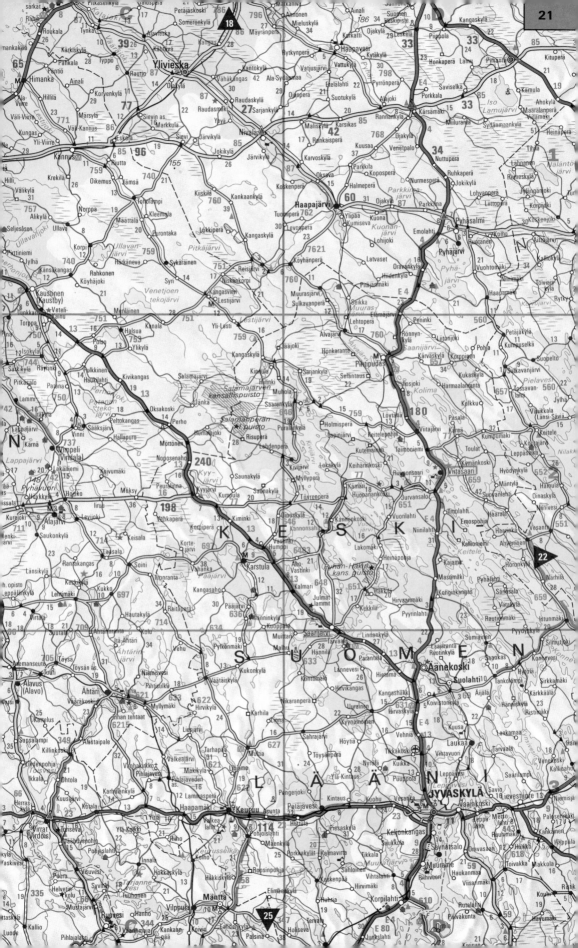

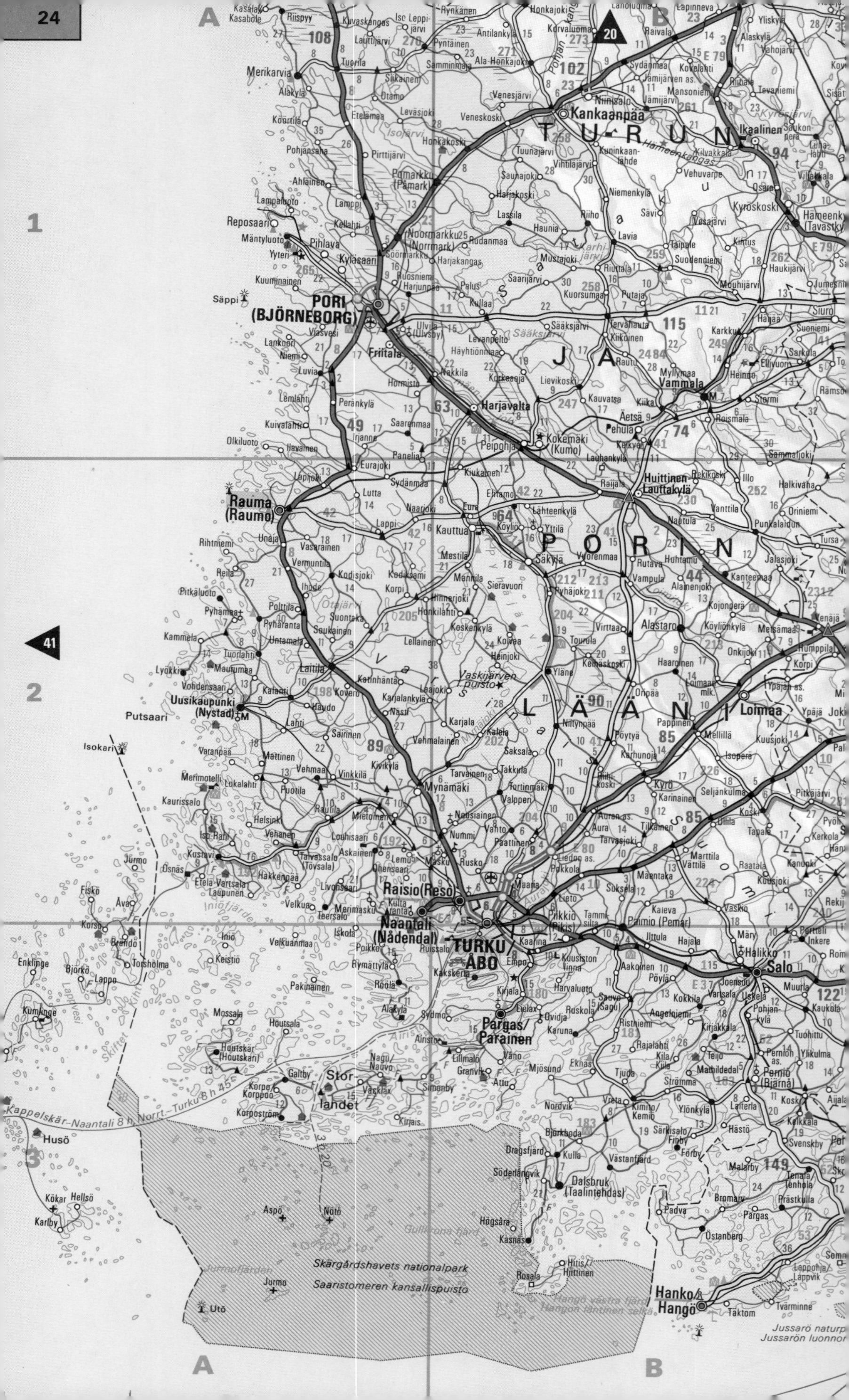

A B

1

2

3

Merikarvia
Kasabóle
Riispyy

Reposaari
Mäntyluoto
Yyteri
Kuuminainen
Säppi

PORI (BJÖRNEBORG)

Pihlava
Kyläsaari
Noormarkku (Norrmark)

Frititala

Luvia
Lankoori
Niemi
Lemlähti
Kuivalahti
Olkiluoto
Iisalmen

Rauma (Raumo)
Rihtniemi
Unaja
Reila
Pitkäluoto
Pyhämaa
Kammela
Lyökki
Vohdensaari

Uusikaupunki (Nystad)
Putsaari
Isokari
Varanpää
Merimotelli
Lokalahti
Kaurissalo
Kustavi (Gustavs)
Iso-Heikki
Jurmo
Osnäs
Fisko
Åva

Harjavalta
Kokemäki (Kumu)
Huittinen
Lauttakylä

Kankaanpää
Ikaalinen

Vammala

Loimaa

PORIN LÄÄNI

TURUN JA

Laitila
Mynämäki
Nousiainen
Masku
Raisio (Reso)
Naantali (Nädendal)
TURKU ÅBO
Lieto
Kaarina
Piikkiö
Paimio (Pemar)
Salo
Halikko
Muurla

Pargas Parainen

Nagu Nauvo
Korpo Korppoo
Korpoström
Galtby
Stor landet

Houtskär (Houtskari)
Mossala

Enklinge
Björkö
Lappo
Kumlinge
Kökar
Hellsö
Karlby
Husö

Kimito Kemiö
Dragsfjärd
Söderlångvik
Dalsbruk (Taalintehdas)
Kasnäs
Rosala
Högsåra

Pernió (Bjärnä)

Hanko Hangö
Täktom

Skärgårdshavets nationalpark
Saaristomeren kansallispuisto

Jurmo
Utö

20

41

A B

A   B

1

Skarv-flesan
Burøya
Gjæsingen
Sula
Mausundvær
Sulsfjorden
Norddyrøy
Nord-Frøya
Uttian
Inntian
Nordskaget
Kløven
14
Sistranda
7167
Frøya
Hatval
Ulvan
Sel
Sør-Frøya
20'
Tittan
Kjerringvåg
8
Ansnes
Fillingsnes
Fillan
Fjell
Hestnes
21   7
Brottinos
Frøyfjorden
Smogasjøen
Kvenvær
10
Gryta 11
Straum
714
Veidholmen
Hummelvik   346
Laksåvik
Hattvik
Hitra
713
Søds
Smøla
Hopen
Bekkvikdal
Hamn
Dyrnesvågen
18
Gjengstøa
Brattvær   36
Nordvika
Forsnes
Bakken
Heim
Ramsøyfjorden
Rønsvik
Vihals
Kjørsvik
Storødden
669
Nelvik
Grisvåg
Seternes
Vikan
711
Jøstølen
Straumen
Svinvik
Vean
680
14 13
Rosvoll
Edøy
Stemshaug
Kyrk
Korsvoll
Ånes
Aure
Todalskjølen
Vinsternes 13
821   12
680
Grip
Nerd heim
Fuglvik
Ervik
Todal
Sinnes
Vinjeøra
18 Gull-steint
Leira
Ertvågøy
Tømmervåg
Tustna
Bendal
15'
Rodal
Engdal
Stabben
Aresvik
Kristiansund
Hals
Liaba
Hendset
Seivika
Betna
Engjan
149
Bremsnes
Arsundfjorden
Halsanaustan
71
Øye
Averøya
20'
Kvisvik
Grimstad
65
Hjelmen
Bøverdjord
Mo
65
711
Frei
Kvalvåg
15'
.973
20'
Skei
Honnstad 31
Farstad
Tøvik
Kvitnes
Saksnes
Brøske
Kvernes
Aspa
Torjut
Støknes
Surnadalsøra
670
Hustad
Ørjavik
10
Kornstad
Høgset
Sandvika
Hamnes
Stangvik
664   663
18
Eide
25
Aksnes
16
Bud   18 Elnesvågen
Troilkirke   67   6
Torvikbukt
73
Nes
Kvanne
Melhus
Ona
Indre Fræna
24
666
Tingvoll
Rakkum
Todal
Rindarøy
Ytre Fræna
23
Batnfjordsøra
665
Angvik
20'
Alvund-foss
Sandøy
Gossen
Småge
Hollingsholm
67
Lønset
Steinløysa
666
Meisingset
Rottås
Hafstad
21
Kårvatn
Steinshamn
Aukra
Kleiva
96
Tjelle
22 Eidsvåg
Haraøya
Sundsbø
662
Molde
240
62
Eidsøra
Alvundeid
Nerdal
Myklebost
Harøyfjorden
10'
Grønnes
Buvik
Sunndalsjorden
Åfarnes
37
Fjørtoft
Sør-Aukra
Horsgard
Vistdal
49
Nausta
16
Storli
Drynaholmen
45'
Solsnes
Mittet
660
Øksendalsøra
Austnes
Rødven
Holm
Eresfjord
62
Sunndalsøra
Ørsnes
Midsund
Fiksdal
Setnes
10'
Dale
Øverås
Skjelten
Vestnes
45'
Vikebukt
Afarnes
MØRE
Brandstad
Dalen
Romo
Sevik
Vatne
(Helland)
Vågstranda
34
Isfjorden
Grøvdalsli
32
Hoff
Havnsund
661
20
6
Eid
Eikesdals-
Vangshaugen
Brattvåg
33
19
44
vatnet
Spjelkavik
Tomra
E69
80
E69
Mandalen
Veblungsnes
1h 30'
Røymoen
Magerheim
Sjøholm
Andalsnes
Hoemsbu
Jens
Aursnes
Søvik
Tresfjord
Innfjorden
Mardals-
Rauberg-
Sortevåg
Sykkylven
Stordal
Mo
Fokhaugstova
Troll-
1788
Marstein
fossen
(X-V)
hytta
Festøy
58
stigen
Troll-
Kors
Reitan
Osbu-
Storvollseter
14
Hundeidvik
(X-V)
Øvstestøl
850 tinndane
Flatmark
vatnet
Amotsdal
1463 Standal
OG   ROMSDAL
Finnset
(X-V)
Aursjøhytta
blåstinden
121
Stranda
'Gra-
Liabygda
56
Verma
1950
Sørelihø
60 35
vanes
Opshaug-
Vakkerstøylen
Naustvika
Gåsbu
Sæbø
1571
vika
Eidsdal
Linge
Valldal
Stuguflaten
Gautsjø
Brekketind
Norddal
Bjorli
Skamsdalshytta
Leknes
Øye
Svora
Tafjord
Pyttbua
Lesjaskog
Lesjaskogs-
Gautsjø
(X-V)
Ørneveien
Tungaseter
vatnet
151
3
655
Viddal
624
25
Rindalsseter
Torsvatn
Lesjaverk
E69
Vatne Bondalseidet
655
Kaldhus-
633
Rusteseter
Lesja
Garc
Hunnes
Bjørka
seter
Digerkampen
Tverrfjellet
Natu
1945
Austefjord
Hellesylt
Geiranger
Torsbua
Nyseter
Lørdalen
Ekra
Bøsetrene
Kalvatn
Dalsnibba
1h
Krosshø
191
Bispen
(X-V) Geirang(X-V)
1476
1857
Billingen
Stamseter
Teigen
Navelsaker
60
Djupvasshytta
1038
870
Pollfoss
582
60
Sterring
Melheim
15/60
Oppstryn
1139 (X-V)
Nordberg
Kjølen
18 7
14
Videdalen
Bispa
Randabygd
M
Stryn
Hjelle
Otta
Skjåk
Lefinnlia
Blakstøer
Loen
39
Strynsvatn
Nordborg
Stafyfnn
Grøna
Nos
Faleide
19
Skridulaupbu
Lomsegga
Gróffer 26
Olden
36
Brennseter
Ulvik
60
Bødal
Sotaseter
Lomsegga
Ottadalen

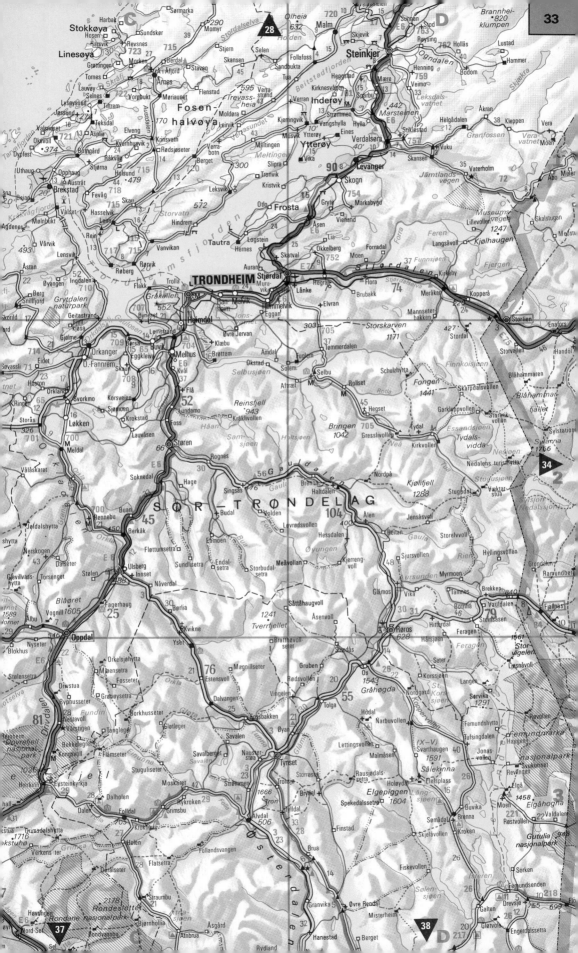

A
Ålesund
Spjelkavik
Giske
Valkve
Godøy
Runde
Hareid-landet
Hareid
Ulsteinvik
Fosnavåg
Gurskøy
Sula
Ørsta
Volda
Stadlandet
Selje
Vanylven
Åheim
Vågsøy
Måløy
Bremanger-landet
Frøya
Kalvåg
Svelgen
Florø
Hovden
Skorpa
Kinnakyrkja
Askrova
Svanøy
Nordfjordeid
Sandane
Stryn
Loen
Olden
Hellesylt
Geiranger
Stranda
Sykkylven
Sunnmøre
Storfjorden
Nordfjord
Hornindalsvatn
Ålfotbreen
Jostedalsbreen
Lodalskåpa
2083
Naustdal
Førde
Sunnfjord
Atløy
Askvoll
Dale
Værlandet
Sula
SOGN OG
FJORDANE
Høyanger
Vadheim
Lavik
Balestrand
Vangsnes
Vik
Sognefjord
Sognefjorden
Sogndal
Kaupanger
Fjærland
Gaupne
Jostedalen
Flåm
Aurland
Gudvangen
Nærøy
Myrdal
Voss
Vossevangen
Stalheim
Dale
Vaksdal
Osterøy
Radøy
Holsnøy
Askøy
BERGEN
Store
Sotra
Fedje
Nordhordland
Hardangerfjorden
Norheimsund
Øystese
Ålvik
Kvanndal
Granvin
Ulvik
Eidfjord
Kinsarvik
Lofthus
Jondal
HORDALAND
Hardanger
Tysse
32
42
80
E 68
E 69

Pohjansalo

Lampaluoto
Reposaari
Mäntyluoto
Yyteri
265

1

Kuuminainen

Säppi

Lankoori
Niemi

Lemlähti

Kuivalahti

Olkiluoto   Ilavainn

**Rauma
(Raumo)**
Unaja
Rihtniemi   8
Reila   27   21   Ve
Pitkäluoto
Pyhämaat   7   10   Pyhäranti
Kammela   8
14   Tuorlahti
Lyökki   Maurumaa
Vohdensaari   13   9
**Uusikaupunki
(Nystad)** M
Putsaari
24   Mattir
Varanpää
Merimotell   Lukalähti
Isokari   Kaurissalo   Helsin
15
Isp-Rahi
Kustavi
Jurmo
Etelä-Vartsala
Ösnäs   Laupunen
Iniöfjärden
Fisko
Avä
Korsö
Brändö   Inio
Tofsholma   Keistio

Åland
(Ahvenanmaa)

Mossala
L A N D S K A P E T   Å L A N D
Enklinge   Houtskär
Björkö   Lappe   (Houtskär)
Söderа
Kvarken   Geta   Simskäla   13
Skarpnätö   12   14
11   Käsberg
Strömma   Ödkarby   Kumlinge   Teili
Eckerö   Sahvik   18   Hulta
Bovik   16   Finström   Sund   Finby   Vårdö   Seglinge
Storby   14   Hammarland   5   Godby   Grundsunda
M   Eckerö   Godby   Kastelhol   Prasto   Busö   Sottanga   Kappelskär-Naantali
6   Torp   Torp   Bjärström   Gölby   Tranvik   Norrboda   Husö
Skeppsvik   Godt   Jomala   Lumparn   Långnäs
Gotth   Önninge-   Överö   Norrt.-Turku
by   Lumparland
Mariehamn   Lemland   14
(Maarianhamina)   Granboda
13   3   Flaka   Degerby   Sandö
Väster anga   Hästersboda
Brätto   Kökar   Hellsö
Herröskatan   Föglö   Karlby
Kappelskär

Stockholm- Turku

Utö

3

Ålands hav

Grisslehamn
avik   16
roda
Väddö
Väddö
Almsta
Lingslätö (Barnens ö)
283
Söderby Karl
Simpnäs
Björko-Arholma
una   **Vätö**
Rådmanso   Grädd
E3   Söderarm
25   Kappelskär
Spillersboda
Furusund
Blidö
Angso
nationalp.   Blido
Blidö
Svartlöga

ROGALAND

VEST-AGDER

STAVANGER
Sandnes
Haugesund
Karmøy
Egersund
Flekkefjord
Farsund
Mandal
Odda
Sauda
Stord
Bømlo
Tysnesøy
Reksteren

Newcastle
Hirtshals

A   B

1
2
3

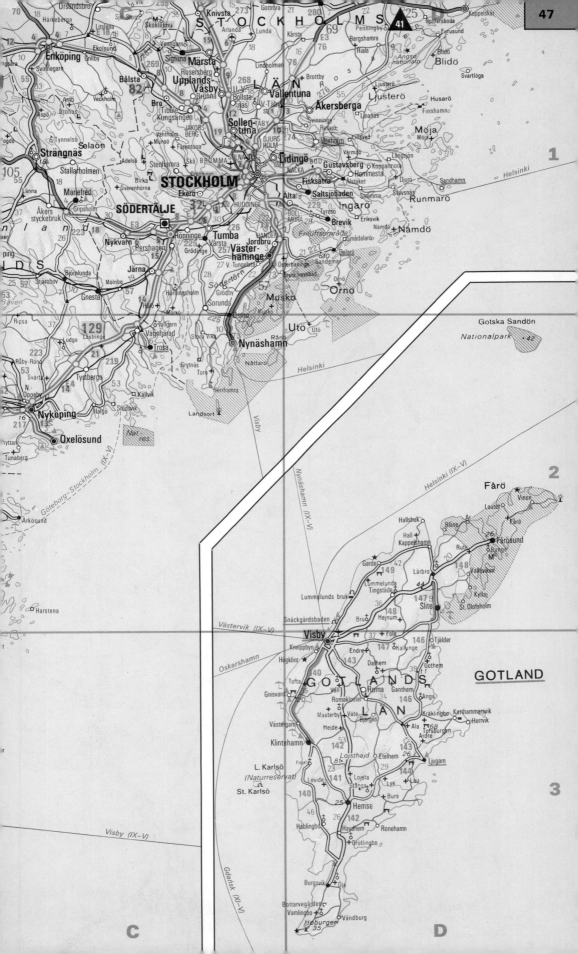

DANMARK / M A R K

Samsø · Sjællands odde · Overby · Hundested · Frederiksværk · Hillerød

Sejerby · Sejerø · Nykøbing · Hornsved · Jægerspris · Frederikssund · Slangerup · Birkerød · Vedbæk · Skodsborg

Endelave · Fyns Hoved · Kalundborg · Holbæk · Ballerup · **KØBENHAVN** · Amager · Dragør

Kerteminde · **SJÆLLAND** · ROSKILDE · Hedehusene · Greve Str. · Karlslunde Strand · Solrød Strand

Nyborg · Slagelse · Sorø · Ringsted · Køge · Køge Bugt

Korsør · Skælskør · Næstved · Haslev · Fakse · St. Heddinge · Stevns Klint

Svendborg · Tåsinge · Agersø · Omø · Knudshoved · Præstø · Fakse Bugt · Fakse Ladeplads

Ærøskøbing · Marstal · Langeland · Vejrø · Femø · Vordingborg · Kalvehave · Stege · Møn · Store Klint · Liselund

Bagenkop · Nakskov · Maribo · Sakskøbing · Nykøbing · **Falster** · Travemünde–Trelleborg

Lolland · Rødby · Nysted · Marielyst · Travemünde–Helsinki · Gdańsk

Rødbyhavn · Gedser · Travemünde–Malmö · Guldborg Sund · Kedertrinne

Fehmarn · Puttgarden · Femer Bælt · Darßer Ort · Prerow · **Darß** · Born

Heiligenhafen · Großenbrode · Fehmarnsundbrücke · Ostseebad Wustrow · Ostseebad Dierhagen

Oldenburg · Dahme · Mecklenburger Bucht · R.-Warnemünde · Ribnitz-Damgarten

Malente · Eutin · Grömitz · Kellenhusen · Ostseebad Kühlungsborn · Bad Doberan · **ROSTOCK** · Marlow · Bad Sülze

Neustadt · Poel · Neubukow · Kröpelin · Schwaan · Laage · Teterow

Scharbeutz · Timmendorf Strand · **WISMAR** · Blowatz · Hagebök · Züsow · Neukloster · Güstrow

LÜBECK · Grevesmühlen · Schönberg · Warin · Bützow · Plaaz · Thürkow

Ratzeburg · Gadebusch · Rehna · Mühlen Eichsen · Zickhusen · Brüel · Sternberg · Krakow · Langhagen

Note:
The Nordic countries in particular, have put forward certain reservations to the proposed new E-Road numbering system.

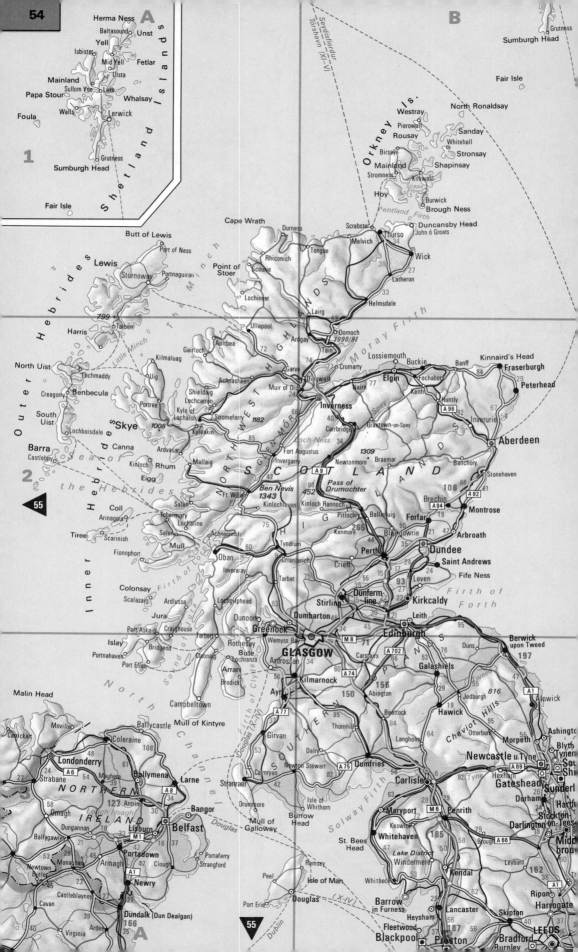

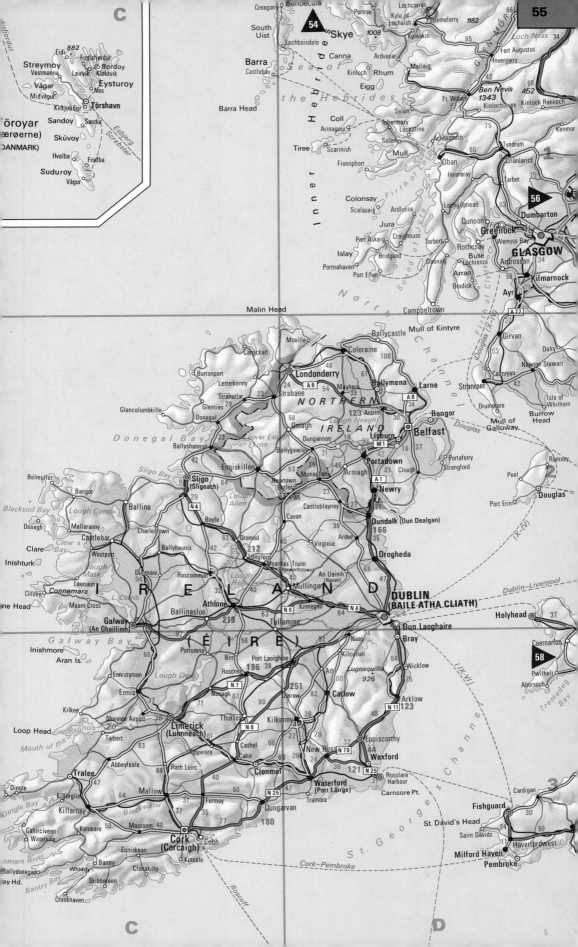

Ostfriesische Inseln

GRONINGEN — EMDEN — WILHELMSHAVEN — OLDENBURG — AURICH — LEER — CLOPPENBURG — MEPPEN — LINGEN — NORDHORN — OSNABRÜCK — MÜNSTER — ENSCHEDE — HENGELO — DEVENTER — BOCHOLT — EMMERICH — COESFELD — HAMM

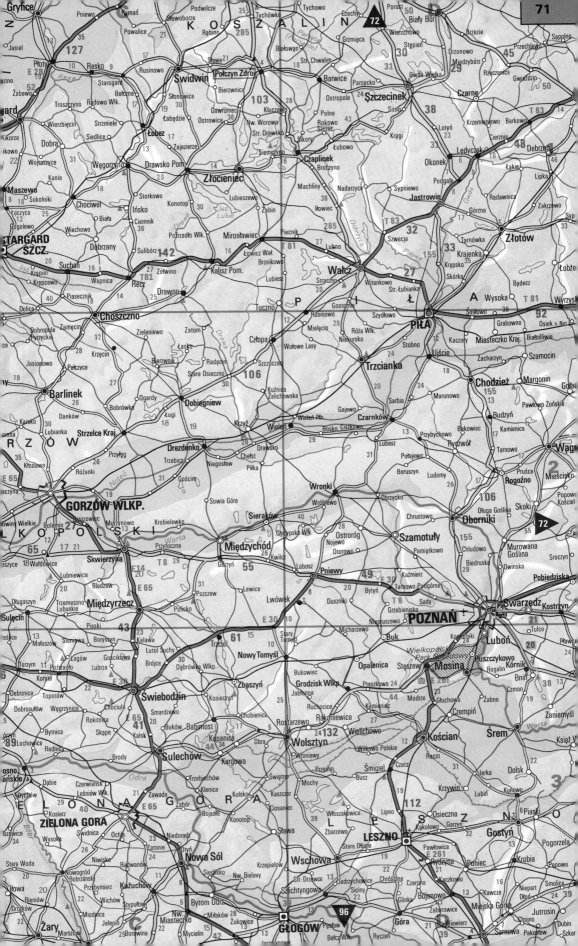

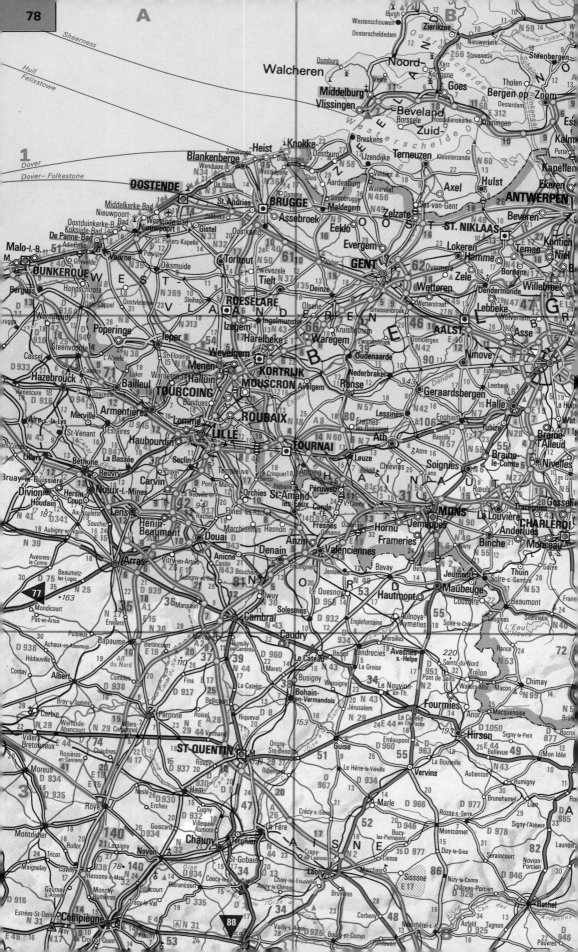

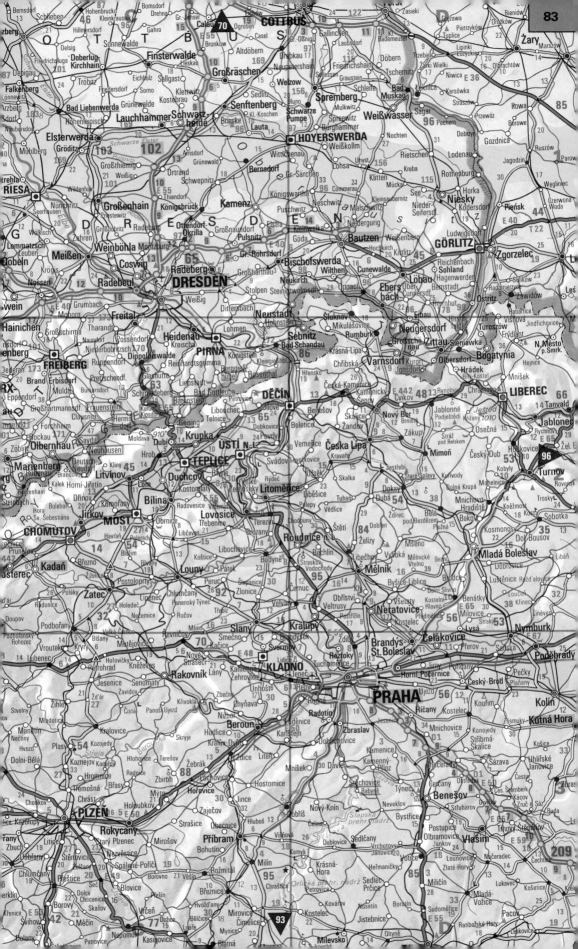

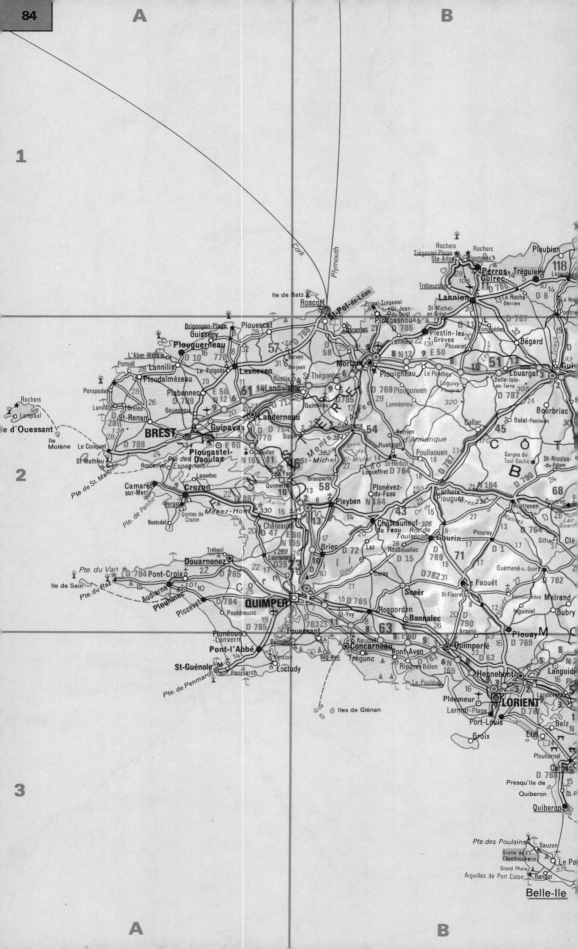

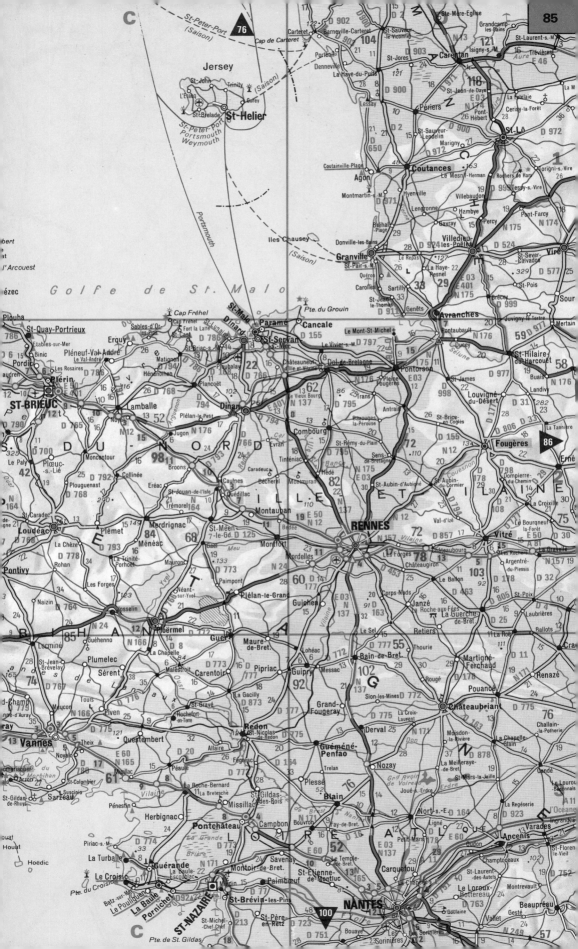

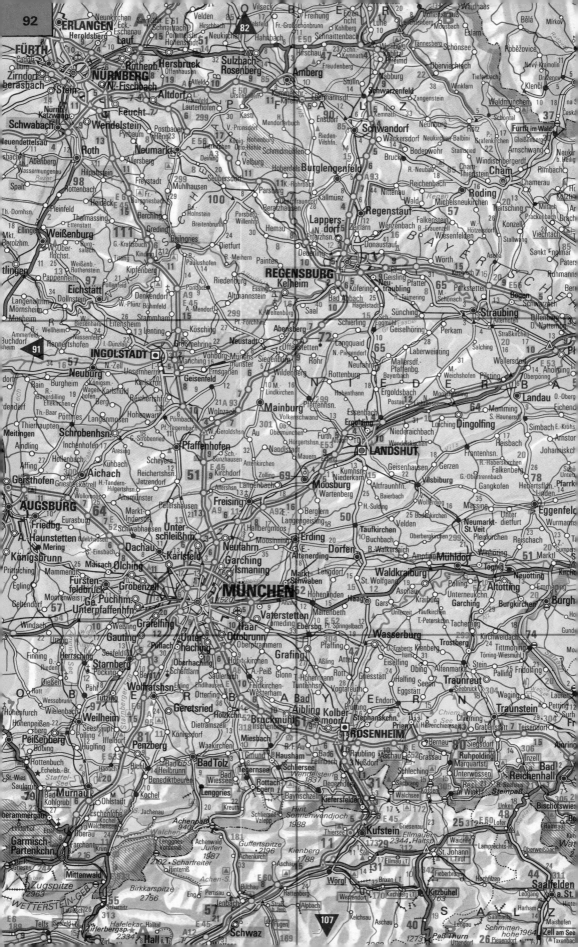

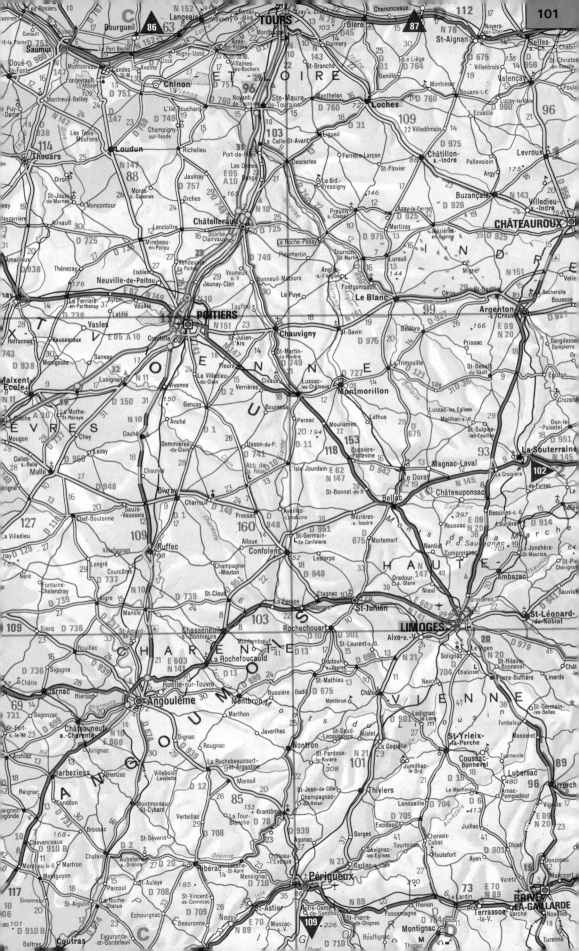

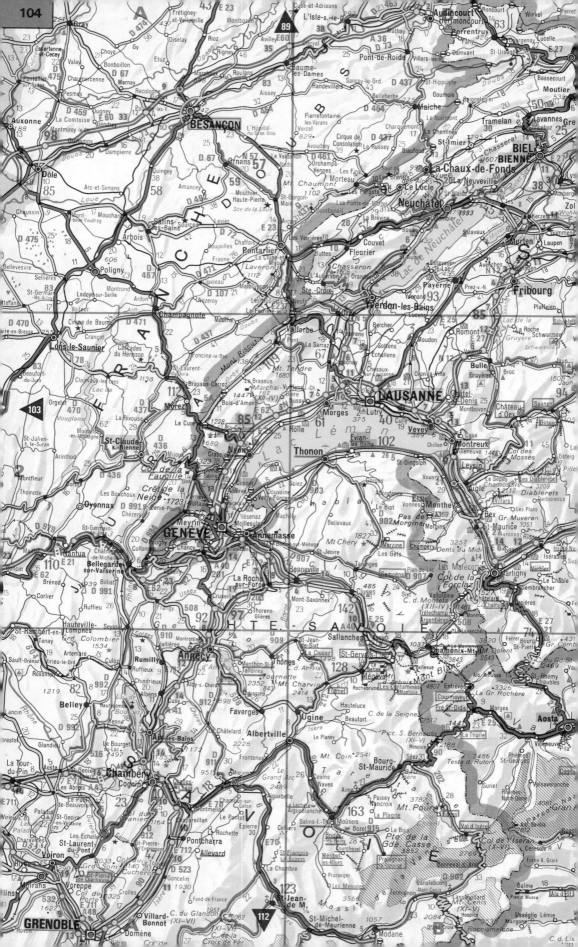

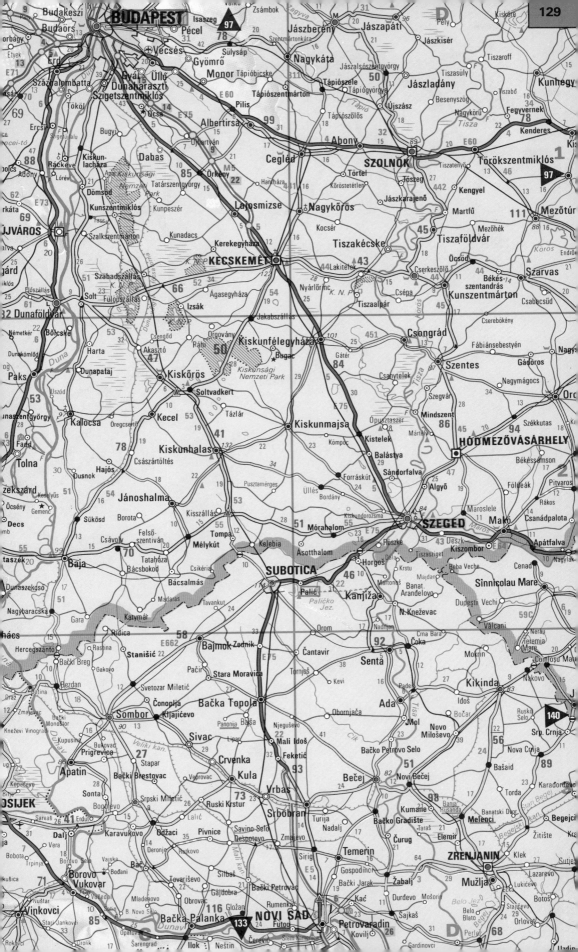

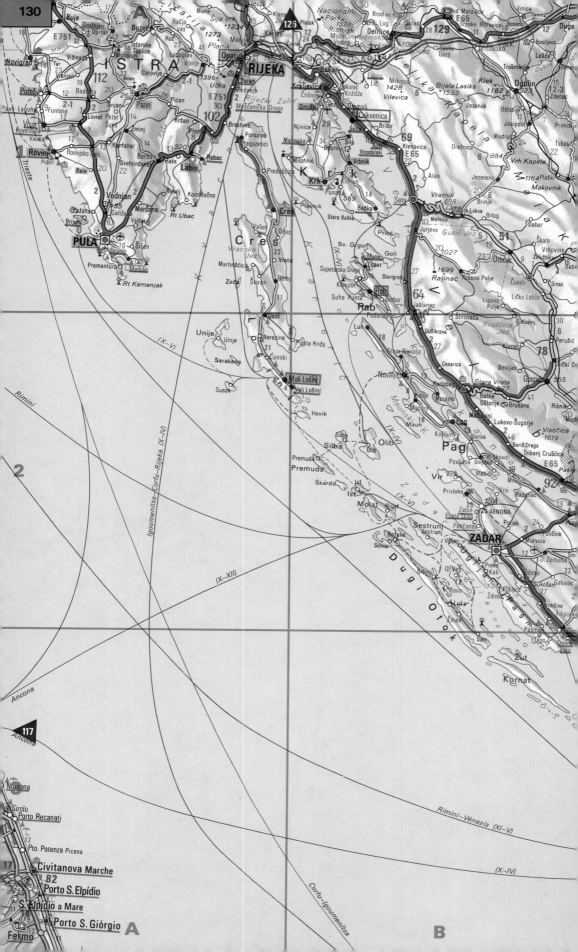

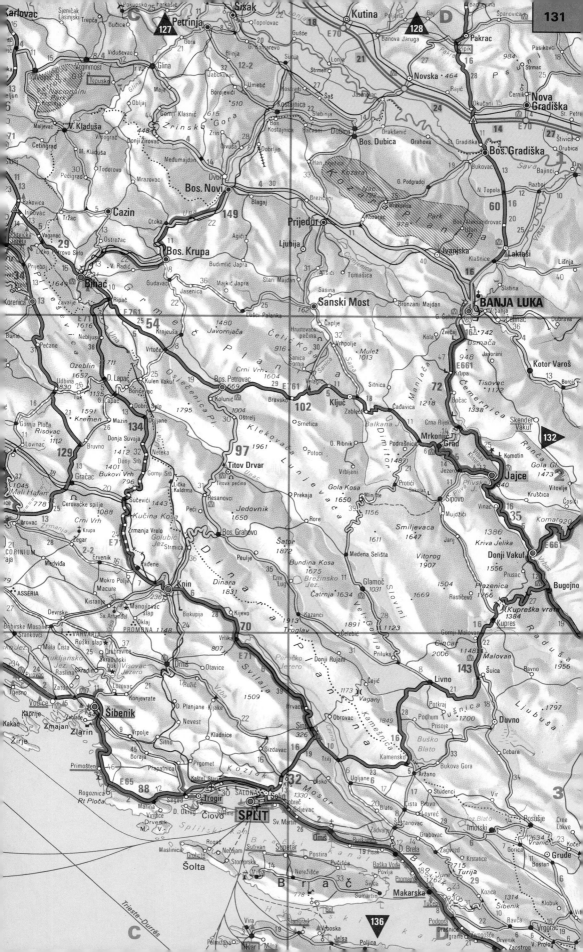

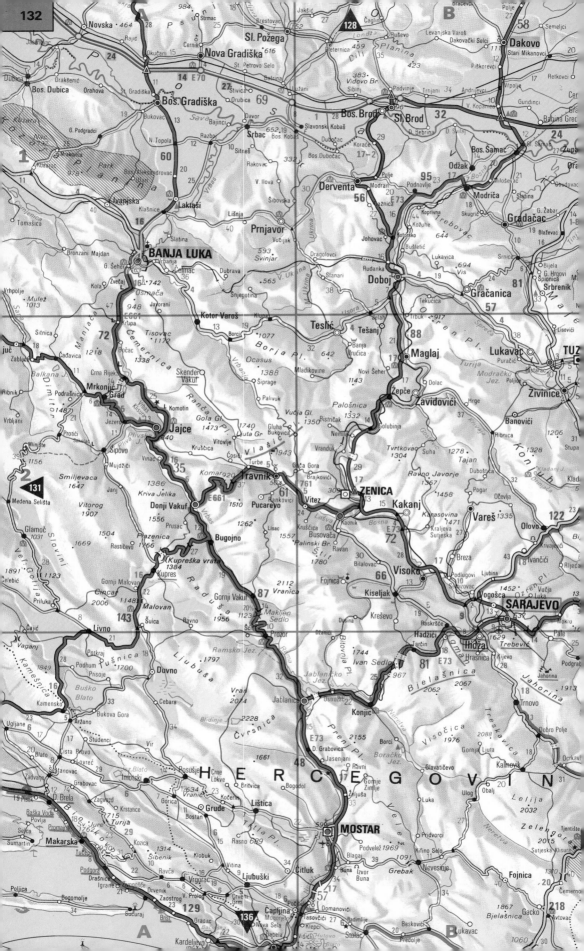

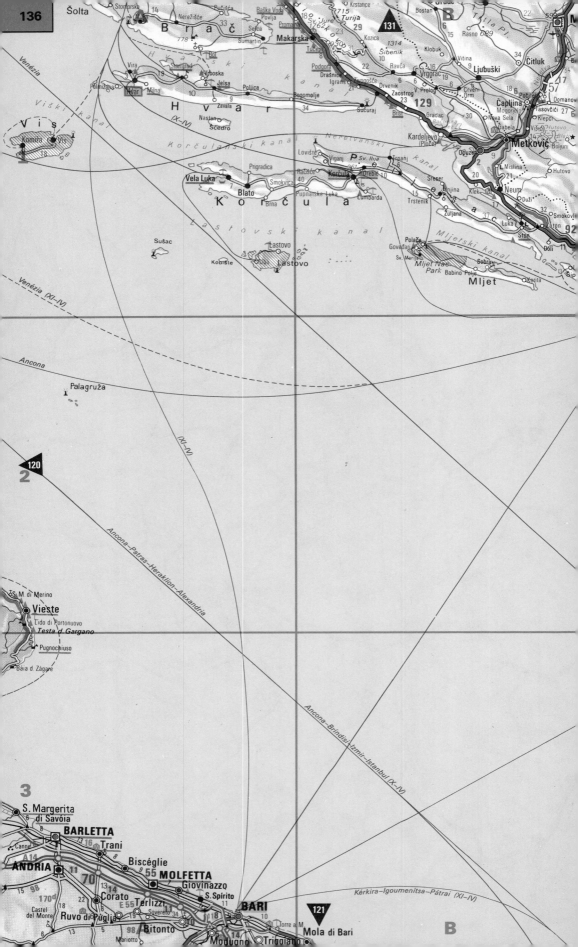

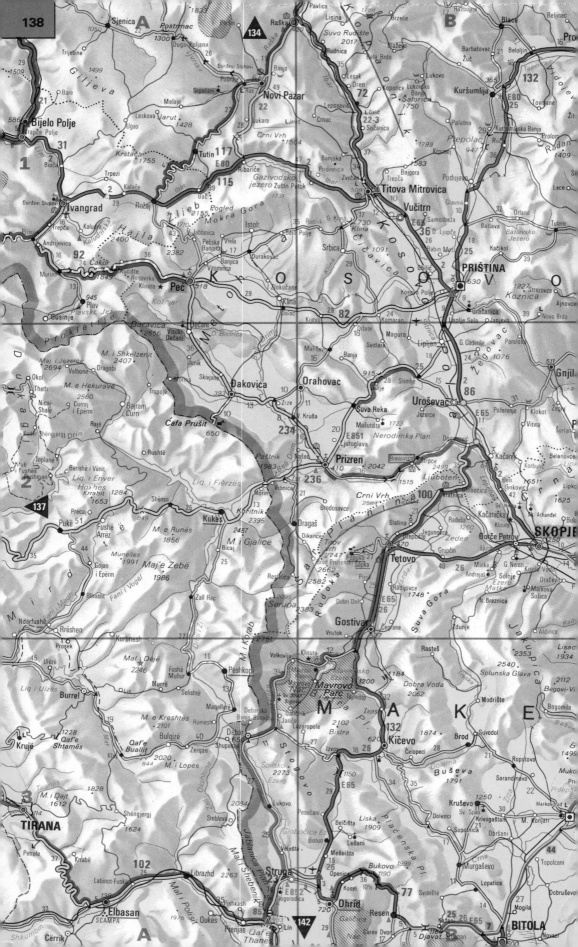

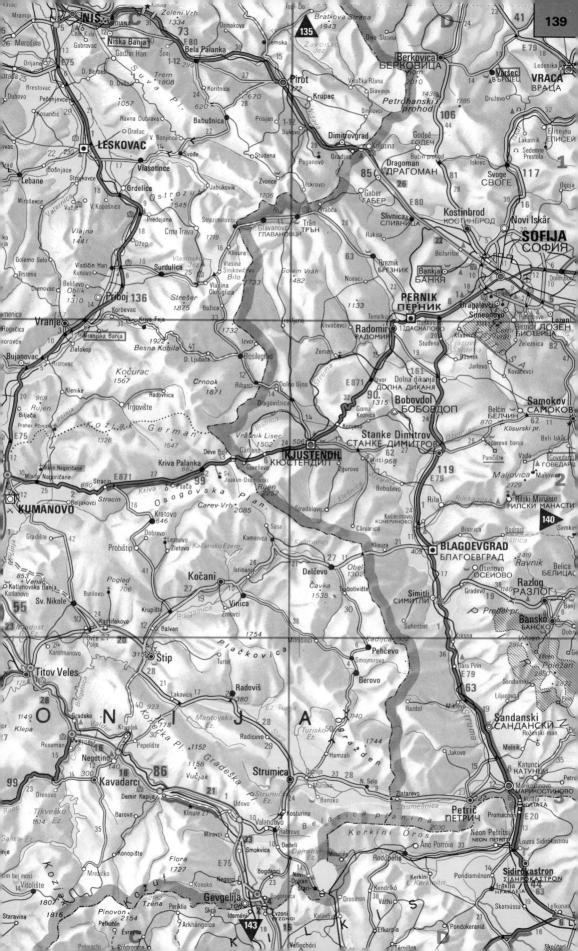

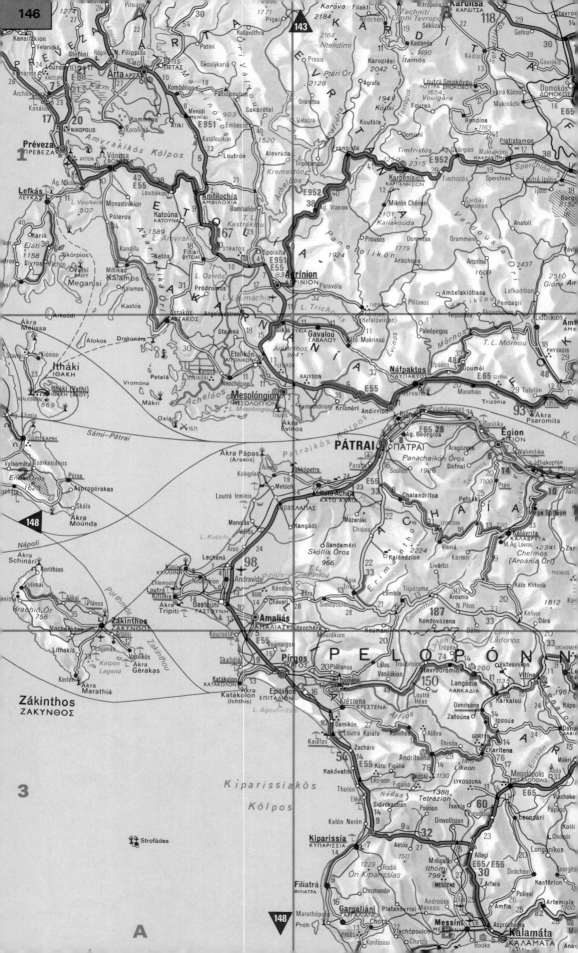

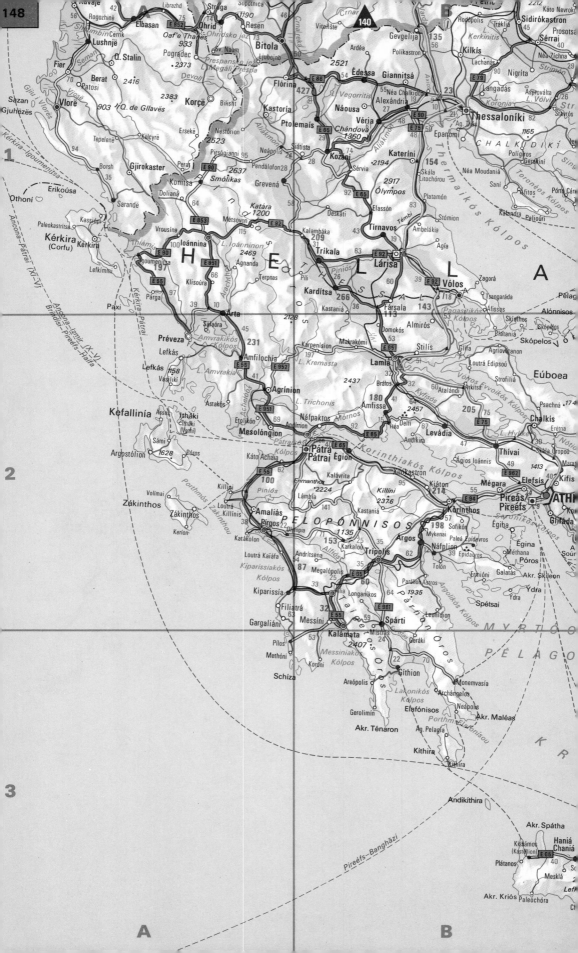

1

DONOSTIA/
S. SEBASTIÁN   Pasaia

Santoña   Laredo

Castro-Urdiales   **GETXO**

SANTURTZI   Leioa   Mungia   Bermeo

PORTUGALETE   Trapaga   **BILBO/BILBAO**   Gernika L.

BARAKALDO/BARACALDO   **BASAURI**   Galdakao   Zornotza

Ondarroa   Mutriku   Deba

Elgoibar   Eibar   Ermua   Azkoitia   Azpeitia   Andoain

Laudio   Durango   Bergara   Zumarraga   Urnieta   Hernani

Arrasate   Legazpi   Ordizia   Tolosa

Amurrio   Aretxabaleta   Oñati   Beasain   Lazkao

Urduña   Alsasua

GASTEIZ VITORIA

Pto. de Orduña   Murgia

Medina de Pomar   Estella

Miranda de E.   Los Arcos

Briviesca   Haro   LOGROÑO   Lodosa   Lerín

Belorado   Sto. Domingo de la C.   Nájera   Mendavia   **154**

BURGOS   Ezcaray   Arnedo

Calahorra

Puerto de Piquetas

Soria

ARANDA de DUERO   El Burgo de Osma   **161**

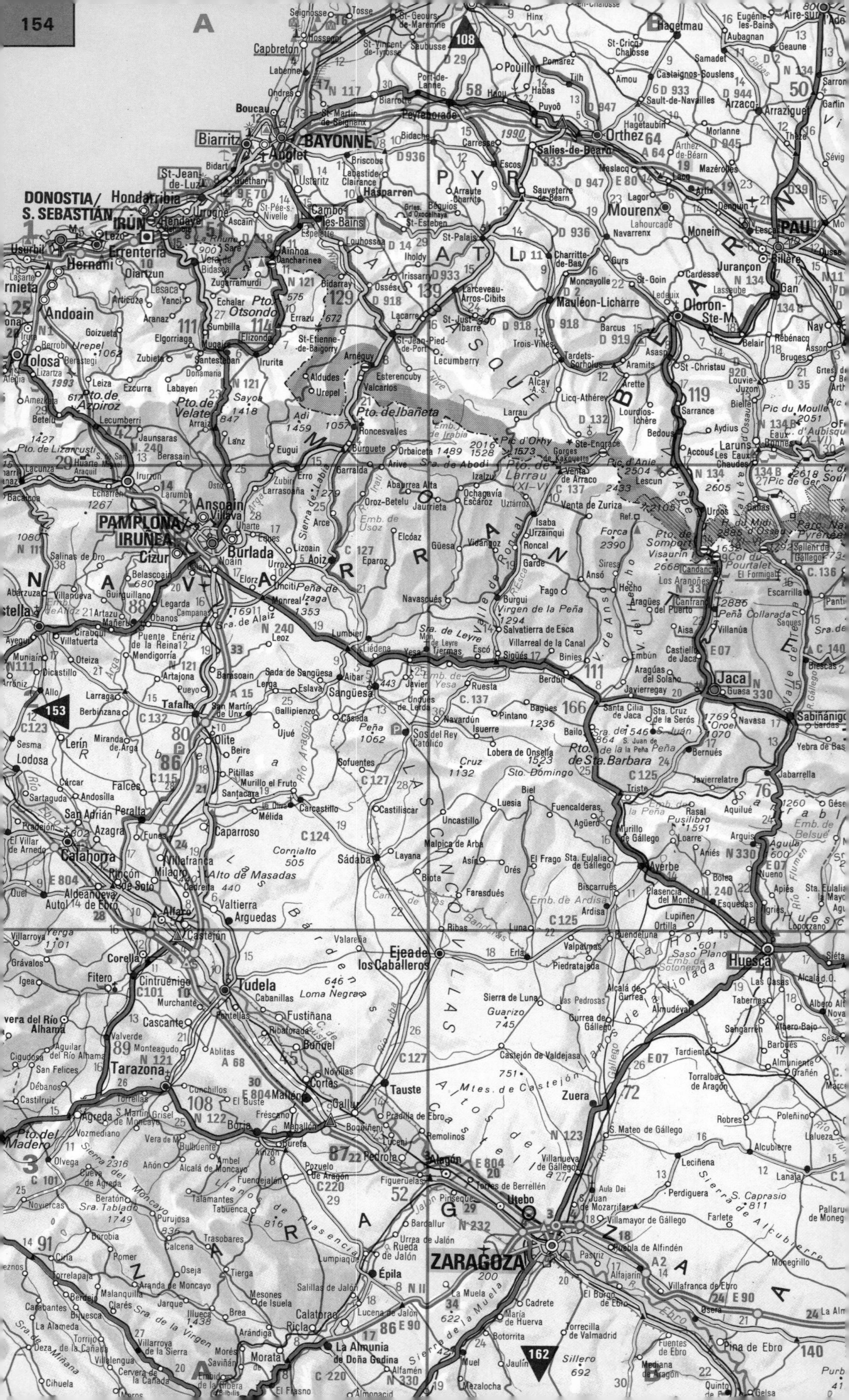
108
153
162
Capbreton
Hossegor
Seignosse
Tosse
St-Geours-de-Maremne
St-Vincent-de-Tyrosse
Saubusse
Labenne
Ondres
Boucau
St-Martin-de-Seignanx
Biarritz
BAYONNE
Anglet
Bidart
St-Jean-de-Luz
Guéthary
Hondarribia
DONOSTIA/ S. SEBASTIÁN
IRÚN
Hendaye
Urrugne
Ascain
St-Pée-s.-Nivelle
Cambo-les-Bains
Espelette
Ustaritz
Hasparren
Briscous
Labastide-Clairance
Bidache
Peyrehorade
Port-de-Lanne
Pouillon
Pomarez
Habas
Tilh
Puyoô
Orthez
Salies-de-Béarn
Hagetmau
Amou
Castaignos-Souslens
Sault-de-Navailles
Arzacq-Arraziguet
Geaune
Aire-sur-l'Adour
Aubagnan
Samadet
Morlanne
Arthez-de-Béarn
Mazerolles
Lacq
Artix
Mourenx
Lagor
Navarrenx
Monein
Lescar
PAU
Billère
Jurançon
Gan
Nay
Oloron-Ste-M.
Sauveterre-de-Béarn
St-Palais
Mauléon-Licharre
Tardets-Sorholus
Arette
Lescun
Bedous
Laruns
Eaux-Bonnes
Pic du Midi d'Ossau
Col du Pourtalet
Sallent de Gállego
Candanchú
Canfranc
Jaca
Sabiñánigo
Huesca
Ayerbe
Zuera
ZARAGOZA
Utebo
Alagón
Pedrola
Gallur
Tauste
Ejea de los Caballeros
Sádaba
Sos del Rey Católico
Sangüesa
Lumbier
Aoiz
PAMPLONA IRUÑEA
Burlada
Villava
Ansoain
Cizur
Noáin
Puente la Reina
Estella
Tafalla
Olite
Peralta
Calahorra
Azagra
San Adrián
Lodosa
Lerín
Falces
Caparroso
Villafranca
Milagro
Rincón de Soto
Alfaro
Castejón
Arguedas
Valtierra
Corella
Cintruénigo
Fitero
Tudela
Cascante
Tarazona
Ágreda
Borja
Mallén
Cortes
Magallón
Ablitas
Buñuel
Fustiñana
Ribaforada
Épila
La Almunia de Doña Godina
Calatorao
Ricla
Illueca
Brea
Morata
La Muela
Cadrete
María de Huerva
Pina de Ebro
Villafranca de Ebro
Alfajarín
Pastriz
Puebla de Alfindén
Villamayor de Gállego
San Juan de Mozarrifar
Villanueva de Gállego
Almudévar
Tardienta
Grañén
Alcubierre
Leciñena
Perdiguera
Monegrillo
Tolosa
Andoain
Hernani
Errenteria
Lezo
Usurbil
Lecumberri
Irurzun
Echarren
Huarte
Alsasua
Elizondo
Sumbilla
Santesteban
Zugarramurdi
Ainhoa
Dancharinea
Bidarray
Ossès
St-Jean-Pied-de-Port
Arnéguy
Valcarlos
Pto. de Ibañeta
Roncesvalles
Burguete
Esterencuby
Larrau
Pic d'Orhy
Ochagavía
Ezcároz
Isaba
Roncal
Burgui
Ansó
Hecho
Pto. de Somport
Villanúa
Yesa
Liédena
Javier
Sigüés
Berdún
Puente la Reina de Jaca
Pto. de Sta. Barbara
Biel
Luesia
Uncastillo
Murillo de Gállego
Loarre
Bolea
Esquedas
Las Casas
Sierra de Luna
Castejón de Valdejasa
Mtes. de Castejón
Sierra de Alcubierre
Loma Negra
Sierra del Moncayo
Llanos de Plasencia
PAYS BASQUE
PYRÉNÉES ATLANTIQUES
BÉARN
NAVARRA
ARAGÓN
ZARAGOZA
LAS BARDENAS
LAS CINCO VILLAS
ALTOS DE CASTELLAR
E 80
E 70
E 07
E 804
E 90
A 15
A 64
A 68
A 2
N 121
N 240
N 330
N 232
N 122
N 123
N 111
N 134
N II

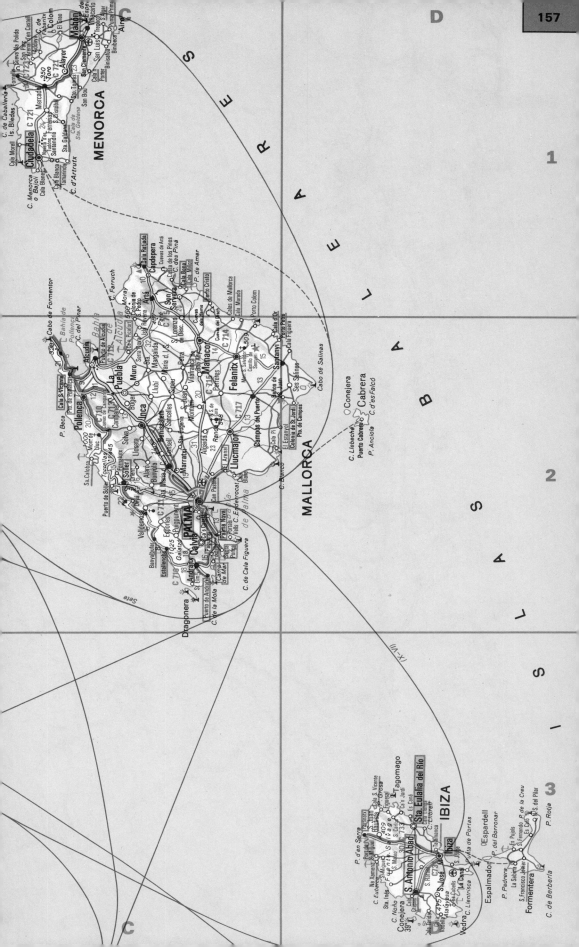

150
164
1
2
3
Verín
Chaves
Braga
Guimarães
Viana do Castelo
Póvoa de Varzim
Vila do Conde
Leça da Palmeira
Matosinhos
PORTO
VILA NOVA DE GAIA
Gondomar
Valongo
Espinho
S. João da Madeira
Ovar
Aveiro
Ílhavo
Vagos
Mira
Águeda
Viseu
Vila Real
Régua
Lamego
Amarante
Penafiel
Felgueiras
Fafe
Barcelos
Esposende
Ponte de Lima
Ponte da Barca
Arcos de Valdevez
Caminha
Montalegre
Boticas
Vila Pouca de Aguiar
Murça
Mondim de Basto
Celorico de Basto
Cabeceiras de Basto
Peneda-Gerês
Serra das Alturas
Serra do Marão
Marco de Canaveses
Baião
Resende
Cinfães
Cast. de Paiva
Arouca
Oliveira de Azeméis
Vale de Cambra
S. Pedro do Sul
Vouzela
Oliveira de Frades
Tondela
Mangualde
Nelas
Celorico da Beira
Guarda
Trancoso
Moimenta da Beira
Sernancelhe
Tarouca
Castro Daire
Sátão
Penalva do Castelo
Fornos de Algedres
Gouveia
Seia
Manteigas
Torre
1991
Covilhã
Fundão
Belmonte
Serra da Estrela
Serra da Gardunha
Castelo Branco
Oliveira do Hospital
Tábua
Arganil
Lousã
Coimbra
Mealhada
Luso
Buçaco
Penacova
Mortágua
Sta. Comba Dão
Anadia
Cantanhede
Tocha
Figueira da Foz
Montemor-o-Velho
Condeixa a Nova
Soure
Penela
Miranda do Corvo
Pombal
Ansião
Figueiró dos Vinhos
Pedrógão Grande
Castanheira de Pera
Pampilhosa
Sertã
Oleiros
Proença a Nova
Sobreira Formosa
Vila Velha de Rodão
Sarzedas
Alvaiázere
Leiria
Marinha Grande
Batalha
Vila Nova de Ourém
Ferreira do Zêzere
Serra do Caramulo
Serra da Lousã
Barragem do Cabril
Ria d'Aveiro
Mondego
Rio Tejo
DOURO
MINHO
TRÁS-OS-MONTES
BEIRA

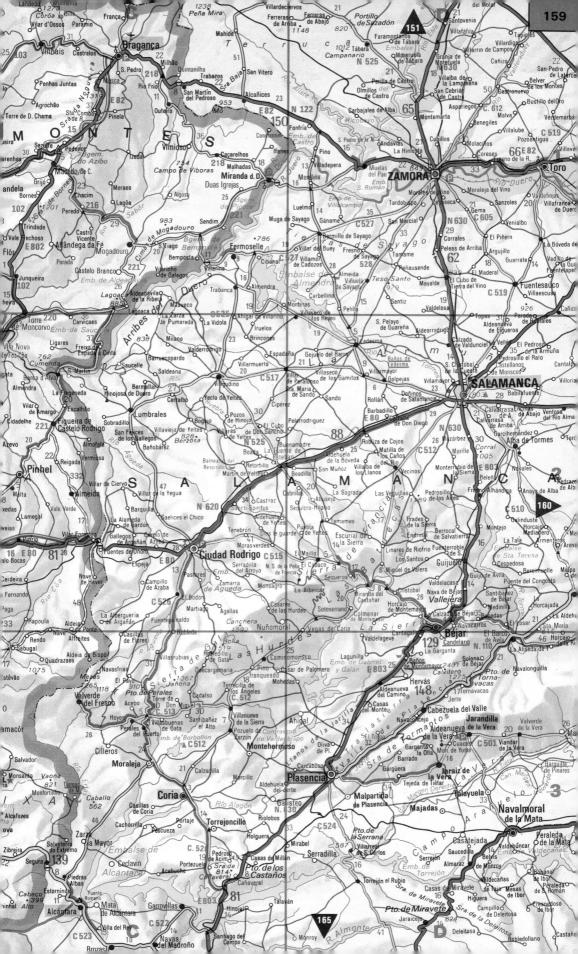

153
Soria
S O R I A
El Burgo de Osma
Almazán
Sigüenza
G U A D A L A J A R A
Guadalajara
Alcalá de Henares
Torrejón de Ardoz
Arganda
Chinchón
Colmenar de Oreja
Villarejo de Salvanés
Aranjuez
Ocaña
Tarancón
Huete
Cuenca
Arcos de Jalón
Medinaceli
Molina de Aragón
Ariza
Pto. de Maranchón
Pto. del Madero
Pto. de Lubia
Pto. de Somosierra
Pto. de Cabrejas
Pto. de Tórdiga
Pastrana
Brihuega
Sacedón
Priego
S. Lorenzo de la Parrilla
Corral de Almaguer
Quintanar de la Orden
162
167
N 234
N 122
N 111
N II
N 320
N 400
N III
N 301
E 90
E 901

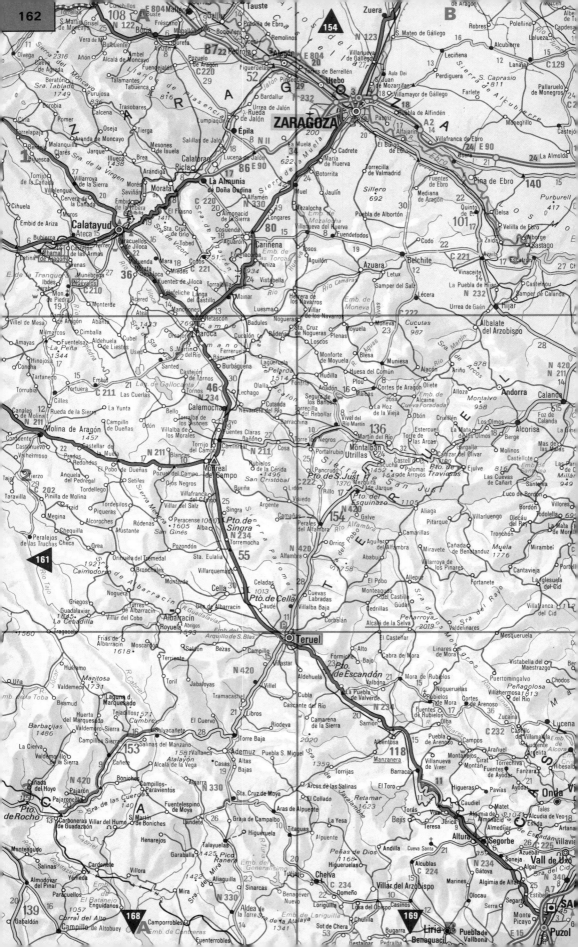

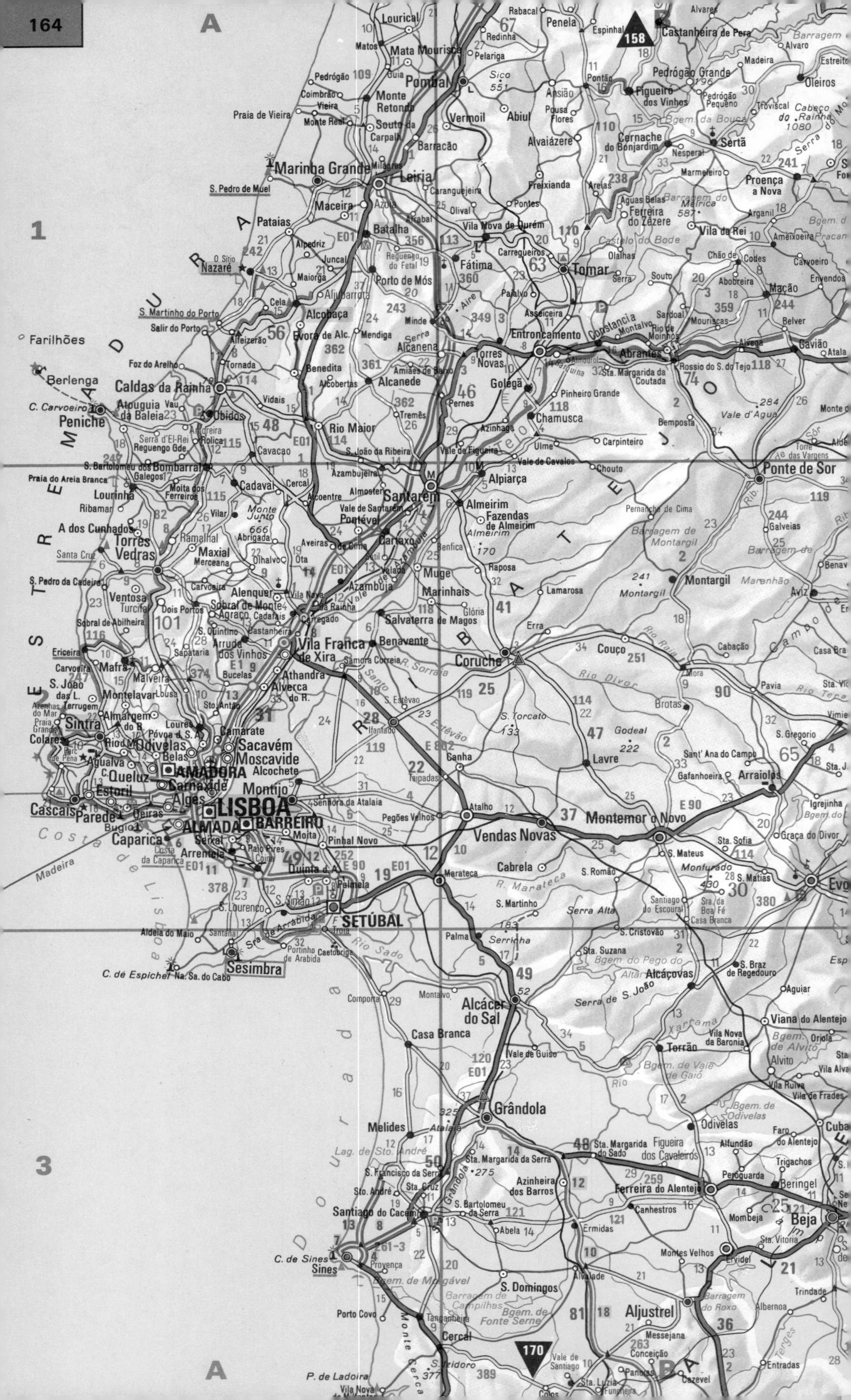

A

1

2

3

Farilhões
Berlenga
C. Carvoeiro
Peniche
Praia do Areia Branca
Lourinhã
Ribamar
A dos Cunhados
Santa Cruz
S. Pedro da Cadeira
Ventosa
Sobral de Abilheira
Ericeira
Carvoeira
Mafra
S. João das L.
Montelavar
Praia Grande
Colares
Sintra
Aguaiva
C. Queluz
Estoril
Cascais
Parede
Oeiras
Algés
Caparica
Costa da Caparica
Arrentela
Aldeia do Maio
C. de Espichel
Sesimbra
Na. Sa. do Cabo

Nazaré
O Sítio
Marinha Grande
S. Pedro de Muel
Maceira
Pataias
Alpedriz
Cela
Alcobaça
S. Martinho do Porto
Salir do Porto
Foz do Arelho
Caldas da Rainha
Atouguia da Baleia
Óbidos
Serra d'El-Rei
Reguengo Gde.
Vidais
Rio Maior
Bombarral
Cadaval
Rolliça
Vilar
Monte Junto
Ramalhal
Maxial
Merceana
Olhalvo
Dois Portos
Torres Vedras
Turcifal
Sapataria
Malveira
Almargem do B.
Belas
Odivelas
Amadora
Carnaxide
Oeiras
Almada
Barreiro
Seixal
Moita
Pinhal Novo
Palmela
Quinta d.A.
S. Simão
S. Lourenço
Setúbal
Tróia
Santana
Sa. da Arrábida
Portinho de Arrábida
Caetobriga

Pombal
Leiria
Batalha
Porto de Mós
Fátima
Alcanena
Tomar
Abrantes
Entroncamento
Santarém
Torres Novas
Golegã
Chamusca
Alpiarça
Almeirim
Cartaxo
Azambuja
Alenquer
Vila Franca de Xira
Benavente
Coruche
Montemor o Novo
Vendas Novas
Alcochete
Montijo
Lisboa

Ponte de Sor
Montargil
Aviz
Montargil
Brotas
Lavre
Arraiolos
Évora
Alcáçovas
Viana do Alentejo
Alvito
Cuba
Beringel
Beja
Ferreira do Alentejo
Aljustrel
Grândola
Santiago do Cacém
Sines
C. de Sines
Alcácer do Sal
Casa Branca
Melides
Santo André
S. Domingos

ESTREMADURA

RIBATEJO

ALTO ALENTEJO

BAIXO ALENTEJO

Rio Tejo
Rio Sado
Rio Sorraia

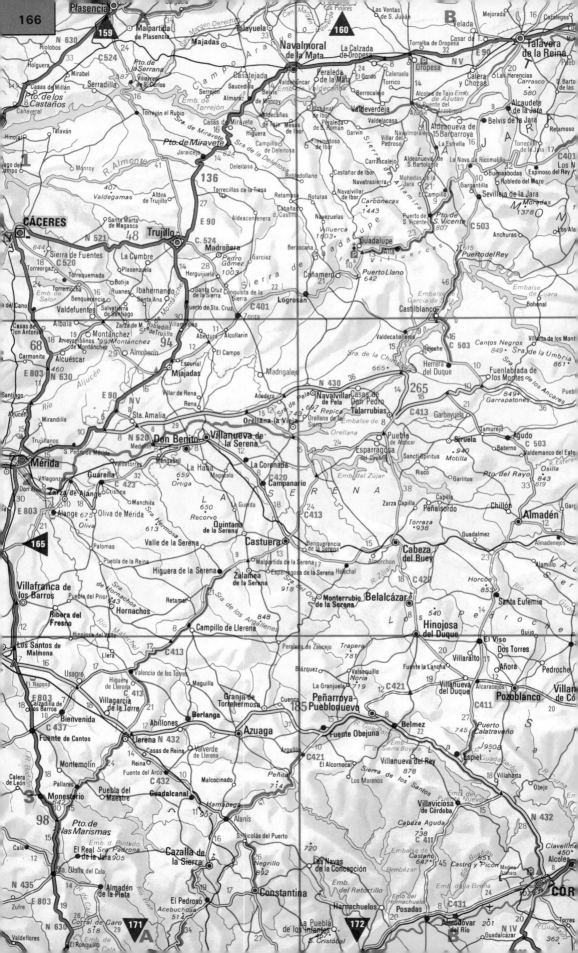

Lag. de Sto André
do Sado   dos Cavaleiros   13
Sta. Margarida da Serra   50
Trigachos   Orada
275   Peroguarda   S. Matias   B
S. Francisco da Serra   Azinheira   Beringel   164   Atalaia Gorda
Sto. André   Sta. Cruz   dos Barros   12   Ferreira do Alentejo   259   Mombeja   S. Matias   Baleizão   386
Santiago do Cacém   19   S. Bartolomeu   121   Canhestros   16   Brinches   265   Pias
13   8   da Serra   13   Ermidas   121   Abela 14   Beja   25 121   Vale de Vargo
7   261-3   Sta. Vitória   d   Quintos   E52   Serpa   260   Aldeia Nova
C. de Sines   Provença   22   120   Sta. Clara   Salvada   18   de S. Bento
Sines   Montes Velhos   13   de Louredo   21   S. Braz   Sta. Iria   Boa Vista   20   262
P. de Ladoira   Tanganheira   S. Domingos   Ervidel   Cabeça Gorda
Porto Covo   Barragem de   Alvalade   Albernoa   Trindade
Cercal   Campilhas   Bgem. de   81   19   Aljustrel   36
Fonte Serne   Messejana   122
1   P. de Ladoira   377   263   Vale de   Conceição   Entradas   28   Asinhal   Corte do Pinto
Vila Nova   55   389   S. Luís   Santiago 10   Sta. Luzia   Gazevel   S. Marcos   123   Alcaria Ruiva   122
de Milfontes   E01   Reliquias   Colos   Panoias   da Ataboeira   Alcaria Ruiva   Mina de
23   263   27   Castro Verde   32   S. Domingos
Fonte Bôa   Mte. da Rocha   20   123   Mértola   Sta. Ana
P. do Cavaleiro   Delheira   S. Martinho   Ourique   15   S. Barbara de Padrões   de Cambas   Moreanes
Vigia 393   das Amoreiras   Rosário   21   Sra. da Graça   267   Pomarão   El Granado
Odemira   Aldeia dos Palheiros   dos Padrões   28   S. Sebastião   122
12   Barragem de   Cola   2   dos Carros   Espirito Santo   Villa
Zambujeira do Mar   120   Sta. Clara   264   S. Sebastião   S. Miguel do Pinheiro   Alcoutim   de la
S. Teotónio   Sabóia   Sta. Clara-a-Velha   de Gomes Aires   Almodôvar   Quinta   54   de Guadiana
Odeceixe   335   Santana da Serra   S. Pedro de Solis 334   R. Vascão   Pereiro
29   Sra. de Mezquita   Sta. Clara a Nova   34   Martim Longo   25
30   266   74   Sta. Cruz   24   Cumeada   Pereirão   16   122
Mte. Clérigo   Destilhadeiro   S. Barnabé 589   Ameixial   Cumeada   Foupana
P. de Atalaia   48   dos Matões   S. Marcos   Mũ   124   Vaqueiros
Aljezur   Alferce   da Serra   361   Odeleite
7   E07   Monchique   14   Cachopo   Azinhal
Alfambras   Marmelete   Sra. de   Caldas de Monchique   Barranco do Velho   124   Peralva   Castro
Bgem. da   Monchique   541   Feiteira   Alcaria do Cume   Marim
Bravura   A   Casais   S. Bartolomeu   Salir   Zebro   525   397   E Vila Real de Sto.
Pontal   L   Porto   G   de Messines   Benafim   Barranco do Velho   40   E António   Ayar
Carrapateira   125   24   de Lagos   Alte   Querença   12   22   23   Cacela   Isla
27   Bensafrim   Mexilhoeira   270   A   S. Brás   Sta. Catarina da   E01
Bordeira   249   16   Grande   Tunes   Paderne   36   V   Loulé   de Alportel   Fonte do Bispo   18   P. de
Vila do Bispo   Odiáxere   Portimão   Estombar   Alcantarilha   Boliqueime   Sta. Bárbara   Sto. Estêvão   25   Conceição   S. Antonio
Barão de S. Miguel   Alvor   Lagoa   Porches   Gula   de Nexe   Estôi   Tavira
10   Burgau   Rudens   Praia   Ferragudo   Armação   Carvoeiro   10   Almansil   Pechão   Luz   Fuseta
Raposeira   Luz   Lagos   da Rocha   46   de Pera   Albufeira   Quarteira   S. João   Quelfes   30
2   Vila do Bispo   P. da Piedade   34   da Venda   Olhão
Sagres   Faro   8
A   C. de Sta. Maria
I   g   a   r   V
3   A   B

2

City Approach Maps

Plans de villes synoptiques

Stadtübersichtspläne

Piante di città sinottiche

Planos de ciudades sinópticos

To find the city approach map you want turn to the map on pages 2 and 3, locate the city and turn to the map number shown in the red circle.

Afin de trouver le plan de ville synoptique de la ville desirée, veuillez consulter la carte aux pages 2 et 3, localiser la ville, vous reporter aux numéros de la carte indiqués dans le cercle rouge.

Um die Zufahrtenkarte zur gewünschten Stadt zu finden, suchen Sie zuerst die Stadt auf der Uebersichtskarte Seiten 2-3 und schlagen nachher die Kartennummer auf, welche im roten Kreis angegeben ist.

Afine di trovare la carta dei accessi alla città desiderate, trovate la città sulla carta su pagine 2 e 3 e poi riforitevi alla carta del numero indicato nel cercio rosso.

Para encontrar el mapa de acceso a la ciudad deseada, vaya al mapa en las páginas 2 y 3, localice la ciudad y entonces busque el número del mapa mostrado dentro del círculo rojo.

Legend Légende Zeichenerklärung
Leggenda Signos Convencionales

Motorway
Autoroute
Autobahn
Autostrada
Autopista

Dual carriageway
Semi-autoroute
Autostrasse
Superstrada
Carretera de doble calzada

Through road
Route de transit
Durchgangsstrasse
Strada di attraversamento
Carretera de tránsito

Secondary road
Route de communication
Verbindungsstrasse
Strada di comunicazione
Carretera secundaria

Delft
Centr.
Motorway junction
Sortie d'autoroute
Autobahnanschluss
Uscita dall'autostrada
Salida de la autopista

E 81
A 107
647
Road numbering
Numérotage des routes
Strassennummerierung
Numerazione delle strade
Numeración de carreteras

Railway with station
Chemin de fer avec station
Eisenbahn mit Station
Ferrovia con stazione
Vía férrea con estación

Cable railway, cable car
Funiculaire, téléphérique
Stand- und Luftseilbahn
Funicolare, teleferica
Funicular, teleférico

Car ferry
Bac pour automobiles
Autofähre
Traghetto per automobili
Transbordador de automóviles

State frontier
Frontière d'Etat
Landesgrenze
Frontiera di stato
Frontera entre Estados

Urban area
Terrain bâti
Überbaute Fläche
Terreno costruito
Area urbana

City centre, old part of the city
Cité, vieille ville
Stadtkern, Altstadt
Nucleo urbano, città vecchia
Centro de la ciudad, parte vieja de la ciudad

Park
Parc
Parkanlage
Parco
Parque

Forest
Forêt
Wald
Bosco
Bosque

Nature reserve, country park
Réserve naturelle, parc naturel
Naturschutzgebiet, Naturpark
Regione protezione della natura
Reserva natural, Parque natural

Restricted area
Zone interdite
Sperrzone
Zona proibita
Area restringida

Place of interest
Curiosité
Sehenswurdigkeit
Curiosita
Lugar de interés

Viewpoint
Point de vue
Aussichtspunkt
Punto panoramico
Punto panorámico

Car park
Possibilité de stationnement (sélection)
Parkmoglichkeit (Auswahl)
Possibilita di parcheggio (selezione)
Parqueadero de automóviles

Motorway restaurant
Restaurant sur autoroute
Restaurant an Autobahn
Ristorante sull'autostrada
Restaurante en la autopista

Motorway petrol station
Station service sur autoroute
Tankstelle an Autobahn
Stazione di servizio sull'autostrada
Gasolinera en la autopista

Frontier crossing
Passage frontalier
Grenzübergang
Passaggio di frontiera
Cruce de fronteras

Airport
Aéroport
Flughafen
Aeroporto
Aeropuerto

Airfield
Aérodrome
Flugplatz
Campo di aviazione
Campo de aviación

Cathedral, church
Cathédrale, église
Kathedrale, Kirche
Cattedrale, chiesa
Catedral, iglesia

Pilgrimage church, monastery
Eglise de pèlerinage, couvent
Wallfahrtskirche, Kloster
Santuario, convento
Santuario, monasterio

Mosque
Mosquée
Moschee
Moschea
Mezquita

Castle
Château
Schloss, Burg
Castello
Castillo

Fort
Fort
Fort
Forte
Fuerte

Television tower
Tour de télévision
Fernsehturm
Torre di televisiva
Torre de televisión

Lighthouse
Phare
Leuchtturm
Faro
Faro

Windmill
Moulin à vent
Windmühle
Mulino a vento
Molino de viento

Stadium
Stade
Stadion
Stadio
Estadio

Motel
Môtel
Motel
Motel
Motel

Leisure park
Parc de loisirs
Freizeitpark
Parco di svaghi
Parque de diversiones

Zoological garden
Jardin zoologique
Zoologischer Garten
Giardino zoologico
Zoológico

Botanical garden
Jardin botanique
Botanischer Garten
Giardino botanico
Jardín botánico

Tourist information office
Poste d'information
Informationsstelle
Posto d'informazione
Oficina de información turística

Hammerfest
Kirkenes
Tromsø
Murmansk
Ivalo
Narvik
Kiruna
Gällivare
Rovaniemi
Archangelsk
Mo i Rana
Tornio
Belomorsk
Oulu
Umeå
Petrozavodsk
Vaasa
Trondheim
Jyväskylä
Sundsvall
Ålesund
Dombås
Tampere
Čerepovec
Turku
21 Helsinki
LENINGRAD
Lærdalsöyra
Bergen
Tallinn
Novgorod
Oslo
35
41
Karlstad
STOCKHOLM
Pskov
Kalinin
Stavanger
Norrköping
MOSKVA
Kristiansand
Uddevalla
Göteborg
Jönköping
20
Riga
Vjazma
Frederikshavn
Daugavpils
Vitebsk
Smolensk
Kalmar
Århus
Helsingborg
KØBENHAVN
24
Malmö
Kaliningrad
(Königsberg)
Kaunas
wcastle
Odense
MINSK
Słupsk
(Stolp)
Gdańsk
(Danzig)
Gomel
ull
Kiel
Rostock
ester
Białystock
18 HAMBURG
Toruń
Groningen
Szczecin
(Stettin)
WARSZAWA
Bremen
Brest
Amsterdam
2
BERLIN
7
Poznań
KIJEV
Den Haag
11
Hannover
Rovno
Magdeburg
Łódź
DON
40 Rotterdam
Essen
Leipzig
Lublin
Calais
3 Antwerpen
Kassel
Wrocław
(Breslau)
Lvov
ghton
10
23 Köln
Dresden
Katowice
BRUXELLES
Kraków
Krivoj Rog
Bonn
17
39 PRAHA
Ostrava
Le Havre
Luxembourg
Frankfurt/M.
Plzeň
26
Brno
36
PARIS
Karlsruhe
Bratislava
ODESSA
Strasbourg
Stuttgart
WIEN
43
Bacău
St-Dizier
BUDAPEST
Linz
MÜNCHEN
31
8
Cluj
urs
42 Salzburg
Basel 4
Zürich
15
45
22
Innsbruck
Graz
Galati
Pécs
Arad
9 Bern
Bolzano/
Bozen
Ljubljana
Ploești
Constanța
Clermont-F.
16 Genève
Zagreb
Novi Sad
27
MILANO
30
Venezia
Trieste
5
BUCUREȘTI
Lyon
Grenoble
Rijeka
Beograd
Craiova
Verona
Varna
44
Banja Luka
Veliko Tărnovo
TORINO
19
Bologna
Burgas
Genova
Niš
Sofija
Nîmes
ulouse
Split
34
14
Ancona
İSTANBUL
Nice
Firenze
Plovdiv
32
Livorno
Marseille
Perugia
Bastia
Skopje
Pescara
37
Kavála
Bandırma
Tirana
6 BARCELONA
ROMA
Thessaloníki
Foggia
33
Bari
NAPOLI
Brindisi
Ioánnina
Lárisa
Sassari
Palma
Cagliari
Catanzaro
1 ATHINAI
Pátrai
Korinthos
38 Messina
Réggio di Calábria
Palermo
Catánia
Béjaïa
(Bougie)
Bizerte
ALGER
Annaba
Iráklion
Tunis
am
Constantine
Valetta
Sousse

PÉRAMA   SKARAMANGÁS   KÓRINTHOS

• 468

E g á l e o   Ó r o s   Moní Dafní

JÓNII NÍSI

N. Ikonio

Amfiali   Keratsíni

Shisto

ÉGINA

Neapoli   Haidári

Drapetsóna

Ág. Varvára

Tampouria   Koridalos

KRITI

Pireás

Níkea

Ág. Vasilios

Kphtika   Kamínia   Ág. Ioánnis Rentís   Egáleo

NÓTII, SPORÁDES, RÓDOS

S a l ó n i k o s

Mosháto

Távros

Votanikós   Kolo

Roúf

K ó l p o s

Kallithéa

Keramikós

Agorá

P. Fáliro

Pláka

KYKLÁDES

Akrópolis

Zápio

N. Smírni

Dafni

Pagráti

LÉSVOS, CHIOS

Kalamáki

Imitós

Kesar

Ág. Dimítrios

Álimos

Vironas

Ilioúpolis

Aerodrómio
Ellinikó

Ellinikó   Argiroúpoli   Moní Karéa

Soúrmena   • 765

Terpsithea   I m i t ó

SOÚNIO

Glifáda

ASPRÓPIRGOS   FILÍ

0 500 1000 1500 2000 2500 m

omata

Kipoúpoli

Áno Liósio

Palatiani

Petroúpoli

Kamatera

Ág. Ierotheos

Anthoúpoli

Zefiri

Peristéri

Aharnés

ATHÍNA

Ág. Anargiri

Kok. Milos

N. Filadelfia

E 92

N. Halkidona

VARIBOMBI THESSALONÍKI

Patísia

Metamorfosi

N1

Kipseli

Galátsi

N. Ionía

giko

Iráklio

Likovrissi

Poligono

Kifisiá

Kalogreza

Gizi

Olympía
Stádio

Filothéi

Maroúsi

Psihikó

N. Filothéi

N. Psihikó

Kefalari

Goúdi

K. Halándri

Halándri

Holargós

Mellisia

Vrilissia

Ág. Paraskevi

sariani

Gargitos

026

Stavros

Glika Nera

PENDÉLI   PENDÉLI   PENDÉLI

5

Amsterdam ②

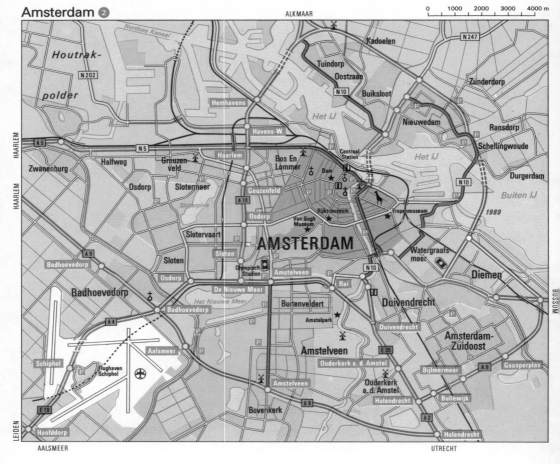

Antwerpen ③ Antwerp

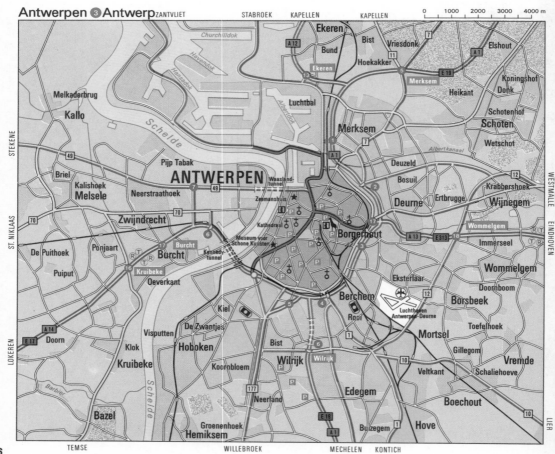

6

Basel ④ Basle

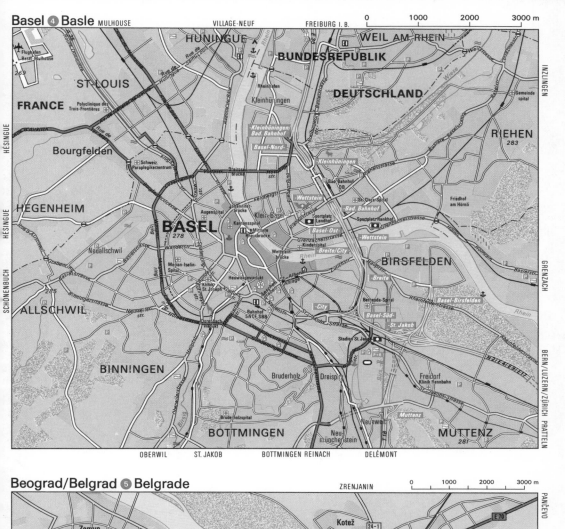

MULHOUSE VILLAGE-NEUF FREIBURG I. B.

0 1000 2000 3000 m

HUNINGUE
WEIL AM RHEIN
BUNDESREPUBLIK
DEUTSCHLAND
ST-LOUIS
Polyclinique des
Trois-Frontières
FRANCE
RIEHEN
283
Bourgfelden
Kleinhüningen
Kleinhüningen
Bad. Bahnhof
Basel-Nord
Schweiz.
Paraplegikerzentrum
Kleinhüningen
HEGENHEIM
Bad. Bahnhof
St. Clara-Spital
Friedhof
am Hörnli
Wettstein
Bad. Bahnhof
Augenspital
Johanniter-
brücke
Sportplatz
Landhof
Merian-Iselin-
Spital
Kantonsspital
Mittlere
Rheinbrücke
Basel-Ost
BASEL
Klein-Basel
278
Wettstein
Wettstein-
brücke
BIRSFELDEN
Breite/City
Heuwaageviadukt
Nedallschwil
Breite
ALLSCHWIL
Klinik
St. Joseph
City
Betnesda-Spital
Basel-Birsfelden
Dorenbach
Viadukt
Bahnhof
SNCF SBB
Basel-Süd
St. Jakob
BINNINGEN
Stadion St. Jakob
Bruderholz
Dreispitz
Freidorf
Klinik Rennbahn
Bruderholzspital
Muttenz
BOTTMINGEN
Neu-
münchenstein
Neuewelt
MUTTENZ
281

OBERWIL ST. JAKOB BOTTMINGEN REINACH DELÉMONT

HÉSINGUE
HÉSINGUE
SCHÖNENBUCH
GRENZACH
BERN/LUZERN/ZÜRICH PRATTELN
INZLINGEN

Beograd/Belgrad ⑤ Belgrade

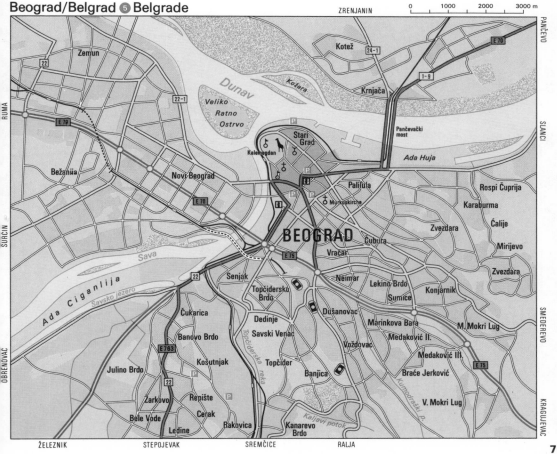

ZRENJANIN

0 1000 2000 3000 m

Zemun
Kotež
Dunav
Kožara
Krnjača
Veliko
Ratno
Ostrvo
Bežanija
Pančevački
most
Novi Beograd
Stari
Grad
Ada Huja
Kalemegdan
Rospi Ćuprija
Palilula
Karaburma
Murkuskirche
Ćalije
Zvezdara
Mirijevo
BEOGRAD
Ćubura
Zvezdara
Vračar
Senjak
Neimar
Lekino Brdo
Konjarnik
Topčidersko
Brdo
Šumice
Čukarica
Dedinje
Dušanovac
Marinkova Bara
M. Mokri Lug
Banovo Brdo
Savski Venac
Medaković II.
Ada Ciganlija
Julino Brdo
Košutnjak
Topčider
Voždovac
Medaković III.
Banjica
Braće Jerković
Žarkovo
Repište
Cerak
Bele Vode
Rakovica
Kanarevo
Brdo
V. Mokri Lug
Ledine

ŽELEZNIK STEPOJEVAK SREMČICE RALJA

RUMA
SURČIN
OBRENOVAC
PANČEVO
SLANCI
SMEDEREVO
KRAGUJEVAC

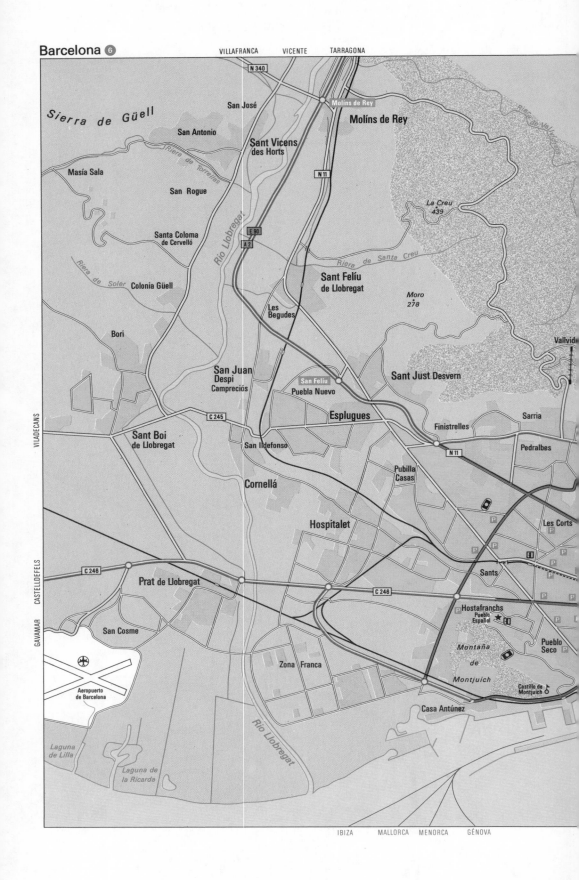

Barcelona ⑥

N 340

Sierra de Güell

San José

San Antonio

Molíns de Rey
Molíns de Rey

Sant Vicens
des Horts

Masía Sala

San Rogue

N 11

Riera de Torrellas

Rio Llobregat

La Creu
439

Santa Coloma
de Cervelló

E 90

A 2

Riera de Santa Creu

Riera de Soler   Colonia Güell

Sant Felíu
de Llobregat

Moro
278

Les
Begudes

Bori

Vallvid

San Juan
Despi
Campreciós

San Felíu

Puebla Nuevo

Sant Just Desvern

C 245

Esplugues

Sarria

Sant Boi
de Llobregat

San Ildefonso

Finistrelles

Pedralbes

N 11

Cornellá

Pubilla
Casas

VILADECANS

Hospitalet

Les Corts

P

P   P   P

P

CASTELLDEFELS

C 246

Sants

GAVAMAR

C 246

P   P

P

Prat de Llobregat

Hostafranchs
Pueblo
Español   ★

San Cosme

**Pueblo
Seco**   P

Montaña

Zona Franca

de

⊕
Aeropuerto
de Barcelona

Montjuich

Castillo de
Montjuich

Casa Antúnez

*Laguna
de Lilla*

*Laguna de
la Ricarda*

Rio Llobregat

8

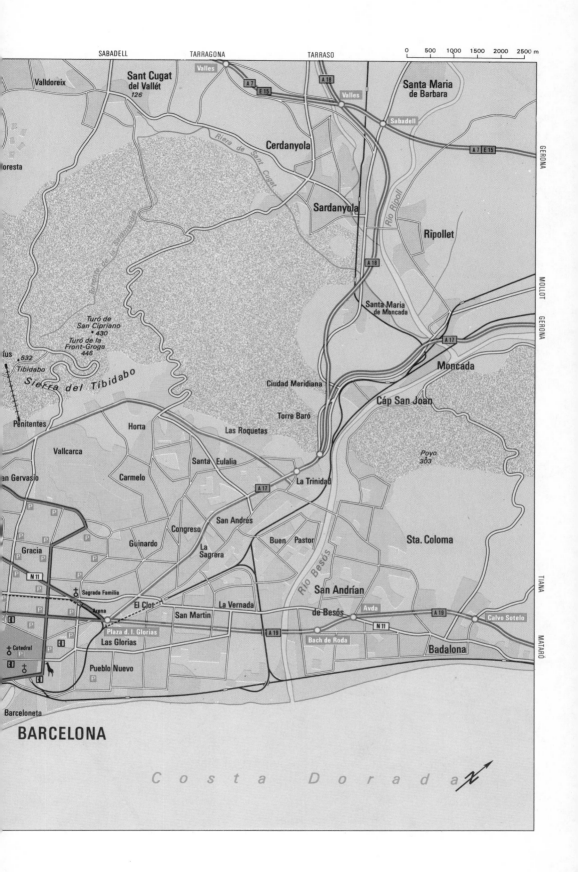

SABADELL   TARRAGONA   TARRASO

0   500   1000   1500   2000   2500 m

Valldoreix

Sant Cugat
del Vallét
126

Valles

A 7
E 15

A 18

Santa Maria
de Barbara

oresta

Riera de Sant Cugat

Cerdanyola

Valles

Sabadell

A 7 E 15

GERONA

Sardanyola

Rio Ripoll

Ripollet

Turó de
San Cipriano
· 430
Turó de la
Front-Groga
446

Santa Maria
de Moncada

A 18

MOLLOT

GERONA

ius · 532

Tibidabo

Sierra del Tibidabo

Ciudad Meridiana

A 17

Moncada

Penitentes

Horta

Torre Baró

Cáp San Joan

Vallcarca

Las Roquetas

Poyo
303

an Gervasio

Santa Eulalia

A 17

La Trinidad

Carmelo

San Andrés

Sta. Coloma

P

Congreso

Guinardo

Buen Pastor

Gracia

P

La
Sagrera

P

N 11

Rio Besós

P

Sagrada Familia

San Andrían

P

El Clot

La Vernada

de Besós

Avda

A 19

Calvo Sotelo

Arena

San Martin

N 11

Catedral

Plaza d. I. Glorias

Las Glorias

A 19

Bach de Roda

Badalona

Pueblo Nuevo

P

Barceloneta

BARCELONA

Costa Dorada

TIANA

MATARÓ

GERONA

9

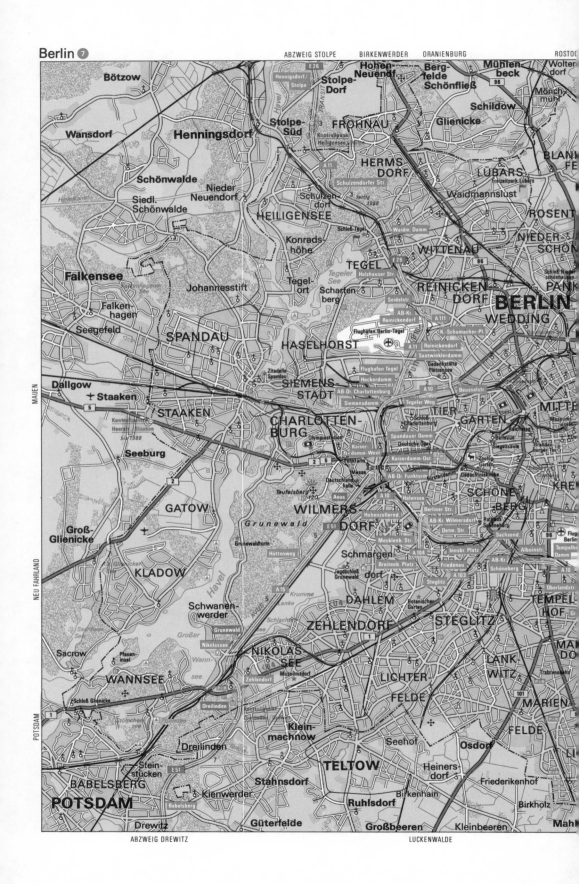

ABZWEIG STOLPE   BIRKENWERDER   ORANIENBURG   ROSTOC

Bötzow

Wandsdorf

Henningsdorf

Schönwalde

Nieder Neuendorf

Siedl. Schönwalde

Falkensee

Falken- hagen

Seegefeld

Johannesstift

SPANDAU

Dallgow   + Staaken

Seeburg

STAAKEN

Groß- Glienicke

GATOW

KLADOW

Sacrow

WANNSEE

BABELSBERG

POTSDAM

Drewitz

Hohen- Neuendf.

Stolpe- Dorf

Stolpe- Süd

Hennigsdorf/ Stolpe

Schulzendorf- str.

HEILIGENSEE

Konrads- höhe

Tegel- ort

Scharfen- berg

Bergfelde Schönfließ

FROHNAU

HERMS DORF

Schildow

Glienicke

Mühlen- beck

Wolter- dorf

Mönch- müh

Waidmannslust

LÜBARS

Tegeler See

Holzhauser Str.

Schloß-Tegel

TEGEL

WITTENAU

Flughafen Berlin-Tegel

HASELHORST

Zitadelle Spandau

SIEMENS- STADT

Flughafen Tegel

Heckerdamm

Siemensdamm

Tegeler Weg

Olympiastadion

CHARLOTTEN- BURG

Kaiser- damm-West

Funkturm

Messe

Deutschland- halle

Teufelsberg

Grunewald

Grunewaldturm

Hüttenweg

WILMERS DORF

Hohenzollernd

Schmargen- dorf

Jagdschloß Grunewald

DAHLEM

Schwanen- werder

Grunewald

Nikolassee

Großer Wann- see

Zehlendorf

NIKOLAS SEE

Museumsdorf

ZEHLENDORF

LICHTER FELDE

Dreilinden

Stein- stücken

Schloß Glienicke

Pfauen- insel

Babelsberg

Kienwerder

Dreilinden

Klein- machnow

Stahnsdorf

TELTOW

Güterfelde

Ruhlsdorf

Seehof

Osdorf

Heiners- dorf

Birkenhain

Großbeeren

REINICKEN DORF

BERLIN

WEDDING

PANK

MITTE

TIER GARTEN

Deutsche Oper

Zoolog. Garten

SCHÖNE BERG

Rathaus Schöneberg

Friedenau

Steglitz

STEGLITZ

Botanischer Garten

TEMPEL HOF

LANK WITZ

MARIEN

FELDE

Friederikenhof

Birkholz

Mah

NIEDER SCHÖN

ROSENT

BLAN FE

KRE

Flugh Berlin

Tempelho Damm

Oberlandstr.

Alboinstr.

MA DO

Trabrennbahn

Schloß Charlottenburg

AB-Dr. Charlottenburg

AB-Kr. Funkturm

AB-Dr. Funkturm

Halensee

Berliner Str.

AB-Kr. Wilmersdorf

Detm. Str.

Mecklenb. Str.

Breitenb. Platz

Innsbr. Platz

AB-Kr. Schöneberg

Sachsend.

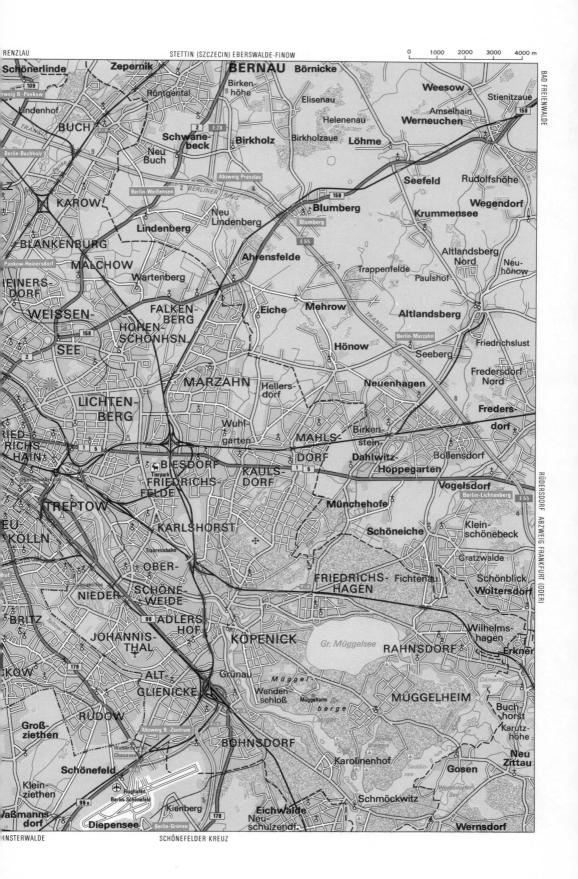

0   1000   2000   3000   4000 m

BAD FREIENWALDE

Schönerlinde

Zepernik

BERNAU   Börnicke

zweig B-Pankow   109

Röntgental

Birken-
höhe

Weesow

Stienitzaue

Lindenhof

158

BUCH

Neu
Buch

Schwane-
beck

Birkholz

Elisenau

Helenenau

Amselhain

Werneuchen

Berlin-Buchholz

2   E28

Birkholzaue

Löhme

KAROW

Berlin-Weißensee

Abzweig Prenzlau

2   BERLINER RING

158

Seefeld

Rudolfshöhe

Blumberg

Wegendorf

Neu
Lindenberg

Blumberg

Krummensee

BLANKENBURG

Lindenberg

E55

Ahrensfelde

Altlandsberg
Nord

Neu-
hönow

Pankow-Heinersdorf

MALCHOW

Wartenberg

Trappenfelde

Paulshof

EINERS-
DORF

FALKEN-
BERG

Eiche

Mehrow

Altlandsberg

WEISSEN-

HOHEN-
SCHÖNHSN.

158

TRANSIT

Berlin-Marzahn

Friedrichslust

2

SEE

Hönow

Seeberg

Fredersdorf
Nord

MARZAHN

Hellers-
dorf

Neuenhagen

8

LICHTEN-
BERG

Wuhl-
garten

Birken-
stein

Freders-

IED
RICHS-
HAIN

1   5

MAHLS-
DORF

dorf

BIESDORF

Tierpark

KAULS-
DORF

Dahlwitz-
Hoppegarten

Bollensdorf

TREPTOW

FRIEDRICHS-
FELDE

1   5

Münchehofe

Vogelsdorf

Berlin-Lichtenberg   E55

EU
KÖLN

KARLSHORST

Schöneiche

Klein-
schönebeck

Trabrennbahn

Gratzwalde

NIEDER-

OBER-
SCHÖNE-
WEIDE

FRIEDRICHS-
HAGEN

Fichtenau

Schönblick

Woltersdorf

BRITZ

96

ADLERS-
HOF

Wilhelms-
hagen

KOW

JOHANNIS-
THAL

KÖPENICK

Gr. Müggelsee

RAHNSDORF

Erkner

179

ALT-
GLIENICKE

Grünau

Müggel

Dämeritz

RUDOW

Abzweig B.-Zentrum

Wenden-
schloß

Müggelturm

berge

MÜGGELHEIM

Buch-
horst

Groß-
ziethen

Wasser-
Chaussee

Karutz-
höhe

Schönefeld

BOHNSDORF

Seddin-
see

Gosen

Neu
Zittau

Klein-
ziethen

96a

Flughafen
Berlin-Schönefeld

Karolinenhof

Wernsdorfer
See

aßmanns-
dorf

Diepensee

Berlin-Grünau

Kienberg

179

Eichwalde

Neu-
schulzendf.

Schmöckwitz

Wernsdorf

RÜDERSDORF   ABZWEIG FRANKFURT (ODER)

11

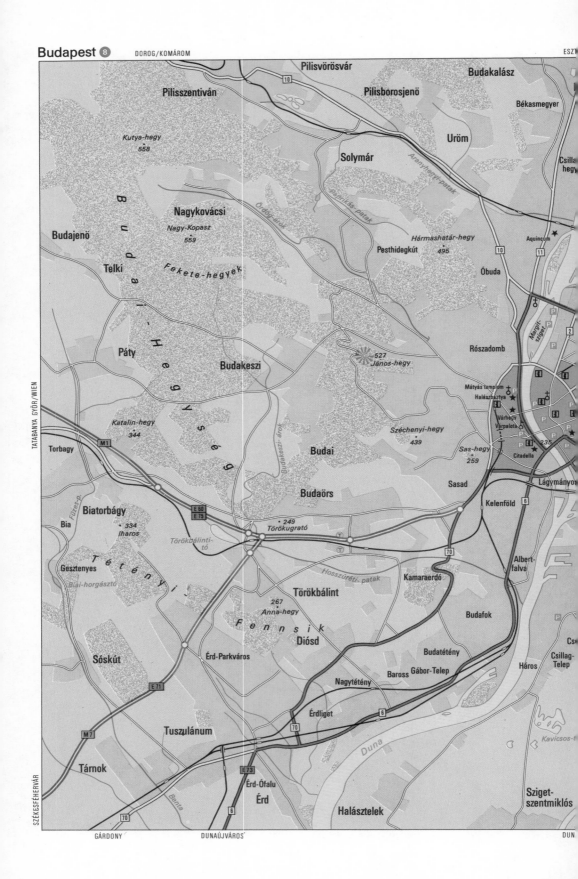

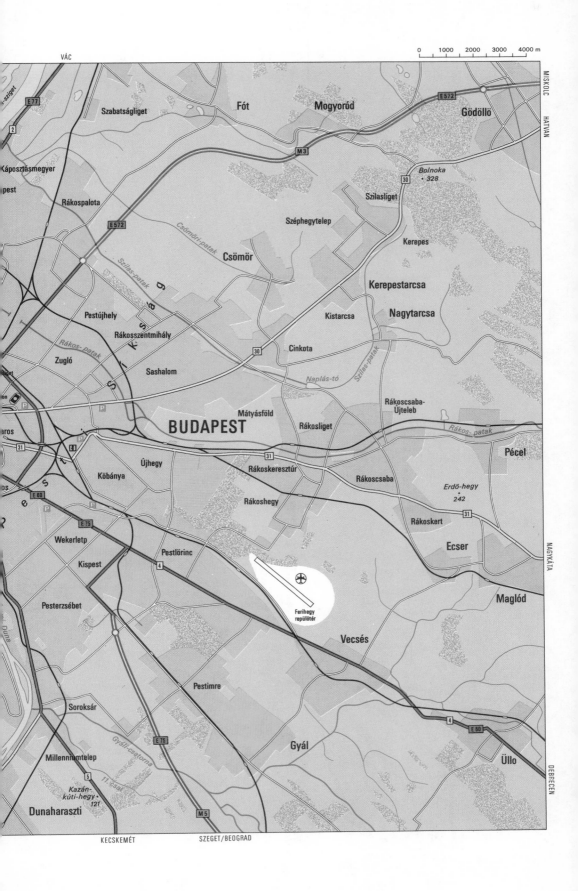

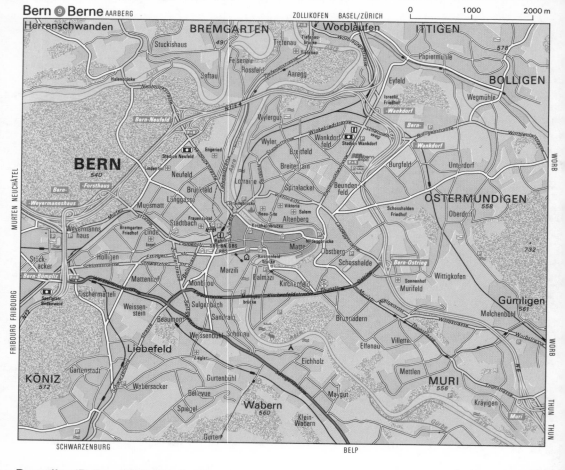

Bern ⑨ Berne

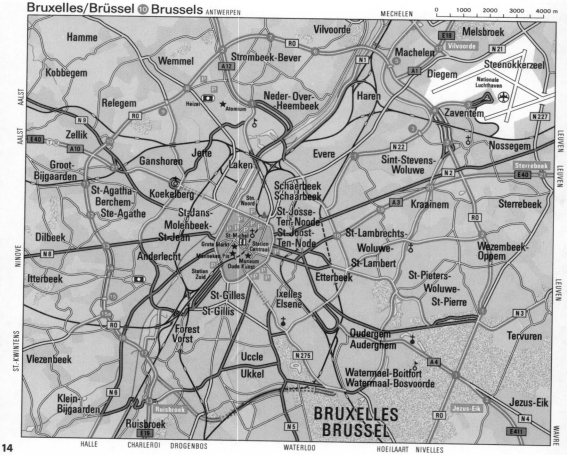

Bruxelles/Brüssel ⑩ Brussels

14

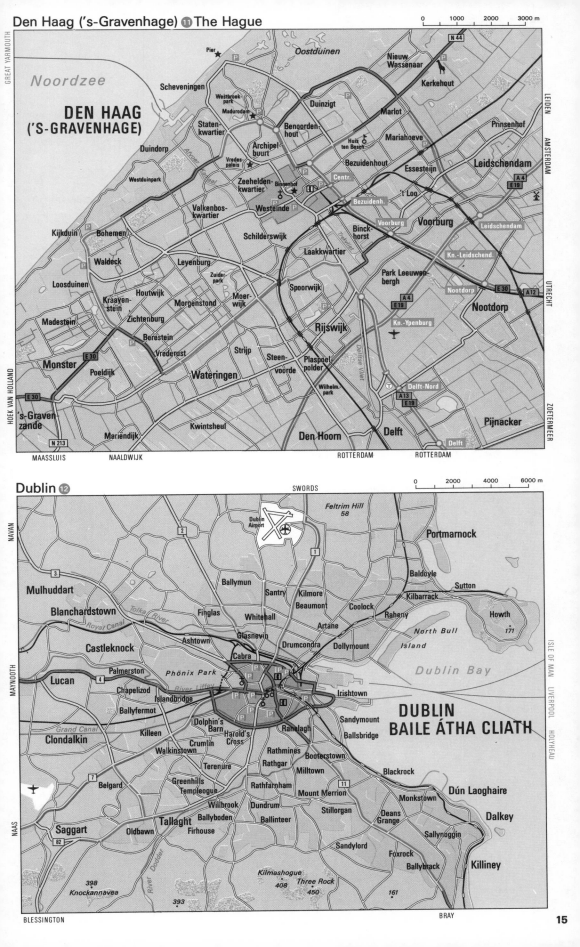

Edinburgh ⑬

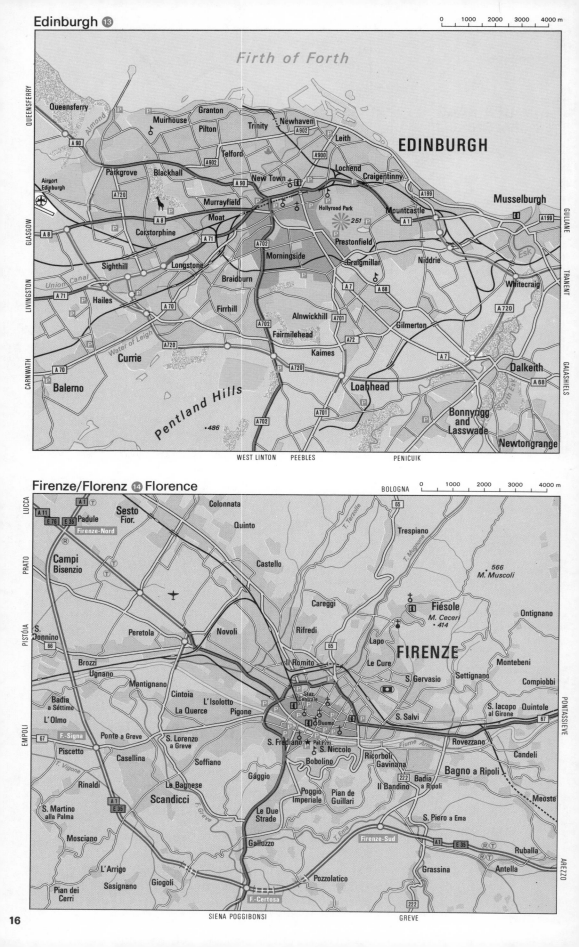

Firth of Forth

0 1000 2000 3000 4000 m

EDINBURGH

Queensferry
Muirhouse
Granton
Pilton
Trinity
Newhaven
Leith
Telford
Lochend
Craigentinny
A 900
A 902
Parkgrove
Blackhall
New Town
Mountcastle
Musselburgh
Airport Edinburgh
Murrayfield
Hollyrood Park
251
Prestonfield
Corstorphine
Moat
Craigmillar
Niddrie
Morningside
Whitecraig
Sighthill
Longstone
Union Canal
Braidburn
Hailes
Firrhill
Alnwickhill
Gilmerton
Water of Leigh
Fairmilehead
Currie
Kaimes
Loanhead
Balerno
Pentland Hills
•486
Bonnyrigg and Lasswade
Newtongrange
Dalkeith

QUEENSFERRY
GLASGOW
LIVINGSTON
CARNWATH
WEST LINTON PEEBLES PENICUIK
GUILANE
TRANENT
GALASHIELS

Firenze/Florenz ⑭ Florence

0 1000 2000 3000 4000 m
BOLOGNA

Colonnata
Padule
Sesto Fior.
Quinto
Firenze-Nord
Trespiano
Campi Bisenzio
Castello
T. Mugnone
566 M. Muscoli
S. Donnino
Careggi
Fiésole
Ontignano
Peretola
Novoli
Rifredi
M. Ceceri •414
Brozzi
Lapo
FIRENZE
Ugnano
Il Romito
Le Cure
Montebeni
Mantignano
S. Gervasio
Settignano
Compiobbi
Cintoia
L'Isolotto
Stazi. Centrale
Badia a Séttimo
La Querce
Pigone
Duomo
S. Salvi
S. Iacopo al Girone
Quintole
L'Olmo
Ponte a Greve
S. Lorenzo a Greve
S. Frediano
Pal.Pitti
S. Niccolo
Fiume Arno
Rovezzano
Piscetto
Casellina
Soffiano
Bobolino
Ricorboli Gavinana
Candeli
Rinaldi
Gággio
Il Bandino
Badia a Ripoli
Bagno a Ripoli
Scandicci
Poggio Imperiale
Pian de Guillari
Meoste
S. Martino alla Palma
Le Due Strade
S. Piero a Ema
Mosciano
Galluzzo
Firenze-Sud
Ruballa
L'Arrigo
Grassina
Antella
Pian dei Cerri
Sasignano
Giogoli
Pozzolatico
F.-Certosa

LUCCA
PRATO
PISTÓIA
EMPOLI
SIENA POGGIBONSI
GREVE
PONTASSIEVE
AREZZO

Graz 15

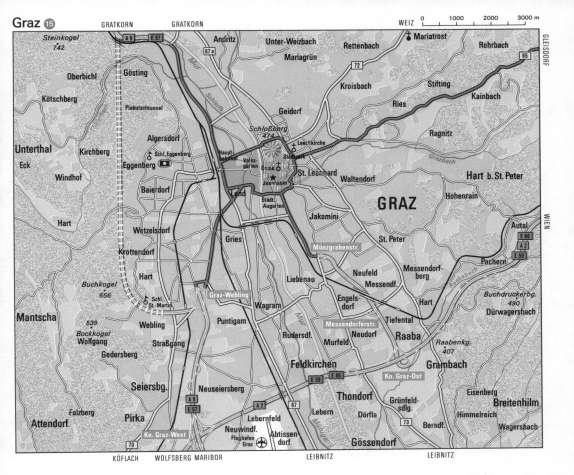

WEIZ

| GRATKORN | GRATKORN |

Steinkogel 742 · Oberbichl · Kötschberg · Unterthal · Eck · Windhof · Hart · Mantscha · Buchkogel 656 · 539 · Bockkogel · Wolfgang · Gedersberg · Attendorf · Falzberg · Pirka · Seiersbg. · Neuseiersberg · A 9 · E 57 · A 2 · 67 · Kn. Graz-West · 70 · Lebenfeld · Neuwindf. · Flughafen Graz · Abtissendorf · Gössendorf

Gösting · Algersdorf · Eggenberg · Schl. Eggenberg · Baierdorf · Wetzelsdorf · Krottendorf · Hart · Schl. St.-Martin · Webling · Straßgang · Puntigam · Gries · Graz-Webling · Wagram · Rudersdf. · Murfeld · Neudorf · Feldkirchen · E 59 · E 66 · Thondorf · Lebern · Dörfla · Grünfeldsdlg.

A 9 · E 57 · Plabutschtunnel · Mur · Schleifb. · Hauptbahnhof · Lend · Städt. Augarten · Jakomini · Liebenau · Messendf. · Engelsdorf · Tiefental · Raaba · Kn. Graz-Ost · Berndf.

Andritz · Unter-Weizbach · Mariagrün · Geidorf · Schloßberg 474 · Leechkirche · Stadtpark · St. Leonhard · Waltendorf · St. Peter · Neufeld · Messendorfberg · Hart · Raabenkg. 407 · Grambach · Eisenberg · Himmelreich · Wagersbach · Breitenhilm

Mariatrost · Rettenbach · Kroisbach · Ries · Stifting · Ragnitz · Kainbach · Hohenrain · Hart b. St. Peter · Buchdruckerbg. 490 · Dürwagersbach

GRAZ

Münzgrabenstr. · Messendorferstr. · Autal · E 66 · A 2 · E 59 · Pachern

Rohrbach · 65 · 72 · Grazbach · Raabbach

GLEISDORF · WIEN

KÖFLACH · WOLFSBERG MARIBOR · LEIBNITZ · LEIBNITZ

Genève 16 Geneva

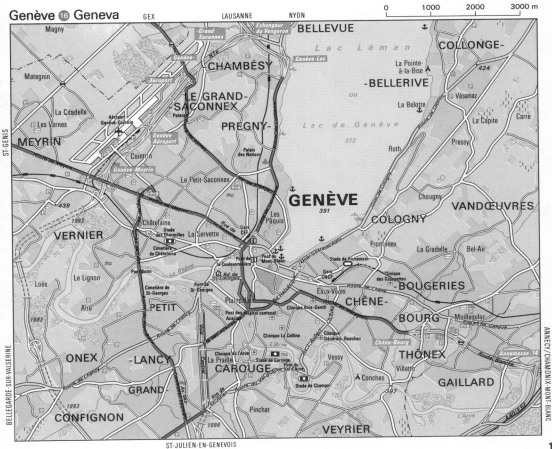

GEX · LAUSANNE · NYON

Magny · Grand Saconnex · Géneve-Lac · Échangeur du Vengeron · BELLEVUE · COLLONGE- · CHAMBÉSY · La Pointe-à-la-Bise · 424 · Matégnin · Aéroport · LE GRAND-SACONNEX · -BELLERIVE · ou · La Belotte · Vésenaz · La Capite · Carre · La Citadelle · Aéroport Genève-Cointrin · PREGNY- · Lac de Genève · 372 · La Gradelle · Les Vernes · Géneve Aéroport · Palais des Nations · Ruth · Pressy

MEYRIN · ST-GENIS · Cointrin · Géneve-Meyrin · Le Petit-Saconnex · GENÈVE 391 · Chougny · VANDŒUVRES · 439 · 1993 · Châtelaine · Stade des Charmilles · La Servette · Les Pâquis · COLOGNY · Bel-Air · VERNIER · Cimetière de Châtelaine · Rue de · Gare CFF · Frontenex · La Gradelle · Pont du Mont-Blanc · Stade de Richemont · Clinique des Grangettes · BOUGERIES · Loëx · Le Lignon · Pont Butin · Le Rhône · Pont de la Coulouvrenière · Gare SNCF · CHÊNE- · Le Rhône · Bd du St-Georges · Eaux-Vives · Route de Chêne · BOURG · Moillesulaz · 1993 · Cimetière de St-Georges · Pont de St-Georges · Plainpalais · Clinique Bois-Gentil · Clinique Générale-Beaulieu · Chêne-Bourg · THÔNEX · PETIT · Hôpital cantonal · Pont des Acacias · Clinique La Colline · Vessy · Villette · ONEX · -LANCY · L'Arve · GAILLARD · Clinique de l'Arve · Stade de Carouge · Pont du Val d'Arve · ANNECY/CHAMONIX-MONT-BLANC · Annemasse 14 · La Praille · CAROUGE · Stade de Champel · Conches · 397 · GRAND- · Pinchat · VEYRIER · 1993 · 1998 · CONFIGNON · BELLEGARDE-SUR-VALSERINE

Lac Léman · Lac de Genève · L'Arve

ST-JULIEN-EN-GENEVOIS

17

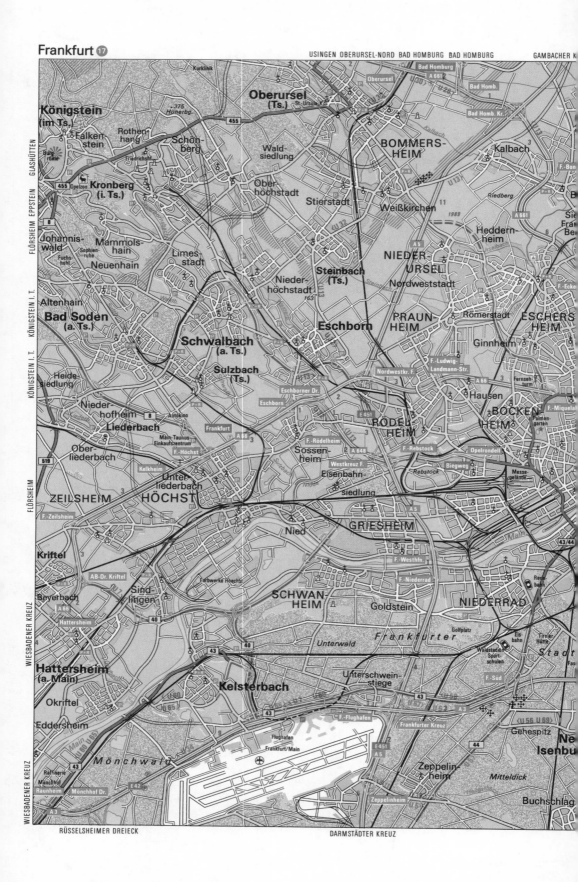

Königstein
(im Ts.)

Falken-
stein

Rothen-
hang

Schön-
berg

·375
Hünerbg.

Kurklinik

Oberursel
(Ts.)
St.-Ursula-K.

Oberursel

Bad Homburg
A 661

Bad Homb.

Bad Homb. Kr.

455

BOMMERS-
HEIM

Kalbach

F-Bon

Burg-
ruine

GLASHÜTTEN

455 Opelzoo

Kronberg
(i. Ts.)

Friedrichshf.

Wald-
siedlung

Ober-
höchstadt

Stierstadt

Weißkirchen

Riedberg

11

1989

A 661

Sie
Frä
Be

8

FLÖRSHEIM EPPSTEIN

Johannis-
wald

Mammols-
hain

Sophien-
ruhe

Fuchs-
hghf.

Neuenhain

Limes-
stadt

Nieder-
höchstadt

Steinbach
(Ts.)

163

NIEDER-
URSEL
Nordweststadt

Heddern-
heim

Urselbach

F-Ecke

Altenhain

KÖNIGSTEIN I. T.

Bad Soden
(a. Ts.)

Schwalbach
(a. Ts.)

Eschborn

PRAUN
HEIM

Römerstadt

ESCHERS
HEIM

Ginnheim

Heide-
siedlung

KÖNIGSTEIN I. T.

Sulzbach
(Ts.)

Eschborner Dr.

Nordwestkr. F.

A 66

Hausen

Fernseh-
turm

F.-Ludwig-
Landmann-Str.

Nieder-
hofheim

8

Autokino

Eschborn

E 451

A 5

RÖDEL
HEIM

BOCKEN
HEIM

F.-Miquela

Palmen-
garten

Liederbach

Frankfurt

A 66

3

F.-Rödelheim

A 648

F.-Rebstock

Opelrondell

FLÖRSHEIM

519

Ober-
liederbach

F.-Höchst

Main-Taunus-
Einkaufszentrum

Sossen-
heim

Rebstock

Biegweg

Messe-
gelände

Kelkheim

Westkreuz F.

Unter-
liederbach

Eisenbahn-
siedlung

A 5

ZEILSHEIM

HÖCHST

Nidda

GRIESHEIM

43/44

F.-Zeilsheim

Nied

Main

F.-Westhfn.

WIESBADENER KREUZ

Kriftel

AB-Dr. Kriftel

Farbwerke Hoechst

F.-Niederrad

Rem-
bach

NIEDERRAD

Beyerbach

A 66

Sind-
lingen

Golfplatz

Goldstein

Eis-
bahn

Tiroler
Hütte

Hattersheim

40

SCHWAN-
HEIM

Frankfurter

Waldstadion
Sport-
schulen

Stadt

Fas

Okriftel

40

43

Unterwald

43

Hattersheim
(a. Main)

Kelsterbach

Unterschwein-
stiege

F.-Süd

WIESBADENER KREUZ

U 80

U 65

43

F.-Flughafen

Frankfurter Kreuz

A 3

(U 56 U 69)

Gehespitz

Ne
Isenbu

Eddersheim

9

E 451

A 5

44

Mönchwald

E 42

Flughafen
Frankfurt/Main

Zeppelin-
heim

Mitteldick

Raffinerie
Mönchhof

Raunheim
Mönchhof Dr.

Zeppelinheim

Buchschläg

A 3

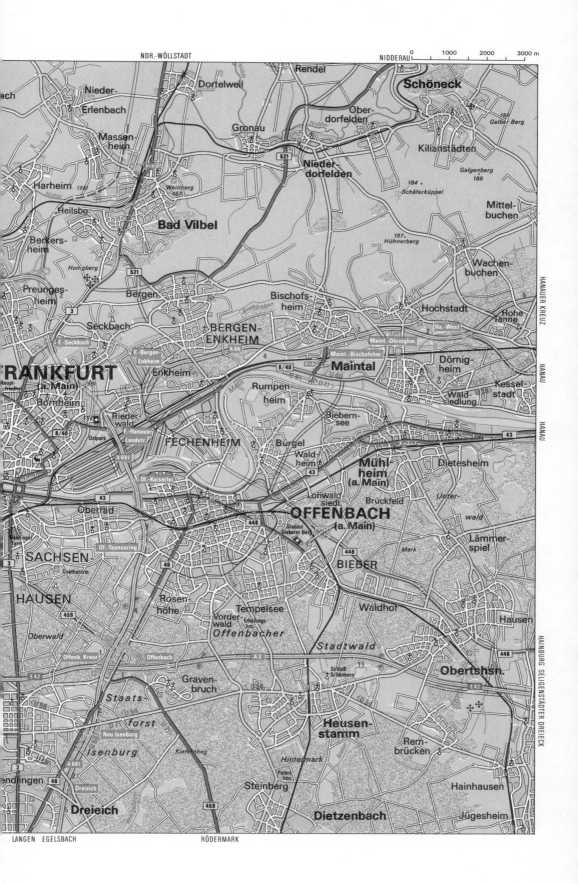

0 1000 2000 3000 m

Rendel
Schöneck
Dortelweil
Nieder-
Erlenbach
Ober-
dorfelden
188
Gelber Berg
Gronau
Massen-
heim
Kilianstädten
521
Galgenberg
188
Nieder-
dorfelden
Harheim 199
184
Schäferküppel
Weinberg
157
Heilsbg.
Nidda
Mittel-
buchen
Berkers-
heim
197
Hühnerberg
Wachen-
buchen
Honigberg
521
Preunges-
heim
Bischofs-
heim
Hochstadt
Hohe
Tanne
3
Bergen
Ha.-West
Seckbach
BERGEN-
ENKHEIM
A 66
Maint.-Dörnighm.
Dörnig-
heim
F.-Seckbach
Maint.-Bischofshm.
F.-Bergen-
Enkheim
4
8/40
Maintal
Kessel-
stadt
FRANKFURT
(a. Main) 98
Enkheim
Main
Rumpen-
heim
Wald-
siedlung
Bornheim
Haupt-
friedhof
Biebern-
see
43
FSV
Rieder-
wald
Bürgel
Wald-
heim
Dietesheim
8/40
F.-Hanauer
Landstr.
FECHENHEIM
43
Mühl-
heim
(a. Main)
Ostpark
A 661
Of.-Kaiserlei
Lohwald-
siedl.
Brückfeld
Unter-
Oberrad
43
OFFENBACH
(a. Main)
wald
Lämmer-
spiel
448
Stadion
Bieber Berg
Mark
Wehrheim-
Turm
Of.-Taunusring
SACHSEN
3
46
448
BIEBER
Goetheturm
Hausen
HAUSEN
Rosen-
höhe
Tempelsee
Waldhof
459
Vorder-
wald
Erholungs-
hm.
Oberwald
Offenbacher
Stadtwald
448
Offenb. Kreuz
Offenbach
A 3
11
Schloß
Schönborn
Obertshsn.
E 42
Gravenbruch
E 42
Staats-
Neu Isenburg
Heusen-
stamm
Rem-
brücken
forst
Kiefernheg
Hintermark
Isenburg
Peters-
hsn.
3
A 661
46
Dreieich
Steinberg
Hainhausen
459
Dreieich
Dietzenbach
Jügesheim

HANAUER KREUZ
HANAU
HANAU
HAINBURG SELIGENSTÄDTER DREIECK

19

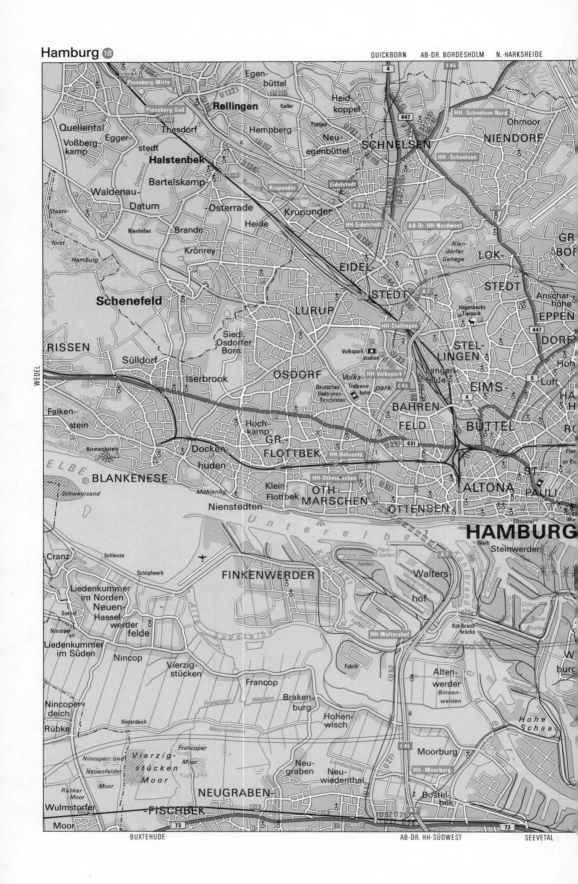

Pinneberg-Mitte
Egen-
büttel
Heid-
koppel
Keller
Pütjen
Neu-
egenbüttel
SCHNELSEN
HH.-Schnelsen-Nord
Ohmoor
NIENDORF
Pinneberg-Süd
Rellingen
Hempberg
447
HH.-Schnelsen
Quellental
Thesdorf
Voßberg-
kamp
Egger-
stedt
Krupunder
Eidelstedt
A 23
AB-Dr. HH-Nordwest
Halstenbek
Bartelskamp-
See
HH-Eidelstedt
Kollau
GR
BOR
Waldenau-
Datum
Osterrade
Krupunder
Nien-
dorfer
Gehege
LOK-
Staats-
Nienhöfen
Heide
EIDEL-
STEDT
forst
Brande
A 7
STEDT
Hamburg
Krönrey
Anschar-
höhe
EPPEN
Schenefeld
LURUP
Hagenbecks
Tierpark
HH-Stellingen
STEL-
LINGEN
447
DORF
Siedl.
Osdorfer
Born
Volkspark
stadion
Langen-
felde
Hoh
5
Luft
RISSEN
Sülldorf
OSDORF
Volks-
Trabrennf.-
bahn
park
HH-Volkspark
EIMS-
HA
H
Iserbrook
Deutsches
Elektronen-
Synchroton
BAHREN
Falken-
stein
Hoch-
kamp
FELD
BÜTTEL
RC
Bismarckstein
GR.
FLOTTBEK
HH-Bahrenfd.
431
Docken-
huden
ELBE
BLANKENESE
HH-Othma-schen
Klein-
Flottbek
OTH-
MARSCHEN
St
ALTONA
PAULI
Mühlenbg.
Nienstedten
OTTENSEN
Elbtunnel
Unterelbe
HAMBURG
Werft
Steinwerder
Cranz
Schleuse
Park-
hafen
A 7
Schöpfwerk
FINKENWERDER
Petroleum
hafen
Walters-
Liedenkummer
im Norden
hof
Oder
hfn
Neuen-
Hassel-
werder
felde
Dradenau
hafen
HH-Waltershof
Kohlbrand
brücke
Trave
hafen
Liedenkummer
im Süden
Nincop
Fabrik
Alten-
werder
Binnen-
weiden
W
burg
Nincoper-
deich
Vierzig-
stücken
Francop
Wettern
Braken-
burg
Rübke
Hinterdeich
Hohen-
wisch
Hohe
Schaa
Moorwetten
Francoper
Moor
Moorburg
Vierzig-
stücken
Moor
Nincoper und
Neuenfelder
Moor
Neu-
graben
Landscheide
E 45
HH.-Moorburg
Rübker
Moor
NEUGRABEN-
Neu-
wiedenthal
Bostel-
bek
Wulmstorfer
Moor
FISCHBEK
73
A 7
73

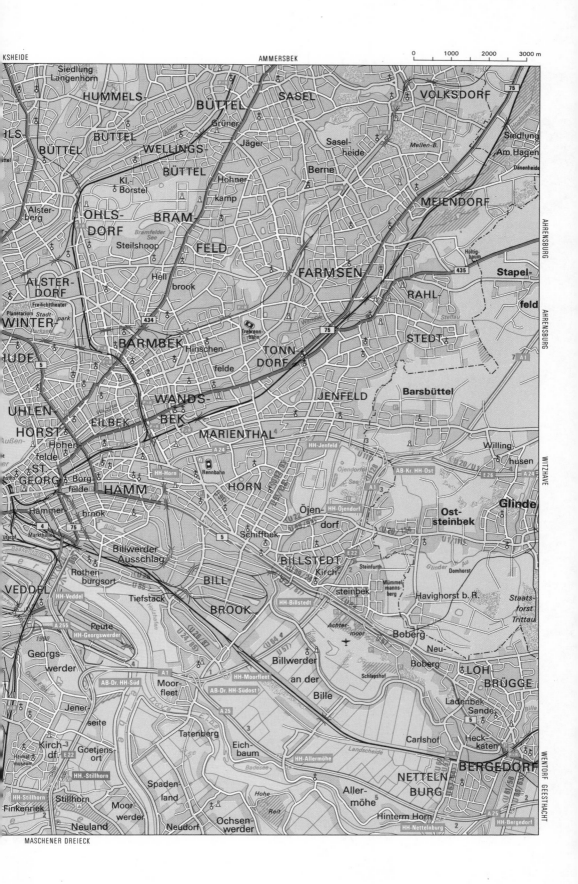

0   1000   2000   3000 m

Siedlung Langenhorn

HUMMELS-
BÜTTEL   SASEL   VOLKSDORF

ILS-   75
BÜTTEL
BÜTTEL   Grüner   Siedlung
           BÜTTEL   Jäger   Sasel-   Am Hagen
                WELLINGS-   heide   Mellen-B.
                     BÜTTEL   Hohner   Berne   Dänenheide
           Kl.-   kamp
Alster-   Borstel   MEIENDORF
berg   OHLS-   BRAM-
           DORF   FELD   435
                Bramfelder   Höltig-
                See   Steilshoop   baum   Stapel-
                                              FARMSEN
ALSTER-   Hell   RAHL-   feld
DORF   brook   STEDT   7 A1
                                       434
WINTER Planetarium Stadt-
        Freilichttheater park   Trabrenn- 75
HUDE   BARMBEK   Hinschen   bahn   STEDT
        5   felde   TONN-
                                        DORF
UHLEN-   WANDS-   JENFELD   Barsbüttel
HORST   EILBEK BEK
             MARIENTHAL   HH-Jenfeld   Willing-
Hohen-   A24   husen
felde   Öjendorfer   AB-Kr. HH-Ost   E 26   A 24
Außen-   See   A1
ST.   Borg-   HH-Horn Rennbahn   Glinde
GEORG felde   HORN   Ost-
       HAMM   HH-Öjendorf steinbek
Hammer   brook   Öjen-   dorf
4   75   Schiffbek   Steinfurth   Havighorst b. R.
     Markthalle Bille   5   Mummel-   Staats-
            Billwerder   BILLSTEDT   manns- Domhorst forst
VEDDEL   Ausschlag   Kirch-   berg   Trittau
       HH-Veddel Rothen-   steinbek
            burgsort   Tiefstack   BILL-   Boberg
A 255   Peute   BROOK HH-Billstedt
       HH-Georgswerder   Achter- moor   Neu-
Georgs-   Boberg   LOH-
werder   Billwerder Schlapshof   BRÜGGE
            AB-Dr. HH-Süd A1   an der   Ladenbek
                           Moor-   Bille   Sande
       Jener-   AB-Dr. HH-Südost   fleet HH-Moorfleet   Heck-
       seite   A 25   Carlshof   käten
Kirch- Goetjens- Tatenberg Eich-   BERGEDORF
df E22 ort   baum   HH-Allermöhe   Landscheide
Heimat-   NETTELN-
museum HH-Stillhorn Spaden-   Badesee Hohe   Aller- BURG
HH-Stillhorn Stillhorn land   möhe
Finkenriek   Reit   Hinterm Horn HH-Bergedorf
       Neuland Moor- Neudorf Ochsen-   HH-Nettelnburg A 25
                werder   werder

AHRENSBURG   AHRENSBURG   WITZHAVE   WENTORF GEESTHACHT

Génova/Genua ⑲ Genoa

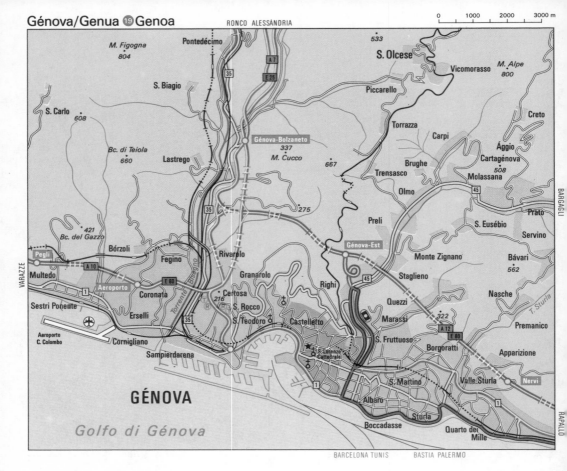

RONCO ALESSÁNDRIA

0   1000   2000   3000 m

M. Figogna 804
Pontedécimo
533
S. Olcese
Vicomorasso
M. Alpe 800

S. Biagio
Piccarello
Creto
S. Carlo 608
A 7
E 25
35
Torrazza
Carpi
Ággio
Cartagénova 508
Bc. di Teiola 660
Lastrego
Génova-Bolzaneto 337
M. Cucco
Brughe
Molassana
Trensasco
Olmo
45
Prato
667
275
Preli
S. Eusébio
Servino
421
Bc. del Gazzo
Bórzoli
Rivarolo
Génova-Est
Monte Zignano
Bávari 562
Pegli
Fegino
Granarolo
Righi
45
Staglieno
Nasche
Multedo
A 10
E 80
Coronata
Certosa
216
Quezzi
Premanico
Aeroporto
S. Rocco
S. Teodoro
Castelletto
Marassi
322
A 12
E 80
Borgóratti
Apparizione
Sestri Ponente
Erselli
35
S. Lorenzo Cattedrale
S. Fruttuoso
Aeroporto C. Colombo
Cornigliano
Sampierdarena
Valle Sturla
Nervi
S. Martino
GÉNOVA
1
Albaro
Stúrla
1
Golfo di Génova
Boccadasse
Quarto dei Mille

VARAZZE
BARGAGLI
RAPALLO
T. Sturla

BARCELONA TUNIS   BASTIA PALERMO

Göteborg ⑳ Gothenburg

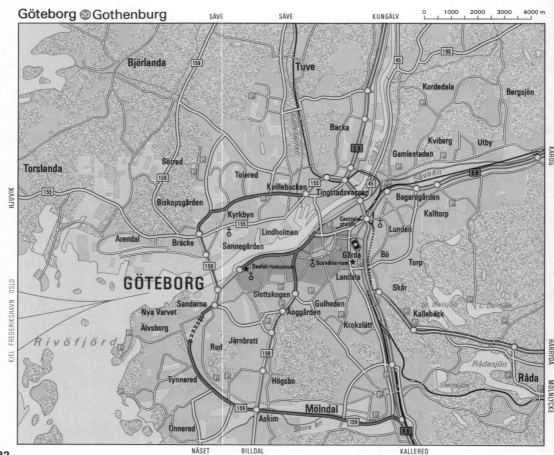

SÄVE   SÄVE   KUNGÄLV

0   1000   2000   3000   4000 m

Björlanda
159
Tuve
45
190
Kordedala
Bergsjön
Backa
E 6
Kviberg
Utby
Sörred
Gamlestaden
E 6
Torslanda
159
Tolered
Kvillebäcken
155
Tingstadsvassen
45
Bagaregården
155
Kalltorp
Biskopsgården
Kyrkbyn
155
Lindholmen
Central station
Lunden
Arendal
Bräcke
Sannegården
Bö
Torp
Scandinavium
Gårda
Landala
Skår
GÖTEBORG
Seefahrtsmuseum
St. Delsjön
L. Delsjön
Sandarna
Slottskogen
Gulheden
Kallebäck
Nya Varvet
Änggården
Krokslätt
Älvsborg
Rud
Järnbrott
158
Rådasjön
Råda
Rivöfjörd
Tynnered
Högsbo
Stensjön
159
Mölndal
Önnered
Askim
Stora ån
159
E 6

HJUVIK
KIEL FREDERIKSHAVN OSLO
HÄRRYDA
MÖLNLYCKE
KÅHOG
Göta Älv
Säveån
Kållebäcken

NÄSET   BILLDAL   KÄLLERED

22

Helsinki ㉑

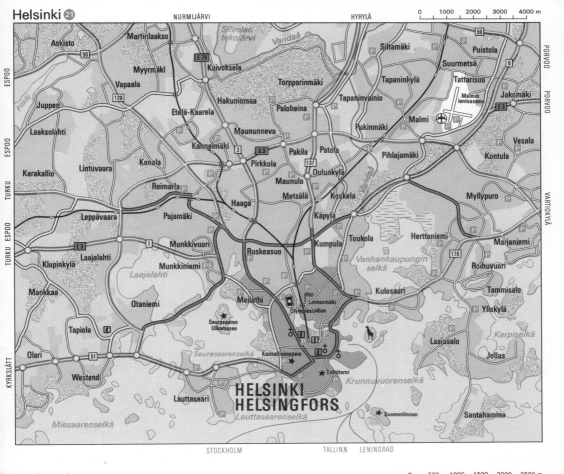

Innsbruck ㉒

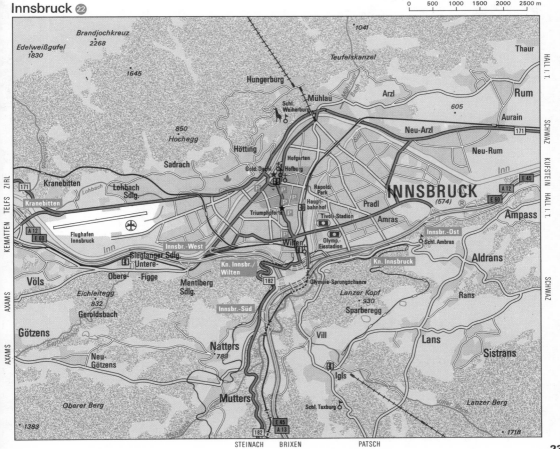

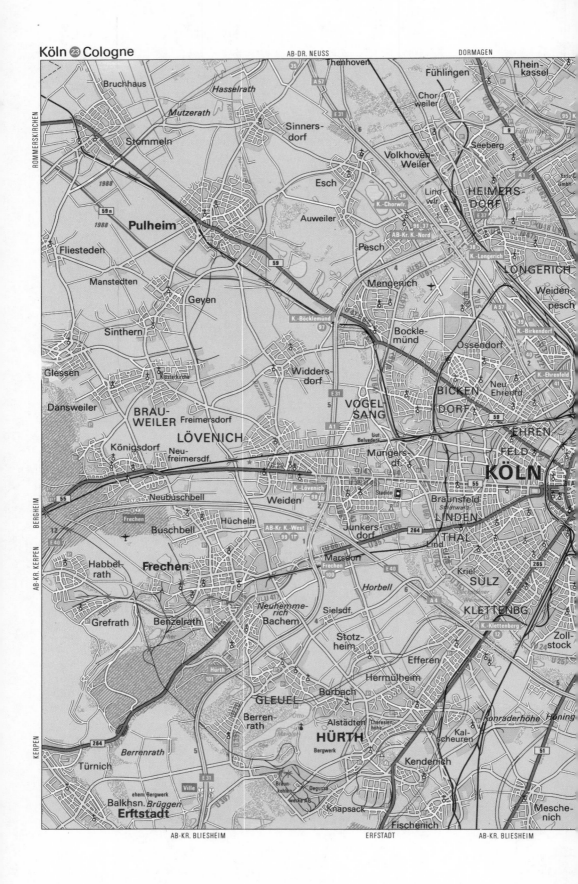

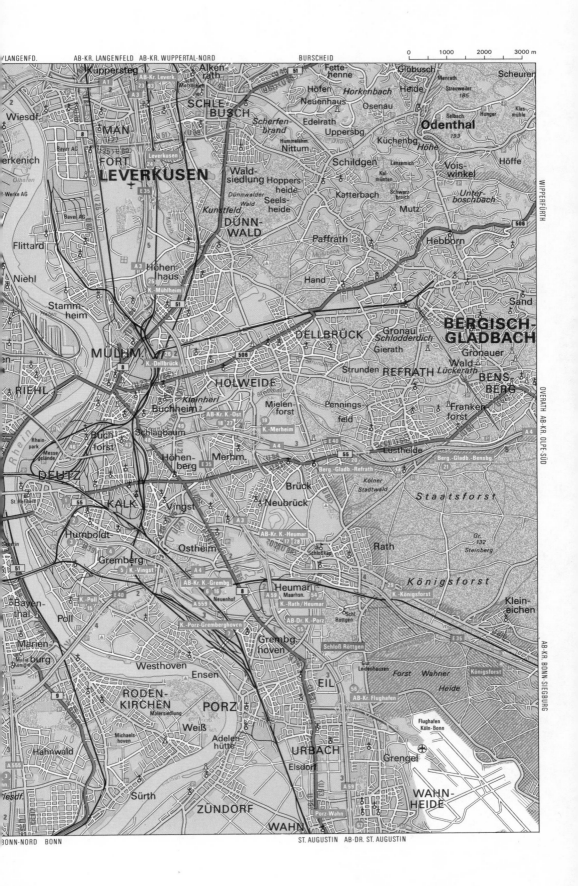

0   1000   2000   3000 m

Kupppersteg
AB-Kr. Leverk.
Alken-rath
Fette-henne
Glöbusch
Menrath
Strauweiler 185
Scheuren

Wiesdf.
Schl. Morsbroich
Höfen
Horkenbach
Heide
Selbach
Hunger
Klas-mühle

MAN
SCHLE-BUSCH
Neuenhaus
Osenau

erkenich
FORT
Leverkusen
Scherfen-brand
Edelrath
Uppersbg.
Küchenbg.
Höhe
Odenthal 193

Werke AG
LEVERKUSEN
Wald-siedlung
Hoppers-heide
Hummelshm.
Nittum
Schildgen
Lanzemich
Vois-winkel
Höffe

Flittard
Dünnwalder Wald
Kunstfeld
Seels-heide
Paffrath
Kal-münten
Schwarz-breich
Katterbach
Unter-boschbach

Niehl
DÜNN-WALD
Mutz

Stamm-heim
Hebborn
Sand

Höhen-haus
K.-Mühlheim
Hand

MÜLHM.
K.-Dellbrück
DELLBRÜCK
Gronau
Schlodderdich
Gierath
BERGISCH-GLADBACH
Gronauer Wald
Lückerath

RIEHL
Kleinherl
Strunden
REFRATH
BENS-BERG

Buchheim
Mielen-forst
Pennings-feld
Franken-forst

Buch-forst
Schlägbaum
AB-Kr. K.-Ost
K.-Merheim

Rhein-park
Messe-gelände
Höhen-berg
Merhm.
Lustheide

DEUTZ
St. Heribert
Brück
Kölner Stadtwald
Berg.-Gladb.-Bensbg.

KALK
Vingst
Neubrück
Berg.-Gladb.-Refrath
Staatsforst

Humboldt-
Ostheim
AB-Kr. K.-Heumar
Rath
Gr. 132 Steinberg

Gremberg
K.-Vingst
Schloßkan
Königsforst

Bayen-thal
AB-Kr. K.-Gremb.
Heumar
Maarhsn.
K.-Königsforst
Klein-eichen

Poll
K.-Poll
Neuenhof
K.-Rath/Heumar
Schl. Röttgen

K.-Porz-Gremberghoven
AB-Dr. K.-Porz

Marien-burg
Grembg.-hoven
Schloß Röttgen

Westhoven
Ensen
EIL
Gut Leidenhausen
Forst Wahner Heide
Königsforst

RODEN-KIRCHEN
PORZ
AB-Kr. Flughafen

Weiß
Malersiedlung
Flughafen Köln-Bonn

Hahnwald
Michaels-hoven
Adelen-hütte
URBACH
Grengel

Sürth
Elsdorf
WAHN-HEIDE

ZÜNDORF
WAHN
Porz-Wahn

WIPPERFÜRTH

OVERATH   AB-KR. OLPE-SÜD

AB-KR. BONN-SIEGBURG

København/Kopenhagen ㉔ Copenhagen

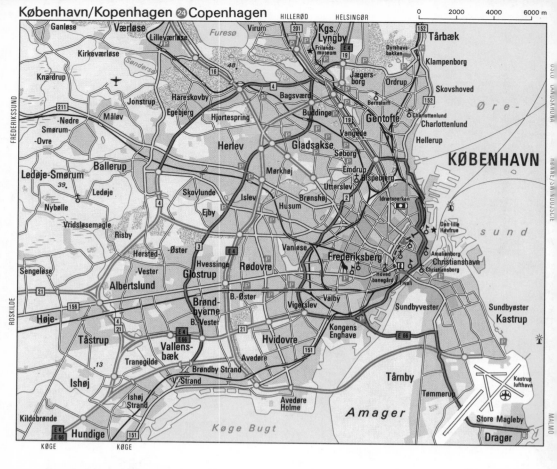

Lisboa/Lissabon ㉕ Lisbon

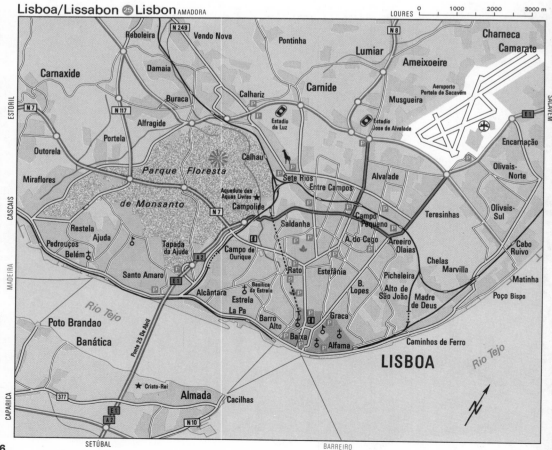

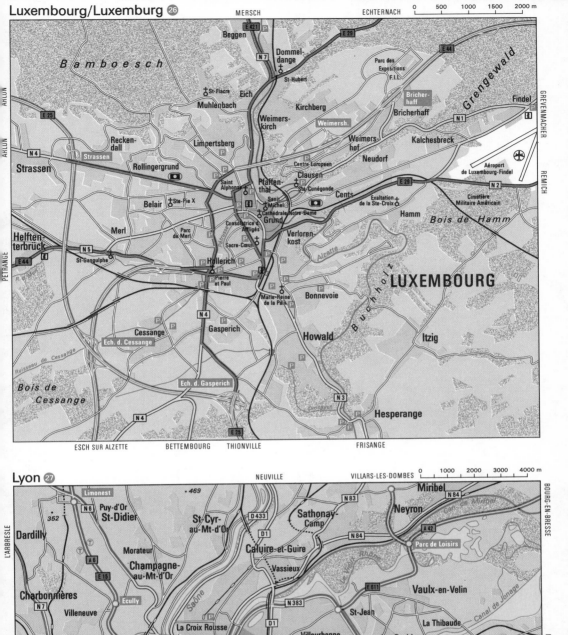

Lyon 27

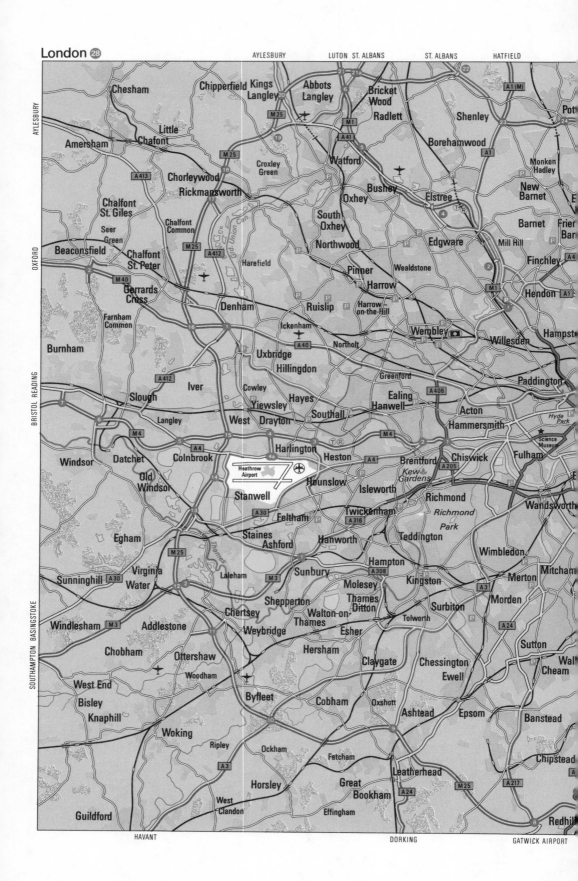

AYLESBURY

OXFORD

BRISTOL READING

SOUTHAMPTON BASINGSTOKE

Chesham
Chipperfield
Kings Langley
Abbots Langley
Bricket Wood
Radlett
Shenley
Pott
Little Chafont
Amersham
Watford
Borehamwood
Monken Hadley
New Barnet
Chorleywood
Croxley Green
Bushey
Oxhey
Elstree
Barnet
Frier Bar
Chalfont St. Giles
Rickmansworth
South Oxhey
Edgware
Mill Hill
Finchley
Seer Green
Chalfont Common
Northwood
Hendon
Beaconsfield
Chalfont St. Peter
Harefield
Pinner
Wealdstone
Harrow
Gerrards Cross
Denham
Ruislip
Harrow-on-the-Hill
Wembley
Willesden
Hampst
Farnham Common
Ickenham
Northolt
Burnham
Uxbridge
Hillingdon
Greenford
Paddington
Iver
Cowley
Hayes
Ealing
Hanwell
Acton
Slough
Yiewsley
Southall
Hammersmith
Langley
West Drayton
Hyde Park
Windsor
Datchet
Colnbrook
Harlington
Heston
Brentford
Chiswick
Fulham
Science Museum
Heathrow Airport
Hounslow
Kew Gardens
Old Windsor
Stanwell
Isleworth
Richmond
Wandsworth
Feltham
Twickenham
Richmond Park
Egham
Staines
Ashford
Hanworth
Teddington
Wimbledon
Virginia Water
Laleham
Sunbury
Hampton
Kingston
Merton
Mitcham
Sunninghill
Shepperton
Molesey
Surbiton
Morden
Windlesham
Addlestone
Chertsey
Walton-on-Thames
Thames Ditton
Tolworth
Esher
Sutton
Chobham
Ottershaw
Weybridge
Hersham
Claygate
Chessington
Ewell
Wal Cheam
West End
Woodham
Byfleet
Cobham
Oxshott
Ashtead
Epsom
Banstead
Bisley
Knaphill
Ashtead
Chipstead
Woking
Ripley
Ockham
Fetcham
Leatherhead
Horsley
Great Bookham
Guildford
West Clandon
Effingham
Redhil

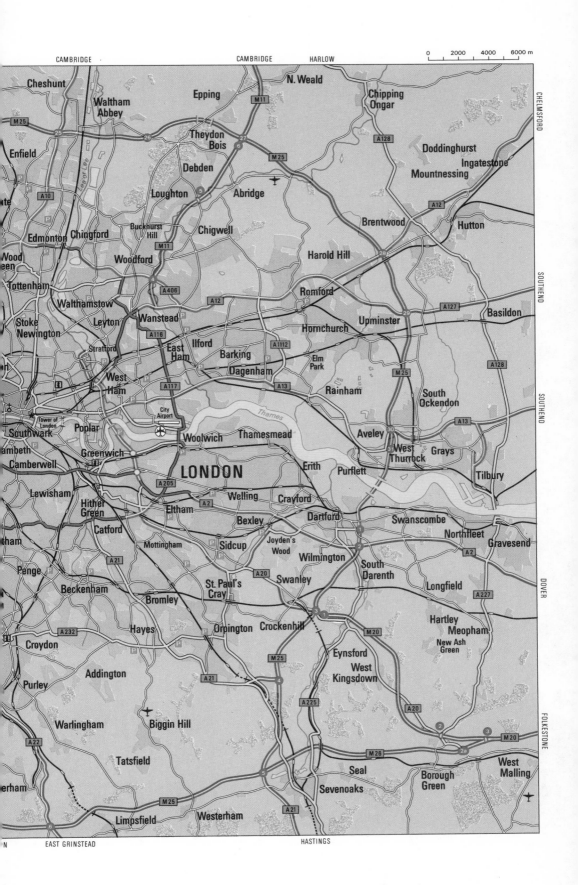

0   2000   4000   6000 m

CHELMSFORD

SOUTHEND

SOUTHEND

DOVER

FOLKESTONE

Cheshunt

Waltham Abbey

Epping

N. Weald

Chipping Ongar

Doddinghurst

Ingatestone

Mountnessing

Enfield

Theydon Bois

Debden

Loughton

Abridge

Brentwood

Hutton

Edmonton

Chingford

Buckhurst Hill

Chigwell

Harold Hill

Woodford

Wood

een

Tottenham

Walthamstow

Leyton

Wanstead

Romford

Upminster

Basildon

Stoke Newington

Stratford

East Ham

Ilford

Hornchurch

Barking

Elm Park

West Ham

Dagenham

Rainham

South Ockendon

Tower of London

City Airport

Poplar

Southwark

ambeth

Camberwell

Greenwich

Woolwich

Thamesmead

Aveley

West Thurrock

Grays

LONDON

Erith

Purfleet

Tilbury

Lewisham

Hither Green

Eltham

Welling

Crayford

Catford

Bexley

Dartford

Swanscombe

Northfleet

Gravesend

Mottingham

Sidcup

Joyden's Wood

Wilmington

Penge

Beckenham

St. Paul's Cray

Swanley

South Darenth

Longfield

Bromley

Hayes

Orpington

Crockenhill

Hartley

Meopham

Croydon

Addington

Eynsford

West Kingsdown

New Ash Green

Purley

Warlingham

Biggin Hill

West Malling

Tatsfield

Borough Green

erham

Seal

Sevenoaks

Limpsfield

Westerham

EL PARDO   EL PARDO   COLMENAR

C 601

A 1

Monte de El Pardo

Fuencarra

Mirasierra

Peña Grande

El Pilar

ARÉVALO

El Plantío

Ciudad de
Puerta de Hierto

Tetuán

A 6   N VI

Alfar

Aravaca

Hipodr.
d. la
Zarzuela

Benitez

Ciudad
Universitaria

Cuatro
Caminos

San José

La Estación

MAJADAHONDA

Pozuelo
de Alarcón

Valladares

*Garabitas
677*

Arguelles

Chamberí

Húmera

Casa de Campo

Templo
de Debod

Centro

Bibli.
y Mu

Somosaguas

Palacio
Real

Museo
del Prado

La Cabaña

Campo
del Moro

BOADILLA.DEL.MONTE

Prado
del Rey

Los Angeles

C 602

Latina
San F. el Grande

Lavapiés

Retamares

El Lucero

Embajadores

Arganzuela

Parque
de San Isidro

Campamento

Cármenes

Aluche

Legazpi

Carabanchel
Bajo

Usera

San Vicente
Paul

San Ignacio de Loyola

Orcasitas

San F

Carabanchel
Alto

E 90

A 5

VILLAVICIOSA DE ODÓN

C 501

La Fortuna

C 602

N 401

NAVALCARNERO

Villaverde

N IV
E 5

Alcorcón

Leganés

GETAFE   GRIÑÓN   TOLEDO   ARANJUEZ

Río Manzanares

0   1000   2000   3000 m

E 5
A 1
N I

MADRID

San Antonio

Manoteras

Hortaleza

Barajas

Canillas

El Corralejo

Ciudad Lineal

Río Jarama

Las Palomas

Aeropuerto Int.
de Madrid-Barajas

eridad

Canillejas

Colonia Llorente

N II   A 2   E 90

La Conception

Ventas

San Blas

Coslada

San Fernando
de Henares

Moratalaz

Vicálvaro

E 901   A 3

726
Almodóvar

Puente Vallecas

ías

Santa
Eugenia

Vallecas

Parque
de Entrevías

C 602

Granja La Nova

N III
E 901

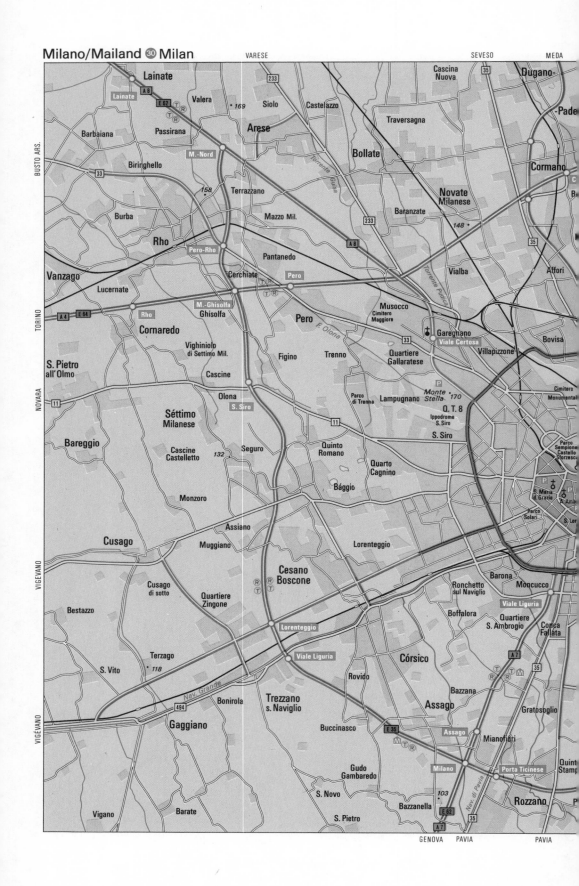

VARESE   SEVESO   MEDA

Lainate
Dugano-
-Pade

Cascina
Nuova

Lainate
E 62
A 8
Valera
Siolo
Castelazzo
Traversagna
Cormano
C

Barbaiana
Passirana
Arese
Bollate

M.-Nord
Biringhello
Novate
Milanese

158
Terrazzano
Mazzo Mil.
Baranzate
148

Burba
233
Cormano
B

Rho
Pero-Rho
Pantanedo
Vialba
Affori

Vanzago
Cerchiate
Pero
A 8

Lucernate
M.-Ghisolfa
Musocco
Gareghano
Bovisa

Rho
Ghisolfa
Pero
Cimitero
Maggiore
Viale Certosa

A 4
E 64
Villapizzone

Cornaredo
Vighiniolo
di Settimo Mil.
Figino
Trenno
Quartiere
Gallaratese

S. Pietro
all'Olmo
Cascine
Cimitero
Monumental

Olona
Parco
di Trenna
Lampugnano
Monte
Stella
170
Q.T. 8

S. Siro
Ippodromo
S. Siro

Séttimo
Milanese
11
S. Siro
Parco
Sempione
Castello
Sforzesc

Bareggio
Cascine
Castelletto
132
Seguro
Quinto
Romano
Quarto
Cagnino

Monzoro
Bàggio
P
S. Maria
d. Grazie
A. Amb

Assiano
Parco
Solari
S. Lor

Cusago
Muggiano
Lorenteggio

Bestazzo
Cusago
di sotto
Quartiere
Zingone
Cesano
Boscone
Barona

Ronchetto
sul Naviglio
Moncucco

Viale Liguria

Lorenteggio
Boffalora
Quartiere
S. Ambrogio
Conca
Fallàta

Terzago
118
Viale Liguria
Córsico
A 7

S. Vito
Rovido
Bazzana
35

Nav. Grande
494
Bonirola
Trezzano
s. Naviglio
Assago
Gratosoglio

Gaggiano
Buccinasco
E 35
Assago
Mianofiori

Gudo
Gambaredo
Milano
Porta Ticinese
Quint
Stamp

Vigano
Barate
S. Novo
Bazzanella
103
Rozzano
P

S. Pietro
E 62
A 7
35

GENOVA PAVIA   PAVIA

BUSTO ARS.
TORINO
NOVARA
VIGEVANO
VIGEVANO

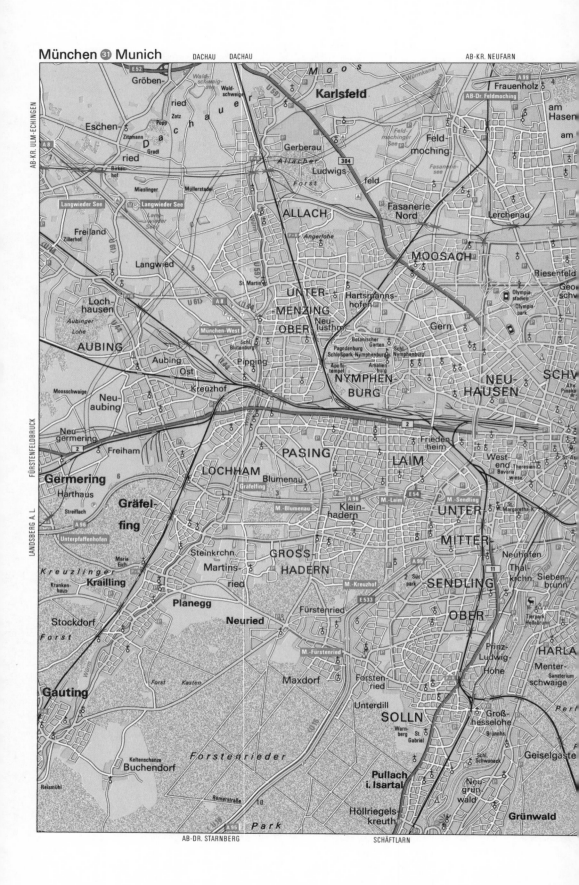

DACHAU   DACHAU

AB-KR. NEUFARN

AB-KR. ULM-ECHINGEN

FÜRSTENFELDBRUCK

LANDSBERG A. L.

Gröben-
ried
Zetz
Popp
Zitzmann
Gradl
Eschen-
ried
Birken-
hof
Mieslinger
Müllerstadel

Waldschweig-
see
Wald-
schweige
D a c h a u e r

E 52

U 59

Karlsfeld

Wurmkanal

Moos

am
Hasen
am

Frauenholz
A 99

AB-Dr. Feldmoching

Feld-
mochinger
See

Feld-
moching

Fasanerie-
see

Gerberau
304

Ludwigs-
feld

Allacher
Forst

Fasanerie
Nord

Lerchenau

A 8

Langwieder See
M8
Langwieder See
Lang-
wieder
See

Freiland
Zillerhof

Langwied

ALLACH

Angerlohe

MOOSACH

Riesenfeld

Geo-
schw

Olympia-
stadion
Olympia-
park

Alte
Pinako

Loch-
hausen
Aubinger
Lohe

AUBING

Moosschwaige

Neu-
aubing

U 61
A 8

St. Martin

München-West
Schl.
Blutenburg

Aubing
Ost

Kreuzhof

UNTER-
MENZING
OBER-

Neu-
lusthm

Pipping

Hartmanns-
hofen

Botanischer
Garten
Schloßpark Nymphenburg
Pagodenburg
Apollo-
tempel
Amalien-
burg

Gern

Schl.
Nymphenburg

NYMPHEN-
BURG

NEU-
HAUSEN

SCH

U 59

Neu-
germering
2
Freiham

Germering
6
Harthaus
Streiflach
A 96
Unterpfaffenhofen

PASING

LOCHHAM
Gräfelfing
Blumenau
3

LAIM

Frieden-
heim

West-
end
Bavaria
Theresien-
wiese

2

St.-K

A 96
M.-Laim
E 54
M-Sendling

M.-Blumenau

Klein-
hadern

Margarethe-K

UNTER-

MITTER-

Gräfel-
fing

Maria
Eich

Steinkrchn.
Martins-
ried

GROSS-
HADERN

M.-Kreuzhof

A 95

Neuhofen
Thal-
krchn.
Sieben-
brunn

Kranken-
haus
Krailling

Planegg

Neuried

Fürstenried

E 533

2
Süd-
park

SENDLING

OBER-

Tierpark
Hellabrunn

HARLA

Stockdorf

Forst

Forst
Kasten

M.-Fürstenried

Maxdorf

Forsten-
ried

Prinz-
Ludwig-
Höhe

Menter-
Sanatorium-
schwaige

Perl

Gauting

Keltenschanze
Buchendorf
Reismühl

Römerstraße
10

Unterdill

Warn-
berg
St.
Gabriel

SOLLN

Groß-
hesselohe
Brünnh.

Geiselgaste

Forstenrieder

Pullach
i. Isartal

Schl.
Schwaneck

Neu-
grün-
wald

Höllriegels-
kreuth

Grünwald

Wurm

A 95

Park

U 6

11

AB-DR. STARNBERG

SCHÄFTLARN

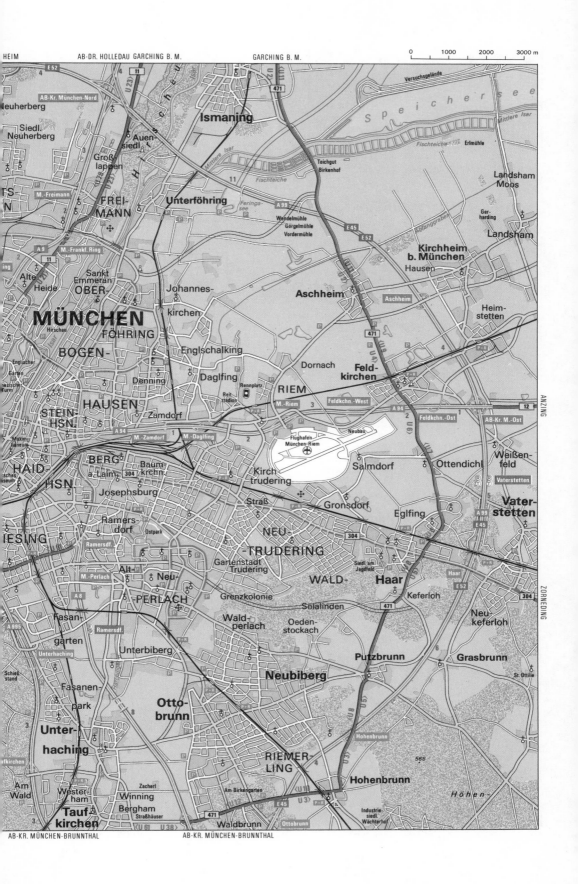

0   1000   2000   3000 m

Neuherberg

AB-Kr. München-Nord

Siedl.
Neuherberg

Groß-
lappen

Ismaning

S p e i c h e r s e e

Mittlere Isar

Fischteiche   Erlmühle

Versuchsgelände

Teichgut
Birkenhof

Auen-
siedl.

M.-Freimann

FREI-
MANN

Unterföhring

Feringa-
see

Mittlere Isar

Fischteiche

Landsham
Moos

Ger-
harding

Landsham

Wendelmühle
Görgelmühle
Vordermühle

Kirchheim
b. München

Hausen

Alte
Heide

Sankt
Emmeran

Johannes-
kirchen

Aschheim

Aschheim

Heim-
stetten

MÜNCHEN

OBER-
FÖHRING

Hirschau

BOGEN-

Englschalking

Dornach

Feld-
kirchen

Englischer
Garten

Chinesischer
Turm

Denning

Daglfing

Rennplatz.

RIEM

M.-Riem

3

Feldkchn.-West

Feldkchn.-Ost

AB-Kr. M.-Ost

12

ANZING

HAUSEN

STEIN-
HSN.

Zamdorf

Reit-
stadion

Neubau

Flughafen
München-Riem

Salmdorf

Ottendichl

Weißen-
feld

Maximil-
laneum

HAID-
HSN.

BERG
a. Laim

Baum-
krchn.

M.-Zamdorf

M.-Daglfing

2

Kirch-
trudering

Vaterstetten

Vater-
stetten

Josephsburg

Straß

Gronsdorf

Eglfing

IESING

Rämers-
dorf

Ramersdf.

Ostpark

NEU-
TRUDERING

304

HSN.

Alt-

Neu-

PERLACH

M.-Perlach

Grenzkolonie

Gartenstadt
Trudering

WALD-

Siedl. am
Jagdfeld

Keferloh

Haar

Haar

Neu-
keferloh

St. Ottilie

Fasan-
garten

Ramersdf.

Wald-
perlach

Oeden-
stockach

Solalinden

Putzbrunn

Grasbrunn

Schieß-
stand

Unterbiberg

Neubiberg

Fasanen-
park

Otto-
brunn

Hohenbrunn

Unter-
haching

RIEMER-
LING

Hohenbrunn

Höhen-

566

Am
Wald

Wester-
ham

Zacherl

Winning
Bergham
Straßhäuser

Am Birkengarten

Industrie
siedl.
Wächterhof

Tauf-
kirchen

Waldbrunn

Ottobrunn

ZORNEDING

35

Marseille ㉜

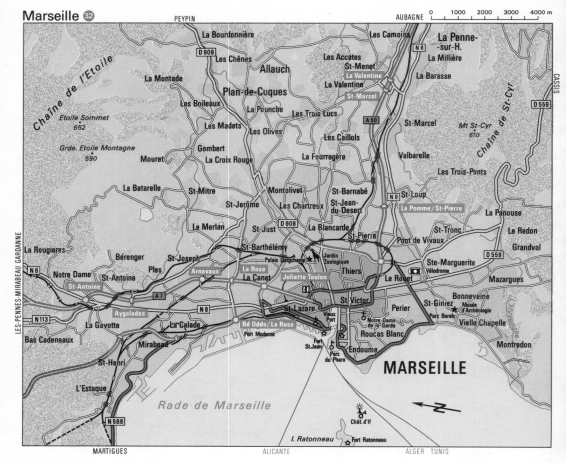

PEYPIN   AUBAGNE

0   1000   2000   3000   4000 m

La Bourdonnière
Les Camoins
La Penne-sur-H.
La Millière
Chaîne de l'Etoile
La Montade
Les Chênes
Les Accates
St-Menet
La Barasse
CASSIS
Allauch
Plan-de-Cuques
La Valentine
La Valentine
St-Marcel
D 559
Les Boileaux
La Pounche
Les Trois Lucs
Étoile Sommet 652
Les Madets
Les Olives
Les Caillols
St-Marcel
Mt St-Cyr 610
Grde. Etoile Montagne 590
Gombert
La Croix Rouge
La Fourragère
Valbarelle
Chaîne de St-Cyr
Mouret
La Batarelle
St-Mitre
Montolivet
St-Barnabé
Les Trois-Ponts
St-Jérôme
Les Chartreux
St-Jean-du-Desert
N 8
St-Loup
La Panouse
Le Merlan
St-Just
La Blancarde
La Pomme / St-Pierre
St-Tronc
Le Redon
D 908
St-Pierre
Pont de Vivaux
Grandval
La Rougiers
St-Barthélémy
Ste-Marguerite
D 559
Bérenger
St-Joseph
Ples
Palais Longchamp
Jardin Zoologique
Vélodrome
Mazargues
Notre Dame
Arnavaux
La Rose
Thiers
N 8
St-Antoine
La Canet
Joliette Toulon
Le Rouet
Bonneveine
Musée d'Archéologie
A 7
St-Lazare
St-Victor
Perier
St-Giniez
Parc Borely
Vielle Chapelle
Aygalades
Bd Oddo / La Rosa
Vieux Port
Notre-Dame de-la-Garde
Roucas Blanc
Montredon
La Gavotte
La Calade
Port Moderne
Fort St-Jean
Endoume
N 113
Bas Cadeneaux
Mirabeau
Parc du Pharo
N 8
St-Henri
MARSEILLE
L'Estaque
N 568

Rade de Marseille

N

Chât. d'If
I. Ratonneau
Fort Ratonneau

MARTIGUES   ALICANTE   ALGER TUNIS

Nápoli/Neapel ㉝ Naples

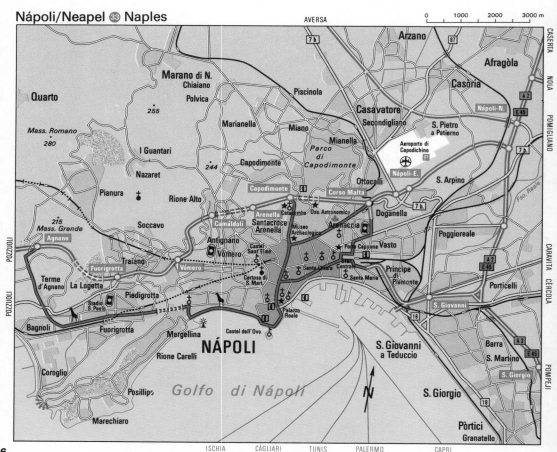

AVERSA

0   1000   2000   3000 m

7 b
Arzano
CASERTA
NOLA
87
Afragòla
Marano di N.
Chiaiano
Piscinola
Casavatore
Casòria
A 2
Quarto
Polvica
Nápoli-N.
E 45
255
Marianella
Miano
Secondigliano
S. Pietro a Patierno
POMIGLIANO
Mass. Romano 280
I Guantari
Mianella
Aeroporto di Capodichino
7 b
Parco di Capodimonte
Nazaret
Capodimonte
Ottocalli
Nápoli-E.
S. Arpino
244
Pianura
Rione Alto
Capodimonte
Corso Malta
Doganella
7 b.
215 Mass. Grande
Soccavo
Arenella
Catacombe
Oss. Astronomico
Poggioreale
Agnano
Camáldoli
Santacroce Arenella
Museo Archeologico
Aremaccia
A 2 E 45
Fuorigrotta
Antignano
Castel Sant'Elmo
Porta Capuana
Vasto
CARAVITA
Traiano
Vómero
Vómero
Santa Chiara
Centrale
Principe di Piemonte
CÈRCOLA
Terme d'Agnano
La Logetta
Certosa di S. Mart.
Santa Maria
Porticelli
Stadio S. Paolo
Piedigrotta
Palazzo Reale
S. Giovanni
Bagnoli
Fuorigrotta
Mergellina
Castel dell'Ovo
18
Barra
A 3
Rione Carelli
NÁPOLI
S. Giovanni a Teduccio
S. Martino
E 45
Coroglio
S. Giorgio
POMPEJI
Posillipo
Golfo di Nápoli
N
S. Giorgio
18
Marechiaro
Pòrtici
Granatello

ISCHIA   CÁGLIARI   TUNIS   PALERMO   CAPRI

Nice/Nizza ㉞

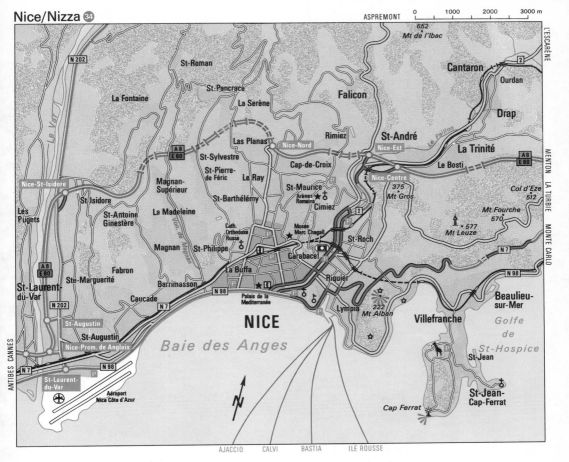

Oslo ㉟

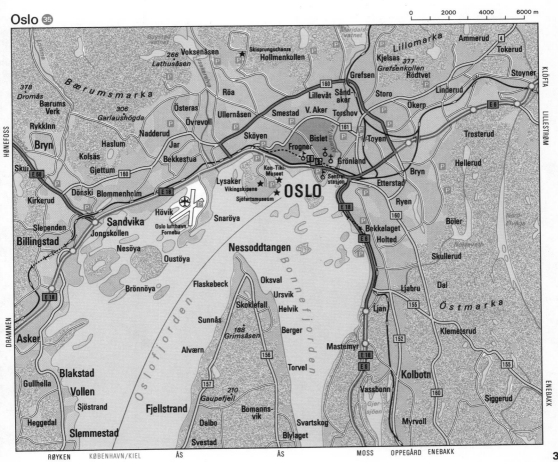

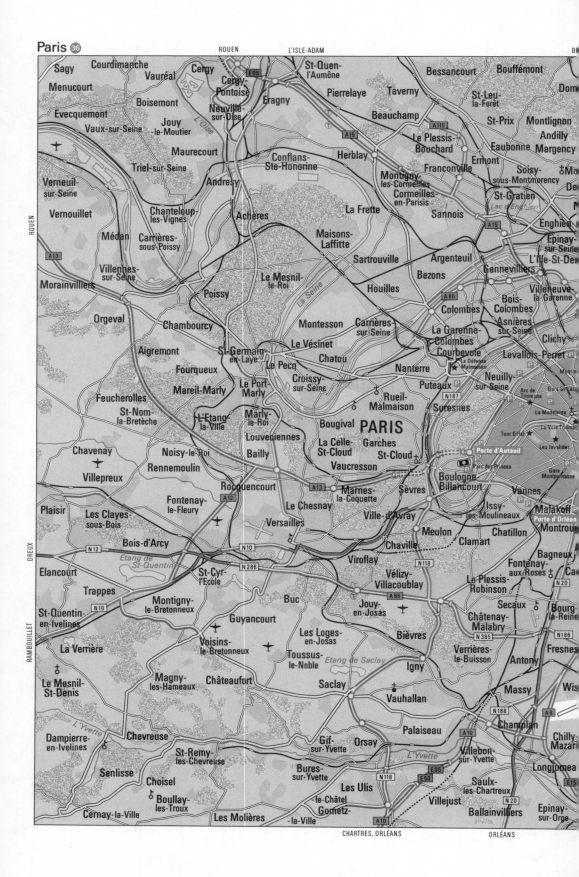

Sagy
Courdimanche
Vauréal
Cergy
St-Quen-l'Aumône
Bessancourt
Bouffémont
Menucourt
Cergy-Pontoise
Pierrelaye
Taverny
St-Leu-la-Forêt
Boisemont
Neuville-sur-Oise
Eragny
Beauchamp
St-Prix
Montlignon
Andilly
Evecquemont
Jouy-le-Moutier
Herblay
Le Plessis-Bouchard
A115
Eaubonne
Margency
Vaux-sur-Seine
Maurecourt
Conflans-Ste-Honorine
Franconville
Ermont
Soisy-sous-Montmorency
Triel-sur-Seine
Andrésy
Montigny-les-Cormeilles
St-Gratien
Lac d'Enghien
Verneuil-sur-Seine
Chanteloup-les-Vignes
Achères
La Frette
Cormeilles-en-Parisis
Sannois
A15
Enghien
Vernouillet
Maisons-Laffitte
Sartrouville
Argenteuil
Gennevilliers
Epinay-sur-Seine
L'Île-St-De
Médan
Carrières-sous-Poissy
Le Mesnil-le-Roi
Bezons
Houilles
Bois-Colombes
Villeneuve-la-Garenne
Villennes-sur-Seine
Colombes
Asnières-sur-Seine
Morainvilliers
Poissy
La Seine
Montesson
Carrières-sur-Seine
La Garenne-Colombes
Clichy
Orgeval
Chambourcy
Le Vésinet
Courbevoie
Levallois-Perret
Aigremont
St-Germain-en-Laye
Chatou
La Défense Malmaison
Fourqueux
Le Pecq
Croissy-sur-Seine
Nanterre
Neuilly-sur-Seine
Arc de Triomphe
Gare St-Laze
Feucherolles
Mareil-Marly
Le Port-Marly
Rueil-Malmaison
Puteaux
A187
La Madeleine
St-Nom-la-Bretèche
L'Etang-la-Ville
Marly-le-Roi
Bougival
PARIS
Suresnes
La Voie-Triomph
Chavenay
Louveciennes
La Celle St-Cloud
Garches
St-Cloud
Tour Eiffel
Les Invalides
Noisy-le-Roi
Bailly
Vaucresson
Porte d'Auteuil
Villepreux
Rennemoulin
Parc des Princes
Rocquencourt
A13
Marnes-la-Coquette
Sèvres
Boulogne-Billancourt
Gare Montparnasse
Plaisir
Les Clayes-sous-Bois
Fontenay-le-Fleury
Le Chesnay
Ville-d'Avray
Vannes
A12
Versailles
Meulon
Issy-les-Moulineaux
Malakoff
Bois-d'Arcy
Chaville
Chatillon
Porte d'Orléan
Montrou
N12
Viroflay
Clamart
Bagneux
Elancourt
Etang de St-Quentin
N286
N118
Vélizy-Villacoublay
Fontenay-aux-Roses
Ca
Trappes
St-Cyr-l'Ecole
A86
Le Plessis-Robinson
N20
St-Quentin-en-Ivelines
Montigny-le-Bretonneux
Buc
Jouy-en-Josas
Secaux
Bourg-la-Reine
N10
Guyancourt
Châtenay-Malabry
La Verrière
Voisins-le-Bretonneux
Les Loges-en-Josas
Bièvres
N385
N186
Fresnes
Le Mesnil-St-Denis
Magny-les-Hameaux
Toussus-le-Noble
Etang de Saclay
Igny
Verrières-le-Buisson
Antony
Dampierre-en-Ivelines
Châteaufort
Saclay
Massy
Wis
L'Yvette
Chevreuse
Vauhallan
N188
A6
Senlisse
St-Remy-les-Chevreuse
Gif-sur-Yvette
Orsay
Palaiseau
A10
Champlan
Choisel
Bures-sur-Yvette
L'Yvette
Villebon-sur-Yvette
Chilly-Mazar
Boullay-les-Troux
N118
E05
Longjumea
Cernay-la-Ville
Les Molières
Les Ulis
le-Châtel
Gometz-la-Ville
E50
Saulx-les-Chartreux
E15
Villejust
Ballainvilliers
Epinay-sur-Orge
A10
N20

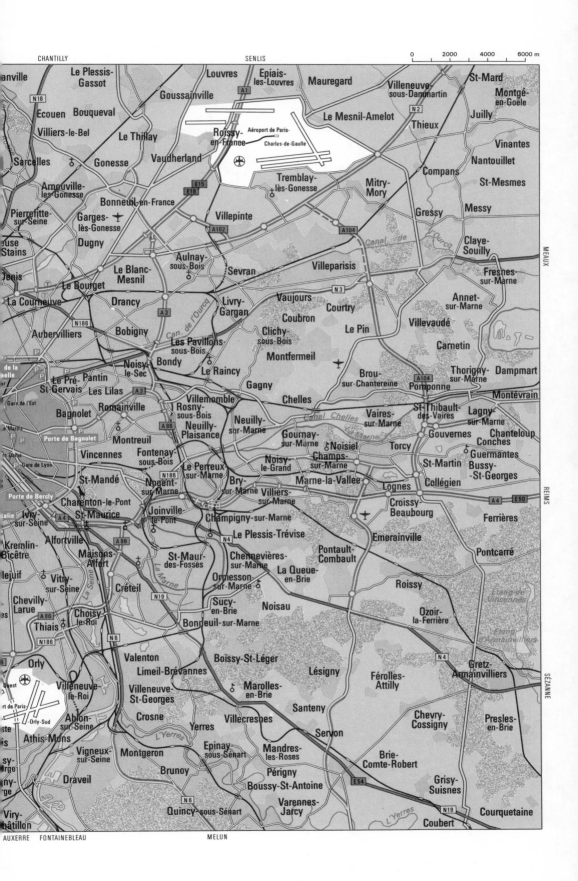

0   2000   4000   6000 m

Le Plessis-Gassot

Louvres

Epiais-les-Louvres

Mauregard

Villeneuve-sous-Dammartin

St-Mard

Montgé-en-Goële

N16

Ecouen

Bouqueval

Goussainville

A1

Le Mesnil-Amelot

Thieux

N2

Juilly

Villiers-le-Bel

Le Thillay

Roissy-en-France

Aéroport de Paris-Charles-de-Gaulle

Vinantes

Nantouillet

Sarcelles

Gonesse

Vaudherland

Compans

St-Mesmes

Arnouville-lès-Gonesse

Bonneuil-en-France

Tremblay-lès-Gonesse

Mitry-Mory

Gressy

Messy

Pierrefitte-sur-Seine

E15

Garges-lès-Gonesse

Villepinte

E19

A102

A104

Claye-Souilly

Dugny

Fresnes-sur-Marne

euse Stains

Le Blanc-Mesnil

Aulnay-sous-Bois

Sevran

Villeparisis

Canal de

l'Ourcq

Annet-sur-Marne

enis

Le Bourget

Drancy

Livry-Gargan

Vaujours

Courtry

N3

Villevaudé

La Courneuve

N186

Coubron

Le Pin

Aubervilliers

Bobigny

Can. de l'Ourcq

A3

Clichy-sous-Bois

Carnetin

Les Pavillons-sous-Bois

Montfermeil

Thorigny-sur-Marne

Dampmart

de la elle

Noisy-le-Sec

Bondy

Le Raincy

Brou-sur-Chantereine

A104

Pomponne

Montévrain

Le Pré-Pantin St-Gervais

Les Lilas

Villemomble

Gagny

Chelles

Canal Chelles

Vaires-sur-Marne

St-Thibault-des-Vaires

Lagny-sur-Marne

Gare de l'Est

A3

Romainville

Rosny-sous-Bois

Marne

Gouvernes

Chanteloup

Bagnolet

e Marais

Neuilly-Plaisance

Neuilly-sur-Marne

Gournay-sur-Marne

Torcy

St-Martin

Conches

re Gare de Lyon

Porte de Bagnolet

Montreuil

Noisiel

Guermantes

Vincennes

Fontenay-sous-Bois

Le Perreux-sur-Marne

Noisy-le-Grand

Champs-sur-Marne

Bussy-St-Georges

Notre-Dame

St-Mandé

Nogent-sur-Marne

N186

Bry-sur-Marne

Marne-la-Vallée

Lognes

Collégien

A4

E50

Porte de Bercly

Charenton-le-Pont

Villiers-sur-Marne

Croissy-Beaubourg

talie

Ivry-sur-Seine

St-Maurice

Joinville-le-Pont

A4

Champigny-sur-Marne

N4

Ferrières

Alfortville

A86

Le Plessis-Trévise

Emerainville

Kremlin-Bicêtre

Maisons-Alfort

St-Maur-des-Fossés

Chennevières-sur-Marne

Pontault-Combault

Pontcarré

lejuif

Vitry-sur-Seine

La Marne

Ormesson-sur-Marne

La Queue-en-Brie

Roissy

Chevilly-Larue

Créteil

Sucy-en-Brie

Noisau

A86

Choisy-le-Roi

N19

Etang de ncennes

Thiais

Bonneuil-sur-Marne

Ozoir-la-Ferrière

N186

La Seine

N6

Orly

Valenton

Boissy-St-Léger

N4

Gretz-Armainvilliers

st

Villeneuve-le-Roi

Limeil-Brévannes

Lésigny

Férolles-Attilly

Etang d'Armainvilliers

rt de Paris-Orly-Sud

Villeneuve-St-Georges

Marolles-en-Brie

Chevry-Cossigny

Presles-en-Brie

Athis-Mons

Ablon-sur-Seine

Crosne

Yerres

Villecresnes

Santeny

Servon

Brie-Comte-Robert

y-rge ny-ge

Vigneux-sur-Seine

Montgeron

L'Yerres

Epinay-sous-Sénart

Mandres-les-Roses

Viry-hâtillon

Draveil

Brunoy

Périgny

Boussy-St-Antoine

E54

Grisy-Suisnes

N6

Quincy-sous-Sénart

Varennes-Jarcy

N19

Courquetaine

L'Yerres

Coubert

MEAUX

REIMS

SÉZANNE

TRAGLIATA

151
M. Lascone

M. Procvio
116

La Giustiniana

Cassia Bis

Flaminia

Cassia

Volusia

Boccea

Ottavia

Tba. di Nerone

Tor
di Quinto

S. Onofrio

Della
Vittoria

Flaminio

Stadio
Flaminio

Monte Mario

Pinciano

Primavalle

Trionfale

PALO

Boccea

Casalotti

Città del
Vaticano

Castel
S. Angelo

San Pietro
Basilica

Galoppatóio
Mausoleo
di Augusto

La Monachina

Valcanuta

G.R.A.

1

Porta
Aurelia

Foro
Romano

Malagrotta

1

Aurelia

Circo
Massimo

Monteverde
Nuovo

Gianicolense

Terme
di Caracalla

Piramide

Garbatell

Portuense

M. Ficone
57

La Pisana

La Parrocchietta

Basilica di
S. Paolo

Ostiense

CIVITAVECCHIA

F. Tevere

60
M. Lumacaro

Magliana

Magliana

8

Ponte Galèria

A12
E80

A12 E80

Cecc

FIUMICINO

Ostiense

F. Tevere

Castel Fusano

Laurentin

Pontina

Vitinia

8 bis

148

MAGLIANO MENTANA

0 1000 2000 3000 m

GUIDONIA

TIVOLI

L'AQUILA

GALICANO

COLONNA

FROSINONE

ARTENA

Bufalotta

Inviolata

Nomentana

Monte Sacro
Alto

San Basilio

5

Monte
Sacro

Ponte Mammolo

Settecamini

Albuccione

F. Aniène

Tiburtina

Lunghezza

Roma-Est
Lunghezza

E80

Trieste

ROMA

5

Agnese

F. Aniène

Cassalone

Tor
Cervata

E80
A24

Cervelletta

Salone Vecchio

A24

Pietralata

Basilica di
S. Lorenzo

omentano

Tor Sapienza

Collatino

Prenestina

Ost d. Osa

Porta
Maggiore

P

Labicano

Centocelle

Porta
S. Giovanni

Tor
Pignattara

G.R.A.

Tuscolano

6

Alessandrina

Finocchio

Appio-Latino

Don Bosco

Casilina

6

eatino

Appio-Claudio

Quadraro

Torrenova

Gaia

Catacombe

7

Appio-Pignatelli

T R

T R

A2
E45

Tuscolana

Roma Torrenova

Anagnina

T R

Romanella

215

T R

Appia

511

Frascati

Ardeatina

G.R.A.

Clampino

7

CASTEL DI LEVA ALBANO

41

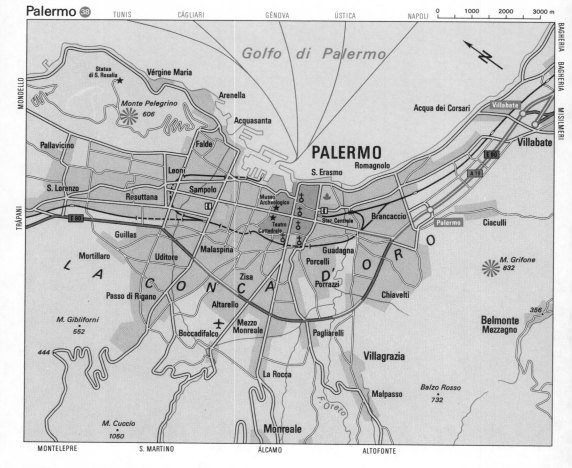

TUNIS   CÁGLIARI   GÉNOVA   ÚSTICA   NAPOLI   0   1000   2000   3000 m

BAGHERIA
BAGHERIA
MISILMERI

Golfo di Palermo

MONDELLO

Statua
di S. Rosalia ★   Vérgine Maria

Monte Pelegrino
606

Arenella

Acquasanta

Acqua dei Corsari   Villabate

Villabate

Pallavicino   Falde

Leoni   Romagnolo   A 19

S. Erasmo

TRAPANI   S. Lorenzo   Sampolo   **PALERMO**

Resuttana   Museo
Archeologico   Staz. Centrale   Brancaccio   Palermo   Ciaculli

E 90   Guillas   Teatro
Cattedrale

Malaspina   Guadagna   M. Grifone
832

Mortillaro   Uditore   Zisa   Porcelli

L A   C O N C A   Porrazzi   D '   O R O

Passo di Rigano   Altarello   Chiavelti

M. Gibliforni
552   Mezzo
Monreale   356

Boccadifalco   Pagliarelli   **Belmonte**
Mezzagno

444   Villagrazia

La Rocca

Malpasso   *Balzo Rosso*
732

F. Oreto

M. Cuccio
1050   **Monreale**

MONTELEPRE   S. MARTINO   ÁLCAMO   ALTOFONTE

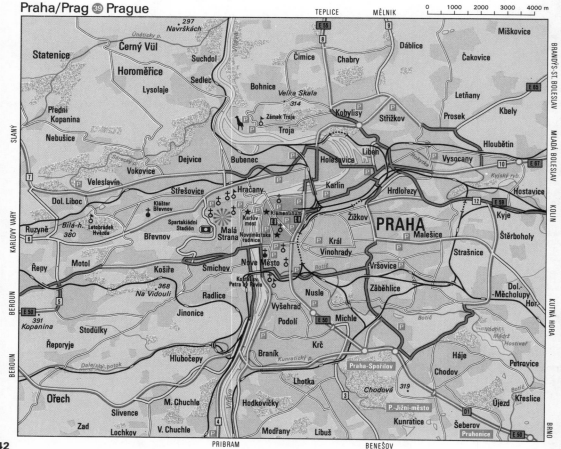

TEPLICE   MĚLNIK   0   1000   2000   3000   4000 m

297
Navrškách   E 55   8   9   Miškovice

BRANDÝS-ST. BOLESLAV

Statenice   Černý Vůl   Suchdol   Čimice   Chabry   Dáblice   Čakovice

Horoměřice   Sedlec   Bohnice   *Velká Skála*   Letňany   Kbely   E 65

Lysolaje   *314*   Kobylisy   Prosek   E 67

Přední
Kopanina   Zámek Troja   Střížkov   10

Nebušice   Troja   Vysočany   Hloubětín   MLADÁ BOLESLAV

Vokovice   Dejvice   Bubeneč   Holešovice   Libeň   *Rokytka*   Hostavice   KOLÍN

SLANÝ   Veleslavín   Střešovice   Hračany   Karlín   Hrdlořezy   Kyjský ryb.   12   E 59   Kyje

Dol. Liboc   Klášter
Břevnov   Spartakiádní
Stadión   Klementinum   Žižkov   **PRAHA**   Štěrboholy

KARLOVY VARY   Ruzyně   Bílá h.
380   Letohrádek
Hvězda   Malá
Strana   Karlův
most   Novoměstská
radnice   Král   Malešice   Strašnice   KUTNÁ HORA

Řepy   Motol   Břevnov   Košíře   Smíchov   Nové Město   Vinohrady   Vršovice   Dol.-
Měcholupy
Hor.

BEROUN   E 50   5   Na Vidouli
368   Radlice   Kostel sv.
Petra a Pavla   Nusle   Zaběhlice   *Botič*

391
Kopanina   Jinonice   Vyšehrad   Michle   *Botič*   Háje   Petrovice

BEROUN   Řeporyje   Stodůlky   Podolí   E 50   Krč   *Vodní*
nádrž
Hostivař   Chodov

Hlubočepy   Praha-Spořilov   Chodová   Kreslice   BRNO

Ořech   *Dalejský potok*   M. Chuchle   Braník   Lhotka   *319*   Újezd

Zad   Slivence   V. Chuchle   Hodkovičky   Kunratický p.   P.-Jižní-město   Šeberov

Lochkov   4   Modřany   Libuš   Kunratice   3   Pruhonice   E 50   01

PRIBRAM   BENEŠOV

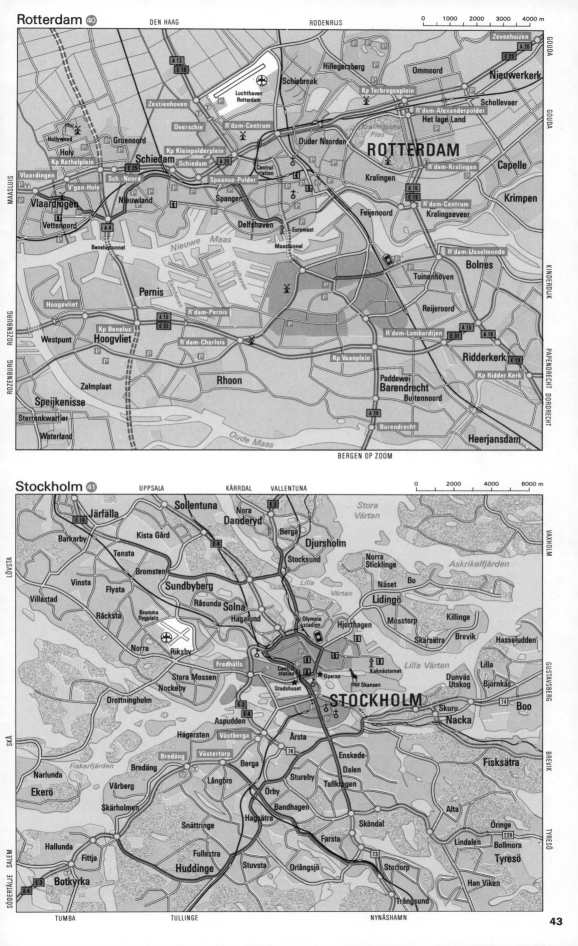

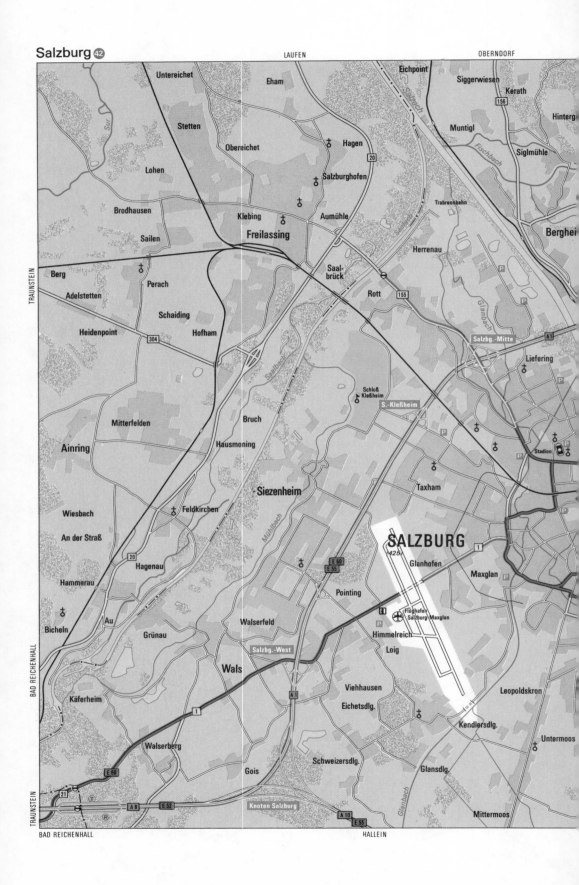

LAUFEN   OBERNDORF

Eichpoint

Siggerwiesen

Kerath

156

Hinterg

Muntigl

Siglmühle

Untereichet

Eham

Stetten

Hagen

20

Obereichet

Salzburghofen

Berghei

Lohen

Salzburgerhofen

Trabrennbahn

Brodhausen

Klebing

Aumühle

Freilassing

Herrenau

Sailen

Saal-
brück

TRAUNSTEIN

Berg

Perach

Rott

155

Salzbg.-Mitte

A1

Adelstetten

Liefering

Schaiding

Heidenpoint

Hofham

304

Schloß
Kleßheim

S.-Kleßheim

Stadion

Mitterfelden

Bruch

Ainring

Hausmoning

Taxham

Feldkirchen

Siezenheim

Wiesbach

An der Straß

20

E 60
E 55

SALZBURG
(425)

Glanhofen

Maxglan

Hagenau

Hammerau

Pointing

Flughafen
Salzburg-Maxglan

Bicheln

Au

Grünau

Walserfeld

Himmelreich

Loig

Leopoldskron

Salzbg.-West

BAD REICHENHALL

Wals

Viehhausen

Käferheim

Eichetsdlg.

Kendlersdlg.

Untermoos

1

Walserberg

Schweizersdlg.

Glansdlg.

E 60

Gois

Knoten Salzburg

Mittermoos

TRAUNSTEIN

21

A 8

E 52

A 10
E 55

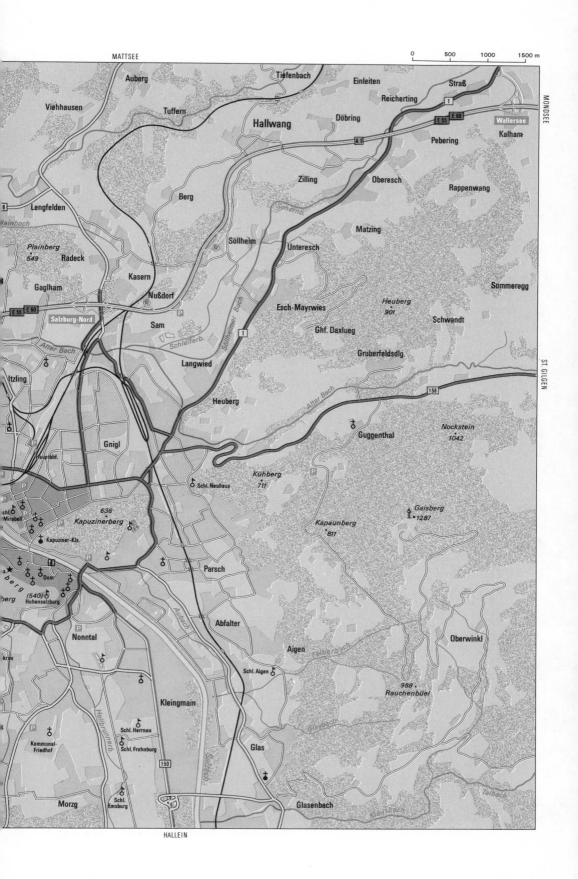

0   500   1000   1500 m

MONDSEE

Auberg

Tiefenbach

Einleiten

Straß

Reicherting

1

Viehhausen

Tuffern

Döbring

E 55   E 60

Hallwang

Wallersee

Pebering

Kalham

ST. GILGEN

Zilling

Oberesch

Rappenwang

Berg

A 1

Schernb.

Lengfelden

Matzing

6

lainbach

Söllheim

Unteresch

Sommeregg

Plainberg
549

Radeck

Heuberg
901

Kasern

Esch-Mayrwies

Schwandt

E 55   E 60

Gaglham

Nußdorf

Söllheimer Bach

Ghf. Daxlueg

Salzburg-Nord

Sam

1

Gruberfeldsdlg.

Alter Bach

Schleiferb.

Langwied

Alter Bach

158

Heuberg

Itzling

Guggenthal

Nockstein
1042

Gnigl

Kühberg
711

Hauptbhf.

Gaisberg
1287

636

Kapaunberg
811

chl.
Mirabel

Kapuzinerberg

Schl. Neuhaus

Kapuziner-Kls.

Parsch

berg

Dom

Oberwinkl

(540)
Hohensalzburg

berg

Abfalter

Aubach

Nonntal

Aigen

Schl. Aigen

kron

988
Rauchenbüel

Kleingmain

Schl. Herrnau

Glas

Kommunal-
Friedhof

Schl. Frohnburg

150

Glasbach

Morzg

Schl.
Emsburg

Heilbrunner b.

Salzach

Talbach

Glasenbach

Klausbach

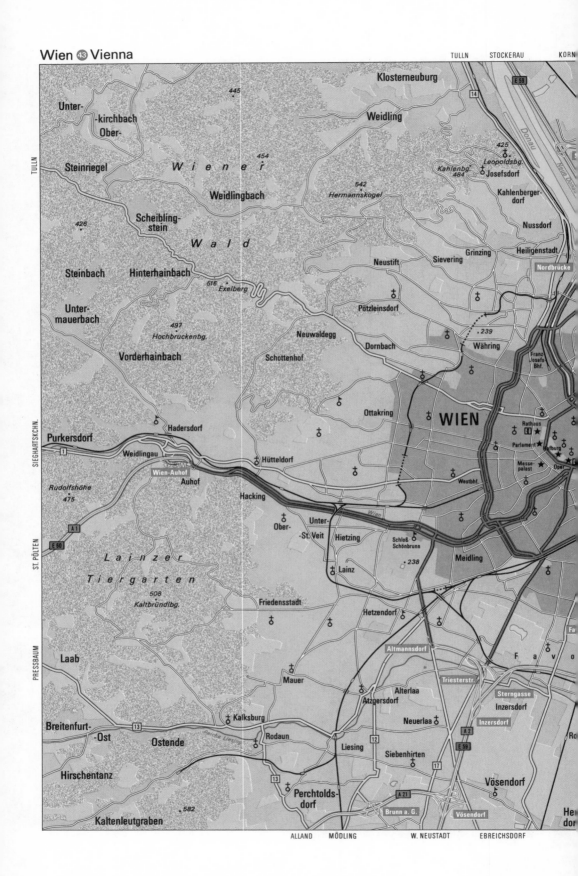

Klosterneuburg

Unter-
-kirchbach
Ober-

Weidling

14

E 59

Donau

TULLN

Steinriegel

Wiener

454

425
Leopoldsbg.

Kahlenbg. *484*
Josefsdorf

Neue Donau

Weidlingbach

542
Hermannskogel

Kahlenberger-
dorf

Scheibling-
stein

426

Wald

Nussdorf

Sievering   Grinzing   Heiligenstadt

Steinbach   Hinterhainbach

516
Exelberg

Neustift

Pötzleinsdorf

Währing

Nordbrücke

Untermauerbach

497
Hochbruckenbg.

Neuwaldegg

239

Vorderhainbach

Schottenhof

Dornbach

Franz
Josefs
Bhf.

Hadersdorf

Ottakring

WIEN

Rathaus ★
Parlament ★ Hofburg

Purkersdorf

1

Weidlingau

Hütteldorf

Messe-
palast

Oper

SIEGHARTSKCHN.

Wien-Auhof

Auhof

Westbhf.

Hacking

Wien

Rudolfshöhe
475

A 1

Ober-

Unter-
-St. Veit   Hietzing

Schloß
Schönbrunn

Meidling

ST. PÖLTEN

E 60

Lainzer

Lainz

238

Tiergarten

508
Kaltbründlbg.

Friedensstadt

Hetzendorf

PRESSBAUM

Laab

Altmannsdorf

F a v o

Mauer

Triesterstr.

Alterlaa

Sterngasse

Atzgersdorf

Inzersdorf

Breitenfurt-
-Ost   Ostende

Kalksburg

Neuerlaa

Inzersdorf

13

Reiche Liesing

Rodaun

Liesing

12

A 2

E 59

Ro

Hirschentanz

Siebenhirten

17

Vösendorf

13

582

Perchtolds-
dorf

A 21

Brunn a. G.

Vösendorf

He
dor

Kaltenleutgraben

0   1000   2000   3000 m

Stammersdorf

Streberdorf

Gerasdorf
b. Wien

Deutsch-
Wagram

Oberlisse

E461

Gross-
Jedlerdorf

Nordrand-
siedlung

Neu.-
Süßenbrunn

Aderklaa

8

7   163

8

Großfeldsdlg.

M a r c h f e l d

Floridsdorf   Leopoldau

Paxsiedlung

Invaliden-
sdlg.

3

Stadtrand-
siedlung

Neueßling

Floridsdorf
brücke   Donaufeld

Kagran

Breitenlee

Raasdorf

Nordbahn-
brücke   Alte Donau

Donaupark
Donaupark

Neukagran

Hirschstetten

LEOPOLDSDORF   ORTH

Brigittenauer
Brücke

UNO-
City

Nordbhf.

Kaiser-
mühlen   Reichsbrücke

Stadlau   3

D o n a u s t a d t

★ Riesenrad

Aspern

Messegelände

Prater
Stadion   Praterbrücke

Kaisermühlen

Essling   3

Handelskai

Mitte

Stadlauer
Brücke

Gross-
Enzersdorf

A 20

10

L   Projektierter   Donau-Oder   Kanal   o   b   a

Prater

St. Marx

andstr.

Donaukanal

Simmeringer Heide

Mühl-
leiten

3

S i m m e r i n g

A 4

u

Donau

Kaiserebers-
dorf   Albern

Schwechat

152

Zentral-
friedhof   Mannswörth

Kurzzentrum

E 58

Oberlaa   Liesing

Unterlaa   9

Flughafen
Wien-Schwechat

Kledering   Ranners-
dorf   10   A 4

Rustenfeld   11

15   E 60

Zwölfaxing   Aichhof

Flughafen
Wien-Schwechat

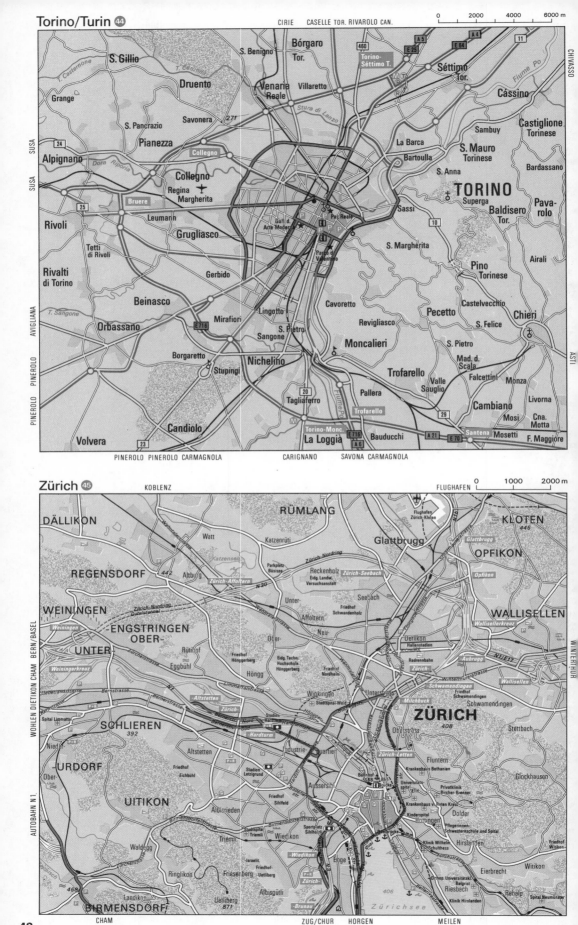

Torino/Turin ㊹

CIRIE · CASELLE TOR. RIVAROLO CAN.

0 2000 4000 6000 m

CHIVASSO

S. Gillio
Druento
Grange
S. Pancrazio
Pianezza
Alpignano
Collegno
Collegno
Regina Margherita
Bruere
Leumann
Rivoli
Tetti di Rivoli
Grugliasco
Rivalti di Torino
Beinasco
Orbassano
Gerbido
Mirafiori
Lingotto
S. Pietro Sangone
Borgaretto
Stupingi
Nichelino
Candiolo
Volvera
Tagliaferro
Trofarello
Torino-Monc.
La Loggia
Bauducchi

S. Benigno
Bórgaro Tor.
Venaria Reale
Villaretto
Savonera
271
Torino-Séttimo T.
Séttimo Tor.
Cássino
Castiglione Torinese
Sambuy
La Barca
Bartoulla
S. Mauro Torinese
S. Anna
Bardassano
TORINO
Superga
Baldisero Tor.
Pavarolo
Sassi
S. Margherita
Pino Torinese
Airali
Cavoretto
Revigliasco
Pecetto
Castelvecchio
S. Felice
Chieri
Moncalieri
S. Pietro
Mad. d. Scala
Falcettini
Monza
Trofarello
Valle Sáuglio
Livorna
Cambiano
Mosi
Cna. Motta
Mosetti
Santena
F. Maggiore
Pallera

SUSA
SUSA
24
25
AVIGLIANA
PINEROLO
PINEROLO
23
E 716
20
M
Torino-Monc.
E 716
A 6
A 21
E 70
29
10
460
A 5
E 25
E 64
A 4
11
Parco d. Valentino
Pal. Reale
Gall. d. Arte Moderna
ASTI

PINEROLO PINEROLO CARMAGNOLA   CARIGNANO   SAVONA CARMAGNOLA

Zürich ㊺

KOBLENZ

FLUGHAFEN

0 1000 2000 m

DÄLLIKON
REGENSDORF
WEININGEN
ENGSTRINGEN OBER-
UNTER-
Weiningen
Weiningerkreuz
SCHLIEREN
URDORF
UITIKON
BIRMENSDORF

Watt
Katzenrüti
Altburg
Zürich-Affoltern
Unter-
Affoltern
Rütihof
Eggbühl
Höngg
Albisrieden
Triemli
Waldegg
Ringlikon
Uetliberg
Landikon

RÜMLANG
Parkplatz Büsisee
Reckenholz
Eidg. Landw. Versuchsanstalt
Zürich-Seebach
Seebach
Zürich-Nordring
Neu-
Ober-
Friedhof Hönggerberg
Eidg. Techn. Hochschule Hönggerberg
Friedhof Nordheim
Winkingen
Unterstrass
Stadtspital Waid
Friedhof Schwandenholz
Friedhof Sihlfeld
Zürich
Stadion Letzigrund
Stadion Hardturm
Hardturm
Industrie-Quartier
Aussersihl
Sportplatz Sihlhölzli
Wiedikon
Enge
Israelit. Friedhof-Uetliberg
Albisgütli
Friesenberg

FLUGHAFEN
Flughafen Zürich-Kloten
KLOTEN
OPFIKON
Glattbrugg
Glattbrugg
Opfikon
WALLISELLEN
Wallisellerkreuz
Uerlikon Hallenbahn
Radrennbahn
Aubrugg
Zürich
Schwamendingen
Friedhof Schwamendingen
Schwamendingen
Stettbach
Milchbuck
ZÜRICH
Oberstrass
Zürich-Letten
Fluntern
Krankenhaus Bethanien
Glockhausen
Bahnhof SBB
Universitätsspital ETH
Krankenhaus v. Roten Kreuz
Privatklinik Bircher-Benner
Dolder
Kinderspital
Pflegerinnen-Schwesternschule und Spital
Klinik Wilhelm Schulthess
Hirslanden
Friedhof Witikon
Witikon
Riesbach
Rehalp
Orthop. Universitätsklinik Balgrist
Klinik Hirslanden
Spital Neumünster
Eierbrecht

WINTERTHUR
N 1
N 20
442
446
408
392
468
871
406

AUTOBAHN N 1.
WOHLEN DIETIKON CHAM BERN/BASEL

Zürichsee

CHAM   ZUG/CHUR HORGEN   MEILEN

48

3

Index of place names

Localités citées

Ortsverzeichnis

Località citate

Localidades citadas

Place names and other places of interest are in alphabetical order according to the spelling of the country concerned. Each name is followed by a page number referring to the road maps in section 1, and then by the grid reference letter and number.

Example: Lausanne 74 B2 = page 74, grid B2.

Les noms des localités ou d'autres endroits intéressants figurent en ordre alphabétique selon la langue du pays en question. Chaque nom est suivi par le numéro de page se référant aux cartes routières en section 1 et après par la lettre et la chiffre du quadrillage.

Par example: Lausanne 74 B2 = page 74, quadrillage B2.

Namen von Ortschaften und anderen Sehenswürdigkeiten sind in alphabetischer Reihenfolge in der Schreibweise des jeweiligen Landes aufgeführt. Jedem Namen folgt die Seitenzahl einer Strassenkarte in Teil 1 und anschliessend Buchstabe und Ziffer des Rasters.

Beispiel: Lausanne 74 B2 = Seite 74, Raster B2.

Nomi di luoghi ed altri posti di interosse son elencati in ordine alfabetico nella lingus del paese in questione. Ogni nome è seguito dal numero di pagina che si riferisce alle carte stradali in sezione I, e dalla lettere e chifro del quadranto.

Esempio: Lausanne 74 B2 = pagina 74, quadranto B2.

Los nombres de los principales lugares de interés y de otros importantes sitios turísticos están ordenados, alfabéticamente según el país correspondiente. Cada nombre es seguido de un número de página correspondiente al mapa de carreteras en la sección I y por una coordenada conformada por una letra y un número, para la exacta ubicación del lugar.

Ejemplo: Lausana 74 B2 = página 74, coordenada B2.

74	A	B
1		1
2		• Lausanne 2
3		3
	A	B

International distinguishing signs

Signaux de distinction internationaux

Internationale Unterscheidungszeichen

Segnali distintivi internazionale

Senãles internacionales distintivas

A	Österreich/Austria	F	France	MC	Monaco
AL	Shqipëria/Albania	FL	Liechtenstein	N	Norge/Norway
AND	Andorra	GB	Great Britain and Northern Ireland	NL	Nederland/Netherlands
B	Belgique/Belgium	GBA	Alderney	P	Portugal
BG	Bålgarija/Bulgaria	GBG	Guernsey Channel Islands	PL	Polska/Poland
CH	Suisse/Switzerland	GBJ	Jersey	RO	România/Romania
CS	Ceskoslovensko/Czechoslovakia	GBM	Isle of Man	RSM	San Marino
CY	Cyprus	GBZ	Gilbraltar	SF	Suomi/Finland
D	Bundesrepublik Deutschland/West Germany	GR	Hellás/Greece	SU	Sojuz Sovetskich Socialističeskich Republik/Union of Soviet Socialist Republics
		H	Magyarország/Hungary		
DDR	Deutsche Demokratische Republik/East Germany	I	Itália/Italy		
		IRL	Ireland	TR	Türkiye/Turkey
DK	Danmark/Denmark	L	Luxembourg	V	Città del Vaticano/Vatican City
E	España/Spain	M	Malta	YU	Jugoslavija/Yugoslavia

A

Å 9 C1
Å 8 A3
Å 9 C/D1/2
Å 33 C2
Å 46 B2
Aach 91 B/C3
Aachen 79 D2
Aachen-Eilendorf 79 D2
Aadorf 91 B/C3
Aakoinen 24 B3
Aalen 91 D2
Aalen-Ebnat 91 D2
Aalen-Wasseralfingen 91 D1/2
Aalsmeer 66 A/B3
Aalst 78 B1/2
Aalten 67 C3
Aalter 78 A/B1
Åan 37 C3
Äänekoski 21 D3, 22 A3
Aapajärvi 12 B2
Aapajärvi 17 D2, 18 A1
Aapua 17 D1
Aarau 90 B3, 105 C1
Aarberg 104 B1
Aarbergen 80 B2/3
Aarburg 105 C1
Aardenburg 78 A/B1
Aareavaara 11 C3
Aareschlucht 105 C1/2
Aatsinki 13 C3
Aavasaksa 17 D2
Aba 128 B1
Ababuj 162 B2
Abades 160 B2
Abadiano 153 D1
Abadín 150 B1
Abadino 153 D1
Abaliget 128 B2
Abalos 153 D2
A Baña 150 A2
Abánades 161 D2
Abanilla 169 C3
Abanto 162 A1/2
Abanto 153 C1
Abarán 169 D3
Abárzuza 153 D2, 154 A2
Abaurrea Alta 108 B3, 155 C2
Abbadía San Salvatore 116 B3
Abbasanta 123 C2
Abbaye 79 B/C2
Abbaye de Chaalis 87 D1
Abbaye de la Réau 101 C2
Abbaye de Montmajour 111 C2
Abbaye de Senanque 111 C2
Abbaye d'Orval 79 C3
Abbaye du Thoronet 112 A3
Abbazia Casamari 119 C2
Abbazia di Fossanova 118 B2
Abbazia di Monte Oliveto Maggiore 115 C3, 116 B2
Abbazia di Montecassino 119 C2
Abbazia di Piona 105 D2, 106 A2
Abbazia di Práglia 107 C3
Abbazia di Valvisciolo 118 B2
Abbazia San Vincenzo al Volturno 119 C2
Abbekås 50 B3
Abbendorf 69 D2
Abbeville 77 D2
Abbey 59 D1, 61 C2
Abbeyfeale 55 C3
Abbey Town 57 C3, 60 A/B1
Abbiategrasso 105 D3
Abborberg 15 C/D3
Abborrträsk 16 A3
Abborrträsk 31 C1
Abbots Bromley 59 D3, 61 C3, 64 A1
Abbotsbury 63 D3
Abbotsford 57 C2

Abbotts Ann 64 A3, 76 A1
Abegondo 150 B1
Abejar 153 C/D3, 161 C1
Abela 164 B3, 170 A1
Abella de la Conca 155 D2/3
Abelnes 42 B3
Abelvær 28 B1
Abenberg 91 D1, 92 A1
Abenberg-Wassermungenau 91 D1, 92 A1
Abengibre 169 B/C2
Abenójar 167 C2
Åbenrå 52 B2
Abensberg 92 A/B2
Abensberg-Offenstetten 92 A/B2
Aberaeron 59 B/C3
Aberargie 57 C1
Aberdare 63 C1
Aberdaron 58 B3
Aberdeen 54 B2
Aberdovey 59 C3
Aberdur 57 C1
Aberfeldy 56 B1
Aberffraw 58 B2
Aberfoyle 56 B1
Abergavenny 63 C1
Abergele 59 C2, 60 A3
Åberget 16 A2
Abergynolwyn 59 C3
Aberlady 57 C1/2
Abernethy 57 C1
Aberporth 62 B1
Abersoch 58 B3
Abersoch 55 D3
Abertillery 63 C1
Abertura 166 A1/2
Aberystwyth 59 C3
Abetone 114 B2, 116 A1
Abiada 152 B1/2
Abia de la Obispalía 161 D3
Abia de las Torres 152 B2
Abide 149 C1
Abiego 155 C3
Abild 49 D2, 50 A1
Abîme du Bramabiau 110 B2
Abingdon 65 C3
Abington 57 B/C2
Abington 54 B3
Abiskojaurestugan 9 D2
Abiskoturiststation 9 D2
Abiul 158 A3, 164 B1
Abla 173 D2
Ablagão 158 A1/2
Ablanque 161 D2
Ablis 87 C2
Ablitas 154 A3
Abmelaseter 4 B3, 10 A/B1
Åbo 28 B3, 33 D1, 34 A1
Åbo 39 D1, 40 A1
Abobreira 164 B1
Aboim 150 A3
A Bola 150 B3
Abondance 104 B2
Abony 129 D1
Åbosjö 30 B2, 35 D1
Åbränna 29 C3, 34 A1
Abrantes 164 B1
Abraur 16 A2
Abraveses 158 B2
Abreiro 158 B1
Abreschwiller 89 D2, 90 A2
Abriès 112 B1
Abrigada 164 A2
Abrigos 162 A2/3
Abrucena 173 D2
Abrud 97 D3, 140 B1
Abtenau 93 C3
Abtsgmünd 91 C/D1/2
Abtsgmünd-Untergröningen 91 C1/2
Abusejo 159 D2
Åby 46 B2
Åbybro 48 B1
Åbyggeby 40 A/B2
Abytorp 46 A1
A Caniza 150 B3
Acate 125 C3
Accadía 120 A2
Accéglio 112 B2
Accettura 120 B3
Acciarella 118 B2
Acciaroli 120 A3
Accous 108 B3, 154 B1/2
Accrington 59 D1/2, 60 B2

Accúmoli 117 D3, 119 B/C1
Acebo 159 C3
Acebuche 171 C2
Acedera 166 A2
Acehuche 159 C3, 165 D1
Acered 162 A1/2
Acerenza 120 B2
Acerno 119 D3, 120 A2
Acerra 119 D3
Aceuchal 165 D2
Ach 92 B2
Acharnaí 147 D2
Achenkirch 92 A3
Achenwald 92 A3
Achern 90 B2
Achern-Wagshurst 90 B2
Acheux-en-Amiénois 78 A3
Achíllion 143 D3
Achíllion 142 A3
Achim 68 A2
Achinós 147 C1
Achladochórion 144 A/B1
Achladókambos 147 C3
Achnacroish 56 A1
Achnasheen 54 A2
Achstetten 91 C2
Aci Castello 125 D2
Aci Catena 125 D2
Acireale 125 D2
Acle 65 D1/2
A Coruna 150 A/B1
Acquacadda 123 C3
Acquacalda 125 C/D1
Acqua-Doria 113 D3
Acquafredda 106 B3
Acqualagna 115 D3, 117 C2
Acquanegra Cremonese 106 A3, 114 A1
Acquanegra sul Chiese 106 B3
Acquapendente 116 B3, 118 A1
Acquarossa [Biasca] 105 D2
Acquasanta Terme 117 D3, 119 C1
Acquasparta 117 C3, 118 B1
Acquaviva 115 C3, 116 B2
Acquaviva delle Fonti 121 C2
Acquaviva Picena 117 D2/3
Acquedolci 125 C2
Acquigny 76 B3, 86 A/B1
Acqui Terme 113 C1
Acri 122 B1
Ács 95 C3
Acsád 94 B3, 127 D1, 128 A1
Ada 129 D3
Ada 140 A1
Adahuesca 155 C2/3
Adak 16 A3
Adakgruvan 16 A3
Adalsbruk 38 A2
Ådalsvollen 28 B3, 33 D1, 34 A1
Adamuz 167 C3, 172 B1
Adanero 160 A/B2
Adaševci 133 C1
Ådbodarna 39 C1
Addaya 157 C1
Addington 65 C3
Adé 108 B3, 155 C1
Adelboden [Frutigen] 105 C2
Adelebsen 81 C1
Adelfia 121 C2
Ådelfors 51 C1
Adelmannsfelden 91 C/D1
Adelöv 46 A3
Adelsdorf 81 D3
Adelsheim 91 C1
Adelshofen-Tauberzell 91 D1
Adelsö 47 C1
Adelsried 91 D2
Ademuz 163 C2
Adenau 80 A2
Aderstedt 69 C3
Adinkerke 78 A1
Adjud 141 D2
Adliswil 105 C/D1
Admont 93 D3

Ådnekvam 36 A3
Ådneram 42 B2
Adolfsberg (Örebro) 46 A1
Adolfsström 15 C/D2
Adony 129 C1
Adorf 82 B2
A dos Cunhados 164 A2
Adra 173 C/D2
Adradas 161 D1
Adrall 155 C2
Adrano 125 C2
Ádria 115 C1
Aduanas 169 D2
Aduard 67 C1
Adzaneta 162 B3
Aerzen 68 A/B3
Aesch 90 A3
A Estrada 150 A2
Aetós 146 A1
Aetós 146 B3
Aetós 143 C2
Aetsä 24 B1
Åfar 32 B2
Åfarnes 32 A3
Affden 67 B/C3, 79 D1
Affing 91 D2, 92 A2
Affoltern am Albis 105 C/D1
Áfidnai 147 D2
Afife 150 A3, 158 A1
Áfissos 144 A3
Áfitos 144 A2
Áfitos 148 B1
Aflenz Kurort 94 A3
A Fonsagrada 151 C1
Åfors 16 B3
Afragola 119 D3
Afritz 126 B1/2
Afsluitdijk 66 B2
Aftraet 28 B3, 33 D1
Aga 36 B3
Aga 82 B2
Agallas 159 C2
Ågård 29 C2
Ågård 129 B/C1
Ágasegyháza 129 C1
Agay 112 B3
Agazzano 113 D1, 114 A1
Agde 110 B3
Agdenes 28 A3, 33 C1
Agen 109 C2
Ager 155 C3
Agerbæk 48 A3, 52 A1
Agérola 119 D3
Agerskov 52 B1/2
Agger 48 A2
Aggersund 48 B1/2
Ággius 123 D1
Aggösundet 31 C3
Aggsbach Markt 94 A2
Aggstein 94 A2
Agiá 143 D3, 144 A3
Agiá 148 B1
Agía Ánna 147 D1
Agía Marína 147 D3
Agía Marína 147 D3
Agía Marína 147 C1
Agía Paraskeví 142 B2
Agía Pelagía 148 B3
Agía Sofía 147 D1
Agiásos 149 C2
Agía Triás 146 B2
Agía Triás 147 C2
Agići 131 C1
Agighiol 141 D2
Ágii Anárgiri 143 D3
Ágii Apóstoli 147 D2
Ágii Apóstoli 147 D2
Ágii Theódori 147 C2
Agiófillon 143 C3
Agiókambos 143 D3, 144 A3
Ágios Achíllios 142 B1/2
Ágios Andréas 147 C3
Ágios Athanásios 145 C1
Ágios Athanásios 143 C1
Ágios Charálambos 145 C/D1
Ágios Charálambos 149 C1
Ágios Dimítrios 147 C2
Ágios Dimítrios 143 D2
Ágios Efstrátios 145 C3
Ágios Efstrátios 149 C1
Ágios Geórgios 146 B1
Ágios Geórgios 147 D3
Ágios Germanós 143 B/C1
Ágios Harálampos 143 D3

Ágios Ioánnis 144 A3
Ágios Ïoánnis 148 B1
Ágios Kírikos 149 C2
Ágios Konstantínos 147 C1
Ágios Loukás 147 D2
Ágios Matthéos 142 A3
Ágios Nikólaos 147 C3
Ágios Nikólaos 142 B3
Ágios Nikólaos 146 A1
Ágios Nikólaos 144 B2
Ágios Nikólaos 147 D1
Ágios Nikoláos 146 B3
Ágios Pandeleímon 143 C1/2
Ágios Pétros 143 D1
Ágios Pétros 147 C3
Ágios Pródromos 144 A2
Ágios Stéfanos 147 D2
Ágios Thomás 147 D2
Ágios Vasílios 147 C3
Ágios Vlásios 146 B1
Ágios Zacharías 142 B2
Agira 125 C2
Aglapsvik 4 A3
Aglasterhausen 91 C1
Aglen 28 C2
Agliana 114 B2, 116 A/B1
Agliano 113 C1
Agliè 105 C2
Aglientu 123 D1
Agnana Cálabra 122 A/B3
Agnanda 142 B3
Agnanda 148 A1
Agnanderón 143 C3
Agnås 31 C2
Agnita 140 B1
Agnone 119 D2
Agnone Bagni 125 D3
Agon 85 D1
Agonac 101 D3
Agoncillo 153 D2
Ágordo 107 C2
Agost 169 C3
Ågotnes 36 A3
Ágrafa 146 B1
Agramón 168 B3
Agramunt 155 D3, 163 D1
Agras 143 C1
Ágreda 153 D3, 154 A3, 162 A1
Agreliá 143 C3
Agri 49 C2/3
Agriá 144 A3
Agrigento 124 B3
Agrínion 146 A1
Agrínion 148 A/B2
Agriovótanon 148 B2
Agriovótanon 147 C/D1
Agrochão 151 C3, 159 C1
Agrón 173 C2
Agrópoli 120 A3
Ågskaret 14 B1
Agua Amarga 174 A2
Aguada de Baixo 158 A2
Aguadulce 173 D2
Aguadulce 172 A2
Agualva 164 A2
A Guarda 150 A3
Aguarón 163 C1
Aguas 154 B2
Aguas Belas 158 A3, 164 B1
Aguas Cándidas 153 C2
Aguas de Busot 169 D2/3
Aguaviva 162 B2
Aguaviva de la Vega 161 D1
A Gudiña 151 C3
Agudo 166 B2
Águeda 158 A2
Agüero 154 B2
Aguessac 110 B2
Aguiar 164 B3
Aguiar da Beira 158 B2
Aguilafuente 160 B1
Aguilar 172 B1
Aguilar de Anguita 161 D2
Aguilar de Bureba 153 C2
Aguilar de Campoo 152 B2
Aguilar de Campos 152 A3
Aguilar de Codés 153 D2
Aguilar del Alfambra 162 B2
Aguilar del Río Alhama 153 D3, 154 A3
Águilas 174 A1
Aguilón 162 A/B1

Aguinaliu **155** C3
Agullent **169** D2
Agunnaryd **50** B2
Agurain **156** A/B1
Aha **15** B/C3
Aha **15** D3
Ahaus **67** C3
Ahaus-Alstätte **67** C3
Ahaus-Ottenstein **67** C3
Ahaus-Wessum **67** C3
Äheim **36** A1
Ahigal **159** D3
Ahigal de Villarino **159** C1/2
Ahillones **166** A3
Ahjola **19** C2
Ahkiolahti **22** B2
Ahlbeck **70** B1
Ahlen **67** D3
Ahlerstedt **68** B1
Ahmas **18** B3
Ahmoo **25** C2
Ahmovaara **23** C/D2
Ahmovaara **23** D1/2
Aho **13** C3
Ahoinen **25** C2
Ahokylä **21** D1, **22** A/B1
Ahola **19** D1
Ahola **19** D2
Ahola **19** D3
Aholahti **27** C1
Aholanvaara **13** C3
Aholming **92** B2
Aho-Nikki **26** B2
Ahonperä **18** A3
Ahorn **81** D2/3, **82** A2
Ahorntal **82** A3
Aho-Västinki **21** D2, **22** A2
Ahrbrück **80** A2
Ahrensbök **53** C3
Ahrensburg **52** B3, **68** B1
Ahrensdorf **70** B3
Ahrenshagen **53** D3
Ähtäri **21** C3
Ähtärinranta **21** C2/3
Ähtävä **20** B1
Ahtiala **25** D2, **26** A2
Ahtopol **141** C/D3
Ahun **102** A2
Åhus **50** B3
Åhus **72** A1/2
Ahvemnen **23** D2
Ahveninen **21** D2, **22** A2
Ahvenisto **26** B1
Ahvensalmi **23** C3
Ahvenselkä **13** C3
Ahvio **26** B2
Å i Åfjord **28** A2, **33** C1
Åibar **155** C2
Aich **93** C3
Aicha **93** C2
Aichach **92** A2
Aichach-Griesbeckerzell **91** D2, **92** A2
Aichstetten **91** D3
Aichtal **91** C2
Aichwald **91** C2
Aiddejavrre **11** C2
Aidenbach **93** C2
Aidone **125** C2
Aidonochórion **144** B1
Aiello Cálabro **122** A2
Aiffres **101** B/C2
Aigen im Mühlkreis **93** C2
Aigle **104** B2
Aignan **108** B2
Aignay-le-Duc **88** B3
Aigre **101** C2
Aigrefeuille-sur-Maine **101** C1
Aigrefeuille-d'Aunis **100** B2
Aiguablava **156** B2
Aiguafreda **156** A3
Aiguebelle **104** A3
Aigueblanche **104** A/B3
Aigueperse **102** B2
Aigues-Mortes **111** C3
Aigues-Vives **110** A3, **156** B1
Aiguilles de Port Colon **84** B3
Aiguilles-en-Queyras **112** B1
Aiguillon **109** C2
Aiguines **112** A2/3

Aigurande-sur-Bouzanne **102** A2
Äijäjoki **11** C2
Äijälä **21** D3, **22** A3
Äijälä **24** B3
Äijävaara **17** C1
Äike **15** C2
Ailefroide **112** A1
Aillant-sur-Tholon **88** A2/3
Aillas **108** B1/2
Aillevillers-et-Lyaumont **89** C/D2/3
Ailly-le-Haut-Clocher **77** D2
Ailly-sur-Noye **77** D3
Aimé **104** B3
Ainali **18** A3
Ainali **21** C1
Aindling **91** D2, **92** A2
Ainhoa **108** A3, **154** A1
Ainring **92** B3
Aínsa **155** C2
Aintala **20** B2
Ainzón **154** A3, **162** A1
Airaines **77** D2
Airaksela **22** B2/3
Airasca **112** B1
Airdrie **56** B2
Aire-sur-l'Adour **108** B2
Aire-sur-la-Lys **77** D2, **78** A2
Airola **119** D3
Airolo **105** D2
Airvault **101** C1
Aísa **154** B2
Aisey-sur-Seine **88** B3
Aissey **89** C/D3, **104** A/B1
Aisy-sur-Armançon **88** B3
Aitakumpu **18** B1
Aitamännikkö **12** A2/3, **17** D1
Aiterhofen **92** B1/2
Aitolahti **25** C1
Aitona **155** C3, **163** C1
Aitoniemi **25** C1
Aitoo **25** C1
Aitrach **91** D3
Aitrang **91** D3
Aittaniemi **13** C3
Aittojärvi **18** B2
Aittojärvi **21** D1, **22** A1
Aittokoski **22** B1
Aittokylä **19** C2
Aittokylä **18** B2
Aittolahti **27** D1
Aittovaara **19** D2
Aittovaara **23** C2
Aiud **97** D3, **140** B1
Aix-en-Othe **88** A2
Aix-en-Provence **111** D3
Aixe-sur-Vienne **101** C2/3
Aix-les-Bains **104** A3
Aix-Noulette **78** A2
Aizarnazabal **153** D1
Aizenay **100** A1
Aizpute **73** C1
Ajac **110** A3, **156** A1
Ajaccio **113** D3
Ajain **102** A2
Ajalvir **161** C2
Ajanki **12** A3, **17** D1/2
Ajankijärvi **12** A3, **17** D1/2
Ajaur **31** C1
Ajaureforsen **15** C3
Ajdovac **134** B3
Ajdovščina **126** B2/3
Ajka **96** B3
Ajnazi **74** A1/2
Ajnovce **138** B1
Ajo **153** C1
Ajofrín **160** B3, **167** C1
Ajos **19** D3, **18** A1
Ajtos **141** C3
Åkarp **50** A3
Äkäsjoensuu **11** C3
Äkäskero **11** C3, **12** A2
Äkäslompolo **11** C3, **12** A2
Akasztó **129** C2
Aken **69** D3
Åker **50** B1
Åkerbäk **20** A1, **31** D2
Åkerbränna **30** A/B2, **35** D1
Åkerby **40** B2
Åkerby **16** B2
Åkerholmen **16** B2
Åkerland **30** A1/2

Åkernäs **15** C3
Åkersberga **47** D1
Åkersjön **29** C/D3, **34** B1
Åkers styckebruk **47** C1
Åkervik **14** B3
Akhisar **149** D2
Åkirkeby **72** A2
Åkirkeby **51** D3
Akkala **23** D3
Akkarfjord **5** C1
Akkarvik **4** B2
Akkastugorna **9** D3
Akkavare **16** A3
Akköy **149** D2
Akkrum **66** B2
Akland **43** C2/3, **44** A2
Akmaçizi **133** D3, **134** A3
Åknes **42** B2
Akonpohja **27** D1
Åkra **42** A1
Åkra **39** C2
Akrai **125** C3
Åkran **28** B2/3, **33** D1
Akréfnion **147** C2
Åkrehamn **42** A2
Akrogiáli **144** B1/2
Åkroken **30** B3, **35** D2
Åkroken **16** B3
Akropótamos **144** B1
Aksla **36** A/B2
Aksnes **32** B2
Aktion **146** A1
Aktsestugorna **15** D1, **16** A1
Åkulla **49** D1, **50** A1
Åkullsjön **31** D2
Åkvåg **43** C/D2/3, **44** A2
Åkvisslan **30** B3, **35** D2
Ål **37** C3
Ala **47** D3
Ala **107** B/C3
Ålabodarna **49** D3, **50** A3
Alacón **162** B2
Alà dei Sardi **123** D1/2
Ala di Stura **104** B3
Alaejos **160** A1
Alafors **45** C3
Alagna Valsésia **105** C3
Alagón **154** A/B3, **162** A1
Alahärmä **20** B2
Ala-Honkajoki **24** B1
Alainenjoki **24** B2
Alájar **165** D3, **171** C1
Alajärvi **21** C2
Alajärvi **23** C1
Alajoki **21** D1, **22** A1
Alaköngäs **6** B2
Ala-Kuona **23** C3
Alakylä **12** A2
Alakylä **18** B2
Alakylä **19** C2
Alakylä **24** A/B3
Alakylä **24** A1
Ala-Livo **18** B2
Alalkomenai **146** A2
Alaló **161** C1
A Lama **150** A2
Alameda **172** B2
Alameda de Cervera **167** D1/2, **168** A1/2
Alamedilla **173** C1
Alamillo **166** B2
Álamo **171** C1
Alan **130** B1
Ala-Näljänkä **19** C2
Ala-Nampa **12** B3
Alanäs **30** A2
Alandroal **165** C2
Ålandsbro **35** D2
Alange **165** D2, **166** A2
Alaniemi **18** A1
Alanís **166** A3, **171** D1
Ala-Paakkola **17** D2, **18** A1
Ala-Pitkä **22** B2
Ala-Postojoki **12** B2
Alaraz **160** A2
Alarcón **168** B1
Alar del Rey **152** B2
Alarilla **161** C2
Alaró **157** C2
Alasehir **149** D2
Ålåsen **29** D2/3, **34** B1
Ala-Siurua **18** B2
Alássio **113** C2
Alastaipale **21** C3
Alastaro **24** B2

Ala-Sydänmaa **18** A3, **21** D1, **22** A1
Ala-Temmes **18** A/B3
Alatoz **169** D2
Alatri **119** C2
Ala-Valli **20** B3
Alavattnet **29** D2, **30** A2, **35** C1
Ala-Vieksi **19** D3
Alavieska **18** A3, **21** C1
Ala-Viirre **21** C1
Alavo **21** C3
Ala-Vuokki **19** D3
Ala-Vuotato **18** B2
Alavus (Alavo) **21** C3
Alayor **157** C1
Alba **163** C2
Alba **113** C1
Alba Adriática **117** D3
Albacete **168** B2
Albacken **35** C2
Alba de Tormes **159** D2
Alba Fucensis **119** C1/2
Albaida **169** D2
Albaina **153** D2
Alba Iulia **140** B1
Ålbæk **44** A/B3, **49** C1
Albala **165** D1/2, **166** A1/2
Albaladejo **167** D2, **168** A2
Albalat dels Sorélls **169** D1
Albalate de las Nogueras **161** D2/3
Albalate de Cinca **155** C3, **163** C1
Albalate de Zorita **161** C3
Albalate del Arzobispo **162** B2
Albalatillo **155** B/C3, **162** B1
Alban **110** A2
Albánchez **173** D2, **174** A2
Albanchez de Ubeda **167** D3, **173** C1
Albanella **122** A3
Albano Laziale **118** B2
Albanyà **156** B2
Albaredo d'Adige **107** C3
Albarellos **150** B3
Albares **161** C3
Albaron **111** C3
Albarracín **162** A2
Albarreal de Tajo **160** B3, **167** C1
Albas **108** B1/2
Albatana **169** B/C2
Albatàrrec **155** C3, **163** C1
Albatera **169** C3
Albbruck **90** B3
Albedin **172** B1
Albelda **153** D2
Albelda **155** C3
Albendea **161** D2
Albendiego **161** C1
Albenga **113** C2
Albens **104** A3
Albentosa **162** B3
Ålberga **46** B2
Albergaria-a-Nova **158** A2
Albergaria-a-Velha **158** A2
Albergo Val Martello **106** B2
Alberique **169** D2
Alberite **153** D2
Albernoa **164** B3, **170** B1
Albero Alto **154** B3
Albero Bajo **154** B3
Alberobello **121** C2
Alberona **119** D2, **120** A1
Albersdorf **52** B3
Albert **78** A3
Albertacce **113** D3
Albertirsa **129** C1
Albertkázmérpuszta **94** B3
Albertville **104** A/B3
Alberuela de Tubo **155** B/C3
Albesa **155** C3, **163** C1
Albestroff **89** D1, **90** A1
Albi **109** D2, **110** A2
Albias **109** D2
Albidona **120** B3, **122** B1
Albínia **116** B3
Albino **106** A3
Albires **152** A2/3
Albisola Marina **113** C2
Albisola Superiore **113** C2
Alblasserdam **66** A3

Albocácer **163** C2/3
Alböke **51** D1
Albolodúy **173** D2
Albolote **173** C2
Albondón **173** C2
Alborache **169** C1
Alboraya **169** D1
Alborea **169** D1/2
Ålborg **48** B1
Alborge **162** B1
Albosággia **106** A2
Albox **174** A1/2
Albrechtice nad Vltavou **93** D1
Albstadt **91** C2
Albstadt-Ebingen **91** C2
Albstadt-Lautlingen **91** B/C2
Albstadt-Onstmettingen **91** C2
Albstadt-Tailfingen **91** C2
Ålbu **33** C2/3
Albudeite **169** D3
Albufeira **170** A2
Albufereta **169** D3
Albujón **174** B1
Albuñol **173** C2
Albuñuelas **173** C2
Alburquerque **165** C2
Alby **51** D2
Alby **35** C3
Alby-sur-Chéran **104** A3
Alcabídeche **164** A2
Alcácer do Sal **164** B3
Alcáçovas **164** B3
Alcadozo **168** B2
Alcafozes **159** C3, **165** C1
Alcaine **162** B2
Alcains **158** B3, **165** C1
Alcala De Chivert **163** C3
Alcalá de Guadaira **171** D1/2
Alcalá de Gurrea **154** B3
Alcalá de Henares **161** C2
Alcalá del Júcar **169** C2
Alcalá de la Selva **162** B2/3
Alcalá de la Vega **162** A3
Alcalá del Río **171** D1
Alcalá del Valle **172** A2
Alcalá del Obispo **154** B3
Alcalá de los Gazules **171** D3
Alcalá de Moncayo **154** A3, **162** A1
Alcalá la Real **173** B/C1
Álcamo **124** A2
Alcampel **155** C3
Alcanadre **153** D2
Alcanar **163** C2
Alcanede **164** A1
Alcanena **164** A/B1
Alcañices **151** D3, **159** C3
Alcañiz **163** B/C2
Alcañizo **160** A3, **166** B1
Alcanó **155** C3, **163** C1
Alcántara **159** C3, **165** C1
Alcántara de Júcar **169** C/D2
Alcantarilha **170** A2
Alcantarilla **169** D3
Alcantud **161** D2
Alcaracejos **166** B3
Alcaraz **168** A2
Alcaria Ruiva **170** B1
Alcarràs **155** C3, **163** C1
Alcaucín **172** B2
Alcaudete **172** B1
Alcaudete de la Jara **160** A3, **166** B1
Alcázar de San Juan **167** D1, **168** A1
Alcazarén **160** A/B1
Alceda **152** B1
Alcester **64** A2
Alcira **169** D2
Alcoba **167** C1/2
Alcobaça **164** A1
Alcobendas **161** C2
Alcobertas **164** A1
Alcocéber **163** C3
Alcocer **161** D2
Alcochete **164** A2
Alcoentre **164** A1/2
Alcofra **158** A/B2
Alcolea **166** B3, **172** B1

Alcolea **173** D2
Alcolea de Calatrava
167 C2
Alcolea de Cinca **155** C3,
163 C1
Alcolea del Río **171** D1
Alcolea del Pinar **161** D2
Alcolea de las Peñas
161 C1
Alcolea de Tajo **160** A3,
166 B1
Alcollarín **166** A1/2
Alconaba **153** D3, **161** D1
Alconchel **165** C2/3
Alconchel de Ariza **161** D1
Alconchel de la Estrella
161 D3, **168** A1
Alconera **165** D3
Alcóntar **173** D2
Alcora **162** B3
Alcorisa **162** B2
Alcorlo **161** C2
Alcoroches **162** A2
Alcoutim **170** B1
Alcover **163** C1
Alcoy **169** D2
Alcsútdoboz **95** D3,
128 B1
Alcubierre **154** B3, **162** B1
Alcubilla de Avellaneda
153 C3, **161** C1
Alcubillas **167** D2, **168** A2
Alcubillas de las Peñas
161 D1
Alcublas **162** B3, **169** C1
Alcudia **157** C2
Alcudia de Carlet **169** D2
Alcudia de Guadix **173** C2
Alcudia de Veo **162** B3,
169 D1
Alcuéscar **165** D2, **166** A2
Alcuneza **161** D2
Aldbrough **61** D2
Aldeacentenera **166** A1
Aldeadávila de la Ribera
159 C1
Aldeade la Torre **163** C3,
169 D1
Aldea del Cano **165** D1/2,
166 A1/2
Aldea del Fresno **160** B3
Aldea del Rey **167** C2
Aldea de San Esteban
153 C3, **161** C1
Aldea de Trujillo **166** A1
Aldealafuente **153** D3,
161 D1
Aldealpozo **153** D3,
161 D1
Aldeanueva de Atienza
161 C1/2
Aldeanueva de Barbarroya
160 A3, **166** B1
Aldeanueva de Guadalajara
161 C2
Aldeanueva de la Serrezuela
160 B1
Aldeanueva del Camino
159 D3
Aldeanueva de San Barto-
lomé **160** A3, **166** B1
Aldeanueva de Ebro
153 D2/3, **154** A2
Aldeanueva de la Vera
159 D3
Aldeanueva de Figueroa
159 D1/2, **160** A1/2
Aldeanueva del Codonal
160 B2
Aldeaquemada **167** D3
Aldea Real **160** B1/2
Aldearrodrigo **159** D2
Aldeaseca de la Frontera
160 A2
Aldeavieja **160** B2
Aldeburgh **65** D2
Aldehuela **162** A/B3
Aldehuela de Yeltes
159 C/D2
Aldehuela del Jerte
159 C/D3
Aldehuela de la Bóveda
159 D2
Aldehuela de Liestos
162 A2
Aldeia da Mata **165** B/C1/2

Aldeia da Ponte **159** C2/3
Aldeia do Bispo **159** C3
Aldeia do Maio **164** A2/3
Aldeia dos Palheiros
170 A1
Aldeia Nova de São Bento
165 C3, **170** B1
Aldeire **173** C2
Aldenhoven **79** D2
Aldeno **107** B/C2
Aldernäset **30** A2
Aldersbach **93** C2
Aldershot **64** B3, **76** B1
Aldince **138** B2/3
Aldudes **108** A3, **154** A1
Ale **17** B/C3
Åled **50** A2
Aledo **168** B3, **174** A1
Alegia **153** D1/2
Alegrete **165** C1/2
Aleko **139** D1/2
Aleksandrija **99** D3
Aleksandrija **99** D3
Aleksandrovac **134** B2
Aleksandrovac **134** B3
Aleksin **75** D3
Aleksinac **140** A2/3
Aleksinac **135** C3
Ålem **51** D1
Ålem **72** B1
Ålen **33** D2
Alençon **86** B2
Alenquer **164** A2
Alentisque **161** D1
Aleria **113** D3
Alès **111** C2
Åles **123** C2/3
Alesð **97** D3, **140** B1
Alesjaurestugorna **9** D2
Alessándria della Rocca
124 B2
Alessándria **113** C1
Alessándria del Carretto
120 B3, **122** B1
Alessano **121** D3
Alesso **107** D2, **126** A2
Ålestrup **48** B2
Ålesund **36** B1
Alet-les-Bains **110** A3,
156 A1
Alevráda **146** A/B1
Alexain **86** A2
Alexándria **143** D2
Alexandria **141** C2
Alexandroúpolis **149** C1
Alexandroúpolis **145** D1,
145 D3
Alf **80** A3
Alfacar **173** C2
Alfajarín **154** B3, **162** B1
Alfambra **162** A/B2
Alfambras **170** A2
Alfamén **155** C3, **163** C1
Alfândega da Fé **159** C1
Alfántega **155** C3, **163** C1
Alfara de Carles dels Ports
163 C2
Alfarela **158** B1
Alfarnate **172** B2
Alfaro **154** A2/3
Alfarrás **155** C3, **163** C1
Alfatar **141** C2
Alfaz del Pi **169** D2
Alfdorf **91** C1/2
Alfedena **119** C2
Alfeizerão **164** A1
Alfeld **92** A1
Alfeld **68** B3
Alfena **158** A1
Alferce **170** A2
Alfés **155** C3, **163** C1
Alfhausen **67** D2
Alfonsine **115** C1/2
Alford **61** D3, **65** C1
Alforja **163** D1
Ålfoten **36** A1
Alfoz **151** B/C1
Alfreites **159** C2/3
Alfreton **61** D3, **65** C1
Alfta **40** A1
Alfundão **164** B3
Algaida **157** C2
Algajola **113** D2
Algalé **165** C2
Algámitas **172** B2
Algar **171** D2
Algar **174** B1

Algar **162** B3, **169** D1
Álgarås **45** D2, **46** A2
Ålgård **42** A2
Algarinejo **172** B2
Algarra **162** A3
Algarrobo **172** B2
Algatocín **172** A3
Algeciras **172** A3
Algemesí **169** D2
Algenstedt **69** C2
Ålgered **35** D3
Algerri **155** C3, **163** C1
Alges **164** A2
Algete **161** C2
Alghero **123** C2
Alghult **51** C1
Ålghult **30** B2
Algimia de Alfara **162** B3,
169 D1
Algimia de Almonacid
162 B3, **169** D1
Alginet **169** D1/2
Algodonales **172** A2
Algora **161** D2
Algorta **153** C1
Algoz **170** A2
Ålgsjö **30** B2
Alguaire **155** C3, **163** C1
Alguazas **169** D3
Algueña **169** C3
Algutsrum **51** D2
Algyõ **129** D2
Alhadas **158** A3
Alhama de Almería **173** D2
Alhama de Aragón **161** D1,
162 A1
Alhama de Granada **172** B2
Alhama de Murcia **169** C3,
174 B1
Alhambra **167** D2, **168** A2
Alhamn **17** C3
Alhandra **164** A2
Alhaurín de la Torre **172** B2
Alhaurín el Grande
172 B2/3
Alhendín **173** C2
Alhojärvi **25** D1, **26** A1
Ålholm **53** D2
Alhóndiga **161** C2
Ålhus **36** B2
Ália **124** B2
Alía **166** B1
Aliaga **162** B2
Aliaguilla **163** C3, **169** D1
Aliano **120** B3
Alíartos **147** C2
Alibunar **134** B1
Alibunar **140** A2
Alicante **169** D2
Alicún de Ortega **173** C1
Alife **119** D2
Alifira **146** B3
Alijó **158** B1
Alikaí **146** A2
Alikaí **143** D2
Alikí **145** C2
Alikí **146** A1
Alikylä **21** C1
Alimena **125** C2
Alingsås **45** C3
Alíns **155** C2
Alinya **155** D2/3
Aliseda **165** D1
Ališići **131** C1
Alistráti **144** B1
Alì Terme **125** D2
Aliud **153** D3, **161** D1
Alivérion **147** D2
Alixan **111** C/D1
Aljaraque **171** C2
Aljažev dom **126** B2
Aljezur **170** A2
Aljubarrota **164** A1
Aljucén **165** D2, **166** A2
Aljustrel **164** B3, **170** A/B1
Alkkia **20** B3
Alkmaar **66** A/B2
Alkoven **93** C/D2
Allagí **146** B3
Állai **123** C2
Allaines **87** C2
Allaire **85** C3
Allanche **102** B3
Alland **94** A2/3
Allariz **150** B3
Allarmont **89** D2, **90** A2

Alleen **42** B3
Álleghe **107** C2
Allègre **103** C3
Allemagne-de-Provence
112 A2/3
Allemalehto **12** B2
Allemont **112** A1
Allendale Town **57** D3,
60 B1
Allendorf **80** B1/2
Allendorf (Dillkreis) **80** B2
Allenstedt **69** C2
Ållered **35** D3
Aller **151** D1, **152** A1
Allersberg **92** A1
Allershausen **92** A2
Alleuze **110** B1
Allevard **104** A3
Allex **111** C1
Allgunnen **51** D1
Allingåbro **49** B/C2
Allinge **51** D1
Allinge **72** A2
Allmendingen **91** C2
Allo **153** D2, **154** A2
Alloa **57** B/C1
Allogny **87** D3, **102** A1
Alloluokta kapell **16** A1
Allonnes **87** C2
Allos **112** A2
Alloue **101** C2
Alloway **56** B2
Alloza **162** B2
Allsån **17** C2
Allschwil [Basel SBB]
90 A3
Allstakan **38** B3
Allstedt **82** A1
Allumiere **118** A1
Ally **102** A3
Almacelles **155** C3, **163** C1
Almáchar **172** B2
Almada **164** A2
Almadén **166** B2
Almadén de la Plata
165 D3, **166** A3, **171** D1
Almadenejos **166** B2
Almagro **167** C2
Almajano **153** D3
Almaluez **161** D1
Almansa **169** C2
Almansil **170** B2
Almanza **152** A2
Almarail **153** D3, **161** D1
Almaraz **159** D3, **166** A1
Almargem do Bispo **164** A2
Almargen **172** A2
Almarza **153** D3
Almásfüzitö **95** C3
Almásneszmely **95** C/D3
Almatret **163** C1
Almazán **161** D1
Almazora **163** C3, **169** D1
Almedíjar **162** B3, **169** D1
Almedina **167** D2, **168** A2
Almedinilla **172** B1/2
Almeida **159** D1
Almeida **159** C2
Almeirim **164** A/B2
Almelo **67** C2/3
Almenar **155** C3, **163** C1
Almenara **162** B3, **169** D1
Almenar de Soria **153** D3,
161 D1
Almendra **159** C1
Almendra **159** C2
Almendral **165** C/D2
Almendral de la Cañada
160 A3
Almendralejo **165** D2
Almendros **161** C3,
167 D1, **168** A1
Almería **173** D2
Almesåkra **46** A3
Ålmhult **50** B2
Ålmhult **72** A1
Almirós **148** B1/2
Almirós **147** C1
Almkerk **66** B3
Almodôvar **170** B1
Almodóvar del Río **166** B3,
172 A1
Almodóvar del Campo
167 C2
Almodóvar del Pinar
161 D3, **162** A3, **168** B1
Almofala **159** C2

Almogía **172** B2
Almoguera **161** C3
Almoharín **165** D2, **166** A2
Almonacid de Toledo
160 B3, **167** C1
Almonacid del Marquesado
161 C/D3, **168** A1
Almonacid de la Sierra
163 B/C1
Almonacid de Zorita
161 C3
Almonaster **165** D3,
171 C1
Almondsbury **63** D3
Almonte **171** C2
Almoradí **169** C3
Almorchon **166** B2
Almorox **160** B3
Almoster **164** A1/2
Almourol **164** B1
Almsele **30** B1/2
Almsjönäs **30** B3, **35** D2
Ålmsta **41** C3
Almudévar **154** B3
Almundsryd **51** C2
Almundsryd **72** A1
Almuñécar **172** C2
Almunge **40** B3
Almunia de San Juan
155 C3
Almuniente **154** B3
Almuradiel **167** D2/3
Almurfe **151** D1
Almvik **46** B3
Alnaryd **51** C2
Alnmouth **57** D2
Alnwick **57** D2
Alnwick **54** B3
Alocén **161** C/D2
Aloja **73** D1, **74** A2
Alónia **149** C1
Alónia **145** C2
Alónnisos **147** D1
Alora **172** B2
Alós de Gil **155** D2
Alosno **171** C1
Alozaina **172** A2
Alpalhão **165** C1
Alpandeire **172** A2/3
Alpanseque **161** D1
Alpas **16** B2
Alpbach **92** A/B3, **107** C1
Alpe del Trucco **105** B/C3
Alpe Dévero **105** C2
Alpe di Mera **105** C3
Alpedrinha **158** B3
Alpedriz **164** A1
Alpedroches **161** C1
Alpen **67** C3, **79** D1
Alpens **156** A2
Alpera **169** D2
Alphen aan de Rijn **66** A3
Alpiarça **164** B1/2
Alpignano **112** A1
Alpirsbach **90** B2
Alpua **18** A3
Alpuente **162** A/B3,
169 C1
Alqueva **165** C3
Alquézar **155** C2/3
Alquife **173** C2
Als **91** B/C2
Alsasua **153** D2
Alsdorf **79** D2
Alsdorf-Höngen **79** D2
Alsen **29** C3, **34** B1/2
Alseno **114** A1
Alsenz **80** B3
Alset **28** A3, **33** C1
Alsfeld **81** C2
Alsfeld-Eifa **81** C2
Alsheim **80** B3
Ålshult **51** C2
Alsleben **69** C/D3, **82** A1
Alsódabas **129** C1
Alsónémedi **95** D3, **129** C1
Alsónemesapáti **128** A1
Alsóörs **128** B1
Alsószölnök **127** D1
Alstad **50** A/B3
Alstad **8** B2
Ålstad **9** B/C3
Alstadhaug **28** B3, **33** D1
Alstahaug **14** A2
Ålstäket **47** D1
Alsterbro **51** D1
Alsterbro **72** B1

Alstermo **51** C1
Alston **57** C/D3, **60** B1
Alsvik **14** B1
Alta **5** C2
Älta **47** C/D1
Altamura **120** B2
Altare **113** C2
Altarejos **161** D3, **168** B1
Altaussee **93** C3
Altavilla Irpina **119** D3
Altavilla Silentina **120** A2/3
Altdöbern **70** B3, **83** C1
Altdorf **92** A1
Altdorf **105** D1
Altdorf (Landshut) **92** B2
Alt Duvenstedt **52** B2/3
Alte **170** A/B2
Altea **169** D2
Alte Ceccato **107** C3
Altedo **115** B/C1
Alteidet **5** C2
Altena **80** A/B1
Altenahr **80** A2
Altenau **69** B/C3
Altenbeken **68** A3
Altenberge **67** D3
Altenbuch (Marktheiden-
  feld) **81** C3
Altenburg **82** B1/2
Altenburg **94** A2
Altenglan **80** A3, **90** A1
Altenhagen **70** A1
Altenholz **52** B2/3
Altenkirchen **80** A/B2
Altenmarkt **92** B3
Altenmarkt an der Triesting
  94 A2/3
Altenmarkt bei Sankt Gallen
  93 D3
Altenmarkt im Yspertal
  93 D2
Altenmedingen-Bostelwie-
  beck **69** C2
Altenmünster-Zusamzell
  91 D2
Altenriet **91** C2
Altenstadt **91** D2
Altenstadt **81** C2
Altensteig **90** B2
Altensteig-Berneck **90** B2
Altentreptow **70** A1
Alter do Chão **165** C2
Altfraunhofen **92** B2
Altfriedland **70** B2
Altheim **91** C/D2
Altheim **93** C2
Althofen **126** B1
Althorpe **61** C/D2/3
Althütte **91** C1/2
Altin **28** B2
Altinoluk **149** D1
Altipiani di Arcinazzo
  118 B2
Altkirch **89** D3, **90** A3
Altkünkendorf **70** B2
Altlandsberg **70** A/B2
Altlewin **70** B2
Altmannstein **92** A1/2
Altmannstein-Mendorf
  92 A1/2
Altmannstein-Pondorf
  92 A1
Alt-Meteln **53** C3, **69** C1
Altmünster **93** C3
Altnes **5** C2
Altofonte **124** B2
Altomonte **122** A1
Altomünster **92** A2
Altomünster-Wollomoos
  92 A2
Alton **64** B3, **76** A1
Altopáscio **114** B2, **116** A1
Altorricón **155** C3, **163** C1
Altötting **92** B2
Altranft **70** B2
Altrincham **59** D2, **60** B3
Altrip **90** B1
Altruppin **70** A2
Alt Schadow **70** B3
Altscheid **79** D3
Alt-Schönau **69** D1, **70** A1
Altshausen **91** C3
Altstätten **91** C3
Altuna **40** A3
Altura **162** B3, **169** D1
Altusried **91** D3

Altusried-Kimratshofen
  91 D3
Altusried-Krugzell **91** D3
Altwarp **70** B1
Altwigshagen **70** B1
Alunda **40** B3
Ålundsby **16** B3
Aluskije **74** A/B2
Alustante **162** A2
Alva **56** B1
Alvaiázere **158** A3, **164** B1
Alvajärvi **21** D1/2, **22** A1/2
Alvalade **164** B3, **170** A1
Alvaneu Bad **106** A1/2
Alvängen **45** C3
Alvarenga **158** A/B2
Alvares **158** A/B3
Alvaro **158** B3
Alvastra **46** A2
Alvdal **33** C3
Älvdalen **39** C1
Alvega **164** B1
Alverca do Ribatejo **164** A2
Alversund **36** A3
Alvesta **51** B/C1
Alvesta **72** A1
Alvettula **25** C2
Ålvho **39** D1
Alviano **117** C3, **118** A/B1
Alvignac **109** D1
Alvik **17** C3
Ålvik **36** B3
Alviksträsk **17** C3
Alvito **119** C2
Alvito **164** B3
Älvkarleby **40** B2
Älvkarleö bruk **40** B2
Ålvkarlhed **39** D1, **40** A1
Alvnes **15** C1
Alvnes **9** C1
Alvøen **36** A3
Alvôr **170** A2
Alvøy **36** A3
Älvros **38** B1
Älvros **34** B1
Älvsbacka **39** C3, **45** D1
Älvsbacka **16** A2
Älvsbyn **16** B3
Älvsered **49** D1, **50** A1
Älvsnäs **41** B/C3
Ålvundeid **32** B2
Ålvundfoss **32** B2
Alwalton **64** B2
Alwinton **57** D2
Alyth **57** C1
Alytus **73** D2, **74** A3
Alzano Lombardo **106** A3
Alzenau in Unterfranken
  81 C3
Alzey **80** B3
Alzo **105** C3
Alzon **110** B2
Alzonne **110** A3, **156** A1
Amadora **164** A2
Amailloux **101** C1
Åmål **45** C1/2
Amalfi **119** D3
Amaliápolis **147** C1
Amaliás **146** A2/3
Amaliás **148** A2
Amance **89** C3
Amancey **104** A1
Amándola **115** D3,
  117 D2/3
Amantea **122** A2
Amantia **142** A2
Amárandon **143** C3
Amárandos **142** B2
Amarante **158** B1
Amareleja **165** C3
Amares **150** A/B3, **158** A1
Amárinthos **147** D2
Amaseno **119** C2
Amatrice **117** D3,
  119 B/C1
Amaxádes **145** C1
Amayas **161** D2
Ambarès **108** B1
Ambasaguas **152** A2
Ambazac **101** C2
Ambel **154** A3, **162** A1
Ambelákia **143** D3
Ambelákia **147** D2
Ambelakiótissa **146** B1
Ambelón **164** B1
Amberg **82** A3, **92** A/B1

Ambérieu-en-Bugey
  103 D2
Ambérieux-en-Dombes
  103 D2
Ambert **103** C3
Ambialet **110** A2
Ambierle **103** C2
Ambjörby **39** C2
Amblainville **77** D3, **87** C1
Amble-by-the-Sea **57** D2
Ambleside **59** C/D1, **60** B1
Amblève **79** D2
Ambleville **77** D3, **87** C1
Amboise **86** B3
Ambra **115** C3, **116** B2
Ambrault **102** A1
Ambrières-le-Grand **86** A2
Ambrógio **115** C1
Ambrona **161** D1/2
Ambronay **103** D2
Amdal **28** A/B3, **33** C/D2
Åmdalsverk **43** C2
Amden **105** D1, **106** A1
Ameixial **170** B1/2
Ameixoeira **164** B1
Amel **79** D2
Amélia **117** C3, **118** B1
Amélie-les-Bains-Palalda
  156 B2
Amelinghausen **68** B2
Amendolara **120** B3,
  122 B1
Amer **156** B2
A Merca **150** B3
America **79** D1
Amerongen **66** B3
Amersfoort **66** B3
Amersham **64** B3
Ames **150** A2
Amesbury **64** A3, **76** A1
Amezketa **153** D1/2
A Mezquita **151** C3
Amfíklia **147** C1
Amfilochía **146** A1
Amfilochía **148** A2
Amfípolis **149** B/C1
Amfípolis **144** B1
Åmfissa **147** B/C2
Åmfissa **148** B2
Amiães de Baixo **164** A1
Amieira **164** B1
Amieira **165** C3
Amiens **77** D2/3
Amigdaléai **143** C2
Amíndeon **143** C2
Åminne **50** B1
Aminne **20** B1
Amiterno **117** D3, **119** C1
Amla **36** B2
Åmli **43** C2
Åmliden **31** C1
Amlwch **58** B2, **60** A3
Ammälä **20** B3
Ammanford **63** C1
Åmmänsaari **19** C/D2
Ammarnäs **15** C2
Åmmätsä **25** C1, **26** A1
Åmmeberg **46** A2
Ammensleben **69** C3
Ammer **35** C2
Ammer **30** A3, **35** C2
Ammerbuch **91** B/C2
Ammern **81** D1
Ammerön **35** C2
Amoeiro **150** B2
Amöneburg **81** C2
Amorbach **81** C3
Amoreanes **170** B1
Amoreira **164** A1
Amorosa **150** A3, **158** A1
Amorosi **119** D3
Åmot **40** A2
Åmot **38** A1/2
Åmot **37** D3
Åmot **43** C1
Åmot **36** B2
Åmot **43** C1
Åmotfors **38** B3, **45** C1
Åmotsdal **43** C1
Åmotsdalshytta **33** B/C3,
  37 D1
Amou **108** B3, **154** B1
Ampezzo **107** D2, **126** A2
Ampfing **92** B2
Amphiareion **147** D2
Ampiaslantta **16** B1
Amplepuis **103** C2

Amposta **163** C2
Ampthill **64** B2
Ampudia **152** A/B3
Ampuero **153** C1
Ampuis **103** D3
Amriswil **91** C3
Amroth **62** B1
Åmsele **31** C1
Amsteg **105** D1
Amstelveen **66** B2/3
Amsterdam **66** B2/3
Amstetten **93** D2
Amstetten **96** A2/3
Amtzell **91** C3
Amulree **56** B1
Amurrio **153** C1/2
Amusco **152** B3
Amusquillo **152** B3,
  160 B1
Åmynnet **31** B/C3
Ån **29** C3, **34** B2
Anacapri **119** C/D3
Anadia **158** A2
Anadón **162** B2
Anafonítria **146** A2
Anagni **118** B2
Añana-Gesaltza **153** C2
Anan'ev **99** C3
Anarisstugan **34** A2
Anåset **31** D2
Anåset **31** C2
Åna-Sira **42** A/B3
Anatolí **146** B1
Anatolikón **143** C2
Anáttila **19** C3
Anávissos **147** D3
Anávra **147** C1
Anaya de Alba **159** D2,
  160 A2
Ancà **158** A3
Ancenis **86** A3
Ancerville-Guë **88** B2
Anché **101** C2
Anchuela del Campo
  161 D2
Anchuras **166** B1
Ancín **153** D2
Ancona **117** D2
Ancroft **57** D2
Ancy-le-Franc **88** A/B3
Anda **36** B1
Åndalo **107** B/C3
Åndalsnes **32** A/B2/3
Andaluz **153** C/D3, **161** C1
Andau **94** B3
Andaval **165** C2
Andavías **151** D3, **159** D1
Andebol **46** B2
Andebu **43** D2, **44** A1
Andeer [Thusis] **105** D2,
  106 A2
Andelfingen **90** B3
Andelot **89** C2
Andenes **9** C1
Andenne **79** C2
Anderberget **30** A3, **35** D2
Anderlues **78** B2
Andermatt **105** D2
Andernach **80** A2
Andernos-les-Bains
  108 A1
Anderslöv **50** B3
Anderstorp **50** B1
Andijk **66** B2
Andilla **162** B3, **169** C1
Andlau **90** A2
Andoain **153** D1, **154** A1
Andocs **128** B2
Andolsheim **90** A2/3
Andørja **9** C1
Andorra **162** B2
Andorra la Vieja **155** D2,
  156 A2
Andosilla **153** D2, **154** A2
Andover **64** A3, **76** A1
Andrå **38** A1
Andraitx **157** C2
Andravída **146** A2
Andreapol' **75** C2
Andrejaš **138** B2
Andrest **108** B3, **155** C1
Andretta **120** A2
Andrezieux **103** C3
Åndria **120** B2, **136** A3
Andrijevci **132** B1
Andrijevica **137** D1,
  138 A1

Andrítsena **146** B3
Andrítsena **148** B2
Androniáni **147** D1
Androúsa **146** B3
Andselv (Bardufoss) **4** A3,
  9 D1
Andsnes **4** B2
Andújar **167** C3, **172** B1
Anduze **111** B/C2
Andviken **29** D3, **34** B1
Andviken **29** D3, **34** B1
Aneby **46** A3
Åneby **38** A3
Anemorráchi **146** A1
Ænes **42** A1
Ånes **32** B2
Ånessletta **9** C1
Ånestad **38** A2
Anet **87** C1
Anetjärvi **19** C1
Anfo **106** B3
Ang **45** C2
Ång **46** A3
Anga **47** D3
Ånge **15** D2
Ånge **29** C/D3, **34** B1
Ånge **35** C3
Ångebo **35** C3
Angeja **158** A2
Angelbachtal **90** B1
Angelburg-Lixfeld **80** B2
Ängelholm **49** D2, **50** A2
Ängelholm **72** A1
Angeli **6** A3, **11** D1
Angelniemi **24** B3
Angelókastron **142** A3
Angelókastron **147** C3
Angelókastron **146** A1/2
Ångelsberg **40** A3
Angen **28** A2
Anger **127** C/D1
Angera **105** C3
Angermünde **70** B2
Angermünde **72** A3
Angern **69** D3
Angern **94** B2
Angern **107** B/C1
Angers **86** A3
Ångersjö **34** B3
Angervikko **23** C1/2
Angerville **87** C2
Ångesån **17** C1
Ångesbyn **17** C3
Anghiari **115** C3, **117** B/C2
Angístrion **147** D3
Angle **62** B1
Anglès **110** A3
Anglès **156** B2
Anglesola **155** D3, **163** D1
Angles-sur-l'Anglin
  101 D1
Anglure **88** A2
Ango **77** C2/3
Ångom **35** D3
Angoulême **101** C3
Ångskär **40** B2
Ängsnäs **40** A2
Ångsö **47** C1
Angüés **155** B/C3
Anguiano **153** C/D2/3
Anguillara Véneta **107** C3,
  115 C1
Anguita **161** D2
Angvik **32** B2
Anholt **49** C2
Aniane **110** B2/3
Aniche **78** A2
Anières [Genève] **104** A2
Aniés **154** B2
Anikščiai **73** D2, **74** A3
Ånimskog **45** C2
Anina **135** C1
Anina **140** A2
Anizy-le-Château **78** A/B3
Anjala **26** B2
Anjalankoski-Inkeroinen
  26 B2
Anjans fjällstation **29** C3,
  34 A1
Anjony **102** A/B3, **110** A1
Anjum **67** C1
Ankaran **126** B3
Ankarede kapell **29** D1
Ankarsrum **46** B3
Ankarsund **15** C/D3
Ankarsvik **35** D3
Ankarvatnet **29** D1

Ankele 22 B3
Ankerlia 4 B3, 10 B1
Anklam 70 A/B1
Anklam 72 A2
Ankum 67 D2
Anlezy 102 B1
Ånn 29 C3, 34 A2
Annaberg 94 A3
Annaberg-Buchholz 82 B2
Annaberg im Lammertal 93 C3
Annaburg 70 A3
Annalong 58 A1
Annamoe 58 A2
Annan 57 C3, 60 A/B1
Anndalsvågen 14 A3
Anneberg 46 A3
Annecy 104 A2/3
Annefors 40 A1
Annemasse 104 A2
Annerstad 50 B2
Annevoie-Rouillon 79 C2
Anneyron 103 D3
Annonay 103 D3
Annonen 18 A3
Annone Véneto 107 D3, 126 A3
Annopol 97 C1, 98 A2
Annot 112 A/B2
Annœullin 78 A2
Annula 25 C2
Annweiler am Trifels 90 B1
Anola 27 C2
Añón 154 A3, 162 A1
Áno Porróia 139 D3, 143 D1, 144 A1
Anor 78 B3
Añora 166 B3
Anost 103 C1
Añover de Tajo 160 B3
Anquela del Pedregal 162 A2
Anquela del Ducado 161 D2
Anröchte 80 B1
Ans 48 B2
Ansager 48 A3, 52 A1
Ansbach 91 D1
Anse 103 D2
Ansedónia 116 B3
Anserall 155 D2
Ansfelden 93 D2
Ansião 158 A3, 164 B1
Ansignan 156 B1
Ansjö 30 A3, 35 C2
Ansnes 32 B1
Ansnes 4 A3
Ansó 154 B2
Ansoain 154 A2
Ånstad 8 B3
Anstruther 57 C1
Ansvar 17 C1/2
Antas 158 B2
Antas 174 A2
Antas de Ulla 150 B2
Antegnate 106 A3
Anten 45 C3
Antequera 172 B2
Anterselva/Antholz 107 C/D1
Antey-Saint-André 105 C3
Anthée 79 C2
Anthéor-Cap-Roux 112 B3
Anthering 93 B/C3
Anthótopos 147 C1
Antibes 112 B3
Antícoli Corrado 118 B2
Antignac 102 A/B3
Antignano 114 A3, 116 A2
Antigonea 142 A2
Antigüedad 152 B3
Antillo 125 D2
Antillón 155 B/C3
Antipatra 142 A2
Antnäs 17 C3
Antoing 78 A/B2
Antoñana 153 D2
Antraigues-sur-Volane 111 C1
Antrain 85 D2
Antrefftal 81 C2
Antrim 54 A3, 55 D2
Antrodoco 117 D3, 118 B1
Antronapiana 105 C2
Anttila 6 B3
Anttila 26 B2
Anttola 27 C/D1

Antwerpen 78 B1
Antzuola 153 D1
Anundshogen 40 A3, 47 B/C1
Anutkaski 16 B2
Anversa degli Abruzzi 119 C2
Anvin 77 D2
Anya 155 D3
Anzano di Púglia 120 A2
Anzasco 105 C3
Anzat-le-Luguet 102 B3
Anzi 120 B2/3
Anzin 78 A/B2
Anzing 92 A2
Ánzio 118 B2
Anzola dell'Emília 114 B1
Aoíz 155 C2
Aosta 104 B3
Aoste 103 D3, 104 A3
Aouste-sur-Sye 111 C/D1
Aovaniemi 12 A/B3
Apahida 97 D3, 140 B1
Apaj 129 C2
Apátfalva 129 D2
Apatin 129 C3
Apatóac 127 D2
Apchon 102 B3
Ape 74 A2
Apécchio 115 C3, 117 C2
Apeldoorn 67 B/C3
Apelern 68 B3
Apen 67 D1
Apenburg 69 C2
Apensen 68 B1
A Peroxa 150 B2
Apfelstädt 81 D2, 82 A2
Aphaia 147 D2/3
Ápice 119 D3, 120 A2
Apiés 154 B2
Apiro 115 D3, 117 D2
Apolda 82 A1/2
Apollonía 144 A2
Apollonía 149 C3
Apolonia 142 A1/2
A Pontenova 151 C1
A Porqueira 150 B3
Äppelbo 39 C2
Appelscha 67 C2
Appen 52 B3, 68 B1
Appenweier 90 B2
Appenzell 91 C3, 105 D1, 106 A1
Appiano/Eppan 107 C2
Appignano 115 D3, 117 D2
Appingedam 67 C2
Appleby 57 C/D3, 60 B1
Appledore 62 B2
Appletreewick 59 D1, 61 C2
Appoigny 88 A2/3
Aprelevka 75 D3
Apremont-la-Forêt 89 C1
Aprica 106 B2
Apricena 120 A1
Aprília 118 B2
Ápsalos 143 C1
Apt 111 D2
Aquiléia 126 A3
Aquilónia 120 A2
Aquilué 154 B2
Aquino 119 C2
Ar 47 D2
Arabba 107 C2
Aracena 165 D3, 171 C1
Arachnéon 147 C3
Aráchova 146 B1
Aráchova 147 C2
Aračinovo 138 B2
Arad 97 C3, 140 A1
Arådalens fjällstation 34 B2
Aragona 124 B2/3
Aragoncillo 161 D2
Aragózena 146 B2
Aragúas del Solano 154 B2
Aragüés del Puerto 154 B2
Åraksbø 43 B/C2
Aram 36 A1
Aramaio 153 D1/2
Aramiñon 153 C2
Aramits 108 B3, 154 B1
Aramon 111 C2
Arana-San Bixenti 156 A/B1
Aranaz 153 D3, 161 D1

Aranda de Duero 153 C3, 161 B/C1
Aranda de Moncayo 154 A3, 162 A1
Aranđelovac 133 D2, 134 A/B2
Aranđelovac 138 B2
Arándiga 154 A3, 162 A1
Arandilla 153 C3, 161 C1
Aranga 150 B1
Aranjuez 161 C3
Arañuel 162 B3
Aranzueque 161 C2
Arapei 149 D2
Aras 153 D2
Aras de Alpuente 163 C3, 169 D1
Arasluoktastugan 9 C3
Áratos 145 D2
Arauzo de Miel 153 C3, 161 C1
Aravaca 160 B2
Aravissós 143 D1
Arazede 158 A3
Arbancón 161 C2
Arbas 109 C3, 155 D1
Arbatax 123 D2
Arbeca 155 D3, 163 D1
Arbesbach 93 D2
Arbesbach 96 A2
Arbeteta 161 D2
Arbneš 137 D2
Arbo 150 B3
Arboga 46 B1
Arbois 104 A1
Arboleas 174 A1/2
Arbon 91 C3
Arborea 123 C2/3
Arbório 105 C3
Årbostad 9 D1
Årbotten 38 B3
Arbrå 40 A1
Arbroath 57 C1
Arbroath 54 B2
Arbúcies 156 B2/3
Árbus 123 C3
Árbyn 17 C2
Arcachon 108 B1
Arčar 135 D3
Arčar 140 B2
Arcas 161 D3
Arce 155 C2
Arce 119 C2
Arcen 79 D1
Arc-en-Barrois 88 B2
Arces 88 A2
Arc-et-Senans 104 A1
Arcévia 115 D3, 117 C2
Archángelos 139 C3, 143 D1
Archángelos 146 A1
Archánion 146 B1
Archena 169 D3
Arches 89 D2
Archiac 101 C3
Archidona 172 B2
Archivel 168 B3, 174 A1
Arcicóllar 160 B3
Arcidosso 116 B3
Arcille 116 B3
Arcis-sur-Aube 88 A/B2
Arciz 141 D1
Arco 106 B2/3
Arçon 104 A/B1
Arconada 152 B2
Arcos 153 B/C2/3
Arcos de Jalón 161 D1
Arcos de la Frontera 171 D2
Arcos de la Sierra 161 D2/3
Arcos de las Salinas 162 A/B3
Arcos de Valdevez 150 A3, 158 A1
Arc-sur-Tille 89 B/C3
Arcusa 153 D2
Arcy-sur-Cure 88 A3
Årdal 42 A2
Årdala 47 C1/2
Ardales 172 A2
Årdalstangen 37 C2
Árdara 123 C1/2
Ardaúli 123 C2
Ardbeg 56 A2
Ardea 118 B2
Ardee 58 A1
Ardee 54 A3, 55 D2
Arden 48 B2

Ardenicës 142 A1
Ardentes 102 A1
Ardes-sur-Couze 102 B3
Ardez 106 B1
Ardgay 54 A/B2
Ardglass 58 A1
Ardino 140 B3
Ardisa 154 B2
Ardlussa 56 A1
Ardlussa 54 A2, 55 D1
Ardminish 56 A2
Ardón 151 D2, 152 A2
Ardon 104 A1
Ardore 122 A3
Ardre 47 D3
Ardres 47 D3
Ardrishaig 56 A1
Arduaine 56 A1
Ardvasar 54 A2, 55 D1
Åre 29 C3, 34 A1/2
Areatza 153 C/D1
Areias 158 A3, 164 B1
Aremark 45 B/C1
Arén 155 C2
Arena 122 A2/3
Arenal d'en Castel 157 C1
Arenales del Sol 169 D3
Arenas 172 B2
Arenas de Iguña 152 B1
Arenas del Rey 173 B/C2
Arenas de San Juan 167 D2
Arenas de San Pedro 160 A3
Arendal 43 C3
Arendonk 79 C1
Arendsee 69 C2
Arengosse 108 A/B2
Arenillas 161 C1
Areños 152 B1/2
Aréns de Lledó 163 C2
Arenys de Mar 156 B3
Arenys de Munt 156 B3
Arenzano 113 C/D2
Ares 150 B1
Arès 108 B1
Ares del Maestre 163 B/C2
Aresing 92 A2
Arespalditza 153 C1
Åresvik 32 B2
Areta 153 C1
Aréthousa 144 A/B1/2
Aretí 146 A2
Arette 108 B3, 154 B1
Aretxabaleta 153 D1/2
Areu 155 C2
Arevalillo 159 D2, 160 A2
Arévalo 160 A2
Arevattnet 14 B3
Arez 165 B/C1
Arezzo 115 C3, 116 B2
Arfará 146 B3
Arfeuilles 103 C2
Arfons 110 A3
Argalastí 144 A3, 147 C1
Argallón 166 A/B3
Argamasilla de Alba 167 D2, 168 A2
Argamasilla de Calatrava 167 C2
Arganda 161 C3
Arganil 158 B3
Arganil 158 B3, 164 B1
Argantzun 153 C/D2
Arganza 151 C2
Årgård 28 B2
Argásion 146 A2/3
Argecilla 161 C2
Argegno 105 D2/3, 106 A3
Argelaguer 156 B2
Argelès-Gazost 108 B3, 155 C1
Argelès-sur-Mer 156 B2
Argelita 162 B3
Argenbühl-Eglofs 91 C3
Argenschwang 80 A/B3
Argenta 115 C1
Argentan 86 A/B1
Argentat 102 A3, 109 D1
Argente 163 C2
Argentella 113 D2/3
Argentera 112 B2
Argenthal 80 A3
Argentière 104 B2
Argentière-la-Bessée 112 A1
Argentona 156 A/B3

Argenton-Château 100 B1
Argenton-sur-Creuse 101 D1/2
Argentré 86 A2
Argentré-du-Plessis 86 A2
Argent-sur-Sauldre 87 D3
Argeriz 151 B/C3, 158 B1
Argés 160 B3, 167 C1
Argetoaia 135 D2
Argirádes 142 A3
Argiropoúlion 143 D3
Argomariz 153 D2
Árgos 147 C3
Árgos 148 B2
Árgos Orestikón 143 C2
Argostólion 148 A2
Arguedas 154 A2/3
Arguis 154 B2
Argujillo 159 D1
Argy 101 C2
Arhípovka 75 C3
Århus 48 B3
Ariano Ferrarese 115 C1
Ariano Irpino 119 D3, 120 A2
Ariano nel Polésine 115 C1
Arienzo 119 D3
Arild 49 D2, 50 A2
Arilje 133 D3, 134 A3
Arinagour 54 A2, 55 D1
Åringen 14 A2
Aríñiz 153 D2
Ariño 162 B2
Arinthod 103 D2, 104 A2
Arisgotas 160 B3, 167 C1
Arísti 142 B2/3
Aritzo 123 D2
Arive 108 B3, 155 C1/2
Ariz 158 B2
Ariza 161 D1
Årjäng 45 C1
Arjeplog 15 D2
Arjona 167 C3, 172 B1
Arjonilla 167 C3, 172 B1
Arkala 18 A3
Arkelstorp 50 B2
Arkítsa 147 C1
Arkkukari 18 A3
Arklow 58 A3
Arklow 55 D3
Arkösund 47 C2
Ärla 46 B1
Àrla 47 B/C1
Arlanc 103 C3
Arlanda 40 B3, 47 C1
Arlanzón 153 C2
Arlempdes 110 B1
Arles 111 C2/3
Arles 156 B2
Arleuf 103 C1
Arlon 79 D3
Armação de Pera 170 A2
Armadale 57 B/C2
Arma di Tággia 113 C2
Armagh 54 A3, 55 D2
Armallones 161 D2
Armamar 158 B2
Armasjärvi 17 D2
Arménion 143 D3
Armeno 105 C/D3
Armenteros 159 D2, 160 A2
Armilla 173 C2
Armintza 153 C1
Armo 122 A3, 125 D2
Armutlu 149 D1
Arnáccio 114 A/B3, 116 A2
Arnac-Pompadour 101 C3
Arnafjord 36 B2/3
Arnage 86 B2/3
Arnager 51 D3
Årnäs 45 D2
Arnäsvall 31 C3
Arnaville 89 C1
Arnavutköy 145 D1/2
Arnay-le-Duc 103 C1
Arnbach 107 D3
Arnberg 31 C1
Arnborg 48 A/B3
Arnbruck 93 B/C1
Arnéa 144 A/B2
Arneberg 38 B2
Arneburg 69 D2
Arnedillo 153 D2/3
Arnedo 153 D2/3

Arnéguy **108** B3, **155** C1
Årnes **28** A2, **33** C1
Arnes **163** C2
Årnes **38** B2/3
Årnes **38** A3
Arnfels **127** C2
Arnhem **66** B3
Árnissa **143** C1
Arnö **47** C1
Arnoga **106** B2
Arnoia **150** B2/3
Arnön **40** B1
Arnoyhamn **4** B2
Arnsberg **80** B1
Arnsberg-Neheim-Hüsten **80** B1
Arnschwang **92** B1
Arnsdorf **83** C1
Arnside **59** D1, **60** B2
Arnstadt **81** D2, **82** A2
Arnstein **81** D3
Arnstorf **92** B2
Arnuero **153** C1
Arnum **52** A/B1
Aroania **146** B2
Aroche **165** C3, **171** C1
Arões **158** A2
Aroffe **89** C2
Arola **7** C2
Arolla [Sion] **105** C2
Arolsen **81** C1
Arolsen-Mengeringhausen **81** C1
Aron **86** A2
Arona **105** D3
Aronkylä **20** B3
Åros **38** A3, **43** D1, **44** B1
Arosa **106** A1
Årosjåkk **10** A3
Ærøskøbing **53** C2
Årøsund **52** B1
Arouca **158** A2
Årøybukt **4** B3
Årøysund **43** D2, **44** A/B1
Arpáia **119** D3
Arpajon **87** C/D2
Arpajon-sur-Cère **110** A1
Árpás **95** C3
Arpela **17** D2, **18** A1
Arpino **119** C2
Arquà Petrarca **107** C3
Arquata del Tronto **117** D3, **119** B/C1
Arquata Scrívia **113** D1
Arques **77** D1
Arques **110** A3, **156** A/B1
Arques-la-Bataille **76** B2/3
Arquillos **167** D3
Arrabal **158** A3, **164** A/B1
Arrabal del Portillo **160** B1
Arracourt **89** D1/2
Arraiolos **164** B2
Arraiz **108** A3, **154** A1
Arrakoski **25** D1, **26** A1
Arrankorpi **25** C/D2, **26** A2
Arras **78** A2
Arraute-Charritte **108** A3, **154** B1
Arrázola **153** D1
Årre **48** A3, **52** A1
Arreau **109** C3, **155** C2
Arredondo **153** C1
Årrenjarka **15** D1
Arrens **108** B3, **154** B1/2
Arrentela **164** A2
Arriate **172** A2
Arrie **50** A3
Arrifana **158** A2
Arrigorriaga **153** C1
Arrild **52** A/B1/2
Arriondas **152** A1
Arro **155** C2
Arroba **167** C2
Arrochar **56** B1
Arromanches-les-Bains **76** B3, **86** A1
Arronches **165** C2
Arróniz **153** D2
Arròs **155** C2
Arroyo de Cuéllar **160** B1
Arroyo de la Luz **165** D1
Arroyo de San Serván **165** D2
Arroyomolinos de Montánchez **165** D2, **166** A2

Arroyomolinos de León **165** D3, **171** C1
Arruda dos Vinhos **164** A2
 Års **48** B2
Årsandøy **28** B1
Årsdale **51** D3
Ars-en-Ré **100** A2
Arsiè **107** C2
Arsiero **107** C3
Årslev **53** C1
Ársoli **118** B2
Ars-sur-Formans **103** D2
Ars-sur-Mozelle **89** C1
Årsta havsbad **47** C/D1
Årstein **9** D2
Årsunda **40** A2
Arsuni **123** C/D2
Arsy **78** A3
Árta **146** A1
Artá **157** C1
Årta **148** A1/2
Artajona **154** A2
Artana **162** B3, **169** D1
Arta Terme **107** D2, **126** A2
Artazu **154** A2
Arteaga **153** C/D1
Arteaga **153** D1
Artedó **155** D2, **156** A2
Artegna **126** A2
Arteixo **150** A1
Artemare **104** A2/3
Artemisía **146** B3
Artemísion **147** C1
Arten **107** C2
Artena **118** B2
Artenay **87** C2
Artern **82** A1
Artés **156** A2/3
Artesa de Segre **155** D3
Arthez-d'Asson **108** B3, **154** B1
Arthez de-Béarn **108** B3, **154** B1
Arthon-en-Retz **85** C/D3, **100** A1
Arthonnay **88** B2/3
Articuza **154** A1
Arties **155** C/D2
Artix **108** B3, **154** B1
Artjärvi (Artsjö) **25** D2, **26** A/B2
Artlenburg **69** B/C1
Artotína **146** B1
Artsjö **25** D2, **26** A/B2
Artziniega **153** C1
A Rúa **151** C2
Arundel **76** B1
Arundel Castle **76** B1
Årup **52** B1
Aruskila **23** C2/3
Årvåg **32** B1/2
Arvaja **25** D1, **26** A1
Arvet **39** D1/2
Arveyres **108** B1
Arvidsjaur **16** A3
Arvidsträsk **16** B3
Årvik **36** A1
Årvik **42** A1
Arvika **38** B3, **45** C1
Årviksand **4** B2
Årvikstrand **42** A1
Åryd **51** C1/2
Arzachena **123** D1
Arzacq-Arraziguet **108** B3, **154** B1
Arzano **84** B2/3
Aržano **131** D3, **132** A3
Arzbach **80** B2
Arzberg **82** B3
Arzberg **83** C1
Arzignano **107** C3
Arzon **85** C3
Arzúa **150** B2
Ås **46** A1
Aš **82** B2/3
Ås **29** D3, **34** B2
Ås **33** D2
As **79** C1
Ås **38** B3
Åsa **49** D1, **50** A1
Asa **45** D3
Åså **49** C1
Åsamati **142** B1
Åsan **28** B2
Åsäng **35** D2/3
Ašanja **133** D1, **134** A1
Åsarna **34** B2/3

Åsarp **45** D3
Asarum (Karlshamn) **51** C2
Asarum (Karlshamn) **72** A1
Asasp **108** B3, **154** B1
Asbach **80** A2
Åsberget **35** C2
Åsbro **46** A1/2
Asby **46** A3
Ascain **108** A3, **154** A1
Ascha **92** B1
Aschach an der Donau **93** C2
Aschaffenburg **81** C3
Aschau **92** B3
Aschau bei Kraiburg **92** B2
Aschau im Chiemgau **92** B3
Aschau-Sachrang **92** B3
Aschbach Markt **93** D2/3
Ascheberg **67** D3
Ascheberg (Holstein) **53** B/C3
Aschersleben **69** C3
Asciano **115** C3, **116** B2
Asco **113** D2/3
Ascó **163** C1/2
Áscoli Piceno **117** D3
Áscoli Satriano **120** A2
Ascona [Locarno] **105** D2
Ascot **64** B3
Ascoux **87** D2
Ascq **78** A3
Åse **9** C1
Aséa **146** B3
Åseda **51** C1
Åseda **72** B1
Åsele **30** B2
Åselet **16** B3
Asemakylä **18** A2
Asemakylä **18** A/B2
Asemanseutu **21** C3
Åsen **39** C1
Åsen **35** C2
Åsen **9** C/D2
Åsen **28** B3, **33** D1
Åsen **39** C1
Åsen **29** D3, **34** B2
Asendorf (Hoya) **68** A2
Åsenhöga **50** B1
Asenovgrad **140** B3
Åsensbruk **45** C2
Asentopalo **12** B2
Åsenvoll **33** D2/3
Åseral **42** B3
Åserud **38** B3
Asfåka **142** B3
Asfeld **78** B3
Åsgård **33** C3, **37** D1
Åsgårdstrand **43** D2, **44** B1
Åshammar **40** A2
Ashbourne **61** C3, **64** A1
Ashbourne **58** A2
Ashburton **63** C3
Ashby de la Zouch **64** A1
Ashford **65** C3, **77** C1
Ashfordby **64** B1
Ashington **57** D2
Ashington **54** B3
Ashkirk **57** C2
Ashton-under-Lyne **59** D2, **60** B3
Asiago **107** C2/3
Asige **49** D2, **50** A1
Asikkala **25** D1/2, **26** A1/2
Asín **154** B2
Asinhal **170** B1
Asíni **147** C3
Ask **50** A/B3
Ask **38** A3
Aska **12** B2
Askainen **24** A2
Askanmäki **19** C2
Askeby **46** B2
Asker **38** A3, **43** D1
Askersund **46** A2
Askesta **40** A/B1
Åskhult **49** D1, **50** A1
Askim **38** A3, **44** B1
Askim (Göteborg) **45** C3, **49** D1
Åskloster **49** D1, **50** A1
Askøby **53** C/D2
Åskogen **17** C2
Askola **25** D2, **26** A2
Asköping **46** B1
Askós **144** A1/2
Askov **48** A/B3, **52** B1
Askøy **36** A3

Askra **147** C2
Askrigg **59** D1, **60** B2
Askvik **42** A1
Askvoll **36** A2
Aslaksrud **43** D1
Aslestad **43** C2
Ásli **37** D3
Åsljunga **50** B2
Åsmark **38** A2
Asmunti **18** B1
Åsnes **38** B2
As Neves **150** A/B3
As Nogais **151** C2
Asnœs **49** C3, **53** C/D1
Ásola **106** B3
Ásolo **107** C3
Asón **153** C2
Asopía **147** D2
Ásotthalom **129** D2
Aspa **32** B2
Aspach **91** C1
Aspang Markt **94** A3
Aspariegos **151** D3, **152** A3, **159** D1
Asparn an der Zaya **94** B2
Aspås **29** D3, **34** B2
Aspatria **57** C3, **60** A1
Aspberg **45** D1
Aspe **167** C3
Åspeå **30** B3, **35** D1/2
Aspeboda **39** D2
Aspenes **29** C2
Asperg **91** C1/2
Asperget **38** C2
Asperup **48** B3, **52** B1
Aspet **109** C3, **155** C/D1
Aspli **32** B2
Asplia **28** A2/3, **33** C1
Aspliden **17** B/C2
Aspnäs **35** D2
Aspö **47** C1
Aspö **24** A3
As Pontes de García Rodríguez **150** B1
Aspremont **111** D1
Aspres-sur-Buëch **111** D1, **112** A1/2
Aspróchoma **146** B3
Asprógerakas **146** A2
Asprókambos **147** C2
Asprópirgos **147** D2
Asproválta **144** B1/2
Aspsele **30** B2
Assago **105** D3, **106** A3
Assamstadt **91** C1
Asse **78** B1/2
Assebakte **5** D3, **6** A3, **11** D1
Asseiceira **164** B1
Assels **48** A2
Assémini **123** C/D3
Assen **67** C2
Assens **48** B2
Assens **52** B1
Assergi **117** D3, **119** C1
Asseria **131** C2
Assisi **115** D3, **117** C2
Assling **92** B3
Asson **108** B3, **154** B1
Assoro **125** C2
Assumar **165** C2
Astaffort **109** C2
Astakós **146** A1/2
Astakós **148** A1/2
Åstan **28** A3, **33** C1
Åstdalseter **38** A1
Asteasu **153** C1
Asten **79** C/D1
Asten **93** D2
Asti **113** C1
Astillero **153** B/C1
Astipálea **149** C3
Aston **59** D2, **60** B3
Astorga **151** D2
Åstorp **49** D3, **50** A2
Åstorp **72** A1
Åstrand **39** C3
Åsträsk **31** C1
Ástros **147** C3
Astudillo **152** B3
Asunta **21** C/D3
Asvestópetra **143** C2
Aszófő **128** B1

Atalaia **164** B1
Atalánti **147** C1
Atalánti **148** B2
Atalaya **165** D3
Atalaya de Cañavate **168** B1
Atalho **164** B2
Atapuerca **153** C2
Ataquines **160** A1
Atarfe **173** C2
Ataun **153** D1/2
Atauta **153** C3, **161** C1
Atea **162** A1/2
Ateca **162** A1
Atei **158** B1
A Teixeira **150** B2
Ateleta **119** C/D2
Atella **120** A/B2
Átena Lucana **120** A3
Atessa **119** D1/2
Ath **78** B2
Atherstone **64** A2
Athíkia **147** C2/3
Athína/Athínai **147** D2
Athína/Athínai **148** B2
Athis-Mons **87** D1/2
Athlone **55** C2
Áthos **144** A3
Athy **55** D3
Atienza **161** C1
Atina **119** C2
Atnbrua **33** C3, **37** D1
Åtniksstugan **14** B3, **29** D1
Atnosen **38** A1
Atostugan **14** B3
Atouguia da Baleia **164** A1
A Toxa **150** A2
Åtrafors **49** D1, **50** A1
Åtran **49** D1, **50** A1
Åträsk **16** B3
Åträsk **31** C/D1/2
Atrå (Tinn) **43** C1
Atri **119** C1
Atripalda **119** D3, **120** A2
Attendorn **80** B1
Attenkirchen **92** A3
Attersee **93** C3
Attersee **96** A3
Attichy **78** A3
Attigliano **117** C3, **118** A/B1
Attigny **79** B/C3
Attleborough **65** C/D2
Attmar **35** D3
Åttonträsk **30** B1
Attre **78** B2
Attu **24** B3
Åtvidaberg **46** B2/3
Atzara **123** D2
Atzendorf **69** C/D3
Au **106** A/B1
Aub **81** D3, **91** C/D1
Aubagnan **108** B2/3
Aubagne **111** D3
Aubange **79** D3
Au bei Bad Aibling **92** A/B3
Aubel **79** D2
Aubenas **111** C1
Aubenton **78** B3
Auberive **88** B3
Auberives-sur-Varèze **103** D3
Auberson, L' [Ste-Croix] **104** B1
Aubeterre-sur-Dronne **101** C3
Aubiet **109** C2/3, **155** C/D1
Aubigny **100** A/B1/2
Aubigny-au-Bac **78** A2
Aubigny-en-Artois **78** A2
Aubigny-sur-Nère **87** D3
Aubin **110** A1
Auboue **89** C1
Aubrac **110** A/B1
Aubusson **102** A2
Auce **73** D1
Auch **109** C2/3, **155** C1
Auchmithie **57** C1
Auchterarder **57** B/C1
Auchtermuchty **57** C1
Auchy-au-Bois **77** D2, **78** A2
Audenge **108** A1
Audenhain **82** B1
Audeux **89** C3, **104** A1
Audierne **84** A2

Audincourt **89** D3, **90** A3
Audlem **59** D2, **60** B3, **64** A1
Audnedal **42** B3
Audresselles **77** D1
Audruicq **77** D1
Audun-le-Roman **89** C1
Aue **82** B2
Auenheim **90** B2
Auerbach **82** A3
Auerbach **82** B2
Auerbach-Michelfeld **82** A3
Auffach **92** B3
Aufsess **82** A3
Aughrim **58** A3
Augsburg **91** D2
Augsburg-Göggingen **91** D2
Augsburg-Haunstetten **91** D2, **92** A2
Augusta **125** D3
Augustdorf **68** A3
Augustenborg **52** B2
Augustów **73** D2/3
Auho **19** C2
Aukra **32** A2
Aukrug **52** B3
Auktsjaur **16** A3
Aulanko **25** C2
Aulendorf **91** C3
Aulis **147** D2
Aulla **114** A2
Aullène **113** D3
Aulnay **101** B/C2
Aulnoye-Aymeries **78** B2
Ault **77** D2
Aultbea **54** A2
Aulus-les-Bains **155** C2
Auma **82** A/B2
Aumale **77** D3
Aumetz **79** D3
Aumont-Aubrac **110** B1
Aunay-en-Bazois **103** C1
Aunay-sur-Odon **86** A1
Aune **28** A/B2
Auneau **87** C2
Auneuil **77** D3, **87** C1
Auning **49** C2
Aups **112** A3
Aura **24** B2
Aura im Sinngrund **81** C2/3
Auran **28** A/B3, **33** C1
Auran asema **24** B2
Auray **85** B/C3
Aure **32** B2
Aurejärvi **21** B/C3
Auriac-sur-Vendinelle **109** D3
Auribeau-sur-Siagne **112** B3
Aurich **67** D1
Aurich-Tannenhausen **67** D1
Aurignac **109** C3, **155** D1
Aurillac **110** A1
Aurland **36** B3
Aurolzmünster **93** C2
Auron **112** B2
Auronzo di Cadore **107** D2
Auros **108** B1
Auroux **110** B1
Aursfjordbotn **4** A3, **9** D1
Aursjøhytta **32** B3, **37** C1
Aurskog **38** A3
Aursmoen **38** A1/2
Aursnes **32** A3, **36** B1
Áusa-Corno **126** A3
Ausejo **153** D2
Ausónia **119** C2
Austad **42** B2
Austafjord **28** B1
Austefjord **32** A3, **36** B1
Austertana (Leirpollen) **7** C1
Austevoll **42** A1
Aústis **123** D2
Austmarka **38** B3
Austnes **32** A2
Austråt **28** A3, **33** C1
Austrumdal **42** A/B2/3
Auterive **109** D3, **155** D1
Autheuil **86** A/B1
Authon **86** B3
Authon **112** A2
Authon-du-Perche **86** B2

Authon-la-Plaine **87** C2
Autio **18** B2/3
Autio **17** C1
Autol **153** D2/3, **154** A2
Autrèche **86** B3
Autreville **89** C2
Autrey-lès-Gray **89** C3
Autricourt **88** B2
Autry-le Châtel **87** D3
Autti **12** B3
Auttoinen **25** D1, **26** A1
Autun **103** C1
Auve **88** B1
Auvers **110** B1
Auvila **27** C1
Auvillars **109** C2
Auxerre **88** A3
Auxey-Duresses **103** D1
Auxi-le-Château **77** D2
Auxon **88** A3
Auxonne **89** C3, **103** D1, **104** A1
Auzances **102** A/B2
Auzat **155** D2
Auzon **102** B3
Åva **24** A2/3, **41** D2
Ava **31** C3
Avaborg **31** D1
Avafors **17** C2
Avaheden **17** B/C2/3
Availles-Limouzine **101** C/D2
Avala **133** D1, **134** A1/2
Avaldsnes **42** A2
Avallon **88** A3
Avan **17** C3
Avanca **158** A2
Åvas **145** D1, **145** D3
Avasjö **30** A/B2
Avaträsk **30** A1/2
Avaviken **16** A3
Avdejevka **99** D1/2
Ávdira **149** C1
Ávdira **145** C1
Avebury Circle **63** D2, **64** A3
A Veiga **151** C2/3
Aveinte **160** C2
Aveiras de Cima **164** C2
Aveiro **158** A2
Avelãs do Caminho **158** A2
Avelengo/Hafling **107** C2
Avelgem **78** A/B2
Avellaneda **153** D3
Avellino **119** D3
Aven Armand **110** B2
Avenches **104** B1
Aven de Marzal **111** C2
Aven d'Orgnac **111** C2
Avène **119** C2
Averbode **79** C1
Avernak By **53** B/C2
Aversa **119** C/D3
Avesnes-le-Comte **78** A2
Avesnes-sur-Helpe **78** B2/3
Avesta **40** A3
Avetrana **121** D3
Avezzano **119** C2
Aviano **107** D2
Avidagos **158** B1
Avigliana **112** B1
Avigliano **120** A/B2
Avignon **111** C2
Avignonet-Lauragais **109** D3, **156** A1
Ávikebruk **35** D3
Ávila **160** A2
Avilés **151** D1
Avilley **89** C/D3
Avintes **158** A2
Avinyó **156** A2
Ávio **106** B3
Avión **150** B2
Avioth **79** C3
Åvist **20** B2
Aviz **164** B2
Avize **88** A1
Avliótai **142** A3
Avlón **147** D2
Avlonárion **147** D2
Avlum **48** A2
Avö **158** B3
Avoca **58** A3
Avoine **86** B3, **101** C1
Ávola **125** D3
Avonmouth **63** D1/2

Avord **102** B1
Avoriaz **104** B2
Avoudrey **104** B1
Avradsberg **39** C2
Avranches **86** A/B1/2
Avren **145** D1
Avricourt **89** D2, **90** A2
Avrillé **100** A2
Avrillé **86** A3
Avtovac **132** B3, **137** C1
Avžže **11** C1
Axat **156** A1
Axbridge **63** D2
Axel **78** A3
Äxelfors **50** A/B1
Axelsvik **17** C/D3
Axiat **155** D2, **156** A1
Axioúpolis **143** D1
Axmarby **40** A/B2
Axmarsbruk **40** A/B1/2
Axminster **63** C/D2
Axvall **45** D2
Ayamonte **170** B2
Aycliffe **57** D3, **61** C1
Ayegui **153** D2, **154** A2
Ayelo de Malferit **169** C/D2
Ayen **101** C3
Ayerbe **154** B2
Ayer [Sierre] **105** C2
Ayguafreda **156** A3
Aylesbury **64** B2/3
Ayllón **161** C1
Aylsham **61** D3, **65** C1
Ayna **168** B2
Aynac **109** D1
Aynho **65** C2
Ayódar **162** B3
Ayora **169** C2
Ayr **56** B2
Ayr **54** A/B3, **55** D1/2
Äyrinmäki **18** A3
Ayron **101** C2
Äyskoski **22** B2
Ay-sur-Moselle **89** C1
Ayton **57** D2
Aytré **100** B2
Ayvacik **149** C1
Ayvalik **149** D1/2
Aywaille **79** C2
Azagra **153** D2, **154** A2
Azaila **162** B1
Azambuja **164** A2
Azambujeira **164** A1/2
Azanja **134** B2
Azannes-et-Soumazannes **89** C1
Azañón **161** D2
Azanúy **155** C2
Azaruja **165** B/C2
Azay-le-Ferron **101** D1
Azay-le-Rideau **86** B3, **101** C1
Azay-sur-Cher **86** B3
Azenhas do Mar **164** A2
Azevo **159** C2
Azinhaga **164** B1
Azinhal **170** B2
Azinheira dos Barros **164** B3
Azkoitia **153** D1
Aznalcázar **171** D2
Aznalcóllar **171** C/D2
Azóia **158** A3, **164** A1
Azpeitia **153** D1
Azuaga **166** A3
Azuara **162** B1
Azuébar **162** B3, **169** D1
Azuqueca de Henares **161** C2
Azur **108** B2
Azurara **158** A1
Azután **160** A3, **166** B1
Azzano Décimo **107** D2/3, **126** A2/3

B

Baad **106** B1
Baamonde **150** B1
Baar **105** C/D1

Baarle-Hertog **79** C1
Baarn **66** B3
Babadag **141** D2
Babaevo **75** D1
Babenhausen **81** C3
Babenhausen **91** D2
Babigoszcz **70** B1
Babilafuente **159** D2, **160** A2
Babimost **71** C3
Babina Greda **132** B1
Babin Most **138** B1
Babino Polje **136** B1
Babin Potok **131** B/C1
Babke **70** A1
Babljak **137** D1
Babócsa **128** A2
Babušnica **139** C1
Bač **138** A1
Bač **129** C3
Bacáicoa **153** D2
Bacarés **173** C2
Bacău **141** C1
Baccarat **89** D2
Baceno **105** C2
Bach **109** D2
Bacharach **80** B3
Bačina **134** B3
Bäckan **35** C3
Bäckarna **34** B3
Backaryd **51** C2
Bäckaskog **50** B2
Bačka Palanka **129** C3, **133** C1
Bačka Topola **129** C3
Bačka Topola **140** A1
Backe **30** A2, **35** C1
Bäckebo **51** D1
Bäckefors **45** C2
Backgränd **25** C3
Bäckhammar **45** D1, **46** A1
Bački Breg **129** C3
Bački Brestovac **129** C3
Bački Jarak **129** D3, **134** A1
Bački Monoštor **129** C3
Bački Petrovac **129** C3
Backnang **91** C1
Bäcknäs **16** A3
Bačko Gradište **129** D3
Bačko Novo Selo **129** C3, **133** C1
Bačko Petrovo Selo **129** D3
Bacoli **119** C3
Bacqueville-en-Caux **77** C3
Bácsalmás **129** C2
Bácsbokod **129** C2
Bacup **59** D1/2, **60** B3
Bačvani **131** D1
Baczyna **71** C2
Bada **39** B/C3
Bad Abbach **92** B1
Badacsonytomaj **128** A1
Bad Aibling **92** B3
Badajoz **165** C2
Badalona **156** A3
Badalucco **113** C2
Badarán **153** C/D2·
Bad Aussee **93** C3
Bad Bentheim **67** C/D2/3
Badbergen **67** D2
Bad Bergzabern **90** B1
Bad Berka **82** A2
Bad Berleburg **80** B1/2
Bad Berleburg-Raumland **80** B1/2
Bad Berleburg-Aue **80** B1/2
Bad Berneck **82** A3
Bad Bertrich **80** A3
Bad Bevensen **69** C2
Bad Bibra **82** A1
Bad Blankenburg **82** A2
Bad Bleiberg ob Villach **126** B2
Bad Bocklet **81** D2
Bad Brambach **82** B2
Bad Bramstedt **52** B3
Bad Breisig **80** A2
Bad Brückenau **81** C2
Bad Buchau **91** C2/3
Bad Camberg **80** B2
Badderen **5** B/C2
Bad Deutsch Altenburg **94** B2
Bad Doberan **53** D3
Bad Driburg **68** A3

Bad Driburg-Neuenheerse **68** A3, **81** C1
Bad Driburg-Dringenberg **68** A3, **81** C1
Bad Düben **82** B1
Bad Düben **72** A3
Bad Dürkheim **80** B3, **90** B1
Bad Dürrenberg **82** B1
Bad Dürrheim **90** B3
Bądecz **71** D1
Bad Eilsen **68** A3
Bad Elster **82** B2
Bad Ems **80** B2
Baden **94** B3
Baden **90** B3
Bádenas **162** A2
Baden-Baden **90** B2
Bad Endbach **80** B2
Badenweiler **90** A3
Baderna **126** B3, **130** A1
Badersleben **69** C3
Bad Essen **68** A3
Bad Feilnbach **92** B3
Bad Feilnbach-Au **92** A/B3
Bad Fischau **94** A/B3
Bad Frankenhausen **82** A1
Bad Freienwalde **70** B2
Bad Freienwalde **72** A3
Bad Friedrichshall **91** C1
Bad Füssing **93** C2
Bad Gandersheim **68** B3
Badgastein **107** D1, **126** A1
Bad Gleichenberg **127** D1
Bad Goisern **93** C3
Bad Gottleuba **83** C2
Bad Grund **68** B3
Bad Hall **93** D3
Bad Harzburg **69** C3
Bad Heilbrunn **92** A3
Bad Herrenalb **90** B2
Bad Hersfeld **81** C2
Bad Hofgastein **107** D1, **126** A1
Bad Homburg von der Höhe **80** B2/3
Bad Honnef **80** A2
Bad Hönningen **80** A2
Badia Calavena **107** C3
Badia Polésine **115** B/C1
Badia Pratáglia **115** C2, **116** B1
Badia Tedalda **115** C2/3, **117** C2
Bad Iburg **67** D3
Bad Imnau **90** B2
Bad Innerlaterns **106** A1
Bad Ischl **93** C3
Bad Ischl **96** A3
Bad Karlshafen **68** B3, **81** C1
Bad Kissingen **81** D2/3
Bad Kleinen **53** C3, **69** C1
Bad Kleinkirchheim **126** B1
Bad Klosterlausnitz **82** A/B2
Bad Kohlgrub **92** A3
Bad König **92** C3
Bad Königshofen **81** D2
Bad Kösen **82** A1
Bad Köstritz **82** B2
Bad Kreuzen **93** D2
Bad Kreuznach **80** B3
Bad Krozingen **90** A3
Bad Laasphe-Holzhausen **80** B2
Bad Laasphe **80** B2
Bad Laer **67** D3
Bad Laer-Glandorf **67** D3
Bad Langensalza **81** D1
Bad Lauchstädt **82** A/B1
Bad Lausick **82** B1
Bad Lauterberg **69** B/C3, **81** D1
Bad Lauterberg-Bartolfelde **81** D1
Bad Liebenstein **81** D2
Bad Liebenwerda **83** C1
Bad Liebenwerda **96** A1
Bad Liebenzell **90** B2
Bad Lippspringe **68** A3
Bad Marienberg **80** B2
Bad Mergentheim **81** C3, **91** C1
Bad Mergentheim-Herbsthausen **91** C1

Bad Mergentheim-Stup-
pach 91 C1
Bad Münder-Hachmühlen
68 B3
Bad Münder 68 B3
Bad Münder-Bakede 68 B3
Bad Münstereifel-Schönau
79 D2, 80 A2
Bad Münster-Ebernberg
80 B3
Bad Münstereifel 79 D2,
80 A2
Bad Münstereifel-Mut-
scheid 80 A2
Bad Muskau 83 D1
Bad Nauheim 81 B/C2
Bad Nenndorf 68 B3
Bad Neuenahr-Ahrweiler
80 A2
Bad Neuenahr-Ahrweiler-
Ramersbach 80 A2
Bad Neustadt 81 D2
Bad Oeynhausen 68 A3
Badolato 122 B2/3
Badolatosa 172 B2
Bad Oldesloe 53 C3, 68 B1
Badonviller 89 D2, 90 A2
Bad Orb 81 C2/3
Bad Peterstal 90 B2
Bad Pirawarth 94 B2
Bad Pyrmont 68 A/B3
Bad Radkersburg 127 D1/2
Bad Ragaz 105 D1, 106 A1
Bad Rappenau 91 C1
Bad Reichenhall 92 B3
Bad Rippoldsau 90 B2
Bad Saarow-Pieskow
70 B3
Bad Sachsa 81 D1
Bad Säckingen 90 B3
Bad Salzdetfurth-Boden-
burg 68 B3
Bad Salzdetfurth 68 B3
Bad Salzschlirf 81 C2
Bad Salzuflen 68 A3
Bad Salzungen 81 D2
Bad Sankt Leonhard im La-
vanttal 127 C1
Bad Sassendorf 67 D3,
80 B1
Bad Schallerbach 93 C2
Bad Schandau 83 C2
Bad Schmiedeberg 69 D3,
70 A3, 82 B1
Bad Schönau 94 B3
Bad Schönborn-Langen-
brücken 90 B1
Bad Schussenried 91 C3
Bad Schwalbach 80 B3
Bad Schwartau 53 C3
Bad Segeberg 53 B/C3
Bad Soden 80 B3
Bad Soden 81 C2
Bad Soden-Salmünster
81 C2
Bad Sooden-Allendorf
81 C/D1
Bad Steben 82 A2
Bad Sulza 82 A1
Bad Sülze 53 D3
Bad Tatzmannsdorf
94 A/B3, 127 D1
Bad Teinach-Zavelstein
90 B2
Bad Tennstedt 81 D1,
82 A1
Bad Tölz 92 A3
Bad Überkingen 91 C2
Badules 163 C1/2
Bad Urach 91 C2
Bad Vellach 126 B2
Bad Vilbel 81 B/C2/3
Bad Vöslau 94 B3
Bad Waldsee 91 C3
Bad Wiessee 92 A3
Bad Wildungen 81 C1
Bad Wilsnack 69 D2
Bad Wimpfen 91 C1
Bad Windsheim 81 D3,
91 D1
Bad Wörishofen 91 D3
Bad Wurzach-Arnach
91 C3
Bad Wurzach 91 C3
Bad Wurzach-Unterschwar-
zach 91 C3
Bad Zell 93 D2

Bad Zwischenahn 67 D1
Baélls 155 C3
Baena 172 B1
Baesweiler 79 D2
Baeza 167 D3, 173 C1
Båfjelldalen 14 B3
Bagà 156 A2
Bagaladi 122 A3, 125 D2
Bågede 29 D2
Bâgé-le-Châtel 103 D2
Bagenkop 53 C2
Bagergue 155 D2
Bages 156 B1/2
Baggård 31 C2
Bagheria 124 B2
Bagn 37 D3
Bagnacavallo 115 C2,
117 B/C1
Bagnac-sur-Celé 109 D1,
110 A1
Bagnàia 117 C3, 118 A1
Bagnara Cálabra 122 A3,
125 D1
Bagnasco 113 C2
Bagnères-de-Luchon
155 C2
Bagnères-de-Bigorre
109 B/C3, 155 C1
Bagni 114 A2, 116 A1
Bagni Contursi 120 A2
Bagni di Bórmio 106 B2
Bagni di Lucca 114 B2,
116 A1
Bagni di Másino 106 A2
Bagni di Petriolo 114 B3,
116 B2
Bagni di Rabbi 106 B2
Bagni di Tívoli 118 B2
Bagni di Vinádio 112 B2
Bagno a Rípoli 114 B2,
116 B1/2
Bagno di Romagna 115 C2,
116 B1
Bagnoles-de-l'Orne 86 A2
Bagnoli del Trigno 119 D2
Bagnoli di Sopra 107 C3
Bagnoli Irpino 119 D3,
120 A2
Bagnolo in Piano 114 B1
Bagnolo Mella 106 B3
Bagnolo Piemonte 112 B1
Bagnolo San Vito 114 B1
Bagnols-en-Forêt
112 A/B3
Bagnols-les-Bains 110 B1
Bagnols-sur-Cèze 111 C2
Bagnone 114 A2
Bagnorégio 117 C3,
118 A1
Bagod 128 A1
Bagolino 106 B3
Bagrdan 134 B2
Bagshot 64 B3, 76 B1
Báguena 163 C2
Bagüés 154 B2
Bahabón de Esgueva
153 C3
Bahillo 152 B2
Bahmač 99 D2
Bahrendorf 69 C3
Baia 119 C3
Baia de Aramă 135 D1
Baia de Aramă 140 B2
Báia delle Zágare 120 B1,
136 A3
Baia Domízia 119 C3
Baia Mare 97 D3, 98 A3
Baiano 119 C3
Baião 158 B1/2
Baiardo 113 B/C2
Baia Sardinia 123 D1
Baienfurt 91 C3
Baierbach 92 B2
Baiersbronn-Klosterreichen-
bach 90 B2
Baiersbronn 90 B2
Baignes-Sainte-Radegonde
101 C2
Baigneux-les-Juifs 88 B3
Băile Herculane 135 C1
Băile Herculane 140 A/B2
Bailén 167 C3
Băile Olănești 140 B2
Băilești 140 B2
Băilești 135 D2
Bailleau-le-Pin 86 A/B2
Bailleul 77 C3

Bailleul 78 A2
Bailo 154 B2
Bain-de-Bretagne 85 D2/3
Bains 110 B1
Bains de Préchacq 108 A2
Bains d'Escouloubre
156 A1
Bains-d'Huchet 108 B2
Bains-les-Bains 89 C/D2
Baio 150 A1
Baiona 150 A3
Bais 86 A2
Baisieux 78 A2
Baiso 114 B1/2
Baixas 156 B1
Baja 129 C2
Baja 96 B3
Bajánsenye 96 A/B3
Bajánsenye 127 D1
Bajgora 138 B1
Bajina Bašta 133 C2
Bajinci 131 D1, 132 A1
Bajmok 129 C2/3
Bajna 95 D3
Bajovo Polje 137 C1
Bajram Curri 138 A2
Bajram Curri 140 A3
Bajša 129 C3
Bajzé 137 C2
Bak 128 A1/2
Bak 96 B3
Bakar 126 B3, 130 B1
Bakarac 126 B3, 130 B1
Bakel 79 C/D1
Bakewell 61 C3, 64 A1
Bakio 153 C/D1
Bække 48 B3, 52 B1
Bakke 42 B3
Bakke 44 B2
Bakkejord 4 A3
Bakken 38 B1/2
Bakken 29 C/D2
Bakken 38 B2
Bakken 32 B1
Bakketun 14 B2/3
Bakko 43 C1
Bækmarksbro 48 A2
Bákoca 128 B2
Bakonybél 128 B1
Bakonycsernye 95 C3,
128 B1
Bakonygyepes 128 A1
Bakonyjákó 128 A/B1
Bakonykcppány 95 C3,
128 B1
Bakonypéterd 95 C3
Bakonysárkány 95 C3,
128 B1
Bakonyszentkirály 95 C3,
128 B1
Bakonyszombathely 95 C3
Bakov nad Jizerou 83 D2
Baksa 128 B2/3
Baksjöliden 30 B2
Baktsjaur 16 A3
Bakum 67 D2, 68 A2
Bakvattnet 29 C/D2/3,
34 B1
Bala 59 C2/3, 60 A3
Balabankoru 145 D3
Balaci 140 B2
Bălăcița 135 D2
Balaguer 155 C/D3,
163 C1
Balaruc-les-Bains 110 B3
Balassagyarmat 95 D2
Balassagyarmat 97 C3
Balata di Baida 124 A2
Balatonakali 128 B1
Balatonalmádi 128 B1
Balatonederics 128 A1
Balatonfőkajár 128 B1
Balatonföldvár 128 B1
Balatonfüred 128 B1
Balatonfüred 96 B3
Balatonfüzfő 128 B1
Balatonkenese 128 B1
Balatonkeresztúr 128 A2
Balatonkeresztúr 96 B3
Balatonlelle 128 B1/2
Balatonmagyaród 128 A2
Balatonszemes 128 B1
Balatonvilágos 128 B1
Bălăușeri 97 D3, 140 B1
Balazote 168 B2
Balbacil 161 D2
Balbigny 103 C2/3

Balboa 151 C2
Balbriggan 58 A2
Balčik 141 D3
Balconete 161 C2
Balcons de la Mescla
112 A2/3
Baldellou 155 C3
Balderschwang 91 D3
Baldichieri d'Asti 113 C1
Baldock 65 B/C2
Baldos 158 B2
Bale 130 A1
Baleira 151 C1/2
Balerno 57 C2
Balestrand 36 B2
Balestrate 124 A2
Balf 94 B3
Balfron 56 B1
Balikesir 149 D1
Bälinge 50 B2
Balingen 90 B2
Balingen-Weilstetten
91 B/C2
Balizac 108 B1
Balje 52 A/B3, 68 A1
Bäljom 29 C3, 34 A1
Balk 66 B2
Balkbrug 67 C2
Ballabani 142 B2
Ballachulish 56 A1
Ballangen 9 C2
Ballangen-Bjørnkåsen 9 C2
Ballan-Miré 86 B3
Ballantrae 56 A/B3
Ballao 123 D2
Ballasalla 58 B1
Ballaugh 58 B1
Ballcaire d'Urgell 155 D3,
163 D1
Balle 49 C2
Ballebro 52 B2
Ballen 49 C3, 53 C1
Ballenstedt 69 C3
Balleroy 76 A/B3, 85 D1,
86 A1
Ballerup 49 D3, 50 A3,
53 D1
Ballestar 163 C2
Ballesteros de Calatrava
167 C2
Ballina 55 C1
Ballinasloe 55 C2/3
Balling 48 A2
Ballingslöv 50 B2
Ballinluig 57 C1
Ballinluig 54 B2
Ballino 106 B2
Ballobar 155 C3, 163 C1
Balloch 56 B1/2
Ballon 86 B2
Ballószög 129 C1
Ballots 85 D2
Ballsh 142 A2
Ballstad 8 B2/3
Ballstädt 81 D1/2
Ballum 52 A2
Ballycanew 58 A3
Ballycarry 56 A3
Ballycastle 54 A3, 55 D2
Ballyclare 56 A3
Ballydonegan 55 C3
Ballygalley 56 A3
Ballygawley 54 A3, 55 D2
Ballygowan 56 A3
Ballyhalbert 56 A3
Ballyhaunis 55 C2
Ballymena 54 A3, 55 D2
Ballynahinch 58 A1
Ballynaskeagh 58 A1
Ballynure 56 A3
Ballyshannon 55 C2
Ballywalter 56 A3
Balmaseda 153 C1
Balme 104 B3
Balmúccia 105 C3
Balneario de Pozo Amargo
172 A2
Balquhidder 56 B1
Balrath 58 A2
Balsa 158 B1
Balsa de Ves 169 D1/2
Balsareny 156 A2/3
Balsby 50 B2

Balsfjord 4 A3, 10 A1
Balsicas 169 C3, 174 B1
Balsièges 110 B1/2
Balsorano 119 C2
Bålsta 40 B3, 47 C1
Balsthal 105 C1
Balta 135 C/D1
Balta 99 C3
Baltanás 152 B3
Baltar 150 B3
Baltasound 54 A1
Baltijsk (Pillau) 73 C2
Baltrum 67 D1
Balugães 150 A3, 158 A1
Bælum 48 B2
Balvano 120 A2
Balve 80 B1
Balvi 74 B2
Balzers [Trübbach] 105 D1,
106 A1
Balzhausen 91 D2
Balzo 117 D3
Bambálion 146 A1
Bamberg 81 D3, 82 A3
Bamble 43 D2, 44 A2
Bamburgh 57 D2
Bampton 63 C2
Bampton 64 A3
Bana 95 C3
Bañares 153 C2
Banatska Palanka 134 B1
Banatsk Aranđelovo
129 D2
Banatski Brestovac 134 B1
Banatski Dvor 129 D3
Banatski Karlovac 134 B1
Banatsko Novo Selo
134 B1
Banbridge 58 A1
Banbury 65 C2
Banchory 54 B2
Bande 150 B3
Bandeira 150 B2
Bandelow 70 B1
Bandirma 149 D1
Bando 115 C1
Bandol 111 D3
Băneasa 141 C2
Bañeres 169 C2
Banff 54 B2
Bångbro 39 D3
Bangor 56 A3
Bangor 59 C2, 60 A3
Bangor 84 B3
Bangor 54 A3, 55 D2
Bangor Erris 55 C2
Bangsund 28 B2
Banhos da Curia 158 A2/3
Banie 70 B2
Banja 133 D3, 134 A3,
138 A1
Banja 133 D2, 134 A/B2
Banja 138 B2
Banja 133 D3
Banja Koviljača 133 C2
Banja Luka 131 D1, 132 A1
Banjani 133 D2, 134 A2
Banja Rusanda 129 D3
Banja Vrućica 132 B2
Banjica 138 A1
Banjišta 138 A3
Banjole 130 A1
Banjska 138 B1
Bánk 95 D3
Banka 95 C2
Bankeryd 45 D3, 46 A3
Bankfoot 57 C1
Bankja 139 D1
Banloc 134 B1
Bannalec 84 B2
Bannedsdorf 53 C2
Bannesdorf-Puttgarden
53 C2
Bannockburn 56 B1
Baño bárez 159 C2
Banon 111 D2
Bañón 163 C2
Baños de Alicún de las Tor-
res 173 C1
Baños de Gigonza 171 D3
Baños de Ledesma 159 D2
Baños de la Encina 167 C3
Baños de Molgas 150 B3
Baños de Montemayor
159 D3
Baños de Panticosa 154 B2

Baños de Río Tobía **153** D2
Baños de San Juan **157** D2
Baños de Tus **168** A/B3
Baños de Valdearados **153** C3, **161** C1
Baños de Zújar **173** D1
Baños Fuensante **174** A1
Bánov **95** C2/3
Banova Jaruga **128** A3
Bánovce nad Bebravou **95** C2
Banovići **132** B2
Banská Bystrica **95** D2
Banská Bystrica **97** B/C2
Banská Štiavnica **95** D2
Bansko **139** D3, **143** D1, **144** A1
Bansko **139** D2
Bantheville **88** B1
Bantry **55** C3
Bantzenheim **90** A3
Banyalbufar **157** C2
Banyoles **156** B2
Banyuls-sur-Mer **156** B2
Banzi **120** B2
Baorationovsk **73** C2
Bapaume **78** A2/3
Bapukkátan **9** D3
Baqueira **155** D2
Bár **129** C2
Bar **137** D2
Barahona **161** D1
Barajas **161** C2
Barajas del Melo **161** C3
Barajevo **133** D1/2, **134** A2
Barakaldo/Baracaldo **153** C1
Baralla **151** C2
Baranbio **153** C1/2
Baranjsko Petrovo Selo **128** B3
Barano d'Íschia **119** C3
Baranovići **98** B1
Barão de São Miguel **170** A2
Baraolt **141** C1
Bar-ar-Lan **84** A2
Barásoain **154** A2
Barbacena **165** C2
Barbadás **150** B2/3
Barbadillo **159** D2
Barbadillo de Herreros **153** C3
Barbadillo del Mercado **153** C3
Barbadillo del Pez **153** C3
Barban **130** A1
Bárbara **115** D3, **117** C/D2
Barbarano Romano **117** C3, **118** A1
Barbarano Vicentino **107** C3
Barbaros **149** D1
Barbaste **109** C2
Barbastro **155** C3
Barbate de Franco **171** D3
Barbatovac **134** B3, **138** B1
Barbâtre **100** A1
Barbazan **109** C3, **155** C1
Barbele **73** D1, **74** A2
Barbens **155** D3, **163** D1
Barberà de la Conca **163** C1
Barberino di Mugello **114** B2, **116** B1
Bárbo **47** C2
Barbonne-Fayel **88** A2
Barbotan-les-Thérmes **108** B2
Barbués **154** B3
Barbullushi **137** D2
Barbuñales **155** C3
Barby **69** D3
Barca **161** D1
Bárcabo **155** C2
Barca d'Alva **159** C2
Barcarrota **165** C/D2/3
Barcellona Pozzo di Gotto **125** D1/2
Barcelona **156** A3
Barcelonnette **112** A/B2
Barcelos **150** A3, **158** A1
Bárcena del Monasterio **151** C1
Barcheta **169** D2
Barchi **115** D2/3, **117** C2
Barcial **151** D3

Barcillonnette **111** D1/2, **112** A2
Barcina de los Montes **153** C2
Bárcis **107** D2
Barco **158** B3
Barcones **161** C1
Barcos **158** B2
Barcs **128** A2/3
Barcus **108** A/B3, **154** B1
Bard **105** C3
Bardal **14** B2
Bardallur **155** C3, **163** C1
Bardejov **97** C2
Bardi **114** A1
Bardolino **106** B3
Bardonécchia **112** A/B1
Bardowick **68** B1
Bare **133** C3
Bare **133** D2, **134** A/B2
Bare **133** C/D3, **134** A3, **137** D1, **138** A1
Barèges **108** B3, **155** C2
Barenburg **68** A2
Barendorf **69** C1
Bärenklau **70** B3
Bärenstein **83** B/C2
Bärenstein **83** C2
Barentin **77** C3
Barenton **85** D2, **86** A2
Barfleur **76** B3
Barga **114** A/B2, **116** A1
Bargas **160** B3, **167** C1
Barge **112** B1
Bargemon **112** A3
Bargen [Schaffhausen] **90** B3
Barghe **106** B3
Bargoed **63** C1
Bargrennan **56** B3
Bargteheide **52** B3, **68** B1
Bargum **52** A2
Barham **65** C3, **76** B1
Bari **121** C2, **136** A3
Barić Draga **130** B2
Bárig **169** D2
Barigazzo **114** B2, **116** A1
Bari Santo Spírito **121** C2, **136** A3
Bari Sardo **123** D2
Barisciano **117** D3, **119** C1
Barjac **111** C2
Barjac **110** B1
Barjols **112** A3
Barkarö **40** A3, **46** B1
Barkow **69** D1
Barkowo **71** D1
Barleben **69** C/D3
Bar-le-Duc **88** B1
Barletta **120** B1/2, **136** A3
Barlieu **87** D3
Barlinek **71** C2
Barlinek **72** A3
Barmouth **59** C3
Barmstedt **52** B3, **68** B1
Barnard Castle **57** D3, **61** C1
Bärnau **82** B3
Barneveld **66** B3
Barneville-Carteret **76** A3
Barnewitz **69** D2
Barnoldswick **59** D1, **60** B2
Barnówko **70** B2
Barnsley **61** C2/3
Barnstaple **63** C2
Barnstorf **68** A2
Barntrup-Alverdissen **68** A3
Baron **87** D1
Barone Canavese **105** C3
Baronissi **119** D3
Baronville **89** D1
Barösund **25** C3
Barovo **139** C3, **143** C/D1
Barquilla **159** C2
Barquilla de Pinares **159** D3, **160** A3
Barquinha **164** B1
Barr **56** B2/3
Barr **90** A2
Barra **158** A2
Barracão **158** A3, **164** A/B1
Barracas **162** B3
Barrachina **163** C2
Barraco **160** A/B2
Barrado **159** D3

Barrafranca **125** C2/3
Barrage de Sarrans **110** A1
Barrage de Serre-Ponçon **112** A2
Barrage de Tignes **104** B3
Barrage du Chambon **112** A1
Barranco do Velho **170** B2
Barrancos **165** C3
Barranda **168** B3, **174** A1
Barraqueville **110** A2
Barrax **168** B2
Barrea **119** C2
Barreiros **151** C1
Barrême **112** A2
Barrhill **56** B3
Barrière-de-Champlon **79** C3
Barrillos **152** A2
Barrio **150** A3, **158** A1
Barrio de San Pedro **165** C1
Barriomartín **153** D3
Barro **152** A1
Barro **150** A2
Barrô **158** B2
Barroca **158** B3
Barrocas e Taias **150** A3
Barromán **160** A2
Barrow-in-Furness **59** C1, **60** A/B2
Barrow-in-Furness **54** B3
Barruecopardo **159** C2
Barruelo de Santullán **152** B2
Barry **63** C2
Bârse **53** D2
Barsebäckshamn **50** A3
Barsinghausen **68** B3
Barssel **67** D1
Barssel-Harkebrügge **67** D1/2
Bar-sur-Aube **88** B2
Bar-sur-Seine **88** B2
Barsviken **35** D3
Barth **53** D2/3
Barth **72** A2
Bartholomä **91** C/D2
Barton **59** D1, **60** B2
Barton-upon-Humber **61** D2
Bartošova Lehôtka **95** D2
Bartoszyce (Bartenstein) **73** C2
Bartow **70** A1
Baruchella **115** B/C1
Barúmini **123** C/D3
Baruth **70** A3
Barvaux **79** C2
Barver **68** A2
Bårvik **5** C1/2
Barwice (Bärwalde) **71** D1
Barwinek **97** C2, **98** A3
Bárzana **151** D2
Bárzio **105** D2/3, **106** A2
Basagliapenta **107** D2, **126** A2
Bašaid **129** D3
Basardilla **160** B2
Basauri **153** C1
Bàscara **156** B2
Baschi **117** C3, **118** A1
Basconcillos del Tozo **152** B2
Basdahl **68** A1
Basedow **53** D3, **69** D1, **70** A1
Basel **90** A3
Baselga di Pinè **107** C2
Baselice **119** D2, **120** A1
Basella **155** C3
Bas-en-Basset **103** C3
Basepohl **70** A1
Bàsheim **43** D1
Basiana **133** D1, **134** A1
Basicò **125** D2
Basildon **65** C3
Basingstoke **64** B3, **76** A1
Baška **130** B1
Baška Voda **131** D3, **132** A3
Baskemölla **50** B3

Baške Oštarije **130** B2
Bäskjö **30** B1
Baslow **61** C3, **64** A1
Bäsna **39** D2
Bassacutena **123** D1
Bassai **146** B3
Bassano del Grappa **107** C3
Basse-Bodeux **79** D2
Bassecourt **89** D3, **90** A3, **104** B1
Bassignana **113** C1
Bassilly **78** B2
Bassou **88** A2/3
Bassoues **109** C3, **155** C1
Bassum **68** A2
Bassum-Bramstedt **68** A2
Bassum-Neubruchhausen **68** A2
Båstad **49** D2, **50** A2
Båstad **72** A1
Båstad (Heiås) **38** A3, **44** B1
Bastahovine **133** C2
Bastardo **117** C3
Bastelica **113** D3
Basterud **39** C3
Bastheim **81** D2
Bastia **113** D2
Bastía **107** C3
Bastida **153** C/D2
Bastida **158** A2
Bastogne **79** C/D3
Bastunäs **31** C1/2
Bastuträsk **31** C1
Batajnica **133** D1, **134** A1
Batak **140** B3
Batalha **158** A3, **164** A1
Bátaszék **129** C2
Bátaszék **96** B3
Baté **128** B2
Batea **163** C2
Bateckij **74** B1
Batelov **94** A1
Baterno **166** B2
Bath **63** D2, **64** A3
Bathgate **57** C2
Bathmen **67** C3
Batignano **116** B3
Batina **129** C3
Batlava **138** B1
Batley **61** C2
Batnfjordsøra **32** A/B2
Batočina **134** B2
Bátovce **95** D2
Batres **160** B3
Batrina **132** A/B1
Båtsfjord **7** C1
Båtsfjord **5** C1
Båtsjaur **15** D2
Båtskärsnäs **17** C/D2/3
Battáglia Terme **107** C3
Battenberg-Dodenau **80** B1/2
Battice **79** D2
Battipáglia **119** D3, **120** A2
Battle **77** C1
Battonya **97** C3, **140** A1
Baturin **99** D2
Baturino **75** C3
Båtvik **25** C3
Batz-sur-Mer **85** C3
Baud **85** B/C2/3
Baudenbach-Mönchsberg **81** D3
Baudreville **87** C2
Baugé **86** A3
Baugy **102** B1
Bauladu **123** C2
Bauma **91** B/C3, **105** D1
Baume-les-Dames **89** D3, **104** A/B1
Baumgarten **93** B/C2
Baumgarten **69** D1, **70** A1
Baumholder **80** A3
Baunach **81** D2
Baunei **123** D2
Bausendorf **80** A3
Bauska **73** D1, **74** A2
Bautzen **96** A1
Bautzen **83** D1
Bavanište **134** B1
Bavay **78** B2
Bäverhult **31** C1
Bäverträsk **30** B1
Bäverudden **16** B2
Bavorov **93** C1

Bawdeswell **65** C/D1
Bawdsey **63** D1
Bawinkel **67** D2
Bawtry **61** C3
Bayárcal **173** D1
Bayerbach bei Ergoldsbach **92** B2
Bayerdilling **91** D2, **92** A2
Bayerisch Eisenstein **93** C1
Bayeux **76** B3, **86** A1
Bayindir **149** D2
Bayon **89** C/D2
Bayonne **108** A3, **154** A1
Bayramiç **149** C/D1
Bayreuth **82** A3
Bayrischzell **92** B3
Baythorn End **65** C2
Bayubas de Abajo **153** C3, **161** C1
Baza **173** D1
Bazas **108** B1/2
Baziaş **134** B1
Baziaş **140** A2
Baziège **109** D3, **155** D1
Bazoches **88** A1
Bazoches-les-Gallerandes **87** C2
Bazoches-sur-Hoëne **86** B2
Bazoges-en-Paillers **101** C1
Bazolles **103** B/C1
Bazouges-la-Pérouse **85** D2
Bâzovec **135** D3
Bazsi **128** A1
Bazuel **78** B3
Bazzano **114** B1/2
Beaconsfield **64** B3
Beade **150** B2
Beaminster **63** D2
Beamud **161** D3, **162** A3
Beariz **150** B2
Beas **171** C1
Beasain **153** D1/2
Beas de Segura **167** D3, **168** A3
Beateberg **45** D2, **46** A2
Beatenberg [Interlaken] **105** C1/2
Beattock **57** C2
Beattock **54** B3
Beaubery **103** C2
Beaubru **79** C3
Beaucaire **111** C2
Beaucens **108** B3, **155** C1/2
Beaufays **79** C2
Beaufort **104** B3
Beaufort-du-Jura **103** D1/2, **104** A2
Beaufort-en-Vallée **86** A3
Beaufort-sur-Gervanne **111** D1
Beaugency **87** C3
Beaujeu **103** C/D2
Beaulac **108** B2
Beaulieu **76** A1
Beaulieu Abbey **76** A1
Beaulieu-sous-la-Roche **100** A1
Beaulieu-sur-Loire **87** D3
Beaulieu-sur-Dordogne **109** D1
Beaulieu-sur-Mer **112** B3
Beaumarchés **108** B3, **155** C1
Beaumaris **59** C2, **60** A3
Beaumes-de-Venise **111** C/D2
Beaumesnil **86** B1
Beaumetz-lès-Loges **78** A2
Beaumont **109** C1
Beaumont **78** B2
Beaumont-de-Lomagne **109** C2
Beaumont-du-Gâtinais **87** D2
Beaumont-en-Argonne **79** C3
Beaumont-Hague **76** A3
Beaumont-la-Ferrière **88** A3, **102** B1
Beaumont-la-Ronce **86** B3
Beaumont-le-Roger **86** B1
Beaumont-les-Autels **86** B2

Beaumont-sur-Oise 77 D3, 87 D1
Beaumont-sur-Sarthe 86 B2
Beaumont-sur-Vesle 88 B1
Beaune 103 D1
Beaune-la-Rolande 87 D2
Beaupréau 85 D3, 100 B1
Beaurising 79 C3
Beauregard 86 A/B3
Beaurepaire-en-Bresse 103 D1, 104 A1/2
Beaurepaire 103 D3
Beaurières 111 D1
Beauronne 101 C3, 109 C1
Beauvais 77 D3
Beauvallon 112 A3
Beauville 109 C2
Beauvoir-sur-Niort 100 B2
Beauvoir-sur-Mer 100 A1
Beauzée-sur-Aire 89 B/C1
Beba Veche 129 D2
Bebra 81 C2
Bebra-Breitenbach 81 C2
Beccles 65 D2
Becedas 159 D2/3
Beceite 163 C2
Bečej 129 D3
Bečej 140 A1/2
Beceni 141 C2
Becerreá 151 C2
Becerril de Campos 152 B3
Bečevinka 75 D1
Bech 79 D3
Bécherel 85 C2
Bechet 140 B2
Bechhofen 91 D1
Bechhofen (Zweibrücken) 89 D1, 90 A1
Bechí 162 B3, 169 D1
Běchovice 83 D3
Bechyně 93 D1
Bečići 137 C2
Becilla de Valderaduey 152 A3
Beckenried 105 C/D1
Beckhampton 63 D2, 64 A3
Beckingen-Düppenweiler 79 D3, 90 A1
Beckov 95 C2
Beckum 67 D3
Beclean 97 D3, 140 B1
Bécon-les-Granits 86 A3
Bečov nad Teplou 82 B3
Becsehely 128 A2
Becsvölgye 127 D1, 128 A1/2
Bedale 61 C2
Bedale 112 B2
Bédar 174 A2
Bédarieux 110 B3
Bedburg 79 D1/2, 80 A1/2
Bedburg-Hau 67 C3
Bedburg-Kaster 79 D1
Beddgelert 59 C2, 60 A3
Beddingestrand 50 B3
Bédée 85 C2
Bederkesa 52 A3, 68 A1
Bedford 64 B2
Bedlington 57 D3
Bedmar 167 D3, 173 C1
Bednja 127 D2
Bedoin 111 D2
Bédole 106 B2
Bedónia 113 D2, 114 A1
Bedous 108 B3, 154 B1
Bedretto [Airolo] 105 C/D2
Bedrule 57 C2
Bedsted 48 A2
Beduido 158 A2
Bedum 67 C1
Bedworth 64 A2
Beelen 67 D3
Beelitz 70 A3
Beelitz 72 A3, 96 A1
Beendorf 69 C3
Beenz 70 A1
Beerfelde 70 B3
Beerfelden 81 C3, 91 C1
Beerta 67 C1
Beeskow 70 B3
Beeskow 72 A3, 96 A1
Beesten 67 D2
Beetsterzwaag 67 C2
Beetz 70 A2

Beetzendorf 69 C2
Begaljica 133 D1/2, 134 B2
Bégard 84 B1/2
Begejci 129 D3
Begíjar 167 D3, 173 C1
Begis 162 B3, 169 C1
Beg-Meil 84 B2/3
Begna 37 D3
Begndalen 37 D3
Begoml' 74 B3
Begonte 150 B1
Begues 156 A3
Begunicy 74 B1
Begunje 126 B2
Begur 156 B2
Behlow 70 B3
Beho 79 D2
Béhobie 154 A1
Behramkale 149 C1
Behren-Lübchin 53 D3
Behringen 81 D1/2
Beian 28 A3, 33 C1
Beiarn 14 B1
Beichlingen 82 A1
Beidendorf 53 C3, 69 C1
Beijos 158 B2
Beilen 67 C2
Beilngries 92 A1
Beilngries-Paulushofen 92 A1
Beilrode 83 B/C1
Beilstein 80 B2
Beinette 112 B2
Beinwil am See 105 C1
Beire 154 A2
Beires 173 D2
Beisfjord 9 D2/3
Beith 56 B2
Beitostølen 37 C2
Beius 97 D3, 140 B1
Beja 164 B3, 170 B1
Béjar 159 D2/3
Bejís 162 B3, 169 C1
Béke 95 C2/3
Békéscsaba 97 C3, 140 A1
Békéssámson 129 D2
Békésszentandrás 129 D1
Bekkarfjord 6 B1
Bekkelegret 33 C3, 37 D1
Bekken 38 B1
Bekkjarvik 42 A1
Bekkvikdal 32 B1
Belá 95 D1
Bélábre 101 C2
Bela Crkva 134 B1
Bela Crkva 133 C2
Bela Crkva 140 A2
Belair 108 B3, 154 B1
Belaja Cerkov' 99 C2
Bel'ajevka 141 D1
Belalcázar 166 B2
Bělá nad Radbuzou 82 B3
Belanovce 138 B2
Belanovica 133 D2, 134 A2
Bela Palanka 135 C3, 139 C1
Bela Palanka 140 A/B3
Bělá pod Bezdězem 83 D2
Belas 164 A2
Belascoáin 154 A2
Bélavár 128 A2
Belazaima 158 A2
Belcaire 156 A1
Belchite 162 B1
Bělčice 83 C3, 93 C1
Belčin 139 D2
Belčišta 138 B3, 142 B1
Bel'cy 99 C3
Bełczna 71 C1
Belebelka 75 C2
Belecska 128 B2
Beled 94 B3
Belegiš 133 D1, 134 A1
Belej 130 A1
Beleña 159 D2
Beleña 161 C2
Beleño 152 A1
Bélesta 109 D3, 156 A1
Belev 75 D3
Belfast 54 A3, 55 D2
Belfast 56 A3
Belford 57 D2
Belfort 89 D3, 90 A3
Belgern 83 C1
Bélgida 169 D2

Belgioioso 105 D3, 106 A3, 113 D1
Belgirate 105 D3
Belgodère 113 D2
Belgorod Dnestrovskij 141 D1
Belhade 108 B2
Belianes 155 D3, 163 D1
Beliet 108 A/B1
Beli Iski 139 D2
Beli Manastir 128 B3
Belimel 135 D3
Belin 108 A/B1
Belinchón 161 C3
Beli Potok 135 D3
Belišče 128 B3
Beliševo 139 C1
Bel Iskŭr 139 D2
Beljakovci 139 C2
Beljina 133 D2, 134 A2
Bella 120 A2
Bellac 101 D2
Bellágio 105 D2, 106 A2
Bellano 105 D2, 106 A2
Bellária-Igea Marina 115 C/D2, 117 C1
Belle Croix 79 D2
Bellegarde 111 C2
Bellegarde-du-Loiret 87 D2
Bellegarde-en-Marche 102 A2
Bellegarde-sur-Valserine 104 A2
Belleherbe 89 D3, 104 B1
Belle-Isle-en-Terre 84 B2
Bellême 86 B2
Bellenaves 102 B2
Bellencombre 76 B3
Bellerive-sur-Allier 102 B2
Bellevaux 104 B2
Bellevesvre 103 D1
Belleville 103 D2
Belleville-sur-Vie 100 A/B1
Bellevue 104 B2/3
Bellevue 78 B3
Bellevue-la-Montagne 103 C3
Belley 104 A3
Bellheim 90 B1
Bellicourt 78 A3
Bellingen 90 A3
Bellingham 57 D3
Bellino 112 B1/2
Bellinzona 105 D2
Bellizzi 119 C3, 120 A2
Bell-lloc d'Urgell 155 C/D3, 163 C1
Bello 162 A2
Bellö 46 A/B3
Bellpuig 155 D3, 163 D1
Bellreguart 169 D2
Belluno 107 D2
Bellús 169 D2
Bellver 155 C3, 163 C1
Bellvik 30 A1/2
Bellvis 154 B3, 162 B1
Belm 67 D2/3
Belmez 166 B3
Belmez de la Moraleda 173 C1
Belmont-de-la-Loire 103 C2
Belmonte 158 B3
Belmonte 151 D1
Belmonte 168 A1
Belmonte de Tajo 161 C3
Belmonte de Mezquín 163 C2
Belmont-sur-Rance 110 A2
Belmullet 55 C2
Belo Blato 129 D3, 133 D1, 134 A1
Belo Brdo 134 B3, 138 B3
Belobresca 134 B1
Belogradčik 135 D3
Belogradčik 140 B2
Belœil 78 B2
Beloljin 134 B3, 138 B3
Belo Polje 138 A1
Belorado 153 C2
Belosavci 133 D2, 134 B2
Belotinci 135 D3
Belovo 140 B3
Belp 105 C1
Belpasso 125 C/D2
Belpech 109 D3, 155 D1, 156 A1

Belper 61 C3, 64 A1
Belsey 57 D3
Belsh 142 A1
Beltheim 80 A3
Beltinci 127 D2
Beluša 95 C/D1
Belušić 134 B3
Belvédère du Cirque 112 B1
Belvédère-Campomoro 113 D3
Belvedere Maríttimo 122 A1
Belvedere Ostrense 115 D3, 117 D2
Belver 164 B1
Belver de los Montes 152 A3, 159 D1, 160 A1
Belvès 109 C1
Belvis de la Jara 160 A3, 166 B1
Belvis de Monroy 159 D3, 166 A1
Belvoir Castle 61 C/D3, 64 B1
Belyj 75 C2/3
Belyniči 74 B3
Belz 84 B3
Belzig 69 D3
Belzig 72 A3
Bembibre 151 C/D2
Bembridge 76 A1/2
Bemmel 66 B3
Bemposta 164 B1
Bemposta 159 C1
Bempton 61 D2
Benabarre 155 C3
Benacazón 171 D1/2
Benadalid 172 A2/3
Benafigos 162 B3
Benafim 170 A/B2
Benagéver Nuevo 162 A3, 169 C1
Benaguacil 169 C/D1
Benahadux 173 D2
Benahavís 172 A3
Benalmádena 172 B2/3
Benalúa de Guadix 173 C2
Benalúa de las Villas 173 C1/2
Benalup de Sidonia 171 D3
Benamargosa 172 B2
Benamaurel 173 D1
Benamejí 172 B2
Benamocarra 172 B2
Benasal 163 B/C2/3
Benasau 169 D2
Benasque 155 C2
Benátky nad Jizerou 83 D2
Benavent de la Conca 155 D3
Benavente 151 D3
Benavente 164 A2
Benavides 151 D2
Benavila 164 B2
Bencatel 165 C2
Bendeleben 81 D1, 82 A1
Bendery 141 D1
Bendorf 80 A2
Benedikt 127 D2
Benediktbeuern 92 A3
Benedita 164 A1
Benegiles 151 D3, 152 A3, 159 D1
Benejama 169 C2
Benejúzar 169 C3, 174 B1
Benesat 97 D3, 140 B1
Benešov 96 A2
Benešov 83 D3
Benešov nad Ploučnicí 83 D2
Benešov nad Černou 93 D2
Benestare 122 A3
Bénestroff 89 D1
Benet 100 B2
Benetuser 169 D1
Benetutti 123 D2
Beneuvre 88 B3
Bene Vagienna 113 C1/2
Bénévent-l'Abbaye 101 D2, 102 A2
Benevento 119 D3
Benfeld 90 A2
Benfica 164 A/B2
Bengesti 135 D1
Bengtsby 25 D3, 26 A3

Bengtsfors 45 C2
Bengtsheden 39 D2, 40 A2
Beniaján 169 C3, 174 B1
Beničanci 128 B3
Benicarló 163 C2
Benicasim 163 C3
Benidorm 169 D2
Beniel 169 C3, 174 B1
Benifallet 163 C2
Benifallim 169 D2
Benifayó 169 D1/2
Beniflá 169 D2
Benigánim 169 D2
Beniloba 169 D2
Benimarfull 169 D2
Benínar 173 C/D2
Benisa 169 D2
Benissalem 157 C2
Benitayo 169 D1/2
Benítsai 142 A3
Benizalón 173 D2, 174 A2
Benkovac 131 C2
Benllech 59 B/C2, 60 A3
Benlloch 163 C3
Bennebo 40 A3
Benneckenstein 69 C3, 81 D1
Bennekom 66 B3
Bennstedt 82 A1
Bénodet 84 A/B2/3
Bénouville 76 B3, 86 A1
Benquerenca de Cima 158 B3, 165 C1
Benquerencia 165 D1, 166 A1
Benquerencia de la Serena 166 A/B2
Bensafrim 170 A2
Bensbyn 17 C3
Bensheim 80 B3
Bensheim-Auerbach 80 B3
Bensjö 35 C2
Benzo 172 A3
Beočin 129 C/D3, 133 C/D1, 134 A1
Beograd 133 D1, 134 A1
Beograd 140 A2
Beram 126 B3, 130 A1
Beranturi 153 C2
Berasáin 154 A1/2
Berastegi 153 D1, 154 A1
Berat 142 A2
Bérat 108 B3, 155 C1
Berat 148 A1
Beratón 154 A3, 161 D1, 162 A1
Beratshausen-Oberpfraundorf 92 A1
Beratzhausen 92 A1
Bérbaltavár 128 A1
Berbegal 155 C3
Berberana 153 C2
Berbinzana 154 A2
Bercedo 153 C1
Berceo 153 C2
Berceto 114 A1
Bercher [Lausanne] 104 B1/2
Berchidda 123 D1
Berching 92 A1
Berching-Holnstein 92 A1
Berchtesgaden 93 B/C3
Bérchules 173 C2
Bercial de Zapardiel 160 A2
Bercimuel 161 C1
Bercimuelle 159 D2
Berck-sur-Mer 77 D2
Bercu 78 A2
Berdal 28 A2, 33 C1
Berdejo 153 D3, 154 A3, 161 D1, 162 A1
Berdičev 99 C2
Berdún 154 A2
Beregovo 97 D2/3, 98 A3
Bereguardo 105 D3, 113 D1
Berek 128 A3
Beremend 128 B3
Berendshagen 53 D3
Bere Regis 63 D2
Berestečko 97 D1/2, 98 B2
Beretinec 127 D2
Berettyóújfalu 97 C3, 140 A1
Berëza 73 D3, 98 B1
Berezan' 99 D2
Berežany 97 D2, 98 B2

Berezino 74 B3, 99 C1
Berezna 99 D2
Berg 29 C2
Berg 14 A3
Berg 28 A3, 33 C1
Berg 29 D3, 34 B1
Berg 126 B1
Berg 34 B2
Berg 30 A3, 35 C2
Berg 51 C1
Berg 29 D3, 34 B1
Berga 51 D1
Berga 50 B1
Berga 51 D2
Berga 156 A2
Berga 81 D1, 82 A1
Berga 82 B2
Bergaland 42 A2
Bergama 149 D2
Bergantino 114 B1
Bergantzu 153 C/D2
Bergara 153 D1
Bergasa 153 D2/3
Bergatreute 91 C3
Bergatreute-Rossberg
  91 C3
Bergbacka 16 B3
Bergby 40 A/B2
Berge 67 D2
Berge 34 B2
Berge 69 D2, 70 A2
Berge 162 B2
Berge 35 D3
Berge 43 C2
Bergeby 7 C2
Bergeforsen 35 D3
Bergen 66 A2
Bergen 36 A3
Bergen 69 C2
Bergen 68 B2
Bergen 72 A2
Bergen aan Zee 66 A2
Bergen-Belsen 68 B2
Bergen-Eidsvåg 36 A3
Bergen op Zoom 78 B1
Bergen-Sülze 68 B2
Bergentheim 67 C2
Bergen-Wardböhmen
  68 B2
Berger 43 D1, 44 B1
Bergerac 109 C1
Bergères-lès Vertus 88 A1
Bergesserin 103 C2
Berget 38 A1
Berget 28 A3, 33 C3
Berggiesshübel 83 C2
Berghaupten 90 B2
Bergheim 79 D1/2,
  80 A1/2
Bergheim-Quadrath-Ichen-
  dorf 79 D1/2, 80 A1/2
Berghülen 91 C2
Berg im Gau 92 A2
Bergisch-Gladbach
  80 A1/2
Bergisch-Glattbach-Bens-
  berg 80 A1/2
Bergkarlås 39 D2
Bergkvara 51 D2
Bergkvara 72 B1
Bergland 15 C3
Berglen 91 C1/2
Bergli 32 B1
Berglia 29 C2
Berglund 4 B2
Berglund 31 C/D1
Berglunda 31 C1
Bergnäs 30 D1
Bergnäs 15 D3
Bergnäset 17 C3
Bergneustadt 80 A/B1/2
Bergö 20 A2, 31 D3
Bergondo 150 B1
Bergsäng 39 D2
Bergsäng 39 C3
Bergsbotn 9 D1
Bergsfjord 4 B2
Bergshamra 41 C3, 47 D1
Bergsjö 35 D3
Bergsjö 30 A2, 35 C1
Bergsjö 37 C3
Bergsjöåsen 30 A2, 35 C1
Bergsmo 28 B2
Bergsnov 28 A/B1
Berg (Starnberg) 92 A3
Bergstjärn 34 B2

Bergsund 15 C3
Bergsviken 16 B3
Bergtheim 81 D3
Bergua 155 B/C2
Berguenda 153 C2
Bergues 77 D1, 78 A1
Bergün/Bravuogn 106 A2
Bergvik 40 A1
Bergwitz 69 C3
Bergzow 69 D2/3
Berhida 128 B1
Beringel 164 B3, 170 B1
Beringen 79 C1
Berishë i Vënit 138 A2
Berja 173 D2
Berka 81 D2
Berkatal-Frankershausen
  81 C/D1
Berkeley 63 D1, 64 A3
Berkenbrück 70 B2/3
Berkenthin 53 C3, 69 C1
Berkhamsted 64 B3
Berkheim 91 D2
Berknes 36 A/B1
Berkón 17 C3
Berkovica 135 D3, 139 D1
Berkovica 140 B3
Berlanga 166 A3
Berlanga de Duero 161 C1
Berlevåg 7 C1
Berlin (-Ost) 70 A2
Berlin (-Ost) 72 A3
Berlin (West) 72 A3
Berlin (West) 70 A2
Berlstedt 82 A1
Bermellar 159 C2
Bermeo 153 D1
Bermillo de Sayago 159 D1
Bern 105 B/C1
Bernalda 121 C3
Bernardin 126 A/B3
Bernardos 160 B1/2
Bernartice 93 D1
Bernau 70 A2
Bernau 92 B3
Bernau 72 A3
Bernau (Hochschwarzwald)
  90 B3
Bernaville 77 D2
Bernay 86 B1
Bernburg 69 D3
Berndorf 94 A3
Berndorf 96 A/B3
Berne 68 A1/2
Berneau 79 C/D2
Bernedo 153 D2
Berneval-le-Grand 76 B2
Berninches 161 C2
Bernkastel-Kues 80 A3
Bernried 92 B1/2
Bernried-Egg 92 B1/2
Bernsdorf 70 A3
Bernsdorf 83 C1
Bernstadt 83 D1
Bernstein 94 B3, 127 D1
Bernués 154 B2
Bernuy-Salinero 160 A/B2
Beromünster 105 C1
Beroun 83 C3
Beroun 96 A2
Berovo 140 B3
Berovo 139 D3
Berra 115 C1
Berre-l'Étang 111 D3
Berrien 84 B2
Berrobi 153 D1, 154 A1
Berrocal 171 C1
Berrocal de Salvatierra
  159 C2
Berrocalejo 160 A3,
  166 B1
Bersbo 46 B2
Bersenbrück 67 D2
Berthelming 89 D1, 90 A2
Bertincourt 78 A3
Bertinoro 115 C2, 117 C1
Bertogne 79 C3
Bertrix 79 C3
Berven 84 A/B2
Berwang 91 D3
Berwick upon Tweed 57 D2
Berwick upon Tweed
  54 B2/3
Berzasca 135 C2
Berzence 128 A2
Berzocana 166 B1

Berzosa 161 C2
Berzosa 153 C3, 161 C1
Berzovia 140 A2
Beša 95 D2
Besalú 156 B2
Besançon 89 C3, 104 A1
Bescanó 156 B2
Besednice 93 D2
Bešenkoviči 74 B3
Besenyszög 129 D1
Běšiny 93 C1
Beška 133 D1, 134 A1
Beskovići 132 B3, 137 C1
Besni Fok 133 D1, 134 A1
Bespén 155 B/C3
Bessaker 28 A2
Bessan 110 B3
Bessarabka 141 D1
Bessay-sur-Allier 102 B2
Bessbrook 58 A1
Besse-en-Chandesse
  102 B3
Bessèges 111 C2
Bessé-sur-Braye 86 B3
Bessheim 37 C2
Bessines-sur-Gartempe
  101 C2
Besson 102 B2
Best 79 C1
Bestensee 70 A3
Bestorp 46 B2
Bestul 43 D1/2, 44 A1
Bestwig-Nuttlar 80 B1
Bestwig-Ramsbeck 80 B1
Betanzos 150 B1
Bétera 169 C2
Beteta 161 D2
Béthenville 88 B1
Bethesda 59 C2, 60 A3
Bethmale 109 C3, 155 D2
Béthune 78 A2
Betna 32 B2
Bettelainville 89 C/D1
Bettembourg 79 D3
Betten [Mörel] 105 C2
Bettignies 78 B2
Bettingen 79 D3
Bettmeralp [Mörel] 105 C2
Bettna 46 B2
Béttola 113 D1, 114 A1
Bettystown 58 A2
Betws-y-Coed 59 C2,
  60 A3
Betz 87 D1
Betzdorf 80 B2
Betzenstein 82 A3
Betzenstein-Spies 82 A3
Beuil 112 A2
Beuron 91 C3
Beuvry 78 A2
Beuzeville 77 C3, 86 B1
Bevagna 115 D3, 117 C2/3
Beveren 78 B1
Beverley 61 D2
Bevern 68 B3
Bevernungen-Dalhausen
  68 A/B3, 81 C1
Beverstedt 68 A1
Beverungen 68 B3, 81 C1
Beverwijk 66 A2
Bevilácqua 107 C3
Béville-le-Comte 87 C2
Bevtoft 52 B1/2
Bex 104 B2
Bexhill 77 C1
Beychac-et-Caillau 108 B1
Beydağ 149 D2
Beynac-et-Cazenac 108 B1
Beynat 102 A3, 109 D1
Bezas 163 C3
Bezau 91 C3
Bezdan 129 C3
Bezděz 83 C2
Bezdružice 82 B3
Bèze 89 C3
Bežeck 75 D2
Bézenet 102 B2
Bezenye 95 B/C3
Béziers 110 B3, 156 B1
Bezmisht 142 B1
Béznar 173 C2
Bezno 83 D2
Bezvěrov 83 B/C3
Bezzecca 106 B2/3
Biała 71 C1

Biała Podlaska 73 D3,
  97 D1, 98 A1
Białogard (Belgard) 72 B2
Białośliwie 71 D2
Białowąs 71 C1
Białowieża 73 D3, 98 A1
Białystok 73 D3, 98 A1
Biancavilla 125 C2
Bianco 122 A3
Biandrate 105 C/D3
Biar 169 C2
Biarritz 108 A3, 154 A1
Biarrotte 108 B3, 155 C1
Bias 108 B2
Bias 69 D3
Biasca 105 D2
Biasteri 153 D2
Biatorbágy 95 D3
Biaufond [La Chaux-de-
  Fonds] 89 D3, 104 B1
Bibbiena 115 C2/3, 116 B2
Bibbona 114 B3, 116 A2
Biberach 80 B3
Biberach 91 C2/3
Biberbach 91 D2
Bibinje 130 B2
Bibione 107 D3, 126 A3
Biblis 80 B3
Biblis-Nordheim 80 B3
Bibury 63 D1, 64 A3
Bicaj 138 A2
Bicaz 141 C1
Bíccari 120 A1
Bicester 65 C2
Bichl 92 A3
Bichlbach 91 D3
Bicorp 169 C2
Bicske 95 D3
Bidache 108 B3, 155 C1
Bidania 153 D1
Bidarray 108 B3, 155 C1
Bidart 108 A3, 154 A1
Bideford 62 B2
Bidjovagge 5 C3, 11 B/C1
Bie 46 B1
Biebergmünd-Bieber 81 C3
Biebersdorf 70 B3
Biebertal 80 B2
Biebertal-Frankenbach
  80 B2
Biebesheim 80 B3
Biedenkopf 80 B2
Biedenkopf-Wallau 80 B2
Biedrusko 71 D2
Biegen 70 B3
Biel 154 B2
Biel/Bienne 89 D3, 104 B1
Bielefeld 68 A3
Bielefeld-Senne 68 A3
Bielefeld-Sennestadt 68 A3
Biella 105 C2
Bielle 108 B3, 154 B1
Biellojaure 15 C2/3
Bielmonte 105 C3
Bielsa 155 C2
Bielsko-Biała 97 B/C2
Bielsk Podlaski 73 D3,
  98 A1
Bienenbüttel 69 B/C2
Bieniów 71 C3
Bienno 106 B2
Bienservida 168 A2
Biéntina 114 B2/3, 116 A2
Bienvenida 165 D3,
  166 A3
Bière 104 A/B2
Biere 69 C/D3
Bierge 155 C2/3
Bierné 86 A3
Bierwart 79 C2
Bierzwnica 71 C1
Bierzwnik 71 C2
Biescas 154 B2
Biesenthal 70 A2
Biessenhofen 91 D3
Bietigheim 90 B1/2
Bietigheim-Bissingen
  91 C1
Bièvre 79 C3
Biga 149 D1
Bigadiç 149 D1
Biganos 108 A1
Bigastro 169 C3, 174 B1
Biggar 57 C2
Biggleswade 64 B2
Bignasco [Ponte Brolla]
  105 D2

Bigorne 158 B2
Bihać 131 C1
Bijela 132 B1
Bijele Poljane 137 C1/2
Bijeljina 133 C1
Bijelo Polje 137 D1,
  138 A1
Bijörnvik 25 D3, 26 B3
Bijuesca 153 D3, 154 A3,
  161 D1, 162 A1
Bikova 74 A/B2
Bílá 95 D1
Bilalovac 132 B2
Bilbilis 162 A1
Bilbo/Bilbao 153 C1
Bileća 137 C2
Bílina 83 C2
Biłgoraj 97 D1, 98 A2
Bílisht 142 B2
Bílisht 148 A1
Biljača 139 C2
Biljanovac 134 B3
Bilje 129 C3
Billabona 153 D1, 154 A1
Billdal 45 C3, 49 D1
Billerbeck 67 D3
Billesdon 64 B1/2
Billesholm 50 A2/3
Billiat 104 A2
Billigheim 91 C2
Billinge 50 B3
Billingen 32 B3, 37 C1
Billingsfors 45 C2
Billingshurst 76 B1
Billom 102 B3
Billsta 30 A2
Billund 48 B3, 52 B1
Billy 102 B2
Bílovice 95 C1
Bilshausen 81 D1
Bilston 59 D3, 64 A2
Bilto 4 B3, 10 B1
Bílý Kostel nad Nisou
  83 D2
Bilzen 79 C2
Biña 95 D3
Binaced 155 C3, 163 C1
Binas 87 C2/3
Binasco 105 D3, 106 A3
Binbrook 61 D3
Binche 78 B2
Bindalseidet 14 A3, 28 B1
Bindlach 82 A3
Bindslev 44 A3, 48 B1
Binéfar 155 C3, 163 C1
Bingen 43 D1
Bingen 91 C2/3
Bingen am Rhein 80 B3
Bingham 61 C3, 64 B1
Bingley 59 D1, 61 C2
Bingsjö 39 D2
Binibeca 157 C1
Binic 85 C2
Biniés 154 B2
Binisafúa 157 C1
Binisalem 157 C1
Binn [Fiesch] 105 C2
Binsfeld 79 D3, 80 A3
Binswangen 91 D2
Biođa 137 D1, 138 A1
Bioče 137 D2
Biograd 130 B2/3
Biol 103 D3
Bionaz 105 B/C3
Biosca 155 C3, 163 C1
Bioska 133 C2
Biota 155 C2
Bippen 67 D2
Birchington 65 C3, 76 B1
Birdlip 63 D1, 64 A2/3
Birgel 79 D2, 80 A2
Birgi 124 A2
Biri 38 A2
Birka 47 C3
Birkeland 43 C3
Birkenfeld (Calw) 90 B1/2
Birkenfeld 80 A3
Birkenhain 81 C2/3
Birkenhead 59 C/D2,
  60 B3
Birkenwerder 70 A2
Birkerød 49 D3, 50 A3,
  53 D1
Birkestrand 7 C1
Birkfeld 94 A3, 127 C/D1
Bîrlad 141 C1
Birmingham 59 D3, 64 A2

Birnbach 93 C2
Biron 109 C1
Birr 55 C3
Birresborn 79 D2/3, 80 A2/3
Birsay 54 B1
Bîrseşti 135 D1
Birstein 81 C2
Biržai 73 D1, 74 A2
Bisáccia 120 A2
Bisacquino 124 B2
Bisaurri 155 C2
Biscarrosse 108 B2
Biscarrués 154 B2
Biscéglie 120 B2, 136 A3
Bischoffen-Niederweidbach 80 B2
Bischofsgrün 82 A3
Bischofsheim 81 D2
Bischofshofen 93 C3
Bischofsmais-Hochdorf 93 C1/2
Bischofswerda 83 C1
Bischofswerda 96 A1
Bischofswiesen 92 B3
Bischofszell 91 C3
Bischwiller 90 B2
Bisegna 119 C2
Bisenti 117 D3, 119 C1
Bishop Auckland 57 D3, 61 C1
Bishop's Castle 59 C/D3
Bishop's Stortford 65 C2/3
Bishops Waltham 76 B1
Bisignano 122 A/B1
Bisingen 91 B/C2
Bisko 131 D3
Biskupiec (Bischofsburg) 73 C2/3
Bismark 69 C2
Bismo 32 B3, 37 C1
Bispberg 39 D2, 40 A2
Bispfors 30 A3, 35 C2
Bispgården 30 A3, 35 C2
Bispingen 68 B2
Bispingen-Wilsede 68 B1/2
Bissendorf 67 D3, 68 A3
Bissingen-Diemantstein 91 D2
Bistagno 113 C1
Bistarac 132 B2
Bistret 135 D2/3
Bistret 140 B2
Bistrica 139 D1/2
Bistrica 133 C/D3
Bistrica 139 D2
Bistrica 137 D1
Bistrica 127 C/D2
Bistričak 132 B2
Bistrita 97 D3, 140 B1
Bitburg 79 D3
Bitche 90 A1
Bítem 163 C2
Bitetto 121 C2
Bitola 143 C1
Bitola 148 A/B1
Bitonto 121 C2, 136 A3
Bitschwiller-lès-Thann 89 D3, 90 A3
Bitterfeld 82 B1
Bitti 123 D2
Bivio [St. Moritz] 106 A2
Bivona 124 B2
Bize-Minervois 110 A3, 156 B1
Bizovac 128 B3
Bjåen 42 B1
Bjala 141 C/D3
Bjala 141 C3
Bjännfors 31 D2
Bjærangen 14 B1
Bjäresjö 50 B3
Bjärges 47 D3
Bjärka-Säby 46 B2
Bjarkøy 9 D2
Bjärlöv 50 B2
Bjärnå 24 B3
Bjärnum 50 B2
Bjärred 50 A3
Bjarsjölagard 50 B3
Bjärström 41 C3
Bjärten 31 C2
Bjärträsk 30 B3, 35 D2
Bjästa 30 B3
Bjæverskov 49 D3, 50 A3, 53 D1

Bjelland 42 B3
Bjelovar 128 A3
Bjergby 48 B1
Bjerkreim 42 A3
Bjerkvik 9 D2
Bjernede Kirke 53 C/D1
Bjerre 48 B3, 52 B1
Bjerregård 48 A3
Bjerringbro 48 B2
Bjøberg 37 C3
Bjolderup 52 B2
Bjøllånes 15 C2
Bjølstad 37 D1/2
Bjønnes 43 D2, 44 A1/2
Bjørbo 39 D2
Bjorboholm 45 C3
Bjordal 42 B2/3
Bjordal 36 A2
Bjoreidalshytta 37 B/C3
Bjørholmen 44 B3
Bjørk 37 C2
Bjørkås 10 A1
Björkås 15 C3
Bjørkbacken 15 C3
Bjorkberg 39 D1
Bjørkberg 16 B2
Björkberg 30 B1
Bjørkboda 24 B3
Bjørke 40 B2
Bjørke 32 A3, 36 B1
Bjørkelangen 38 A/B3
Bjørketorp 49 D1, 50 A1
Björkfors 46 B3
Björkfors 15 C2/3
Björkfors 17 C/D2
Björkhöjden 30 A3, 35 C1/2
Björkholmen 16 A1
Björkliden 16 A3
Björkliden 9 D2
Björklinge 40 B3
Björklinge 40 A/B3
Björklund 16 A3
Bjørkmo 9 D2
Bjørkneset 28 B1
Björkö 24 A3, 41 D2
Björkö 46 A3, 51 C1
Björkö 45 B/C3
Björkö-Arholma 41 C3
Björköby 20 A2, 31 D3
Björkön 35 D3
Björksele 31 B/C1
Björksele 30 B2, 35 D1
Björksjön 39 D3
Björkvattnet 29 C2
Björkvik 46 B2
Björlanda 45 C3, 49 D1
Bjorli 32 B3, 37 C1
Bjørn 14 A2
Björna 31 B/C3
Björnänge 29 C3, 34 A1/2
Bjørnås 32 B2
Bjørnåsbrua 38 A1
Björnbäck 30 B3, 35 D1
Björnbäck 30 B3, 35 D1
Björnberg 35 B/C3
Björnböle 30 B3, 35 D2
Bjørneborg 45 D1, 46 A1
Bjørneborg 24 A1
Bjørnes 14 B2
Bjørnestad 42 B3
Bjørnevasshytta 42 B2
Bjørnevatn 7 C2
Bjørnhollia 33 C3, 37 D1
Björnlunda 47 C1
Bjørnset 5 C2
Bjørnset 36 A2
Björnsholm 46 B3
Björnsjö 30 B3
Bjørnskar 4 A2
Bjørnskinn 9 C1
Bjørnsletta 9 D1/2
Björsarv 35 C3
Björsäter 46 B2
Björsjö 39 D3
Bjørsvik 36 A3
Bjurånäs 17 C2
Bjurbekkdalen 14 B2
Bjurberget 38 B2
Bjurfors 31 D1
Bjurholm 31 C2
Bjuröklubb fiskeläge 31 D1
Bjursås 39 D2
Bjurselefors 31 C1
Bjursund 46 B3
Bjurtjärn 45 D1, 46 A1
Bjurträsk 30 B1

Bjurvattnet 31 C2
Bjuv 50 A2
Blace 134 B3
Blackbo 40 A3
Black Bull 58 A2
Blackburn 59 D1/2, 60 B2
Blacke 31 D1
Black Mount 56 B1
Blackpool 59 C1, 60 B2
Blackpool 54 B3
Blackrock 58 A1
Blacksnäs 20 A2/3
Blackstad 46 B3
Blackwater 58 A3
Blackwaterfoot 56 A2
Bladåker 40 B3
Bladon 65 C2/3
Blaenau Ffestiniog 59 C2, 60 A3
Blaenavon 63 C1
Blåfjellhytta 42 B2
Blagaj 131 C1
Blagaj 132 B3, 136 B1
Blagdon 63 D2
Blagodatnoe 99 D3
Blagoevgrad 140 B3
Blagoevgrad 139 D2
Blagojev Kamen 135 C2
Blåhammaren 28 B3, 33 D2, 34 A2
Blaiken 15 D3
Blain 85 D3
Blairgowrie 57 C1
Blairgowrie 54 B2
Blaise 88 B2
Blaj 97 D3, 140 B1
Blajan 109 C3, 155 C1
Blakeney 65 C/D1
Blakeney 63 D1
Blaker 38 A3
Blaksæter 32 A3, 36 B1
Blakstad 38 A3, 42 B3
Blåmont 89 D2, 90 A2
Blanca 169 D3
Blancas 162 A2
Blancos 150 B3
Blandford Forum 63 D2
Blanes 156 B3
Blangy-sur-Bresle 77 D2
Blankaholm 46 B3
Blankenberge 78 A1
Blankenburg 69 C3
Blankenfelde 70 A3
Blankenhain 82 A2
Blankenheim 79 D2, 80 A2
Blankensee 70 A1
Blansko 94 B1
Blansko 96 B2
Blanzac 101 C3
Blanzy 103 C1
Blascomillán 160 A2
Blascosancho 160 A/B2
Bläse 47 D2
Blåsmark 16 B3
Blatná 93 C1
Blatná na Ostrove 95 C3
Blatné 95 C2
Blatnice 95 C1
Blato 131 D3, 132 A3
Blato 136 A1
Blatten b. Naters [Naters] 105 C2
Blatten (Lötschen) [Goppenstein] 105 C2
Blattnicksele 15 D3
Blaubeuren 91 C2
Blaufelden 91 C1
Blaufelden-Wiesenbach 91 C/D1
Blaustein 91 C2
Blåvand 48 A3, 52 A1
Blåvik 46 A3
Blaye-et-Sainte-Lucie 100 B3, 108 B1
Blaye-les-Mines 109 D2, 110 A2
Blažejovice 93 C1
Blaževac 132 B1
Blaževo 134 B3, 138 B1
Blázquez 166 B3
Bleckede 69 C1
Blecua 155 B/C3
Bled 126 B2
Bledzew 71 C2
Bléharies 78 A/B2
Bleialf 79 D2

Bleibach 90 B2/3
Bleiburg 127 C2
Bleicherode 81 D1
Bleik 9 C1
Bleikvassli 14 B2
Blekendorf 53 C3
Bleket 44 B3
Blendija 135 C3
Bléneau 87 D3
Blenheim Palace 65 C2/3
Blénod-lès-Toul 89 C2
Blera 117 B/C3, 118 A1
Blérancourt 78 A3
Bléré 86 B3
Bleriksstugan 15 C3, 29 D1
Blesa 162 B2
Blesje stadmoen 42 B1
Blesle 88 A3
Blesme 88 B1/2
Blessington 58 A2
Blestua 43 D1
Blet 102 B1
Bletchley 64 B2
Bletterans 103 D1, 104 A1
Blickling Hall 61 D3, 65 C1
Blidö 41 C3, 47 D1
Blidsberg 45 D3
Bliecos 153 D3, 161 D1
Blieskastel 89 D1, 90 A1
Blieskastel-Breitfurt 89 D1, 90 A1
Bligny-sur-Ouche 103 C/D1
Blinisht 138 A2
Blinja 127 D3, 131 C1
Blodelsheim 90 A3
Bloemendaal 66 A2
Blois 86 A/B3
Blokhus 33 C2/3
Blokhus 48 B1
Blokzijl 67 B/C2
Blomberg 67 D1
Blomberg 68 A3
Blomberg-Grossenmarpe 68 A3
Blomhöjden 29 D1/2
Blomsholm 44 B2
Blomstermåla 51 D1
Blomvåg 36 A3
Blönsdorf 70 A3
Blonville-sur-Mer 76 B3, 86 A/B1
Blosenberg 82 B2
Bloška Polica 126 B3
Blötberget 39 D3
Błotno 71 C1
Blotzheim 90 A3
Blovice 83 C3, 93 C1
Blowatz 53 C/D3
Blšany 83 C2/3
Bludenz 106 A1
Blumberg 90 B3
Blumberg 70 A2
Blyberg 39 C1/2
Blyth 61 C3
Blyth 57 D3
Blyth 54 B3
Bnin 71 D3
Bo 46 B2
Bø 43 C2
Bø 8 B2
Bø 43 D2, 44 A1
Boada 159 C2
Boadilla 159 C/D2
Boadilla de Rioseco 152 A3
Boadilla del Monte 160 B2
Boal 151 C1
Boalhosa 150 A3, 158 A1
Boan 137 D1
Bobadilla 153 D2
Bobadilla 172 B2
Bobadilla del Campo 160 A1
Bóbbio 113 D1
Bóbbio Péllice 112 B1
Boberg 30 A3, 35 C2
Böbing 91 D3, 92 A3
Bobingen 91 D2
Böblingen 91 C2
Bobolice 72 B2
Boborás 150 B2
Boboševo 139 D2
Bobova 129 C3
Bobova 133 C/D2, 134 A2
Bobovdol 139 D2
Bobovol 140 B3
Böbrach 93 B/C1

Bobrinec 99 D3
Bobrka 97 D2, 98 A2/3
Bobrowice 71 C3
Bobrówko 71 C2
Bobrujsk 99 C1
Bočac 131 D2, 132 A2
Boca do Inferno 164 A2
Bocairente 169 C/D2
Bočar 129 D3
Bocchigliero 122 B1
Boceguillas 161 C1
Bochnia 97 C2
Bocholt 67 C3
Bochov 83 B/C3
Bochum 80 A1
Bocigas de Perales 153 C3, 161 C1
Bockara 51 D1
Bockenem 68 B3
Bockfliess 94 B2
Bockhorn 67 D1
Bockhorn 92 A/B2
Bockhorst 67 D2
Böckstein 107 D1, 126 A1
Bockswiese 68 B3
Bocognano 113 D3
Bocsa 135 C1
Boczów 71 B/C3
Boda 40 A1
Boda 30 A3, 35 C/D2
Boda 45 C1
Boda 39 D2
Böda 51 D1
Böda 72 B1
Bodafors 72 A1
Bodafors 46 A3, 51 C1
Bodajk 95 C3, 128 B1
Bødal 36 B1/2
Boðani 129 C3
Bodåsgruvan 40 A2
Bodbacka 20 A2/3
Bodbyn 20 A1, 31 D2
Boddin 69 C1
Boden 17 B/C2/3
Boden 31 C1
Bodenburg 68 B3
Bodenkirchen 92 B2
Bodenkirchen-Aich 92 B2
Bodenmais 93 C1
Bodenteich 69 C2
Bodenwerder 68 B3
Bodenwöhr 92 B1
Bodiam Castle 77 C1
Bodilis 84 A/B2
Bodin 14 B1
Bodiosa Queirã 158 B2
Bodman 91 C3
Bodmin 62 B3
Bodø 14 B1
Bodom 28 B2, 33 D1
Bodön 17 C3
Bodonal de la Sierra 165 D3
Bodrost 139 D2
Bodrum 149 D2/3
Bodsjö 34 B2
Bodträskfors 16 B2
Boechout 78 B1
Boecillo 152 A/B3, 160 A1
Boek 91 D1, 70 A1
Boën-sur-Lignon 103 C3
Boeza 151 D2
Bofors 46 A1
Bogádmindszent 128 B3
Bogajo 159 C2
Bogan 28 B1
Bogarra 168 B2
Bogatić 133 C1
Bogatynia 83 C2
Bogatynia 96 A1
Boğaz 149 D1
Bogdanci 139 C/D3, 143 D1
Bogdaniec 71 C2
Bogdanovo 75 C3
Bogë 137 D2
Bogen 92 B1/2
Bogen 9 C2
Bogen 38 B3
Bogense 48 B3, 52 B1
Bogetići 137 C/D1
Boggsjö 35 C2
Bogholm 9 D2
Boglárielle 128 B1/2
Boglárlelle 96 B3
Bognanco Fonti 105 C2
Bognelv 5 C2

Bognes 9 C2
Bogno [Lugano] 105 D2, 106 A2
Bognor Regis 76 B1
Bogodol 132 A3
Bogojevo 129 C3
Bogomila 138 B3
Bogomolje 132 A3, 136 A/B1
Bogorojca 139 C/D3, 143 D1
Bögöte 128 A1
Bogovina 135 C2/3
Bogøy 8 B3
Bøgsetsetran 29 C2
Boguševsk 74 B3
Boguslav 99 D3
Bogutovac 133 D3, 134 A3
Bogutovačka Banja 133 D3, 134 A3
Bogyoszló 94 B3
Bohain-en-Vermandois 78 A/B3
Bohdalice 94 B1
Bohdalov 94 A1
Böheimkirchen 94 A2
Bohinjska Bistrica 126 B2
Böhl-Iggelheim 90 B1
Böhlitz-Ehrenberg 82 B1
Böhmenkirch 91 C2
Böhmfeld 92 A1/2
Bohmte 67 D2, 68 A2/3
Bohmte-Hunteburg 67 D2, 68 A2
Bohonal 166 B1
Bohonal de Ibor 159 D3, 166 A/B1
Böhönye 128 A2
Böhönye 96 B3
Bohunice 95 D2
Bohuslavice u Gottwaldova 95 C1
Boí 155 C/D2
Boiano 119 D2
Boimorto 150 B2
Boiro 150 A2
Bois-d'Amont 104 A2
Boismont 89 C1
Bois Sir Amé 102 A/B1
Boissy-Saint-Léger 87 D1
Boitzenburg 70 A1
Bóixols 155 C2/3
Boizenburg 69 C1
Bojadła 71 C3
Bojana 139 D1
Bojanowo 71 D3
Bojar 163 C2
Bojarka 99 C2
Bojčinovci 135 D3
Bøjden 52 B2
Bojkovice 95 C1
Bojnica 135 C2
Bojtiken 15 C3
Boka 134 B1
Bokel 52 B3, 68 B1
Bokel 68 A1
Bökemåla 51 C2
Bokenäs 44 B2/3
Böklund 52 B2
Bokn 42 A2
Bokod 95 C3
Boksel 16 A3
Böksholm 51 C1
Boksitogorsk 75 C1
Bol 131 D3, 136 A1
Bölan 40 A1
Bolaños de Campos 152 A3
Bolaños de Calatrava 167 C/D2
Bolbec 77 C3
Bölcske 129 C1/2
Bolderslev 52 B2
Böle 17 C2
Böle 29 D3, 34 B3
Böle 34 B3
Bolea 154 B2
Bölebyn 16 B3
Bolemin 71 C2
Bölen 30 A2/3, 35 C1
Böleseter 28 A2
Bolesławiec (Bunzlau) 96 A1
Boleszkowice 70 B2
Bólgheri 114 B3, 116 A2
Bolgrad 141 D1/2
Boliden 31 D1
Boliqueime 170 A/B2

Boljanići 133 C3
Boljetin 135 C2
Boljevac 135 C3
Boljevac 140 A2
Boljevci 133 D1, 134 A1/2
Bolkesjø A/C/D1, 44 A1
Bölkow 53 D3
Boll 91 C2
Bollate 105 D3, 106 A3
Bollebygd 45 C3, 49 D1
Bollendorf 79 D3
Bollène 111 C2
Bollensdorf 70 A3
Bollerup 50 B3
Bollesetra 5 C2
Bólliga 161 D3
Bollmora 47 D1
Bollnäs 40 A1
Bollstabruk 30 B3, 35 D2
Bollstanäs (Upplands-Väsby) 47 C1
Bollullos de la Mitación 171 D1/2
Bollullos par del Condado 171 C1/2
Bolman 128 B3
Bolmen 50 B1/2
Bolmsö 50 B1
Bolmstad 50 B1
Bologna 114 B1/2
Bologne 88 B2
Bolognetta 124 B2
Bolognola 115 D3, 117 D2/3
Bologoe 75 C1/2
Bologovo 75 C2
Bol'šaja Novinka 75 D1
Bol'šakovo 73 C2
Bolsena 111 B/C3, 118 A1
Bolsover 61 D3, 65 C1
Bolstad 45 C2
Bolsward 66 B2
Boltaña 155 C2
Boltigen 105 B/C2
Bolton 59 D2, 60 B2/3
Bolton Bridge 59 D1, 61 C2
Bolventor 62 B3
Bolvir 156 A2
Bóly 128 B2/3
Bolzaneto 113 D2
Bolzano/Bozen 107 C2
Bomarsund 41 D3
Bomba 119 D2
Bombarón 173 C2
Bombarral 164 A1/2
Bömenzien 69 C2
Bom Jesus 150 A/B3, 158 A1
Bomlitz 68 B2
Bomlitz-Bommelsen 68 B2
Bømlo 42 A1
Bompart 111 D3
Bomsdorf 70 A3
Bomsund 30 A3, 35 C2
Bona 102 B1
Bonaduz 105 D1, 106 A1
Bonaguil 109 C1
Bönan 40 B2
Bonansa 155 C2
Bonanza 171 C/D2
Boñar 152 A2
Bonárcado 123 C2
Bonares 171 C2
Bönäs 39 C/D1/2
Bönäset 29 D2, 35 C1
Bonassola 113 D2, 114 A2
Bonastre 163 D1
Bonboillon 89 C3, 104 A1
Boncourt 89 D3, 90 A3
Bondal 43 C1
Bondalseidet 32 A3, 36 B1
Bondeno 114 B1
Bonderup 48 B1
Bondstorp 45 D3
Bondues 78 A2
Bonefro 119 D2, 120 A1
Bönen 67 D3, 80 B1
Bones 9 D2
Bo'ness 57 C1/2
Bonete 169 D2
Bönhamn 30 B3
Boniches 162 A3
Bonifacio 123 D1
Boniswil 105 C1
Bonn 80 A2
Bonnåsjøen 9 C3

Bonnat 102 A2
Bonn-Bad Godesberg 80 A2
Bonndorf 90 B3
Bønnerup Strand 49 C2
Bonne-sur-Ménoge 104 A/B2
Bonnétable 86 B2
Bonneuil-Matours 101 C1
Bonneval 86 A/B2
Bonneval-sur-Arc 104 B3
Bonneville 104 A/B2
Bonnières-sur-Seine 87 C1
Bonnieux 111 D2
Bonny-sur-Loire 87 D3
Bono 123 D2
Bono 155 C2
Bonorva 123 C2
Bonrepos 109 D2
Bon Secours 78 B2
Bon Secours 79 C2/3
Bønsnes 43 D1
Bønsvig 53 D2
Bontveit 36 A3
Bonyhád 128 B2
Bönyrétalap 95 C3
Boock 70 B1
Boofzheim 90 A2
Booischot 79 C1
Boom 78 B1
Boos 76 B3, 86 A/B1
Boossen 70 B2/3
Boostedt 52 B3
Boothby Graffoe 61 D3, 64 B1
Bootle 59 C/D2, 60 B3
Bootle 59 C1, 60 A2
Bopfingen 91 D1/2
Boppard 80 A/B2
Boqueijón 150 A2
Boquiñeni 155 C3, 163 C1
Bor 135 C2
Bor 50 B1
Bor 82 B3
Bor 140 A2
Borač 133 D2, 134 A/B2
Boraja 131 C3
Borås 45 C3
Borås 72 A1
Borba 165 C2
Borbela 158 B1
Borbona 117 D3, 118 B1
Borča 133 D1, 134 A1
Borchen 68 A3, 81 B/C1
Borci 131 D2, 132 A2
Borculo 67 C3
Bordalba 161 D1
Bordány 129 D2
Bordeaux 108 B1
Bordeira 170 A2
Bordères-Louron 155 C2
Bordes 109 D3, 155 C1
Bordeshom 52 B3
Bordighera 112 B2/3
Bording Stationsby 48 B3
Bordón 162 B2
Bordvedaven 14 B2
Borek Wielkopolski 71 D3
Borello 115 C2, 117 C1
Borelva 15 B/C1
Borensberg 46 A/B2
Borgafjäll (Avasjö) 29 D1
Borgan 28 B1
Bórgaro Torinese 105 C3, 113 B/C1
Borge 44 B2
Borgen 30 B2
Borgentreich 81 C1
Borgentreich-Bühne 81 C1
Börger 67 D2
Borger 67 C2
Borgestad 43 D2, 44 A1
Borggård 46 B2
Borghamn 46 A2
Borghetto 117 C3, 118 B1
Borghetto di Vara 114 A2
Borghetto Santo Spírito 113 C2
Borgholm 51 D1
Borgholm 72 B1
Borgholzhausen 67 D3, 68 A3
Bórgia 122 B2
Borgloon 79 C2
Børglum kloster 48 B1
Borgo alla Collina 115 C2, 116 B1/2

Borgo a Mozzano 114 B2, 116 A1
Borgoforte 114 B1
Borgofranco 105 C3
Borgo Grappa 118 B2
Borgo le Taverne 120 A2
Borgo Libertà 120 A/B2
Borgomanero 105 C/D3
Borgonovo Lígure 113 D2
Borgonovo Val Tidone 113 D1
Borgo Pace 115 C2/3, 117 C2
Borgo Piave 118 B2
Borgoricco 107 C3
Borgo San Dalmazzo 112 B2
Borgo San Lorenzo 114 B2, 116 B1
Borgosésia 105 C3
Borgo Túfico 115 D3, 117 C/D2
Borgo Val di Taro 114 A1/2
Borgo Valsugana 107 C2
Borgo Vercelli 105 C/D3
Borgsjö 35 C3
Borgsjö 30 B2
Borgstena 45 C/D3
Borgund 37 C2
Borgvattnet 30 A3, 35 C1/2
Borgvik 45 C1
Borhaug 42 B3
Boriç 137 D2
Boričevac 131 C2
Borines 152 A1
Bořislav 83 C2
Borislav 97 D2, 98 A3
Borisov 74 B3
Borispol' 99 D2
Borja 154 A3, 162 A1
Börjelsbyn 17 C2
Börjelslandet 17 C3
Borkan 16 C3, 29 D1
Borken 67 C3
Borken 81 C1/2
Borkenes 9 C2
Borken-Kleinenglis 81 C1
Borken-Weseke 67 C3
Borkheide 70 A3
Borkhusseten 33 C3, 37 D1
Børkop 48 B3, 52 B1
Borkum 67 C1
Borlänge 39 D2
Borlaug 37 C2
Børlia 33 C2
Borlova 135 C1
Borlu 149 D2
Bormes-les-Mimosas 112 A3
Bórmio 106 B2
Born 53 D2/3
Born 69 C2/3
Borna 82 B1
Borne 67 C2/3
Borne 69 C3
Borne 103 C3, 110 B1
Bornem 78 B1
Bornes 159 C1
Bornheim (Bonn) 80 A2
Bornhöved 52 B3
Börnicke 70 A2
Borno 106 B2
Bornos 171 D2
Bornova 149 D2
Bornstedt 82 A1
Borobia 153 D3, 154 A3, 161 D1, 162 A1
Borodjanka 99 C2
Borojevići 127 D3, 131 C1
Borotín 83 D3, 93 D1
Boroughbridge 61 D2
Borovan 140 B2/3
Borovany 93 D1/2
Borovci 135 D3
Borovići 75 C1
Borovnica 126 B2/3
Borovo 129 C3
Borovo Selo 129 C3
Borovsk 75 D3
Borowe 83 D1
Borowina 71 C3
Borrby 50 B3
Borrby 72 A2
Borrby strandbad 50 B3
Borre 53 D2

Borre 43 D2, 44 B1
Borreby 53 C1/2
Borredà 156 A2
Borrentin 70 A1
Borriol 163 C3
Borris 48 A3
Börrum 46 B2
Børsa 28 A3, 33 C2
Borščev 98 B3
Børselv 5 D2, 6 A2
Borsfa 128 A2
Borsh 142 A2
Borsh 148 A1
Borssele 78 B1
Börssum 69 C3
Borstel 69 D2
Borth 59 C3
Borthwick Castle 57 C2
Bortígali 123 C2
Bort-les-Orgues 102 A/B3
Börtnan 34 B2
Bortnen 36 A1
Borum 48 B2/3
Borup 49 D3, 53 D1
Boruszyn 71 D2
Boryszyn 71 C3
Borzna 99 D2
Borzonasca 113 D2
Bosa 123 C2
Bosa Marina 123 C2
Bosanci 127 C3
Bosanska Dubica 131 D1, 132 A1
Bosanska Gradiška 131 D1, 132 A1
Bosanska Kostajnica 127 D3, 131 C/D1
Bosanska Krupa 131 C1
Bosanska Mezgraja 133 C1/2
Bosanska Rača 133 C1
Bosanski Aleksandrovac 131 D1, 132 A1
Bosanski Brod 132 B1
Bosanski Dubočac 132 B1
Bosanski Kobaš 132 A/B1
Bosanski Novi 131 C1
Bosanski Petrovac 131 C2
Bosanski Šamac 132 B1
Bosansko Grahovo 131 C2
Bosansk Rača 133 C2
Bösárkány 95 B/C3
Bosau 53 C3
Boscastle 62 B2/3
Bosco 115 C/D3, 117 C2
Bosco Chiesanuova 107 B/C3
Bosco/Gurin [Ponte Brolla] 105 C/D2
Bösel 67 D2
Bösel-Petersdorf 67 D2
Bøseter 38 A1
Bøsetrene 32 B3, 37 C1
Bosilegrad 139 C2
Bosiljevo 127 C3, 130 B1
Bosjökloster 50 B3
Bosjön 39 C3
Boskoop 66 A3
Boskovice 94 B1
Boskovice 96 B2
Bosnek 139 D2
Bošnjace 139 C1
Bošnjaci 133 B/C1
Bosost 155 C2
Bössbo 39 C1
Bossbu 42 B2
Bossolasco 113 C1/2
Bøstad (Borge) 8 B2
Bostan 131 D3, 132 A3
Bostanj 127 C2
Böste 50 B3
Boston 61 D3, 65 C1
Bostrak 43 C2
Bosut 133 C1
Böszénfa 128 B2
Bot 163 C2
Boteå 30 B3, 35 D2
Botesdale 65 C/D2
Botevgrad 140 B3
Bothel 57 C3, 60 A/B1
Boticas 150 B3, 158 B1
Botija 165 D1, 166 A1
Botley 76 B1
Botn 5 B/C2
Botn 4 A/B2/3
Botn 14 A2

Botn **4** A2
Botngård **28** A3, **33** C1
Botnlia **33** D2
Bötom **20** A3
Botorrita **154** B3,
 162 A/B1
Botoš **129** D3, **133** D1,
 134 R1
Botosani **98** B3
Botsmark **31** C/D2
Bottarvegården **47** D3
Bottesford **61** C3, **64** B1
Böttingen (Tuttlingen)
 90 B2/3
Bottnaryd **45** D3
Botun **138** B3, **142** B1
Bouayé **85** D3, **100** A1
Boubínský prales (Urwald)
 93 C1
Boucau **108** A3, **154** A1
Boucé **86** A2
Bouchain **78** A2
Bouchoir **78** A3
Boucoiran **111** C2
Boucq **89** C1
Boudrac **109** C3, **155** C1
Bouessay **86** A2/3
Bouesse **101** D1/2,
 102 A1/2
Bouillon **79** C3
Bouilly **88** B2
Bouin **100** A1
Boujailles **104** A1
Boulay-Moselle **89** D1
Bouleternère **156** B1/2
Bouloc **110** A2
Boulogne-sur-Gesse
 109 C3, **155** C1
Boulogne-sur-Mer
 77 D1/2
Bouloire **86** B2
Boulouris-sur-Mer **112** B3
Boulzicourt **79** C3
Boumois **86** A3
Bourbon-Lancy **103** C1/2
Bourbonne-les-Bains
 89 C2
Bourbourg **77** D1
Bourbriac **84** B2
Bourdeaux **111** D1
Bouresse **101** C2
Bourg-Achard **77** C3,
 86 B1
Bourganeuf **102** A2
Bourg-Argental **103** C3
Bourg-de-Péage **111** C/D1
Bourg-de-Visa **109** C2
Bourg-d'Oueil **155** C2
Bourg-en-Bresse **103** D2
Bourges **102** A1
Bourg-et-Comin **78** B3,
 88 A1
Bourg-Lastic **102** A/B3
Bourg-Madame **156** A2
Bourgneuf-en-Retz **100** A1
Bourgneuf-en-Mauges
 86 A3
Bourgoin-Jallieu **103** D3
Bourg-Saint-Maurice
 104 B3
Bourg-Saint-Andéol
 111 C2
Bourg-St-Pierre [Orsières]
 104 B2
Bourg-sur-Gironde **108** B1
Bourgtheroulde **77** C3,
 86 B1
Bourgueil **86** B3, **101** C1
Bourmont **89** C2
Bournazel **110** A1
Bourne **64** B1
Bournemouth **63** D2/3,
 76 A1
Bournezeau **101** C1/2
Bouro **150** B3, **158** A1
Bourret **108** B2
Boussac **102** A2
Bousse **89** C1
Bouttencourt **77** D2
Bouvellemont **79** B/C3
Bouvières **111** D1
Bouvron **85** D3
Bouxwiller **90** A2
Bouzonville **89** D1
Bova **122** A3
Bovalino **122** A3
Bovalino Marina **122** A3

Bovallstrand **44** B2
Bova Marina **122** A3
Bovan **135** C3
Bovec **126** A/B2
Bóveda **150** B2
Bóvegno **106** B3
Bovenden **81** C/D1
Bovense **53** C1
Bøverdal **37** C2
Bøverfjord **32** B2
Bóves **112** B2
Boves **77** D2/3
Bovey Tracey **63** C3
Bovik **41** C2/3
Bovino **120** A2
Bøvlingbjerg **48** A2
Bovolenta **107** C3
Bovolone **107** C3
Bovrup **52** B2
Bowes **57** D3, **61** B/C1
Box **63** D2, **64** A3
Box **25** C3
Box **25** D3, **26** A3
Boxberg **81** C3, **91** C1
Boxholm **46** A2/3
Boxmeer **67** B/C3, **79** D1
Boxtel **66** B3, **79** C1
Boyardville **101** C2
Boyle **55** C2
Boynes **87** D2
Božaj **137** D2
Božava **130** B2
Bozcaada **149** C1
Bozdoğan **149** D2
Božejov **93** D1, **94** A1
Bozel **104** B3
Boževac **134** B2
Bozhigradi **142** B2
Božica **139** C1
Božice **94** B1/2
Boži Dar **82** B2
Bozouls **110** A1/2
Bozovici **135** C1
Bozsok **94** B3, **127** D1
Božurište **139** D1
Bózzolo **114** A/B1
Bra **113** C1
Braås **51** C1
Bråbo **51** D1
Brabova **135** D2
Braccagni **116** B3
Bracciano **118** A1/2
Braćevac **135** C2
Bračvici **128** B3
Bracieux **87** C3
Bräcke **35** C2
Brackel **68** B1
Brackenheim **91** C1
Brackley **65** C2
Bracknell **64** B3
Braco **56** B1
Brad **97** D3, **140** B1
Bradford **54** B3
Bradford **61** C2
Bradford on Avon **63** D2,
 64 A3
Brädikow **69** D2, **70** A2
Brading **76** B1/2
Brådland **42** A/B2
Bradninch **63** C2
Brædstrup **48** B3
Bradwell Waterside **65** C3
Bradworthy **62** B2
Braemar **54** B2
Bràfim **163** C1
Braga **150** A3, **158** A1
Bragada **150** B3, **158** B1
Bragança **151** C3, **159** C1
Brager **37** D3, **38** A2
Bragin **99** C2
Brahestad **18** A3
Brahetrolleborg **53** C2
Brahmenau **82** B2
Bråila **141** C/D2
Braine-l'Alleud **78** B2
Braine-le-Comte **78** B2
Braintree **65** C2
Brajković **132** B2
Brake **68** A3, **81** C1
Brakel-Bökendorf **68** A3
Brakkstad **28** B1/2
Bräkne-Hoby **51** C2
Brålanda **45** C2
Bralitz **70** B2
Brallo **113** D1
Brålos **147** C1

Brålos **148** B2
Braloştiţa **135** D2
Bramminge **48** A3, **52** A1
Brampton **57** C3, **60** B1
Bramsche **67** D2
Bramsche-Achmer **67** D2
Bramsche-Engter **67** D2
Bramsche-Hesepe **67** D2
Bramsche-Ueffeln **67** D2
Brånaberg **15** C3
Branäs **38** B2
Branca **115** D3, **117** C2
Brancaleone **122** A3
Branchewinda **81** D2,
 82 A2
Brand **82** A/B3
Brand **106** A1
Brandal **36** A/B1
Brändåsen **34** A3
Brändberg **16** B2
Brändbo **35** C3
Brandbu **38** A2
Brände **31** C1/2
Brande **48** B3
Brandenberg **92** A3
Brandenburg **69** D2
Brandenburg **72** A3
Brand-Erbisdorf **83** C2
Brandis **82** B1
Brandizzo **105** C3, **113** C1
Brändö **24** A2/3, **41** D2
Brandomil **150** A1/2
Brändön **17** C3
Brandon **65** C2
Brändövik **20** A2, **31** D3
Brandstad **32** B2
Brandstorp **45** D3, **46** A3
Brandval **38** B2
Brandvoll **9** D1/2
Brandýsek **83** C2/3
Brandýs nad Labem-Stará
 Boleslav **83** D2/3
Brandýs nad Labem-Stará
 Boleslav **96** A2
Braničevo **134** B1/2
Braniewo (Braunsberg)
 73 C2
Branišovice **94** B1
Brankovice **94** B1
Brankovina **133** D2,
 134 A2
Brännaby **30** A1
Brännåker **30** A1
Brännan **31** D1
Brännäs **16** B3
Brännau **16** A3
Brännberg **16** A3
Branne **108** B1
Brännforsliden **31** C1
Brännland **31** C2
Brännö **45** C3, **49** D1
Brännvattnet **31** D1
Brañosera **152** B2
Branston **61** D3, **64** B1
Brantevik **50** B3
Brantôme **101** C/D3
Branzi **106** A2
Braojos **161** C2
Braskereidfoss **38** B2
Braslav **74** A/B3
Braşov **141** C1/2
Brasparts **84** B2
Brassac **110** A2/3
Brasschaat **78** B1
Bras-sur-Meuse **89** C1
Brassus, Le **104** A2
Brassy **88** A3, **103** C1
Brastad **44** B2
Brataj **142** A2
Bråte **38** A3, **44** B1
Brăteşti **135** D1/2
Bratina **127** D3
Bratislava **94** B2
Bratislava **96** B2/3
Bratronice **83** C3
Brattåker **15** C/D3
Brattås **15** C3, **29** D1
Brattås **14** A3
Brattbäcken **30** A2
Bratten **30** B1
Bratteng **14** B3
Brattfjell **4** A2/3
Brattfjord **94** A3
Brattfors **39** C3, **45** D1
Brattfors **31** C2
Bratthøvollseter **33** C/D2/3
Brattknabben **16** B3

Brattland **14** A/B2
Bråttö **41** D3
Brattsbacka **31** C2
Brattset **32** B2
Brattvåg **32** A2/3
Brattvær **32** B1
Bratunac **133** C2
Bråtveit **42** B1
Braubach **80** A/B2
Braunau am Inn **93** B/C2
Braunlage **69** C3
Braunlage-Hohengeiss
 69 C3, **81** D1
Bräunlingen **90** B3
Braunsbach **91** C1
Braunsbedra **82** A/B1
Braunschweig-Waggum
 69 C3
Braunschweig **69** C3
Bräunsdorf **83** C2
Braunton **63** B/C2
Braunwald [Linthal]
 105 D1, **106** A1
Brauron **147** D2
Bravães **150** A3, **158** A1
Bravsko **131** D2
Bray **58** A2
Bray **55** D2/3
Braye **63** D3
Bray-sur-Seine **87** D2,
 88 A2
Bray-sur-Somme **78** A3
Brazatortas **167** C2
Brazey-en-Plaine **103** D1
Brazuelo **151** D2
Brbinj **130** B2
Brčko **133** C1
Brea **154** A3, **162** A1
Brea de Tajo **161** C3
Breared **50** A/B2
Breaza **141** C2
Bréban **88** B2
Brécey **86** A1
Brechin **54** B2
Breckerfeld **80** A1
Břeclav **94** B2
Břeclav **96** B2
Brecon **63** C1
Brécy **102** A2
Breda **66** A/B3, **79** C1
Bredåker **16** B2
Bredåkra **51** C2
Bredared **45** C2
Bredaryd **50** B1
Bredballe **48** B3, **52** B1
Bredbyn **30** B3, **35** D1
Breddin **69** D2
Bredebro **52** A2
Bredenfelde **70** A1
Bredereiche **70** A1/2
Bredestad **46** A3
Bredevad **52** B2
Bredevoort **67** C3
Bredkälen **29** D2/3, **35** C1
Bredsätra **51** D1/2
Bredsel **16** B2
Bredsjö **39** D3
Bredstedt **52** A/B2
Bredsten **48** B3, **52** B1
Bredstrup **48** B3, **52** B1
Bredträsk **31** B/C2
Bredvik **31** C2/3
Bree **79** C1
Breganze **107** C3
Bregenz **91** C3
Breginj **126** A2
Bregovo **135** C/D2
Bregovo **140** B2
Breguzzo **106** B2
Bréhal-Plage **85** D1
Brehna **82** B1
Breidablikk **42** A/B1
Breidenbach **80** B2
Breifonn **42** B1
Breil-sur-Roya **112** B2
Breim **36** B2
Breisach **90** A3
Breistein **36** A3
Breistølen **37** C2/3
Breistrand **9** C2
Breitenbach **81** C2
Breitenbrunn **94** B3
Breitenbrunn **91** D2
Breitenbrunn **92** A1
Breitenfelde **69** C1
Breitengüßbach **81** D3

Breitenworbis **81** D1
Breitscheid **80** B2
Breitstetten **94** B2
Breitungen **81** D2
Breive **42** B1
Breivik **7** C1
Breivik **9** C2
Breivik **8** B2
Breivik **15** C1
Breivik **9** C2
Breivikbotn **5** C1
Breivikeidet **4** A3
Brejning **48** B3, **52** B1
Brejtovo **75** D1
Brekke **36** A2/3
Brekken **14** B2
Brekken **33** D2
Brekkestø **43** C3
Brekkhus **36** B3
Brekksillan **28** B1/2
Breklum **52** A/B2
Brekstad **28** A3, **33** C1
Brélès **84** A2
Bremanger **36** A1
Bremen **68** A2
Bremerhaven **68** A1
Bremervörde **68** A/B1
Bremervörde-Elm **68** A/B1
Bremervörde-Hesedorf
 68 A/B1
Bremgarten **90** B3, **105** C1
Bremnes **42** A1
Bremsdorf **70** B3
Bremsnes **32** A/B2
Brenderup **48** B3, **52** B1
Brenes **171** D1
Brenets, Les [Le Locle]
 104 B1
Brenna **8** B2
Brenna **33** D2
Brenna **38** A1
Brennberg-Frauenzell
 92 B1
Brénnero/Brenner **107** C1
Brennes **4** B3, **10** A1
Brennfjell **4** B3, **10** A1
Brenngam **6** B1
Brennhaug **33** C3, **37** D1
Brennseter **32** B3, **37** C1
Brennvik **8** B3
Breno **106** B2
Brénod **103** D2, **104** A2
Brensbach **81** C3
Brensvik **5** C/D1, **6** A1
Brentónico **106** B3
Brentwood **65** C3
Brescello **114** B1
Bréscia **106** B3
Bresewitz **53** D2/3
Brésimo **106** B2
Breskens **78** B1
Bresles **77** D3
Bressana Bottarone **113** D1
Bressanone/Brixen
 107 C1/2
Bressuire **100** B1
Brest **84** A2
Brest **73** D3, **97** D1, **98** A1
Brestanica **127** C2
Brestova **126** B3, **130** A1
Brestovac **135** C2
Brestovac **128** A/B3
Brestovac **139** C1
Brestovac **139** B/C1
Brestovačka Banja **135** C2
Bretenoux **109** D1
Breteuil **86** B1
Breteuil-sur-Noye **77** D3
Brétignolles-sur-Mer
 100 A1/2
Bretningen **37** D1/2, **38** A1
Bretten **90** B1
Brettesnes **8** B2
Bretteville-sur-Laize **86** A1
Breuil-Barret **100** B1
Breuil-Cervínia **105** C2/3
Breuilpont **87** C1
Breuna **81** C1
Brevens bruk **46** B1/2
Brevik **47** D3
Breviken **45** C1
Brévine, La [Les Verrières]
 104 B1
Breza **132** B2
Brežde **133** D2, **134** A2
Brezičani **131** D1
Brežice **127** C2/3

Březina 83 B/C2/3
Brezna 133 D3, 134 B3
Breznica 127 D2
Březnice, 83 C3, 93 C1
Březnice 96 A2
Breznik 140 B3
Breznik 139 D1
Březno 83 C2
Brezno 97 C2
Brezoi 140 B2
Brézolles 87 B/C1/2
Brezová pod Bradlom
   95 C2
Brezovica 134 B3
Brezovica 138 B2
Brezovica 127 D3
Brezovo Polje 133 C1
Briançon 112 A/B1
Briare 87 D3
Briático 122 A2
Bribir 127 C3, 130 B1
Bričany 98 B3
Bricherásio 112 B1
Bricon 88 B2
Bricquebec 76 A3
Brides 62 B1
Brides-les-Bains 104 B3
Bridgend 63 C1/2
Bridgend 54 A2/3, 55 D1
Bridge of Allan 56 B1
Bridge of Cally 57 C1
Bridge of Earn 57 C1
Bridge of Orchy 56 B1
Bridgnorth 59 D3, 64 A2
Bridgwater 63 C/D2
Bridlington 61 D2
Bridport 63 D2/3
Briec 84 B2
Brie-Comte-Robert
   87 D1/2
Briedel 80 A3
Brielle 66 A3
Brienne-le-Château 88 B2
Brienon-sur-Armançon
   88 A2
Brienz 105 C1
Brienza 120 A3
Brieselang 70 A2
Briesen 70 B3
Brieske 83 C1
Brieskow-Finkenheerd
   70 B3
Brietlingen 69 B/C1
Brieva de Cameros
   153 C/D3
Brieves 151 C/D1
Briey 89 C1
Brig 105 C2
Brigg 61 D2/3
Brighouse 61 C2
Brightlingsea 65 C/D2/3
Brighton 76 B1
Brignais 103 D3
Brignogan-Plage 84 A1/2
Brignoles 112 A3
Brigstock 64 B2
Brihuega 161 C2
Briksdal 36 B2
Brill 64 B2/3
Brillon-en-Barrois 88 B1/2
Brilon 80 B1
Brilon-Alme 80 B1
Brilon-Messinghausen
   80 B1
Brimnes 36 B3
Briñas 153 C/D2
Brinches 165 C3, 170 B1
Brincones 159 C2
Bríndisi 121 D2
Bringsinghaug 36 A1
Brinje 130 B1
Brinon-sur-Beuvron 88 A3,
   102 B1
Brinon-sur-Sauldre 87 D3
Brintbodarne 39 C2
Brínzio 105 D2/3
Brión 150 A2
Brione (Verzasca) [Tenero]
   105 D2
Brioni 130 A1
Brionne 77 C3, 86 B1
Brion-sur-Ource 88 B2/3
Brioude 102 B3
Briouze 86 A1/2
Briscous 108 B3, 155 C1
Brisighella 115 C2, 116 B1
Brissac-Quincé 86 A3

Brissago [Locarno] 105 D2
Brist 132 A3, 136 B1
Bristol 63 D2
Briton Ferry 63 C1
Brittas 58 A2
Brittas Bay 58 A3
Britvica 132 A3
Britz 70 B2
Brive-la-Gaillarde 101 D3
Briviesca 153 C2
Brixen in Tirol 92 B3
Brixham 63 C3
Brixlegg 92 A3
Bříza 83 C/D2
Brka 133 B/C1
Brløg 130 B1
Brna 136 A1
Brnjica 135 C1/2
Brno 94 B1
Brno 96 B2
Bro 72 B1
Bro 47 C1
Bro 47 D2/3
Bro 44 B2
Broadstairs 65 C3, 76 B1
Broadway 63 D1, 64 A2
Broager 52 B2
Broaryd 50 B1
Broby 50 B2
Broby 72 A1
Bročanac 131 C1
Broc [Broc-Village] 104 B2
Bröckel 68 B2
Brockenhurst 76 A1
Broczyno 71 D1
Brod 133 B/C3
Brod 138 B3
Brod 140 A3
Brodarevo 133 C/D3,
   134 A3, 137 D1, 138 A1
Broddbo 40 A3
Broddebo 46 B3
Brodek u Prostějova 94 B1
Brodersby 52 B2
Brodersby-Schönhagen
   52 B2
Brodica 135 C2
Brodick 56 A2
Brodick 54 A3, 55 D1
Brod Moravice 127 C3
Brod na Kupi 127 C3
Brodnica 73 C3
Brodosavce 138 B2
Brod Prizrenski 138 B2
Brod Prizrenski 140 A3
Brody 97 D2, 98 B2
Brody 70 B3
Brody 71 C3
Broek 79 D1
Broglie 86 B1
Brójce 71 C3
Brokind 46 B2/3
Brokstedt 52 B3
Brolo 125 C1/2
Bromarv 24 B3
Brome 69 C2
Bromley 65 C3, 76 B1
Bromma 47 C1
Bromma 37 D3
Brommösund 45 D2
Bromnes 4 A2
Bromölla 51 B/C2/3
Bromölla 72 A1
Brompton 61 D2
Brömsebro 51 D2
Bromsgrove 59 D3, 64 A2
Bromyard 59 D3, 63 D1
Bronchales 162 A2
Brønderslev 48 B1
Broni 113 D1
Bronikowo 71 C/D1
Bronkow 70 B3, 83 C1
Brønnøysund 14 A3
Brøns 52 A1/2
Bronte 125 C2
Bronzani Majdan 131 D1,
   132 A1
Broons 85 C2
Broquiès 110 A2
Brørup 48 A/B3, 52 A/B1
Brösarp 50 B3
Brösarp 72 A2
Brøske 32 B2
Brossac 101 C3
Brøstadbotn 9 D1
Broşteni 135 D1
Broşteni 140 B2

Brøstrud 37 C3
Brotas 164 B2
Brötjemark 46 A3
Broto 155 C2
Brottby 40 B3, 47 D1
Brøttem 28 A3, 33 C2
Brotterode 81 D2
Brøttingsvåg 32 B1
Brøttum 38 A2
Brou 86 A/B2
Brough 57 D3, 60 B1
Brough 54 B3
Broughshane 56 A3
Broughton 57 C2
Broughton in Furness
   59 C1, 60 A/B2
Broughty Ferry 57 C1
Broumov 82 B3
Broumov 96 B1
Brouwersdam 66 A3
Brouwershaven 66 A3
Brouzet-lès-Alès 111 C2
Brovallen 40 A3
Brovary 99 C/D2
Brovès 112 A3
Brovst 48 B1
Brownhills 59 D3, 64 A1/2
Brozas 165 D1
Brozzo 106 B3
Brtnice 94 A1
Brtonigla 126 A/B3,
   130 A1
Bru 36 A2
Bru 42 A2
Brua 33 D3
Bruay-en-Artois 78 A2
Brubakk 28 B3, 33 D1
Bruca 124 A2
Bruchhausen-Vilsen 68 A2
Bruchmühlbach-Miesau
   90 A1
Bruchsal 90 B1
Bruck 92 B1
Brück 69 D3, 70 A3
Bruck an der Grossglockner-
   strasse 107 D1, 126 A1
Bruck an der Mur 94 A3
Bruck an der Leitha 94 B3
Bruck an der Mur 96 A3
Bruck an der Leitha 96 B3
Brücken 80 A3
Brückl 126 B1
Bruckmühl 92 A/B3
Brúcoli 125 D3
Brüel 53 D3, 69 C/D1
Bruère-Allichamps 102 A1
Brués 160 B2
Bruflat 37 D3
Bruges 108 B3, 154 B1
Brugg 90 B3
Brugge 78 A1
Brüggen 79 D1
Brüggen 68 B3
Brühl 80 A2
Bruksvallarna 34 A2/3
Brûlon 86 A2
Brûly 78 B3
Brumath 90 A2
Brummen 67 C3
Brumunddal 38 A2
Brumund sag 38 A2
Bruna 117 C3
Brunau 69 C2
Brunehamel 78 B3
Brunella 123 D1
Brunete 160 B2
Brunflo 34 B2
Brunheda 158 B1
Brunico/Bruneck 107 C1
Bruniquel 109 D2
Brunkeberg 43 C2
Brunna 40 B3
Brunna 47 C1
Brunnbach 93 D3
Brunnberget 39 C2
Brunnen 105 D1
Brunnsberg 39 C1
Brunsbüttel 52 A/B3
Brunskog 38 B3, 45 C1
Brunssum 79 D1/2
Bruntál 96 B2
Bruntveit 42 A1
Bruravik 36 B3
Brus 134 B3
Brusago 107 C2
Brusali 42 A3
Brusand 42 A3

Brušane 130 B2
Brusarci 135 D3
Brusasco 113 C1
Brusino Arsízio [Capolago-
   Riva s. Vitale] 105 D2/3
Brúsio 106 B2
Brusnik 135 C2
Brusno 95 D1/2
Brusson 105 C3
Brüssow 70 B1
Brutelles 77 D2
Bruton 63 D2, 64 A3
Bruttig-Fankel 80 A3
Bruvik 36 A3
Bruvno 131 C2
Bruvoll 38 A2
Bruxelles/Brussel 78 B2
Bruyéres 89 D2
Bruyères-et-Montbérault
   78 B3
Bruzaholm 46 A3
Břvany 83 C2
Brydal 33 D3
Bryn 38 A3, 43 D1
Brynamman 63 C1
Bryne 42 A2
Bryngelhögen 34 B3
Bryn-Hoffnant 62 B1
Brynje 29 D3, 34 B2
Brynjegård 29 D3, 35 C2
Brynmawr 63 C1
Bryrup 48 B3
Brzan 134 B2
Brza Palanka 135 C2
Brzeće 134 B3
Brzeg (Brieg) 96 B1
Brzezie 71 D1
Brzozowiec 71 C2
Bua 49 D1, 50 A1
Bua 72 A1
Buais 85 D2, 86 A2
Buan 33 C2
Buarcos 158 A3
Buavåg 42 A1
Bubany 128 A3
Bubari 142 A2/3
Búbbio 113 C1
Bubenreuth 82 A3
Buberget 31 C2
Buberow 70 A2
Bubierca 161 D1, 162 A1
Bubry 84 B2
Bučač 98 B3
Buçaco 158 A2/3
Buccheri 125 C3
Bucchiánico 119 C1
Buccino 120 A2
Bucelas 164 A2
Buchbach 92 B2
Buchbach-Walkersaich
   92 B2
Buchboden 106 A/B1
Buchdorf 91 D2
Bücheloh 81 D2, 82 A2
Buchen 81 C3, 91 C1
Büchen 69 C1
Buchenau (Lahn) 80 B2
Buchenbach (Freiburg)
   90 B3
Buchenhain 70 A1
Buchères 88 A/B2
Buchholz 70 A3
Buchholz 81 D1, 82 A1
Buchholz in der Nordheide
   68 B1
Buchholz-Sprötze 68 B1
Buchloe 91 D3
Buchlov 95 C1
Buchlovice 95 C1
Buchlyvie 56 B1
Buch-Obenhausen 91 D2
Buchs 95 D1, 106 A1
Buchy 76 B3
Bučica 127 D3
Bučin prohod 139 D1
Bučje 135 C3
Bučje 133 C3
Buckden 65 B/C2
Bückeburg 68 A3
Bücken 68 A2
Buckfastleigh 63 C3
Buckhaven 57 C1
Buckie 54 B2
Buckingham 64 B2
Bucklers Hard 76 A1
Buckow 70 B2

Bückwitz 69 D2
Bučovice 94 B1
Bucsu 127 D1
Bucureşti 141 C2
Bucy-les-Pierrepont 78 B3
Bucz 71 D3
Bud 32 A2
Buda 83 D3
Budakalász 95 D3
Budakeszi 95 D3
Budal 33 C2
Budanovci 133 D1, 134 A1
Budaörs 95 D3, 129 C1
Budapest 95 D3
Budapest 97 B/C3
Budča 95 D2
Buddbyn 17 B/C2
Büddenstedt-Neu Büdden-
   stedt 69 C3
Buddusò 123 D2
Bude 62 B2
Budeč 94 A1
Büdelsdorf 52 B3
Budenheim 80 B3
Budens 170 A2
Büderich 67 C3, 79 D1,
   80 A1
Büderscheid 79 D3
Büdesheim 79 D2
Budeşti 141 C2
Budia 161 C/D2
Budimlić Japra 131 C1
Büdingen 81 C2
Budišov 94 A1
Budleigh Salterton 63 C3
Budmerice 95 C2
Budogošč 75 C1
Budoni 123 D1
Búdrio 115 C1
Budva 137 C2
Budyně nad Ohří 83 C2
Budzyń 71 D2
Bue 42 A2/3
Bueña 163 C2
Buenache de la Sierra
   161 D3
Buenache de Alarcón
   161 D3, 168 B1
Buenamadre 159 C/D2
Buenasbodas 160 A3,
   166 B1
Buenaventura 160 A3
Buenavista de Valdavia
   152 B2
Buendía 161 C/D2/3
Buer 45 B/C1
Bueu 150 A2
Bugarach 156 A/B1
Bugarra 169 C1
Bugeat 102 A3
Buger 157 C2
Buggerru 123 C3
Buggingen 90 A3
Buglose 108 A2
Bugnara 119 C2
Bugojno 131 D2, 132 A3
Bugøyfjord 7 C2
Bugøynes 7 C2
Bugyi 129 C1
Bühl 90 B2
Bühlertal 90 B2
Bühlertann 91 C1
Bühlerzell 91 C1
Buhuşi 141 C1
Búia 126 A2
Builth Wells 63 C1
Buis-les-Baronnies 111 D2
Buitenpost 67 C1
Buitrago 153 C2
Buitrago del Lozoya 161 C2
Bujalance 167 C3, 172 B1
Bujanovac 139 C2
Bujanovac 140 A3
Bujaraloz 155 B/C3,
   163 B/C1
Bujarrabal 161 D2
Buje 126 B3, 130 A1
Buk 71 D2/3
Bükkösd 128 B2
Bukovac 131 D1, 132 A1
Bukovac 129 C3
Bukova Gora 131 D3,
   132 A3
Bukovi 133 D2, 134 A2
Bukovje 126 B3
Buków 71 C3
Bukowiec 71 D2

Bukowiec **71** D3
Bulačani **138** B2
Bülach **90** B3
Bulat-Pestivien **84** B2
Bulbuente **154** A3, **162** A1
Buldan **149** D2
Bulgnéville **89** C2
Bulinac **128** A3
Bulken **36** B3
Bullas **168** B3, **174** A1
Bullay **80** A3
Bulle **104** B2
Büllingen **79** D2
Bulqizë **138** A3
Bultei **123** D2
Bulwell **61** D3, **65** C1
Bumbesti-Jiu **135** D1
Buna **132** B3, **136** B1
Bünde **68** A3
Bunde **67** D1
Bunessan **56** A1
Bungay **65** D2
Bunge **47** D2
Bunić **131** C2
Buniel **153** B/C2
Bunkeflostrand **50** A3
Bunkris **39** C1
Bunleix **102** A2/3
Bunnerviken **29** C3, **34** A2
Buñol **169** C1
Buntingford **65** C2
Buñuel **154** A3
Bunyola **157** C2
Buollannjargga **5** D3, **6** A3, **11** D1
Buonabitácolo **120** A3
Buonalbergo **119** D3, **120** A2
Buonconvento **115** B/C3, **116** B2
Burbach-Niederdresselndorf **80** B2
Burbage **64** A3, **76** A1
Burbáguena **163** C2
Burcei **123** D3
Bureå **31** D1
Bureåborg **30** B3, **35** D1
Burela **151** B/C1
Büren **80** B1
Büren an der Aare **104** B1
Büren-Steinhausen **80** B1
Bures **65** C2
Bureta **154** A3, **162** A1
Burfjord **5** B/C2
Burford **64** A2/3
Burg **69** D3
Burg **70** B3
Burg **53** C2/3
Burg **52** B3
Burgas **141** C3
Burgau **170** A2
Burgau **127** D1
Burgau **91** D2
Burgbernheim **81** D3, **91** D1
Burgbrohl **80** A2
Burgdorf **68** B2
Burgdorf **105** C1
Burgdorf-Ramlingen-Ehlershausen **68** B2
Burgebrach **81** D3
Bürgel **82** A2
Bürgeln **90** A3
Bürgeln **81** B/C2
Burgelo **153** D2
Burgess Hill **76** B1
Burgh **66** A3
Burghammer **83** D1
Burghaslach **81** D3
Burghaun **81** C2
Burghausen **92** B2
Burgheim **91** D2, **92** A2
Burgh le Marsh **61** D3, **65** C1
Burghley House **64** B1/2
Búrgio **124** B2
Burgkirchen **92** B2
Burgkunstadt **82** A3
Burglengenfeld **92** B1
Burgohondo **160** A2
Burgos **153** C2
Búrgos **123** C/D2
Burgsalach **92** A1
Burgschwalbach **80** B2
Burgsinn **81** C3
Burgstädt **82** B2
Burgstall **69** C/D2/3

Burg-Stargard **70** A1
Burgsteinfurt **67** D3
Burg Strechau **93** D3
Burgsvik **47** D3
Burgsvik **72** B1
Burguete **108** B3, **155** C1/2
Burgui **154** B2
Burguillos **171** D1
Burguillos del Cerro **165** D3
Burguillos de Toledo **160** B3, **167** C1
Burgwald-Ernsthausen **80** B1/2
Burgwedel **68** B2
Burgwedel-Wettmar **68** B2
Burgwindheim **81** D3
Burhaniye **149** D1
Buriasco **112** B1
Burie **101** B/C3
Burjasot **169** D1
Burk **91** D1
Burkardroth **81** D2
Burkardroth-Waldfenster **81** C/D2
Burkersdorf **83** C2
Burkhardsdorf **82** B2
Burlada **154** A2
Burladingen-Stetten **91** C2
Burladingen-Hausen **91** C2
Burladingen **91** C2
Burnham Market **65** C1
Burnham-on-Crouch **65** C3
Burnham-on-Sea **63** C/D2
Burnley **59** D1, **60** B2
Burnley **54** B3
Burntisland **57** C1
Burón **152** A1/2
Buronzo **105** C3
Burøy **32** B1/2
Burøysund **4** A2
Burrel **138** A3
Burriana **163** C3, **169** D1
Burry Port **62** B1
Burs **47** D3
Burscheid **80** A1
Bürserberg **106** A1
Burseryd **50** B1
Bursnäs **34** B3
Burstad **5** D1, **6** A1
Bürstadt **80** B3
Burtenbach **91** D2
Burton **59** D1, **60** B2
Burton Agnes **61** D2
Burtonport **55** C2
Burton upon Trent **61** C3, **64** A1
Burträsk **31** D1
Buru **97** D3, **140** B1
Buruen **38** A1
Burujón **160** B3, **167** C1
Burvik **31** D1
Burwell **65** C2
Burwick **54** B1
Bury **59** D2, **60** B2
Bury Saint Edmunds **65** C2
Burzet **111** C1
Busachi **123** C2
Busalla **113** D1/2
Busana **114** A2, **116** A1
Busca **112** B2
Busche **107** C2
Buseck-Beuern **81** B/C2
Busenberg **90** A/B1
Buseto Palizzolo **124** A2
Buševac **127** D3
Bushat **137** D2
Busigny **78** A/B3
Busjön **31** C1
Busk **97** D2, **98** B2
Busko-Zdrój **97** C1/2
Bušletić **132** B1
Busot **169** D2/3
Busovača **132** B2
Bussang **89** D2/3, **90** A3
Busset **102** B2
Busseto **114** A1
Bussière-Badil **101** C3
Bussière-Poitevine **101** D2
Bussò **41** D3
Bussolengo **106** B3
Bussoleno **112** B1
Büssü **128** B2
Bussum **66** B3
Bussy [Cugy FR] **104** B1

Bustares **161** C1/2
Bustarviejo **161** B/C2
Bustillo del Páramo **151** D2
Bustillo del Oro **152** A3, **159** D1, **160** A1
Bustnes **14** A2
Busto Arsízio **105** D3
Busto de Bureba **153** C2
Bustos **158** A2
Büsum **52** A3
Butan **140** B2
Butera **125** C3
Bütgenbach **79** D2
Buthroton **142** A3
Butjadingen-Langwarden **52** A3, **67** D1, **68** A1
Butjadingen-Burhave **67** D1, **68** A1
Butjadingen-Eckwarden **67** D1, **68** A1
Butjadingen-Stollhamm **67** D1, **68** A1
Butrinti **142** A3
Bütschwil **91** C3, **105** D1, **106** A1
Buttapietra **107** B/C3
Buttelstedt **82** A1
Buttenheim **82** A3
Buttenwiesen **91** D2
Buttermere **57** C3, **60** A/B1
Buttes **104** B1
Buttlar **81** C/D2
Buttstädt **82** A1
Butzbach **80** B2
Butzen **70** B3
Bützow **53** D3, **69** D1
Buvåg **9** C2
Buvassbrenna **37** C3
Buvatn Fjellstue (Engene Fjellstue) **37** D3
Buvik **28** A3, **33** C2
Buvik **14** B2
Buvik **32** A/B2
Buvika **33** D3
Buxières-les-Mines **102** B2
Buxtehude **68** B1
Buxton **59** D2, **61** C3, **64** A1
Buxy **103** D1
Buzançais **101** D3
Buzancy **79** C3
Buzău **141** C2
Buzet **126** B3, **130** A1
Buziaş **140** A1/2
Byberget **35** C3
Bybjerg **49** D3, **53** D1
Bydalen **34** B2
Bydgoszcz **72** B3
Byerum **51** D1
Byfield **65** C2
Bygd **36** B3
Bygdeå **20** A1, **31** D2
Bygdeträsk **31** D1
Bygdin **37** C2
Bygdsiljum **31** D1/2
Bygget **50** B1/2
Bygland **43** C2
Byglandsfjord **43** B/C2/3
Bygstad **36** A2
Byhleguhre **70** B3
Byholma **50** B2
Byhov **99** C1
Bykle **42** B2
Bylderup **52** B2
Bylnice **95** C1
Byn **35** D3
Byneset **28** A3, **33** C1
Byremo **42** B3
Byrkjedal **42** A/B2
Byrkjelo **36** B2
Byrknes **36** A3
Byrum **49** C1
Byšice-Liblice **83** D2
Byske **31** D1
Byškovice **95** C1
Byssträsk **31** C1/2
Bystrica **97** D2, **98** A3
Bystřice **83** D3
Bystřice nad Pernštejnem **94** B1
Bystřice pod Hostýnem **95** C1
Bytča **95** D1
Bytča **96** B2
Bytnica **71** C3
Bytom **96** B2

Bytom Odrzański (Beuthen) **71** C3
Bytów **72** B2
Bytyń **71** D2
Byvalla **40** A2
Bywell **57** D2/3
Byxelkrok **51** D1
Byxelkrok **72** B1
Bzenec **95** C1
Bzovík **95** D2

C

Cabação **164** B2
Caballar **160** B1/2
Cabana **150** A1
Cabanas **150** B1
Cabañas de Yepes **161** C3, **167** C1
Cabañas de la Sagra **160** B3
Cabañas de Virtus **152** B1/2
Cabañas del Castillo **166** A/B1
Cabanes **163** C3
Cabanillas **161** C2
Cabanillas **154** A3
Cabanne **113** D2
Čabar **127** B/C3
Cabdella **155** D2
Cabeça Gorda **164** B3, **170** B1
Cabeceiras de Basto **158** B1
Cabeço de Vide **165** C2
Cabella **113** D2
Cabeza del Buey **166** B2
Cabeza de Vaca **165** D3
Cabezamesada **161** C3, **167** D1, **168** A1
Cabezarados **167** C2
Cabezarrubias **167** C2
Cabezas del Villar **160** A2
Cabezas Rubias **171** C1
Cabezón **152** B3, **160** A/B1
Cabezón de la Sal **152** B1
Cabezuela del Valle **159** D3
Cabo de Palos **174** B1
Cabolafuente **161** D1
Cabo Roig **169** C3, **174** B1
Cabourg **76** B3, **86** A1
Cabra **172** B1
Cabra **158** B2
Cabra del Camp **163** C1
Cabra del Santo Cristo **173** C1
Cabra de Mora **162** B3
Cábras **123** C2
Cabredo **153** D2
Cabreiro **150** A3
Cabreiroá **151** B/C3
Cabreiros **150** B1
Cabrejas del Campo **153** D3, **161** D1
Cabrejas del Pinar **153** C/D3, **161** C1
Cabrela **164** B2
Cabrerets **109** D1
Cabril **158** B3
Cabril **158** A/B2
Cabrillanes **151** D2
Cabrillas **159** D2
Cabuérniga **152** B1
Cacabelos **151** C2
Čačak **133** D2, **134** A2/3
Čačak **140** A2
Caçarelhos **151** C/D3, **159** C1
Cáccamo **124** B2
Caccuri **122** B2
Cacela **170** B2
Cáceres **165** D1, **166** A1
Cachopo **170** B2
Cachorrilla **159** C3, **165** D1
Čachrov **93** C3
Čachtice **95** C2
Cacia **158** A2
Čačinci **128** B3
Cadafais **164** A2
Cadalso **159** C3

Cadalso de los Vidrios **160** B3
Cadaqués **156** B2
Cadaval **164** A1/2
Cadavedo **151** C/D1
Čadavica **131** D2, **132** A2
Čadca **95** D1
Čadca **96** B2
Cadelbosco di Sotto **114** B1
Cadelbosco di Sopra **114** B1
Cadenazzo **105** D2
Cadenberge **52** A/B3, **68** A1
Cadenet **111** D2
Cadeo **114** A1
Cadeuil **100** B3
Cádiar **173** C2
Cadillac **108** B1
Cadillon **108** B3, **155** B/C1
Cadima **158** A3
Cádiz **171** D3
Čadjavica **128** B3
Cadolzburg **81** D3, **91** D1, **92** A1
Cadouin **109** C1
Cadours **109** C2
Cadreita **154** A2
Cadrete **154** B3, **162** B1
Čadyr-Lunga **141** D1
Caen **76** B3, **86** A1
Caër **86** A/B1
Caerano di San Marco **107** C3
Caergwrle **59** C2, **60** B3
Caerlaverock Castle **57** C3, **60** A1
Caerleon **63** C/D1
Caernarfon **59** B/C2, **60** A3
Caerphilly **63** C1
Caersws **59** C2
Caëstre **78** A2
Caetobriga **164** A2/3
Cagli **115** D3, **117** C2
Cágliari **123** D3
Cágliari **123** D3
Čaglin **128** B3
Cagnano Varano **120** B1
Cagnes-sur-Mer **112** B3
Čagoda **75** D1
Cahir **55** C3
Cahors **109** D1/2
Cahuzac-sur-Vère **109** D2
Caiazzo **119** D3
Cain Picafort **157** C2
Caiolo **106** A2
Caión **150** A1
Cairnryan **56** A/B3
Cairnryan **54** A3, **55** D2
Cáiro Montenotte **113** C2
Caister-on-Sea **65** D1/2
Caistor **61** D3
Caivano **119** D3
Cajarc **109** D1
Čajetina **133** C/D3, **134** A3
Čajić **131** D3, **132** A2/3
Čajniče **133** C3
Čakovec **127** D2
Čakovec **96** B3
Cala **133** D3, **166** A3, **171** C/D1
Calabernardo **125** D3
Cala Blanca **157** C1
Cala Blanes **157** C1
Cala Blava **157** C2
Cala Bona **157** C1
Calabor **151** C3
Calaceite **163** C2
Calacuccia **113** D3
Cala d'Oliva **123** C1
Cala d'Or **157** C/D1/2
Caladrones **155** C3
Calaf **155** D3, **156** A3, **163** C1
Calafat **135** D2
Calafat **140** B2
Calafell La Platja **156** A3, **163** C1
Cala Figuera **157** D2
Cala Gonone **123** D2
Cala Grassió **169** D2
Calahonda **172** B3
Calahonda **173** C2
Calahorra **153** D2, **154** A2
Calahorra de Boedo **152** B2
Calais **77** D1

Cala Llonga 157 D3
Calambrone 114 A3,
 116 A2
Cala Millor 157 C1
Calamita 124 A2
Calamocha 163 C2
Calamonte 165 D2
Cala Morell 157 C1
Calañas 171 C1
Calanda 162 B2
Calangiánus 123 D1
Cala'n Porter 157 C1
Cala Pi 157 D2
Cala Ratjada 157 C1
Cala San Vicente 157 D3
Cala San Vicente 157 C2
Calasanz 155 C3
Calascibetta 125 C2
Calas de Mallorca 157 C1/2
Calasetta 123 C3
Calatafimi 124 A2
Calatañazor 153 C/D3,
 161 C1
Cala Tarida 169 D2
Calatayud 162 A1
Calatorao 155 C3, 163 C1
Calau 70 B3
Cala Vadella 169 D2
Calavino 106 B2
Calbe 69 D3
Calcena 154 A3, 162 A1
Calcinelli 115 D2,
 117 C1/2
Calco 105 D3, 106 A3
Caldaro/Kaltern 107 C2
Caldarola 115 D3, 117 D2
Caldas da Felgueira 158 B2
Caldas da Rainha 164 A1
Caldas de Besaya 152 B1
Caldas de Cavaca 158 B2
Caldas de Monchique
 170 A2
Caldas de Nocedo 152 A2
Caldas de Reis 150 A2
Caldas de San Adrián
 152 A2
Caldas de Vizela 158 A1
Caldas do Gerez 150 B3,
 158 A/B1
Caldbeck 57 C3, 60 B1
Caldelas 150 A/B3, 158 A1
Calden 81 C1
Calderari 125 C2
Calders 156 A3
Caldes de Bohí 155 C/D2
Caldes de Malavella
 156 B2/3
Caldes de Montbui 156 A3
Caldetes 156 B3
Caldiero 107 C3
Caldirola 113 D1
Caldonazzo 107 C2
Calella de Mar 156 B3
Calella de Palafrugell
 156 B2
Calenzana 113 D2/3
Calera de León 165 D3
Calera y Chozas 160 A3,
 166 B1
Caleruega 153 C3, 161 C1
Caleruela 160 A3, 166 B1
Calestano 114 A1
Calgary 56 A1
Cálig 163 C2
Calivelos 158 B2
Calizzano 113 C2
Callac 84 B2
Callander 56 B1
Calliano 113 C1
Callington 62 B3
Callione 107 B/C2
Callosa de Ensarriá 169 D2
Callosa de Segura 169 C3
Čalma 133 C1
Calne 63 D2, 64 A3
Calolziocorte 105 D3,
 106 A3
Calonge de les Gavarres
 156 B2
Calore 119 D3, 120 A2
Calov 108 B2
Čalovo 95 C3
Calpe 169 D2

Caltabellotta 124 B2
Caltagirone 125 C3
Caltanissetta 125 B/C2
Caltavuturo 124 B2
Caltojar 161 C/D1
Caluso 105 C3
Calvaire 85 C2/3
Calvarrasa de Abajo 159 D2
Calvarrasa de Arriba 159 D2
Calvello 120 B3
Calvera 155 C2
Calvi 113 D2
Calvia 157 C2
Calvi dell'Úmbria 117 C3,
 118 B1
Calvinet 110 A1
Calvisson 111 C2
Calvörde 69 C2/3
Calvos de Randín 150 B3
Calw 90 B2
Calw-Hirsau 90 B2
Calw-Stammheim 90 B2
Calzada de Calatrava
 167 C2
Calzada de Don Diego
 159 D2
Calzada del Coto 152 A2
Calzada de los Molinos
 152 B2
Calzada de Valdunciel
 159 D2
Calzadilla 159 C3
Calzadilla de los Barros
 165 D3, 166 A3
Calzadilla de la Cueza
 152 A/B2
Camaiore 114 A2, 116 A1
Camáldoli 115 C2, 116 B1
Camañas 163 C2
Camarasa 155 D3
Camarate 164 A2
Camarena de la Sierra
 162 A/B3
Camarès 110 A2
Camaret-sur-Mer 84 A2
Camargo 152 B1
Camarillas 162 B2
Camariñas 150 A1
Camarma de Esteruelas
 161 C2
Camarmeña 152 A1
Camarzana de Tera 151 D3
Camas 171 D1
Cambados 150 A2
Cambeo 150 B2
Camberley 64 B3, 76 B1
Cambil 173 C1
Cambo-les-Bains 108 B3,
 155 C1
Camborne 62 A/B3
Cambra 158 A/B2
Cambrai 78 A2/3
Cambre 150 B1
Cambridge 65 C2
Cambrils de Mar 163 D2
Cambron 77 D2
Cambs 53 C/D3, 69 C1
Camburg 82 A1
Cámedo 105 D2
Camelford 62 B3
Camelle 150 A1
Camerino 115 D3, 117 D2
Camerota 120 A3
Camigliatello Silano
 122 B1/2
Camin 69 C1
Caminha 150 A3
Caminomorisco 159 C3
Camineal 163 C2
Camisano Vicentino 107 C3
Cammarata 124 B2
Cammer 69 D3, 70 A3
Cammin 53 D3
Camogli 113 D2
Camoins-les-Bains 111 D3
Camon 109 D3, 156 A1
Campagna 119 D3, 120 A2
Campagne 109 C1
Campagne 108 B2
Campan 109 B/C3, 155 C1
Campana 122 B1
Campanario 166 A2
Campanas 154 A2
Campanet 157 C2
Campano 171 D3
Campaspero 152 B3,
 160 B1

Campbeltown 56 A2
Campbeltown 54 A3,
 55 D1/2
Campbon 85 C3
Campdevànol 156 A2
Campeã 158 B1
Campello 169 D3
Campello Monti 105 C2/3
Campese 116 A3
Campi Bisénzio 114 B2,
 116 B1
Campíglia 105 C3
Campíglia dei Fosci 114 B3,
 116 B2
Campíglia Maríttima
 114 B3, 116 A2
Campillo 163 C3
Campillo de Deleitosa
 159 D3, 166 A1
Campillo de Aragón
 161 D1/2, 162 A1/2
Campillo de Altobuey
 168 B1
Campillo de Llerena
 166 A2/3
Campillo de Dueñas 162 A2
Campillo de Azaba 159 C2
Campillo de Aranda
 153 C3, 160 B1
Campillo de Arenas 173 C1
Campillos 172 A2
Campillos-Paravientos
 162 A3
Campillos-Sierra 162 A3
Campione 105 D2
Campione del Garda
 106 B3
Campisábalos 161 C1
Campi Salentina 121 D3
Campitello 114 B1
Campitello Matese 119 D2
Campli 117 D3, 119 C1
Campmany 156 B2
Campo 155 C2
Campo 105 D2, 106 A2
Campo 165 C3
Campo 158 A1/2
Campobasso 119 D2
Campobecerros 151 C3
Campobello di Licata
 124 B3
Campobello di Mazara
 124 A2
Campocologno 106 B2
Campodársego 107 C3
Campo de Caso 152 A1
Campo de Criptana 167 D1,
 168 A1
Campo di Giove 119 C2
Campo di Trens/Freienfeld
 107 C1
Campodolcino 105 D2,
 106 A2
Campodónico 115 D3,
 117 C2
Campofelice di Roccella
 124 B2
Campofelice di Fitália
 124 B2
Campofiorito 124 B2
Campofórmido 126 A2
Campotorogna 117 C/D3,
 118 B1
Campofrío 165 D3, 171 C1
Campogalliano 114 B1
Campo Lameiro 150 A2
Campolasta/Astfeld
 107 C1/2
Campolattaro 119 D2/3
Campo Ligure 113 C/D1/2
Campo Maior 165 C2
Campomanes 151 D1
Campomarino 119 D2,
 120 A1
Campomarino 121 C/D3
Campo Molino 112 B2
Câmpora San Giovanni
 122 A2
Campo Real 161 C3
Camporeale 124 A/B2
Camporells 155 C3
Camporredondo de Alba
 152 A/B2
Camporredondo 160 B1
Camporrobles 163 C3,
 169 D1
Campos 162 B2

Campos 150 B3, 158 B1
Camposampiero 107 C3
Camposanto 114 B1
Campos del Puerto 157 C2
Campos del Río 169 D3
Campotéjar 173 C1
Campo Túres/Sand in Tirol
 107 C1
Campoverde 118 B2
Camprodón 156 A/B2
Camps-en-Amiénois
 77 D2/3
Camucia 115 C3, 116 B2
Camugnano 114 B2,
 116 B1
Camuñas 167 D1
Çan 149 D1
Canach 79 D3
Cañada de Calatrava
 167 C2
Cañada de Benatanduz
 162 B2
Cañada del Hoyo 161 D3,
 162 A3
Cañadajuncosa 168 B1
Cañada-Rosal 172 A1
Čanak 131 B/C1/2
Çanakkale 149 C1
Canale 113 C1
Canalejas del Arroyo
 161 D2/3
Canales de Molina 161 D2
Canals 169 C/D2
Canal San Bovo 107 C2
Cañamero 166 B1
Canas de Senhorim 158 B2
Cañaveral 159 C3, 165 D1
Cañaveral de León 165 D3,
 171 C1
Cañaveras 161 D2/3
Cañaveruelas 161 D2/3
Canazei 107 C2
Cancale 85 C/D1/2
Cancellara 120 B2
Cancello Arnone 119 C3
Cancon 109 C1
Candal 158 A/B2
Candanchú 154 B2
Candasnos 155 C3, 163 C1
Candé 85 D3
Candela 120 A2
Candelario 159 D2/3
Candeleda 160 A3
Candemil 158 B1
Candes-Saint-Martin
 86 A/B3, 101 C1
Cándia Lomellina 105 D3,
 113 C1
Candilichera 153 D3,
 161 D1
Candín 151 C2
Caneças 164 A2
Canelli 113 C1
Canero 151 C1
Canet 156 B1
Canet de Mar 156 B3
Cañete 162 A3
Cañete de las Torres
 167 C3, 172 B1
Cañete la Real 172 A2
Canet lo Roig 163 C2
Canet-Plage 156 B1
Canfranc 154 B2
Cangas 150 A2/3
Cangas de Narcea 151 C1
Cangas de Onís 152 A1
Canha 164 B2
Canhestros 164 B3, 170 A1
Canicattì 124 B2/3
Canicattini Bagni 125 D3
Canicosa de la Sierra
 153 C3
Caniles 173 D1/2
Canillas de Aceituno
 172 B2
Canillas de Esgueva
 152 B3, 160 B1
Canillas de Albaida 172 B2
Canillo 155 D2, 156 A2
Canino 116 B3, 118 A1
Cañizal 159 D1/2, 160 A1
Cañizar 161 C2
Cañizar del Olivar 162 B2
Cañizares 161 D2
Cañizo 152 A3, 159 D1,
 160 A1
Čanj 137 D2

Canjáyar 173 D2
Ca'N Jordí 157 D3
Canna 120 B3, 122 B1
Canne 120 B2
Cánnero Riviera 105 D2
Cannes 112 B3
Canneto 125 C/D1
Canneto 114 B3, 116 A2
Canneto sul Óglio 106 B3,
 114 A/B1
Cannigione 123 D1
Cannóbio 105 D2
Cannock 59 D3, 64 A1
Cano 165 B/C2
Canonbie 57 C2
Canosa di Púglia 120 B2
Canósio 112 B2
Canossa 114 A/B1
Canove 107 C2/3
Canove 113 C1
Can Pastilla 157 C2
Canredondo 161 D2
Cansano 119 C2
Cantagallo 159 D2/3
Cantalapiedra 160 A1/2
Cantalejo 160 B1
Cantallops 156 B2
Cantalojas 161 C1
Cantalpino 159 D2, 160 A2
Cantanhede 158 A2/3
Cantavieja 162 B2
Čantavir 129 D2
Canterbury 65 D3, 77 C1
Cantiano 115 D3, 117 C2
Cantillana 171 D1
Cantimpalos 160 B2
Cantin 78 A2
Cantiveros 160 A2
Cantoral 152 B2
Cantoria 173 D2, 174 A1/2
Cantù 105 D3, 106 A3
Canvey 65 C3
Cany-Barville 77 C3
Canyelles 156 A3, 163 D1
Canyon 5 C2/3
Canzo 105 D3, 106 A2/3
Caoria 107 C2
Cáorle 107 D3, 126 A3
Caorso 114 A1
Caoulet 109 C2
Capáccio 120 A3
Capaci 124 B1/2
Capafóns 163 D1
Capafonts La Mussara
 163 D1
Capálbio 116 B3, 118 A1
Capanne 115 C3, 117 C2
Capánnole 115 C3, 116 B2
Capánnoli 114 B3, 116 A2
Capannori 114 A2, 116 A1
Caparde 133 C2
Capareiros 150 A3, 158 A1
Capari 138 B3, 143 B/C1
Caparica 164 A2
Caparroso 154 A2
Capbreton 108 A2/3,
 154 A1
Capdenac-Gare 109 D1,
 110 A1
Capdepera 157 C1
Cap-de-Pin 108 A2
Capdesaso 155 B/C3,
 162 B1
Capel 64 B3, 76 B1
Capela 150 B1
Capel Curig 59 C2, 60 A3
Capel'ka 74 B1/2
Capella 155 C2/3
Capellades 153 D3, 161 D1
Capellen 79 D3
Capendu 110 A3, 156 B1
Capens 108 B3, 155 C1
Capestang 110 A/B3,
 156 B1
Capestrano 117 D3,
 119 C1
Cap Fréhel 85 C1/2
Capileira 173 C2
Capilla 166 B2
Capillas 152 A3
Capinha 158 B3
Capistrello 119 C2
Čaplje 131 D1/2
Čapljina 132 A3, 136 B1
Capodimonte 116 B3,
 118 A1
Capo di Ponte 106 B2

Capo d'Orlando **125** C1/2
Capolago [Capolago-Riva S. Vitale] **105** D2/3
Capolíveri **116** A3
Čapor **95** C2
Capo Rizzuto **122** B2
Capoterra **123** C/D3
Capovalle **106** B3
Cappadócia **119** B/C2
Cap Pelat **108** B2
Cappelle **119** C1/2
Cappelle sul Tavo **119** C1
Capracotta **119** C/D2
Capráia **114** A3
Capránica **117** C3, **118** A1
Caprarola **117** C3, **118** A1
Caprese Michelángelo **115** C2/3, **117** B/C2
Capri **119** C/D3
Capriati a Volturno **119** C2
Capríccioli **123** D1
Caprile **107** C2
Caprino Bergamasco **106** A3
Caprino Veronese **106** B3
Căpruta **140** A1
Captieux **108** B2
Cápua **119** C/D3
Capurso **121** C2
Capvern **109** C3, **155** C1
Carabaña **161** C3
Carabanchel **160** B2/3
Carabantes **153** D3, **154** A3, **161** D1
Caracal **140** B2
Caracena **161** C1
Caracenilla **161** D3
Caracuel **167** C2
Caradeuc **85** C2
Caráglio **112** B2
Caraman **109** D3, **155** D1
Caramánico Terme **119** C1
Caramulo **158** A/B2
Caranga **151** D1
Caranguejeira **158** A3, **164** A/B1
Caransebeş **140** A/B2
Carantec **84** B1/2
Carasco **113** D2
Caraşova **135** C1
Caraula **135** D2
Caravaca de la Cruz **168** B3, **174** A1
Caravággio **106** A3
Carazo **153** C3
Carbajales de Alba **151** D3, **159** D1
Carbajo **165** C1
Carballeda **151** C2
Carballeda de Avia **150** B2
Carballedo **150** B2
Carballiño **150** B2
Carballo **150** A1
Carbellino **159** D1
Carbonara di Po **114** B1
Carbonare di Folgaria **107** C2
Carbon-Blanc **108** B1
Carboneras **174** A2
Carboneras de Guadazaón **162** A3, **168** B1
Carbonero el Mayor **160** B1/2
Carboneros **167** C/D3
Carbónia **123** C3
Carbonin/Schluderbach **107** D2
Carbonne **108** B3, **155** C1
Carbuccia **113** D3
Carcaboso **159** C/D3
Carcabuey **172** B1
Carcagente **169** D2
Carcans **100** B3, **108** A1
Carcans-Plage **101** C3, **108** B1
Cárcar **153** D2, **154** A2
Cárcare **113** C2
Carcassonne **110** A3, **156** A/B1
Carcastillo **154** A2
Carcelén **169** D2
Carcès **112** A3
Carchel **173** C1
Carchelejo **173** C1
Cardedeu **156** A/B3
Cardejón **153** D3, **161** D1

Cardeña **167** C3
Cárdenas **153** C/D2
Cardenete **162** A3, **168** B1
Cardeñosa **160** A2
Cardesse **108** B3, **154** B1
Cardiff **62** B1
Cardigan **62** B1
Cardigan **55** D3
Cardó **163** C2
Cardona **155** D3, **156** A2
Carei **97** D3, **98** A3
Carenas **162** A1
Carennac **109** D1
Carentan **76** B3, **86** A/B1
Carentoir **85** C3
Carevdar **127** D2, **128** A2
Carev Dvor **138** B3, **142** B1
Cargèse **113** D3
Carhaix-Plouguer **84** B2
Caria **158** B3
Cariati **122** B1
Cariċin Grad **139** C1
Caridade **165** C3
Carignan **79** C3
Carignano **113** B/C1
Carina **142** B2
Cariñena **163** C1
Carini **124** A/B1/2
Cariño **150** B1
Carínola **119** C3
Carisbrooke Castle **76** B1/2
Carisolo **106** B2
Carlentini **125** D3
Carlet **169** D2
Carling **89** D1
Carlingford **58** A1
Carlisle **57** C3, **60** B1
Carlisle **54** B3
Carloforte **123** C3
Carlópoli **122** B2
Carlow **53** C3, **69** C1
Carlow **55** D3
Carlsberg **80** B3, **90** B1
Carlsfeld **82** B2
Carlton-in-Lindrick **61** C3
Carluke **56** C1
Carmagnola **113** B/C1
Carmarthen **62** B1
Carmaux **109** D2, **110** A2
Carmena **160** B3, **167** C1
Cármenes **151** D2, **152** A2
Carmiano **121** D3
Carmona **171** D1, **172** A1
Carmonita **165** D2, **166** A2
Carnac **84** B3
Carnaxide **164** A2
Carnew **58** A3
Carnforth **59** D1, **60** B2
Cárnia **126** A2
Carnlough **56** A3
Carno **59** C3
Carnon-Plage **110** B3
Carnota **150** A2
Carnoules **112** A3
Carnoustie **57** C1
Carnwath **57** C2
Carolei **122** A2
Carolles **85** D1
Carona **106** A2
Caronía **125** C2
Caronia Marina **125** C2
Carovigno **121** D2
Carovilli **119** D2
Carpaneto Piacentino **114** A1
Carpegna **115** C2, **117** C1/2
Carpenédolo **106** B3
Carpentras **111** C/D2
Carpi **114** B1
Carpineti **114** B1/2
Carpineto Romano **118** B2
Cărpiniş **135** D1
Carpino **120** B1
Carpinone **119** D2
Carpinteiro **164** B1/2
Carpio de Azaba **159** C2
Carquefou **85** D3, **100** A/B1
Carqueiranne **112** A3
Carradale **56** A2
Carral **150** A/B1
Carrapateira **170** A2
Carrapichana **158** B2
Carrara **114** A2, **116** A1
Cărrascal del Río **160** B1

Carrascalejo **160** A3, **166** B1
Carrascosa **161** D2
Carrascosa del Campo **161** C/D3
Carrascosa de Abajo **161** C1
Carrascosa de Haro **168** A1
Carratraca **172** A/B2
Carrazeda de Anciães **158** B1
Carrazedo **151** B/C3, **158** B1
Carrbridge **54** B2
Carreço **150** A3, **158** A1
Carrefour-Saint-Jean **86** A/B1
Carregado **164** A2
Carregal do Sal **158** B2
Carrega Lígure **113** D1
Carregueiros **164** B1
Carreña **152** A1
Carreño **151** D1
Carresse **108** A3, **154** B1
Carrickart **55** C/D2
Carrickfergus **56** A3
Carrión de los Condes **152** B2
Carrión de los Céspedes **171** C/D1/2
Carrión de Calatrava **167** C2
Carrizo de la Ribera **151** D2
Carrizosa **167** D2, **168** A2
Carronbridge **57** B/C2
Carrouges **86** A2
Carrù **113** C2
Carry-le-Rouet **111** D3
Carskiey **56** A2
Carsóli **118** B1/2
Carsphairn **56** B2/3
Carstairs **57** B/C2
Carstairs **54** B3
Cartagena **174** B1
Cártama **172** B2
Cartaxo **164** A2
Cartaya **171** C2
Cartelle **150** B2/3
Carteret **76** A3
Cartoceto **115** D3, **117** C2
Carúnchio **119** D2
Carvajal **172** B2
Carvalhal **158** B2
Cârvarica **139** D2
Carviças **159** C1/2
Carvin **78** A2
Carvoeira **164** A2
Carvoeira **164** A2
Carvoeiro **170** A2
Carvoeiro **164** B1
Caryduff **56** A3
Carzig **70** B2
Casabermeja **172** B2
Casa Branca **164** A3
Casa Branca **164** B2/3
Casa Branca **164** B2
Casacalenda **119** D2, **120** A1
Casa de Uceda **161** C2
Casaio **151** C2
Casais **170** A2
Casa l'Abate **121** D2/3
Casalánguida **119** D1/2
Casalarreina **153** C2
Casalbordino **119** D1
Casalborgone **113** C1
Casalbuono **120** A/B3
Casalbuttano **106** A/B3
Casal Cermelli **113** C1
Casal di Príncipe **119** C3
Casalécchio di Reno **114** B1/2
Casale Monferrato **113** C1
Casalgrande **114** B1
Casalgrasso **112** B1
Casalmaggiore **114** A/B1
Casalmorano **106** A3
Casalnuovo **122** A3
Casalnuovo Monterotaro **119** D2, **120** A1
Casaloldo **106** B3
Casalpusterlengo **106** A3, **113** D1
Casalromano **106** B3
Casalvécchio di Púglia **119** D2, **120** A1

Casalvieri **119** C2
Casamássima **121** C2
Casamícciola Terme **119** C3
Casamozza **113** D2
Casarabonela **172** A2
Casarano **121** D3
Casar de Cáceres **165** D1
Casar de Palomero **159** C/D3
Casar de Talavera **160** A3, **166** B1
Casares **172** A3
Casares de las Hurdes **159** C/D2
Casariche **172** A/B2
Casarrubios del Monte **160** B3
Casarsa della Delízia **107** D2, **126** A2
Casas Altas **163** C3
Casasana **161** D2
Casas Bajas **163** C3
Casasbuenas **160** B3, **167** C1
Casas de Don Antonio **165** D1/2, **166** A1/2
Casas de Don Pedro **166** B2
Casas de Fernando Alonso **168** B1
Casas de Haro **168** B1
Casas de Juan Núñez **168** B2
Casas de Lázaro **168** B2
Casas del Monte **159** D3
Casas de los Pinos **168** B1
Casas de los Muneras **168** A2
Casas del Puerto de Villatoro **160** A2
Casas de Millán **159** C3, **165** D1, **166** A1
Casas de Miravete **159** D3, **166** A1
Casas de Reina **166** A3
Casas de Ves **169** D1/2
Casaseca **159** D1
Casas-Ibáñez **169** B/C1/2
Casasimarro **168** B1
Casasola de Arión **152** A3, **160** A1
Casasuertes **152** A1
Casatejada **159** D3, **166** A1
Casavieja **160** A3
Casazza **106** A3
Casbas de Huesca **155** B/C2/3
Cascades du Hérisson **104** A2
Cascais **164** A2
Cascante **154** A3
Cascante del Río **162** A/B3
Cascata del Toce **105** C2
Ca'S Catalá **157** C2
Casei Gerola **113** D1
Casekow **70** B1/2
Casel **70** B3, **83** C1
Casella **113** D1/2
Caselle in Píttari **120** A3
Caselle Torinese **105** C3, **112** B1
Casemurate **115** C2, **117** C1
Case Perrone **121** C3
Caseres **163** C2
Caserío de Llanos de Don Juan **172** B1/2
Caserta **119** C3
Caserta vécchia **119** D3
Cashel **55** C3
Cashlie **56** B1
Casillas **160** A/B3
Casillas de Flores **159** C2/3
Casillas de Coria **159** C3
Casina **114** A/B1
Casinina **115** D2, **117** C1
Casinos **162** B3, **169** C1
Časkel **5** D2, **6** A2
Casla **161** B/C1/2

Čáslav **96** A2
Čašniki **74** B3
Cásola Valsénio **115** C2, **116** B1
Cásole d'Elsa **114** B3, **116** A/B2
Cásoli **119** D1
Casória **119** D3
Caspe **163** C1
Caspóggio **106** A2
Caspueñas **161** C2
Cassà de la Selva **156** B2
Cassagnes-Bégonhès **110** A2
Cassana **115** C1
Cassaniouze **110** A1
Cassano allo Iónio **122** A/B1
Cassano d'Adda **106** A3
Cassano delle Murge **121** C2
Cassano Spínola **113** D1
Cássaro **125** C/D3
Cassel **77** D1, **78** A2
Casserres **156** A2
Cassíbile **125** D3
Cassine **113** C1
Cassino **119** C2
Cássio **114** A1
Cassis **111** D3
Cassuéjouls **110** A1
Castagnaro **114** B1
Castagneto Carducci **114** B3, **116** A2
Castaignos-Souslens **108** B3, **154** B1
Castalla **169** C2
Castañar de Ibor **160** A3, **166** B1
Castañares de Rioja **153** C2
Castanheira **164** A2
Castanheira de Pera **158** A3
Castanheira do Vouga **158** A2
Cástano Primo **105** D3
Castasegna [St. Moritz] **106** A2
Castéggio **113** D1
Castejón **154** A2/3
Castejón **161** D2/3
Castejón de Sobrarbe **155** C2
Castejón del Puente **155** C3
Castejón de las Armas **162** A1
Castejón de Valdejasa **154** B3
Castejón de Monegros **154** B3, **162** B1
Castejón de Sos **155** C2
Castejón de Tornos **162** A2
Castel Baronia **120** A2
Castelbelforte **106** B3
Castel Bolognese **115** C2, **116** B1
Castelbuono **125** C2
Castel d'Aiano **114** B2, **116** A/B1
Castel d'Ário **106** B3
Castel de Cabra **162** B2
Casteldelfino **112** B1/2
Castel del Monte **117** D3, **119** C1
Castel del Monte **120** B2, **136** A3
Castel del Piano **116** B3
Castel del Rio **115** B/C2, **116** B1
Castel di Iúdica **125** C2
Castel di Lagopésole **120** A/B2
Castel di Sangro **119** C2
Casteleiro **159** B/C3
Castel Euriaio **125** D3
Castelfiorentino **114** B3, **116** A2
Castelflorite **155** C3, **163** C1
Castelforte **119** C2/3
Castelfranc **108** B1
Castelfranco Emília **114** B1
Castelfranco Véneto **107** C3
Castelfranco in Miscano **119** D2/3, **120** A1/2
Castel Fusano **118** A/B2
Castel Gandolfo **118** B2

Castelgrande **120** A2
Casteljaloux **108** B2
Castellabate **120** A3
Castelladral **156** A2
Castellafiume **119** C2
Castellammare di Stábia **119** D3
Castellammare del Golfo **124** A2
Castellamonte **105** C3
Castellana Grotte **121** C2
Castellane **112** A2
Castellaneta **121** C2
Castellanos de Moriscos **159** D2
Castellarano **114** B1
Castellar de Santisteban **167** D3, **168** A3
Castellar de la Ribera **155** C3
Castellar de la Frontera **172** A3
Castellar de Santiago **167** D2
Castellar del Vallès **156** A3
Castellar de N'Hug **156** A2
Castellar de la Muela **162** A2
Castell'Arquato **114** A1
Castell'Azzara **116** B3
Castellazzo Bormida **113** C1
Castellbó **155** C2
Castelldans **155** C/D3, **163** C1
Castell de Cabres **163** C2
Castell de Castells **169** D2
Castell de Ferro **173** C2
Castelldefels **156** A3
Castelleone **106** A3
Castelletto di Brenzone **106** B3
Castellfollit de la Roca **156** B2
Castellfort **162** B2
Castelli **117** D3, **119** C1
Castellina in Chianti **114** B3, **116** B3
Castellina Maríttima **114** B3, **116** A2
Castelló d'Empúries **156** B2
Castelló de Farfanya **155** C3, **163** C1
Castello di Annone **113** C1
Castello di Fiemme **107** C2
Castello di Quirra **123** D3
Castellolí **155** D3, **156** A3, **163** C1
Castellón de Rugat **169** D2
Castellón de la Plana **163** C3
Castellote **162** B2
Castello Tesino **107** C2
Castellserà **155** D3, **163** D1
Castellterçol **156** A3
Castellúcchio **106** B3, **114** B1
Castellúccio Inferiore **120** B3, **122** A1
Castellúccio de'Sáuri **120** A1/2
Castellúccio Valmaggiore **120** A1/2
Castellúccio Superiore **120** B3, **122** A1
Castell'Umberto **125** C2
Castelluzzo **124** A2
Castel Maggiore **114** B1
Castelmassa **114** B1
Castelmáuro **119** D2
Castelmoron-sur-Lot **109** C1
Castelnau **108** B2
Castelnau **109** D1
Castelnau-Barbarens **109** C3, **155** C1
Castelnau-d'Estrétefonds **108** B2
Castelnaudary **109** D3, **156** A1
Castelnau-de-Médoc **108** A/B1
Castelnau-de-Montmiral **109** D2
Castelnau-Magnoac **109** C3, **155** C1

Castelnau-Montratier **108** B2
Castelnau-Rivière-Basse **108** B3, **155** C1
Castelnou **162** B1
Castelnovo di Sotto **114** B1
Castelnovo ne'Monti **114** A1/2, **116** A1
Castelnuovo di Val di Cécina **114** B3, **116** A2
Castelnuovo Scrívia **113** D1
Castelnuovo della Daúnia **119** D2, **120** A1
Castelnuovo di Garfagnana **114** A2, **116** A1
Castelnuovo Berardenga **115** B/C3, **116** B2
Castelnuovo Don Bosco **113** C1
Castelnuovo del Garda **106** B3
Castelo Branco **159** C1
Castelo Branco **158** B3, **165** C1
Castelo de Paiva **158** A2
Castelo de Vide **165** C1
Castelraimondo **115** D3, **117** D2
Castel San Giovanni **113** D1
Castel San Giórgio **119** D3
Castel San Gimignano **114** B3, **116** A/B2
Castel San Pietro Terme **115** C2, **116** B1
Castelsantángelo **117** D3
Castelsaraceno **120** B3
Castelsardo **123** C1
Castelserás **163** B/C2
Casteltérmini **124** B2
Castelvécchio **107** C3
Castelvécchio Subéquo **119** C1
Castelvétere in Valfortore **119** D2, **120** A1
Castelvetrano **124** A2
Castel Volturno **119** C3
Castenédolo **106** B3
Castéra-Verduzan **109** C2
Castets **108** B2
Castiádas **123** D3
Castiello de Jaca **154** B2
Castigaleu **155** C2/3
Castiglioncello **114** A3, **116** A2
Castiglione Olona **105** D3
Castiglione di Garfagnana **114** A2, **116** A1
Castiglione delle Stiviere **106** B3
Castiglione d'Órcia **115** C3, **116** B2/3
Castiglione Chiavarese **113** D2
Castiglione d'Adda **106** A3, **113** D1
Castiglione Messer Marino **119** D2
Castiglione Mantovano **106** B3
Castiglione di Sicília **125** D2
Castiglione della Pescáia **116** A3
Castiglione dei Pépoli **114** B2, **116** B1
Castiglione del Lago **115** C3, **117** B/C2
Castiglion Fibocchi **115** C3, **116** B2
Castiglion Fiorentino **115** C3, **116** B2
Castignano **117** D2/3
Castilblanco de los Arroyos **171** D1
Castilblanco **166** B1/2
Castildelgado **153** C2
Castil de Peones **153** C2
Castilfalé **152** A2/3
Castiliscar **155** C2
Castillazuelo **155** C3
Castilleja del Campo **171** C/D1/2
Castilleja de la Cuesta **171** D1/2
Castilléjar **173** D1

Castillejo de Iniesta **168** B1
Castillejo de Mesleón **161** C1
Castillejo del Romeral **161** D3
Castillejo de Robledo **153** C3, **161** C1
Castillo de Bayuela **160** A3
Castillo de Locubín **173** B/C1
Castillo de Villamalefa **162** B3
Castillon-en-Couserans **109** C3, **155** D1/2
Castillon-la-Bataille **108** B1
Castillonnès **109** C1
Castillonroy **155** C3
Castilnuevo **161** D2, **162** A2
Castilruiz **153** D3
Castione [Castione-Arbedo] **105** D2, **106** A2
Castione della Presolana **106** B2/3
Castions di Strada **126** A2/3
Castlebar **55** C2
Castlebay **54** A2, **55** D1
Castlebellingham **58** A1
Castleblayney **54** A3, **55** D2
Castlebridge **58** A3
Castle Cary **63** D2
Castle Douglas **56** B3, **60** A1
Castleford **61** D2
Castleton **61** C3
Castletown **58** B1
Castletown **58** A3
Castlewellan **58** A1
Casto **106** B3
Castraz **159** C2
Castrejón **160** A1
Castrelo de Miño **150** B2/3
Castrelo do Val **151** B/C3
Castrelos **151** C3, **159** C1
Castres **110** A3
Castricum **66** A2
Castril **168** A3, **173** D1
Castrillo **153** B/C3, **160** B1
Castrillo de la Reina **153** C3
Castrillo de Villavega **152** B2
Castrillo de Duero **152** B3, **160** B1
Castrillo de Murcia **152** B2
Castrillo de Don Juan **152** B3, **160** B1
Castrillo de Onielo **152** B3
Castrillo Matajudíos **152** B2
Castrillón **151** C1
Castrillon **151** D1
Castrillo-Tejeriego **152** B3, **160** B1
Castrocalbón **151** D3
Castro Caldelas **151** B/C2
Castrocaro Terme **115** C2, **116** B1
Castrocontrigo **151** D3
Castro Daire **158** B2
Castro dei Volsci **119** C2
Castro del Río **172** B1
Castro de Rei **151** B/C1
Castrodeza **152** A3, **160** A1
Castrofilippo **124** B2/3
Castrofuerte **151** D2/3, **152** A2/3
Castrojeriz **152** B2
Castro Laboreiro **150** B3
Castro Marim **170** B2
Castromocho **152** A3
Castromonte **152** A3, **160** A1
Castronuevo **151** D3, **152** A3, **159** D1, **160** A1
Castronuño **160** A1
Castropol **151** C1
Castrop-Rauxel **80** A1
Castroreale Terme **125** D1/2
Castro Urdiales **153** C1
Castroverde de Campos **152** A3
Castroverde **151** C1/2

Castroverde de Cerrato **152** B3, **160** B1
Castro Verde **170** B1
Castro Vicente **159** C1
Castrovíllari **120** B3, **122** A1
Castuera **166** A2
Čata **95** D3
Catadau **169** C/D1/2
Catalca **149** D1
Catane **135** D2
Catánia **125** D2
Catanzaro **122** B2
Catanzaro Lido **122** B2
Catarroja **169** D1
Catelrotto/Kastelruth **107** C2
Catenanuova **125** C2
Cateraggio **113** D3
Caterham **65** C3, **76** B1
Čateške Toplice **127** C2/3
Čatež **127** C2/3
Catí **163** C2
Cá Tiepolo **115** C1
Catignano **119** C1
Catlowdy **57** C3
Catoira **150** A2
Catral **169** C3
Cattaéggio **106** A2
Cattenom **79** D3
Catterick **61** C1/2
Cattólica **115** D2, **117** C1
Cattólica Eraclea **124** B2
Catus **108** B1
Caudé **163** C2
Caudebec-en-Caux **77** C3
Caudete **169** C2
Caudete de las Fuentes **169** D1
Caudiel **162** B3, **169** C/D1
Caudiès-de-Fenouillèdes **156** A/B1
Caudos **108** A1
Caudry **78** A/B2/3
Caujac **109** D3, **155** D1
Caulnes **85** C2
Caulónia **122** B3
Caumont-l'Évente **86** A1
Caunes-Minervois **110** A3, **156** B1
Cauro **113** D3
Caussade **109** D2
Causse-de-la-Selle **110** B2
Čausy **75** C3, **99** C/D1
Cauterets **155** C2
Cauville-sur-Mer **76** B3
Caux [Montreux] **104** B2
Cavacao **164** A1
Cava d'Aliga **125** C3
Cava de Tirreni **119** D3
Cava d'Íspica **125** C3
Cavaglià **105** C2
Cavaillon **111** C/D2
Cavalaire-sur-Mer **112** A3
Cavalese **107** C2
Cavalière **112** A3
Cavallermaggiore **113** B/C1
Cávalo **106** B3
Cavan **54** A3, **55** D2
Cavareno **107** C2
Cavárzere **107** C/D3, **115** C1
Cave del Predil **126** A/B2
Ca'Venier **115** C1
Cavernães **158** B2
Cavezzo **114** B1
Cavignac **101** B/C3, **108** B1
Cavle **126** B3, **130** A/B1
Cavo **116** A3
Cavour **112** B1
Cavtat **137** C2
Caya **165** C2
Caya **165** C2
Cayeux-sur-Mer **77** D2
Caylus **109** D2
Cayres **110** B1
Cayrols **110** A1
Cazalegas **160** A3
Cazalilla **167** C3, **173** B/C1
Cazalla de la Sierra **166** A3, **171** D1
Cazals **108** B1
Cazane **135** C2
Cazaubon **108** B2
Cazaux **108** B1

Cazaux-Savès **109** C3, **155** D1
Cazères-sur-Garonne **109** C3, **155** D1
Cazères-sur-l'Adour **108** B2
Cazevel **164** B3, **170** A/B1
Cazin **131** C1
Cazorla **167** D3, **168** A3, **173** C/D1
Cazouls-lès-Béziers **110** B3
Cá Zuliani **115** C1
Cdeynia **70** A2
Cdeynia **72** A3
Cea **152** A2
Ceánuri **153** C/D1
Céaucé **86** A2
Cebanico **152** A2
Cebara **131** D3, **132** A3
Cebas **167** D3, **168** A3, **173** D1
Cebolais de Cima **158** B3, **165** C1
Cebolla **160** A/B3, **167** B/C1
Čebovce **95** D2
Cebreros **160** B2
Cebrikovo **141** D1
Cebrones del Río **151** D2/3
Ceccano **119** C2
Cece **129** B/C1/2
Cece **96** B3
Čečersk **99** D1
Čečeviči **99** C1
Čechtice **83** D3
Čechtín **94** A1
Cécina **114** A/B3, **116** A2
Ceclavín **159** C3, **165** D1
Cecos **112** B3
Cedégolo **106** B2
Cedeira **150** B1
Cedillo **158** B3, **165** C1
Cedillo de la Torre **161** C1
Cedovim **158** B3
Cedrillas **162** B2
Cée **150** A2
Cefalù **125** B/C2
Céggia **107** D3, **126** A3
Ceglé d **129** D1
Cegléd **97** C3, **140** A1
Céglie Messápico **121** C2
Čegrane **138** B2
Cehegín **168** B3, **174** A1
Cehnice **93** C1
Čehov **75** D3
Ceilhes-et-Rocozels **110** B2
Ceillac **112** B1
Ceinos de Campos **152** A3
Ceira **158** A3
Čejč **94** B1
Čejkovice **94** B1
Čekalin **75** D3
Čekanje **137** C2
Cela **164** A1
Celada de Roblecedo **152** B2
Celadas **163** C2
Čeladná **95** C/D1
Čelákovice **83** D2/3
Celano **119** C1/2
Celanova **150** B3
Celbridge **58** A2
Čelebić **131** D2/3
Celei **135** D1
Cele Kula **135** C3
Celenza Valfortore **119** D2, **120** A1
Čelić **133** C1
Čelije **133** D2, **134** A2
Čelije **140** A2
Čelinac **131** D1/2, **132** A1
Celje **127** C2
Čelje **96** A3
Cella **114** B1
Cella **163** C2
Celldömölk **128** A1
Celle **68** B2
Celle-Garssen **68** B2
Celle-Gross Hehlen **68** B2
Celle Lígure **113** C2
Celle-Scheuen **68** B2
Celles-sur-Belle **101** C2
Celles-sur-Ource **88** B2
Celliers **104** A/B3
Cellino San Marco **121** D3

Čelopeci **138** B3
Celorico da Beira **158** B2
Celorico de Basto **158** B1
Céltigos **151** B/C2
Cemaes Bay **58** B2
Cembra **107** C2
Čemerno **132** B3, **137** C1
Cenad **129** D2
Cenarth **62** B1
Cencenighe **107** C2
Cendejas de la Torre **161** C2
Cenicero **153** D2
Cenicientos **160** B3
Cenizate **168** B1/2
Cenlle **150** B2
Cenon **108** B1
Censeau **104** A1
Čenta **133** D1, **134** A1
Centallo **112** B2
Centelles **156** A2/3
Cento **114** B1
Centúripe **125** C2
Cepagatti **119** C1
Čepelare **140** B3
Cépet **109** D2
Čepin **128** B3
Čepinci **145** C1
Čepinski Martinci **128** B3
Cepões **158** B2
Čepovan **126** B2
Ceppo **117** D3, **119** C1
Čeralije **128** B3
Cerami **125** C2
Cérans-Foulletourte **86** A/B3
Cerbáia **114** B2/3, **116** B2
Cerbère **156** B2
Cercal **164** A1/2
Cercal **164** A/B3, **170** A1
Cerceda **150** A1
Cerceda **160** B2
Cercedilla **160** B2
Cercemaggiore **119** D2
Cerchiara di Calábria **120** B3, **122** B1
Cercs **156** A2
Cercy-la-Tour **103** C1
Cerda **124** B2
Cerdedo **150** A/B2
Cerdeira **158** B3
Cerdeira **159** C2
Cerdeira **158** B3
Cerdido **150** B1
Cérdigo **153** C1
Cerdon-du-Loiret **87** D3
Cerea **107** C3
Ceremošnia **135** C2
Cerenskoe **75** D1
Cerénzia **122** B2
Čerepovec **75** D1
Céres **105** B/C3
Cerese **114** B1
Ceresole Alba **113** C1
Ceresole Reale **104** B3
Céreste **111** C2
Céret **156** B2
Čerević **129** C/D3, **133** C1, **134** A1
Cerezo de Abajo **161** C1
Cerezo de Arriba **161** C2
Cerezo de Riotirón **153** C2
Ceriale **113** C2
Cerignola **120** B2
Čerikov **99** D1
Cérilly **102** B1/2
Čerín **95** D2
Cerisano **122** A2
Cerisiers **88** A2
Cerisy-la-Forêt **76** A3, **85** D1, **86** A1
Cerizay **100** B1
Čerkassy **99** D3
Cerklje **126** B2
Cerknica **126** B3
Cerkno **126** B2
Cerler **155** C2
Cerna **133** B/C1
Cernache do Bonjardim **158** A3, **164** B1
Cernadoi **107** C2
Černá Hora **94** B1
Cernavodă **141** C/D2
Černá v Pošumaví **93** C/D2
Cernay **89** D3, **90** A3

Cernay-en-Dormois **88** B1
Cerne Abbas **63** D2
Cernégula **153** C2
Černičevo **145** D1
Černigov **99** D2
Černík **95** C2
Cernik **128** A3, **131** D1, **132** A1
Černjahov **99** C2
Černjahovsk (Insterburg) **73** C2
Černóbbio **105** D3, **106** A3
Černobyl' **99** C2
Černošin **82** B3
Černovcy **98** B3
Černovice **93** D1
Černuc **83** C/D2
Cerollera **163** C2
Cérons **108** B1
Cerósimo **120** B3, **122** B1
Cerovac **127** C3, **131** C1
Cerovac **134** B2
Cerovac **133** C/D1, **134** A1/2
Cerováčke spilje **131** C2
Cerovlje **126** B3, **130** A1
Cerovo **95** D2
Cerralbo **159** C2
Cerrédolo **114** B2, **116** A1
Cerreto d'Esi **115** D3, **117** C/D2
Cerreto Sannita **119** D2/3
Cërrik **138** A3, **142** A1
Certaldo **114** B3, **116** A/B2
Certosa di Pésio **113** B/C2
Certosa di Pavia **105** D3, **106** A3, **113** D1
Certosa San Lorenzo **120** A3
Cerva **158** B1
Cervantes **151** C2
Cervarolo **114** A/B2, **116** A1
Cervatos **152** B2
Cervatos de la Cueza **152** A/B2
Červen' **99** C1
Červen brjag **140** B3
Červený Kameň **95** C2
Cervera **155** C3, **163** C1
Cervera de Buitrago **161** C2
Cervera del Río Alhama **153** D3, **154** A3
Cervera del Maestre **163** C2
Cervera de los Montes **160** A3
Cervera del Llano **161** D3, **168** A/B1
Cervera de la Cañada **154** A3, **162** A1
Cervera de Pisuerga **152** B2
Cervéteri **118** A2
Cérvia **115** C2, **117** C1
Cerviá de les Garrigues **163** C/D1
Cerviá de Ter **156** B2
Cervignano del Friuli **126** A3
Cervinara **119** D3
Cervione **113** D3
Cervo **113** C2
Cervo **151** B/C1
Cervon **88** A3, **103** C1
Červonoarmejsk **97** D2, **98** B2
Červonograd **97** D1/2, **98** A2
Červonoznamenka **141** D1
Cerzeto **122** A1
Cesana Torinese **112** B1
Cesarica **130** B2
Cesarò **125** C2
Cesena **115** C2, **117** C1
Cesenático **115** C2, **117** C1
Cēsis **73** D1, **74** A2
Česká Kamenice **83** D2
Česká Kubice **92** B1
Česká Lípa **83** D2
Česká Lípa **96** A1
České Budějovice **96** A2
České Budějovice **93** D1
České Velenice **93** D1
Český Brod **83** D3
Český Dub **83** D2
Český Krumlov **93** D2
Český Krumlov **96** A2
Český Šternberk **83** D3

Český Těšín **96** B2
Češljeva Bara **134** B2
Çeşme **149** C2
Cespedosa **159** D2
Cessalto **107** D3
Cessenon **110** A/B3
Cestereg **129** D3
Čestín **83** D3
Cesuras **150** B1
Cesvaine **74** A2
Cetate **135** D2
Cetina **161** D1
Cetingrad **131** C1
Cetinje **137** C2
Četirci **139** D2
Cetraro **122** A1
Ceutí **169** D3
Ceva **113** C2
Cevico de la Torre **152** B3
Cevico Navero **152** B3
Cevins **104** B3
Cevio [Ponte Brolla] **105** D2
Čevo **137** C2
Ceyrat **103** D2
Ceyzériat **103** D2
Chabanais **101** D2
Chabeuil **111** C/D1
Châble, Le **104** B2
Chablis **88** A3
Chabreloche **103** C2
Chabris **87** C3, **101** D1, **102** A1
Chacim **159** C1
Chaffois **104** A1
Chagny **103** D1
Chaillé-les-Marais **100** B2
Chailley **88** A2
Chailly-en-Brie **87** D1, **88** A1
Chailly-en-Bière **87** D2
Chalabre **109** D3, **156** A1
Chalais **101** C3
Chalamera **155** C3, **163** C1
Chalamont **103** D2
Chalandrítsa **146** B2
Chalet de Peñalara **160** B2
Chalíkion **143** B/C3
Chálki **143** D3
Chalkiádes **143** D3
Chalkidón **143** D1/2
Chalkís **147** D2
Chalkís **148** B2
Challain-la-Potherie **85** D3
Challans **100** A1
Challes-les-Eaux **104** A3
Chalmazel **103** C3
Chalonnes-sur-Loire **86** A3
Châlons-sur-Marne **88** B1
Châlons-sur-Vesle **88** A1
Chalon-sur-Saône **103** D1
Châlus **101** D3
Chalusset **101** C3
Cham **105** C/D1
Cham **92** B1
Chamalières-sur-Loire **103** C2
Chamberet **102** A3
Chambéry **104** A3
Chambilly **103** C2
Chamblet **102** B2
Chambley-Bussières **89** C1
Chambly **77** D3, **87** C/D1
Chambois **86** B1
Chambon-Sainte-Croix **102** A2
Chambon-sur-Voueize **102** A2
Chambon-sur-Lac **102** B3
Chambord **87** C3
Chamboulive **102** A3
Chamerau **92** B1
Chamonix-Mont-Blanc **104** B2/3
Chamoux-sur-Gelon **104** A3
Champagnac-de-Belair **101** C/D3
Champagnac-le-Vieux **102** B2
Champagne-Mouton **101** C2
Champagney **89** D3
Champagnole **104** A1
Champaubert **88** A1

Champ de Bataille **77** C3, **86** B1
Champdeniers **101** B/C2
Champdieu **103** C3
Champeaux **87** D2
Champeix **102** B3
Champenoux **89** C/D1
Champéry **104** B2
Champex [Orsières] **104** B2
Champier **103** D3
Champigné **86** A3
Champignelles **87** D3
Champigny-sur-Veude **101** C1
Champillet **102** A2
Champlitte-et-le-Prélot **89** C3
Champoluc **105** C3
Champoly **103** C2
Champorcher **105** C3
Champrond-en-Gatine **87** B/C2
Champs-sur-Tarentaine **102** A/B3
Champtoceaux **86** A/B3
Chamrousse **104** A3, **112** A1
Cham-Thierlstein **92** B1
Chamusca **164** B1
Cham-Windischbergerdorf **92** B1
Chanac **110** B1/2
Chanas **103** D3
Chancy [Pougny-Chancy Ain] **104** A2
Chandai **86** B1
Chandrexa de Queixa **151** B/C2/3
Changy **103** C2
Chaniótis **144** A/B2
Chantada **150** B2
Chantelle **102** B2
Chantelouve **111** D1, **112** A1
Chantemerle **112** A/B1
Chantilly **87** D1
Chantonnay **100** B1
Chão de Codes **164** B1
Chaource **88** A/B2
Chapa **158** B1
Chapaize **103** D2
Chapareillan **104** A3
Chapel-en-le-Frith **59** D2, **61** C3
Chapelle-Royale **86** B2
Charavgí **143** C2
Charavines-les-Bains **103** D3, **104** A3
Charches **173** D2
Chard **63** C/D2
Charenton-du-Cher **102** B1
Charing **65** C3, **77** C1
Charlbury **64** A2/3
Charleroi **78** B2
Charlestown **55** C2
Charleville-Mézières **79** C3
Charlieu **103** C2
Charlottenberg **38** B3
Charly **87** D1, **88** A1
Charmeil **102** B2
Charmes **89** C/D2
Charmes-sur-Rhône **111** C1
Charmoille **89** C3
Charny **87** D2/3
Charny-sur-Meuse **89** C1
Charolles **103** C2
Chârost **102** A1
Charquemont **89** D3, **104** B1
Charritte-de-Bas **108** A3, **154** B1
Charron **100** B2
Charroux **101** C2
Chars **77** D3, **87** C1
Chartres **87** C2
Chásia Óri **143** C3
Chasseneuil-sur-Bonnieure **101** C2/3
Chastellux **88** A3
Château-Arnoux **112** A2
Châteaubourg **86** A/B2
Châteaubriant **86** A3
Château-Chinon **103** C1
Château-d'Oex **104** B2

Château d'Ô **86** B2
Château d'If **111** D3
Château-du-Loir **86** B3
Châteaudun **86** A/B2
Châteaugay **102** B2
Châteaugiron **85** D2
Château-Gontier **86** A3
Château-l'Évêque **101** C/D3
Château-la-Vallière **86** B3
Château-Landon **87** D2
Châteaulin **84** A/B2
Châteaumeillant **102** A1/2
Châteauneuf-sur-Loire **87** C/D2/3
Châteauneuf-en-Thymerais **86** A/B2
Châteauneuf-du-Faou **84** B2
Châteauneuf-de-Chabre **111** D2, **112** A2
Châteauneuf **88** B3, **103** C/D1
Châteauneuf **103** C2
Châteauneuf-du-Pape **111** C2
Châteauneuf-sur-Charente **101** C3
Châteauneuf-les-Bains **102** B2
Châteauneuf-la-Forêt **101** D3, **102** A3
Châteauneuf-d'Ille-et-Vilaine **85** C/D2
Châteauneuf-de-Randon **110** B1
Châteauneuf-Val-de-Bargis **88** A3, **102** B1
Châteauneuf-sur-Sarthe **86** A3
Châteauneuf-sur-Cher **102** A1
Château-Porcien **78** B3
Châteauponsac **101** C2
Château-Queyras **112** B1
Château-Renault **86** B3
Châteauredon **112** A2
Châteaurenard **87** D2
Châteaurenard **111** C2
Châteauroux-les-Alpes **112** A1
Châteauroux **101** D1, **102** A1
Château-Salins **89** D1
Château-Thierry **88** A1
Châteauvert **112** A3
Châteauvillain **88** B2
Châtel **104** B2
Châtelaillon-Plage **100** B2
Châtelard, Le [Le Châtelard-Frontière] **104** B2
Châtel-Censoir **88** A3
Châtel-de-Neuvre **102** B2
Châteldon **102** B2
Châtelet **78** B2
Châtel-Guyon **102** B2
Châtelineau **78** B2
Châtellerault **101** C1
Châtel-Montagne **103** C2
Châtel-St-Denis **104** B2
Châtel-sur-Moselle **89** D2
Châtelus-Malvalaix **102** A2
Châtenois **89** C2
Châtillon-de-Michaille **104** A2
Châtillon-Coligny **87** D3
Châtillon-en-Diois **111** D1
Châtillon-sur-Seine **88** B3
Châtillon-la-Palud **103** D2
Châtillon-sur-Chalaronne **103** D2
Châtillon-sur-Sèvre **100** B1
Châtillon **105** C3
Châtillon-en-Bazois **103** C1
Châtillon-sur-Loire **87** D3
Châtillon-sur-Indre **101** C1
Châtillon-sur-Marne **88** A1
Châtre **101** C3
Chatsworth **61** C3, **64** A1
Chatteris **65** C2
Chauchina **173** C2
Chaudes-Aigues **110** A/B1
Chau de Ventadour **102** A3
Chaudieu **104** A3
Chaudrey **88** B2

Chauffailles **103** C2
Chaulnes **78** A3
Chaumercenne **89** C3, **104** A1
Chaumont **88** B2
Chaumont-en-Vexin **77** D3, **87** C1
Chaumont-sur-Loire **86** A/B3
Chaumont-sur-Tharonne **87** C3
Chaunay **101** C2
Chauny **78** A3
Chaussin **103** D1, **104** A1
Chauvency-le-Château **79** C3
Chauvigny **101** C/D2
Chaux-de-Fonds, La **104** B1
Chavanges **88** B2
Chávarion **146** A2
Chaves **150** B3, **158** B1
Chazelles-sur-Loyn **103** C3
Cheadle **59** D2, **61** B/C3, **64** A1
Cheb **82** B3
Checa **162** A2
Cheddar **63** D2
Chedgrave **65** D2
Chef-Boutonne **101** C2
Cheffois **100** B1
Chéggio **105** C2
Cheles **165** C2/3
Chella **169** C2
Chelle-Debat **109** C3, **155** C1
Chelles **87** D1
Chełm **97** D1, **98** A2
Chelmós **146** B3
Chelmsford **65** C3
Chełmża **73** B/C3
Chełst **71** C2
Cheltenham **63** D1, **64** A2
Chelva **162** B3, **169** C1
Chéméré-le-Roi **86** A2
Chémery-sur-Bar **79** C3
Chemillé **86** A3, **100** B1
Chemillé-sur-Dême **86** B3
Chemin **103** D1
Chemiré-le-Gaudin **86** A/B2/3
Chemnitz **70** A1
Chénérailles **102** A2
Cheniménil **89** D2
Chenoise **87** D2, **88** A2
Chenonceaux **87** B/C3
Chepstow **63** D1
Chequilla **161** D2, **162** A2
Chera **169** C1
Cherain **79** D2/3
Cherasco **113** C1
Cheray **101** C2
Cherbourg **76** A3
Chercos **173** D2, **174** A2
Chérisy **87** C1
Cherónia **147** C2
Chéroy **87** D2
Chert **163** C2
Chertsey **64** B3, **76** B1
Cherveix-Cubas **101** C3
Cheseaux-sur-Lausanne [Lausanne] **104** B2
Chesham **64** B3
Cheshunt **65** C3
Chéssy-les-Mines **103** C/D2
Chessy-les-Près **88** A2
Cheste **169** C1
Chester **59** D2, **60** B3
Chesterfield **61** C3, **64** A/B1
Chester le Street **57** D3, **61** C1
Chesters **57** C2
Chételaudren **85** B/C2
Chevagnes **103** B/C1/2
Chevanceaux **101** C3
Cheverny **87** C3
Chevillon **88** B2
Chevilly **87** C2
Chevreuse **87** C1/2
Chevron **79** C/D2
Chey **101** C2
Cheylade **102** B3
Chezal-Benoît **102** A1
Chézery-Forens **104** A2
Chialamberto **104** B3

Chiampo **107** C3
Chianale **112** B1
Chianciano Terme **115** C3, **116** B2
Chianni **114** B3, **116** A2
Chiappera **112** B2
Chiappi **112** B2
Chiaramonte Gulfi **125** C3
Chiaramonti **123** C1
Chiaravalle **115** D3, **117** D2
Chiaravalle Centrale **122** B2
Chiaréggio **106** A2
Chiari **106** A3
Chiaromonte **120** B3
Chiasso **105** D3
Chiávari **113** D2
Chiavenna **105** D2, **106** A2
Chiché **101** B/C1
Chichester **76** B1
Chiclana de la Frontera **171** D3
Chiclana de Segura **167** D3, **168** A3
Chieming **92** B3
Chieri **113** C1
Chiesa in Valmalenco **106** A2
Chiesina Uzzanese **114** B2, **116** A1
Chieti **119** C1
Chiéuti **120** A1
Chièvres **78** B2
Chigwell **65** C3
Chilbolton **64** A3, **76** A1
Chilches **162** B3, **169** D1
Chilham **65** C/D3, **77** C1
Chilia Veche **141** D2
Chiliomódion **147** C2/3
Chilivani **123** C/D1/2
Chillarón de Cuenca **161** D3
Chilleurs-aux-Bois **87** C2
Chillón **166** B2
Chillon [Villeneuve] **104** B2
Chiloeches **161** C2
Chimay **78** B3
Chimeneas **173** C2
Chinchilla de Monte Aragón **168** B2
Chinchón **161** C3
Chinon **86** B3, **101** C1
Chióggia **107** D3
Chiomonte **112** B1
Chióna **146** B2
Chipiona **171** C2
Chippenham **63** D2, **64** A3
Chipping Campden **64** A2
Chipping Norton **64** A2
Chipping Ongar **65** C3
Chipping Sodbury **63** D1/2, **64** A3
Chiprana **163** B/C1
Chirivel **173** D1, **174** A2
Chirivella **169** D1
Chirk **59** C/D2/3, **60** B3
Chirnside **57** D2
Chisa **113** D3
Chiusa di Pésio **113** B/C2
Chiusaforte **126** A2
Chiusa/Klausen **107** C2
Chiusa Scláfani **124** B2
Chiusi **115** C3, **116** B2
Chiusi della Verna **115** C2/3, **116** B2
Chiva de Morella **163** B/C2
Chivasso **105** C3, **113** C1
Chivy-les-Etouvelles **78** B3
Chizé **101** B/C2
Chlebowo **70** B3
Chludowo **71** D2
Chlumec **83** C2
Chlum u Třeboně **93** D1
Chobienice **71** C3
Chociule **71** C3
Chociwel **71** C3
Chodos **162** B3
Chodov **82** B2
Chodová Planá **82** B3
Chodzież **71** D2
Choisy-le-Roi **87** D1
Chojna **70** B2
Chojnice **72** B2/3
Chojno **71** D3
Cholet **100** B1
Chomérac **111** C1
Chomutov **83** C2

Chomutov **96** A1
Chóra **146** B3
Choranche **103** D3, **111** D1
Chorefton **144** A3
Chorges **112** A1/2
Chorin **70** B2
Choristí **144** B1
Chorley **59** D2, **60** B2
Chortiátis **144** A2
Chospes **168** A/B2
Choszczno **71** C1/2
Choszczno **72** A/B3
Chotěšov **83** C2
Chouilly **88** A1
Choumnikón **144** A/B1
Choustník **93** D1
Chouto **164** B1/2
Chouvigny **102** B2
Choye **89** C3, **104** A1
Chrást **83** C3
Chrastava **83** D2
Chřibská **83** D2
Chrísafa **147** C3
Chrisochórion **145** C1
Chrisón **147** C2
Chrisoúpolis **145** C1
Christchurch **76** A1
Christiáni **144** B1
Christianón **146** B3
Christiansfeld **52** B1
Chropyně **95** C1
Chróscina **71** D3
Chroúsou **144** B2/3
Chrudim **96** A2
Chrustowo **71** D2
Chrzypsko Wielkie **71** D2
Chudleigh **63** D2
Chueca **160** B3, **167** C1
Chulilla **162** B3, **169** C1
Chulmeigh **63** C2
Chur **106** A1
Church Stretton **59** D3
Churchtown **58** A2
Churwalden [Chur] **106** A1
Chvalovice **94** A2
Chvalšiny **93** D1/2
Chyňava **83** C3
Chynorany **95** C2
Chýnov **93** D1
Chyše **83** C3
Ciadoncha **152** B3
Ciadoux **109** C3, **155** C1
Cianciana **124** B2
Ciano d'Enza **114** A1
Cibanal **159** C1
Cicagna **113** D2
Cicciano **119** D3
Cićevac **134** B3
Ćićevo **137** C1/2
Čičmany **95** D1
Cicognolo **106** B3
Ciconicco **107** D2, **126** A2
Cidadelhe **159** C2
Cidones **153** D3, **161** D1
Ciechanów **73** C3
Ciemnik **71** C2
Ciempozuelos **161** C3
Cierp **109** C3, **155** C2
Cierznie **71** D1
Cieszyn **96** B2
Cieza **169** C3
Cífer **95** C2
Cifuentes **161** C2
Cigales **152** B3, **160** A1
Čigirin **99** D3
Cigliano **105** C3
Cigudosa **153** D3
Cihuela **154** A3, **161** D1
Čineni **140** B2
Čilipi **137** C2
Cillamayor **152** B2
Cillán **160** A2
Cillas **161** D2, **162** A2
Cilleros **159** C3
Cilleruelo de Arriba **153** C3
Cilleruelo de Abajo **153** B/C3
Cillorigo-Castro **152** B1
Cima Cogna **107** D2
Cimalmotto [Ponte Brolla] **105** C/D2
Cimanes del Tejar **151** D2
Cimballa **162** A2
Ciminna **124** B2
Čimišlija **141** D1
Cimoláis **107** D2

Cîmpeni **97** D3, **140** B1
Cîmpu lui Neag **140** B2
Cîmpu lui Neag **135** D1
Cîmpulung **141** B/C2
Cîmpulung Moldovenesc **141** C1
Cinctorres **162** B2
Cinderford **63** D1
Cine **149** D2
Čiňeves **83** D2
Ciney **79** C2
Cinfães **158** B2
Cíngia de'Botti **114** A1
Cíngoli **115** D3, **117** D2
Cinigiano **116** B3
Cinisello Bálsamo **105** D3, **106** A3
Cínovec **83** C2
Cintegabelle **109** D3, **155** D1
Cintrey **89** C3
Cintruénigo **154** A3
Cional **151** D3
Ciordia **153** D2
Cioroiasi **135** D2
Ciosaniec **71** C3
Ciovîrnăsani **135** D1
Cipérez **159** C/D2
Čiprovci **135** D3
Cirák **94** B3
Cirat **162** B3
Cirauqui **153** D2, **154** A2
Cirella **122** A1
Cirencester **63** D1, **64** A3
Cirey-sur-Vezouze **89** D2, **90** A2
Ciria **153** D3, **154** A3, **161** D1
Cirie **105** C3, **112** B1
Cirigliano **120** B3
Cîrlibaba **141** B/C1
Cirò **122** B1
Cirò Marina **122** B1/2
Ciron **101** C1/2
Cîrpan **141** C3
Cirque d'Archiane **111** D1
Cirque de Consolation **104** B1
Cirque de Gavarnie **155** C2
Cirque de Navacelles **110** B2
Cirque de Troumouse **155** C2
Ciruelos **161** C3, **167** C/D1
Ciry-le-Noble **103** C1/2
Cismon del Grappa **107** C2/3
Cisnădie **140** B1/2
Cisneros **152** A2/3
Čistá **82** B3
Čistá **83** C3
Cisterna di Latina **118** B2
Cisternino **121** C2
Cistierna **152** A2
Ciszkowo **71** D2
Čitluk **135** C3
Čitluk **132** A/B3, **136** B1
Cítov **83** D2
Città della Pieve **115** C3, **117** B/C2/3
Cittadella **107** C3
Cittadella del Capo **122** A1
Città del Vaticano **118** B2
Città di Castello **115** C3, **117** C2
Cittaducale **117** C3, **118** B1
Cittanova **122** A3
Cittareale **117** D3, **118** B1
Città Sant'Ángelo **119** C1
City Airport **65** C3
Ciucea **97** D3, **140** B1
Ciuchesu **123** D1
Ciucurova **141** D2
Ciudadela **157** C1
Ciudad Encantada **161** D3
Ciudad Real **167** C2
Ciudad Rodrigo **159** C2
Ciupercenii-Noi **135** D2/3
Civaux **101** C/D2
Cividale del Friuli **126** A2
Cividate Camuno **106** B2
Civitacampomarano **119** D2

Cívita Castellana **117** C3, **118** B1
Civitanova del Sánnio **119** D2
Civitanova Marche **117** D2, **130** A3
Civitavécchia **118** A1/2
Civitella Casanova **117** D3, **119** C1
Civitella d'Agliano **117** C3, **118** A1
Civitella del Tronto **117** D3, **119** C1
Civitella di Romagna **115** C2, **116** B1
Civitella Maríttima **114** B3, **116** B2/3
Civitella Roveto **119** C2
Civray **101** C2
Civrieux-d'Azergues **103** D2
Cizur **154** A2
Clachan **56** A2
Clacton-on-Sea **65** C3
Clairac **109** C2
Clairvaux-les-Lacs **104** A2
Clamecy **88** A3
Clapham **59** D1, **60** B2
Clare **65** C2
Clarés **154** A3, **161** D1, **162** A1
Clausholm **48** B2
Clausnitz **83** C2
Clausthal-Zellerfeld **68** B3
Cláut **107** D2
Claviere **112** B1
Clavière **112** B1
Clavijo **153** D2
Claydon **65** D2
Claye-Souilly **87** D1
Cleanov **135** D2
Cleanov **140** D2
Clécy **86** A1
Cleethorpes **61** D2/3
Cleeve Abbey **63** C2
Clefmont **89** C2
Cléguérec **84** B2
Clelles-en-Trièves **111** D1
Clémont **87** D3
Clenze **69** C2
Cleobury Mortimer **59** D3, **64** A2
Cléon-d'Andran **111** C1
Cléré-les-Pins **86** B3
Clères **77** C3
Clergoux **102** A3
Clermain **103** C/D2
Clermont **77** D3, **87** D1
Clermont-Créans **86** A/B3
Clermont-en-Argonne **88** B1
Clermont-Ferrand **102** B2/3
Clermont-l'Hérault **110** B3
Clerval **89** D3, **104** B1
Clervaux (Clerf) **79** D3
Cléry-Saint-André **87** C3
Cles **107** B/C2
Clevedon **63** D2
Cleveleys **59** C1, **60** B2
Cley **65** C/D1
Clifden **55** C2
Cliffe **65** C3
Clisson **101** C1
Clitheroe **59** D1, **60** B2
Cliveden **64** B3
Clogherhead **58** A1
Cloghy **56** A2
Clonakilty **55** C3
Clondalkin **58** A2
Clonee **58** A2
Clonmel **55** C/D3
Clophill **64** B2
Clopodia **134** B1
Cloppenburg **67** D2
Closani **135** D1
Clough **58** A1
Clough **54** A3, **55** D2
Clovelly **62** B2
Cloyes-sur-le-Loir **86** A/B2
Clue d'Aiglun **112** B2
Clugnat **102** A2
Cluis **102** A1/2
Cluj-Napoca **97** D3, **140** B1
Clun **59** C/D3
Cluny **103** C/D2

Cluses 104 B2
Clusone 106 A/B2/3
Clydebank 56 B2
Clynnog-fawr 58 B2
Coalville 65 C1
Coaña 151 C1
Coarraze 108 B3, 154 B1
Coatbridge 56 B2
Cobadin 141 D2
Cóbdar 173 D2, 174 A2
Cobertelada 161 D1
Cobeta 161 D2
Cobh 55 C3
Cobham 65 C3, 77 C1
Cobisa 160 B3, 167 C1
Cobos de Cerrato 152 B3
Coburg 81 D2, 82 A2
Coburg-Creidlitz 81 D2/3,
    82 A2
Coca 160 B1
Cocaali 145 D2
Coccau 126 A/B2
Cocentaina 169 D2
Cochem 80 A3
Cockburnspath 57 D2
Cockermouth 57 C3, 60 A1
Coclois 88 B2
Coculina 152 B2
Codaruina 123 C1
Codes 161 D2
Codigoro 115 C1
Codlea 141 C1/2
Codo 162 B1
Codognè 107 D2/3
Codogno 106 A3, 113 D1,
    114 A1
Codos 163 C1
Codróipo 107 D2, 126 A2
Coentral 158 A3
Coesfeld 67 C/D3
Coesfeld-Lette 67 C/D3
Coevorden 67 C2
Cofrentes 169 C2
Cogeces de Monte 152 B3,
    160 B1
Coggeshall 65 C2/3
Cognac 101 C3
Cogne 104 B3
Cognin 104 A3
Cogoleto 113 C2
Cogolin 112 A3
Cogollos 153 C2
Cogollos de Guadix 173 C2
Cogollos Vega 173 C2
Cogolludo 161 C2
Cógolo 106 B2
Cohade 102 B3
Coimbra 158 A3
Coimbrão 158 A3, 164 A1
Coín 172 B2
Coirós 150 B1
Coja 158 B3
Čoka 129 D2/3
Col 126 B2/3
Cola 170 A1
Colares 164 A2
Colaret 135 D2
Cölbe 81 B/C2
Cölbe-Bürgeln 81 B/C2
Cölbe-Schönstadt 81 B/C2
Colbitz 69 C/D3
Colchester 65 C2
Coldingham 57 D2
Colditz 82 B1
Coldstream 57 D2
Coleford 63 D1
Colembert 77 D1
Colera 156 B2
Coleraine 54 A3, 55 D2
Coles 150 B2
Coleshill 64 A2
Colfiorito 115 D3, 117 C2
Cólico 105 D2, 106 A2
Coligny 103 D2
Colindres 153 C1
Collado Hermoso 160 B2
Collado Villalba 160 B2
Collagna 114 A2, 116 A1
Collanzo 151 D1, 152 A1
Collarmele 119 C1/2
Colldejou 163 D2
Coll de Nargó 155 C2/3
Collebarucci 114 B2,
    116 B1
Collécchio 114 A1
Colle di Tora 117 C3,
    118 B1

Colle di Val d'Elsa 114 B3,
    116 B2
Colleferro 118 B2
Collegno 112 B1
Colle Isarco/Gossensass
    107 C1
Collelongo 119 C2
Collenberg 81 C3
Collepardo 119 C2
Collepasso 121 D3
Collesalvetti 114 A/B3,
    116 A2
Colle Sannita 119 D2,
    120 A1
Collesano 124 B2
Colletorto 119 D2, 120 A1
Colli a Volturno 119 C2
Colli di Montebove
    118 B1/2
Collinas 123 C3
Collinée 85 C2
Cóllio 106 B3
Collioure 156 B2
Collobrières 112 A3
Collon 58 A1
Collonges 104 A2
Colmar 90 A2/3
Colmars 112 A2
Colmberg 91 D1
Colmenar 172 B2
Colmenar de la Sierra
    161 C2
Colmenar de Oreja 161 C3
Colmenar de Montemayor
    159 D2/3
Colmenar del Arroyo
    160 B2
Colmenar Viejo 160 B2
Colmonell 56 B3
Colne 59 D1, 60 B2
Colobraro 120 B3
Cologna 115 C1
Cologna Véneta 107 C3
Cologne-du-Gers 109 C2
Cologno al Sério 106 A3
Cologno Monzese 105 D3,
    106 A3
Colombey-les-deux-Eglises
    88 B2
Colombey-les-Belles 89 C2
Colombier 104 B1
Colombiès 110 A2
Colomby 76 A3
Colomera 173 C2
Colomers 156 B2
Colonia de San Pedro
    157 C1/2
Colonia de Sant Jordi
    157 D2
Colonne 113 D1
Colorno 114 A1
Colos 170 A1
Cölpin 70 A1
Colsey 65 C3
Colsterworth 61 D3, 64 D1
Colunga 152 A1
Colungo 155 C2/3
Colwyn Bay 59 C2, 60 A3
Colyton 63 C2
Coma 115 D2/3, 156 A2
Comácchio 115 C1
Comănești 141 C1
Comano Terme 106 B2
Comares 172 B2
Coma-ruga 163 D1
Combarros 151 D2
Combeaufontaine 89 C3
Combe Martin 63 C2
Comber 56 A3
Combles 78 A3
Combourg 85 D2
Combres 87 B/C2
Combronde 102 B2
Comeglians 107 D2,
    126 A2
Comillas 152 B1
Cómiso 125 C3
Comlosu Mare 129 D3
Commana 84 B2
Commensacq 108 A/B2
Commentry 102 B2
Commequiers 100 A1
Commerau 83 D1
Commercy 89 C1
Commessággio 114 B1
Como 105 D3, 106 A3
Comorîste 134 B1

Cómpeta 172 B2
Compiègne 78 A3
Comporta 164 A3
Compreignac 101 C2
Comps-sur-Artuby 112 A3
Comrie 56 B1
Comunanza 117 D2/3
Cona 107 C3
Conca 113 D3
Concarneau 84 B2/3
Conceição 164 B3, 170 A1
Conceição 170 B2
Conceição 170 B2
Concerviano 117 C/D3,
    118 B1
Concha 161 D2
Conches-en-Ouche 86 B1
Concórdia sulla Sécchia
    114 B1
Concots 109 D1/2
Condado 153 C2
Condamine-Châtelard
    112 B2
Condat-en-Féniers 102 B3
Condat-lès-Monboissier
    102 B3
Condè-en-Brie 88 A1
Condeixa a Nova 158 A3
CONDEON 101 C3
Condé-sur-l'Escaut 78 B2
Condé-sur-Noireau 86 A1
Condé-sur-Vesgre 87 C1/2
Condino 106 B2/3
Condofuri 122 A3
Condom 109 C2
Condove 112 B1
Condrieu 103 D3
Conegliano 107 D2/3
Conflans-en-Jarnisy 89 C1
Conflans-Sainte-Honorine
    87 C1
Conflans-sur-Lanterne
    89 C3
Conflenti 122 A/B2
Confolens 101 C/D2
Confrides 169 C2
Congleton 59 D2, 60 B3,
    64 A1
Congosto de Valdavia
    152 B2
Coniale 115 B/C2, 116 B1
Conil de la Frontera 171 D3
Conimbriga 158 A3
Coniston 59 C1, 60 B1/2
Conlie 86 A/B2
Conlig 56 A3
Connah's Quay 59 C2,
    60 B3
Connantre 88 A1/2
Connaux 111 C2
Connel 56 A1
Connerré 86 B2
Čonoplja 129 C3
Conques 110 A1
Conques-sur-Orbiel
    110 A3, 156 A/B1
Conquista 167 C3
Conquista de la Sierra
    166 A1
Consélice 115 C1
Consell 157 C2
Conselve 107 C3
Consenvoye 89 C1
Consett 57 D3, 61 C1
Constancia 164 B1
Constanța 141 D2
Constantí 163 C1/2
Constantim 151 D3,
    159 C/D1
Constantina 166 A3,
    171 D1, 172 A1
Consuegra 167 D1
Consuma 115 C2,
    116 B1/2
Contada 119 D3
Contadero 167 C3
Contarina 115 C1
Contay 78 A3
Contessa Entellina
    124 A/B2
Conthil 89 D1
Contigliano 117 C3,
    118 B1
Contis-Plage 108 B2
Contres 87 D2
Contrexéville 89 C2
Contrisson 88 B1

Controne 120 A2/3
Contursi 120 A2
Contwig 90 A1
Conty 77 D3
Convento de la Rábida
    171 C2
Convento di Fonte Colombo
    117 C3, 118 B1
Conversano 121 C2
Conweiler 90 B1/2
Conwy 59 C2, 60 A3
Cookham 64 B3
Coombe Hill 63 D1, 64 A2
Coombes 63 C2
Copertino 121 D3
Copons 155 D3, 156 A3,
    163 D1
Copparo 115 C1
Coppenbrügge 68 B3
Coppet 104 A2
Copplestone 63 C2
Corabia 140 B2
Córaci 122 B2
Corato 120 B2, 136 A3
Coray 84 B2
Corbalán 162 B2/3
Corbeil-Essonnes 87 D2
Corbeilles-du-Gâtinais
    87 D2
Corbera de Alcira 169 D2
Corbera d'Ebre 163 C2
Corbie 78 A3
Corbigny 88 A3, 103 C1
Corbridge 57 D3, 61 B/C1
Corby 64 B2
Corchiano 117 C3, 118 B1
Corciano 115 C3, 117 C2
Corcieux 89 D2, 90 A2
Córcoles 161 D2
Corconne 110 B2
Corconte 152 B1/2
Corcova 135 D1/2
Corcoya 172 B2
Corcubión 150 A2
Cordenòns 107 D2, 126 A2
Cordes 109 D2
Cordesse 103 C1
Cordignano 107 D2
Córdoba 166 B3, 172 B1
Córdobilla de Lácara
    165 D2
Cordovado 107 D2/3,
    126 A3
Corduente 161 D2
Corella 154 A3
Corera 153 D2
Coreses 151 D3, 152 A3,
    159 D1
Corga 158 A2
Corgo 151 B/C2
Cori 118 B2
Coria 159 C3
Coria del Río 171 D2
Coriano 115 D2, 117 C1
Corigliano Cálabro 122 B1
Corinaldo 115 D2/3,
    117 C/D2
Corinium 131 C2
Coripe 172 A2
Cork (Corcaigh) 55 C3
Corlătel 135 D2
Corlay 84 B2
Corleone 124 B2
Corleto Perticara 120 B3
Corlier 103 D2, 104 A2
Çorlu 149 D1
Cormainville 87 C2
Cormatin 103 D2
Cormeilles 77 C3, 86 B1
Corme-Porto 150 A1
Cormery 86 B3, 101 D1
Cormons 126 A2
Cormoz 103 D2
Cornago 153 D3
Cornaredo 105 D3
Cornberg 81 C1
Cornea 135 C1
Cornelian d'Alba 113 C1
Cornella 156 A3
Cornellà del Terri 156 B2
Cornellana 151 D1
Cornereva 135 C1
Corníglio 114 A1/2
Cornimont 89 D2, 90 A3
Corniolo 115 C2, 116 B1
Cornštejn 94 A1

Cornuda 107 C3
Cornudella de Montsant
    163 D1
Cornudilla 153 C2
Cornus 110 B2
Corny-sur-Moselle 89 C1
Coronado 158 A1
Çorovoda 142 A/B2
Corpa 161 C2
Corps 111 D1, 112 A1
Corps Nuds 85 D2
Corral de Almaguer 161 C3,
    167 D1, 168 A1
Corral de Ayllón 161 C1
Corral de Cal 167 C2
Corrales 159 D1
Corrales 171 C2
Corral-Rubio 169 C2
Corre 89 C2/3
Corredoiras 150 B1/2
Corréggio 114 B1
Corrèze 102 A3
Corridónia 117 D2
Corrie 56 A2
Corsavy 156 B2
Corsham 63 D2, 64 A3
Corsicana 113 D3
Córsico 105 D3, 106 A3
Čortanovci 133 D1, 134 A1
Corte 113 D3
Corteconcepción 165 D3,
    171 C1
Corte de Peleas 165 D2
Corte do Pinto 170 B1
Cortegada 150 B2
Cortegada 150 B3
Cortegana 165 C/D3,
    171 C1
Cortelazor 165 D3, 171 C1
Cortemaggiore 114 A1
Cortemília 113 C1/2
Córteno Golgi 106 B2
Corteolona 105 D3,
    106 A3, 113 D1
Corteraso/Kurzras 106 B1
Cortes 154 A3
Cortes de Aragón 162 B2
Cortes de Arenoso 162 B3
Cortes de Baza 173 D1
Cortes de la Frontera
    172 A2/3
Cortes de Pallás 169 C1/2
Cortiguera 151 C2
Cortina d'Ampezzo
    107 C/D2
Čortkov 98 B3
Cortona 115 C3, 117 B/C2
Coruche 164 B2
Corullón 151 C2
Coruña del Conde 153 C3,
    161 C1
Corvara in Badia 107 C2
Corvera de Asturias 151 D1
Corvey 68 B3
Corwen 59 C2/3, 60 A3
Coryton 65 C3
Corzu 135 D2
Cosa 116 B3
Cosa 163 C2
Cosenza 122 A/B2
Cosham 76 A1
Čosići 132 A2
Coslada 161 C2
Cosne-d'Allier 102 B2
Cosne-sur-Loire 87 D3
Cospeito 150 B1
Cossato 105 C3
Cossé-le-Vivien 85 D2,
    86 A2
Cossonay 104 B2
Costa da Caparica 164 A2
Costa de los Pinos 167 D1
Costa Nova 158 A2
Costaros 110 B1
Costeán 155 C3
Costesti 140 B2
Costigliole Saluzzo
    112 B1/2
Costigliole d'Asti 113 C1
Costur 163 B/C3
Cosuenda 163 C1
Coswig 69 D3
Coswig 83 C1
Cotehele House 62 B3
Cotillas 168 A3
Cotobade 150 A2
Cotronei 122 B2

Cottanello **117** C3, **118** B1
Cottbus **70** B3
Cottbus **72** A3, **96** A1
Cottendorf **81** D2, **82** A2
Coubert **87** D1/2
Couches-les-Mines **103** C1
Couço **164** B2
Coucouron **110** B1
Coucy-le-Château Auffrigue **78** A3
Coudes **102** B3
Coudons **156** A1
Couflens **155** C2
Couhé **101** C2
Couilly-Pont-aux-Dames **87** D1
Couiza **110** A3, **156** A1
Coulange-la-Vineuse **88** A3
Coulanges-sur-Yonne **88** A3
Coulans-sur-Gée **86** A/B2
Coullons **87** D3
Coulmier-le-Sec **88** B3
Coulmiers **87** C2/3
Coulommiers **87** D1
Coulon **100** B2
Coulonges-en-Tardenois **88** A1
Coulonges-sur-l'Autize **100** B2
Coulport **56** B1
Coupar Angus **57** C1
Couptrain **86** A2
Coura **150** A3
Courances **87** D2
Courcelles-Chaussy **89** D1
Courcelles-sur-Nied **89** C/D1
Courchaton **89** D3
Courchevel **104** B3
Cour-Cheverny **87** C3
Courcité **86** A2
Courcôme **101** C2
Courçon **100** B2
Cour-et-Buis **103** D3
Courgains **86** B2
Courgenard **86** B2
Courgenay **89** D3, **90** A3, **104** B1
Courmangoux **103** D2
Courmayeur **104** B3
Courniou **110** A3
Courpière **103** B/C3
Cours **103** C2
Coursan **110** A/B3, **156** B1
Coursegoules **112** B2/3
Courseulles-sur-Mer **76** B3, **86** A1
Courson-les-Carrières **88** A3
Courtacon **88** A1/2
Courtalain **86** A/B2
Courteilles **86** B1
Courtenay **87** D2
Courthézon **111** C2
Courtomer **86** B2
Courtown Harbour **58** A3
Court-Saint-Étienne **79** B/C2
Courville-sur-Eure **86** A/B2
Cousolre **78** B2
Coussac-Bonneval **101** C3
Coussegrey **88** A2
Coussey **89** C2
Coustellet **111** D2
Coustouges **156** B2
Coutainville-Plage **85** D1
Coutances **85** D1
Couterne **86** A2
Couthenans **89** D3
Coutras **108** B1
Couvent de Corbara **113** D2
Couvent Sainte-Marie **113** D3
Couvet **104** B1
Couvin **78** B3
Couzan **103** C3
Couze-et-Saint-Front **109** C1
Covadonga **152** A1
Covaleda **153** C3
Covanera **153** B/C2
Covarrubias **153** C3
Covas **158** A1
Covasna **141** C1

Coveiu **135** D2
Covelães **150** B3, **158** B1
Covelo **150** A/B2/3
Coventry **64** A2
Coverack **62** B3
Čoviči **130** B1
Covide **150** B3, **158** A1
Covigliáio **114** B2, **116** B1
Covilhã **158** B3
Cowbridge **63** C2
Cowdenbeath **57** C1
Cowes **76** B1
Cowley **65** C3
Cox **109** C2
Coxwold **61** D2
Cózar **167** D2, **168** A2
Cozes **100** B3
Cozvíjar **173** C2
Cozzano **113** D3
Craco **120** B3
Crăguești **135** D1
Craighouse **56** A2
Craighouse **54** A2/3, **55** D1
Craignure **56** A1
Crail **57** C1
Crailsheim **91** D1
Crailsheim-Jagstheim **91** C/D1
Craiova **140** B2
Cranborne **63** D2, **76** A1
Cranbrook **65** C3, **77** C1
Crançot **104** A1/2
Cranleigh **64** B3, **76** B1
Cransac **110** A1
Crans-sur-Sierre [Sierre] **105** C2
Cranwell **61** D3, **64** B1
Craon **85** D2/3, **86** A2/3
Craponne-sur-Arzon **103** C3
Crasna **141** C1
Crassier [Nyon] **104** A2
Craster **57** D2
Crato **165** C1/2
Cravant **87** C3
Craven Arms **59** D3
Crawford **57** C2
Crawinkel **81** D2
Crawley **65** B/C3, **76** B1
Creagorry **54** A2
Crecente **150** B3
Crécy-en-Brie **87** D1
Crécy-en-Ponthieu **77** D2
Crécy-sur-Serre **78** B3
Crediton **63** C2
Creetown **56** B3, **60** A1
Creglingen **81** D3, **91** C/D1
Creil **87** D1
Crema **106** A3
Crémieu **103** D3
Cremlingen **69** C3
Cremona **114** A1
Čbrensovci **127** D2
Créon **108** B1
Crepaja **133** D1, **134** B1
Crépey **89** C2
Crépy-en-Laonnois **78** A/B3
Crépy-en-Valois **87** D1
Cres **130** A1
Crescentino **105** C3, **113** C1
Crespadoro **107** C3
Crespino **115** C1
Crespos **160** A2
Cressensac **109** D1
Crest **111** C/D1
Cresta, Avers- [Thusis] **106** A2
Cretas **163** C2
Creully **76** B3, **86** A1
Creussen **82** A3
Creussen-Seidwitz **82** A3
Creutzwald **89** D1
Creuzburg **81** D1
Crevalcore **114** B1
Crèvecoeur-le-Grand **77** D3
Crevedia Mare **141** C2
Crevillente **169** C3
Crevola d'Óssola **105** C2
Crewe **59** D2, **60** B3, **64** A1
Crewkerne **63** D2
Crézancy **88** A1
Crianlarich **56** B1
Crianlarich **54** A/B2, **55** D1
Criccieth **59** B/C2/3, **60** A3

Crickhowell **63** C1
Cricklade **63** D1, **64** A3
Crieff **56** B1
Crieff **54** B2
Criel-Plage **76** B2
Criel-sur-Mer **76** B2
Crikvenica **127** C3, **130** B1
Crillon **77** D3
Crimmitschau **82** B2
Crinan **56** A1
Criquetot-l'Esnéval **77** B/C3
Crišnjevo **126** B3, **130** B1
Crispiano **121** C2
Crissolo **112** B1
Cristina **165** D2, **166** A2
Cristóbal **159** D2
Cristuru Secuiesc **141** B/C1
Crivaia **135** C1
Crivillén **162** B2
Crivitz **69** C/D1
Črmošnjice **127** C3
Crna **127** C2
Crna Bara **133** C1
Crnac **133** D3, **138** A/B1
Crnac **128** B3
Crna Rijeka **131** D2, **132** A2
Crna Trava **139** C1
Crne Lokve **132** A3
Crniljevo **133** C2
Crni Lug **127** C3, **130** B1
Crni Lug **131** D2
Črni Vrh nad Idrija **126** B2/3
Črnkovci **128** B3
Črnomelj **127** C3
Črnuče **126** B2
Crock **81** D2, **82** A2
Crocketford **56** B3, **60** A1
Crocq **102** A2
Crodo **105** C2
Croft **57** D3, **61** C1
Croglin **57** C3, **60** B1
Croix de Chamrousse **104** A3, **112** A1
Croix-Valmer **112** A3
Crolles **104** A3
Cromarty **54** B2
Cromer **61** D3, **65** C1
Crosmières **86** A3
Crosscar **58** A1
Crossmaglen **58** A1
Crossmichael **56** B3, **60** A1
Crotone **122** B2
Crottendorf **82** B2
Croutelle **101** C2
Crowborough **76** B1
Crowland **65** B/C1
Crowle **61** C2
Croxton Kerrial **61** C/D3, **64** B1
Croydon **65** C3, **76** B1
Crozant **101** D2, **102** A2
Crozon **84** A2
Cruas **111** C1
Crúcoli Torretta **122** B1
Crulai **86** B1/2
Cruseilles **104** A2
Crussol **111** C1
Cruz **158** A1
Cruzy **110** A3, **156** B1
Cruzy-le-Châtel **88** B3
Crveni Grm **132** A3, **136** B1
Crvenka **129** C3
Crvljivac **133** C3
Crymmych Arms **62** B1
Csabacsüd **129** D1
Csabrendek **128** A1
Csákánydoroszló **127** D1
Csákberény **95** C/D3, **128** B1
Csákvár **95** D3, **128** B1
Csanytelek **129** D2
Csapod **94** B3
Császár **95** C3
Császártöltés **129** C2
Csávoly **129** C2

Csengöd **129** C2
Csépa **129** D1
Csepreg **94** B3, **128** A1
Cserdi **128** B2
Cserebökény **129** D1/2
Cserkeszölö **129** D1
Csesztreg **127** D1/2
Csokonyavisonta **128** A2
Csömend **128** A2
Csongrád **129** D2
Csopak **128** B1
Csór **128** B1
Csorna **95** B/C3
Csót **95** C3, **128** A/B1
Csurgó **128** A2
Csurgó **96** B3
Cuacos **159** D3
Cuadros **151** D2, **152** A2
Cualedro **150** B3
Cuart de Poblet **169** D1
Cuatretonda **169** D2
Cuba **164** B3
Cubel **162** A2
Cubelles **150** A3, **163** D1
Cubells **155** D3
Cubières **156** B1
Cubillas de Cerrato **152** B3, **160** B1
Cubillas de los Oteros **151** D2, **152** A2
Cubillos **153** C3, **161** C1
Cubillos **151** D3, **159** D1
Cubla **162** A/B3
Cubo de Bureba **153** C2
Cubo de la Solana **153** D3, **161** D1
Cucalón **163** C2
Cucho **153** C/D2
Cuckfield **76** B1
Cudillero **151** D1
Cuéllar **160** B1
Cuenca **166** A3
Cuenca **161** D3
Cuenca de Campos **152** A3
Cuers **112** A3
Cuerva **160** B3, **167** C1
Cueva de Ágreda **154** A3, **161** D1, **162** A1
Cueva de Altamira **152** B1
Cueva de Canalobre **169** D2/3
Cueva de la Vieja **169** D2
Cueva de la Pileta **172** A2
Cueva del Aguila **160** A3
Cueva del Hierro **161** D2
Cueva de los Chorros **168** A/B3
Cueva dels Civils y dels Cavalls **163** C2/3
Cueva de Minateda **168** B3
Cueva de Montesino **167** D2, **168** A2
Cueva de Valporquero **151** D2, **152** A2
Cueva Na Polida **157** C1
Cueva Remigia **163** B/C2
Cueva Rosegador **163** C2
Cueva Santa **162** B3, **169** C1
Cuevas Bajas **172** B2
Cuevas de Amaya **152** B2
Cuevas de Artá **157** C1
Cuevas de Campanet **157** C2
Cuevas del Almanzora **174** A2
Cuevas del Becerro **172** A2
Cuevas del Drach **157** C1/2
Cuevas del Valle **160** A3
Cuevas de Nerja **173** C2
Cuevas de San Clemente **153** C3
Cuevas de San Marcos **172** B2
Cuevas de Santimaminie **153** D1
Cuevas de Velasco **161** D3
Cuevas de Vinromá **163** C3
Cuevas Labradas **161** D2
Cuevas Labradas **162** A/B2
Cuevas Minadas **161** D2
Cuges-les-Pins **111** D3
Cúglieri **123** C2

Cugny **78** A3
Cuijk **66** B3
Cuiseaux **103** D2, **104** A2
Cuisery **103** D2
Cujmir **135** D2
Cujmir **140** B2
Čukljenik **139** C1
Culan **102** A2
Culemborg **66** B3
Culgaith **57** C3, **60** B1
Culine **133** C2
Culjković **133** C1
Culla **162** B3
Cúllar-Baza **173** D1
Cullera **169** D2
Culleredo **150** A1
Cullompton **63** C2
Cully **104** B2
Culoz **104** A3
Cuma **119** C3
Cumbernauld **56** B2
Cumbres de Enmedio **165** D3
Cumbres de San Bartolomé **165** D3
Cumbres Mayores **165** D3, **171** C1
Cumiana **112** B1
Cumieira **158** B1
Cumnock and Holmhead **56** B2
Cumrew **57** C3, **60** B1
Cumwhitton **57** C3, **60** B1
Cunault **86** A3, **101** C1
Cunchillos **154** A3
Cunèges **109** C1
Cúneo **112** B2
Cunewalde **83** D1
Cunfin **88** B2
Cunlhat **103** B/C3
Čunski **130** A2
Cuntis **150** A2
Cuorgnè **105** C3
Cupar **57** C1
Cupello **119** D1/2
Cupra Maríttima **117** D2
Cupramontana **115** D3, **117** D2
Čuprene **135** C/D3
Čuprija **134** B2/3
Curalha **150** B3, **158** B1
Čurilovo **74** B2/3
Curinga **122** A/B2
Curon Venosta/Graun im Vinschgau **106** B1
Curraj i Epërm **138** A2
Curtarolo **107** C3
Curtatone **106** B3, **114** B1
Curtea de Arges **140** B2
Curtis **150** B1
Curtis-Estación **150** B1
Čurug **129** D3
Cusano Mutri **119** D2
Cuse-et-Adrisans **89** D3
Cushendall **56** A3
Cushendun **56** A3
Cusiano **106** B2
Cusset **102** B2
Cussy-les-Forges **88** A3
Custines **89** C1
Cusy **104** A3
Cutanda **163** C2
Cutigliano **114** B2, **116** A1
Cutro **122** B2
Cutrofiano **121** D3
Cuvilly **78** A3
Cuxac-d'Aude **110** A/B3, **156** B1
Cuxhaven **52** A3, **68** A1
Cuxhaven-Altenbruch **52** A3, **68** A1
Cuxhaven-Altenwalde **52** A3, **68** A1
Cuzago **105** C2
Cuzzola **123** D1
Cvikov **83** D2
Čvrstec **127** D2, **128** A2
Cwmbran **63** C1
Cybinka **71** D1
Cynwyl Elfed **62** B1
Cysoing **78** A2
Czacz **71** D2
Czaplinek **71** D1
Czarne **71** D1
Czarnków **71** D2
Czarnków **72** B3
Czempiń **71** D3

Czernina 71 D3
Czersk 72 B2/3
Czerwieńsk 71 C3
Czerwona Woda 83 D1
Częstochowa 97 B/C1
Człopa 71 C/D2
Człuchów 72 B3
Czmon 71 D3

D

Daaden 80 B2
Dåasdammen 39 D1
Dabar 130 B1
Dabas 129 C1
Dabel 53 D3, 69 D1
Dąbie 71 C3
Dabilja 139 D3
Dabo 89 D2, 90 A2
Dąbrowa Tarnowska
97 C2
Dąbrówka Wielkopolska
71 C3
Dachau 92 A2
Dachsenhausen 80 B2
Dačice 94 A1
Dad 95 C3
Dådesjö 51 C1
Dadiá 145 D1, 145 D3
Dåfjord 4 A2
Dáfnai 146 B2
Dáfni 144 B2
Dáfni 146 B2/3
Dáfni 149 C1
Dagali 37 C3
Daganzo de Arriba 161 C2
Dagarn 39 D3
Dagda 74 B2
Dagebüll 52 A2
Daggrø 43 C1
Dagmersellen 105 C1
Dagsmark 20 A3
Dahlem 79 D2
Dahlem-Schmidtheim
79 D2
Dahlen 82 B1
Dahlen 70 A1
Dahlen 69 D2
Dahlenburg 69 C1/2
Dahlewitz 70 A3
Dahme 70 A3
Dahme 53 C3
Dahn 90 A/B1
Dähre 69 C2
Dailly 56 B2
Daimiel 167 D2
Dajkanberg 15 C3
Dajkanvik 15 C3
Đakovački Selci 128 B3,
132 B1
Đakovica 138 A2
Đakovica 140 A3
Đakovo 128 B3, 132 B1
Daksbruk (Taalintehdas)
24 B3
Dal 30 B3, 35 D2
Dal 38 A3
Dala 30 B3, 35 D2
Đala 129 D2
Dalaas 30 A/B1
Dalabojegoatte 5 D3, 6 A3,
11 D1
Dalarö 47 D1
Dalåsen 34 B2
Dalasjö 30 A/B1
Dalavardo 15 C2
Dalbeattie 56 B3, 60 A1
Dalby 50 B3
Dalby 38 B2
Dalby 58 B1
Dalby 72 A2
Dalbyn 39 D1/2
Dale 62 B1
Dale 9 C1
Dale 36 A3
Dale 36 A2
Dale 43 C2
Dale 43 C2
Dale 32 A/B2
Dalen 67 C2
Dalen 43 C2
Dalen 33 C3, 37 D1

Dalen 32 B2/3
Dalešice 94 A/B1
Dalfors 39 D1
Dalfsen 67 C2
Dalgard 9 D1
Dâlgopol 141 C3
Dalhem 72 B1
Dalhem 46 B3
Dalhem 47 D3
Dalías 173 D2
Dalj 129 C3
Dalkeith 57 C2
Dalkey 58 A2
Dallgow 70 A2
Dallmin 69 D1/2
Dalmally 56 B1
Dalmellington 56 B2
Dálmine 106 A3
Dalmose 53 C1
Dalry 56 B3
Dalry 56 B2
Dalry 54 B3
Dalrymple 56 B2
Dalseter 37 D2
Dalseter 33 C2
Dalsfjord 36 A/B1
Dals Högen 45 B/C2
Dalsjöfors 45 C/D3
Dals Rostock 45 C2
Dalston 57 C3, 60 B1
Dalstuga 39 D2
Dalsvallen 34 A/B3
Dalton-in-Furness 59 C1,
60 A/B2
Daluis 112 B2
Dalvangen 33 C3, 37 D1
Damásion 143 D3
Damaskiná 143 B/C2
Damazan 109 C2
Damerow 70 B1
Damice 82 B2
Dammartin-en-Goële
87 D1
Damme 67 D2, 68 A2
Damme 78 A1
Damnatz-Landsatt 69 C2
Dampierre 104 A1
Dampierre 87 C1/2
Dampierre-en-Burly 87 D3
Dampierre-sous-Bouhy
87 D3
Dampierre-sur-Boutonne
101 B/C2
Dampierre-sur-Salon 89 C3
Damp-Zweitausend 52 B2
Damsdorf 53 B/C3
Damsdorf 69 D2/3,
70 A2/3
Damshagen 53 C3
Damüls 106 A1
Damvant [Porrentruy]
89 D3, 90 A3, 104 B1
Damville 87 B/C1
Damvillers 89 C1
Damwoude 67 B/C1
Danasjö 15 C/D3
Danby 61 C1
Dancharinea 108 A3,
154 A1
Dangé 101 C1
Dangeau 86 A/B2
Dangers 86 A/B2
Dangu 77 D3, 87 C1
Danholm 39 D2, 40 A2
Danilovgarad 137 D2
Danków 71 C2
Dannäs 50 B1
Dannemare 53 C2
Dannemarie 89 D3, 90 A3
Dannemora 40 B3
Dannenberg / Elbe 69 C2
Dannenberg-Schaafhausen
69 C2
Dannenwalde 70 A2
Dänschendorf-Westermar-
kelsdorf 53 C2
Danzé 86 B2/3
Daon 86 A3
Daoulas 84 A2
Darabani 98 B3
Darány 128 A/B2/3
Daránypuszta 128 B1/2
Dáras 146 B2/3
Darchau 69 C1
Darda 129 B/C3
Dardha 142 B2

Darfo-Boário Terme
106 B2/3
Darlington 57 D3, 61 C1
Darlington 54 B3
Darlowo 72 B2
Darméni 145 D1
Darmstadt 80 B3
Darney 89 C2
Darníus 156 B2
Daroca 162 A2
Darque 150 A3, 158 A1
Darro 173 C2
Dærtahytta 10 A1/2
Dartford 65 C3
Darthus 37 C/D1/2
Dartmouth 63 C3
Dartsel 16 B3
Darvel 56 B2
Darwen 59 D2, 60 B2
Darze 69 D1
Dasburg 79 D3
Dašev 99 C3
Daskalovo 139 D1/2
Dassel 68 B3
Dassel-Lauenberg 68 B3
Dassel-Marakoldendorf
68 B3
Dassow 53 C3
Datça 149 D3
D'atlovo 98 B1
Datteln 67 D3, 80 A1
Dáttilo 124 A2
Daugård 48 B3, 52 B1
Daugavpils 74 A2/3
Daumeray 86 A3
Daumitsch 82 A2
Daun 79 D2/3, 80 A2/3
Dautphetal-Allendorf
80 B2
Dautzschen 70 A3, 82 B1
Daventry 65 C2
Daviá 146 B3
David-Gorodok 98 B1
Davle 83 D3
Dávlia 147 C2
Davor 132 A1
Davos Dorf 106 A1
Davos Platz 106 A1
Dawlish 63 C3
Dax 108 A2
Dažnica 132 B1
Deal 65 C3, 76 B1
Deão 150 A3, 158 A1
Deauville 76 B3, 86 B1
Deba 153 D1
Débanos 153 D3, 154 A3
Debar 138 A3
Debar 140 A3
Debeli Lug 135 C2
Debeljača 133 D1,
134 A/B1
Debenham 65 C2
Dębica 97 C2
Dęblin 97 C1, 98 A2
Dębno 70 B2
Debrc 133 D1/2, 134 A2
Debrecen 97 C3, 140 A1
Debrznica 71 C3
Debrzno 71 D1
Dečani 138 A1/2
Decazeville 110 A1
Dechtice 95 C2
Decimomannu 123 C/D3
Děčín 83 C/D1
Děčín 96 A1
Decize 102 B1
Deckenpfronn 90 B2
De Cocksdorp 66 B1/2
Decollatura 122 B2
Decs 129 C2
Dedaj 137 D2
Deddington 65 C2
Dedeleben 69 C3
Dedeli 139 C/D3, 143 D1
Dedelow 70 B1
Dedemsvaart 67 C2
Deetz 69 D2, 70 A2
Deetz 69 D3
Défilé de l'Inzecca 113 D3
Dég 128 B1
Degaña 151 C2
Degeberga 50 B3
Degerby 41 D3
Degerby 25 C3
Degerfors 45 D1, 46 A1
Degerfors 31 C2

Degerhamn 51 D2
Degerndorf 92 B3
Degernes 44 B1
Degerselet 17 C2
Degerträsk 16 B3
Deggendorf 92 B1/2
Deggendorf-Natternberg
92 B2
Deggenhausertal 91 C3
Degolados 165 C2
De Haan 78 A1
De Haar 66 B3
Dehesa de Campoamor
169 C3, 174 B2
Dehesas de Guadix 173 C1
Dehesas Viejas 173 C1
Deibow 69 C1/2
Deidesheim 90 B1
Deifontes 173 C2
Deining 92 A2
Deinste 68 B1
Deinze 78 B1
Déiva Marina 113 D2,
114 A2
Dej 97 D3, 140 B1
Deje 39 C3, 45 D1
Dekani 126 B3
Dekanovec 127 C2
Dekélia 147 D2
Deknepollen 36 A1
De Koog 66 A/B1/2
De Kooi 66 A/B2
De Krim 67 C2
Delary 50 B2
Del'atin 97 D2, 98 A/B3
Delbrück 68 A3
Delbrück-Boke 68 A3,
80 B1
Delbrück-Ostenland 68 A3
Delbrück-Westenholz
68 A3
Delčevo 139 D2
Delčevo 140 B3
Delébio 105 D2, 106 A2
Deleitosa 159 D3, 166 A1
Đelekovec 128 A2
Delémont 90 A3, 104 B1
Delfi 147 C2
Delfí 148 B2
Delft 66 A3
Delfzijl 67 C1
Delgany 58 A2
Délia 124 B2/3
Delianuova 122 A3
Deliblato 134 B1
Deliceto 120 A2
Deligrad 134 B3
Delitzsch 82 B1
Delle 89 D3, 90 A3
Delligsen 68 B3
Delligsen-Grünenplan
68 B3
Dello 106 B3
Delme 89 D1
Delmenhorst 68 A2
Delnice 127 C3, 130 B1
Delvina 142 A2/3
Delvinákion 142 B2/3
Demandice 95 D2
Demetrias 143 D3, 144 A3
Demidov 75 C3
Demigny 103 D1
Demirci 149 D2
Demir Kapija 140 A3
Demir Kapija 139 C3,
143 D1
Demjansk 75 C2
Demmin 72 A2
Demonte 112 B2
Dému 109 B/C2
Denain 78 A2
Denbigh 59 C2, 60 A3
Den Burg 66 A/B2
Dendermonde 78 B1
Denekamp 67 C2
Đeneral Janković 138 B2
Den Haag ('s-Gravenhage)
66 A3
Den Ham 67 C2
Den Helder 66 A/B2
Den Hoorn 66 A/B2
Denia 169 D2
Denkendorf 92 A1
Denklingen (Kaufbeuren)
91 D3
Denneville 76 A3, 85 D1
Denno 107 B/C2

Denny 56 B1/2
Densow 70 A1/2
Dent 59 D1, 60 B2
Dentlein 91 D1
Denzlingen 90 B2/3
De Panne-Bad 78 A1
Deptford 63 D2, 64 A3,
76 A1
Deràs 28 B2
Derbent 149 D2
Derborence [Sion] 104 B2
Derby 61 C3, 64 A1
Derenburg 69 C3
Derendingen 105 C1
Dermbach 81 D2
Dermulo 80 B/C2
Derome 49 D1, 50 A1
Deronje 129 C3
Dersenow 69 C1
Deruta 115 C3, 117 C2/3
Dervaig 56 A1
Derval 85 D3
Dervénion 147 C2
Derventa 132 B1
Dérvio 105 D2, 106 A2
Dervíziana 142 B3
Desa 135 D2/3
Desborough 64 C2
Descargamaría 159 C3
Descartes 102 B1
Desenzano del Garda
106 B3
Desfína 147 C2
Dési 143 C3
Desláti 143 C2/3
Dešov 94 A1
Despotovac 134 B2
Despotovac 140 A2
Despotovo 129 C3
Dessau 69 D3
Dessau-Mosigkau 69 D3
Deštná 93 D1
Destriana 151 D2
Désulo 123 D2
Desvres 77 D1/2
Deszk 129 D2
Deta 134 B1
Deta 140 A2
Detčino 75 D3
Detern 67 D1
Detmold 68 A3
Dettelbach 81 D3
Dettingen 91 C2
Dettingen an der Erms
91 C2
Dettmannsdorf 53 D3
Dettwiller 90 A2
Deuerling 92 A/B1
Deurne 79 D1
Deutschfeistritz 127 C1
Deutschkreutz 94 B3
Deutschlands 127 C1
Deutsch Neudorf 83 C2
Deutsch-Wagram 94 B2
Deux-Chaises 102 B2
Deva 140 B1
Devecser 128 A1
Deventer 67 C3
Devesset 103 C3, 111 C1
Devil's Bridge 59 C3
Devín 94 B2
Devin 140 B3
Devínska Nová Ves 94 B2
Devizes 63 D2, 64 A3,
76 A1
Devojački Bunar 134 B1
Devonport 63 B/C3
Devrske 131 C2
Dewsbury 61 C2
Deyá 157 C2
Deza 161 D1
Dezzo 106 B2
Dhërmiu 142 A2
Dhuizon 87 C3
Diablerets, Les 104 B2
Diakoptón 146 B2
Diakovce 95 C2
Diamante 122 A1
Dianalund 49 C3, 53 C/D1
Diano 113 C2
Diano d'Alba 113 C1
Diano Marina 113 C2
Diarville 89 C2
Diavatá 143 D2, 144 A2
Diavolítsion 146 B3
Dicastillo 153 D2, 154 A2
Dichálion 144 B1

Dicomano 115 C2, 116 B1
Didcot 65 C3
Dídima 147 C3
Didimótichon 145 D3
Die 111 D1
Dieburg 81 C3
Diekholzen 68 B3
Diekirch 79 D3
Diélette 76 A3
Dielmissen 68 B3
Dielsdorf 90 B3
Diemelsee-Adorf 81 B/C1
Diemelstadt 81 C1
Diemitz 69 D1/2, 70 A1/2
Dienne 102 B3
Dienstedt 82 A2
Dienten am Hochkönig
　93 B/C3, 107 D1,
　126 A1
Diepenau-Essern 68 A2
Diepenau-Lavelsloh
　68 A2/3
Diepenheim 67 C3
Diepenveen 67 C3
Diepholz 68 A2
Diepholz-Aschen 68 A2
Dieppe 77 C2
Dierberg 70 A2
Dierdorf 80 A/B2
Dieren 67 C3
Diesdorf 69 C2
Diessen am Ammersee
　92 A3
Diessenhofen 90 B3
Diessen-Rieden 92 A3
Diest 79 C1/2
Dietenheim 91 D2
Dietenhofen 91 D1
Dietfurt 92 A1
Dietikon 90 B3, 105 C1
Dietingen 90 B2
Dietramszell 92 A3
Dietzenbach 81 B/C3
Dietzhölztal-Ewersbach
　80 B2
Dieulefit 111 C/D1
Dieulouard 89 C1
Dieuze 89 D1
Diever 67 C2
Diez 80 B2
Diezma 173 C2
Differdange 79 D3
Digerberg 34 B3
Digerberget 39 D1/2
Digermulen 8 B2
Dignac 101 C3
Dignano 107 D2, 126 A2
Digne 112 A2
Digny 86 A/B2
Digoin 103 C2
Dijon 88 B3
Dikanäs 15 C3
Dikance 138 A/B2
Dikili 149 D2
Diksmuide 78 A1
Dílar 173 C2
Dillenburg 80 B2
Dillingen an der Donau
　91 D2
Dillingen/Saar 89 D1
Dima 153 D1
Dimaro 106 B2
Dimbach 93 D2
Dímena 147 C3
Dimitrievka 99 D2
Dimitrovgrad 140 B3
Dimitrovgrad 141 D3
Dimitrovgrad 139 D1
Dimitsána 146 B3
Dimmelsvik 42 A1
Dimovo 135 D3
Dinami 122 A2/3
Dinan 85 C2
Dinant 79 C2
Dinard 85 C1/2
Dinas Mawddwy 59 C3
Dine 151 C3
Dingden 67 C3
Dingelstädt 81 D1
Dingle 44 B2
Dingle 55 C3
Dingolfing 92 B2
Dingtuna 40 A3, 46 B1
Dingwall 54 A/B2
Dinjiška 130 B2
Dinkelsbühl 91 D1
Dinklage 67 D2

Dinslaken-Bottrop 79 D1,
　80 A1
Diö 50 B2
Dion 143 D2
Diósjenő 95 D3
Dios le Guarde 159 C2
Diou 103 D2
Dipótamos 145 B/C1
Dippen 56 A2
Dipperz 81 C2
Dippoldiswalde 83 C2
Diragușan 145 D3
Dirdal 42 A2
Dirinella 105 D2
Dirinella [Ranzo-S. Abbon-
　dio] 105 D2
Dirleton 57 C1
Dirlewang 91 D2
Dirmstein 80 B3, 90 B1
Dirráchion 146 B3
Dischingen 91 D2
Dischingen-Ballmertshofen
　91 D2
Disemont 77 D2
Disenå 38 A/B3
Disentis/Mustér 105 D1/2
Disna 74 B3
Diso 121 D3
Dispílion 143 C2
Diss 65 D2
Dissay-sous-Courcillon
　86 B3
Dissen am Teutoburger
　Wald 67 D3, 68 A3
Distad 36 B2
Distington 57 C3, 60 A1
Dístomon 147 C2
Distos 147 C3
Dístraton 142 B2
Dittelbrunn-Hambach
　81 D3
Dittersbach 83 C1
Dittersdorf 82 A2
Dittrichshütte 82 A2
Ditzingen 91 C2
Diustes 153 D3
Divača 126 B3
Diva Slatina 135 D3
Divci 133 D2, 134 A2
Divčibare 133 D2, 134 A2
Dives-sur-Mer 76 B3,
　86 A1
Diviakë 142 A1
Dividalshytta 10 A2
Divieto 125 D1
Divišov 83 D3
Divonne-les-Bains 104 A2
Divuša 127 D3, 131 C1
Dixmont 88 A2
Dizy-le-Gros 78 B3
Dizy-Magenta 88 A1
Djäkneböle 31 C2
Djatlovo 98 B1
Djønno 36 B3
Djup 37 C3
Djupa 40 B2/3
Djupdal 30 A1
Djupfjord 9 C2
Djupfors 15 C2
Djuping 9 C3
Djupsjön 29 C3, 34 A1
Djuptjärn 31 C2
Djupvasshytta 32 A3,
　36 B1
Djupvik 4 B2/3
Djupvik 9 C3
Djuramåla 51 C2
Djuras 39 D2
Djurö 47 D1
Djurpark 46 B2
Djurröd 50 B2/3
Djursholm 47 C/D1
Dłoń 71 D3
Długa Goślina 71 D2
Długoszyn 71 C2
Dmitrov 75 D2
Dno 74 B2
Doagh 56 A3
Dobanovci 133 D1, 134 A1
Dobbertin 69 D1
Dobbiaco/Toblach 107 D1
Dobele 73 D1
Döbeln 96 A1
Döbeln 83 B/C1
Doberlug-Kirchhain 83 C1
Döbern 83 D1

Dobersberg 94 A1
Doberschütz 82 B1
Dobiegniew 71 C2
Dobiegniew 72 B3
Doboj 132 B1
Dobra 135 C2
Dobra 71 C1
Dobrá Niva 95 D2
Dobřany 83 C3
Dobrá Voda 95 C2
Dobre Miasto (Guttstadt)
　73 C2
Dobřen 83 D2
Dobrevo 139 C2
Dobrica 134 B1
Dobričevo 134 B1
Dobřichovice 83 D3
Dobri Dol 138 B2
Dobrinci 133 D1, 134 A1
Dobrinj 130 B1
Dobříš 83 C/D3
Dobritz 69 D3
Dobrljin 127 D3, 131 C1
Dobrna 127 C2
Dobrnič 127 C3
Dobrodzień 96 B1
Döbrököz 128 B2
Dobromirci 145 C1
Dobro Polje 132 B3
Dobroselica 133 C/D3,
　134 A3
Dobro Selo 131 C2
Dobrovice 83 D2
Dobrovnik 127 D2
Dobrun 133 C3
Dobruš 99 D1
Dobruševo 138 B3, 143 C1
Dobrzany 71 C1
Dobrzyń 83 D1
Dockasberg 17 C2
Docking 65 C2
Dockmyr 30 A3, 35 C2
Docksta 30 B3
Dockweiler 79 D2, 80 A2
Doclea 137 D2
Doclin 135 B/C1
Döderhult 51 D1
Dodewaard 66 B3
Dödismorän 34 A3
Dodona 142 B3
Dodóni 142 B3
Dödre 34 B2
Dodro 150 A2
Doesburg 67 C3
Doetinchem 67 C3
Doganović 138 B2
Dogliani 113 C1/2
Dogna 126 A2
Dognecea 135 C1
Dois Portos 164 A2
Dokka 37 D3
Dokkas 16 B1
Dokkum 67 B/C1
Doksany 83 C2
Dokšicy 74 B3
Doksy 83 D2
Dolac 138 A/B1/2
Dolac 132 B2
Dol'any 95 C2
Dólar 173 C/D2
Dolceácqua 112 B2
Dol-de-Bretagne 85 D2
Dôle 103 D1, 104 A1
Dølemo 43 C2/3
Dolenci 138 B3, 142 B1
Dolenja Vas 127 C3
Dolenjske Toplice 127 C3
Dolga Vas 127 D2
Dolgellau 59 C3
Doli 136 B1
Dolianá 142 B3
Dolianá 148 A1
Dolianova 123 D3
Dolice 71 C1/2
Dolina 97 D2, 98 A3
Dolinskaja 99 D3
Dolinskoe 141 D1
Doljane 131 C2
Döllach im Mölltal 107 D1,
　126 A1
Dollar 57 B/C1
Dollart-Bunderhammrich
　67 D1
Dolle 69 C/D2/3
Döllnitz 82 B1
Dollnstein 91 D1, 92 A1/2

Döllstädt 81 D1
Dolna dikanöa 139 D2
Dolná Poruba 95 C1
Dolné Orešany 95 C2
Dolné Saliby 95 C2
Dolné Vestenice 95 C/D2
Dolni Balvan 139 C2/3
Dolni Bělá 83 C3
Dolni Bogrov 139 D1
Dolni Bousov 83 D2
Dolni Dâbnik 140 B3
Dolní Dvořiště 93 D2
Dolni Kounice 94 B1
Dolni Lom 135 D3
Dolni Poustevna
　83 C/D1/2
Dolni Žandov 82 B3
Dolno Cerovene 135 D3
Dolno Ujno 139 C/D2
Dolný Kubín 95 D1
Dolný Kubín 97 C2
Dolný Ohaj 95 C2/3
Dolný Turček 95 D2
Dolo 107 C/D3
Dolores 169 C3
Dolovo 134 B1
Dölsach 107 D1, 126 A1
Dolsk 71 D3
Dołuje 70 B1
Dolus-d'Oléron 101 C2
Domanevka 99 D3
Dománico 122 A2
Domaniža 95 D1
Domanovići 132 B3,
　136 B1
Domart-en-Ponthieu 77 D2
Domaševo 137 C1
Domașnea 135 C1
Domaso 105 D2, 106 A2
Domats 87 D2
Domažlice 92 B1
Dombås 32 B3, 37 D1
Dombasle-en-Argonne
　89 B/C1
Dombóvár 128 B2
Dombóvár 96 B3
Dombrot-le-Sec 89 C2
Domburg 78 B1
Domène 104 A3, 112 A1
Doménikon 143 C/D3
Domeño 155 C2
Domeño 162 B3, 169 C1
Domèvre-en-Haye 89 C1
Domèvre-sur-Vezouze
　89 D2, 90 A2
Domfessel 89 D1, 90 A1
Domfront 86 A2
Domianí 146 B1
Domingo Pérez 160 B3,
　167 C1
Dömitz 69 C2
Dommartin 103 C1
Dommartin-Dampierre
　88 B1
Dommartin-la-Planchette
　88 B1
Dommartin-le-Franc 88 B2
Dommartin-sur-Yèvre
　88 B1
Domme 108 B1
Dommitzsch 70 A3, 82 B1
Domnanpirtti 19 D3
Domnița 146 B1
Domodóssola 105 C2
Domokós 146 B1
Domoravče 139 B/C2
Dömös 95 D3
Dompaire 89 C2
Dompierre-du-Chemin
　86 A2
Dompierre-sur-Besbre
　103 C2
Dompierre-sur-Mer 100 B2
Dompierre-sur-Veyle
　103 D2
Domptail 89 D2
Domrémy-la-Pucelle 89 C2
Dom Savica 126 B2
Domsjö 31 C3
Dömsöd 129 C1
Dómus de Maria 123 C3
Domusnóvas 123 C3
Domžale 127 B/C2
Donabate 58 A2
Donado 151 D3
Donaghadee 56 A3

Don Álvaro 165 D2,
　166 A2
Doña María Ocaña 173 D2
Donamaría 108 A3, 154 A1
Doña Mencía 172 B1
Donaueschingen-Wolter-
　dingen 90 B3
Donaueschingen 90 B3
Donaustauf 92 B1
Donauwörth 92 A2
Don Benito 166 A2
Doncaster 61 C2/3
Donegal 55 C2
Dongen 66 B3, 79 C1
Dongo 105 D2, 106 A2
Donhierro 160 A1/2
Donington 61 D3, 65 B/C1
Doñinos de Salamanca
　159 D2
Donja Badanja 133 C2
Donja Bebrina 132 B1
Donja Brela 131 D3,
　132 A3
Donja Brezna 137 C1
Donja Bukovica 137 D1
Donja Dubrava 128 A2
Donja Grabovica 132 A/B3
Donja Kamenica 135 C3
Donja Konjščina 127 D2
Donja Ljubata 139 C2
Donja Mutnica 134 B3
Donja Omašnica 134 B3
Donja Sabanta 134 B2
Donja Stubičke Toplice
　127 D2
Donja Suvaja 131 C2
Donja Trnava 135 C3
Donje Ljupče 138 B1
Donje Plananjane 131 C3
Donje Vukovije 133 B/C2
Donji Barbeš 135 C3,
　139 C1
Donji Dragonožec 127 D3
Donji Dušnik 135 C3,
　139 C1
Donji Krčin 134 B3
Donji Lapac 131 C2
Donji Miholjac 128 B3
Donji Milanovac 135 C2
Donji Okrug 131 C3
Donji Rujani 131 D3
Donji Skugrić 132 B1
Donji Svilaj 132 B1
Donji Vakuf 131 D2,
　132 A2
Donji Zemunik 130 B2
Donji Žirovac 131 C1
Donkerbroek 67 C2
Donnalucata 125 C3
Donnemarie-Dontilly
　87 D2, 88 A2
Donnersbach 93 C/D3
Donnersbachwald
　93 C/D3, 126 B1
Donnersdorf 81 D3
Dønnes 14 A2
Dønnesfjord 5 C1
Donorático 114 B3, 116 A2
Donostia/San Sebastián
　153 D1, 154 A1
Donovaly 95 D1/2
Donsö 45 C3, 49 D1
Dont 107 C/D2
Dont Forno di Zoldo
　107 D2
Donville-les-Bains 85 D1
Donzdorf 91 C2
Donzenac 101 D3
Donzère 111 C1/2
Donzy 87 D3
Dooagh 55 C2
Doorn 66 B3
Dørålseter 33 C3, 37 D1
Đorče Petrov 138 B2
Dorchester 63 D2/3
Dørdal 43 D2/4, 44 A2
Dordrecht 66 A3
Dörentrup 68 A3
Dörentrup-Bega 68 A3
Dorfen 92 B2
Dorfgastein 107 D1,
　126 A1
Dorgali 123 D2
Dorkás 144 A1
Dorking 64 B3, 76 B1
Dormagen 79 D1, 80 A1
Dormans 88 A1

Dornach [Dornach-Arlesheim] **90** A3
Dornauberg **107** C1
Dornberk **126** B2/3
Dornbirn **91** C3
Dornburg **80** B2
Dornburg **82** A1/2
Dorndorf **81** D2
Dornecy **88** A3
Dornelas **150** B3, **158** B1
Dornes **102** B1
Dornoch **54** B2
Dornstadt **91** C2
Dornstetten **90** B2
Dornum **67** D1
Dorog **95** D3
Dorog **96** B3
Dorogobuž **75** C3
Dorohoi **98** B3
Dorotea **30** A2
Dörpen **67** D2
Dörrenbach **90** B1
Dorsten **67** C3, **80** A1
Dorsten-Lembeck **67** C3
Dorsten-Rhade **67** C3
Dorsten-Wulfen **67** C3
Dortan **104** A2
Dortmund **80** A1
Dorum **52** A3, **68** A1
Dörverden **68** A/B2
Dörzbach **91** C1
Dos Aguas **169** C1/2
Dosante **153** B/C1/2
Dosbarrios **161** C3, **167** D1
Dos Hermanas **171** D2
Dósolo **114** B1
Dospat **140** B3
Dos Torres **166** B3
Dötlingen **68** A2
Dotsikón **143** B/C2
Döttingen **80** A2
Douai **78** A2
Douarnenez **84** A2
Doubravník **94** B1
Douchy **87** D2
Doudeville **77** C3
Doué-la-Fontaine **86** A3,
    101 C1
Douglas **56** B2
Douglas **58** B1
Douglas **54** A/B3, **55** D2
Doulaincourt **89** B/C2
Doulevant-le-Château
    88 B2
Doullens **77** D2
Doune **56** B1
Dounreay **54** B1
Doupov **83** C2
Dourdan **87** C2
Dourgne **110** A3
Douvaine **104** A2
Douvres-la-Délivrande
    76 B3, **86** A1
Douzy **79** C3
Dovádola **115** C2, **116** B1
Dover **65** C3, **76** B1
Døviken **34** B2
Dovre **33** B/C3, **37** D1
Dovregubbens hall **33** C3,
    37 D1
Dovsk **99** C1
Dowlais **63** C1
Downham Market **65** C1/2
Downpatrick **58** A1
Doxáton **144** B1
Doyet **102** B2
Dozón **150** B2
Drac **137** D3
Dračevo **137** C1
Dračevo **138** B2
Drachhausen **70** B3
Drachten **67** C1/2
Drag **9** C2/3
Drag **28** B1
Dragalevci **139** D1
Drăgănești-Vlasca **141** C2
Drăgănești-Olt **140** B2
Draganovo **141** C3
Drăgăsani **140** B2
Dragaš **138** A/B2
Draginac **133** C2
Draginje **133** C/D2, **134** A2
Dragland **9** C2
Dragobi **138** A2
Dragocvet **134** B2/3

Dragoištica **139** C/D2
Dragolovci **132** B1
Dragoman **139** D1
Dragomiresti **141** C1
Dragoni **119** D2/3
Dragør **49** D3, **50** A3,
    53 D1
Dragoš **143** C1
Dragovac **134** B2
Dragovac **139** C1
Dragozetići **130** A1
Dragsfjärd **24** B3
Dragsholm **49** C3, **53** C1
Dragsvik **36** A/B2
Draguignan **112** A3
Drahnsdorf **70** A3
Drahonice **93** C1
Drahovce **95** C2
Drákia **144** A3
Drakótripa **143** C3
Drakótripa **148** B1
Drakšenić **128** A3, **131** D1,
    132 A1
Dráma **144** B1
Dramalj **127** B/C3, **130** B3
Drammen **43** D1, **44** A/B1
Drangedal **43** C2, **44** A1
Drängsered **50** A1
Drangstedt **52** A3, **68** A1
Dransfeld **81** C1
Draschwitz **82** B1
Drasenhofen **94** B2
Drašnice **131** D3, **132** A3,
    136 B1
Drassburg **94** B3
Drassmarkt **94** B3
Dravagen **34** A/B3
Drávaszabolcs **128** B3
Dravasztára Zaláta **128** B3
Drávasztára **128** B3
Dravískos **144** B1
Dravograd **127** C2
Dravograd **96** A3
Drawno **71** C1/2
Drawsko **71** C2
Drawsko Pomorskie **71** C1
Draž **129** C3
Draženov **82** B3, **92** B1
Draževac **133** D2, **134** A2
Drebkau **70** B3, **83** C/D1
Drée **103** C2
Dreetz **69** D2
Drégelypalánk **95** D2/3
Dreglin **73** C3
Drehna **70** A/B3
Dreieich-Sprendlingen
    80 B3
Dreileben **69** C3
Dreis (Wittlich) **79** D3,
    80 A3
Drejø **53** C2
Dren **138** B1
Drena **106** B2
Drénchia **126** A/B2
Drenovac **139** C1
Drenovci **133** C1
Drenovec **135** D3
Drenovo **139** C3, **143** C1
Drensteinfurt **67** D3
Drensteinfurt-Rinkerode
    67 D3
Dresden **83** C1
Dresden **96** A1
Dreux **86** A/B1
Drevdalen **38** B1
Drevja **14** B2
Dřevohostice **95** C1
Drevsjø **33** D3
Drewen **69** D2
Drewitz **69** D3
Drezdenko **71** C2
Drezdenko **72** B3
Drežnica **130** B1
Drhovy **83** C/D3
Driebergen **66** B3
Driebes **161** C3
Driedorf **80** B2
Dries **78** B1/2
Drijber **67** C2
Drimnin **56** A1
Drimós **143** D1, **144** A1
Drinjača **133** C2
Drionville **77** D1/2
Drist **137** D2
Drivstua **33** C3, **37** D1
Drlače **133** C2
Drnholec **94** B1/2

Drniš **131** C3
Drò **106** B2
Drøbak **38** A3, **44** B1
Drobeta-Turnu Severin
    135 C/D2
Drobeta-Turnu Severin
    140 B2
Drobin **73** C3
Drobrovo **126** A2
Drochtersen **52** B3, **68** B1
Drochtersen-Assel **52** B3,
    68 B1
Drogeham **67** C1
Drogheda **58** A1/2
Drogheda **55** D2
Drogičin **73** D3, **97** D1,
    98 B1
Drogobyč **97** D2, **98** A3
Drogomin **71** C2
Drögsnäs **46** B3
Droisy **86** A/B1
Droitwich **59** D3, **64** A2
Drokija **99** C3
Dromara **58** A1
Drömme **30** B3
Dromod **55** C2
Dromore **56** A3, **58** A1
Dronero **112** B2
Dronfield **61** C3, **64** A/B1
Dronninglund **49** B/C1
Dronten **66** B2
Drosáton **139** D3, **143** D1,
    144 A1
Drosendorf Stadt **94** A1/2
Drösing **94** B2
Drosopigí **143** C2
Drosopigí **143** B/C3
Drøsselbjerg **49** C3, **53** C1
Drottningholm **47** C1
Drottningkär **51** C2
Droué **87** B/C2
Drożków **71** C3, **83** D1
Dr Petru Groza **97** D3,
    140 B1
Drubravice **131** C2/3
Druento **112** B1
Druid **59** C2/3, **60** A3
Druja **74** B2/3
Drulingen **89** D1, **90** A1/2
Drumgoft **58** A2/3
Drummore **56** B3
Drummore **54** A3, **55** D2
Drusenheim **90** B2
Druten **66** B3
Druyes-les-Belles-Fontai-
    nes **88** A3
Družba **99** D1
Družba **141** C/D3
Družetići **133** D2, **134** A2
Druževo **139** D1
Drvenik **132** A3, **136** B1
Dryburgh Abbey **57** C2
Drymen **56** B2
Drynaholmen **32** A2
Drzonowo **71** D1
Dualchi **123** C2
Duas-Igrejas **159** C1
Dub **137** C2
Dub **133** C2
Dubá **83** D2
Dubac **137** C1/2
Dubci **133** D2, **134** A2/3
Duben **70** B3
Dübendorf **90** B3, **105** D1
Dubica **128** A3, **131** D1,
    132 A1
Dubin **71** D3
Dublin (Baile Átha Cliath)
    58 A2
Dublin (Baile Átha Cliath)
    55 D2
Dublje **133** C1
Dubna **75** D2
Dub nad Moravou **95** B/C1
Dubňany **94** B1
Dubnica nad Váhom **95** C1
Dubník **95** D3
Dubno **98** B2
Duboĉac **132** B1
Dubossary **141** D1
Duboštica **132** B2
Dubovac **134** B1
Dubovo **139** C1
Dubraja **131** C2
Dubrava **127** D3
Dubrava **131** D1/2, **132** A1
Dubrava **137** C1/2

Dubravčak **127** D3
Dubravica **134** B1/2
Dubrovica **98** B2
Dubrovka **74** B2
Dubrovka **99** B/C2
Dubrovnik **137** C1/2
Ducaj **137** D2
Ducey **86** A2
Duchcov **83** C2
Ducherow **70** B1
Duči **73** D1
Duclair **77** C3
Dudar **95** C3, **128** B1
Duddington **64** B2
Dudelange **79** D3
Dudeldorf **79** D3, **80** A3
Duderstadt **81** D1
Duderstadt-Mingerode
    81 D1
Dudeştii Vechi **129** D2
Düdingen **104** B1
Dudley **59** D3, **64** A2
Dueñas **152** B3
Duerne **103** C3
Dueso **152** A2
Dueville **107** C3
Duffel **79** B/C1
Duffield **61** C3, **64** A1
Duga Poljana **133** D3,
    134 A3, **138** A1
Duga Resa **127** C3
Dugenta **119** D3
Dugi Selo **127** D3
Duhovščina **75** C3
Duinbergen **78** A1
Duingen **68** B3
Duingt **104** A3
Duino-Aurisina **126** A/B3
Duisburg **79** D1, **80** A1
Duisburg-Rheinhausen
    79 D1, **80** A1
Duisburg-Walsum **79** D1,
    80 A1
Dukati **142** A2
Dukovany **94** A/B1
Dukštas **74** A3
Dulantzi **153** D2
Duleek **58** A2
Dulje **138** B2
Dülmen **67** D3
Dülmen-Buldern **67** D3
Dülmen-Merfeld **67** D3
Dulovo **141** C2
Dulpetorpet **38** B2
Dulverton **63** C2
Dumača **133** C/D1, **134** A1
Dumbarton **56** B2
Dumbarton **54** A/B2/3,
    55 D1
Dumbrava de Sus **135** D2
Dumbría **150** A2
Dumfries **57** C3
Dumfries **54** B3
Dummer **65** C3, **76** B1
Dümmer **69** C1
Dümpelfeld **80** A2
Duna **28** B2
Dunaalmás **95** C/D3
Dunaföldvár **129** C1
Dunaföldvár **96** B3
Dunaharaszti **95** D3,
    129 C1
Dunajevcy **98** B3
Dunajská Streda **96** B3
Dunajská Streda **95** C3
Dunakeszi **95** D3
Dunakömlőd **129** C2
Dunapataj **129** C2
Dunaszekcső **129** C2
Dunaszentgyörgy **129** C2
Dunaújváros **129** C1
Dunaújváros **96** B3
Dunavățu de Jos **141** D2
Dunavci **135** D2
Dunbar **57** C1/2
Dunblane **56** B1
Duncombe **59** D1, **60** B2
Dundalk **58** A1
Dundalk **54** A3, **55** D2
Dundee **54** B2
Dundee **57** C1
Dundonald **56** A3
Dundrum **58** A1
Dunfermline **57** C1
Dunfermline **54** B2
Dungannon **54** A3, **55** D2

Dungarvan **55** C/D3
Dunholme **61** D3, **64** B1
Dunières **103** C3
Đunis **134** B3
Dunje **139** C3, **143** C1
Dunkeld **57** C1
Dunker **47** C1
Dunkerque **77** D1, **78** A1
Dún Laoghaire **58** A2
Dún Laoghaire **55** D2/3
Dunleer **58** A1
Dun-le-Palestel **101** D2,
    102 A2
Dunlop **56** B2
Dunmore **55** C2
Dunmurry **56** A3
Dunningen **90** B2
Dunoon **56** B1/2
Dunoon **54** A2/3, **55** D1
Duns **54** B3
Duns **57** D2
Dunshaughlin **58** A2
Dunstable **64** B2
Dunster **63** C2
Dun-sur-Auron **102** B1
Dun-sur-Meuse **89** B/C1
Dunwich **65** D2
Đurakovac **138** A2
Durance **109** B/C2
Durango **153** D1
Duras **109** B/C1
Đuravci **137** D2
Durban-Corbières **110** A3,
    156 B1
Durbe **73** C1
Durbuy **79** C2
Dúrcal **173** C2
Durdat-Larequille **102** B2
Đurđevac **128** A2
Đurđevi Stupovi **137** D1,
    138 A1
Đurđevića Tara **133** C3,
    137 D1
Đurđevo **129** D3, **134** A1
Düren **79** D2
Düren-Gürzenich **79** D2
Durfort **108** B2
Durham **57** D3, **61** C1
Durham **54** B3
Đurinci **133** D2, **134** A/B2
Đurmanec **127** D2
Đurmanec **96** A3
Dürmentingen **91** C2/3
Durmersheim **90** B1
Durness **54** A1
Dürnfeld **126** B1
Dürnkrut **94** B2
Dürnstein **94** A2
Durón **161** C/D2
Dürrboden [Dovos-Platz]
    106 A1
Dürrenboden [Schwyz]
    105 D1
Durrës **137** D3, **142** A1
Durrow **55** D3
Dürrwangen **91** D1
Dursley **63** D1, **64** A3
Durston **63** C/D2
Dursunbey **149** D1
Durtal **86** A3
Duruelo de la Sierra **153** C3
Dushman **137** D2, **138** A2
Dušikrava **130** B1/2
Dusina **132** B2
Dusnok **129** C2
Düsseldorf **79** D1, **80** A1
Düssnitz **70** A3
Dussoi **107** C2
Duszniki **71** D2
Dutovlje **126** B3
Duvberg **34** B3
Duved **29** C3, **34** A1/2
Duvno **131** D3, **132** A3
Duži **136** B1
Duži **137** C1
Dužica **127** D3
Dvärsätt **29** D3, **34** B2
Dverberg **9** C1
Dvor **131** C3
Dvorníky **95** C2
Dvorovi **133** C2
Dvory nad Žitavou **95** C3
Dwingeloo **67** C2
Dybbøl **52** B2
Dybvad **49** B/C1
Dymchurch **77** C1
Dymer **99** C2

Dynäs 30 B3, 35 D2
Dypfest 28 A3, 33 C1
Dyranut 37 B/C3
Dyreborg 52 B2
Dyrnesvågen 32 B1
Džanići 132 B3
Džep 139 C1
Džepčište 138 B2
Dzeržinsk 98 B1
Działdowo 73 C3
Džigolj 135 B/C3
Džurin 99 C3

E

Ea 153 D1
Eándion 147 D2
Eaní 143 C2
Eardisley 63 C1
Earith 65 C2
Earls Colne 65 C2
Earlston 57 C2
Easdale 56 A1
Easington 61 D1
Easington 61 D2
Easingwold 61 D2
East Aberthaw 63 C2
Eastbourne 77 B/C1
Eastchurch 65 C3, 77 C1
East Cowes 76 B1
East Dereham 65 C1
East Grinstead 65 C3,
   76 B1
East Harling 65 C2
East Kilbride 56 B2
Eastleigh 76 B1
East Linton 57 C1/2
East-Looe 62 B3
East Retford 61 C3, 64 B1
Eastry 65 C3, 76 B1
Eastwood 61 D3, 65 C1
Eaton Socon 64 B2
Eaux-Bonnes 108 B3,
   154 B1/2
Eauze 108 B2
Ebbw Vale 63 C1
Ebeleben 81 D1
Ebelsbach 81 D3
Ebeltoft 49 C2/3
Ebenfurth 94 B3
Ebensee 93 C3
Ebensee 96 A3
Ebensfeld 81 D3, 82 A3
Ebenweiler 91 C3
Eberbach 81 C3, 91 C1
Ebergötzen 81 C2
Eberhardzell 91 C3
Ebermannsdorf 92 B1
Ebermannstadt 82 A3
Ebern 81 D3
Eberndorf 127 B/C2
Ebersbach 83 D1/2
Ebersbach 96 A1
Ebersbach-Musbach 91 C3
Ebersberg 92 A/B2/3
Ebersburg-Schmalnau
   81 C2
Eberschwang 93 C2
Ebersdorf 68 A1
Eberstein 126 B1
Eberswalde-Finow 70 B2
Eberswalde-Finow 72 A3
Ebnat (-Kappel) [Ebnat-
   Kappel] 105 D1, 106 A1
Éboli 119 D3, 120 A2
Ebrach 81 D3
Ébreuil 102 B2
Ebsdorfergrund-Dreihausen
   81 C2
Ebstorf 69 B/C2
Ecclefechan 57 C3,
   60 A/B1
Eccleshall 59 D3, 60 B3,
   64 A1
Eceabat 149 C1
Echalar 108 A3, 154 A1
Echallens [Lausanne]
   104 B2
Echarren 153 D2, 154 A1/2
Echarrí-Aranaz 153 D2
Échauffour 86 B1/2
Echevarría 153 D1

Eching 92 B2
Échiré 101 B/C2
Échourgnac 101 C3,
   109 C1
Echt 79 D1
Echtenbrug 66 B2
Echternach 79 D3
Echzell 81 C2
Écija 172 A1
Ečka 129 D3, 133 D1,
   134 A1
Eckartsberga 82 A1
Eckental 82 A3
Eckental-Eschenau 82 A3,
   92 A1
Eckernförde 52 B2
Eckerö 41 C3
Eckington 61 D3, 65 C1
Ecommoy 86 B3
Écouché 86 A1/2
Écouen 87 D1
Écouis 77 D3, 87 C1
Écouviez 79 C3
Écs 95 C3
Écueillé 101 C1
Ed 30 B3, 35 D2
Eda 38 B3
Eda glasbruk 38 B3
Edalund Milla 46 B2
Edam 66 B2
Edane 38 B3, 45 C1
Eddelak 52 B3
Edderitz 69 D3, 82 A/B1
Eddleston 57 C2
Eddystone Lighthouse
   62 B3
Ede 35 D3
Ede 29 D3, 35 C1
Ede 66 B3
Edebäck 39 C3
Edefors 16 B2
Edefors 29 D3, 35 C1
Edefors Harads 16 B2
Edeköy 145 D1, 145 D3
Edelschrott 127 C1
Edelsfeld 82 A3, 92 A1
Edemissen 68 B2/3
Eden 30 A/B2, 35 D1
Edenbridge 65 C3, 76 B1
Edenkoben 90 B1
Edermünde-Besse 81 C1
Edertal 81 D3
Edertal-Gellershausen
   81 C1
Edertal-Hemfurth-Edersee
   81 C1
Edertal-Mehlen 81 C1
Édessa 143 C1
Édessa 148 B1
Edevik 29 C2, 34 A1
Edewecht 67 D1/2
Edinburgh 57 C2
Edinburgh 54 B2/3
Edincy 98 B3
Edincy 98 B3
Edingen 78 B2
Edipsós 147 C1
Edirne 145 D2
Edirne 141 C3
Edland 42 B1
Edlitz im Burgenland
   127 D1
Edlitz Markt 94 A/B3
Édolo 106 B2
Edremit 149 D1
Edsbro 40 B3
Edsbruk 46 B3
Edsbyn 39 D1, 40 A1
Edsele 30 A3, 35 C1/2
Edshult 46 A3
Edsleskog 45 C1/2
Edsvalla 45 D1
Eefde 67 C3
Eeklo 78 B1
Eelde-Paterswolde 67 C1/2
Eemshaven 67 C1
Eferding 93 C2
Eferding 96 A2
Effeltrich 82 A3
Effiat 102 B2
Éfira 146 A/B2
Efirie Sud 141 D2
Efpálion 146 B2
Efringen-Kirchen 90 A3
Efteløt 43 D1, 44 A1

Egebjerg 49 D3, 53 D1
Egebjerg Gård 49 B/C3,
   53 C1
Egeln 69 C3
Egeløkke 53 C2
Egenäs 45 C1
Eger 97 C3
Egersund 52 B2
Egersund 42 A3
Egervár 128 A1
Egeskov 53 C1/2
Egestorf 68 B1/2
Egestorf-Evendorf 68 B2
Egg 91 C3
Eggan 28 A3, 33 C1/2
Eggenburg 94 A2
Eggenthal 91 D3
Eggesin 70 B1
Eggingen 90 B3
Eggkleiva 28 A3, 33 C2
Egglham 93 B/C2
Eggstätt 92 B3
Eggum 8 B2
Egham 64 B3
Eghezée 79 C2
Égletons 102 A3
Egling 91 D2, 92 A2
Egling 92 A3
Egling-Endlhausen 92 A3
Eglisau 90 B3
Égliseneuve-d'Entraigues
   102 B3
Egloffstein 82 A3
Egmond aan Zee 66 A2
Egna/Neumarkt 107 C2
Egnázia 121 C2
Egósthena 147 C2
Egremont 57 C3, 60 A1
Égreville 87 D2
Egton 61 D/C1
Egtved 48 B3, 52 B1
Éguilly-sous-Bois 88 B2
Éguzon 102, 102 A2
Egyházasrádóc 127 D1,
   128 A1
Egyptinkorp 23 C1
Ehäjärvi 26 B2
Ehekirchen 92 A2
Ehingen 91 C2
Ehningen 91 B/C2
Ehra-Lessien 69 C2
Ehrenberg 81 D2
Ehrenburg 68 A2
Ehrenburg-Schweringhau-
   sen 68 A2
Ehrenfriedersdorf 82 B2
Ehrenhain 82 B2
Ehrenhausen 127 C1/2
Ehrenkirchen-Kirchhofen
   90 A3
Ehringshausen 80 B2
Ehrwald 91 D3
Ehtamo 24 B2
Eibar 153 D1
Eibau 83 D1/2
Eibenstock 82 B2
Eibergen 67 C3
Eibesbrunn 94 B2
Eibiswald 127 C1/2
Eibiswald 96 A3
Eichelsachsen 81 C2
Eichenberg 81 D2
Eichendorf 92 B2
Eichendorf-Kröhstorf 92 B2
Eichenzell 81 C2
Eichholz 83 C1
Eichow 70 B3
Eichstätt 92 A1/2
Eichstetten 90 A2/3
Eichwalde 70 A2/3
Eich (Worms) 80 B3
Eicklingen 68 B2
Eid 32 A2/3
Eidbukta 14 B2
Eide 42 A/B3
Eide 32 A2
Eidem 14 A3
Eidet 28 A3, 33 C2
Eidet 125 D2
Eidfjord 36 B3

Eidhaugen 14 B2
Eidi 55 C1
Eidkjosen 4 A3
Eidsborg 43 C1/2
Eidsbotn 36 A3
Eidsbugarden 37 C2
Eidsdal 32 A3, 36 B1
Eidsfjord 8 B2
Eidsfoss 43 D1, 44 A1
Eidshaug 28 B1
Eidslandet 36 A3
Eidsøra 32 B2
Eidssund 42 A2
Eidstå 43 C2
Eidsvåg 32 B2
Eidsvold 38 A2/3
Eidsvoll 38 A2/3
Eidsvoll verk 38 A2/3
Eidvågeid 5 C1/2
Eigeltingen 91 B/C3
Eikanger 36 A3
Eikefjord 36 A2
Eiken 42 B3
Eikenes 36 A2
Eiksund 36 A/B1
Eilenburg 82 B1
Eimisjärvi 23 D3
Eimke 68 B2
Eina 38 A2
Einbeck 68 B3
Einbeck-Salzderhelden
   68 B3
Einbeck-Wenzen 68 B3
Eindhoven 79 C1
Eines 28 B3, 33 D1
Einsiedeln 105 D1
Einvika 28 A/B2
Einville-au-Jard 89 D2
Eisdorf 68 B3
Eiselfing 92 B2/3
Eisenach 81 D1/2
Eisenbach-Schollach 90 B3
Eisenberg 80 B3, 90 B1
Eisenberg 82 A/B1/2
Eisenerz 93 D3
Eisenerz 96 A3
Eisenhüttenstadt 72 A3,
   96 A1
Eisenhüttenstadt 70 B3
Eisenkappel 126 B2
Eisenkappel 96 A3
Eisenstadt 96 B3
Eisenstadt 94 B3
Eisfeld 81 D2, 82 A1
Eisgarn 93 D1/2
Eisleben 82 A1
Eisleben-Helfta 82 A1
Eislingen 91 C2
Eisriesenwelt 93 C3
Eitensheim 92 A2
Eiteråga 14 B2
Eiterelvmoen 9 C/D2
Eiterfeld 81 C2
Eitorf 80 A2
Eivik 14 B1
Eixo 158 A2
Eizeringen 78 B2
Ejby 52 B1
Ejea de los Caballeros
   155 C3
Ejheden 39 D1
Ejsing 48 A2
Ejstrup 48 B3
Ejulve 162 B2
Ekáli 147 D2
Ekängen 46 B2
Ekeberg 45 D3
Ekeby 45 D3
Ekeby 50 A3
Ekebyholm 40 B3
Ekedalen 45 D3
Ekenäs 45 D2
Ekenässjön 46 A3, 51 C1
Ekenäs/Tammisaari 24 B3
Ekeren 78 B1
Ekerö 47 C1
Eketånga 49 D2, 50 A2
Ekfors 17 C/D2
Ekkerøy 7 C/D2
Eknäs 24 B3
Ekne 28 B3, 33 D1
Ekolsund 40 B3, 47 C1
Ekora 153 D2
Ekorrsele 31 C1
Ekorrsjö 31 C1
Ekorrträsk 31 C1
Ekra 32 B3, 37 C1
Ekshärad 39 C3

Eksingedal 36 A3
Eksjö 46 A3
Eksjö 72 A/B1
Ekträsk 31 C1
El Abalario 171 C2
Eläinpuisto 18 B1
El Álamo 160 B3
El Alcornocal 166 B3
El Almendro 171 B/C1
El Almicerán 167 D3,
   168 A3, 173 D1
El Alquián 173 D2
Elämäjärvi 21 D1/2,
   22 A1/2
Elanec 99 D3
Elantxobe 153 D1
El Arahal 171 D2, 172 A2
El Arenal 157 C2
El Arenal 160 A3
Elassón 143 D3
Elassón 148 B1
Elateia 147 C1
Eláti 143 C3
Elátia 147 C1
Elátia 143 D3
Elatochórion 142 B3
El Ballestero 168 A/B2
El Barco de Avila 159 D2/3
Elbasan 138 A3, 142 A1
El Berrón 151 D1, 152 A1
El Berrueco 161 C2
Elbeuf 77 C3, 86 B1
Elbingerode 69 C3
Elblag (Elbing) 73 C2
El Bodón 159 C2
El Bohodón 160 A2
El Bonillo 168 A2
El Bosque 172 A2
El Bruc 156 A3, 163 D1
El Brull 156 A2/3
Elburg 66 B2
El Burgo 172 A2
El Burgo de Ebro 154 B3,
   162 B1
El Burgo de Osma 153 C3,
   161 C1
El Burgo Ranero 152 A2
El Buste 154 A3
El Cabaco 159 D2
El Cabo de Gata 173 D2,
   174 A2
El Campillo 160 A1
El Campillo 166 B1
El Campo 166 A2
El Campo de Peñaranda
   160 A2
El Cañavate 168 B1
El Cardoso de la Sierra
   161 C2
El Carpio 167 C3, 172 B1
El Carpio de Tajo 160 B3,
   167 C1
El Casar de Talamanca
   161 C2
El Casar de Escalona
   160 B3
El Castellar 162 B2/3
El Castillo de las Guardas
   171 D1
El Centenillo 167 C3
El Cerro de Andévalo
   171 C1
Elche 169 C3
Elche de la Sierra 168 B2/3
Elcili 145 C2
Elcóaz 155 C2
El Collado 162 A/B3,
   169 C1
El Collado 153 D3
El Colmenar 172 A3
El Coronil 171 D2
El Cubillo 161 C2
El Cubo de Don Sancho
   159 C2
El Cubo de Tierra del Vino
   159 D1
El Cuervo 171 D2
El Cuervo 163 C3
Elda 169 C2/3
Eldagsen 68 B3
Eldalsosen 36 B2
Eldena 69 C1
Eldforsen 39 C2
Eléa 86 B3
Elefsís 147 D2
Elefsís 148 B2
Elefthériani 146 B1/2

Elefthérion **143** D3
Eleftherochórion **143** C2
Eléftheron **142** B2
Eleftheroúpolis **144** B1
Eleja **73** D1, **74** A2
El Ejido **173** D2
Elektrénai **73** D2, **74** A3
Elemir **129** D3
Elena **141** C3
Elenheimen **5** C1/2
Eleochória **144** A2
Eleoúsa **142** B3
El Escorial **160** B2
El Espinar **160** B2
El Estanyol **157** D2
Eleutherai **147** D2
El Formigal **154** B2
El Frago **154** B2
El Franco **151** C1
El Frasno **154** A3, **162** A1
Elgå **33** D3
Elgå **33** D3
El Garrobo **171** D1
El Gastor **172** A2
Elgeta **153** D1
Elgin **54** B2
Elgoibar **153** D1
El Gordo **160** A3, **166** B1
Elgorriaga **108** A3, **154** A1
El Grado **155** C2/3
El Granado **170** B1
El Grao **169** D1
El Grao de Gandía **169** D2
Elgsnes **9** C1
El Herrada **160** B2
El Herrumblar **168** B1
El Higueral **172** B2
El Hito **161** C/D3, **168** A1
El Horcajo **167** C2/3
El Hornillo **160** A3
Elhovo **141** C3
El Hoyo **167** C3
El Hoyo de Pinares **160** B2
Elïaen **38** B1
Elie **57** C1
Elijärvi **17** D2/3, **18** A1
Elimäenkylä **21** C/D3
Elimäki **26** B2
Elin Pelin **140** B3
Elis **146** A2
Eliseyna **139** D1
Elizondo **108** A3, **154** A1
Eljaröd **50** B3
Ełk (Lyck) **73** D2/3
Elland **59** D2, **61** C2
Ellefsplass **33** D3
Ellenberg **91** D1
Ellesmere **59** D2/3, **60** B3
Ellesmere Port **59** D2, **60** B3
Elling **49** C1
Ellingen **91** D1, **92** A1
Ellinikón **147** D2
Ellmau **92** B3
Ellös **44** B3
El Losar **159** D2/3
Ellrich **81** D1
Ellwangen **91** D1
Ellwangen-Rindelbach **91** D1
Elzee **91** D2
El Maderal **159** D1
El Madroño **171** C1
El Maíllo **159** D2
El Masnou **156** A3
El Masroig **163** C1/2
Elmelunde **53** D2
El Molar **161** C2
El Molinillo **167** C1
El Moral **168** B3, **173** D1, **174** A1
El Moralico **168** A2/3
Elmshorn **52** B3, **68** B3
Elmstein **90** B1
El Musel **151** D1, **152** A1
Elne **156** B1/2
Elnesvågen **32** A2
Elorrio **153** D1
Elorz **154** A2
Előszállás **129** C1
El Palmar **169** D3
El Palmar **169** D1/2
El Palo **172** B2
El Payo **159** C3
El Pedernoso **168** A1
El Pedroso **166** A3, **171** D1

El Pedroso de la Armuña **159** D2, **160** A2
El Peral **168** B1
El Perello **163** C2
El Perelló **169** D1/2
El Picazo **168** B1
El Piñero **159** D1
El Pla de Cabra **163** C1
El Plantío **160** B2
El Pobo **162** B2
El Pobo de Dueñas **162** A2
El Pont d'Armentera **163** C1
El Portal **171** D2/3
El Port de la Selva **156** B2
El Portil **171** C2
El Poyo **163** D2
El Pozuelo **171** C1
El Prat de Llobregat **156** A3
El Provencio **168** A1
El Puente del Arzobispo **160** A3, **166** B1
El Puerto de Santa María **171** D2/3
El Quintanar **153** C/D3
El Raposo **165** D3, **166** A3
El Rasillo **153** D3
El Real de la Jara **165** D3, **166** A3, **171** D1
El Real de San Vicente **160** A3
El Recuenco **161** D2
El Redal **153** D2
El Rocío **171** C2
El Rompido **171** C2
El Ronquillo **171** D1
El Royo **153** D3
El Rubio **172** A2
El Sabinar **168** B3
El Saler **169** D1
El Salobral **168** B2
El Saucejo **172** A2
Elsdorf **79** D2, **80** A2
Elsegårde **49** C2/3
Elsenborn **79** D2
Elsenfeld **81** C3
El Serrat **155** D2, **156** A1/2
Elsfjord **14** B2
Elsfleth **68** A1
Elsfleth-Moorriem **67** D1, **68** A1
Elshø **38** B1
Elsloo **67** C2
El Soleràs **163** C1
Elspe-Cobbenrode **80** B1
Elspeet **66** B3
Els Prats de Rei **155** D3, **156** A3, **163** D1
Elsrud **37** D3
Elst **66** B3
Elster **70** A3
Elsterberg **82** B2
Elsterwerda **83** C1
Els Torms **163** C1
Elstra **83** C1
Eltdalen **38** B1
El Tejar **172** B2
Eltendorf **127** D1
El Tiemblo **160** B2
El Toboso **167** D1, **168** A1
El Tormillo **155** C3
El Torno **159** D3
El Toro **162** B3
El Tosalet **169** D2
El Tranco **168** A3
Eltravåg **42** A1
Eltville am Rhein **80** B3
Eltziego **153** D2
El'uja **75** C3
Elva **74** A1
Elva **112** B1/2
Elvanfoot **57** C2
Elvas **165** C2
Elvåsen **28** B1
Elvdal **38** B1
Elve **42** B3
Elvebakken **6** B1
Elvekrok **6** B1
Elven **85** C3
El Vendrell **156** A3, **163** D1
Elvenes **7** C/D2
Elveng **28** A3, **33** C1
Elverum **38** A/B2
Elveseter **37** C2
Elvestad **38** A3, **44** B1
Elvevollen **4** A/B3, **10** A1
El Villar **167** C2
El Villar de Arnedo **153** D2

El Vilosell **163** D1
El Viso **169** D1/2
El Viso **166** B2/3
El Viso del Alcor **171** D1/2
Elvran **28** B3, **33** D1
Elxleben **81** D2, **82** A2
Elxleben **81** D1, **82** A1
Ely **65** C2
Elz **80** B2
Elzach **90** B2
Elzach-Prechtal **90** B2
Elze **68** B3
Emådalen **39** D1
Embesós **146** A1
Embid **162** A2
Embid de Ariza **161** D1
Embid de la Ribera **154** A3, **162** A1
Embleton **57** D2
Emborión **149** C3
Embrun **112** A1/2
Embún **154** B2
Emden **67** C/D1
Emersacker **91** D2
Emkarby **41** C3
Emkendorf **52** B3
Emlichheim **67** C2
Emmaboda **51** C2
Emmaboda **72** B1
Emmaljunga **50** B2
Emmeloord **66** B2
Emmelshausen **80** A3
Emmen **105** C1
Emmen **67** C2
Emmenbrücke **105** C1
Emmendingen **90** A/B2
Emmer-Compascuum **67** C2
Emmerich **67** C3
Emmerich-Elten **67** C3
Emmersdorf an der Donau **94** A3
Emmerthal **68** B3
Emmerthal-Emmern **68** B3
Emmerthal-Grohnde **68** B3
Emmerting **92** B2
Emolahti **21** D1, **22** A1
Emospohja **21** D2, **22** A2
Empo **24** B3
Émpoli **114** B2, **116** A2
Emptinne **79** C2
Emsbüren **67** D2
Emsbüren-Elbergen **67** D2
Emsdetten **67** D3
Emsfors **51** D1
Emskirchen **81** D3, **91** D1
Emstal **81** C1
Emstek **67** D2, **68** A2
Emsworth **76** A/B1
Ena **154** B2
Enafors **28** B3, **33** D2, **34** A2
Enånger **40** A/B1
Enanlahti **27** D1
Enare **6** B3
Enarsvedjan **29** C/D3, **34** A1
Enåsen **35** C3
Encamp **155** D2, **156** A2
Encausse-les-Thermes **109** C3, **155** C1
Encinacorba **163** C1
Encinas de Abajo **159** D2, **160** A2
Encinasola **165** C/D3
Encinas Reales **172** B2
Encío **153** C2
Enciso **153** D3
Endalsetra **33** C2
Endelave By **49** B/C3, **53** B/C1
Enden **37** D1/2, **38** A1
Enden **37** C1
Éndine **106** A/B3
Endingen **90** A2
Endorf **92** B3
Endre **47** D3
Endresplass **14** B3, **29** C1
Endrinal **159** D2
Enebakk **38** A3, **44** B1
Enebakkneset **38** A3
Eneby **46** B3
Enériz **154** A2
Enese **95** C2
Enez **145** D1/2
Enez **149** C1
Enfield **65** C3

Engan **14** A2
Engdal **32** B2
Engelberg **105** C1
Engelhartszell **93** C2
Engelhartszell **96** A2
Engelia **37** D3, **38** A2
Engeln **68** A2
Engelskirchen **80** A1/2
Engelskirchen-Ründeroth **80** A1/2
Engelsviken **44** B1
Engen **90** B3
Engen-Talmühle **90** B3
Enger **68** A3
Engerda **82** A2
Engerdal **38** B1
Engerdalssetra **33** D3
Engerneset **38** B1
Enghien (Edingen) **78** B2
Engjan **32** B2
Englefontaine **78** B2
Engstingen-Grossengstingen **91** C2
Enguera **169** C2
Enguídanos **162** A3, **168** B1
Engvik **4** A2
Enix **173** D2
Enkenbach-Alsenborn **80** B3, **90** B1
Enkhuizen **66** B2
Enkirch **80** A3
Enklinge **24** A3, **41** D2
Enköping **40** A/B3, **47** C1
Enmoerr **33** C2
Enna **125** C3
Ennepetal **80** A1
Ennezat **102** B2
Ennigerloh **67** D3
Ennigerloh-Enniger **67** D3
Ennigerloh-Westkirchen **67** D3
Enningdal **44** B2
Ennis **55** C3
Enniscorthy **55** D3
Enniskean **55** C3
Enniskerry **58** A2
Enniskillen **54** A3, **55** C/D2
Ennistimon **55** C3
Enns **96** A2/3
Enns **93** D2
Eno **23** D2
Enokunta **25** C1
Enonkoski **23** C3
Enonkylä **18** B3
Enonlahti **26** B1
Enontekiö/Hetta **11** C2, **12** A1
Ens **66** B2
Enschede **67** C3
Ensdorf **92** A/B1
Ensisheim **89** D2/3, **90** A3
Enskogen **35** C3
Enstaberga **47** C2
Enter **67** C3
Entlebuch **105** C1
Entrácque **112** B2
Entradas **164** B3, **170** B1
Entraigues **111** D1, **112** A1
Entrains-sur-Nohain **88** A3
Entrambasmestas **152** B1
Entraunes **112** B2
Entraygues-sur-Truyère **110** A1
Entrechaux **111** D2
Entrena **153** C2
Entre-os-Rios **158** A2
Entrevaux **112** B2
Entrèves **104** B3
Entrimo **150** B3
Entrín Bajo **165** D2
Entroncamento **164** B1
Entzheim **90** A2
Envendos **164** B1
Envermeu **76** B2/3
Enviken **39** D2, **40** A3
Enying **128** B1
Enzersdorf im Thale **94** B2
Enzinger Boden **107** D1, **126** A1
Enzklösterle **90** B2
Eosazia **113** D3
Épaignes **77** C3, **86** B1
Épannes **100** A2
Epanomí **143** D2, **144** A2
Epanomí **148** B1

Epároz **155** C2
Epe **67** B/C2/3
Épernay **88** A1
Épernon **87** C2
Epfig **90** A2
Ephesos **149** D2
Epidamnus **137** D3, **142** A1
Epidauros (Hieron Asklepiou) **147** D3
Epidauros (Hieron Asklepiou) **148** B3
Epidaurum **137** C2
Épierre **104** A3
Épila **155** C3, **163** C1
Épinal **89** D2
Episcopía **120** B3, **122** A1
Epískepsis **142** A3
Episkopí **147** D3
Epitálion **146** A/B3
Époisses **88** A/B3
Epoo/Ebbo **25** D3, **26** A3
Épouville **77** B/C3
Eppelborn **90** A1
Eppelheim **90** B1
Eppenbrunn **90** A1
Eppendorf **83** C2
Epping **65** C3
Eppingen **91** B/C1
Eppingen-Richen **91** B/C1
Eppishausen-Mörgen **91** D2
Épreville **77** C3
Eptachórion **142** B2
Eptálofos **147** C1/2
Epworth **61** C2/3
Eques **54** A2
Équi Terme **114** A2, **116** A1
Eracléa **107** D3, **126** A3
Eraclea Mare **107** D3, **126** A3
Eraclea Minoa **124** B2/3
Eräjärvi **25** C1
Eräjärvi **27** C1
Erásmion **145** C1
Eratiní **146** B2
Eratinón **145** C1
Erátira **143** C2
Erba **105** D3, **106** A3
Erbach **81** C3
Erbach **91** C2
Erbach-Ebersberg **81** C3
Erbalunga **113** D2
Erbendorf **82** B3
Erbendorf-Grötschenreuth **82** B3
Ercé **155** D2
Ercheu **78** A3
Érchie **121** D3
Ercolano **119** D3
Ercsi **129** C1
Ercsi **96** B3
Érd **96** B3
Érd **95** D3, **129** C1
Erdek **149** D1
Erdevik **133** C1
Erding **92** A/B2
Erding-Langengeisling **92** A/B2
Erdut **129** C3
Éreac **85** C2
Éremo dei Cárceri **115** D3, **117** C2
Eresfjord **32** B2
Eretria **147** D2
Erétria **147** D2
Erezée **79** C2
Erfde **52** B3
Erftstadt **79** D2, **80** A2
Erfurt **81** D1/2, **82** A1/2
Ergersheim-Ermetzhofen **81** D3, **91** D1
Ergersheim-Neuherberg **81** D3, **91** D1
Ergli **73** D1, **74** A3
Ergolding **92** B2
Ergoldsbach **92** B2
Érice **124** A2
Ericeira **164** A2
Eriksberg **46** B2
Eriksbu **43** C/D1
Erikslund **35** C3
Eriksmåla **51** C2
Eriksvik **47** D1
Erímanthos Óros **146** B2
Eringsboda **51** C2
Erithraí **147** C/D2
Érize-la-Petite **89** B/C1

Erkelenz **79** D1
Erkheim **91** D3
Erkner **70** A/B2/3
Erkrath **80** A1
Erla **154** B3
Erlangen **82** A3
Erlau **81** D2
Erlenbach(am Main) **81** C3
Erlensee **81** C3
Erli **113** C2
Erlsbach **107** D1
Ermelo **66** B2/3
Ermenoville **87** D1
Ermidas **164** B3, **170** A1
Ermióni **147** C/D3
Ermióni **148** B2
Ermoúpolis **149** C2
Ermsleben **69** C3
Ermua **153** D1
Erndtebrück **80** B1/2
Ernée **85** D2, **86** A2
Ernestinovo **129** B/C3
Ernsgaden **92** A2
Ernstbrunn **94** B2
Eroles **155** C/D2/3
Erolzheim **91** D2/3
Erpfendorf **92** B3
Erquy **85** C1/2
Erra **164** B2
Errazu **108** A3, **154** A1
Errenteria **153** D1, **154** A1
Errezil **153** D1
Errindlev **53** C/D2
Erro **108** A3, **154** A1/2
Ersekë **142** B2
Ersekë **148** A1
Érsekvadkert **95** D3
Ershausen **81** D1
Ersmark **31** D1
Ersnäs **17** C3
Erstein **90** A2
Erstfeld **105** D1
Ersvik **14** B1
Ertebølle **48** B2
Ertenvåg **14** B1
Ertingen **91** C2/3
Erto **107** D2
Ertsjärv **17** C1/2
Ervalla **46** A/B1
Ervas Tenras **159** B/C2
Ervasti **19** C2
Ervedal **158** B2/3
Ervedal **164** B2
Ervedosa **158** B1/2
Ervenik **131** C2
Ervidel **164** B3, **170** B1
Ervik **36** A1
Ervik **32** B2
Ervillers **78** A2
Ervy-le-Châtel **88** A2
Erwitte **80** B1
Erwitte-Bad Westernkotten **68** A3, **80** B1
Erxleben **69** C3
Esbjerg **48** A3, **52** A1
Escalada **153** B/C2
Escalaplano **123** D3
Escalhão **159** C2
Escaló **155** C2
Escalona **160** B3
Escalonilla **160** B3, **167** C1
Escalos de Baixo **158** B3, **165** C1
Escalos de Cima **158** B3, **165** C1
Escamilla **161** D2
Es Caná **157** D3
Escañuela **167** C3, **172** B3
Escariche **161** C2
Escároz **154** A/B2
Escarrilla **154** B2
Escatrón **162** B1
Eschach **91** C3
Eschau **81** C3
Eschede **68** B2
Eschede-Starkshorn **68** B2
Eschede-Weyhausen **68** B2
Eschenbach in der Oberpfalz **82** A3
Eschenburg-Eibelshausen **80** B2
Eschenlohe **92** A3
Eschershausen **68** B3
Esch-sur-Alzette **79** D3
Esch-sur-Sûre **79** D3
Eschwege **81** D1

Eschweiler **79** D2
Escó **154** B2
Escobosa de Almazán **161** D1
Escombreras **174** B1
Escos **108** A3, **154** B1
Escosse **109** D3, **155** D1, **156** A1
Escource **108** A2
Es Cubells **169** C2
Escucha **162** B2
Escúllar **173** D2
Escurial **166** A2
Escurial de la Sierra **159** D2
Esens **67** D1
Esens-Bensersiel **67** D1
Esfiliana **173** C2
Esgos **150** B2
Esgueira **158** A2
Esher **64** B3, **76** B1
Eskdale **59** C1, **60** A1/2
Eskeland **42** A1
Eskelinkosi **22** B3
Eskiköy **145** D3
Eskilsäter **45** C/D2
Eskilstrup **53** D2
Eskilstuna **46** B1
Eskola **21** C1
Eskön **40** B2
Eskoriatza **153** D1/2
Eslarn **82** B3, **92** B1
Eslava **154** A2
Eslida **162** B3, **169** D1
Eslohe **80** B1
Eslohe-Reiste **80** B1
Eslöv **50** B3
Eslöv **72** A1/2
Esnanqes **100** B2
Espadaña **159** C2
Espalion **110** A1
Esparragal **172** B1
Esparragalejo **165** D2
Esparragosa de Caudillo **166** B2
Esparragosa de la Serena **166** A2
Esparreguera **156** A3
Esparron **111** D3, **112** A3
Espeja **156** C2
Espejo **153** C2
Espejo **172** B1
Espejón **153** C3, **161** C1
Espeland **36** A3
Espelette **108** A3, **154** A1
Espelkamp **68** A2/3
Espelúy **167** C3, **173** C1
Espera **171** D2
Espéraza **110** A3, **156** A1
Espergærde **49** D3, **50** A2/3
Espéria **119** C2
Esperstoft **52** B2
Espiel **166** B3
Espierba **155** C2
Espinama **152** A/B1
Espinhal **158** A3
Espinho **158** A2
Espinilla **152** B1/2
Espinosa de Cerrato **152** B3
Espinosa de Cervera **153** C3
Espinosa de Villagonzalo **152** B2
Espinosa de Henares **161** C2
Espinosa de los Monteros **153** C1
Espinoso del Rey **160** A3, **166** B1
Espírito Santo **170** B1
Esplantas **110** B1
Esplegares **161** D2
Esplús **155** C3, **163** C1
Espolla **156** B2
Espondeilhan **110** B3
Esponellá **156** B2
Espoo/Esbo **25** C3
Esporles **157** C2
Esposende **150** A3, **158** A1
Espot **155** D2
Esprels **89** D3
Espronceda **153** D2
Es Pujols **157** D3
Esquedas **154** B2
Esquivias **160** B3
Esrange **10** B3
Essai **86** B2
Esse (Ähtävä) **20** B1

Essen **80** A1
Essen **78** B1
Essen-Kettwig **80** A1
Esserteaux **77** D3
Essertenne-et-Cecey **89** C3
Essing **92** A1
Essingen **91** C/D2
Esslingen **91** C2
Essômes-sur-Marne **88** A1
Essoyes **88** B2
Essvik **35** D3
Estació d'Amposta **163** C2
Estada **155** C3
Estadilla **155** C3
Estagel **156** B1
Estaing **110** A1
Estaires **78** A2
Estallenchs **157** C2
Estang **108** B2
Estavayer-le-Lac **104** B1
Este **107** C3
Estebanvela **161** C1
Estela **158** A1
Estella **153** D2, **154** A2
Estensvoll **33** C3, **37** D1
Estepa **172** A2
Estépar **152** B2/3
Estepona **172** A3
Esterasa de Medina **161** D1/2
Estercuel **162** B2
Estérencuby **108** B3, **155** C1
Esternay **88** A1
Esterri d'Àneu **155** C2
Estertal-Bösingfeld **68** A3
Esterwegen **67** D2
Esterzili **123** D2
Esthal **90** B1
Estibella **162** B3, **169** D1
Estiche **155** C3, **163** C1
Estissac **88** A2
Estivareilles **102** B2
Estoi **170** B2
Estômbar **170** A2
Estopiñán **155** C3
Estorf **68** A/B1
Estoril **164** A2
Estorninos **159** C3, **165** C1
Estrées-Saint-Denis **78** A3
Estreito **158** B3, **164** B1
Estremera **161** C3
Estremoz **165** C2
Estriégana **161** D2
Estuna **41** C3
Estvad **48** A/B2
Esztergom **95** D3
Esztergom **96** B3
Étables **101** C1
Étables-sur-Mer **85** C1/2
Étagnac **101** D2
Étain **89** C1
Étais-la Sauvin **88** A3
Étalle **79** C3
Étampes **87** C2
Étang-sur-Arroux **103** C1
Étaples **77** D2
Étaules **100** B3
Étauliers **100** B3
Étel **84** B3
Eteläinen **25** C2
EteläIahti **18** A3, **21** D1, **22** A1
Etelämaa **24** A1
Etelä-Vartsala **24** A2, **41** D2
Etelhem **47** D3
Étival-Clairefontaine **89** D2, **90** A2
Etnedal **37** D2/3
Etnesjøen **42** A1
Étoges **88** A1
Etolikón **146** A2
Eton **64** B3
Étréaupont **78** B3
Étréchy **87** C/D2
Étrépagny **77** D3, **87** C1
Étretat **77** C/D1
Étropole **140** B3
Étroubles **104** B3
Ettal **92** A3
Ettelbrück **79** D3
Ettenheim **90** A/B2
Etten-Leur **79** C1
Ettenstatt **91** D1, **92** A1
Ettington **64** A2
Ettlingen **90** B1
Ettringen **91** D2

Étuz **89** C3, **104** A1
Etxebarri **153** D1
Etxebarri **110** A3, **156** B1
Etyek **95** D3, **129** C1
Etzenricht **82** B3
Eu **77** C/D2
Euerdorf **81** D2
Eugénie-les-Bains **108** B2
Eúgenikon **145** D3
Eugmo **20** B1
Eugui **108** A3, **154** A1/2
Eulate **153** D2
Eupen **79** D2
Eura **24** B2
Eurajoki **24** A1/2
Eurasburg **92** A2
Eursinge **67** C3
Euskirchen **79** D2, **80** A2
Eutin **53** C1
Eutresis **147** C2
Eväjärvi **25** C1, **26** A1
Evanger **36** A/B3
Évaux-les-Bains **102** A/B2
Evenesdal **15** C1
Évenos **111** D3, **112** A3
Evenskjær **9** C2
Evenstad **38** A1
Evergem **78** B1
Everöd **50** B3
Everswinkel **67** D3
Evertsberg **39** C1/2
Evesham **63** D1, **64** A2
Évians-les-Bains **104** B2
Evijärvi **21** C2
Evinochórion **146** B2
Evínos **146** B2
Évisa **113** D3
Evitskog **25** C3
Evje **43** C3
Evjen **14** B1
Evolène [Sion] **105** C2
Evora **164** B2
Évora de Alcobaça **164** A1
Evoramonte **165** C2
Évran **85** C2
Évrange **79** D3
Évrecy **86** A1
Évreux **86** B1
Évron **86** A2
Évropos **139** C3, **143** C/D1
Evrostína **147** B/C2
Evry **87** D2
Évzoni **139** C/D3, **143** D1
Ewijk **66** B3
Exaplátanos **143** C/D1
Exaplátanos **145** C1
Éxarchos **147** C1/2
Excideuil **101** D3
Exeter **63** C2/3
Exmes **86** B1
Exmouth **63** C3
Exochí **144** B1
Extertal **68** A3
Extremo **150** A3
Eydehamn **43** C3
Eye **65** C2
Eye **65** B/C1/2
Eyemouth **57** D2
Eyguians **111** D2, **112** A2
Eyguières **111** C/D2
Eygurande **102** A3
Eygurande-et-Gardefeuil **101** C3, **108** B1
Eylie **155** D2
Eymet **109** C3
Eymoutiers **102** A3
Eysteinkyrkja **33** C3, **37** D1
Eystrup **68** A/B2
Ézaro **150** A2
Ezcaray **153** C2
Ezcurra **154** A1
Ezeris **135** C1
Ezerišče **74** B2/3
Ezine **149** C1

F

Fabara **163** C1/2
Fabas **109** C3, **155** D1
Fåberg **37** D2, **38** A1
Fåbergstølen **36** B2
Fabero **151** C2

Fabian **155** C2
Fåbodliden **30** B1
Fåborg **53** B/C2
Fabrègues **110** B3
Fabrezan **110** A3, **156** B1
Fabriano **115** D3, **117** C2
Fabrízia **122** A/B3
Facha **150** A3, **158** A1
Facheca **169** D2
Facinas **171** D3
Facture **108** A1
Fadagosa **165** C1
Fadd **129** C2
Faédis **126** A2
Faenza **115** C2, **116** B1
Faeto **120** A1/2
Fafe **158** A/B1
Fågåras **140** B1
Fågelberget **29** D2
Fågelfors **51** C/D1
Fågelmara **51** D2
Fågelsjö **39** D1
Fågelsta **46** A2
Fågelsundet **40** B2
Fågelvik **47** B/C3
Fagerhaug **33** C2
Fagerhøi **37** D2
Fagerholt **44** B1/2
Fagerhult **44** B2
Fagerhult **51** C1
Fagernes **4** A3
Fagernes **37** D2/3
Fagersanna **45** D2, **46** A2
Fagersta **39** D3, **40** A3
Fagerstrand **38** A3, **44** B1
Fagervik **25** C3
Fagervika **14** A2
Fåget **140** A/B1
Fäggeby **39** D2, **40** A2
Fåglavik **45** C/D3
Fagnano Castello **122** A1
Fago **154** B2
Fahrenhorst **68** A2
Fahrenzhausen-Grossnö- bach **92** A2
Fahrland **70** A2
Fahy [Porrentruy] **89** D3, **90** A3
Faia **158** B1
Fai della Paganella **107** B/C2
Faido **105** D2
Faimes **79** C2
Fairford **64** A3
Fairlie **56** B2
Faissault **78** B3
Fajão **158** B3
Fakenham **65** C1
Fåker **34** B2
Fakovići **133** C2
Fakse **53** D1
Fakse Ladeplads **53** D1/2
Falaise **86** A1
Falaise d'Aval **76** B3
Fålasjø **30** B3, **35** D2
Falcade **107** C2
Falces **154** A2
Falconara Maríttima **115** D3, **117** D2
Falcone **125** D1/2
Faleide **32** A3, **36** B1
Falerna **122** A2
Falerum **46** B3
Falešty **99** C3
Falešty **141** C1
Falirákion **149** D3
Falkenberg **72** A1
Falkenberg **82** B3
Falkenberg **49** D2, **50** A1
Falkenberg **92** B2
Falkenberg **83** C1
Falkenhagen **69** D1/2
Falkenhain **82** B1
Falkenrehde **70** A2
Falkensee **70** A2
Falkenstein **82** B2
Falkenstein **92** B1
Falkenthal **70** A2
Falkirk **57** B/C1/2
Falkland **57** C1
Falköping **45** D3
Fall **37** D3, **38** A2
Fallet **34** A/B3
Fällfors **20** A1, **31** D2
Fällfors **16** B3
Fallingbostel **68** B2

Fallingbostel-Dorfmark
68 B2
Fällkäl 30 B2, 35 D1
Fällkäl 30 B2, 35 D1
Fällsvikshamnen 30 B3
Falltorp 38 B2
Falmouth 62 B3
Falset 163 C/D1/2
Falstone 57 C/D2/3
Fälticeni 141 C1
Fältjägarstugan 34 A2
Falträsk 31 B/C1
Falun 39 D2
Fana 36 A3
Fanano 114 B2, 116 A1
Fanári 147 C/D3
Fanárion 143 C3
Fanárion 145 C1
Fanefjord Kirke 53 D2
Fangel 53 C1
Fanghetto 112 B2
Fanjeaux 109 D3, 156 A1
Fankel 80 A3
Fannrem (Orkanger) 28 A3,
33 C2
Fano 115 D2, 117 C/D1
Fanø Vesterhavsbad 52 A1
Fantoft 36 A3
Fanzara 162 B3
Fão 150 A3, 158 A1
Fara 127 C3
Faråd 95 B/C3
Fara in Sabina 118 B1
Faraján 172 A2/3
Faramontanos de Tábara
151 D3, 159 D1
Fara Novarese 105 C/D3
Fara San Martino
119 C/D1/2
Farasdués 154 B2
Fårbo 51 D1
Fårbo 72 B1
Farchant 92 A3
Farcheville 87 D2
Fardella 120 B3
Færder 44 B1/2
Fareham 76 B1
Färentuna 47 C1
Fårevejle 49 C3, 53 C1
Fargau-Pratjau 53 C3
Färgelanda 45 C2
Faringdon 64 A3
Faringe 40 B3
Färingtofta 50 B2/3
Farini d'Olmo 113 D1,
114 A1
Färjestaden 51 D2
Färjestaden 72 B1
Farkadón 143 C3
Farlete 154 B3, 162 B1
Färlöv 50 B2/3
Farná 95 D3
Färnäs 39 D2
Farnborough 65 C3, 76 B1
Farnborough 64 B3, 76 B1
Farnese 116 B3, 118 A1
Farnham 64 B3, 76 B1
Farningham 65 C3,
77 B/C1
Farnworth 59 D2, 60 B2/3
Fårö 47 D2
Faro 170 B2
Faro do Alentejo 164 B3
Fårösund 47 D2
Fårösund 73 C1
Farra d'Alpago 107 D2
Farrington Gurney 63 D2
Farrou 109 D1/2
Fársala 143 D3
Fársala 148 B1/2
Farsaliótis 143 C/D3
Farsø 48 B3
Farstad 32 A2
Farsund 42 B3
Farum 49 D3, 50 A3,
53 D1
Fårup 48 B2
Fasano 121 C2
Fassberg 68 B2
Fassberg-Müden 68 B2
Fåssjö 35 B/C3
Fasterholt 48 B3
Fastov 99 C2
Fátima 164 A/B1
Fatmomakke 29 D1
Fättjaur 15 C3
Faucogney 89 D3

Faugères 110 B3
Fauguerolles 109 C1/2
Faulenrost 69 D1, 70 A1
Faulquemont 89 D1
Faulungen 81 D1
Fauquembergues 77 D2
Fáurei 141 C1/2
Fauske 15 C1
Fauville-en-Caux 77 C3
Fauvillers 79 C3
Fåvang 37 D2, 38 A1
Favara 124 B3
Favareta 169 D2
Faverges 104 A3
Faverney 89 C3
Faverolles 87 C1/2
Faversham 65 C3, 77 C1
Favignana 124 A2
Favone 113 D2
Fawley 76 B1
Fay-aux-Loges 87 C2/3
Fay-de-Bretagne 85 D3
Fayence 112 A/B3
Fayet 110 A2
Fayl-Billot 89 C3
Fayón 163 C1
Fay-sur-Lignon 111 C1
Fažana 130 A1
Fazendas de Almeirim
164 B2
Fécamp 77 C3
Feces de Abajo 151 B/C3,
158 B1
Feda 42 B3
Fedje 36 A3
Fefor 37 D2
Fegen 50 A1
Fégréac 85 C3
Fegyvernek 129 D1
Fehérvárcsurgó 95 C3,
128 B1
Fehrbellin 69 D2, 70 A2
Fehring 127 D1
Feichten 106 B1
Feigefossen 36 B2
Feios 36 B2
Feira 158 A2
Feiring 38 A2
Feistritz am Wechsel 94 A3
Feiteira 170 B2
Feitos 150 A3, 158 A1
Feketić 129 C/D1
Fekjan 37 D3
Felanitx 157 C2
Felchow 70 B2
Feldbach 127 D1
Feldbach 96 A3
Feldberg 90 B3
Feldberg 70 A1
Felde 52 B3
Feldkirch 106 A1
Feldkirchen in Kärnten
126 B1/2
Feldkirchen-Westerham
92 A3
Feldkirchen in Kärnten
96 A3
Felgueiras 158 A/B1
Feliceto 113 D2
Felina 114 A/B1/2
Félines-Termenès 110 A3,
156 B1
Felino 114 A1
Felísio 115 C2, 116 B1
Felitto 120 A3
Félix 173 D2
Felixstowe 65 C2
Felizzano 113 C1
Fell 79 D3, 80 A3
Fellbach 91 C2
Felletin 102 A2
Fellingfors 14 B3
Fellingsbro 46 B1
Felsberg 81 C1
Felsörajk 128 A2
Felsöszentiván 129 C2
Felsted 52 B2
Felton 57 D2
Feltre 107 C2
Femanger 42 A1
Femsjö 50 B1
Femundsenden 33 D3
Femundshytta 33 D3
Fendeille 109 D3, 156 A1
Fene 150 B1
Fenékpuszta 128 A2
Fener 107 C2/3

Fenes 9 C1
Fenestrelle 112 B1
Fénétrange 89 D1, 90 A1/2
Fengersfors 45 C2
Fenny Stratford 64 B2
Fensmark 53 D1
Feolin Ferry 56 A2
Feragen 33 D2/3
Ferchland 69 D2
Ferdinandovac 128 A2
Ferdinandshof 70 B1
Fère-Champenoise 88 A1
Fère-en-Tardenois 88 A1
Ferentillo 117 C3, 118 B1
Ferentino 119 B/C2
Férento 117 C3, 118 A1
Férez 168 B3
Feria 165 D2
Feričanci 128 B3
Ferla 125 C/D3
Ferlach 126 B2
Fermignano 115 D2/3,
117 C2
Fermo 117 D2
Fermoselle 159 C1
Fermoy 55 C3
Fernancaballero 167 C2
Fernán Núñez 172 B1
Ferney-Voltaire 104 A2
Fernhurst 76 B1
Ferns 58 A3
Ferragudo 170 A2
Férrai 145 D1, 145 D3
Férrai 149 C1
Ferrals-les-Corbières
110 A3, 156 B1
Ferrandina 120 B3
Ferrara 115 C1
Ferrara di Monte Baldo
106 B3
Ferreira do Alentejo
164 B3, 170 A/B1
Ferreira do Zêzere 158 A3,
164 B1
Ferreiros 150 A3, 158 A1
Ferreras de Abajo 151 D3
Ferreras de Arriba 151 D3
Ferrerías 157 C1
Ferreruela 163 C2
Ferret [Orsières] 104 B2/3
Ferrette 89 D3, 90 A3
Ferriere 113 D1
Ferrière-Larçon 101 D1
Ferrières 100 B2
Ferrières 108 B3, 154 B1
Ferrières-en-Gâtinais
87 D2
Ferrières-Saint-Mary
102 B3
Ferrières-sur-Sichon
103 C2
Ferring 48 A2
Ferrol 150 B1
Fertília 123 C1/2
Fertöd 94 B3
Fertöszentmiklós 94 B3
Fervença 158 B1
Ferwerd 66 B1
Festøy 32 A3, 36 B1
Festvåg 8 B2
Festvåg 8 B3
Feteşti 141 C/D2
Fetsund 38 A3
Feucht 92 A1
Feuchtwangen 91 D1
Feudingen 80 B2
Feugarolles 109 C2
Feurs 103 C3
Fevåg 28 A3, 33 C1
Fevik 43 C3
Ffestiniog 59 C2/3, 60 A3
Fiamignano 117 D3,
118 A1
Fiane 43 C3
Fiano 105 C3, 112 B1
Fiastra 115 D3, 117 D2
Ficarolo 115 B/C1
Fichtelberg 82 A3
Fichtenau-Wildenstein
91 D1
Fichtenberg 91 C1
Fichtenwalde 70 A3
Ficulle 117 C3
Fidenza 114 A1
Fidjeland 42 B2
Fiè allo Scíliar/Völs am
Schlern 107 C2

Fieberbrunn 92 B3
Fienvillers 77 D2
Fier 142 A1/2
Fier 148 A1
Fiera di Primiero 107 C2
Fierbinți Tîrg 141 C2
Fierbinți 141 C2
Fiesch 105 C2
Fiésole 114 B2, 116 B1
Figalía 146 B3
Figeac 109 D1
Figeholm 51 D1
Figline Valdarno 115 B/C3,
116 B2
Figueira da Foz 158 A3
Figueira de Castelo Rodrigo
159 C2
Figueira dos Cavaleiros
164 B2
Figueiredo de Alva 158 B2
Figueiro 158 B2
Figueiró dos Vinhos
158 A3, 164 B1
Figueiró do Campo 158 A3
Figuera 155 D3, 156 A3,
163 D1
Figueral 157 D3
Figueres 156 B2
Figuerola d'Orcau
155 D2/3
Figueruelas 155 C3,
163 B/C1
Fiholm 47 B/C1
Fiksdal 32 A2/3
Filadélfia 142 A/B2
Filadélfion 144 A1/2
Filáki 143 D3, 147 C1
Filákion 145 D2/3
Filákion 141 C3
Filaktí 143 C3
Filettino 119 C2
Filey 61 D2
Filí 147 D2
Fília 146 B3
Fília 148 B2
Filiași 140 B2
Filiași 135 C3
Filiátai 142 B3
Filiatrá 146 B3
Filiatrá 148 A/B2
Filipjakov 130 B2
Filipstad 39 C3, 45 D1
Filiriá 143 D1
Filitosa 113 D3
Fillan 32 B1
Fillingsnes 32 B1
Fillsta 29 D3, 34 B2
Filótas 143 C2
Filottrano 115 D3, 117 D2
Filskov 48 A/B3, 52 B1
Filsum 67 D1
Filton 63 D1/2
Filtvet 44 B1
Filzmoos 93 C3
Finale di Rero 115 C1
Finale Emília 114 B1
Finale Lígure 113 C2
Fiñana 173 D2
Finbo 41 C2
Finby 41 D3
Findon 76 B1
Fines 173 D1/2, 174 A1/2
Finja 50 B2
Finnanger 28 B1/2
Finnart 56 B1
Finnäs 30 B1
Finnbacka 39 D2
Finnberget 39 C1
Finnbyen 8 A2/3
Finneby 35 C3
Finneidfjord 14 B2
Finnemisj kapell 5 C/D2,
6 A2
Finnentrop 80 B1
Finnerödja 45 D2, 46 A2
Finnes 9 C/D1
Finnes 14 B1
Finnfjordeidnet 9 D1
Finngruvan 39 C2
Finnhamn 47 D1
Finning 91 D2/3, 92 A3
Finnjord 4 A3, 10 A1
Finnkroken 4 A2
Finnmyren 16 B3
Finnøy 42 A2
Finnøy 9 C3
Finnsäter 29 C3, 34 B1

Finnset 32 B3, 37 C1
Finnskog 38 B2
Finnsnes 9 D1
Finntorp 45 C1
Finnträsk 16 B3
Finnvik 42 A1/2
Finnvik 5 C1
Finnvollan 29 C1
Fino Mornasco 105 D3,
106 A3
Fins 78 A3
Finsand 37 D3
Finse 37 B/C3
Finsjö 51 D1
Finsland 42 B3
Finspång 46 B2
Finstad 33 D3
Finstad 38 B2
Finsterwalde 70 A/B3,
83 C1
Finsterwalde 72 A3, 96 A1
Finström 41 C2/3
Fintel 68 B1/2
Fintry 56 B1
Fionnay [Le Châble]
104 B2
Fionnphort 54 A2, 55 D1
Fiorano Modenese 114 B1
Fiorenzuola d'Arda 114 A1
Fiquefleur 77 C3
Firenze 114 B2, 116 B1/2
Firenzuola 117 C3, 118 B1
Firenzuola 114 B2, 116 B1
Firminy 103 C3
Firmo 122 A1
Firovo 75 C2
Fiscal 155 C2
Fischach 91 D2
Fischamend Markt 94 B2
Fischamend Markt 96 B3
Fischbach 94 A3
Fischbach 90 A1
Fischbach (Birkenfeld)
80 A3
Fischen 91 D3
Fishguard 62 B1
Fishguard 55 D3
Fiskåhaugen 28 B1
Fiskarheden 39 C2
Fiskari/Fiskars 25 B/C3
Fiskbæk 48 B2
Fiskebäckskil 44 B3
Fiskebøl 8 B2
Fiskeby 46 B2
Fiskefjord 9 C2
Fiskeläge 31 D1
Fiskevollen 33 D3
Fiskö 24 A2/3, 41 D2
Fiskøy 9 C2
Fisksätra 47 D1
Fisksjölandet 35 C2
Fisktjønnmoen 14 B2
Fismes 88 A1
Fisterra 150 A2
Fitero 154 A3
Fitíai 146 A1
Fitjar 42 A1
Fiuggi 118 B2
Fiuggi Fonte 118 B2
Fiumalbo 114 B2, 116 A1
Fiumata 117 D3, 118 B1
Fiumefreddo di Sicília
125 D2
Fiumefreddo Brúzio 122 A2
Fivizzano 114 A2, 116 A1
Fix-Saint-Geneys 103 C3,
110 B1
Fjägesund 43 C2
Fjäl 29 D3, 34 B2
Fjälbyn 31 D1
Fjälkinge 50 B2/3
Fjällandet 29 D3, 35 C2
Fjällåsen 10 A3
Fjällbacka 44 B2
Fjällbosjö 15 D3
Fjällnäs 33 D2, 34 A2/3
Fjällsjönäs 15 D3
Fjällskäfte 46 B1
Fjälltuna 30 B2, 35 D1
Fjand Gårde 48 A2
Fjæra 42 A/B1
Fjärås 49 D1, 50 A1
Fjärdhundra 40 A3
Fjære 43 C3
Fjærland 36 B2
Fjelberg 42 A1
Fjell 36 A3

Fjell 28 B2
Fjellerup 49 C2
Fjellkjøsa 28 A3, 33 C1/2
Fjellsrud 38 A3
Fjellstad 9 D1
Fjellstøl 43 C1
Fjellvær 32 B1
Fjelstrup 52 B1
Fjerritslev 48 B1
Fjølvika 28 B1
Fjørtoft 32 A2
Fjugesta 46 A1
Flå 37 D3
Flå 28 A3, 33 C2
Flaach [Henggart] 90 B3
Fladungen 81 D2
Flaka 41 D3
Flakaträsk 15 D3
Flakaträsk 31 B/C2
Flakk 28 A3, 33 C1
Flakkebjerg 53 C1
Flakstad 8 A/B2/3
Flåm 36 B3
Flamatt 104 B1
Flammersfeld 80 A2
Flåmseter 33 C3, 37 D1
Flärke 31 C2/3
Flarken 31 D1/2
Flassans-sur-Issole 112 A3
Flata 5 D2, 6 A2
Flatabø 42 A/B1
Flatdal 43 C1
Flåte 42 A1
Flateby 38 A3
Flateland 42 B2
Flaten 43 C3
Flåten 4 B2
Flatford Mill 65 C/D2
Flatholmen 44 B3
Flatøydegard 37 D2/3
Flatråker 42 A1
Flått 28 B1
Flattach 107 D1, 126 A1
Flattnitz 126 B1
Flatval 32 B1
Flatvoll 37 D3
Flauenskjold 49 B/C1
Flavigny-sur-Moselle 89 C2
Flawil 91 C3
Flayat 102 A2/3
Flechtingen 69 C3
Fleckeby 52 B2
Flecken Zechlin 69 D1/2, 70 A1/2
Fleet 64 B3, 76 B1
Fleetmark 69 C2
Fleetwood 59 C/D1, 60 B2
Flekke 36 A2
Flekkefjord 42 B3
Flemløse 52 B1
Flen 39 D2/3
Flen 46 B1
Flensburg 52 B2
Flenstad 28 A2, 33 C1
Fléres/Pflersch 107 C1
Flermoen 38 B1
Flers 86 A1
Flesberg 43 D1
Flesje 36 B2
Flesnes 9 C2
Flessau 69 C/D2
Flesvik 33 B/C1
Fleurance 109 C2
Fleuré 101 C2
Fleurey-lès-Faverney 89 C3
Fleurie 103 D2
Fleurier 104 B1
Fleurus 79 B/C2
Fleurville 103 D2
Fleury 77 D3, 87 C1
Fleury-en-Bière 87 C2
Fleury-sur-Andelle 76 B3, 86 B1
Flez 88 A3
Flickerbäcken 38 B1
Flieden 81 C2
Flims Dorf [Trin] 105 D1, 106 A1
Flims Waldhaus [Valendas-Sagogn] 105 D1, 106 A1
Flines-les-Râches 78 A2
Flins-sur-Seine 87 C1
Flint 59 C2, 60 B3
Flintbek 52 B3
Flirsch 106 B1

Flisa 38 B2
Flisby 46 A3
Fliseryd 51 D1
Flivik 46 B3
Flix 163 C1
Flize 79 C3
Flø 36 A1
Floby 45 D3
Floda 31 C/D1
Floda 45 C3
Floda 46 B1
Floda 39 D2
Flogny 88 A2
Flöha 83 B/C2
Floirac 108 B1
Flor 34 B3
Flora 28 B3, 33 D1
Florac 110 B2
Flôr da Rosa 165 C1/2
Florejachs 155 C3, 163 C1
Florennes 79 B/C2
Florensac 110 B3
Florentin 135 D2
Florenville 79 C3
Flores de Ávila 160 A2
Floridia 125 D2
Flórina 143 C1/2
Florínas 123 C1/2
Florø 36 A2
Flörsbach 81 C3
Flörsbachtal 81 C3
Florstadt-Niederflorstadt 81 C2
Florvåg 36 A3
Floss 82 B3
Flossenbürg 82 B3
Flosta 43 C3
Flostrand 14 B2
Flötningen 33 D3
Fløttumsetra 33 C2
Flovika 8 B2
Fluberg 37 D3, 38 A2
Flüelen 105 D1
Flüh 90 A3
Flumet 104 B3
Flúmini 123 D3
Fluminimaggiore 123 C3
Flums 105 D1, 106 A1
Fluorn-Winzeln 90 B2
Flurkmark 31 C/D2
Flyggsjö 31 C2
Flyinge 50 B3
Flykälen 29 D2/3, 34 B1
Flyn 30 A2, 35 C1
Flystveit 42 B3
Flytsåsen 39 D1
Fobello 105 C2/3
Foča 133 C3
Foça 149 D2
Fochabers 54 B2
Focsani 141 C1/2
Foeni 140 A1/2
Fogdö 47 C1
Fóggia 120 A1
Foglianise 119 D3
Föglö 41 D3
Fogueteiro 164 A2
Fohnsdorf 127 C1
Foiano della Chiana 115 C3, 116 B2
Foiano Valfortore 119 D2, 120 A1
Foix 109 D3, 155 D1/2, 156 A1
Fojnica 132 B2
Fojnica 132 B3, 137 C1
Fokovci 127 D1/2
Fokstua 33 B/C3, 37 D1
Foldereid 28 B1
Foldingbro 52 A/B1
Fole 47 D2/3
Folelli 113 D2/3
Folgaria 107 C2/3
Folgosa 158 B1/2
Folgoso de la Ribera 151 D2
Folgoso do Caurel 151 C2
Foligno 115 D3, 117 C2/3
Folkärna 40 A3
Folkestad 36 A/B1
Folkestone 65 C3, 76 B1
Folkingham 61 D3, 64 B1
Follafoss 28 B2, 33 D1
Follandsvangen 33 C3, 37 D1
Folldalsverk 33 C3, 37 D1
Follebu 37 D2, 38 A1

Follina 107 C/D2
Föllinge 29 D3, 34 B1
Follónica 116 A3
Fombelaux 101 D3
Fombellida 152 B3, 160 B1
Foncea 153 C2
Foncine-le-Bas 104 A2
Foncouverte 110 A2
Fondamente 110 B2
Fondi 119 C2
Fondo 107 C2
Fondón 173 D2
Fonelas 173 C1/2
Fonfría 162 A/B2
Fonfría 151 D3, 159 D1
Fonn 36 B2
Fonnebostsjøn 36 A3
Fonnes 36 A3
Fonni 123 D2
Fonó 128 B2
Fons 111 C2
Fontainebleau 87 D2
Fontaine-Chalendray 101 C2
Fontaine-de-Vaucluse 111 D2
Fontaine-Française 89 C3
Fontaine Henry 76 B3, 86 A1
Fontaine-la-Soret 77 C3, 86 B1
Fontaine-le-Dun 77 C3
Fontaine-le-Comte 88 B1
Fontana Liri 119 C2
Fontanarejo 167 C2
Fontane 113 C2
Fontanellato 114 A1
Fontanelle 114 A1
Fontanelle 107 D3
Fontanetto Po 105 C3, 113 C1
Fontaniva 107 C3
Fontannes 103 C3
Fontanosas 167 C2
Fonte Blanda 116 B3
Fonte Bôa 170 A1
Fontécchio 117 D3, 119 C1
Fontellas 154 A3
Fontenay-le-Comte 100 B2
Fontenay-sur-Loing 87 D2
Fontenay-Trésigny 87 D1/2
Fontet 108 B1
Fontevrault-l'Abbaye 86 A/B3, 101 C1
Fontfroide 110 A3, 156 B1
Fontgombault 101 D1
Fontibre 152 B1/2
Fonti del Clitunno 117 C3
Fontiveros 160 A2
Font Romeu 156 A2
Fontvieille 111 C3
Fonyód 128 A1/2
Fonz 155 C3
Fonzaleche 153 C2
Fonzaso 107 C2
Fóppolo 106 A2
Föra 51 D2
Foradada 155 D3
Foradada de Tosca 155 C2
Foråsen 29 D3, 34 B1
Forbach 90 B2
Forbach 89 D1, 90 A1
Forbach-Schönmünzach 90 B2
Förby 24 B3
Forcall 162 B2
Forcalqueiret 112 A3
Forcalquier 111 D2, 112 A2
Forchheim 82 A3
Forchheim 83 C2
Forchtenau 94 B3
Forchtenberg 91 C1
Førde 36 B2
Førde 36 A2
Førde 42 A1
Förderstedt 69 C/D3
Fordingbridge 76 A1
Fordongiánus 123 C2
Fore 14 B1
Forenza 120 B2
Foresta Búrgos 123 C/D2
Forest-Montiers 77 D2

Føresvik 42 A2
Forfar 57 C1
Forfar 54 B2
Forges-les-Eaux 77 D3
Forheim-Aufhausen 91 D2
Foria 120 A3
Forío 119 C3
Forjães 150 A3, 158 A1
Forland 42 B3
Førland 42 B3
Forlì 115 C2, 117 B/C1
Forlì del Sánnio 119 C2
Forlimpópoli 115 C2, 117 C1
Formby 59 C2, 60 B2/3
Formerie 77 D3
Fórmia 119 C3
Formiche Alto 162 B3
Formiche Bajo 162 B3
Formiche di Grosseto 116 A3
Formícola 119 C/D3
Formigal 154 B2
Formigaleso 155 C2
Formigine 114 B1
Formigliana 105 C3
Formignana 115 C1
Formiguères 156 A1/2
Fornalutx 157 C2
Fornebu 38 A3
Fornelli 123 C1
Fornells 157 C2
Fornells de la Muntanya 156 A2
Fornelos de Montes 150 A2
Fornes 173 C2
Fornes 9 C1/2
Fornes 9 D1
Forneset 43 C2
Forni Avoltri 107 D2, 126 A2
Forni di Sopra 107 D2
Forni di Sotto 107 D2, 126 A2
Forno 112 B3
Forno Allione 106 B2
Forno Alpi Gráie 104 B3
Forno di Zoldo 107 D2
Fórnoles 163 C2
Fornols 155 D2, 156 A2
Fornos de Algedres 158 B2
Fornovo di Taro 114 A1
Forradal 28 B3, 33 D1
Forráskút 129 D2
Fors 40 A3
Fors 31 B/C3
Forsa 40 A1
Forsand 42 A2
Forsbacka 15 D2/3
Forsed 30 A3, 35 D2
Forserum 46 A3
Forshaga 45 D1
Forsheda 50 B1
Forsland 14 A2
Förslövsholm 49 D2, 50 A2
Forsmark 40 B2
Forsmark 15 C3
Forsmo 30 A2/3, 35 C1
Forsmo 30 A2/3, 35 C1
Forsmo 30 B3, 35 D2
Forsnacken 15 C3
Forsnäs 30 A/B2
Forsnäs 16 A2
Forsnäs 16 B2
Forsnes 32 B1
Forsøl 5 C1, 6 A1
Forssa 25 C2
Forssjö 46 B2
Forst 70 B3
Forst 72 A3, 96 A1
Forstau 93 C3, 126 A/B1
Forsvik 46 A2
Fortanete 162 B2
Fort Augustus 54 A2, 55 D1
Forte dei Marmi 114 A2, 116 A1
Forte di Bibbona 114 A/B3, 116 A2
Förtha 81 D2
Fortingall 56 B1
Fortino 120 A/B3
Fort la Latte 85 C1/2
Fort-Mahon-Plage 77 D2
Fortun 37 C2
Fortuna 169 C3

Fortuneswell 63 D3
Fort William 54 A2, 55 D1
Forvik 14 A3
Fos 155 C2
Fosdinovo 114 A2
Foskros 34 A3
Fosmark 42 A2
Fosnavåg 36 A1
Foss 33 C2
Foss 28 B2
Fossacésia 119 D1
Fossacésia Marina 119 D1
Fossano 113 B/C1/2
Fossbakken 33 C3
Fossbakken 9 D2
Fossbua 10 A2
Fosse 37 D2
Fossé 86 A/B3
Fossemagne 101 D3, 109 C1
Fosser 38 A3
Fosses-la-Ville 79 C2
Fossestølen 36 A3
Fossestrand 5 D2, 6 A2
Fosseter 33 C3, 37 D1
Fossheim 37 C/D2
Fossholt 37 D3
Fossli 36 B3
Fosso Ghiáia 115 C2, 117 C1
Fóssoli 114 B1
Fossombrone 115 D2/3, 117 C2
Fos-sur-Mer 111 C3
Fót 95 D3
Fotheringhay 64 B2
Fotolívos 144 B1
Foucarmont 77 D3
Fouesnant 84 B2/3
Fougères 86 A/B2
Fougères-sur-Bièvre 86 A/B3
Fougerolles 89 D2/3
Foulain 89 B/C2
Foulsham 65 C/D1
Fountains Abbey 61 C2
Fouras 100 B2
Fourchambault 102 B1
Fourfourás 149 C2/3
Foúrka 142 A2
Fourmies 78 B3
Fourná 146 B1
Fournels 110 B2
Fournols 103 B/C3
Fourques 156 B1/2
Fourquet 109 C2
Fours 103 C1
Fours 112 A/B2
Fovant 63 D2, 76 A1
Foz 151 C1
Foz de Arouce 158 A3
Foz de Calanda 162 B2
Foz do Arelho 164 A1
Frabosa Soprana 113 C2
Fraddon 62 B3
Frades 150 B1/2
Frades de la Sierra 159 D2
Fraeyming-Merlebach 89 D1, 90 A1
Frafjord 42 A2
Fraga 155 C3, 163 C1
Fragagnano 121 C3
Fragneto Monforte 119 D2/3
Frahier-et-Chatebier 89 D3
Frailes 173 C1
Fraire 78 B2
Fraize 89 D2, 90 A2
Frameries 78 B2
Framlingham 65 C2
Främlingshem 40 A2
Frammersbach 81 C3
Främmestad 45 C2/3
Framnäs 16 A1
França 151 C3
Francardo 113 D3
Francavilla Fontana 121 C2/3
Francavilla di Sicília 125 D2
Francavilla al Mare 119 C/D1
Francavilla in Sinni 120 B3, 122 A1
Franco 158 B1
Francofonte 125 C3
Francorchamps 79 D2
Frändefors 45 C2

Franeker 66 B1
Frangy 104 A2
Frankenau 81 C1
Frankenberg 81 B/C1
Frankenberg 83 B/C2
Frankenburg am Hausruck 93 C2/3
Frankenfels 94 A3
Frankenfels 96 A3
Frankenhardt-Gründelhardt 91 C1
Frankenheim 81 D2
Frankenmarkt 93 C3
Frankenstein 90 B1
Frankenthal 80 B3, 90 B1
Frankershausen 81 C/D1
Frankfurat-Markendorf 70 B3
Frankfurt 70 B3
Frankfurt 72 A3
Frankfurt am Main 80 B3
Frankrike 29 C3, 34 A/B1
Frånö 30 B3, 35 D2
Fránscia 106 A/B2
Fränsta 35 C3
Františkovy Lázně 82 B3
Frascati 118 B2
Frascineto 120 B3, 122 A/B1
Fraserburgh 54 B2
Frashëri 142 B2
Frasne 104 A1
Frasnes-lez-Buissenal 78 B2
Fratel 165 B/C1
Frauenau 93 C1
Frauenfeld 91 B/C3
Frauenkirchen 94 B3
Frauenstein 83 C2
Fraugde 53 C1
Frayssinet 109 D1
Frayssinet-le-Gélat 108 B1
Frechas 159 B/C1
Frechen 79 D2, 80 A2
Frechilla 152 A3
Frechilla de Almazán 161 D1
Freden 68 B3
Fredensborg 49 D3, 50 A3
Fredericia 48 B3, 52 B1
Frederikshavn 49 C1
Frederiksoord 67 C2
Frederikssund 49 D3, 50 A3, 53 D1
Frederikssund 72 A1/2
Frederiksværk 49 D3, 50 A3
Fredes 163 C2
Fredrika 30 B2
Fredriksberg 39 C3
Fredriksdal 46 A3
Fredrikshamn 26 B2
Fredrikstad 44 B1
Fredros 38 B3
Fredvang 8 A2/3
Fregenal de la Sierra 165 D3
Freginals 163 C2
Frehne 69 D1
Frei 32 B2
Freiamt-Ottoschwanden 90 B2
Freiberg 83 C2
Freiberg 96 A1
Freiberg am Neckar 91 C1
Freiburg 52 B3, 68 A/B1
Freiburg im Breisgau 90 A/B3
Freiburg-Tiengen 90 A3
Freiensteinau 81 C2
Freigericht 81 C2
Freihung 82 A/B3
Freila 173 D1
Freiland 94 A3
Freilassing 93 B/C3
Freilingen 80 B2
Freisen 80 A3, 90 A1
Freising 92 A2
Freistadt 93 D2
Freistadt 96 A2
Freistatt 68 A2
Freital 83 C1/2
Freixedas 159 B/C2
Freixenet de Segarra 155 C3, 163 C1
Freixianda 158 A3, 164 B1
Freixiosa 158 B2
Freixo 165 C2
Freixo de Espada a Cinta 159 C2
Fréjus 112 A/B3
Frekhaug 36 A3
Frelsdorf 68 A1
Fremdingen 91 D1
Frensdorf 81 D3
Frenštát pod Radhoštěm 95 C1
Freren 67 D2
Fréscano 154 A3
Freshwater 76 A1/2
Fresnay-sur-Sarthe 86 A/B2
Fresneda de Altarejos 161 D3, 168 B1
Fresneda de la Sierra 161 D2/3
Fresneda de la Sierra Tirón 153 C2
Fresnedillas 160 B2
Fresnedo 151 C2
Fresnedoso de Ibor 159 D3, 166 A/B1
Fresne-Saint-Mamès 89 C3
Fresnes-en-Woëvre 89 C1
Fresnes-sur-Apance 89 C2/3
Fresnes-sur-Escaut 78 B2
Fresnillo de las Dueñas 153 C3, 161 B/C1
Fresno-Alhandiga 159 D2
Fresno de Cantespino 161 C1
Fresno de Caracena 161 C1
Fresno de la Ribera 151 D3, 152 A3, 159 D1
Fresno de Riotirón 153 C2
Fresno de Sayago 159 D1
Fresno de Torote 161 C2
Fresnoy-Folny 77 C/D2/3
Fressonneville 77 D2
Fresvik 36 B2
Frétigney-et-Velloreille 89 C3
Frettes 89 C3
Freudenberg 82 A/B3, 92 B1
Freudenberg 80 B2
Freudenberg 81 C3
Freudenstadt 90 B2
Frévent 77 D2
Freyburg 82 A1
Freyenstein 69 D1
Freystadt 92 A1
Freystadt-Burggriesbach 92 A1
Freyung 93 C2
Frías 153 C2
Frías de Albarracín 162 A3
Fribourg/Freiburg 104 B1
Frick 90 B3
Frickenhausen 91 C2
Frickenhausen am Main 81 D3
Frickingen 91 C3
Fridafors 51 C2
Fridaythorpe 61 D2
Fridingen 91 B/C3
Fridolfing 92 B3
Frieda 81 D1
Friedberg 81 B/C2
Friedberg 91 D2, 92 A2
Friedberg 94 A3
Friedburg 93 C3
Friedeburg 82 A1
Friedeburg 67 D1
Friedeburg-Horsten 67 D1
Friedenfels 82 B3
Friedenshorst 69 D2, 70 A2
Friedersdorf 83 C1
Friedersdorf 70 A/B3
Friedewald (Bad Hersfeld) 81 C2
Friedland 81 C/D1
Friedland 70 B3
Friedland 70 A1
Friedland-Stockhausen 81 C/D1
Friedrichroda 81 D2
Friedrichsbrunn 69 C3
Friedrichshafen 91 C3
Friedrichshain 83 D1
Friedrichskoog 52 A3
Friedrichsluga 70 A3, 83 C1
Friedrichsruhe 69 D1
Friedrichstadt 52 A/B2/3
Friedrichsthal 89 D1, 90 A1
Friedrichsthal 70 B1/2
Friedrichswalde 70 A/B2
Frielendorf 81 C1/2
Friesach 126 B1
Friesach 96 A3
Friesack 69 D2
Friesenheim 90 B2
Friesenried 91 D3
Friesoythe 67 D2
Friesoythe-Edewechter-damm 67 D1/2
Friesoythe-Gehlenberg 67 D2
Friesoythe-Markhausen 67 D2
Friesoythe-Neuscharrel 67 D2
Friggesby 25 C3
Friggesund 35 C3
Friitala 24 A1
Frijsenborg 48 B2
Frilandsmuseum Hjerl Hede 48 A2
Frillesås 49 D1, 50 A1
Frillesås 49 D1, 50 A1
Frillesås 72 A1
Frinnaryd 46 A3
Frinton 65 C2/3
Friockheim 57 C1
Friol 150 B1/2
Fristad 45 C/D3
Fristad 15 D3
Fritsla 45 C3, 49 D1
Fritzlar 81 C1
Froan 32 B1
Frodba 55 C1
Frogner 38 A3
Frognerseteren 38 A3
Frohburg 82 B1
Frohnhausen (Dillkreis) 80 B2
Frohnleiten 127 C1
Frohnleiten 96 A3
Froidos 88 B1
Froissy 77 D3
Fröjel 47 D3
Fröjel 72 B1
Froland 43 C3
Frome 63 D2, 64 A3
Fromentel 86 A1/2
Fromentine 100 A1
Frómista 152 B2/3
Frönäs 20 A2/3
Fronhausen-Bellnhausen 81 B/C2
Fronreute-Blitzenreute 91 C3
Fronsac 108 B1
Fronteira 165 C2
Frontenay-Rohan-Rohan 100 B2
Frontenex 104 A3
Frontenhausen 92 B2
Frontignan 110 B3
Fronton 108 B2
Frøsendal 28 B2
Frosinone 119 C2
Frosolone 119 D2
Frosta 28 A3, 33 C1
Frostavallen 50 B3
Frostkåge 31 D1
Frøstup 48 A/B1
Frövi 46 B1
Frøyrak 43 B/C2
Fruges 77 D2
Frunzovka 141 D1
Frutak 137 D2
Frutigen 105 C2
Frýdek-Místek 96 B2
Frýdlant 96 A1
Frýdlant 83 D2
Fryele 50 B1
Fryksås 39 C/D1
Fryksta 45 D1
Frymburk 93 D2
Fryšták 95 C1
Fthiótis 146 B1
Fubine 113 C1
Fucécchio 114 B2, 116 A1/2
Fuencalderas 154 B2
Fuencaliente 167 C3
Fuencaliente 167 C2
Fuencarral 161 B/C2
Fuencubierta 172 A1
Fuendejalón 154 A3, 162 A1
Fuendetodos 162 B1
Fuengirola 172 B3
Fuenlabrada 160 B3
Fuenlabrada de los Montes 166 B2
Fuenllana 167 D2, 168 A2
Fuenmayor 153 D2
Fuensalida 160 B3
Fuensanta 168 B1/2
Fuensanta de Martos 173 B/C1
Fuente-Álamo 169 C2
Fuente-Alamo de Murcia 174 B1
Fuentealbilla 168 B1/2
Fuente Amarga 171 D3
Fuentebravia 171 D2/3
Fuentecambrón 153 C3, 161 C1
Fuentecén 152 B3, 160 B1
Fuente de Cantos 165 D3, 166 A3
Fuente del Arco 166 A3
Fuente del Maestre 165 D2
Fuente de Pedro Naharro 161 C3, 167 D1, 168 A1
Fuente de Piedra 172 B2
Fuente de Santa Cruz 160 A/B1
Fuente el Fresno 167 C2
Fuente el Olmo de Iscar 160 B1
Fuente el Olmo de Fuentidu-eña 160 B1
Fuente el Saz 161 C2
Fuente el Saz de Jarama 161 C2
Fuente el Sol 160 A1
Fuenteguinaldo 159 C2
Fuente la Higuera 169 C2
Fuente la Lancha 166 B3
Fuentelárbol 153 D3, 161 C1
Fuentelespino de Haro 161 D3, 168 A1
Fuentelespino de Moya 162 A3, 169 C1
Fuentelmonje 161 D1
Fuentelsaz 161 D2, 162 A2
Fuentemilanos 160 B2
Fuentenovilla 161 C2/3
Fuente Obejuna 166 B3
Fuente Palmera 172 A1
Fuentepelayo 160 B1
Fuentepinilla 153 D3, 161 C1
Fuenterrebollo 160 B1
Fuenterroble de Salvatierra 159 D2
Fuenterrobles 169 D1
Fuentes 161 D3
Fuente Salvage 169 B/C2
Fuente Santa 151 D1, 152 A1
Fuentesaúco de Fuentidu-eña 160 B1
Fuentesaúco 159 D1, 160 A1
Fuentes Claras 163 C2
Fuentes de Andalucía 172 A1
Fuentes de Ayódar 162 B3
Fuentes de Cesna 172 B2
Fuentes de Ebro 154 B3, 162 B1
Fuentes de Jiloca 162 A1
Fuentes de León 165 D3
Fuentes de Magaña 153 D3
Fuentes de Nava 152 A/B3
Fuentes de Oñoro 159 C2
Fuentes de Ropel 151 D3, 152 A3
Fuentes de Rubielos 162 B3
Fuentes de Valdepero 152 B3
Fuentesoto 160 B1
Fuentespina 153 C3, 161 B/C1
Fuente-Tójar 172 B1
Fuentidueña de Tajo 161 C3
Fuentidueña 160 B1
Fuerte del Rey 167 C3, 173 C1
Fuertescusa 161 D2
Fugelsta 30 A3, 35 C2
Fügen 92 A3, 107 C1
Fuglafjørdhur 55 C1
Fugleberg 9 C1/2
Fuglebjerg 53 C/D1
Fuglefjell 5 D1
Fuglefjell 4 B2
Fuglefjell 28 B1
Fuglefjell 4 B2
Fuglefjell 8 A3
Fuglefjell 7 D1
Fuglefjell 5 B/C1
Fuglefjell 7 C1
Fuglefjell 4 A/B2
Fuglefjell 7 C/D2
Fuglefjell 6 B1
Fuglefjell 7 C/D1
Fuglefjell 8 A3
Fuglefjell 5 D1, 6 B1
Fuglefjell 6 B1
Fuglefjell 7 C1
Fuglefjell 7 D1
Fuglefjellet 14 A2
Fuglem 28 A/B3, 33 D2
Fuglstad 29 C1
Fuglvik 32 B2
Fulda 81 C2
Fuldera [Zernez] 106 B2
Fulleda 155 D3, 163 D1
Fullerö 40 A3, 46 B1
Fullsjön 30 A3, 35 C1
Fullsjön 30 A3, 35 C1
Fülöpszállás 129 C1
Fulpmes 107 C1
Fulunäs 39 B/C1
Fumay 79 C3
Fumel 109 C1
Funäs 34 B2
Funäsdalen 34 A3
Funcheira 170 A1
Fundão 158 B3
Fúndres/Pfunders 107 C1
Fundulea 141 D2
Funes 154 A2
Fünfstetten 91 D2
Funtana 126 A/B3, 130 A1
Furadouro 158 A2
Furci 119 D2
Fure 36 A2
Furenes 36 A3
Furnace 56 A1
Furnes 38 A2
Fürstenau 68 A/B3
Fürstenau 67 D2
Fürstenau-Schwagstorf 67 D2
Fürstenberg 70 A1/2
Fürstenfeldbruck 92 A2
Fürstenfeld 127 C1
Fürstenfeld 96 A/B3
Fürstenstein 93 C2
Fürstenwalde 70 B2/3
Fürstenwalde 72 A3
Fürstenwerder 70 A1
Fürstenzell 93 C2
Fürstenzell-Sandbach 93 C2
Fürth 81 B/C3
Fürth 82 A3, 91 D1, 92 A1
Furth 92 B2
Furth im Wald 92 B1
Furtwangen 90 B3
Furuberg 35 C3
Furudal 39 C2
Furudalseter 28 B2
Furuflaten 4 A/B3, 10 A1
Furuhult 35 D2
Furunäs 16 B2
Furuögrund 31 D1
Furusjö 45 D3
Furusund 41 C3, 47 D1
Furutangvik 29 C1
Furuvik 40 B2
Fuscaldo 122 A1
Fusch an der Grossglock-nerstrasse 107 D1, 126 A1
Fuseta 170 B2
Fushë Arrëz 138 A2
Fushë Muhur 138 A3
Fush Krujë 137 D3

Fusine Laghi 126 B2
Fúsio [Ponte Brolla] 105 D2
Füssen 91 D3
Fussy 87 D3, 102 A1
Fustiñana 154 A3
Futog 129 C/D3, 133 C1, 134 A1
Futrikelv 4 A2
Füzesabony 97 C3
Fužine 127 C3, 130 B1
Fynshav 52 B2
Fyns Hoved 49 C3, 53 C1
Fyrås 29 D3, 35 C1
Fyresdal 43 C2
Fyrkat 48 B2

G

Gaaldorf 127 B/C1
Gabaldón 161 D3, 168 B1
Gabarret 108 B2
Gabas 108 B3, 154 B2
Gabasa 155 C3
Gabbro 114 A/B3, 116 A2
Gabčíkovo 95 C3
Gabela 136 B1
Gabellino 114 B3, 116 A/B2
Gaber 139 D1
Gabicce Mare 115 D2, 117 C1
Gablingen 91 D2
Gabøl 52 B1
Gabriac 110 A1/2
Gabrica 140 A3
Gabrovac 135 C3
Gabrovo 141 C3
Gaby 105 C3
Gacé 86 B1
Gacko 132 B3, 137 C1
Gadbjerg 48 B3, 52 B1
Gäddträsk 31 C1
Gadebusch 53 C3, 69 C1
Gædgenjarga 6 B2
Gadmen [Meiringen] 105 C1/2
Gádor 173 D2
Gádoros 129 D2
Gadžin Han 135 C3, 139 C1
Gaël 85 C2
Gaerwen 58 B2, 60 A3
Găeşti 141 C2
Gaeta 119 C3
Gafanha da Nazaré 158 A2
Gafanhoeira 164 B2
Gáfete 165 C1
Gaflenz 93 D3
Gagarin 75 D3
Gägelow 53 C3
Gaggenau 90 B2
Gaggi 125 D2
Gággio Montano 114 B2, 116 A1
Gagliano Castelferrato 125 C2
Gagliano del Capo 121 D3
Gagnef 39 D2
Gagsmark 16 B3
Gahro 70 A/B3
Gaibana 115 C1
Gæidno 7 B/C2
Gaienhofen-Hemmenhofen 91 C3
Gaildorf 91 C1
Gailey 59 D3, 64 A1
Gailingen 90 B3
Gaillac 109 D2
Gaillefontaine 77 D3
Gaillon 76 B3, 86 A/B1
Gainsborough 61 C/D3
Gaiole in Chianti 115 B/C3, 116 B2
Gairloch 54 A2
Gáiro 123 D2
Gáiro Scalo 123 D2
Gais 91 C3, 105 D1, 106 A1
Gaishorn 93 D3
Gaj 128 A3
Gaj 134 B1

Gajary 94 B2
Gajewo 71 D2
Gajsin 99 C3
Gajvoron 99 C3
Gakovo 129 C3
Gala 158 A3
Galambok 128 A2
Galan 109 C3, 155 C1
Galanito 11 C1
Galanta 95 C2
Galapagar 160 B2
Galápagos 161 C2
Galar 154 A2
Galaroza 165 D3, 171 C1
Galashiels 57 C2
Galashiels 54 B3
Galatás 148 B2
Galatás 147 D3
Galaţi 141 C/D2
Galatina 121 D3
Galatiní 143 C2
Galátone 121 D3
Galaxidion 147 B/C2
Galbarra 153 D2
Galdakao 153 C1
Galeata 115 C2, 116 B1
Galegos 165 C1
Galenbeck 70 A/B1
Galera 168 A3, 173 D1
Galeria 113 D3
Galgojavrre 4 B3, 10 B1
Galič 97 D2, 98 B3
Galičnik 138 A/B3
Galíndez 153 C2
Galinduste 159 D2
Galipsós 144 B1
Galisteo 159 C/D3
Galižana 130 A1
Gallardon 87 C2
Gällared 49 D1, 50 A1
Gallareto 113 C1
Gallegos de Argañán 159 C2
Gallejaur 16 A3
Galliate 105 D3
Gallicano 114 A/B2, 116 A1
Gällinge 49 D1, 50 A1
Gállio 107 C2/3
Gallipienzo 155 C2
Gallípoli 121 D3
Gällivare 16 B1
Gallneukirchen 93 D2
Gällö 35 C2
Gallo 115 D2, 117 C1/2
Gallspach 93 C2
Gällstad 45 D3
Gallúccio 119 C2
Gallur 155 C3
Galovac 130 B2
Gålsjö bruk 30 B3, 35 D2
Galston 56 B2
Galtabäck 49 D1, 50 A1
Galtby 24 A3
Galten 33 D3
Galten 5 C1
Galten 48 B3
Galtisjaur 15 D2
Gåltjärn 35 D3
Galtström 35 D3
Galtür 106 B1
Galugnano 121 D3
Galve 162 B2
Galve de Sorbe 161 C1
Galveias 164 B2
Galven 40 A1
Gálvez 160 B3, 167 C1
Galway (Gaillimh) 55 C2/3
Gama 153 C1
Gamaches 77 D2
Gamarde-les-Bains 108 A2
Gambach (Friedberg) 80 B2
Gámbara 106 B3
Gambarana 113 C/D1
Gambárie 122 A3
Gambassi Terme 114 B3, 116 A2
Gambatesa 119 D2, 120 A1
Gambolò 105 D3, 113 D1
Gamfoss 15 C1
Gamil 150 A3, 158 A1
Gaming 93 D3
Gaming 96 A3

Gaminiz 153 C1
Gamlakarleby 20 B1
Gamleby 46 B3
Gamleby 72 B1
Gammalvallen 34 A/B3
Gammelboliden 16 B3
Gammelby 25 D2, 26 A2
Gammel Estrup 49 B/C2
Gammel Skagen 44 B3
Gammelstad (Nederluleå) 17 C3
Gammelvær 5 B/C2
Gammertingen 91 C2
Gams bei Hieflau 93 D3
Gams [Haag-Gams] 105 D1, 106 A1
Gamvik 5 C1
Gamvik 7 C1
Gamvik 5 C2
Gamzigrad 135 C2/3
Gåmzovo 135 D2
Gan 108 B3, 154 B1
Gáname 159 D1
Gancevichi 98 B1
Ganda di Martello/Gand 106 B2
Ganddal 42 A2
Ganderkesee-Brink 68 A2
Ganderkesee 68 A2
Gandesa 163 C2
Gandía 169 D2
Gandino 150 A3
Gandra 150 A3, 158 A1
Gándria [Lugano] 105 D2
Gandvik 7 C2
Gangelt 79 D1/2
Ganges 110 B2
Gånghester 45 C/D3
Gangi 125 C2
Gangkofen 92 B2
Gankofen-Obertrennbach 92 B2
Gan'kovo 75 C1
Gannat 102 A2
Gannay-sur-Loire 103 C1
Gånsager 52 A1
Gansdalen 38 A3
Gänserndorf 94 B2
Gänserndorf 96 B2/3
Gånsvik 35 D2/3
Gánt 95 D3, 128 B1
Ganthem 47 D3
Ganton 61 D2
Gaočići 133 C2
Gap 112 A1/2
Gapohytta 4 B3, 10 A1
Gara 129 C2
Garaballa 163 C3, 169 D1
Garaguso 120 B2/3
Gara Hitrino 141 C3
Garaño 151 D2
Gara Pirin 139 D3
Garavan 112 B2/3
Garbagna 113 D1
Garbayuela 166 B2
Garbom 25 D2, 26 A2
Garbsen 68 B2/3
Garching 92 B2
Garching bei München 92 A2
García 163 C1/2
Garcíaz 166 A1
Garcihernández 159 D2, 160 A2
Garcinarro 161 C/D3
Garda 106 B3
Gardanne 111 D3
Gårdås 39 C2
Gårdby 51 D2
Gärde 29 C3, 34 B1
Garde 47 D2
Garde 154 B2
Gardelegen 69 C2
Gardermoen 38 A3
Gardíkion 146 B1
Gardíkion 142 B3
Gardíkion 143 C3
Garding 52 A2/3
Gardinovci 129 D3, 133 D1, 134 A1
Gärdnäs 29 D2
Gardno 70 B1
Gardone Riviera 106 B3
Gardone Val Trómpia 106 B3
Gardonne 109 C1
Gårdony 129 B/C1

Gardouch 109 D3, 155 D1
Gårdsby 51 C1
Gardsenden 32 B3, 37 D1
Gårdsjö 45 D2, 46 A2
Gardsjönäs 15 C3
Gårdskär 40 B2
Gårdslösa 51 D1/2
Garein 108 B2
Garelochhead 56 B1
Garešnica 128 A3
Garéssio 113 C2
Gargaliáni 146 B3
Gargaliáni 148 A/B2/3
Gargallo 162 B2
Garganta El Chorro 172 A2
Garganta la Olla 159 D3
Gargantiel 166 B2
Gargantilla 166 B1
Gargellen 106 A/B1
Garggogæcce 7 B/C1
Gárgia 5 C2/3
Gargilesse-Dampierre 101 D2, 102 A2
Gargnano 106 B3
Gargnås 15 D3
Gárgoles de Abajo 161 D2
Gargüera 159 D3
Gargždai 73 C2
Garijp 67 B/C1/2
Garitz 69 D3
Garkleppvollen 33 D2
Garlasco 105 D3, 113 D1
Garlieston 56 B3, 60 A1
Garlin 108 B3, 154 B1
Garlitos 166 B2
Gârljano 139 C/D2
Garlstorf 68 B1
Garmisch-Partenkirchen 92 A3
Garmisch-Partenkirchen-Griesen 91 D3, 92 A3
Garnat-sur-Engièvre 103 C1/2
Garpenberg 40 A2
Garphytte nationalpark 46 A1
Garrafe de Torío 151 D2, 152 A2
Garralda 108 B3, 155 C1/2
Garray 153 D3, 161 D1
Garrel 67 D2
Garrigil 57 D3, 60 B1
Garriguella 156 B2
Garristown 58 A2
Garrovillas 159 C3, 165 D1
Garrow 56 B1
Garrucha 174 A2
Gars am Inn 92 B2
Gars am Kamp 94 A2
Garsås 39 C2
Gärsnäs 50 B3
Garstang 59 D1, 60 B2
Garten 28 A3, 33 C1
Garth 63 C1
Gartow 69 C2
Gartz 70 B1/2
Garvão 170 A1
Garve 54 A/B2
Garvín 160 A3, 166 B1
Garwolin 73 C3, 97 C1, 98 A1/2
Garzyn 71 D3
Gasa 15 D3
Gåsborn 39 C3
Gåsbu 32 B3, 37 C1
Gaschurn 106 B1
Gascueña 161 C3
Gåsenstugan 34 A2
Gåsholma 40 B2
Gaskashytta 10 A2
Gaskeluokt 15 D3
Gasny 87 C3
Gaspoltshofen 93 C2
Gassano 114 A2, 116 A1
Gasselsdorf 127 C1/2
Gasselte 67 C2
Gássino Torinese 113 C1
Gässjön 30 A3, 35 C2
Gasteiz/Vitoria 153 D2
Gasteren 67 C2
Gastoúni 146 A2
Gastoúrion 142 A3
Gata de Gorgos 169 D2
Gatčina 74 B1
Gatehouse of Fleet 56 B3, 60 A1

Gateshead 57 D3, 61 C1
Gateshead 54 B3
Gátova 162 B3, 169 D1
Gattendorf 94 B3
Gatteo al Mare 115 C/D2, 117 C1
Gattières 112 B2/3
Gattinara 105 C3
Gau-Algesheim 80 B3
Gaucín 172 A3
Gaukheihytta 42 B2
Gau-Odernheim 80 B3
Gaupne 36 B2
Gausdal 37 D2
Gautefall 43 C2
Gautelishytta 9 D3
Gauting 92 A2/3
Gautsbu 32 B3, 37 C1
Gautsjø 32 B3, 37 C1
Gavà 156 A3
Gavaloú 146 B1/2
Gavardo 106 B3
Gavarnie 155 C2
Gavi 113 D1
Gavião 164 B1
Gavirate 105 D3
Gävle 40 B2
Gavnø 53 D1/2
Gavoi 123 D2
Gavorrano 114 B3, 116 A2/3
Gavrákia 146 B1
Gavray 86 A/B1
Gávrion 149 C2
Gávros 143 B/C2
Gavsele 30 B2, 35 D1
Gävunda 39 C2
Gaweinstal 94 B2
Gawroniec 71 C1
Gåxsjö 29 D3, 35 B/C1
Gazoldo degli Ippóliti 106 B3
Gázoros 144 B1
Gazzuolo 114 B1
Gbelce 95 D3
Gdańsk (Danzig) 73 B/C2
Gdov 74 B1
Gdynia 72 B2
Gea de Albarracín 163 C2
Geaune 108 B2/3, 154 B1
Geay 101 C1
Gebhardshain-Elkenroth 80 B2
Gebhardshain 80 B2
Gebra 81 D1
Gebra 81 D1
Gedern 81 C2
Gedinne 79 C3
Gedney Drove End 61 D3, 65 C1
Gèdre 155 C2
Gedser 53 D2
Gedsted 48 B2
Gedved 48 B3
Geel 79 C1
Geertruidenberg 66 B3
Geeste 67 D2
Geeste-Dalum 67 C/D2
Geeste-Gross-Hespe 67 C/D2
Geeste-Osterbrock 67 D2
Geesthacht 68 B1
Gefell 82 A2
Géfira 143 D1/2
Gefíria 143 D3
Gefrees 82 A3
Gehrden 68 B3
Gehren 81 D2, 82 A2
Geijersholm 39 C3
Geilenkirchen 79 D1/2
Geilo 37 C3
Geiranger 32 A3, 36 B1
Geisa 81 C/D2
Geiselhöring 92 B2
Geiselwind 81 D2
Geisenfeld 92 A2
Geisenhausen 92 B2
Geisenheim 80 B3
Geising 83 C2
Geisingen 90 B3
Geislingen 91 C2
Geisnes 28 C1
Geistthal 127 C1
Geitastrand 28 A3, 33 C1/2
Geiterygghytta 37 C3
Geithain 82 B1
Geithus 43 D1

Gejuelo del Barro 159 D2
Gela 125 C3
Geldermalsen 66 B3
Geldern 79 D1
Geldrop 79 C1
Geleen 79 D1/2
Gelenau 82 B2
Gelibolu 149 C/D1
Gelida 156 A3
Gellershausen 81 C1
Gel'm'azov 99 D2
Gelnhausen 81 C2/3
Gelsa 162 B1
Gelse 128 A2
Gelsenkirchen 80 A1
Gelsted 52 B1
Geltendorf 91 D2, 92 A2
Gelting 52 B2
Gema 159 D1
Gembloux 79 C2
Gemenc 129 C2
Gémenos 111 D3
Gemert 79 C/D1
Gémir 109 D2
Gemla 51 C1/2
Gemona del Friuli 126 A2
Gémozac 100 B3
Gemünden 81 C2
Gemünden 80 A3
Gemünden am Main 81 C3
Gemünden am Main-Wern-
feld 81 C3
Gemünden-Ehringshausen
81 C2
Gemuño 160 A2
Genarp 50 B3
Genazzano 118 B2
Gençay 101 C2
Gendrey 89 C3, 104 A1
Gendringen 67 C3
Génelard 103 C1/2
Genemuiden 67 C2
Generalski Stol 127 C3,
130 B1
General-Toševo 141 C/D2
Genêts 85 D1/2
Genevad 50 A2
Genève 104 A2
Gengenbach 90 B2
Génicourt-sur-Meuse
89 C1
Genillé 87 B/C3, 101 D1
Genk 79 C1/2
Genlis 89 B/C3, 103 D1
Gennep 67 B/C3
Genner 52 B2
Gennes 86 A3
Gennes-sur-Glaize 86 A3
Genola 112 B1/2
Génolhac 110 B2
Genouilly 103 C1
Génova 113 D2
Génova-Dória 113 D2
Génova-Nervi 113 D2
Génova-Pegli 113 D2
Génova-Voltri 113 C/D2
Gensingen 80 B3
Gent 78 B1
Genthin 69 D2/3
Gentioux 102 A2/3
Genzano di Lucánia 120 B2
Genzano di Roma 118 B2
Geolooginen tutkimusasema
12 B1
Georgenthal 81 D2
Georgítsion 146 B3
Georgsheil 67 D1
Georgsmarienhütte 67 D3
Gepatschhaus 106 B1
Ger 108 B3, 155 C1
Ger 108 B3, 155 C1
Ger 86 A1/2
Ger 156 A2
Gera 82 B2
Geraardsbergen 78 B2
Gerabronn 91 C1
Gerace 122 A3
Gerakaroú 144 A2
Gerakiní 144 A2
Gerakiní 148 B1
Gera Lário 105 D2, 106 A2
Gérardmer 89 D2, 90 A2/3
Geras 94 A2
Gerb 155 C/D3, 163 C1
Gerbéviller 89 D2

Gerbini 125 C2
Gerbstedt 69 C/D3, 82 A1
Gerca 98 B3
Gerdau 69 B/C2
Gereméas 123 D3
Gerena 171 D1
Geretsried 92 A3
Gérgal 173 D2
Gergei 123 D3
Gerhardshofen-Birnbaum
81 D3
Geria 158 A3
Gerichshain 82 B1
Gerindote 160 B3, 167 C1
Geringswalde 82 B1
Gerlé 109 C3, 155 C1/2
Gerlos 107 C1
Germaringen 91 D3
Germay 89 C2
Germering-Unterpfaffenho-
fen 92 A2
Germersheim 90 B1
Germigny-des-Prés 87 D3
Germont 79 C3
Gernay-la-Ville 87 C1/2
Gernika Lumo 153 D1
Gernrode 69 C3
Gernsbach 90 B2
Gernsheim 80 B3
Gerola Alta 106 A2
Geroldsbach-Strobenried
92 A2
Geroldsgrün 82 A2
Geroldstein 80 B3
Gerolimín 148 B3
Gerolzhofen 81 D3
Geroplátanos 142 B2/3
Gerovo 127 B/C3
Gerri de la Sal 155 D2
Gersau 105 C/D1
Gersfeld 81 C/D2
Gersheim 89 D1, 90 A1
Gersten 67 D2
Gerstetten 91 C/D2
Gerstungen 81 D2
Gerswalde 70 A/B1/2
Gerthausen 81 D2
Gerwisch 69 D3
Gerzen (Vilsbiburg) 92 B2
Gescher 67 C2
Geseke 68 A3, 80 B1
Gésera 154 B2
Geslau 91 D1
Gessertshausen 91 D2
Gestalgar 169 C1
Gesté 85 D3, 100 B1
Gesten 48 B3, 52 B1
Gesualdo 119 D3, 120 A2
Gesunda 39 C/D2
Geta 41 C2
Getafe 160 B3
Getan 29 C3, 34 A/B1
Getan 29 C3, 34 B1
Getaria 153 D1
Getbo 39 D3
Getinge 49 D2, 50 A1/2
Getinge 72 A1
Gettorf 52 B2/3
Getxo 153 C1
Gevelsberg 80 A1
Gevgelija 139 C3, 143 D1
Gevrey-Chambertin 88 B3,
103 D1
Gex 104 A2
Geyer 82 B2
Gföhl 94 A2
Ghedi 106 B3
Gheorghe Gheorghiu-Dej
141 C1
Gheorghieni 141 C1
Gherla 97 D3, 140 B1
Ghiffa 105 D2
Ghigo 112 B1
Ghilarza 123 C2
Ghirla 105 D2/3
Ghislarengo 105 C3
Ghisonaccia 113 D3
Ghisoni 113 D3
Ghyvelde 78 A1
Giáltra 147 C1
Giâmos 33 D2
Giannitsá 143 D1
Giants Ring 56 A3
Giardinetto 120 A1/2
Giardini-Náxos 125 D2
Giarole 113 C1

Giarratana 125 C3
Giarre 125 D2
Giat 102 A/B2/3
Giaveno 112 B1
Giazza 107 C3
Giba 123 C3
Gibellina 124 A2
Gibostad 9 D1
Gibraleón 171 C1/2
Gibraltar 172 A3
Gic 95 C3, 128 B1
Gic 96 B3
Gideå 31 C2/3
Giebelstadt 81 C/D3
Gieboldehausen 81 D1
Giekerk 66 B1
Gielow 69 D1, 70 A1
Gien 87 D3
Giengen 91 D2
Giens 112 A3
Gières 104 A3, 112 A1
Giessen 80 B2
Giessübel 81 D2, 82 A2
Gieten 67 C2
Giethoorn 67 C2
Gievnjegoikka 5 C3, 11 C1
Giffaumont 88 B2
Gifford 57 C2
Gifhorn 69 C2
Gifhorn-Kästorf 69 C2
Gifhorn-Wilsche 69 B/C2
Gif-sur-Yvette 85 C1/2
Gige 128 A/B2
Gigean 110 B3
Gigen 140 B2
Gíglio Porto 116 A3
Gignac 110 B2/3
Gijón 151 D1, 152 A1
Gil 155 D2
Gilău 97 D3, 140 B1
Gildeskål 14 B1
Gilena 172 A2
Gillberga 45 C1
Gilleleje 49 D3, 50 A2
Gilleleje 72 A1
Gillenfeld 80 A3
Gillhovs Kapell 34 B2
Gillingham 63 D2
Gillingham 65 C3, 77 C1
Gillstad 45 C2
Gilserberg 81 C2
Gilserberg-Moischeid
81 C2
Gimat 109 C2
Gimdalen 30 A3, 35 C2
Gimigliano 122 B2
Gimileo 153 C/D2
Gimnón 147 C2/3
Gimo 40 B3
Gimont 109 C2/3,
155 C/D1
Gimsøy 8 B2
Ginasservis 111 D2/3,
112 A3
Ginestar 163 C2
Ginestra degli Schiavoni
119 D2/3, 120 A2
Ginosa 121 C2
Ginostra 125 D1
Gioi 120 A3
Gióia dei Marsi 119 C2
Gióia del Colle 121 C2
Gióia Sannítica 119 D2/3
Gióia Táuro 122 A3
Gioiosa Iónica 122 B3
Gioiosa Marea 125 C1/2
Giornico 105 D2
Giovinazzo 121 B/C2,
136 A3
Gîrbovu 135 D1
Girecourt-sur-Durbion
89 D2
Girifalco 122 B2
Gîrnic 135 C1
Giromagny 89 D3, 90 A3
Girona/Gerona 156 B2
Gironella 156 A2
Gironnville-sous-les-Côtes
89 C1
Girvan 56 B2
Girvan 54 A3, 55 D2
Gisburn 59 D1, 60 B2
Gisira Pagana 125 C3
Gislaved 50 B1
Gislaved 72 A1
Gislev 53 C1/2
Gisløy 9 B/C1

Gisors 77 D3, 87 C1
Gisselås 29 D3, 35 C1
Gisselfeld 53 D1
Gissi 119 D2
Gisslarbo 39 D3, 40 A3,
46 B1
Gissträsk 31 C1
Gistad 46 B2
Gistain 155 C2
Gistel 78 A1
Gistrup 48 B1/2
Giswil 105 C1
Gíthion 148 B3
Gittelde 68 B3
Giubega 135 D2
Giubega 140 B2
Giulești 140 B2
Giulianova 119 C1
Giurgeni 141 C/D2
Giurgiu 141 C2
Giussano 105 D3, 106 A3
Give 48 B3, 52 B1
Givet 79 C2/3
Givors 103 D3
Givry 103 D1
Givry 78 B2
Givry-en-Argonne 88 B1
Givskud 48 B3, 52 B1
Gizdavac 131 C/D3
Gizeux 86 A2
Giżycko (Lötzen) 73 C2
Gizzeria 122 A2
Gizzeria Lido 122 A2
Gjælen 14 B1
Gjæsingen 28 B2
Gjendebu 37 C2
Gjendesheim 37 C2
Gjengedal 36 A2
Gjengstøa 32 B1
Gjerdvik 36 A2
Gjerlev 48 B2
Gjermundshamn 42 A1
Gjern 48 B2/3
Gjerrild 49 C2
Gjerstad 43 C2
Gjersvik 29 C1
Gjesås 38 B2
Gjestal 42 A2
Gjesvær 5 D1
Gjevillvasshytta 33 C2
Gjeving 42 C/D3, 44 A2
Gjorslev 50 A3, 53 D1
Gjøvdal 43 C2
Gjøvik 38 A2
Gjøvik 9 D1
Gjueševo 139 C2
Gjueševo 140 A/B3
Gla (Arne) 147 C2
Gladbeck 80 A1
Gladdenstedt 69 C2
Gladenbach 80 B2
Gladstad 14 A2
Glaisin 69 C1
Glamis 57 C1
Glamis Castle 57 C1
Glamoč 131 D2, 132 A2
Glamsbjerg 52 B1
Glandieu 104 A3
Glan-Münchweiler 80 A3,
90 A1
Glanshammar 46 B1
Glarus 105 D1, 106 A1
Glasgow 56 B2
Glasgow 54 B2/3, 55 D1
Glashütte 83 C2
Glashütten 127 C1
Glassdrummond 58 A1
Glastonbury 63 D2
Glauchau 82 B2
Glava 45 C1
Glava Glasbruk 45 C1
Glavanovci 139 C1
Glavatičevo 132 B3
Glavnik 138 B1
Gledić 134 B3
Gledica 133 D3, 134 A3
Gleichen-Bremke 81 D1
Glein 14 A2
Gleina 82 A1
Gleinstätten 127 C1
Gleisdorf 127 C/D1
Gleisdorf 96 A3
Gleissenberg 92 B1

Glen 34 A/B2
Glenariffe 56 A3
Glenarm 56 A3
Glenbarr 56 A2
Glencoe 56 A/B1
Glencolumbkille 55 C2
Glendalough 58 A2
Glenluce 56 B3
Glenrothes 57 C1
Glenties 55 C2
Gleschendorf 53 C3
Glesne 43 D1
Gletsch 105 C2
Glienicke 70 B3
Glifa 147 C1
Glifa 148 B2
Glifáda 148 B2
Glifáda 147 D2
Gliki 142 B3
Glimåkra 50 B2
Glimminge 50 B2
Glimmingehus 50 B3
Glina 127 D3, 131 C1
Glinka 71 D3
Glissjöberg 34 A3
Glitterheim 37 C2
Gliwice (Gleiwitz) 96 B2
Globino 99 D3
Globočica 138 B2
Glod'any 99 B/C3
Gloggnitz 94 A3
Glogovac 138 B1
Glogovica 135 C2
Glogovica 127 D2
Głogów (Glogau) 71 C/D3
Głogów (Glogau) 96 A/B1
Glomfjord 14 B1
Glommen 49 D2, 50 A1
Glommen 72 A1
Glommersträsk 16 A3
Glömminge 51 D2
Glonn 92 A3
Glória 164 A/B2
Glösa 29 C/D3, 34 B1/2
Gløshaug 29 B/C2
Glos-la-Ferrière 86 B1
Glóssa 147 D1
Glóssbo 40 A1
Glossop 59 D2, 61 B/C3
Glöte 34 A3
Gløtleger 33 C3, 37 D1
Glottertal 90 B2/3
Gløtvola 33 D3
Gloucester 63 D1, 64 A2
Glöwen 69 D2
Gložan 129 C3, 133 C1
Głubczyce (Leobschütz)
96 B2
Glubokoe 74 B3
Gluchowo 71 D3
Glücksburg 52 B2
Glückstadt 52 B3, 68 B1
Glud 48 B3, 52 B1
Gluggvatnet 14 B3
Gluha Bukovica 132 A/B2
Gluhov 99 D1/2
Glumsø 53 D1
Glun 111 C1
Glušci 133 C1
Glusk 99 C1
Glyngøre 48 A2
Glynn 56 A3
Glypha 146 B2
Gmünd 126 A/B1
Gmünd 93 D2
Gmünd 96 A2
Gmund am Tegernsee
92 A3
Gmunden 93 C3
Gmunden 96 A3
Gnarp 35 D3
Gnarrenburg-Kuhstedt
68 A1
Gnarrenburg-Karlshöfen
68 A1
Gnarrenburg 68 A1
Gnas 127 D1
Gnesta 47 C1
Gnevsdorf 69 D1
Gniew 98 B/C2/3
Gniezno 72 B3
Gnisvärd 47 C/D3
Gnjilane 138 B2
Gnjilane 140 A3
Gnocchetta 115 C1
Gnoien 53 D3
Gnosjö 50 B1

Goathland 61 D1
Goatteluobbal 10 B1/2
Goč 134 B3
Goce Delčev 140 B3
Goch 67 C3, 79 D1
Gochsheim 81 D3
Göd 95 D3
Göda 83 D1
Godall 162 B2
Godalming 64 B3, 76 B1
Godby 41 C/D3
Godeč 139 D1
Godeč 140 B3
Godegård 46 A2
Godejord 29 C2
Godelleta 169 C1
Goderville 77 C3
Godiascò 113 D1
Godisa 128 B2
Godmanchester 65 B/C2
Gödöllő 95 C3
Godovič 126 B2
Gödre 128 B2
Godshill 76 B2
Godstone 65 C3, 76 B1
Godus 133 C2
Goes 78 B1
Góglio 105 C2
Gogolewo 71 C1
Göhlsdorf 69 D2/3,
   70 A2/3
Göhrde 69 C2
Göhren 82 B2
Goirle 79 C1
Góis 158 A/B3
Goizueta 153 D1, 154 A1
Gojan i Epërm 138 A2
Gokels 52 B3
Göksholm 46 B1
Gol 37 C/D3
Golâ 37 D2
Gola 128 A2
Golada 150 B2
Gołańcz 71 D2
Gölby 41 C/D3
Golchen 70 A1
Golczewo 71 B/C1
Gołdap 73 C/D2
Goldbach 81 D1/2
Goldbeck 69 D2
Goldberg 69 D1
Goldelund 52 B2
Goldenbaum 70 A1
Goldenstedt 68 A2
Golegã 164 B1
Golemo Selo 139 C1
Golenice 70 B2
Goleniów (Gollnow) 70 B1
Goleniów (Gollnow) 72 A3
Golfe Juan 112 B3
Golfo Aranci 123 D1
Gölle 128 B2
Göllersdorf 94 A/B2
Gollhofen 81 D3, 91 D1
Gollin 70 A2
Golling an der Salzach
   93 C3
Göllingen 81 D1, 82 A1
Gollmitz 70 A/B1
Gollonboc 142 B1
Golmayo 153 D3, 161 D1
Golmés 155 D3, 163 D1
Golpejas 159 D2
Golssen 70 A3
Golubac 135 B/C2
Golubac 140 A2
Golubińci 133 D1, 134 A1
Golubinja 132 B2
Golubovec 127 D2
Golzow 69 D3
Golzow 70 B2
Golzow 70 B2
Gomadingen 91 C2
Gomagoi 106 B2
Gómara 153 D3, 161 D1
Gomaringen 91 C2
Gombrén 156 A2
Gomel' 99 C/D1
Gomesende 150 B3
Gomeznarro 161 C1
Gomezserracín 160 B1
Gommern 69 D3
Gomolava 133 C/D1,
   134 A1
Gompertshausen 81 D2
Gomphoi 143 C3

Gonçalo Bocas 159 B/C2
Goncelin 104 A3
Gondelsheim 90 B1
Gondershausen 80 A3
Gondifelos 158 A1
Gondo [Brig] 105 C2
Gondomar 158 A1/2
Gondomar 150 A3
Gondrecourt-le-Château
   89 C2
Gönen 149 D1
Gonesse 87 D1
Gonfaron 112 A3
Goni 123 D3
Gonnesa 123 C3
Gönnheim 90 B1
Gónni 143 D3
Gonnord 86 A3, 100 B1
Gónnos 143 D3
Gonnosfanádiga 123 C3
Gonnostramatza 123 C2/3
Gontinhães 150 A3,
   158 A1
Gönyü 95 C3
Gonzaga 114 B1
Goodwood House 76 B1
Goole 61 C2
Goor 67 C3
Göpfritz an der Wild 94 A2
Goppenstein 105 C2
Göppingen 91 C2
Goppollen 38 A1
Gopshus 39 C2
Gor 173 D2
Góra 71 D3
Gora 71 D3, 131 C1
Goračići 133 D2/3, 134 A3
Gorafe 173 C/D1
Goraiolo 114 B2, 116 A1/2
Goraioio 114 B2, 116 A1
Góra Kalwaria 73 C3, 97 C1
Goražde 133 C3
Görcsöny 128 B2/3
Gördalen 38 B1
Gordaliza del Pino 152 A2
Gordes 111 D2
Gördes 149 D2
Górdola 105 D2
Gordon 57 C2
Gordona 105 D2, 106 A2
Gordoncillo 152 A3
Gordoxola 153 C1
Gorebridge 57 C2
Gorey 63 D3, 85 C1
Gorey 58 A3
Gorga 169 D2
Gorga 118 B2
Gorges de Daluis 112 B2
Gorges de Galamus 156 B1
Gorges de Kakouetta
   108 A/B3, 154 B1
Gorges de l'Asco 113 D2/3
Gorges de l'Ardèche
   111 C2
Gorges de la Restonica
   113 D3
Gorges du Daoulas 84 B2
Gorges du Fier 104 A2/3
Gorges du Lot 110 A1
Gorges du Toul Gonlic
   84 B2
Gorges Supérieures du
   Cians 112 B2
Görgeteg 128 A2
Gorgómilos 142 B3
Gorgonzola 105 D3,
   106 A2
Gorgopótamos 147 B/C1
Gorica 130 B2
Gorica 131 D3, 132 A3
Goričan 127 D2, 128 A2
Goriče 126 B2
Goricy 75 D2
Gorinchem 66 B3
Goring 65 C3
Gorino Ferrarese 115 C1
Göritz 69 D3
Göritz 70 B1
Gorízia 126 A/B2
Gorki 75 C3
Gorleben 69 C2
Gorleston 65 D1/2
Gørlev 49 C3, 53 C1
Gorlice 97 C2
Görlitz 96 A1
Görlitz 83 D1
Gormaz 153 C3, 161 C1

Gorna Koznica 139 D2
Gorni Cibâr 135 D3
Gornja Briska 137 D2
Gornja Bukovica 133 C/D2,
   134 A2
Gornja Čadjavica 133 C1
Gornjak 134 B2
Gornja Klina 138 B1
Gornja Ljubovida 133 C2
Gornja Ljuta 132 B3
Gornjane 135 C2
Gornja Radgona 127 D2
Gornja Radgona 96 A3
Gornja Stubičke Toplice
   127 D2
Gornja Toplica-Vrujci
   133 D2, 134 A2
Gornja Trepča 133 D2,
   134 A2/3
Gornja Tuzla 133 B/C2
Gornje Gadimlje 138 B2
Gornje Jelenje 127 B/C3,
   130 B1
Gornje Morakovo 137 D1
Gornje Zimlje 132 B3
Gornji Banjani 133 D2,
   134 A2
Gornji Grad 127 C2
Gornji Hrgovi 132 B1
Gornji Klasnić 127 D3,
   131 C1
Gornji Kneginec 127 D2
Gornji Kokoti 137 D2
Gornji Komarevo 127 D3,
   131 C1
Gornji Kosinj 130 B1/2
Gornji Lapac 131 C2
Gornji Malovan 131 D2/3,
   132 A2
Gornji Milanovac 133 D2,
   134 A2
Gornji Podgradci 131 D1,
   132 A1
Gornji Ribnik 131 D2,
   132 A2
Gornji Šeher 131 D1,
   132 A1
Gornji Vakuf 132 A2
Gornji Žabar 132 B1
Gorno Nerezi 138 B2
Goro 115 C1
Gorodec 98 B2
Gorodenka 98 B3
Gorodišče 99 D3
Gorodnja 99 D1/2
Gorodok 98 B3
Gorodok 97 D2, 98 A2/3
Gorohov 97 D1, 98 B2
Górowo Iławeckie (Landsberg) 73 C2
Gorredijk-Kortezwaag
   67 C2
Gorron 86 A2
Gorsium 128 B1
Gorssel 67 C3
Gortyn 86 A2
Gortyn 146 B3
Görvik 30 A2/3, 35 C1
Görzke 69 D3
Górzna 71 D1
Gorzów Wielkopolski
   (Landsberg) 71 C2
Gorzów Wielkopolski
   (Landsberg) 72 A3
Górzyca 70 B2
Gorzyń 71 C2
Gosaldo 107 C2
Gosau 93 C3
Göschenen 105 D1/2
Goscikowo 71 C3
Gościm 71 C2
Gosdorf 127 D1/2
Gosforth 59 C1, 60 A1
Gösing an der Mariazellerbahn 94 A3
Goslar 69 B/C3
Goslar-Hahndorf 69 B/C3
Goslar-Hahnenklee 68 B3
Goslar-Oker 69 B/C3
Gospić 130 B2
Gospodinci 129 D3
Gosport 76 B1
Gossa 69 D3, 82 B1
Gössäter 45 D2
Gossau 91 C3
Gössenheim 81 C3
Gössl 93 C3
Gössnitz 82 B2

Gössweinstein 82 A3
Gössweinstein-Behringersmüle 82 A3
Gostivar 138 B2/3
Gostivar 140 A3
Göstling an der Ybbs 96 A3
Göstling an der Ybbs 93 D3
Gostomia 71 D1/2
Gostyń 71 D3
Gostyń 72 B3, 96 B1
Goszczanowo 71 C2
Göta 45 C3
Götafors 50 B1
Göteborg 45 C3
Göteborg 72 A1
Götene 45 D2
Gotha 81 D2
Gothem 47 D3
Gotlunda 46 B1
Gottby 41 C3
Gotthun 69 D1, 70 A1
Gotthun 69 D1, 70 A1
Göttingen 81 C/D1
Gottlob 129 D2/3
Gottne 30 B3
Gottröra 40 B3
Gottwaldov 95 C1
Gottwaldov 96 B2
Götzendorf an der Leitha
   94 B3
Götzis 91 C3, 106 A1
Gouarec 84 B2
Gouda 66 A3
Goudargues 111 C2
Gouesnou 84 A2
Gouffre de Padirac 109 D1
Goulaine 86 A/B3, 101 C1
Gouméi 146 B2
Gouménissa 143 D1
Goumois 89 D3, 104 B1
Gouneau 109 C2
Goúra 147 B/C2
Gourdon 108 B1
Gourin 84 B2
Gournay 87 D1
Gournay-en-Bray 77 D3
Gournay-sur-Aronde 78 A3
Gourock 56 B1/2
Gouveia 158 B2
Gouveias 159 B/C2
Gouviá 142 A3
Gouvinhas 158 B1/2
Gouzon 102 A2
Govedarci 139 D2
Govedari 136 B1
Govérnolo 114 B1
Goviller 89 C2
Goyatz 70 B3
Gozd 126 B2
Gozdnica 83 D1
Gozdowice 70 B2
Gozée 78 B2
Gozón 151 D1
Gozzano 105 C/D3
Grab 133 C3, 137 D1
Grab 137 C2
Gräben 69 D3
Graben-Neudorf 90 B1
Grabenstätt 92 B3
Gråbo 45 C3
Gråborg 51 D2
Grabovac 131 D3, 132 A3
Grabovac 133 D1/2,
   134 A2
Grabovci 133 D1, 134 A1
Grabovica 135 C2
Grabovica 131 D3, 132 A3
Grabow 69 C1
Grabowhöfe 69 D1, 70 A1
Grabowno 71 D1/2
Grabrovnica 128 A2/3
Gračac 131 C2
Gračac 134 B3
Graça do Divor 164 B2
Gračanica 138 B1/2
Gračanica 132 B1
Gračanica 133 C2
Graçay 102 A1
Grad 127 D1
Gradac 132 A3, 136 B1
Gradac 133 D3, 134 A3
Gradac 133 C3
Gradačac 132 B1
Gradani 137 D2
Gradara 115 D2, 117 C1
Graddis fjellstue 15 C1
Gräddö 41 C3

Gradec 127 D2/3
Gradec 135 D2
Gradefes 152 A2
Grades 126 B1
Gradevo 139 D2
Gradignan 108 B1
Grådinari 135 B/C1
Gradine 139 D1
Gradisca d'Isonzo
   126 A2/3
Gradišče 127 D2
Gradište 128 B3
Gradište 133 B/C1
Gradište 139 C2
Gradižsk 99 D3
Grado 126 A3
Grado 151 D1
Grádoli 116 B3, 118 A1
Gradsko 139 C3
Gradskovo 135 C2
Graena 173 C2
Gräfelfing 92 A2/3
Grafenau 93 C1/2
Grafenau-Haus 93 C2
Gräfenberg 82 A3
Gräfenhainichen 69 D3
Grafenhausen 90 B3
Grafenrheinfeld 81 D3
Gräfenroda 81 D2
Grafenschlag 93 D2, 94 A2
Gräfentonna 81 D1
Grafenwöhr 82 A/B3
Graffer 82 B3, 37 C1
Grafing 92 A/B2/3
Gräfsnäs 45 C3
Gráglia 105 C3
Gragnano 119 D3
Grahovo 126 B2
Grahovo 137 C1/2
Graine 65 C3
Graja de Campalbo 163 C3,
   169 D1
Grajal de Campos 152 A2
Grajewo 73 D3, 98 A1
Gram 52 B1
Gramada 135 C/D3
Gramais 106 B1
Gramat 109 D1
Gramkow 53 C3
Grammatikón 147 D2
Gramméni Oxiá 146 B1
Grammichele 125 C3
Grampound 62 B3
Gramsbergen 67 C2
Gramsh 142 A/B1
Gramzow 70 B1/2
Gran 38 A2
Granabeg 58 A2
Granada 173 C2
Granäs 15 C3
Gransäsen 30 A2, 35 C/D1
Granåtula de Calatrava
   167 C2
Granberget 31 D2
Granberget 30 A1/2
Granbergsliden 16 A3
Granbergsträsk 16 A3
Granboda 41 D3
Grancey-le-Château 88 B3
Grandas de Salime 151 C1
Grandcamp-les-Bains
   76 A3, 86 A1
Grand Canyon du Verdon
   112 A2/3
Grand Champ 85 C3
Grand-Couronne 77 C3,
   86 B1
Grand Croix 104 B3,
   112 B1
Grandes Grottes 84 A2
Grand-Fougeray 85 D3
Grândola 164 B3
Grand Phare 84 B3
Grandrieu 110 B1
Grand-Rozoy 88 A1
Grands Goulets 111 D1
Grandson 104 B1
Grandvillars 89 D3, 90 A3
Grandvilliers 77 D3
Grane 14 B3
Grañén 154 B3
Granera 156 A3
Grangärde 39 D2
Grangemouth 57 B/C1/2
Grange-over-Sands
   59 C/D1, 60 B2
Grängesberg 39 D3

Granges-de-Crouhens 109 C3, 155 C1/2
Granges-sur-Vologne 89 D2
Granges-sur-Aube 88 A2
Grängshyttan 39 D3
Grängsjö 35 D3
Grängsjö 40 A1
Granheim 37 C3
Granhult 51 C1
Granhult 17 C1
Granieri 125 C3
Graninge 30 A/B3, 35 D2
Gräningen 69 D2
Granitsa 146 B1
Granja 158 A2
Granja 165 C3
Granja de Iniesta 168 B1
Granja de Moreruela 151 D3, 159 D1
Granja de Torrehermosa 166 A3
Granjinha 158 B2
Grankulla 25 C3
Grankullavik 51 D1
Granliden 31 D1
Gränna 46 A3
Grannäs 15 C3
Grannäs 15 D3
Granollers 156 A3
Grañón 153 C2
Granön 31 C2
Granön 29 D2, 30 A1
Granschütz 82 B1
Granschütz-Grimma 82 B1
Gransee 70 A2
Gransee 72 A3
Gränsgård 15 D3
Gransherad 43 C1, 44 A1
Gransjö 30 A3, 35 D2
Gransjö 30 B1
Gransjö 16 B2
Gransjön 38 B2/3
Gransjöriset 30 B1
Gränssjö 15 B/C3
Grantham 61 D3, 64 B1
Grantown-on-Spey 54 B2
Granträsk 17 C2
Granträsk 16 B3
Granträskmark 16 B3
Grantshouse 57 D2
Granvik 24 B3
Granvika 33 D3
Granville 85 D1
Granvin 36 B3
Granyena de les Garrigues 155 C3, 163 C1
Grao de Sagunto 162 B3, 169 D1
Grasbakken 7 C2
Gräsberg 39 D3
Grasellenbach-Wahlen 81 C3
Gräsgård 51 D2
Grasleben 69 C3
Grasleben-Twülpstedt 69 C2/3
Gräslotten 29 C3, 34 A/B1
Gräsmark 38 B3
Grasmere 57 C3, 60 B1
Gräsmyr 31 C2
Gräsö 40 B2
Grassano 120 B2
Grassau 92 B3
Grasse 112 B3
Gråssjö 35 C2
Græsted 49 D3, 50 A2
Gråsten 52 B2
Grästorp 45 C2
Gratangen 9 D2
Gratens 109 C3, 155 D1
Gråtneset 14 B2
Gråträsk 16 A3
Gratteri 124 B2
Gratwein 127 C1
Graulhet 109 D2
Graus 155 C2/3
Graustein 83 D1
Grautheller 42 B2
Grávalos 153 D3, 154 A3
Gravanes 32 A3, 36 B1
Gravberget 38 B2
Gravdal 8 B2
Gravdal 42 A3
Grave 66 B3
Gravedona 105 D2, 106 A2
Gravéggia 105 C/D2

Graveide 43 C1
Gravelines 77 D1
Gravellona Toce 105 C/D2/3
Gravelotte 89 C1
Gravendal 39 C/D3
Grävenwiesbach 80 B2
Gravesend 65 C3
Gravfjorden 14 A3, 29 B/C1
Graviá 147 C1
Gråvika 36 A3
Gravina di Catánia 125 D2
Gravina in Púglia 120 B2
Gravmark 20 A1, 31 D2
Gravoúna 145 C1
Gray 89 C3
Grayan-et-l'Hôpital 100 B3
Grays 65 C3
Graz 127 C1
Graz 96 B3
Grazalema 172 A2
Grčarice 127 C3
Grdelica 139 C1
Gréalou 109 D1
Great Ayton 61 C1
Great Driffield 61 D2
Great Dunmow 65 C2/3
Great Harwood 59 D1, 60 B2
Great Malvern 63 D1, 64 A2
Great Missenden 64 B3
Great Rowsley 61 C3, 64 A1
Great Shelford 65 C2
Great Torrington 63 B/C2
Great Witley 59 D3, 64 A2
Great Yarmouth 65 D1/2
Grebbestad 44 B2
Grebenac 134 B1
Grebenau 81 C2
Grebenstein 81 C1
Gréccio 117 C3, 118 B1
Greda 127 D2
Greding 92 A1
Greding-Kraftsbuch 92 A1
Gredstedbro 52 A1
Greencastle 58 A1
Greenlaw 57 C/D2
Greenloaning 56 B1
Greenock 56 B2
Greenock 54 A2/3, 55 D1
Greenore 58 A1
Grefrath 79 D1
Grefsgård 37 C3
Gréggio 105 C3
Greifenburg 126 A1
Greifenstein-Allendorf 80 B2
Greiffenberg 70 B2
Greifswald 72 A2
Greillenstein 94 A2
Grein 93 D2
Grein 96 A2/3
Greipstad 43 B/C3
Greiz 82 B2
Gremersdorf 53 C3
Grenå 49 C2
Grenade 108 B2
Grenade-sur-l'Adour 108 B2
Grenås 29 D3, 35 C1
Grenåskilen 29 D3, 30 A2, 35 C1
Grenchen 105 B/C1
Grenier-Montgon 102 B3
Greningen 29 D3, 35 C2
Grenoble 104 A3
Grense-Jakobselv 7 D2
Gréoux-les-Bains 111 D2, 112 A2/3
Gresenhorst 53 D3
Gressåmoen 29 C2
Gresse 69 D2
Gresslivollen 33 D2
Gressoney-la Trinité 105 C3
Gressoney-Saint-Jean 105 C3
Gressvik 44 B1
Gresten 93 D3
Gretna Green 57 C3, 60 B1
Grettstadt 81 D2
Greussen 81 D1, 82 A1
Greux 89 C2
Grevbäck 45 D2, 46 A2

Greve 114 B3, 116 B2
Greven 69 C1
Greven 67 D3
Grevená 143 C2
Grevená 148 A/B1
Grevenbroich-Gustorf 79 D1, 80 A1
Grevenbroich 79 D1, 80 A1
Grevenítion 142 B3
Grevenka 99 D2
Grevenmacher 79 D3
Greven-Reckenfeld 67 D3
Grevesmühlen 53 C3, 69 C1
Greve Strand 49 D3, 50 A3, 53 D1
Grevie 49 D2, 50 A2
Grey Abbey 56 A3
Greystoke 57 C3, 60 B1
Greystones 58 A2
Grez-en-Bouère 86 A2/3
Grèzes 109 D1
Grgar 126 B2
Grieben 69 D2
Griegos 162 A2
Gries 126 A1
Griesalp [Reichenbach im Kandertal] 105 C2
Gries am Brenner 107 C1
Griesbach 93 C2
Griesen 91 D3, 92 A3
Griesheim 80 B3
Gries in Sellrain 107 C1
Grieskirchen 93 C2
Griesstätt 92 B3
Griffen 127 C1/2
Grignan 111 C1/2
Grigno 107 C2
Grignols 108 B2
Grigoriopol' 141 D1
Grijó 159 C1
Grijó 158 A2
Grijota 152 B3
Grijpskerk 67 C1
Grillby 40 B3, 47 C1
Grimaldi 122 A/B2
Grimaud 112 A3
Grimdalen 43 C2
Grimentz [Sierre] 105 C2
Grime's Grave 65 C2
Grimeton 49 D1, 50 A1
Grimma 82 B1
Grimmared 49 D1, 50 A1
Grimmialp, Kurheim [Oey-Diemtigen] 105 C2
Grimsås 50 B1
Grimsbu 33 C3, 37 D1
Grimsby 61 D2/3
Grimsdalshytta 33 C3, 37 D1
Grimslöv 51 B/C2
Grimsmark 31 D1/2
Grimsmyrheden 39 C2
Grimstad 43 C3
Grimstad 32 B2
Grindaheim 37 C2
Grinde 36 B2
Grindheim 42 B3
Grindjord 9 D2
Grindsted 48 A3, 52 A/B1
Grinkiškis 73 D2
Grinneröd 45 C3
Griñón 160 B3
Grip 32 A/B2
Gripenberg 46 A3
Gripport 89 C2
Gripsholm 47 C1
Grisel 154 A3
Grisignano di Zocco 107 C3
Grisolles 108 B2
Grisslehamn 41 C3
Grisvåg 32 B2
Grizzana 114 B2, 116 B1
Grjaznovo 75 D3
Grljan 135 C3
Grljevac 131 D3
Grøbæk 48 B2
Gröbenzell 92 A2
Gröbers 82 B1
Grobjina 73 C1
Gröbming 93 C3
Gröbzig 69 D3, 82 A/B1
Grocka 133 D1, 134 B1/2
Gródby 47 C1

Grödig 93 B/C3
Grödinge 47 C1
Gröditsch 70 B3
Gröditz 83 C1
Grodno 73 D2/3, 98 A1
Grodzisk Mazowiecki 73 C3, 97 C1
Grodzisk Wielkopolski 71 D3
Groenlo 67 C3
Groesbeek 67 B/C3
Grohote 131 C3
Groitzsch 82 B1
Groix 84 B3
Grójec 73 C3, 97 C1
Grolanda 45 D3
Groléjac 108 B1
Grolloo 67 C2
Grömbach 90 B2
Grömitz 53 C3
Grömitz-Cismar 53 C3
Gromo Santa Maria 106 A2
Grøna 32 B3, 37 C1
Grönahög 45 D3
Gronau 67 C3
Gronau-Epe 67 C3
Gronau (Leine) 68 B3
Grönbo 16 B3
Grønbua 37 C2
Grøndal 36 A2
Grøndalen 38 A/B1
Grøndalen 33 D2, 34 A2
Grönenbach 91 D3
Grong 28 B2
Grönhögen 51 D2
Grönhögen 72 B1
Gröningen 91 C/D1
Groningen 67 C1
Gröningen 69 C3
Grønlia 14 B3
Grønligrotten 14 B2
Grønnes 32 A2
Grønningen 28 A3, 33 C1
Grono [Castione-Arbedo] 105 D2, 106 A2
Grønøysetra 33 C3, 37 D1
Grönskåra 51 C1
Grönskåra 72 B1
Grønvik 42 A2
Grönviken 35 C2
Grønvollfoss 43 C/D1, 44 A1
Groomsport 56 A3
Grootegast 67 C1
Gropello Cairoli 105 D3, 113 D1
Groppo San Giovanne 114 A1
Grorud 43 D2, 44 A1
Grosbois-en-Montagne 88 B3
Grosbreuil 100 A2
Grósio 106 B2
Grošnica 134 B2
Grossa 113 D3
Grossalmerode 81 C1
Grossalsleben 69 C3
Grossarl 126 A1
Grossbodungen 81 D1
Grossbothen 82 B1
Grossbottwar 91 C1
Gross Buchholz 69 D2
Grossdobritz 83 C1
Gross-Dölln 70 A2
Grossefehn 67 D1
Grossefehn-Bagband 67 D1
Grossefehn-Strackholt 67 D1
Grossenbrode 53 C2/3
Grossenehrich 81 D1, 82 A1
Grossengottern 81 D1
Grossenhain 83 C1
Grossenhain 96 A1
Grossenkneten 67 D2, 68 A2
Grossenkneten-Sage 67 D2, 68 A2
Grossenlüder 81 C2
Grossenlupnitz 81 D1/2
Grossensee 68 B1
Grossenstein 82 B2
Grossenwiehe 52 B2
Gross-Enzersdorf 94 B2
Grossereix 101 C2
Grosserlach 91 C1

Grosser Rachel 93 C1
Grosseto 116 B3
Grossfurra 81 D1
Gross Gastrose 70 B3
Gross-Gerau 80 B3
Gross-Gerungs 93 D2
Grosshansdorf 53 B/C3, 68 B1
Grossharthau 83 C1
Grosshartmannsdorf 83 C2
Grosshartmannsdorf 127 D1
Grossheide 67 D1
Grossheimschuh 127 C1
Grossheubach 81 C3
Grosshöchstetten 105 C1
Grosskayna 82 A/B1
Grosskirchheim 107 D1, 126 A1
Gross Köris 70 A3
Gross-Kreutz 69 D2/3, 70 A2/3
Grosskrut 94 B2
Gross-Leine 70 B3
Gross Lieskow 70 B3
Grosslittgen 79 D3, 80 A3
Grossmehring 92 A2
Gross-Miltzow 70 A1
Grossmugl 94 B2
Grossnaundorf 83 C1
Gross-Nemerow 70 A1
Gross Oesingen 69 B/C2
Gross-Ossnig 70 B3, 83 D1
Grossostheim 81 C3
Gross-Pankow 69 D2
Grosspertholz 93 D2
Grosspetersdorf 127 D1
Grossraming 93 D3
Grossräschen 83 C1
Grossreifling 93 D3
Gross Reken 67 C3
Gross Rietz 70 B3
Grossrinderfeld 81 C3
Grossröhrsdorf 83 C1
Grossrosenburg 69 D3
Grossrosseln 89 D1, 90 A1
Gross-Salitz 53 C3, 69 C1
Gross Sankt Florian 127 C1
Gross Särchen 83 C/D1
Grossschirma 83 C2
Gross Schönebeck 70 A2
Grossschönau 83 D2
Grossschweinbarth 94 B2
Gross Schwülper 69 B/C3
Gross-Siegharts 94 A2
Grosssölk 93 C3
Grosssolt 52 B2
Grossthiemig 83 C1
Gross-Umstadt 81 C3
Grosswarasdorf 94 B3
Gross Warnow 69 C1
Grossweikersdorf 94 A2
Gross-Welle 69 C1
Gross-Welzin 69 C1
Gross-Werzin 69 D2
Grosswilfersdorf 127 D1
Gross-Wittensee 52 B2/3
Gross Wokern 53 D3, 69 D1
Grosswudicke 69 D2
Gross-Ziethen 70 B2
Grostenquin 89 D2
Grosuplje 127 B/C2/3
Grøtavær 9 C1
Grøtfjord 4 C1
Grötingen 35 C2
Grotli 32 A/B3, 37 C1
Grötlingbo 47 D3
Grøtnesdalen 4 A2
Grotta Azzurra 119 C/D3
Grotta di Bossea 113 C2
Grotta di Nettuno 123 C2
Grotta di Tibério 119 C3
Grottáglie 121 C2/3
Grottaminarda 119 D3, 120 A2
Grottammare 117 D2/3
Grotta Zinzulusa 121 D3
Grotte 124 B2/3
Grotte de Clamouse 110 B2
Grotte de Dargilan 110 B2
Grotte de l'Apothicairerie 84 B3
Grotte de la Sainte Baume 111 D3
Grotte de Labouiche 109 D3, 155 D1, 156 A1

Grotte de Médous **109** B/C3, **155** C1
Grotte de Niaux **155** D2, **156** A1
Grotte de Pech Merle **109** D1
Grotte des Demoiselles **110** B2
Grotte di Catullo **106** B3
Grotte di Castro **116** B3, **118** A1
Grotte du Loup **108** B3, **155** C1
Grotteria **122** A/B3
Grotte Santo Stéfano **117** C3, **118** A1
Grottes de Bétharram **108** B3, **155** B/C1
Grottes de Crozon **84** A2
Grottes de Trabuc **110** B2
Grottes d'Oxocelhaya **108** B3, **155** C1
Grøttingen **28** A2, **33** C1
Gróttole **120** B2
Grouw **66** B1/2
Grova **43** C2
Grøvdalsbu **32** B2/3
Gröveldalsvallen **34** A3
Grövels fjellstation **34** A3
Grovfjord **9** C/D2
Grøvseter **37** C2
Grožnjan **126** B3, **130** A1
Grua **38** A3
Grubbe **40** A1
Grubbe **30** B2, **35** D1
Grubben **14** B3
Gruben **33** D3
Grubišno Polje **128** A3
Grubo **69** D3
Gruda **137** C2
Grude **131** D3, **132** A3
Grudovo **141** C3
Grudziądz **73** B/C3
Grue Finnskog **38** B2
Gruffelingen **79** D2
Gruissan **103** B3, **156** B1
Gruja **135** D2
Grumbach **83** C1/2
Grumento Nova **120** B3
Grumo Appula **121** C2
Grums **45** C/D1
Grünau im Almtal **93** C3
Grünbach am Schneeberg **94** A3
Grünberg **81** C2
Grünburg **93** D3
Grundagssätern **34** A3
Grundfors **15** C3, **29** D1
Grundfors **30** B1
Grundforsen **38** B1
Grundsjö **35** C3
Grundsjö **30** A2
Grundsund **44** B3
Grundsunda **31** C3
Grundsunda **41** D3
Grundtjärn **30** B3, **35** D1
Grundträsk **16** B3
Grundträsk **16** A3
Grundträsk **16** A3
Grundträskliden **16** A3
Grundvattnet **16** B2/3
Grüneberg **70** A2
Grünendeich **68** B1
Grünewald **83** C1
Grünewalde **83** C1
Grungedal **42** B1
Grünhain **82** B2
Grünheide **70** B2/3
Grünkraut **90** A3
Grunnfarnes **9** C1
Grunnfjord **4** A2
Grunnførfjorden **8** B2
Grunow **70** B3
Grünsfeld **81** C3
Grünstadt **80** B3, **90** B1
Grüntal **70** A/B2
Gruomba **15** D1/2
Grupčin **138** B2
Grutness **54** A1
Gruvberget **40** A1/2
Gruyères **104** B2
Gruža **134** B2/3
Grycksbo **39** D2
Gryfice **72** A/B2
Gryfino **72** A3
Gryfino **70** B1
Gryllefjord **9** C1

Grymyr **38** A2/3
Grynberget **30** A2
Gryt **47** C2/3
Gryta **32** B1
Gryte **28** B3, **33** D1
Grytgöl **46** B2
Grythyttan **39** C/D3
Grytnäs **47** C3
Grytsjö **29** D1
Grytstorp **46** B2
Grzebienisko **71** D2
Grzmiąca **71** D1
Gschwend **91** C1
Gstaad **104** B2
Gsteig b. Gstaad [Gstaad] **104** B2
Guadahortuna **173** C1
Guadalajara **161** C2
Guadalaviar **162** A2/3
Guadalcanal **166** A3
Guadalcázar **172** A1
Guadalest **169** D2
Guadalix de la Sierra **161** B/C2
Guadalmez **166** B2
Guadalmina **172** A3
Guadalupe **166** B1
Guadamur **160** B3, **167** C1
Guadarrama **160** B2
Guadix **173** C2
Guagno **113** D3
Guájar Alto **173** C2
Gualchulain **56** A/B1
Gualchos **173** C2
Gualda **161** D2
Gualdo Tadino **115** D3, **117** C2
Gualtieri **114** B1
Guarcino **119** C2
Guarda **158** B2
Guardamar del Segura **169** C3, **174** B1
Guardamíglio **113** D1, **114** A1
Guardas Viejas **173** D2
Guardavalle **122** B3
Guardea **117** C3, **118** A/B1
Guárdia **120** A2
Guardia de Ares **155** C2
Guardia de Noguera **155** D3
Guardiagrele **119** C/D1
Guardialfiera **119** D2, **120** A1
Guárdia Perticara **120** B3
Guárdia Sanframondi **119** D2/3
Guardiola de Berga **156** A2
Guardistallo **114** B3, **116** A2
Guardo **152** A2
Guareña **165** D2, **166** A2
Guarrate **159** D1, **160** A1
Guarromán **167** C/D3
Guasa **154** B2
Guasila **123** D3
Guastalla **114** B1
Gúbbio **115** D3, **117** C2
Gubbträsk **15** D3
Guberevac **134** B3
Gubin **70** B3
Gubin **72** A3, **96** A1
Guča **133** D3, **134** A3
Guča Gora **132** A/B2
Guchen **155** C2
Gúdar **162** B2
Gudavac **131** C1
Guddal **36** A2
Gudensberg **81** C1
Gudhem **45** D2/3
Gudhjem **51** D3
Gudhjem **72** A2
Gudme **53** C2
Gudmuntorp **50** B3
Gudow **69** C1
Gudsø **48** B3, **52** B1
Gudumbro **48** A2
Gudvangen **36** B3
Guebwiller **89** D2/3, **90** A3
Gué-d'Hossus **78** B3
Guéhenno **85** C2/3
Güeñes **153** C1
Guer **85** C2/3

Guérande **85** C3
Guéret **102** A2
Guérigny **102** B1
Güesa **154** B2
Guéthary **108** A3, **154** A1
Gueugnon **103** C1/2
Gúglia **166** B2/3
Gúglia **114** B1/2, **116** A/B1
Güglingen **91** C1
Guglionesi **119** D2, **120** A1
Gugutka **145** D1, **145** D3
Gühlen Glienicke **69** D2, **70** A2
Guia **170** A2
Guia **158** A3, **164** A1
Guichen **85** D2
Guide Post **57** D2/3
Guidizzolo **106** B3
Guidónia-Montecélio **118** B2
Guíglia **114** B1/2, **116** A/B1
Guignes **87** D2
Guijo **166** B2/3
Guijo de Ávila **159** D2
Guijuelo **159** D2
Guildford **64** B3, **76** B1
Guillaumes **112** B2
Guillena **171** D1
Guillestre **112** A/B1
Guimara **153** B/C3
Guimarães **158** A1
Guimiliau **84** B2
Guînes **77** D1
Guingamp **84** B2
Guintanilla **151** D2
Guipavas **84** A2
Guipry **85** D3
Guirguillano **153** D2, **154** A2
Guisando **160** A3
Guisborough **61** C1
Guiscard **78** A3
Guise **78** B3
Guisséry **84** A1/2
Guissona **155** C3, **163** C1
Guitiriz **150** B1
Guîtres **108** B1
Gujan-Mestras **108** A1
Gulbene **74** A2
Gulboviken **34** B2
Guldborg **53** D2
Gulen **36** A2/3
Gulgofjorden **7** C1
Gullabo **51** C/D2
Gullane **57** C1
Gullänget **31** C3
Gullaskruv **51** C1
Gullbrø **36** B3
Gulleråsen **39** D2
Gullholmen **9** C2
Gullholmen **44** B3
Gullön **16** A3
Gullringen **46** B3
Gullspång **45** D2, **46** A1/2
Gullstein **32** B2
Güllük **149** D2
Gulpen **79** D2
Gulsele **30** B2, **35** D1
Gulsvik **37** D2
Gültz **70** A1
Gülze **69** C1
Gützow **53** D3, **69** D1
Gumboda **31** D1
Gumiel de Hizán **153** C3, **161** B/C1
Gummark **31** D1
Gummarksnoret **31** D1
Gümmenen **104** B1
Gummersbach **80** A1/2
Gummersbach-Derschlag **80** A/B1/2
Gumpelstadt **81** D2
Gumpersdorf **92** B2
Gumpoldskirchen **94** B2/3
Gumtow **69** D2
Gümüldür **149** D2
Gunarasfürdö **128** B2
Gundelfingen **91** D2
Gundelsheim **91** C1
Gundertshausen **93** B/C2/3
Gundheim **80** B3
Gundinci **132** B1
Gunnar **30** B1
Gunnarsberg **15** D3
Gunnarsbyn **17** C2
Gunnarskog **38** B3

Gunnarvattnet **29** C/D2
Gunnebo **46** B3
Gunnilbo **39** D3, **40** A3
Günselsdorf **94** B3
Gunsleben **69** C3
Gunsta **40** B3
Güntersberge **69** C3, **81** D1, **82** A1
Guntersblum **80** B3
Guntersdorf **94** A2
Guntín de Pallares **150** B2
Guntramsdorf **94** B2/3
Günzburg **91** D2
Gunzenhausen **91** D1
Günzerode **81** D1
Gurahonţ **97** D3, **140** A/B1
Gura Humorului **141** C1
Guralätsch-Alp [Ilanz] **105** D2, **106** A2
Gura Văii **135** C1/2
Gura Zlata **135** D1
Gurgazo **123** D3, **123** D1
Guri i zi **137** D2
Gurk **126** B1
Gurrea de Gállego **154** B3
Gurs **108** B3, **154** B1
Gusborn **69** C2
Gušče **127** D3, **131** C/D1
Gusendos de los Oteros **152** A2
Gusev **73** C/D2
Gusinje **137** D2, **138** A1/2
Gusmar **142** A2
Gúspini **123** C3
Gussago **106** B3
Gusselby **39** D3, **46** A/B1
Güssing **127** D1
Gussola **114** A1
Gusswerk **94** A3
Gustav Adolf **39** C3
Gustavsberg **45** C2
Gustavsberg **47** D1
Gustavsfors **45** C1
Güsten **69** C/D3
Gustorf **79** D1, **80** A1
Güstrow **53** D3, **69** D1
Gusum **46** B2
Gütenbach **90** B2/3
Gutengermendorf **70** A2
Gutenstein **94** A3
Gütersloh **68** A3
Gutierre Muñoz **160** A/B2
Guttannen [Innertkirchen] **105** C1/2
Guttaring **126** B1
Guvåg **92** B2
Guyhirn **65** C1/2
Gvardejsk (Tapiau) **73** C2
Gvarv **43** C/D2, **44** A1
Gvozd **137** D1
Gwda Wielka **71** D1
Gwieżdzin **71** D1
Gy **89** C3
Gyál **95** D3, **129** C1
Gyékényes **128** A2
Gyldensten **48** B3, **52** B1
Gyljen **17** C2
Gyllene Uttern **46** A3
Gylling **48** B3, **52** B1
Gyltvik **9** C3
Gyömrő **129** C1
Gyöngyös **97** C3
Gyönk **128** B2
Györ **95** C3
Györ **96** B3
Györvár **128** A1
Gysinge **40** A2/3
Gyttorp **46** A1
Gyula **97** C3, **140** A1
Gyulafirátót **128** B1
Gyulakeszi **128** A1
Gyülevész **128** A1
Gyvasshytta **42** B2

H

Haacht **79** C1/2
Häädemeeste **74** A1
Haag **92** B2
Haag **93** D2/3
Haag am Hausruck **93** C2
Haahainen **22** B1

Haaksbergen **67** C3
Haan **80** A1
Haapajärvi **21** D1, **22** A1
Haapajärvi **27** C2
Haapa-Kimola **25** D2, **26** B2
Haapakoski **20** B2
Haapakoski **22** B3
Haapakumpu **13** C2/3
Haapala **26** B2
Haapala **27** C1
Haapalahti **23** D2
Haapaloso **23** D3
Haapaluoma **20** B3
Haapamäki **21** D1/2, **22** A1/2
Haapamäki **21** C3
Haapamäki **22** B2
Haapamäki **23** C3
Haaparanta **13** C3
Haapasaari **26** B3
Haapasalmi **23** C3
Haapavaara **23** D1
Haapavesi **18** A3, **21** D1, **22** A1
Haapovaara **23** D2/3
Haapsalu **74** A1
Haar **92** A2/3
Haaraaoja **18** B3
Haarada **21** D2, **22** A2
Haarajoki **22** B3
Haarajoki **25** D2, **26** A2
Haarasaajo **12** A3, **17** D2
Haarbach **93** C2
Haarinka **21** D2, **22** A2
Haarlem **66** A2
Haaroinen **24** B2
Haataja **19** C1
Haavisto **25** C3
Habach **92** A3
Habartice **83** D1/2
Habas **108** A3, **154** B1
Habay-la-Neuve **79** C3
Habkern [Interlaken-West] **105** C1/2
Hablingbo **47** D3
Habo **45** C2
Håbol **45** C2
Habsburg [Schinznach Bad] **90** B3
Habscheid **79** D2/3
Håby **44** B2
Hachenburg **80** B2
Hacinas **153** C3
Hackås **34** B2
Hadamar **80** B2
Hädanberg **30** B2/3, **35** D1
Haddenham **65** C2
Haddington **57** C1/2
Haddon Hall **61** C3, **64** A1
Hademstorf **68** B2
Hadersdorf am Kamp **94** A2
Haderslev **52** B1
Haderup **48** A/B2
Hadleigh **65** C/D2
Hadmersleben **69** C3
Hadrian's Wall **57** C/D3, **60** B1
Hadsel **8** B2
Hadselsand **8** B2
Hadsten **48** B2
Hadsund **48** B2
Hadžići **132** B2/3
Haedington **65** C3
Haeggeriset **38** B1
Haelen **79** D1
Haffkrug-Scharbeutz **53** C3
Hafslo **36** B2
Hafstad **32** B2
Haga **38** A2
Haga **34** B2
Hagafoss **37** C3
Haganj **127** D2/3
Hagaström **40** A/B2
Hagby **51** D2
Hage **33** C2
Hage **67** D1
Hagebök **53** C/D3
Hægebostad **42** B3
Hægeland **43** B/C3
Hagelstadt **92** B1/2
Hagen **80** A1
Hagen **67** D3
Hagen **68** A1
Hagen-Hohenlimburg **80** A2

Hagenow 69 C1
Hagenwerder 83 D1
Hagétaubin 108 B3, 154 B1
Hagetmau 108 B2/3
Hagfors 39 C3
Häggås 30 A1
Häggåsen 30 B3, 35 D2
Häggdånger 35 D3
Häggenås 29 D3, 34 B1/2
Häggnäset 29 D2
Häggsåsen 34 B2
Häggsjöbränna 29 C3, 34 A1
Häggsjömon 30 B2, 35 D1
Häggsjön 29 D2, 34 B1
Haglebu 37 D3
Hagley 59 D3, 64 A2
Hagnillseter 33 C3
Hagondange 89 C1
Hagshult 50 B1
Hagsta 40 A/B2
Haguenau 90 A/B2
Håhellerhytta 42 B2
Hahn 80 A3
Hahnbach 82 A3, 92 A1
Hahnenklee-Bockswiese 68 B3
Hahót 128 A2
Haiger 80 B2
Haigerloch 90 B2
Häijää 24 B1
Haikela 23 D1
Hailsham 77 B/C1
Hailuoto 18 A2
Haina-Löhlbach 81 C1
Hainburg an der Donau 94 B2
Hainburg an der Donau 96 B2/3
Hainfeld 96 A3
Hainfeld 94 A2/3
Hainichen 83 B/C2
Hajala 24 B2/3
Hajdúböszörmény 97 C3
Hajdučica 134 B1
Hajnówka 73 D3, 98 A1
Hajós 129 C2
Hakadal 38 A3
Håkafot 29 D2
Håkantorp 45 C2/3
Hakasuo 19 C3
Hakenberg 70 A2
Hakenstedt 69 C3
Håkjerringnes 9 D1
Hakkas 16 B1
Hakkenpää 24 A2
Häkkilä 21 D2, 22 A2
Häkkilä 22 B3
Häkkiskylä 21 C3
Hakkstabben 5 C2
Håknäs 31 C2/3
Hakokylä 19 D3
Hakulinranta 18 B2
Halaesa 125 C2
Hålaforsen 30 A2/3, 35 D1
Halámky 93 D1/2
Hålandsosen 42 A/B2
Halastelki iskola 129 C/D2
Halászi 95 C3
Halbe 70 A/B3
Halbenrain 127 D1/2
Hålberg 16 A3
Halberstadt 69 C3
Halblech-Buching 91 D3
Halblech-Trauchgau 91 D3
Halbturn 94 B3
Halbturn 96 B3
Hald Ege 48 B2
Halden 44 B1
Haldensleben 69 C3
Haldenwang 91 D3
Halesworth 65 D2
Halfing 92 B3
Hålgö 47 C2
Halhjem 42 A1
Halifax 59 D1/2, 61 C2
Halikarnassos 149 D2/3
Halikko 24 B3
Hälilä 23 C1
Haljala 74 A1
Halk 52 B1/2
Halkia 25 D2, 26 A2
Halkivaha 24 B2
Halkokumpu 22 B3
Halkosaari 20 B2
Hall 47 D2

Hälla 30 B2, 35 D1
Hällabrottet 46 A1
Hålland 29 C3, 34 A2
Hallapuro 21 C2
Hallaryd 50 B2
Hallaskar 36 B3
Hallavaara 19 C2/3
Hallbergmoos 92 A2
Hällbo 40 A1
Hällbybrunn 46 B1
Hälle 44 B1/2
Halle 82 B1
Halle 68 A3
Halle 78 B2
Hällefors 39 C/D3
Hälleforsnäs 46 B1
Halle-Hörste 67 D3, 68 A3
Hallein 93 C3
Hällekis 45 D2
Hallen 29 C/D3, 34 B2
Hallen 29 D3, 30 A2, 35 C1
Hallen 34 B2
Hallenberg 80 B1
Hallenberg-Hesborn 80 B1
Hallencourt 77 D2
Halle-Neustadt 82 A/B1
Hallerud 45 D2, 46 A2
Hällesjö 30 A3, 35 C2
Hällestad 46 B2
Hällevadsholm 44 B2
Hällevik 51 C2/3
Hälleviksstrand 44 B3
Hållfjället 29 C3, 34 A2
Hällfors 16 B3
Halli 25 C1, 26 A1
Hallila 25 D2, 26 A2
Hallingby 37 D3
Hallingskeid 36 B3
Hällinmäki 22 B3
Hall in Tirol 107 C1
Hällnäs 15 D2
Hållnäs 40 B2
Hällnäs 31 C1/2
Hallsberg 46 A1
Hallschlag 79 D2
Hallshuk 47 D2
Hällsjö 30 B3, 35 D2
Hällstad 45 D3
Hallstahammar 40 A3, 46 B1
Hallstatt 93 C3
Hallstatt 96 A3
Hallstavik 41 B/C3
Hällstugan 39 C1
Halltal 107 C1
Halluin 78 A2
Hällvattnet 30 A2, 35 C1
Hallviken 29 D3, 35 C1
Halma 79 C3
Halmeniemi 26 B1/2
Halmeperä 21 D1, 22 A1
Halmeu 97 D3, 98 A3
Halmrast 37 D3, 38 A2
Halmstad 49 D2, 50 A2
Halmstad 72 A1
Halna 45 D2, 46 A2
Halne 37 C3
Halos 147 C1
Halosenniemi 18 A2
Hals 32 B2
Hals 49 B/C1/2
Hals 9 C1
Hals 28 B2
Halsa 14 B1
Halsanaustan 32 B2
Hälsingfors 31 C2
Halskov 53 C1
Halsnøykloster 42 A1
Halstead 65 C2
Halstedkloster 53 C2
Halstenbek 52 B3, 68 B1
Halsua 21 C1/2
Hålta 45 C3
Haltdalen 33 D2
Haltern 67 C/D3
Haltern-Hamm 67 C/D3
Halttula 18 A1/2
Haltwhistle 57 C/D3, 60 B1
Hälvä 27 D1
Halver 80 A1
Ham 78 A3
Hämäläinen 12 B2
Hamar 38 A2
Hamarhaug 42 A1
Hamarinperä 18 A1
Hamarneset 14 B2

Hamarøy 14 A/B2
Hamarøy 9 C2/3
Hambergen 68 A1
Hambühren 68 B2
Hamburg 68 B1
Hamburg-Kirchwerder 68 B1
Hamburgsund 44 B2
Hambye 86 A/B1
Hamdorf 52 B3
Hämeenkyrö (Tavastkyrö) 24 B1
Hämeenlinna (Tavastehus) 25 C2
Hämelerwald 68 B3
Hameln 68 B3
Hamersleben 69 C3
Hamidiye 145 D3
Hamilton 56 B2
Hamina (Fredrikshamn) 26 B2
Haminalahti 22 B2
Haminanmäki 25 D1, 26 A/B1
Hamlagrø 36 A/B3
Hamlagrøosen 36 A/B3
Hamleperä 21 D1, 22 A1
Hamm 67 D3, 80 B1
Hammar 46 A2
Hammarby 40 A2
Hammarland 41 C3
Hammarn 39 C/D3, 45 D1
Hammarnäs 29 D3, 34 B2
Hammarö 45 D1
Hammarsbyn 39 C2
Hammarstrand 30 A3, 35 C2
Hammaslahti 23 D3
Hamm-Bockum-Hövel 67 D3, 80 B1
Hamme 78 B1
Hammel 48 B2/3
Hammelburg 81 C/D3
Hammelburg-Gauaschach 81 C/D3
Hammelspring 70 A2
Hamme-Mille 79 C2
Hammenhög 50 B3
Hammer 28 B2, 33 D1, 34 A1
Hammer 28 B2
Hammer 28 B2
Hammerdal 29 D3, 35 C1
Hammerfest 5 C1, 6 A1
Hammershøj 48 B2
Hammershus 51 D3
Hammerum 48 A/B2
Hamm-Heessen 67 D3, 80 B1
Hamminkeln 67 C3
Hamminkeln-Brünen 67 C3
Hamminkeln-Dingden 67 C3
Hamm-Pelkum 67 D3, 80 B1
Hamn 32 B1
Hamnbukt 5 D2, 6 A2
Hamneidet 4 B2
Hamnes 28 B2
Hamnes 4 B2/3
Hamningberg 7 D1
Hamnøy 8 A3
Hamnsund 9 C2/3
Hamnsundet 14 A3
Hamnvågernes 4 A3, 9 D1, 10 A1
Hamnvik 9 C/D2
Hamoir 79 C2
Hampetorp 46 B1
Hamra 39 D1
Hamrångefjärden 40 A/B2
Hamremoen 43 D1
Hamstreet 77 C1
Hamula 22 A/B2
Hamula 22 B2
Hamzali 139 D3
Hån 45 C1
Hana 7 C2
Hanau 81 C3
Hanau-Grossauheim 81 C3
Hanau-Steinheim 81 C3
Handen 47 C/D1
Handewitt 52 B2
Handlová 95 D2
Handlová 96 B2
Handog 29 D3, 34 B2
Handöl 29 B/C3, 34 A2

Handrup 67 D2
Handsjö 36 B3
Handstein 14 A2
Handsverk 37 C/D2
Hanerau-Hademarschen 52 B3
Hanestad 33 D3
Hangaskylä 20 B3
Hangasmäki 25 C2
Hangastenmaa 26 B1
Hangelsberg 70 B2/3
Hånger 50 B1
Hanhikoski 12 B3
Hanhimaa 11 D3, 12 A1/2
Hanhivirta 23 C3
Hanho 21 C3
Haniá/Chaniá 149 B/C3
Hani i Hotit 137 D2
Hankamäki 23 C2
Hankamäki 22 B3
Hankasalmen asema 22 A/B3
Hankasalmi 22 A3
Han Knežica 131 D1
Hankø bad 44 B1
Hanko/Hangö 24 B3
Hannäs 46 B3
Hännilä 27 C1
Hännilä 21 D3, 22 A2/3
Hänninen 19 D1
Hänniskylä 21 D3, 22 A3
Hannover 68 B2/3
Hannukainen 11 C3, 12 A2
Hannumäki 17 C1
Hannusperä 18 B2
Hannusranta 19 C3
Hannut 79 C2
Hanö 51 C2/3
Hanøy kapell 9 B/C2
Han Pijesak 133 C2
Hanshagen 53 C3, 69 C1
Hansjö 39 C/D1/2
Hansnes 4 A2
Hanstedreservatet 48 A1
Hanstedt (Harburg) 68 B1
Hanstedt-Velgen 68 B2
Hanstholm 48 A1
Han-sur-Lesse 79 C2/3
Han-sur-Nied 89 D1
Häntälä 24 B2
Hanthâza 129 C/D1
Haou 108 A3, 154 B1
Haparanda/Haaparanta 17 D2/3, 18 A1
Haparanda hamn 17 D3, 18 A1
Häppälä 21 D3, 22 A3
Hapträsk 16 B2
Hara 39 C3
Hara 74 A1
Häradsbygden 39 D2
Haranes 28 B1
Haras du Pin 86 B1
Harbach 93 D2
Harbak 28 A2
Härbergsdalen 29 D1
Harbo 40 B3
Harboøre 48 A2
Harburg 91 D2
Harburg-Ebermergen 91 D2
Hårby 52 B1/2
Harcourt 77 C3, 86 B1
Hardegarijp 67 B/C1
Hardegsen 68 B3, 81 C1
Hardelot-Plage 77 D2
Hardenberg 67 C2
Harderwijk 66 B2/3
Hardeshøj 52 B2
Hardheim 81 C3
Hardheim-Bretzingen 81 C3, 91 °C1
Hardom 25 D2, 26 A/B2
Hardt (Rottweil) 90 B2
Hareid 36 A/B1
Harelbeke 78 A2
Haren 67 C/D2
Haren 67 C1/2
Haren-Rütenbrock 67 C2
Haren-Wesuwe 67 C/D2
Hareskov 49 D3, 50 A3, 53 D1
Harestad 45 C3
Harestua 38 A3
Harewood 61 C2
Harewood House 61 C2
Harfleur 77 B/C3

Harg 40 B3
Hargnies 79 C3
Hargshamn 40 B3
Harhala 25 C1
Haringvlietdam (Uitwateringssluizen) 66 A3
Harivaara 23 D2
Harjakangas 24 A/B1
Harjakopski 24 B1
Harjankylä 20 B3
Härjänvatsa 25 C3
Harjavalta 24 B1
Harjula 18 B1
Harjumaa 26 B1
Harjunkylä 20 A/B2
Harjunmaa 22 B3
Harjunpää 24 A1
Harjunsalmi 25 D1, 26 A1
Härkäneva 21 C1
Harkány 128 A2
Härkeberga 40 A/B3
Härkinvaara 23 C2/3
Härkmeri 20 A3
Härkmyran 16 B2
Härkönen 17 D2, 18 A1
Harlech 59 C3, 60 A3
Harleston 65 C2
Härlev 50 A3, 53 D1
Harlingen 66 B1/2
Harlösa 50 B3
Harlow 65 C3
Härlunda 51 B/C2
Härmä 20 B2
Härmä 19 D1
Harmaalamranta 21 D2, 22 A2
Harmainen 25 D1, 26 A1
Harmanec 95 D1/2
Harmånger 35 D2
Härmänkylä 19 D3
Harmanli 141 C3
Härmänmäki 19 C3
Härmas 129 C1
Harmer Hill 59 D3
Harndrup 48 B3, 52 B1
Harnekop 70 B2
Hårnes 28 A2
Hårnes 32 A2
Härnösand 35 D2/3
Haro 153 C2
Háromfa 128 A2
Härpe 25 D3, 26 A3
Harpefoss 37 D2
Harpenden 64 B2/3
Harplinge 49 D2, 50 A2
Harpstedt 68 A2
Harrejaure 16 B1
Harrelv 7 C1/2
Harrogate 61 C2
Harrogate 54 B3
Harrold 64 B2
Harrow 64 B3
Harrsjö 15 C3
Harrsjöhöjden 29 D2, 30 A1
Harrsjön 29 D2
Harrström 20 A2/3
Harrvik 15 C3
Härryda 45 C3, 49 D1
Harsa 39 D1, 40 A1
Harsefeld 68 B1
Harsewinkel 67 D3, 68 A3
Hårsjøen 33 D2/3
Harskirchen 89 D1, 90 A1
Harsleben 69 C3
Harsprånget 16 A/B1
Harstad 9 C2
Harsum 68 B3
Harsvik 28 A2
Harta 129 C2
Hartberg 127 D1
Hartberg 96 A3
Hårte 35 D2
Hartenholm 52 B3
Hartennes-et-Taux 88 A1
Hartha 82 B1
Hartland 62 B2
Hartlepool 61 D1
Hartmannsdorf 82 B2
Hartola 25 D1, 26 A1
Hartola 26 B2
Hartosenpää 26 B1
Harvaluoto 24 B3
Harvasstua 14 B3, 29 D1
Harwich 65 C3
Harzgerode 82 A1
Hasborn 80 A3

Haseldorf **68** B1
Häselgehr **106** B1
Haselund **52** B2
Haselünne **67** D2
Håsjö **30** A3, **35** C2
Håsjö Gamla **30** A3, **35** C2
Haskovo **141** C3
Haslach **90** B2
Haslach an der Mühl **93** C2
Hasle **51** D3
Hasle [Hasle-Rüegsau] **105** C1
Haslemere **64** B3, **76** B1
Haslemoen **38** B2
Haslev **53** D1
Haslev **72** A2
Hasmark **49** C3, **53** C1
Hasnon **78** A2
Hasparren **108** B3, **155** C1
Hassel **35** C/D3
Hassela **35** C/D3
Hasselfelde **69** C3, **81** D1, **82** A1
Hasselfors **46** A1
Hassel (Hoya) **68** A/B2
Hasselö **47** B/C3
Hasselt **79** C1/2
Hasselt **67** C2
Hasselvik **28** A3, **33** C1
Hassfurt **81** B3
Hassi **25** D1, **26** A1
Hässjö **35** D3
Hassleben **81** D1, **82** A1
Hässleholm **50** B2
Hässleholm **72** A1
Hasslerör **45** D2
Hasslö **51** C2
Hassloch **90** B1
Hæstad **14** A2
Hästbacka **21** B/C1
Hästbo **40** A/B2
Hastersboda **41** D3
Hästholmen **46** A2
Hastière-Lavaux **79** C2
Hastings **77** C1
Hästö **24** B3
Hästveda **50** B2
Hasvik **5** C2
Hatě **94** A2
Hateg **140** B1/2
Hatfield **61** C2/3
Hatfield **65** B/C3
Hatherleigh **63** C2
Hathersage **61** C3, **64** A1
Hatsola **27** C1
Hattem **67** C2
Hatten **90** B1/2
Hatten-Kirchhatten **67** D2, **68** A2
Hattevik **32** B1
Hattfjelldal **14** B3
Hatting **48** B3, **52** B1
Hattingen **80** A1
Hattlinghus **28** B2
Hattstedt **52** A/B2
Hattula **25** C2
Hattuselkonen **23** D1
Hattuvaara **23** D2
Hattuvaara **23** D1
Hatulanmäki **22** B1
Hatvan **97** C3
Hatzfeld **80** B1/2
Haubourdin **78** A2
Haudères, Les [Sion] **105** C2
Haudo **24** A2
Hauenstein **90** B1
Haugastøl **37** C3
Hauge **42** A3
Haugen **37** D2
Haugen **33** D3
Haugesund **42** A2
Haugfoss **43** D1
Haugfoss **43** C2
Haughom **42** B3
Haugnes **9** C1
Haugsdorf **94** A2
Haugseter **37** C/D2
Hauho **25** C2
Haukå **36** A2
Haukanmaa **21** D3, **22** A3
Haukedal **36** B2
Haukeland **36** A3
Haukeligrend **42** B1
Haukeliseter **42** B1
Haukijärvi **24** B1
Haukijärvi **19** C2

Haukilahti **21** C2
Haukilahti **19** D3
Haukimäki **22** B1/2
Haukiniemi **23** B/C2
Haukipudas **18** A2
Haukitaipale **12** A3, **18** A/B1
Haukivouri asema **22** B3
Haukivuori **22** B3
Hauklappi **27** C1
Hauknes / Andfiska **14** B2
Haundorf-Obererlbach **91** D1
Haunetal **81** C2
Haunia **24** B1
Haurida **46** A3
Haus **36** A3
Haus **93** C3
Hausach **90** B2
Häusern **90** B3
Hausham **92** A3
Hausjärvi **25** C/D2, **26** A2
Hauske **42** A2
Hausmannstätten **127** C1
Haustreisa **14** B3
Hausvik **42** B3
Hautajärvi **13** C3
Hautakylä **21** C2
Hautecombe **104** A3
Hautefort **101** C3
Hauteluce **104** B3
Haute-Nendaz [Sion] **104** B2
Hauterives **103** D3
Hauteville-Lompnès **103** D2, **104** A2
Hautjärvi **25** D2, **26** A2
Hautmont **78** B2
Hautomäki **22** B2
Hauzenberg **93** C2
Hauzenberg-Germannsdorf **93** C2
Hauzenberg-Oberneureuth **93** C2
Havant **76** A1
Håvberget **39** D3
Havdhem **47** D3
Havdrup **49** D3, **50** A3, **53** D1
Havelange **79** C2
Havelberg **69** D2
Havelte **67** C2
Havelterberg **67** C2
Håven **39** D1
Haverdal **49** D2, **50** A2
Haverfordwest **62** B1
Haverfordwest **55** D3
Haverhill **65** C2
Haverö **35** B/C3
Häverödal **41** B/C3
Håvered **45** C2
Håvilsrud **38** B3
Havířov **96** B2
Havixbeck **67** D3
Hävla **46** B2
Havlíčkův Brod **96** A2
Hävlingstugan **34** A3
Havnbjerg **52** B2
Havndal **48** B2
Havneby **52** A2
Havnsø **49** C3, **53** C1
Havnsund **32** A3
Havola **27** B/C2
Havøysund **5** D1, **6** A1
Havsa **141** C3
Havsnäs **30** A2
Havsnäs **30** A2, **35** C1
Havstenssund **44** B2
Havtorsbygget **39** C1
Havumäki **21** D3, **22** A3
Hawarden **59** C/D2, **60** B3
Hawes **59** D1, **60** B2
Hawick **57** C2
Hawick **54** B3
Hawkhurst **77** C1
Haworth **59** D1, **61** B/C2
Hayange **89** C1
Haydon Bridge **57** D3, **60** B1
Hayfield **59** D2, **61** B/C3
Hayingen **91** C2
Hayle **62** A3
Hay-on-Wye **63** C1
Haywards Heath **76** B1
Hazas de Cesto **153** C1
Hazebrouck **78** A2
Hazlov **82** B3

Headcorn **65** C3, **77** C1
Heager **48** A3
Heanor **61** D3, **65** C1
Heathfield **77** B/C1
Heathrow **64** B3
Hebnes **42** A2
Heby **40** A3
Hèches **109** C3, **155** C1
Hechingen **91** C2
Hecho **154** B2
Hechtel **79** C1
Hechthausen **52** B3, **68** A/B1
Heckelberg **70** B2
Heckington **61** D3, **64** B1
Hecklingen **69** C3
Hedalen **37** D3
Hedared **45** C3
Hédauville **78** A3
Hedberg **16** A3
Hedby **39** D2
Heddal **43** C/D1, **44** A1
Hedderen **42** B2
Hede **34** A3
Hede **45** B/C2
Hédé **85** D2
Hedehusene **49** D3, **50** A3, **53** D1
Hedemora **40** A2/3
Heden **15** D3
Hedenäset **17** D2
Hedensted **48** B3, **52** B1
Hedersleben **82** A1
Hedersleben **69** C3
Hédervár **95** C3
Hedesunda **40** A2
Hedeviken **34** A/B3
Hedlo **36** B3
Hedmark **30** B1
Hedon **61** D2
Hee **48** A3
Heede **67** D2
Heek **67** C3
Heemstede **66** A2/3
Heer **79** C/D2
Heer-Agimont **79** C2/3
Heerbrugg **91** C3
Heerde **67** C2
Heerenveen **66** B2
Heerhugowaard **66** A/B2
Heerlen **79** D2
Heesch **66** B3
Heeslingen **68** B1
Heestrand **44** B2
Heeze **79** C1
Hegge **37** C/D2
Heggenes **37** D2
Heggmo **14** B2
Heggstad **28** B2, **33** D1
Hegrø **28** B3, **33** D1
Hegset **33** D2
Hegyeshalom **94** B3
Hegyfalu **94** B3, **128** A1
Heia **4** A3, **9** D1, **10** A1
Heia **28** B2
Heidal **37** D1/2
Heiddorf **69** C1/2
Heide **52** A/B3
Heideck **92** A1
Heidelberg **90** B1
Heiden **67** C3
Heiden **91** C3
Heidenau **68** B1
Heidenau **83** C1/2
Heidenheim **91** D2
Heidenheim (Gunzenhausen) **91** D1
Heidenheim-Hechlingen **91** D1
Heidenreichstein **93** D1/2, **94** A1/2
Heidenrod **80** B3
Heidenrod-Geroldstein **80** B3
Heidenrod-Laufenselden **80** B2/3
Heiderscheid **79** D3
Heigenbrücken **81** C3
Heikendorf **52** B2/3
Heikkilä **19** D1
Heikkurila **27** C1
Heiland **43** C2
Heilbronn **91** C1
Heiligenberg **91** C3
Heiligenblut **107** D1, **126** A1
Heiligengrabe **69** D1/2

Heiligenhafen **53** C2/3
Heiligenhaus **80** A1
Heiligenkreuz im Lafnitztal **127** D1
Heiligenkreuz **94** A/B2/3
Heiligenstadt-Burggrub **82** A3
Heiligenstadt **81** D1
Heiligkreuzsteinach **81** B/C3, **90** B1
Heiloo **66** A2
Heilsbronn **91** D1
Heiltz-le-Maurupt **88** B1
Heim **32** B1
Heimbach **80** A3
Heimbach (Schleiden) **79** D2
Heimburg **69** C3
Heimdal **28** A3, **33** C1/2
Heimertingen **91** D2/3
Heimola **13** B/C2
Heimseta **36** A2
Heinäaho **22** B2
Heinälammi **25** B/C1
Heinämaa **25** D2, **26** A2
Heinäperä **22** B1
Heinäpohja **21** D2, **22** A2
Heinävaara **23** C2
Heinävaara **23** D3
Heinäveden asema **23** C3
Heinävesi **23** C3
Heinersdorf **70** B2
Heinersreuth (Bayreuth) **82** A3
Heiniemi **26** B1
Heinijärvi **18** A3
Heinikoski **18** A1
Heinisuo **18** B1
Heinjoki **24** B2
Heinlahti **26** B2/3
Heino **67** C2
Heinola **25** D1/2, **26** A1/2
Heinolan maalaiskunta **25** D1/2, **26** B1/2
Heinolanperä **18** A3
Heinoniemi **23** C3
Heinoo **24** B1
Heinsberg **79** D1
Heinsberg-Karken **79** D1
Heinsburg-Randerath **79** D1
Heintaival **22** A/B2/3
Heist-op-den-Berg **79** C1
Heitersheim **90** A3
Heituinlahti **26** B2
Hejde **47** D3
Hejlsminde **52** B1
Hejnice **83** D2
Hejnsvig **48** A/B3, **52** A/B1
Hejnum **47** D2
Hekal **142** A2
Hel **73** B/C1
Helags fjällstation **34** A2
Helbra **82** A1
Heldburg **81** D2
Helden **79** D1
Heldrungen **82** A1
Helechal **166** B2
Helfenberg **93** C/D2
Helfštýn **95** C1
Helgådalen **28** B3, **33** D1
Helgeli **4** B2/3
Helgenäs **46** B3
Helgenäs Kirke **49** C3
Helgeroa **43** D2, **44** A2
Helgheim **36** B2
Helgøy **4** C2
Helgøy **38** A2
Helgum **30** A3, **35** D2
Helgum **30** A/B3, **35** D2
Heligfjäll **30** A1
Heliport (Scilly Isles) **62** A3
Hell **28** A/B3, **33** C/D1
Hella **36** B2
Helland **32** B2
Helland **32** A2/3
Helland **42** A2
Helland **9** C3
Hellandsbygd **42** B1
Hellanmaa **20** B2
Hellarmo **15** C1
Helle **43** D2, **44** A2
Helle **42** B2
Helle **8** A3
Helle **42** A2
Helleland **42** A3

Hellemobotn **9** C3
Hellendoorn **67** C2
Hellenthal **79** D2
Hellenthal-Hollerath **79** D2
Hellenthal-Losheim **79** D2
Hellenthal-Reifferscheid **79** D2
Hellesøy **36** A3
Hellested **50** A3, **53** D1
Hellesvik **14** A2
Hellesylt **32** A3, **36** B1
Hellevad **52** B2
Hellevik **36** A2
Hellevoetsluis **66** A3
Helligvær **8** B3
Hellín **168** B2/3
Hellmonsödt **93** D2
Hellnes **4** B2
Hellsö **24** A3, **41** D3
Hellvik **42** A3
Helmbrechts **82** A2/3
Helmdon **65** C2
Helmond **79** C1
Helmsdale **54** B1/2
Helmsley **61** C2
Helmstedt **69** C3
Helnæs By **52** B2
Helnessund **8** B3
Helppi **12** A2, **17** D1
Helsingborg **49** D3, **50** A2/3
Helsingborg **72** A1
Helsinge **49** D3, **50** A2/3
Helsingør **49** D3, **50** A2/3
Helsingør **72** A1
Helsinki **24** A2
Helsinki/Helsingfors **25** C/D3, **26** A3
Helsinki-Kivenlahti **25** C3
Helsinki-Soukka **25** C3
Helsinki-Tapiola **25** C3
Helsinki-Vuosaari **25** D3, **26** A3
Helston **62** A/B3
Heltersberg **90** A1
Helvécia **129** C1
Hemau **92** A1
Hemel Hempstead **64** B3
Hemer **80** B1
Hemfurt-Edersee **81** C1
Hemhofen **81** D3, **82** A3
Héming **89** D1/2, **90** A2
Hemingbrough **61** C2
Hemling **31** B/C2
Hemmesta **47** D1
Hemmet **48** A3, **52** A1
Hemmingen **68** B3
Hemmingen **31** C1
Hemmingsmark **16** B3
Hemmonranta **23** B/C2
Hemmoor **52** A/B3, **68** A1
Hemnebygda **36** B1
Hemnes **38** A3, **44** B1
Hemnesberget **14** B3
Hemsbach **80** B3
Hemse **47** D3
Hemse **72** B1
Hemsedal **37** C3
Hemsjö **35** C2
Hemsjö **51** C2
Hemslingen **68** B2
Hemsön **35** D2
Henån **45** B/C3
Hénanbihen **85** C2
Henarejos **162** A3, **169** B/C1
Hendaye **154** A1
Hendset **32** B2
Hendy **63** C1
Hengelo **67** C3
Hengelo **67** C3
Hengersberg **93** B/C2
Hénin-Liétard **78** A2
Henley-in-Arden **64** A2
Henley on Thames **64** B3
Hennan **35** C3
Henndorf am Wallersee **93** C3
Henneberg **81** D2
Hennebont **84** B3
Hennef **80** A2
Hennef-Uckerath **80** A2
Henne Strand **48** A3, **52** A1
Hennickendorf **70** A3
Hennigsdorf **70** A2
Henning **28** B2, **33** D1
Henningen **69** C2

Henningsvær **8** B2
Hennstedt **52** B3
Hennstedt **52** B3
Hénoville **77** D2
Henri-Chapelle **79** D2
Henrichemont **87** D3
Henriksfjäll **15** C3, **29** D1
Hensås **37** C2
Henstedt-Ulzburg **52** B3, **68** B1
Henstridge **63** D2
Henvålen **34** A2
Hepolanperä **17** D3, **18** A1
Heppenheim **80** B3
Herad **42** B3
Heradsbygd **38** A/B2
Heraion **147** C2
Heraion **147** C3
Herajärvi **25** C/D1, **26** A1
Herajoki **25** C2
Herajoki **23** D2
Heraklea **143** C1
Herálec **94** A1
Herand **36** B3
Heraniemi **23** D2
Herbault **86** A/B3
Herbertingen **91** C2/3
Herbés **163** C2
Herbesthal **79** D2
Herbignac **85** C3
Herbitzheim **89** D1, **90** A1
Herbolzheim **90** A/B2
Herborn **80** B2
Herbrechtingen-Hausen **91** D2
Herbrechtingen **91** D2
Herbstein **81** C2
Herce **153** D2/3
Herceg Novi **137** C2
Hercegovac **128** A3
Hercegszántó **129** C2/3
Herdla **36** A3
Herdorf **80** B2
Herdwangen-Schönach **91** C3
Héréchou **109** C3, **155** C1
Hereford **63** D1
Herefoss **43** C3
Herencia **167** D1
Herend **128** B1
Herentals **79** C1
Hérépian **110** B3
Herfølge **50** A3, **53** D1
Herford **68** A3
Herguijuela **166** A2
Héricourt **89** D3
Héricourt-en-Caux **77** C3
Hérimoncourt **89** D3, **90** A3
Heringen **81** D1, **82** A1
Heringen-Widdershausen **81** D2
Heringsdorf **53** C3
Herisau **91** C3, **105** D1
Hérisson **102** B2
Herk-de-Stad **79** C1/2
Herland **36** A2
Herlesheusen-Nesselröden **81** D1/2
Herleshausen **81** D1/2
Herlufmagle **53** D1
Hermagor **126** A2
Hermannsburg **68** B2
Hermannshof **53** D3
Hermansjö **30** B3, **35** D1
Hermansjö **30** B3, **35** D1
Hermansverk **36** B2
Hérmedes de Cerrato **152** B3, **160** B1
Herment **102** A/B3
Hermeskeil **80** A3
Hermisende **151** C3
Hermitage Castle **57** C2
Hermsdorf **82** A/B2
Hermsdorf **83** C2
Hernani **153** D1, **154** A1
Herne **80** A1
Herne Bay **65** D3, **77** C1
Hernes **28** A3, **33** C1
Herning **48** A/B3
Heroldsberg **82** A3, **92** A1
Heroldstatt-Ennabeuren **91** C2
Herøy **14** A2
Herpf **81** D2
Herråkra **51** C1
Herrala **25** D2, **26** A2

Herramélluri **153** C2
Herräng **41** C3
Herraskylä **21** C3
Herre **43** D2, **44** A1
Herredsgrensen **14** B1
Herrenberg **91** B/C2
Herrenchiemsee **92** B3
Herrera **172** A/B2
Herrera de Alcántara **165** C1
Herrera del Duque **166** B2
Herrera de los Navarros **162** A/B1
Herrera de Pisuerga **152** B2
Herrera de Valdecañas **152** B3
Herreros **153** D3, **161** C/D1
Herreros **151** D2/3
Herreros de Suso **160** A2
Herreruela **165** C1
Herrestad **45** C2
Herrhamra **47** C1/2
Herrieden **91** D1
Herrieden-Neunstetten **91** D1
Herringbotn **14** B2/3
Herrischried **90** B3
Herrlslev **53** D2
Herrljunga **45** C3
Herrnhut **83** D1/2
Herrö **34** B3
Herröskatan **41** D3
Herrsching **92** A3
Herrskog **30** B3, **35** D2
Herrstein **80** A3
Herrvik **47** D3
Herry **87** D3, **102** B1
Hersbruck **82** A3, **92** A1
Herschbach **80** B2
Herschbach **80** B2
Herscheid **80** B1
Herselt **79** C1
Hersin-Coupigny **78** A2
Herstal **79** C2
Herstmonceux Castle **77** C1
Hersvik **36** A2
Herte **40** A1
Herten **67** C/D3, **80** A1
Hertford **65** C3
Hervás **159** D3
Hervideros de Fuensanta **167** C2
Herxheim **90** B1
Herxheim **80** B3, **90** B1
Herzberg **68** B3, **81** D1
Herzberg **70** A3, **83** C1
Herzberg **69** D1
Herzberg **70** A2
Herzberg **72** A3, **96** A1
Herzberg-Scharzfeld **81** D1
Herzberg-Sieber **69** B/C3, **81** D1
Herzebrock **67** D3, **68** A3
Herzfelde **70** B2
Herzlake **67** D2
Herzogenaurach **81** D3, **91** D1, **92** A1
Herzogenbuchsee **105** C1
Herzogenburg **94** A2
Herzsprung **69** D2
Hesdin **77** D2
Hesel **67** D1
Heskestad **42** A/B3
Hesnæs **53** D2
Hesperange **79** D3
Hessdalen **33** D2
Hesselagergård **53** C2
Hessen **69** C3
Hesseneck-Kailbach **81** C3, **91** C1
Hessisch Lichtenau **81** C1
Hessisch Oldendorf-Hemeringen **68** A/B3
Hessisch Oldendorf **68** A/B3
Hessisch Oldendorf-Fischbeck **68** A/B3
Hessvik **42** A1
Hestedt **69** C2
Hestenesøyri **36** A/B1
Hestmon **14** A2
Hestnes **32** B1
Hestøy **14** A2
Hestra **50** B1
Hestra **46** A3
Hestvika **32** B1

Hetekylä **18** B2
Hetlevik **36** A3
Hettstedt **69** C3, **82** A1
Hetzerath **79** D3, **80** A3
Heubach **91** C2
Heubach **81** D2, **82** A2
Heudebouville **76** B3, **86** A/B1
Heusden **79** C1
Heustreu **81** D2
Heusweiler **89** D1, **90** A1
Heves **97** C3
Héviz **128** A1/2
Hevlín **94** B2
Hevosoja **26** B2
Hexham **57** D3, **60** B1
Hexham **54** B3
Heyrieux **103** D3
Heysham **59** C/D1, **60** B2
Heysham **54** B3
Heytesbury **63** D2, **64** A3
Hidasnémeti **97** C2
Hiddenhausen **68** A3
Hieflau **93** B3
Hiendelaencina **161** C2
Hiersac **101** C3
Hiers-Brouage **100** B3
Hietakangas **13** B/C2
Hietakylä **22** B3
Hietama **21** D3, **22** A3
Hietana **25** D2, **26** A/B2
Hietanen **26** B1
Hietanen **17** D1
Hietaniemi **13** C2
Hietaniemi **19** C1
Hietaniemi **11** D2/3, **12** B1
Hietaniemi **26** B1
Hietaperä **19** D3
Hietoinen **25** D2, **26** A2
Hiettanen **17** D1
Higham Ferrers **64** B2
Highworth **64** A3
High Wycombe **64** B3
Higrav **21** C2
Higuera **159** D3, **166** A1
Higuera de Arjona **167** C3, **172** B1
Higuera de Calatrava **167** C3, **172** B1
Higuera de la Serena **166** A2
Higuera de la Sierra **165** D3, **171** C1
Higuera de las Dueñas **160** A/B3
Higuera de Llerena **165** D3, **166** A3
Higuera de Vargas **165** C2/3
Higuera la Real **165** D3
Higueras **162** B3
Higueruela **169** C2
Higueruela **163** C3, **169** D1
Higueruelas **162** B3, **169** C1
Hihnavaara **13** C2
Hiidenkirnut **12** A3
Hiidenkylä **21** D1, **22** A1
Hiilinki **21** C/D2
Hiirikylä **23** C1
Hiirola **26** B1
Hiisijärvi **19** C3
Hiiskoski **23** D2
Hiitelä **25** D2, **26** A2
Híjar **162** B1/2
Hikiä **25** C/D2, **26** A2
Hilchenbach **80** B1/2
Hildburghausen **81** D2
Hilden **80** A1
Hildesheim **68** B3
Hilgertshausen-Tandern-Hilgertshausen **92** A2
Hilgertshausen-Tandern **92** A2
Hillared **45** D3
Hille **68** A3
Hillebola **40** B2
Hillegom **66** A2/3
Hiller **28** B1
Hillerød **49** D3, **50** A3
Hillerød **72** A1/2
Hillerse **68** B2/3
Hillerstorp **50** B1
Hilleshamn **9** D2
Hillesheim **79** D2, **80** A2
Hillestad **43** D1, **44** A1

Hilli **21** C1
Hillilä **21** C1
Hillmersdorf **70** A3
Hillosensalmi **26** B2
Hillringsberg **45** C1
Hillsborough **56** A3
Hilltown **58** A1
Hilpoltstein **92** A1
Hilter **67** D3
Hiltunen **19** D1
Hilvarenbeek **79** C1
Hilversum **66** B3
Hilzingen **90** B3
Himalansaari **27** B/C1
Himanka **21** C1
Himankakylä **21** C1
Himara **142** A2
Himberg **94** B2/3
Himbergen **69** C2
Himesháza **128** B2
Himki **75** D2
Himmelberg **126** B1
Himmelpforten **68** B1
Hinckley **65** C2
Hindås **45** C3
Hindås **72** A1
Hindelang **91** D3
Hindelbank **105** C1
Hindeloopen **66** B2
Hindenberg **70** A2
Hindersby **25** D2, **26** B2
Hinderson **17** C3
Hinderwell **61** C1
Hindhead **64** B3, **76** B1
Hindley **59** D2, **60** B2/3
Hindon **63** D2, **64** A3
Hindrem **28** A3, **33** C1
Hindseter **37** C2
Hinganmaa **12** B2
Hingham **65** C/D2
Hinkaperä **18** B3, **21** D1, **22** A1
Hinnerjoki **24** A/B2
Hinnerup **48** B2
Hinneryd **50** B2
Hinojal **159** C3, **165** D1, **166** A1
Hinojales **165** D3, **171** C1
Hinojos **171** C/D2
Hinojosa **161** D2, **162** A2
Hinojosa de la Sierra **153** D3
Hinojosa de Duero **159** C2
Hinojosa de San Vicente **160** A3
Hinojosa del Valle **165** D2/3, **166** A2/3
Hinojosa del Duque **166** B2/3
Hinojosas de Calatrava **167** C2
Hinova **135** D2
Hinrichshagen **53** D3
Hinrichshagen **70** A1
Hinte **67** C/D1
Hinte-Loppersum **67** C/D1
Hinterhornbach **91** D3, **106** B1
Hinterrhein [Thusis] **105** D2, **106** A2
Hinterriss **92** A3
Hintersee **93** C3
Hintersee **70** B1
Hinterstoder **93** C/D3
Hinterthal **92** B3, **126** A1
Hintertux **107** C1
Hinterzarten **90** B3
Hinthaara/Hindhår **25** D2/3, **26** A3
Hinx **108** A2
Hio **150** A2/3
Hippolytushoef **66** B2
Hîrlău **141** C1
Hirrlingen **91** B/C2
Hirschaid **81** D3, **82** A3
Hirschau **82** A/B3, **92** A/B1
Hirschbach **82** A3, **92** A1
Hirschberg **82** A2
Hirschfelde **83** D2
Hirschhorn **81** B/C1
Hirsilä **25** C1
Hirsingue **89** D3, **90** A3
Hirsjärvi **25** C2
Hirson **78** B3
Hîrşova **141** C/D2
Hirtshals **44** A3, **48** B1

Hirvaanmäki **21** D2, **22** A2
Hirvas **12** A3
Hirvaskoski **19** C2
Hirvaskylä **21** D3, **22** A3
Hirvasperä **18** A2/3
Hirvasvaara **13** C3
Hirveäkuaru **12** B2
Hirvelä **18** B2
Hirvelä **19** D3, **23** D1
Hirvelä **26** B2
Hirvenlahti **25** D1, **26** B1
Hirvensalmi **26** B1
Hirviäkuru **12** B2
Hirvihaara **25** D2, **26** A2
Hirvijärvi **20** B3
Hirvijärvi **25** C1
Hirvijärvi **22** B1
Hirvijärvi **17** C2
Hirvijoki **20** B2
Hirvikylä **21** C3
Hirvilahti **22** B2
Hirvimäki **21** D3, **22** A3
*Hirvirangas **21** D3, **22** A3
Hirvisalo **25** D1/2, **26** B1/2
Hirvivaara **23** D2
Hirvlax **20** B2
Hirwaun **63** C1
Hirzenhain **81** C2
Hisar **149** D2
Hishult **50** B2
Hisøy **43** C3
Hissjön **31** C/D2
Hita **161** C2
Hitchin **64** B2
Hitis/Hiittinen **24** B3
Hittarp **49** D3, **50** A2
Hitterdal **33** D2
Hittisau **91** C/D3
Hitzacker **69** C2
Hitzendorf **127** C1
Hitzkirch **105** C1
Hiukkajoki **27** D1
Hjäggsjö **31** C2
Hjallerup **48** B1
Hjälmset **14** A3, **28** B1
Hjältanstorp **35** C3
Hjältevad **46** A/B3
Hjardemal Klit **48** A1
Hjartdal **43** C1
Hjelle **37** C2
Hjelle **32** A3, **36** B1
Hjelle **36** B1
Hjellebotn **28** B2
Hjellestad **36** A3
Hjelmelandsvågen **42** A2
Hjelmset **14** A3, **28** B1
Hjerkinn **33** C3, **37** D1
Hjerm **48** A2
Hjerpsted **52** A2
Hjerting **48** A3, **52** A1
Hjo **50** B2/3, **46** A2
Hjøllund **48** B3
Hjølmo **36** B3
Hjørring **48** B1
Hjorte **52** B1
Hjorted **46** B3
Hjortkvarn **46** B2
Hjortnäs **39** C2
Hjortsberga **51** B/C1
Hjortskarmoen **14** B3
Hjulsjö **39** D3
Hlinky **82** B3
Hlohovec **95** C2
Hlohovec **96** B2
Hluboká nad Vltavou **93** D1
Hluboš **83** C3
Hluk **95** C1
Hmel'nickij **98** B3
Hmelnik **99** C3
Hnanice **94** A2
Hoberg **29** C3, **34** A1
Hobøl **38** A3, **44** B1
Hobro **48** B2
Hoburgen **47** C/D3
Höchberg **81** C/D3
Hochdonn **52** B3
Hochdorf **105** C1
Höchenschwand **90** B3
Höchenschwand-Tiefenhäusern **90** B3
Hochfelden **90** A2
Hochfilzen **92** B3
Höchheim-Irmelshausen **81** D2
Hochkirch **83** D1
Hochosterwitz **126** B1
Hochsölden **107** B/C1
Hochspeyer **90** B1

Höchst **81** C3
Hochstadt **90** B1
Höchstädt **91** D2
Höchstädt **82** B3
Höchstadt an der Aisch **81** D3
Höchstenbach **80** B2
Hochwolkersdorf **94** B3
Hockenheim **90** B1
Hockeroda **82** A1
Hocksjö **30** A2, **35** C1
Hodal **33** D3
Hoddesdon **65** C3
Hoddevika **36** A1
Hodenhagen **68** B2
Hodkovice nad Mohelkou **83** D2
Hódmezővásárhely **129** D2
Hódmezővásárhely **97** C3, **140** A1
Hodnet **59** D3, **60** B3
Hodonín **94** B1/2
Hodonín **96** B2
Hodorov **97** D2, **98** A3
Hodoš **96** A/B3
Hodoš **127** D1
Hodošan **127** D2, **128** A2
Hoedekenskerke **78** B1
Hoek van Holland **66** A3
Hoemsbu **32** B3
Hoenderloo **66** B3
Hoensbroek **79** D2
Hof **82** A/B2
Hof **80** B2
Hof **38** B2
Hof am Leithagebirge **94** B3
Hofbieber **81** C2
Hofbieber-Kleinsassen **81** C2
Höfer **68** B2
Hofgeismar **81** C1
Hofgeismar-Hümme **81** C1
Hofheim **81** D3
Hofheim **80** B3
Hofkirchen im Mühlkreis **93** C2
Hofles **28** B1
Hofors **40** A2
Höganäs **49** D2/3, **50** A2
Höganäs **72** A1
Högberget **16** A3
Högbo **40** A2
Hogboda **45** C1
Högby **51** D1
Högby **72** B1
Högbynäs **29** D2, **30** A2
Högerud **45** C1
Högfjällshotellet **39** C1
Högfors **39** D3
Högfors **40** A3
Höggnabba **21** B/C1/2
Högheden **15** D2
Högheden **16** A3
Höghult **46** B3
Högklint **47** D3
Högkulla **31** C1
Högland **31** C2
Höglekardalen **34** B2
Höglunda **30** A3, **35** C2
Högnäset **30** A1
Hogndalen **15** B/C1
Hognerud **45** C1
Hognes **28** B1
Hognfjord **9** C2
Högsåra **24** B3
Högsäter **38** B3
Högsäter **45** C1
Högsäter **45** C2
Högsby **51** D1
Högsby **72** B1
Høgset **32** A/B2
Högsjö **46** B1
Högsta **29** C/D3, **34** B2
Högvålen **34** A3
Högyész **128** B2
Hohberg **90** B2
Hohburg **82** B1
Höheinöd **90** A1
Hohenaltheim **91** D2
Hohenaspe **52** B3
Hohenau **94** B2
Hohenberg **94** A3
Hohenberg-Krusemark **69** D2
Hohenbrünzow **70** A1
Hohenbucko **70** A3

Hohenburg **92** A1
Hohenburg-Mendorferbuch **92** A1
Hohenems **91** C3, **106** A1
Hohenfels **92** A1
Hohenfurch **91** D3
Hohengüstow **70** B1
Hohenhameln **68** B3
Höhenkirchen **92** A3
Hohenleipisch **83** C1
Hohenleuben **82** B2
Hohenlinden **92** A/B2
Hohenlockstedt **52** B3
Hohenmölsen **82** B1
Hohen Neuendorf **70** A2
Hohenpeissenberg **91** D3, **92** A3
Hohenpolding-Sulding **92** B2
Hohenpriessnitz **82** B1
Hohenroda **81** C/D2
Hohensaaten **70** B2
Hohenschwangau **91** D3
Hohenseeden **69** D3
Hohenseefeld **70** A3
Hohenstein-Bernloch **91** C2
Hohenstein-Ernstthal **82** B2
Hohentauern **93** D3
Hohenthann **92** B2
Hohenwarsleben **69** C3
Hohenwarth **82** B2
Hohenwarth **94** A2
Hohenwarthe **69** D3
Hohenwart (Schrobenhausen) **92** A2
Hohenwestedt **52** B3
Hohenziatz **69** D3
Hohn **52** B3
Höhn **80** B2
Hohne **68** B2
Höhnstedt **82** A1
Hohnstein **83** C1/2
Hohnstorf **69** C1
Höhr-Grenzhausen **80** A/B2
Hohwacht **53** C3
Hoilola **23** D3
Hoisko **21** C2
Højby **49** C/D3
Højer **52** A2
Højerup **50** A3, **53** D1
Hojniki **99** C1/2
Hojreby **53** C2
Hojslev Stationsby **48** B2
Hojsova Stráž **93** C1
Hok **45** D3, **46** A3, **50** B1
Hökåsen **40** A3, **46** B1
Hokka **26** B1
Hokkaskylä **21** C3
Hokksund **43** D1
Hökmark **31** D1
Hökön **50** B2
Hököpinge **50** A3
Hokovce **95** D2
Hokstad **28** B3, **33** D1
Hol **37** C3
Hol **45** C3
Holaforsen **30** A2/3, **35** D1
Holand **15** B/C1
Holand **29** C2
Holand **14** A/B2
Holand **9** C2
Holbæk **49** D3, **53** D1
Holbeach **61** D3, **65** C1
Holckenhavn **53** C1
Holdorf **67** C2
Holdorf-Gramke **67** D2
Høle **42** A2
Hole **43** D1
Holeby **53** C2
Hølen **44** B1
Holen **33** C3, **37** D1
Holešov **95** C1
Holevik **36** A2
Holguera **159** C3, **165** D1, **166** A1
Holíč **94** B2
Hölick **40** B1
Holja **25** C1
Höljäkkä **23** C2
Höljes **38** B2
Holkestad **8** B3
Hollabrunn **94** A2
Hollabrunn **96** A/B2
Holland-on-Sea **65** C3

Hollandsche Veld **67** C2
Hollandse brug **66** B2/3
Hollås **28** B2, **33** D1
Holle **68** B3
Holleben **82** A/B1
Høllen **43** B/C3
Hollenbach **92** A2
Hollenegg **127** C1
Hollenstedt **68** B3
Hollenstedt **68** B1
Hollfeld **82** A3
Hollingsholm **32** A2
Hölloch **105** D1
Hollola **25** D2, **26** A2
Hollsand **29** D2
Hollum **66** B1
Höllviksnäs **50** A3
Holm **57** C2
Holm **20** B1/2
Holm **14** B2
Holm **35** C2
Holm **30** B3, **35** D1/2
Holm **9** B/C1/2
Holm **52** B2
Holm **14** A3, **28** B1
Holm **32** A2
Holm **75** C2
Holmajärvi **10** A3
Holmbukt **4** B2
Holme **36** A/B1/2
Holme **65** B/C2
Holmec **127** C2
Holmedal **42** A1
Holmegård **53** D1
Holmegil **45** B/C1
Holmen **37** D3, **38** A2
Holmen **4** B3, **10** B1
Holmenkollen **38** A3
Holmes Chapel **59** D2, **60** B3, **64** A1
Holmesletta **4** A2
Holmestrand **43** D1/2, **44** A/B1
Holmfirth **61** C2/3
Holmfors **16** B3
Holmisperä **21** D2, **22** A2
Holmön **20** A1, **31** D2
Holmsbu **43** D1, **44** B1
Holmsjö **51** C2
Holmsjö **30** B2, **35** D1
Holmsta **30** A3, **35** C/D2
Holmstad **8** B2
Holmstrand **30** A3, **35** C/D2
Holmsund **20** A1, **31** D2
Holmsvattnet **31** D1
Holmsveden **40** A1
Holmträsk **30** B2, **35** D1
Holmträsk **31** C1
Holmträsk **31** C1
Holmträsk **16** B3
Holmvassdalen **14** B3
Holm-Žirkovskij **75** C3
Hölö **47** C1/2
Holopeniči **74** B3
Holøydal **33** D2
Holsbybrunn **46** A3, **51** C1
Holsen **36** B2
Holsengsetra **28** B2
Holsljunga **49** D1, **50** A1
Holstebro **48** A2
Holsted **48** A3, **52** A/B1
Holsteinborg **53** C1/2
Holsworthy **62** B2
Holt **65** C1
Holt **59** D2, **60** B3
Holte **49** D3, **50** A3, **53** D1
Holten **38** B2
Holtet **44** B2
Holtinkylä **18** B2
Holubov **93** D1/2
Holum **42** B3
Holungen **81** D1
Holungsøyi **33** B/C3, **37** D1
Holvik **28** B2
Holvik **43** C1
Holwerd **66** B1
Holyhead **58** B2
Holyhead **55** D2/3
Holywell **59** C2, **60** A/B3
Holywood **56** A3
Holzappel **80** B2
Holzdorf **70** A3
Holzengel **81** D1, **82** A1
Holzgau **106** B1

Holzgerlingen **91** C2
Holzhausen (Hofgeismar) **81** C1
Holzheim **91** D2
Holzkirchen **92** A3
Holzminden **68** B3
Holzminden-Neuhaus **68** B3
Holzthaleben **81** D1
Holzweissig **82** B1
Homberg **79** D1, **80** A1
Homberg **81** C1/2
Homberg **81** C2
Homborsund **14** A3
Homburg **89** D1, **90** A1
Homburg-Einöd **89** D1, **90** A1
Homesh **138** A3
Hommelstø **14** A3
Hommelvik **28** A/B3, **33** C1
Hommersåk **42** A2
Homps **110** A3, **156** B1
Homstad **28** B2
Hondarribia **154** A1
Hondón de las Nieves **169** C3
Hondón de los Frailes **169** C3
Hondschoote **78** A1
Hønefoss **38** A3, **43** D1
Honfleur **77** B/C3
Høng **49** C3, **53** C1
Hongsand **28** A2
Hongset **14** A3
Honigsee **52** B3
Honiton **63** C2
Honkajärvi **20** A3
Honkajoki **20** B3
Honkakoski **24** B1
Honkakoski **22** B1/2
Honkalahti **27** C2
Honkamukka **13** C2
Honkaranta **21** D2, **22** A2
Honkilahti **24** B2
Honko **20** B3
Honkola **25** B/C2
Honningsvåg **36** A1
Honningsvåg **5** D1, **6** B1
Honnstad **32** B2
Hönö **45** B/C3, **49** C/D1
Honrubia **168** B1
Honrubia de la Cuesta **153** C3, **161** B/C1
Hønseby **5** C1/2
Hontalbilla **160** B1
Hontanar **160** B3, **167** C1
Hontanaya **161** C3, **167** D1, **168** A1
Hontangas **153** B/C3, **160** B1
Hontianska Vrbica **95** D2
Hontianske Nemce **95** D2
Hontianske Nemce **96** B2/3
Hontianske Tesáre **95** D2
Hontoba **161** C2
Hontomín **153** C2
Höntönvaara **23** D2
Hontoria de la Cantera **153** C3
Hontoria del Pinar **153** C3, **161** C1
Hönttö **23** D2
Hoofddorp **66** A2/3
Hoogersmilde **67** C2
Hoogeveen **67** C2
Hoogezand-Sappemeer **67** C1
Hoogkerk **67** C1
Hoog-Soeren **66** B3
Hoogstede **67** C2
Hoogstraten **79** C1
Hook **64** B3, **76** A/B1
Höör **50** B3
Höör **72** A1/2
Hoorn **66** B2
Hopelandsjøen **36** A3
Hopen **32** B1
Hopen **9** C3
Hopen **28** A2
Hoppegarten **70** B2
Hoppenrade **53** D3, **69** D1
Hopperstad **36** B2
Hoppula **12** B3
Hopseidet **6** B1
Hopsten **67** D2
Hopsten-Schale **67** D2
Hoptrup **52** B1/2

Hora Svatého Šebestiána **83** C2
Horažďovice **93** C1
Horb am Neckar **90** B2
Horb-Dettingen **90** B2
Horbelev **53** D2
Hørby **49** C1
Hörby **50** B3
Hörby **72** A1/2
Horcajada de la Torre **161** D3
Horcajo de las Torres **160** A2
Horcajo de los Montes **166** B1
Horcajo de la Rivera **159** D2/3, **160** A2/3
Horcajo de Montemayor **159** D2/3
Horcajo de Santiago **161** C3, **167** D1, **168** A1
Horcajo-Medianero **159** D2, **160** A2
Horche **161** C2
Horda **50** B1
Hordabø **36** A3
Hořelice **83** C/D3
Hořesedly **83** C3
Høreslia **37** D3
Horezu **140** B2
Horgen **105** D1
Hörgertshausen **92** A/B2
Horgoš **129** D2
Horgoš **140** A1
Horhausen **80** A2
Horia **141** D2
Hořice na Šumavě **93** C/D2
Höringhausen **81** C1
Horjul **126** B2
Horka **83** D1
Hörken **39** D3
Horley **65** B/C3, **76** B1
Hormakumpu **11** D3, **12** A3
Hormigos **160** B3
Hormilleja **153** D2
Hormisto **24** A/B1
Horn **46** B3
Horn **14** A2
Horn **14** A3
Horn **37** D3, **38** A2
Horn **94** A2
Horn **96** A2
Hornachos **165** D2, **166** A2
Hornachuelos **166** B3, **172** A1
Horná Mariková **95** C1
Horná Štubňa **95** D1/2
Hornbach **89** D1, **90** A1
Horn-Bad Meinberg **68** A3
Hornbæk **49** D3, **50** A2
Hornberg **90** B2
Hornberga **39** C/D1
Hornburg **69** C3
Horncastle **61** D3, **65** C1
Horndal **40** A2/3
Horndal **9** C2
Horndean **76** A1
Horne **52** B2
Horneburg **68** B1
Hörnefors **31** C2
Horné Lefantouce **95** C2
Hornhausen **69** C3
Horní Bečva **95** C1
Horní Bobrová **94** A1
Horní Cerekev **94** A1
Horní Jiřetín **83** C2
Horní Lideč **95** C1
Horní Lomná **95** D1
Hornindal **32** A3, **36** B1
Hørning **48** B3
Hörningsholm **47** C1
Horní Planá **93** C2
Horní Slavkov **82** B3
Horní Stropnice **93** D2
Horní Vltavice **93** C1
Hornmyr **30** B1
Hornnes **43** B/C3
Horno **70** B3
Hornos **168** A3
Hornoy **77** D3
Hornsea **61** D2
Hornsjø **38** A1
Hörnsjö **31** C2
Hornslet **49** B/C2
Hornsved **49** D3
Hornu **78** B2

Hornum 48 B2
Horný Tisovník 95 D2
Horo 20 A3
Horol 99 D2
Horonkylä 21 D2, 22 A2
Hořovice 83 C3
Hořovičky 83 C3
Horred 49 D1, 50 A1
Horrmundsvalla 39 C1
Horschen Althorschen 81 C1
Horsdal 14 B1
Horsens 48 B3, 52 B1
Horsforth 61 C2
Horsgard 32 A/B2
Horsham 76 B1
Horsham Saint Faith 65 C1
Hørsholm 49 D3, 50 A3, 53 D1
Hörsingen 69 C3
Horská Kvilda 93 C1
Horsmaanaho 23 C2
Horsnes 4 A/B3, 10 A1
Horšovský Týn 82 B3, 92 B1
Horst 79 D1
Horst 52 B3, 68 B1
Hörstel 67 D2/3
Hörstel-Dreierwalde 67 D2/3
Horstmar 67 D3
Horta 158 B2
Horta de Sant Joan 163 C2
Horten 43 D2, 44 B1
Hortigüela 153 C3
Hortlax 16 B3
Horton 59 D1, 60 B2
Horton 63 C/D2
Hørve 49 C3, 53 C1
Hörvik 51 C2/3
Hosanger 36 A3
Hösbach 81 C3
Hoscheid 79 D3
Hosen 28 A2
Hosenfeld 81 C2
Hosenfeld-Hainzell 81 C2
Hosingen 79 D3
Hosio 18 B1
Hosjö 39 D2, 40 A2
Hospental 105 D2
Hospice de France 155 C2
Hospital 155 C2
Hospital de Órbigo 151 D2
Hospitalet de Llobregat 156 A3
Hossa 19 D2
Hossa 11 D3, 12 A2
Hossegor 108 A2/3
Hössjö 31 C2
Hössjön 30 A2, 35 C1
Hossmo 51 D2
Hössna 45 D3
Hostalric 156 B3
Höstanäs 25 C3
Hostens 108 B1
Hostěradice 94 B1
Hosterias de Ordesa 155 C2
Hostikka 27 C2
Hostomice 83 C3
Hoston 28 A3, 33 C2
Höstoppen 29 D2, 35 C1
Hostouň 82 B3, 92 B1
Hostrup 48 B1
Hotagen 29 D2, 34 B1
Hotedršica 126 B2/3
Hötensleben 69 C3
Hotimsk 99 D1
Hotin 98 B3
Hoting 30 A2
Hotkovo 75 D2
Hotton 79 C2
Hou 49 C1
Houdain 78 A2
Houdan 87 C1
Houdelaincourt-sur-Ornair 89 C2
Houdremont 79 C3
Houécourt 89 C2
Houeillès 108 B2
Houffalize 79 C/D3
Houghton le Spring 57 D3, 61 C1
Houlgate 76 B3, 86 A/B1
Hourtin 100 B3
Hourtin-Plage 101 C3
Houthalen 79 C1
Houtsala 24 A3

Houtskär 24 A3, 41 D3
Houtskari 24 A3, 41 D3
Hov 48 B3
Hov 46 A2
Hov 14 A2
Hova 45 D2, 46 A2
Høvåg 43 C3
Hovdala 50 B2
Hovde 43 C2/3
Hovden 8 B1/2
Hovden 42 B1/2
Hove 48 A2
Hove 76 B1
Hovedgård 48 B3
Hövelhof 68 A3
Hoven 48 A3, 52 A1
Hovenäset 44 B2
Hoverport 77 D1
Hovet 42 B2
Hovet 37 C3
Hovězí 95 C1
Höviksnäs 45 C3
Hoviland 37 D3, 38 A2
Hovin 43 C1
Hovlös 17 C2
Hovmantorp 51 C2
Hovmantorp 72 A/B1
Høvreslia 37 D3
Hovslätt 45 D3, 46 A3
Howard 61 C2
Howden 61 C2
Howth 58 A2
Höxter 68 B3
Höxter-Fürstenau 68 A/B3
Höxter-Godelheim 68 B3, 81 C1
Hoya 68 A2
Hoya-Gonzalo 168 B2
Hoya Gonzalo 160 B2
Høyanger 36 A/B2
Høydal 36 B1
Høydal 36 A2
Høydalsmo 43 C1/2
Hoyerswerda 83 C/D1
Hoyerswerda 96 A1
Høyholm 14 A3
Høykkylä 21 C2
Hoylake 59 C2, 60 A/B3
Høylandet 28 B1/2
Hoym 69 C3
Hoyocasero 160 A2
Hoyos 159 C3
Hoyos del Espino 160 A2/3
Höytiä 21 D3, 22 A3
Hoyuelos de la Sierra 153 C3
Hrachoviště 93 D1
Hradec Králové 96 A2
Hrádek 94 B2
Hrádek nad Nisou 83 D2
Hranice 82 B2
Hranice 95 C1
Hranice 96 B2
Hrasnica 132 B3
Hrastnik 127 C2
Hrastovlje 126 B3
Hřensko 83 D2
Hrge 132 B2
Hrob 83 C2
Hroboňovo 95 C3
Hronov 95 D1/2
Hronská Dúbrava 95 D2
Hronský Beňadik 95 D2
Hrotovice 94 A1
Hroznětín 82 B2
Hrtkovci 133 C/D1, 134 A1
Hrubieszów 97 D1, 98 A2
Hrubý Šúr 95 C2
Hrušovany nad Jevišovkou 94 B1/2
Hrustovaća pečina 131 D1/2
Hrvace 131 D3
Huaröd 50 B3
Huarte Araquil 153 D2, 154 A1/2
Hubberholme 59 D1, 60 B2
Huben 107 D1
Hückelhoven 79 D1
Hückeswagen 80 A1
Hucknall 61 D3, 65 C1
Hucksjöåsen 30 A3, 35 C2
Hucqueliers 77 D2
Huddersfield 61 C2
Huddinge 47 C1
Huddunge 40 A3
Hude 68 A2

Hude-Wüsting 68 A2
Hudiksvall 40 B1
Huecas 160 B3
Huedin 97 D3, 140 B1
Huélago 173 C1/2
Huélamo 162 A3
Huelgoat 84 B2
Huelma 173 C1
Huelva 171 C2
Huelves 161 C2
Huéneja 173 D2
Huercal-Overa 174 A1/2
Huérmeces 153 B/C2
Huerta de Arriba 153 C3
Huerta del Marquesado 162 A3
Huerta del Rey 153 C3, 161 C1
Huerta de Valdecarábanos 161 C3, 167 C/D1
Huertahernando 161 D2
Huérteles 153 D3
Huertezuela 167 C2/3
Huerto 155 B/C3
Huesa 167 D3, 168 A3, 173 C1
Huesa del Común 162 B2
Huesca 154 B3
Huéscar 168 A3, 173 D1
Huete 161 D3
Huétor-Tájar 172 B2
Hüfingen 90 B3
Huglfing 92 A3
Hugulia 37 D2
Huhdasjärvi 26 B2
Huhmarkoski 20 B2
Huhtamo 24 B2
Huhtiankylä 21 D3
Huhtilampi 23 D3
Huhus 23 D2
Huikko 21 D3, 22 A3
Huikola 18 B3
Huissinkylä 20 B2
Huittinen 24 B2
Huizen 66 B3
Hukanmaa 11 C3
Hukkajärvi 23 D1
Hukkula 23 C2
Hulån 39 C2
Hulín 95 C1
Huljala 25 D2, 26 A2
Hullaryd 46 A3
Hüllhorst-Schnathorst 68 A3
Hullsjön 35 C/D3
Hulsig 44 B3, 49 C1
Hulst 78 B1
Hulsund 28 A3, 33 C1
Hult 46 A3
Hulta 41 D2/3
Hultafors 45 C3
Hultanäs 51 C1
Hulterstad 51 D2
Hultsbruck 46 B2
Hultsfred 46 B3, 51 C/D1
Hultsjö 51 C1
Hum 135 C3
Hum 137 C2
Humada 152 B2
Humalajoki 21 C2
Humanes 161 C2
Humbécourt 88 B2
Humble 53 C2
Humenné 97 C2, 98 A3
Humes 89 C2/3
Humilladero 172 B2
Humlebæk 49 D3, 50 A3
Humlum 48 A2
Hummelholm 31 C2
Hummelshain 82 A2
Hummeltal 82 A3
Hummelvik 32 B1
Hummelvik 4 B2
Humppi 21 C/D2
Humppila 24 B2
Hundåla 14 A2
Hundberg 4 A3, 10 A1
Hundeidvik 32 A3, 36 B1
Hundeluft 69 C3
Hundested 49 D3
Hundested 72 A1
Hundholmen 9 C2
Hundisburg 69 C3
Hundorp 37 D2
Hundslund 48 B3
Hundsnes 42 A2
Hundvik 36 A1

Hundvin 36 A3
Hunedoara 140 B1/2
Hünengräber 67 D2, 68 A2
Hünfeld 81 C2
Hünfelden 80 B2
Hünfelden-Kirberg 80 B2
Hunge 35 B/C2
Hungen 81 C2
Hungen-Villingen 81 C2
Hungerford 64 A3
Huningue 90 A3
Hunmanby 61 D2
Hunnebostrand 44 B2
Hunnes 36 A1
Hunstanton 65 C1
Huntingdon 65 B/C2
Huntly 54 B2
Hünxe 67 C3, 79 D1, 80 A1
Huopanankoski 21 D2, 22 A2
Huorso 9 C3
Huotari 22 B1
Hüpstedt 81 D1
Hurbanovo 95 C3
Hurdal 38 A2
Hures-la-Parade 110 B2
Hurezani 140 B2
Huriel 102 A/B2
Hurissalo 27 C1
Hurskaala 22 B3
Hurst Green 77 C1
Hürtgenwald 79 D2
Hürth 80 A2
Hurttala 27 C2
Huruksela 26 B2
Hurum 37 C2
Hurup 48 A2
Hurva 50 B3
Huså 29 C3, 34 A1
Husaby 45 D2
Husbands Bosworth 64 B2
Huşi 141 C/D1
Husinec 93 C1
Huskasnäs 35 C3
Husnes 42 A1
Husøy 36 A2
Hust 97 D2/3, 98 A3
Hustad 32 A2
Hustopeče 94 B1
Husu 27 C2
Husum 31 C3
Husum 52 A/B2
Husvik 28 B2
Husvika 14 A2/3
Hutisko Solanec 95 C1
Hutovo 136 B1
Hüttau 93 C3
Hüttenberg 127 B/C1
Hüttenberg-Rechtenbach 80 B2
Hutthurm 93 C2
Hutton Cranswick 61 D2
Hutton Rudby 61 D1
Hüttschlag 126 A1
Huttula 27 B/C1
Huttula 27 C2
Huttula 21 D3
Huttwil 105 C1
Hutunvaara 23 D2
Huuhanaho 27 B/C1
Huuhkaala 27 C1
Huuki 11 C3
Huutijärvi 25 C1
Huutokoski 22 B3
Huutokoski 23 C2
Huutoniemi 6 B3
Huuvari 25 D2, 26 A2
Huy 79 C2
Hvalba 55 C1
Hvalpsund 48 B2
Hvar 131 C3, 136 A1
Hvaščevka 75 D3
Hverringe 49 C3, 53 C1
Hvidbjerg 48 A2
Hvide Sande 48 A3
Hvitsten 38 A3, 44 B1
Hvittingfoss 43 D1/2, 44 A1
Hvojnaja 75 C/D1
Hvožďany 83 C3, 93 C1
Hycklinge 46 B3
Hyde 59 D2, 60 B3
Hyen 36 A2

Hyenville 85 D1
Hyères 112 A3
Hylestad 42 B2
Hylla 28 B2/3, 33 D1
Hyllekrog 53 C/D2
Hyllestad 36 A2
Hyllinge 53 D1
Hyllinge 50 A2
Hyllingsvollen 33 D2
Hyltebruk 50 B1
Hyltebruk 72 A1
Hynnekleiv 43 C3
Hyödynknylä 21 D2, 22 A2
Hyönölä 25 C2/3
Hypämäki 23 C3
Hypiö 12 B3
Hyppeln 44 B3
Hyrakäs 18 B2/3
Hyrlä 25 D3, 26 A3
Hyrov 97 D2, 98 A3
Hyry 18 A/B1
Hyrynsalmi 19 C3
Hyssna 45 C3, 49 D1
Hythe 77 C1
Hythe 76 A1
Hytölä 21 D3, 22 A3
Hytti 27 C2
Hyttikoski 18 B3
Hyttön 40 B2
Hyväniemi 19 C1
Hyvikkälä 25 C2
Hyvinkää (Hyvinge) 25 C2, 26 A2
Hyvölänranta 18 B3
Hyypiänniemi 23 C3
Hyypiö 12 B3
Hyyppä 20 B3
Hyyrylä 25 C1

I

Iacobeni 141 C1
Iam 134 B1
Iaşi 141 C1
Iasmos 145 C2
Ibahernando 166 A1
Ibarrangelu 153 D1
Ibbenbüren 67 D3
Ibdes 161 D1, 162 A1
Ibeas de Juarros 153 C2
Ibestad 9 C/D2
Ibi 169 C2
Ibieca 155 B/C2/3
Ibiza 157 D3
Ibriktepe 145 D3
Ibros 167 D3, 173 C1
Ichenhausen 91 D2
Ichtershausen 81 D2, 82 A2
Ickworth House 65 C2
Ičnja 99 D2
Idanha a Nova 159 B/C3, 165 C1
Idar-Oberstein 80 A3
Idbacka 30 A2
Idd 44 B1/2
Iden 69 D2
Idiazabal 153 D1/2
Idivuoma 10 B2
Idkerberget 39 D2
Idoméni 139 C3, 143 D1
Idra 147 D3
Ídra 148 B2
Idre 34 A3
Idrija 126 B2
Idse 42 A2
Idstein 80 B2/3
Idstein-Wörsdorf 80 B2/3
Idvattnet 30 A1
Idvor 133 D1, 134 A/B1
Iecava 73 D1, 74 A2
Ielsi 119 D2, 120 A1
Ieper 78 A2
Ierissós 144 B2
Ierissós 149 B/C2
Ieropigi 142 B2
Iérzu 123 D2
Ieşelniţa 135 C1/2
Iesi 115 D3, 117 D2
Ifanes 151 D3, 159 C/D1
Iffeldorf 92 A3
Iffezheim 90 B2
Ifjord 6 B1

Ifta 81 D1
Igal 128 B2
Igalo 137 C2
Iga Vas 126 B3
Igea 153 D3, 154 A3
Igelfors 46 B2
Igensdorf 82 A3
Igerøy 14 A3
Iggelheim 90 B1
Iggesund 40 A/B1
Iggön 40 B2
Iglesias 152 B2
Iglésias 123 C3
Igling 91 D2/3
Igls 107 C1
Ignaberga 50 B2
Igorre 153 C/D1
Igoumenítsa 142 A/B3
Igoumenítsa 148 A1
Igrane 131 D3, 132 A3,
136 B1
Igrejinha 164 B2
Igrexa 151 B/C1
Igriés 154 B2
Igualada 155 D3, 156 A3,
163 D1
Igualeja 172 A2/3
Igüeña 151 D2
Iguerande 103 C2
Ihamaniemi 23 C3
Iharosberény 128 A2
Ihlienworth 52 A3, 68 A1
Ihlow 67 D1
Ihode 24 A2
Iholdy 108 B3, 155 C1
Ihotunlahti 22 B1
Ihringen 90 A2/3
Ii 18 A2
Iijärvi 6 B3
Iinattijärvi 19 C2
Iironranta 21 C2
Iiruu 21 C2
Iisalmi 22 B1
Iisvesi 22 B3
Iittala 25 C2
Iitti 26 B2
Iitto 10 B2
Iittula 24 B3
Iivantiira 19 D3
IJmuiden 66 A2
IJsselmuiden 67 B/C2
IJzendijke 78 B1
Ika 126 B3, 130 A1
Ikaalinen 24 B1
Ikast 48 B3
Ikervár 128 A1
Ikkala 21 C3
Ikkala 25 C2/3
Ikkeläjärvi 20 B3
Ikornnes 32 A3, 36 B1
Ikosenniemi 18 B2
Ilandža 134 B1
Ilanz 105 D1, 106 A1
Ilava 95 C1
Ilavainen 24 A1/2
Iława 73 C3
Il Bívio 114 B2, 116 B1
Il Castagno 114 B3, 116 A2
Ilche 155 C3
Ilchester 63 D2
Ile d'Aix 101 C2
Ilfracombe 63 B/C2
Ílhavo 158 A2
Ilia 140 B1
Il'ičevsk 141 D1
Ilidža 132 B2/3
Iliókastron 147 C/D3
Ilirska Bistrica 126 B3
Iljanvaara 23 D1
Iljino 75 C2
Ilkeston 61 D3, 65 C1
Ilkley 59 D1, 61 C2
Illana 161 C3
Illano 151 C1
Illar 173 D2
Illats 108 B1
Illereichen-Altenstadt
91 D2
Illerkirchberg 91 C/D2
Illertissen 91 D2
Illescas 160 B3
Ille-sur-Têt 156 B1
Illfeld-Wiegersdorf 81 D1
Illfurth 89 D3, 90 A3
Illiers 86 A/B2
Illingen 91 B/C1

Illkirch Graffenstaden
90 A2
Illmitz 94 B3
Illo 24 B1/2
Illora 173 B/C2
Illueca 154 A3, 162 A1
Ilmajoki 20 B2/3
Ilmenau 81 D2, 82 A2
Ilminster 63 D2
Ilmola 17 D2, 18 A1
Ilmolahti 21 D2, 22 A2
Ilok 129 C3, 133 C1
Ilola/Illby 25 D2/3,
26 A2/3
Ilomantsi 23 D2/3
Ilosjoki 21 D2, 22 A2
Ilowa 83 D1
Iłowiec 71 D1
Ilsede 68 B3
Ilsenburg 69 C3
Ilseng 38 A2
Ilshofen 91 C1
Ilskov 48 B2/3
Ilvesjoki 20 B3
Ilveskorpi 18 A3
Ilz 127 D1
Imatra 27 C2
Imeno 127 C2
Imera 124 B2
Imera 143 C2
Imeron 145 C1
Imfors 30 A2/3, 35 C1
Imingen 37 C3
Immala 27 C1/2
Immeln 50 B2
Immenhausen-Holzhausen
81 C1
Immenreuth 82 A3
Immenstaad 91 C3
Immenstadt 91 D3
Immingham 61 D2
Ímola 115 C2, 116 B1
Imón 161 C/D1/2
Imotski 131 D3, 132 A3
Impéria 113 C2
Imphy 102 B1
Impiö 9 B/C1
Impruneta 114 B2/3,
116 B2
Imsenden 38 A1
Imst 106 B1
Ina 21 C3
Inari 23 D2
Inari (Anar) 6 B3
Inarinköngäs 5 D3, 6 A3,
11 D1
Inca 157 C2
Inchenhofen 92 A2
Incisa in Val d'Arno
115 B/C2/3, 116 B2
Incisioni rupestri (Parco Na-
zionale) 106 B2
Indal 35 D3
Inden 79 D2
Inderdalen 14 B2
Indija 133 D1, 134 A1
Indija 140 A2
Indre Arna 36 A3
Indre Billefjord 5 D2,
6 A1/2
Indre Brenna 5 D1/2,
6 A/B1
Indre Fræna 32 A2
Indre Leirpollen 5 D2,
6 A1/2
Indre Matre 42 A1
Ineu 97 C3, 140 A1
Infantado 164 A2
Ingå/Inkoo 25 C3
Ingå station 25 C3
Ingatestone 65 C3
Ingatorp 46 A/B3
Ingdalen 28 A3, 33 C1
Ingedal 44 B1
Ingelfingen 91 C1
Ingelheim 80 B3
Ingelmunster 78 A1/2
Ingelstad 51 C2
Ingelstad 72 A/B1
Ingersheim 89 D2, 90 A2/3
Ingleton 59 D1, 60 B2
Ingliston 57 C2
Ingolstadt 92 A2
Ingolstadt-Dünzlau 92 A2
Ingolstadt-Unsernherrn
92 A2
Ingøy 5 C1

Ingrandes-sur-Loire 85 D3,
86 A3
Inguiniel 84 B2
Ingulec 99 D3
Ingulsvatn 29 C1/2
Ingurtosu 123 C3
Ingvallsbenning 39 D3,
40 A2/3
Ingwiller 90 A1/2
Inha 21 C3
Iniesta 168 B1
Iniö 24 A3, 41 D2
Inke 128 A2
Inkee 19 C1
Inkere 24 B2/3
Inkerilä 26 B2
Innala 21 C3
Innansjön 31 D1
Inndyr 14 B1
Innerkrems 126 B1
Innerleithen 57 C2
Innertällmo 30 B2, 35 D1
Innertavle 20 A1, 31 D2
Innerthal [Siebnen-Wan-
gen] 105 D1
Innertkirchen 105 C1/2
Innervillgraten 107 D1
Innfjorden 32 A3
Innhavet 9 C3
Innset 33 C2
Innset 9 D2
Inntorget 14 A3
Innvik 32 A3, 36 B1
Inói 147 D2
Inowrocław 72 B3
Ins 104 B1
Inseros 45 C3, 49 D1
Insingen 91 D1
Insjön 39 D2
Insjön 30 B1
Ińsko 71 C1
Instefjord 36 A2/3
Ínsurăţei 141 C2
Interlaken 105 C1/2
Întorsura Buzăului
141 C1/2
Intra 105 D2/3
Intróbio 105 D2, 106 A2
Inveraray 56 A/B1
Inveraray 54 A2, 55 D1
Invergarry 54 A2, 55 D1
Inverkeilor 57 C1
Inverkeithing 57 C1
Inverness 54 B2
Inveruno 105 D3
Inverurie 54 B2
Inviken 29 D2
Inzell 92 B3
Inzersdorf im Kremstal
93 C3
Ioánnina 142 B3
Ioánnina 148 A1
Ioniškis 73 D1
Íos 149 C3
Ipáti 146 B1
Ipazter 153 D1
Ipel'ský Sokolec 95 D2/3
Iphofen 81 D3
Ipolytarnóc 97 C2/3
Ípsala 149 C1
Ipsala 145 D1, 145 D3
Ipsheim 81 D3, 91 D1
Ipsos 142 A3
Ipsoús 146 B3
Ipswich 65 C2
Iráklia 139 D3, 144 A1
Iráklio/Iráklion 149 C3
Irañeta 153 D2, 154 A1/2
Irdning 93 C/D3
Iregszemcse 128 B2
Irig 133 D1, 134 A1
Irinovac 131 C1
Irissarry 108 B3, 155 C1
Irixo 150 B2
Irixoa 150 B1
Irjanne 24 A1/2
Irninniemi 19 D1
Ironbridge 59 D3, 64 A1/2
Irrel 79 D3
Iršava 97 D2/3, 98 A3
Irschenberg 92 A/B3
Irsina 120 B2
Iruecha 161 D1/2
Iruelos 159 C2
Irún 154 A1
Irura 153 D1, 154 A1

Irurita 108 A3, 154 A1
Irurzun 154 A1/2
Irvine 56 B2
Irxleben 69 C3
Isaba 154 B2
Isaccea 141 D2
Isane 36 A1
Ísaris 146 B3
Isbister 54 A1
Isbre 5 B/C2
Iscar 160 B1
Isca sullo Iónio 122 B2
Ischgl 106 B1
Íschia 119 C3
Íschia di Castro 116 B3,
118 A1
Ischitella 120 B1
Iscroni 135 D1
Isdes 87 D3
Ise 44 B1
Iselle 105 C2
Iseltwald 105 C1/2
Isenbüttel 69 C2/3
Iseo 106 A/B3
Isérables [Riddes] 104 B2
Iserlohn 80 B1
Iserlohn-Letmathe 80 A/B1
Isernhagen 68 B2
Isérnia 119 C/D2
Isfjorden 32 B2/3
Ishëm 137 D3
Isigny-sur-Mer 76 A3,
85 D1
Ísili 123 D2/3
Iskola 24 A2/3
Iskrec 139 D1
Iskrovci 139 D1
İşkuras 5 D3, 6 A3, 11 D1
Isla Canela 170 B2
Isla Cristina 170 B2
Isla Ravena 157 C1/2
Isle of Whithorn 56 B3,
60 A1
Isle of Whithorn 54 A/B3,
55 D2
Isles-sur-Suippes 88 B1
Ismaning 92 A2
Ismantorpsborg 51 D2
Isnäs 25 D2/3, 26 A3
Isnestoften 5 C2
Isny 91 D3
Iso-Äiniö 25 D1/2,
26 A1/2
Iso-Evo 25 C/D2, 26 A2
Isohaara 17 D2/3, 18 A1
Isohalme 13 C3
Isojoki (Storå) 20 B3
Isokumpu 19 C1/2
Isokylä 20 B2
Isokylä 18 A/B3
Isokylä 17 C1
Isokylä 13 B/C3
Isokylä 21 C2
Isokyrö (Storkyrö) 20 B2
Isola 112 B2
Isoláccia 106 B2
Ísola d'Asti 113 C1
Ísola del Cantone 113 D1
Ísola del Gran Sasso d'Itália
117 D3, 119 C1
Ísola del Liri 119 C2
Ísola della Scala 107 B/C3
Ísola delle Fémmine 124 B1
Ísola di Capo Rizzuto
122 B2
Ísola Dovarese 106 B3
Ísola Fossara 115 D3,
117 C2
Ísola Rossa 123 C1
Isona 155 D3
Isoniemi 20 B3
Isoperä 24 B2
Iso-Rahi 24 A2, 41 D2
Isorella 106 B3
Isòvol 156 A2
Ispagnac 110 B2
Isperih 141 C2
İspica 125 C/D3
Ispra 105 D3
Ispringen 90 B1/2
Issakka 23 B/C1
Isselburg 67 C3
Isselburg-Werth 67 C3
Issenheim 89 D2/3, 90 A3
Issigeac 109 C1
Íssime 105 C3
Issogne 105 C3

Issoire 102 B3
Issoncourt 89 C1
Issoudun 102 A1
Íssum 79 D1
Is-sur-Tille 88 B3
Issy-l'Évêque 103 C1
Ist 130 B2
Istán 172 A3
Istanbul 149 D1
Istarske Toplice 126 B3,
130 A1
Isterberg-Wengsel
67 C/D2/3
Isthmía 147 C2
Ístia d'Ombrone 116 B3
Istiaia 147 C1
Istibanja 139 C2
Istiéa 147 C1
Istok 138 A1
Istra 75 D2
Isträsk 16 B2/3
Istres 111 C/D3
Istunmäki 22 A/B2/3
Istvándi 128 A/B2
Isuerre 154 B2
Itä-Áhtäri 21 C2/3
Itä-Aure 21 B/C3
Itä-Karttula 22 B2
Itäkoski 22 B1/2
Itäkylä 21 C2
Itálica 171 D1
Itäranta 19 B/C3, 22 B1
Itéa 147 C2
Itéa 143 D3
Itháki (Vathí) 146 A2
Itháki (Vathí) 148 A2
Iti 147 B/C1
Íti Óros 146 B1
Ítrabo 173 C2
Itri 119 C2/3
Ittenhausen 91 C2
Ittenheim 90 A2
Itterbeck 67 C2
Ittervoort 79 D1
Ittireddu 123 C/D2
Íttiri 123 C1/2
Itzehoe 52 B3
Itzgrund-Kaltenbrunn
81 D3, 82 A3
Ivacevići 98 B1
Ivajlovgrad 141 C2
Ivajlovgrad 145 D3
Ivalon Matti 11 D2, 12 B1
Iván 94 B3, 128 A1
Ivančice 94 B1
Ivančici 132 B2
Ivanec 127 D2
Ivangorod 74 B1
Ivangrad 137 D1, 138 A1
Ivanić Grad 127 D3
Ivanjci 127 D2
Ivanjica 133 D3, 134 A3
Ivanjica 140 A2
Ivanjska 131 D1, 132 A1
Ivanka pri Nitre 95 C2
Ivankovo 129 B/C3,
132 B1
Ivano-Frankovsk 97 D2,
98 B3
Ivanovice na Hané 94 B1
Ivanovka 141 D1
Ivanovo 97 D1, 98 B1
Ivanovo Selo 128 A3
Ivanska 128 A3
Ivarrud 14 B3
Ivars de Noguera 155 C3
Ivars d'Urgell 155 D3,
163 D1
Iveland 43 C3
Iven 70 A1
Ivenack 70 A1
Iversfjord 7 B/C1
Ívira 144 B1
Ivje 74 A3
Ivla 50 B2
Ivorra 155 C3, 163 C1
Ivoy-le-Pré 87 D3
Ivrea 105 C3
Ivry-en-Montagne
103 C/D1
Ivry-la-Bataille 87 C1
Ivybridge 63 C3
Iwuy 78 A2
Ixworth 65 C2
Izalzu 108 A3, 154 B2
Izarra 153 C2
Izbište 134 B1

Izborsk **74** B2
Izeda **151** C3, **159** C1
Izegem **78** A1/2
Izjaslav **98** B2
Izmail **141** D2
Izmir **149** D2
Iznájar **172** B2
Iznalloz **173** C1/2
Iznatoraf **167** D3, **168** A3
Izola **126** A/B3
Izsák **129** C1
Iž Veli **130** B2
Izvor **139** C2
Izvor **139** D2
Izvor **139** C3
Izvor **138** B3
Izvor **140** A3
Izvor **140** A3
Izvor Buna **132** B3,
 137 B/C1
Izzetiyve **145** D3

J

Jäähdyspohja **21** C3
Jääjoki **21** C/D2
Jääkärikämppä **18** B1
Jaakonvaara **23** D2
Jaala **26** B2
Jaalanka **19** C2
Jaalanka **19** B/C3
Jaama **23** D3
Jaama **74** B1
Jääskönkylä **12** A2/3,
 17 D1
Jaatila **12** A3
Jabalera **161** C/D3
Jabaloyas **163** C3
Jabalquinto **167** C3,
 173 C1
Jabarella **154** B2
Jabbeke **78** A1
Jablanac **130** B1/2
Jablan Do **137** C2
Jablanica **132** A/B3
Jablanica **135** C3
Jablanovac **127** D2/3
Jablonec nad Nisou **83** D2
Jablonica **95** C2
Jabłonna **71** D3
Jablonné v Podještědí
 83 D2
Jablonov **97** D2, **98** B3
Jabugo **165** D3, **171** C1
Jabuka **133** D1, **134** A/B1
Jabuka **133** C3
Jabukovac **135** C2
Jabukovac **127** D3, **131** C1
Jabukovik **139** C1
Jaca **154** B2
Jachenau **92** A3
Jáchymov **82** B2
Jackarby **25** D3, **26** A3
Jäckvik **15** D2
Jade **67** D1, **68** A1
Jäder **47** B/C1
Jäderfors **40** A2
Jade-Schweiburg **67** D1,
 68 A1
Jädraås **40** A2
Jadraque **161** C2
Jaén **167** C3, **173** C1
Jagel **52** B2
Jægerspris **49** D3, **53** C1
Jægervatn **4** A2/3
Jagnjilo **134** B2
Jagodzin **83** D1
Jagotin **99** D2
Jagow **70** B1
Jagsthausen **91** C1
Jagstzell **91** D1
Jahkola **25** C/D2, **26** A2
Jahnsfelde **70** C2
Jahodná **95** C2/3
Jahorina **132** B3
Jahroma **75** D2
Jajce **131** D2, **132** A2
Ják **127** D1
Jakabszállás **129** C1/2
Jäkälävaara **19** C1
Jakimovo **135** D3
Jakkukylä **18** B2
Jakkula **20** B2

Jäkna **16** A2
Jákó **128** A2
Jakobsbakken **15** C1
Jakobsberg **47** C1
Jakobstad/Pietarsaari
 20 B1
Jakokoski **23** D2/3
Jakoruda **140** B3
Jakovo **139** D3
Jakšić **128** B3
Jalance **169** C2
Jalasjärvi **20** B3
Jalasjoki **24** B2
Jalhay **79** D2
Jaligny **103** B/C2
Jalkala **22** B3
Jallais **86** A3, **100** B1
Jalón **169** D2
Jaluna **22** B2
Jamali **23** D2
Jämäs **19** D3, **23** C1
Jambol **141** C3
Jameln **33** D2
Jamena **133** C1
Jametz **79** C3
Jämijärven asema **24** B1
Jämijärvi **24** B1
Jamikow **70** B1/2
Jäminkipohja **25** C1
Jämjö **51** C/D2
Jämjö **21** D1
Jamm **74** B1
Jammerdal **38** B3
Jamnička Kiselica **127** D3
Jämnvallen **34** B3
Jamoigne **79** C3
Jampol' **98** B2
Jampol' **99** C3
Jämpsä **19** D1
Jämsä **25** D1, **26** A1
Jämsä **21** C1
Jämsänkoski **25** D1, **26** A1
Jämshög **51** B/C2
Jämtkrogen **35** C2/3
Jämtön **17** C2/3
Jamu Mare **134** B1
Janakkala **25** C2
Jančė **138** A/B3
Jandelsbrunn **93** C2
Jäniskylä **26** B1
Janiszowice **71** C3
Janj **131** D2, **132** A2
Janja **133** C1/2
Janjevo **138** B1/2
Janjina **136** B1
Jänkä **21** C2
Jänkälä **13** C2
Jänkänalusta **10** A3
Jänkisjärvi **17** C2
Jankkila **7** C2/3
Jankov **83** D3
Jánoshalma **129** C2
Jánoshalma **97** C3
Jánosháza **96** B3
Jánosháza **128** A1
Janossomorja **94** B3
Janovice nad Úhlavou
 93 C1
Janów Lubelski **97** C/D1,
 98 A2
Jänschwalde **70** B3
Jansjö **30** A/B3, **35** D1
Jansjö **30** A/B3, **35** D1
Jänsmässholmen **29** C3,
 34 B1
Janzé **85** D2
Jäpåsen **39** D1/2
Jäppilä **22** B3
Jaraba **161** D1, **162** A1/2
Jaraco **169** D2
Jarafuel **169** C2
Jaraicejo **159** D3, **166** A1
Jaraiz de la Vera **159** D3
Jarak **133** C/D1, **134** A1
Jarandilla de la Vera **159** D3
Jaray **153** D3, **161** D1
Järbo **40** A2
Jarcevo **75** C3
Jard-sur-Mer **100** A2
Jaren **38** A2
Jarfjordbotn **7** D2
Jargeau **87** C2/3
Jarhoinen **12** A3, **17** D1
Jarkovac **134** B1
Järkvissle **35** C/D2
Järlåsa **40** B3

Jarlovo **139** D2
Jarmolincy **98** B3
Järna **39** C2
Järna **47** C1
Jarnac **101** C3
Järnäs **31** C3
Järnäsklubb **31** C3
Järnboås **39** D3, **46** A1
Järnforsen **51** C1
Järnmalm gruvor **10** B3
Järnskog **38** B3, **45** C1
Jarny **89** C1
Jarocin **72** B3, **96** B1
Jaromér **96** A/B1/2
Jaroméřice **94** A1
Jaroslavice **94** B2
Jarosław **97** D2, **98** A2
Jarošov nad Nežárkou
 93 D1
Järpås **45** C2
Järpen **29** C3, **34** A/B2
Järpliden **38** B2
Jarplund **52** B2
Jarplund-Weding **52** B2
Jarque **154** A3, **162** A1
Jarrow **57** D3, **61** C1
Järsnäs **46** A3
Järvberget **30** B2, **35** D1
Järvelä **25** D2, **26** A2
Järvelänranta **19** D3
Järvenpää **25** D2, **26** A2
Järvenpää **20** A/B3
Järvenpää **22** B1
Järvenpää **27** C1
Järvenpää **22** B1
Järvenpää **23** D2
Järvenpää **11** C3, **12** A2
Järvensuu **17** C3
Järvikylä **18** B3
Järvikylä **21** C/D1
Järvikylä **21** C1
Järvinen **25** D2, **26** A/B2
Järvirova **12** A2, **17** D1
Järvsjö **30** B1
Järvsö **40** A1
Järvtjärn **31** D1
Jarzé **86** A3
Jasakső **41** C2
Jasenak **127** C3, **130** B1
Jasenica **131** C1
Jasenice **131** C2
Jasenjani **132** B3
Jasenovac **128** A3, **131** D1,
 132 A1
Jasenovo **133** D3, **134** A3
Jasenovo **134** B1
Jasień **71** C3
Jasika **134** B3
Jasin'a **97** D2, **98** A3
Jaskyňa Izbica **95** D1/2
Jasło **97** C2
Jastrebarsko **127** C/D3
Jastrowie **71** C1
Jastrowie **72** B3
Jastrzębie-Zdrój **96** B2
Jászalsószentgyörgy
 129 D1
Jászberény **97** C3
Jászladány **129** D1
Jatabe **153** C1
Játar **173** B/C2
Játiva **169** D2
Jättendal **35** D3
Jättensjö **35** C3
Jättölä **25** C3
Jatuni **11** C2
Jatznik **70** B1
Jauge **108** B1
Jaulín **154** B3, **162** B1
Jaulnay **101** C1
Jaunay-Clan **101** C1
Jaun [Broc-Fabrique]
 104 B2
Jaunjelgava **73** D1, **74** A2
Jaunpiebalga **74** A2
Jaunsaras **154** A1
Jaurakainen **18** B2
Jaurakkajärvi **19** C2
Jaurrieta **155** C2
Jausiers **112** A/B2
Jåvall **38** A/B3, **44** B1
Javarus **12** B3
Jávea **169** D2
Jävenitz **69** C2
Javerlhac **101** C3
Javier **155** C2

Javierregay **154** B2
Javierrelatre **154** B2
Javorani **131** D2, **132** A1/2
Javorov **97** D2, **98** A2
Jävre **16** B3
Jävrebodarna **16** B3
Javron **86** A2
Jawor (Jauer) **96** B1
Jaworzno **97** B/C2
Jayena **173** C2
Jazak **133** C/D1, **134** A1
Jazbina **127** D2
Jaželbicy **75** C1/2
Jebjerg **48** A/B2
Jedburgh **57** C2
Jedburgh **54** B3
Jedlina **82** B3
Jedl'ové Kostol'any **95** D2
Jedovnice **94** B1
Jędrzejów **97** C1
Jędrzychowice **71** D3
Jeesiö **11** D3, **12** B2
Jeesiöjärvi **11** D3, **12** A2
Jegunovce **138** B2
Jekabpils **74** A2
Jekimoviči **75** C3
Jektevik **42** A1
Jelah **132** B1/2
Jelašnica **135** C3
Jelenec **95** D2
Jelenia Góra (Hirschberg)
 96 A1
Jelenin **71** C3
Jelgava **73** D1, **74** A2
Jelling **48** B3, **52** B1
Jels **52** B1
Jelsa **42** A2
Jelsa **136** A1
Jelšane **126** B3
Jemappes **78** B2
Jemgum **67** D1
Jemgum-Ditzum **67** D1
Jemnice **94** A1
Jena **82** A2
Jenbach **92** A3
Jeneč **83** C/D3
Jenikowo **71** C1
Jenlain **78** B2
Jenneret **78** B2
Jensåsvoll **33** D2
Jenzat **102** B2
Jeppo/Jepua **20** B2
Jeresa **169** D2
Jeres del Marquesado
 173 C2
Jerez de la Frontera **171** D2
Jerez de los Caballeros
 165 D3
Jerggul (Holmestrand)
 5 D3, **6** A3, **11** D1
Jergucati **142** A/B2/3
Jérica **162** B3, **169** C/D1
Jerichow **69** D2
Jerka **71** D3
Jerši **75** C/D3
Jerslev **48** B1
Jerstad **8** B2
Jerte **159** D3
Jerup **44** B3, **49** C1
Jérusalem **78** B3
Jerxheim **69** C3
Jesberg **81** C1/2
Jesenice **126** B2
Jesenice **83** D3
Jesenice **83** C3
Jesenice **96** A3
Jeseník **96** B2
Jeseritz **69** C2
Ješín **83** C/D2
Jésolo **107** D3
Jessen **70** A3
Jessheim **38** A3
Jessnitz **69** D3, **82** B1
Jesteburg **68** B1
Jestřebí **83** D2
Jetnemsstugan **29** D1
Jettingen **90** B2
Jettingen-Scheppach
 91 D2
Jetzendorf **92** A2
Jeumont **78** B2
Jevenstedt **52** B3
Jever **67** D1
Jevišovice **94** A1
Jevnaker **38** A3
Jevremovac **133** C1,
 134 A1/2

Jezerane **130** B1
Jezerce **138** B2
Jezero **131** D2, **132** A2
Jezersko **126** B2
Jiana **135** D2
Jibou **97** D3, **140** B1
Jičín **96** A1/2
Jieprenjåkkstugan **9** D2
Jieznas **73** D2, **74** A3
Jihlava **96** A2
Jihlava **94** A1
Jijona **169** D2/3
Jillesnåle **15** D2/3
Jílové u Prahy **83** D3
Jiltjer **15** D3
Jimbolia **140** A1
Jimena **167** D3, **173** C1
Jimena de la Frontera
 172 A3
Jince **83** C3
Jindřichovice **82** B2
Jindřichovice pod Smrkem
 83 D1/2
Jindřichův Hradec **93** D1
Jindřichův Hradec **96** A2
Jinošov **94** B1
Jiřetín pod Jedlovou **83** D2
Jiříkov **83** D1/2
Jirkov **83** C2
Jirueque **161** C2
Jistebnice **83** D3, **93** D1
Joachimshof **69** D2
Joachimsthal **70** A/B2
Joachimsthal **93** D2
Jochberg **92** B3
Jock **17** C1
Jockas **27** C1
Jódar **167** D3, **173** C1
Jodoigne **79** C2
Joensuu **23** D3
Joesjö **14** B3
Joeström **15** C3
Jõgeva **74** A1
Johannelund **31** C1/2
Johannestorp **16** B2
Johanngeorgenstadt **82** B2
Johannisfors **40** B2
Johannisholm **39** C2
Johanniskirchen **92** B2
Johansfors **51** C2
Johnsbach **93** D3
Johnstone **56** B2
Johovac **132** B1
Jöhstadt **83** B/C2
Joigny **88** A2
Joinville **88** B2
Jokela **25** C/D2, **26** A2
Jokela **25** C1, **26** A1
Jokela **12** A3, **17** D1
Jokela **12** B3
Jokela **22** B1
Jøkelfjord **5** B/C2
Jokijärvi **22** B2
Jokijärvi **19** C3
Joki-Kokko **18** B2
Jokikunta **25** C2/3
Jokikylä **18** A1
Jokikylä **21** D1, **22** A1
Jokikylä **20** A2, **31** D3
Jokikylä **21** C1
Jokikylä **19** C3
Jokikylä **20** B3
Jokilampi **19** C1
Jokiniemi **25** C2
Jokioinen **25** B/C2
Jokiperä **20** B2
Jokipii **20** B3
Jokitörmä **6** B3
Jokivarsi **21** C3
Jokkmokk **16** A/B1/2
Jokue **25** D2, **26** B2
Jolanda di Savóia **115** C1
Jolanki **12** A3, **17** D1
Jøldalshytta **33** C2
Joloskylä **18** B2
Jomala **41** C/D3
Jømna **38** B2
Jonåker **47** B/C2
Jonasvollen **33** D2
Jonava **73** D2, **74** A3
Jonchery-sur-Vesle **88** A1
Joncy **103** C1/2
Jondal **36** B3
Jönköping **45** D3, **46** A3
Jönköping-Huskvarna
 45 D3, **46** A3

Jönköping-Norahammar 45 D3
Jönköping 72 A1
Jönköping-Huskvarna 72 A1
Jonku 19 C2
Jonquières 111 C2
Jons 103 D2/3
Jonsa 22 B2
Jonsberg 47 C2
Jonstorp 49 D2, 50 A2
Jonzac 100 B3
Jorairátar 173 C2
Jorba 155 D3, 156 A3, 163 D1
Jordbru 9 B/C3
Jordbru 47 C/D1
Jordbrugrotten 14 B2
Jördenstorf 53 D3
Jordet 38 B1
Jordfallet 5 C2
Jorgastak 5 D3, 6 A3, 11 D1
Jork 68 B1
Jörlanda 45 C3
Jormlien 29 C1
Jormua 19 C3
Jormvattnet 29 C/D1
Joroinen 22 B3
Jørpeland 42 A2
Jorquera 169 B/C2
Jørstad 28 B2
Josa 162 B2
Jošanica 135 C3
Jošanica 134 B2
Jošanička Banja 134 B3
Josipdol 127 C3, 130 B1
Josipovac 128 B3
Josnes 87 C3
Jössefors 38 B3, 45 C1
Josselin 85 C2
Jossgrund-Burgjoss 81 C2/3
Jøssinghamn 42 A/B3
Jøssund 28 A/B2
Jøssund 28 A2/3, 33 C1
Jostedal 36 B2
Jøstølen 32 B1/2
Jotkajavrre 5 C/D2/3, 6 A2
Jou 158 B1
Joucou 156 A1
Joué-sur-Erdre 85 D3
Jouet-sur-l'Aubois 102 B1
Jougné-Remouchamps 79 C/D2
Joukio 27 D1
Joukokylä 19 C2
Joure 66 B2
Jöusen 20 B1
Jou-sous-Monjou 110 A1
Joutsa 25 D1, 26 A/B1
Joutsenmäki 23 C3
Joutseno 27 C2
Joutsijärvi 13 C3
Joux-la-Ville 88 A3
Jouy-le-Châtel 87 D1/2, 88 A1/2
Jouy-le-Potier 87 C3
Jovan 30 B1
Jøvik 4 A3
Joyeuse 111 C1/2
Juånäset 35 C3
Juankoski 23 C2
Juan-les-Pins 112 B3
Jübek 52 B2
Jubera 153 D2
Jublains 86 A2
Jubrique 172 A3
Jüchen 79 D1
Jüchsen 81 D2
Judaberg 42 A2
Judenau 94 A2
Judenburg 127 B/C1
Judenburg 96 A3
Judinsalo 25 D1, 26 A1
Juelsminde 48 B3, 52 B1
Juf [Thusis] 106 A2
Juggijaur 16 B1
Jugorje 127 C3
Juhnov 75 D3
Juhtimäki 25 B/C1
Juillac 101 C3
Juist 67 C1
Jukajärvi 27 C1
Jukkasjärvi 10 A/B3
Juktfors 15 D3

Jukua 19 C1
Julåsen 35 C3
Jule 29 C2
Jülich 79 D2
Juliénas 103 D2
Julita 46 B1
Julmatt lammit 21 D2, 22 A2
Jumaliskylä 19 D3
Jumeaux 102 B3
Jumesniemi 24 B1
Jumièges 77 C3
Jumilhac-le-Grand 101 D3
Jumilla 169 D2/3
Juminen 22 B1/2
Jumisko 13 C3
Jumkil 40 B3
Juncal 164 A1
Juncosa de les Garrigues 163 C1
Juneda 155 C/D3, 163 C/D1
Jung 45 C/D2
Jungdalshytta 37 C3
Junget 48 B3, 52 B1
Jungfraujoch BE/VS 105 C2
Jungsund 20 A2, 31 D3
Junik 138 A2
Juniville 78 B3, 88 B1
Junkerdal 15 C1
Junkerträsk 16 B2
Junnikkala 27 C1
Junnonoja 18 B3
Junosuando 11 B/C3
Junqueira 159 C1
Junsele 30 A/B2, 35 D1
Junttilanvaara 19 D2
Juntusranta 19 D2
Juojärvi 23 C3
Juoksengi 17 D1/2
Juoksenki 12 A3, 17 D1/2
Juokslahti 26 A1
Juokuanvaara 17 D2/3, 18 A1
Juonto 19 D3
Juorkuna 18 B2
Juornaankylä 25 D2, 26 A2
Juotasniemi 12 B3
Jurançon 108 B3, 154 B1
Junik 138 A2
Jurbarkas 73 D2
Juré 103 C2
Jurignac 101 C3
Jurilovca 141 D2
Jurjevo 130 B1
Jūrmala 73 D1, 74 A2
Jurmo 24 A2, 41 D2
Jurmo 24 A3
Jurmu 19 C2
Juromenha 165 C2
Jur pri Bratislave 95 B/C2
Jurques 86 A1
Jurunbron 15 C1
Jurva 20 B2/3
Jurvala 27 C2
Jurvansalo 21 D2, 22 A2
Jussac 110 A1
Jussey 89 C3
Juta 128 B2
Jüterbog 70 A3
Jüterbog 72 A3, 96 A1
Jutis 15 D2
Jutrosin 71 D3
Juujärvi 12 B3
Juuka 23 C2
Juuma 19 C3
Juupajoki 25 C1
Juupakylä 21 B/C3
Juurikka 23 D3
Juurikkalahti 23 C1
Juurikkamäki 23 C2
Juustovaara 12 A2, 17 D1
Juutinen 22 B1
Juutinva A 19 C3
Juva (Jockas) 27 C1
Juvigny-le-Tertre 85 D1/2, 86 A1/2
Juvigny-sous-Andaine 86 A2
Juvola 23 C3
Juvvasshytta 37 C2
Juzennecourt 88 B2
Jyderup 49 C3, 53 C1
Jylängänjoki 21 D1, 22 A1
Jylhä 22 A/B2
Jylhä 19 C1

Jylhämä 18 B3
Jyllinge 49 D3, 50 A3, 53 D1
Jyllinkoski 20 B3
Jyrkänkoski 19 D1
Jyrkkä 22 B1
Jyväskylä 21 D3, 22 A3

K

Kaakamo 17 D2/3, 18 A1
Kaalimaa 11 D2, 12 B1
Kaamanen 6 B3
Kaamasen Kievari 6 B3
Kaamasmukka 6 B3
Kaanaa 25 C1
Kaanaa 25 D2, 26 A2
Kääpälä 26 B2
Kaarakkala 22 B1
Kaaresuvanto 11 B/C2
Kaarina 24 B2/3
Käärmelehto 12 A/B2
Kaarnalampi 23 C3
Kaarnijärvi 12 B3
Kaarssen 69 C1/2
Kaarst 79 D1, 80 A1
Kaartilankoski 27 C1
Kaava 6 B2
Käävänkulä 26 B2
Kaavi 23 C2
Kabböle 25 D3, 26 A/B3
Kåbdalis 16 A/B2
Kabelvåg 8 B2
Kać 129 D3, 133 D1, 134 A1
Kačanička Klisura 138 B2
Kačanik 138 B2
Kačarevo 133 D1, 134 B3
Kačikol 138 B1
Kácov 83 D3
Kaczkowo 71 D3
Kaczory 71 D2
Kadań 83 C2
Kadarkút 128 A/B2
Kåddis 31 D2
Kadrifakovo 139 C2/3
Käenkoski 23 D2
Kåfjord 5 C2
Kåfjord 5 D1, 6 A/B1
Kåfjord 4 B3
Kåfjordbotn 4 B3, 10 B1
Kagarlyk 99 D2
Kåge 31 D1
Kågeröd 50 A2/3
Kagul 141 D1
Kahl 81 C3
Kahla 82 A2
Kähtävä 18 A3, 21 C1
Kaiafas 146 B3
Kaibing 127 C1
Kaidankylä 25 C1
Kainach bei Voitsberg 127 C1
Kainasto 20 B3
Kaindorf 127 D1
Kainulasjärvi 17 C1
Kainuunkylä 17 D2
Kainuunmäki 22 B1
Kaipiainen 26 B2
Kaipola 25 D1, 26 A1
Kairala 12 B3
Kaisajoki 17 D2, 18 A1
Kaisepakte 10 A2
Kaisers 106 B1
Kaisersbach 91 C1
Kaisersesch 80 A2/3
Kaiserslautern 90 A/B1
Kaiserstuhl [Weiach-Kaiser-stuhl] 90 B3
Kaiser-Wilhelm-Koog 52 A3
Kaisheim 91 D2
Kaitainen 27 C2
Kaitainen 22 B3
Kaitainsalmi 19 C3
Kaitajärvi 12 A3, 17 D2
Kaitjärvi 26 B2
Kaitsor 20 B2
Kaitum 10 A3
Kaitumjaurestugorna 9 D3
Kaivanto 19 B/C3
Kaivomäki 26 B1
Kajaani 19 C3

Kajama 21 D2, 22 A2
Kajanki 11 C2/3
Kajava 19 D1
Kajo 23 C2
Kakanj 132 B2
Kakavi 142 B3
Käkelä 19 C2
Kakerbeck 69 C2
Käkilahti 18 B3
Kakolewo 71 D3
Kakoúri 147 B/C3
Kakóvatos 146 B3
Kakriala 26 B1
Kakskerta 24 B3
Kälä 25 D1, 26 B1
Kalače 138 A1
Kalak 6 B3
Kalakoski 20 B3
Kalamákion 143 D3, 144 A3
Kalamákion 144 A3
Kalamariá 143 D2, 144 A2
Kalámata 146 B3
Kalámata 148 B2/3
Kalambáka 148 B1
Kalambáka 143 C3
Kalambákion 144 A3
Kalamítsion 144 B2
Kálamos 147 D2
Kálamos 146 A1
Kalándra 144 A2/3
Kalándra 148 B1
Kalá Nerá 144 A3
Kalanti 24 A2
Kalapódion 147 C1
Kalaraš 141 D1
Kálarne 30 A3, 35 C2
Kalávrita 146 B2
Kalávrita 148 B2
Kalawa 71 C2/3
Kalax 20 A3
Kalbach-Veitsteinbach 81 C2
Kalbe 69 C2
Kalce 126 B2/3
Káld 128 A1
Kaldfarnes 9 C1
Kaldfjord 4 A3
Kaldhusseter 32 A3, 36 B1
Kaldjord 9 C2/3
Kaldvåg 9 C2/3
Kalefeld-Echte 68 B3
Kalek 83 C2
Kaleköy 149 C1
Kalela 24 B2
Kälen 35 C3
Kaléndzion 146 B2
Kaléndzion 142 B3
Kalenić 134 B3
Kalesija 133 C2
Kaleva 24 B2/3
Kalhovd 43 C1
Kalí 143 C/D1
Kali 130 B2
Kaliáni 147 C2
Kálimnos 149 D3
Kalindría 139 D3, 143 D1, 144 A1
Kalinin 75 D2
Kaliningrad (Königsberg) 73 C2
Kalinkoviči 99 C1
Kalinovik 132 B3
Kalinovka 99 C3
Kalisz 72 B3, 96 B1
Kalisz Pomorski 71 C1
Kalíves 145 C1/2
Kalívia 146 B2/3
Kalix 17 C2/3
Kalixforsbron 10 A3
Kaljazin 75 D2
Kalje 127 C3
Kaljula 27 C1
Kaljunen 27 D1
Kalkar 67 C3
Kalkar-Grieth 67 C3
Kalkberget 30 A2
Kalkbruk 25 D3, 26 A3
Kalkhorst 53 C3
Kalkkiainen 13 C3
Kalkkimaa 17 D2, 18 A1
Kalkkinen 25 D1, 26 A1
Kall 79 D2
Kall 29 C3, 34 A1
Källa 51 D1
Kallax 17 C3
Kallbäck 25 D3, 26 A3

Källby 45 D2
Källebäcken 45 D3, 46 A3
Kallenhardt 80 B1
Källered 45 C3, 49 D1
Källerstad 50 B1
Källeryd 50 B1
Kalletal 68 A3
Kalletal-Langenholzhausen 68 A3
Kallinge 51 C2
Kallioaho 22 A3
Kalliokylä 21 D1, 22 A/B1
Kalliola 25 D2, 26 A2
Kallioniemi 21 D2, 22 A2
Kalliosalmi 12 B3
Kallipéfki 143 D2/3
Kallislahti 27 C1
Kallithéa 143 D2/3
Kallithéa 144 A2
Kallithéa 146 B3
Kallmora 39 D1
Kallmünz 92 A/B1
Kallmünz-Rohrbach 92 A/B1
Kallo 11 D3, 12 A2
Källom 30 B3, 35 D2
Kallön 15 D3
Kalloní 147 C/D3
Kalloní 149 C1/2
Kallrör 29 C3, 34 A1
Kallsedet 29 C3, 34 A1
Källsjö 49 D1, 50 A1
Kallsta 29 D3, 34 B1/2
Kallträsk 20 A3
Källunge 47 D3
Kallunki 13 C3
Källvik 47 C2
Källvik 40 B1
Källvik 9 C2
Kallviken 31 D1/2
Kalmankaltio 11 D2, 12 A1
Kalmar 51 D2
Kalmar 72 B1
Kalmari 21 D2
Kalmavirta 21 D3, 22 A3
Kalmomäki 23 B/C1
Kalmthout 78 B1
Kalna 135 C2
Kálna nad Hronom 95 D2
Kalnciems 73 D1, 74 A2
Kalnik 127 D2
Kaló 49 C2
Kalochórion 143 B/C2
Kalocsa 129 C2
Kalocsa 96 B3
Kalógria 146 A2
Kalókastron 144 A1
Kalonérion 143 C2
Kalón Nerón 146 B3
Kalótichon 145 C1
Kalotina 139 C2
Kalovka 75 C2
Káloz 128 B1
Kalpáki 142 B3
Kalpio 19 C3
Kals 107 D1, 126 A1
Kalsdorf bei Graz 127 C1
Kälsjärv 17 C2
Kalsk 71 C2
Kaltbrunn 105 D1, 106 A1
Kaltenkirchen 52 B3, 68 B1
Kaltennordheim 81 D2
Kaluđerovo 134 B1
Kaludra 138 A1
Kaluga 75 D2
Kalundborg 49 C3, 53 C1
Kaluš 97 D2, 98 A/B3
Kalvåg 36 A1/2
Kalvarija 73 D2
Kalvatn 32 A3, 36 B1
Kalvbäcken 30 B2, 35 D1
Kalvehave 53 D2
Kalvhögen 30 A2, 35 C1
Kälviä 21 B/C1
Kalvitsa 26 B1
Kalvola 25 C2
Kalvsvik 51 C2
Kalvträsk 31 C1
Kalwang 93 D3
Kalydon 146 B2
Kám 128 A1
Kämäränkylä 19 D3, 23 C/D1
Kämäri 21 D2, 22 A2
Kamári 143 D3, 144 A3
Kamarína 146 A1
Kamen 67 D3, 80 A/B1

Kamen' 74 B3
Kamenari 137 C2
Kámena Voúrla 147 C1
Kamenec 73 D3, 98 A1
Kamenec-Podol'skij 98 B3
Kamenica 133 C/D2, 134 A2
Kamenica 135 C3
Kamenica 139 C/D2
Kamenica 138 B1/2
Kamenice nad Lipou 93 D1
Kamenický Šenov 83 D2
Kameničná 95 C3
Kamenka 99 C3
Kamenka 99 D3
Kamenka 141 D1
Kamenka-Bugskaja 97 D2, 98 A/B2
Kamen'-Kaširskij 73 D3, 97 D1, 98 B2
Kamenný Újezd 93 D1/2
Kameno Pole 140 B3
Kamenščak 127 D2
Kamensko 131 D3, 132 A3
Kamensko 128 A3
Kamenz 83 C1
Kami 81 B/C1
Kamienica 71 D2
Kamieniec 71 D3
Kamień Pomorski 72 A2
Kamlunge 17 C2
Kammela 24 A2, 41 D2
Kämmenniemi 25 C1
Kammerforst 81 D1
Kamnik 127 B/C2
Kamnik 96 A3
Kamøyvær 5 D1, 6 B1
Kampen 52 A2
Kampen 66 B2
Kampevoll 9 D1
Kamp-Lintfort 79 D1, 80 A1
Kampor 130 B1
Kamsjön 31 C1/2
Kamula 21 D1, 22 A1
Kamýk nad Vltavou 83 D3
Kanal 126 A/B2
Kanala 21 C1/2
Kanália 143 D3, 144 A3
Kanálion 146 A1
Kanallákion 146 A1
Kanan 15 C3
Kandel 90 B1
Kandern 90 A3
Kandersteg 105 C2
Kandestederne 44 A/B3, 49 C1
Kándia 147 C3
Kandíla 146 A1
Kandíla 147 B/C3
Kanev 99 D2/3
Kanfanar 130 A1
Kangaasvieri 21 C1
Kangádion 146 A/B2
Kangas 18 A3, 21 C1
Kangas 20 B2
Kangasaho 21 C2
Kangasala 25 C1
Kangashäkki 21 D3, 22 A3
Kangaskylä 18 B3
Kangaskylä 21 C1
Kangaskylä 21 C/D2
Kangaslahti 23 B/C2
Kangaslampi 23 C3
Kangasniemi 22 A/B3
Kangasvieri 21 C1
Kangosfors 11 C3
Kangosjärvi 11 C3
Kania 71 C1
Kanina 142 A2
Kanjiža 129 D2
Kankaankylä 21 C1
Kankaanpää 24 B1
Kankaanpää 21 C3
Kankainen 22 B3
Kankainen 21 D3, 22 A3
Kankari 18 B3
Kankari 20 B3
Kankenseter 38 B2
Kånna 50 B2
Kännäkkä 19 C1
Kannas 19 C/D2
Kannonkoski 21 D2, 22 A2
Kannonsaha 21 D2, 22 A2
Kannus 21 C1
Kannusjärvi 26 B2
Kannuskoski 26 B2

Kanona 133 D3, 134 A3
Kanpezu-Santi Kurtz 153 D2
Känsäkangas 21 C1
Kanstad 9 C2
Kantala 22 B3
Kanteemaa 24 B2
Kantokylä 18 A3, 21 C1
Kantola 19 C3
Kantomaanpää 12 A3, 17 D2
Kantornes 4 A3, 10 A1
Kantti 20 B3
Kantvik 25 C3
Kanunki 24 B2
Kánya 128 B2
Kaonik 132 B2
Kapandrítion 147 D2
Kaparéllion 147 C2
Kapela 128 A2/3
Kapellen 94 A3
Kapellen 78 B1
Kapelln 94 A2
Kapfenberg 94 A3
Kapfenberg 96 A3
Kapfenstein 127 D1
Kapitan Andreevo 145 D2
Kaplice 93 D2
Kaplice 96 A2
Kaporin 134 B2
Kaposfő 128 A/B2
Kaposszekcső 128 B2
Kaposvár 128 B2
Kaposvár 96 B3
Kapp 38 A2
Kapparmora 47 D1
Kappel 53 C2
Kappel 80 A3
Kappel am Albis [Baar] 105 C/D1
Kappel-Grafenhausen 90 A2
Kappeln 52 B2
Kappelshamn 47 D2
Kappelshamn 73 B/C1
Kappelskär 41 C3
Kapperapalo 11 D2, 12 A1
Kappl 106 B1
Käpponis 16 B2
Kaprun 107 D1, 126 A1
Kápsas 147 B/C3
Kapsochóra 144 A/B2
Káptalanfa 128 A1
Kaptol 128 B2
Kapusta 12 A3, 17 D2
Kapuvár 94 B3
Kapuvár 96 B3
Käpylä 18 A3
Käpysalo 22 B2
Karabiga 149 D1
Karaburun 149 C/D2
Karacabey 149 D1
Karacasu 149 D2
Karaincirli 145 D2
Karakasim 145 D3
Karan 133 D2, 134 A2/3
Karankamäki 22 B1
Karaova 149 D2/3
Karasjok 5 D3, 6 A3, 11 D1
Karatmanovo 139 C2/3
Karats 16 A1
Karatu 25 C3
Káravos 147 D2
Karavukovo 129 C3
Karbäcken 30 A1/2
Karben 81 B/C2/3
Karbenning 40 A3
Kårberg 46 A1/2
Kårböle 35 C3
Karby 48 A2
Karcag 97 C3, 140 A1
Kardámila 149 C2
Kardašova Řečice 93 D1
Kardeljevo (Ploče) 136 B1
Karden 80 A2/3
Kardis 17 D1
Karditsa 143 C3
Karditsa 148 B1
Kardoskút 129 D2
Kårdžali 141 C3
Kåremo 51 D1/2
Karesuando 11 B/C2
Kargowa 71 C3
Kårhamn 5 C1/2
Karhe 25 B/C1
Karhi 21 B/C1
Karhila 21 C3

Karhujärvi 13 C3
Karhukangas 18 A3
Karhula 26 B2
Karhulankylä 21 C3
Karhunoja 24 B2
Karhunpesäkivi 6 B3
Kariá 143 D2/3
Kariá 147 C2
Kariá 146 A1
Kariá 147 C3
Kariaí 147 C1
Kariaí 144 B2
Kariaí 147 C3
Karianí 144 B1/2
Karifaí 144 B1
Karigasniemi 5 D3, 6 A/B3, 11 D1
Karihaug 9 C2
Karijoki 20 A3
Karilanmaa 25 D1, 26 A1
Karinainen 24 B2
Käringön 44 B3
Karinkanta 18 A2
Karinusbua 38 A/B1
Karise 50 A3, 53 D1
Karisjärvi 25 C2/3
Karis/Karjaa 25 C3
Karítena 146 B3
Karítsa 143 D3, 144 A3
Karjala 24 A/B2
Karjalaisenniemi 19 C1
Karjalohja 25 C3
Karjanlahti 20 B2
Kärjenkoski 20 A3
Kärjenniemi 25 C1/2
Karjula 25 C1
Kärkäjoki 12 B2
Karkalmpi 25 D1, 26 A1
Karkaloú 146 B3
Karkaloú 148 B2
Kärkiskylä 21 C1
Kärkkäälä 21 D3, 22 A3
Karkkila (Högfors) 25 C2
Karkku 24 B1
Kärkölä 25 C2
Kärkölä 25 D2, 26 A2
Karlå 20 A3
Karlby 24 A3, 41 D3
Karlebotn 7 C2
Karleby/Kaarlela 20 B1
Karlholmsbruck 40 B2
Karl-Marx-Stadt (Chemnitz) 82 B2
Karlobag 130 B2
Karlovac 127 C3
Karlovásion 149 D2
Karlovčić 133 D1, 134 A1
Karlovo 140 B3
Karlovy Vary 82 B2/3
Karlsbad-Langensteinbach 90 B1/2
Karlsberg 39 D1
Karlsborg 17 C2/3
Karlsborg 46 A2
Karlsby 46 A2
Karlsfeld 92 A2
Karlshamn 51 C2
Karlshamn 72 A1
Karlshausen 79 D3
Karlshöfen 68 A1
Karlshuld 92 A2
Karlskoga 46 A1
Karlskron 92 A2
Karlskrona 51 C2
Karlskrona 72 B1
Karlskron-Pobenhausen 92 A2
Karlslunde Strand 49 D3, 50 A3, 53 D1
Karlsøy 4 A/B2
Karlsro 16 B2
Karlsruhe 90 B1
Karlstad 45 D1
Karlstadt 4 A3, 9 D1
Karlstadt 81 C3
Karlstadt-Wiesenfeld 81 C3
Karlstein 94 A1/2
Karlštejn 83 C/D3
Karlsten 15 D3
Karlstift 93 D2
Karlstift 96 A2
Karmacs 128 A1
Karmanovo 75 D2/3
Karmansbo 39 D3
Kärnä 21 D2, 22 A2
Kärnä 21 C2

Kârnare 140 B3
Karnevaara 11 C3
Karnin 70 B1
Karnobat 141 C3
Karoro 126 A3
Karow 69 D1
Kärpänkylä 19 D1
Karpenísion 146 B1
Karperón 143 C2/3
Kärra 49 D1, 50 A1
Karrantza 153 C1
Kärrbo 40 A3, 47 B/C1
Karrebæksminde 53 D1/2
Kärrgruvan 40 A3
Karsaikkovvara 22 B1
Kärsämä 18 B3
Kärsämäki 21 D1, 22 A1
Karsanlahti 22 B2
Kärsava 74 B2
Karsbo 51 D2
Karsikas 21 D1, 22 A1
Karsko 71 C2
Kårsta 40 B3, 47 D1
Karstädt 69 D2
Kårstø 42 A2
Karstorp 51 C2
Karstula 21 C2
Kartavoll 42 A3
Kartérion 142 B3
Kårtjevuolle 9 D3
Karttula 22 B2
Karuna 24 B3
Karungi 17 D2, 18 A1
Karunki 17 D2, 18 A1
Karup 48 B2
Karvala 21 C2
Karvasselkä 11 D2, 12 B1
Kärväskylä 21 D2, 22 A2
Kårvatn 32 B2
Karvia 20 B3
Karvik 9 D1
Karvik 4 B2
Karvila 23 C3
Karvio 23 C3
Karvoskylä 21 D1, 22 A1
Karvsor 20 B2
Kås 48 B1
Kasala/Kasaböle 20 A3
Käsatakka 9 C3
Kåseberga 50 B3
Kasejovice 83 C3, 93 C1
Kasendorf 82 A3
Kasfjord 9 C1/2
Kašin 75 D2
Kašina 127 D2/3
Kasiniemi 25 C1, 26 A1
Kaskei 27 C2
Kasker 15 D2
Kaskii 27 C1
Kaskinen (Kaskö) 20 A3
Kaskö 20 A3
Käsmä 19 C/D1
Kasnäs 24 B3
Káspakas 145 C3
Kašperské Hory 93 C1
Kassa 17 D1
Kassándria 144 A2
Kassel 81 C1
Kässijärvi 7 C3
Kassiópi 142 A3
Kassiterá 145 D1
Kassope 146 A1
Kastanéa 143 D2
Kastanéa 143 C/D2
Kastanéa 147 B/C2
Kastanéa 147 B/C2
Kastanéa 143 C3, 146 B1
Kastanéa 148 B2
Kastanéa 148 B3
Kastanéa 148 B1/2
Kastanéai 145 D2
Kastaní 142 B3
Kastav 126 B3, 130 A1
Kastellaun 80 A3
Kastéllion 147 C3
Kaštel Stari 131 C3
Kastélyosdombó 128 A/B2/3
Kasterlee 79 C1
Kastl 92 A1
Kastlösa 51 D2
Kastorf 53 C3, 69 C1
Kästorf (Gifhorn) 69 C2
Kastoría 143 C2
Kastoría 148 A/B1
Kastórion 146 B3

Kástron 147 C2
Kástron 147 D1
Kástron 147 C2
Kástron tís Oréas 143 D3
Kastrup 49 D3, 50 A3, 53 D1
Kasukkala 27 C2
Kaszczor 71 C/D3
Katafa 127 D1, 128 A1
Katajamäki 23 C1/2
Katajamäki 22 B3
Katajamäki 22 B2
Katákolon 146 A3
Katákolon 148 A2
Kataloinen 25 C/D2, 26 A2
Katápola 149 C3
Kåtaselet 16 A/B3
Katavothra 143 C3
Katelbogen 53 D3, 69 D1
Kateríni 143 D2
Katerma 19 D3, 23 D1
Katholm 49 C2
Katinhäntä 24 A2
Kätkäsuvanto 11 C2/3
Kätkävaara 12 A3, 17 D2
Kätkesuando 11 C2/3
Katlanovo 139 C2
Katlanovska Banja 139 C2
Káto Achaïa 146 B2
Káto Achaïa 148 A/B2
Káto Alepochórion 143 D3, 144 A3
Kató Alepochórion 147 C2
Káto Almirí 147 C2
Katochí 146 A2
Káto Drosíni 145 D1
Káto Figália 146 B3
Káto Gotzéa 144 A3
Káto Klinaí 143 C1
Káto Makrinoú 146 B2
Káto Nevrokópion 144 B1
Káto Orfaná 143 C3
Káto Tithoréa 147 C1
Katoúna 146 A1
Káto Vérmion 143 C2
Katovice 93 C1
Katowice 96 B2
Katrineberg 40 A1/2
Katrineholm 46 B1/2
Kats 66 A3, 78 B1
Katsikás 142 B3
Katsikko 12 B2
Kattarp 49 D2/3, 50 A2
Kättbo Norra 39 C2
Kattelus 21 C2
Katthammarsvik 47 D3
Kattila-aho 23 D3
Kattilainen 26 B2
Kattilanmäki 23 C3
Kattilasaari 17 D2
Kattisavan 30 B1
Kattisberg 31 C1
Kattiträsk 31 C1
Katunci 139 D3
Katusice 83 D2
Katwijk 66 A3
Katymár 129 C2
Katzelsdorf 94 B3
Katzenelnbogen 80 B2
Katzhütte 82 A2
Katzweiler 80 A/B3, 90 A1
Kaub 80 B3
Kaufbeuren 91 D3
Kaufbeuren-Neugablonz 91 D3
Kaufering 91 D2/3
Kaufungen 81 C1
Kauhajärvi 21 B/C2
Kauhajärvi 20 B3
Kauhajoki 20 B3
Kauhava 20 B2
Kaukalampi 25 D2, 26 A2
Kauklahti 25 C3
Kaukola 24 B3
Kaukonen 11 D3, 12 A2
Kaukuri 24 B3
Kaulinranta 17 D2
Kaulio 26 B2
Kaulsdorf 82 A2
Kaunas 73 D2, 74 A3
Kauniainen/Grankulla 25 C3
Kaunissaari 26 B3
Kaupanger 36 B2
Kauppila 20 A3
Kauppila 22 B/B3

Kauppilanmäki **22** B1
Kaurajärvi **20** B2
Kaurissalo **24** A2, **41** D2
Kauronkylä **19** D3
Kausala **25** D2, **26** B2
Kaušany **141** D1
Kaustby **21** C1
Kaustinen (Kaustby) **21** C1
Kautokeino **11** C1
Kauttua **24** B2
Kautzen **94** A1
Kavadarci **139** C3, **143** C1
Kavadarci **140** A3
Kavajë **137** D3
Kavak **149** D1
Kavála **149** C1
Kavála **144** B1
Kavarna **141** D3
Kavcik **145** D3
Kávlinge **50** A3
Kávos **142** A3
Kavoúri **147** D2
Kawcze **71** D3
Kaxäs **29** C3, **34** B1
Kaxholmen **45** D3, **46** A3
Käylä **13** C3
Käymäjärvi **11** C3
Kayna **82** B1/2
Käyrämö **12** B2
Käyrämö **12** B3
Kaysersberg **89** D2, **90** A2
Kazanci **131** D2
Kažani **138** B3, **143** B/C1
Kazanlâk **141** C3
Kazatin **99** C2/3
Kazincbarcika **97** C2/3
Kaźmierz **71** D2
Kbely **83** D3
Kdyně **93** B/C1
Kéa **149** C2
Kebnekaise fjällstation **9** D3
Kecel **129** C2
Kecskemét **129** C/D1
Kecskemét **97** C3, **140** A1
Kédainiai **73** D2, **74** A3
Kédange-sur-Canner **89** C/D1
Kédros **143** C3, **146** B1
Kędzierzyn-Koźle **96** B2
Kefalárion **147** C2
Kefalárion **147** C3
Kéfalos **149** D3
Kefenrod **81** C2
Kefermarkt **93** D2
Kehl **90** A/B2
Kehl-Bodersweier **90** B2
Kehl-Goldscheuer **90** A/B2
Kehnert **69** D3
Kehrig **80** A2
Kehrigk **70** B3
Kehro **25** B/C2
Keighley **59** D1, **61** C2
Keihärinkoski **21** D2, **22** A2
Keihäskoski **24** B2
Keikyä **24** B1/2
Keila **74** A1
Keills **56** A1/2
Keimola **25** C3, **26** A3
Keinäsperä **18** B2
Keipene **73** D1, **74** A2
Keisala **21** C2
Keisanmäki **26** B2
Keistiö **24** A3, **41** D2
Keitele **21** D2, **22** A2
Keitelepohja **21** D2, **22** A2
Keith **54** B2
Kekäleniemi **27** D1
Kekkilä **21** D2, **22** A2
Kelankylä **18** B1
Kelberg **80** A2
Kelbra **81** D1, **82** A1
Kelč **95** C1
Kelchsau **92** B3
Këlcyrë **142** A2
Këlcyrë **148** A1
Keléd **128** A1
Kelevíz **128** A2
Kelheim **92** A/B1
Kelheim-Weilenburg **92** A1/2
Keljonkangas **21** D3, **22** A3
Kelkheim (Taunus) **80** B3
Kelkkala **24** B3
Kell **80** A3
Kella **81** D1
Kélla **143** C1/2
Kellahti **24** A1

Kellarpelto **27** C1
Kellenhusen **53** C3
Kellinghusen **52** B3
Kellmünz **91** D2
Kello **18** A2
Kellokoski **25** D2, **26** A2
Kelloniemi **13** B/C3
Kelloselkä **13** C3
Kelmë **73** D2
Kelontekemä **11** D3, **12** A/B2
Kelso **57** C/D2
Kelsterbach **80** B3
Kelstrup Strand **52** B1
Keltiäinen **25** C2
Keltti **26** B2
Kelujärvi **12** B2
Kelvä **12** B3
Kelvedon **65** C2/3
Kemberg **69** D3
Kembs **90** A3
Kemence **95** D2/3
Kemeneshögyész **95** C3, **128** A1
Kemer **149** D2
Kémes **128** B3
Kemi **17** D3, **18** A1
Kemihaaran rajavartioasema **13** C1
Kemijärvi **12** B3
Kemilä **19** D1
Keminmaa **17** D2/3, **18** A1
Keskijärvi **23** D3
Kemin maalaiskunta **17** D2/3, **18** A1
Keminvaara **19** C2
Kemnath **92** B1
Kemnath **82** A3
Kempele **18** A/B2
Kempen-Hülsd **79** D1
Kempenich **80** A2
Kempen-Niederrhein **79** D1
Kempfeld-Katzenloch **80** A3
Kempten (Allgäu) **91** D3
Kempten-Sankt Mang **91** D3
Kemptthal **90** B3
Kendal **59** D1, **60** B1/2
Kendal **54** B3
Kenderes **129** D1
Kendríkón **139** D3, **143** D1, **144** A1
Kéndron **146** A/B2
Kenespahta **6** B2
Kengis **17** C/D1
Kengyel **129** D1
Kenilworth **64** C3
Kenmare **55** C3
Kenmore **54** B2
Kenmore **54** B1
Kennacraig **56** A2
Kenraalinkylä **23** D3
Kentford **65** C2
Kenton **63** C3
Kenzingen **90** A/B2
Kępno **96** B1
Kepsut **149** D2
Keramídion **143** D3, **144** A3
Keramítsa **142** B3
Keramotí **145** C1
Keräntöjärvi **11** C3
Kerasëa **143** C2
Kerasóna **142** B3
Keräs-Sieppi **11** C2/3, **12** A1
Keratéa **147** D2/3
Kerava (Kervo) **25** D3, **26** A3
Kérazan **84** A3
Kerdílion Óros **144** A/B1
Kerekegyháza **129** C1
Kerepes **95** D3
Kerimäki **27** D1
Keriniemi **27** C1
Kériolet **84** B2/3
Keríon **146** A3
Kerión **148** A2
Kerisalo **22** B3
Kerjean **84** A/B2
Kerken-Nieukerk **79** D1
Kerketión Óros **143** C3
Kerkhove **78** B2
Kerkineon **143** D3
Kerkíni **139** D3, **144** A1
Kérkira **142** A3

Kérkira **148** A1
Kerkkoo **25** D2/3, **26** A2/3
Kerkola **24** B2
Kerkonkoski **22** B2
Kerkrade **79** D2
Kerma **23** C3
Kermaria **85** B/C1/2
Kernascléden **84** B2
Kernhof **94** A3
Kernovo **74** B1
Kerns [Kerns-Kägiswil] **105** C1
Kernuz **84** A3
Kerpen **79** D2, **80** A2
Kerpen-Blatzheim **79** D2, **80** A2
Kerpen-Türnich **79** D2, **80** A2
Kershopefoot **57** C3
Kersilö **12** B2
Kerta **128** A1
Kerteminde **53** C1
Kértezi **146** B2
Kertuuankylä **21** B/C2
Kervo **25** D3, **26** A3
Kesälahti **27** D1
Keşan **145** D3
Keşan **149** C/D1
Kesäranta **27** C1
Kesariani **147** D2
Keselyüs **129** C2
Kesilö **25** D1, **26** B1
Keskijärvi **23** D3
Keskikylä **18** A2/3
Keskikylä **21** C2
Keskikylä **20** B3
Keskikylä **18** B3
Keskikylä **18** A3
Keskinen **19** B3
Keskipiiri **18** A2
Keski-Posio **19** C1
Kes'ma **75** D1
Kesova Gora **75** D2
Kesseli **23** D1
Kesti **20** A/B3
Kestilä **18** B3
Kestilä **18** A2
Keswick **57** C3, **60** B1
Keswick **54** B3
Keszeg **95** D3
Keszthely **128** A1/2
Keszthely **96** B3
Ketomella **11** C2, **12** A1
Keträvaara **19** D2
Kętrzyn (Rastenburg) **73** C2
Ketsch **90** B1
Kettering **64** B2
Kettershausen **91** D2
Kettlewell **59** D1, **60** B2
Kéty **128** B2
Ketzin **70** A2
Keula **81** D1
Keuruu **21** C3
Kevelaer **67** C3, **79** D1
Kevelaer-Winnekendonk **67** C3, **79** D1
Kevi **129** D3
Kevo **6** B1
Keynsham **63** D2
Keyritty **23** B/C2
Kežmarok **97** C2
Kianí **145** D1, **145** D3
Kiannanniemi **19** D2
Kiáton **147** C2
Kiáton **148** B2
Kibæk **48** A3
Kiberg **7** D2
Kičevo **138** B3
Kičevo **140** A3
Kidderminster **59** D3, **64** A2
Kidlington **65** C2/3
Kidwelly **62** B1
Kiefersfelden **92** B3
Kiehtäjä **19** C2
Kiekinkoski **23** D1
Kieksiäisvaara **17** C/D1
Kiel **52** B3
Kielajoki **6** B3
Kielce **97** C1
Kielder **57** C2
Kiellatupa **6** B3
Kienberg **92** B3
Kienitz **70** B2
Kiental [Reichenbach im Kandertal] **105** C2

Kieri **17** D2
Kierinki **12** A/B2
Kierspe **80** A/B1
Kierun **15** C/D1
Kiesen **105** C1
Kiesilä **26** B1/2
Kiesima **22** A/B2
Kietävälä **27** C1
Kietävälä **27** C1
Kietz **70** B2
Kiev **99** C2
Kifíno Selo **132** B3, **137** C1
Kifisiá **147** D2
Kifisiá **148** B2
Kifísos **148** B2
Kifísos **147** C2
Kifjord **6** B1
Kihlanki **11** C3
Kihniö **20** B3
Kihniön asema **20** B3
Kiihtelysvaara **23** D3
Kiikala **25** C2/3
Kiikka **24** B1
Kiikoinen **24** B1
Kiilisjärvi **17** C2
Kiilopään-Eräkeskus **12** B1
Kiimavaara **19** D3
Kiiminki **18** B2
Kiiskilä **21** C1
Kiiskilä **27** C1
Kiistala **11** D3, **12** A1/2
Kijevo **132** B3
Kijevo **131** C2
Kijevo **138** B1/2
Kikinda **129** D3
Kikinda **140** A1
Kikorze **71** C1
Kil **46** A1
Kil **45** D1
Kil **43** D2, **44** A2
Kila **46** B2
Kila **45** C1
Kilafors **40** A1
Kila/Kiila **24** B3
Kilás **147** C3
Kilb **94** A2
Kilberget **16** B3
Kilberry **56** A2
Kilboghamn **14** B2
Kilbotn **9** C2
Kilbride **58** A2
Kilchattan **56** A/B2
Kilchrenan **56** A1
Kilcreggan **56** B1/2
Kilcullen **55** D3
Kile **44** B2
Kilebygd **43** D2, **44** A1
Kilen **43** C2
Kilija **141** D2
Kilingi-Nömme **74** A1
Kilkinkylä **26** B1
Kilkis **143** D1, **144** A1
Kilkenny **55** D3
Killarney **55** C3
Killearn **56** B1
Killeberg **50** B2
Killin **56** B1
Killiney **58** A2
Killingi **10** A3
Killíni **146** A2
Killinkoski **21** C3
Killnick **58** A3
Killorglin **55** C3
Killough **58** A1
Killyleagh **58** A1
Kilmacolm **56** B2
Kilmaluag **54** A2
Kilmarnock **54** A/B3, **55** D1
Kilmarnock **56** B2
Kilmartin **56** A1
Kilmelford **56** A1
Kilmory **56** A2
Kilmory **56** A2
Kilmuckridge **58** A3
Kilninver **56** A1
Kilpisjärvi **10** B1
Kilpua **18** A3
Kilsmo **46** B1
Kilsyth **56** B1/2
Kilvakkala **24** B1
Kilvenaapa **18** B1
Kilvo **16** B1
Kilwinning **56** B2
Kimbolton **64** B2

Kími **147** D1
Kími **149** B/C2
Kiminki **21** C2
Kimito/Kemiö **24** B3
Kimméria **145** C1
Kimo **20** B2
Kimola **25** D2, **26** B2
Kimonkylä **25** D2, **26** B2
Kimry **75** D2
Kimstad **46** B2
Kinahmo **23** C2
Kincardine on Forth **57** B/C1
Kindberg **94** A3
Kindelbrück **81** D1, **82** A1
Kinderåsen **34** B2
Kinding **92** A1
Kinéta **147** D2
Kineton **64** A2
Kingarth **56** A/B2
Kinghorn **57** C1
Kingisepp **74** B1
Kingsbarn **57** C1
Kingsberg **40** A2
Kingsbridge **63** C3
Kingsclere **65** C3, **76** B1
King`s Lynn **65** C1
Kings Thorn **63** D1
Kingston **64** B3, **76** B1
Kingston upon Hull **61** D2
Kingswear **63** C3
Kington **59** C/D3, **63** C1
Kinisjärvi **12** A2, **17** D1
Kinkton **56** A1
Kinloch **54** A2, **55** D1
Kinlochleven **54** A2, **55** D1
Kinloch Rannoch **54** B2, **55** D1
Kinn **37** D3
Kinn **9** C1
Kinna **49** D1, **50** A1
Kinna **72** A1
Kinnared **50** A/B1
Kinnarp **45** D3
Kinnarumma **45** C3, **49** D1
Kinna-Skene **49** D1, **50** A1
Kinna-Skene **72** A1
Kinnegad **55** D2
Kinni **26** B1
Kinnula **21** C/D2
Kinnulanlahti **22** B2
Kinrooi-Kessenich **79** D1
Kinross **57** C1
Kinsale **55** C3
Kinsarvik **36** B3
Kintaus **21** D3, **22** A3
Kintus **24** B1
Kiónion **146** A2
Kiosque **155** C2
Kiparissía **146** B3
Kipárissos **143** D3
Kipfenberg **92** A1
Kípi **142** B3
Kipinä **18** B2
Kipouríon **143** C2/3
Kippel [Goppenstein] **105** C2
Kippford **56** B3, **60** A1
Kippinge **53** D2
Kirakkajärvi **7** C2/3
Kirakkaköngäs **6** B3
Kirakka-Olli **7** C2
Kirazli **149** D1
Kirbymoorside **61** C2
Kirchardt **91** C1
Kirchbach **126** A2
Kirchbach in Steiermark **127** C1
Kirchberg **91** C/D1
Kirchberg **80** A3
Kirchberg **82** B2
Kirchberg am Wagram **94** A2
Kirchberg am Wechsel **94** A3
Kirchberg am Walde **93** D2
Kirchberg an der Pielach **94** A2/3
Kirchberg an der Raab **127** C/D1
Kirchberg in Tirol **92** B3
Kirchberg [Kirchberg-Alchenflüh] **105** C1
Kirchberg (Regen) **93** C1/2
Kirchdorf **68** A2
Kirchdorf **93** B/C2
Kirchdorf **94** A3, **127** C1

Kirchdorf 53 C3
Kirchdorf an der Krems 93 C/D3
Kirchdorf an der Krems 96 A3
Kirchdorf (Freising) 92 A2
Kirchdorf im Wald 93 C1
Kirchehrenbach 82 A3
Kirchenlamitz 82 A/B3
Kirchen-Sieg 80 B2
Kirchhain 81 C2
Kirchheilingen 81 D1
Kirchheim 91 C1
Kirchheim 81 C3
Kirchheim-Bolanden 80 B3
Kirchheim (Hersfeld) 81 C2
Kirchheim im Innkreis 93 C2
Kirchheim unter Teck 91 C2
Kirchhundem 80 B1
Kirchhundem-Oberhundem 80 B1
Kirchhundem-Rahrbach 80 B1/2
Kirchhundem-Albaum 80 B1
Kirchlauter 81 D3
Kirchlinteln-Sehlingen 68 B2
Kirchlinteln 68 B2
Kirchroth 92 B1
Kirchschlag in der Buckligen Welt 94 B3
Kirchweidach 92 B2/3
Kirchzarten 90 B3
Kircubbin 56 A3
Kiriákion 147 C2
Kiriši 75 C1
Kirjais 24 A/B3
Kirjakkala 24 B3
Kirjala 24 B3
Kirkağaç 149 D2
Kirkambeck 57 C3, 60 B1
Kirkbride 57 C3, 60 A/B1
Kirkby in Ashfield 61 D3, 65 C1
Kirkby Lonsdale 59 D1, 60 B2
Kirkby Stephen 57 D3, 60 B1
Kirkcaldy 57 C1
Kirkcaldy 54 B2
Kirkcolm 56 A3
Kirkconnel 56 B2
Kirkcowan 56 B3
Kirkcudbright 56 B3, 60 A1
Kirkeby 52 A2
Kirkeby 28 B3, 33 D1
Kirkehamn 42 B3
Kirkehavn 53 C1/2
Kirke Hvalsø 49 D3, 53 D1
Kirkenær 38 B2
Kirkenes (Kirkkoniemi) 7 C/D2
Kirkham 59 D1, 60 B2
Kírki 145 D1
Kirkintilloch 56 B2
Kirkjubøur 55 C1
Kirkkonummi/Kyrkslätt 25 C3
Kirkkopahta 11 C3, 12 A2
Kirk Michael 58 B1
Kirknesvågen 28 B2, 33 D1
Kirkoswald 57 C3, 60 B1
Kirkoswald 56 B2
Kirkpatrick 57 C3, 60 B1
Kirkton 57 C2
Kirkton of Largo 57 C1
Kirkvollen 33 D2
Kirkwall 54 B1
Kirkwhelpington 57 D3
Kirn 80 A3
Kirnički 141 D1/2
Kirnujärvi 17 C1
Kirov 75 D3
Kirovograd 99 D3
Kirovsk 75 C1
Kirra 147 C2
Kirriemuir 57 C1
Kirton-in-Lindsey 61 D3
Kirtorf 81 C2
Kiruna 10 A3
Kiruna-Tuolluvaara 10 A3
Kisa 46 B3
Kisbér 95 C3
Kisbér 96 B3

Kisela Voda 138 B2
Kiseljak 132 B2
Kiseljak 133 C2
Kishajmás 128 B2
Kisiljevo 134 B1/2
Kišiněv 141 D1
Kiskassa 128 B2/3
Kisko 25 B/C3
Kiskomárom 128 A2
Kiskörös 129 C2
Kiskőrös 97 C3
Kiskundorozsma 129 D2
Kiskunfélegyháza 129 D1/2
Kiskunfélegyháza 97 C3, 140 A1
Kiskunhalas 97 C3, 140 A1
Kiskunhalas 129 C2
Kiskunlacháza 129 C1
Kiskunmajsa 129 C/D2
Kiskunmajsa 97 C3, 140 A1
Kismaros 95 D3
Kisoroszi 95 D3
Kissakoski 26 B1
Kissala 27 D1
Kissámos (Kastéllion) 148 B3
Kissanlahti 23 C1/2
Kisslegg 91 C3
Kisslegg-Waltershofen 91 C3
Kistanje 131 C2
Kistelek 129 D2
Kisterenye 97 C3
Kistrand 5 D2, 6 A1
Kisújszállás 129 D1
Kisújszállás 97 C3, 140 A1
Kisurisstugan 9 D3
Kisvárda 97 C/D2/3, 98 A3
Kiszkowo 71 D2
Kiszombor 129 D2
Kitee 83 D2
Kiteenlahti 23 D3
Kitinoja 20 B2
Kitka 19 C/D1
Kitkiöjärvi 11 C3
Kitkiojoki 11 C3
Kitrinópetras 145 D1, 145 D3
Kítros 143 D2
Kitsi 23 D2
Kittelfjäll 15 C3, 29 D1
Kittilä 11 D3, 12 A2
Kittlitz 83 D1
Kittsee 94 B2/3
Kitula 25 C3
Kitupera 18 B3, 22 B1
Kitzbühel 92 B3
Kitzingen 81 D3
Kitzscher 82 B1
Kiukainen 24 B1/2
Kiuruvesi 22 B1
Kivarinjärvi 19 C2
Kivercy 98 B2
Kivérion 147 C3
Kivesjärvi 19 C3
Kiveslahti 19 B/C3
Kivijärvi 21 D2, 22 A2
Kivijärvi 18 B2
Kivik 50 B3
Kivik 72 A2
Kivikangas 21 C2
Kivikylä 24 A2
Kivilahti 23 D2
Kivilompolo 12 A3, 17 D2
Kiviöli 74 A/B1
Kivipaja 27 C1
Kiviperä 19 D1
Kiviranta 19 D1
Kivisuo 26 A1
Kivivaara 23 D1
Kivivaara 19 C2
Kivivaara 23 D3
Kivotós 143 C2
Kjækan 5 C2/3
Kjärnes 9 C3
Kjeldebotn 9 C2
Kjeldobu 37 B/C3
Kjellerup 48 B2
Kjengsnes 9 C2
Kjennsvasshytta 14 B2
Kjerret 38 B3
Kjerringøy 8 B3
Kjerringvåg 32 B1
Kjerringvik 9 C2

Kjerringvik 43 D2, 44 A/B1/2
Kjerringvik 28 B3, 33 D1
Kjerstivika 28 B2
Kjevik 43 C2
Kjølen 44 B1
Kjøli turisthytte 33 D2
Kjøllefjord 6 B1
Kjølsdal 36 A1
Kjølstad 28 B1
Kjoltan 15 C1
Kjøpmannskjer 43 D2, 44 B1
Kjøpsvik 9 C2/3
Kjørsvik 32 B1
Kjorvihytta 15 C1
Kjosen 43 C2, 44 A1
Kjul 14 A3
Kjulaås 47 B/C1
Kjustendil 139 D2
Kjustendil 140 B3
Klåbu 28 B2
Kl'ačno 95 D1
Kladanj 133 B/C2
Kläden 69 C/D2
Klädesholmen 44 B3
Kladnica 133 D3, 134 A3
Kladnica 139 D1/2
Kladnice 131 C3
Kladno 83 C3
Kladno 96 A2
Kladovo 135 C/D2
Kladruby 82 B3
Klagenfurt 126 B2
Klagenfurt 96 A3
Klågerup 50 A/B3
Klagstorp 50 B3
Klaipėda (Memel) 73 C2
Klaksvík 55 C1
Klamila 26 B2
Klampenborg 49 D3, 50 A3, 53 D1
Klana 126 B3
Klanac 130 B2
Klanjec 127 D2
Klanxbüll 52 A2
Kläppe 34 B2
Kläppen 16 A3
Kläppsjö 30 B2, 35 D1
Kläppsjö 30 B2, 35 D1
Klarabro 38 B2
Klarup 48 B1/2
Klašnice 131 D1, 132 A1
Klašterec 83 C2
Kláštor pod Znievom 95 D1
Klatovy 93 C1
Klatovy 96 A2
Klaukkala 25 C3
Klaus an der Pyhrnbahn 93 C/D3
Klausenleopoldsdorf 94 A2/3
Klauvnes 4 B2
Klazienaveen 67 C2
Kleemola 21 C1
Klegod 48 A3
Kleinarl 126 A1
Kleinau 69 C2
Klein Bademeusel 70 B3, 83 D1
Klein Berssen 67 D2
Kleinblittersdorf 89 D1, 90 A1
Kleingiesshübel 82 A2
Kleinglödnitz 126 B1
Kleinhaugsdorf 94 A2
Klein-Koschen 83 C1
Kleinkrausnik 70 A3
Klein Lüben 69 D2
Klein-Machnow 70 A2/3
Klein-Muckrow 70 B3
Klein-Mühlingen 69 D3
Kleinmünchen 93 D2
Klein Oschersleben 69 C3
Kleinpaschleben 69 D3
Kleinrinderfeld 81 C3
Kleinsaubernitz 83 D1
Kleinwelka 83 D1
Kleinwusterwitz 69 D2
Kleiv 37 D3
Kleiva 9 B/C2
Kleive 32 A/B2
Kleivegrend 43 C2
Klek 129 D3
Klek 136 B1
Klemensker 51 D3
Klemetinvaara 19 C3

Klemetsrud 38 A3
Klemetstad 5 D2, 6 A2
Klenak 133 C1, 134 A1
Klenčí 92 B1
Klenica 71 C3
Klenike 139 C2
Klenovica 130 B1
Klepci 132 A/B3, 136 B1
Klepp 42 A2
Kleppen 28 B3, 33 D1, 34 B1
Kleppestø 36 A3
Kleptow 70 B1
Kletnja 99 D1
Klettbach 82 A2
Klettgau-Bühl 90 B3
Klettgau-Erzingen 90 B3
Klettwitz 83 C1
Klevar 43 D1, 44 A1
Kleve 67 C3
Klevshult 50 B1
Kličev 99 C1
Kličevac 134 B1
Kliening 127 C1
Klietz 69 D2
Klimatiá 142 B3
Kliment 141 C2/3
Klimovići 99 D1
Klimovo 99 D1
Klimovsk 75 D3
Klimpfjäll 29 D1
Klin 75 D2
Klina 138 A1
Klinča Selo 127 D3
Klincy 99 D1
Klinga 28 B2
Klingenberg 9 C3
Klingenmünster 90 B1
Klingenthal 82 B2
Klintebjerg 49 C3, 53 C1
Klintehamn 47 D3
Klintehamn 72 B1
Klintholm 53 D2
Kliplev ‘52 B2
Klippan 50 A2
Klippan 72 A1
Klippen 15 C2
Klis 131 C/D3
Klisoúra 143 C2
Klisoúra 142 B3
Klisoúra 148 A1
Klisura 139 C1
Klisura 139 D2
Klitmøller 48 A1/2
Klitten 83 D1
Klitten 39 C1
Kljaci 131 C3
Kljajičevo 129 C3
Kljake 131 C3
Kljasticy 74 B2/3
Ključ 131 D2, 132 A2
Klobouky 94 B1
Klobuck 96 B1
Klobuk 131 D3, 132 A3, 136 B1
Klockarberg 39 D2
Klockow 69 D1, 70 A1
Klockow 70 A/B1
Klockrike 46 A/B2
Kłodawa 71 C2
Klöden 70 A3
Kłodzko (Glatz) 96 B1/2
Kløfta 38 A3
Klokkarstua 38 A3, 43 D1, 44 B1
Klokočevac 135 C2
Klokočevci 128 B3
Klokočov 95 D1
Klokot 138 B2
Kloosterburen 67 C1
Kloosterhaar 67 C2
Kloosterzande 78 B1
Kłopot 70 B3
Klos 138 A3
Klöse 31 C2
Kloštar 128 A2/3
Kloštar Ivanić 127 D3
Kloster-Birnau 91 C3
Klosterfelde 70 A2
Klostermansfeld 82 A1
Klosterneuburg 94 B2
Klosterreichenbach 90 B2
Klosters 106 A1
Kloster Sankt Trudpert 90 A/B3
Kloster Zinna 70 A3
Kloten 39 D3

Kloten 90 B3
Klotten 80 A3
Klötze 69 C2
Klovborg 48 B3
Kløven 32 B1
Klöverträsk 16 B3
Klöveskog 45 C2
Kløvfors 14 B3
Klövsjö 34 B3
Klubbfors 16 B3
Klubbukt 5 C/D1/2, 6 A1
Kluczbork 96 B1
Kluczewo 71 C/D1
Kluess 53 D3, 69 D1
Klukshåckren 29 C3, 34 A/B2
Klupe 132 A1/2
Klüsserath 80 A3
Klutmark 31 D1
Klütz 53 C3
Knaben gruver 42 B2/3
Knåda 39 D1, 40 A1
Knaften 31 C1
Knap-dale 56 A2
Knapstad 38 A3, 44 B1
Knäred 50 B2
Knaresborough 61 C2
Knarrevik 36 A3
Knarsdale 57 C3, 60 B1
Knarvik 36 A3
Knebel 49 C2/3
Kneippbyn 47 D3
Knetzgau 81 D3
Kneža 140 B2/3
Knežak 126 B3
Kneževi Vinogradi 129 C3
Kneževo 128 B3
Knežina 133 B/C2
Kněžmost 83 D2
Knić 134 B2/3
Kničanin 129 D3, 133 D1, 134 A1
Knighton 59 C/D3
Knin 131 C2
Knislinge 50 B2
Knittelfeld 127 C1
Knittelfeld 96 A3
Knittlingen 90 B1
Knivsta 40 B3
Knížecí Pláně 93 C1
Knjaževac 135 C3
Knjaževac 140 A2
Knock 57 C/D3, 60 B1
Knokke-Heist 78 A1
Knoppe 35 D2
Knott End 59 C/D1, 60 B2
Knowle 64 A2
Knüllwald 81 C1/2
Knüllwald-Remsfeld 81 C1/2
Knutby 40 B3
Knuthenborg 53 C/D2
Knutsford 59 D2, 60 B3, 64 A1
Knutsvik 42 A2
Koarholanmäki 19 C3, 22 B1
Kobarid 126 A/B2
Kobbevåg 4 A3, 10 A1
Kobbfoss 7 C3
København 49 D3, 50 A3, 53 D1
København 72 A2
Kobenz 127 C1
Koberg 45 C3
Kobern-Gondorf 80 A2
Koblenz 80 A/B2
Koblenz 90 B3
Kobrin 73 D3, 97 D1, 98 A/B1
Kobylanka 70 B1
Kobylin 71 D3
Kočani 139 C2
Kočani 140 A/B3
Koceljevo 133 D2, 134 A2
Kočerin 132 A3
Kočerinovo 139 D2
Kočerov 99 C2
Kočevje 127 C3
Kočevska Reka 127 C3
Kochel am See 92 A3
Kochel-Walchensee 92 A3
Kočov 82 B3
Kocs 95 C3
Kocsér 129 D1
Kocsola 128 B2
Kodal 43 D2, 44 A1

Kode **45** C3
Kodër Shëngjergij **137** D2, **138** A2
Kodesjärvi **20** B3
Kodiksalm **24** A/B2
Kodisjoki **24** A2
Ködnitz **82** A3
Koekange **67** C2
Köfering (Regensburg) **92** B1
Köflach **127** C1
Köflach **96** A3
Køge **72** A2
Køge **49** D3, **50** A3, **53** D1
Kogel **69** D1
Kohiseva **22** B3
Kohlberg **82** B3
Kohma **23** C2
Kohtavaara **23** C1/2
Koijärvi **25** C2
Koikkala **27** C1
Koikul **16** B2
Köinge **49** D1, **50** A1
Koirakoski **22** B1
Koiramännikkö **12** A2/3
Koiravaara **23** C1
Koisjärvi **25** C3
Koitila **19** C1
Koitsanlahti **27** D1
Koivistonkylä **21** D3, **22** A3
Koivu **18** A1
Koivula **13** C2
Koivumaa **12** A2/3, **17** D1
Koivumäki **21** C2
Koivumäki **23** C3
Koivumäki **22** B2
Koivuniemi **18** A/B1
Koivuvaara **23** D2/3
Koja **10** A3
Köjan **29** C3, **34** A2
Kojanlahti **23** C2/3
Kojetín **95** C1
Kojola **20** B2
Kojonperä **24** B2
Kojsko **126** A/B2
Kökar **24** A3, **41** D3
Kokašice **82** B3
Kokava nad Rimavicou **97** C2
Kokelv **5** D1, **6** A1
Kokemäki (Kumo) **24** B1/2
Kokheden **16** B2
Kokin Brod **133** D3, **134** A3
Kokkila **24** B3
Kokkila **25** C2
Kókkini Ekklisía **143** B/C3
Kokkinókastro **147** D1
Kókkino Neró **143** D3, **144** A3
Kokkinopilós **143** D2
Kokkokylä **18** B1
Kokkola **25** C1
Kokkolahti **23** C3
Kokkoniemi **19** D2
Kokkosenlahti **27** B/C1
Kokkovaara **12** A2
Koklë **142** B1
Köklot **20** A2, **31** D3
Kokonvaara **23** C2
Kokořín **83** D2
Kokory **95** C1
Kokra **126** B2
Kokseby **53** D2
Koksijde-Bad **78** A1
Kokträsk **16** A3
Köla **38** B3
Kola **131** D1/2, **132** A1
Kolan **130** B2
Kolari **134** B2
Kolari **12** A2
Kolárovo **95** C3
Kolárovo **96** B3
Kolåsen **29** C3, **34** A1
Kolašin **137** D3
Kolbäck **40** A3, **46** B1
Kołbaskowo **70** B1
Kolbermoor **92** B3
Kolbnitz **126** A1
Ko^lbu **38** A2
Kolby Kås **49** C3, **53** C1
Kolchikón **144** A1/2
Koldby **48** A2
Kolding **48** B3, **52** B1
Koler **16** B3
Kolerträsk **16** B3

Kölesd **128** B2
Kolho **21** C3
Koli **23** D2
Kolín **83** D3
Kolín **96** A2
Kolind **49** C2
Kolindrós **143** D2
Kolinec **93** C1
Kölingared **45** D3
Kolka **73** C/D1
Kolkanranta **27** C1
Kolkonjärvi **19** C1
Kolkonpää **27** C1
Kolkontaipale **23** B/C3
Kolkwitz **70** B3
Kollaja **18** B2
Kölleda **82** A1
Kollerschlag **93** C2
Kollerud **39** B/C3
Kollínai **147** B/C3
Kolltveit **36** A3
Kollum **67** C1
Kolma **22** B3
Kolmikanta **18** B3
Kölmjärv **17** C2
Kolm-Saigurn **107** D1, **126** A1
Köln **80** A2
Kolno **73** C3, **98** A1
Köln-Porz **80** A2
Köln-Rondorf **80** A2
Koło **73** B/C3, **96** B1
Kolodistoe **99** C3
Kolomyja **97** D2, **98** B3
Kolonjë **142** A2
Kolovec **83** C3, **93** C1
Kolovrat **133** C3
Kolpino **75** B/C1
Kolppi **20** B1
Kolsätter **34** B3
Kölsillre **35** B/C3
Kölsjön **35** C3
Kolsko **71** C3
Kølstrup **53** C1
Kolsva **39** C3, **40** A3, **46** B1
Kolta **95** D3
Kolu **21** C2/3
Kolunić **131** C2
Kolvaa **24** B2
Kolvereid **28** B1
Kølvrå **48** B2
Komádi **97** C3, **140** A1
Komagfjord **5** C2
Komagvær **7** D2
Komagvik **4** A2
Koman **137** D2, **138** A2
Komarin **99** C2
Komárno **96** B3
Komárno **95** C3
Komárom **95** C3
Komárom **96** B3
Kombótion **146** A1
Komen **126** B3
Komi **25** B/C1
Komin **127** D2
Komiža **136** A1
Komjatice **95** C2
Komló **128** B2 *
Kömlőd **95** C3
Kommelhaug **9** C2
Komménon **146** A1
Kommerniemi **27** C1
Komniná **143** C2
Komninón **143** C2
Komoran **138** B1/2
Komorniki **71** D3
Komossa **20** B2
Kompakka **23** D3
Kompelusvaara **17** C1
Kömpöc **129** D2
Komrat **141** D1
Komsomol'skoe **99** C2/3
Komu **21** D1, **22** A1
Komula **23** C1
Komulanköngäs **19** C3
Konak **134** B1
Konakovo **75** D2
Konarevo **133** D3, **134** A/B3
Konäs **29** C3, **34** A1
Končanica **128** A3
Kondiás **145** C3
Kondopoúli **145** C3
Kondovázena **146** B2/3

Kondrovo **75** D3
Konēprusy **83** C3
Kong **53** D2
Konga **51** C2
Köngäs **5** D3, **6** A/B3, **11** D1
Köngäs **6** B2
Köngäs **12** B3
Köngäs **11** D3, **12** A1/2
Kongasmäki **19** C3
Kongens gruve **43** D1, **44** A1
Kongenshus Hede **48** B2
Kongensvoll **28** A3, **33** C1
Kongeparken **42** A2
Konginkangas **21** D2, **22** A2
Kongsberg **43** D1, **44** A1
Kongsbergseter **43** C1
Kongselva **9** B/C2
Kongsfjord **7** C1
Kongsli **10** A1
Kongsmoen **29** B/C1
Kongsness **36** B2
Kongsvinger **38** B3
Kongsvoll **33** C3, **37** D1
Koniarovce **95** C2
Königerode **82** A1
Königsberg **81** D3
Königsbronn **91** D2
Königsbrück **83** C1
Königsbronn **91** D2
Königsdorf **92** A3
Königsee **82** A2
Königsfeld im Schwarzwald **90** B2
Königshütte **69** C3
Königslutter **69** C3
Königsmoos-Wagenhofen **92** A2
Königstein **80** B2/3
Königstetten **94** A/B2
Königswartha **83** D1
Königswiesen **93** D2
Königswinter **80** A2
Königswinter-Oberpleis **80** A2
Königs-Wusterhausen **70** A3
Königs-Wusterhausen **72** A3
Konin **72** B3, **96** B1
Koningsbosch **79** D1
Konispoli **142** A3
Kónitsa **142** B2
Kónitsa **148** A1
Konjavo **139** D2
Konjevrate **131** C3
Konjic **132** B3
Konjsko **137** C1/2
Konken **80** A3, **90** A1
Könnern **69** D3, **82** A1
Konnersreuth **82** B3
Konnerud **43** D1, **44** A1
Konnevesi **21** D3, **22** A3
Könni **20** B2
Konnuslahti **22** B3
Könölä **17** D2, **18** A1
Konolfingen **105** C1
Konopiště **83** D3
Konopiště **139** C3, **143** C1
Konotop **71** C3
Konotop **71** C1
Konotop **99** D2
Konradsreuth **82** A2
Końskie **97** C1
Konsko **139** C3, **143** D1
Konsmo **42** B3
Konstanz **91** C3
Konstanz-Dettingen **91** C3
Kontich **78** B1
Kontinjoki **19** C3, **22** B1
Kontiolahti **23** D2
Kontiomäki **19** C3
Kontiomäki **23** D2
Kontioranta **23** D2/3
Kontiovaara **23** D2
Kontiovaara **23** D2
Kontkala **23** C3
Kontojärvi **12** A3
Kontókalion **142** A3
Konttajärvi **12** A3, **17** D1
Konttila **18** B1
Konttimäki **21** D3
Konz **79** D3
Konzell **92** B1
Köörtilä **24** A1

Kopačevo **129** C3
Kopanica **71** C3
Kopardal **14** A2
Koparnes **36** A1
Koper **126** B3
Köpernitz **70** A2
Kopervik **42** A2
Kópháza **94** B3
Kopidlno **83** D2
Kopilovci **135** D3
Köping **46** B1
Köpinge **50** B3
Köpingebro **50** B3
Köpingsvik **51** D1
Kopisto **18** A3
Koplik **137** D2
Köpmanholmen **31** B/C3
Köpmannebro **45** C2
Koporice **138** B1
Koposperä **21** D1, **22** A1
Koppang **38** A1
Koppangen **4** B3
Kopparberg **39** D3
Koppelo **23** C2
Kopperå **28** B3, **33** D1
Koppom **38** B3, **45** C1
Kopravaara **23** C/D2
Koprivna **132** B1
Koprivnica **135** C2
Koprivnica **128** A2
Koprivnica **96** B3
Koprivnik **127** C3
Kopsa **18** A3
Kopti **99** D2
Koraće **132** B1
Korahosenniemi **19** C/D1
Koraj **133** C1
Korakiána **142** A3
Korapela **11** D3, **12** A1
Koravenkylä **21** C1
Korbach **81** C1
Korbevac **139** C1/2
Korbovo **135** D2
Korbulič **138** B2
Korçë **142** B2
Korçë **148** A1
Korčula **136** B1
Korczyców **71** B/C3
Kordel **79** D3, **80** A3
Korec **98** B3
Korentokylä **19** C2
Korentovaara **23** D1
Kórfos **147** C2/3
Korgen **14** B2
Koria **26** B2
Koridallós **143** C3
Korifí **143** C2
Korinth **53** C2
Kórinthos **147** C2
Kórinthos **147** C2
Kórinthos **148** B2
Koriseva **23** D2
Korissós **143** C2
Korita **136** B1
Korita **137** C1
Korithion **146** A2
Koritnica **135** C3, **139** C1
Koritnik **133** D3, **134** A3
Korjukovka **99** D1/2
Korkana **19** D3
Korkatti **18** A3
Korkea **23** D1
Korkeakangas **23** D3
Korkeakoski **25** C1
Korkeaoja **24** B1
Korkeela **25** C/D1, **26** A1
Korkeporten **5** D1
Korkiamaa **17** D2, **18** A1
Körle **81** C1
Körmend **127** D1
Körmend **96** B3
Kormu **25** C2
Kormu **18** B3
Korneuburg **94** B3
Kórnik **71** D3
Kornsjø **45** B/C2
Kornstad **32** A2
Kornwestheim **91** C1/2
Környe **95** C/D3
Koromačno **130** A1
Koróni **148** B3
Korónia **147** C2
Koronisiá **146** A1
Koronoúda **143** D1, **144** A1
Koronowo **72** B3
Koropíon **148** B2

Koropíon **147** D2
Kőröshegy **128** B1
Korospohja **25** D1, **26** A1
Korosten' **99** C2
Kőröstetétlen **129** D1
Korostyšev **99** C2
Korotovo **75** D3
Korovatiči **99** C1
Korpela **11** D3, **12** A1
Körperich **79** D3
Korpi **21** C1
Korpi **24** A2
Korpi **24** B2
Korpijärvi **26** B1
Korpijoki **21** D1, **22** A1
Korpikå **17** C2
Korpikoski **26** B1
Korpikylä **17** D2, **18** A1
Korpilahti **21** D3, **22** A3
Korpilombolo **17** C1
Korpilompolo **12** A3, **17** D1
Korpimäki **23** C2
Korpinen **22** B2
Korpierä **21** D2
Korpo/Korppoo **24** A3
Korpoström **24** A3
Korppinen **21** D2, **22** A2
Kors **32** B3, **37** C1
Korså **40** A2
Korsbäck **20** A2
Korsberga **45** D2/3, **46** A3
Korsberga **51** C1
Korsbyn **31** B/C2
Korsen **28** B2
Korsfjord **5** C2
Korshamn **42** B3
Korshavn **44** B1/2
Korsholm/Mustasaari **20** A2
Korsmo **38** A/B3
Korsmyrbränna **29** D3, **35** C1/2
Korsnäs **39** D2
Korsnäs **20** A2
Korsnes **9** C2
Korsö **24** A2/3, **41** D2
Korsør **53** C1
Korssjøen **33** D3
Korssjön **31** D1/2
Korsträsk **16** B3
Korsu **23** D1
Korsun'-Ševčenkovskij **99** D3
Korsveien **28** A3, **33** C2
Korte **21** B/C3
Kortejärvi **21** C2
Kortekangas **22** B1
Kortesalmi **25** D1, **26** B1
Kortesjärvi **20** B2
Kortevaara **19** D3, **23** D1
Kortgene **78** B1
Kortrijk **78** A2
Kortteinen **23** C2
Kor'ukovka **99** D1/2
Korvala **12** B3
Korvanniemi **19** C3
Korvenkylä **18** A/B2
Korvenkylä **21** C1
Korweiler **80** A3
Koryčany **94** B1
Korytnica-kúpele **95** D1
Kos **149** D3
Kosančić **139** C1
Košava **135** D2
Kösching **92** A2
Kościan **71** D3
Kościan **72** B3, **96** B1
Kościerzyna **72** B2
Kose **74** A1
Kosel **138** B3, **142** B1
Košetice **83** D3, **93** D1
Košice **83** D3
Košice **97** C2
Kosieczyn **71** C3
Kosierz **71** C3
Kosjerić **133** D2, **134** A2
Kosjerić **140** A2
Koška **128** B3
Koskama **11** D3, **12** A/B2
Koskeby/Koskenkylä **20** B2
Koskela **18** B3
Koskenjoki **21** D1, **22** A/B1
Koskenkorva **20** B2/3
Koskenkylä/Forsby **25** D2, **26** A2
Koskenkylä **24** B2
Koskenkylä **25** B/C2

Koskenkylä **17** D2, **18** A1
Koskenlaskupaikka **19** D3
Koskenmäki **19** D3
Koskenmylly **25** D1,
  26 A/B1
Koskenniska **6** B3, **11** D1
Koskenpää **21** D3, **22** A3
Koskenperä **21** D1, **22** A1
Koski **24** B2
Koski **24** B3
Koski **25** D2, **26** A2
Koski **25** C3
Koskimäki **20** B2/3
Koskue **20** B3
Koskullskulle **16** B1
Kosman **133** C3
Kosmás **147** C3
Kosmonosy **83** D2
Kosola **20** B2
Kosola **27** C/D1
Kosov **97** D2, **98** B3
Kosovo Polje **138** B1
Kosovrasti **138** A3
Kosovska Kamenica
  138 B1/2
Kóspallag **95** D3
Kossdorf **83** C1
Kössen **92** B3
Kost **83** D2
Kosta **51** C1/2
Kósta **147** C3
Kosta **72** B1
Kostajnica **127** D3,
  131 C/D1
Košt'álkov **94** A1
Kostamo **12** B3
Kostanjevac **127** C3
Kostanjevica **127** C3
Kostebrau **83** C1
Kostelec **93** D1
Kostelec na Hané **94** B1
Kostelec nad Černými Lesy
  83 D3
Kostelec nad Labem
  83 D2/3
Kostenec **140** B3
Koštice **83** C2
Kostinbrod **139** D1
Kostojevići **133** C2, **134** A2
Kostolac **134** B1/2
Kostrina **97** D2, **98** A3
Kostrzyn **70** B2
Kostrzyn **71** D2/3
Kost'ukoviči **99** D1
Kosturino **139** C/D3,
  143 D1
Kosula **23** C3
Koszalin (Köslin) **72** B2
Kőszeg **94** B3, **127** D1
Koszyce **71** D1/2
Kotajärvi **19** D3, **23** D1
Kotajärvi **18** B2
Kotala **13** C2
Kotala **21** C3
Kotalanperä **18** B2
Kotamaa **12** B2
Kótas **143** B/C2
Kotasalmi **23** B/C2
Kotel **141** C3
Köthen **69** D3
Kotikylä **22** B2
Kotila **19** C3
Kotiranta **19** D2
Kotka **26** B2/3
Kotor **137** C2
Kotoriba **128** A2
Kotorsko **132** B1
Kotor Varoš **131** D2,
  132 A1/2
Kotovsk **99** C3
Kotovsk **141** D1
Kotrónia **145** D1, **145** D3
Kötschach **107** D1/2,
  126 A1/2
Köttsjön **30** A3, **35** C2
Kötz **91** D2
Kötzting **92** B1
Koufália **143** D1
Koufós **144** B2/3
Kouhi **21** D3, **22** A3
Koúkoura **147** C2
Koúmanis **146** B2/3
Koura **20** B2/3
Kouřim **83** D3
Kouroútas **146** A2/3
Koutaniemi **19** C3

Koutojärvi **17** D2
Koutsochéra **146** B2/3
Koutsócheron **143** D3
Koutus **12** A3, **17** D1
Kouva **19** C1
Kouvola **26** B2
Kovačevci **139** D2
Kovačica **133** D1,
  134 A/B1
Kovačica **140** A2
Kovářská **83** B/C2
Kovel' **97** D1, **98** B2
Kovelahti **24** B1
Kovero **23** D3
Kovero **24** A2
Kovero **24** B1
Koversada **130** A1
Kovilj **129** D3, **133** D1,
  134 A1
Kovin **134** B1
Kovin **140** A2
Kovjoki **20** B1/2
Kövra **34** B2
Köyceğiz **149** D3
Köyhäjoki **21** C1
Köyhänperä **21** D1, **22** A1
Köyliö **24** B2
Köyliönkylä **24** B2
Kozáni **143** C2
Kozáni **148** B1
Kozarac **129** B/C3
Kozarac **131** D1, **132** A1
Kozármisleny **128** B2
Kozelec **99** D2
Kozel'sk **75** D3
Kozica **131** D3, **132** A3,
  136 B1
Kozienice **97** C1, **98** A2
Kozí Hrádek **93** D1
Kozina **126** B3
Kozluk **133** C2
Kožlany **83** C3
Kozluk **133** C2
Kozly **83** C2
Kozmice **83** D3
Kozojedy **83** C3
Kozolupy **83** C3
Kożuchów **71** C3
Kožuhe **132** B1
Krääkkiö **24** B1/2
Kräckelbäcken **39** C1
Krackow **70** B2
Kraddsele **15** C/D2/3
Kraftsdorf **82** A/B2
Kragenæs **53** C2
Kragerø **43** D2, **44** A2
Krągi **71** D1
Kragujevac **134** B2
Kragujevac **140** A2
Krahne **69** D3
Kraiburg **92** B2
Kraichtal **90** B1
Krajenka **71** D1
Krajková **82** B2/3
Krajkovac **135** B/C3
Krajn **137** D2
Krajné **95** C2
Krajnik Dolny **70** B2
Kråkberget **8** B2
Kråken **31** C3
Krakhella **36** A2
Kraekkjahytta **37** C3
Kräklingbo **47** D3
Kråklivollen **33** C2
Kråkmo **9** C3
Krakovec **83** C3
Kraków **97** C2
Krakow am See **53** D3,
  69 D1
Kråkshult **46** B3
Kråkstad **38** A3, **44** B1
Králíky **96** B2
Kraljeva Sutjeska **132** B2
Kraljevica **126** B3, **130** B1
Kraljevo **134** B3
Kraljevo **140** A2
Kral'ovany **95** D1
Král'ov Brod **95** C2/3
Kralovice **83** C3
Kralupy nad Vltavou
  83 D2/3
Kralupy nad Vltavou **96** A2
Králův Dvůr **83** C3
Kramfors **30** B3, **35** D2
Kramnitse **53** C2
Krampen **94** A3
Krampenes **7** C/D2

Krampfer **69** D2
Kråmvik **43** C1
Kramvik **7** D2
Kranéa **143** C3
Kranéa Deskátis **143** C2/3
Kranenburg **67** B/C3
Kranevo **141** D3
Krångede **30** A3, **35** C2
Kranichfeld **82** A2
Kranídion **147** C3
Kranj **126** B2
Kranj **96** A3
Kranjska Gora **96** A3
Kranjska Gora **126** B2
Kransvik **14** B1
Krąpiel **71** C1
Krapina **127** D2
Krapinske Toplice **127** D2
Krapkowice **96** B1/2
Kraselov **93** C1
Krašic **127** C3
Krasilov **98** B3
Kräslava **74** A/B2/3
Kraslice **82** B2
Krásná Hora **83** D3
Krásná Lípa **83** D2
Krasník **97** C/D1, **98** A2
Krásno **82** B3
Krasnoe **75** C3
Krasnogorodskoe **74** B2
Krasnoil'sk **98** B3
Krasnoje Selo **74** B1
Krásno nad Kysucou **95** D1
Krasnopole **99** D1
Krasnopolje **74** B3
Krasno Polje **130** B1
Krasnye Okny **141** D1
Krasnyj **75** C3
Krasnyj Holm **75** D1
Krasnystaw **97** D1, **98** A2
Kratovo **140** A3
Kratovo **139** C2
Kraubath **127** C3
Krauchenwies **91** C3
Krautheim **91** C1
Krautscheid (Prüm) **79** D3
Kravaře **83** D2
Kravarsko **127** D3
Krčedin **133** D1, **134** A1
Kreba **83** D1
Krefeld **79** D1, **80** A1
Kreien **69** D1
Kreien **69** D1
Kreiensen **68** B3
Kreischa **83** C2
Krej Lura **138** A2
Krekilä **21** C1
Křelovice **83** D3, **93** D1
Kremenčug **99** D3
Kremenec **98** B2
Kremenica **143** C1
Kremges **99** D3
Kremikovci **139** D1
Kremincy **97** D2, **98** A/B3
Kremmen **70** A2
Kremna **133** C2/3
Kremnica **95** D2
Krems an der Donau **94** A2
Krems an der Donau **96** A2
Kremsbrücke **126** A/B1
Kremsmünster **93** C/D2/3
Křemže **93** D1
Krepoljin **135** B/C2
Krępsko **71** D1
Kreševo **132** B2/3
Kresna **139** D2/3
Kressberg-Mariäkappel
  91 D1
Kressbronn **91** C3
Krestcy **75** C1
Kréstena **146** B3
Kretinga **73** C2
Kreuth **92** A3
Kreuzau **79** D2
Kreuzen **126** A/B2
Kreuzen **93** D2
Kreuzenstein **94** B2
Kreuzlingen **91** C3
Kreuztal **80** B2
Kreuztal-Krombach
  80 B1/2
Kreuzwirt **94** A3, **127** D1
Kría Vrísi **143** D2
Kričev **99** D1
Kričevci **127** D2
Kriebstein **82** B1
Krieglach **94** A3

Kriegsfeld **80** B3
Krien **70** A1
Kriezá **147** D2
Krimml **107** D1
Krimpen aan de Lek **66** A3
Křinec **83** D3
Kringlevasshytta **42** B2
Krionéri **146** B2
Krionérion **147** C2
Kripan **153** D2
Kristallopigí **142** B2
Kristdala **51** D1
Kristdala **72** B1
Kristianopel **72** B1
Kristianopel **51** D2
Kristiansand **43** C3
Kristiansand-Randesund
  43 C3
Kristianstad **50** B2/3
Kristianstad **72** A1
Kristiansund **32** A/B2
Kristiinankaupunki **20** A3
Kristineberg **39** B/C1
Kristineberg **16** A3
Kristinefors **38** B2
Kristinehamn **45** D1, **46** A1
Kristinehov **50** B3
Kristinestad (Kristiinankau-
  punki) **20** A3
Kristóni **143** D1, **144** A1
Kristvalla **51** D1/2
Kristvik **28** A/B3, **33** C/D1
Kriva Feja **139** C1/2
Krivajevići **132** B2
Kriváň **97** C2
Kriva Palanka **140** A3
Kriva Palanka **139** C2
Krivelj **135** C2
Krivi Vir **135** C3
Krivodol **135** D3
Krivoe Ozero **99** C3
Krivogaštani **138** B3,
  143 C1
Krivoj Rog **99** D3
Křivoklát **83** C3
Krivolak **139** C3
Križ **127** D3
Křižanov **94** A/B1
Križevci **127** D2
Križevci **127** D2
Križišče **127** B/C3, **130** B1
Krk **130** B1
Krka **127** C3
Krmčine **130** B2
Krnjeuša **131** C1/2
Krnjevo **134** B2
Krnov **96** B2
Krobia **71** D3
Krobielewko **71** C2
Krøderen **43** D1
Krögis **83** C1
Krognes **7** D1
Krogsbølle **49** C3, **53** C1
Krokan **43** C1
Krokedal **38** A3, **44** B1
Krokek **46** B2
Krokelv **5** D1, **6** A1
Kroken **14** B3
Kroken **4** A3
Kroken **36** A2
Kroken **43** C/D2, **44** A2
Kroken **36** B2
Kroken **33** D2
Kroken **36** D3
Krokfors **15** C3
Krokhaug **33** C3, **37** D1
Kroknäs **34** B3
Krokom **29** D3, **34** B2
Kroksätra **38** B2
Krokselvmoen **14** B2
Kroksjö **31** C/D2
Kroksjö **30** B1
Krokstad **28** A3, **33** C2
Krokstadelva **43** D1, **44** A1
Krokstrand **44** B2
Krokträsk **17** C2
Krokvåg **30** A3, **35** C2
Krokvik **10** A3
Krolevec **99** D2
Królpa **82** A2
Kroměříž **95** C1
Kroměříž **96** B2
Krompachy **97** C2
Kronach **82** A2/3
Kronberg **80** B2/3
Kronburg **91** D3
Kronoberg **51** C1
Kronoby/Kruunupyy **20** B1

Kronogård **16** A3
Kronogård **14** A2
Kronsågen **16** A/B1
Kronshagen **52** B3
Kronstorf **93** D2
Kröpelin **53** D3
Kropp **52** B2/3
Kroppenstedt **69** C3
Kropstädt **69** D3, **70** A3
Krościenko **97** D2, **98** A3
Krośniewice **73** C3,
  97 B/C1
Krosno **97** C2, **98** A2/3
Krosno Odrzańskie (Cros-
  sen) **72** A3, **96** A1
Krosno Odrzańskie (Cros-
  sen) **71** C3
Krossbu **37** C2
Krostitz **82** B1
Krotoszyn **96** B1
Kröv **80** A3
Krovíli **145** D1
Krpimen **138** B1
Krrabë **138** A3, **142** A1
Kršan **126** B3, **130** A1
Krško **127** C2
Krstac **137** C1
Krstatice **131** D3, **132** A3
Krstinja **127** D3, **131** C1
Krstu **129** D2
Křtiny **94** B1
Krüden **69** C/D2
Krue i Fushës **137** D2
Kruft **80** A2
Kruishoutem **78** B1/2
Krujë **97** D3, **138** A3
Krumbach **91** D2
Krumbach Markt **94** A/B3
Krummesse **53** C3, **69** C1
Krummhörn **67** C2
Krummhörn-Greetsiel
  67 C1
Krummhörn-Rysum **67** C1
Krün **92** A3
Krupa **131** C2
Krupa **131** D2, **132** A1/2
Krupac **139** D1
Krupaja **135** B/C2
Krupanj **133** C2
Krupina **95** D2
Krupište **139** C2
Krupka **83** C2
Krupki **74** B2
Krušá **52** B2
Kruščica **132** B2
Kruščica **134** B1
Kruščica **131** D2, **132** A2
Kruse **137** D2
Krušedol Selo **133** D1,
  134 A1
Kruševac **134** B3
Kruševac **140** A2
Kruševo **138** B3, **143** C1
Krutå **14** B3
Kruth **89** D2/3, **90** A3
Krutvatn **14** B3
Kruusila **25** B/C3
Kryckeltjärn **31** C2
Krylbo **40** A3
Krynica **97** C2
Krystallgrotten **14** B2
Krzęcin **71** C2
Krzemieniewo **71** D1
Krzepielow **71** C/D3
Krzeszyce **71** C2
Krzystkowice **71** C3
Krzywin **71** D3
Krzyż **71** C2
Ksiąz Wielkopolski **71** D3
Kšinná **95** C/D2
Kuaejoki **21** C1
Kubbe **30** B3, **35** D1
Kubinka **75** D3
Küblis **106** A1
Kubrat **141** C2
Kučevo **140** A2
Kučevo **135** C2
Kuchen **91** C2
Kuchl **93** C3
Kuçi **142** A2
Kučište **138** A1
Kuddby **46** B2
Kuerlinkant **11** C3, **12** A2
Kufstein **92** B3
Kuggeboda **51** C2
Kuggören **40** B1
Kuha **18** B1

Kuhakoski 27 C1
Kuhala 27 C1/2
Kuhlhausen 69 D2
Kuhmalahti 25 C1
Kuhmo 19 D3, 23 C1
Kuhmoinen 25 D1, 26 A1
Kühren 82 B1
Kühtai 107 B/C1
Kuikka 21 D3, 22 A3
Kuikkaperä 18 B2
Kuikkavaara 19 C2/3
Kuikooaho 22 B2
Kuinre 66 B2
Kuisma 23 D2
Kuittila 23 D1
Kuitula 26 B1
Kuivainen 27 C1
Kuivajärvi 19 D3
Kuivajärvi 25 D1, 26 B1
Kuivakangas 17 D2
Kuivalahti 24 A1
Kuivaniemi 18 A1/2
Kuivanto 25 D2, 26 A2
Kuivasjärvi 18 A/B2
Kuivasjärvi 20 B3
Kukasjärvi 12 A/B2
Kukasjärvi 17 C/D2
Kukaskylä 21 D2, 22 A2
Kukës 138 A2
Kukës 140 A3
Kukkalampi 23 D2
Kukko 21 C2
Kukkola 17 D2, 18 A1
Kukkolankoski 17 D2, 18 A1
Kukljica 130 B2
Kukonkylä 21 C3
Kukujevci 133 C1
Kula 129 C3
Kula 135 C2/3
Kula 140 A/B2
Kula 149 D2
Kulata 139 D3, 144 A1
Kuldiga 73 C1
Kulennoinen 27 D1
Kulen Vakuf 131 C2
Kulho 23 D3
Kulhuse 49 D3
Kulina 135 B/C3
Kulju 25 C1
Kulla 24 B3
Kullaa 24 B1
Kulladal 50 A3
Kullavik 45 C3, 49 D1
Kullo 25 D3, 26 A3
Küllstedt 81 D1
Kulltorp 50 B1
Kulmbach 82 A3
Kuloharju 19 C1
Kuløyholmen 42 A1
Külsheim 81 C3
Kultala 12 B1
Kultima 11 C2
Kulvemäki 22 B1
Kumane 129 C3
Kumanica 133 D3, 134 A3
Kumanovo 139 C2
Kumanovo 140 A3
Kumhausen-Niederkam 92 B2
Kumiseva 21 D1, 22 A1
Kumla 40 A3
Kumla 46 A1
Kumlinge 24 A3, 41 D2/3
Kummelby 46 B2
Kummerow 69 D1, 70 A1
Kümmersbruck-Köfering 92 A/B1
Kumo 24 B1/2
Kumpula 21 C2
Kumpumäki 21 D2, 22 A2
Kumpuranta 23 C3
Kumpuselkä 21 D2, 22 A2
Kumpuvaara 18 B1
Kumrovec 127 C/D2
Kunda 74 A/B1
Kundl 92 A/B3
Kunes 6 B1/2
Kungälv 45 C3
Kungas 21 C1
Kungsängen 47 C1
Kungsåra 40 A3, 47 C1
Kungsäter 49 D1, 50 A1
Kungsbacka 49 D1, 50 A1
Kungsbacka 72 A1
Kungsfors 40 A2
Kungshamn 44 B2

Kungslena 45 D3
Kungsör 46 B1
Kunhegyes 129 D1
Kunhegyes 97 C3, 140 A1
Kuni 20 B2
Kuninkaanlähde 24 B1
Kun'ja 75 C2
Kunna 14 B1
Kunnasniemi 23 C/D2
Kunovice 95 C1
Kunovo 139 C1
Kunowo 71 D3
Kunrau 69 C2
Kunštát 94 B1
Kunszentmárton 129 D1
Kunszentmárton 97 C3, 140 A1
Kunszentmiklós 129 C1
Kunžak 93 D1, 94 A1
Künzelsau 91 C1
Künzing 93 C2
Kuohatti 23 C1
Kuohenmaa 25 C1
Kuohijoki 25 C1, 26 A1
Kuohu 21 D3, 22 A3
Kuoksjärvi 12 A/B3
Kuoksu 10 B3
Kuolio 19 C1
Kuollejaur 16 A2
Kuomiokoski 26 B1
Kuona 21 D1, 22 A1
Kuopio 22 B2
Kuoppala 21 C/D2/3
Kuoppaniva 5 D3, 6 A/B3, 11 D1
Kuoppilasjoki 6 B2
Kuora 23 D2
Kuorasjärvi 20 B3
Kuorevaara 23 C2
Kuorpak 16 A1
Kuorsumaa 24 B1
Kuortane 21 C2
Kuortti 26 B1
Kuosku 13 C2
Kup 128 A1
Kupari 137 C1/2
Kupci 134 B3
Kupferzell 91 C1
Kupinovo 133 D1, 134 A1/2
Kupiškis 73 D1/2, 74 A2/3
Küplü 145 D1, 145 D3
Kuppenheim 90 B2
Kupres 131 D2, 132 A2
Küps 82 A2/3
Kupusina 129 C3
Kurbnesh 138 A2/3
Kurd 128 B2
Kurejoki 21 C2
Kurenlahti 27 C2
Kurgolovo 74 B1
Kurhila 25 D2, 26 A2
Kurikankylä 20 B3
Kurikka 20 B3
Kuřim 94 B1
Kurisjärvi 25 C2
Kurjala 23 B/C3
Kurjenkylä 21 B/C3
Kurkela 25 B/C3
Kurkikylä 19 C2
Kurkimäki 22 B2
Kurkkio 11 D3, 12 A1
Kürnach 81 D3
Kurolanlahti 22 B2
Kurort Jonsdorf 83 D2
Kurort Kipsdorf 83 C2
Kurów 97 C1, 98 A2
Kurravaara 10 A3
Kurrokvejk 15 D2
Kuršenai 73 D1/2
Kursu 13 C3
Kuršumlija 138 B1
Kuršumlija 140 A3
Kuršumlijska Banja 138 B1
Kurtakko 11 C3, 12 A2
Kurtbey 145 D3
Kürten 80 A1
Kurtti 19 C2
Kurtto 19 C2/3
Kuru 25 C1
Kuru 25 C/D2, 26 A2
Kurujärvi 12 B2
Kurvinen 19 D2
Kusadak 134 B2
Kuşadası 149 D2
Kušalino 75 D2
Kusel 80 A3, 90 A1

Kusey 69 C2
Kusmark 31 D1
Küsnacht 105 D1
Kussjön 31 C2
Küssnacht am Rigi 105 C1
Kustavi 24 A2, 41 D2
Kutas 128 A2
Kutemainen 21 D2, 22 A2
Kutemajärvi 22 B3
Kutenholz 68 B1
Kutila 25 C2
Kutina 128 A3
Kutjaurestugan 9 C/D3
Kutjevo 128 B3
Kutlovo 134 B2
Kutná Hora 83 D3
Kutno 73 C3, 97 C1
Kutrikko 13 C3
Kuttanen 11 C2
Kuttanen 11 C2
Kuttura 12 B1
Kuttusoja 13 C2
Kúty 94 B2
Kutzleben 81 D1, 82 A1
Kuukasjärvi 18 B1
Kuuksenvaara 23 D2/3
Kuuminainen 24 A1
Kuumu 19 D3
Kuurila 25 C2
Kuurtola 19 C/D2
Kuusaa 21 D1, 22 A1
Kuusaa 21 D3, 22 A3
Kuusajärvi 11 D3, 12 A2
Kuusajoki 11 D3, 12 A2
Kuusamo 19 D1
Kuusankoski 26 B2
Kuusijärvi 18 B1
Kuusijärvi 19 C2
Kuusijärvi 21 C3
Kuusikko 17 D2, 18 A1
Kuusilahti 17 C1
Kuusiranta 18 B3
Kuusivaara 12 B3
Kuusjärvi 23 C2/3
Kuusjoki 24 B2
Kuuskanlahti 19 C3
Kuuslathi 22 B2
Kuvansi 22 B3
Kuvšinovo 75 C/D2
Kuženkino 75 C2
Kuzma 127 D1
Kuzmin 133 C1
Kuznecovka 74 B1
Kuźnica Żelichowska 71 C2
Kvål 28 A3, 33 C2
Kvåle 42 B3
Kvalfjord 5 C2
Kvalnes 15 B/C1
Kvalnes 8 B3
Kvalnes 8 B2
Kvalnesodden 14 A2
Kvaløyhamn 14 A2
Kvaløyseter 28 A2
Kvaløysletta 4 A2/3
Kvalsund 5 C1/2, 6 A1
Kvalsund 36 A1
Kvalsvik 36 A1
Kvalvåg 42 A1
Kvalvåg 32 B2
Kvam 37 D2
Kvam 28 B2
Kvammen 36 A2
Kvammen 32 A2
Kvamskogen 36 A3
Kvamsøy 36 B2
Kvænangsbotn 5 C3
Kvænangsseua 5 C2/3
Kvanløse 49 D3, 53 D1
Kvannås 9 D1
Kvanndal 36 B3
Kvanne 32 B2
Kvannli 14 B3, 29 C1
Kvänum 45 D2/3
Kvarnåsen 31 C1
Kvarnberg 39 D1
Kværndrup 53 C1/2
Kvarnsjö 34 B3
Kvarntorp 46 A/B1
Kvarsebo 47 B/C2
Kvås 42 B3
Kvelde 43 D2, 44 A1
Kvelia 29 C2
Kvellandstrand 42 B3
Kvemoen 29 C2
Kvenvær 32 B1
Kvernaland 42 A2
Kvernes 32 A/B2

Kvernhusvik 28 A3, 33 C1
Kvernland 28 A2
Kverrestad 50 B3
Kvevlax/Koivulahti 20 A/B2
Kvicksund 46 B1
Kvig 8 B3
Kvikkjokk 15 D1
Kvikne 33 C2/3
Kvikne 37 D2
Kvilda 93 C1
Kvillsfors 51 C1
Kvimo 20 B2
Kvinen 42 B2
Kvinesdal 42 B3
Kvinlog 42 B3
Kvipt 43 C2
Kvissle 30 B3, 35 D2
Kvissleby 35 D3
Kvistbro 46 A1
Kvisvik 32 B2
Kvitberget 5 C2, 6 A1
Kviteseid 43 C2
Kviting 14 A2
Kvitingen 36 A3
Kvitnes 7 C1
Kvitsand 14 B3
Kvitsøy 42 A2
Kvittingen 42 B3
Kwidzyń (Marienwerder) 73 C2/3
Kwilcz 71 C2
Kyarnåsen 31 C1
Kybartai 73 D2
Kycklingvattnet 29 C/D2
Kyellmyra 38 B2
Kyjov 94 B1
Kyjov 96 B2
Kyläinpää 20 B2
Kylämä 25 D1, 26 A1
Kyläniemi 27 C1/2
Kylänlahti 23 C/D2
Kyläsaari 24 A1
Kyleakin 54 A2, 55 D1
Kyle of Lochalsh 54 A2, 55 D1
Kyllaj 47 D2
Kyllburg 79 D3
Kylmäkoski 25 C2
Kylmälä 18 B3
Kylmämäki 22 B3
Kylören 31 C3
Kymbo 45 D3
Kymentaka 25 D2, 26 B2
Kymönkoski 21 D2, 22 A2
Kyngäs 18 B2
Kynsiperä 19 C1
Kynsivaara 19 C1
Kynšperk nad Ohří 82 B3
Kypäräjärvi 23 C3
Kypärävaara 19 C/D3
Kypäsjärvi 17 C2
Kyritz 69 D2
Kyritz 72 A3
Kyrkås 29 D3, 34 B2
Kyrkesund 44 B3
Kyrkhult 51 C2
Kyrkjebø 36 A2
Kyrkjestølane 37 C2
Kyrksæterøra 32 B2
Kyrö 24 B2
Kyrönlahti 25 B/C1
Kyröskoski 24 B1
Kyrping 42 A1
Kyrsyä 27 C1
Kysucké Nové Mesto 95 D1
Kysucký Lieskovec 95 D1
Kytäjä 25 C2
Kytäkylä 18 A/B3, 21 D1, 22 A1
Kytömäki 19 C3
Kyyjärvi 21 D2
Kyynämöinen 21 D3, 22 A3
Kyynärö 25 C1, 26 A1
Kyynelniemi 7 C3

L

Laa an der Thaya 94 B2
Laaben 94 A2
La Adrada 160 A/B3
Laage 53 D3

La Aguilera 153 B/C3, 160 B1
Laaja 19 C2
Laajaranta 21 D2/3, 22 A2/3
Laajoki 24 B2
Laakamäki 22 B3
Laakirchen 93 C3
La Alameda 153 D3, 161 D1
La Alameda 167 C2
La Alameda de la Sagra 160 B3
La Alameda de Gardón 159 C2
La Alberca 159 D2
La Albergueria de Argañán 159 C2/3
La Albuera 165 C/D2
La Aldehuela 159 D2, 160 A2
La Algaba 171 D1
La Aliseda de Tormes 159 D3, 160 A2/3
La Almarcha 161 D3, 168 B1
La Almolda 155 B/C3, 162 B1
La Almunia de Doña Godina 155 C3, 163 C1
Laamala 27 C1
Laamala 27 C1
Laanila 12 B1
La Antilla 171 B/C2
Laasala 21 C2
Laatzen 68 B3
Laax [Valendas-Sagogn] 105 D1, 106 A1
La Baconnière 85 D2, 86 A2
Labajos 160 B2
La Balme-les-Grottes 103 D2
La Baña 151 C2/3
La Bañeza 151 D2
La Barca de la Florida 171 D2
Labarde 108 B1
La Barraque-Saint-Jean 110 A2
La Barre-de-Monts 100 A1
La Barre-en-Ouche 86 B1
La Barrosa 171 D3
La Barthe-de-Neste 109 C3, 155 C1
La Bassée 78 A2
Labastide-Beauvoir 109 D3, 155 D1
Labastide-Clairence 108 B3, 155 C1
La Bastide-des-Jourdans 111 D2
Labastide-d'Anjou 109 D3, 156 A1
La Bastide-de-Bousignac 109 D3, 156 A1
La Bastide-de-Sérou 109 D3, 155 D1
Labastide-Murat 109 D1
La Bastide-Puylaurent 110 B1
Labastide-Rouairoux 110 A3
Labastide-Saint-Pierre 108 B2
La Bastie 111 D2
Labata 155 B/C2/3
La Bâtie-Neuve 112 A1/2
Lábatlan 95 D3
La Baule 85 C3, 100 A1
La Baule-Escoublac 85 C3
Labayen 154 A1
La Bazoché-Gouët 86 B2
Łabędzie 71 C1
L'Abeele 78 A2
La Bégude-Blanche 112 A2
La Bégude-de-Mazenc 111 C1
Labejau 109 D2
La Belle Étoile 88 A2
Labenne 108 A3, 154 A1
La Bérarde 112 A1
Laberweinting 92 B2
Laberweinting-Hofkirchen 92 B2
L'Aber-Wrac'h 84 A2
Labin 130 A1

Labinot-Fushë **138** A3, **142** A1
La Bisbal d'Empordà **156** B2
La Bisbal de Falset **163** C1
Lablachère **111** C1/2
Lábod **128** A2
Laboe **52** B2/3
Labouheyre **108** A2
La Bouille **77** C3, **86** B1
La Bourboule **102** B3
Laboutarié **109** D2, **110** A2
La Bouteille **78** B3
La Bóveda de Toro **159** D1, **160** A1
Labrède **108** B1
La Bresse **89** D2, **90** A3
La Bretagne **77** C3, **86** B1
La Bretesche **85** C3
La Brillanne **111** D2, **112** A2
Labrit **108** B2
Labroye **77** D2
Labruguière **110** A3
L'Absie **100** B1/2
Laburgade **109** D2
Laç **137** D3
La Cabrera **161** C2
La Caillère **100** B1/2
La Caletta **123** C3
La Caletta **123** D1/2
Lacalm **110** A1
La Calmette **111** C2
La Calzada de Béjar **159** D2/3
La Calzada de Oropesa **160** A3, **166** B1
La Campana **172** A1
La Canal **169** D2
Lacanau **108** A1
Lacanau-Océan **108** B1
La Canourgue **110** B1/2
La Canya **156** B2
La Capelle **78** B3
Lacapelle-Marival **109** D1
Laćarak **133** C1
La Carlota **172** A1
La Carolina **167** D3
Lacarre **108** B3, **155** C1
Lacaune **110** A2
La Cava **163** C2
La Cavalerie **110** B2
Lacave **109** D1
La Caze **110** B2
Lacco Ameno **119** C3
Lacedónia **120** A2
La Celle **102** A3
La Celle-en-Morvan **103** C1
La Cellera de Ter **156** B2
La Celle-Saint-Avant **101** C1
La Cerca **153** C2
La Chaise-Dieu **103** C3
La Chaize-le-Vicomte **101** C1
La Chamba **103** C3
La Chambre **104** A3
Lachamp **101** D3, **102** A3
Lachanás **144** A1
Lachanás **148** B1
La Chapelaude **102** A/B2
La Chapelle-Gauthier **87** D2
La Chapelle-Saint Blaise **86** B3, **101** C1
La Chapelle-en-Serval **87** D1
La Chapelle-Glain **86** A/B3
La Chapelle-Laurent **102** B3
La Chapelle **79** C3
La Chapelle d'Angillon **87** D3
La Chapelle-la-Reine **87** D2
La Chapelle **85** C2/3
La Chapelle-en-Vercors **111** D1
La Chapelle-sur-Erde **85** D3, **100** A1
La Chapelle-en-Valgaudemard **112** A1
La Chapelle-Rainsouin **86** A2
La Chapelle-Saint-Laurent **100** B1

Lachapelle-sous-Rougemont **89** D3, **90** A3
Láchar **173** C2
La Charce **111** D1/2
La Charité-sur-Loire **87** D3, **102** B1
La Chartre-sur-le-Loir **86** B3
La Châtaigneraie **100** B1
La Châtre **102** A1/2
La Chaussée-sur-Marne **88** B1
La Cheminée **89** D3, **104** B1
Lachen **105** D1
Lachendorf **68** B2
La Cheppe **88** B1
La Chèze **85** C2
La Cierva **161** D3, **162** A3
La Ciotat **111** D3
Laćisled **134** B3
La Cité **110** A3, **156** A/B1
Läckeby **51** D2
Läckö **45** D2
La Clayette **103** C2
La Clusaz **104** A/B2/3
La Cluse-et-Mijoux **104** A/B1
Lacock **63** D2, **64** A3
La Codoñera **163** B/C2
La Codosera **165** C2
La Colle-Saint-Michel **112** A2
La Coma **155** D2/3, **156** A2
Lacona **116** A3
Láconi **123** D2
La Coquille **101** D3
La Coronada **166** A2
La Corte **165** D3, **171** C1
La Côte-Saint-André **103** D3
La Couarde **100** A/B2
La Coucourde **111** C1
La Couronne **111** C/D3
Lacourt **108** B3, **155** C1/2
La Courtine-le Trucq **102** A3
La Couvertoirade **110** B2
Lacq **108** B3, **154** B1
La Crèche **101** C2
La Croisière **101** C2
Lacroix-Bàrrez **110** A1
La Croix-Haute **111** D1
La Croixille **85** D2
La Croix-Laurent **85** D3
La Croix-Saint-Ouen **87** C1
La Crosetta **107** D2
Lacrouzette **110** A2/3
La Cumbre **165** D1, **166** A1
Lacunza **153** D2, **154** A1/2
La Cure **104** A2
Lad **128** A/B2
Ladánybene **129** C1
Ladapeyre **102** A2
Ladbergen **67** D3
Ladby **53** C1
Lâddejåkkstugan **9** C3
Ladelund **52** A/B2
Ladenburg **80** B3, **90** B1
Ladendorf **94** B2
Ladero **153** D2
Ladignac-le-Long **101** D3
Ladíspoli **118** A2
Ladne Vode **134** B2
Ladoeiro **158** B3, **165** C1
Ladon **87** D2
Ladoye-sur-Seille **104** A1
La Drée **103** C1
Laer **67** D3
Laerru **123** C1
La Espina **151** D1
La Estrella **160** A3, **166** B1
La Fajolle **156** A1
La Farga de Moles **155** D2
La Fatarella **163** C1/2
La Felguera **151** D1, **152** A1
La Felipa **168** B2
La Fère **78** A3
La Ferrière-sous-Jougne **104** A/B1
La Ferrière **101** C1
La Ferrière-sur-Risle **86** B1
La Ferrière-en-Parthenay **101** C1
La Ferté-Alais **87** D2
La Ferté-Bernard **86** B2

La Ferté-Beauharnais **87** C3
La Ferté-Fresnel **86** B1
La Ferté-Gaucher **88** A1
La Ferté-Imbault **87** C3
La Ferté-Macé **86** A2
La Ferté-Milon **87** D1, **88** A1
La Ferté-Saint-Aubin **87** C3
La Ferté-Saint-Cyr **87** C3
La Ferté-sous Jouarre **87** D1, **88** A1
La Ferté-Vidame **86** B2
La Feuillie **77** D3
Laffrey **111** D1, **112** A1
La Flèche **86** A3
La Florida **151** C/D1
Lafnitz **94** A3, **127** D1
La Fotelaie **76** A3, **85** D1
La Fouillade **109** D2
La Fourche **86** B2
Lafrançaise **108** B2
La Franqui **110** A/B3, **156** B1
La Fregeneda **159** C2
La Fresneda **163** C2
La Frette **103** D3
La Frontera **161** D2/3
La Frua **105** C2
La Fuliola **155** D3, **163** D1
La Gacilly **85** C3
La Galera del Pla **163** C2
Laganadi **122** A3, **125** D1/2
La Garde **110** B1
La Garde-Freinet **112** A3
Lagares **158** B2/3
Lagares **158** A2
La Garganta **159** D3
La Garnache **100** A1
Lagaro **114** B2, **116** B1
La Garonnette **112** A/B3
La Garriga **156** A3
La Garrovilla **165** D2
Lage **68** A3
La Gendretière **87** C3, **101** D1, **102** A1
Lageosa **158** B2
Lägerdorf **52** B3, **68** B1
Lagfors **35** D2
Laggars **20** B2
Laginá **143** D1/2, **144** A1/2
La Ginebrosa **163** B/C2
La Gineta **168** B2
Lagnieu **103** D2
Lagny-sur-Morin **87** D1
Lago **122** A2
Lagôa **170** A2
Lagôa **99** C1
Lagoaça **159** C1/2
Lagonegro **120** B3
Lagonísi **147** D2/3
Lagor **108** B3, **154** B1
Lagorce **111** C1/2
Lagos **170** A2
Lagosanto **115** C1
Łagów **71** C3
La Grafouillère **102** A3, **109** D1
Lagran **153** D2
La Granada **165** D3, **171** C1
La Granadella **163** C1
La Grand'Combe **111** B/C2
La Grand Croix **103** C3
La Grande Motte **111** C3
La Granja d'Escarp **163** C1
La Granjuela **166** B3
Lagrasse **110** A3, **156** B1
La Grave-en-Oisans **112** A1
La Gravelle **85** D2
La Groise **78** B3
Lägsta **30** B2, **35** D1
La Guarda **166** A2
La Guàrdia Lada **155** C3, **163** C1
La Guardia **161** C3, **167** D1
La Guardia de Jaén **173** C1
Laguarres **155** C2/3
Laguarta **155** C2
Laguenne **102** A3
Laguépie **109** D2
La Guerche-de-Bretagne **86** A2/3
Lagueruela **163** C2

Laguiole **110** A1
Laguna de Cameros **153** D3
Laguna de Duero **152** A/B3, **160** A1
Laguna del Marquesado **162** A3
Laguna de Negrillos **151** D2/3
Lagunarrota **155** C3
Lagunilla **159** D3
Lagunilla del Jubera **153** D2
La Haba **166** A2
La Haye-Descartes **101** C/D1
La Haye-du-Puits **76** A3, **85** D1
La Haye-Pesnel **86** A/B1
Lähdejänkkä **12** A3, **17** D2
Lähden **67** D3
Lahdenkylä **21** C3
Lahdenperä **21** C/D2
Lahenpää **17** C1
La Hermida **152** B1
La Herrera **167** D3, **168** A3
La Herrería **168** B2
Laheycourt **88** B1
La Higuera **169** D2
La Hiniesta **151** D3, **159** D1
La Hinojosa **161** D3, **168** A/B1
Lahn **67** D2
Lahnajärvi **17** C1
Lahnajärvi **25** C3
Lahnakoski **21** B/C1
Lahnalahti **22** B3
Lahnanen **21** D1, **22** A1
Lahnasjärvi **22** B1
Lahnasuando **17** C1
Lahntal **80** B2
Lahntal-Caldern **80** B2
Laholm **50** A2
Laholm **72** A1
Laholuoma **20** B3
La Horcajada **159** D2, **160** A2
La Horra **152** B3, **160** B1
La Houssoye **77** D3, **87** C1
Lahovaara **23** C2
La Hoz de la Vieja **162** B2
Lahr-Reichenbach **90** B2
Lahr/Schwarzwald **90** B2
Lahstedt **68** B3
Lähteenkylä **24** B2
Lahti **25** D2, **26** A2
Lahti **24** A2
Lahtiranta **18** A3
Lahtolahti **23** C2
La Huerce **161** C1/2
La Hulpe **78** B2
La Hutte **86** B2
Laichingen **91** C2
Laichingen-Feldstetten **91** C2
Laichingen-Machtolsheim **91** C2
L'Aigle **86** B1
La Iglesuela **160** A3
La Iglesuela del Cid **162** B2
Laignes **88** B3
Laiguéglia **113** C2
L'Aiguillon-sur-Mer **101** C2
Laihia **20** B2
Laikko **27** D1
Laimbach am Ostrong **93** D2
Laimoluokta **10** A2
Lainate **105** D3
Lainio **10** B3
Lairg **54** A/B1/2
La Iruela **167** D3, **168** A3, **173** C/D1
Laisbäck **15** D3
La Isla **152** A1
La Isleta de Escullos **174** A2
Laissac **110** A2
Laisstugan **15** C2
Laïsta **142** B2/3
Laisvall **15** D2
Laisvallsby **15** D2
Laiterla **24** B3
Laitiala **25** D2, **26** A2
Laitikkala **25** C1/2
Laitila **24** A2
Laivajärvi **17** D2, **18** A1

Laives **103** D1
Láives/Leifers **107** C2
La Jana **163** C2
La Javie **112** A2
Lajkovac **133** D2, **134** A2
Lajksjö **30** A2
La Jonchère-Saint-Maurice **101** D2
La Joncosa **163** C1
La Jonquera **156** B2
Lajosmizse **129** C1
Lakaluoma **21** B/C2
Lakaniemi **21** C2
Lakasjö **30** B2, **35** D1
Lakatnik **139** D1
Lakaträsk **16** B2
Lakavica **139** C3
Łąkie **71** D1
Lákion **149** D2/3
Lákka **142** A3
Lakkópetra **146** A/B2
Lakócsa **128** B3
Lakolk **52** A1/2
Lakomäki **21** D2, **22** A2
Laksåvik **32** B1
Lakselv **5** D2, **6** A2
Lakshola **9** C3
Laktaši **131** D1, **132** A1
La Lantejuela **172** A2
La Lapa **165** D2/3
Lálas **146** B3
L'Albagés **155** C3, **163** C1
L'Albenc **103** D3
Lalbenque **109** D2
La Léchère **105** C2/3
Lalić **129** C3
La Lima **114** B2, **116** A1
Lalín **150** B2
Lalinci **133** D2, **134** A2
Lalinde **109** C1
La Línea de la Concepcion **172** A3
La Llacuna **155** D3, **156** A3, **163** C1
Lalley **111** D1
Lalling **93** C1/2
Lalm **37** D1
La Lóggia **113** B/C1
La Losilla **153** D3
La Loupe **86** B2
Lalouvesc **103** C3, **111** C1
La Louviére **78** B2
L'Alpe-d'Huez **112** A1
Laluenga **155** C3
Lalueza **154** B3, **162** B1
La Luisiana **172** A1
Laluque **108** A2
Lam **93** B/C1
Lama **150** A3, **158** A1
La Machine **102** B1
La Maddalena **123** D1
Lama dei Peligni **119** C2
Lamagistère **109** C2
Lamaids **102** A2
La Maielletta **119** C1
La Mailleraye-sur-Seine **77** C3
La Malène **110** B2
Lamalou-les-Bains **110** A/B3
Lama Mocogno **114** B2, **116** A1
Lamanère **156** B2
Lamanon **111** D2
Lamarche **89** C2
La Marina **169** C3
Lamarosa **164** B2
Lamarque **100** B3, **108** B1
La Martella **120** B2
Lamas de Mouro **150** B3
Lamas d'Olo **158** B1
Lamastre **111** C1
La Mata **160** B3, **167** C1
La Mata **169** C3, **174** B1
La Mata de los Olmos **162** B2
La Mata de Monteagudo **152** A2
La Mata de Morella **162** B2
La Matilla **160** B1/2
La Maurarrière **101** C1
Lambach **93** C2/3
Lamballe **85** C2
Lambesc **111** D2/3
Lámbia **146** B3
Lámbia **148** B2
Lamborn **39** D2, **40** A2

Lambourn 64 A3
Lambrecht 90 B1
Lamegal 159 C2
Lamego 158 B2
La Membrolle-sur-Choisille 86 B3
L'Ametlla de Mar 163 C/D2
L'Ametlla de Montsec 155 C/D3
Lamézia Terme 122 A/B2
Lamía 147 C1
La Mierla 161 C2
La Mine 76 A/B3, 85 D1, 86 A1
Lamington 57 C2
Lamland 41 C/D3
Lamlash 56 A2
Lammasaho 22 B2
Lammasperä 21 C3
Lammhult 51 C1
Lammhult 72 A1
Lammi 21 C2
Lammi 25 C/D2, 26 A2
Lamminmäki 22 B3
Lamminperä 18 B1/2
Lammu 23 C3
La Molina 164 C2
La Mongie 109 B/C3, 155 C2
La Monnerie-le-Montel 103 B/C2
La Morera 165 D2
La Morte 111 D1, 112 A1
Lamorteau 79 C3
La Mothe 110 B1/2
La Mothe-Achard 100 A1/2
Lamothe-Cassel 109 D1
La Mothe-Saint-Héraye 101 C2
Lamotte-Beuvron 87 C3
La Motte-Chalancon 111 D1
La Motte-du-Caire 112 A2
Lampaanjärvi 22 B2
Lampaluoto 24 A1, 41 D1
Lampaul 84 A2
Lampeland 43 D1
Lamperila 22 B2
Lampertheim 80 B3
Lampeter 63 C1
Lampinsaari 18 A3
Lampiselkä 12 B2
L'Ampolla 163 C2
Lamposaari 27 C2
Lamppi 24 A1
Lamprechtshausen-Kirchendorf 92 B3
Lämsänkylä 19 D1
Lamsfeld 70 B3
Lamspringe 68 B3
Lamstedt 52 A/B3, 68 A1
Lamstedt-Grossenhain 68 A1
Lamu 18 B3, 21 D1, 22 A1
La Muda 107 C/D2
La Mudarra 152 A3, 160 A1
La Muela 154 A/B3, 162 A1
La Mure 111 D1, 112 A1
Lamure-sur-Azergues 103 C2
La Musara 163 D1
Lana 107 C2
Lanabukt 7 D2
Lanaja 154 B3, 162 B1
Lanarce 111 B/C1
Lanark 57 B/C2
La Nava 165 D3, 171 C1
La Nava de Ricomalillo 160 A3, 166 B1
La Nava de Santiago 165 D2
Láncara 151 C2
Lancaster 59 D1, 60 B2
Lancaster 54 B3
Lanchester 57 D3, 61 C1
Lanciano 119 D1
Lancin 103 D3
Landåsen 37 D3, 38 A2
Landau 92 B2
Landau in der Pfalz 90 B1
Landcross 62 B2
Landeck 106 B1
Landedo 151 C3
Landensberg 91 D2

Landerneau 84 A2
Landersfjorden 6 B1
Landeryd 50 B1
Landesbergen 68 A2
Landete 163 C3, 169 D1
Landévant 84 B3
Landin 69 D2
Landivisiau 84 A/B2
Landivy 85 D2
Landkirchen 53 C2
Landl 92 B3
Landön 29 D3, 34 B1
Landrecies 78 B2/3
Landres 89 C1
Landriano 105 D3, 106 A3
Landsberg 82 B1
Landsberg am Lech 91 D2/3
Landsbro 51 C1
Landshut 92 B2
Landskrona 49 D3, 50 A3
Landskrona 72 A1/2
Landstuhl 90 A1
Landvetter 45 C3, 49 D1
Lanestosa 153 C1
La Neuville 78 A2
Laneuville-sur-Meuse 79 C3
Langa 160 A2
Långå 34 A3
Långå 48 B2
Langådás 144 A1/2
Langa de Duero 153 C3, 161 C1
Langa del Castillo 163 C1
Langádia 146 B3
Langadíkia 144 A2
Långåminne 20 A2
Langangen 43 D2, 44 A1/2
Långared 45 C3
Långaröd 50 B3
Långås 49 D1/2, 50 A1
Långasjö 51 C2
Langau 94 A1/2
Langayo 152 B3, 160 B1
Långbäcken 30 B1/2
Langballig 52 B2
Långban 39 C3
Långbergsöda 41 D2/3
Långbo 39 D1, 40 A1
Langdorf 93 C1
Langeac 102 B3, 110 B1
Langeais 86 B3
Langebæk 53 D2
Langedijk 66 A/B2
Långedrag 45 C3, 49 D1
Längelmäki 25 C1
Langelsheim 68 B3
Langen 80 B3
Langen 52 A3, 68 A1
Langen 106 B1
Langen 33 D3
Langenaltheim 91 D1/2, 92 A1/2
Langenargen 91 C3
Langenau 91 D2
Langenbach (Freising) 92 A2
Langenberg 68 A3
Langenburg 91 C1
Langeneichstädt 82 A1
Langenenslingen 91 C2
Langenes 8 B1
Langenfeld 80 A2
Langenfeld 80 A1
Langenfeld (Scheinfeld) 81 D2
Längenfeld 106 B1
Langenhagen 68 B2
Langenhahn 80 B2
Langenhorn 52 A2
Langenlois 94 A2
Langenmosen 92 A2
Langen-Neuenwalde 52 A3, 68 A1
Langenneufnach 91 D2
Langenselbold 81 C2/3
Langenthal 105 C1
Langenwang 94 A3
Langenwetzendorf 82 B2
Langenzenn 81 D3, 91 D1
Langeoog 67 D1
Langernyw 59 C2, 60 A3
Langerwehe 79 D2
Langesi 36 A1
Langeskov 53 C1

Langesø 53 B/C1
Langesund 43 D2, 44 A2
Langevåg 36 B1
Langevåg 42 A1
Langewahl 70 B3
Langewiesen 81 D2, 82 A2
Langfjell 14 B2
Langfjord 5 C2
Langfjordbotn 7 C2
Långflon 38 B2
Långforsselet 17 C2
Langhamn 9 D1
Långhed 40 A1
Langhirano 114 A1
Langholm 57 C3
Langholm 54 B3
Langhuso 36 B3
Länglingen 30 A2, 35 C1
Långlöt 51 D2
Långnäs 40 A2
Långnäs 41 D3
Langnes 9 D1
Langø 53 C2
Langogne 110 B1
Langon 108 B1
Langør 49 C3
Langport 63 D2
Languaid 92 B2
Langraiz 153 C/D2
Langreo 151 D1
Langres 89 C3
Långron 31 C3
Langrune-sur-Mer 76 B3, 86 A1
Långsådalen 29 C3, 34 A1
Långsåvoll 28 B3, 33 D1
Langschlag 93 D2
Långsel 17 C2
Långsel 17 C2
Långsele 30 A1
Långsele 31 C/D1
Långsele 30 B3, 35 D1
Långsele 30 A3, 35 D1
Långsele 30 A/B3, 35 D2
Långserud 45 C3
Långset 14 A/B2
Långshyttan 40 A2
Långsjön 16 B2
Långsjön 47 D1
Långskog 35 D3
Langstrand 5 C1
Långträsk 16 B3
Långträsk 31 C1
Långträsk 17 B/C3
Långträsk 17 D2
Långudden 15 D2
Languidic 84 B3
Languilla 161 C1
Langula 81 D1
Langvatn 14 B3
Långvattnet 15 D3
Långvattnet 30 B2, 35 D1
Långvattnet 31 C1
Langvattnet 31 C2
Långvik 25 C3
Långviksmon 31 C2
Långvinds bruk 40 B1
Langwedel 68 A2
Langwedel-Etelsen 68 A2
Langweid 91 D2
Langwies 106 A1
Lanhezes 150 A3, 158 A1
Lanildut 84 A2
Lanivet 62 B3
Lanjarón 173 C2
Lånke 28 A/B3, 33 C/D1
Länkipohja 25 C1, 26 A1
Lanklaar 79 C/D1
Lankojärvi 12 A3, 17 D1
Lankoori 24 A1
Lanmeur 84 B1/2
Länna 47 C1
Länna 46 A1
Lännahom 40 B3
Lannavaara 10 B3
Lannéanou 84 B2
Lannemezan 109 C3, 155 C1
Lannevesi 21 D3, 22 A3
Lannilis 84 A2
Lannion 84 B1
La Nocle-Maulaix 103 C1
Lanouaille 101 C3
Lansån 17 C2
Länsi-Aure 21 B/C3
Länsikoski 19 D1
Länsikoski 17 D2, 18 A1

Länsikylä 21 C2
Länsi-Teisko 25 C1
Länsi-Vuokko 23 C2
Lansjärv 17 C1
Lanslebourg-Mont-Cenis 104 B3
Lanslevillard 104 B3
Lanta 109 D3, 155 D1
Lantadilla 152 B2
Lantto 19 D3
Lanuéjols 110 B2
La Nuncia 169 D2
Lanusei 123 D2
Lanvéoc 84 A2
Lanvollon 85 B/C1/2
Lány 83 C3
Lanz 69 C2
Lanz 108 A3, 154 A1
Lanza 150 B1/2
Lanzahita 160 A3
Lanžhot 94 B2
Lanzo d'Intelvi 105 D2, 106 A2
Lanzo Torinese 105 C3
Laon 78 B3
Laons 86 A/B1/2
La Paca 168 B3, 174 A1
La Pacaudière 103 C2
Lapad 137 C1
Lápafö 128 B2
Lapajärvi 13 C3
Lapalisse 103 C2
La Pallice 101 C2
Lapalluoto 18 A3
La Palma del Condado 171 C1/2
La Palud-sur-Verdon 112 A2/3
Lapani 142 B2
La Parra 165 D2
La Parra de las Vegas 161 D3, 168 B1
La Parrilla 152 B3, 160 B1
Lápas 146 A/B2
La Patte-d'Oie 87 C/D1
La Pedraja de Portillo 160 A/B1
La Pedriza 173 B/C1/2
La Peraleja 161 D3
Laperdiguera 155 C3
La Pernelle 76 B3
La Péruse 101 C2
La Pesquera 168 B1
La Petite-Pierre 89 D1, 90 A1/2
La Petrízia 122 B2
Lapeyrade 108 B2
Lapeyrouse 103 D2
Lapeza 173 C2
Lapford 63 C2
Lapinhelvetti 11 C3
La Pinilla 161 C1
Lapinjärvi/Lappträsk 25 D2, 26 B2
Lapinjärvi 21 D2, 22 A2
Lapinjoki 24 A1/2
Lapinkylä 25 C3
Lapinlahti 22 B2
Lapinneva 20 B3
La Plagne 104 B3
La Plama 174 B1
La Plama d'Ebre 163 C1
La Platja d'Aro 156 B2/3
La Plaza 173 D1
Laplje Selo 138 B1/2
Laplume 109 C2
Lapoblación 153 D2
La Pobla de Cérvoles 163 D1
La Pobla de Lillet 156 A2
La Pobla de Massaluca 163 C1/2
La Pobleta de Bellveí 155 D2
La Pola de Gordón 151 D2, 152 A2
La Portella 155 C3, 163 C1
La Portellada 163 C2
Lapoutroie 89 D2, 90 A2
La Póveda de Soria 153 D3
Lapovo 134 B2
Lappago/Lappach 107 C1
Lappajärvi 21 C2
Lappalaisten kesätuvat 11 C2

Läppe 46 B1
Lappea 17 D1
Lappeenranta (Villmanstrand) 27 C2
Lappers 25 C3
Lappersdorf 92 B1
Lappersdorf-Hainsacker 92 B1
Lappfjärd/Lappväärtti 20 A3
Lappfors 20 B1/2
Lapphaugen 9 D2
Lappi 24 A2
Lappi 19 D2
Lappila 25 D2, 26 A2
Lappo 20 B2
Lappo 24 A3, 41 D2
Lappohja/Lappvik 24 B3
Lappoluobbal 5 C3, 11 C1
Lapporten 9 D2, 10 A2
Lappträsk 16 A3
Lappvattnet 31 D1
Laprade 110 A3
Lapradelle 156 A1
La Preste 156 A/B2
La Primaube 110 A2
Laprugne 103 C2
Låpseki 149 D1
Lapua (Lappo) 20 B2
La Puebla 157 C2
La Puebla de los Infantes 166 B3, 172 A1
La Puebla de Montalbán 160 B3, 167 C1
La Puebla de Valdavia 152 B2
La Puebla de Híjar 162 B1
La Puebla de Fantova 155 C2
La Puebla de Roda 154 B2
La Puebla de Cazalla 171 D2
La Puebla de Almoradiel 167 D1, 168 A1
La Puebla de Valverde 162 B3
La Puebla del Río 171 D2
La Puerta 161 D2
La Puerta de Segura 168 A3
La Punta 113 D3
La Punta 123 C3
Lăpuşna 141 C1
Lăpuşnicel 135 C1
La Puye 101 D1
Lapväärtti 20 A3
Łapy 73 D3, 98 A1
Laqueuille 102 B3
L'Áquila 117 D3, 119 C1
La Rábita 173 C2
Laracha 150 A1
Laragh 58 A2
Laragne-Montéglin 111 D2, 112 A2
La Rambla 172 B1
Larbert 56 B1/2
L'Arboç 166 A3, 163 D1
L'Arbresle 103 C/D2/3
Lärbro 47 D2
Lärbro 73 B/C1
Larceveau-Arros-Cibits 108 A3, 154 B1
Larchant 87 C2
Larche 101 D3, 109 D1
Larche 112 B2
Lårdal 43 C2
Lærdalsøyri 37 B/C2
Lardaro 106 B2
Larderello 114 B3, 116 A2
Lardero 153 D2
Lárdos 149 D3
Lardosa 158 B3
La Reale 123 C1
Laredo 153 C1
Laredorte 87 C1
Laredorte 110 A3, 156 B1
La Regeserie 86 A3
Laren 67 C3
Laren 66 B3
La Réole 108 B1
Largentière 111 C1
Largs 56 B2
La Riaille 112 B1
Lariano 118 B2
La Riba 163 C1
La Riba de Escalote 161 C1
La Riera de Gaià 163 C1/2
Lárimna 147 C/D1/2

La Rinconada 171 D1
Larino 119 D2, 120 A1
Lárisa 143 D3
Lárisa 148 B1
La Rixouse 104 A2
Larkhall 56 B2
Larkollen 44 B1
L'Armentera 156 B2
Larmor-Plage 84 B3
Larne 56 A3
Larne 54 A3, 55 D2
La Robla 151 D2, 152 A2
La Roca de la Sierra 165 D2
La Roche-aux-Fées
86 A/B2/3
La Rochebeaucourt-et-Ar-
gentine 101 C3
La Roche-Bernard 85 C3
La Roche-Chalais 101 C3
La Rochecourbon
100 B2/3
La Roche-Derrien 84 B1
La Roche-des-Arnauds
111 D1, 112 A1/2
La Roche-en-Brénil
88 A/B3
La Roche-en-Ardenne
79 C2/3
La Rochefoucauld 101 C3
La Roche-Jagu 84 B1
La Rochelle 101 C2
La Roche-Posay 101 D1
La Rochepot 103 C/D1
La Rocherolle 101 D1,
102 A1
La Roche-sur-Yon
100 A/B1
La Roche-sur-Foron
104 A2
La Rochette 104 A3
Larochette 79 D3
La Roche-Vineuse 103 D2
La Roda 168 B2
La Roda 151 C1
La Roda de Andalucía
172 A/B2
La Roë 85 D2
Laroles 173 C/D2
La Romana 169 C3
La Romieu 109 C2
Laroquebrou 109 D1,
110 A1
Laroque-d'Olmes 109 D3,
156 A1
La Roque-Sainte-Margu-
erite 110 B2
Laroque-Timbaut 109 C2
Larouco 151 C2
Larraga 154 A2
Larraona 153 D2
Larrasoaña 108 A3, 154 A2
Larrate 153 C2
Larrau 108 A3, 154 B1
Larrazet 109 C2
Larrêt 89 C3
Larseng 4 A3
Larsmo/Luoto 20 B1
Larsnes 36 A1
Larumbe 154 A1/2
Laruns 108 B3, 154 B1/2
Larv 45 C/D3
Larva 167 D3, 168 A3,
173 C1
Larvik 43 D2, 44 A1/2
Larvik 42 A2
Lärz 69 D1, 70 A1
La Sabina 157 D3
La Sagrada 159 D2
La Sainte-Baume 111 D3
Lasalle 110 B2
La Salvetat-sur-Agout
110 A3
La Salvetat-Peyralès
110 A2
Läsänkoski 26 B1
Las Arenas 152 A/B1
Lasarte 153 D1, 154 A1
La Saulce 111 D1/2,
112 A2
La Sauve-Majeure 108 B1
Las Bordas 155 C2
Låsby 48 B3
Las Cabezadas 161 C2
Las Cabezas de San Juan
171 D2
Las Caldas 151 D1
Las Casas 154 B3

Lascaux (fermées) 108 B1
Lascellas 155 C3
Lascelle 110 A1
Lascuarre 155 C2/3
Las Cuerlas 162 A2
Las Cuevas de Cañart
162 B2
La Seca 160 A1
Lasel 79 D3
La Selle-sur-le-Bied 87 D2
La Selva 119 C2
La Selva 163 C1
La Sénia 163 C2
La Sentiu de Suó 155 D3,
163 C/D1
La Serre 102 A3
La Seu d'Urgell 155 D2
La Seyne-sur-Mer 111 D3,
112 A3
Las Fraguas 153 D3,
161 C/D1
Lasgraisses 109 D2
Las Herencias 160 A3,
166 B1
Las Illas 156 B2
Lasinja 127 D3
Łasko 71 C2
Laško 127 C2
Las Labores 167 D1/2
Las Machorras 110 B3
Las Majadas 161 D3
Las Mesas 168 A1
Las Navas del Marqués
160 B2
Las Navas de la Concepción
166 A/B3, 172 A1
Las Negras 174 A2
La Solana 167 D2, 168 A2
La Source 87 C3
La Souterraine 101 D2
Lasovo 135 C3
Las Parras de Castellote
162 B2
Laspaúles 155 C2
Las Pedroñeras 168 A1
Las Pedrosas 154 B3
Las Peralosas 167 C2
La Spézia 114 A2
Las Presas 156 B2
Las Rotas 169 D2
Las Rozas 152 B2
Las Rozas de Madrid
160 B2
Lassahn 69 C1
Lassay 86 A2
Lassee 94 B2
Lassekrog 35 C3
Lasseube 108 B3, 154 B1
Lassigny 78 A3
Lassila 24 B1
Lassing 93 D3
Lassnitz 126 B1
Lasswade 57 C2
Lastanosa 155 C3,
163 B/C1
Lastebasse 107 C2/3
Lastic 102 A/B3
Las Torcas 161 D3
Lastours 110 A3, 156 A/B1
Lastovo 136 A1
Lastra a Signa 114 B2,
116 B1/2
Lastras de Cuéllar 160 B1
Lastres 152 A1
Lästringe 47 C2
Lastrup 67 D2
Lastukoski 23 C2
Lastva 137 C1
La Suze-sur-Sarthe
86 A/B2/3
Las Veguillas 159 D2
Las Ventas 153 C2
Las Ventas con Peña Agui-
lera 167 C1
Las Ventas de San Julián
160 A3
Las Ventas de Retamosa
160 B3
Las Vertientes 173 D1
Las Vilás de Tubó 155 C2
Las Villas de Benicasim
163 C3
La Tala 159 D2
La Talaudière 103 C3
La Terrasse-sur-Dorlay
103 C/D3
Laterza 121 C2

La Teste 103 C/D3
La Teste 108 B1
Lathen 67 D2
Latheron 54 B1
La Thuile 104 B3
Lathus 101 D2
Latiana 121 D2/3
Latikberg 30 B1
Latillé 101 C1/2
Latina 118 B2
Latisana 107 D3, 126 A3
La Toba 161 C2
Latorps-bruk 46 A1
La Torre 160 A2
La Torre de Esteban Ham-
brán 160 B3
La Torre de Cabdella
155 D2
La Torre de l'Espanyol
163 C1/2
La Torresaviñan 161 D2
La Tour-Blanche 101 C3
La Tour-d'Aigues 111 D2
La Tour-d'Auvergne
102 B3
Latour-de-France 156 B1
La Tour-du-Pin 103 D3,
104 A3
Latovaino 25 B/C2
La Tranche-sur-Mer
100 A/B2
La Tremblade 101 C3
Latresne 108 B1
La Trimouille 101 D2
La Trinité-sur-Mer 85 B/C3
La Trinité-Porhoët 85 C2
La Trinité 63 D3, 85 C1
La Trique 100 B1
Latrónico 120 B3, 122 A1
Latronquière 109 D1,
110 A1
Latschau 106 A1
Latterbach [Oey-Diemti-
gen] 105 C2
Lattuna 13 C2
La Tuca 155 C/D2
La Turballe 85 C3
Latva 18 A/B3
Latva 19 B/C2
Latvaset 21 D1, 22 A1
Lau 47 D3
Laubach 80 A3
Laubach 81 C2
Laubrières 85 D2
Laubsdorf 70 B3, 83 D1
Laucha 82 A1
Lauchhammer 83 C1
Lauchhammer 96 A1
Lauda-Königshofen 81 C3,
91 C1
Laudal 42 B3
Lauder 57 C2
Laudio 153 C1
Lauenbrück 68 B1/2
Lauenburg 69 C1
Lauenen [Gstaad] 104 B2
Lauf 82 A3, 92 A1
Laufach 81 C2
Laufen 90 A3
Laufen 92 B3
Laufenburg 90 B3
Laufenburg 90 B3
Lauffen am Neckar 91 C1
Laugerie 109 C1
Laugharne 62 B1
Laugnac 109 C2
Lauhankylä 24 B1/2
Lauhovd 43 C1
Lauingen 91 D2
Laujar de Andarax 173 D2
Laukaa 21 D3, 22 A3
Laukansalo 23 C3
Lauker 16 A/B3
Laukka 18 B2/3
Laukka-aho 23 C2
Laukkala 22 A/B2
Laukuluspa 10 A3
Laukvik 8 B3
Laukvik 4 A2
Laukvik 8 B2
Laukvik 5 C2
La Umbría 165 D3, 171 C1
Launceston 62 B3
La Unión 174 B1
La Unión de Campos
152 A3
Launois 78 B3

Launonen 25 C2
Laupen 104 B1
Laupheim 91 C2
Laurbjerg 48 B2
Laureana di Borrello
122 A3
Laurenburg 80 B2
Laurenzana 120 B3
Lauria 120 B3, 122 A1
Laurière 101 D2
Laurino 120 A3
Lauris-sur-Durance 111 D2
Laurito 120 A3
Lauritsala 27 C2
Lausanne 104 B2
Lauscha 82 A2
Laussonne 111 B/C1
Lauta 83 C1
Lautamaa 17 D2, 18 A1
Lautaporras 25 C2
Lautela 25 B/C2
Lautenbach 89 D2, 90 A3
Lautenbach 90 B2
Lauter 47 D2
Lauter 82 B2
Lauterbach 81 C2
Lauterbourg 90 B1
Lauterbrunnen 105 C2
Lauterecken 80 A3
Lauterhofen 92 A1
Lauterhofen-Traunfeld
92 A1
Lauterstein 91 C2
Lautertal 81 D2, 82 A2
Lautertal 81 C2
Lautertal-Gadernheim
81 B/C3
Lautiosaari 17 D3, 18 A1
Lautrec 109 D2, 110 A2
Lauttakulma 25 C1
Lauttavaara 19 C2
Lauvareid 42 A1
Lauvåsen 37 D2
Lauvåsen 37 D2
Lauve 43 D2, 44 A1/2
Lauvnes 42 B3
Lauvøy 28 A2, 33 C1
Lauvsjøla 29 C2
Lauvsnes 28 B2
Lauvstad 36 A/B1
Lauvuskylä 23 C1
Lauzerte 108 B2
Lauzun 109 C1
La Vachey 104 B3
Lavagna 113 C2
La Vaivre-de-Seveux 89 C3
Laval 86 A2
Lavala 19 C2
Laval-Atger 110 B1
Lavamünd 127 C2
Lavamünd 96 A3
Lavangen 9 D2
La Vansa 155 D2
Lávara 145 D1, 145 D3
Lavardac 109 C2
Lavardin 86 B3
Lavau 87 D3
Lavaur 109 D2
Lavaveix-les-Mines 102 A2
La Vecilla 152 A2
La Vega 152 B3
Lavelanet 109 D3, 156 A1
La Vellés 159 D2
Lavello 120 B2
Laven 48 B3
Lavena-Ponte Tresa
105 C2
Lavenham 65 C2
Laveno-Mombello
105 D2/3
La Ventosa 161 D3
La Veredilla 167 C2
Lavergne 108 B1
La Verna 115 C2/3, 116 B2
Lavezzola 115 C1
Lavia 24 B1
Laviana 151 D1, 152 A1
Laviano 120 A2
La Victoria 172 A/B1
La Vid 153 C3, 161 C1
Lavid de Ojeda 152 B2
La Vídola 159 C1/2
La Vieille-Lyre 86 B1
Lavik 36 A/B3
Lavik 36 A2
Lavik 9 D1
La Vilella Baixa 163 C1

La Villa 116 A3
La Villa 107 C2
La Villa de Don Fadrique
167 D1, 168 A1
La Villa/Stern 107 C2
La Villedieu-en-Fontenette
89 C3
La Villedieu 101 C2
La Villedieu 102 A3
La Villedieu-du-Clain
101 C2
La Villetelle 102 A2
Lavínio Lido di Enea
118 B2
Lavis 107 C2
La Visaille 104 B3
Lavit 109 C2
Låvong 14 A/B2
Lavos 158 A3
La Voulte-sur-Rhône
111 C1
Lavoûte-Chilhac 102 B3
Lavra 159 C1
Lavre 164 B2
Lávrion 147 D3
Lávrion 149 B/C2
Lavry 74 B2
Lavsjö 30 A2
La Wantzenau 90 A/B2
Ławy 71 B/C2
Laxå 46 A1/2
Laxbäcken 30 A1
Laxe 150 A1
Laxede 16 B2
Laxenburg 94 B2/3
Laxey 58 B2
Laxo 54 A1
Laxsjö 29 D3, 34 B1
Laxsjön 35 D2
Laxtjärn 39 C3
Laxton 61 C3, 64 B1
Laxvik 49 D2, 50 A2
Laxviken 29 D3, 34 B1
Layana 155 C2
La Yesa 162 B3, 169 C1
Läyliäinen 25 C2
Layna 161 D2
Layos 160 B3, 167 C1
Layrac 109 C2
Laytown 58 A2
La Yunta 162 A2
Laz 84 B2
Laza 150 B3
La Zaida 162 B1
Lazarádes 143 C2
Lazarevac 133 D2, 134 A2
Lazarevo 129 D3, 134 A1
Lazaropole 138 A/B3
La Zarza de Pumareda
159 C1/2
La Zenia 169 C3, 174 B1
Lazici 133 C2/3
Lazise 106 B3
Lazkao 153 D1/2
Lázně-Kynžvart 82 B3
Laznica 135 C2
Lazonby 57 C3, 60 B1
Lazzaro 122 A3, 125 D2
Leadenham 61 D3, 64 B1
Leadhills 57 B/C2
Leányvár 95 D3
Leatherhead 64 B3, 76 B1
Łeba 72 B2
Lebach 89 D1, 90 A1
Lebane 139 C1
Le Barcarès 156 B1
Le Barp 108 B1
Lebbeke 78 B1
Le Béage 111 C1
Le Beausset 111 D3,
112 A3
Le Bec-Hellouin 77 C3,
86 B1
Lebeña 152 B1
Lébénymiklós 95 C3
Lebesby 6 B1
Le Bettex 104 B3
Le Biot 86 A1/2
Le Biot 104 B2
Le Blanc 101 C1
Le Bleymard 110 B1/2
Le Bois 104 B3
Le Boisle 108 B2
Le Bonhomme 89 D2,
90 A2
Le Boréon 112 B2

Lębork (Lauenburg) **72** B2
Le Boulou **156** B2
Le Bourg **109** D1
Le Bourg-d'Oisans **112** A1
Le Bourget **87** D1
Le Bourget-du-Lac **104** A3
Le Bourgneuf-la-Forêt **85** D2, **86** A2
Le Bourg-Saint-Léonard **86** B1
Le Breuil **103** C2
Lebrija **171** D2
Le Brugeron **103** C3
Le Bugue **109** C1
Le Buisson **110** B1
Le Buisson-Cussac **109** C1
Lebus **70** B2/3
Le Busseau **100** B1/2
Leca da Palmeira **158** A1
Le Canadel-sur-Mer **112** A3
Le Castella **122** B2
Le Cateau **78** B3
Le Catelet **78** A3
Le Caylar **110** B2
Lecce **121** D3
Lecco **105** D3, **106** A2/3
Lece **138** B1
Lécera **162** B1
Lech **106** B1
Lechago **163** C2
L'Échalp **112** B1
Le Chambon-Feugerolles **103** C3
Le Chambon-sur-Lignon **103** C3, **111** C1
Le Champ-Saint-Père **101** C2
Le Château-d'Oléron **101** C2
Le Châtelard **104** A3
Le Châtelet-en-Brie **87** D2
Le Châtelet-en-Berry **102** A1
Le Châtellier **86** A1/2
Lechbruck **91** D3
Lechená **146** A2
Le Cheylard **111** C1
Le Chiâviche **114** B1
Lechlade **64** A3
Lechovice **94** B1/2
Leči **73** C1
Leciñena **154** B3, **162** B1
Leck **52** A/B2
Le Collet-de-Dèze **110** B2
Le Colombier **111** C1
Le Conquet **84** A2
Le Creusot **103** C1
Le Croisic **85** C3
Le Crotoy **77** D2
Lectoure **109** C2
Lecumberri **153** D1/2, **154** A1
Lecumberry **108** B3, **155** C1
Łęczyca **71** C1
Łęczyca **73** C3, **97** B/C1
Ledaña **168** B1
Ledanca **161** C2
Ledbury **63** D1, **64** A2
Ledeč nad Sázavou **83** D3
Ledenika **135** D3, **139** D1
Lederzeele **77** D1
Le Désert **112** A1
Ledesma **159** D2
Ledesma de Soria **153** D3, **161** D1
Ledeuix **108** B3, **154** B1
Lédignan **111** C2
Leding **31** B/C3
Lednice **94** B2
Lednické Rovne **95** C1
Le Donjon **103** C2
Le Dorat **101** D2
Lędyczek **71** D1
Lee **48** B2
Leeds **61** C2
Leeds **54** B3
Leegebruch **70** A2
Leek **59** D2, **61** B/C3, **64** A1
Leek **67** C1/2
Leenane **55** C2
Leende **79** C1
Leer **67** D1
Leerbeek **78** B2
Leerdam **66** B3

Leer-Loga **67** D1
Leese **68** A2
Leeuwarden **66** B1
Leezen **52** B3, **68** B1
Le Faou **84** A2
Le Faouët **84** B2
Le Ferriere **118** B2
Lefinnlia **32** B3, **37** C1
Lefka **145** D2
Lefkadítion **146** B1
Lefkás **146** A1
Lefkás **148** A2
Lefkímmi **148** A1
Lefkímmi **142** A3
Lefkón **139** D3, **144** A1
Léfktra **146** B3
Léfktrá **147** C2
Léfktra **148** A/B2
Le Fleix **109** C1
Le Folgoët **84** A2
Le Fond-de-France **104** A3
Le Fossat **109** D3, **155** D1
Le Fousseret **109** C3, **155** D1
Le Fromental **110** B1
Leganes **160** B2/3
Leganiel **161** C3
Legarda **153** D2
Legarda **154** A2
Legau **91** D3
Le Gault-Perche **86** B2
Legazpi **153** D1/2
Legden **67** C3
Légé **100** A1
Legionowo **73** C3
Legnago **107** C3
Legnano **105** D3
Legnica (Liegnitz) **96** B1
Légny **103** C/D2
Legoland **48** B3, **52** B1
Legorreta **153** D1
Legrad **128** A2
Le Grand-Bourg **101** D2, **102** A2
Le Grand-Lemps **103** D3
Le Grand-Lucé **86** B2/3
Le Grand-Pressigny **101** D1
Le Grau-du-Roi **111** C3
Legrená **147** D3
Le Gua **100** B3
Léguevin **108** B3, **155** C1
Legutio **153** D2
Le Havre **76** B3
Lehčevo **135** D3
Le Hérie-la-Viéville **78** B3
Lehesten **82** A2
Lehmäjoki **20** B2
Lehmen **80** A2
Lehmikumpu **17** D2, **18** A1
Lehmivaara **23** C1
Lehmo **23** D3
Lehndorf **82** B2
Lehnice **95** C2/3
Lehnin **69** D3, **70** A3
Le Hohwald **89** D2, **90** A2
Le Houga **108** B2
Lehrberg **91** D1
Lehre **69** C3
Lehre-Flechtorf **69** C3
Lehrte **68** B2/3
Lehrte-Hämelerwald **68** B3
Lehrte-Immensen **68** B2/3
Lehtimäki **21** C2
Lehtiniemi **13** C3
Lehtoi **23** D3
Lehtola **19** C/D3
Lehtoperä **21** D1/2, **22** A1/2
Lehtovaara **19** C1/2
Lehtovaara **12** B2
Lehtovaara **23** D2, **23** D1
Lehtovaara **19** D2
Lehtovaara **19** C3, **22** B1
Lehva **98** B1
Leibnitz **96** A3
Leibnitz **127** C1
Leicester **65** C1/2
Leiden **66** A3
Leidenborn **79** D3
Leiferde **69** B/C2/3
Leigh **59** D2, **60** B3
Leighton Buzzard **64** B2
Leikanger **36** A1
Leikanger **36** A1
Leikanger **36** B2
Leimen **90** B1
Leimrieth **81** D2

Leine **37** C2
Leinefelde **81** D1
Leinesodden **14** A2
Leinfelden-Echterdingen **91** C2
Leingarten **91** C1
Leinì **105** C3, **113** B/C1
Leino **19** C2
Leino **27** C2
Leinovaara **23** C/D3
Leinstrand **28** A3, **33** C1/2
Leioa **153** C1
Leipämäki **23** C3
Leipheim **91** D2
Leipivaara **19** C2
Leipojärvi **16** B1
Leipzig **82** B1
Leira **32** B2
Leira **28** A3, **33** C1
Leira **37** D2/3
Leiranger **8** B3
Leirbakk **29** C2
Leirbotn **5** C2
Leiret **38** A/B2
Leirfjord **14** A2
Leirvåg **9** C1
Leirvassbu **37** C2
Leirvik **36** A2
Leirvik **28** B1
Leirvik **28** A2/3, **33** C1
Leirvik **42** A1
Leirvík **55** C1
Leirvika **14** B2
Leisnig **82** B1
Leissigen **105** C2
Leiston **65** D2
Leith **57** C1/2
Leitzersdorf **94** B2
Leitzkau **69** D2
Leivonmäki **26** A/B1
Leivonmäki **23** C3
Leixlip **58** A2
Leiza **153** D1, **154** A1
Leizen **69** D1
Leka **14** A3, **28** B1
Lekåsa **45** C3
Lekeitio **153** D1
Lekenik **127** D3
Lekeryd **46** A3
Leknes **32** A3, **36** B1
Leknes **8** B2
Le Lardin **101** C3, **108** B1
Le Lauzet-Ubaye **112** A2
Le Lavandou **112** A3
Lel'čicy **99** C2
Le Levancher **104** B2
Le Liège **87** B/C3, **101** D1
Le Lion-d'Angers **86** A3
Lelkendorf **53** D3, **69** D1, **70** A1
Lellainen **24** B2
Le Locle **104** B1
Le Logis du Pin **112** A2/3
Le Lonzac **102** A3
Le Loroux-Bottereau **86** A3, **101** C1
Le Louroux-Béconnais **85** D3, **86** A3
Le Luc **112** A3
Le Lude **86** B3
Lelystad **66** B2
Lem **48** A3
Lem **48** A2
Le Malzieu-Ville **110** B1
Le Mans **86** B2
Le Mas **112** B2
Le Mas-d'Agenais **109** B/2
Le Mas-d'Azil **108** B3, **155** C1
LEMASNAUMA **110** A2
Le Mayet-de-Montagne **103** C2
Le May-sur-Evre **85** D3, **86** A3, **100** B1
Lembach **90** A/B1
Lemberg **89** D1, **90** A1
Lemberk **83** D2

Lembeye **108** B3, **155** C1
Lembruch **68** A2
Le Mechenin **101** C3
Le Mêle-sur-Sarthe **86** B2
Le Ménil **89** C2
Le Merlerault **86** B1/2
Lemesjö **31** C2
Le Mesnil-Herman **86** A/B1
Lemförde **68** A2
Lemgo **68** A3
Lemgow-Schmarsau **69** C2
Lemi **27** C2
Lémié **104** B3, **112** B1
Lemierzyce **71** B/C2
Le Mirandol **109** D1
Lemke (Nienburg-Weser) **68** A2
Lemlahti **24** A1
Lemland **41** D3
Lemmenjoki **6** B3, **11** D2
Lemmer **66** B2
Lemnia **141** C1
Le Moline **113** D1, **114** A1
Le Monastier-sur-Gazeille **111** B/C1
Le Monêtier-les-Bains **112** A1
Le Monêtier-Allemont **111** D2, **112** A2
Le Mont-Dore **102** B3
Le Montenvers **104** B2/3
Le Montet **102** B2
Le Mont-Saint-Michel **85** D1/2
Le Moustier **109** C1
Lempäälä **25** C1
Lempdes **102** B3
Lempyy **22** B3
Lemu **24** A/B2
Le Muret **108** A/B1/2
Le Muy **112** A3
Lemvig **48** A2
Lena **38** A2
Lena **151** D1
Lenart **127** D2
Lencloître **101** C1
Lencouacq **108** B2
Lend **107** D1, **126** A1
Lendava **127** D2
Lendinara **115** C1
Lendinez **167** C3, **172** B1
Lendrup Strand **48** B2
Lendum **49** B/C1
Le Neubourg **77** C3, **86** B1
Lengau **92** B3, **107** D3
Lengdorf **92** B2
Lengefeld **83** C2
Lengenfeld **81** D1
Lengenfeld **94** A2
Lengenfeld **82** B2
Lengenwang **91** D3
Lengerich **67** D3
Lengerich **67** D2
Lenggries **92** A3
Lenggries-Vorderriss **92** A3
Lengronne **86** A1
Lengyeltóti **128** A/B2
Lenhovda **51** C1
Lenhovda **72** B1
Leningrad **74** B1
Lenk im Simmental **105** D2
Lenkovcy **98** B2
Lennartsfors **45** C1
Lennestadt-Altenhundem **80** B1
Lennestadt-Elspe **80** B1
Lennestadt-Kirchveischede **80** B1
Lenningen-Schopfloch **91** C2
Lennoxtown **56** B1/2
Leno **106** B3
Lénola **119** C2
Le Nouvion-en-Thiérache **78** B3
Lenovac **135** C3
Lens **78** A3
Lens **78** A2
Lensahn **53** C3
Lensvik **28** A3, **33** C1
Lenti **127** D2
Lentiira **19** D3
Lenting **92** A2
Lentini **125** D3
L'Enveja **163** C2
Lenvik **9** D1

Lenzburg **90** B3, **105** C1
Lenzen **69** C2
Lenzerheide/Lai [Tiefenca- stel] **106** A1
Lenzkirch **90** B3
Leoben **93** D3, **127** C1
Leoben **94** A3
Leobersdorf **94** B3
Leofreni **118** B1
Léogang **92** B3
Léognan **108** B1
Leominster **59** D3
Léon **108** B2
León **151** D2, **152** A2
Leonberg **91** C2
Léoncel **111** D1
Leondárion **146** B3
Leonding **93** D2
Leonessa **117** C/D3, **118** B1
Leonforte **125** C2
Leonídion **147** C3
Leonídion **148** B2/3
Leonstein **93** D3
Leonte **150** B3, **158** A/B1
Leontion **146** B2
Leopoldov **95** C2
Leopoldsburg **79** C1
Leopoldshagen **70** B1
Leovo **141** D1
Leoz **154** A2
Lepaa **25** C2
Le Palais **84** B3
Le Paly **85** C2
Le Pas **110** A2
Lepe **171** D2
Le Péage-de-Roussillon **103** D3
Lepel' **74** B3
Lepenski Vir **135** C2
Le Perray-en-Yvelines **87** C1/2
Le Perrier **100** A1
Le Perron **86** B2
Le Perthus **156** B2
Lepetane **137** C2
Lepikkomäki **23** C3
Lepikontorppa **22** B2
L'Épine **88** B1
Le Pin-en-Mauges **85** D3, **86** A3, **100** B1
Le Pin-la-Garenne **86** B2
Lepistönmäki **20** B2
Le Planey **104** B3
Le Plessis-Belleville **87** D1
Lepoglava **127** D2
Le Poiré-sur-Vie **100** A1
Le Pondy **102** B3
Le Pont-de-Beauvoisin **104** A3
Le Pont-de-Claix **111** D1
Le Pont-de-Montvert **110** B2
Le Pont du Travo **113** D3
Le Pontet **100** B3
Le Pontet **111** C2
Le Pontet **104** A3
Le Ponthou **84** B2
Le Porge **108** A1
Le Port-Boulet **86** B3, **101** C1
Le Portel **77** D1/2
Leposaviči **138** B1
Le Pouldu **84** B3
Le Pouliguen **85** C3, **100** A1
Lépoura **147** D2
Lépoura **149** B/C2
Le Pouzin **111** C1
Leppäjärvi **11** C2
Leppäkoski **25** C1, **26** A1
Leppäkoski **25** C2
Leppälä **27** C2
Leppälahti **23** C3
Leppälahti **22** B2
Leppälahti **21** D3, **22** A3
Leppälänkylä **21** C2
Leppämäki **23** B/C3
Leppärinne **23** D1
Leppäselkä **21** D2, **22** A3
Leppävesi **21** D3, **22** A3
Leppävirta **22** B3
Leppiaho **18** B1
Leppin **69** C2
Leppiniemi **18** B2/3
Le Prada **109** B/C2

Lépreon 146 B3
Lepşa 141 C1
Lepsala 25 D1, 26 B1
Lepsény 128 B1
Leptokariá 143 D2
Le Puy 110 B1
Le Puy-Notre-Dame 101 C1
Le Quesnoy 78 B2
Léquile 121 D3
Lerbäck 46 A1/2
Lerberg 43 D1
Lerberget 49 D2/3, 50 A2
Lercara Friddi 124 B2
Lerchenborg 49 C3, 53 C1
Lerdal 45 C2
Lerdala 45 D2
L'Erée 63 D3
Le Repas 85 D1
Lerga 154 A2
Lérici 114 A2
Lérida / Lleida 155 C3, 163 C1
Lerín 153 D2, 154 A2
L'Erkelsbrugge 77 D1, 78 A1/2
Lerkil 49 D1, 50 A1
Lerma 153 B/C3
Lermon 29 C2
Lermoos 91 D3
Lerna 147 C3
Le Rocher-Mézangers 86 A2
Lérouville 89 C1
Le Roux 112 B1
Le Rozier 110 B2
Lerrain 89 C2
Lerum 45 C3
Lerum 72 A1
Le Russey 89 D3, 104 B1
Lerwick 54 A1
Les 155 C2
Les Abrets 103 D3, 104 A3
Lesaca 108 A3, 154 A1
Les Aix-d'Angillon 87 D3, 102 B1
Les Ajustons 110 B1
Lešak 134 B3, 138 B1
Les Ancizes-Comps 102 B2
Les Andelys 77 C/D3, 87 C1
Lešani 138 B3, 142 B1
Les Arcs 104 B3
Les Arcs-sur-Argens 112 A3
Le Saret 108 B3, 155 C1
Les Aubiers 100 B1
Le Sauze 112 A/B2
Les Avellanes 155 C3
Les Baux 111 C2
Les Bertins 87 D3, 102 B1
Les Billaux 108 B1
Les Bordes 87 D3
Les Borges Blanques 155 D3, 163 C/D1
Les Borges del Camp 163 D1/2
Les Bouchoux 104 A2
Lesbury 57 D2
Les Cabanes-de-Lapalme 110 A/B3, 156 B1
Les Cabannes 155 D2, 156 A1
Les Cabòries 156 A3
L'Escala 156 B2
Les Calanche 113 D3
Les Cammazès 109 D3
Lescar 108 B3, 154 B1
L'Escarène 112 B2
Lesce 126 B2
Lešće 127 C3, 130 B1
Les Clots 112 A1
Les Contamines-Montjoie 104 B3
Les Cortalets 156 B2
Lescun 108 B3, 154 B1/2
Les Deux Alpes 112 A1
Les Eaux-Chaudes 108 B3, 154 B1/2
Les Échelles 104 A3
Le Sel-de-Bretagne 85 D2
Lesencefalu 128 A1
Les Escaldes 155 D2, 156 A2
Les Essarts 101 C1
Les Estables 111 C1
Les Étangs 89 C/D1
Les Eyzies-de-Tayac 109 C1
Les Farguettes 110 A2
Les Fins 104 B1
Les Forges 85 D2
Les Forges 85 C2
Les Fourgs 104 B1
Les Gets 104 B2
Les Goudes 111 D3
Les Halles 103 C3
Les Hayons 76 B3
Les Herbiers 100 B1
Les Hôpitaux-Neufs 104 A/B1
Lésina 120 A1
Les Islettes 88 B1
Lesja 32 B3, 37 C1
Lesjaskog 32 B3, 37 C1
Lesjaverk 32 B3, 37 C1
Lesjöfors 39 C3
Leskelä 18 B3
Leskova 138 A1
Leskovac 139 C1
Leskovac 140 A3
Leskovice 83 D3, 93 D1, 94 A1
Leskovik 135 C3
Leskoviku 142 B2
Les Lèches 109 C1
Leslie 57 C1
Les Llosses 156 A2
Les Lucs-sur-Boulogne 100 A1
Lesmahagow 56 B2
Les Matelles 110 B2
Les Mazures 79 B/C3
Les Mées 111 D2, 112 A2
Les Ménuires 104 B3
Les Mesnuls 87 C1
Lesmont 88 B2
Les Moutiers-les-Mauxfaits 100 A/B2
Leśna 83 D1/2
Lešná 95 C1
Lešnica 133 C1/2
Leśniów Wielki 71 C3
Lesnoe 141 D1
Lesnoe 75 D1
Les Ollières-sur-Eyrieux 111 C1
Les Oluges 155 C3, 163 C1
Les Ormes 101 C1
Lesovaara 19 D2
Les Pargots 104 B1
Lesparre-Médoc 100 B3
L'Espérou 110 B2
Les Pieux 76 A3
Les Pilles 111 D2
Les Planes d'Hostoles 156 B2
L'Espluga Calba 155 D3, 163 D1
L'Espluga de Francolí 163 D1
Les Ponts-de-Cé 86 A3
L'Espunyola 156 A2
Les Quatre-Bras 78 B2
Lesquin 78 A2
L'Esquirol 156 A/B2
Les Riceys-Haut 88 B2
Les Rochers 86 A2
Les Rosaires 85 C2
Les Rosiers 86 A3
Les Rousses 104 A2
Les Sables-d'Olonne 100 A2
Lessach 126 B1
Les Salles-du-Gardon 111 B/C2
Les Salles-sur-Verdon 112 A2/3
Lessay 76 A3, 85 D1
Lessebo 51 C2
Lessebo 72 A/B1
Les Settons 88 A3, 103 C1
Les Sièges 88 A2
Lessines 78 B2
Les Sorinières 85 D3, 100 A1
L'Estany 156 A2
L'Estartit 156 B2
Lestelle-Bétharram 108 B3, 154 B1
Les Ternes 110 A/B1
Lesterps 101 D2
Les Thilliers-en-Vexin 77 D3, 87 C1
Lestijärvi 21 C1
L'Estréchure 110 B2
Les Trois Moutiers 101 C1
Lesund 32 B2
Lesura 135 D3
Les Vans 111 C2
Les Vignes 110 B2
Leszno 71 D3
Leszno 72 B3, 96 B1
L'Etac 63 D3, 85 C1
Letchworth 65 B/C2
Le Teil 111 C1
Le Teilleul 85 D2, 86 A2
Le Temple-de-Médoc 108 A1
Le Temple-de-Bretagne 85 D3
Letenye 128 A2
Le Theil-sur-Huisne 86 B2
Le Thillot 89 D2/3
Le Thor 111 C/D2
Le Thoronet 112 A3
Letičev 99 B/C3
Letino 119 C/D2
Letkés 95 D3
Letku 25 C2
Le Touquet-Paris-Plage 77 D2
Le Tourne 108 B1
Le Touvet 104 A3
Letovanić 127 D3
Letovice 94 B1
Le Translay 77 D2
Le Trayas 112 B3
Le Tréport 76 B2
Le Truel 110 A2
Letsbo 35 C3
Letschin 70 B2
Letter 68 B2/3
Letterkenny 55 C/D2
Lettingsvollan 33 D3
Letur 168 B3
Letuš 127 C2
Letux 162 B1
Letzlingen 69 C2
Leuben 83 C1
Leubingen 82 A1
Léuca 121 D3
Leuchars 57 C1
Leuglay 88 B3
Leugnies 78 B2
Leukerbad [Leuk] 105 C2
Leuk Stadt 105 C2
Leuna 82 B1
Leušen' 141 D1
Leutenbach 91 C1/2
Leutenberg 82 A2
Leutershausen 91 D1
Leutkirch 91 C/D3
Leutkirch-Friesenhofen 91 D3
Leutkirch-Gebrazhofen 91 C/D3
Leutkirch-Herlazhofen 91 C/D3
Leutschach 127 C2
Leuven 79 C2
Leuze 78 B2
Levadiá 147 C2
Levajok fjellstue 6 B2
Leväkylä 22 B3
Le Val André 85 C2
Le Val Richer 76 B3, 86 B1
Levan 142 A2
Lévane 115 C3, 116 B2
Levänen 27 C2
Levang 43 D2, 44 A2
Levanger 28 B3, 33 D1
Levanjska Varoš 128 B3, 132 B1
Levanpelto 24 B1
Levanto 25 D2, 26 A2
Lévanto 113 D2, 114 A2
Lévanzo 124 A2
Leväranta 12 B3
Leväsjoki 24 A1
Leveld 37 C3
Leven 57 C1
Leven 54 B2
Levene 45 C2
Levens 112 B2
Levens Hall 59 D1, 60 B2
Leverano 121 D3
Leveråsvallen 34 B3
Le Verdon-sur-Mer 100 B3
Leverkusen 80 A1/2
Leverkusen-Opladen 80 A1
Le Vernet 112 A2
Le Vernet-la-Varenne 102 B3
Levet 102 A1
Le Veurdre 102 B1
Levice 95 D2
Levice 96 B2/3
Lévico Terme 107 C2
Levide 47 D3
Levídion 146 B3
Levie 113 D3
Levier 104 A1
Le Vieux Bourg 85 C/D2
Le Vigan 110 B2
Le Vigean 108 B1
Le Vigen 101 C3
Lévignac 108 B2/3
Levignen 87 D1
Levijoki 21 C2
Le Ville 115 C3, 117 C2
Le Vivier-sur-Mer 85 D2
Levonperä 21 C/D1, 22 A1
Levo oja 18 B2
Levroux 101 D1, 102 A1
Levski 141 B/C3
Lewes 76 B1
Lewice 71 C2
Leyburn 59 D1, 61 C2
Leyburn 54 B3
Leymen 90 A3
Leysin 104 B2
Leżajsk 97 C/D2, 98 A2
Lezama 153 C1/2
Lezardrieux 84 B1
Lézat-sur-Lèze 108 B3, 155 C1
Lezay 101 C2
Lezhë 137 D3
Lézignan-Corbières 110 A3, 156 B1
Ležimir 133 C1
Lézinnes 88 A/B3
Lezo 153 D1, 154 A1
Lezoux 102 B2/3
Lezuza 168 B2
LGuardia 150 A3
L'Herbaudière 100 A1
L'Herbergement 101 C1
L'Hermet 110 A2
L'Hôpital-du-Grosbois 89 C3, 104 A1
L'Hospitalet 156 A1/2
L'Hospitalet de l'Infant 163 D2
Lia 28 B3, 33 D1
Lia 9 B/C1/2
Liabø 32 B2
Liabygda 32 A3, 36 B1
Liancourt 87 D1
Lianokládian 146 B1
Liapádes 142 A3
Liart 78 B3
Liarvåg 42 A2
Liatorp 50 B2
Liatorp 72 A1
Liaunet 28 B1
Libáň 83 D2
Libčeves 83 C2
Liběchov 83 D2
Libeliče 127 C2
Liber 151 C2
Liberec 83 D2
Liberec 96 A1
Liběšice 83 D2
Líbeznice 83 D2/3
Libin 79 C3
Libochovice 83 C2
Libofshë 142 A1
Libohova 142 A/B2
Libourne 108 B1
Liboussou 109 C1
Librazhd 138 A3, 142 B1
Librilla 169 D3
Libros 163 C3
Libuň 83 D2
Lič 127 C3, 130 B1
Licata 124 B3
Licenza 118 B1/2
Liceras 161 C1
Lich 81 B/C2
Lichás 147 C1
Lichères-près-Aigremont 88 A3
Lichfield 64 A1
Lichtenau 94 A2
Lichtenau 90 B2
Lichtenau 81 C1
Lichtenau-Atteln 81 B/C1
Lichtenau-Kleinenberg 81 C1
Lichtenberg 82 A2
Lichtenborn 79 D3
Lichtenegg 94 A/B3
Lichtenfels-Goddelsheim 81 B/C1
Lichtenfels 82 A3
Lichtenfels-Sachsenberg 81 B/C1
Lichtensteig 105 D1, 106 A1
Lichtenstein-Unterhausen 91 C2
Lichtenstein 82 B2
Lichtenstein 91 C2
Lichtenvoorde 67 C3
Lička Kaldrma 131 C2
Lički Jasenica 130 B1
Lički Osik 130 B2
Ličko Lešće 130 B1
Ličko Petrovo Selo 131 C1
Licodía Eubéa 125 C3
Licq-Atherey 108 A3, 154 B1
Licques 77 D1
Lid 42 B1
Lid 39 C3
Lida 73 D2, 74 A3
Lidar 37 C/D2
Liden 35 D2
Liden 30 A1
Lidgatu 30 A/B3, 35 D1/2
Lidhult 50 B1/2
Lidhult 72 A1
Lidice 83 C/D3
Lidingö 47 C/D1
Lidköping 45 D2
Lido Azzurro 121 C3
Lido degli Estensi 115 C1
Lido dei Pini 118 B2
Lido delle Nazioni 115 C1
Lido di Camaiore 114 A2, 116 A1
Lido di Copanello 122 B2
Lido di Jésolo 107 D3, 126 A3
Lido di Metaponto 121 C3
Lido di Mortelle 122 A3, 125 D1
Lido di Portonuovo 120 B1, 136 A2/3
Lido di Siponto 120 B1
Lido di Tarquínia 118 A1
Lido di Volano 115 C1
Lidón 162 A2
Lidoríkion 146 B1/2
Lido Silvana 121 C3
Lidsjöberg 29 D2
Lidzbark Warmiński (Heilsberg) 73 C2
Liebenau 93 D2
Liebenau (Nienburg-Weser) 68 A2
Liebenthal 70 A2
Liebenwalde 70 A2
Liebertswolkwitz 82 B1
Lieboch 127 C1
Liebschütz 82 A2
Liebstadt 83 C2
Liechtensteinklamm 126 A1
Liedakkala 17 D2, 18 A1
Liédena 155 C2
Liedenpohja 21 C3
Liedon asema 24 B2
Lieg 80 A3
Liège 79 C2
Liehittäjä 17 C/D2
Liekokylä 18 B1
Lieksa 23 D2
Lielax 24 B3
Lien 29 C3, 34 B1
Lienen 67 D3
Lienen-Kattenvenne 67 D3
Lienz 107 D1, 126 A1
Liepäja 73 C1
Liepimä 11 C3, 12 A1
Liepimäjärvi 11 C3, 12 A1
Lièpvre 89 D2, 90 A2
Lier 79 B/C1
Lierbyen 43 D1
Liérganes 153 B/C1
Lierstall 80 A2
Liesa 154 B2/3
Liesborn 67 D3, 68 A3, 80 B1

Liesjärvi 21 C3
Lieskau 83 C1
Lieskovec 95 D2
Lieso 25 C2, 26 A2
Liesse 78 B3
Liessel 79 D1
Liestal 90 A3
Liesti 141 C2
Lieteksavo 10 A3
Lietlahti 22 B3
Lieto 24 B2
Liétor 168 B2
Lietzen 70 B2
Lieurey 77 C3, 86 B1
Lieusaint 87 D2
Lievestuore 21 D3, 22 A3
Lievikoski 24 B1
Lievoperä 18 B3
Liezen 93 D3
Liezen 96 A3
Liffol-le-Grand 89 C2
Lifjell Turisthotell 43 C1/2, 44 A1
Lifton 62 B3
Ligardes 109 C2
Ligares 159 C2
Ligatne 73 D1, 74 A2
Ligescourt 77 D2
Lignan 105 C3
Lignano Pineta 126 A3
Lignano Sabbiadoro 126 A3
Ligné 86 A3
Ligneuville 79 D2
Lignières 102 A1
Ligny-en-Barrois 89 C1/2
Ligny-en-Brionnais 103 C2
Ligny-le-Châtel 88 A2/3
Ligny-le-Ribault 87 C3
Ligónchio 114 A2, 116 A1
Ligourion 147 C3
Ligueil 101 D1
Lihjamo 21 C3
Lihme 48 A2
Lihostavl' 75 D2
Lihula 74 A1
Liikasenvaara 13 C/D3
Liikavaara 16 B1
Liimattala 22 B3
Liinamaa 20 B2
Liinanki 12 A3, 17 D1/2
Liipantönkkä 20 B2
Liittoperä 21 D1, 22 A1
Lijeva Rijeka 137 D1/2
Likenäs 39 B/C2
Liléa 147 C1
L'Île Bouchard 101 C1
L'Île Rousse 113 D2
Lilienfeld 94 A2/3
Lilienthal 68 A2
Lilienthal-Worpswede 68 A1/2
Liljanovo 139 D3
Liljedal 45 C/D1
Liljendal 25 D2, 26 A2
Lillå 16 B2
Lilla Edet 45 C3
Lillåfors 16 B2
Lilland 9 C2
Lillby 20 B1/2
Lille 78 A2
Lillebonne 77 C3
Lillefjord 5 D1, 6 A1
Lillehammer 38 A1/2
Lillehamn 42 B3
Lilleidet 8 B2
Lille Lerresfjord 5 C2
Lilleng 9 C2
Lillerød 49 D3, 50 A3, 53 D1
Lillers 77 D2, 78 A2
Lillesand 43 C3
Lille Skensved 49 D3, 50 A3, 53 D1
Lillestrøm 38 A3
Lillevollen 28 B3, 33 D1
Lillholmsjön 29 D3, 34 B1
Lillholmträsk 31 C1
Lillkågeträsk 31 D1
Lillkyro 20 B2
Lillmälö 24 B3
Lillmörtsjö 35 C3
Lillo 161 C3, 167 D1, 168 A1
Lillögda 30 B1/2
Lillpite 16 B3

Lillsaivis 17 C2
Lillselet 17 C1/2
Lillström 35 D3
Lillsved 47 D1
Lillviken 15 C2
Lillviken 29 D2, 30 A2
Lima 39 C2
Limanowa 97 C2
Limátola 119 D3
Limay 87 C1
Limbach (Mosbach) 81 C3, 91 C1
Limbach-Oberfrohna 82 B2
Limbaži 73 D1, 74 A2
Limburg an der Lahn 80 B2
Limedsforsen 39 C2
Limenária 145 B/C2
Limenária 149 C1
Limerick (Luimneach) 55 C3
Limes 106 B2
Limhamn 50 A3
Limín 144 B1
Liminka 18 A2/3
Limín Litochórou 143 D2
Liminpuro 19 B/C3
Limmared 45 D3
Limmared 72 A1
Limmen 66 A2
Límni 147 C/D1
Límni Ilíki 147 C/D2
Límni Ioánninon 144 A1/2
Límni Kerkínis 139 D3, 144 A1
Limoges 101 C2/3
Limogne 109 D1/2
Limoise 102 B1
Limone Piemonte 112 B2
Limonest 103 D2/3
Limone sul Garda 106 B3
Limours 87 C2
Limoux 110 A3, 156 A1
Limpias 153 C1
Lin 138 A/B3, 142 B1
Lina älv 16 B1
Linards 101 D3
Linanäs 47 D1
Linares 167 D3, 173 C1
Linares de la Sierra 165 D3, 171 C1
Linares de Mora 162 B3
Linares de Riofrío 159 D2
Linás de Broto 155 B/C2
Lincluden Abbey 57 C3
Lincoln 61 D3, 64 B1
Linda 82 A2
Lindärva 45 D2
Lindås 36 A3
Lindåskroken 43 D1, 44 A1
Lindau 69 D3
Lindau 52 B2/3
Lindau (Bodensee) 91 C3
Linde 48 A2
Lindelse 53 C2
Linden 81 D2
Lindenberg im Allgäu 91 C3
Lindenberg 48 B2
Lindenfels 81 B/C3
Lindenhayn 82 B1
Lindern 67 D2
Linderöd 50 B3
Lindesberg 39 D3, 46 A/B1
Lindesnäs 39 C/D2/3
Lindesnes 42 B3
Lindfors 39 C3, 45 D1
Lindholmen 40 B3, 47 C/D1
Lindholm Høje 48 B1
Lindisfarne 57 D2
Lindlar 80 A1/2
Lindö 46 B2
Lindome 45 C3, 49 D1
Líndos 149 D3
Lindoso 150 B3, 158 A/B1
Lindow 70 A2
Lindsdal 51 D2
Lindwedel-Hope 68 B2
Líně 83 C3
Lingbo 40 A1/2
Linge 32 A3, 36 B1
Lingen 67 D2
Lingen-Brögbern 67 D2
Lingen-Estringen 67 D2
Linghed 39 D2, 40 A2
Lingslätö (Barnens ö) 41 C3

Linguaglossa 125 D2
Linhamari 25 C3
Linkenheim-Hochstetten 90 B1
Linka 17 D2
Linkôping 46 B2
Linkuva 73 D1, 74 A2
Linlithgow 57 C1/2
Linna 21 C/D3
Linnankylä 20 B3
Linnankylä 21 D2/3, 22 A2/3
Linnerud 38 A/B2
Linneryd 51 C2
Linnes 38 B1
Linnes 29 C/D2, 34 B1
Linnés Hammarby 40 B3
Linnich 79 D1/2
Linsell 34 B3
Linthal 105 D1, 106 A1
Linthe 69 D3, 70 A3
Linton 65 C2
Lintorpet 38 B2
Lintula 11 D3, 12 A1/2
Linxe 108 B2
Linyola 155 D3, 163 D1
Linz 93 D2
Linz 96 A3
Linz am Rhein 80 A2
Lion 76 B3, 86 A1
Lioni 120 A2
Lípari 125 C/D1
Lipe 134 B2
Lipenec 83 C2
Liperi 23 C3
Lipiany 71 B/C2
Lipica 126 B3
Lipik 128 A3
Lipinki Łużyckie 71 C3, 83 D1
Lipinvaara 23 C1
Lipka 71 D1
Lipkany 98 B3
Lipkovo 138 B2
Lipljan 138 B2
Lipník nad Bečvou 95 C1
Lipno 71 D3
Lipno 73 C3
Lipno nad Vltavou 93 D2
Lipolist 137 C1
Lipomo 105 D3, 106 A3
Liposthey 108 A2
Lipova 140 A1
Lipovac 135 C3
Lipovac 133 C1
Lipovec 99 C3
Lipovo Polje 130 B1/2
Lippetal 67 D3, 80 B1
Lippetal-Herzfeld 67 D3, 80 B1
Lippetal-Lipporg 67 D3, 80 B1
Lippó 128 B3
Lippstadt 68 A3, 80 B1
Lippstadt-Benninghausen 67 D3, 68 A3, 80 B1
Lippstadt-Hörste 68 A3, 80 B1
Liptál 95 C1
Liptovská Lúžna 95 D1
Liptovská Osada 95 D1
Liptovská Teplá 95 D1
Liptovský Mikuláš 97 C2
Lipůvka 94 B1
Liqenas 142 B1/2
Liria 162 B3, 169 C/D1
Lirkía 147 C3
Lis 138 A3
Lisac 132 A3
Lisboa 164 A2
Lisburn 56 A3
Lisburn 54 A3, 55 C2
Liseleje 49 D3
Liselund 53 D2
Lišeň 94 B1
Lisiera 107 C3
Lisieux 77 B/C3, 86 B1
Lisina 134 B3
Liskeard 62 B3
L'Isle-Adam 87 C/D1
L'Isle d'Abeau 103 D3
L'Isle-de-Noé 109 C3, 155 C1
L'Isle-en-Dodon 109 C3, 155 C/D1
L'Isle-Jourdain 101 C/D2

L'Isle-Jourdain 109 C2/3, 155 D1
L'Isle-sur-la-Sorgue 111 C/D2
L'Isle-sur-le-Doubs 89 D3
L'Isle-sur-Serein 88 A3
Lisle-sur-Tarn 109 D2
Lisma 11 D2, 12 A/B1
Lismanaapa 12 B2
Lišnja 131 D1, 132 A1
Lišov 93 D1
Lisovići 132 B1/2
Lispeszentadorján 127 D2, 128 A2
Lisse 66 A3
Lisskogsåsen 39 C2
Lissus 137 D3
List 52 A2
Lísta 142 B3
Listed 51 D3
Listerby 51 C2
Lištica 132 A3
Listrac-Médoc 100 B3, 108 A/B1
Lit 29 D3, 34 B2
Litava 95 D2
Litcham 65 C1
Litchfield 65 C3, 76 B1
Liteň 83 C3
Lit-et-Mixe 108 B2
Lithakiá 146 A3
Lití 143 D1/2, 144 A1/2
Litice 83 C3
Litija 127 C2
Litlos 42 B1
Litmaniemi 23 C2/3
Litobratřice 94 B1
Litochoron 143 D2
Litoměřice 83 C2
Litoměřice 96 A1
Litschau 93 D1
Litslena 40 B3, 47 C1
Litsnäset 29 D3, 34 B2
Littiäinen 17 D2
Littlehampton 76 B1
Little Moreton Hall 59 D2, 60 B3, 64 A1
Little Petherick 62 B3
Littleport 65 C2
Little Walsingham 65 C1
Litvínov 83 C2
Litvínov 96 A1
Liubcova 135 C2
Liukkunen 23 D2
Liumseter 37 D2
Livaderón 143 C2
Livádion 144 A2
Livádion 143 C/D2
Livanátai 147 C1
Livarot 86 B1
Livártzion 146 B2
Livata 118 B2
Livek 126 A/B2
Liverá 143 C2
Livernon 109 D1
Liverpool 59 C/D2, 60 B3
Livigno 106 B2
Livingston 57 C2
Liviöjärvi 17 C1
Livno 131 D3, 132 A2/3
Livo 18 B2
Livø 48 B2
Livold 127 C3
Livonniska 19 C1
Livorno 114 A3, 116 A2
Livorno Antignano 114 A3, 116 A2
Livorno Ferráris 105 C3
Livorno Quercianella 114 A3, 116 A2
Livron-sur-Drôme 111 C1
Livry-Gargan 87 D1
Lixheim 89 D1, 90 A2
Lizartza 153 D1, 154 A1
Lizoáin 154 A2
Lizy-sur-Ourcq 87 D1
Lizzano 121 C3
Lizzano in Belvedere 114 B2, 116 A1
Lizzola 106 A/B2
Ljady 74 B1
L'jalovo 75 D2
Ljig 133 D2, 134 A2
Ljønes 15 C1
Ljørdal 38 B1
Ljøsheim 38 A1/2

Ljosland 42 B2
Ljuban' 75 C1
Ljubaništa 142 B1
Ljubaševka 99 C3
Ljuben 140 B3
Ljubija 131 D1
Ljubimec 145 D2
Ljubimec 141 C3
Ljubin 138 B2
Ljubina 132 B2
Ljubinić 133 D2, 134 A2
Ljubinje 137 C1
Ljubiš 133 D3, 134 A3
Ljubljana 126 B2
Ljubno 127 C2
Ljubojno 143 B/C1
Ljubojno 148 A1
Ljuboml' 97 D1, 98 A2
Ljuboml' 97 D1, 98 A2
Ljubostinja 134 B3"
Ljubovija 133 C2
Ljubuški 132 A3, 136 B1
Ljubytino 75 C1
Ljudinovo 75 D3
Ljugarn 73 B/C1
Ljugarn 47 D3
Ljung 45 C/D3
Ljungå 35 C2
Ljungaverk 35 C3
Ljungby 50 B1/2
Ljungby 72 A1
Ljungbyhed 50 A/B2/3
Ljungbyholm 51 D2
Ljungbyholm 72 B1
Ljungdalen 34 A2
Ljungsarp 45 C2
Ljungsbro 46 B2
Ljungskile 45 C3
Ljuså 17 B/C2
Ljusfallshammar 46 B2
Ljusfors 46 B2
Ljusliden 15 C3, 29 D1
Ljusne 40 A/B1
Ljusnedalen 34 A3
Ljusterö 47 D1
Ljustorp 35 D2
Ljusträsk 16 A/B2/3
Ljusvattnet 31 D1
Ljutice 133 D2, 134 A2
Ljutoglava 138 B2
Ljutomer 127 D2
Lladorre 155 C2
Lladurs 155 D3, 156 A2
Llafranc 156 B2
Llagostera 156 B2/3
Llamas de la Ribera 151 D2
Llanarmon Dyffryn Ceiriog 59 C3, 60 A3
Llanbadarn-Fynydd 59 C3
Llanberis 59 C2, 60 A3
Llancà 156 B2
Llandeilo 63 C1
Llandinabo 63 D1
Llandovery 63 C1
Llandrindod Wells 59 C3
Llandudno 59 C2, 60 A3
Llandyssul 62 B1
Llanelli 63 B/C1
Llanera 151 D1
Llanerchymedd 58 B2
Llanes 152 A/B1
Llanfaethlu 58 B2
Llanfair Caereinion 59 C3
Llanfairfechan 59 C2, 60 A3
Llanfarian 59 C3
Llanfihangel Ystrad 63 B/C1
Llanfyllin 59 C3
Llangadock 63 C1
Llangefni 58 B2
Llangoed 59 C2, 60 A3
Llangollen 59 C2/3, 60 A/B3
Llangranog 62 B1
Llangurig 59 C3
Llanidloes 59 C3
Llanrhystyd 59 C3
Llanrwst 59 C2, 60 A3
Llansteffan 62 B1
Llanthaedr ym Mochnant 59 C3, 60 A3
Llanthony Priory 63 C1
Llantrisant 63 C1/2
Llanwrda 63 C1
Llanwrtyd Wells 63 C1
Llanymynech 59 C3

Llardecans 163 C1
Llavorsí 155 C2
Lledó 156 B2
Lleida/Lérida 155 C3, 163 C1
Llera 165 D2/3, 166 A3
Llerena 165 D3, 166 A3
Llers 156 B2
Lles 155 D2, 156 A2
Llessui 155 D2
Llimiana 155 D3
Llinars de l'Aigua d'Ora 155 D2/3, 156 A2
Llivia 156 A2
Lloret de Mar 156 B3
Lloseta 157 C2
Llovio 152 A1
Llubi 157 C2
Llucmajor 157 C2
Llwyngwril 59 C3
Llyswen 63 C1
Lnáře 83 C3, 93 C1
Lo 80 B3, 35 D2
Lo 78 A1
Löa 39 D3
Loanhead 57 C2
Loano 113 C2
Loarre 154 B2
Löbau 83 D1
Löbau 96 A1
Lobbach-Waldwimmersbach 91 B/C1
Lobbæk 51 D3
Lobeira 150 B3
Löbejün 69 D3, 82 A/B1
Lobenstein 82 A2
Lobera de Onsella 154 B2
Löberöd 50 B3
Łobez 71 C1
Lobios 150 B3
Lobn'A 75 D2
Löbnitz 82 B1
Löbnitz 53 D3
Lobón 165 D2
Lobor 127 D2
Loburg 69 D3
Łobzenica 71 D1
Locana 105 B/C3
Locarno 105 D2
Locate di Triulzi 105 D3, 106 A3
Lochaline 56 A1
Lochaline 54 A2, 55 D1
Lochboisdale 54 A2, 55 D1
Lochbuie 56 A1
Lochcarron 54 A2
Lochdonhead 56 A1
Lochearnhead 56 B1
Lochem 67 C3
Loches 101 D1
Lochgelly 57 C1
Lochgilphead 56 A1
Lochgilphead 54 A2, 55 D1
Lochgoilhead 56 B1
Lochinver 54 A1/2
Lochmaben 57 C3
Lochmaddy 54 A2
Łochowice 71 C3
Lochranza 56 A2
Lochwinnoch 56 B2
Lockerbie 57 C3
Lockne 34 B2
Locknevi 46 B3
Löcknitz 70 B1
Locksta 30 B2
Locmaria 84 B3
Locmariaquer 85 C3
Locminé 85 C2/3
Locorotondo 121 C2
Locri 122 A/B3
Locri Epizefiri 122 A3
Locronan 84 A2
Loctudy 84 A2/3
Lodares de Osma 153 C3, 161 C1
Lodby 46 B2
Löddeköpinge 50 A3
Lødding 28 B1
Lodè 123 D2
Lodenau 83 D1
Loděnice 83 C3
Lodersleben 82 A1
Loderup 50 B3
Loderups strandbad 50 B3
Lodève 110 B2
Lodi 106 A3
Lødingen 9 C2

Lodosa 153 D2
Lödöse 45 C3
Łódź 73 C3, 97 C1
Loeches 161 C2/3
Loen 32 A3, 36 B1
Loenen 67 B/C3
Løfallstrand 42 A1
Lofer 92 B3
Löffingen 90 B3
Lofsdalen 34 A3
Loftahammar 47 B/C3
Lofthouse 59 D1, 61 C2
Lofthus 36 B3
Lofthus 9 C3
Loftus 61 C1
Loga 42 B3
Logatec 126 B2/3
Lögdeå 31 C2/3
Logišin 98 B1
Logodaš 139 D2
Lögow 69 D2
Log pod Mang 126 A/B2
Lograto 106 A/B3
Logron 86 A/B2
Logroño 153 D2
Logrosán 166 A/B1
Logstein 28 A3, 33 C1
Løgstør 48 B2
Loguivy-Plougras 84 B2
Løgumkloster 52 A/B2
Lohals 53 C2
Lohärad 41 B/C3
Lohberg 93 C1
Lohéac 85 C/D2/3
Lohiaanta 19 C1
Lohijärvi 12 A3, 17 D2
Lohijoki 21 D1, 22 A1
Lohikoski 27 C1
Lohiniva 12 A2, 17 D1
Lohja (Lojo) 25 C3
Lohjan asema 25 C3
Lohmar 80 A2
Lohmar-Wahlscheid 80 A2
Lohmen 83 C1/2
Lohmen 53 D3, 69 D1
Löhnberg 80 B2
Löhnberg-Niederhausen 80 B2
Löhne 68 A3
Lohne 67 D2, 68 A2
Lohnsburg 92 B2
Lohnsfeld 80 B3, 90 B1
Loholm 15 D2
Lohr 81 C3
Lohra 80 B2
Lohsa 83 D1
Lohtaja 21 C1
Lohvica 99 D2
Loiano 114 B2, 116 B1
Loiching 92 B2
Loiching-Wendelskirchen 92 B2
Loimaa 24 B2
Loimaan maalaiskunta 24 B2
Lóiri 123 D1
Loivos 150 B3, 158 B1
Loja 172 B2
Lojev 99 C/D1/2
Lojsta 47 D3
Løjt Kirkeby 52 B2
Loka Brunn 39 C/D3, 45 D1, 46 A1
Lokakylä 21 D2, 22 A2
Lokalahti 24 A2
Lokca 95 D1
Loke 34 B2
Løken 37 D2
Løken 38 A3
Løkeng 5 B/C2
Loker 78 A2
Lokeren 78 B1
Loket 82 B2/3
Lokka 13 C2
Løkken 28 A3, 33 C2
Løkken 48 B1
Lokkiperä 21 C1
Loknja 74 B2
Loksa 74 A1
Lokve 126 B2
Lokve 127 C3, 130 B1
Lollar 80 B2
Lom 37 C1
Lom 135 D3
Lom 140 B2
Lomajärvi 11 D3, 12 B2
Lomåsen 29 D3, 34 B1

Lomåsen 29 D3, 34 B1
Lombardore 105 C3, 113 B/C1
Lombez 109 C3, 155 D1
Lombheden 17 C2
Lomello 113 D1
Lomen 37 C2
Lominchar 160 B3
Lomma 50 A3
Lommatzsch 83 C1
Lomme 78 A2
Lommel 79 C1
Lomnice 82 B2/3
Lomnice nad Lužnicí 93 D1
Lompolo 11 D2/3, 12 A1
Lomsjö 3 A/B2
Łomża 73 C/D3, 98 A1
Lonato 106 B3
Lončari 132 B1
Lončarica 128 A3
Londinières 76 B3
London 65 C3
Londonderry (Derry) 54 A3, 55 D2
Lonevåg 36 A3
Longaníkos 146 B3
Longaníkos 148 B2
Longare 107 C3
Longares 163 C1
Long Compton 64 A2
Long Eaton 61 D3, 65 C1
Longeau 89 C3
Longega/Zwischenwasser 107 C1/2
Longeville 100 A2
Longeville-les-Saint-Avold 89 D1
Longford 55 C/D2
Longformacus 57 C2
Longhorsley 57 D2
Longjumeau 156 A1
Longlaville 79 C/D3
Longleat House 63 D2, 64 A3
Longlier 79 C3
Long Melford 65 C2
Longnes 87 C1
Longnor 59 D2, 61 C3, 64 A1
Longny-au-Perche 86 B2
Longobucco 122 B1
Longpont 87 D1, 88 A1
Longpré-les-Corps-Sainte 77 D2
Longré 101 C2
Longridge 59 D1, 60 B2
Longroiva 159 B/C2
Long Stratton 65 C2
Long Sutton 65 C1
Longton 59 D2, 60 B3, 64 A1
Longtown 57 C3, 60 B1
Longué 86 A3
Longueville-sur-Scie 77 C3
Longuyon 79 C3
Longvic 88 B3, 103 D1
Longwy 79 C/D3
Lonigo 107 C3
Lonin 28 A2
Löningen 67 D2
Löningen-Wachtum 67 D2
Lonja 128 A3, 131 D1
Lonkka 19 C2
Lönne 79 B/C3
Lönsboda 50 B2
Lönsboda 72 A1
Lønsdal 15 C1
Lønset 33 C2/3
Lønset 32 A2
Lons-le-Saunier 103 D1, 104 A1/2
Lønstrup 48 B1
Loon op Zand 66 B3, 79 C1
Loon-Plage 77 D1
Loosdorf 94 A2
Lopar 130 B1
Lopare 133 C1/2
Lopătari 141 C2
Lopatica 138 B3, 143 C1
Lopera 167 C3, 172 B1
Loporzano 154 B2/3
Loppa 4 B2
Loppersum 67 C1
Loppi 25 C2
Loqueffret 84 B2

Lora de Estepa 172 A/B2
Lora del Río 171 D1, 172 A1
Loranca del Campo 161 D3
Loranca de Tajuña 161 C2
Lorås 29 D3, 35 C1
Lorca 174 A1
Lorch 91 C2
Lorch 80 B3
Lordosa 158 B2
Loreley 80 B3
Lorentzweiler 79 D3
Lorenzago di Cadore 107 D2
Lorenzana 151 D2, 152 A2
Lorenzo 113 D3
Loreo 115 C1
Loreto 117 D2, 130 A3
Loreto Aprutino 119 C1
Lórév 129 C1
Lorgues 112 A3
Lórica 122 B2
Lorient 84 B3
Loriga 158 B3
Loriguilla 162 B3, 169 C1
Loriol-sur-Drôme 111 C1
Lormes 88 A3, 103 C1
Loro Ciuffenna 115 C3, 116 B2
Loro Piceno 115 D3, 117 D2
Lorqui 169 D3
Lorquin 89 D1/2, 90 A2
Lörrach 90 A3
Lorrez-le-Bocage 87 D2
Lorris 87 D2/3
Lorsch 80 B3
Lörudden 35 D3
Lorup 67 D2
Lorvão 158 A3
Los 39 D1
Losa del Obispo 162 B3, 169 C1
Los Alares 166 B1
Los Alcázares 174 B1
Los Arañones 154 B2
Los Arcos 153 C2
Los Balbases 152 B2/3
Los Barrios de Bureba 153 C2
Los Barrios 172 A3
Los Berengueles 173 C2
Los Cerralbos 160 A/B3
Los Corrales 172 A2
Los Corrales de Buelna 152 B1
Los Cortijos 167 C1/2
Loscos 162 A/B2
Løset 38 A1
Loshamn 42 B3
Losheim 79 D3, 80 A3, 90 A1
Los Hinojosos 167 D1, 168 A1
Loshult 50 B2
Los Marines 165 D3, 171 C1
Los Martínez 169 C3, 174 B1
Los Molares 171 D2
Los Molinos 160 B2
Los Morenos 166 B3
Los Navalmorales 160 A/B3, 166 B3
Los Navalucillos 160 A/B3, 166 B1
Løsning 48 B3, 52 B1
Los Olmos 162 B2
Losomäki 23 C2
Losovaara 19 C2
Los Palacios y Villafranca 171 D2
L'Ospedale 113 D3
Los Rábanos 153 D3, 161 D1
Lossa / Finne 82 A1
Los Santos 158 B3
Los Santos de la Humosa 161 C2
Los Santos de Maimona 165 D2/3
Lossburg 90 B2
Losse 108 B2
Losser 67 C3
Lossiemouth-Branderburgh 54 B2
Lössnitz 82 B2

Lossvik 9 C3
Lostwithiel 62 B3
Los Valencianos 174 A/B1
Los Villares 173 C1
Los Villares de Soria 153 D3
Los Yebenes 167 C1
Löt 51 D1
Lote 36 B1
Loten 42 A2
Løten 38 A2
Lotorp 46 B2
Lotte 67 D2/3
Lottefors 40 A1
Löttorp 51 D1
Lotyń 71 D1
Lotzorai 123 D2
Louargat 84 B2
Loubeyrat 102 B2
Loučeň 83 C2
Loučim 93 C1
Loučka 95 C1
Loudéac 85 C2
Loudes 103 C3, 110 B1
Loudun 101 C1
Loué 86 A2
Loue 17 D2, 18 A1
Louejärvi 12 A3
Louejoki 12 A3, 17 D2
Loughborough 65 C1
Loughbrickland 58 A1
Loughgall 58 A1
Loughor 63 C1
Lougratte 109 C1
Louhans 103 D1
Louhossoa 108 B3, 155 C1
Loukee 26 B1
Loukeinen 23 C2
Louko 20 B3
Loukolampi 22 B3
Loukusa 19 C1
Loulay 100 B2
Loulé 170 B2
Louny 83 C2
Louny 96 A1/2
Lourdes 108 B3, 155 C1
Lourdios-Ichère 108 B3, 154 B1
Louredo 150 B3, 158 A/B1
Lourenzá 151 C1
Loures 164 A2
Loures-Barousse 109 C3, 155 C1
Lourical 158 A3
Lourinhã 164 A1/2
Loúros 146 A1
Lourosa 158 B3
Lourosa 158 A2
Loury 87 C2
Lousã 158 A3
Lousa 164 A2
Lousada 158 A1
Lousame 150 A2
Louth 58 A1
Louth 61 D3
Loutrá 145 D2
Loutrá 144 A/B2/3
Loutrá 144 A1/2
Loutrá Aridéas 143 C1
Loutrá Edipsoú 147 C1
Loutrá Eleftherón 144 B1/2
Loutrá Eleftherón 149 C1
Loutrá Ipátis 146 A2
Loutrá Irmínis 146 A2
Loutrá Kaïtsis 146 B1
Loutrá Kaïáfas 146 B3
Loutrá Kaïáfas 148 A/B2
Loutrá Killínis 146 A2
Loutrákion 147 C2
Loutrákion 146 A1
Loutrá Sidirókastrou 139 D3, 144 A1
Loutrá Smokóvou 146 B1
Loutrá Vólvis 144 A2
Loutrón 146 A1
Loutrón Elénis 147 C2
Loutrós 145 D1, 145 D3
Loutrós 143 D3
Loútsa 147 D2
Louveigné 79 C/D2
Louvie-Juzon 108 B3, 154 B1
Louviers 76 B3, 86 B1
Louvigné du-Désert 86 A/B2
Louvois 88 A/B1

Louvres 87 D1
Lövånger 31 D1
Lovanperä 21 D1, 22 A1
Lövås 30 B2
Løvås 43 D1/2, 44 A1
Lovasbereny 95 D3,
 128 B1
Lövåsen 30 A3, 35 C2
Lovászpatona 95 C3,
 128 A/B1
Lövberg 29 D1
Lövberga 30 A2, 35 C1
Lövdalen 34 A/B2
Loveč 140 B3
Løvenborg 49 C/D3,
 53 C/D1
Lóvere 106 B3
Lóvero 106 B2
Lövestad 50 B3
Loviisa/Lovisa 25 D2/3,
 26 B2/3
Lovinac 131 C2
Lovište 136 A/B1
Lövnäs 39 C1
Lövnäs 30 A1
Lövö 94 B3
Lovosice 83 C2
Løvøyen 33 D2
Lovran 126 B3, 130 A1
Lovreč 126 B3, 130 A1
Lovreć 131 D3, 132 A3
Lovrenc na Pohorju 127 C2
Løvrødsvollen 33 C/D2
Lövsjön 39 D2/3
Lövsta 39 B/C2
Lövstabruk 40 B2
Lövstrand 30 A1
Lövtjärn 40 A2
Lovund 14 A2
Lövvattnet 31 D1
Lövvik 35 D2
Lövvik 30 A2
Lövvik 35 D2
Lowdham 61 C3, 64 B1
Löwenberg 70 A2
Löwenstein 91 C1
Lowestoft 65 D2
Łowicz 73 C3, 97 C1
Łowicz Wałecki 71 C1
Loxstedt 68 A1
Loxstedt-Bexhövede 68 A1
Loxstedt-Dedesdorf 68 A1
Loxstedt-Stotel 68 A1
Löytana 21 D2, 22 A2
Löytövaara 19 C1
Löyttymäki 25 C/D2, 26 A2
Löytynmäki 22 B2
Lož 126 B3
Lozen 139 D1
Łozice 70 B2
Loznica 133 C2
Loznicy 75 C2
Lozöac 131 C3
Lozovik 134 B2
Lozoya 160 B2
Lozoyuela 161 C2
Lozzo di Cadore 107 D2
Luarca 151 C1
Lubań (Lauban) 83 D1
Lubań (Lauban) 96 A1
Lubanowo 70 B2
L'ubar 99 C2
Lübars 69 D3
Lubartów 97 D1, 98 A2
Lubasz 71 D2
Lübbecke 68 A3
Lübben 70 B3
Lübben 72 A3, 96 A1
Lübbenau 70 B3
Lubczyna 70 B1
Lübeck 53 C3, 69 C1
Lübeck-Travemünde 53 C3
Lubenec 83 C3
Lubersac 101 C3
Lubia 153 D3, 161 D1
Lubiatowo 71 C1/2
Lubiesz 71 C/D1
Lubieszewo 71 C1
Lubiń 71 D1
Lubin 96 B1
Lublin 97 D1, 98 A2
Lubliniec 96 B1
Lubniewice 71 C2
Lubno 71 D1
Lubny 99 D2
Lubochňa 95 D1
Luboń 71 D2/3

Lubosz 71 C/D2
Łubowo 71 D1
Lubrín 174 A2
Lubrza 71 C3
Lubsko 71 B/C3
Lübtheen 69 C1
Luby 82 B2
Lübz 69 D1
Lucainena 173 C/D2
Lucainena de las Torres
 173 D2, 174 A2
Lucan 58 A2
Lúcar 173 D1/2
Luçay-le-Mâle 101 D1
Lucca 114 A/B2, 116 A1
Luče 127 C2
Lucelle [Alle] 89 D3, 90 A3
Lucena 172 B1/2
Lucena de Jalón 155 C3,
 163 B/C1
Lucena del Cid 162 B3
Lucena del Puerto 171 C2
Lucenay-l'Évêque 103 C1
Luc-en-Diois 111 D1
Lučenec 97 C2/3
Luceni 155 C3, 163 B/C1
Lucens 104 B1/2
Lucera 120 A1
Luchente 169 D2
Luché-Pringé 86 A/B3
Lüchow 69 C2
Luciana 167 C2
Lučice 133 D3, 134 A/B3
Lucignano 115 C3, 116 B2
Lucillo 151 D2
Lucillos 160 A/B3
Lucito 119 D2
Luck 97 D1, 98 B2
Lucka 82 B1
Luckau 70 A/B3
Luckau 72 A3, 96 A1
Luckenwalde 72 A3, 96 A1
Luckenwalde 70 A3
Lucksta 35 D3
Lückstedt 69 C2
Lüćky Kúpele 95 D1
Luco de Bordón 162 B2
Luco dei Marsi 119 C2
Luçon 101 C2
Ludbreg 127 D2
Lüdenscheid 80 A/B1
Lüderitz 69 D2
Lüdersdorf 53 C3, 69 C1
Lüdge-Elbrinxen 68 A/B3
Lüdge-Rischenau 68 A/B3
Ludgershall 64 A3, 76 A1
Ludgo 47 C2
Ludiente 162 B3
Lüdinghausen 67 D3
Ludlow 59 D3
Ludomy 71 D2
Ludus 92 D3, 140 B1
Ludvika 39 D3
Ludwigsau 81 C2
Ludwigsau-Ersrode 81 C2
Ludwigsburg 91 C1/2
Ludwigschorgast 82 A3
Ludwigsdorf 83 D1
Ludwigsfelde 70 A3
Ludwigshafen am Rhein
 80 B3, 90 B1
Ludwigshafen am Bodensee
 91 C3
Ludwigslust 69 C1
Ludwigsstadt 82 A2
Ludza 74 B2
Luelmo 159 D1
Luesia 154 B2
Luesma 163 C1/2
Lug 137 C1
Lug 129 C3
Lug 133 C1
Luga 74 B1
Lugagnano Val d'Arda
 114 A1
Lugán 152 A2
Lugano 105 D2
Lugar Nuevo 167 C3
Lugar Nuevo de Fenollet
 169 D2
Lugau 82 B2
Lügde 68 A/B3
Lugendorf 94 A2
Lugi 71 C2
Lugnano in Teverina
 117 C3, 118 A/B1
Lugnarohögen 50 A2

Lugnås 45 D2
Lugnvik 30 B3, 35 D2
Lugnvik 29 D3, 34 B2
Lugny 103 D2
Lugo 115 C2, 116 B1
Lugo 150 B2
Lugoj 140 A1/2
Lugones 151 D1
Lugros 173 C2
Lugueros 152 A2
Lugugnana 107 D3,
 126 A3
Luhačovice 95 C1
Luhalahti 24 B1
Luhanka 25 D1, 26 A1
Luhe-Wildenau 82 B3,
 92 B1
Luhtapohja 23 D2
Luhtikylä 25 D2, 26 A2
Luikonlahti 23 C2
Luino 105 D2
Luiro 13 B/C2
Luisenthal 81 D2
Lújar 173 C2
Luka 132 B3
Lúka 95 C2
Luka 136 B1
Luka 136 B1
Luka 130 B2
Luka 135 C2
Luka-Barskaja 99 C3
Lukácsháza 94 B3, 127 D1
Lukare 133 D3, 138 A1
Lukavac 132 B2
Lukavac 132 B3, 137 C1
Lukavec 83 D3, 93 D1
Lukavica 132 B1
Lukićevo 129 D3, 134 A1
Lukkarila 22 B2
Lukkaroinen 18 A3
Lukovica 127 C2
Lukovit 140 B3
Lukovo 135 C3
Lukovo 134 B3, 138 B1
Lukovo 138 A3, 142 B1
Lukovo-Šugarje 130 B2
Lukovska Banja 134 B3,
 138 B1
Łuków 73 D3, 97 C/D1,
 98 A1/2
Luksefjell 43 D2, 44 A1
Lula 123 D2
Luleå 17 C3
Lumbarda 136 B1
Lumbier 155 C2
Lumbrales 159 C2
Lumbreras 153 D2
Lumbres 77 D1/2
Lumijoki 18 A2/3
Lumio 113 D2
Lummelunda 47 D2
Lummelunds bruk 47 D2
Lummimetsä 18 A3
Lummukka 21 B/C2
Lumparland 41 D3
Lumpiaque 155 C3, 163 C1
Lumsheden 40 A2
Luna 154 B2/3
Lunano 115 C2, 117 C1/2
Lunas 110 B2
Lund 50 A/B3
Lund 28 B1
Lund 53 D1/2
Lund 72 A2
Lunda 40 B3, 47 C1
Lundbäck 31 D1
Lunde 30 B3, 35 D2
Lunde 37 D2
Lunde 43 C/D2, 44 A1
Lunde 37 D3
Lunde 36 B2
Lundeborg 53 C2
Lundeby 44 B1
Lundebyvollen 38 B2
Lunden 52 A/B3
Lundenes 9 C1
Lunderseter 38 B3
Lunderskov 48 B3, 52 B1
Lundkälen 29 D3, 34 B2
Lundmoen 37 D2/3
Lundsberg 45 D1, 46 A1
Lundsbrunn 45 D2
Lundsjön 29 D3, 34 B1
Lüneburg 68 B1
Lunel 111 C2/3

Lunestedt 68 A1
Lunéville 89 D2
Lungern 105 C1
Lungro 122 A1
Lungsjön 30 A3, 35 C1
Luninec 98 B1
Lunkkaus 13 C2
Lunnäset 34 A3
Lünne 67 D2
Lunow 70 B2
Lunz am See 93 D3
Luogosanto 123 D1
Luoma-aho 21 C2
Luopa 20 B3
Luopajärvi 20 B3
Luopioinen 25 C1
Luoppoperä 19 C2
Luostanlinna 23 C2
Luosu 11 C3, 12 A2
Luotola 27 B/C2
Luovankylä 20 A/B3
Lupac 135 C1
Lupeni 135 D1
Lupeni 140 B2
Lupiac 109 B/C2/3
Lupiana 161 C2
Lupiñen 154 B2/3
Lupión 167 D3, 173 C1
Lupoglav 127 D3
Lupoglav 126 B3, 130 A1
Luppa 82 B1
Luque 172 B1
Lúras 123 D1
Lurbe-Saint-Christau
 108 B3, 154 B1
Lurçy-Lévy 102 B1
Lure 89 D3
Lureuil 101 D1
Lurgrotte 127 C1
Luri 113 D2
Lurøy 14 A2
Lury-sur-Arnon 102 A1
Lušci Palanka 131 C1/2
Lüsens 107 C1
Luserna San Giovanni
 112 B1
Lusévera 126 A2
Lushnjë 142 A1
Lushnjë 148 A1
Lusi 25 D1, 26 A/B1
Lusiana 107 C3
Lusignan 101 C2
Lusigny-sur-Barse 88 B2
Lus-la-Croix-Haute 111 D1
Lusminki 19 D1
Luso 158 A2/3
Lusón/Lüsen 107 C1
Luspa 10 B2
Luss 56 B1
Lussac 108 B1
Lussac-les-Châteaux
 101 C/D2
Lussac-les-Eglises 101 C2
Lussan 111 C2
Lustad 28 B2, 33 D1,
 34 A1
Lustenau 91 C3
Luštěnice 83 D2
Luster 36 B2
Lutago/Luttach 107 C1
Lutherstadt-Wittenberg
 69 D3
Lutherstadt-Wittenberg
 72 A3
Lütjenburg 53 C3
Lutnes 38 B2
Lutol Suchy 71 C3
Luton 64 B2
Luton Hoo 64 B2/3
Lutry 104 B2
Lutta 24 A2
Lütte 69 D3
Lutter am Barenberge
 68 B3
Lutterworth 65 C2
Lutzelbourg 89 D1, 90 A2
Lützen 82 B1
Lutzerath 80 A3
Lutzmannsburg 94 B3
Lützow 53 C3, 69 C1
Luujoki 18 A1
Luukkola 27 C1
Luukkonen 27 C1
Luumäen asema 27 C2
Luumäki 27 C2
Luupujoki 22 B1

Luupuvesi 22 B1
Luusniemi 22 B3
Luusua 12 B3
Luutalahti 23 D3
Luvia 24 A1
Luvos 16 A1
Luxembourg 79 D3
Luxeuil-les-Bains 89 D3
Luxey 108 B2
Luyego 151 D2
Luyères 88 B2
Luynes 86 B3
Luz 170 B2
Luz 170 A2
Lužani 132 A/B1
Luzarches 87 D1
Luzás 155 C2/3
Luzenac 155 D2, 156 A1
Luzern 105 C1
Lužki 74 B3
Luzo 158 A2/3
Luzón 161 D2
Luz-Saint-Sauveur 155 C2
Luzy 103 C1
Luzzara 114 B1
Luzzi 122 A/B1
L'vov 97 D2, 98 A2
Lwówek 71 C/D2
Lychen 70 A1/2
Lycke 45 D2
Lyckeby 51 C2
Lyčkovo 75 C1/2
Lycksele 31 C1
Lydd 77 C1
Lydham 59 C/D3
Lydney 63 D1
Lye 47 D3
Lyestad 45 D2, 46 A2
Lygna 38 A2
Lykintö 23 C1
Lykkja 37 C2
Lykkja 37 C3
Lykosoura 146 B3
Lyly 25 C1
Lylykylä 19 C2
Lylyvaara 23 D2
Lyme Regis 63 C/D2/3
Lymington 76 A1
Lyndhurst 76 A1
Lyne 48 A3, 52 A1
Lyngdal 43 D1
Lyngdal 42 B3
Lyngør 43 C/D3, 44 A2
Lyngseidet 4 B3
Lyngsnes 28 B1
Lyngvær 8 B2
Lynton 63 C2
Lyø 52 B2
Lyökki 24 A2, 41 D2
Lyon 103 D2
Lyons-la-Forêt 77 D3,
 87 C1
Lysá nad Labem 83 D2/3
Lysá pod Makytou 95 C1
Lysebotn 42 B2
Lysekil 44 B2/3
Lysekloster 36 A3
Lysnes 9 D1
Lysøysund 28 A2/3, 33 C1
Lyss 104 B1
Lystrup 48 B2/3
Lysvik 39 C3
Lysvoll 9 C2
Lytham 59 C/D1/2, 60 B2
Lytham Saint Anne's
 59 C1/2, 60 B2
Lyxaberg 30 B1

M

Maakeski 25 D1, 26 A1
Maalahti 20 A2, 31 D3
Maalismaa 18 B2
Maam Cross 55 C2
Maaninka 22 B2
Maaninkavaara 13 C3
Maanselkä 23 C1
Maarala 27 C1
Maaria 24 B2
Maarianhamina 41 C/D3
Maarianvaara 23 C2
Maarlanperä 21 D1, 22 A1
Maarssen 66 B3

Maaseik 79 D1
Maaselka 19 D3
Maasholm 52 B2
Maasholm-Maasholm-Bad 52 B2
Maasmechelen 79 C/D1/2
Maassluis 66 A3
Maastricht 79 C/D2
Määttälä 21 C1
Määttälänvaara 19 D1
Maavesi 22 B3
Mablethorpe 61 D3, 65 C1
Macael 173 D2, 174 A1/2
Mação 164 B1
Maccagno 105 D2
Macchiagódena 119 D2
Macchiareddu 123 D3
Macclesfield 59 D2, 60 B3, 64 A1
Maceda 150 B2/3
Macedo de Cavaleiros 151 C3, 159 C1
Maceira 158 B2
Maceira 158 A3, 164 A1
Macelj 127 D2
Macerata 117 D2
Maceráta Féltria 115 C2, 117 C1
Machault 88 B1
Machecoul 100 A1
Macherádon 146 A2/3
Machilly 104 A/B2
Machliny 71 D1
Machrihanish 56 A2
Machynlleth 59 C3
Macieira 158 A1
Măcin 141 D2
Macinaggio 113 D2
Mácine 115 D3, 117 D2
Mačkat 133 C/D3, 134 A3
Macken 80 A2/3
Mackenrode 81 D1
Mačkovci 127 D1
Macocha 94 B1
Macomér 123 C2
Mâcon 103 D2
Macon 78 B3
Macotera 160 A2
Macquenoise 78 B3
Macroom 55 C3
Macugnaga 105 C2
Mačul'niki 75 C3
Macure 131 C2
Madängsholm 45 D3
Madaras 129 C2
Maddalena 112 B1
Maddalena Spiággia 123 D3
Maddaloni 119 D3
Made 66 A/B3
Madeira 158 B3, 164 B1
Madekoski 18 B2
Maderuelo 161 C1
Madésimo 105 D2, 106 A2
Madetkoski 12 B1/2
Madlan 42 A2
Madona 74 A2
Madonna del Bosco 115 C1
Madonna delle Grázie 112 B2
Madonna della Neve 117 D3, 118 B1
Madonna della Pace 118 B2
Madonna di Campíglio 106 B2
Madonna di Ponte [Brissago] 105 D2
Madonna di Tirano 106 B2
Madrid 161 B/C2/3
Madridejos 167 D3
Madrid El Pardo 160 B2
Madrigal 161 C1
Madrigal de la Vera 159 D3, 160 A3
Madrigal de las Altas Torres 160 A2
Madrigalejo 166 A2
Madrigalejo del Monte 153 C3
Madriguera 161 C1
Madrigueras 168 B1/2
Madrona 160 B2
Madroñera 166 A1
Madžarovo 145 D2
Maella 163 C1/2

Mäenkylä 21 C/D3
Mäentaka 24 B2
Maesteg 63 C1
Maeztu 153 D2
Mafalda 119 D2
Mafjordhamn 5 C1
Mafra 164 A2
Magacela 166 A2
Magalas 110 B3
Magallón 154 A3, 162 A1
Magán 160 B3, 167 C1
Magaña 153 D3
Magasa 106 B3
Magaz de Cepeda 151 D2
Magdala 82 A2
Magdeburg 69 C/D3
Magenta 105 D3
Magerholm 32 A3, 36 B1
Magesq 108 B2
Maggia [Ponte Brolla] 105 D2
Maghera 54 A3, 55 D2
Magione 115 C3, 117 C2
Maglaj 132 B2
Maglavit 135 D2
Magleby 53 C2
Maglehem 50 B3
Magliano de'Marsi 119 C1/2
Magliano in Toscana 116 B3
Magliano Sabina 117 C3, 118 B1
Maglić 133 D3, 134 A3
Máglie 121 D3
Magnac-Laval 101 C2
Magnières 89 D2
Magnor 38 B3
Magny-Cours 102 B1
Magny-en-Vexin 77 D3, 87 C1
Mágocs 128 B2
Magolsheim 91 C2
Magouládes 142 A3
Maguelone 110 B3
Maguilla 166 A3
Magura 135 C/D3
Magura 138 B2
Magusteiro 150 B3, 158 B1
Magyaratád 128 B2
Magyaregregy 128 B2
Magyarfalva 94 B3
Magyarkeszi 128 B1/2
Magyarmecske 128 B2/3
Magyarnándor 95 D3
Magyarszék 128 B2
Mahide 151 D3, 159 C1
Mahlsdorf 69 C2
Mahora 168 B2
Mahovo 127 D3
Mähring 82 B3
Maials 163 C1
Măicănești 141 C2
Maicas 162 B2
Maïche 89 D3, 104 B1
Máida 122 B2
Máida Marina 122 A/B2
Maiden Castle 63 D2/3
Maidenhead 64 B3
Maiden Newton 63 D2
Maidstone 65 C3, 77 C1
Maienfeld 106 A1
Maiero 115 C1
Mäieruş 141 C1
Maignelay 78 A3
Maijanen 12 A2/3, 17 D1
Mailhac-sur-Benaize 101 C2
Maillat 103 D2, 104 A2
Maillezais 100 B2
Mailly-la-Ville 88 A3
Mailly-le-Camp 88 B2
Mainar 163 C1
Mainburg 92 A2
Mainburg-Lindkirchen 92 A2
Mainhardt 91 C1
Mainiemi 26 B1
Mainleus 82 A3
Mainleus-Buchau 82 A3
Mainsat 102 A2
Maintenon 87 C2
Mainua 19 C3, 22 B1
Mainz 80 B3
Maiorca 158 A3
Maiorga 164 A1

Maiori 119 D3
Mairena del Aljarafe 171 D1/2
Mairena del Alcor 171 D1/2
Mairos 151 C3, 158 B1
Maisach 92 A2
Maisey-le-Duc 88 B3
Maison Forestière 113 D2/3
Maison-Rouge 87 D2, 88 A2
Maisons-Laffitte 87 C1
Maissau 94 A2
Maisse 87 D2
Maissin 79 C3
Maitenbeth 92 B2
Maivala 27 C1
Maizières-lès-Vic 89 D1/2
Maizières-lès-Metz 89 C1
Maja 127 D3, 131 C1
Majadahonda 160 B2
Majadas 159 D3, 166 A1
Majaelrayo 161 C2
Majava 19 C1
Majavasuvanto 13 C2
Majavatn 14 B3, 29 C1
Majdan 129 D2
Majdanpek 135 C2
Majilovac 134 B1/2
Majkić Japra 131 C1
Majovakylä 18 B1
Makarska 131 D3, 132 A3, 136 A/B1
Makeevskoe 75 D2
Mäkelä 25 D2, 26 A2
Mäkikylä 21 C3
Makkola 21 D3, 22 A3
Makó 129 D2
Makó 97 C3, 140 A1
Makole 127 C/D2
Makov 95 D1
Makov 96 B2
Makovac 138 B1
Makovo 139 B/C3, 143 C1
Makrakómi 146 B1
Makrakómi 148 B2
Mákri 145 D1
Makríammos 145 C1/2
Makrinoú 146 B2
Makriráchi 146 B1
Maksama 20 B2
Maksatiha 75 D2
Maksniemi 17 D3, 18 A1
Mæl 43 C1
Malå 16 A3
Malá 173 C2
Mala Bršljanica 128 A3
Mala Čista 131 C2/3
Malacky 94 B2
Malacky 96 B2
Málaga 172 B2
Málaga del Fresno 161 C2
Malagón 167 C2
Malaguilla 161 C2
Malahide 58 A2
Malahvianvaara 19 D3
Malaja Višera 75 C1
Malaja Viska 99 D3
Mala Kladuša 131 C1
Mala Krsna 134 B2
Malalbergo 115 C1
Mala Mitrovica 133 C1
Malanquilla 154 A3, 161 D1, 162 A1
Malarby 24 B3
Mälarhusens strandbad 50 B3
Mäläskä 18 B3
Mala Subotica 127 D2
Malaucène 111 D2
Malaunay 77 C3
Mälävaara 13 C3
Malax (Maalahti) 20 A2, 31 D3
Malborghetto 126 A2
Malbork (Marienburg) 73 C2
Malborn 80 A3
Malbuisson 104 A1
Malcésine 106 B3
Malchin 69 D1, 70 A1
Malching 93 C2
Malchow 69 D1
Malcocinado 166 A3
Maldegem 78 B1
Maldon 65 C3
Malè 106 B2

Malefougasse 111 D2, 112 A2
Malemort-sur-Corrèze 101 D3
Mælen 28 B2
Malente 53 C3
Målerås 51 C1
Malesco 105 C/D2
Malesherbes 87 D2
Malesina 147 C1
Malestroit 85 C3
Maletićevo 134 B1
Malexander 46 A3
Malfa 125 C1
Malga Mare 106 B2
Malgrat de Mar 156 B3
Malhadas 151 D3, 159 C1
Malham 59 D1, 60 B2
Malhu 21 D3
Mali Borak 133 D2, 134 A2
Malicorne-sur-Sarthe 86 A3
Mali Đerdap 135 C1/2
Mali Idoš 129 C/D3
Malijai 112 A2
Málilla 51 C/D1
Mălilla 72 B1
Mali Lošinj 130 A/B2
Malín 83 D3
Malin 99 C2
Malingsbo 39 D3
Malinska 130 B1
Maliq 142 B1/2
Mališevo 138 B2
Maliskylä 21 D1, 22 A1
Mali Zvornik 133 C2
Maljasalmi 23 C2/3
Maljevac 127 D3, 131 C1
Maljovica 139 D2
Malkara 149 D1
Malkenes 42 A1
Malkkila 23 C3
Malko Gradište 145 D2
Malko Tărnovo 141 C3
Mallaig 54 A2, 55 D1
Mållångssta 39 D1, 40 A1
Mallemort 111 D2
Mallén 154 A3
Mallersdorf-Pfaffenberg 92 B2
Málles Venosta/Mals 106 B1/2
Malling 48 B3
Mallinkainen 25 C2, 26 A2
Malliss 69 C1/2
Mallnitz 126 A1
Mallow 55 C3
Mallusjoki 25 D2, 26 A2
Malm 28 B2
Malmåsen 38 B1
Malmbäck 46 A3
Malmberget 16 B1
Malmédy 79 D2
Malmesbury 63 D1, 64 A3
Malmköping 47 B/C1
Malmö 50 A3
Malmö 72 A2
Malmön 44 B2
Malmslätt 46 B2
Malnate 105 D3
Malnes 8 B2
Malo 107 C2
Malojaroslavec 75 D3
Maloja [St.-Moritz] 106 A2
Malo Konjari 138 B3, 143 C1
Malo-les-Bains 77 D1, 78 A1
Malonty 93 D2
Malorita 73 D3, 97 D1, 98 A2
Malovățu 135 D1/2
Måløy 36 A1
Malpartida 160 A2
Malpartida de Cáceres 165 D1
Malpartida de la Serena 166 A2
Malpartida de Plasencia 159 D3
Malpartida de Corneja 159 D2, 160 A2
Malpas 59 D2, 60 B3
Malpica 160 B3, 167 B/C1
Malpica 158 B3, 165 C1
Malpica de Arba 154 A/B2

Malpica de Bergantiños 150 A1
Malsch 90 B1/2
Malschwitz 83 D1
Målselv 4 A3, 9 D1
Målsetsløl 36 B2/3
Malsfeld 81 C1
Malšice 93 D1
Malsjö 45 C1
Målsnes 4 A3, 9 D1
Målsryd 45 C/D3
Malstedt 68 A/B1
Malta 126 A/B1
Malta 159 C2
Maltat 103 C1
Maltbränna 31 C1
Maltby 61 D3
Malterdingen 90 A/B2
Malterhausen 70 A3
Maltesholm 50 B3
Malton 61 C2
Maluenda 162 A1
Mælum 43 D2, 44 A1
Malung 39 C2
Malungen 35 D3
Malungen 38 A2
Malungsfors 39 C2
Małuszów 71 C2/3
Malva 152 A3, 159 D1, 160 A1
Malveira 164 A2
Malveira da Serra 164 A2
Malvik 28 A3, 33 C1/2
Malý Krtíš 95 D2
Malženice 95 C2
Mamaia Băi 141 D2
Mamarrosa 158 A2
Mambrillas de Lara 153 C3
Mamers 86 B2
Mammendorf 92 A2
Mamming 92 B2
Mámmola 122 A/B3
Mamoiada 123 D2
Mamolar 153 C3
Mamone 123 D2
Mamonovo (Heiligenbeil) 73 C2
Mamuras 137 D3
Manacor 157 C/D2
Manacore 120 B1
Manamansalo 19 B/C3
Mañaria 153 D2
Manasija 134 B2
Mănăstirea Tismana 135 D1
Manastir Morača 137 D1
Mancera de Arriba 160 A2
Mancera de Abajo 160 A2
Mancha Real 167 D3, 173 C1
Manchester 59 D2, 60 B3
Manchita 165 D2, 166 A2
Manchones 162 A1/2
Manciano 116 B3, 118 A1
Manciet 108 B2
Mancourt-sur-Orne 89 C1
Mandal 42 B3
Måndalen 32 A3
Mandanici 125 D2
Mándas 123 D3
Mandatoríccio 122 B1
Mandayona 161 C/D2
Mandello del Lário 105 D2/3, 106 A2/3
Manderscheid 80 A3
Mandling 93 C3, 126 A/B1
Mandø 52 A1
Mandoúdion 147 D1
Mándras 147 D2
Mandres-la-Côte 89 C2
Mandrica 145 D1, 145 D3
Manduária 121 D3
Mane 111 D2
Mane 109 C3, 155 D1
Manerba del Garda 106 B3
Mañeru 154 A2
Mânset 28 B1
Mánesis 146 B3
Manětín 83 C3
Manevici 98 B3
Mánfa 128 B2
Manfredónia 120 B1
Mangalia 141 D2
Mángana 145 C1
Mangen 38 B3
Mångsbodarna 39 C2
Mangskog 38 B3, 45 C1

Mangualde **158** B2
Manhay **79** C2
Manheulles **89** C1
Maniago **107** D2, **126** A2
Maninghem-au-Mont **77** D2
Manisa **149** D2
Manises **169** D1
Manjärv **16** B3
Manjaur **31** C1
Mank **94** A2
Mankala **25** D2, **26** B2
Månkarbo **40** B3
Mankila **18** A/B3
Manlleu **156** A2
Mánna **147** C2
Mannersdorf an der Rabnitz **94** B3
Mannersdorf am Leithagebirge **94** B3
Mannervaara **23** D3
Mannheim **80** B3, **90** B1
Männikkö **17** C1
Männikkövaara **19** B/C1
Mannila **24** B2
Manningtree **65** D2
Mannseterbakken **33** D3
Manojlovac slap **131** C2
Manolás **146** A2
Manoppello **119** C1
Manosque **111** D2, **112** A2
Manresa **156** A3
Mansares **158** A2
Månsåsen **34** B2
Manschnow **70** B2
Mansfeld **82** A1
Mansfield **61** D3, **65** C1
Mansilla **153** C3
Mansilla de las Mulas **152** A2
Mansle **101** C2
Mansoniemi **24** B1
Månsta **39** C1
Månsträsk **16** A3
Manteigas **158** B2/3
Mantel **82** B3
Mantes **87** C1
Mantgum **66** B1/2
Manthelan **101** D1
Mantiel **161** D2
Mantila **20** B3
Mantineia **147** B/C3
Mäntlahti **26** B2
Mantorp **46** A/B2
Måntorp **30** A1
Måntova **106** B3, **114** B1
Mäntsälä **25** D2, **26** A2
Mänttä **21** C3
Mäntyharju **26** B1
Mäntyharjun asema **26** B1
Mäntyjärvi **19** C1
Mäntyjärvi **12** A3, **17** D1
Mäntylahti **22** B2
Mäntylänperä **18** A3
Mäntylärvi **23** C2
Mäntyluoto **24** A1, **41** D1
Mäntypää **12** B1
Mäntyvaara **17** C1
Manzac-sur-Vern **101** C3, **109** C1
Manzalvos **151** C3
Manzanal de Arriba **151** C/D3
Manzanares **167** D2
Manzanares el Real **160** B2
Manzaneda **151** C2
Manzaneque **160** B3, **167** C1
Manzanera **162** B3
Manzanilla **171** C1/2
Manzat **102** B2
Manziana **118** A1
Maoča **132** B1
Maqellarë **138** A3
Maqueda **160** B3
Mara **162** A1
Maracena **173** C2
Maradik **133** D1, **134** A1
Maråkerby **40** A/B1
Maranchón **161** D2
Maranello **114** B1
Marano **114** B2, **116** A/B1
Marano di Nápoli **119** C/D3
Marano Lagunare **126** A3
Marans **100** B2
Mǎrǎșești **141** C1

Marateca **164** A/B2
Marathéa **143** C3
Marathías **146** B2
Marathón **147** D2
Marathópolis **146** B3
Maraye-en-Othe **88** A2
Marazion **62** A3
Marazoleja **160** B2
Marazovel **161** C/D1
Marbach **91** C1
Marbach an der Donau **93** D2, **94** A2
Marbache **89** C1
Mårbacka **39** C3
Marbella **172** A3
Marboz **103** D2
Mårbu **43** C1
Marburg **81** B/C2
Marburg-Cappel **81** B/C2
Marby **34** B2
Marc **155** D2
Marça **163** C1/2
Marcali **128** A2
Marcaltő **95** C3, **128** A1
Marčana **130** A1
Marcaria **114** B1
Marcelová **95** C3
Marcén **154** B3
Marcena **107** B/C2
Marcenais **101** C3, **108** B1
Marcenat **102** B3
Mârčevo **135** D3
March **65** C2
Marchais **78** B3
Marchamalo **161** C2
Marchaux **89** C3, **104** A1
Marche-en-Famenne **79** C2/3
Marchegg **94** B2
Marchegg **96** B2/3
Marchena **172** A2
Marchenoir **86** A/B3
Marcheprime **108** A/B1
March-Hugstetten **90** A/B2/3
Marchiennes **78** A2
Marchtrenk **93** C/D2
Marciac **109** B/C3, **155** C1
Marciana **116** A3
Marciana Marina **116** A3
Marcianise **119** D3
Marcigny **103** C2
Marcilhac-sur-Celé **109** D1
Marcillac-la-Croze **109** D1
Marcillac-la-Croisille **102** A3
Marcillac-Vallon **110** A1/2
Marcillat-en-Combraille **102** B2
Marcilloles **103** D3
Marcilly-en-Gault **87** C3
Marcilly-sur-Eure **86** A/B1
Marcilly-sur-Seine **88** A2
Marck **77** D1
Marckolsheim **90** A2
Marco **107** B/C3
Marco de Canaveses **158** A/B1/2
Marcoing **78** A2/3
Mårdaklev **50** A1
Mar de Cristal **174** B1
Marden **63** D1
Mardie **87** C2/3
Mårdsel **16** B2
Mårdsjö **30** A1/2
Mårdsund **29** C/D3, **34** B2
Mære **28** B2, **33** D1
Marécottes, Les **104** B2
Marèges **102** A3
Mareilly-en-Villette **87** C3
Mareilly-le-Hayer **88** A2
Marennes **100** B2/3
Maresquel **77** D2
Maretz **78** A3
Mareuil **101** C3
Mareuil-en-Brie **88** A1
Mareuil-le-Port **88** A1
Mareuil-sur-Ourcq **87** D1
Mareuil-sur-Ay **88** A1
Mareuil-sur-Arnon **102** A1
Mareuil-sur-Lay **101** C2
Marevo **75** C2
Margam **63** C1
Margarítion **142** B3
Margate **65** C3, **76** B1
Margaux **108** B1
Margerie **88** B2

Margès **103** D3
Margherita di Savóia **120** B1, **136** A3
Marghita **97** D3, **140** B1
Margone **104** B3, **112** B1
Margonin **71** D2
Margut **79** C3
María **173** D1, **174** A1
Maria Alm am Steinernen Meer **92** B3, **126** A1
María de Huerva **154** B3, **162** B1
María de la Salud **157** C2
Maria Elend **126** B2
Mariager **48** B2
Marialva **159** B/C2
Maria Neustift **93** D3
Marianka **94** B2
Mariannelund **46** B3
Mariannelund **72** B1
Marianópoli **124** B2
Mariánské Lázně **82** B3
Mariapfarr **126** B1
Maria Saal **126** B1/2
Maria Taferl **93** D2, **94** A2
Maria-ter-Heide **79** B/C1
Maria Wörth **126** B2
Maiazell **146** A3
Mariazell **96** A3
Maribo **53** C/D2
Maribor **127** C/D2
Marica **141** C3
Marieberg **17** C2
Marieberg **46** A1
Marieby **34** B2
Mariedamm **46** A2
Mariefred **47** C1
Mariehamn (Maarianhamina) **41** C/D3
Marieholm **50** A/B3
Marieholm **50** B1
Marielyst **53** D2
Mariembourg **78** B3
Marienberg **83** C2
Marienborg **53** D2
Marienhagen **68** B3
Marienheide **80** A1
Marienmünster Bredenborn **68** A3
Marienmünster **68** A3
Mariental **69** C3
Mariënvelde **67** C3
Mariestad **45** D2
Marifjøra **36** B2
Marignane **111** D3
Marigny **86** A/B1
Marigny-le-Châtel **88** A2
Marija Bistrica **127** D2
Marikostinovo **139** D3, **144** A1
Marín **150** A2
Marina **131** C2
Marina del Cantone **119** D3
Marina di Alberese **116** A/B3
Marina di Amendolara **120** B3, **122** B1
Marina di Andora **113** C2
Marina di Badolato **122** B2/3
Marina di Belvedere **122** A1
Marina di Castagneto Donorático **114** B3, **116** A2
Marina di Carrara **114** A2
Marina di Camerota **120** A3
Marina di Campo **116** A3
Marina di Castellaneta **121** C3
Marina di Cécina **114** A/B3, **116** A2
Marina di Chiéuti **119** D2, **120** A1
Marina di Fuscaldo **122** A1
Marina di Gáiro **123** D2
Marina di Gioiosa Iónica **122** B3
Marina di Grosseto **116** A3
Marina di Lícola **119** C3
Marina di Mancaversa **121** D3
Marina di Maratea **120** A/B3, **122** A1
Marina di Massa **114** A2, **116** A1
Marina di Nováglie **121** D3

Marina di Orosei **123** D2
Marina di Palma **124** B3
Marina di Pisa **114** A2/3, **116** A2
Marina di Pietrasanta **114** A2, **116** A1
Marina di Ragusa **125** C3
Marina di Sant'António **122** B3
Marina di Sorso **123** C1
Marina di Torre Grande **123** C2
Marina di Vasto **119** D1/2
Mar'ina Gorka **99** C1
Marina San Giovanni **121** D3
Marina San Vito **119** D1
Marina Schiavonea **122** B1
Marine d'Albo **113** D2
Marine de Meria **113** D2
Marine De Porticciolo **113** D2
Marine de Sisco **113** D2
Marineo **124** B2
Marines **77** D3, **87** C1
Marines **162** B3, **169** D1
Mæringsdalen **33** B/C2
Maringues **102** B2
Marinha Grande **158** A3, **164** A1
Marinhais **164** A/B2
Marinkainen **21** B/C1
Marino **118** B2
Mariol **102** B2
Mariotto **120** B2
Maristova **37** C2
Marjaliza **167** C1
Märjamaa **74** A1
Marjaniemi **18** A2
Marjoniemi **25** D1, **26** A1/2
Marjotaipale **25** D1, **26** B1
Marjovaara **23** D3
Mark **30** A1
Marka **14** B1
Markabygd **28** B3, **33** D1
Markaryd **50** B2
Markaryd **72** A1
Markdorf **91** C3
Markee **70** A2
Markelo **67** C3
Marken **20** B2
Markersdorf **82** B2
Market Deeping **64** B1
Market Drayton **59** D2/3, **60** B3, **64** A1
Market Harborough **64** B2
Markethill **58** A1
Market Rasen **61** D3
Market Weighton **61** D2
Markgrafneusiedl **94** B2
Markgrafpieske **70** B3
Markgröningen **91** C1/2
Markina Xemein **153** D1
Markiniz **153** D2
Märkisch Buchholz **70** A/B3
Markitta **17** B/C1
Markkina **10** B2
Mark-Kleeberg **82** B1
Markkleeberg **82** B1
Markkula **21** C1
Marklohe-Lemke **68** A2
Marknesse **66** B2
Markneukirchen **82** B3
Márkó **128** B1
Markópoulon **147** D2
Markovac **134** B1
Markovac **134** B2
Markovgrad **138** B3, **143** C1
Markovićevo **134** B1
Markranstädt **82** B1
Marksuhl **81** D2
Markt Allhau **127** D1
Marktbergel **81** D3, **91** D1
Markt Berolzheim **91** D1
Markt Bibart **81** D3
Markt Erlbach **81** D3, **91** D1
Marktheidenfeld **81** C3
Markt Indersdorf **92** A2
Marktjärn **35** C2/3
Marktl **92** B2
Marktleugast **82** A2/3
Marktleuthen **82** B3
Markt Nordheim-Herbolzheim **81** D3, **91** D1

Marktoberdorf **91** D3
Marktoberdorf-Leuterschach **91** D3
Markt Piesting **94** A/B3
Marktredwitz **82** B3
Markt Rettenbach **91** D3
Marktrodach **82** A2
Markt Sankt Martin **94** B3
Markt Sankt Florian **93** D2
Markt Schwaben **92** A/B2
Markušica **129** B/C3
Markvarec **94** A1
Marl **67** C3, **80** A1
Marlborough **64** A3
Marle **78** B3
Marlieux **103** D2
Marlishausen **81** D2, **82** A2
Marlow **64** B3
Marlow **53** D3
Marma **40** B2
Marmagne **103** C1
Marmande **109** B/C1
Marmara **149** D1
Marmaris **149** D3
Marmaverken **40** A1
Marmeleiro **158** B3, **164** B1
Marmelete **170** A2
Marmirolo **106** B3
Marmolejo **167** C3, **172** B3
Marmorbyn **46** B1
Marmore **117** C3, **118** B1
Marmoutier **89** D1/2, **90** A2
Marnach **79** D3
Marnay **89** C3, **104** A1
Marne **52** A3
Marne-la-Vallée **87** D1
Mårnes **14** B1
Marnheim **80** B3
Marnitz **69** D2
Maroilles **78** B2/3
Maroldsweisach **81** D2/3
Marolles-les-Braults **86** B2
Maromme **77** C3
Marone **106** B3
Marónia **145** C/D1
Mårosjö **30** A3, **35** C2
Maroslele **129** C2
Maróstica **107** C3
Marotta **115** D2, **117** D1/2
Mårøyfjord **6** B1
Marpingen **80** A3, **90** A1
Marquartstein **92** B3
Marquion **78** A2
Marquise **77** D1
Marradi **115** C2, **116** B1
Marrasjärvi **12** A3, **17** D1
Marraskoski **12** A3
Marratxi **157** C2
Mars **111** C1
Marsac-en-Livradois **103** C3
Marságlia **113** D1
Marsala **124** A2
Marsango **107** C3
Marsannay-la-Côte **88** B3, **103** D1
Marsanne **111** C1
Marsberg-Bredelar **81** B/C1
Marsberg-Essentho **81** B/C1
Marsberg-Meerhof **81** C1
Marsberg-Westheim **81** C1
Marsciano **117** C3
Marseillan **110** B3
Marseille **111** D3
Marseille-en-Beauvaisis **77** D3
Marseilles-les-Aubigny **102** B1
Marshfield **63** D1/2, **64** A3
Mársia **117** D3
Mársico **120** A/B3
Mársico Nuovo **120** A/B3
Marsjärv **17** C2
Mars-la-Tour **89** C1
Marsliden **29** D1
Maršovice **83** D1
Marssac-sur-Tarn **109** D2
Märsta **40** B3, **47** C1
Marstal **53** C2
Marstein **32** B3, **37** C1
Marstrand **44** B3
Marsvinsholm **50** B3
Märsylä **21** C1

Marszow **71** C3, **83** D1
Marta **116** B3, **118** A1
Martano **121** D3
Martel **109** D1
Martelange **79** C/D3
Mártély **129** D2
Mårtensboda **31** D1
Martfeld **68** A2
Martfü **129** D1
Marthon **101** C3
Martiago **159** C2
Martignacco **126** A2
Martigné **86** A2
Martigné-Briand **86** A3,
101 B/C1
Martigné-Ferchaud **86** A3
Martigny **104** B2
Martigny-les-Bains **89** C2
Martigues **111** C/D3
Martiherrero **160** A2
Martikkala **22** B2
Martim Longo **170** B1
Martimo **17** D2, **18** A1
Martímporra **151** D1,
152 A1
Martin **95** D1
Martin **96** B2
Martina Franca **121** C2
Martina (Martinsbruck)
[Scuol-Tarasp] **106** B1
Martinci **133** C1
Martín de la Jara **172** A2
Martín del Río **162** B2
Martín de Yeltes **159** C/D2
Martinet **155** D2, **156** A2
Martínez **160** A2
Martín Muñoz de las Posa-
das **160** A/B2
Martinniemi **18** A2
Martiñon **147** C1/2
Martinroda **81** D2, **82** B2
Martinsberg **93** D2, **94** A2
Martinščica **130** A1
Martinsicuro **117** D3
Martinska **131** C3
Mártis **123** C1
Martizay **101** D1
Martjanci **127** D1/2
Mart'janovo **75** B/C2
Martock **63** D2
Martofte **49** C3, **53** C1
Martonoš **129** D2
Martonvaara **23** C2
Martonvásár **95** D3,
129 C1
Martorell **156** A3
Martos **172** B1
Martres-de-Veyre **102** B3
Martres-Tolosane **109** C3,
155 D1
Martron **101** C3
Martti **13** C2
Marttila **25** C2
Marttila **24** B2
Marttisenjärvi **22** B1
Marum **67** C1/2
Marunowo **71** D2
Marvão **165** C1
Marvejols **110** B1
Marvik **42** A2
Marxheim **91** D2, **92** A2
Marxwalde **70** B2
Marxzell **90** B1/2
Máry **24** B2/3
Maryport **57** C3, **60** A1
Maryport **54** B3
Marzabotto **114** B2,
116 B1
Marzahna **69** D3, **70** A3
Marzahne **69** D2
Marzocca **115** D2/3,
117 D2
Masalcolreig **155** C3,
163 C1
Masamagrell **169** D1
Mas-Cabardes **110** A3,
156 A/B1
Máscali **125** D2
Mascalucia **125** D2
Mascaraque **160** B3,
167 C1
Mascarenhas **151** C3,
159 C1
Mas de Barberans **163** C2
Mas de las Matas **162** B2
Masdenverge **163** C2
Masegoso **168** B2

Masegoso de Tajuña
161 D2
Maselheim **91** C2
Masella **156** A2
Måsenes **5** D1, **6** B1
Masera **105** C2
Masevaux **89** D3, **90** A3
Masfjorden **36** A3
Masham **61** C2
Masi **5** C3, **11** C1
Maside **150** B2
Masi Torello **115** C1
Måskenåive **15** D3
Maskjok **7** C2
Masku **24** A/B2
Maslacq **108** B3, **154** B1
Maslenica **131** B/C2
Maslinica **131** C3
Masllorenç **163** D1
Maso Corto **106** B1
Masomäki **21** D2, **22** A2
Måsøy **5** D1, **6** A1
Masquefa **156** A3
Massa **114** A2, **116** A1
Massa Fiscáglia **115** C1
Massafra **121** C2
Massagettes **102** B3
Massa Lombarda **115** C1/2,
116 B1
Massa Lubrense **119** D3
Massalubrense **119** D3
Massa Maríttima **114** B3,
116 A2
Massa Martana **117** C3,
118 B1
Massanet de la Selva
156 B3
Massanet de Cabrenys
156 B2
Massarosa **114** A2, **116** A1
Massat **155** C2
Massay **87** C3, **102** A1
Massbach-Poppenlauer
81 D2/3
Massello **112** B1
Masseret **101** D3
Masseria **107** C1
Masseria/Maiern **107** C1
Masseria Piede Rocca
119 C2
Masseube **109** C3, **155** C1
Massiac **102** B3
Massing **92** B2
Mässlingen **34** A2
Mästerby **47** D3
Masterelv **5** D1, **6** A1
Mästocka **50** B2
Masua **123** C3
Masueco **159** C1/2
Masungsbyn **10** B3
Måsvik **4** A2
Maszewo **71** B/C3
Maszewo **71** C1
MATABUENA **160** B2
Mata de Alcántara **159** C3,
165 C/D1
Mata de Cuéllar **160** B1
Matala **18** A1
Matalalahti **22** B1
Matalascañas **171** C2
Matamala de Almazán
153 D3, **161** D1
Mata Mourisca **158** A3,
164 A1
Matanza **152** A2/3
Matanza de Soria **153** C3,
161 C1
Matapozuelos **160** A1
Matara **23** C2
Mataramäki **22** B3
Mataraselkä **12** B2
Mataró **156** B3
Matarredonda **172** A1/2
Mataruška Banja **133** D3,
134 A/B3
Mätäsvaara **23** C2
Matejče **139** B/C2
Matélica **115** D3,
117 C/D2
Matera **121** B/C2
Materija **126** B3
Matešévo **137** D1
Mátészalka **97** D3, **98** A3
Matet **162** B3, **169** D1
Mateus **158** B3
Matfen **57** D3, **61** B/C1
Matfors **35** D3

Matha **101** C2
Mathay **89** D3
Mathildedal **24** B3
Mathopen **36** A3
Mathry **62** B1
Máti **147** D2
Matignon **85** C2
Matilla de los Caños del Río
159 D2
Matino **121** D3
Mátion **145** D3
Mátion **147** B/C2/3
Matka **138** B2
Matkakoski **17** D2, **18** A1
Matkaniva **18** A3
Matkavaara **19** C3
Matku **25** B/C2
Matlock **61** C3, **64** A1
Matnäset **34** B2
Matočina **145** D2
Matojärvi **17** D2
Matos **158** A3
Matosinhos **158** A1/2
Matour **103** C2
Matrand **38** B3
Matre **36** A3
Matrei am Brenner **107** C1
Matreier Tauernhaus
107 D1
Matrei in Osttirol **107** D1
Mätsäkansa **25** C1/2
Matsdal **15** C3
Mattaincourt **89** C2
Mattarello **107** C2
Matteröd **50** B2
Mattersburg **94** B3
Mattighofen **93** C2/3
Mattila **19** D1
Mattilanmäki **13** C3
Mattilanperä **18** A3
Mattinata **120** B1
Mattinen **24** A2
Mattisudden **16** B1/2
Mattmar **29** C3, **34** B2
Mattön **40** A2/3
Mattsmyra **39** D1
Måttsund **17** C3
Matulji **126** B3, **130** A1
Matute **153** C/D2
Matvejevskaja-Harčevn'a
75 C1
Maubeuge **78** B2
Maubourguet **108** B3,
155 C2
Maubranche **102** A/B1
Mauchline **56** B2
Mauer **90** B1
Mauerkirchen **93** C2
Mauern **92** A/B2
Mauguio **111** B/C3
Maukkula **23** D3
Maula **17** D2, **18** A1
Maulbronn **90** B1
Maulde **78** A/B2
Maule **87** C1
Mauléon-Licharre **108** A3,
154 B1
Maulévrier **100** B1
Maunola **27** C1
Maunu **10** B2
Maunu **10** B2
Maunujärvi **12** A2
Maunula **18** A/B2
Maura **38** A3
Maurach **92** A3, **107** C1
Maure-de-Bretagne
85 C2/3
Maureilhan **110** B3,
156 B1
Mauriac **102** A3
Maurnes **9** C2
Mauron **85** C2
Maurs **110** A1
Maurset **36** B3
Maurstad **36** A1
Mauru **18** B1
Maurumaa **24** A2, **41** D2
Maury **156** B1
Mausoléo **113** D2
Maussac **102** A3
Maussane **111** C2
Mausundvær **32** B2
Mautern an der Donau
94 A2
Mauterndorf **126** B1
Mauterndorf **96** A3

Mautern in Steiermark
93 D3, **127** C1
Mauth **93** C1/2
Mauthausen **93** D2
Mauth-Finsterau **93** C1
Mauvezin **109** C2
Mauzé-sur-le-Mignon
100 B2
Mauzun **102** B3
Mavas **15** C1
Mavrélion **143** C3
Mavrodéndrion **143** C2
Mavrothálassa **144** B1
Mavrovo **138** B3
Mavrovi Hanovi **138** B3
Mavrovoúnion **143** D3
Maxhütte-Haidhof **92** B1
Maxial **164** A2
Maxmo (Maksamaa) **20** B2
Mayalde **159** D1
Maybole **56** B2
Mayen **80** A2
May-en-Multien **87** D1
Mayenne **86** A2
Mayerhofen **107** D1,
126 A1
Mayet **86** B3
Mayorga **152** A3
Mäyränperä **18** A3
Mayrhofen **107** C1
Mäyry **21** C2
Mazagón **171** C2
Mazaleón **163** C2
Mazamet **110** A3
Mazara del Vallo **124** A2
Mazarákia **142** B3
Mazarambroz **160** B3,
167 C1
Mazarete **161** D2
Mazaricos **150** A2
Mazarulleque **161** C/D3
Mázaszászvár **128** B2
Mazaterón **153** D3, **161** D1
Maze **86** A3
Mažeikiai **73** C/D1
Mazères **109** D3, **155** D1,
156 A1
Mazérolles **108** B3, **154** B1
Mazeyrolles **109** C1
Mazières-en-Gâtine **101** C2
Mazin **131** C2
Mázion **142** B2
Mazirbe **73** C/D1
Mazsalaca **73** D1, **74** A2
Mazuecos **161** C3
Mazuelo de Muñó
152 B2/3
Mažurani **130** B2
Mazzarino **125** C3
Mazzarrá Sant'Andrea
125 D2
Mazzarrone **125** C3
Mchy **71** D3
Mealhada **158** A2/3
Méan **79** C2
Meana Sardo **123** D2
Meaño **150** A2
Meåstrand **30** A3, **35** C2
Meathas Truim (Edgeworth-
stown) **55** C/D2
Meaulne **102** B1/2
Meaux **87** C1
Meåvollan **33** D2
Mebygda **29** C2
Mecerreyes **153** C3
Mechelen **78** B1
Mechernich **79** D2, **80** A2
Mecina **173** C2
Meckenbeuren **91** C3
Meckenheim **80** A2
Mecklenburg **53** C3, **69** C1
Meco **161** C2
Mêda **158** B2
Medak **131** B/C2
Medåker **46** B1
Meddo **67** C3
Mede **113** C/D1
Medebach **80** B1
Medeja **126** B3, **130** A1
Medelby **52** B2
Medelim **159** B/C3
Medellín **165** D2, **166** A2
Medemblik **66** B2
Medena Selišta **131** D2
Mêdênec **83** C2
Medesano **114** A1
Medevi **46** A2

Medewitz **69** D3
Medgidia **141** D2
Medhamn **45** D1
Mediana **135** C3
Mediana de Aragón
154 B3, **162** B1
Mediaş **97** D3, **140** B1
Medicina **115** C1/2
Medina Azahara **166** B3,
172 A1
Medinaceli **161** D1/2
Medina de las Torres
165 D3
Medina del Campo **160** A1
Medina de Pomar **153** C2
Medina de Ríoseco **152** A3
Medina-Sidonia **171** D3
Medinci **128** B3
Medinilla **159** D2
Mediona **155** D3, **156** A3,
163 D1
Medjurečje **133** D3,
134 A3
Medkovec **135** D3
Medle **31** D1
Médole **106** B3
Medrano **153** D2
Medskogen **38** B2
Medskogsbygget **34** A3
Medstugan **29** B/C3,
33 D1, **34** A1
Medulin **130** A1
Medumajdan **131** C1
Meduno **107** D2, **126** A2
Medveda **134** B3
Medveđa **139** B/C1
Medveđa **140** A3
Medved'ov **95** C3
Medvida **131** C2
Medvode **126** B2
Medvodje **126** B2
Medyn' **75** D3
Medzibrod **95** D1/2
Medzilaborce **97** C2, **98** A3
Medžitlija **143** C1
Meeder **81** D2, **82** A2
Meerane **82** B2
Meerbeck **68** A3
Meerbusch **79** D1, **80** A1
Meerle **79** C1
Meersburg **91** C3
Meerssen **79** C/D2
Mefjordbotn **9** D1
Megála Kalívia **143** C3
Megáli Panagiá **144** B2
Megáli Vólvi **144** A1/2
Megalochórion **143** C3
Megalopolis **146** B2
Mégara **147** D2
Mégara **148** B2
Mégaron **143** C2
Mégève **104** B3
Megina **161** D2, **162** A2
Meglecy **75** D1
Mehadia **135** C1
Mehamn **7** B/C1
Mehedeby **40** B2
Méhoudin **86** A2
Mehringen **69** C3
Mehring (Trier) **80** A3
Mehrstetten **91** C2
Mehun-sur-Yèvre **87** C/D3,
102 A1
Mehus **9** C1
Meigle **57** C2
Meijel **79** D1
Meilen **105** D1
Meilhan **108** A2
Meillant **102** A/B1
Meimoa **159** B/C3
Méina **105** D3
Meine **69** C2/3
Meinersen **68** B2
Meinerzhagen **80** A/B1
Meinerzhagen-Valbert
80 B1
Meineweh **82** B1
Meinhardt-Frieda **81** D1
Meiningen **81** D2
Meira **151** C1
Meiringen **105** C1/2
Meis **150** A2
Meisburg **79** D3, **80** A3
Meisenheim **80** A/B3
Meisingset **32** B2
Meissen **83** C1
Meissen **96** A1

Meitingen **91** D2
Mejorada **160** A3
Mejorada del Campo
   161 C2/3
Mel **107** C/D2
Melago/Melag **106** B1
Melaje **133** D3, **138** A1
Melalahti **19** C3
Melangseidet **4** A3, **9** D1,
   10 A1
Melás **143** C2
Melbeck **68** B1/2
Melbourne **61** C3, **64** A/B1
Melbu **8** B2
Melby **49** D3
Meldal **33** C2
Méldola **115** C2, **117** C1
Meldorf **52** A/B3
Melegnano **105** D3,
   106 A3
Melen **29** B/C3, **34** A1
Melen **29** B/C3, **34** A1
Melenci **129** D3
Melendugno **121** D3
Meleta **114** B3, **116** A/B2
Meleti **114** A1
Mélezet **112** A/B1
Melfi **120** A/B2
Melfjorden **14** B2
Melgaço **150** B3
Melgar de Arriba **152** A2/3
Melgar de Fernamental
   152 B2
Melgar de Tera **151** D3
Melgar de Yuso **152** B2/3
Melhus **32** B2
Melhus **28** A3, **33** C2
Melick **79** D1
Mélida **154** A2
Melide **150** B2
Melides **164** A3
Meligalás **146** B3
Melíki **143** D2
Melilli **125** D3
Mélisey **89** D3
Mélissa **145** C1
Melíssi **143** C2/3
Melissourgós **144** A2
Melíti **143** C1
Mélito di Porto Salvo
   122 A3, **125** D2
Melívia **145** C1
Melívia **143** D3, **144** A3
Melk **94** A2
Melk **96** A2/3
Melkoniemi **27** D1
Melksham **63** D2, **64** A3
Mellajärvi **12** A3, **17** D2
Mellakoski **12** A3, **17** D2
Mellansel **30** B3
Mellansjö **35** C3
Mellansjö **17** C3
Mellansvartbäck **31** C2
Mellbystrand **50** A2
Melle **68** A3
Melle **101** C2
Melle-Buer **68** A3
Mellen **69** C2
Melle-Neuenkirchen **68** A3
Mellensee **70** A3
Melleray **86** B2
Melle-Riemsloh **68** A3
Mellerud **45** C2
Mellerup **48** B2
Mellifont Abbey **58** A1/2
Mellilä **24** B2
Mellingen **82** A2
Mellingen **90** B3
Mellingsmoen **29** C1
Mellösa **46** B1
Mellrichstadt **81** D2
Mellrichstadt-Bahra **81** D2
Melnica **134** B2
Melnice **130** B1
Mělnické Vtelno **83** D2
Mělník **83** D2
Melnik **139** D3
Mělník **96** A1/2
Melo **158** B2
Melón **150** B2/3
Melpers **81** D2
Melrand **84** B2
Melrose **57** C2
Melsomvik **43** D2, **44** A/B1
Melsträsk **16** B3
Melsungen **81** C1
Meltaus **12** A3

Meltausjoki **12** A/B3
Meltingen **28** A/B3, **33** C1
Meltola **25** C3
Meltola **27** C2
Melton Mowbray **64** B1
Meltosjärvi **12** A3, **17** D2
Melun **87** D2
Melun-Sénart **87** D2
Melvich **54** B1
Mélykút **129** C2
Melzo **105** D3, **106** A3
Mem **46** B2
Memaliaj **142** A2
Membrilla **167** D2
Membrio **165** C1
Memešïsti **142** B1
Memmelsdorf **81** D3,
   82 A3
Memmingen **91** D3
Memmingen-Steinheim
   91 D3
Memurubu **37** C2
Menággio **105** D2, **106** A2
Menai Bridge **59** B/C2,
   60 A3
Menàrguens **155** C3,
   163 C1
Menars **86** A/B3
Menasalbas **160** B3,
   167 C1
Menat **102** B2
Menata **115** C1
Mendavia **153** D2
Mende **110** B1
Mende **129** C1
Menden **80** B1
Mendenítsa **147** C1
Menden-Lendringsen
   80 B1
Mendibieu **108** A/B3,
   154 B1
Mendig **80** A2
Mendiga **164** A1
Mendigorría **154** A2
Mendrisio **105** D2/3
Ménéac **85** C2
Menemen **149** D2
Menen **78** A2
Menetou-Salon **87** D3,
   102 A/B1
Ménétréol-sur-Sauldre
   87 D3
Ménétréol-sur-Sancerre
   87 D3
Menfi **124** A2
Ménfőcsanak **95** C3
Mengabril **166** A2
Mengamuñoz **160** A2
Mengara **115** D3, **117** C2
Mengen **91** C3
Mengerskirchen **80** B2
Mengeš **126** B2
Mengíbar **167** C3, **173** C1
Mengkofen-Weichshofen
   92 B1
Menídion **146** A1
Menigoute **101** C2
Menkijärvi **21** C2
Mennecy **87** D2
Menonen **25** B/C2
Mens **111** D1, **112** A1
Mensignac **101** C3
Menslage **67** D2
Mentana **118** B2
Menthon-Saint-Bernard
   104 A3
Menton **112** B2/3
Méntrida **160** B3
Menz **70** A2
Méounes-les-Montrieux
   112 A3
Meppel **67** C2
Meppen **67** D2
Meppen-Helte **67** D2
Meppen-Versen **67** C/D2
Mequinenza **163** C1
Mer **87** C3
Mera **150** B1
Meráker **28** B3, **33** D1
Meranges **156** A2
Merano/Meran **107** C1/2
Merate **105** D3, **106** A3
Mercadal **157** C1
Mercatale **115** C3, **117** C2

Mercatino Conca
   115 C/D2, **117** C1
Mercato San Severino
   119 D3
Mercato Saraceno **115** C2,
   117 C1
Merceana **164** A2
Mercus **155** D2, **156** A1
Merdrignac **85** C2
Mere **63** D2, **64** A3
Merelim **150** A3, **158** A1
Merenlahti **27** C2
Mérens-les-Vals **156** A1/2
Méréville **87** C2
Mergozzo **105** C/D2
Méribel-les-Allues **104** B3
Meric **145** C2
Mérida **165** D2, **166** A2
Mérigon **108** B3, **155** C1
Merijärvi **18** A3
Merikarvia **24** A1
Meriläinen **21** C1/2
Merimasku **24** A2
Merkenes **15** C1
Merkine **73** D2, **74** A3
Merklín **83** C3, **93** C1
Merlara **107** C3, **115** B/C1
Merlimont-Plage **77** D2
Mern **53** D2
Mernye **128** B2
Merošina **135** C3
Mersch **79** D3
Merseburg **82** B1
Mersevát **128** A1
Mers-les-Bains **76** B2
Mertajärvi **10** B2
Mertendorf **82** A1
Merthyr Tydfil **63** C1
Mertingen **91** D2
Mértola **170** B1
Merton **63** C2
Mertzwiller **90** A1/2
Méru **77** D3, **87** C1
Merufe **150** A/B3
Mervans **103** D1
Merville **78** A2
Merxheim **80** A3
Méry-sur-Oise **87** C/D1
Méry-sur-Seine **88** A2
Merzamemi **125** D3
Merzdorf **70** A3
Merzenich **79** D2
Merzenstein **93** D2
Merzig **79** D3, **80** A3
Merzig-Besseringen **79** D3
Merzig-Brotdorf **79** D3,
   80 A3
Mes **137** D2
Mesagne **121** D2/3
Mesão Frio **158** B1/2
Mesas de Ibor **159** D3,
   166 A/B1
Meschede **80** B1
Meschede-Calle **80** B1
Meschede-Eversberg **80** B1
Meschede-Freienohl **80** B1
Meschede-Remblinghausen
   80 B1
Meschers-sur-Gironde
   100 B3
Mescoules **109** C1
Meščovsk **75** D3
Mesegar **160** B3, **167** C1
Mešeišta **138** B3, **142** B1
Meselefors **30** A/B1
Mesenikólas **143** C3
Mesía **150** B1
Mesić **134** B1
Mesinge **49** C3, **53** C1
Meskjer **4** A3, **9** D1
Meskusvaara **19** C/D1
Meslay-du-Maine **86** A2
Mesnalien **38** A1/2
Mesnières-en-Bray **76** B3
Mesocco [Castione-Ar-
   bedo] **105** D2, **106** A2
Mesochóra **143** C3
Mésola **115** C1
Mesolóngion **146** A/B2
Mesón do Vento **150** A/B1
Mesones **161** C2
Mesones de Isuela **154** A3,
   162 A1
Mesopótamon **142** B3

Mesoraca **122** B2
Mespelbrunn **81** C3
Messac **85** D3
Messaure **16** B1
Messdorf **69** C2
Messei **86** A1/2
Messejana **164** B3, **170** A1
Messel **81** B/C3
Messelt **38** A1
Messene **146** B3
Méssia **144** B1
Messigny **88** B3
Messina **122** A3, **125** D1
Messina Divieto **125** D1
Messina Mili Marina
   122 A3, **125** D2
Messina Sparta **122** A3,
   125 D1
Messina Torre Faro **122** A3,
   125 D1
Messíni **146** B3
Messíni **148** B2/3
Messkirch **91** C3
Messkirch-Rohrdorf **91** C3
Messtetten **91** C2
Mestanza **167** C2
Mestilä **24** B2
Mestlin **69** D1
Město-Touškov **83** C3
Mestrino **107** C3
Mesvres **103** C1
Metajna **130** B2
Metaljka **133** C3
Metallikón **143** D1, **144** A1
Metamórfosis **144** A/B2
Metanópoli **105** D3,
   106 A3
Metapontum **121** C3
Metaxás **143** C2
Metelen **67** C/D3
Meteóra **143** C3
Méthana **147** D3
Methil **57** C1
Methóni **143** D2
Methven **57** C1
Metković **136** B1
Metlika **127** C3
Metnitz **126** B1
Metnitz **96** A3
Mętno **70** A3
Metóchion **146** A2
Metovnica **135** C2
Metsäkylä **19** C3
Metsäkylä **25** C2
Metsäkylä **18** A3
Metsäkylä **26** B2
Metsälä **19** C1/2
Metsälä **20** A3
Metsämaa **24** B2
Metsolahti **21** D3, **22** A3
Métsovon **143** B/C3
Mettälä **26** B2
Mettendorf (Bitburg)
   79 D3
Mettet **79** C2
Mettingen **67** D2/3
Mettlach **79** D3
Mettlach-Orscholz **79** D3
Mettlach-Weiten **79** D3
Mettmann **80** A1
Metz **89** C1
Metzdorf **70** B2
Metzervisse **89** C1
Metzingen **91** C2
Meucon **85** C3
Meulan **87** C1
Meung-sur-Loire **87** C3
Meurville **88** B2
Meuselwitz **82** B1
Mevagissey **62** B3
Mevassvika **28** B2
Mexborough **61** D3
Mexilhoeira Grande **170** A2
Meximieux **103** D2
Meyenburg **69** D1
Meymac **102** A3
Meyrargues **111** D2/3
Meyrin [Vernier-Meyrin]
   104 A2
Meyrueis **110** B2
Meyssac **102** A3, **109** D1
Mezalocha **154** A/B3,
   162 A/B1
Mezdra **140** B3
Mèze **110** B3
Mežgorje **97** D2, **98** A3
Mézidon **86** A1

Mézières-en-Brenne
   101 C1
Mézières-sur-Issoire
   101 D2
Mézilhac **111** C1
Mézilles **87** D3, **88** A3
Mézin **109** C2
Mezöberény **97** C3, **140** A1
Mezöcsokonya **128** A/B2
Mezöfalva **129** C1
Mezöhék **129** D1
Mezökövesd **97** C3
Mezöörs **95** C3
Mezöszilas **128** B1
Mezötúr **129** D1
Mezötúr **97** C3, **140** A1
Mezquita de Jarque **162** B2
Mezzana **106** B2
Mezzani **114** A1
Mezzano **107** C2
Mezzaselva/Mittewald
   107 C1
Mezzoiuso **124** B2
Mezzoldo **106** A2
Mezzolombardo **107** B/C2
Miajadas **166** A2
Mialet **101** D3
Miami Platja **163** D2
Miasteczko Krajeńskie
   71 D2
Miastko **72** B2
Michalovce **97** C2, **98** A3
Michalovy Hory **82** B3
Michelau im Steigerwald
   81 D3
Michelau in Oberfranken
   82 A2/3
Michelbach Markt **94** A2
Micheldorf in Oberöster-
   reich **93** C/D3
Michelfeld (Schwäbisch
   Hall) **91** C1
Michelsneukirchen **92** B1
Michelstadt **81** C3
Michendorf **70** A3
Michíon **146** B2
Michorzewo **71** D2/3
Mickelsträsk **31** C/D2
Mičurin **141** C/D3
Mid-Calder **57** C1
Middalsbu **42** B1
Middelburg **78** B1
Middelfart **48** B3, **52** B1
Middelharnis **66** A3
Middelharnis-Sommelsdijk
   66 A3
Middelkerke-Bad **78** A1
Middelstum **67** C1
Middenmeer **66** B2
Middleham **59** D1, **61** C2
Middlesbrough **61** D1
Middleton **59** D1, **60** B2
Middleton **59** D2, **60** B2/3
Middleton-in-Teesdale
   57 D3, **60** B1
Middleton Stoney **65** C2
Middlewich **59** D2, **60** B3,
   64 A1
Midéa **147** C3
Midhurst **76** B1
Midlum **52** A3, **68** A1
Midões **158** B2/3
Midsund **32** A2
Midtgulen **36** A1/2
Midtleger **42** B1
Midtli **38** B1/2
Midtskogberget **38** B1/2
Midvágur **55** C1
Mid Yell **54** A1
Miechów **97** C1/2
Miedes **162** A1
Miedes de Atienza **161** C1
Międzybórz **71** D1
Międzychód **71** C2
Międzyrzecz **71** C3
Międzyrzecz Podlaski
   73 D3, **97** D1, **98** A1
Międzyzdroje **72** A/B3
Miehikkälä **27** C2
Miehlen **80** B2/3
Miejska Górka **71** D3
Miekojärvi **17** C2
Miélan **109** C3, **155** C1
Mielec **97** C2
Mielęcin **71** D2
Mielęcin **71** B/C2
Mielslahti **19** C3

Mieluskylä **18** A3, **21** D1
Miengo **152** B1
Mierasjärvi **6** B2/3
Mieraslompolo **6** B2
Miercurea-Ciuc **141** C1
Mieres **156** B2
Mieres **151** D1
Mierlo **79** C1
Miesakjaurestugan **9** D2
Miesbach **92** A3
Mieste **69** C2
Miesterhorst **69** C2
Mieszkowice **70** B2
Mietingen **91** C2
Mietinkylä **27** C1/2
Mieto **20** B3
Mietoinen **24** A2
Miettilä **27** D1
Mifol **142** A2
Migennes **88** A2
Migliarino **114** A2, **116** A1/2
Migliaro **115** C1
Migliónico **120** B2/3
Migné **101** C1
Miguelánez **160** B1/2
Miguel Esteban **167** D1, **168** A1
Miguelturra **167** C2
Mihai-Viteazu **141** D2
Mihajlovac **134** B2
Mihajlovac **135** C2
Mihajlovgrad **135** D3
Mihal'kovo **75** D1
Mihályfa **128** A1
Mihályi **94** B3
Mihla **81** D1
Miiluranta **21** D1, **22** A1
Mijares **160** A3
Mijas **172** B2/3
Mijoux **104** A2
Mikaševiči **99** B/C1
Mikínai **147** C3
Mikkeli (Sant Michel) **26** B1
Mikkelvik **4** A2
Mikkola **12** B2
Mikleuš **128** B3
Míkonos **149** C2
Mikosszéplak **128** A1
Mikrevo **139** D3
Mikrókambos **143** D1, **144** A1
Mikromiliá **144** B1
Mikrón Chórion **146** B1
Mikrón Dérion **145** D1, **145** D3
Mikrópolis **144** B1
Mikrothívai **143** D3, **147** C1
Mikróvalton **143** C2
Mikulášovice **83** D1/2
Mikulincy **98** B3
Mikulino **75** D2
Mikulov **96** B2
Mikulov **94** B2
Mikulov **83** C2
Mikulovice **96** B2
Milagres **158** A3, **164** A1
Milagro **154** A2
Milaków **71** C3
Milano **159** C2
Milano **105** D3, **106** A3
Milano Maríttima **115** C2, **117** C1
Milâs **149** D2
Milatovac **135** C2
Milazzo **125** D1
Milborne Port **63** D2
Mildenhall **65** C2
Miléai **144** A3
Milena **124** B2
Mileševo **133** C/D3
Miletići **130** B2
Mileto **122** A2
Miletos **149** D2
Milevsko **83** D3, **93** D1
Milford **64** B3, **76** B1
Milford Haven **62** B1
Milford Haven **55** D3
Milhão **151** C3, **159** C1
Míli **147** C3
Míli **147** D1
Milići **133** C2
Milíčin **83** D3
Milín **83** C3
Milína **147** C1

Mílis **123** C2
Militello in Val di Catánia **125** C3
Miljutino **74** B1
Mill **66** B3
Millana **161** D2
Millançay **87** C3
Millares **169** C1/2
Millas **156** B1
Millau **110** B2
Millésimo **113** C2
Millevaches **102** A3
Millisle **56** A3
Millom **59** C1, **60** A/B2
Millom **54** B3
Millport **56** B2
Millstatt **126** A/B1
Milly **87** D2
Milmarcos **161** D2, **162** A2
Milmersdorf **70** A2
Milna **131** C/D3
Milna **131** C/D3, **136** A1
Milnathort **57** C1
Milngavie **56** B2
Milnthorpe **59** D1, **60** B2
Miločer **137** C2
Milohnić **130** A/B1
Milos **59** C1
Miloševac **132** B1
Miloševa Kula **135** C2
Miloševa Kula **140** A2
Milošev Do **133** D3, **134** A3, **137** D1
Miloševo **135** C2
Miloslavci **139** C1
Milot **137** D3
Milovidy **98** B1
Milow **69** D2
Miltach **92** B1
Miltenberg **81** C3
Milton Keynes **64** B2
Milutinovac **135** C2
Milverton **63** C2
Mimizan **108** B2
Mimizan-Plage **108** B2
Mimoň **83** D2
Minack Theatre **62** A3
Mina de São Domingos **170** B1
Miñana **153** D3, **161** D1
Minas de Oro Romanas **151** C1
Minas de Rio Tinto **171** C1
Mînăstirea **141** C2
Minaya **168** B1/2
Minde **164** A/B1
Mindelheim **91** D2/3
Minden **68** A3
Mindin **85** C3, **100** A1
Mindnes **14** A3
Mindszent **129** D2
Mindtangen **14** A2/3
Minehead **63** C2
Mineo **125** C3
Minerbe **107** C3
Minérbio **115** B/C1
Minerbio **113** D2
Minerve **110** A3, **156** B1
Minervino Murge **120** B2
Minfeld **90** B1
Minglanilla **168** B1
Mingorría **160** A/B2
Miniato **114** B2/3, **116** A2
Minićevo **135** C3
Minkiö **25** B/C2
Minne **35** B/C3
Minnesund **38** A2
Miño **150** B1
Miño de San Esteban **153** C3, **161** C1
Minsk **74** B3
Mińsk Mazowiecki **73** C3, **97** C1, **98** A1
Minster **65** C3, **76** B1
Minsterley **59** D3
Minturnae **119** C3
Minturno **119** C3
Miodnica **71** C3
Miokovićevo **128** A3
Miolans **104** A3
Mionica **133** D2, **134** A2
Mionnay **103** D2
Mios **108** A1
Mira **107** D3
Mira **143** D3
Mira **162** A3, **169** C1
Mira **158** A2

Mirabeau **111** D2
Mirabel **159** C/D3, **165** D1, **166** A1
Mirabella **119** D3, **120** A2
Mirabella Imbáccari **125** C3
Mirador Fito **152** A1
Miradoux **109** C2
Miraflores de la Sierra **160** B2
Miralrío **161** C2
Miramar **158** A2
Miramare **115** D2, **117** C1
Miramas **111** C/D3
Mirambeau **100** B3
Mirambel **162** B2
Miramont-de-Guyenne **109** C1
Miranda de Arga **154** A2
Miranda de Ebro **153** C2
Miranda del Castañar **159** D2
Miranda do Corvo **158** A3
Miranda do Douro **159** C/D1
Mirande **109** C3, **155** C1
Mirandela **159** B/C1
Mirandilla **165** D2, **166** A2
Mirándola **114** B1
Mirano **107** C/D3
Mirantes **151** D2
Miravci **139** C3, **143** D1
Miraveche **153** C2
Miravet **163** C2
Miravete **162** B2
Miré **86** A3
Mirebeau-en-Poitou **101** C1
Mirebeau-sur-Bèze **89** C3
Mirecourt **89** C2
Mirepoix **109** D3, **156** A1
Mireval **110** B3
Mirgorod **99** D2
Miribel **103** D2/3
Miŕkov **82** B3
Mirna **127** C2/3
Mirna Peč **127** C3
Mironovka **99** D2/3
Mirosławiec **71** C1
Mirošov **83** C3
Mirotice **93** C1
Mirovice **83** C3, **93** C1
Mirow **69** D1, **70** A1
Mirtíski **145** D1
Mirto Crosia **122** B1
Mirtófion **144** B1
Mirueña **160** A2
Misano Adriático **115** D2, **117** C1
Misburg **68** B2/3
Misi **12** B3
Misilmeri **124** B2
Miske **129** C2
Miskolc **97** C3
Miškovići **130** B2
Mislata **169** D1
Mislina **136** B1
Mišnjak **130** B1/2
Missanello **120** B3
Missilä **22** B1
Missillac **85** C3
Mistelbach **94** B2
Mistelbach **96** B2
Misten **8** B3
Misterbianco **125** D2
Misterhem **33** D3
Misterhult **46** B3, **51** D1
Mistorf **53** D3, **69** D1
Mistrás **147** B/C3
Mistrás **148** B2/3
Mistretta **125** C2
Místros **147** D2
Misurina **107** D2
Misvær **15** C1
Mitanderfors **38** B3
Mítikas **146** A1
Mitilíni **149** C/D2
Mitrašinci **139** D2/3
Mitrópolis **143** C3
Mitrovac **133** C2
Mittådalen **34** A2
Mittelberg **106** B1
Mittelberg **91** D3, **106** B1
Mittelbiberach **91** C2/3
Mittel-Neufnach **91** D2
Mittenwald **92** A3
Mittenwalde **70** A3
Mittenwalde **70** A/B1/2

Mitterbach am Erlaufsee **94** A3
Mitterding **93** C2
Mitterdorf an der Raab **127** C1
Mitterndorf im Steir.Salz-kammergut **93** C3
Mittersheim **89** D1, **90** A1/2
Mittersill **107** D1
Mitterteich **82** B3
Mitterweissenbach **93** C3
Mittet **32** A/B2
Mittewald an der Drau **107** D1, **126** A1
Mittweida **82** B1/2
Mizil **141** C2
Mjällby **51** C2/3
Mjällom **30** B3
Mjåvatn **43** C2
Mjåvatn **43** C3
Mjöbäck **49** D1, **50** A1
Mjøensetra **33** C3
Mjöhult **49** D2/3, **50** A2
Mjölan **17** C2
Mjölby **46** A2
Mjølfjell **36** B3
Mjølkarlia **14** B3
Mjölkbäcken **15** B/C2
Mjømna **36** A3
Mjøndalen **43** D1, **44** A1
Mjørlund **38** A2
Mjösebo **51** D1
Mjösjöby **31** C2
Mjösund **24** B3
Mjöträsk **17** C2
Mladá Boleslav **83** D2
Mladá Boleslav **96** A1/2
Mladá Vožice **83** D3, **93** D1
Mladenovac **133** D2, **134** B2
Mladenovac **140** A2
Mladenovo **129** C3, **133** C1
Mladikovine **132** B2
Mlado Nagoričane **139** C2
Mladotice **83** C3
Mława **73** C3
Mlini **137** C1/2
Mlinište **131** D2, **132** A2
Mnich **93** D1
Mnichov **82** B3
Mnichovice **83** D3
Mnichovo Hradiště **83** D2
Mníšek **83** C2
Mníšek pod Brdy **83** D3
Mo **30** A3, **35** C1
Mo **44** B2
Mo **32** B2
Mo **30** A3, **35** D2
Mo **45** C1/2
Mo **36** A3
Mo **37** D2, **38** A1/2
Mo **43** C1/2
Mo **38** A/B2
Moan **29** C3, **34** B2
Moaña **150** A2/3
Moarottaja **19** C1
Moat of Urr **56** B3, **60** A1
Moča **95** D3
Mocejón **160** B3, **167** C1
Mochales **161** D2
Mochov **83** D3
Mochtín **93** C1
Mochy **71** C/D3
Möckern **91** C1
Mockfjärd **39** D2
Möckmühl **91** C1
Möckmühl-Züttlingen **91** C1
Mockrehna **82** B1
Mockträsk **17** B/C3
Moclín **173** C2
Modane **104** B3, **112** A/B1
Modbury **63** C3
Módena **114** B1
Módica **125** C3
Modigliana **115** C2, **116** B1
Mödling **94** B2/3
Modra **95** C2
Modran **132** B1
Modřany **83** D3
Modrava **93** C1
Modriča **132** B1
Modrište **138** B3

Modruš **130** B1
Modrý Kameň **95** D2
Modrze **71** D3
Modugno **121** C2
Moeche **150** B1
Moelingen **79** C/D2
Moelv **38** A2
Moen **28** B3, **33** D1, **34** A1
Moen **28** B3, **33** D1
Moen **4** A3, **9** D1
Moena **107** C2
Moers **79** D1, **80** A1
Mofalla **45** D2, **46** A2
Moffat **57** C2
Mogadouro **159** C1
Møgeltønder **52** A2
Mogen **43** C1
Mogente **169** C2
Móggio Udinese **126** A2
Mögglingen **91** C2
Mogila **138** B3, **143** C1
Mogilev **74** B3
Mogilëv-Podol'skij **99** C3
Móglia **114** B1
Mogliano Véneto **107** D3
Moglica **142** B1/2
Mogón **167** D3, **168** A3, **173** C/D1
Mogor **150** B1
Mogorić **131** B/C2
Mógoro **123** C3
Mohács **129** B/C2/3
Moharras **168** B2
Moheda **51** C1
Mohedas **159** D3
Mohedas de la Jara **166** B1
Mohelnice **96** B2
Möhkö **23** D1
Möhne-Günne **80** B1
Möhnesee-Körbecke **80** B1
Moholm **45** D2, **46** A2
Mohorn **83** C1/2
Mohorte **161** D3
Mohrkirch **52** B2
Moi **42** B3
Moi **42** B3
Moi **135** D1
Moià **156** A2/3
Móie **115** D3, **117** D2
Moikipää **20** A2, **31** D3
Moimenta **151** C3
Moimenta da Beira **158** B2
Moimenta de Mac Dão **158** B2
Mo i Rana **14** B2
Moirans **103** D3, **104** A3
Moirans-en-Montagne **104** A2
Mõisaküla **74** A1
Moisdon-la-Rivière **86** A3
Moisiovaara **19** D3
Moissac **109** C2
Moisselles **87** D1
Moisund **43** B/C3
Moíta **113** D3
Moita **164** A2
Moita **158** A/B3
Moita dos Ferreiros **164** A1/2
Möja **47** D1
Mojácar **174** A2
Mojados **160** A/B1
Mojkovac **137** D1
Mojstrana **126** B2
Møklevika **29** C1
Möklinta **40** A3
Mokošica **137** C1
Mokra Gora **133** C3
Mokreš **135** D3
Mokrice **127** C/D3
Mokrin **129** D2/3
Mokro **132** B2
Mokronog **127** C2/3
Mokro Polje **131** C2
Mokrós **144** B1
Möksy **21** C2
Mol **129** D3
Mol **79** C1
Molacillos **151** D3, **159** D3
Mola di Bari **121** C2
Molare **113** C1
Molaretto **104** B3, **112** B1
Molat **130** B2
Molbergen **67** D2
Mold **59** C2, **60** B3

Moldava v Krušných horách **83** C2
Molde **32** A2
Moldøra **28** A2/3, **33** C1
Moldova Nouă **135** C1/2
Moldova Nouă **140** A2
Moldova Veche **135** B/C1/2
Møldrup **48** B3, **52** B1
Moldvik **5** B/C2
Molesme **88** B2/3
Molesworth **64** B2
Molezuelas de la Carballeda **151** D3
Molfetta **121** B/C2, **136** A3
Moliden **30** B3
Molières **108** B2
Moliets-et-Maa **108** B2
Molina Aterno **119** C1
Molina de Aragón **161** D2, **162** A2
Molina de Segura **169** D3
Molina di Ledro **106** B2/3
Molinella **115** C1
Molinicos **168** B2/3
Molini di Túres/Mühlen **107** C1
Molino **112** B3
Molinos **162** B2
Molinos de Duero **153** C/D3
Molins de Rei **156** A3
Moliterno **120** B3
Molitg **156** A/B1/2
Molivdosképastos **142** B2
Möljeryd **51** C2
Molkojärvi **12** A2
Molkoköngäs **12** A2/3, **17** D1
Molkom **39** C3, **45** D1
Mollans-sur-Ouveze **111** D2
Möllbrücke **126** A1
Mölle **49** D2, **50** A2
Mollebogen **28** B1
Molledo **152** B1
Möllenbeck **70** A1
Möllenhagen **70** A1
Mollerussa **155** D3, **163** C/D1
Mollet del Vallès **156** A3
Móllia **105** C3
Molliens-Vidame **77** D2/3
Mollina **172** B2
Mollišjok **5** D3, **6** A2
Mollis [Näfels-Mollis] **105** D1, **106** A1
Mölln **69** C1
Molló **156** A/B2
Mollösund **44** B3
Mölltorp **45** D2, **46** A2
Molnári **128** A2
Mølnarodden **8** A3
Mölnbo **47** C1
Mølnbukt **28** A3, **33** C1
Mölndal (Göteborg) **45** C3, **49** D1
Mölndal (Göteborg) **72** A1
Mölnlycke **45** C3, **49** D1
Molodečno **74** A3
Mólos **147** C1
Moloy **88** B3
Molpe (Moikipää) **20** A2, **31** D3
Molschleben **81** D1/2
Molsheim **90** A2
Molunat **137** C2
Molve **128** A2
Molveno **106** B2
Molvízar **173** C2
Mománo **112** B3
Momarken **38** A3, **44** B1
Mombaróccio **115** D2, **117** C1
Mombaruzzo **113** C1
Mombeja **164** B3, **170** B1
Mombeltrán **160** A3
Momblona **161** D1
Mömbris **81** C3
Mombuey **151** D3
Momčilgrad **141** C3
Mömlingen **81** C3
Mommark **52** B2
Mommila **25** D2, **26** A2
Momo **105** D3
Momrak **43** C2
Momyr **28** A2

Moná **20** B2
Monachil **173** C2
Monaco **112** B2/3
Monaghan **54** A3, **55** D2
Monamolin **58** A3
Monäs **20** B1/2
Monasterace Marina **122** B3
Monasterio de Rodilla **153** C2
Monasterio de Cristo **151** C1
Monasterio de Lluc **157** C2
Monasterio de Poblet **163** D1
Monasterio de Yuste **159** D3
Monasterio de las Huelgas **153** C2
Monasterio de Vega **152** A2/3
Monasterio de Leyre **155** C2
Monasterio de Piedra **161** D1, **162** A1
Monasterio El Paular **160** B2
Monasterio Montserrat **156** A3
Monasterio San Salvador **157** C2
Monasterio Santes Creus **163** C1
Monasterio San Miguel de Escalade **152** A2
Monastir **123** D3
Monastirákion **146** A1
Monastyriska **97** D2, **98** B3
Monbahus **109** C1
Monbrun **109** C2/3
Moncada **169** D1
Moncalieri **113** B/C1
Moncalvillo de Huete **161** D3
Moncalvo **113** C1
Monção **150** A3
Moncarapacho **170** B2
Monceau **78** B2
Mönchdorf **93** D2
Mönchengladbach **79** D1
Mónchio delle Corti **114** A2, **116** A1
Monchique **170** A2
Monchy-Humières **78** A3
Monclar-de-Quercy **109** D2
Moncófar **163** B/C3, **169** D1
Moncontour-de-Bretagne **85** C2
Moncontour-de-Poitou **101** C1
Moncoutant **100** B1
Monda **172** A/B2/3
Mondariz **150** A2/3
Mondariz-Balneario **150** A3
Mondéjar **161** C3
Mondicourt **77** D2, **78** A2
Mondim de Basto **158** B1
Mondolfo **115** D2, **117** D1/2
Mondoñedo **151** B/C1
Mondorf-les-Bains **79** D3
Mondoubleau **86** B2
Mondoví **113** C2
Mondragon **111** C2
Mondragone **119** C3
Mondsee **93** C3
Monéglia **113** D2
Monegrillo **154** B3, **162** B1
Monein **108** B3, **154** B1
Monemvasía **148** B3
Moneo **153** C2
Monesi **113** C2
Monesíglio **113** C2
Monesterio **165** D3, **166** A3
Monestier-de-Clermont **111** D1
Monestiès **109** D2, **110** A2
Moneva **162** B1/2
Monfalcone **126** A3
Monfero **150** B1
Monflanquin **109** C1
Monfort **109** C2
Monforte **165** C2

Monforte **158** B3, **165** C1
Monforte de Lemos **150** B2
Monforte de Moyuela **162** B2
Monforte del Cid **169** C3
Monforte San Giórgio **125** D1/2
Monghidoro **114** B2, **116** B1
Mongiana **122** A/B3
Mongiardino Lígure **113** D1
Mongstad **36** A3
Monguelfo/Welsberg **107** C/D1
Monguillem **108** B2
Monheim **80** A1
Moní Agías Lávras **146** B2
Moniaive **56** B2/3
Monica **133** D2, **134** A2
Moní Chiliandaríou **144** B2
Mönichkirchen **94** A3
Mon Idée **78** B3
Moní Elónis **147** C3
Monifieth **57** C1
Moniga del Garda **106** B3
Moní Ikosifiníssis **144** B1
Monikie **57** C1
Moní Loukoú **147** C3
Moní Megístis Lávras **144** B2
Moní Osíou Louká **147** C2
Monistrol **156** A3
Monistrol-d'Allier **110** B1
Monistrol-sur-Loire **103** C3
Mönkebude **70** B1
Monmouth **63** D1
Monnai **86** B1
Monnaie **86** B3
Mönni **23** D2/3
Monni **25** C2, **26** A2
Monnickendam **66** B2
Monninkylä **25** D2, **26** A2
Monó Àgios Ioánnis **144** A/B1
Monola **47** B2/C2
Monópoli **121** C2
Monor **129** C1
Monor **97** C3, **140** A1
Monóvar **169** C3
Monpazier **109** C1
Monreal **154** A2
Monreal **80** A2
Monreal del Campo **163** C2
Monreal del Llano **168** A1
Monreale **124** B2
Monroy **165** D1, **166** A1
Monroyo **163** C2
Mons **78** B2
Mons **112** A/B3
Monsagro **159** C/D2
Monsanto **159** C3
Monsaraz **165** C3
Monschau **79** D2
Monschau-Imgenbroich **79** D2
Monschau-Kalterherberg **79** D2
Monségur **108** B1
Monsélice **107** C3
Monsheim **80** B3
Mönsheim **91** B/C1/2
Monsols **103** C2
Mønsted **48** B2
Mönsterås **51** D1
Mönsterås **72** B1
Monsteroy **42** A2
Monsummano Terme **114** B2, **116** A1
Montabaur **80** B2
Montaberner **169** D2
Montagnac **110** B3
Montagnana **107** C3
Montagny **103** C2
Montagut de Fluviá **156** B2
Montaigu **101** C2
Montaigu-de-Quercy **109** C2
Montaiguët-en-Forez **103** C2
Montaigut-en-Combraille **102** B2
Montaigut-sur-Save **108** B2
Montalba-d'Amélie **156** B2
Montalba-le-Château **156** B1

Montalbán **162** B2
Montalbán de Córdoba **172** B1
Montalbanejo **161** D3, **168** A/B1
Montalbano Elicona **125** D2
Montalbano Iónico **120** B3
Montalbo **161** D3, **168** A1
Montalbos **168** B2
Montalcino **115** B/C3, **116** B2
Montaldo di Cósola **113** D1
Montalegre **150** B3, **158** B1
Montalivet-les-Bains **101** C2
Montallegro **124** B2/3
Montalto delle Marche **117** D2/3
Montalto di Castro **116** B3, **118** A1
Montalto Marina **116** B3, **118** A1
Montalto Pavese **113** D1
Montalto Uffugo **122** A1
Montalvão **165** C1
Montalvo **164** B1
Montalvo **164** A/B3
Montamarta **151** D3, **159** D1
Montán **162** B3
Montañana **155** C2/3
Montanara **106** B3, **114** B1
Montanaro **105** C3, **113** C1
Montana [Sierre] **105** C2
Montánchez **165** D2, **166** A2
Montanejos **162** B3
Montaner **108** B3, **155** C1
Montano Antília **120** A3
Montargil **164** B2
Montargis **87** D2
Montari **25** D2, **26** A2
Montastruc **109** C3, **155** C1
Montastruc-la-Conseillère **109** D2
Montauban **108** B2
Montauban-de-Bretagne **85** C2
Montauriol **109** D3, **155** D1
Montázzoli **119** D2
Montbard **88** B3
Montbazens **110** A1
Montbazon **106** B3, **101** C/D1
Montbéliard **89** D3
Montbenoît **104** B1
Montblanc **163** C1
Montbovon **104** B2
Montbozon **89** C/D3
Montbras **89** C2
Montbrison **103** C3
Montbron **101** C3
Montbrun **101** D3
Montbrun-les-Bains **111** D2
Montceau-les-Mines **103** C1
Montceaux-les-Provins **88** A1/2
Montcenis **103** C1
Montchanin-les-Mines **103** C1
Montcornet **78** B3
Montcuq **108** B2
Montdardier **110** B2
Mont-de-Marsan **108** B2
Montdidier **78** A3
Monteagudo **161** D3, **162** A3, **168** B1
Monteagudo **154** A3
Monteagudo de las Vicarías **161** D1
Monteagudo del Castillo **162** B2
Montealegre **152** A3
Montealegre del Castillo **169** C2
Montearagón **160** A/B3, **166** B1
Monte Argentário **116** B3
Montebello Iónico **122** A3, **125** D2

Montebello Veronese **107** C3
Montebelluna **107** C/D3
Montébilloy **87** D1
Montebourg **76** B3
Montebruno **113** D1/2
Montecalvo Irpino **119** D3, **120** A2
Monte Carlo **112** B2/3
Montecarotto **115** D3, **117** D2
Montecastrilli **117** C3, **118** B1
Montecatini Terme **114** B2, **116** A1
Montecatini Val di Cécina **114** B3, **116** A2
Montécchio Emília **114** A/B1
Montécchio Maggiore **107** C3
Montécchio **115** D2, **117** C1
Monte Cerignone **115** C2, **117** C1
Montech **108** B2
Montechiaro d'Asti **113** C1
Monte Claro **165** C1
Monte Clérigo **170** A2
Monte Colombo **115** D2, **117** C1
Montecorvino Rovella **119** D3, **120** A2
Montecreto **114** B2, **116** A1
Monte da Pedra **165** B/C1
Monterderramo **150** B2/3
Monterderramo **150** B2/3
Monte de Trigo **165** C3
Monte di Prócida **119** C3
Montedoro **124** B2
Montefalco **117** C3
Montefalcone di Val Fortore **119** D2, **120** A1/2
Montefalcone nel Sánnio **119** D2
Montefano **117** D2
Montefiascone **117** B/C3, **118** A1
Montefiorino **114** B2, **116** A1
Monteflávio **118** B1/2
Monteforte d'Alpone **107** C3
Monteforte Irpino **119** D3
Montefrío **172** B2
Montegalda **107** C3
Montegiordano Marina **120** B3, **122** B1
Montegiórgio **117** D2
Monte Gordo **158** B3, **165** B/C1
Montegranaro **117** D2, **130** A3
Montegrotto Terme **107** C3
Montehermoso **159** C3
Montejaque **172** A2
Montejicar **173** C1
Montejo **153** C2
Montejo **159** D2
Montejo De La Vega **153** C3, **161** B/C1
Montejo de la Sierra **161** C2
Montejo de Tiermes **161** C1
Montelánico **118** B3
Montelavar **164** A2
Montel-de-Gelat **102** B2
Monteleone di Púglia **120** A2
Monteleone d'Orvieto **117** B/C3
Monteleone di Spoleto **117** C/D3, **118** B1
Montelepre **124** A/B2
Montélimar **111** C1
Montella **119** D3, **120** A2
Montellano **171** D2, **172** A2
Montelupo Fiorentino **114** B2, **116** A/B1/2
Montemaggiore Belsito **124** B2
Montemagno **113** C1
Montemarano **119** D3, **120** A2
Montemarcello **114** A2
Montemayor **172** B1

Montemayor de Pililla 152 B3, 160 B1
Montemboeuf 101 C3
Montemerano 116 B3, 118 A1
Montemésola 121 C2/3
Montemiletto 119 D3, 120 A2
Montemilone 120 B2
Montemolín 165 D3, 166 A3
Montemónaco 117 D3
Montemor o Novo 164 B2
Montemor-o-Velho 158 A3
Montemurlo 114 B2, 116 A/B1
Montemurro 120 B3
Montendre 101 B/C3
Montenegro de Cameros 153 D3
Montenero 114 A3, 116 A2
Montenero di Bisáccia 119 D2, 120 A1
Montenero Sabino 117 C3, 118 B1
Montepiano 114 B2, 116 B1
Monte Picayo 162 B3, 169 D1
Montépilloy 87 D1
Montepulciano 115 C3, 116 B2
Monteras 159 C/D1/2
Monterchi 115 C3, 117 C2
Monterde 162 A1/2
Monterde 162 A2
Monte Real 158 A3, 164 A1
Montereale 117 D3, 119 B/C1
Montereale Valcellina 107 D2, 126 A2
Montereau-Faut-Yonne 87 D2
Monte Redondo 158 A3, 164 A1
Monterénzio 114 B2, 116 B1
Monteriggioni 114 B3, 116 B2
Monte Romano 116 B3, 118 A1
Monteroni d'Árbia 114 B3, 116 B2
Monteroni di Lecce 121 D3
Monterosi 118 A/B1
Monterosso al Mare 114 A2
Monterosso Almo 125 C3
Monterotondo 118 B1/2
Monterotondo Maríttimo 114 B3, 116 A2
Monterrei 151 B/C3
Monterroso 150 B2
Monterrubio de Demanda 153 C3
Monterrubio de la Serena 166 B2
Monterrubio de la Sierra 159 D2
Monterubbiano 117 D2
Montesa 169 C2
Monte Salgueiro 150 B1
Monte San Biágio 119 C2
Monte San Giovanni Incárico 119 C2
Montesano Salentino 121 D3
Montesano Scalo 120 A/B3
Montesano sulla Marcellana 120 A/B3
Monte San Savino 115 C3, 116 B2
Monte Sant'Ángelo 120 B1
Monte San Vito 115 D3, 117 D2
Montesárchio 119 D3
Montescaglioso 121 B/C2/3
Montesclaros 160 A3
Montese 114 B2, 116 A1
Montesilvano Marina 119 C1
Montespértoli 114 B3, 116 A/B2
Montespluga 105 D2, 106 A2

Montesquieu-Volvestre 108 B3, 155 C1
Montesquiou-sur-Losse 109 C3, 155 C1
Montes Velhos 164 B3, 170 A/B1
Monteux 111 C/D2
Montevarchi 115 C3, 116 B2
Montevécchio 123 C3
Montevécchio 123 C3
Monteverde 120 A2
Monteverdi Maríttimo 114 B3, 116 A2
Montezémolo 113 C2
Montfaucon 85 D3, 100 B1
Montfaucon 88 B1
Montfaucon-en-Velay 103 C3
Montferrat 112 A3
Montfleur 103 D2, 104 A2
Montfort 79 D1
Montfort-en-Chalosse 108 A/B2
Montfort-l'Amaury 87 C1
Montfort-sur-Boulzane 156 A1
Montfort-sur-Meu 85 C2
Montfort-sur-Risle 77 C3, 86 B1
Montfranc 110 A2
Montgai 155 D3, 163 D1
Montgaillard 108 B3, 155 C1
Montgenèvre 112 A/B1
Montgomery 59 C3
Montguyon 101 C3
Monthermé 79 C3
Monthey 104 B2
Monthois 88 B1
Monthureux-sur-Saône 89 C2
Monti 123 D1
Montícchio Bagni 120 A2
Monticelli d'Ongina 114 A1
Monticelli Terme 114 A1
Montichiari 106 B3
Monticiano 114 B3, 116 B2
Montiel 167 D2, 168 A2
Montier-en-Der 88 B2
Montieri 114 B3, 116 A/B2
Montiers-sur-Saulx 89 C2
Montíglio 113 C1
Montignac 101 C3, 108 B1
Montigny 89 D2, 90 A2
Montigny-le-Roi 89 C2
Montigny-sur-Canne 103 C1
Montigny-sur-Aube 88 B2
Montijo 165 D2
Montijo 164 A2
Montilla 172 B1
Montillana 173 C1
Montivilliers 77 B/C3
Montizón 167 D3, 168 A3
Montjay 111 D2
Montjean-sur-Loire 86 A3
Montlhéry 87 D2
Montlieu-la-Garde 101 C3
Mont-Louis 156 A2
Montluçon 102 B2
Montluel 103 D2
Montmarault 102 B2
Montmartin-sur-Mer 85 D1
Montmédy 79 C3
Montmélian 104 A3
Montmeyan 112 A3
Montmeyran 111 C1
Montmirail 86 B2
Montmirail 88 A1
Montmirey-le-Château 89 C3, 103 D1, 104 A1
Montmoreau-Saint-Cybard 101 C3
Montmorency 87 D1
Montmorillon 101 D2
Montmort 88 A1
Montmuran 85 C/D2
Montóggio 113 D1/2
Montoir-de-Bretagne 85 C3
Montoire-sur-le-Loir 86 B3
Montoito 165 C2/3
Montolieu 110 A3, 156 A1
Montorio 153 B/C2

Montório al Vomano 117 D3, 119 C1
Montório nei Frentani 119 D2, 120 A1
Montoro 167 C3, 172 B1
Montpellier-le-Vieux 110 B2
Montpellier 110 B3
Montpézat 109 C3, 155 D1
Montpezat 111 C2
Montpezat-de-Quercy 109 D2
Montpezat-sous-Bauzon 111 C1
Montpon-Ménestérol 109 B/C1
Montpont-en-Bresse 103 D2
Montrdon-Labessonnié 110 A2
Montréal 110 A3, 156 A1
Montréal-de-Gers 109 B/C2
Montréjeau 109 C3, 155 C1
Montrésor 86 A/B3, 101 C1
Montresta 123 C2
Montret 103 D1
Montreuil-aux-Lions 87 D1, 88 A1
Montreuil-Bellay 101 C1
Montreuil-sur-Mer 77 D2
Montreux 104 B2
Montrevault 85 D3, 100 B1
Montrevel-en-Bresse 103 D2
Montrichard 86 A/B3
Montricoux 109 D2
Montroc 104 B2
Mont-roig del Camp 163 D2
Montrond 104 A1
Montrond-les-Bains 103 C3
Montrose 54 B2
Montrottier 104 A2/3
Montroy 169 C/D1
Mont-Saint-Vincent 103 C1
Montsalvy 110 A1
Montsauche 88 A3, 103 C1
Montsaunès 109 C3, 155 D1
Mont-Saxonnex 104 B2
Montsecret 86 A1
Montségur 156 A1
Montseny 156 A/B3
Montsoreau 86 A/B3, 101 C1
Mont-sous-Vaudrey 103 D1, 104 A1
Monts-sur-Guesnes 101 C1
Montsûrs 86 A2
Montuenga 160 A/B2
Montuïri 157 C2
Monturque 172 B1
Monumento a Colón 171 C2
Monza 105 D3, 106 A3
Monze 110 A3, 156 B1
Monzón 155 C3
Monzón de Campos 152 B3
Moorenweis 92 A2
Moormerland-Warsingsfehn 67 D1
Moormerland 67 D1
Moormerland-Oldersum 67 D1
Moormerlland-Neermoor 67 D1
Moosbach 82 B3
Moosbrunn 94 B3
Moosburg 92 A/B2
Moosinning 92 A2
Moos-Langenisarhofen 92 B2
Moosthenning 92 B2
Mór 95 C3, 128 B2
Mór 96 B3
Mora 160 B3, 167 C1
Mora 164 B2
Mora 39 C/D2
Mora 39 D2
Moracz 70 B1

Móra d'Ebre 163 C2
Mora de Rubielos 162 B3
Mora de Santa Quiteria 168 B2
Moradillo de Roa 153 B/C3, 160 B1
Moraes 159 C1
Morag 73 C2
Mórahalom 129 D2
Moraira 169 D2
Moraïtika 142 A3
Moral 161 C1
Móra la Nova 163 C2
Moral de Calatrava 167 D2
Moral de la Reina 152 A3
Moraleda de Zafayona 172 B2
Moraleja 159 C3
Moraleja del Vino 159 D1
Morales 161 C1
Morales del Vino 159 D1
Morales de Toro 152 A3, 160 A1
Morales de Valverde 151 D3
Moralina 159 D1
Moralzarzal 160 B2
Moraña 150 A2
Morannes 86 A3
Morano Cálabro 120 B3, 122 A1
Morano sul Po 105 C3, 113 C1
Morasverdes 159 C/D2
Morata 174 B1
Morata de Jalón 154 A3, 162 A1
Morata de Jiloca 162 A1
Morata de Tajuña 161 C3
Moratalla 168 B3
Moratilla de los Meleros 161 C2
Moravče 127 C2
Moravita 134 B1
Moravská Nová Ves 94 B2
Moravské Budějovice 94 A1
Moravské Budějovice 96 A2
Moravské Lieskové 95 C1/2
Moravské Toplice 127 D1/2
Moravský Ján 94 B2
Moravský Krumlov 94 B1
Morbach 80 A3
Morbach-Gonzerath 80 A3
Morbegno 106 A2
Mörbisch am See 94 B3
Mörbylånga 51 D2
Mörbylånga 72 B1
Morcenx 108 A2
Morciano di Romagna 115 D2, 117 C1
Morcillo 159 C3
Morcone 119 D2
Morcote 105 D2/3
Morcuera 161 C1
Mordelles 85 D2
Morecambe 59 D1, 60 B2
Moreda 173 C1/2
Morée 86 A/B2/3
Morehampstead 63 C3
Moreira 158 A1
Moreira do Rei 158 A/B1
Mørekvam 37 C2/3
Morella 163 B/C2
Moreni 141 C2
Moreruela de Tábara 151 D3, 159 D1
Morés 154 A3, 162 A1
Móres 123 C2
Morestel 103 D3, 104 A3
Moreton in Marsh 64 A2
Moret-sur-Loing 87 D2
Moretta 112 B1
Moreuil 78 A3
Morez 104 A2
Morfasbukten 9 D2/3
Morfasso 113 D1, 114 A1
Mörfion 142 B3
Morgat 84 A2
Morgedal 43 C1/2
Morges 104 B2
Morgex 104 B3
Morgins [Troistorrents] 104 B2

Morgny 77 D3, 87 C1
Morgongåva 40 A3
Morgovejo 152 A2
Morhange 89 D1
Mørholmen 43 C3
Mori 106 B3
Moriani-Plage 113 D3
Møriaunet 28 A2, 33 C1
Morienval 87 D1
Moriles 172 B1/2
Morillas Zubilana 153 C2
Morille 159 D2
Morillejo 161 D2
Morillo de Monclus 155 C2
Morin 138 A2
Morina 138 A2
Morina 140 A3
Moringen 68 B3, 81 C1
Moringen-Fredelsloh 68 B3
Moripen 43 C3
Moritzburg 83 C1
Moriville 89 D2
Morjärv 17 C2
Morkarla 40 B3
Mørke 49 C2
Morken 28 A2, 33 C1
Morkkaperä 12 B3
Mörkö 47 C1/2
Mørkøv 49 C3, 53 C/D1
Morkovice 95 B/C1
Mörkret 38 B1
Mørkri 37 B/C2
Morl 82 A/B1
Morlaàs 108 B3, 154 B1
Morlaix 84 B2
Morlanne 108 B3, 154 B1
Mörlen 80 B2
Morley 61 C2
Mörlunda 51 C/D1
Mörlunda 72 B1
Mormanno 120 B3, 122 A1
Mormant 87 D2
Mornant 103 D3
Mornay-Berry 102 B1
Mornesi 113 C/D1
Mörnsheim 91 D1/2, 92 A1/2
Moročno 98 B2
Mörön 17 C3
Morón de Almazán 161 D1
Morón de la Frontera 172 A2
Moror 155 C/D3
Moros 161 D1, 162 A1
Morosaglia 113 D2/3
Morovič 133 C1
Morozzo 113 B/C2
Morpeth 57 D2/3
Morpeth 54 B3
Morrfällsviken 30 B3
Morriston 63 C1
Mörrum 51 C2
Morsains 88 A1
Morsbach 80 B2
Mörsch 90 B1
Mörsil 29 C3, 34 A/B2
Mørsvikbotn 9 C2
Mortagne-au-Perche 86 B2
Mortagne-sur-Sèvre 100 B1
Mortagne-sur-Gironde 100 B3
Mortágua 158 A2/3
Mortain 85 D1/2, 86 A1/2
Mortara 105 D3, 113 C/D1
Mörtberg 16 B2
Morteau 104 B1
Mortegliano 126 A2
Mortemart 101 C2
Mortenshals 4 A3, 9 D1
Mortensjordet 5 D1, 6 A/B1
Mortenslund 29 C2
Mörtfors 46 B3, 51 D1
Mortrée 86 B2
Mörtsjön 29 D3, 34 B1
Mortsund 8 B2/3
Mörtträsk 16 B2
Morup 49 D2, 50 A1
Morups Tånge 49 D2, 50 A1
Moryń 70 B2
Morzine 104 B2
Morzyczyn 71 B/C1
Mos 150 A3
Mosa 26 B2

Mosätt **34** B3
Mosbach **91** C1
Mosbach-Neckarelz **91** C1
Mosby **43** C3
Mosca **151** C3, **159** C1
Moscardón **162** A3
Moscavide **164** A2
Mošćenička Draga **126** B3, **130** A1
Moschendorf **127** D1
Moschófiton **143** C3
Moschopótamos **143** D2
Mosel **82** B2
Mosina **71** D3
Mosiny **71** B1
Mosjøen **14** A/B2/3
Moskaret **33** C3, **37** D1
Moskog **36** A/B2
Moskosel **16** A2
Moskuvaara **12** B2
Moskva **75** D2/3
Moso in Passíria/Moos in Passeiert. **107** C1
Mosonmagyaróvár **95** B/C3
Mosonmagyaróvár **96** B3
Mosonszolnok **94** B3
Mošorin **129** D3, **133** D1, **134** A1
Mošovce **95** D1
Mosqueruela **162** B2/3
Moss **44** B1
Mossala **24** A3
Mossaträsk **30** B2, **35** D1
Mossebo **50** B1
Mossiberg **39** C1
Mössingen **91** C2
Mössingen-Bad Sebastiansweiler **91** C2
Mosso Santa Maria **105** C3
Møsstrand **43** C1
Most **83** C2
Most **96** A1
Mostad **8** A3
Mostar **132** B3
Moste **126** B2
Moster **42** A1
Mosterhamn **42** A1
Mosterøy **42** A2
Mostiska **97** D2, **98** A2
Most na Soči **126** B2
Mostøl **42** B1
Móstoles **160** B3
Mostrim **55** C/D2
Mosty **73** D3, **98** B1
Mosty **71** B/C1
Mosty u Jablunkova **95** D1
Mosvik **28** B3, **33** D1
Mota de Altarejos **161** D3, **168** B3
Mota del Cuervo **167** D1, **168** A1
Mota del Marqués **152** A3, **160** A1
Motala **46** A2
Motešice **95** C1/2
Motherwell **56** B2
Möthlow **69** D2, **70** A2
Motilla del Palancar **168** B1
Motilleja **168** B2
Mötingselberget **30** A/B1
Motjärnshyttan **39** C3
Motnik **127** C2
Motovun **126** B3, **130** A1
Motril **173** C2
Motru **135** D1
Motta **107** C3
Motta di Livenza **107** D3
Motta Montecorvino **119** D2, **120** A1
Motta San Giovanni **122** A3, **125** D2
Motta Visconti **105** D3
Motten-Kothen **81** C2
Möttingen **91** D2
Móttola **121** C2
Möttönen **21** C2
Mötzing-Schönach **92** B1/2
Mou **48** B2
Mouchamps **100** B1
Mouchan **109** C2
Mouchard **104** A1
Moudon **104** B1/2
Moúdros **145** C3
Mouflers **77** D2
Mougon **101** C2

Mouhijärvi **24** B1
Mouilleron-en-Pareds **100** B1
Moulay **86** A2
Mouleydier **109** C1
Mouliherne **86** A/B3
Moulin-Mage **110** A2
Moulin-Neuf **109** D3, **156** A1
Moulins **102** B1/2
Moulins-Engilbert **103** C1
Moulins-la-Marche **86** B2
Moulismes **101** D2
Moult **86** A1
Mountain Ash **63** C1
Moura **165** C3
Mourão **165** C3
Moure **150** A3, **158** A1
Mourenx **109** C3, **155** C1
Mouriés **139** D3, **143** D1, **144** A1
Mouriès **111** C2/3
Mouríkion **147** D2
Mouriscas **164** B1
Mourmelon-le-Grand **88** B1
Mouronho **158** B3
Mourujärvi **13** C3
Mouscron (Moeskroen) **78** A2
Moussey **89** D1/2, **90** A2
Moustey **108** B2
Moustier **109** C1
Moustiers-Sainte-Marie **112** A2
Mouthe **104** A1/2
Mouthier-Haute-Pierre **104** A1
Mouthoumet **110** A3, **156** B1
Moutier **104** B1
Moûtiers **104** B3
Moutiers-au-Perche **86** B2
Mouton **100** B3
Moux **88** A/B3, **103** C1
Moux **110** A3, **156** B1
Mouy-de-l'Oise **77** D3, **87** D1
Mouzákion **146** B2/3
Mouzákion **143** C3
Mouzay **79** C3
Mouzon **79** C3
Møvik **36** A3
Moville **54** A3, **55** D2
Moxhe **79** C2
Moyenvic **89** D1
Moyeuvre-Grande **89** C1
Möykky **20** B3
Möykkylä **18** A3
Möykkylänperä **18** B3
Moyuela **162** B1/2
Možajsk **75** D3
Mozárbez **159** D2
Mozgovo **135** C3
Mózia **124** A3
Mozirje **127** C2
Mozoncillo **160** B1/2
Mozyr' **99** C1
Mozzánica **106** A3
Mrągowo **73** C2/3
Mrakovica **131** D1, **132** A1
Mramor **135** C3
Mramorak **134** B1
Mratinje **133** C3, **137** C1
Mrazovac **131** C1
Mrčajevci **133** D2, **134** A2/3
Mrežičko **139** C3, **143** C1
Mrkalji **133** C2
Mrkonjić Grad **131** D2, **132** A2
Mrkopalj **127** C3, **130** B1
Mrzla Vodice **127** C3, **130** B1
Mšec **83** C2/3
Mšené-lázně **83** C2
Mšeno **83** D2
Mstislavl' **75** C3
Mszczonów **73** C3, **97** C1
Múccia **115** D3, **117** C/D2
Much **80** A2
Muchamiel **169** D3
Mücheln **82** A1
Much Wenlock **59** D3
Mucientes **152** A/B3, **160** A1

Mücka **83** D1
Mücke-Flensungen **81** C2
Mücke-Nieder-Ohmen **81** C2
Mudanya **149** D1
Mudau **81** C3, **91** C1
Müddersheim **79** D2, **80** A2
Müden (Aller) **68** B2
Muel **154** A/B3, **162** A/B1
Muelas del Pan **151** D3, **159** D1
Mués **153** D2
Muga de Sayago **159** C/D1
Mugaire **108** A3, **154** A1
Mugardos **150** B1
Muge **164** A/B2
Mügeln **83** B/C1
Mügeln **70** A3
Muggensturm **90** B1/2
Múggia **126** B3
Mugła **149** D2/3
Mugron **108** B2
Mühlacker **90** B1
Mühlbach am Hochkönig **93** C3, **107** D1, **126** A1
Muhlbach-sur-Munster **89** D2, **90** A3
Mühlbeck **69** D3, **82** B1
Mühlberg **83** C1
Mühlberg **81** D2
Mühldorf **94** A2
Mühldorf **92** B2
Mühlen Eichsen **53** C3, **69** C1
Mühlhausen (Höchstadt) **81** D3
Mühlhausen **81** D2
Mühlhausen (Neumarkt) **92** A1
Mühlhausen **81** D1
Mühlingen **91** C3
Mühltal **80** B3
Mühltroff **82** A/B2
Muhola **21** D2, **22** A2
Muhos **18** B2/3
Muhr **126** A1
Muhr **91** D1
Muiden **66** B2/3
Muides-sur-Loire **87** C3
Muiños **150** B3
Muirkirk **56** B2
Muir of Ord **54** A/B2
Muittan **21** D2
Mujdžići **131** D2, **132** A2
Mujejärvi **23** C1
Mukačevo **97** D2, **98** A3
Mukařov **83** D3
Mukkajärvi **17** C1/2
Mukkavaara **16** B1
Mukkavaara **13** C2
Mula **14** B2
Mula **169** B/C3, **174** A/B1
Mulda **83** C2
Mulfingen **91** C1
Mülheim **80** A1
Mulhouse **89** D3, **90** A3
Muljula **23** D3
Mulkwitz **83** D1
Mullaghboy **56** A3
Mullerup **49** C3, **53** C1
Müllheim **90** A3
Mullhyttan **46** A1
Mullingar **55** D2
Mullsjö **45** D3
Mullsjö **31** C2
Mulrany **55** C2
Mulsanne **86** B2/3
Multia **21** C3
Multra **30** B3, **35** D2
Munakka **20** B2
Munapirtti **26** B2/3
Münchberg **82** A2/3
Müncheberg **70** B2
Müncheberg **72** A3
München **92** A2
Münchenbernsdorf **82** A/B2
Münchhausen (Marburg) **80** B2
Münchsmünster **92** A2
Münchweiler an der Rodalbe **90** A2
Mundaca **153** D1
Mundal **36** B2
Münden **81** C1

Münden-Hedemünden **81** C1
Munderfing **93** C2/3
Munderkingen **91** C2
Mundesley **65** D1
Mundford **65** C2
Mundheim **42** A1
Mune **126** B3
Munébrega **162** A1
Munera **168** A2
Mungia **153** C1
Muniesa **162** B2
Munilla **153** D3
Munka-Ljungby **50** A2
Munkbyn **35** C3
Munkedal **45** B/C2
Munkedals bruk **45** B/C2
Munkflohögen **29** D3, **34** B1
Munkfors **39** C3
Munktorp **40** A3, **46** B1
Munne **26** B2
Münnerstadt **81** D2
Muñogalindo **160** A2
Muñopedro **160** B1/2
Muñopepe **160** A2
Muñotello **160** A2
Muñoveros **160** B1/2-
Munsala **20** B2
Münsingen **91** C2
Münsingen **105** C1
Münsingen-Bremelau **91** C2
Münsingen-Buttenhausen **91** C2
Munsö **47** C1
Munster **68** B2
Münster **67** D3
Münster **105** C2
Munster **89** D2, **90** A2/3
Munster-Alvern **68** B2
Munster-Breloh **68** B2
Münster-Hiltrup **67** D3
Münstermaifeld **80** A2
Münster-Nienberge **67** D3
Munster-Oerrel **68** B2
Münster-Sprakel **67** D3
Münstertal **90** B3
Münster-Wolbeck **67** D3
Munsvattnet **29** D2
Muntele Mic **135** C1
Münzkirchen **93** C2
Muodoslompolo **11** C3
Muonio **13** C3, **12** A1
Muotkajärvi **11** C2
Muotkan Ruoktu **6** B3
Muotkavaara **11** C3, **12** A1/2
Murakeresztúr **128** A2
Murakka **25** D1, **26** A/B1
Muráň **97** C2
Muras **150** B1
Muraszemenye **127** D2
Murat **102** B3, **110** A1
Murata **119** C2
Muratli **149** D1
Murat sur-Vèbre **110** A2
Murau **126** B1
Murau **96** A3
Muravera **123** D3
Murazzano **113** C2
Murazzo **112** B2
Murça **159** B/C2
Murça **158** B1
Murchante **154** A3
Murci **116** B3, **118** A1
Murcia **169** C3, **174** B1
Mur-de-Barrez **110** A1
Mur-de-Bretagne **85** B/C2
Mur-de-Sologne **87** C3
Mureck **127** D1/2
Mureşenii Bîrgăului **97** D3, **140** B1
Muret **108** B3, **155** C1
Murg **101** D1, **106** A1
Murgaševo **138** B3, **143** C1
Murgeni **141** C/D1
Murgia **153** C/D2
Muri **105** C1
Murias de Paredes **151** D2
Muriel Viejo **153** C3, **161** C1
Murieta **153** D2
Murillo de Gállego **154** B2
Murillo de Río Leza **153** D2
Murillo el Fruto **154** A2
Murino **137** D1, **138** A1

Mürlenbach **79** D2/3, **80** A3
Murnau am Staffelsee **92** A3
Muro **157** C2
Muro **113** D2
Muro de Aguas **153** D3
Muro de Alcoy **169** D2
Muro en Cameros **153** D2/3
Murol **102** B3
Murole **25** C1
Muro Lucano **120** A2
Muron **100** B2
Muros **150** A2
Muros de Nalón **151** D1
Murowana Goślina **71** D2
Murrë **138** A3
Murrhardt **91** C1
Murronkylä **18** B3
Murska Sobota **127** D1/2
Murska Sobota **96** A/B3
Mursko Središče **127** D2
Murtas **173** C2
Murtede **158** A2/3
Murten **104** B1
Murter **131** C3
Murtfü **129** D1
Murtino **139** D3, **143** D1, **144** A1
Murto **18** B2
Murtoinen **22** A/B3
Murtolahti **22** B2
Murtomäki **22** B1
Murtomäki **22** A/B2
Murtosa **158** A2
Murtovaara **19** D1
Murueta **153** D1
Murum **45** D2
Muruvik **28** A/B3, **33** C/D1
Murvica **130** B2
Murviel-les-Beziers **110** B3
Mürzsteg **94** A3
Murzynowo **71** C2
Mürzzuschlag **94** A3
Mürzzuschlag **96** A3
Müsch **79** D2, **80** A2
Musetesti **135** D1
Musetrene **37** D2
Museums-Jernbane **28** A3, **33** C2
Musile di Piave **107** D3
Muskiz **153** C1
Muskö **47** C/D1/2
Mušov **94** B1
Mussalo **26** B2/3
Musselburgh **57** C2
Musselkanaal **67** C2
Mussidan **109** C1
Mussomeli **124** B2
Mussy-sur-Seine **88** B2
Mustafa Kemalpaşa **149** D1
Müstair [Zernez] **106** B2
Mustajärvi **21** C2
Mustajärvi **20** B3
Mustajärvi **25** D1/2, **26** A1/2
Mustajoki **24** B1
Mustamaa **20** B2
Mustamaa **18** B3
Mustavaara **19** C2
Mustila **26** B2
Mustinlahti **23** C2/3
Mustio **25** C3
Mustion asema **25** C3
Mustla **74** A1
Mustolanmäki **23** C1
Mustolanmutka **19** C3, **23** D/C1
Mustvee **74** A/B1
Mušutište **138** B2
Muta **127** C2
Mutala **25** C1
Mutalahti **23** D3, **23** D1/2
Mutanj **133** D2, **134** A2
Mutriku **153** D1
Mutterstadt **90** B1
Mutzig **90** A2
Mutzschen **82** B1
Muuga **74** A1
Muurame **21** D3, **22** A3
Muurasjärvi **21** D1, **22** A1
Muurikkala **27** C2
Muurla **24** B3
Muurola **12** A3
Muurola **27** B/C2
Muuruvesi **23** C2

Muusko 12 B3
Muxagata 159 B/C2
Muxía 150 A1
Muzillac 85 C3
Mužla 95 D3
Mužlja 129 D3, 134 A1
Muzzana del Turgnano 126 A3
Mycielin 71 C3
Myckelasen 34 B2
Myckelgensjö 30 B2/3, 35 D1
Myckelsjö 35 D2/3
Myckle 31 D1
Mycklebostad 9 D1
Myckling 35 D3
Myennes 87 D3
Myggenäs 45 B/C3
Myggsjö 39 C/D1
Myhinpää 22 B3
Myjava 95 C2
Mykenai 147 C3
Mykland 36 B2
Mykland 43 C3
Myklebostad 8 B3
Myklebust 36 B2
Myllperä 21 D2, 22 A2
Myllyklä 25 C2
Myllykoski 26 B2
Myllykoski 20 B2
Myllykylä 25 C3
Myllykylä 12 B2
Myllylahti 19 D2
Myllymaa 24 B1
Myllymäki 21 C3
Myllyperä 18 A3
Myllyperä 21 D2, 22 A2
Mynämäki 24 A/B2
Mynttilä 26 B1
Myössäjärvi 6 B3
Myran 38 B3, 45 C1
Myrdal 36 B3
Myre 8 B1
Myreng 37 D2
Myrheden 16 B2
Myrheden 16 B3
Myrholen 39 D2
Myrkky 20 A3
Myrland 9 C2
Myrland 8 A/B2
Myrlandshaugen 9 D2
Myrlia 4 A3, 10 A1
Myrmoen 33 D2
Myrskylä/Mörskom 25 D2, 26 A2
Myrvang 9 C2
Myrviken 34 B2
Mysen 44 B1
Myślenice 97 C2
Myślibórz 70 B2
Myssjö 34 B2
Myssjön 35 D3
Mysuseter 37 D1/2
Mýto 83 C3

N

Nå 36 B3
Naamanka 19 C1/2
Naamankylä 18 B3
Naamijoki 12 A3, 17 D1
Naantali (Nådendal) 24 A/B2/3
Naappila 25 C1
Naarajärvi 22 B3
Naarden 66 B2/3
Näärinki 27 B/C1
Naarjoki 24 A/B2
Naartijärvi 17 D2
Naarva 23 D2
Naas 55 D2/3
Näätämö 7 C2
Näätänmaa 23 C3
Näätävaara 19 D2
Naatula 24 B2
Nabbelund 51 D1
Nabburg 82 B3, 92 B1
Načeradec 83 D3
Náchod 96 A/B1/2
Nacimiento 173 D2
Nacka 47 D1
Näckådalen 39 C1
Näcksåsen 29 D2

Nådab 97 C3, 140 A1
Nadalj 129 D3
Nadarzyce 71 D1
Nádasdladány 128 B1
Naddvik 37 C2
Nadela 150 B2
Nådendal 24 A/B2/3
Nädlac 140 A1
Nadrljan 129 D2
Nadvornaja 97 D2, 98 A/B3
Näfels [Näfels-Mollis] 105 D1, 106 A1
Náfpaktos 146 B2
Náfplion 147 C3
Náfplion 148 B2
Nafría la Llana 153 D3, 161 C1
Naggen 35 C3
Nago 106 B2/3
Nagold 90 B2
Nagold-Hochdorf 90 B2
Nagu/Nauvo 24 A3
Nagyargencs 95 C3, 128 A1
Nagyatád 128 A2
Nagyatád 96 B3
Nagybajom 128 A2
Nagybaracska 129 C2
Nagycenk 94 B3
Nagydorog 129 B/C2
Nagygyimót 95 C3, 128 A/B1
Nagyhalász 97 C3, 98 A3
Nagyharsány 128 B3
Nagyigmánd 95 C3
Nagykanizsa 128 A2
Nagykanizsa 96 B3
Nagykapornak 128 A1
Nagykáta 129 C/D1
Nagykáta 97 C3, 140 A1
Nagykörös 129 C/D1
Nagykörü 129 D1
Nagylak 129 D2
Nagylengyel 128 A1/2
Nagymágocs 129 D2
Nagymaros 95 D3
Nagyoroszi 95 D3
Nagyszénás 129 D2
Nagyvázsony 128 B1
Naharros 161 D3
Nahrstedt 69 C/D2
Nahwinden 82 A2
Naidăş 135 B/C1
Naila 82 A2
Nailloux 109 D3, 155 D1, 156 A1
Nailsworth 63 D1, 64 A3
Nairn 54 B2
Naisjärv 17 C2
Naizin 85 C2
Najac 109 D2
Nájera 153 D2
Näkkälä 11 C2
Naklo 126 B2
Nakło nad Notecią 72 B3
Nakovo 129 D3
Nakskov 53 C2
Nalda 153 D2
Nälden 29 D3, 34 B2
Näljänkä 19 C2
Nalkki 19 C3
Nálles/Nals 107 C2
Nalliers 100 B2
Naltijärvi 11 D2, 12 A1
Nalzen 109 D3, 155 D1/2, 156 A1
Nalžovské Hory 93 C1
Namborn 80 A3, 90 A1
Nambroca 160 B3, 167 C1
Namdalseid 28 B2
Námdö 47 D1
Náměšť nad Oslavou 94 A/B1
Namlos 91 D3, 106 B1
Namnå 38 B2
Nampont-Saint-Martin 77 D2
Namsos 28 B2
Namsvassgardan 29 C1
Namur 79 C2
Namysłów 96 B1
Nancy 89 C1/2
Nandlstadt 92 A2
Nangis 87 D2
Nannestad 38 A3

Nans-les-Pins 111 D3
Nantes 85 D3, 100 A1
Nanteuil-le-Haudoin 87 D1
Nantiat 101 C2
Nantrow 53 D3
Nantua 103 D2, 104 A2
Nantwich 59 D2, 60 B3, 64 A1
Náousa 143 C/D2
Náousa 148 B1
Napajedla 95 C1
Napapiiri 12 A3
Nápola 124 A2
Nápoli 119 C/D3
Napp 8 A/B2
Nárai 127 D1
Narberth 62 B1
Nårbo 42 A2/3
Nærbø 42 A2/3
Narbonne 110 A/B3, 156 B1
Narbonne-Plage 110 B3, 156 B1
Narbuvollen 33 D3
Narcao 123 C3
Narcy 87 D3, 102 B1
Nard 128 B3
Nardò 121 D3
Närhilä 21 D2, 22 A2
Narila 22 B3
Narkaus 12 B3
Narken 17 C1
Narni 117 C3, 118 B1
Naro 124 B3
Naroč 74 A3
Narodiči 99 C2
Naro-Fominsk 75 D3
Narón 150 B1
Nærøy 28 B1
Nåroy 36 B3
Nærø 36 B3
Närpes (Närpiö) 20 A3
Närpiö 20 A3
Narppa 21 C1
Narrillos de Rebollar 160 A2
Narros del Castillo 160 A2
Närsäkkälä 27 D1
Närsen 39 C2/3
Nærsnes 38 A3, 43 D1, 44 B1
Narta 128 A3
Närtesalo 27 C1
Närunga 45 C3
Naruska 13 C2
Narva 25 B/C1
Närvä 25 D1, 26 A1
Narva 74 B1
Närvijoki 20 A3
Narvik 9 D2
Narvik-Ankenes 9 D2
Narzole 113 C1/2
Näs 41 C/D2
Näs 34 B2
Näs 30 A/B3, 35 D2
Næs 53 D2
Näsåker 30 A3, 35 D1/2
Näsåud 97 D3, 140 B1
Näsberg 39 D1
Näs bruk 40 A3
Näsby 51 D2
Našec 138 A/B2
Näset 35 C3
Näset 29 D2
Näset 45 C3, 49 D1
Näset 39 D1
Näshult 51 C1
Našice 128 B3
Näske 30 B3
Näsland 31 C2
Naso 125 C1/2
Nassau 80 B2
Nassenfels 92 A2
Nassenheide 70 A2
Nassereith 91 D3, 106 B1
Nässja 46 A2
Nässjö 46 A3
Nässjö 30 A2/3, 35 C1
Nässjö 72 A1
Nässundet 45 D1, 46 A1
Nastan 136 A1
Nästangsjö 30 A1
Nastätten 80 B2/3
Nästelsjö 34 B3
Nästi 24 A2
Nastola 25 D2, 26 A2
Næstved 53 D1/2

Näsum 51 B/C2
Näsviken 40 A1
Natalinci 134 B2
Naters 105 C2
Nattavaara by 16 B1
Nattavaara station 16 B1
Nattheim 91 D2
Nättraby 51 C2
Naturno/Naturns 107 B/C1/2
Naturreservatet 49 C2
Naucelle 110 A2
Nauders 106 B1
Nauen 70 A2
Nauen 72 A3
Naul 58 B2
Naulaperä 19 C2
Naulavaara 23 C1
Naumburg 82 A1
Naumburg 81 C1
Naundorf 83 C2
Naundorf 70 A3, 82 B1
Naunhof 82 B1
Naurua 18 B2
Naustbukt 4 A2
Naustbukta 28 B1
Naustdal 36 A2
Nauste 32 B2
Nausterstøa 33 C3
Naustvilla 32 B3, 37 C1
Nauthella 42 A1
Nautijaur 16 A1
Nautsund 36 A2
Nauviale 110 A1
Näva 38 B3, 45 C1
Nava 151 D1, 152 A1
Navacarros 159 D2/3
Navacepeda de Tormes 160 A2/3
Navacepedilla de Corneja 160 A2
Navacerrada 167 C2
Navacerrada 160 B2
Navaconcejo 159 D3
Nava de Arévalo 160 A2
Nava de Béjar 159 D2
Nava de la Asunción 160 B1/2
Nava del Rey 160 A1
Nava de Roa 152 B3, 160 B1
Nava de Sotrobal 160 A2
Navafría 160 B2
Navahermosa 160 B3, 167 C1
Naval 155 C2/3
Navalacruz 160 A2
Navalagamella 160 B2
Navalcaballo 153 D3, 161 D1
Navalcán 160 A3
Navalcarnero 160 B3
Navaleno 153 C3, 161 C1
Navales 159 D2, 160 A2
Navalilla 160 B1
Navalmanzano 160 B1
Navalmoral de la Mata 159 D3, 166 A/B1
Navalmoralejo 160 A3, 166 B1
Navalón 169 C2
Navalonguilla 159 D3
Navalperal de Pinares 160 B2
Navalpino 167 B/C2
Navaluenga 160 A2
Navalvillar de Ibor 166 B1
Navalvillar de Pela 166 A/B2
Navamorcuende 160 A3
Navan (An Uaimh) 55 D2
Navarcles 156 A3
Navardún 155 C2
Navares de las Cuevas 160 B1
Navarredondilla 160 A2
Navarrenx 108 B3, 154 B1
Navarrés 169 C2
Navarrete 153 D2
Navarrete del Río 163 C2
Navàs 156 A2
Navasa 154 B2
Navascués 154 A/B2
Navas de Estena 167 C1
Navas de Jorquera 168 B1/2
Navas del Madroño 165 D1

Navas del Rey 160 B2/3
Navas de Oro 160 B1
Navas de San Juan 167 D3
Navas de Tolosa 167 D3
Navasfrías 159 C3
Navata 156 B2
Navatrasierra 166 B1
Nave 106 B3
Nave 159 C2/3
Nave de Haver 159 C2
Nävekvarn 47 C2
Navelli 117 D3, 119 C1
Navelsaker 32 A3, 36 B1
Nåverdal 33 C2
Näverede 29 D3, 35 C2
Näverkärret 39 D3, 46 B1
Näverliden 16 A3
Näverrys 18 B1
Naverstad 44 B2
Naves 104 B3
Navès 155 D3, 156 A2
Naves 102 A3
Naveta d'Es Tudóns 157 C1
Navezuelas 166 B1
Navia 151 C1
Navia de Suarna 151 C2
Navilly 103 D1
Navioci 133 B/C1/2
Navis 107 C1
Navit 5 B/C2/3
Năvodari 141 D2
Na Xamena 169 D2
Náxos 149 C2/3
Nay 108 B3, 154 B1
Nayland 65 C2
Nazaré 164 A1
Nazija 75 C1
Nazilli 149 D2
Ndërfushë 137 D3, 138 A2/3
Ndroq 137 D3, 142 A1
Néa Anchíalos 143 D3, 144 A3
Néa Artáki 147 D2
Néa Epídavros 147 C3
Néa Fókea 144 A2
Néai Kariaí 143 D3
Néa Iraklítsa 144 B1
Néa Kallikrátia 144 A2
Néa Kallísti 145 C1
Néa Karváli 145 B/C1
Néa Kerdília 144 B1
Néa Máditos 144 A/B2
Néamákri 147 D2
Néa Messángala 143 D2/3
Néa Michanióna 143 D2, 144 A2
Néa Moudaniá 144 A2
Néa Moudaniá 148 B1
Néant-sur-Yvel 85 C2
Néa Péramos 144 A1
Néa Plagiá 144 A2
Neápolis 143 C2
Neápolis 148 A/B1
Néa Potídea 144 A2
Néa Psará 147 D2
Néa Psará 148 B2
Néa Róda 144 B2
Néa Sánda 145 D1
Néa Sánda 149 C1
Néa Skióni 144 A2/3
Néa Ténedos 144 A2
Neath 63 C1
Néa Tríglia 144 A2
Néa Víssi 145 D2/3
Néa Zíchni 144 B1
Néa Zíchni 149 B/C1
Nebel 52 A2
Nebelin 69 C/D2
Nebljusi 131 C2
Nebolči 75 C1
Nebra 82 A1
Nebreda 153 C3
Nečemice 83 C2
Neckarbischofsheim 91 C1
Neckargemünd 90 B1
Neckargerach 91 C1
Neckarsulm 91 C1
Neckartailfingen 91 C2
Neckenmarkt 94 B3
Necrópoli Etrusca 114 B2, 116 B1
Necrópoli Pantálica 125 D3
Necrópolis Romana 171 D1
Nečtiny 83 C3
Nečujam 131 C3
Neda 150 B1

Nedalens turisthytta **33** D2
Nedansjö **35** D3
Nedaški **99** C2
Neded **95** C3
Nedelišče **127** D2
Nederbrakel **78** B2
Nederby **48** A/B2
Nedervetil/Alaveteli **21** B/C1
Nederweert **79** C/D1
Nedlitz **69** D3
Nedre Eggedal **43** D1
Nedre Flåsjøn **17** C2
Nedrefosshytta **5** B/C3, **10** B1
Nedre Gärdsjö **39** D2
Nedre Heimdalen **37** C/D2
Nedre Kuouka **16** B1/2
Nedre Parakka **10** B3
Nedre Soppero **10** B3
Nedre Tollådal **15** B/C1
Nedre Voljakkala **17** D2, **18** A1
Nedstrand **42** A2
Neede **67** C3
Needham Market **65** D2
Neerpelt **79** C1
Nees By **48** A2
Neetze **69** C1
Nefyn **58** B2/3
Negádes **142** B3
Negenborn **68** B3
Negorci **139** C3, **143** D1
Negotin **135** C2
Negotin **140** B2
Negotino **139** C3
Negovanovci **135** D2
Negredo **161** C2
Negreira **150** A2
Nègrepelisse **109** D2
Negresti-Oaş **97** D3, **98** A3
Negru Vodă **141** D2
Nehvonniemi **23** D1/2
Neiden **7** C2
Neila **153** C3
Neistenkangas **12** A3, **17** D1
Neitisuando **10** B3
Neittävä **18** B3
Nejdek **82** B2
Neksø **51** D3
Neksø **72** A/B2
Nelas **158** B2
Nelidovo **75** C2
Neljäntuulen tupa **6** B3
Nellimö **7** C3
Nellingen **91** C2
Nellingen **91** C2
Nelson **59** D1, **60** B2
Nelvik **32** B1/2
Neman (Ragnit) **73** C2
Němčice **93** B/C1
Neméa **147** C2/3
Neméa **147** C2/3
Nemesszalók **128** A1
Nemesvid **128** A2
Németkér **129** C2
Nemila **132** B2
Nemirov **99** C3
Nemours **87** D2
Nemšová **95** C1
Nenagh **55** C3
Nendeln **106** A1
Nennhausen **69** D2
Nensjö **30** B3, **35** D2
Nentershausen **81** C/D1/2
Nentershausen **80** B2
Nenthead **57** D3, **60** B1
Nenzing **106** A1
Neochórion **143** C3
Neochórion **146** A2
Neochórion **144** A3
Neochórion **146** A2
Neochórion **145** D1, **145** D3
Néon Ginekókastron **143** D1, **144** A1
Néon Kavaklíon **145** C1
Néon Monastírion **143** D3, **146** B1
Néon Petrítsi **139** D3, **144** A1
Néos Marmarás **144** B2
Neós Páos **146** B2
Nepas **153** D3, **161** D1
Nepi **117** C3, **118** B1

Nepomuk **83** C3, **93** C1
Nepomuk **96** A2
Nérac **109** C2
Neráida **143** C2
Neráida **142** B3
Neratovice **83** D2
Nerău **129** D2/3
Nerdal **32** B2
Néré **101** C2
Neresheim **91** D2
Neresnica **135** C2
Nereta **73** D1, **74** A2
Nereto **117** D3
Nerezine **130** A2
Nerežišče **131** D3
Neringa **73** C2
Néris-les-Bains **102** B2
Nerja **173** C2
Nerkoo **22** B2
Nermo **38** A1
Néronde **103** C2/3
Nérondes **102** B1
Nerpio **168** B3
Nersingen **91** D2
Nerskogen **33** C2
Nerva **171** C1
Nervesa della Battáglia **107** D3
Nes **36** A/B2
Nes **38** A2
Nes **9** C2
Nes **29** B/C2
Nes **66** B1
Nes **37** D3
Nes **37** D3
Nes **36** B2
Nes **38** A3
Nes **29** C2
Nes **42** A1/2
Nes **32** B2
Nes **55** C1
Nesan **29** C1
Nesaseter **29** C1
Nesbøsjøen **36** A3
Nesbyen **37** D3
Neschholz **69** D3, **70** A3
Neschwitz **83** D1
Nesebâr **141** C3
Neset **4** B2
Nesflaten **42** B1
Nesheim **36** B3
Nesland **43** C2
Nesland **42** B2
Nesland **8** A3
Neslandsvatn **43** C/D2, **44** A2
Nesna **14** A/B2
Nesodden **38** A3
Nesoddtangen **38** A3
Nesperal **158** A/B3, **164** B1
Nespereira **158** A/B2
Nespereira **158** B2
Nes Røstlandet **8** A3
Nesseby **7** C2
Nesselwang **91** D3
Nesse-Nessmersiel **67** D1
Nesso **105** D2/3, **106** A2
Nestáni **147** C3
Nestar **152** B2
Nestavoll **33** C3, **37** D1
Nestelbach bei Graz **127** C1
Nesterov **97** D2, **98** A2
Neštin **129** C3, **133** C1
Neston **59** C2, **60** B3
Nestórion **142** B2
Nestórion **148** A1
Nesttun **38** A3
Nesviž **98** B3
Neteka **131** C2
Netlandsnes **42** B3
Netolice **93** D1
Netphen **80** B2
Netretić **127** C3
Nettancourt **88** B1
Nettersheim-Tondorf **79** D2, **80** A2
Nettersheim **79** D2, **80** A2
Nettetal **79** D1
Nettetal-Kaldenkirchen **79** D1
Nettetal-Lobberich **79** D1
Nettlebed **64** B3
Nettuno **118** B2
Netvořice **83** D3
Netzschkau **82** B2
Neualbenreuth **82** B3

Neubörger **67** D2
Neubrandenburg **70** A1
Neubrandenburg **72** A3
Neubrück **70** B3
Neubrunn (Marktheidenfeld) **81** C3
Neu Büddenstedt **69** C3
Neubukow **53** D3
Neubulach **90** B2
Neuburg **92** A2
Neuburg am Inn **93** C2
Neuburg-Zell **92** A2
Neuburxdorf **83** C1
Neuchâtel **104** B1
Neudau **127** D1
Neudenau **91** C1
Neudingen **90** B3
Neudorf **82** B2
Neudorf-Platendorf **69** C2
Neudrossenfeld **82** A3
Neuenbürg **90** B1/2
Neuendettelsau **91** D1
Neuendorf **79** D2
Neuenhagen **70** A/B2
Neuenhaus **67** C2
Neuenkirchen **68** A2
Neuenkirchen **67** D2
Neuenkirchen **68** B2
Neuenkirchen **67** D3
Neuenkirchen-Vörden **67** D2
Neuenkirchen **52** A3
Neuenmarkt **82** A3
Neuenrade **80** B1
Neuensalz **82** B2
Neuenstein **91** C1
Neuenstein-Aua **81** C2
Neuental-Zimmersrode **81** C1/2
Neuenweg **90** A/B3
Neuerburg **79** D3
Neue Schleuse **69** D2
Neufahrn **92** B2
Neufahrn (Freising) **92** A2
Neufahrn-Piegendorf **92** B2
Neuf-Brisach **90** A3
Neufchâteau **89** C2
Neufchâteau **79** C3
Neufchâtel-en-Bray **77** D3
Neufchâtel-sur-Aisne **78** B3
Neufelden **93** C2
Neugattersleben **69** D3
Neugersdorf **83** D1/2
Neuharlingersiel **67** D1
Neuhaus **82** A3
Neuhaus **52** A/B3, **68** A1
Neuhaus **69** C1
Neuhaus **82** A2
Neuhausen **83** C2
Neuhausen am Rheinfall **90** B3
Neuhausen ob Eck **91** B/C3
Neuhaus-Schierschnitz **82** A2
Neuhof **81** C2
Neuhofen an der Krems **93** D2
Neuillé-Pont-Pierre **86** B3
Neuilly-le-Réal **102** B2
Neuilly-l'Evêque **89** C2/3
Neuilly-Saint-Front **87** D1, **88** A1
Neu-Isenburg **80** B3
Neukalen **69** D1, **70** A1
Neukirch **83** D1
Neukirchen **52** A2
Neukirchen **81** C2
Neukirchen am Walde **93** C2
Neukirchen an der Enknach **93** B/C2
Neukirchen bei Sulzbach-Rosenberg **82** A3, **92** A1
Neukirchen bei Heilig Blut **92** B1
Neukirchen-Balbini **92** B1
Neukirchen-Vluyn **79** D1, **80** A1
Neukloster **53** D3, **69** C/D1
Neu Kosenow **70** A/B1
Neulengbach **94** A2
Neulietzegöricke **70** B2
Neulikko **19** C2
Neulingen-Bauschlott **90** B1

Neulise **103** C2
Neu Lübbenau **70** B3
Neulussheim **90** B1
Neum **136** B1
Neumagen-Dhron **80** A3
Neumarkt **92** A1
Neumarkt am Wallersee **93** C3
Neumarkt an der Ybbs **93** D2
Neumarkt an der Raab **127** D1
Neumarkt im Mühlkreis **93** D1
Neumarkt im Hausruckkreis **93** C2
Neumarkt in Steiermark **126** B1
Neumarkt-Sankt Veit **92** B2
Neu-Moresnet **79** D2
Neumünster **52** B3
Neunagelberg **93** D2
Neunburg **92** B1
Neunburg-Kemnath **92** B1
Neung-sur-Beuvron **87** C3
Neunkirch **90** B3
Neunkirchen **94** A3
Neunkirchen **80** B2
Neunkirchen **81** C3
Neunkirchen-Seelscheid **80** A2
Neunkirchen-Wiebelskirchen **89** D1, **90** A1
Neunkirchen **89** D1, **90** A1
Neunkirchen am Brand **82** A3
Neunkirchen **96** A/B3
Neuötting **92** B2
Neupetershain **83** C1
Neupölla **94** A2
Neureichenau-Altreichenau **93** C2
Neuried-Ichenheim **90** A/B2
Neuruppin **69** D2, **70** A2
Neuruppin **72** A3
Neusäss **91** D2
Neuschoo **67** D1
Neuschwanstein **91** D3
Neusiedl am See **94** B3
Neuss **79** D1, **80** A1
Neussargues **102** B3, **110** A/B1
Neustadt **81** C2
Neustadt **81** C3
Neustadt **53** C3
Neustadt **80** A2
Neustadt **83** C/D1/2
Neustadt **82** A2
Neustadt **69** D2
Neustadt am Rennsteig **81** D2, **82** A2
Neustadt am Rübenberge-Schneeren **68** B2
Neustadt am Rübenberge-Mandelsloh **68** B2
Neustadt am Rübenberge-Mardorf **68** A/B2
Neustadt am Rübenberge **68** B2
Neustadt am Kulm **82** A3
Neustadt am Rübenberge-Eilvese **68** B2
Neustadt am Rübenberge-Dudensen **68** B2
Neustadt an der Waldnaab **82** B3
Neustadt an der Weinstrasse **90** B1
Neustadt an der Donau **92** A2
Neustadt an der Aisch **81** D3
Neustadt bei Coburg **82** A2
Neustadt-Geinsheim **90** B1
Neustadt-Glewe **69** C1
Neustift im Stubaital **107** C1
Neu St. Johann [Nesslau-Neu St. Johann] **105** D1, **106** A1
Neustrelitz **70** A1
Neustrelitz **72** A3
Neustupov **83** D3
Neu-Ulm **91** C/D2
Neu-Ulm-Pfuhl **91** C/D2
Neuves-Maisons **89** C2

Neuveville, La **104** B1
Neuvic **101** C3, **109** C1
Neuvic-d'Ussel **102** A3
Neuville **78** B2/3
Neuville-aux-Boix **87** C2
Neuville-de-Poitou **101** C1
Neuville-en-Condroz **79** C2
Neuville-lès-Decize **102** B1
Neuville-sur-Saône **103** D2
Neuville-sur-Ain **103** D2
Neuvilly-en-Argonne **88** B1
Neuvola **22** B3
Neuvosenniemi **19** C3
Neuvy-Pailloux **102** A1
Neuvy-Saint-Sépulchre **102** A1/2
Neuvy-Sautour **88** A2
Neuvy-sur-Barangeon **87** D3
Neuvy-sur-Loire **87** D3
Neu-Wendischthun **69** C1
Neuwied **80** A2
Neuwiller **90** A2
Neu Wulmstorf **68** B1
Neuzelle **70** B3
Neu-Zittau **70** A/B2/3
Névache **112** A1
Nevade **140** A2
Nevegal **107** D2
Neveklov **83** D3
Nevel' **74** B2
Nevernes **14** A3
Nevers **102** B1
Nevesinje **132** B3, **137** C1
Nevest **131** C3
Neviano **121** D3
Neviano degli Arduini **114** A1
Nevlunghavn **43** D2, **44** A2
New Abbey **57** C3, **60** A1
New Alresford **65** C3, **76** B1
Newark-on-Trent **61** C/D3, **64** B1
Newbiggin-by-the-Sea **57** D2/3
Newborough **58** B2
Newbridge **63** C1
Newbridge-on-Wye **59** C3, **63** C1
Newburgh **57** C1
Newbury **65** C3, **76** B1
Newby Bridge **59** C/D1, **60** B2
Newcastle **58** A1
Newcastle **58** A2
Newcastle Emlyn **62** B1
Newcastleton **57** C2/3
Newcastle-under-Lyme **59** D2, **60** B3, **64** A1
Newcastle upon Tyne **57** D3, **61** C1
Newcastle upon Tyne **54** B3
New Cumnock **56** B2
Newenden **77** C1
Newent **63** D1, **64** A2
New Galloway **56** B3
Newgrange **58** A1/2
Newhaven **76** B1
New Holland **61** D2
New Luce **56** B3
Newlyn East **62** B3
Newmarket **65** C2
New Mills **59** D2, **61** B/C3
Newnham **63** D1, **64** A2/3
Newport **62** B1
Newport **59** D3, **64** A1
Newport **65** C2
Newport **63** C/D1
Newport **76** B1/2
Newport-on-Tay **57** C1
Newport Pagnell **64** B2
Newquay **62** B3
New Quay **58** B3, **62** B1
New Radnor **59** C3
New Romney **77** C1
New Ross **55** D3
Newry **54** A3, **55** D2
Newry **58** A1
New Scone **57** C1
Newstead Abbey **61** D3, **65** C1
Newton **59** D2, **60** B3
Newtonabbey **56** A3
Newton Abbot **63** C3

Newton Ferrers 63 C3
Newton Hamilton 58 A1
Newtonmore 54 B2, 55 D1
Newton Stewart 54 A/B3, 55 D2
Newton Stewart 56 B3
Newtown 59 C3
Newtownards 56 A3
Newtownbutler 54 A3, 55 D2
Nexon 101 C3
Nezavertajlovka 141 D1
Nežin 99 D2
Nianfors 40 A1
Niannoret 40 A1
Niaux 155 D2, 156 A1
Nibbiano 113 D1
Nibe 48 B1/2
Nicaj-Shalë 137 D2, 138 A2
Nicastro 122 A/B2
Niccone 115 C3, 117 C2
Nice 112 B3
Nichelino 112 B1
Nickelsdorf 94 B3
Nickelsdorf 96 B3
Nicolint 134 B1
Nicolosi 125 D2
Nicosia 125 C2
Nicótera 122 A2/3
Nicótera Marina 122 A2/3
Nidda 81 C2
Nidda-Eichelsdorf 81 C2
Nidderau 81 C2/3
Nideck 89 D2, 90 A2
Nideggen 79 D2
Nidrí 146 A1
Nidríon 146 A1
Nidzica (Neidenburg) 73 C3
Niebla 171 C1/2
Niebüll 52 A2
Niederaichbach 92 B2
Niederanven 79 D3
Niederaula 81 C2
Niederbipp 105 C1
Niederbobritzsch 83 C2
Niederbronn-les-Bains 90 A1
Niederfell 80 A2
Niederfeulen 79 D3
Niederfinow 70 B2
Niedergurig 83 D1
Niederheimbach 80 B3
Niederkassel 80 A2
Niederkrüchten 79 D1
Niederlahnstein 80 A/B2
Niederlandin 70 B2
Niedernai 90 A2
Niederndodeleben 69 C3
Nieder-Olm 80 B3
Niederorschel 81 D1
Nieder-Ramstadt 80 B3
Niedersachswerfen 81 D1
Nieder-Seifersdorf 83 D1
Niederstetten 91 C1
Niederstotzingen 91 D2
Niedersulz 94 B2
Niederurnen [Nieder- und Oberurnen] 105 D1, 106 A1
Niederviehbach-Lichtensee 92 B2
Niederwölz 126 B1
Niederzier 79 D2
Niederzissen 80 A2
Niedoradz 71 C3
Niegosław 71 C2
Nieheim 68 A3
Niekursko 71 D2
Niel 78 B1
Niella Tánaro 113 C2
Niemegk 69 D3, 70 A3
Niemelä 13 C3
Niemelä 8 B2
Niemelä 7 B/C2
Niemenkylä 20 B2/3
Niemenkylä 24 B1
Niemi 24 A1, 41 D1
Niemica 71 B/C1
Niemis 17 D2
Niemisel 17 C2
Niemisjärvi 21 D3, 22 A3
Niemistenkylä 25 D1, 26 A/B1
Niemisvesi 21 C3
Nienborstel 52 B3

Nienburg 68 A/B2
Nienburg 69 D3
Nienburg-Holtorf 68 A/B2
Nienburg-Langendamm 68 A/B2
Nienhagen 68 B2
Niepart 71 D3
Niepruszewo 71 D2/3
Nierstein 80 B3
Niesi 12 B2/3
Niesky 83 D1
Niesky 96 A1
Niestetal 81 C1
Nietsak 16 B1
Nieul 101 C2
Nieul-le-Dolent 100 A1/2
Nieul-sur-l'Autise 100 B2
Nieuw-Amsterdam 67 C2
Nieuweburg 66 B2
Nieuwe-Pekela 67 C2
Nieuwerbrug 66 A/B3
Nieuwerkerk 66 A3, 78 B1
Nieuweschans 67 C/D1
Nieuw-Heeten 67 C2/3
Nieuwkoop 66 A/B3
Nieuwleusen 67 C2
Nieuwolda 67 C1
Nieuwpoort 66 B3
Nieuwpoort 78 A1
Nieuwpoort-Bad 78 A1
Nieuw-Schoonebeek 67 C2
Nieva 160 B2
Niewisch 70 B3
Nigrán 150 A3
Nigríta 144 A1
Nigríta 148 B1
Nihajlovgrad 140 B2/3
Nihajlovgrad 135 D3
Niinikoski 25 D2, 26 A2
Niinilahti 21 D2, 22 A2
Niinimäki 23 C3
Niinimäki 21 D1, 22 A1
Niinisaari 27 C1
Niinisalo 24 B1
Niinivesi 22 A/B2
Niirala 23 D3
Niittylahti 23 D3
Niitynpää 24 B2
Níjar 173 D2, 174 A2
Nijbroek 67 C2/3
Nijemci 133 C1
Nijeveen 67 C2
Nijkerk 66 B3
Nijmegen 66 B3
Nijverdal 67 C2/3
Nikaranperä 21 D3, 22 A3
Níkea 143 D3
Níki 143 D3
Nikifóros 144 B1
Nikinci 133 D1, 134 A1
Nikísiani 144 B1
Nikísiani 149 C1
Nikítas 144 B2
Nikitsch 94 B3
Nikkala 17 D2/3, 18 A1
Nikkaluokta 10 A3
Nikkaroinen 25 D1, 26 A1
Nikkeby 4 B2
Nikkilä 25 D3, 26 A3
Nikolaev 97 D2, 98 A3
Nikolaevo 74 B1
Nikoličevo 135 C2
Nikolince 134 B1
Nikol'skoe 75 D1
Nikopol 140 B2
Nikopolis 146 A1
Nikopolis 144 A1
Nikopolis 146 A1
Nikšić 137 C/D1
Nilakkavuoma 10 A3
Nilivaara 17 B/C1
Nilivaara 11 D3, 12 A2
Nilsebu 42 B2
Nilsiä 23 B/C2
Nîmes 111 C2
Nímis 126 A2
Nin 130 B2
Nine 158 A1
Ninfa 118 B2
Ninove 78 B2
Niort 100 B2
Nipen 9 C2
Nipivatn 5 C2
Niš 135 C3
Niš 140 A3
Nisa 165 C1
Nisákion 142 A3

Niscemi 125 C3
Niška Banja 135 C3
Niskalehto 19 C1
Niskankorpi 21 C1
Niskanpää 17 D2
Niskanperä 12 A/B3
Niska-Pietilä 27 C/D1/2
Nisko 97 C1/2, 98 A2
Niskos 20 B3
Nissan-lez-Enserune 110 B3, 156 B1
Nissedal 43 C2
Nissinvaara 19 D1
Niton 76 B2
Nitra 95 C2
Nitra 96 B2/3
Nitrianske Pravno 95 D1/2
Nitrianske Rudno 95 D2
Nitry 88 A3
Nittedal 38 A3
Nittel 79 D3
Nittenau 92 B1
Nittendorf-Etterzhausen 92 B1
Nittkvarn 39 D3
Nittsjö 39 D2
Nittylahti 22 B2
Niukkala 27 D1
Nivå 49 D3, 50 A3
Niva 19 D3
Niva 18 B2
Nivankylä 12 A/B3
Nivelles 78 B2
Nivnice 95 C1
Niwica 83 D1
Niwiska 71 C2
Nizy-le-Comte 78 B3
Nizza Monferrato 113 C1
Njakaure 16 B2
Njallejaur 16 A/B3
Njavve 15 D1, 16 A1
Njegušovo 129 C/D3
Njetsavare 16 B1
Njivice 126 B3, 130 B1
Njunjes 16 A1
Njunjesstugan 15 D1
Njurundabommen 35 D3
Njutånger 40 A/B1
Noailles 77 D3, 87 C/D1
Noailles 101 D3, 109 D1
Noáin 154 A2
Noasco 104 B3
Nöbbele 51 C2
Noblejas 161 C3
Nocé 86 B2
Noceda 151 C/D2
Nocera Inferiore 119 D3
Nocera Tirinese 122 A2
Nocera Umbra 115 D3, 117 C2
Noceto 114 A1
Nochten 83 D1
Noci 121 C2
Nociglia 121 D3
Nocina 153 C1
Nocito 154 B2
Nódalo 153 D3, 161 C/D1
Nodeland 43 C3
Nödinge 45 C3
Nods 104 A/B1
Noépoli 120 B3, 122 B1
Noeux-les-Mines 78 A2
Noevci 139 D2
Noez 160 B3, 167 C1
Nofuentes 153 C2
Nogales 165 D2
Nogara 107 B/C3
Nogaro 108 B2
Nogent-en-Bassigny 89 C2
Nogent-l'Artaud 88 A1
Nogent-le-Roi 87 C2
Nogent-le-Rotrou 86 B2
Nogent sur Oise 87 D1
Nogent-sur-Seine 88 A2
Nogent-sur-Vernisson 87 D3
Nógrád 95 D3
Nograles 161 C3
Nogueira de Ramuin 150 B2
Noguera 162 A2
Nogueras 162 A/B1/2
Nogueruelas 162 B3
Nohant 102 A1
Nohfelden 80 A3

Noia 150 A2
Noidans-le-Ferroux 89 C3
Noirétable 103 C2/3
Noirmont, Le 89 D3, 104 B1
Noirmoutier-en-l'Île 100 A1
Noja 153 C1
Nojamaa 27 C1
Nojewo 71 D2
Nokia 25 B/C1
Nokka 25 D1, 26 B1
Nol 45 C3
Nola 119 D3
Nolay 153 D3, 161 D1
Nolay 103 C/D1
Noli 113 C2
Nolmyra 40 B3
Nolvik 15 C3
Nombela 160 B3
Nomécourt 88 B2
Nomény 89 C1
Noméxy 89 D2
Nomparedes 153 D3, 161 D1
Nompatelize 89 D2, 90 A2
Nonancourt 86 A/B1
Nonant-le-Pin 86 B1/2
Nonántola 114 B1
Nonaspe 163 C1
None 112 B1
Nonnenhorn 91 C3
Nonnweiler 80 A3
Nonnweiler-Primstal 80 A3, 90 A1
Nontron 101 C/D3
Nonza 113 D2
Noordbergum 67 B/C1
Noordeinde 66 B2
Noordwijk 66 A3
Noordwijkerhout 66 A3
Noordwolde 67 C2
Noormarkku (Norrmark) 24 A1
Nopala 26 B2
Nopankylä 20 B2/3
Noposenaho 21 C2
Noppo 25 C2
Nor 40 A1
Nor 35 C2
Nor 38 B2/3
Nora 30 B3, 35 D2
Nora 46 A1
Nora 123 D3
Nørager 48 B2
Norainkylä 20 B3
Norberg 40 A3
Nórchia 116 B3, 118 A1
Nórcia 117 D3
Nordagutu 43 D2, 44 A1
Nordana 35 D2
Nordanå 35 D3
Nordanåker 30 A3, 35 C1/2
Nordanås 15 C3
Nordanås 30 B2
Nordanholen 39 D2
Nordankäl 30 A2, 35 C1
Nordansjö 30 A1
Nordansjö 30 A1
Nordausques 77 D1
Nordberg 32 B3, 37 C1
Nordborg 52 B2
Nordbotn 32 B1
Nordby 38 A/B1
Nordby 48 A3, 52 A1
Nordby 49 C3
Nordby Bruk 38 A3
Nördbyn 16 B3
Norddal 32 A3, 36 B1
Norddal 36 A2
Norddyrøy 32 B1
Nordeide 36 A/B2
Norden 16 A/B2
Norden 67 C/D1
Nordendorf 91 D2
Nordenham 68 A1
Nordenham-Esenshamm 68 A1
Norden-Norddeich 67 C1
Norderåsen 29 D3, 34 B1
Norderhov 38 A3, 43 D1
Norderney 67 C1
Norderö 29 D3, 34 B2
Norderstapel 52 B2/3
Norderstedt 52 B3, 68 B1

Nordfjordbotn 4 A3, 9 D1, 10 A1
Nordfjordeid 36 A/B1
Nordfold 9 B/C3
Nord-Frøya 32 B1
Nordgard 33 D3
Nordhalben 82 A2
Nordhallen 29 C3, 34 A1
Nordhallen 29 C3, 34 A1
Nordhastedt 52 B3
Nordhausen 81 D1
Nordheim 32 B2
Nordheim vor der Rhön 81 D2
Nordholz 52 A3, 68 A1
Nordholz-Spieka 52 A3, 68 A1
Nordhorn 67 C2
Nordhorn-Brandlecht 67 C2
Nordhus 5 C2
Nordingrå 30 B3
Nordkisa 38 A3
Nordkjosbotn 4 A3, 10 A1
Nordkrekling 28 B1
Nordland 8 A3
Nordlandskorsen 28 B1
Nord-Lenangen 4 B2
Nordli 14 B3
Nördlingen 91 D1/2
Nordlysobservatoriet 4 A3
Nordmaling 31 C2/3
Nordmannset 5 D1, 6 A1
Nordmannset 5 D1, 6 B1
Nordmannvik 6 B1
Nordmark 39 C3
Nordmela 9 C2
Nordnesøy 14 A1/2
Nord-Odal 38 A/B2
Nordomsjön 39 C1
Nordre Osen 38 B1
Nordsand 15 C3
Nord-Sel 33 C3, 37 D1
Nordseter 38 A1
Nordsinni 37 D3
Nordsjö 40 A1
Nordsjö 40 A1
Nordsjö 30 A2, 35 C1
Nordsjona 14 B2
Nordskaget 32 B1
Nordskot 8 B3
Nord-Statland 28 B2
Nordstemmen 68 B3
Nörd-Stensvattnet 30 A2, 35 C1
Nordstrand-Süden 52 A2
Nordstrand-Süderhafen 52 A2
Nordvågen 5 D1, 6 B1
Nordværnes 14 B1
Nordvik 24 B3
Nordvik 14 A2
Nordvik 32 B1
Nordvika 32 B1
Nordwalde 67 D3
Nore 43 C1
Norg 67 C2
Norges-la-Ville 88 B3
Norham 57 D2
Norheimsund 36 A/B3
Nørholm 43 C3
Norinkylä 20 B3
Norma 118 B2
Nornäs 39 C1
Noroy-le-Bourg 89 C/D3
Norppa 21 C1
Norra Bergnäs 15 D2
Norra Drängsmark 31 D1
Norra Finnskoga 38 B2
Norra Fjällnäs 15 C3
Norra Flymen 51 C2
Norra Hede 34 A3
Norra Holmnäs 16 A3
Norråker 29 D2, 30 A1
Norra Klagshamn 50 A3
Norra Kölviken 45 C1
Norrala 40 A/B1
Norra Möckleby 51 D2
Norra Nordsjö 31 C2
Norra Ny 39 C2
Norra polcirkeln 17 C2
Norra Rörum 50 B2/3
Norra Sandsjö 46 A3, 51 C1
Norra Sunderbyn 17 C3
Norra Tannflo 30 A/B3, 35 D1/2

Norra Tresund **30** A1
Norra Umstrand **15** D3
Norra Unnaryd **45** D3
Norra Vallgrund **20** A2, **31** D3
Norra Vånga **45** D2/3
Norrbäck **30** B1
Norrbacka **16** A3
Norrboda **40** B2
Norrboda **39** D1/2
Norrboda **41** D3
Norrby **30** B1
Norrby **31** C1
Norrbyn **39** D1
Norrbyn **31** B/C3
Norrbyn **31** C2/3
Nørre Åby **52** B1
Nørre Alslev **53** D2
Nørre Arup **48** A/B1/2
Nørre Broby **53** B/C1
Nørre Knudstrup **48** B2
Nørre Nebel **48** A3, **52** A1
Nørre Snede **48** B3
Nørresundby **48** B1
Nørre Vorupør **48** A2
Norrfjärden **16** B3
Norrfjärden **20** A1, **31** D2
Norrfjärden **35** D3
Norrfors **31** C2
Norrfors **30** B2
Norrgård **31** C1
Norrhult-Klavreström **51** C1
Norrhult-Klavreström **72** A/B1
Norriån **17** C2
Norrköping **46** B2
Norrmark **24** A1
Norrmesunda **30** B3, **35** D1
Norrmjöle **31** C2
Norrnäs **20** A3
Norrow Water Castle **58** A1
Norrsjö **29** D2
Norrskedika **40** B2/3
Norrsunda **40** B3, **47** C1
Norrsundet **40** A/B2
Norrtälje **41** C3
Norrvik **30** B1
Nors **48** A1/2
Norsholm **46** B2
Norsjö **31** C1
Norsjövallen **31** C1
Norsminde **49** B/C3
Nørstedalsseter **37** C2
Nörten-Hardenberg **81** C/D1
Northallerton **61** C1/2
Northam **62** B2
Northampton **64** B2
North Berwick **57** C1
Northeim **68** B3, **81** C/D1
Northeim-Hohnstedt **68** B3
Northeim-Sudheim **68** B3, **81** C/D1
Northleach **63** D1, **64** A2/3
North Newbald **61** D2
North Petherton **63** C/D2
North Somercotes **61** D3
North Sunderland **57** D2
North Tawton **63** C2
North Tidworth **64** A3, **76** A1
North Walsham **61** D3, **65** C1
Northwich **59** D2, **60** B3, **64** A1
Northwold **65** C2
Nortorf **52** B3
Nortrup **67** D2
Nort-sur-Erde **85** D3
Norvalahti **12** A/B3
Norvasalmi **12** B3
Nörvenich **79** D2, **80** A2
Norwich **65** C1/2
Nos **32** A3, **36** B1
Nøsen **37** C/D3
Nøsenseter **37** C3
Nosovka **99** D2
Nøss **9** C1
Nossa Senhora da Espe-rança **165** C2
Nossa Senhora do Cabo **164** A3
Nossa Senhora d'Ajuda **165** C2
Nossebro **45** C3
Nössemark **45** C1
Nossen **83** C1

Nossentiner Hütte **69** D1
Nösund **44** B3
Noszlop **128** A1
Notaresco **117** D3, **119** C1
Nötbolandet **31** C3
Notmarkskov **52** B2
Nötö **24** A3
Noto **125** D3
Noto Antica **125** D3
Notodden **43** D1, **44** A1
Notre Dame **112** B2
Notre-Dame de la Salette **111** D1, **112** A1
Notre-Dame-de-Monts **100** A1
Notre-Dame-d'Aspres **86** B1/2
Notre-Dame-du-Mai **111** D3, **112** A3
Notre-Dame-de-Sanilhac **101** D3, **109** C1
Notre-Dame des Fontaines **113** B/C2
Nøtterøy **43** D2, **44** B1
Nottingham **61** D3, **65** C1
Nottuln **67** D3
Nottuln-Appelhülsen **67** D3
Nottuln-Darup **67** D3
Nouan-le-Fuzelier **87** C3
Nouans-les-Fontaines **101** C1
Nougaroulet **109** C2
Nousiainen **24** B2
Nousu **13** C2
Nouvion-en-Ponthieu **77** D2
Nova **127** D1/2, **128** A2
Nová Baňa **95** D2
Nova Breznica **138** B2
Nova Bukovica **128** B3
Nová Bystřice **93** D1, **94** A1
Novaci **133** D2, **134** A2
Novaci **143** C1
Novaci **140** B2
Nova Crnja **129** D3
Nová Dubnica **95** C1
Novaféltria **115** C2, **117** C1
Nova Gorica **126** B2
Nova Gradiška **128** A3, **131** D1, **132** A1
Nová Hospoda **93** C1
Novaja Praga **99** D3
Novaja Ušica **98** B3
Nova Kasaba **133** C2
Nováky **95** D2
Novales **154** B3
Nova Levante/Welschnofen **107** C2
Novalja **130** B2
Nova Pazova **133** D1, **134** A1
Nova Pec **93** C2
Nova Ponente/Deutschnofen **107** C2
Novara **105** D3
Novara di Sicília **125** D2
Nová Říše **94** A1
Nova Sela **132** A3, **136** B1
Nova Siri **120** B3
Nova Siri Stazione **121** B/C3
Novate Mezzola **105** D2, **106** A2
Nova Topola **131** D1, **132** A1
Nova Varoš **133** D3, **134** A3
Nova Vas **126** B3
Nova Zagora **141** C3
Nové Hrady **93** D2
Novelda **169** C3
Novellara **114** B1
Nové Mesto nad Váhom **95** C2
Nové Město pod Smrkem **83** D2
Nové Mesto nad Váhom **96** B2
Nové Mitrovice **83** C3, **93** C1
Noventa di Piave **107** D3
Noventa Vicentina **107** C3
Novés **160** B3
Nové Sady **95** C2
Nové Strašecí **83** C3
Nové Zámky **95** C3

Nové Zámky **96** B3
Novgorod **75** C1
Novgorodka **99** D3
Novgorodka **74** B2
Novgorod-Severskij **99** D1
Novi-Bečej **129** D3
Novi di Módena **114** B1
Novi-Dojran **139** D3, **143** D1, **144** A1
Noviercas **153** D3, **161** D1
Novigrad **126** A/B3, **130** A1
Novigrad **131** B/C2
Novigrad Podravski **128** A2
Novi Iskår **139** D1
Novij Bug **99** D3
Novi Karlovci **133** D1, **134** A1
Novi Kneževac **129** D2
Novi Lígure **113** D1
Novillas **155** C3
Novi Marof **127** D2
Novi Marof **96** A/B3
Novion-Porcien **78** B3
Novi Pazar **133** D3, **138** A1
Novi Pazar **140** A3
Novi Pazar **141** C3
Novi Sad **140** A2
Novi Sad **129** D3, **133** D1, **134** A1
Novi Šeher **132** B2
Novi Slankamen **133** D1, **134** A1
Novi Vinodolski **130** B1
Novoarhangel'sk **99** D3
Novo Brdo **138** B1
Novograd-Volynskij **99** B/C2
Novogrudok **98** B1
Novo Korito **135** C3
Nóvoli **114** B2, **116** B1
Novo Mesto **127** C3
Novo Miloševo **129** D3
Novomirgorod **99** D3
Novopetrovskoe **75** D2
Novopolock **74** B3
Novoržev **74** B2
Novoselé **142** A2
Novoselica **98** B3
Novo Selo **135** D2
Novo Selo **139** D3
Novosokol'niki **74** B2
Novoukrainka **99** D3
Novovolynsk **97** D1, **98** A2
Novozavidovskij **75** D2
Novo Zvečevo **128** A3
Novozybkov **99** D1
Novska **128** A3, **131** D1
Nový Bor **83** D2
Nový Hrozenkov **95** C1
Nový Jičin **96** B2
Nový Knín **83** D3
Nový Přerov **94** B2
Novy Rychnov **94** A1
Nowa Dęba **97** C1/2, **98** A2
Nowa Sól (Neusalz) **72** B3, **96** A1
Nowa Sól (Neusalz) **71** C3
Nowe **73** B/C3
Nowe Bielawy **71** C3
Nowe Biskupice **70** B3
Nowe Miasteczko **71** C3
Nowe Warpno **70** B1
Nowe Worowo **71** C1
Nowiny Wielkie **71** C2
Nowogard **71** C1
Nowogard **72** A2/3
Nowogród Bobrżanski **71** C3
Nowy Dwór Gdański **73** C2
Nowy Dwór Mazowiecki **73** C3
Nowy Sącz **97** C2
Nowy Tomyśl **71** C/D3
Noyal **85** C2
Noyalo **85** C3
Noyant **86** B3
Noyant-de-Touraine **101** C1
Noyant-la-Plaine **86** A3, **101** B/C1
Noyelles-sur-Mer **77** D2
Noyen-sur-Sarthe **86** A2/3
Noyers **88** A3
Noyers-sur-Cher **86** A/B3, **101** C1

Noyers-sur-Jabron **111** D2, **112** A2
Noyon **78** A3
Nozay **85** D3
Nozeroy **104** A1
Nuaillé **100** B1
Nuasjärvi **12** A3, **17** D1
Nuasniemi **12** A3, **17** D1
Nueil-sur-Argent **100** B1
Nuenen **79** C1
Nueno **154** B2
Nuestra Señora de Cura **157** C2
Nuestra Señora de la Peña de Fra **159** D2
Nueva **153** C1
Nueva **152** A1
Nueva Carteya **172** B1
Nuévalos **162** A1
Nuevo Baztán **161** C2/3
Nughedu Santa Vittória **123** C/D2
Nuijamaa **27** C2
Nuits **88** B3
Nuits-Saint-Georges **103** D1
Nukari **25** C/D2, **26** A2
Nules **163** B/C3, **169** D1
Nulles **163** C1
Nulvi **123** C1
Numaná **117** D2, **130** A3
Numancia **153** D3, **161** D1
Numansdorp **66** A3
Nümbrecht **80** A2
Nummela **25** C3
Nummenkylä **25** C3
Nummenpää **25** C2/3
Nummi **25** C3
Nummi **24** A/B2
Nummijärvi **20** B3
Nummikoski **20** B3
Numminen **25** D2, **26** A2
Nummi-Pusula **25** C2/3
Nünchritz **83** C1
Nuneaton **64** A2
Nunnanen **11** D2, **12** A1
Nunnanlahti **23** C2
Nunnington **61** C2
Nuño Gómez **160** A/B3
Nuñomoral **159** C/D2/3
Nunsdorf **70** A3
Nunspeet **66** B2
Nuojua **18** B3
Nuoksujärvi **17** C1
Nuoramoinen **25** D1, **26** A1
Nuorgam (Njuorggam) **6** B2
Nuoritta **18** B2
Núoro **123** D2
Nuorpiniemi **6** B2
Nuortikon **16** B1
Nuorunka **19** C1
Nuottionranta **17** D2
Nuraghe Seruci **123** C3
Nuraghe su Nuraxi **123** C/D3
Nurágus **123** D2/3
Nurallao **123** D2
Nuráminis **123** D3
Núria **156** A2
Nurmaa **26** B1
Nurmes **23** C1
Nurmesklyä **23** C1
Nurmesperä **21** D1, **22** A1
Nurmijärvi **23** D1/2
Nurmijärvi **25** C2/3, **26** A2/3
Nurmo **20** B2
Nürnberg **82** A3, **91** D1, **92** A1
Nürnberg-Fischbach **92** A1
Nürnberg-Katzwang **91** D1, **92** A1
Nurri **123** D2/3
Nürtingen **91** C2
Nus **105** D2
Nusco **119** D3, **120** A2
Nusfjord **8** A/B2/3
Nusnäs **39** D2
Nusplingen **91** B/C2
Nussdorf am Inn **92** B3
Nuštar **129** C3, **133** C1
Nüsttal-Morles **81** C2
Nutheim **43** C1
Nuttuperä **21** D1, **22** A1
Nuuatila **18** B3
Nuuksujärvi **11** B/C3

Nuupas **18** B1
Nuutajärvi **25** B/C2
Nuutilanmäki **27** B/C1
Nuvsvåg **5** C2
Nuvvus **6** B2
Nvutånger **40** A/B1
Nya Bastuselet **16** A3
Nyadal **35** D2
Nyåker **31** C2
Nyåkern **34** B3
Nyåkerstjärn **31** C2
Nyalka **95** C3
Nyárlörinc **129** D1
Nybäck **31** D1
Nybble **45** D1, **46** A1
Nybergsund **38** B1
Nyborg **53** C1
Nybro **51** D2
Nybro **72** B1
Nyby **29** D3, **35** B/C2
Nyby **30** B1/2
Nyby **20** A2
Nyby **53** D2
Nybyn **30** B3, **35** D2
Nybyn **17** C2
Nydala **50** B1
Nye **51** C1
Nyergesújfalu **95** D3
Nygård **38** A2
Nygård **9** D1
Nygard **38** A1
Nygården **14** B3
Nyhammar **39** D3
Nyhamnsläge **49** D2, **50** A2
Ny Hellesund **43** C3
Nyhem **30** A3, **35** C2
Ny Hesselager **53** C1/2
Nyhyttan **39** D3, **46** A1
Nyírábrány **97** C/D3, **98** A3, **140** A/B1
Nyírád **128** A1
Nyírbátor **97** C/D3, **98** A3
Nyíregyháza **97** C3
Nykälä **22** B3
Nykarleby (Uusikaarlepyy) **20** B1
Nyker **51** D3
Nykirke **37** D3, **38** A2
Nykirke **43** D2, **44** B1
Nykøbing **53** D2
Nykøbing **48** A2
Nykøbing **49** D3
Nyköping **47** C2
Nykrogen **40** A3
Nykroppa **39** C3, **45** D1, **46** A1
Nyksund **8** B1
Nykvåg **8** B2
Nykvarn **47** C1
Nyland **30** B3, **35** D2
Nyland **31** C3
Nyland **31** C2
Nyland **30** B3, **35** D2
Nyliden **31** C2
Nymburk **83** D2/3
Nymindegab **48** A3, **52** A1
Nymo **4** B2
Nymoen **38** B1
Nymoen **14** B2
Nynäshamn **47** C2
Nyon **104** A2
Nyons **111** C2
Nyord **53** D2
Nyřany **83** C3
Nyrölä **21** D3, **22** A3
Nýrsko **93** C1
Nyrud **7** C3
Nysa (Neisse) **96** B1/2
Nysäter **45** C1
Nysätern **34** A2/3
Nyseter **37** D2
Nyseter **32** B3, **37** C1
Nyseter **33** C2/3
Nyseter **38** B1
Nyskoga **38** B2
Nyskolla **38** A1
Nyslott **27** C1
Nysø **53** D2
Nystad **24** A2, **41** D2
Nysted **53** D2
Nystrand **16** B3
Nysund **45** D1, **46** A1
Nytjärn **30** B2, **35** D1
Nytorp **17** C1
Nyträsk **31** D1
Nyúl **95** C3
Nyvik **30** A3, **35** C2

Nyvik **29** C1
Nyvoll **5** C2

O

Oakengates **59** D3, **64** A1
Oakham **64** B1/2
Oanes **42** A2
Obalj **132** B3
Oban **56** A1
Oban **54** A2, **55** D1
Obanos **154** A2
O Barco **151** C2
Obbola **20** A1, **31** D2
Obdach **127** C1
Obejo **166** B3
Oberammergau **92** A3
Oberasbach **82** A3, **91** D1, **92** A1
Oberau **92** A3
Oberaula **81** C2
Oberaurach-Kirchaich **81** D3
Oberaurach-Unterschleichach **81** D3
Oberbergkirchen **92** B2
Oberbodnitz **82** A2
Ober-Cunnersdorf **83** D1/2
Oberdachstetten **91** D1
Oberderdingen-Flehingen **90** B1
Oberdrauburg **107** D1, **126** A1
Oberelsbach **81** D2
Oberfeistritz **127** C/D1
Obergrafendorf **94** A2
Obergünzburg **91** D3
Oberhaching **92** A3
Oberharmersbach **90** B2
Oberhausen **80** A1
Oberhof **81** D2
Oberhofen am Thunersee **105** C1/2
Oberiberg [Schwyz] **105** D1
Oberkappel **93** C2
Oberkirch **90** B2
Oberkochen **91** D2
Oberkotzau **82** A/B2
Oberlahnstein **80** A/B2
Oberland **81** C2
Oberlungwitz **82** B2
Obermassfeld-Grimmenthal **81** D2
Obermehler **81** D1
Obermodern **90** A1/2
Obernai **90** A2
Obernberg am Brenner **107** C1
Obernberg am Inn **93** C2
Obernburg **81** C3
Oberndorf **90** B2
Oberndorf **52** A/B3, **68** A1
Oberndorf am Lech **91** D2
Oberndorf an der Melk **94** A2/3
Oberndorf bei Salzburg **92** B3
Obernkirchen **68** A3
Obernzenn **81** D3, **91** D1
Oberoderwitz **83** D1/2
Oberort **93** D3
Oberpframmern **92** A3
Oberpöring **92** B2
Ober-Ramstadt **81** B/C3
Oberreute **91** C/D3
Oberriet **106** A1
Oberröblingen **82** A1
Oberrot **91** C1
Oberschweinbach **92** A2
Obersinn **81** C2/3
Oberstaufen **91** C/D3
Oberstdorf **91** D3
Oberstenfeld **91** C1
Obersulm **91** C1
Obersüssbach-Obermünchen **92** A/B2
Obertilliach **107** D1/2, **126** A1/2
Obertrubach **82** A3
Obertrum am See **93** C3
Oberursel **80** B2/3

Obervellach **126** A1
Oberviechtach **82** B3, **92** B1
Oberwart **127** D1
Oberwart **96** A/B3
Oberweiler (Bitburg) **79** D3
Oberweissbach **82** A2
Oberwesel **80** B3
Oberweser-Gieselwerder **81** C1
Oberweser-Oedelsheim **81** C1
Oberwiesenthal **82** B2
Oberwölz **126** B1
Obidos **164** A1
Obilić **138** B1
Obing **92** B3
Obing-Frabertsham **92** B3
Objaljai **74** A2
Objat **101** D3
Obladis **106** B1
Obljaj **127** D3, **131** C1
Obninsk **75** D3
Obod **137** D2
Obodovka **99** C3
O Bolo **151** C2
Obón **162** B2
Oborniki **71** D2
Oborniki **72** B3
Obornjača **129** D3
Oborovo **127** D3
Obory **83** C/D3
Obra **71** C3
Obrenovac **133** D1/2, **134** A2
Obrenovac **140** A2
Obrež **133** D1, **134** A1
Obrigheim **91** C1
Obrov **126** B3
Obrovac **131** C2
Obrovac **131** D3
Obrovac **129** C3, **133** C1
Obršani **138** B3, **143** C1
Obrtići **133** C2/3
Obryta **71** B/C1/2
Obrzycko **71** D2
Obsteig **106** B1
Obudovac **132** B1
Obuhov **99** C/D2
Ocaña **161** C3, **167** D1
Ocana **113** D3
Occhiobello **115** C1
Occimiano **113** C1
Očevlja **132** B2
Ochagavía **108** A3, **154** B2
Ochandiano **153** D1/2
Ochiltree **56** B2
Ochla **71** C3
Ochsenfurt **81** D3
Ochsenfurt-Hopferstadt **81** D3
Ochsenhausen **91** C2/3
Ochtendung **80** A2
Ochtrup **67** C/D3
Očihov **83** C2/3
Ockelbo **40** A2
Ockholm **52** A2
Ocrkavlje **132** B3
Ócsa **95** D3, **129** C1
Öcsény **129** C2
Öcsöd **129** D1
Octeville **76** A3
Octeville-sur-Mer **76** B3
Öd **34** B2
Ödåkra **49** D3, **50** A2
Odda **42** B1
Odden **4** B3
Odder **48** B3
Oddesund **48** A2
Ödeborg **45** C2
Odeceixe **170** A1
Odeleite **170** B2
Odelzhausen **92** A2
Odemira **170** A1
Ödemiş **149** D3
Odén **155** D2/3
Ödena **155** D3, **156** A3, **163** D1
Odensbacken **46** B1
Odensberg **45** D3
Odense **53** C1
Odensjö **50** B1/2
Oderberg **70** B2
Odernheim **80** A/B3
Oderzo **107** D3
Ödeshög **46** A2

Odessa **141** D1
Odestugu **45** D3, **46** A3
Odiáxere **170** A2
Odiham **64** B3, **76** A/B1
Ødis **52** B1
Odivelas **164** A2
Odivelas **164** B3
Odkarby **41** C/D2/3
Ödkarby **41** C/D2/3
Odlandstø **42** A3
Odoev **75** D3
Odón **162** A2
Odoorn **67** C2
Odorheiu Secuiesc **141** C1
Odra **127** D3
Ødsted **48** B3, **52** B1
Odžaci **129** C3
Odžak **133** C3, **137** D1
Odžak **132** B1
Oebisfelde **69** C2
Oechsen **81** D2
Oed **93** D2
Oederan **83** C2
Oeffelt **67** B/C3
Oegstgeest **66** A3
Oeiras **164** A2
Oelde **67** D3
Oelde-Stromberg **67** D3, **68** A3
Oelsig **70** A3, **83** C1
Oelsnitz **82** B2
Oelsnitz **82** B2
Oelze **81** D2, **82** A2
Oelzschau **82** B1
Oensingen **105** C1
Oer-Erkenschwick **67** D3, **80** A1
Oettingen **91** D1
Oetzen-Stöcken **69** C2
Ofärne **40** A1
Ofena **117** D3, **119** C1
Offenbach **90** B1
Offenbach am Main **81** B/C3
Offenbach-Hundheim **80** A3
Offenberg **92** B1/2
Offenburg **90** B2
Offenhausen **82** A3, **92** A1
Offenseealm **93** C3
Offerberg **40** A1
Offerdal **29** C/D3, **34** B1
Offersøy **9** C2
Offida **117** D2/3
Offingen **91** D2
Ofte **43** C1/2
Ofte **42** B3
Ofterschwang **91** D3
Oftringen [Aarburg-Oftringen] **105** C1
Ogardy **71** C2
Ogéviller **89** D2
Oggevatn **43** C3
Oggiono **105** D3, **106** A3
Ogliara **119** D3, **120** A2
Ogliastro Cilento **120** A3
Ogna **42** A3
Ognica **70** B2
Ogoja **139** D1
Ogorele **75** C1
Ogradena **135** C1/2
Ogre **73** D1, **74** A2
Ogrosen **70** B3
O Grove **150** A2
Ogulin **127** C3, **130** B1
Ohanes **173** D2
Ohensaari **24** A/B2
Ohey **79** C2
Ohkola **25** D2, **26** A2
Ohlstadt **92** A3
Öhn **29** D2, **30** A2, **35** C1
Ohrdruf **81** D2
Ohrid **138** B3, **142** B3
Öhringen **91** C1
Ohtaanniemi **23** C2
Ohtanajärvi **17** C1
Ohtinen **25** C2
Ohtola **21** C3
Oia **150** A3
Oiå **158** A2
Oiartzun **153** D1, **154** A1
Oijärvi **18** B1
Oijusluoma **19** D1
Oikarainen **12** B3
Oikemus **21** C1
Oímbra **150** B3
Oinaala **25** C2

Oinas **12** B3
Oinasjärvi **25** C2
Oinasjärvi **22** B1
Oinaskylä **21** D2, **22** A2
O Incio **151** C2
Oiniadai **146** A2
Oinoskylä **21** C/D2
Oion **153** D2
Oiron **101** C1
Oirschot **79** C1
Oiselay-et-Grachaux **89** C3
Oisemont **85** C1/2
Oitti **25** C/D2, **26** A2
Oittila **21** D3
Oix **156** B2
Öja **20** B1
Öja **47** D3
Ojakkala **25** C3
Ojakylä **21** D1, **22** A1
Ojakylä **21** D1, **22** A1
Ojakylä **18** A/B3
Ojakylä **18** A2
Ojakylä **18** A3, **21** C1
Ojakylä **18** B3
Ojala **21** B/C2
Ojanpera **18** B3
Ojanperä **21** D1, **22** A1
Ojarn **29** D2, **35** B/C1
Öje **39** C2
Öjebyn **16** B3
Ojén **172** A3
Ojós **169** D1
Ojos Negros **162** A2
Öjung **39** D1
Ojurås **39** D2
Okehampton **63** C2/3
Okkelberg **28** B3, **33** D1
Okkenhaug **28** B3, **33** D1
Oklaj **131** C2/3
Öknö **51** D1
Okol **137** D2, **138** A2
Okoli **127** D3
Okonek **71** D1
Okruglica **139** C1
Oksajärvi **11** B/C3
Oksakoski **21** C2
Oksava **21** D1, **22** A1
Oksbøl **48** A3, **52** A1
Oksby **48** A3, **52** A1
Økseidet **11** C1
Øksendalsøra **32** B2
Øksendrup **53** C1/2
Øksengard **15** C1
Øksfjord **5** C2
Øksna **38** A2
Øksnes **8** B1
Øksnes **28** B2
Øksneshamn **9** B/C2
Okstad **28** A/B3, **33** C/D2
Oksvoll **28** A3, **33** C1
Okt'abr'skij **99** C1
Okučani **128** A3, **131** D1, **132** A1
Okulovka **75** C1
Olalhas **164** B1
Olalla **163** C2
Olargues **110** A3
Olazagutía **153** D2
Olba **162** B3
Olbernhau **83** C2
Olbersdorf **83** D2
Olbersleben **82** A1
Ólbia **123** D1
Olby **102** B3
Olching **92** A2
Oldeboorn **66** B2
Oldebroek **66** B2
Oldeide **36** A1
Oldemarkt **67** B/C2
Olden **36** B1
Oldenburg **67** D1, **68** A1/2
Oldenburg **53** C3
Oldenswort **52** A2/3
Oldenzaal **67** C/D3
Olderbakken **4** B3, **10** A1
Olderdalen **4** B3
Olderfjord **5** D1/2, **6** A1
Oldernes **5** D2, **6** A1
Oldervik **4** A3, **9** D1, **10** A1
Oldervik **14** B2
Oldervik **4** A2/3
Oldham **59** D2, **60** B2/3
Oldisleben **82** A1
Oldsum **52** A2
Oleby **39** B/C3
Oledo **158** B3
Oléggio **105** D3

Oleiros **158** B3, **164** B1
Oleiros **150** A2
Oleiros **150** B1
Ølen **42** A1
Olesa de Montserrat **156** A3
Oleśnica (Oels) **96** B1
Oletta **113** D2
Olette **156** A2
Olevsk **99** B/C2
Olfen **67** D3, **80** A1
Ølgod **48** A3, **52** A1
Olhain **78** A2
Olhalvo **164** A2
Olhão **170** B2
Olhava **18** A2
Oliana **155** C3
Olías **172** B2
Olías del Rey **160** B3, **167** C1
Olib **130** B2
Oliena **123** D2
Oliete **162** B2
Olígirtos **143** D3
Olimbiás **143** C2
Olimpiás **144** B2
Olimpiás **143** C2
Olingen **79** D2
Olingskog **39** C1
Oliola **155** C3
Olite **154** A2
Olius **155** D3, **156** A2
Oliva **169** D2
Oliva de la Frontera **165** C3
Oliva de Mérida **165** D2, **166** A2
Oliva de Plasencia **159** D3
Olivadi **122** B2
Olival **158** A3, **164** B1
Olivarella **125** D1/2
Olivares **171** D1
Olivares de Duero **152** B3, **160** B1
Olivares de Júcar **161** D3, **168** B1
Oliveira de Frades **158** A/B2
Oliveira de Azeméis **158** A2
Oliveira do Bairro **158** A2
Oliveira do Hospital **158** B3
Olivella **156** A3
Olivenza **165** C2
Olivèse **113** D3
Olivet **87** C2/3
Olivone [Biasca] **105** D2
Olkamangi **17** D1
Olkkajärvi **12** B3
Olkusz **97** C2
Olla de Altea **169** D1
Ollebacken **29** D3, **34** B1
Ollería **169** C/D2
Ollerton **61** C3, **64** B1
Olli **21** C2
Olliergues **103** C3
Ollikkala **26** B1
Ollila **25** B/C2
Ollila **13** C3
Ollilanniemi **19** C/D3
Öllölä **23** D3
Ollsta **29** D3, **35** B/C1
Ollsta **29** D3, **35** B/C1/2
Ölme **45** D1, **46** A1
Olmeda de la Cuesta **161** D3
Olmeda del Rey **161** D3, **168** B1
Olmedilla de Alarcón **168** B1
Olmedilla de Eliz **161** D3
Olmedillo de Roa **152** B3, **160** B1
Olmedo **160** A/B1
Olmedo **123** C1/2
Olmi Cappella **113** D2
Olmillos de Sasamón **152** B2
Olmillos de Castro **151** D3, **159** D1
Olmo **115** C3, **116** B2
Olmo al Brembo **106** A2
Olmos de la Picaza **152** B2
Olney **64** B2
Olocau **162** B3, **169** D1
Olocáu del Rey **162** B2
Olofsbo **49** D2, **50** A1
Olofsfors **31** C2/3
Olofström **51** B/C2
Olofström **72** A1

Olombrada 160 B1
Olomouc 96 B2
Olonne-sur-Mer 100 A2
Olonzac 110 A3, 156 B1
Oloron-Sainte-Marie
108 B3, 154 B1
Olost 156 A2
Olot 156 B2
Olovo 132 B2
Olpe 80 B1/2
Olšany u Prostějova 94 B1
Olsäter 39 C3, 45 D1
Olsberg 80 B1
Olsberg-Bigge 80 B1
Olsborg 4 A3, 9 D1
Olsbrücken 80 A/B3,
90 A1
Olsene 78 A/B1/2
Olseröd 50 B3
Ölserud 45 C/D2
Olshammar 46 A2
Olši 94 B1
Olsker 51 D3
Olsrud 4 A3, 10 A1
Olst 67 C2/3
Olsvik 14 A3, 28 B1
Olsztyn (Allenstein)
73 C2/3
Oltedal 42 A2
Olten 90 B3, 105 C1
Oltenița 141 C2
Oltre Vara 114 A2
Oltyně 93 D1
Olula de Castro 173 D2
Olvasjärvi 18 B2
Ølve 42 A1
Olvega 153 D3, 154 A3,
161 D1
Olveiroa 150 A2
Olvenstedt 69 C3
Olvera 172 A2
Olvés 162 A1
Olympia 146 B3
Olynthos 144 A2
Olzai 123 D2
Omagh 54 A3, 55 D2
Ombersley 59 D3, 64 A2
Omeath 58 A1
Omegna 105 C2/3
Omellóns 155 D3, 163 D1
Omenamäki 23 C1
Omiš 131 D3
Omišalj 126 B3, 130 B1
Ommen 67 C2
Omoljica 133 D1, 134 B1
Omonville-la-Rogue 76 A3
Ōmossa/Metsälä 20 A3
Omsjö 30 B2/3, 35 D1
Omurtag 141 C3
Ön 34 B3
Øn 36 A2
Oña 153 C2
Onano 116 B3, 118 A1
Onara 107 C3
Oñati 153 D1/2
Onchan 58 B1
Onda 162 B3, 169 D1
Ondara 169 D2
Ondarroa 153 D1
Ondřejov 83 D3
Ondres 108 A3, 154 A1
Onéglia 113 C2
Onesse-et-Laharie 108 A2
Ongstad 8 B2
Önhult 46 B3
Onil 169 C2
Onís 152 A1
Onkamaa 26 B2
Onkamo 23 D3
Onkamo 13 C3
Onkeroinen 25 D2, 26 A2
Onkijoki 24 B2
Onkiniemi 25 D1, 26 A/B1
Onnaing 78 B2
Önnesmark 31 D1
Önnestad 50 B2/3
Önningeby 41 C/D3
Onno 105 D2/3, 106 A2
Onøy 14 A2
Onsaker 37 D3, 38 A2/3
Onsevig 53 C2
Önskan 30 B3, 35 D1
Onslunda 50 B3
Onšovice 94 A1
Onstwedde 67 C2
Ontaneda 152 B1
Onteniente 169 C/D2

Ontiñena 155 C3, 163 C1
Ontojoki 19 C/D3, 23 C1
Onttola 23 C/D3
Ontur 169 B/C2
Önusberg 16 B3
Onzonilla 151 D2, 152 A2
Oombergen 78 B2
Ooperi 20 B2
Oostburg 78 B1
Oost-Cappel 78 A1/2
Oostduinkerke-Bad 78 A1
Oostende 78 A1
Oosterbeek 66 B3
Oosterend 66 B1
Oosterhesselen 67 C2
Oosterhout 66 A/B3, 79 C1
Oosterwolde 67 C2
Oosthuizen 66 B2
Oostkamp 78 A1
Oostmalle 79 C1
Oostvleteren 78 A1/2
Oostvoorne 66 A3
Oostwold 67 C1
Ootmarsum 67 C2
Opalenica 71 D3
Opaljenik 133 D3, 134 A3
Opatija 126 B3, 130 A1
Opatovac 129 C3, 133 C1
Opatovská Vez 95 D2
Opava 96 B2
Ope 29 D3, 34 B2
Openica 138 B3, 142 B1
Opi 119 C2
O Pino 150 B2
Oplenac 133 D2, 134 B2
Opočka 74 B2
Opočno 96 B1
Opoul-Périlos 156 B1
Opovo 133 D1, 134 A1
Oppach 83 D1
Oppbodarna 34 B3
Oppdal 33 C2/3
Oppeano 107 C3
Oppeby 46 B3
Oppeby (Nyköping) 47 C2
Oppegård 38 A2
Oppegård 38 A3, 44 B1
Oppeid 9 C2/3
Oppenau 90 B2
Oppenheim 80 B3
Opphaug 28 A3, 33 C1
Oppheim 36 B3
Opphus 38 A1
Óppido Lucano 120 B2
Óppido Mamertina 122 A3
Oppin 82 B1
Opponitz 93 D3
Oppsjö 30 B3, 35 D2
Oppstryn 32 A3, 36 B1
Oppurg 82 A2
Oprișor 135 D2
Oprtalj 126 B3, 130 A1
Opshaugvik 32 A3, 36 B1
Ópusztaszer 129 D2
Opuzen 136 B1
Ör 51 C1
ØR 44 B1/2
Öra 45 D3
Øra 4 B2
Ora/Auer 107 C2
Orada 165 C2
Orada 165 C3
Oradour-sur-Glane 101 D2
Oradour-sur-Vayres
101 D3
Orago 105 D3
Orahova 131 D1, 132 A1
Orahovac 138 A/B2
Orahovac 140 A3
Orahovica 128 B3
Oraison 110 D2, 112 A2
Orajärvi 12 A3, 17 D1
Orajärvi 12 B2
Orakylä 12 B2
Orange 111 C2
Orani 123 D2
Oranienbaum 69 D3
Oranienburg 70 A2
Oranienburg 72 A3
Orašac 139 C1
Orašac 137 B/C1
Orašac 133 D2, 134 A/B2
Orasi 137 D2
Orasi 113 D3
Orašje 133 B/C1
Oraštie 140 B1
Oratoire 112 A1

Orava 20 B2
Oravais/Oravainen 20 B2
Oravala 26 B2
Oravankylä 21 D1, 22 A1
Oravasaan 21 D3, 22 A3
Oravi 23 C3
Oravikoski 22 B3
Oravisalo 23 C3
Oravita 135 C1
Oravita 140 A2
Oravivaara 19 C3
Oravská Lesná 95 D1
Oravská Polhora 95 D1
Oravská Polhora 97 C2
Oravské Veselé 95 D1
Oravský Podzámok 95 D1
Orba 169 D2
Orbaiceta 108 B3,
155 C1/2
Ørbæk 53 C1
Orbaneja del Castillo
153 B/C2
Orbassano 112 B1
Orbe 104 B1/2
Orbec 86 B1
Örberga 46 A2
Orbetello 116 B3
Örby 49 D1, 50 A1
Orca 158 B3
Orcajo 162 A2
Orcau 155 D2/3
Orce 173 D1
Orcera 168 A3
Orchamps 103 D1, 104 A1
Orchamps-Vennes 104 B1
Orches 101 C1
Orcheta 169 D2
Orchies 78 A2
Orchomenós 147 C2
Orchomenos 147 B/C3
Orchomenos 147 C2
Orcières 112 A1
Orcines 102 B2/3
Orcival 102 B3
Ordes 150 A/B1/2
Ordino 155 D2, 156 A2
Ordizia 153 D1/2
Ordona 120 A1/2
Öre 42 B3
Öre 31 C2/3
Öre 39 D1/2
Orea 162 A2
Orebić 136 B1
Örebro 46 A1
Orebygård 53 C/D2
Oredež 74 B1
Öregcsertő 129 C2
Öreglak 128 A/B2
Öregrund 40 B2/3
Orehoved 53 D2
Oreí 147 C1
Orellana de la Sierra
166 A/B2
Orellana la Vieja 166 A/B2
Ören 149 D2/3
Oreovica 134 B2
Öreryd 50 B1
Orés 154 B2
Oreškovica 134 B2
Orestiás 145 D3
Öretjärndalen 30 A3, 35 C2
Orford 65 D2
Organya 155 C2
Orgaz 160 B3, 167 C1
Orgeev 141 D1
Orgelet-le Bourget 103 D2,
104 A2
Ørgenvika 37 D3
Orgères-en-Beauce 87 C2
Orgiano 107 C3
Orgon 111 C/D2
Orgósolo 123 D2
Orgovány 129 C1/2
Orhaneli 149 D3
Ória 121 D2/3
Oria 173 D1, 174 A1
Orient 157 C2
Orihuela 169 C3, 174 B1
Orihuela del Tremedal
162 A2
Orikon 142 A2
Oriku 142 A2
Orimattila 25 D2, 26 A2
Oriniemi 24 B2
Oriniemi 23 C/D3

Orinnoro 22 B3
Orio 153 D1
Oriola 164 B3
Oriolo 120 B3, 122 B1
Oripää 24 B2
Oristano 123 C2
Őriszentpéter 127 D1
Oriveden asema 25 C1
Orivesi 25 C1
Orjães 158 B3
Orjahovo 140 B2
Orjasjärvi 17 D2
Örjavik 32 A2
Ørje 45 B/C1
Orjiva 173 C2
Orkanger 28 A3, 33 C2
Örkelljunga 50 B2
Örkelljunga 72 A1
Orkelsjøhytta 33 C3
Örkény 129 C1
Örkény 97 C3, 140 A1
Orkland 28 A3, 33 C2
Orlamünde 82 A2
Ørland 28 A3, 33 C1
Orlate 138 B2
Orléans 87 C2/3
Orlec 130 A1
Orlík nad Vltavou 83 C/D3,
93 C/D1
Orljane 135 C3, 139 C1
Orljani 138 B1
Orlovat 129 D3, 133 D1,
134 A/B1
Orlu 156 A1
Örma 143 C1
Ormaiztegi 153 D1/2
Ormaryd 46 A3
Ormea 113 C2
Ormemyr 43 C/D1, 44 A1
Orménion 145 D2
Ormes 87 C2/3
Ormhult 50 B2
Ormília 144 A2
Órmos 143 D2, 144 A2
Órmos Panagiás 144 B2
Órmos Prínou 145 B/C1/2
Ormož 127 C2
Ormskirk 59 D2, 60 B2/3
Ornaisons 110 A3, 156 B1
Ornans 104 A1
Ornäs 39 D2
Ørnes 14 B1
Orneta 73 C2
Ørnhøj 48 A2/3
Ornö 47 D1
Örnsköldsvik 31 C3
Ornès 100 B3, 155 C1
Orolik 129 C3, 133 C1
Orom 129 D2/3
Orón 153 C2
Oron-la-Ville [Oron]
104 B2
Oropesa 160 A3, 166 B1
Oropesa de Mar 163 C3
Ororbia 154 A2
Orosei 123 D2
Orosháza 129 D2
Orosháza 97 C3, 140 A1
Oroso 150 A/B2
Oroszlány 95 C/D3
Oroszló 128 B2
Orotelli 123 D2
Oroz-Betelu 108 B3,
155 C2
Orozko 153 C1
Orphin 87 C2
Orpierre 111 C2
Orrefors 51 C1/2
Orrefors 72 B1
Orrestad 42 A3
Orrios 162 B2
Orroli 123 D2/3
Orrskog 40 B2
Orrviken 34 B2
Orsa 39 D1/2
Orša 74 B3
Orsago 107 D2/3
Orsara di Púglia 120 A1/2
Orsay 87 C/D1/2
Örsbäck 31 C2
Örsebo 46 B3
Orsennes 101 D2, 102 A2
Örserum 46 A3
Orsia 105 C3
Orsières 104 B2
Örsjö 51 C2
Ørslev 49 C3, 53 C1

Ørslevkloster 48 B2
Ørsnes 32 A2/3
Orsogna 119 C/D1
Orsoja 135 D3
Orsomarso 120 B3, 122 A1
Orșova 135 C1/2
Orșova 140 A/B2
Örspuszta 128 B1
Ørsta 36 B1
Ørsted 52 B1
Ørsted 49 B/C2
Ørsundsbro 40 B3
Orta 105 C3
Ortaklar 149 D2
Orta Nova 120 A/B1/2
Orte 117 C3, 118 B1
Ortenberg-Selters 81 C2
Ortenburg-Iglbach 92 A1
Ortenburg-Wolfachau
93 C2
Orth an der Donau 94 B2
Orth an der Donau 96 B3
Orthez 108 A/B3, 154 B1
Orthovoúnion 143 C3
Ortigosa 153 D3
Ortigueira 150 B1
Ortilla 154 B2/3
Ortisei/Sankt Ulrich 107 C2
Ortișoara 140 A1
Ortnevik 36 B2
Orto 113 D3
Ortolano 117 D3, 119 C1
Örtomta 46 B2
Orton 57 C3, 60 B1
Ortona 119 D1
Ortona dei Marsi 119 C2
Ortrand 83 C1
Örträsk 31 C2
Ortsjö 35 D3
Ortueri 123 C/D2
Orubica 131 D1, 132 A1
Ørum 49 C2
Ørum 48 B2
Orune 123 D2
Orusco 161 C3
Orvella 43 C1, 44 A1
Orvieto 117 C3, 118 A1
Orville 89 B/C3
Orvínio 118 B1
Orzinuovi 106 A3
Osa 36 B3
Osa de la Vega 161 C/D3,
168 A1
Osanica 135 C2
Osann-Monzel 80 A3
Os Anxeles 150 A2
Osara 24 B1
O Saviñao 150 B2
Osbruk 50 B1
Osburg 79 D3, 80 A3
Osby 50 B2
Osby 72 A1
Oščadnica 95 D1
Oschatz 83 B/C1
Oschatz 96 A1
Oschersleben 69 C3
Óschiri 123 D1
Osdalssetter 38 A/B1
Os de Balaguer 155 C3
Ose 42 B2
Øse 48 A3, 52 A1
Osečina 133 C2
Osečná 83 D2
Oseja 154 A3, 162 A1
Oseja de Sajambre 152 A1
Osek 83 C2
Osenovo 139 D2
Osera 154 B3, 162 B1
Oset 38 A1
Oset 37 C/D3
Osidda 123 D2
Osieczna 71 D3
Osiek nad Notecią 71 D2
Osíglia 113 C2
Osijek 129 B/C3
Osilnica 127 C3
Ósilo 123 C1
Ósimo 117 D3
Osinów Dolny 70 B2
Osipaonica 134 B2
Osipoviči 99 C3
Osječenica 137 C1
Oskar 51 C/D2
Oskarshamn 51 D1
Oskarshamn 72 B1
Oskarström 72 A1
Oskarström 50 A1/2

Oslany 95 D2
Oslättfors 40 A2
Oslavany 94 B1
Oslavička 94 A1
Osli 94 B3
Oslo 38 A3
Osløs 48 A/B1/2
Osma 12 A/B2/3
Osma 153 C2
Osmakova 135 C3
Os Milagres do Medo
  150 B3
Os'mino 74 B1
Ošmjany 74 A3
Ösmo 47 C1/2
Osnabrück 67 D3
Osnäs 24 A2, 41 D2
Ošno Lubuskie 70 B2
Osoppo 107 D2, 126 A2
Osor 130 A1/2
Osor 156 B2
Osorno 152 B2
Ospedaletti 113 B/C2/3
Ospitale di Cadore 107 D2
Ospitaletto 106 B3
Oss 66 B3
Ossa 144 A1
Ossa de Montiel 168 A2
Ossauskoski 18 A1
Össeby-Garn 40 B3, 47 D1
Ossès 108 B3, 155 C1
Ossi 123 C1/2
Ossiach 126 B2
Ossmannstedt 82 A1/2
Osso 155 C3, 163 C1
Ossun 108 B3, 155 C1
Östanå 50 B2
Östanbäck 31 D1
Östanberg 24 B3
Östanbjörke 39 C3
Östansjö 15 D2
Östansjö 39 C1
Östansjö 16 A2
Östansjö 46 A1
Östansjö 40 A/B1
Östanvik 39 D1
Oštarije 127 C3, 130 B1
Ostaškov 75 C2
Ostatija 133 D3, 134 A3
Östavall 35 C3
Ostbevern 67 D3
Østbirk 48 B3
Östbjörka 39 D2
Östby 30 B2, 35 D1
Østby 38 B1
Östbyn 35 C3
Östbyn 35 C2
Östbyn 31 D2
Osted 49 D3, 53 D1
Osteel 67 D1
Ostellato 115 C1
Ostelsheim 90 B2
Ostenfeld 52 B2
Ostenholz 68 B2
Østerbø 37 B/C3
Osterburg 69 D2
Osterburken 91 C1
Østerby 53 C2
Østerby 48 A3
Østerby 49 C1
Østerbybruk 40 B3
Österbymo 46 A3
Österbymo 72 B1
Ostercappeln 67 D2/3,
  68 A2/3
Østerdalsisen 14 B2
Österfärnebo 40 A2/3
Österforse 30 A/B3, 35 D2
Östergraninge 30 B3,
  35 D2
Österhaninge 47 D1
Österhankmo 20 B2
Osterheide-Osternholz
  68 B2
Osterhofen 93 B/C2
Osterhofen-Obergessen-
  bach 92 B2
Osterholz-Scharmbeck
  68 A1
Øster Hurup 49 B/C2
Østerhus 42 A/B2
Østerild 48 A1/2
Øster Karup 50 A2
Østerlars 51 D3
Øster Løgum 52 B2
Österlövsta 40 B2

Östermarie 51 D3
Östermark 20 A3
Ostermiething 92 B3
Östernoret 30 B2
Österö 20 B2
Osterode 68 B3
Osterode-Dorste 68 B3,
  81 D1
Oster-Ohrstedt 52 B2
Øster Ritjemjåkk 9 D3
Östersele 31 C2
Øster Själevad 31 B/C3
Österslöv 50 B3
Öster Sönnarslöv 50 B3
Österströ 35 C/D2/3
Österström 35 C/D2/3
Österstrand 30 B2
Östersund 29 D3, 34 B2
Östersundom 25 D3, 26 A3
Österunda 40 A/B3
Östervåla 40 B3
Östervallskog 38 B3, 45 C1
Øster Vrå 48 B1
Österwieck 69 C3
Osterzell 91 B3
Ostffyasszonyfa 94 B3,
  128 A1
Ostfildern 91 C2
Östhammar 40 B2/3
Ostheim 81 D2
Osthofen 80 B3
Ostia 118 A/B2
Ostiano 106 B3
Ostíglia 114 B1
Ostiz 108 A3, 154 A2
Östloning 35 D2/3
Östmark 38 B2/3
Östmarkum 30 B3
Ostnäs 20 A1, 31 D2
Ostomsjön 39 C1
Ost'or 99 C/D2
Ostoróg 71 D2
Ostra 115 D3, 117 D2
Östra Ämtervik 39 C3,
  45 C/D1
Östraby 50 B3
Ostrach 91 C3
Ostrach-Habsthal 91 C2/3
Östra Ed 47 B/C3
Östra Eknö 47 B/C3
Östra Frölunda 50 A1
Östra Galåbodarna 34 B2
Östra Grevie 50 A3
Östra Hjoggböle 31 D1
Östra Husby 46 B2
Östra Karup 50 A2
Östra Ljungby 50 A2
Östra Malmagen 33 D2/3,
  34 A2/3
Östra Näsberget 39 C2
Östrand 16 B2/3
Östra Ny 46 B2
Östra Ryd 46 B2
Östra Sjulsmark 31 D2
Östra Stugusjö 35 C2/3
Östra Torsås 51 C1/2
Ostrau 83 C1
Ostrau 82 B1
Ostrava 96 B2
Oštrelj 131 C2
Ostriconi 113 D2
Östringen 90 B1
Ostritz 83 D1/2
Ostróda (Osterode) 73 C3
Ostrog 98 B2
Ostrołęka 73 C3, 98 A1
Ostromsjön 39 C1
Ostropole 71 D1
Ostrošickij Gorodok 74 B3
Ostrov 74 B2
Ostrov 141 C2
Ostrov 82 B2
Ostrovačice 94 B1
Ostrov nad Oslavou 94 A1
Ostrov u Macochy 94 B1
Ostrowice 71 C1
Ostrowiec 70 B2
Ostrowiec Świętokrzyski
  97 C1
Ostrów Mazowiecka 73 C3,
  98 A1
Ostrów Wielkopolski 96 B1
Ostrožac 131 C1
Ostružnica 133 D1,
  134 A1/2
Ostryna 73 D2/3, 74 A3,
  98 B1

Ostseebad Ahrenshoop
  53 D2/3
Ostseebad Boltenhagen
  53 C3
Ostseebad Dierhagen
  53 D3
Ostseebad Graal-Müritz
  53 D3
Ostseebad Kühlungsborn
  53 D3
Ostseebad Nienhagen
  53 D3
Ostseebad Prerow 53 D2/3
Ostseebad Prerow 72 A2
Ostseebad Rerik 53 D3
Ostseebad Wustrow 53 D3
Ostseebad Zingst 53 D2/3
Ostuni 121 C/D2
Ostvik 31 D1
Østvika 29 C1
Osuna 172 A2
Oswestry 59 C3, 60 B3
Oszkó 128 A1
Osztopán 128 B2
Ota 164 A2
Otalampi 25 C3
Otamo 24 A1
Otanmäki 18 B3, 22 B1
Otava 26 B1
Otavice 131 C3
Oteiza 153 D2, 154 A2
Oteo 153 C1
Oteren 4 A3, 10 A1
Oterma 18 B3
Otero de Bodas 151 D3
Otero de las Dueñas
  151 D2
Oterstranda 14 B1
Otervik 14 A3, 28 B1
Oteševo 142 B1
Othery 63 D2
Otiñar 173 C1
Otívar 173 C2
Otley 61 C2
Otlo 28 A/B3, 33 C/D1
Otnes 38 A1
Otočac 130 B1
Otočec 127 C3
Otofta 50 A/B3
Otok 133 C1
Otoka 181 C1
Otorowo 71 D2
Otrokovice 95 C1
Otrokovice 96 B2
Otta 37 D1/2
Ottana 123 D2
Ottaviano 119 D3
Ottenby 72 B1
Ottendorf-Okrilla 83 C1
Ottenhöfen 90 B2
Ottenschlag 94 A2
Ottensheim im Mühlkreis
  93 D2
Ottenstein 68 B3
Otterbach 80 B3, 90 A/B1
Otterbäcken 45 D2,
  46 A1/2
Otterberg 80 B3, 90 A/B1
Otterburn 57 D2
Otterburn 54 B3
Otter Ferry 56 A1/2
Otterfing 92 A3
Otterlo 66 B3
Otterndorf 52 A3, 68 A1
Ottersberg 68 A2
Ottersøy 28 B1
Ottersweier 90 B2
Otterup 49 C3, 53 C1
Ottervattnet 31 C2
Ottervik 28 B2
Ottery Saint Mary 63 C2
Ottevény 95 C3
Ottmarsheim 90 A3
Ottnang 93 C2/3
Ottobeuren 91 D3
Ottobiano 105 D3, 113 D1
Ottobrunn 92 A2/3
Ottone 113 D1
Ottonträsk 31 C2
Ottrau 81 C2
Ottsjö 29 C3, 34 A1
Ottsjön 29 D3, 34 B1
Ottweiler 89 D1, 90 A1
Otvöskónyi 128 A2
Otxandio 153 D1/2
Otyń 71 C3
Otzberg-Lengfeld 81 C3

Ötztal-Bahnhof 106 B1
Ouanne 88 A3
Ouarville 87 C2
Oucques 86 A/B3
Ouddorp 66 A3
Oudega 67 B/C1/2
Oudenaarde 78 B2
Oude-Pekela 67 C1/2
Oudeschild 66 B2
Oudeschoot 67 B/C2
Oudewater 66 B3
Oudon 86 B2
Ougney 89 C3, 103 D1,
  104 A1
Oguela 165 C2
Ouistreham 76 B3, 86 A1
Oulainen 18 A3
Oulanka 13 C3
Oulchy-le-Château 88 A1
Oulins 87 C1
Oullins 103 D3
Oulujoki 18 A/B2
Oulunsalo 18 A2
Oulu (Uleåborg) 18 A/B2
Oulx 112 B1
Oundle 64 B3
Oura 150 B3, 158 B1
Ouranópolis 144 B2
Ourense 150 B2
Ourique 170 A1
Ourol 150 B1
Ourondo 158 B3
Ouroux-en-Morvan 88 A3,
  103 C1
Ouroux-sur-Saône 103 D1
Ourville-en-Caux 77 C3
Ousse 108 B3, 154 B1
Ousson-sur-Loire 87 D3
Outakoski 6 B2
Outarville 87 C2
Outeiro 151 C3, 159 C1
Outeiro 151 B/C1
Outeiro 150 A3, 158 A1
Outeiro de Rei 150 B1
Outes 150 A2
Outokumpu 23 C2/3
Outovaara 12 B3
Ouville-la-Rivière 77 C2/3
Ouzouer-le-Marché
  87 C2/3
Ouzouer-sur-Loire 87 D3
Ovada 113 C1
Ovågen 36 A3
Ovanåker 39 D1, 40 A1
Ovanmyra 39 D2
Ovar 158 A2
Ovča 133 D1, 134 A/B1
Ovčar Banja 133 D2,
  134 A2/3
Ovče Polje 139 C2/3
Övedskloster 50 B3
Ovelgönne 68 A1
Ovelgönne-Oldenbrock
  68 A1
Överålive 35 C3
Överammer 30 A3, 35 C2
Överäng 29 C3, 34 A1
Överås 32 B2
Overath 80 A2
Overby 49 C3
Øverbygd 10 A1
Överenhörna 47 C1
Over Feldborg 48 A2
Övergård 48 B2
Övergård 4 A3, 10 A1
Överhogdal 34 B3
Overijse 79 B/C2
Over Jerstal 52 B1/2
Överkalix 17 C2
Överlännäs 30 B3, 35 C2
Överlida 49 D1, 50 A1
Overloon 79 D1
Övermalax 20 A2
Övermark (Ylimarkku)
  20 A3
Overmere 78 B1
Överö 41 D2
Over Simmelkær 48 A/B2
Överste Nyland 31 C2
Overton 59 C/D2/3, 60 B3
Övertorneå 17 D2
Övertorneå 17 D2
Överturingen 34 B3
Överum 46 B3
Ovesholm 50 B3
Ovidiopol' 141 D1
Ovidiu 141 D2

Oviedo 151 D1
Ovíglio 113 C1
Oviken 34 B2
Ovíndoli 119 C1
Ovitsby 25 C3
Ovodda 123 D2
Övra 30 A2, 35 C/D1
Övre Åbyn 31 D1
Øvre Årdal 37 C2
Øvre Åstbru 38 A1
Øvre Björknäs 15 C3
Øvrebø 43 B/C3
Øvrebø 43 B/C3
Övre Brännträsk 16 B2
Øvrebygd 42 A2/3
Øvre Espedal 42 A2
Övre Granberg 16 B3
Övre Grundsel 16 B3
Øvre Kildal 4 B3
Övre Långträsk 16 A3
Øvre Moen 42 B2
Øvrenes 5 D2, 6 A2
Øvre Nyland 31 C2
Övre Parakka 10 B3
Øvre Rendal 33 D3
Øvre Sirdal 42 B2
Övre Soppero 10 B2/3
Övre Svartlå 16 B2
Övre Tväråselet 16 B3
Ovronnaz [Riddes] 104 B2
Ovruč 99 C2
Øvstebo 42 A1
Øvstestøl 32 A3, 37 B/C1
Ovtočiči 137 C/D2
Ovtrup 48 A3, 52 A1
Owen 91 C2
Owingen (Überlingen)
  91 C3
Owinska 71 D2
Owschlag 52 B2/3
Öxabäck 49 D1, 50 A1
Oxberg 39 C1/2
Oxelösund 47 C2
Oxford 65 C3
Oxie 50 A3
Oxílithos 147 D1/2
Oxkangar 20 B2
Oxnered 45 C2
Oxsjön 45 C3
Øy 43 C2
Oyace 104 B3
Øyan 33 C/D3
Øyangen 28 A3, 33 C1
Oyarzún 153 D1, 154 A1
Øye 32 B2
Øye 32 A3, 36 B1
Øyenkilen 44 B1
Øyer 37 D2, 38 A1
Øyestranda 42 B3
Øyfjell 43 C1
Øyhelle 8 B2
Øyjord 8 B3
Oy-Mittelberg 91 D3
Øynan 37 C2/3
Øynes 9 C2
Øynes 15 C1
Oyonnax 104 A2
Øyra 5 C2
Oyrières 89 C3
Øysang 43 D2, 44 A2
Øyslebø 42 B3
Øystad Moskusgård 9 D2
Øystese 36 B3
Oyten 68 A2
Oyten-Bassen 68 A2
Oyten-Schanzendorf 68 A2
Oyteti Stalin (Kuçovë)
  142 A1
Øyungen 38 A1
Øyvatnet 9 C2
Oza dos Ríos 150 B1
Ozalj 127 C3
Ozariči 99 C1
Özd 97 C2/3
Ozeta 153 D2
Ozieri 123 C/D2
Ozora 128 B1/2
Ozzano Monferrato 113 C1

Pääaho 19 C2
Pääjärvi 21 C2

Paaki 19 C3
Paakkila 23 C2
Paakkola 17 D2, 18 A1
Paalasmaa 23 C2
Påarp 49 D3, 50 A2/3
Pääsinniemi 25 D1, 26 A1
Paaso 25 D1, 26 B1
Paatela 27 C1
Paattinen 24 B2
Paatus 6 B2
Paavola 18 A3
Paavonvaara 23 D3
Pabianice 97 C1
Pabillónis 123 C3
Pabneukirchen 93 D2
Påbo 45 D3
Pabradè 74 A3
Paceco 124 A2
Pacentro 119 C1/2
Pachino 125 D3
Pačir 129 C3
Pack 127 C1
Paço de Sousa 158 A1/2
Paços de Ferreira 158 A1
Pacov 83 D3, 93 D1
Pacsa 128 A1/2
Pacy-sur-Eure 86 B1
Padankoski 25 C1, 26 A1
Padasjoki 25 D1, 26 A1
Padborg 52 B2
Padej 129 D3
Padene 131 C2
Padenghe sul Garda 106 B2
Paderborn 68 A3, 81 B/C1
Paderborn-Sande 68 A3
Paderborn-Schloss Neuhaus 68 A3, 80 B1
Paderborn-Wewer 68 A3, 80 B1
Padern 156 B1
Paderne 170 A2
Paderne 150 B1
Paderne de Allariz 150 B2/3
Padiham 59 D1, 60 B2
Padina 133 D1, 134 B1
Padina 141 C2
Padinska Skela 133 D1, 134 A1
Padirac 109 D1
Pádola 107 D2
Pádova 107 C3
Padragküt 128 A/B1
Padrela 158 B3, 158 B1
Padrenda 150 B3
Pádria 123 C2
Padron 150 A2
Padru 123 D1
Padstow 62 B3
Padul 173 C2
Padula 120 A/B3
Paduli 119 D3, 120 A2
Padva 24 B3
Paesana 112 B1
Paese 107 D3
Paestum 120 A3
Pag 130 B2
Pagánica 117 D3, 119 C1
Pagánico 114 B3, 116 B2/3
Pagny-sur-Meuse 89 C1/2
Pagode-de-Chanteloup 86 B3
Pagoúria 145 C1
Pago Veiano 119 D2/3, 120 A2
Paguera 157 C2
Paharova 17 C1
Páhi 129 C2
Pahkakoski 18 B2
Pahkakumpu 13 C3
Pahkala 21 C1
Pahkasalo 18 A3
Pähl 92 A3
Pahtaoja 18 A1
Pahuvaara 19 D2
Paialvo 164 B1
Paião 158 A3
Paide 74 A1
Paijärvi 26 B2
Pailhès 109 D3, 155 D1
Paillart 78 D2
Paimbœuf 85 C3, 100 A1
Paimio (Pemar) 24 B2/3
Paimpol 84 B1
Paimpont 85 C2
Painsalo 22 B1

Painswick 63 D1, 64 A2/3
Painten 92 A1
Paio Pires 164 A2
Paipórta 169 D1
Paisco 106 B2
Paisley 56 B2
Paistivuoma 12 A2, 17 D1
Paisua 22 B1
Paittasjärvi 11 C2
Päiväjoki 12 B3
Päiväkunta 21 D3, 22 A3
Päiviälä 23 C3
Pajala 17 C1
Pajares 153 D3
Pajares 161 C2
Pajares de los Oteros 152 A2
Pajarón 162 A3, 168 B1
Pajaroncillo 162 A3, 168 B1
Pajujärvi 22 B2
Pajukoski 23 C1
Pajulankylä 26 B1
Pajuniemi 18 A2
Pajuskylä 22 B2
Páka 127 D2, 128 A2
Pakaa 25 D2, 26 A2
Pakarila 22 A/B3
Pakinainen 24 A3
Pakisvaara 12 A3, 17 D2
Pakkala 25 C1
Pakola 12 A2
Pakosław 71 D3
Pakoštane 131 B/C2/3
Pákozd 128 B1
Pakrac 128 A3
Paks 129 C2
Paks 96 B3
Paksumaa 6 B3
Paksuniemi 10 A/B3
Palacios de Benaver 152 B2
Palacios de la Sierra 153 C3
Palacios de Sanabria 151 C3
Palacios del Sil 151 C/D2
Palaciosrubios 160 A2
Paladru 103 D3, 104 A3
Palafrugell 156 B2
Palagiano 121 C2
Palagonía 125 C3
Paláia 114 B3, 116 A2
Palaiseau 87 C/D1/2
Palamás 143 C/D3
Palamonastíri 143 C3
Palamós 156 B2/3
Pálàng 17 C2/3
Palanga 73 C1/2
Palanzano 114 A1/2, 116 A1
Palárikovo 95 C2/3
Palas de Rei 150 B2
Palata 119 D2, 120 A1
Palatítsia 143 D2
Palatna 138 B1
Palau 123 D1
Palau Sverdera 156 B2
Palavas-les-Flots 110 B3
Palazuelos 161 C/D2
Palazzo Adriano 124 B2
Palazzo del Pero 115 C3, 117 B/C2
Palazzolo Acréide 125 C/D3
Palazzolo sull'Óglio 106 A3
Palazzolo Vercellese 105 C3, 113 C1
Palazzo San Gervásio 120 B2
Palazzuolo sul Sénio 115 C2, 116 B1
Pålböle 20 A1, 31 D2
Paldiski 74 A1
Pale 132 B2/3
Palea Epídavros 147 C3
Palena 119 C2
Palencia 152 B3
Palenciana 172 B2
Paleochóra 148 B3
Paleochórion 144 B2
Paleokastrítsa 142 A3
Paleokastrítsa 148 A1
Paleómonastíri 143 C3
Paleópirgos 146 B2
Paleópolis 145 C/D2
Palermo 124 B1/2

Palermo Ácqua dei Corsari 124 B2
Palermo-Mondello 124 B1
Páleros 146 A1
Palestrina 118 B2
Palheiros 158 B1
Palheiros da Tocha 158 A3
Palheiros de Quiaios 158 A3
Palhoça 158 A2
Páli 94 B3
Pali 125 C2
Paliano 118 B2
Palič 129 C/D2
Palikkala 24 B2
Palinges 103 C2
Palinuro 120 A3
Palionéllini 143 D2
Paliouriá 143 C2/3
Palioúrion 144 B2/3
Palioúrion 148 B1
Paliseul 79 C3
Palivuk 132 A2
Paljakanpuisto 19 C3
Paljakka 19 C3
Paljakka 19 C2
Paljakka 26 B1/2
Paljakka 19 D1
Paljakka 30 A/B3, 35 D2
Påljorda 14 A/B3
Pälkäne 25 C1
Pälkem (Vitträsk) 17 B/C2
Palkisoja 12 B1
Pallagorío 122 B2
Pallanza 105 D2/3
Pallares 165 D3, 166 A3
Palluelo de Monegros 155 B/C3, 162 B1
Pallastunturi 11 C3, 12 A1
Palling 92 B3
Pallíni 147 D2
Pallonen 23 D2
Palma 164 B2/3
Palma Campánia 119 D3
Pálmaces de Jadraque 161 C2
Palma del Río 172 A1
Palma de Mallorca 157 C2
Palma di Montechiaro 124 B3
Palmanova 126 A2/3
Palma Nova 157 C2
Palmela 164 A2
Palmeral de Elche 169 C3
Palmi 122 A3
Palmižana 131 C3, 136 A1
Pålnostugan 9 D2
Palo 12 A3, 17 D1
Palo 113 C2
Palo del Colle 121 C2
Palojärvi 11 C2
Palojärvi 12 A3, 17 D1
Palojärvi 12 B3
Palojoensuu 11 C2
Palokangas 22 B3
Palokaster 142 A2
Palokki 23 C2
Palolompolo 12 A3, 17 D1
Palomaa 6 B3
Palomäki 23 C2
Palomar de Arroyos 162 B2
Palomares del Campo 161 D3
Palomas 165 D2, 166 A2
Palombara Sabina 118 B1/2
Palomera 161 D3
Palonselkä 11 D3, 12 A2
Palonurmi 23 C2
Paloperä 13 C3
Paloperä 11 C3, 12 A2
Palos de la Frontera 171 C2
Paloselkä 11 D3, 12 A2
Palosenjärvi 22 B1
Palosenmäki 21 D3, 22 A3
Palovaara 18 B1
Pals 156 B2
Palsasuo 10 B2
Palsasuo 6 B3
Pålsboda 46 A/B1
Pålsböle 25 C3
Palsgård 48 B3, 52 B1
Palsselkä 12 B2
Paltamo 19 C3
Paltanen 22 B3
Paltaniemi 19 C3
Pältsastugorna 10 A1

Palù di Férsina 107 C2
Palus 24 A/B1
Paluzza 107 D2, 126 A2
Påmark 24 A/B1
Pambukovica 133 D2, 134 A2
Pamhagen 94 B3
Pamiątkowo 71 D2
Pamiers 109 D3, 155 D1, 156 A1
Pamilo 23 D2
Pamparato 113 C2
Pampelonne 110 A2
Pampilhosa 158 A3
Pampilhosa do Botão 158 A3
Pamplona/Iruñea 154 A2
Panagiá 147 D2
Panagía 145 C1/2
Panagjurište 140 B3
Panajë 142 A2
Panassac 109 C3, 155 C1
Pancalieri 112 B1
Pančarevo 139 D1
Pančevo 133 D1, 134 A/B1
Pančevo 140 A2
Pancorbo 153 C2
Pancrudo 162 A/B2
Pandino 106 A3
Pandrup 48 B1
Panelia 24 A/B1/2
Panenský Týnec 83 C2
Panes 152 B1
Panevéggio 107 C2
Panevėžys 73 D2, 74 A2/3
Pangbourne 64 B3
Paničište 139 D2
Panillo 155 C2
Panissières 103 C2/3
Paniza 163 C1
Panka 22 B2
Pankajärvi 23 D1/2
Pankakoski 23 D2
Pankasz 127 D1
Panker 53 C3
Panni 120 A2
Pannonhalma 95 C3
Panoias 159 B/C2
Panoias 164 B3, 170 A1
Panórama 144 A2
Päntäne 20 B3
Panticosa 154 B2
Pantoja 160 B3
Pantón 150 B2
Panttila 20 B3
Páola 122 A1/2
Pápa 95 C3, 128 A1
Pápa 96 B3
Páparis 146 B3
Paparotti 126 A2
Papasídero 120 B3, 122 A1
Pápatesžér 95 C3, 128 B1
Papenburg 67 D2
Papenburg-Aschendorf 67 D2
Papinniemi 23 D3
Pappás 139 D3, 144 A1
Pappenheim 91 D1, 92 A1
Pappenheim 81 D2
Pappilanvaara 19 C3
Pappinen 25 D1, 26 A1
Pappinen 24 B2
Papracá 133 C2
Papradno 95 C/D1
Papsuso 18 B3, 22 B1
Parábita 121 D3
Paraćin 134 B3
Paraćin 140 A2
Paracuellos de Jiloca 162 A1
Paracuellos 162 A3, 168 B1
Paracuellos de Jarama 161 C2
Parada de Cunhos 158 B1
Parada de Rubiales 159 D1/2, 160 A1/2
Parada do Sil 150 B2
Paradas 171 D2, 172 A2
Paradaseca 151 C2
Paradela 150 B2
Paradela 150 B3, 158 B1
Paradísia 146 B3
Parália 143 D2
Parália 146 B2
Parália Avlídos 147 D2
Parália Iríon 147 C3

Parália Kímis 147 D1
Parália Skotínis 143 D2
Parália Tiroú 147 C3
Parálion Ástros 147 C3
Parálion Ástros 148 B2
Paralovo 138 B1/2
Paramé 85 C1/2
Paramio 151 C3
Paramithiá 142 B3
Páramo 150 B2
Páramo del Sil 151 C2
Paranéstion 145 B/C1
Paranhos 158 B2
Parantala 21 D3, 22 A3
Parapótamos 142 B3
Paravóla 146 B1
Paray-le-Monial 103 C2
Parcent 169 D2
Parcé-sur-Sarthe 86 A3
Parchen 69 D2/3
Parchim 69 D1
Parcoul 101 C3
Parczew 73 D3, 97 D1, 98 A2
Pardilla 153 C3, 161 B/C1
Pardubice 96 A2
Parede 164 A2
Paredes 160 B3
Paredes 158 A1/2
Paredes de Coura 150 A3
Paredes de Nava 152 B3
Paredes de Sigüenza 161 C/D1
Paredes de Viadores 158 A/B2
Pareja 161 D2
Parentis-en-Born 108 A2
Parey 69 D2/3
Párga 142 B3
Párga 148 A1
Pargas 24 B3
Pargas/Parainen 24 B3
Pargny-sur-Saulx 88 B1
Parhalahti 18 A3
Parigné-l'Évêque 86 B2/3
Parikkala 27 D1
Paris 87 C3
Parisot 109 D2
Parissavaara 23 D2
Pärjänsuo 19 B/C2
Parkajoki 11 C3
Parkalompolo 11 C3
Parkano 20 B3
Parkkila 19 C2
Parkkila 26 B1
Parkkila 21 D1, 22 A1
Parkkima 21 D1, 22 A1
Parkku 25 C1
Parkstetten 92 B1/2
Parkua 19 C3, 23 C2
Parla 160 B3
Pärlan 16 A1/2
Parma 114 A1
Parma-San Pancrázio 114 A1
Parndorf 94 B3
Párnica 95 D1
Pärnu 74 A1
Pärnu-Jaagupi 74 A1
Parola 25 C2
Parona di Valpolicella 106 B3
Páros 149 C2/3
Parowa 83 D1
Parque da Pena 164 A2
Parracombe 63 C2
Pårraskårsa 10 A3
Parres 152 A/B1
Parsau 69 C2
Parsberg 92 A1
Parsberg-Willenhofen 92 A1
Parsdorf 92 A2
Parsęcko 71 D1
Parsów 70 B1
Parstein 70 B2
Partaharju 22 B3
Partakko 6 B3
Partakoski 27 C1/2
Partaloa 173 D1/2, 174 A1
Partanna 124 A2
Partenen 106 B1
Partenstein 81 C3
Parthenay 101 C1
Parthénion 147 C3
Partille (Göteborg) 45 C3
Partinello 113 D3

Partinico **124** A/B2
Partizani **133** D2, **134** A2
Partizanske Vode **133** C3, **134** A3
Partizánske **95** C/D2
Partoș **134** B1
Pårup **48** B3
Parviainen **19** C2
Pårvomaj **141** B/C3
Påryd **72** B1
Påryd **51** D2
Parzán **155** C2
Pasaia **153** D1, **154** A1
Pasaköy **145** D1, **145** D3
Pasala **21** D2, **22** A2
Pasayiğit **145** D3
Pascani **141** C1
Pas de Cère **110** A1
Pas-en-Artois **78** A2
Pasewalk **70** B1
Pasewalk **72** A3
Pasi **26** B2
Pasiano di Pordenone **107** D2/3
Pasikovci **128** A3, **131** D1
Påskallavik **51** D1
Påskallavik **72** B1
Pasmajärvi **12** A2, **17** D1
Pašman **130** B2
Passail **127** C1
Passais **86** A2
Passau **93** C2
Passau **96** A2
Passau-Heining **92** B2
Passetto **115** C1
Passignano sul Trasimeno **115** C3, **117** C2
Passò **158** B2
Passopisciaro **125** D2
Passos **158** B1
Passow **69** D1
Passow **70** B1/2
Passugg [Chur] **106** A1
Pástena **119** D2
Pástena **119** D2
Pasto **20** B3
Pastorello **114** A1
Pastores **159** C2
Pastoriza **151** C1
Pastow **53** D3
Pastrana **161** C2
Pastricciola **113** D3
Pastriz **154** B3, **162** B1
Pasvalis **73** D1, **74** A2
Pata **95** C2
Pataholm **51** D1
Pataias **164** A1
Patajoki **25** D1, **26** A1
Patana **21** C2
Påtas **135** C1
Patay **87** C2
Pateley Bridge **61** C2
Pateniemi **18** A2
Patergassen **126** B1
Patergassen **96** A3
Paterna **169** D1
Paterna del Campo **171** C1
Paterna de la Madera **168** B2
Paterna del Río **173** D2
Paterna de Rivera **171** D3
Paternion **126** B1/2
Paternò **125** C2
Paternópoli **119** D3, **120** A2
Patersdorf **93** B/C1
Pathhead **57** C2
Patini **143** B/C3, **146** A1
Patiópoulon **146** A1
Pătîrlagele **141** C2
Patitírion **147** D1
Patokoski **12** A3
Patoniemi **13** C3
Patoniva **6** B2
Patos **142** A2
Patos **148** A1
Patosh Fshat **142** A2
Pátra/Pátrai **146** B2
Pátra/Pátrai **148** B2
Pátrica **119** B/C2
Patrikka **23** D3
Patrington **61** D2
Pattada **123** D2
Pattensen **68** B3
Pattensen-Schulenburg **68** B3
Patterdale **57** C3, **60** B1

Patti **125** C/D1/2
Pattijoki **18** A3
Pättikkä **10** B2
Pättikkäkoski **10** B2
Pătulele **135** D2
Páty **95** D3
Pau **108** B3, **154** B1
Pauillac **100** B3
Paukarlahti **22** B3
Paukkaja **23** D2
Paul **158** B3
Pauland **30** B1
Paularo **107** D2, **126** A2
Paulhac-en-Margeride **110** B1
Paulhaguet **103** B/C3
Paulhan **110** B3
Paullilátino **123** C2
Paulinenaue **69** D2, **70** A2
Paull **61** D2
Paullo **105** D3, **106** A3
Pauls **163** C1
Pausa **82** A/B2
Pausele **30** B1
Pauträsk **30** B1
Pauvres **78** B3
Pavia **105** D3, **106** A3, **113** D1
Pavia **164** B2
Pavías **162** B3, **169** D1
Pavilly **77** C3
Pavilosta **73** C1
Pávliani **147** B/C1
Pavlica **133** D3, **134** A/B3
Pavlíkeni **141** C3
Pavlíkov **83** C3
Pávlos **147** C1/2
Pavlovsk **74** B1
Pavullo nel Frignano **114** B2, **116** A1
Päwesin **69** D2, **70** A2
Pawłowice **71** D3
Pawłowo Zońskie **71** D2
Payerne **104** B1
Paymogo **165** C3, **170** B1
Payrac **109** D1
Pazardžik **140** B3
Pazin **126** B3, **130** A1
Paziols **156** B1
Pazo de Irijoa **150** B1
Pazos de Borbén **150** A2/3
Peacehaven **76** B1
Peal de Becerro **167** D3, **168** A3, **173** C1
Peanía **147** D2
Péaule **85** C3
Peć **138** A1
Peć **140** A3
Pećane **131** C2
Péccioli **114** B3, **116** A2
Pécel **95** D3
Pečenjevce **139** C1
Pechão **170** B2
Pechea **141** C1/2
Pechern **83** D1
Pechina **173** D2
Peći **131** C2
Pećigrad **131** C1
Pećinci **133** D1, **134** A1
Pecka **133** C2
Peckatel **70** A1
Pečky **83** D3
Pęcław **71** D3
Pecorara **113** D1
Pecorone **120** B3, **122** A1
Pečory **74** B2
Pécs **128** B2
Pécska Banja **138** A1
Pécsvárad **128** B2
Pečurice **137** D2
Pedaso **117** D2
Pederoa **107** C1/2
Pederobba **107** C2/3
Pedersöre/Pietarsaaren maalaiskunta **20** B1
Pederstrup **53** C2
Pedescala **107** C3
Pedorido **158** A2
Pedrafita do Cebreiro **151** C2
Pedra Furada **158** A1
Pedrajas **153** D3, **161** D1
Pedrajas de San Esteban **160** B1
Pedralba **169** C1
Pedralva de la Praderia **151** C3

Pedras Salgadas **150** B3, **158** B1
Pedraza **160** B1/2
Pedraza de Alba **159** D2, **160** A2
Pedreguer **169** D2
Pedreira **150** B1
Pedreña **153** B/C1
Pedrera **172** A2
Pedro Abad **167** C3, **172** B1
Pedroche **166** B3
Pedrógão Grande **158** A/B3, **164** B1
Pedrógão **165** C3
Pedrógão **159** B/C3
Pedrógão **158** A3, **164** A1
Pedrola **155** C3, **163** C1
Pedro Martínez **173** C1
Pedro Muñoz **167** D1, **168** A1
Pedrosa de Duero **152** B3, **160** B1
Pedrosa del Rey **152** A2
Pedrosillo de los Aires **159** D2
Pedrosillo el Ralo **159** D2
Pedroso **153** D2
Pedroso de Acim **159** C3, **165** D1
Peebles **57** C2
Peel **58** B1
Peel **54** A3, **55** D2
Peera **10** B1/2
Pefkíon **147** C1
Pefkotón **139** C3, **143** C1
Pega **159** C3
Pegalajar **173** C1
Pegau **82** B1
Peggau **127** C1
Pegnitz **82** A3
Pego **169** D2
Pegões Velhos **164** A/B2
Pegolotte **107** C3
Pehčevo **139** D2/3
Pehula **24** B1
Peine **88** B3
Peine-Stederdorf **68** B3
Peinikanniemi **19** D1
Péio **106** B2
Peipohja **24** B1/2
Peira-Cava **112** B2
Peisey-Nancroix **104** B3
Peissen **69** D3
Peissenberg **92** A3
Peiting **91** D3
Peitz **70** B3
Pekankylä **19** D3
Pekanpää **17** D2
Pekkala **12** B3
Pekkula **23** D3
Peklino **99** D1
Pelahustán **160** A/B3
Pelaria **158** A3
Pelarrodríguez **159** D2
Pelasgía **147** C1
Pelayos de la Presa **160** B2/3
Pełczyce **71** C2
Peleas de Arriba **159** D1
Pélekas **142** A3
Peletá **147** C2
Pelhřimov **83** D3, **94** A1
Pelhřimov **96** A2
Pelilla **159** D1/2
Pelinnaion **143** C3
Pelkkikangas **21** B/C2
Pelkoperä **18** A/B3
Pelkosenniemi **12** B2
Pella **44** B1
Pella **143** D1/2
Pélla **143** D1/2
Pellegrino Parmense **114** A1
Pellegrue **108** B1
Pelléd **128** A2
Pellesmäki **22** B2
Pellevoisin **101** D1
Pellingen **79** D3, **80** A3
Pellinki/Pellinge **25** D3, **26** A3
Pello **12** A3, **17** D1
Pello **12** A3, **17** D1
Pellosniemi **26** B1
Pellossalo **27** C/D1

Pellworm-Ostersiel **52** A2
Pellworm-Waldhusen **52** A2
Peloche **166** B2
Pelso **18** B3
Peltokangas **21** C2
Peltosalmi **22** B1
Peltovuoma **11** C2, **12** A1
Pélussin **103** D3
Pemar **24** B2/3
Pembridge **59** D3
Pembroke **62** B1
Pembroke **55** D3
Pembroke Dock **62** B1
Pemfling-Grafenkirchen **92** B1
Pempelijärvi **17** C1
Penacova **158** A3
Peñafiel **152** B3, **160** B1
Penafiel **158** A1/2
Peñaflor **172** A1
Peñaflor de Hornija **152** A3, **160** A1
Penagos **153** B/C1
Penaguião **158** B1/2
Peñalba **155** C3, **163** C1
Peñalba de San Esteban **153** C3, **161** C1
Peñalén **161** D2
Peñalsordo **166** B2
Penalva do Castelo **158** B2
Peñalver **161** C2
Penamacor **159** B/C3
Peñaranda de Duero **153** C3, **161** C1
Peñaranda de Bracamonte **160** A2
Peñarroya-Pueblonuevo **166** B3
Peñarroya de Tastavins **163** C2
Peñarrubia **172** A2
Peñascosa **168** A/B2
Peñas de San Pedro **168** B2
Peñausende **159** D1
Penc **95** D3
Pencader **62** B1
Penchard **87** D1
Pendagií **146** B1/2
Pendálofos **143** B/C2
Pendápolis **144** B1
Pendine **62** B1
Pendueles **152** B1
Penedono **158** B2
Penela **158** A3
Pénestin **85** C3
Pengerjoki **21** D3
Penhale **62** A/B3
Penhas Juntas **151** C3, **159** C1
Peniche **164** A1
Penicuik **57** C2
Penig **82** B2
Peñíscola **163** C2/3
Penistone **61** C2/3
Penkridge **59** D3, **64** A1
Penkun **70** B1
Penmaenmawr **59** C2, **60** A3
Penmarch **84** A3
Pennabilli **115** C2, **117** C1
Pennala **25** D2, **26** A2
Pennapiedimonte **119** C1
Penne **117** D3, **119** C1
Penne **42** B3
Penningby **41** C3
Peno **75** C2
Pensala **20** B2
Pentinniemi **18** B1
Penttäjä **17** C/D1
Pentti **26** B2
Penttilänlahti **22** B2
Penttilänvaara **19** D1
Pen-y-groes **58** B2, **60** A3
Penzance **62** A3
Penzberg **92** A3
Pénzesgyör **128** B1
Penzlin **70** A1
Pepelište **139** C3

Pépinster **79** D2
Pepovo **71** D3
Peqin **142** A1
Pér **95** C3
Pera Boa **158** B3
Peracense **162** A2
Perachóra **147** C2
Perafita **158** A1
Perafita **156** A2
Perä-Hyyppä **20** B3
Peral **158** B3, **165** B/C1
Perälä **20** A3
Peralada **156** B2
Peralbillo **167** C2
Peral de Arlanza **152** B3
Peraleda de la Mata **159** D3, **160** A3, **166** B1
Peraleda de Zaucejo **166** A2/3
Peraleda de San Román **159** D3, **160** A3, **166** B1
Peralejos de las Truchas **161** D2, **162** A1
Perales del Alfambra **162** B2
Perales del Puerto **159** C3
Perales de Tajuña **161** C3
Peralta **154** A2
Peralta de Alcofea **155** C3
Peralta de la Sal **155** C3
Peraltilla **155** C3
Peralva **170** B2
Peralveche **161** D2
Pérama **147** C2
Pérama **142** B3
Peramola **155** C3
Perä-Musko **23** D3
Peranka **19** D2
Peränkylä **24** A1
Perä-Posio **19** C1
Perarolo **107** C3
Perarolo di Cadore **107** D2
Perarrúa **155** C2
Peräseinäjoki **20** B3
Peräsilta **25** C2
Perast **137** C2
Perat **142** B2
Perat **148** A1
Perazancas **152** B2
Perbál **95** D3
Perchtoldsdorf **94** B2
Percy **86** A/B1
Perdasdefogu **123** D3
Perdiguera **154** B3, **162** B1
Pérdika **142** B3
Pérdika **147** D3
Pérdika **142** B3
Peréa **143** D2, **144** A2
Perečin **97** D2, **98** A3
Peredo **159** C1
Pereg **129** C1
Pereiro **170** B1
Pereiro de Aguiar **150** B2
Perejaslav-Hmel'nickij **99** D2
Perelhal **150** A3, **158** A1
Peremyšľ' **75** D3
Peremyšľ'any **97** D2, **98** A/B2/3
Perevolok **74** B1
Pérfugas **123** C1
Perg **93** D2
Perga **99** C2
Pérgine Valdarno **115** C3, **116** B2
Pérgine Valsugana **107** C2
Pérgola **115** D3, **117** C2
Pergusa **125** C2
Perho **21** C2
Peri **106** B3
Periam **140** A1
Periana **172** B2
Périers **76** A3, **85** D1
Pérignac **100** B3
Périgné **101** C2
Périgueux **101** D3
Períklia **139** C3, **143** D1
Perilla de Castro **151** D3, **159** D1
Perillo **150** A/B1
Perino **113** D1
Perişor **135** D2
Peristerá **144** A2
Perithórion **144** B1
Perivol **139** C/D2
Perivólion **142** B2/3

Perjasica **127** C3,
131 B/C1
Perkam **92** B1/2
Perkáta **129** C1
Perkiömäki **20** B2
Perkupa **97** C2
Perl **79** D3
Perl-Borg **79** D3
Perleberg **69** D2
Perlez **129** D3, **133** D1,
134 A1
Perlez **140** A2
Perly [Genève] **104** A2
Permantokoski **12** B3
Pérmeti **142** B2
Pernancha de Cima **164** B2
Pernå/Pernaja **25** D2/3,
26 A2/3
Pernarec **83** B/C3
Pernek **94** B2
Pernes **164** A/B1
Pernes-les-Fontaines
111 C/D2
Pernik **139** D1/2
Pernik **140** B3
Pernink **82** B2
Perniö (Bjärnå) **24** B3
Perniön asema **24** B3
Pernitz **94** A3
Pernitz **96** A3
Pernoo **26** B2
Pernu **18** A1
Peroguarda **164** B3
Peroniel del Campo
153 D3, **161** D1
Péronne **78** A3
Perorrubio **161** B/C1
Perosa Argentina **112** B1
Pérouges **103** D2
Perpignan **156** B1
Perranporth **62** B3
Perrecy-les-Forges
103 C1/2
Perrero **112** B1
Perreux **103** C2
Perrigny-sur-Loire **103** C2
Perros-Guirec **84** B1
Persac **101** C/D2
Persberg **39** C3, **45** D1
Persenbeug **93** D2
Pershagen **47** C1
Pershore **63** D1, **64** A2
Persi **113** D1
Persnäs **51** D1
Persön **17** C3
Perštejn **83** B/C2
Perstorp **50** B2
Perstorp **72** A1
Pertengo **105** C/D3,
113 C1
Perth **57** C1
Perth **54** B2
Perthes **88** B2
Pertisau **92** A3
Perttaus **12** A/B2/3
Pertteli **24** B2/3
Pertula **25** C2/3
Pertuis **111** D2/3
Pertunmaa **26** B1
Pertusa **155** B/C3
Peruc **83** C2
Perúčac **133** C2
Perúgia **115** C3, **117** C2
Perunkajärvi **12** B3
Perušić **130** B2
Péruwelz **78** B2
Pervijze **78** A1
Pervomajsk **99** D3
Perwez **79** C2
Pesadas de Burgos **153** C3
Pésaro **115** D2, **117** C1
Pescantina **106** B3
Pescányj Brod **99** C/D3
Pescara **119** C/D1
Pescasséroli **119** C2
Péschici **120** B1
Peschiera del Garda **106** B3
Péscia **114** B2, **116** A1
Pescina **119** C2
Pescolanciano **119** D2
Pescopagano **120** A2
Pescopennataro **119** D2
Pesco Sannita **119** D3,
120 A2
Pescueza **159** C3, **165** D1
Peshkëpija **142** A2
Peshkopi **138** A3

Peshkopi **140** A3
Pesiökylä **19** C2
Pesiönranta **19** C2
Pesmes **89** C3, **103** D1,
104 A1
Pesočani **138** B3, **142** B1
Pesoz **151** C1
Pesquera de Duero **152** B3,
160 B1
Pessac **108** B1
Pessalompolo **12** A3,
17 D2
Pessáni **145** D1, **145** D3
Pessegueiro do Vouga
158 A2
Pessione **113** C1
Pessoux **79** C2
Pestá **142** B3
Peštani **142** B1
Pešteana Jiu **135** D1
Peštera **140** B3
Peștișani **135** D1
Pestovo **75** D1
Pešurići **133** C2/3
Peszéradacs **129** C1
Petacciato Marina **119** D2
Petäiskylä **23** C1
Petäjäjärvi **18** B1
Petäjäkangas **18** B2
Petäjäkylä **21** D2, **22** A2
Petäjämäki **22** B3
Petäjäskoski **12** A3
Petäjäskoski **18** A3
Petäjävaara **19** C3
Petäjävesi **21** D3, **22** A3
Petalax (Petolahti) **20** A2,
31 D3
Pétange **79** D3
Petanjci **127** D2
Petar u Sumi **126** B3,
130 A1
Pétas **146** A1
Petäys **22** B1
Peteranec **128** A2
Peterborough **65** B/C2
Peterhead **54** B2
Peterlee **61** D1
Petersberg-Marbach **81** C2
Petersborg **4** A3, **10** A1
Petersfield **76** A/B1
Petershagen-Ovenstädt
68 A2/3
Petershagen-Windheim
68 A2/3
Petershagen **68** A2/3
Petershagen **70** B2/3
Petershausen **92** A2
Peterstow **63** D1
Petiknäs **31** C1
Petikträsk **16** A3
Petília Policastro **122** B2
Petín **151** C2
Petit-Fossard **87** D2
Petit-Mars **85** D3
Petkula **12** B2
Petkus **70** A3
Petlovača **133** C1
Petolahti **20** A2, **31** D3
Pétra **143** D2
Petra **157** C2
Petragalla **120** B2
Petralía Soprana **125** C2
Petralía Sottana **125** C2
Petralóna **144** A2
Petraná **143** C2
Petrčane **130** B2
Petrel **169** C2/3
Petrele **137** D3, **138** A3,
142 A1
Petrella Liri **119** B/C2
Petrella Salto **117** D3,
118 B1
Petrella Tifernina **119** D2
Petreto-Bicchisano **113** D3
Petrič **139** C3, **144** A1
Petrijanec **127** D3
Petrijevci **128** B3
Petrikov **99** C1
Petrinja **127** D3
Petrodvorec **74** B1
Petröec **139** B/C2
Petrokrepost' **75** C1
Pétrola **168** B2
Petroná **122** B2
Petronell-Carnuntum **94** B2
Petroșani **140** B2
Petroúlion **143** C3

Petroússa **144** B1
Petrovaara **23** C2
Petrovac **134** B2
Petrovac **137** C/D2
Petrovac **140** A2
Petrovaradin **129** D3,
133 D1, **134** A1
Petrovčić **133** D1, **134** A1
Petrovice **83** D3, **93** D1
Petrovice **83** C2
Petrovice **93** C1
Petrovice **83** C3, **93** C1
Petrovo **75** D1
Petrovo Selo **135** C2
Petruma **23** C3
Petržalka **94** B2
Petsáki **146** B2
Petschow **53** D3
Petsmo **20** A/B2
Petsund **38** A3
Pettäikkö **18** B3
Pettbol **40** B3
Pettenbach **93** C3
Petting **92** B3
Pettorano sul Gízio **119** C2
Pettorazza Grimani **107** C3,
115 C1
Petworth **76** B1
Peuerbach **93** C2
Peuerbach **96** A2
Peulje **131** C2
Peura **18** A1
Peurajärvi **18** B1
Peuralinna **21** C2
Peurasuvanto **12** B2
Peuravaara **19** C3
Peutaniemi **19** D2
Pevensey **77** C1
Pewsey **64** A3, **76** A1
Peyrat-le-Château
102 A2/3
Peyrebrune **109** D1
Peyrehorade **108** A3,
154 B1
Peyrolles-en-Provence
111 D2/3
Pézenas **110** B3
Pezinok **95** B/C2
Pezuela de las Torres
161 C2
Pfaffendorf **70** B3
Pfaffenhofen **91** D2
Pfaffenhofen-Tegernbach
92 A2
Pfaffenhofen **92** A2
Pfaffenhofen **107** B/C1
Pfaffenhoffen **90** A1/2
Pfäffikon **105** C2
Pfäffikon **90** B3, **105** D1
Pfaffing **92** B2/3
Pfaffing-Springlbach
92 B2/3
Pfafflar **106** B1
Pfalzgrafenweiler **90** B2
Pfarrkirchen **92** B2
Pfatter **92** B1
Pfatter-Geisling **92** B1
Pfeffenhausen **92** A/B2
Pfinztal-Berghausen **90** B1
Pförring-Forchheim
92 A1/2
Pforzheim **90** B1/2
Pfreimd **82** B3, **92** B1
Pfronstetten-Tigerfeld
91 C2
Pfronten **91** D3
Pfullendorf **91** C3
Pfullendorf-Denkingen
91 C3
Pfullingen **91** C2
Pfungstadt **80** B3
Pfyn [Felben-Wellhausen]
91 B/C3
Phalsbourg **89** D1, **90** A1
Phare de Cordouan **100** B3
Phare de Pertusato **123** D1
Pheneos **146** B2
Pherai **143** D3
Philippeville **78** B3
Phílippi **144** B1
Philippsbourg **90** B1
Philippsreut **93** C1/2
Philippsreut **96** A2
Philippsthal-Heimbolds-
hausen **81** C/D2
Philippsthal (Werra)
81 C/D2

Phlious **147** C2
Phoenike **142** A3
Phyäselkä **23** D3
Phyhämaa **24** A2, **41** D2
Physkeis **146** B2
Piacenza **113** D1, **114** A1
Piádena **106** B3, **114** A1
Piagge **115** D2, **117** C1/2
Piamprato **105** C3
Piana **113** D3
Piana Crixia **113** C2
Piana degli Albanesi
124 B2
Pianazzo **105** D2, **106** A2
Piancáldoli **115** B/C2,
116 B1
Pian Castagna **113** C1/2
Piancastagnáio **116** B3
Piandelagotti **114** B2,
116 A1
Pian della Mussa **104** B3
Piandimeleto **115** C2,
117 C2
Pianella **119** C1
Pianella **114** B3, **116** B2
Pianello Val Tidone **113** D1
Pianezza **112** B1
Piano del Re **112** B1
Piano Laceno **119** D3,
120 A2
Pianoro **114** B2, **116** B1
Pianottoli-Caldarello
113 D3
Pians **106** B1
Piansano **116** B3, **118** A1
Pias **165** C3, **170** B1
Piasecznik **71** C1
Piaseczno **70** B2
Piasek **70** B2
Piaski **71** D3
Piastre **114** B2, **116** A1
Piatra-Neamt **141** C1
Piazza **107** C2
Piazza al Sérchio **114** A2,
116 A1
Piazza Armerina **125** C2/3
Piazza Brembana **106** A2
Piazze **116** B3
Piazzola sul Brenta **107** C3
Píbrac **108** B2/3, **155** C1
Pićan **126** B3, **130** A1
Picão **158** B2
Picão **158** B2
Picasent **169** D1
Piccovagia **113** D3
Picerno **120** A2
Picher **69** C1
Pickering **61** C/D2
Pico **119** C2
Picón **167** C2
Picquigny **77** D2
Piecnik **71** D1
Piedicavallo **105** C3
Piédicorte-di-Gaggio
113 D3
Piedicroce **113** D3
Piediluco **117** C3, **118** B1
Piedimonte Etneo **125** D2
Piedimonte Matese **119** D2
Piedimulera **105** C2
Piedipaterno **117** C3,
118 B1
Piedivalle **117** D3
Pie di Via **114** A1
Piedrabuena **167** C2
Piedrafita **151** D2
Piedrahita **160** A2
Piedralaves **160** A3
Piedras Albas **159** C3,
165 C1
Piedratajada **154** B3
Piegaro **115** C3, **117** C2/3
Piehinki **18** A3
Pieksämäki **22** B3
Pieksänlahti **27** C1
Pielavesi **22** B2
Pielppajärven lapin kirkko
6 B3
Pielungo **107** D2, **126** A2
Piène-Basse **112** B2
Pieńsk **83** D1
Pienza **115** C3, **116** B3
Piera **156** A3, **163** D1
Pierowall **54** B1
Pierowall **54** B1
Pierre **103** D1
Pierre-Buffière **101** C3

Pierrefeu-du-Var **112** A3
Pierrefitte-Nestalas **108** B3,
155 C1/2
Pierrefitte-sur-Aire **89** C1
Pierrefonds **87** D1
Pierrefontaine-les-Varans
89 D3, **104** B1
Pierrefort **110** A1
Pierrelatte **111** C2
Pierreton **108** B1
Piertinjaure **16** A1/2
Piesasskylä **21** D3, **22** A3
Piesau **82** A2
Piesjoki **6** B2/3
Pieski **71** C2/3
Piešt'any **95** C2
Piešt'any **96** B2
Pietracamela **117** D3,
119 C1
Pietralba **113** D2
Pietra Lígure **113** C2
Pietralunga **115** C/D3,
117 C2
Pietramelara **119** C/D2/3
Pietramontecorvino
119 D2, **120** A1
Pietraperzía **125** C2
Pietrapórzio **112** B2
Pietraróia **119** D2
Pietrasanta **114** A2, **116** A1
Pieve al Toppo **115** C3,
116 B2
Pieve del Cáiro **113** D1
Pieve di Bono **106** B2
Pieve di Cadore **107** D2
Pieve di Livinallongo
107 C2
Pieve di Soligo **107** D2/3
Pieve di Teco **113** C2
Pievepélago **114** B2,
116 A1
Pieve Santo Stéfano
115 C2/3, **117** B/C2
Pieve Tesino **107** C2
Pieve Torina **115** D3,
117 C/D2
Pieve Vécchia **106** B3
Pigaí **145** C1
Pigaí **143** C3
Pigaí **148** A/B1
Pigna **113** B/C2
Pignataro Maggiore **119** C3
Pignola **120** B2/3
Pihkainmäki **22** B2
Pihkala **18** B3
Pihlajalahti **27** C1
Pihlajalahti **25** C1
Pihlajamäki **19** C3
Pihlajavaara **23** D2, **23** D1
Pihlajaveden-asema **21** C3
Pihlajavesi **21** C3
Pihlava **24** A1
Pihtipudas **21** D2, **22** A2
Pihtisulku **21** C3
Pihtsoskordši **4** B3, **10** B1
Piikkiö (Pikis) **24** B2/3
Piilijärvi **10** B3
Piilo **23** D2
Piippola **18** B3, **22** A1
Piipsjärvi **18** A3
Piispa **23** C2
Piispajärvi **19** D2
Piittisjärvi **18** B1
Pikajärvi **12** A/B3
Pikalevo **75** C1
Pikalji **137** D2
Pikis **24** B2/3
Pikkarala **18** A3
Pikkavaara **13** C3
Pikkujaakko **16** B1
Pikku-Kulus **12** B3
Pila **115** C/D1
Pila **104** B3
Pila Canale **113** D3
Pilas **171** D2
Pila (Schneidemühl)
71 D1/2
Pila (Schneidemühl) **72** B3
Pilastri **114** B1
Pilat-Plage **108** B1
Piléa **92** D2, **144** A2
Pilgrimstad **34** B2
Pili **147** D2
Pílion **147** D1
Pílion Óros **143** D3, **144** A1
Pilis **129** C1
Piliscsaba **95** D3

Pilisszentkereszt 95 D3
Pilisvörösvár 95 D3
Piłka 71 C2
Pille-l'Ardit 108 B2
Pillingsdorf 82 A2
Piloña 152 A1
Pilorí 143 C2
Pilpala 25 C2
Pilsach-Dietkirchen 92 A1
Pilštanj 127 C2
Pilsting 92 B2
Pilträsk 16 A/B2/3
Piña de Campos 152 B2/3
Pina de Ebro 154 B3,
  162 B1
Piñar 173 C1/2
Pinarejo 168 A/B1
Pinarejos 160 B1
Pinarello 113 D3
Pinarhisar 141 C3
Pinay 103 C2
Píncara 115 C1
Pincehely 128 B2
Pineda 161 D3
Pineda de la Sierra
  153 C2/3
Pineda de Mar 156 B3
Pinela 151 C3, 159 C1
Piñel de Arriba 152 B3,
  160 B1
Pinell de Solsonés 155 D3
Pinerolo 112 B1
Pineto 119 C1
Piney 88 B2
Pinggau 94 A3
Pinhal Novo 164 A2
Pinhão 158 B1/2
Pinheiro 150 B3, 158 A1
Pinheiro Grande 164 B1
Pinhel 159 C2
Pinilla de los Barruecos
  153 C3
Pinilla del Olmo 161 D1
Pinilla de los Moros 153 C3
Pinilla de Molina 161 D2,
  162 A2
Pinjainen/Billnäs 25 C3
Pinkafeld 94 A3, 127 D1
Pinneberg 52 B3, 68 B1
Pino 151 D3, 159 D1
Pino 113 D2
Pino del Río 152 A/B2
Pino do Val 150 A2
Pinofranqueado 159 C3
Piñols 102 B3, 110 B1
Piñor 150 B2
Pinos de Miramar 163 D2
Pinoso 169 C3
Pinos Puente 173 C2
Pinsaguel 108 B3, 155 C1
Pinseque 154 A/B3,
  162 A/B1
Pinsk 98 B1
Pintamo 19 C2
Pintano 154 B2
Pinto 161 B/C3
Pinzano al Tagliamento
  107 D2, 126 A2
Pinzio 159 C2
Pinzolo 106 B2
Pióbbico 115 C/D3,
  117 C2
Piojärvi 27 C1
Piombino 116 A3
Pionsat 102 B2
Pioppo 124 B2
Pióraco 115 D3, 117 C/D2
Piossasco 112 B1
Piotrków Trybunalski 97 C1
Piove di Sacco 107 C3
Piovene-Rocchette 107 C3
Póvera 113 C/D1
Pioz 161 C2
Pipriac 85 C/D3
Piqerasi 142 A2
Piqueras 162 A2
Piqueras 161 D3, 168 B1
Piran 126 A/B3
Píras 123 D1/2
Pirciato 125 C1
Pireás/Pireéfs 147 D2
Pireás/Pireéfs 148 B2
Pirgadíkia 144 B2
Pírgi 144 B1
Pírgi 143 C2
Pirgí 149 C2
Pírgos 146 A/B3

Pírgos 143 D2, 144 A2
Pírgos 147 B/C1
Piriac-sur-Mer 85 C3
Pirin 139 D3
Pirjatin 99 D2
Pirkkala 25 C1
Pirmasens 90 A1
Pirna 83 C2
Pirna 96 A1
Pirok 138 B2
Pirompré 79 C3
Pirot 135 C/D3, 139 C/D1
Pirot 140 B3
Pirovac 131 C3
Pirrtitkoski 12 B3
Pirsógianni 142 B2
Pirsógianni 148 A1
Pirttijärvi 24 A1
Pirttijärvi 23 D3
Pirttikoski 18 A3
Pirttikoski 25 C2
Pirttikylä 20 A2/3
Pirttikylä 21 C3
Pirttimäki 23 B/C1
Pirttimäki 22 B1
Pirttimäki 22 B2
Pirttinen 20 B2
Pirttiniemi 21 C1
Pirttiniemi 17 C1
Pirttivaara 19 D2
Pirttivaara 23 D2/3
Pirttivuopio 10 A3
Pisa 12 A3
Pisa 23 C2
Pisa 114 A2, 116 A1/2
Pisak 131 D3, 132 A3
Pisana 107 C3
Pisany 100 B3
Pisarovina 127 D3
Pisa Tirrénia 114 A3,
  116 A2
Pišča 73 D3, 97 D1, 98 A2
Pisciatello 113 D3
Pisciotta 120 A3
Piscu Vechi 135 D2/3
Písek 93 C/D1
Písek 96 A2
Pishkash 138 A3, 142 B1
Písia 147 C2
Piškorevci 128 B3, 132 B1
Pisodérion 143 C1/2
Pisogne 106 B3
Pissos 108 B2
Pisticci 120 B3
Pisto 19 D2
Pistóia 114 B2, 116 A1
Pisz (Johannisburg) 73 C3,
  98 A1
Pitäjänmäki 21 D1, 22 A1
Pitarque 162 B2
Piteå 16 B3
Pite-Altervattnet 16 B3
Piteå-Munksund 16 B3
Pitești 140 B2
Pithagórion 149 D2
Pithiviers 87 C/D2
Pitigliano 116 B3, 118 A1
Pitillas 154 A2
Pitkäaho 26 B1
Pitkäjärvi 24 B2
Pitkälä 27 C/D1
Pitkälahti 22 B2
Pitkälahti 23 C3
Pitkälahti 27 C1
Pitkälahti 22 B2/3
Pitkäluoto 24 A2, 41 D2
Pitkäsalo 21 C1
Pitlochry 54 B2
Pitomača 128 A2/3
Pitres 173 C2
Pitsund 16 B3
Pittenweem 57 C1
Pitvaros 129 D2
Pivka 126 B3
Pivnica 128 A3
Pivnice 129 C3
Pivski Manastir 133 C3,
  137 C1
Pizarra 172 B2
Pizzighettone 106 A3
Pizzo 122 A2
Pizzolato 124 A2
Pizzoli 117 D3, 119 B/C1
Pjätteryd 50 B2
Pjelax 20 A3
Pjesker 16 A3
Pjesörn 31 C1

Plaaz 53 D3, 69 D1
Plabennec 84 A2
Pla de San Tirs 155 C2
Plaffeien [Fribourg] 104 B1
Plaisance 110 A2
Plaisance-du-Gers 108 B3,
  155 C1
Pláka 147 C3
Plameira 150 A2
Plan 155 C2
Plana 137 C1
Planá 82 B3
Plána 144 B2
Planá nad Lužnicí 93 D1
Plaňany 83 D3
Pláncios 107 C1/2
Plancoët 85 C2
Plan-de-Baix 111 D1
Plandište 134 B1
Plan d'Orgon 111 C/D2
Plan-du-Lac 104 B2
Plan-du-Var 112 B2
Planes 169 C2
Planfoy 103 C3
Planica 126 B2
Plánice 93 C1
Planina 127 C2
Planina 126 B3
Planina 126 B2
Planinica 126 C3
Plankenfels 82 A3
Planoles 156 A2
Plános 146 A2
Plans-sur-Bex, Les [Bex]
  104 B2
Plasencia 159 D3
Plasencia del Monte
  154 B2
Plasenzuela 165 D1,
  166 A1
Plasiá 143 D3
Plaški 130 B1
Plassen 38 B1/2
Plášťovce 95 D2
Plasy 83 C3
Plat 137 C1/2
Platak 126 B3
Platamón 143 D2
Platamón 145 B/C1
Platamona Lido 123 C1
Platania 122 A/B2
Plataniá 147 C/D1
Plataniá 148 B1
Plataniá 148 B2
Plátanos 148 B3
Plátanos 147 C1
Plátanos 143 D2
Plátanos 146 B1
Plátanos 146 B3
Platanótopos 144 B1
Platanoúsa 142 B3
Platanóvrisi 146 B3
Platariá 142 A/B3
Plate 69 C1
Plateaí 147 C/D2
Platí 143 D2
Platí 122 A3
Platí 145 C3
Platíčevo 133 C/D1,
  134 A1
Platíkambos 143 D3
Platíschis 126 A2
Platístomon 146 B1
Platta (Medel) [Disentis/
  Mustér] 105 D1/2
Plattling 92 B2
Plau 69 D1
Plau 72 A3
Plaue 81 D2, 82 A2
Plauen 82 B2
Plav 138 A1
Plava Laguna 126 A/B3,
  130 A1
Plavca 130 B1
Plave 126 A/B2
Plavecký Mikuláš 95 C2
Plavisevita 135 C2
Plavna 135 C2
Plavnica 137 D2
Pławce 71 D3
Playa de Oropesa 163 C3
Playa de Pineda 163 C2
Playa de San Juan 169 D3
Playa de Tabernes 169 D2
Pleaux 102 A3, 110 A1
Pleine-Fougères 85 D2
Pleinfeld 91 D1, 92 A1

Pleiskirchen 92 B2
Plélan-le-Grand 85 C2
Plélan-le-Petit 85 C2
Plémet 85 C2
Plenas 162 B2
Pléneuf-Val-André 85 C2
Plenița 135 D2
Plérin 85 C2
Pleš 134 B3
Pleščenicy 74 B3
Plešin 133 D3, 134 A3
Plessé 85 C/D3
Plestin-les Grèves 84 B1/2
Pleszew 72 B3, 96 B1
Pleterje 127 C3
Pleternica 128 B3, 132 B1
Plettenberg 80 B1
Pleubian 84 B1
Pleumartin 101 C1
Pleuron 146 B2
Pleurs 88 A1/2
Pleven 140 B3
Pleyben 84 B2
Pleystein 82 B3
Pliego 169 B/C3,
  174 A/B1
Pliešovce 95 D2
Pliezhausen 91 C2
Plitvice 131 C1
Plitvička Jezera 131 C1
Plitvički Ljeskovac 131 C1
Pljavinjas 73 D1, 74 A2
Pljevlja 133 C2
Ploaghe 123 C1/2
Plobsheim 90 A2
Plochingen 91 C2
Płock 73 C3
Ploemeur 84 B3
Ploërmel 85 C2
Ploieşti 141 C2
Plomárion 149 C2
Plomin 130 A1
Plombières-les-Bains
  89 D2
Plonéour-Lanvern 84 A2/3
Plonévez-du-Faou 84 B2
Płońsk 73 C3
Płośko 71 C2
Plössberg 82 B3
Plössberg-Schönficht
  82 B3
Ploștina 135 D1
Ploty 71 C1
Plou 162 B2
Plouagat 85 B/C2
Plouaret 84 B2
Plouay 84 B2
Ploubalay 85 C2
Plœuc-sur-Lié 85 C2
Ploudalmézeau 84 A2
Plouescat 84 A1/2
Plouézec 85 B/C1
Plougasnou 84 B1/2
Plougonven 84 B2
Plouguenast 85 C2
Plouguerneau 84 A2
Plouha 85 C1/2
Plouharnel 84 B3
Plouhinec 84 A2
Plouigneau 84 B2
Ploumanach 84 B1
Plouray 84 B2
Plovdiv 140 B3
Plozevet 84 A2
Plumelec 85 C3
Plumlov 94 B1
Plumpton 57 C3, 60 B1
Plungê 73 C2
Pluvigner 85 B/C3
Plužina 135 C3
Plužine 133 C3, 137 C1
Plymouth 63 B/C3
Plzeň 83 C3
Plzeň 96 A2
Pniewy 72 B3
Pniewy 71 D2
Pobar 153 D2
Poběžovice 82 B3, 92 B1
Pobla de Claramunt
  155 D3, 156 A3, 163 D1
Pobla del Duc 169 D2
Pobla de Segur 155 D2
Pobladura del Valle 151 D3
Poblete 167 C2
Poboleda 163 C/D1

Pobrdje 133 D3, 134 A3,
  138 A1
Počátky 94 A1
Počep 99 D1
Pöchlarn 94 A2
Počinok 75 C3
Počitelj 132 A/B3, 136 B1
Pockau 83 C2
Pocking 93 C2
Pöcking 92 A3
Pocklington 61 C/D2
Poco do Inferno 158 B2/3
Poćuta 133 C/D2, 134 A2
Podberez'je 75 B/C2
Podbořanský Rohozec
  83 C2/3
Podbořany 83 C2/3
Podborove 75 C/D1
Podbro 126 B2
Podčetrtek 127 C2
Poděbrady 83 D3
Poděbrady 96 A2
Podence 151 C3, 159 C1
Podensac 108 B1
Podersdorf am See 94 B3
Podgajci Posavski 133 C1
Podgajcy 97 D2, 98 B3
Podgaje 71 D1
Podgora 131 D3, 132 A3,
  136 B1
Podgorač 128 B3
Podgorac 135 C2/3
Podgorić 128 A3
Podgorica 127 B/C2
Podgorje 126 B3
Podgrab 133 B/C3
Podgrad 126 B3
Podhum 131 D3, 132 A3
Podivín 94 B1/2
Podkoren 126 B2
Podkova 145 C1
Podlapača 131 C1
Podlugovi 132 B2
Podnanos 126 B3
Podnovlje 132 B1
Podochórion 144 B1
Podol'sk 75 D3
Podpeč 126 B2/3
Podrašnica 131 D2, 132 A2
Podravska Moslavina
  128 B3
Podravska Slatina 128 B3
Podravske Sesvete 128 A2
Podromanija 133 B/C2
Podsreda 127 C2
Podsused 127 D3
Podturen 127 D2
Podujevo 138 B1
Podujevo 140 A3
Podvelež 132 B3
Podvinje 132 B1
Podvoločisk 98 B3
Podvrška 135 C2
Pogar 132 B2
Poggiardo 121 D3
Poggibonsi 114 B3,
  116 B2
Póggio a Caiano 114 B2,
  116 A/B1
Poggiodomo 117 C3,
  118 B1
Póggio Mirteto 117 C3,
  118 B1
Póggio Moiano 118 B1
Póggio Renático 115 B/C1
Póggio Rusco 114 B1
Póggio Valleversa 113 C1
Pöggstall 94 A2
Pogny 88 B1
Pogonianí 142 B2
Pogorzela 71 D3
Pogradec 142 B1
Pogradec 148 A1
Pohja 25 C1
Pohja 21 D2, 22 A2
Pohjälahti 18 B1
Pohjalahti 25 C1
Pohja-Lankila 27 C1
Pohjankylä 24 B3
Pohjansaha 24 A1
Pohja/Pojo 25 B/C3
Pohjasenvaara 12 A2
Pohjaslahti 21 C3
Pohjois-Ii 18 A2
Pohjoislahti 21 C3
Pohjoisranta 18 A1/2
Pohjola 25 D1, 26 A1

Pohořelice **94** B1
Pohořelice **96** B2
Pohoří na Šumavě **93** D2
Pohtimolampi **12** A3
Poiana Mare **135** D2/3
Poiana Teiului **141** C1
Poiares **158** A3
Poijula **19** C2
Poikajärvi **12** A/B3
Poikelus **25** C1
Poikko **24** A2/3
Poikmetsä **25** C/D2, **26** A2
Point Sublime **110** B2
Poio **150** A2
Poirino **113** C1
Poisieuy **102** A1
Poissy **87** C1
Poitiers **101** C1/2
Poix **77** D3
Poix-Terron **79** B/C3
Pojan **142** A1/2
Pojanluoma **20** B2/3
Pojate **134** B3
Pokka **11** D2, **12** B1
Pokkola **24** B2
Pokljuka **126** B2
Pokupsko **127** D3
Pol **151** C1
Pola **75** C1/2
Polače **136** B1
Pola de Allande **151** C1
Pola de Somiedo **151** D1
Połajewo **71** D2
Poláky **83** C2
Polán **160** B3, **167** C1
Polari **130** A1
Polch **80** A2
Połczyn-Zdrój **71** C1
Połczyn-Zdrój **72** B2/3
Poleñino **154** B3
Polesella **115** C1
Polessk (Labiau) **73** C2
Polesskoe **99** C2
Polgár **97** C3
Polgárdi **96** B3
Polgárdi **128** B1
Polhov Gradec **126** B2
Polia **122** A/B2
Poliani **146** B3
Poliçan **142** A2
Poliçani **142** B2
Poliçani **148** A1
Policastrello **122** A1
Police **70** B1
Políchnitos **149** C2
Policko **71** C2
Poličnik **130** B2
Policoro **121** C3
Polídendron **143** D2
Polígiros **144** A2
Polígiros **148** B1
Polignac **103** C3, **110** B1
Polignano a Mare **121** C2
Poligny **104** A1
Políkastron **143** D1
Políkastron **148** B1
Polístena **122** A3
Politiká **147** D1/2
Polizzi Generosa **124** B2
Pölja **22** B2
Poljak **130** B2
Poljana **134** B2
Poljana **127** C2
Poljana **128** A3
Poljanak **131** C1
Poljane Gorenja Vás **126** B2
Poljčane **127** C2
Polje **132** B1
Poljica **136** A1
Poljice **132** B2
Poljice Popovo **137** C1
Polla **120** A2/3
Pölläkkä **22** B3
Pölläkkä **23** C3
Pöllau **94** A3, **127** D1
Polle **68** B3
Polleben **82** A1
Pollença **157** C2
Pollenfeld **92** A1
Pollenzo **113** C1
Pollfoss **32** B3, **37** C1
Pollhagen **68** A2/3
Póllica **120** A3
Polling **92** B2
Polling **92** A3
Pollos **160** A1
Pöllwitz **82** B2

Polmak (Pulmanki) **7** B/C2
Polná **94** A1
Polne **71** D1
Polock **74** B3
Polonkylä **19** D1/2
Polonnoe **99** B/C2
Polopos **173** C2
Polperro **62** B3
Polruan **62** B3
Polsingen-Döckingen **91** D1
Polski Gradec **141** C3
Polski Trâmbeš **141** C3
Polso **21** C2
Pöls ob Judenburg **126** B1
Põltsamaa **74** A1
Polttila **24** A2
Polusperä **18** A3
Polvela **23** C2
Polvenkylä **20** B3
Polverigi **115** D3, **117** D2
Polvijärvi **23** C2
Polviniemi **19** C2
Polz **69** C2
Polzela **127** C2
Pomar **155** C3, **163** C1
Pomarance **114** B3, **116** A2
Pomarão **170** A2
Pomarez **108** A/B2/3, **154** B1
Pomárico **120** B2/3
Pomarkku (Påmark) **24** A/B1
Pomáz **95** D3
Pombal **158** A3, **164** B1
Pomer **154** A3, **161** D1, **162** A1
Pomézia **118** B2
Pomezí nad Ohří **82** B3
Pomigliano d'Arco **119** D3
Pömiö **18** A1
Pommersfelden **81** D3
Pomorie **141** C3
Pomošnaja **99** D3
Pomoy **89** C/D3
Pompei **119** D3
Pompei Scavi **119** D3
Pompignan **110** B2
Pomposa **115** C1
Pomssen **82** B1
Poncé-sur-le-Loir **86** B3
Poncin **103** D2
Pondisménon **139** D3, **144** A1
Pondokeraséa **139** D3, **144** A1
Ponferrada **151** C2
Poniec **71** D3
Ponikovica **133** D2, **134** A2/3
Pons **100** B3
Ponsa **25** C1
Ponsacco **114** B3, **116** A2
Ponso **107** C3
Pont **104** B3
Pontaco **108** B3, **155** C1
Pontailler-sur-Saône **89** C3, **104** A1
Pont-à-Marcq **78** A2
Pont-à-Mousson **89** C1
Pontão **158** A3, **164** B1
Pontardawe **63** C1
Pontarion **102** A2
Pontarlier **104** A/B1
Pontassieve **115** B/C2, **116** B1/2
Pontaubault **86** A/B2
Pont-Audemer **77** C3, **86** B1
Pontaumur **102** B2
Pont-Authou **77** C3, **86** B1
Pont-Aven **84** B2/3
Pontavert **78** B3
Pont Canavese **105** C3
Pont-Carral **108** B1
Pontcharra **104** A3
Pontchâteau **85** C3
Pont-Croix **84** A2
Pont-d'Ain **103** D2
Pont d'Arc **111** C2
Pont-de-Dore **102** B2/3
Pont-de-Labeaume **111** C1
Pont-de-la-Maye **108** B1
Pont-de-l'Arche **76** B3, **86** B1
Pont-de-l'Isère **111** C1
Pont de Molins **156** B2

Pont-de-Pany **88** B3
Pont-de-Rhodes **109** D1
Pont-de-Roide **89** D3, **104** B1
Pont-de-Salars **110** A2
Pont d'Espagne **155** C2
Pont de Suert **155** C2
Pont de Tréboul **110** A1
Pont-de-Vaux **103** D2
Pont-de-Veyle **103** D2
Pont-d'Ouilly **86** A1
Pont-du-Château **102** B2/3
Pont-du-Gard **111** C2
Pont-du-Loup **112** B3
Pont du Roi **155** C2
Ponte **105** C/D2
Ponte a Elsa **114** B2/3, **116** A2
Ponte a Moriano **114** A/B2, **116** A1
Ponte Arche **106** B2
Ponteareas **150** A3
Pontebba **126** A2
Ponte Cáffaro **106** B3
Pontecagnano **119** D3, **120** A2
Ponte-Caldelas **150** A2
Ponte Castirla **113** D3
Ponteceno di sopra **113** D1, **114** A1
Ponte-Ceso **150** A1
Pontecesures **150** A2
Pontecorvo **119** C2
Ponte da Barca **150** A3, **158** A1
Pontedássio **113** C2
Ponte de Lima **150** A3, **158** A1
Ponte dell'Ólio **113** D1, **114** A1
Pontedera **114** B2/3, **116** A2
Ponte de Sor **164** B1/2
Pontedeume **150** B1
Pontedeva **150** A3
Ponte di Barbarano **107** C3
Ponte di Ferro **117** C3
Ponte di Legno **106** B2
Ponte di Nava **113** C2
Ponte di Piave **107** D3
Pontefract **61** D2
Pontegrande **105** C2
Pontelagoscuro **115** C1
Ponteland **57** D3, **61** C1
Pontelandolfo **119** D2/3
Ponte Leccia **113** D2/3
Pontelongo **107** C3
Ponte Nelle Alpi **107** D2
Ponte Nossa **106** A2/3
Pont-en-Royans **103** D3, **111** D1
Ponte-Nuovo **113** D2/3
Pontenure **114** A1
Pontenx-les-Forges **108** A2
Pontepetri **114** B2, **116** A1
Ponterwyd **59** C3
Pontes **158** A3, **164** B1
Ponte Sampaio **150** A2
Ponte San Nicolò **107** C3
Ponte San Pietro **106** A3
Pontesbury **59** C3
Pont-et-Massène **88** B3
Ponte Tresa **105** D2
Pontevedra **150** A2
Pontével **164** A2
Pontevico **106** B1
Pont-Farcy **85** D1, **86** A1
Pontfaverger-Moronvilliers **88** B3
Pontgibaud **102** B2/3
Pont-Hébert **76** B3, **86** A/B1
Ponthierry **87** D2
Ponticino **115** C3, **116** B2
Pontigny **88** A2/3
Pontijou **86** A/B3
Pontínia **118** B2
Pontinvrea **113** C2
Pöntiö **21** C1
Pontivy **85** B/C2
Pont-l'Abbé **84** A2/3
Pont, Le **104** A/B1/2
Pont-l'Evêque **76** B3, **86** B1
Pontlevoy **86** A/B3
Pontoise **87** C1

Ponton **106** B3
Pontones **168** A3
Pontons **155** D3, **156** A3, **163** D1
Pontonx-sur-l'Adour **108** A2
Pontorson **85** D2
Pontrémoli **114** A2
Pontresina **106** A2
Pontrhydfendigaid **59** C3
Pontrieux **84** B1/2
Pontrilas **63** D1
Ponts **155** C3
Pont-Sainte-Maxence **87** D1
Pont-Saint-Esprit **111** C2
Pont-Saint-Martin **105** C3
Pont-Saint-Pierre **76** B3, **86** A/B1
Ponts-de-Martel, Les **104** B1
Ponts-de-Sains **78** B3
Pöntsö **11** D3, **12** A1
Pöntsönlahti **23** C/D3
Pont-sur-Yonne **87** D2, **88** A2
Pontvallain **86** B3
Pontypool **63** C1
Pontypridd **63** C1
Ponza **118** B3
Ponzone **113** C1/2
Poola **20** A/B2
Poole **63** D2/3, **76** A1
Popel'n'a **99** C2
Poperinge **78** A2
Pópoli **119** C1
Popovac **134** B2/3
Popovača **127** C2
Popova Šapka **138** B2
Popovica **135** C2
Popovica **140** B3
Popovo **141** C3
Popowo Kościelne **71** D2
Poppel **79** C1
Poppenhausen **81** D3
Poppenhausen **81** C2
Poppi **115** C2, **116** B2
Poprad **97** C2
Poreč **126** A/B3, **130** A1
Poreč'je **75** D2/3
Porhov **74** B2
Pori (Björneborg) **24** A1
Poříčí nad Sázavou **83** D3
Porjus **16** A/B1
Pörkenäs **20** B1
Porkkakylät **21** D3
Porkkala **25** C3
Pörknäs **20** B1
Porla **46** A1
Porlammi **25** D2, **26** A3
Porlezza **105** D2, **106** A2
Porlock **63** C2
Pornainen **25** D2/3, **26** A2/3
Pornássio **113** C2
Pörnbach **92** A2
Pornic **85** C3, **100** A1
Pornichet **85** C3, **100** A1
Pornóapáti **127** D1
Porokylä **23** C1
Pörölänmäki **22** B3
Póros **147** D3
Porozina **130** A1
Porras **25** C2
Porraskoski **25** C/D1/2, **26** A1/2
Porrassalmi **26** B1
Porrentruy **89** D3, **90** A3
Porreres **157** C2
Porretta Terme **114** B2, **116** A/B1
Porriño **150** A3
Porsangmoen **5** D2, **6** A2
Pörsänmäki **22** B2
Porsgrunn **43** D2, **44** A1
Porsgrunn-Brevik **43** D2, **44** A1/2

Porsgrunn-Eidanger **43** D2, **44** A1
Porsgrunn-Heistad **43** D2, **44** A1/2
Porsifors **16** B2
Porspoder **84** A2
Portadown **58** A1
Portadown **54** A3, **55** D2
Portaferry **54** A3, **55** D2
Portaferry **58** A1
Portaje **159** C3, **165** D1
Portalegre **165** C1/2
Portalrubio de Guadamajud **161** D3
Portalrubio **162** A/B2
Portals Vells **157** C2
Port Appin **56** A1
Portariá **143** D3, **144** A3
Portás **150** A2
Port Askaig **56** A2
Port Askaig **54** A2/3, **55** D1
Porta Westfalica-Barkhausen **68** A3
Portbail **76** A3, **85** D1
Port Barcarès **156** B1
Portbou **156** B2
Port Camargue **111** C3
Port Carlisle **57** C3, **60** A/B1
Port d'Agres **110** A1
Port-de-Bouc **111** C3
Port-de-la-Meule **100** A1
Port-de-Lanne **108** B3, **155** C1
Port-de-Piles **101** C1
Port de San Miguel **157** D3
Port Dinorwic **59** B/C2, **60** A3
Porté **156** A2
Porte de la Creu **157** D3
Portel **165** C3
Portel-des-Corbières **110** A3, **156** B1
Portell de Morella **162** B2
Port Ellen **56** A2
Port Ellen **54** A3, **55** D1
Port-en-Bessin **76** B3, **86** A1
Port'Ércole **116** B3
Port Erin **58** B1
Port Erin **54** A3, **55** D2
Portese **106** B3
Portet-d'Aspet **109** C3, **155** C/D1/2
Portets **108** B2
Port-Eynon **62** B1
Portezuelo **159** C3, **165** D1
Port Glasgow **56** B2
Port-Grimaud **112** A3
Porthcawl **62** C1/2
Porthleven **62** A/B3
Porth Mellin **62** A/B3
Porticcio **113** D3
Pórtici **119** D3
Pórtico di Romagna **115** C2, **116** B1
Portile de fier (Eisernes Tor) **135** C1/2
Portilla de la Reina **111** C3
Portillo **160** B3
Portimão **170** A2
Portimo **18** A1
Portimojärvi **17** D2
Portinatx **157** D3
Portinho da Arabida **164** A2/3
Portishead **63** D1/2
Port-Joinville **100** A1
Port Lamont **56** A/B2
Port-la-Nouvelle **110** A/B3, **156** B1
Port Laoise **55** D3
Port-Leucate **156** B1
Port Logan **56** A/B3
Port-Louis **84** B3
Portmadoc **59** C2/3, **60** A3
Portman **174** B1
Portmarnock **58** A2
Portnacroish **56** A1
Portnaguran **54** A1
Portnahaven **54** A3, **55** D1
Port Navalo **85** C3
Porto **113** D3
Porto **151** C3
Porto **158** A1/2
Porto Azzurro **116** A3
Porto Botte **123** C3

Portobuffolè **107** D2/3
Pórto Cárras **144** B2
Porto Cerésio **105** D2/3
Porto Cervo **123** D1
Porto Cesáreo **121** D3
Pórto Chéli **147** C3
Porto-Colom **157** C1/2
Porto Conte **123** C2
Porto Covo **164** A3,
 170 A1
Porto Cristo **157** C1
Porto d'Áscoli **117** D2/3
Porto de Lagos **170** A2
Porto de Mós **164** A1
Porto di Brenzone **106** B3
Porto do Son **150** A2
Porto Empédocle **124** B3
Portoferráio **116** A3
Portofino **113** D2
Port of Menteith **56** B1
Port of Ness **54** A1
Porto Garibaldi **115** C1
Portogruaro **107** D3,
 126 A3
Pórto Lágo **145** C1
Porto Levante **115** C1
Porto Levante **125** C/D1
Portomaggiore **115** C1
Porto Mantovano **106** B3
Portomarín **150** B2
Porto Maurízio **113** C2
Portomouro **150** A2
Pörtom (Pirttikylä) **20** A2/3
Portonovo **150** A2
Porto Palma **123** C3
Porto Palo **124** A2
Portopalo **125** D3
Porto Petro **157** D2
Porto-Pollo **113** D3
Porto Potenza Picena
 117 D2, **130** A3
Pórto Ráfti **147** D2
Porto Recanati **117** D2,
 130 A3
Portorož **126** A/B3
Porto San Giórgio **117** D2,
 130 A3
Porto Sant'Elpídio **117** D2,
 130 A3
Porto Santo Stéfano
 116 B3
Portoscuso **123** C3
Porto Tolle **115** C1
Porto Tórres **123** C1
Porto-Vecchio **113** D3
Portovénere **114** A2
Portovesme **123** C3
Portpatrick **56** A3
Portree **54** A2
Port-Sainte-Marie **109** C2
Port-Saint-Louis-du-Rhône
 111 C3
Port Saint Mary **58** B1
Port-Saint-Père **85** D3,
 100 A1
Pörtschach am Wörther See
 126 B2
Portsmouth **76** A1
Port Soderick **58** B1
Portsonachan **56** A1
Port-sur-Saône **89** C3
Port Talbot **63** C1
Porttikoski **12** B2
Portugalete **153** C1
Portumna **55** C3
Portunhos **158** A3
Port-Vendres **156** B2
Port William **56** B3
Porvoo/Borgå **25** D3,
 26 A3
Porzuna **167** C2
Posada **152** A1
Posada **123** D1/2
Posada de Valdeón **152** A1
Posadas **166** B3, **172** A1
Posav Bregi **127** D3
Poschiavo **106** B2
Posedarje **131** B/C2
Poseidón **147** D3
Poshnjë **142** A1
Pósina **107** C3
Posio **19** C1
Positano **119** D3
Possagno **107** C3
Possåsen **38** B2
Possendorf **83** C2
Pössneck **82** A2

Posta **117** D3, **118** B1
Póstal **107** C2
Posta Piana **120** B2
Postau **92** B2
Postavy **74** A3
Postbauer-Heng **92** A1
Postiglione **120** A2/3
Postioma **107** D3
Postira **131** D3
Post-mawr **62** B1
Postneset **6** B1
Postojna **126** B3
Postojnska Jama **126** B3
Postoloprty **83** C2
Postřižín **83** D2
Posušje **131** D3, **132** A3
Poteaux **79** D2
Potenza **120** B2
Potenza Picena **117** D2,
 130 A3
Potes **152** B1
Potka **4** B3
Potkraj **131** D3, **132** A3
Potoci **131** D2
Potok **127** D3
Potós **145** C2
Potries **169** D2
Potsdam **70** A2/3
Potsdam **72** A3
Pottendorf **94** B3
Pottenstein **94** A3
Pottenstein **82** A3
Pöttmes **92** A2
Potton **65** B/C2
Potůčky **82** B2
Pouancé **86** A3
Pouan-les-Vallées **88** A/B2
Pougny **104** A2
Pougues-les-Eaux **102** B1
Pouillé **100** B2
Pouilley-les-Vignes **89** C3,
 104 A1
Pouillon **108** A3, **154** B1
Pouilly-en-Auxois **88** B3,
 103 C1
Pouilly-sous-Charlieu
 103 C2
Pouilly-sur-Loire **87** D3,
 102 B1
Pouilly-sur-Saône **103** D1
Poulaines **87** C3, **101** D1,
 102 A1
Pouldreuzic **84** A2
Poule-lès-Écharmeaux
 103 C2
Poúlithra **147** C3
Poullaouen **84** B2
Poulton-le-Fylde **59** C/D1,
 60 B2
Pourcieux **111** D3, **112** A3
Pourión **144** A3
Pourrain **88** A3
Pouru **21** C3
Pousa Flores **158** A3,
 164 B1
Poussu **19** D1
Pouttula **20** B2
Pouxeux **89** D2
Pouyastruc **109** B/C3,
 155 C1
Pouy-de-Touges **109** C3,
 155 D1
Pouzauges **100** B1
Pouzilhac **111** C2
Považská Bystrica **95** D1
Považská Bystrica **96** B2
Poveda de la Sierra **161** D2
Povíglio **114** B1
Povino Polje **133** C3,
 137 D1
Povlja **131** D3, **132** A3
Povljana **130** B2
Povoa **96** B3
Póvoa de Lanhoso **150** B3,
 158 A1
Póvoa de Santo Adrião
 164 A2
Póvoa de Varzim **158** A1
Póvoa e Meadas **165** C1
Powalice **71** C1
Powerscourt Gardens
 58 A2
Poyatos **161** D2
Pöylä **24** B3
Pöyry **26** B1
Poysdorf **94** B2
Pöytä **24** B2

Poza de la Sal **153** C2
Poza de la Vega **152** A/B2
Pozal de Gallinas **160** A1
Pozaldez **160** A1
Pozalmuro **153** D3, **161** D1
Pozán de Vero **155** C3
Pozdeň **83** C2
Požega **133** D2/3,
 134 A2/3
Požega **140** A2
Pożeranje **138** B2
Poznań **71** D2/3
Poznań **72** B3
Pozo Alcón **173** D1
Pozoamargo **168** B1
Pozoantiguo **152** A3,
 159 D1, **160** A1
Pozoblanco **166** B3
Pozo-Cañada **168** B2
Pozo de Guadalajara
 161 C2
Pozo de la Serna **167** D2,
 168 A2
Pozohondo **168** B2
Pozo-Lorente **169** B/C2
Pozondón **162** A2
Pozořice **94** B1
Pozorrubio **161** C3,
 167 D1, **168** A1
Pozos de Hinojo **159** C2
Pózrzadło **71** C3
Pozuel de Ariza **161** D1
Pozuel del Campo **162** A2
Pozuelo **168** B2
Pozuelo de Aragón **154** A3,
 162 A1
Pozuelo de Alarcón **160** B2
Pozuelo de Calatrava
 167 C2
Pozuelo de la Orden
 152 A3, **160** A1
Pozuelo del Rey **161** C2/3
Pozuelo de Zarzón **159** C3
Pozuelos de Calatrava
 167 C2
Pozza di Fassa **107** C2
Poźżadło Wielke **71** C1
Pozzallo **125** C3
Pozzolengo **106** B3
Pozzomaggiore **123** C2
Pozzo San Nicola **123** C1
Pozzuoli **119** C3
Pozzuolo **115** C3, **116** B2
Prača **133** B/C3
Prachatice **93** C1
Prachatice **96** A2
Pracht **80** A/B2
Prackenbach **92** B1
Prada **151** C2
Prádanos de Ojeda **152** B2
Pradejón **153** D2
Pradell de la Teixeta
 163 C/D1/2
Pradelles **110** B1
Prades **163** D1
Prades **156** A/B1/2
Prades-le-Lez **110** B2
Pradiéls **126** A2
Pradilla de Ebro **155** C3
Pradillo **153** D3
Pradléves **112** B2
Prado del Rey **171** D2,
 172 A2
Pradoluengo **153** C2
Prados Redondos **162** A2
Pragelato **112** B1
Pragersko **127** C/D2
Prägraten **107** D1
Praha **83** D1
Praha **96** A2
Prahecq **101** B/C2
Prahovo **135** C2
Práia a Mare **120** B3,
 122 A1
Praia da Rocha **170** A2
Praia de Mira **158** A2
Praia de Vieira **158** A3,
 164 A1
Praia do Areia Branca
 164 A1/2
Praia do Guincho **164** A2
Praia Grande **164** A2
Pralboino **106** B3
Pralognan-la-Vanoise
 104 B3

Pra Loup **112** A2
Prámanda **142** B3
Prameny **82** B3
Pranjani **133** D2, **134** A2
Prapatnica **131** C3
Praranger **104** B3
Praraye **105** C2/3
Prasiá **146** A/B1
Prášily **93** C1
Prästkulla **24** B3
Prästö **41** D3
Praesto **53** D2
Praestø **72** A2
Pratau **69** D3
Prat de Comte **163** C2
Pratdip **163** C/D2
Prat-et-Bonrepaux **109** C3,
 155 D1
Prati di Tivo **117** D3,
 119 C1
Pratjau **53** C3
Prato **114** B2, **116** B1
Prato all'Isarco/Blumau
 107 C2
Prato Cárnico **107** D2,
 126 A2
Prato della Résia **126** A2
Prátola **119** D3, **120** A2
Prátola Peligna **119** C1/2
Pratolino **114** B2, **116** B1
Pratomagno/Prastmann
 107 C/D1
Prato Nevoso **113** C2
Prats de Lluçanès **156** A2
Prats-de-Mollo-la-Preste
 156 B2
Prauthoy **89** C3
Pravdinsk (Friedland)
 73 C2
Pravia **151** D1
Prazzo **112** B2
Prebl **127** C1
Přebuz **82** B2
Préchac **108** B2
Prechtal **90** B2
Précigné **86** A3
Přečistoe **75** C3
Précy-sous-Thil **88** B3
Predáppio **115** C2,
 117 B/C1
Predazzo **107** C2
Preddvor **126** B2
Predeal **141** C2
Predejane **139** C1
Predešti **135** D2
Predgrad **127** C3
Předín **94** A1
Preding **127** C1
Predlitz **126** B1
Predlitz **96** A3
Predmier **95** D1
Přední Výtoň. **93** C/D2
Predolje **137** C1
Predosa **113** C1
Predošćca **130** A1
Pré-en-Pail **86** A2
Preetz **53** C2
Préfailles **85** C3, **100** A1
Pregarten **93** D2
Pregarten **96** A2
Pregnana **105** D3
Pregrada **127** D2
Preignac **108** B1
Preili **74** A2
Preixens **155** D3, **163** D1
Préjano **153** D3
Prekaja **131** C/D2
Preko **130** B2
Prekonoška Pećina **135** C3
Preljina **133** D2, **134** A2/3
Prelog **127** D2
Premana **105** D2, **106** A2
Premantura **130** A1
Premeno **105** D2
Prémery **88** A3, **102** B1
Premià de Mar **156** A/B3
Premnitz **69** D2
Prémontré **78** A3
Premuda **130** B2
Prenčov **95** D2
Prenjas **138** A3, **142** B1
Prenzlau **70** B1
Prenzlau **72** A3
Přerov **96** B2
Přerov **95** C1
Pré-Saint-Didier **104** B3
Prescot **59** D2, **60** B3

Prese, Le **106** B2
Preševo **139** B/C2
Presicce **121** D3
Presjeka **137** C1
Preslav **141** C3
Prešov **97** C3
Prespa **128** A3
Pressac **101** C2
Pressath **82** A/B3
Pressath-Hessenreuth
 82 A/B3
Pressbaum **94** A2
Presseck **82** A2/3
Pressel **82** B1
Pressig **82** A2
Prestatyn **59** C2, **60** A3
Presteigne **59** C/D3
Prestesetra **29** C2
Přeštice **83** C3, **93** C1
Přeštice **96** A3
Preston **59** D1/2, **60** B2
Prestwick **56** B2
Pretor **142** B1
Pretoro **119** C1
Prettin **70** A3, **82** B1
Pretzier **69** C2
Pretzsch **70** A3
Pretzschendorf **83** C2
Preuilly-sur-Claise **101** D1
Preussisch-Oldendorf-
 Holzhausen **68** A3
Preussisch-Oldendorf
 68 A3
Preusslitz **69** D3
Prévenchères **110** B1
Préveranges **102** A2
Préveza **146** A1
Préveza **148** A2
Prezelle **69** C2
Prezid **126** B3
Prez-vers-Noréaz [Rosé]
 104 B1
Prgomet **131** C3
Priaranza del Bierzo **151** C2
Priay **103** D2
Pribeta **95** C/D3
Priboj **133** C3
Priboj **139** C1
Priboj **133** C1/2
Príbovce **95** D1
Příbram **83** C3
Příbram **96** A2
Prichsenstadt **81** D3
Prichsenstadt-Neuses
 81 D3
Pričinović **133** C1, **134** A1
Pridvorci **132** B3
Pridvorica **133** D3, **134** A3
Pridvorica **138** B1
Priego **161** D2
Priego de Córdoba
 172 B1/2
Priekopa **95** D1
Priekule **73** C1
Prienai **73** D2
Prien am Chiemsee **92** B3
Prieros **70** A/B3
Priestewitz **83** C1
Prievidza **95** D2
Prievidza **96** B2
Prignano Cilento **120** A3
Prigradica **136** A1
Prigrevica **129** C3
Prijeboj **131** C1
Prijedor **131** D1
Prijepolje **133** C3
Prilep **138** B3, **143** C1
Prilike **133** D3, **134** A3
Priluka **131** D3, **132** A2
Priluki **99** D2
Přimda **82** B3
Primel-Trégastel **84** B1
Primišlje **127** C3, **131** B/C1
Primolano **107** C2
Primorsko **141** C3
Primošten **131** C3
Princetown **63** C3
Prinsehytta **37** C/D2
Prinzersdorf **94** A2
Príolo Gargallo **125** D3
Prioro **152** A2
Prisad **139** B/C3, **143** C1
Přísečnice **83** C2
Prisjan **139** C1
Prismala **20** B2
Prisoje **131** D3, **132** A3
Prissac **101** C2

Priština **138** B1
Priština **140** A3
Prittriching **91** D2
Pritzerbe **69** D2
Pritzier **69** C1
Pritzwalk **69** D1/2
Privas **111** C1
Priverno **118** B2
Privlaka **130** B2
Privlaka **133** C1
Prizren **138** B2
Prizren **140** A3
Prizzi **124** B2
Prnjavor **132** A/B1
Prnjavor **133** C1
Probištip **139** C2
Probstzella **82** A2
Prócchio **116** A3
Prócida **119** C3
Prodo **117** C3, **118** A/B1
Pródromos **143** D1
Pródromos **146** A1
Pródromos **147** C2
Proença a Nova **158** B3, **164** B1
Proença-a-Velha **158** B3
Proevska Banja **139** C2
Profítis **144** A2
Prohor Pčinjski **139** C2
Prokópion **147** D1
Prokuplje **135** B/C3, **139** B/C1
Prokuplje **140** A3
Prolom **138** B1
Prómachi **143** C1
Promachón **139** D3, **144** A1
Promajna **131** D3, **132** A3
Promírion **147** C/D1
Promona **131** C2
Pronstorf **53** C3
Propiac-les-Bains **111** D2
Propriano **113** D3
Prosek **138** A3
Prosigk **69** D3, **82** B1
Prosiměřice **94** A/B1
Proskinás **147** C1
Prosotsáni (Pirsópolis) **144** B1
Prosotsáni (Pirsópolis) **149** B/C1
Prossedi **119** B/C2
Prosselsheim **81** D3
Prostějov **94** B1
Prostějov **96** B2
Protići **131** D2, **132** A2
Protivanov **94** B1
Protivín **93** D1
Prottes **94** B2
Prötzel **70** B2
Prousós **146** B1
Provadija **141** C3
Provatón **145** D1, **145** D3
Provença **164** A3, **170** A1
Provenchères-lès-Darney **89** C2
Provenchères-sur-Fave **89** D2, **90** A2
Provés/Proveis **107** B/C2
Provins **88** A2
Provo **133** B3, **134** A1/2
Prozor **132** A2/3
Prozoroki **74** B3
Prudhoe **57** D3, **61** C1
Prudnik (Neustadt) **96** B2
Prulláns **155** D2, **156** A2
Prüm **79** D2
Prun **106** B3
Pruna **172** A2
Prunelli di-Fiumorbo **113** D3
Prunéřov **83** C2
Prunetta **114** B2, **116** A1
Prunişor **135** D2
Prusac **131** D2, **132** A2
Prušce **71** D2
Pruszków **73** C3, **97** C1
Prut **141** D1
Prutting **92** B3
Prutz **106** B1
Pružany **73** D3, **98** B1
Prüzen **53** D3, **69** D1
Pružina **95** D1
Przasnysz **73** C3
Przechlewo **71** D1
Przelewice **71** C2
Przemęt **71** D3

Przemocze **71** B/C1
Przemyśl **97** D2, **98** A2
Przewóz **83** D1
Pržno **137** C2
Przybiernów **70** B1
Przybychowo **71** D2
Przybymierz **71** C3
Przyłęg **71** C2
Przytoczna **71** C2
Psača **139** C2
Psachná **147** D1/2
Psárion **146** B3
Psárion **147** C2
Psathópirgos **146** B2
Pskov **74** B2
Pšov **83** C3
Pšovlky **83** C3
Pszczew **71** C2
Ptaszkowo **71** D3
Pteleós **147** C1
Ptéri **146** B2
Ptič' **99** C1/2
Ptoíon **147** C/D2
Ptolemaïs **143** C2
Ptolemaïs **148** B1
Ptuj **96** A3
Ptuj **127** D2
Ptujska Gora **127** D2
Puanunsuo **19** D1
Pucarevo **132** A2
Puchberg am Schneeberg **94** A3
Puchheim **92** A2
Púchov **95** C/D1
Púchov **96** B2
Pucioasa **141** C2
Pučišča **131** D3
Puck **72** B2
Puckeridge **65** C2
Pudarica **130** B1/2
Pudasjärvi Kurenalus **18** B2
Puddletown **63** D2
Puderbach (Neuwied) **80** A/B2
Puebla de Alcocer **166** B2
Puebla de Alfindén **154** B3, **162** B1
Puebla de Almenara **161** C3, **167** D1, **168** A1
Puebla de Albortón **162** B1
Puebla de Arenoso **162** B3
Puebla de Beleña **161** C2
Puebla de Benifasar **163** C2
Puebla de Brollón **151** B/C2
Puebla de Don Rodrigo **167** B/C2
Puebla de Don Fadrique **168** A3, **173** D1
Puebla de Eca **161** D1
Puebla de Guzmán **171** B/C1
Puebla de la Calzada **165** D2
Puebla de la Reina **165** D2, **166** A2
Puebla del Caramiñal **150** A2
Puebla de Lillo **152** A1/2
Puebla del Maestre **165** D3, **166** A3
Puebla del Príncipe **167** D2, **168** A2
Puebla del Prior **165** D2, · **166** A2
Puebla del Salvador **168** B1
Puebla de Obando **165** D2
Puebla de Parga **150** B1
Puebla de Sanabria **151** C3
Puebla de Sancho Pérez **165** D3
Puebla de Trives **151** C2
Puebla de Valles **160** B3
Puebla de Vallbona **169** C/D1
Puebla de Yeltes **159** D2
Pueblanueva **160** A3, **166** B1
Puebla San Miguel **163** C3
Puebla Tornesa **163** C3
Puéchabon **110** B2
Puendeluña **154** B2/3
Puente-Almuhey **152** A2
Puente de Domingo Flórez **151** C2
Puente de Génave **167** D3, **168** A3

Puente de la Reina **154** A2
Puente del Congosto **159** D2
Puente de Montañana **155** C2/3
Puente Duero **152** A3, **160** A1
Puentedura **153** C3
Puente Genil **172** A/B1/2
Puentenansa **152** B1
Puente Nuevo **172** A2
Puente Romano **159** C3, **165** C/D1
Puentevea **150** A2
Puente-Viesgo **152** B1
Puerto Cabrera **157** D2
Puerto de Alcudia **157** C2
Puerto de Andratx **157** C2
Puerto de Burriana **163** C3, **169** D1
Puerto de Campos **157** D2
Puerto de Motril **173** C2
Puerto de Pollença **157** C2
Puerto de Santa Cruz **166** A1
Puerto de San Vicente **166** B1
Puerto de Sóller **157** C2
Puerto de Vega **151** C1
Puerto Lápice **167** D1
Puertollano **167** C2
Puerto Lumbreras **174** A1
Puertomingalvo **162** B3
Puerto Moral **165** D3, **171** C1
Puerto Real **171** D3
Puerto Serrano **171** D2, **172** A2
Puget-Théniers **112** B2
Puget-Ville **112** A3
Pugnac **100** B3, **108** B1
Puhos **23** D3
Puhos **19** C2
Puichéric **110** A3, **156** B1
Puig **169** D1
Puigcerdà **156** A2
Puigpuñent **157** C2
Puig-reig **156** A2
Puigverd de Lleida **155** C3, **163** C1
Puiseaux **87** C2
Puisieux **78** A2/3
Puisserguier **110** A/B3, **156** B1
Puivert **109** D3, **156** A1
Pujerra **172** A2/3
Pujols-sur-Dordogne **108** B1
Pukaro/Pockar **25** D2, **26** B2
Pukavik **51** C2
Pukë **138** A2
Pukiš **133** C1
Pukkila **25** D2, **26** A2
Pula **130** A1
Pula **123** C/D3
Pulaj **137** D2/3
Puławy **97** C1, **98** A2
Pulborough **76** B1
Púlfero **126** A2
Pulgar **160** B3, **167** C1
Pulheim **79** D1/2, **80** A1/2
Pulheim-Sinnersdorf **79** D1, **80** A1/2
Pulheim-Stommeln **79** D1, **80** A1/2
Pulju **11** D2, **12** A1
Pulkau **94** A2
Pulkkaviita **13** C2
Pulkkila **18** B3
Pulkkila **25** D1/2, **26** A1/2
Pulkkinen **21** C2
Pulkonkoski **22** B2
Pullach **92** A2/3
Pullenreuth **82** A/B3
Pulliala **26** B1
Pulpí **174** A1
Pulsa **27** C2
Pulsano **121** C2
Pulsnitz **83** C1
Pułtusk **73** C3
Pułtusk **97** C1, **98** A2
Pulversheim **89** D3, **90** A3
Pumpsaint **63** C1
Punat **130** B1
Punkaharju **27** D1
Punkaharjun asema **27** D1

Punkalaidun **24** B2
Punkasalmi **27** D1
Punkka **26** B1
Punta Ala **116** A3
Punta Križa **130** A/B2
Punta Secca **125** C3
Punta Skala **130** B2
Punta Umbría **171** C2
Punt-Chamues-ch, La **106** A2
Punxín **150** B2
Puokio **19** C3
Puolakkavaara **12** B2
Puolanka **19** C2
Puolitaival **11** C2
Puoliväli **22** B2
Puoltikasvaara **10** B3
Puolusperä **18** A3
Puotila **24** A2
Puottaure **16** B2
Pupnatska Luka **136** A/B1
Puračić **132** B2
Puralankylä **21** D2, **22** A2
Puranuvaara **19** C1
Puras **19** D2
Purchena **173** D2
Pürgen-Stoffen **91** D3
Pürgg **93** C/D3
Purgstall **93** D2/3, **94** A2/3
Purkersdorf **94** A/B2
Purkijaur **16** A1
Purmerend **66** B2
Purmo **20** B1/2
Purmojärvi **21** B/C2
Purnumukka **12** B1
Purnuvaara **10** B3
Purontaka **21** C1
Purroy de la Solana **155** C3
Purujosa **154** A3, **162** A1
Purullena **173** C2
Puschwitz **83** D1
Puškin **74** B1
Puškinskie **74** B2
Püspökládány **97** C3, **140** A1
Pussay **87** C2
Pussemange **79** C3
Pusterwald **126** B1
Pustevny **95** C/D1
Pustoška **74** B2
Pusula **25** C2/3
Puszczykowo **71** D3
Pusztamagyaród **128** A2
Pusztamérges **129** C2/3
Pusztaszabolcs **129** C1
Pusztaszemes **128** B1/2
Pusztaszemes **128** B1/2
Pusztavám **95** C3, **128** B1
Putaja **24** B1
Putanges-Pont-Écrepin **86** A1
Puthossalo **23** D3
Putifígari **123** C2
Putignano **121** C2
Putikko **27** D1
Putivl' **99** D2
Putkela **23** D2/3
Putkilahti **25** D1, **26** A1
Putkivaara **18** B1
Putlitz **69** D1
Putna **98** B3
Putous **6** B2
Putte **78** B1
Puttelange-les-Farschwiller **89** D1, **90** A1
Putten **66** B3
Püttlingen **89** D1, **90** A1
Putula **25** D2, **26** A2
Putzu Idu **123** C2
Puukari **23** C1
Puukkoinen **25** D1, **26** A1
Puukkokumpu **18** A1
Puuluoto **17** D2/3, **18** A1
Puumala **27** C1
Puuppola **21** D3, **22** A3
Puutikkala **25** C1
Puutossalmi **22** B2/3
Puutteenperä **17** D3, **18** A1
Puydrouard **100** B2
Puy-Guillaume **102** B2
Puylagarde **109** D2
Puylaroque **109** D2
Puylaurens **109** D3
Puy-l'Évêque **108** B1
Puymiclan **109** C1
Puymirol **109** C2
Puyôo **108** A3, **154** B1
Puyravault **100** B2

Puzol **169** D1
Pwllheli **58** B3
Pwllheli **55** D3
Pyhäjärvi **12** B2/3
Pyhäjärvi **21** D1, **22** A1
Pyhäjärvi **6** A/B3, **11** D1
Pyhäjoki **24** B2
Pyhäjoki **18** A3
Pyhäkylä **19** C2
Pyhältö **26** B2
Pyhänkoski **18** A3
Pyhäntä **18** B3, **21** D1, **22** A1
Pyhäntä **19** C3
Pyhäntaka **25** D2, **26** A2
Pyhäportti **18** C3
Pyhäranta **24** A2, **41** D2
Pyhäsalmi **21** D1, **22** A1
Pyhäselkä **23** D3
Pyhra **94** A2
Pyhtää/Pyttis **26** B2/3
Pylähti **21** D2, **22** A2
Pyle **63** C1/2
Pylkönmäki **21** C3
Pylvänälä **22** A/B3
Pyntäinen **24** A/B1
Pyöli **24** B2
Pyöli **25** C3
Pyöree **22** B1
Pyörni **20** B2/3
Pyrbaum **92** A1
Pyrrönperä **21** D1, **22** A1
Pyrzyce **70** B1/2
Pyšely **83** D3
Pytalovo **74** B2
Pyttbua **32** B3, **37** C1
Pyydyskylä **21** D2/3, **22** A2/3
Pyykkölänvaara **19** C/D3
Pyyli **23** C3
Pyyrinlahti **21** D2, **22** A2/3

Q

Qeparoi **142** A2
Quadrazaes **159** C3
Quaglietta **120** A2
Quakenbrück **67** D2
Qualiano **119** C3
Quarré-les-Tombes **88** A3
Quart **105** B/C3
Quart d'Onyar **156** B2
Quarteira **170** A/B2
Quarto d'Altino **107** D3
Quartu Sant'Élena **123** D3
Quédillac **85** C2
Quedlinburg **69** C3
Queensferry **57** C1/2
Queijada **150** A3, **158** A1
Queipo **171** D2
Queis **82** B1
Quejo **153** C1
Quel **153** D2/3
Quelaines **86** A2
Quelfes **170** B2
Quellendorf **69** D3
Queluz **164** A2
Quemada **153** C3, **161** C1
Quend **77** D2
Quenstedt **69** C3, **82** A1
Queralbs **156** A2
Quercianella **114** A3, **116** A2
Querença **170** B2
Querfurt **82** A1
Quérigut **156** A1
Quero **167** D1, **168** A1
Querol **163** C1
Quéron **85** D1
Querschied **89** D1, **90** A1
Quesa **169** C2
Quesada **167** D3, **168** A3, **173** C1
Quesnoy-sur-Deûle **78** A2
Questembert **85** C3
Quettehou **76** B3
Quetzdölsdorf **82** B1
Queyrac **100** B3
Quiaios **158** A3
Quiberon **84** B3
Quiberville **77** C2/3
Quickborn **52** B3, **68** B1
Quiévrain **78** B2

Quiévrechain **78** B2
Quiliano **113** C2
Quillan **156** A1
Quillebeuf-sur-Seine **77** C3
Quimerch **84** A/B2
Quimper **84** A/B2
Quimperlé **84** B2/3
Quincoces de Yuso **153** C2
Quinéville **76** B3
Quingey **104** A1
Quinson **112** A3
Quinta do Anjo **164** A2
Quintana de la Serena **166** A2
Quintana del Puente **152** B3
Quintana del Marco **151** D3
Quintanaloranco **153** C2
Quintanapalla **153** C2
Quintanar de la Sierra **153** C3
Quintanar del Rey **168** B1
Quintanar de la Orden **167** D1, **168** A1
Quintana Redonda **153** D3, **161** D1
Quintanarraya **153** C3, **161** C1
Quintana y Congosto **151** D2/3
Quintanilha **151** C3, **159** C1
Quintanilla de Trigueros **152** B3
Quintanilla de Arriba **152** B3, **160** B1
Quintanilla de la Mata **153** B/C3
Quintanilla Sobresierra **153** C2
Quintanilla de las Torres **152** B2
Quintanilla de San García **153** C2
Quintanilla de Abajo **152** B3, **160** B1
Quintela de Leirado **150** B3
Quintin **85** C2
Quinto **162** B1
Quintos **165** C3, **170** B1
Quinzano d'Óglio **106** A/B3
Quiroga **151** C2
Quirra **123** D3
Quissac **111** B/C2
Quistello **114** B1
Qukës **138** A3, **142** B1
Qytet Stalin (Kuçovë) **142** A1
Qytet Stalin (Kuçovë) **148** A1

R

Raaattama **11** C2/3, **12** A1
Raab **93** C2
Raabs an der Thaya **94** A1/2
Raahe (Brahestad) **18** A3
Raajärvi **12** B3
Raakku **13** C3
Rääkkylä **23** C/D3
Raalte **67** C2
Raanujärvi **12** A3, **17** D1
Raappananmäki **19** C3
Raate **19** D2/3
Raattama **11** C2/3, **12** A1
Raatti **23** C2
Rab **130** B1/2
Rabac **130** A1
Rabacal **158** A3
Råbäck **45** D2
Rábade **150** B1
Rábafüzes **127** D1
Rábahidvég **128** A1
Rabanal del Camino **151** D2
Rabanera del Pinar **153** C3
Rábano **152** B3, **160** B1
Rábano de Sanabria **151** C3
Rabastens **109** D2
Rabastens-de-Bigorre **109** B/C3, **155** C1

Rabbalshede **44** B2
R'abcevo **75** C3
Rabenau **81** C2
Rabenstein **94** A2/3
Råberg **30** B1
Rabí **93** C1
Rąbino **71** C1
Rabiša **135** C/D3
Råbjerg Mile **44** A/B3, **49** C1
Rabka **97** C2
Rabrovo **134** B2
Rabrovo **139** C/D3, **143** D1
Rabštejn **94** A/B1
Rabuiese **126** B3
Råby-Rönö **47** C2
Rača **94** B2
Rača **134** B2
Rača **133** C2
Rača **138** B1
Rácale **121** D3
Racalmuto **124** B2
Răcari de Sus **135** D2
Răcăşdia **135** B/C1
Racconigi **113** C1
Rače **127** C/D2
Ráchai **147** C1
Rachecourt-sur-Marne **88** B2
Râches **78** A2
Racibórz (Ratibor) **96** B2
Racimierz **70** B1
Račinovci **133** C1
Račišče **136** A/B1
Račja vas **126** B3
Ráckeve **129** C1
Racksund **15** D2
Racot **71** D3
Råda **39** C3
Råda **45** C/D2
Rada de Haro **168** A1
Radalj **133** C2
Radanovići **137** C2
Rădăuți **98** B3
Radawnica **71** D1
Radcliffe **59** D2, **60** B2/3
Radda in Chianti **114** B3, **116** B2
Raddusa **125** C2
Råde **44** B1
Radeberg **83** C1
Radebeul **83** C1
Radeburg **83** C1
Radeče **127** C2
Radęcin **71** C2
Radehov **97** D1/2, **98** B2
Rådelsbråten **38** B2
Radenbeck (Gifhorn) **69** C2
Radenci **127** D2
Radenthein **126** B1
Radevormwald **80** A1
Radiče **139** C/D3
Radicófani **116** B3
Radicóndoli **114** B3, **116** A/B2
Radijovce **138** B2
Radimlije **132** B3, **136** B1
Radiumbad Brambach **82** B2/3
Radlje ob Dravi **127** C2
Radljevo **133** D2, **134** A2
Rådmansö **41** C3
Radmer an der Hasel **93** D3
Radmirje **127** C2
Radnevo **141** C2/3
Radnica **71** C2
Radnice **83** C3
Radoboj **127** D2
Radoinja **133** C/D3, **134** A3
Radolfzell **91** C3
Rådom **30** A3, **35** D2
Radom **97** C1
Radomir **139** D1/2
Radomsko **97** C1
Radomyšl' **99** C2
Radomyšl **93** C1
Radona **161** D1
Radonice **83** C2
Radošina **95** C2
Radošovce **95** B/C2
Radoszyce **97** C2, **98** A3
Radotín **83** D3
Radovesice **83** C2
Radovići **137** C2

Radoviš **139** C3
Radoviš **140** A/B3
Radovljica **126** B2
Radovnica **139** C2
Radowo Wielkie **71** C1
Radstadt **93** C3, **126** A1
Radstock **63** D2, **64** A3
Raduč **131** C2
Răducăneni **141** C/D1
Radujevac **135** D2
Radun' **73** D2, **74** A3
Raduša **138** B2
Radviliškis **73** D2
Radwanow **71** C3
Radzyń Podlaski **73** D3, **97** D1, **98** A1/2
Raesfeld **67** C3
Ráfales **163** C2
Raffadali **124** B2/3
Rafína **147** D2
Rafjord **7** C1
Rafnes **43** C2
Rafsbotn **5** C2
Raftsjöhöjden **29** D3, **34** B1
Ragazzola **114** A1
Rågeleje **49** D3, **50** A2
Rägelin **69** D2, **70** A2
Raggsjö **31** C1
Raggsteinhytta **37** C3
Raglan **63** D1
Raglicy **75** B/C1
Rágol **173** D2
Ragösen **69** D3
Ragow **70** B3
Rågsveden **39** C2
Raguhn **69** D3
Ragunda **30** A3, **35** C2
Ragusa **125** C3
Råhällan **40** A2
Rahden **68** A2
Rahikka **20** B3
Rahikkala **27** C1
Rahkonen **21** C1
Rahnlavaara **23** C2
Råholt **38** A3
Rahov **97** D2/3, **98** A3
Rahula **26** B1
Raiano **119** C1/2
Raijala **24** B2
Raikuu **23** C3
Räimä **22** B2
Rain **91** D2, **92** A2
Rainbach im Mühlkreis **93** D2
Rain-Bayerdilling **91** D2, **92** A2
Raippaluoto **20** A2, **31** D3
Raippo **27** C2
Rairiz de Veiga **150** B3
Räisälä **13** C3
Raisdorf **52** B3
Raisio (Reso) **24** B2/3
Raisjavrre **5** C3, **11** B/C1
Raiskio **18** B1
Raistimäki **21** D3, **22** A3
Raitapera **21** C2
Raitoo **25** C2
Raittijärvi **10** B1
Raiutula **6** B3
Rajac **133** D3, **134** A3
Rajadell **155** D3, **156** A3, **163** D1
Raja-Jooseppi **13** C1
Rajala **12** B2
Rajalahti **24** B3
Rajamäki **25** C2
Rajavartioasema **19** D1
Rajcza **95** D1
Rajë **138** A2
Rajec **95** D1
Rájec-Jestřebí **94** B1
Rajhrad **94** B1
Rajić **128** A3, **131** D1, **132** A1
Rajka **95** B/C3
Raka **127** C2/3
Rakalj **130** A1
Rakeie **38** B3
Rakek **126** B3
Rakicke **142** B1/2
Rakita **139** D1
Rakitnica **128** A2
Rakkestad **44** B1
Rakneset **14** A2
Rákos **129** D2
Rakov **74** A/B3

Raková **95** D1
Rakova Bara **135** C2
Rakovac **132** A1
Rakovica **131** C1
Rakovica **135** C3
Rakovník **83** C3
Rakovník **96** A2
Rakovski **140** B3
Råkvåg **28** A3, **33** C1
Rakvere **74** A1
Raldon **107** B/C3
Ralja **133** D1/2, **134** A/B2
Ralsko **83** D2
Ram **134** B1
Ramacastañas **160** A3
Ramacca **125** C2/3
Rämälä **26** B1
Ramales de la Victoria **153** C1
Ramalhal **164** A2
Ramanj **15** D1/2
Ramatuelle **112** A3
Ramberg **8** A2/3
Ramberg **90** B1
Rambervillers **89** D2
Rambo **31** C2
Rambouillet **87** C2
Rambucourt **89** C1
Ramerupt **88** B2
Rameški **75** D2
Ramin **70** B1
Ramirás **150** B3
Ramkvilla **51** C1
Ramlingen-Ehlershausen **68** B2
Rämmen **39** C3
Rammsjö **30** A3, **35** C2
Ramnäs **40** A3
Ramne **44** B2
Ramnous **147** D2
Rampillon **87** D2
Ramså **9** C1
Ramsau **92** B3
Ramsberg **39** D3
Ramsbottom **59** D2, **60** B2
Ramsele **30** A2/3, **35** C1
Ramsele **31** C2
Ramsen **80** B3, **90** B1
Ramsey **58** B1, **60** A1/2
Ramsey **65** C2
Ramsey **54** A/B3, **55** D2
Ramsgate **65** C3, **76** B1
Rämshyttan **39** D2/3
Rämshyttan-turist station **39** D2/3
Ramsjö **35** C3
Rämsöö **24** B1
Ramstadlandet **28** A/B1
Ramstein-Miesenbach **90** A1
Ramsund **9** C2
Ramsvik **8** B3
Ramundberget **34** A2
Ramvik **35** D2
Ramygala **73** D2, **74** A3
Råna **42** A3
Råna **9** C2
Råna **9** C3
Ranalt **107** C1
Rånäs **40** B3
Rånåsfoss **38** A3
Rance **78** B2
Ránchio **115** C2, **117** C1
Rancířov **94** A1
Randaberg ferjekai **42** A2
Randabygd **32** A3, **36** B1
Rändalen **34** A3
Randalsvollen **15** C2
Randan **102** B2
Randazzo **125** C/D2
Randbøl **48** B3, **52** B1
Randbøl Hede **48** B3, **52** B1
Randegg **93** D3
Randen **32** B3, **37** C/D1
Randers **48** B2
Randijaur **16** A1
Randín **150** B3
Randsfjord **38** A3
Randsundet **34** A3
Randsverk **37** C/D2
Rånea **17** C2
Ranemsletta **28** B2
Ranes **32** B2
Rånes **86** A2
Ranft **105** C1
Rangendingen **91** B/C2

Rangsby **20** A3
Rangsdorf **70** A3
Ranhados **158** B2
Ranheim **28** A3, **33** C1
Ranis **82** A2
Rankinen **18** A3
Rankovići **132** A/B2
Rankweil **106** A1
Rannankylä **21** D1, **22** A1
Ranna-Pungerja **74** B1
Rännelanda **45** C2
Rannoch Station **56** B1
Rannungen **81** D3
Ranovac **134** B2
Ransarstugan **14** B3, **29** D1
Ransäter **39** C3, **45** D1
Ransbach-Baumbach **80** B2
Ransjö **34** B3
Ranста **40** A3
Ranstadt **81** C2
Ranta **6** B3
Rantajärvi **17** D1
Rantakangas **21** C2
Rantakylä **26** B1
Rantala **26** B2
Rantasalmen asema **23** C3
Rantasalmi **23** C3
Rantsila **18** B3
Ranttila **5** D3, **6** A3, **11** D1
Rantum **52** A2
Rantzau **53** C3
Ranua **18** B1
Ranum **48** B2
Rånvassbotn **9** C2
Ranzo **113** C2
Rao **151** C2
Raon-l'Étape **89** D2, **90** A2
Rapakkojoki **22** B1
Rapala **25** D1, **26** A1
Rapallo **113** D2
Rapla **74** A1
Rapolano Terme **115** C3, **116** B2
Rapolla **120** A/B2
Raposa **164** B2
Raposeira **170** A2
Rapperswil **105** D1
Räpplinge **51** D1/2
Rappy **109** D3, **156** A1
Rapsáni **143** D3
Rapukkåtan **9** C/D3
Ras **133** D3, **134** A3, **138** A1
Rasal **154** B2
Räsälä **22** B2/3
Rasbo **40** B3
Rascafría **160** B2
Rasdorf **81** C2
Raseborg **25** C3
Raseiniai **73** D2
Raševica **134** B3
Rasimäki **22** B1
Rasines **153** C1
Rasinkylä **19** C2/3
Rasinperä **18** B3
Rasivaara **23** D3
Råsjö **35** C3
Raška **133** D3, **134** A/B3
Raška **140** A2/3
Raskršče **132** B2/3
Raslina **131** C3
Rasno **132** A3
Rasovo **135** D3
Rássina **115** C2/3, **116** B2
Rast **135** D2/3
Rastabynes **5** C2
Rastatt **90** B1/2
Rasteby **4** A/B3, **10** A1
Rastede **67** D1, **68** A1
Rastenfeld **94** A2
Rasteš **138** B2
Rasti **11** D3, **12** A2
Rasti **23** D3
Rastičevo **131** D2, **132** A2
Rastina **129** C2/3
Rastinkylä **23** C/D1
Rastovac **137** C/D1
Rastow **69** C1
Råstrand **15** D3
Rasueros **160** A2
Rasvåg **42** B3
Ratan **20** A1, **31** D2
Rätan **34** B3
Ratasjärvi **12** A3, **17** D2

Ratasvuoma 12 A3, 17 D2
Rateče 126 B2
Ratekau 53 C3
Rathcoole 58 A2
Rathdrum 58 A2/3
Rathenow 69 D2
Rathfriland 58 A1
Rath Luirc (Charleville) 55 C3
Rathnew 58 A2
Rathsweiler 80 A3
Ratibořské Hory 83 D3, 93 D1
Ratikylä 20 B3
Ratingen 80 A1
Ratíškovice 94 B1
Ratkovo 129 C3
Ratno 73 D3, 97 D1, 98 A/B2
Ratoath 58 A2
Rattelsdorf 81 D3
Rattenberg 92 A/B3
Rattendorf 126 A2
Rattersdorf 94 B3
Rattersdorf 96 B3
Rattosjärvi 12 A3, 17 D1
Rättvik 39 D2
Ratu 20 A1, 31 D2
Ratula 25 D2, 26 A/B2
Ratula 26 B2
Ratzdorf 70 B3
Ratzeburg 53 C3, 69 C1
Rätzlingen 69 C2/3
Raubling 92 B3
Raudanjoki 12 B3
Raudaskylä 21 C1
Raudasmäki 21 C1
Raudeberg 36 A1
Raudnes 42 A1/2
Rauduskylä 11 D3, 12 A1/2
Raufoss 38 A2
Rauha 27 C2
Rauhala 11 C3, 12 A1/2
Rauhaniemi 27 C1
Rauhellern 37 C3
Rauhenebrach-Untersteinbach 81 D3
Rauland 43 C1
Rauland fjellstoge 43 C1
Rauma (Raumo) 24 A2
Raumo 24 A2
Rauris 107 D1, 126 A1
Rauscedo 107 D2, 126 A2
Rauschenberg (Marburg) 81 C2
Rausjødalssetra 33 D3
Raustøl 43 C3
Rautajärvi 25 C1
Rautalampi 22 B3
Rautaperä 7 C3
Rautas 10 A3
Rautasluspe 10 A2/3
Rautavaara 23 C1/2
Rautila 24 A2
Rautio 18 A3, 21 C1
Rautionmäki 21 D2/3, 22 A2/3
Rautjärvi 27 C/D1
Rautu 24 B1
Rautuvaara 11 C3, 12 A2
Rauvantaipale 23 C2
Rauvatn 14 B2
Rauville-la-Bigot 76 A3
Rava 130 B2
Ravadasköngäs 11 D2
Ravan 132 B2
Ravanica 134 B2
Ravanusa 124 B3
Rava-Russkaja 97 D2, 98 A2
Ravatn 14 B3
Ravattila 27 C2
Ravča 131 D3, 132 A3, 136 B1
Ravel 102 B2/3
Ravello 119 D3
Ravelsnes 4 B2
Raven 127 D2
Ravenglass 59 C1, 60 A1/2
Ravenhorst 53 D3
Ravenna 115 C2, 117 C1
Ravenna Casal Borsetti 115 C1
Ravenna Ghibullo 115 C2, 117 C1

Ravenna Lido di Sávio 115 C2, 117 C1
Ravenna Lido di Classe 115 C2, 117 C1
Ravenna Marina Romea 115 C1
Ravenna Marina di Ravenna 115 C1/2
Ravenna Mezzano 115 C1/2
Ravenna Punta Marina 115 C1/2, 117 C1
Ravenna Sant'Alberto 115 C1
Ravensburg-Eschach 91 C3
Ravensburg-Weingarten 91 C3
Ravensburg-Weingarten-Taldorf 91 C3
Ravijoki 27 B/C2
Ravioskorpi 25 D1, 26 A1
Rävlanda 45 C3, 49 D1
Ravna Dubrava 139 C1
Ravna Gora 127 C3, 130 B1
Ravnastua 5 D3, 6 A2/3
Ravne na Koroškem 127 C2
Ravni 132 B3
Ravniš 134 B3
Ravnje 133 C1
Ravno 131 D3, 132 A2/3
Ravnstrup 48 B2
Ravsted 52 B2
Rawa Mazowiecka 73 C3, 97 C1
Rawicz 96 B1
Rawtenstall 59 D1/2, 60 B2
Rayleigh 65 C3
Räyrinki 21 C2
Räyskälä 25 C2
Ražana 133 D2, 134 A2
Ražanac 130 B2
Razboj 131 D1, 132 A1
Razbojna 134 B3
Razdel'naja 141 D1
Razdol 140 B3
Razdol 139 D3
Razdrto 126 B3
Razgrad 141 C2/3
Ražice 93 C/D1
Razlog 139 D2
Razlog 140 B3
Räzvani 141 C2
Re 105 C2
Reading 64 B3
Real 158 A2
Réalmont 110 A2
Réaumur 100 B1
Réaup 109 B/C2
Rebais 87 D1, 88 A1
Rébénacq 108 B3, 154 B1
Rebild 48 B2
Rebild Bakker Nat. Park 48 B2
Rebirechioulet 109 C3, 155 C1
Rebolledo de la Torre 152 B2
Rebollo de Duero 161 C/D1
Rebollosa de Jadraque 161 C2
Rebordelo 151 C3, 159 B/C1
Recanati 117 D2
Rečane 75 C2
Recas 160 B3
Recco 113 D2
Recea 135 D2
Recey-sur-Ource 88 B3
Rechnitz 94 B3, 127 D1
Rečica 127 C/D3
Rečica 99 C1
Recke 67 D2
Reckendorf 81 D3
Recklinghausen 67 C/D3, 80 A1
Recław 70 B1
Recoaro Terme 107 C3
Recogne 79 C3
Recologne 89 C3, 104 A1
Recoules-Prévinquières 110 A/B2
Recuerda 161 C1
Reculver 65 C3, 76 B1

Recz 71 C1
Redalen 38 A2
Redange 79 D3
Redcar 61 C1
Redditch 59 D3, 64 A2
Redefin 69 C1
Redekin 69 D2
Redessan 111 C2
Redhill 65 B/C3, 76 B1
Redice 137 D1
Rédics 127 D2
Rédics 96 B3
Redinha 158 A3
Redon 85 C3
Redondela 150 A2/3
Redondo 165 C2
Redruth 62 A/B3
Redslared 50 A1
Reedham 65 D2
Rees 67 C3
Reeth 59 D1, 61 B/C1/2
Reetz 69 D3
Reetz 69 D1/2
Reffannes 101 C2
Reftele 50 B1
Refugio Club Alpino 160 A3
Regalbuto 125 C2
Regen 93 C1
Regensburg 92 B1
Regenstauf 92 B1
Reggello 115 C2/3, 116 B2
Réggio di Calàbria Catafório 122 A3, 125 D2
Réggio di Calàbria 122 A3, 125 D1/2
Réggio di Calàbria Péllaro 122 A3, 125 D2
Reggiolo 114 B1
Réggio nell'Emília 114 B1
Reghin 97 D3, 140 B1
Regis Breitingen 82 B1
Regna 46 B2
Regnitzlosau 82 B2
Regny 103 C2
Régua 158 B1/2
Reguengo de Fetal 158 A3, 164 A1
Reguengo Grande 164 A1/2
Reguengos de Monsaraz 165 C3
Rehau 82 B2
Rehberg 69 D2
Rehburg-Loccum 68 A/B2
Rehburg-Loccum-Bad Rehburg 68 A/B2
Rehden 68 A2
Rehlingen 89 D1
Rehlingen-Biringen 79 D3
Rehna 53 C3, 69 C1
Rehula 27 C2
Reichelsheim 81 C3
Reichenau 91 C3
Reichenau an der Rax 94 A3
Reichenau [Reichenau-Tamins] 105 D1, 106 A1
Reichenbach im Kandertal 105 C2
Reichenbach 82 B2
Reichenbach (Roding) 92 B1
Reichenbach-Steegen 80 A3, 90 A1
Reichenbach 83 D1
Reichenberg 70 B2
Reichenberg (Würzburg) 81 C/D3
Reichenfels 127 C1
Reichenthal 93 D2
Reichertshausen 92 A2
Reichertshofen 92 A2
Reichmannsdorf 82 A2
Reichshof-Denklingen 80 A/B2
Reichshof-Eckenhagen 80 B1/2
Reichshoffen 90 A1
Reigada 159 C2
Reigate 65 B/C3, 76 B1
Reignac 100 B3
Reignac 101 C3
Reijolanmäki 23 D3
Reila 24 A2, 41 D1/2
Reillo 161 D3, 162 A3, 168 B1

Reims 88 A1
Rein 28 A3, 33 C1
Reina 166 A3
Reinach 105 C1
Reinbek 68 B1
Reine 8 A3
Reinfeld 53 C3, 69 B/C1
Reinfjord 4 B2
Reingard 14 B1
Reinhardshagen-Veckerhagen 81 C1
Reinhardtsgrimma 83 C2
Reinheim 33 C3, 37 D1
Reinheim 81 B/C3
Reinli 37 D3
Reinosa 152 B1/2
Reinøysund 7 C/D2
Reinsfeld 80 A3
Reinskar 4 A2
Reinskareng 14 B3
Reinsnos 42 B1
Reinsvoll 38 A2
Reisbach 92 B2
Reisbach-Haberskirchen 92 B2
Reischach (Altötting) 92 B2
Reisjärvi 21 C1
Reiskirchen 81 B/C2
Reistad 38 A3, 43 D1
Reitan 32 B3, 37 C1
Reitan 33 D2
Reitano 125 C2
Reite 9 D1/2
Reit im Winkl 92 B3
Reitkalli 26 B2
Reittiö 22 A2
Reitzenhain 83 C2
Rejas 153 C3, 161 C1
Rejmyre 46 B2
Rejsby 52 A1
Rekeland 42 A3
Reken 67 C3
Rekhulet 17 C2
Rekijoki 25 B/C2/3
Rekikoski 24 B2
Rekivaara 23 D3
Rekovac 134 B3
Rekowo 70 B1
Rekvik 4 A2/3
Reliquias 170 A1
Reljinac 134 B3
Relletti 18 A3
Relleu 169 D2
Remagen 80 A2
Rémalard 86 B2
Remchingen 90 B1
Remda 82 A2
Remdalen 14 B3, 29 D1
Remeskylä 21 D1, 22 A/B1
Remich 79 D3
Remiremont 89 D2
Remmarbäcken 30 B2/3, 35 D1
Remmaren 30 B2, 35 D1
Remmen 34 B3
Remolinos 155 C3, 163 B/C1
Remollon 112 A2
Remoulins 111 C2
Remplin 53 D3, 69 D1, 70 A1
Remscheid 80 A1
Rémuzat 111 D2
Rena 38 A1/2
Rena 166 A2
Renaison 103 C2
Renålandet 29 D2, 35 C1
Renåseter 38 A1
Renazé 85 D3
Renchen 90 B2
Rendal 32 B2
Rendalen fjellstue 38 A1
Rende 122 A1/2
Rendína 144 A/B2
Rendína 146 B1
Rendo 159 C2/3
Rendsburg 52 B3
Renedo 152 B3, 160 A/B1
Renedo de Valdavia 152 B2
Renera 161 C2
Renescure 77 D1, 78 A2
Renesse 66 A3
Renfors 31 C1
Renfrew 56 B2
Rengínion 147 C1
Rengonkylä 20 B3

Rengsdorf 80 A2
Rengsjö 40 A1
Reni 141 D2
Renieblas 153 D3, 161 D1
Renko 25 C2
Renkomäki 25 D2, 26 A2
Renkum 66 B3
Rennebu 33 C2
Rennerod 80 B2
Rennertshofen 91 D2, 92 A2
Rennertshofen-Ammerfeld 91 D2, 92 A2
Rennes 85 D2
Rennes-les-Bains 110 A3, 156 A1
Renningen 91 B/C2
Rennweg 126 A/B1
Rens 52 B2
Rensjön 30 A3, 35 C1
Rensjön 10 A2/3
Rensved 34 B2
Rentjärn 16 A2
Renträsk 16 A3
Renvallen 16 A3
Renviken 16 A3
Reocín 152 B2
Répcelak 94 B3, 128 A1
Repki 99 D1/2
Replot/Raippaluoto 20 A2, 31 D3
Repojoki 11 D2, 12 B1
Reposaari 24 A1, 41 D1
Reppen 14 B1
Repušnica 135 C3
Repvåg 5 D1, 6 A/B1
Requejo 151 C3
Requena 169 C1
Réquista 110 A2
Reriz 158 B1
Resana 107 C3
Resanovci 131 C2
Resarö 47 D1
Resavica 135 B/C2
Resavska-pećina 135 C2
Resele 30 B3, 35 D1/2
Resen 138 B3, 142 B1
Resende 158 B2
Résia 106 B1
Résia/Reschen 106 B1
Resița 135 C1
Reșița 140 A2
Resko 71 C1
Resmo 51 D2
Resnik 133 D1, 134 A1/2
Resö 44 B2
Reso 24 B2/3
Ressons-sur-Matz 78 A3
Restábal 173 C2
Restad 45 C2
Restelica 138 A/B2
Resuttano 125 B/C2
Retamal 166 A2
Retamar 173 D2, 174 A2
Retamosa 166 A/B1
Retamoso 160 A3, 166 B1
Retascón 163 C1/2
Rethel 78 B3
Rethem 68 B2
Réthimnon 149 C3
Retiendas 161 C2
Retiers 86 A2/3
Retiro 165 C2
Retjons 108 B2
Retkovci 129 B/C3, 132 B1
Retortillo 159 C2
Retortillo de Soria 161 C1
Retournac 103 C3
Rétság 95 D3
Rettenberg 91 D3
Rettenegg 94 A3
Retuerta 153 C3
Retuerta de Bullaque 167 C1
Retunen 23 C2
Retz 94 A2
Retzow 69 D1
Reuden 69 D3
Reudnitz 82 B2
Reugny 86 B3
Reugny 102 B2
Reuilly 102 A1
Reus 163 D1/2
Reusel 79 C1
Reuterstadt Stavenhagen 70 A1

Reuti (Hasliberg) [Brünig-
Hasliberg] **105** C1/2
Reutlingen **91** C2
Reutlingen-Gönningen
91 C2
Reutte **91** D3
Reutuaapa **18** B1
Rev **51** D2
Revel **109** D3
Reventin-Vaugris **103** D3
Révere **114** B1
Revest-du-Bion **111** D2
Révfülöp **128** A/B1
Revholmen **44** B1
Revigny-sur-Ornain **88** B1
Revilla del Campo
153 C2/3
Revin **79** B/C3
Revine **107** D2
Revište **95** D2
Revlingen **33** D3
Řevnice **83** C/D3
Revò **107** B/C2
Revonlahti **18** A3
Revsnes **36** B2
Revsnes **9** C2
Revsnes **28** A2, **33** C1
Revsneshamn **5** D1, **6** A1
Revsund **35** B/C2
Rexbo **39** D2
Reynel **89** C2
Rēzekne **74** B2
Rezepin **72** A3
Rezepin **70** B3
Rezina **99** C3
Reznos **153** D3, **161** D1
Rezzato **106** B3
Rezzo **113** C2
Rezzoáglio **113** D1/2
Rgošte **135** C3
Rgotina **135** C2
Rgotina **140** A/B2
Rhade **67** C3
Rhälänmäki **22** B1
Rhauderfehn-Westrhauder-
fehn **67** D1/2
Rhauderfehn-Burlage
67 D2
Rhauderfehn-Collinghorst
67 D1
Rhaunen **80** A3
Rhayader **59** C3
Rheda-Wiedenbrück **68** A3
Rhede **67** C3
Rhede (Ems) **67** D2
Rheden **67** C3
Rheinau [Altenburg-Rhei-
nau] **90** B3
Rheinau-Freistett **90** B2
Rheinbach **80** A2
Rheinbach-Hilberath **80** A2
Rheinberg **79** D1, **80** A1
Rheinberg-Borth **67** C3,
79 D1, **80** A1
Rheinböllen **80** A/B3
Rheine **67** D3
Rheineck **91** C3
Rheine-Mesum **67** D3
Rheinfelden **90** A/B3
Rheinfelden **90** A/B3
Rheinhausen **90** A2
Rheinsberg **70** A2
Rheinstetten-Mörsch
90 B1
Rheinzabern **90** B1
Rhêmes-Notre-Dame
104 B3
Rhenen **66** B3
Rhens **80** A/B2
Rhiconich **54** A1
Rhinow **69** D2
Rho **105** D3
Rhosllanerchrugog
59 C/D2, **60** B3
Rhumspringe **81** D1
Rhyl **59** C2, **60** A3
Riace **122** B3
Riace Marina **122** B3
Riaguas de San Bartolomé
161 C1
Riákia **143** D2
Riala **41** B/C3, **47** D1
Rialb de Noguera **155** C2
Riaño **152** A2
Rians **111** D2/3
Rianxo **150** A2
Riaza **161** C1

Ribadavia **150** B2/3
Ribadelago **151** C3
Ribadeo **151** C1
Riba de Saelices **161** D2
Ribadesella **152** A1
Ribadumia **150** A2
Ribaflecha **153** D2
Ribaforada **154** A3
Ribagorda **161** D2/3
Ribamar **164** A2
Ribarce **140** B3
Ribarci **139** C2
Ribare **134** B3
Riba-roja d'Ebre **163** C1
Ribarredonda **161** D2
Ribarroja **169** C/D1
Ribarroja del Turia
169 C/D1
Ribarska Banja **134** B3
Ribas **155** C2/3
Ribas **152** B3
Ribas de Sil **151** C2
Ribatajada **161** D2/3
Ribchester **59** D1, **60** B2
Ribe **52** A1
Ribeauvillé **89** D2, **90** A2
Ribécourt **78** A3
Ribeira **150** A2
Ribeira de Fraguas **158** A2
Ribeira de Pena **158** B1
Ribeira de Piquín **151** C1
Ribeiradio **158** A2
Ribemont **78** A/B3
Ribera **124** B2
Ribera Alta **173** C1
Ribérac **101** C3
Ribera de Cardós **155** C2
Ribera del Fresno **165** D2,
166 A2
Ribesalbes **162** B3
Ribes de Freser **156** A2
Ribnica **132** B2
Ribnica **127** C3
Ribnica **126** B3
Ribnica na Pohorju **127** C2
Ribnik **131** B/C2
Ribnik **127** C3
Ribnitz-Damgarten **53** D3
Ribnitz-Damgarten **72** A2
Ribolla **114** B3,
116 A/B2/3
Ribota **161** C1
Ricadi **122** A2
Říčany **83** D3
Riccall **61** C2
Ríccia **119** D2, **120** A1
Ríccio **115** C3, **117** B/C2
Riccione **115** D2, **117** C1
Richelieu **101** C1
Rich Hill **58** A1
Richisau [Glarus] **105** D1
Richmond **61** C1
Rickenbach-Willaringen
90 B3
Rickleå **20** A1, **31** D2
Rickling **52** B3
Rickmansworth **64** B3
Ricla **55** C3, **163** C1
Ricote **169** D3
Ridasjärvi **25** C/D2, **26** A2
Riddarhyttan **39** D3
Riddes **104** B2
Ridica **129** C2/3
Ridsdale **57** D2/3
Riebnesluspen **15** D2
Riečnica **95** D1
Riec-sur-Bélon **84** B3
Riedau **93** C2
Riede **68** A2
Riedenburg **92** A1
Riedenburg-Meihern **92** A1
Riedenhaim **81** D3,
91 C1
Rieden-Vilshofen **92** B1
Riedhausen **91** C2
Ried im Innkreis **93** C2
Ried im Innkreis **96** A2/3
Ried im Oberinntal **106** B1
Riedlingen **91** C2
Riedstadt-Wolfskehlen
80 B3
Riegelsberg **89** D1, **90** A1
Riegersburg **127** D1
Riegersburg **94** A1/2
Riegersdorf **126** B2
Riego de la Vega **151** D2

Riekofen-Taimering
92 B1/2
Rielasingen-Worblingen
90 B3
Riello **151** D2
Rielves **160** B3, **167** C1
Riemst **79** C2
Rieneck **81** C3
Riénsena **152** A1
Rieponlahti **22** B2
Riepsdorf **53** C3
Riesa **83** C1
Riese **96** A1
Rieseby **52** B2
Riese Pio X **107** C3
Riesi **125** C3
Riessen **70** B3
Rieste **67** D2
Riestedt **82** A1
Rietavas **73** C2
Rietbad [Nesslau-Neu St.
Johann] **105** D1, **106** A1
Rietberg **68** A3
Rietberg-Mastholte **68** A3
Rietheim-Weilheim **90** B3
Rieti **117** C3, **118** B1
Rietschen **83** D1
Rieumes **109** C3, **155** D1
Rieupeyroux **110** A2
Rieutord **111** C1
Rieutort-de-Randon
110 B1
Rieux **108** B3, **155** C1
Rieux-Minervois **110** A3,
156 B1
Rievaulx Abbey **61** C2
Riez **112** A2
Riezlern **91** D3, **106** B1
Rifiano/Riffian **107** C1/2
Rifúgio del Teodulo **105** C2
Rīga **73** D1, **74** A2
Rigács **128** A1
Riggisberg [Thurnen]
105 C1
Rignac **110** A1/2
Rignano Flamínio **118** B1
Rignano Gargánico **120** A1
Rigney **89** C3, **104** A3
Rigny-Ussé **86** B3, **101** C1
Rigolato **107** D2, **126** A2
Rihtniemi **24** A2, **41** D1/2
Riihikoski **24** B2
Riihimäki **25** C2, **26** A2
Riihiniemi **25** D1, **26** B1
Riihivaara **23** D1
Riihivaara **19** D3, **23** D1
Riihivalkama **25** C2
Riihivuori **21** D3, **22** A3
Riiho **24** B1
Riiho **21** C3
Riikonkumpu **11** D3, **12** A2
Riipi **12** B2
Riipi **20** A/B3
Riipisenvaara **12** A3, **17** D1
Riisikkala **25** C2
Riisipere **74** A1
Riistavesi **23** B/C2
Riitiala **24** B1
Rijeka **126** B3, **130** A1
Rijeka **127** C3, **131** C1
Rijeka Crnojevića **137** D2
Rijssen **67** C2/3
Riksgränsen **9** D2
Rila **139** D2
Rillé **86** B3
Rillo **162** B2
Rilly-sur-Loire **86** A/B3
Rilski Manastir **139** D2
Rilski Manastir **140** B3
Rima **105** C3
Rimala **20** A/B2
Rimasco **105** C3
Rimaucourt **89** C2
Rimavská Sobota **97** C2
Rimbach (Kötzting) **92** B1
Rimbo **40** B3
Rimeize **110** B1
Rimella **105** C2/3
Rimforsa **46** B3
Rímini **115** D2, **117** C1
Rímini-Viserba **115** D2,
117 C1
Rimmilä **25** C2
Rîmnicu Sărat **141** C2
Rîmnicu Vîlcea **140** B2

Rimont **108** B3, **155** C1
Rimpar **81** C/D3
Rimske Toplice **127** C2
Rincón de la Victoria
172 B2
Rincón de Soto **154** A2
Rindal **33** B/C2
Rindarøy **32** A2
Rinde **36** B2
Rinella **125** C1
Ringarum **46** B2
Ringe **53** C1
Ringebu **37** D2
Ringelai **93** C2
Ringen **28** A3, **33** C2
Ringkøbing **48** A3
Ringmer **76** B3
Ringnäs **39** C1
Ringnes **37** D3
Ringselet **15** D2
Ringsted **49** D3, **53** D1
Ringvattnet **29** D2
Ringwood **76** A1
Rinkaby **50** B3
Rinna **46** A2
Rinøyvåg **9** C2
Rintala **20** B2
Rinteln **68** A3
Rinteln-Steinbergen **68** A3
Río **151** C2
Riobianco/Weissenbach
107 C1
Riocavado de la Sierra
153 C3
Riocerezo **153** C2
Rio de Mel **158** B2
Rio de Moinhos **164** B1
Rio de Mouro **164** A2
Riodeva **163** C2
Rio di Pusteria/Mühlbach
107 C1
Rio dos Moinhos **165** C2
Riofrío **172** B2
Riofrío **160** A2
Rio Frio **151** C3, **159** C1
Riofrío del Llano **161** C1/2
Riogordo **172** B2
Rioja **173** D2
Riola di Vergato **114** B2,
116 B1
Riola Sardo **123** C2
Riolobos **159** C/D3,
165 D1, **166** A1
Riolo Terme **115** C2,
116 B1
Riom **102** B2
Riomaggiore **114** A2
Rio Maior **164** A1
Riomar **163** C/D2
Rio Marina **116** A3
Rio Mau **158** A2
Riom-ès-Montagnes
102 B3
Ríon **146** B2
Ríon **148** B2
Rion-des-Landes **108** A2
Ríonegro del Puente
151 D3
Rionero in Vúlture
120 A/B2
Rionero Sannítico **119** C2
Ríópar **168** A2/3
Ríós **151** C3
Riosa **151** D1
Rio Saliceto **114** B1
Ríoscuro **151** D2
Ríoseco **153** C/D3, **161** C1
Ríoseco de Tapia **151** D2
Riospaso **151** D1/2
Riotord **103** C3
Riotorto **151** C1
Rio Torto **151** C3, **158** B1
Riovéggio **114** B2, **116** B1
Rioz **89** C3
Říp **83** C/D2
Ripač **131** C1
Ripacándida **120** A/B2
Ripanj **133** D1/2, **134** A2
Riparbella **114** B3, **116** A2
Ripatransone **117** D2
Ripley **61** D3, **65** C1
Ripley **61** C2
Ripoll **156** A2
Ripon **61** C2
Ripon **54** B3
Riposto **125** D2
Rippig **79** D3

Ripsa **47** C1/2
Riqueval **78** A3
Risan **137** C2
Risarven **39** D1, **40** A1
Risbäck **30** B2/3, **35** D1
Risbäck **29** D1, **30** A1
Risberg **39** C2
Risberg **31** C1
Risbrunn **34** B3
Risca **63** C1
Riscle **108** B2/3
Risco **166** B2
Rise **29** D3, **34** B1
Riseberga kloster **46** A1
Riseley Common **64** B3,
76 A/B1
Risliden **31** C1
Risnes **36** A2
Risnes **42** B3
Risnes **36** A3
Rišňovce **95** C2
Risögrund **17** C2/3
Risöhäll **20** B1
Risør **43** D2/3, **44** A2
Risøyhamn **9** C1
Rispéscia **116** B3
Rissna **35** C2
Ristedt **69** C2
Risteli **74** A1
Risti **74** A1
Ristiina **26** B1
Ristijärvi **19** C3
Ristijärvi **25** C1, **26** A1
Ristikangas **22** A3
Ristilä **13** C3
Ristilampi **12** B3
Ristinge **53** C2
Ristinkylä **23** C3
Ristniemi **24** B3
Ristonmännikkö **12** B2
Ristovac **139** C2
Risträsk **30** A1, **31** D2
Risträsk **30** B1
Ristrețu **135** D2/3
Ristrețu **140** B2
Risudden **17** D2
Risulahti **27** C1
Risum-Lindholm **52** A2
Risuperä **21** C2
Ritakoski **6** B3
Rítíni **143** D2
Ritopek **133** D1, **134** B1
Rittarylä **19** C3
Ritterhude **68** A1/2
Rittersdorf **79** D3
Rittersgrün **82** B2
Ritzerow **70** A1
Ritzleben **69** C2
Riudecols **163** D1/2
Riudoms **163** D1/2
Riutta **21** C1
Riuttala **24** B1
Riuttala **22** B2
Riuttaskylä **21** C3
Riutula **6** B3
Riva-Bella **76** B3, **86** A1
Riva del Garda **106** B2/3
Riva di Túres/Rain-Taufers
107 C1
Rivalta di Torino **112** B1
Rivanazzano **113** D1
Rivarolo Canavese **105** C3
Rivarolo Mantovano
114 A1
Rive-de-Gier **103** C/D3
Riverbukt **5** C2
Rivergaro **113** D1, **114** A1
Rives **103** D3, **104** A3
Rivesaltes **156** B1
Rivières-le-Bois **89** C3
Rivière-sur-Tarn **110** B2
Rivignano **107** D2/3,
126 A3
Rivisóndoli **119** C2
Rívoli **112** B1
Rivolta d'Adda **106** A3
Rixheim **90** A3
Rixö **44** B2
Rízai **147** C3
Rizárion **143** C1
Rízoma **143** C3
Rizómata **143** D2
Rjukan **43** C1
Rljeća **132** B2
Rö **35** D2
Roa **38** A3

Røa 38 B1
Roa 152 B3, 160 B1
Roade 64 B2
Roaldkvam 42 A1
Roan 28 A2
Röån 30 A2, 35 C/D1
Roana 107 C2/3
Roanne 103 C2
Roasjö 45 C3, 49 D1
Roavvegiedde 6 B2
Röbäck 31 C/D2
Róbbio 105 D3
Robecco d'Óglio 106 A/B3
Röbel 69 D1, 70 A1
Röbel 72 A3
Røberg 28 A3, 33 C1
Robert-Espagne 88 B1
Robertsfors 31 D2
Robič 126 A/B2
Robin Hood's Bay 61 D1
Rob Koy's Cave 56 B1
Robleda 159 C2/3
Robledillo de Gata 159 C3
Robledillo de Mohernando
   161 C2
Robledillo de Trujillo
   165 D1/2, 166 A1/2
Robledo 168 A/B2
Robledo 151 C2
Robledo de Chavela 160 B2
Robledo de Corpes 161 C2
Robledo del Mazo 160 A3,
   166 B1
Robledollano 166 A/B1.
Robles 151 D2, 152 A2
Röblingen 82 A1
Robliza de Cojos 159 D2
Robregordo 161 C2
Robres 154 B3
Robres del Castillo
   153 D2/3
Roč 126 B3, 130 A1
Rocafort de Queralt
   155 C3, 163 C1
Rocamadour 109 D1
Roccabianca 114 A1
Roccadáspide 120 A3
Rocca di Mezzo 119 C1
Rocca di Neto 122 B2
Rocca di Papa 118 B2
Roccafranca 106 A3
Roccagorga 118 B2
Roccalbegna 116 B3
Roccalumera 125 D2
Rocca Mássima 118 B2
Roccamena 124 A/B2
Roccamonfina 119 C2/3
Roccanova 120 B3
Rocca Pia 119 C2
Rocca Priora 115 D2/3,
   117 D2
Roccaraso 119 C2
Rocca San Casciano
   115 C2, 116 B1
Roccasecca 119 C2
Roccasicura 119 C/D2
Rocca Sinibalda 117 C3,
   118 B1
Roccastrada 114 B3,
   116 B2
Roccaverano 113 C1/2
Roccavione 112 B2
Roccella Iónica 122 B3
Roccelletta del Véscovo di
   Sqvillace 122 B2
Rocchetta Sant'António
   120 A2
Rocha 170 A2
Rochdale 59 D2, 60 B2
Rochebloine 111 C1
Roche-Bonne 111 C1
Rochebrune 104 B3
Rochechouart 101 D2/3
Roche d'Oëtre 86 A1
Rochefort 79 C2/3
Rochefort-en-Terre 85 C3
Rochefort-en-Yvelines
   87 C2
Rochefort-Montagne
   102 B3
Rochefort-sur-Loire 86 A3
Rochefort-sur-Mer 100 B2
Roche, La [Bulle] 104 B1/2
Rochemaure 111 C2
Rochemolles 112 B1
Rochers de Ham 85 D1,
   86 A1

Rocheservière 100 A1
Rochester 65 C3, 77 C1
Rochetaillée-sur-Aujon
   88 B3
Rochetaillée 103 D2
Rochford 65 C3
Rochlitz 82 B1
Rociana del Condado
   171 C2
Rockanje 66 A3
Rockcliffe 56 B3, 60 A1
Rockenhausen 80 B3
Rockesholm 46 A1
Rockhammar 46 B1
Rockmyrheden 15 D3
Rockneby 51 D1/2
Ročov 83 C2
Rocroi 78 B3
Rød 28 B1
Róda 142 A3
Rodach 81 D2
Rodach-Mährenhausen
   81 D2
Roda de Isábena 155 C2
Roda de Ter 156 A2
Rodal 32 B2
Rodalben 90 A1
Rödånäs 31 C2
Rodange 79 D3
Rødberg 28 A3, 33 C1
Rødberg 37 C/D3
Rødby 53 C2
Rødbyhavn 53 C2
Rødding 48 A2
Rødding 52 B1
Rödeby 51 C2
Rodeiro 150 B2
Rødekro 52 B2
Rodel 54 A2
Rodellar 155 C2
Rodelund 48 B3
Roden 67 C1/2
Rødenas 162 A2
Rødenes 38 A/B3, 44 B1
Rodenkirchen 68 A1
Rodenkirchen-Rondorf
   80 A2
Rödental-Oeslau 82 A2
Rödermark-Ober-Roden
   81 B/C3
Rodewisch 82 B2
Rodez 110 A2
Rodheim vor der Höhe
   80 B2
Rødhus 48 B1
Rodiá 143 D3
Rodiá 146 B3
Rodiezmo 151 D2, 152 A2
Rodi Gargánico 120 B1
Roding 92 B1
Rödingbäck 15 C2
Rödinghausen 68 A3
Rödinghausen-Bieren
   68 A3
Roding-Neubäu 92 B1
Rödingsträsk 16 B2
Rödingträsk 31 B/C1
Rødkærsbro 48 B2
Rodleben 69 D3
Rödmyra 40 A1
Rodolívos 144 B1
Rödön 29 D3, 34 B2
Rodópolis 139 D3, 143 D1,
   144 A1
Ródos 149 D3
Rødøy 14 A/B1
Rødsand 9 C1
Rødsjøseter 28 A3, 33 C1
Rødsvollen 33 D3
Rødtangen 43 D1, 44 B1
Rødungstøl 37 C3
Rödvattnet 30 B2, 35·D1
Rødven 32 A2
Rødvig 53 D1
Roermond 79 D1
Roeselare 78 A1/2
Roetgen 79 D2
Ro Ferrara 115 C1
Röfors 46 A1/2
Rogač 131 C3
Rogača 133 D2, 134 A2
Rogačev 99 C1
Rogačica 139 C1/2
Rogačica 133 C2
Rogalin 71 D3
Rogåsen 69 D3
Rogaška Slatina 127 C2

Rogatec 127 C/D2
Rogatica 133 C3
Rogatin 97 D2, 98 A/B3
Rogätz 69 D3
Rogenstugan 34 A3
Roggel 79 D1
Roggenburg 91 D2
Roggiano Gravina 122 A1
Rogliano 122 A/B2
Rognan 32 B1/2
Rognan 15 C1
Rogne 32 A2
Rognes 33 C2
Rogny 87 D3
Rógoi 146 A1
Rogoznica 131 C3
Rogoźno 71 D2
Rogsta 34 B2
Rogsta 40 B1
Rohan 85 C2
Rohr 92 A/B2
Rohr 81 D2
Rohrau 94 B2/3
Rohrbach an der Lafnitz
   94 A3, 127 D1
Rohrbach in Oberösterreich
   93 C2
Rohrbach in Oberösterreich
   96 A2
Rohrbach-les-Bitche
   89 D1, 90 A1
Rohrbach-les-Dieuze
   89 D1, 90 A1/2
Rohrbeck 70 A3
Rohrdorf 90 B2
Röhrnbach 93 C2
Roigheim 91 C1
Rois 150 A2
Roisel 78 A3
Roismala 24 B1
Roitzsch 82 B1
Roitzsch 82 B1
Roivanen 12 B1
Rojales 169 C3, 174 B1
Röjan 34 B3
Rojas 153 C2
Röjdåfors 38 B2
Röjdåsen 38 B2/3
Röjeråsen 39 D2
Röjtökmuzsaj 94 B3
Rok 46 A2
Röke 50 B2
Rokitnica 71 C3
Røkkum 32 B2
Røkland 15 C1
Roknäs 16 B3
Rokovci 129 C3, 133 B/C1
Rokowo Szczecinskie
   71 D1
Röksta 30 B3
Rokuankansallispuisto
   18 B3
Rokycany 83 C3
Rokycany 96 A2
Rokytnice 95 C1
Rolampont 89 C2
Rolandstorpet 29 C/D1/2
Rold 48 B2
Røldal 42 B1
Rolde 67 C2
Rolfs 17 C2/3
Rolfstorp 49 D1, 50 A1
Rolica 164 A1
Rollag 43 D1
Rollán 159 D2
Rolle 104 A/B2
Rolleville 77 B/C3
Rollos de Arriba 168 B3,
   174 A1
Rollot 78 A3
Rollset 28 B3, 33 D2
Rolsvåg 36 A3
Rølvåg 14 A2
Rolvsøy 44 B1
Roma 47 D3
Roma 118 B2
Roma 72 B1
Roma-Fiumicino 118 A2
Roma-Focene 118 A2
Roma-Fregene 118 A2
Romagnano Sésia 105 C3
Romakloster 47 D3
Romaldkirk 57 D3,
   61 B/C1
Roma-Lido di Castel Fusano
   118 A/B2

Roma-Lido di Óstia
   118 A/B2
Roman 141 C1
Romana 123 C2
Romancos 161 C2
Romanillos de Medinaceli
   161 D1
Romano Alto 107 C3
Romanones 161 C2
Romanshorn 91 C3
Romans-sur-Isère 103 D3,
   111 C/D1
Romedal 38 A2
Romenay 103 D2
Romeral 161 C3, 167 D1
Römerstein 91 C2
Romfo 32 B2/3
Romhány 95 D3
Römhild 81 D2
Romilly-sur-Seine 88 A2
Rommenäs 38 B3, 45 C1
Romny 99 C3
Romont 104 B1/2
Romorantin-Lanthenay
   87 C3
Romppala 23 D2
Romrod 81 C2
Romsey 76 A1
Romsila 24 B3
Rømskog 38 B3, 45 C1
Romstad 28 B2
Røn 37 C/D2
Rönäs 14 B2/3
Roncade 107 D3
Roncal 154 B2
Roncegno 107 C2
Ronce-les-Bains 101 C2/3
Roncesvalles 108 B3,
   155 C1
Ronchamp 89 D3
Ronchi dei Legionari
   126 B3
Ronciglione 117 C3,
   118 A1
Ronco 115 C2, 117 C1
Ronco Canavese 105 C3
Ronco Scrívia 113 D1
Ronda 172 A2
Rondablikk 37 D1/2
Rondanina 113 D1/2
Rønde 49 C2
Rondelli 114 B3, 116 A2/3
Rondvassbu 33 C3, 37 D1
Ronehamn 47 D3
Ronfe 158 B2
Rong 36 B3
Rongesund 36 A3
Ronkaisperä 21 D1, 22 A1
Rönkönvaara 23 C3
Rönnäng 44 B3
Rönnäs 16 A3
Rönnberg 16 A3
Rønne 51 D3
Rønne 72 A2
Ronneburg 82 B2
Ronneby 51 C2
Ronneby 72 A/B1
Ronnebyhamn 51 C2
Rønnede 49 C2
Rönneshytta 46 A2
Rönnholm 31 C3
Rönnholm 20 A2
Rönninge 47 C1
Rönnliden 16 A3
Rönnön 29 C3, 34 B1
Ronnynklä 21 D2, 22 A2
Rönö 47 B/C2
Ronsberg 91 D3
Ronse 78 B2
Rønsvik 32 B1/2
Ronta 115 B/C2, 116 B1
Rontsa 22 C2
Roodeschool 67 C1
Röölä 24 A3
Roosendaal 78 B1
Roosinpohja 21 C3
Ropeid 42 A1/2
Ropenkatan 15 B/C3
Roperuelos del Páramo
   151 D2/3
Ropinsalmi 10 B2
Ropotovo 138 B3
Roppen 106 B2
Roquebillière 112 B2
Roquebrun 110 A/B3
Roquecourbe 110 A2/3
Roquefort 108 B2

Roquefort-sur-Soulzon
   110 A/B2
Roquemaure 111 C2
Roquesteron 112 B2
Roquetaillade 108 B1
Roquetas de Mar 173 D2
Roquetes 163 C2
Roquevaire 111 D3
Rörbäck 17 C2/3
Rörbäcksnäs 38 B1/2
Rørby 49 C3, 53 C1
Rore 131 D2
Roreto Chisone 112 B1
Rørholt 43 D2, 44 A2
Röron 44 B3
Rörön 34 B2
Røros 33 D2/3
Rørøy 14 A3
Rorschach 91 C3
Rørstad 9 B/C3
Rörvattnet 29 C/D2, 34 B1
Rørvig 49 D3
Rørvik 28 B1
Rørvik 28 A3, 33 C1
Rosà 107 C3
Rosal 150 A3
Rosala 24 B3
Rösa, La [Ospizio Bernina]
   106 B2
Rosal de la Frontera
   165 C3, 171 B/C1
Rosans 111 D2
Rosário 170 B1
Rosarno 122 A3
Roscanvel 84 A2
Rosche 69 C2
Roscoff 84 B1
Roscommon 55 C2
Roscrea 55 C/D3
Rose 137 A/B1
Rose 137 C2
Rosegg 126 B2
Rosell 163 C2
Roselle 116 B3
Rosenberg 91 C/D1
Rosenburg 94 A2
Rosendahl 67 C/D3
Rosendahl-Darfeld 67 D3
Rosendahl-Holtwick
   67 C/D3
Rosendahl-Höpingen
   67 D3
Rosendahl-Osterwick
   67 C/D3
Rosendal 42 A1
Rosendal 28 B1
Rosenfeld 90 B2
Rosenfors 51 C/D1
Rosengarten 91 C1
Rosengarten 68 C2
Rosenheim 92 B3
Rosenholm 49 B/C2
Rosenow 70 A1
Rosenthal 81 C2
Rosenthal 83 C2
Rosentorp 39 D1
Rosersberg 40 B3, 47 C1
Roses 156 B2
Roseto degli Abruzzi
   119 C1
Roseto Valfortore 119 D2,
   120 A1
Rosheim 90 A2
Rósia 114 B3, 116 B2
Rosia Jiu 135 D1
Rosice 94 B1
Rosières-en-Blois 89 C2
Rosières-en-Santerre 78 A3
Rosiers-d'Égletons 102 A3
Rosignano Maríttimo
   114 A/B3, 116 A2
Rosignano Solvay
   114 A/B3, 116 A2
Rosinedal 31 C2
Roșiorii de Vede 140 B2
Rositz 82 B1/2
Roskilde 49 D3, 50 A3,
   53 D1
Roskilde 72 A2
Roški slap 131 C2/3
Rosko 71 D2
Roskovec 142 A1/2
Röslau 82 A/B3
Roslavl' 75 C3
Roslev 48 A/B2
Roslin 57 C2

Rosmaninhal 159 C3, 165 C1
Røsnæs Kloster 49 C3, 53 C1
Rosnay-l'Hopital 88 B2
Rosny-sur-Seine 87 C1
Rosolina 115 C1
Rosolina Mare 107 D3, 115 C1
Rosolini 125 C/D3
Rosoman 139 C3
Rosporden 84 B2
Rösrath 80 A2
Rossa [Castione-Arbedo] 105 D2, 106 A2
Rossano 122 B1
Rossas 158 A2
Rossenes 36 A3
Rossfjord 4 A3, 9 D1
Rosshaupten 91 D3
Rosshyttan 40 A3
Rossiglione 113 C1/2
Rossillon 103 D2, 104 A3
Rossio do São do Tejo 164 B1
Rossla 81 D1, 82 A1
Rossland 36 A3
Rosslare 58 A3
Rosslare Harbour 58 A3
Rosslare Harbour 55 D3
Rosslau 69 D3
Rossleithen 93 D3
Rossön 30 A2, 35 C1
Ross-on-Wye 63 D1
Rossow 69 D2
Rossow 70 A1
Røssvik 9 C3
Rosswein 83 C1
Røst 36 A1
Rostadalen 10 A1
Rostahytta 10 A1
Röstånga 50 B2/3
Rostarzewo 71 D3
Rostassac 108 B1
Roštín 95 B/C1
Rostock 53 D3
Rostock 72 A2
Rostock-Petersdorf 53 D3
Rostock-Warnemünde 53 D3
Rostrenen 84 B2
Rostrevor 58 A1
Rostrup 48 B2
Rostudel 84 A2
Rösund 25 C3
Røsvassbukt 14 B2
Røsvik 9 C3
Rosvik 17 B/C3
Rosvoll 32 B2
Röszke 129 D2
Rot 39 C1
Rot 91 C/D3
Rota 9 C3
Rota 171 C/D2/3
Rota Greca 122 A1
Rot am See 91 C/D1
Rot am See-Brettheim 91 D1
Roteberg 39 D1, 40 A1
Rotello 119 D2, 120 A1
Rot-Ellwangen 91 C3
Rotenburg 81 C1/2
Rotenburg 68 B2
Rotenburg-Mulmshorn 68 A/B1/2
Rotglá 169 C/D2
Roth 79 D2
Roth 80 B2
Roth 92 A1
Rötha 82 B1
Rotha 82 A1
Rothbury 57 D2
Röthelstein 94 A3, 127 C1
Rothemühl 70 B1
Röthenbach (Allgäu) 91 C/D3
Röthenbach im Emmental [Signau] 105 C1
Rothenbuch 81 C3
Rothenburg 83 D3
Rothenburg ob der Tauber 91 D1
Rothenfels 81 C3
Rothenklempenow 70 B1
Rothenthurm 127 B/C1
Rotherham 61 D3

Rothesay 56 A/B2
Rothesay 54 A2/3, 55 D1
Rotonda 120 B3, 122 A1
Rotondella 120 B3
Rótova 169 D2
Rotsjö 30 A3, 35 C2
Rotsund 4 B2/3
Rott 92 B3
Rott 91 D3, 92 A3
Rottach-Egern 92 A3
Røttangen 9 C3
Rottås 32 B2
Röttenbach 91 D1, 92 A1
Rottenbach 82 A2
Rottenbuch 91 D3, 92 A3
Rottenburg 92 B2
Rottenburg 91 B/C2
Rottenburg-Bad Niedernau 91 B/C2
Rottenburg-Ergenzingen 90 B2
Rottendorf (Würzburg) 81 D3
Rottenmann 93 D3
Rotterdam 66 A3
Rotthalmünster 93 C2
Röttingen 81 C/D3, 91 C1
Rottleberode 81 D1, 82 A1
Rottmersleben 69 C3
Rottne 51 C1
Rottnemon 38 B3
Rottneros 39 B/C3
Rottofreno 113 D1, 114 A1
Rottweil 90 B2
Roturas 166 A/B1
Rötviken 29 C/D2, 34 B1
Rötz 92 B1
Roubaix 78 A2
Rouchovany 94 A/B1
Roudnice nad Labem 83 C/D2
Roudouallec 84 B2
Rouen 77 C3
Rouffach 89 D2, 90 A3
Rouffignac 101 D3, 109 C1
Rougé 85 D3
Rougemont 89 D3
Roughsike 57 C3
Rougnac 101 C3
Rouillac 101 C2/3
Roujan 110 B3
Roukala 21 C1
Roukalahti 23 C3
Roulans 89 C3, 104 A1
Roundwood 58 A2
Roupy 78 A3
Rouravaara 11 D3, 12 A1/2
Rousínov 94 B1
Roussac 101 C2
Rouvignies 78 A/B2
Rouvray 88 A/B3
Rouvroy-sur-Audry 78 B3
Rouy 103 B/C1
Rovakka 17 D1
Rovala 13 C2
Rovala 12 B3
Rovaniemi 12 A/B3
Rovanjska 131 B/C2
Rovanpää 11 D3, 12 A/B2
Rovanpää 12 A3, 17 D1
Rovanperä 11 D3, 12 A2
Rovastinaho 18 B1
Rovato 106 A/B3
Rovensko pod Troskou 83 D2
Roverbella 106 B3
Roveredo in Piano 107 D2, 126 A2
Roveredo [Lugano] 105 D2
Rovereto 107 B/C2/3
Róvere Veronese 107 B/C3
Rövershagen 53 D3
Roverud 38 B3
Roviaí 147 C1
Rovigo 115 C1
Rovinari 135 D1
Rovinj 130 A1
Rovinjsko Selo 130 A1
Rovišče 128 A2/3
Rovisuvanto 5 D3, 6 A/B3, 11 D1
Rovno 98 B2
Rovon 103 D3, 104 A3
Rów 70 B2
Rowardennan 56 B1
Roxburgh 57 C2

Roxenbaden 46 B2
Roxförde 69 C2
Royal Leamington Spa 64 A2
Royal Tunbridge Wells 65 B/C3, 76 B1
Royan 100 B3
Royat 102 B3
Roybon 103 D3
Roye 78 A3
Royères-de-Vassivières 102 A2
Røyken 38 A3, 43 D1, 44 B1
Røykenvik 38 A2
Röykkä 25 C2/3
Røymoen 32 B3
Røyrvik 29 C1
Røysheim 37 C1/2
Røysing 28 B2
Royston 65 C2
Röyttä 17 D3, 18 A1
Røytvoll 14 A3, 28 B1
Royuela 162 A2/3
Rožaj 138 A1
Rožaj 140 A3
Rozalén del Monte 161 C3
Rózan 73 C3, 98 A1
Rózanki 71 C2
Róza Wielka 71 D1/2
Rozay-en-Brie 87 D1/2
Rožďalovice 83 D2
Roženski manastir 139 D3
Rozières-sur-Mouzon 89 C2
Rozkoš 94 A1
Rožmberk nad Vltavou 93 D2
Rožmitál pod Třemšínem 83 C3
Rožňava 97 C2
Rožnov 98 B3
Rožnov pod Radhoštěm 95 C1
Rozoy-sur-Serre 78 B3
Roztoky 83 D2/3
Rozvadov 82 B3
Rrëshen 138 A2/3
Rrogozhinë 137 D3, 142 A1
Ruabon 59 C/D2/3, 60 B3
Ruanes 165 D1, 166 A1
Rubbestad 9 D1
Rubbestadneset 42 A1
Rübenau 83 C2
Rubeži 137 C/D1
Rubiá 151 C2
Rubián 150 B2
Rubí de Bracamonte 160 A1
Rubielos Bajos 168 B1
Rubielos de la Cérida 163 C2
Rubielos de Mora 162 B3
Rubiera 114 B1
Rubik 137 D3
Rubjerg Knude 48 B1
Rublacedo de Abajo 153 C2
Rucava 73 C1
Ruchocice 71 D3
Ruda 51 D1
Rudanka 132 B1
Rudanmaa 24 B1
Rudbøl 52 A2
Ruddington 61 D3, 65 C1
Rude 127 C/D3
Ruden 127 C2
Rüdenhausen 81 D3
Rüdersdorf 70 A/B2
Rüdersdorf 72 A3
Ruderting 93 C2
Rüdesheim 80 B3
Rüdesheim-Assmannshau- sen 80 B3
Rudíkov 94 A1
Rudilla 162 B2
Rudina 135 D1
Rüdingsdorf 70 A3
Rudinice 137 C1
Rudki 97 D2, 98 A2/3
Rudkøbing 53 C2
Rudná 83 C/D3
Rudna Glava 135 C2
Rudnica 133 C3
Rudnica 134 B3, 138 B1
Rudnik 133 D2, 134 A2

Rudnik 138 B1
Rüdnitz 70 A2
Rudnja 75 C3
Rudo 133 C3
Rudolstadt 82 A2
Rudozem 140 B3
Rudsgrend 43 C1
Rudskoga 45 D1/2, 46 A1
Ruds Vedby 49 C3, 53 C1
Rue 77 D2
Rueda 160 A1
Rueda de Jalón 155 C3, 163 C1
Rueda de la Sierra 161 D2, 162 A2
Rueil-Malmaison 87 C/D1
Ruelle-sur-Touvre 101 C3
Ruerrero 152 B2
Ruesta 154 B2
Ruffano 121 D3
Ruffec 101 C2
Ruffieu 104 A2
Ruffieux 104 A3
Rúfina 115 B/C2, 116 B1
Rugby 65 C2
Rugeley 59 D3, 64 A1
Ruggstorp 51 D1
Rugles 86 B1
Rugsund 36 A1
Ruguilla 161 D2
Ruhällen 40 A3
Rühen 69 C2
Ruhkaperä 21 D1, 22 A1
Ruhla 81 D2
Rühlow 70 A1
Ruhmannsfelden 93 B/C1
Ruhpolding 92 B3
Ruhpolding-Seehaus 92 B3
Ruhstorf 93 C2
Ruhstorf-Schmidham 93 C2
Ruhvana 27 D1
Ruidera 167 D2, 168 A2
Ruínas 123 C2
Ruinen 67 C2
Ruinerwold 67 C2
Ruines-en-Margeride 110 B1
Ruissalo 24 B2/3
Ruivães 150 B3, 158 B1
Rūjiena 74 A1/2
Ruka 19 D1
Rukajärvi 19 D1
Rukkisenperä 18 A3
Rullbo 39 D1
Rülzheim 90 B1
Rum 128 A1
Ruma 133 D1, 134 A1
Ruma 140 A2
Rumburk 96 A1
Rumburk 83 D2
Rumenka 129 D3, 133 C/D1, 134 A1
Rumigny 78 B3
Rumilly 104 A2/3
Rumilly-en-Cambrésis 78 A2/3
Rummukkala 23 C3
Rumo 23 C1
Rumont 89 C1
Rumpu 27 C2
Rumšiškes 73 D2, 74 A3
Runcorn 59 D2, 60 B3
Runde 36 A1
Rundhaug 4 A3, 9 D1, 10 A1
Rundmoen 15 B/C2
Rundvik 31 C3
Runemo 40 A1
Rungsted 49 D3, 50 A3, 53 D1
Runkaus 18 A1
Runni 22 B1
Runsten 51 D2
Ruohokangas 13 C1
Ruohola 18 B1/2
Ruokojärvi 12 A2, 17 D1
Ruokojärvi 17 C1/2
Ruokolahti 27 C1/2
Ruokotaipale 27 C1
Ruolahti 25 D1, 26 A1
Ruoms 111 C1/2
Ruona 21 C2
Ruona 18 B1
Ruonajärvi 12 A2/3, 17 D1

Ruoppaköngäs 11 C/D3, 12 A1
Ruopsa 12 B3
Ruorasmäki 25 D1, 26 B1
Ruosniemi 24 A1
Ruotanen 21 D1, 22 A1
Ruoti 120 A/B2
Ruotinkulä 21 D3, 22 A3
Ruotsalo 21 B/C1
Ruotsinkylä 26 B2
Ruotsinpyhtää/Strömfors 26 B2
Ruotten 19 B/C2
Ruovesi 21 C3
Rupa 126 B3
Rupakivi 13 C3
Rupea 141 B/C1
Ruppendorf 83 C2
Ruppichteroth 80 A2
Rupt-sur-Moselle 89 D2/3
Rus 167 D3, 173 C1
Rušani 128 A3
Rúscio 117 C3, 118 B1
Rusdal 42 B3
Ruše 127 C2
Ruse 141 C2
Rusele 30 B1
Rușețu 141 C2
Ruševo 128 B3, 132 B1
Rushden 64 B2
Rushtë 138 A2
Rusi 25 D1, 26 A/B1
Rusinowo 71 C1
Rusinowo 71 D1/2
Ruskamen 131 D3
Ruske 30 A/B2, 35 D1
Ruskeala 25 D1, 26 A1
Ruskeala 25 C3
Ruski Krstur 129 C3
Rusko 24 B2
Ruskola 24 B3
Rusko Selo 129 D3
Rusksele 31 C1
Ruskträsk 31 C1
Rusovce 94 B2/3
Rüsselsheim 80 B3
Russeluft 5 C2
Russelv 4 B2
Russenes 5 D1/2, 6 A1
Russhaugen 9 C2
Russi 115 C2, 117 B/C1
Russkaja 98 B3
Rust 94 B3
Rustefjelbma 7 C1/2
Rusteseter 32 B3, 37 C1
Rustrel 111 D2
Ruszów 83 D3
Rutalahti 21 D3, 22 A3
Rutalahti 25 D1/2, 26 A2
Rutava 24 B2
Rute 172 B2
Rutesheim 91 B/C2
Rüthen 80 B1
Rutherglen 56 B2
Ruthin 59 C2, 60 A3
Ruthwell 57 C3, 60 A1
Rüti 105 D1
Rutigliano 121 C2
Rutino 120 A3
Rutledal 36 A2
Rutna 16 B1
Ruto 20 B2
Rutvik 17 C3
Ruuhijärvi 25 D2, 26 A2
Ruuhijärvi 12 A3, 17 D1
Ruuhimäki 21 D3, 22 A3
Ruukki 18 A3
Ruunaa 23 C3
Ruunala 25 B/C2
Ruurlo 67 C3
Ruutana 22 B1
Ruutana 25 C1
Ruuvaoja 13 C2
Ruvallen 34 A2
Ruvanaho 13 C3
Ruvaslahti 23 C2
Ruvo del Monte 120 A2
Ruvo di Púglia 120 B2, 136 A3
Ruza 75 D2/3
Ružany 73 D3, 98 B1
Ružić 131 C3
Ružin 99 C2/3
Ružinci 135 D3
Ružomberok 95 D1
Ružomberok 97 C2
Ry 48 B3

Rybnica **99** C3
Rybnik **96** B2
Rychnov **83** D2
Rychtářov **94** B1
Ryczywół **71** D2
Rydaholm **50** B1
Rydal **45** C3, **49** D1
Rydboholm **45** C3, **49** D1
Ryde **76** B1/2
Rydet **49** D1, **50** A1
Rydland **38** A1
Rydöbruk **50** A/B1
Rydsgård **50** B3
Rydsnäs **46** A3
Rydzyna **71** D3
Rye **48** B3
Rye **77** C1
Rygg **36** B1/2
Rygge **44** B1
Ryggefjord **5** D1, **6** A1
Ryggesbo **39** D1, **40** A1
Ryhälä **27** C1
Rykene **43** C3
Rykroken **33** C3, **37** D1
Rymättylä **24** A3
Ryningsnäs **51** D1
Rynkäinen **20** B3
Rynkänpuoli **18** B1
Rynoltice **83** D2
Ryönanjoki **22** B1
Ryphusseter **33** C3, **37** D1
Rypin **73** C3
Ryppefjord **5** C1, **6** A1
Ryr **45** C2
Rysjedalsvåg **36** A2
Ryssa **39** C/D2
Ryssby **50** B1/2
Ryssdal **36** B1/2
Rytilahti **13** C3
Rytinki **19** C1
Rytky **22** B1/2
Rytkynperä **18** A3, **21** D1, **22** A1
Ryttylä **25** C2, **26** A2
Ryumgård **49** C2
Rzeczenica **71** D1
Rzęśnica **70** B1
Rzeszów **97** C2, **98** A2
Ržev **75** C/D2

S

Sääksjärvi **21** C2
Sääksjärvi **25** D2, **26** A2
Sääksjärvi **20** B1/2
Sääksjärvi **24** B1
Sääksjärvi **25** D2, **26** B2
Sääksmäki **25** C2
Saal **53** D3
Saal **92** A/B1
Saalbach **92** B3, **126** A1
Saalburg **82** A2
Saaldorf **82** A2
Saaldorf-Surheim **92** B3
Saales **89** D2, **90** A2
Saalfeld **82** A2
Saalfelden am Steinernen
   Meer **92** B3
Saanen **104** B2
Säänjärvi **27** B/C2
Saaramaa **26** B2
Saarbrücken-Dudweiler
   89 D1, **90** A1
Saarbrücken **89** D1, **90** A1
Saarburg **79** D3
Saarela **23** D1
Saarenkirkko **27** D1
Saarenkylä **21** D2, **22** A2
Saarenmaa **24** A1/2
Säärenperä **18** A2
Saaresmäki **22** B1
Saari **27** D1
Saari **25** D2, **26** A2
Saariharju **19** B/C1
Saarijärvi **24** B1
Saarijärvi **21** D2/3, **22** A2/3
Saari-Kämä **18** B1
Saarikas **21** D3, **22** A3
Saarikoski **10** B2
Saarikoski **18** A3
Saarikylä **19** D2
Saarilampi **21** D3, **22** A3
Saarimäki **23** C1

Saario **23** D3
Saaripudas **11** C3
Saariselkä **12** B1
Saarivaara **19** D3
Saarivaara **23** C2
Saarivaara **23** D3
Saarlouis **89** D1, **90** A1
Saarmund **70** A3
Saarwellingen **89** D1,
   90 A1
Saas Almagell [Stalden-
   Saas] **105** C2
Saasenheim **90** A2
Saas Fee [Stalden-Saas]
   105 C2
Saas Grund [Stalden-Saas]
   105 C2
Sääskilahti **19** B/C1
Säävälä **18** B2
Šabac **133** C1, **134** A1
Šabac **140** A2
Sabadell **156** A3
Săbăoani **141** C1
Sabarat **108** B3, **155** C1
Sabáudia **118** B2/3
Sabero **152** A2
Sabile **73** D1
Sabiñánigo **154** B2
Sabinov **97** C2
Sabiote **167** D3, **173** C1
Šabla **141** D2/3
Sables-d'Or-les-Pins
   85 C1/2
Sablé-sur-Sarthe **86** A3
Sablonnières **88** A2
Sæbø **32** A3, **36** B1
Sabóia **170** A1
Sæbø (Øvre Eidfjord) **36** B3
Sæbøvik **42** A1
Sabres **108** B2
Sabrosa **158** B1
Sabugal **159** C3
Sæby **49** C1
Sacavém **164** A2
Sacecorbo **161** D2
Sacedón **161** C/D2
Saceruela **167** B/C2
Sachsenbrunn **81** D2,
   82 A2
Sachsendorf **70** B2
Sachsenhagen **68** A/B2/3
Sachsenheim **91** C1
Sachsenheim-Hohenhas-
   lach **91** C1
Sachy **79** C3
Sacile **107** D2
Sacra di San Michele
   112 B1
Sacramenia **152** B3,
   160 B1
Săcueni **97** C/D3,
   140 A/B1
Sada **150** B1
Sádaba **155** C2
Sada de Sangüesa **155** C2
Sadelkow **70** A1
Sadjem **16** B1
Sadovec **140** B3
Sądów **70** B3
Sadská **83** D3
Sädvaluspen **15** D2
Sady **71** D2
Saelices **161** C3, **167** D1,
   168 A1
Saelices de Mayorga
   152 A2/3
Saelices del Río **152** A2
Saelices el Chico **159** C2
Saepinum **119** D2
Saerbeck **67** D3
Saetre **38** A3, **43** D1, **44** B1
Saeul **79** D3
Safara **165** C3
Šafárikovo **97** C2
Säffle **45** C1
Saffron Walden **65** C2
Safonovo **75** C3
Šafov **94** A1/2
Säfsnäs **39** C3
Saga **28** A3, **33** C1
Sagar **83** D1
S'Agaró **156** B3
Sågen **39** C3
Sagiáda **142** A3
Sagides **161** D1/2
Sågliden **34** A3

Sågmyra **39** D2
Sagone **113** D3
Sagra **169** D2
Sagrado **126** A3
Sagres **170** A2
Sagu **24** B3
Sagunto **162** B3, **169** D1
Sagvåg **42** A1
Ságvár **128** B1
Sahagún **152** A2
Sahalahti **25** C1
Sahankylä **20** B3
Sahinpuro **23** B/C2
Sahloinen **21** D3, **22** A3
Sahrajärvi **21** D3
Sahún **155** D1
Šahovskaja **75** D2
Šahy **95** D2/3
Šahy **96** B3
Saignelégier **89** D3, **104** B1
Saignes **102** A3
Saija **13** C2/3
Säijä **25** C1
Saikari **22** B2
Saillagouse **156** A2
Saillans **111** D1
Šäimen **23** D3
Sain-Bel **103** C/D2/3
Sains-du-Nord **78** B3
Saint-Affrique **110** A2
Saint-Agnan-en-Vercors
   111 D1
Saint-Agnant **100** B2
Saint Agnes **62** B3
Saint-Agrève **111** C1
Saint-Aignan-sur-Cher
   86 A/B3, **101** C1
Saint-Aignan **109** C2
Saint-Aigulin **101** C3
Saint-Alban-sur-Limagnole
   110 B1
Saint Albans **64** B3
Saint-Alvère **109** C1
Saint-Amand-les-Eaux
   78 A/B2
Saint-Amand-de-Vendôme
   86 B3
Saint-Amand-sur-Fion
   88 B1
Saint-Amand-Mont-Rond
   102 A/B1
Saint-Amand-en-Puisaye
   87 D3
Saint-Amans-des-Cots
   110 A1
Saint-Amans-la-Lozère
   110 B1
Saint-Amans-Soult **110** A3
Saint-Amant-Roche-Savine
   103 C3
Saint-Amant-Tallende
   102 B3
Saint-Amant-de-Boixe
   101 C2/3
Saint-Amarin **89** D2/3,
   90 A3
Saint-Ambroix **111** C1
Saint-Amé **89** D2
Saint-Amour **103** D2
Saint-Andiol **111** C2
Saint-André-d'Hébertot
   77 B/C3, **86** B1
Saint-André-de-Valborgne
   110 B2
Saint-André-de-Najac
   109 D2
Saint-André-les-Alpes
   112 A2
Saint-André-de-l'Eure
   86 A/B1
Saint-André-sur-Cailly
   76 B3
Saint-André-le-Bouchoux
   103 D2
Saint-André-de-Corcy
   103 D2
Saint-André-de-Cubzac
   108 B1
Saint-André-de-Sangonis
   110 B2/3
Saint Andrews **57** C1
Saint Andrews **54** B2
Saint-Angel **102** A3
Saint Anne **63** D3
Saint-Anthème **103** C3
Saint-Antoine-de-Ficalba
   109 C2

Saint-Antoine **108** B1
Saint-Antonin **113** D3
Saint-Antonin-Noble-Val
   109 D2
Saint-Août **102** A1
Saint-Arcons-d'Allier
   103 B/C3, **110** B1
Saint-Arnoult-en-Yvelines
   87 C2
Saint Asaph **59** C2, **60** A3
Saint-Astier **101** C3
Saint-Auban-sur-l'Ouvèze
   111 D2
Saint-Auban **112** A/B2
Saint-Aubin-du-Cormier
   86 A/B2
Saint-Aubin-sur-Aire
   89 C1/2
Saint-Aubin-de-Blaye
   100 B3
Saint-Aubin-sur-Mer
   76 A/B2/3
Saint-Aubin-d'Aubigné
   85 D2
Saint-Augustin **102** A3
Saint-Aulaye **101** C3
Saint Austell **62** B3
Saint Austell-Fowey **62** B3
Saint-Avit **102** A/B2
Saint-Avold **89** D1
Saint-Aygulf **112** A/B3
Saint-Bard **102** A2
Saint-Bauzille-de-Putois
   110 B2
Saint-Béat **109** C3, **155** C2
Saint-Beauzély **110** A2
Saint Bees **57** C3, **60** A1
Saint-Benin-d'Azy **102** B1
Saint-Benoît-en-Woëvre
   89 C1
Saint-Benoît-du-Sault
   101 C2
Saint-Benoît-en-Diois
   111 D1
Saint-Benoît-en-Woëvre
   87 D1
Saint-Bertrand-de-Com-
   minges **109** C3, **155** C1
Saint-Blaise-la-Roche
   89 D2, **90** A2
Saint Blazey **62** B3
Saint-Blin **89** C2
Saint-Bonnet-le-Froid
   103 C3
Saint-Bonnet-le-Courreau
   103 C3
Saint-Bonnet-près-Riom
   102 B2
Saint-Bonnet-le-Château
   103 C3
Saint-Bonnet-de-Joux
   103 C2
Saint-Bonnet-en-Champ-
   saur **112** A1
Saint-Bonnet-de-Bellac
   101 D2
Saint-Bonnet-sur-Gironde
   100 B3
Saint Boswells **57** C2
Saint-Branchs **86** B3,
   101 D1
Saint Brelade **63** D3, **85** C1
Saint-Brévin-les-Pins
   85 C3, **100** A1
Saint-Briac-sur-Mer
   85 C1/2
Saint-Brice-en-Coglès
   86 A2
Saint-Brieuc **85** C2
Saint-Broing-les-Moines
   88 B3
Saint-Calais **86** B2/3
Saint-Cannat **111** D2/3
Saint-Caradec **85** C2
Saint-Cast **85** C1/2
Saint-Céré **109** D1
Saint-Cernin **102** A3,
   110 A1
Saint-Cézaire-sur-Siagne
   112 B3
Saint-Chamant **102** A3
Saint-Chamas **111** C/D3
Saint-Chamond **103** C3
Saint-Chély-d'Aubrac
   110 A1
Saint-Chély-d'Apcher
   110 B1

Saint-Chéron **87** C2
Saint-Chinian **110** A3
Saint-Christophe-en-Brion-
   nais **103** C2
Saint-Christoly-Médoc
   100 B3
Saint-Christophe-du-Li-
   gneron **100** A1
Saint-Christol-lès-Alès
   111 C2
Saint-Christophe-le-
   Chaudry **102** A1/2
Saint-Christophe-le-Jajolet
   86 A/B1/2
Saint-Christophe-en-Ba-
   zelle **87** C3, **101** D1,
   102 A1
Saint-Ciers-sur-Gironde
   100 B3
Saint-Cirq-Lapopie **109** D1
Saint-Clair-sur-Epte **77** D3,
   87 C1
Saint-Clar **109** C2
Saint-Clar-de-Rivière
   108 B3, **155** C1
Saint-Claud-sur-le-Son
   101 C2
Saint-Claude-sur-Bienne
   104 A2
Saint Clears **62** B1
Saint Colombier **85** C3
Saint-Côme-d'Olt **110** A1
Saint-Constant **110** A1
Saint-Cosme-en-Vairais
   86 B2
Saint-Cricq-Chalosse
   108 B2/3, **154** B1
Saint-Cyprien **109** C1
Saint-Cyprien-Plage
   156 B1/2
Saint-Cyr-du-Vaudreuil
   76 B3, **86** A/B1
Saint-Cyr-en-Talmondais
   101 C2
Saint-Cyr-l'Ecole **87** C1
Saint-Cyr-les-Vignes
   103 C3
Saint-Cyr-sur-Menthon
   103 D2
Saint-Cyr-sur-Mer **111** D3
Saint-Dalmas-le-Selvage
   112 B2
Saint David's **62** A/B1
Saint David's **55** D3
Saint Day **62** B3
Saint-Denis-de-Gastines
   85 D2, **86** A2
Saint-Denis **110** A3,
   156 A1
Saint-Denis-sur-Sarthon
   86 A2
Saint-Denis **85** C1
Saint-Denis-d'Oléron
   101 C2
Saint-Denis-en-Bugey
   103 D2
Saint-Denis-d'Anjou **86** A3
Saint-Didier-sur-Chalaro-
   nue **103** D2
Saint-Didier-en-Velay
   103 C3
Saint-Dié **89** D2, **90** A2
Saint-Dier-d'Auvergne
   102 B3
Saint-Disdier **111** D1,
   112 A1
Saint-Dizier **88** B2
Saint-Dizier-Leyrenne
   102 A2
Saint Dogmaels **62** B1
Saint-Donat **102** B3
Saint-Dyé-sur-Loire **87** C3
Sainte-Adresse **76** B3
Sainte-Anne-d'Auray
   85 C3
Sainte-Anne **86** B2
Sainte-Bazeille **108** B1
Sainte-Cécile **103** C/D2
Sainte-Croix **111** D1
Sainte-Croix-Volvestre
   108 B3, **155** C1
Sainte-Croix-en-Plaine
   90 A3
Sainte-Engrâce **108** A/B3,
   154 B1
Sainte-Énimie **110** B2

Sainte-Eulalie-en-Born **108** B2

Sainte-Feyre **102** A2

Sainte-Foy-de-Longas **109** C1

Sainte-Foy-l'Argentière **103** C3

Sainte-Foy-la-Grande **109** B/C1

Sainte-Gauburge-Sainte-Colombe **86** B1/2

Sainte-Gemme-la-Plaine **100** B2

Sainte-Geneviève-sur-Argence **110** A1

Sainte-Hélène **108** A/B1

Sainte-Hermine **100** B2

Sainte-Jalle **111** D2

Sainte-Livrade-sur-Lot **109** C2

Saint-Élix-Theux **109** C3, **155** C1

Sainte-Lucie-di-Tallano **113** D3

Sainte-Marguerite **77** C2/3

Sainte-Marie-de-Ré **101** C2

Sainte-Marie-de-Vars **112** A/B1

Sainte-Marie-aux-Mines **89** D2, **90** A2

Sainte-Marie-de-Campan **109** C3, **155** C1

Sainte-Marie-et-Sicché **113** D3

Sainte-Maure-de-Touraine **101** C1

Sainte-Maxime-sur-Mer **112** A3

Sainte-Menehould **88** B1

Sainte-Mère-Eglise **76** B3

Saint-Émilion **108** B1

Sainte-Montaine **87** D3

Sainte-Odile **90** A2

Saintes **100** B3

Sainte-Sévère-sur-Indre **102** A2

Saintes-Maries-de-la-Mer **111** C3

Saint-Esteben **108** B3, **155** C1

Saint-Estèphe **100** B3

Sainte-Suzanne **86** A2

Sainte-Thorette **102** A1

Saint-Étienne-de-Montluc **85** D3, **100** A1

Saint-Étienne-en-Dévoluy **111** D1, **112** A1

Saint-Étienne-les-Orgues **111** D2, **112** A2

Saint-Étienne-de-Baïgorry **108** B3, **155** C1

Saint-Étienne-du-Grès **111** C2

Saint-Étienne-de-Saint-Geoirs **103** D3

Saint-Étienne-de-Tinée **112** B2

Saint-Étienne-de-Lugdarès **110** B1

Saint-Étienne-Vallée-Française **110** B2

Saint-Étienne **103** C3

Saint-Fargeau **87** D3

Saint-Félicien **103** C/D3, **111** C1

Saint-Félix-Lauragais **109** D3

Saint-Félix **100** B2

Saint-Félix-de-Sorgues **110** A/B2

Saint-Fiacre **84** B2

Saintfield **56** A3

Saint Fillans **56** B1

Saint-Firmin-en-Valgodemard **112** A1

Saint-Florent **113** D2

Saint-Florent-le-Vieil **85** D3

Saint-Florent-sur-Cher **102** A1

Saint-Florentin **88** A2

Saint-Florent-des-Bois **101** C1/2

Saint-Flour **110** B1

Saint-Flovier **101** D1

Saint-Fort-sur-le-Né **101** C1

Saint-Fort-sur-Gironde **100** B3

Saint-François-Longchamp **104** A/B3

Saint-Front-sur-Lémance **109** C1

Saint-Fulgent **101** C1

Saint-Gabriel-Brécy **76** B3, **86** A1

Saint-Galmier **103** C3

Saint-Gaudens **109** C3, **155** C1

Saint-Gaultier **101** D1

Saint-Gein **108** B2

Saint-Gély-du-Fesc **110** B2

Saint-Genès-Champespe **102** A3

Saint-Genest-Malifaux **103** C3

Saint-Gengoux-le-National **103** C/D1/2

Saint-Geniès-de-Malgoirès **111** C2

Saint-Geniez-d'Olt **110** A/B1/2

Saint-Genis-Laval **103** D3

Saint-Genis-de-Saintonge **100** B3

Saint-Génis-Pouilly **104** A2

Saint-Génis-des-Fontaines **156** B2

Saint-Genix-sur-Guiers **104** A3

Saint-Geoire-en-Valdaine **104** A3

Saint-Georges-sur-Loire **86** A3

Saint-Georges-de-Luzençon **110** A/B2

Saint-Georges-en-Couzan **103** C3

Saint-Georges-du-Vièvre **77** C3, **86** B1

Saint-Georges de Didonne **100** B3

Saint-Georges-sur-la-Prée **87** C3, **102** A1

Saint-Georges-du-Bois **86** B2

Saint-Georges-de-Reneins **103** D2

Saint-Geours-de-Maremme **108** B2/3

Saint-Gérand-le-Puy **102** B2

Saint-Gérard **79** C2

Saint-Germain-de-Confolens **101** C/D2

Saint-Germain-de-Joux **104** A2

Saint-Germain-l'Herm **103** B/C3

Saint-Germain-de-Calberte **110** B2

Saint-Germain-Laval **103** C2/3

Saint-Germain-Lembron **102** B3

Saint-Germain-des-Fossés **102** B2

Saint-Germain-du-Plain **103** D1

Saint-Germain-du-Bois **103** D1

Saint-Germain-lès-Arlay **103** D1, **104** A1

Saint-Germain-Lespinasse **103** C2

Saint-Germain-les-Belles **101** D3

Saint-Germain-en-Laye **87** C1

Saint Germans **62** B3

Saint-Germé **108** B2/3

Saint-Germer-de-Fly **77** D3

Saint-Gervais-sur-Mare **110** A/B2/3

Saint-Gervais-d'Auvergne **102** B2

Saint-Gervais-les-Bains **104** B2/3

Saint-Gildas-de-Rhuys **85** C3

Saint-Gildas-des-Bois **85** C3

Saint-Gilles **111** C2/3

Saint-Gilles-Croix-de-Vie **100** A1

Saint-Gingolph **104** B2

Saint-Girons **108** B3, **155** C1/2

Saint-Girons **108** B2

Saint-Goin **108** B3, **154** B1

Saint-Gobain **78** A3

Saint-Gondon **87** D3

Saint-Gorgon-Main **104** A/B1

Saint-Gravé **85** C3

Saint-Guénolé **84** A3

Saint-Guilhem-le-Désert **110** B2

Saint-Héand **103** C3

Saint Helens **59** D2, **60** B3

Saint Helier **63** D3, **85** C1

Saint-Herbot **84** A2

Saint-Hilaire **110** A3, **156** A1

Saint-Hilaire-de-Court **87** C3, **102** A1

Saint-Hilaire-du-Harcouët **85** D2

Saint-Hilaire-de-Villefranche **100** B2/3

Saint-Hilaire-des-Loges **100** B2

Saint-Hilaire-Fontaine **103** C1

Saint-Hilaire-Cottes **77** D2, **78** A2

Saint-Hilaire-le-Grand **88** B1

Saint-Hilaire-Bonneval **101** C3

Saint Hippolyte **89** D3, **104** B1

Saint-Hippolyte-du-Fort **110** B2

Saint-Honorat **112** B3

Saint-Honoré-les-Bains **103** C1

Saint-Hubert **79** C3

Saint Ives **62** A3

Saint Ives **65** C2

Saint-James **86** A2

Saint-Jaques **105** C3

Saint-Jean-aux-Bois **87** D1

Saint-Jean-Brévelay **85** C2/3

Saint-Jean-de-Luz **108** A3, **154** A1

Saint-Jean-de-Verges **109** D3, **155** D1, **156** A1

Saint-Jean-d'Angle **100** B2/3

Saint-Jean-de-Bournay **103** D3

Saint-Jean-d'Angély **100** B2

Saint-Jean-de-Côle **101** D3

Saint-Jean-de-Losne **103** D1

Saint Jean-de-Daye **76** B3, **86** A/B1

Saint-Jean-de-Monts **100** A1

Saint-Jean-d'Illac **108** A/B1

Saint-Jean-du-Doigt **84** B1/2

Saint-Jean-du-Gard **110** B2

Saint-Jean-du-Bruel **110** B2

Saint-Jean-de-Sixt **104** A/B2/3

Saint-Jean-de-Maurienne **104** A/B3

Saint-Jean-de Barrou **110** A3, **156** B1

Saint-Jean-de-Maruéjols **111** C2

Saint-Jean-de-Linières **86** A3

Saint-Jean-de-Fos **110** B2

Saint-Jean-en-Royans **111** D1

Saint-Jean-le-Centenier **111** C1

Saint-Jean-le-Priche **103** D2

Saint-Jean-le-Thomas **85** D1

Saint-Jean-les-Deux-Jumeaux **87** D1

Saint-Jean-la-Bussière **103** C2

Saint-Jean-Pied-de-Port **108** B3, **155** C1

Saint-Jean-Rohrbach **89** D1, **90** A1

Saint-Jean-Soleymieux **103** C3

Saint-Jean-sur-Erve **86** A2

Saint-Jeoire **104** B2

Saint-Jeure-d'Ay **103** D3

Saint John **63** D3, **85** C1

Saint John's Chapel **57** D3, **60** B1

Saint Johns **58** B1

Saint-Jores **76** A3, **85** D1

Saint-Jouan-de-l'Isle **85** C2

Saint-Jouin-de-Marnes **101** C1

Saint-Juéry **110** A2

Saint-Julien Boutières **111** C1

Saint-Julien-l'Ars **101** C2

Saint-Julien-du-Sault **88** A2

Saint-Julien-en-Quint **111** D1

Saint-Julien-Molin-Molette **103** C/D3

Saint-Julien-en-Genevois **104** A2

Saint-Julien-de-l'Escap **100** B2

Saint-Julien-sur-le-Suran **103** D2, **104** A2

Saint-Julien-Beychevelle **100** B3

Saint-Julien-le-Faucon **86** B1

Saint-Julien-Chapteuil **111** C1

Saint-Julien-en-Born **108** B2

Saint-Julien-en-Beauchêne **111** D1

Saint-Junien **101** D2

Saint Just **62** A3

Saint-Just-en-Chevalet **103** C2

Saint-Just-en-Chaussée **77** D3

Saint-Juste-Ibarre **108** A3, **154** B1

Saint-Justin **108** B2

Saint-Just-sur-Loire **103** C3

Saint Keverne **62** B3

Saint-Lambert-du-Lattay **86** A3, **100** B1

Saint-Lary **155** C2

Saint-Lary **109** C2

Saint-Laurent-en-Grandvaux **104** A2

Saint-Laurent-sur-Saône **103** D2

Saint-Laurent-des-Eaux **87** C3

Saint-Laurent-du-Pont **104** A3

Saint-Laurent-de-Mûre **103** D3

Saint-Laurent-sur-Gorre **101** D3

Saint-Laurent **89** D2

Saint-Laurent-sur-Mer **76** A/B3, **86** A1

Saint-Laurent-d'Aigouze **111** C2/3

Saint-Laurent-en-Caux **77** C3

Saint-Laurent-de-Neste **109** C3, **155** C1

Saint-Laurent-de-la-Cabrerisse **110** A3, **156** B1

Saint-Laurent-de-Chamousset **103** C3

Saint-Laurent-des-Autels **86** A/B3, **101** C1

Saint-Laurent-de-Cerdans **156** B2

Saint-Laurent-et-Benon **100** B3

Saint-Laurent-sur-Sèvre **100** B1

Saint-Laurent-les-Bains **110** B1

Saint-Laurent-de-la-Salanque **156** B1

Saint-Laurent-en-Gâtines **86** B3

Saint-Léger-sous-Beuvray **103** C1

Saint-Léger-sous-Cholet **85** D3, **100** B1

Saint-Léger-en-Yvelines **87** C1/2

Saint-Léger-des-Vignes **102** B1

Saint-Léger-sur-Dheune **103** C/D1

Saint-Léon **109** D3, **155** D1

Saint-Léonard-de-Noblat **101** D2/3

Saint-Léonard-des-Bois **86** A2

Saint Leonards **77** C1

Saint-Leu-d'Esserent **77** D3, **87** D1

Saint-Lizier **108** B3, **155** C1

Saint-Lô **85** D1

Saint-Louis **90** A3

Saint-Loup-de-Fribois **86** A/B1

Saint-Loup-de-la-Salle **103** D1

Saint-Loup-de-Naud **87** D2, **88** A2

Saint-Loup-du-Dorat **86** A2/3

Saint-Loup-sur-Semouse **89** C/D2/3

Saint-Lunaire **85** C1/2

Saint-Lys **108** B3, **155** C1

Saint-Macaire **108** B1

Saint-Maclou **77** C3, **86** B1

Saint-Magne **108** B1

Saint-Maixent-l'École **101** C2

Saint-Malo **85** C1/2

Saint-Mamest **109** C1

Saint-Mamet-la-Salvetat **110** A1

Saint-Marcel **103** D1

Saint-Marcel-de-Careiret **111** C2

Saint-Marcellin **103** D3

Saint-Marcet **109** C3, **155** C1

Saint-Marc-sur-Seine **88** B3

Saint-Mard-de-Réno **86** B2

Saint-Mars-la-Jaille **86** A/B3

Saint-Martain-la-Rivière **101** C/D2

Saint-Martial-d'Artenset **109** B/C1

Saint-Martin-Osmonville **76** B3

Saint-Martin-de-Ré **101** C2

Saint-Martin-en-Campagne **76** B2

Saint-Martin-en-Haut **103** C3

Saint-Martin-d'Estréaux **103** C2

Saint-Martin-d'Auxigny **87** D3, **102** A1

Saint-Martin **110** B2/3

Saint-Martin-d'Ablois **88** A1

Saint-Martin-du-Puy **88** A3

Saint-Martin-en-Bresse **103** D1

Saint-Martin-de-Londres **110** B2

Saint-Martin-de-Valamas **111** C1

Saint-Martin-de-Seignanx **108** B3, **155** C1

Saint-Martin-de-Crau
111 C2/3
Saint-Martin-Valmeroux
102 A3, **110** A1
Saint-Martin-la-Méanne
102 A3
Saint-Martin-sur-Ouanne
87 D3
Saint-Martin-d'Ardèche
111 C2
Saint-Martin-Vésubie
112 B2
Saint-Martin-des-Besaces
85 D1, **86** A1
Saint-Martin-du-Var
112 B2
Saint-Martin-d'Oney
108 B2
Saint-Martin-d'Oydes
109 D3, **155** D1, **156** A1
Saint-Martin-de-Boscher-
ville **77** C3
Saint-Martin-d'Entraunes
112 B2
Saint-Martory **109** C3,
155 D1
Saint-Mathieu **101** D3
Saint-Mathieu **84** A2
Saint-Mathurin **86** A3
Saint-Matré **108** B2
Saint-Maurice-Navacelles
110 B2
Saint-Maurice-sur-Aveyron
87 D3
Saint-Maurice-de-Ventalon
110 B2
Saint-Maurice-les-Charen-
cey **86** B2
Saint-Maurice-sur-Moselle
89 D2/3, **90** A3
Saint-Maurin **109** C2
Saint Mawes **62** B3
Saint-Maximin-la-Sainte-
Baume **111** D3, **112** A3
Saint-Médard-de-Guizières
108 B1
Saint-Médard-en-Jalles
108 B1
Saint-Méen-le-Grand
85 C2
Saint-Menoux **102** B1/2
Saint-Mesmin **100** B1
Saint Michael's Mount
62 A3
Saint-Michel-en-Grève
84 B1/2
Saint-Michel-Chef-Chef
85 C3, **100** A1
Saint-Michel-de-Castelnau
108 B2
Saint-Michel-de-Maurienne
104 B3, **112** A1
Saint-Michel-en-l'Herm
101 C2
Saint-Michel-Mont Mercure
100 B1
Saint-Michel **109** C3,
155 C1
Saint-Mihiel **89** C1
Saint-Montant **111** C1/2
Saint-Nazaire **85** C3,
100 A1
Saint-Nazaire-le-Désert
111 D1
Saint-Nazaire-en-Royans
103 D3, **111** D1
Saint-Nectaire **102** B3
Saint Neots **64** B2
Saint-Nicolas-du-Pélem
84 B2
Saint-Nicolas-de-la-Grave
109 C2
Saint-Nicolas-de-Port
89 C/D2
Saint-Nicolas-de-Redon
85 C3
Saint-Omer **77** D1
Saint-Pair-sur-Mer **85** D1
Saint-Palais **108** A3,
154 B1
Saint-Palais-sur-Mer
100 B3
Saint-Papoul **109** D3,
156 A1
Saint-Pardoux-la-Rivière
101 D3

Saint-Parres-lès-Vaudes
88 B2
Saint-Paul-Cap-de-Joux
109 D2/3
Saint-Paul-de-Fenouillet
156 B1
Saint-Paul-de-Jarrat
109 D3, **155** D1/2,
156 A1
Saint-Paul-de-Varáx
103 D2
Saint-Paul-des-Landes
110 A1
Saint-Paul-et-Valmalle
110 B2/3
Saint-Paulien **103** C3,
110 B1
Saint-Paul-lez-Durance
111 D2
Saint-Paul-le-Jeune
111 C2
Saint-Paul-lès-Dax **108** A2
Saint-Paul-sur-Ubaye
112 B2
Saint-Paul-Trois-Châteaux
111 C2
Saint-Pé-de-Bigorre
108 B3, **155** B/C1
Saint-Pée-sur-Nivelle
108 A3, **154** A1
Saint-Péravy-la-Colombe
87 C2
Saint-Péray **111** C1
Saint-Père **88** A3
Saint-Père-en-Retz **85** C3,
100 A1
Saint Peter Port **63** D3
Saint-Péver **84** B2
Saint-Pey-d'Armens
108 B1
Saint Philbert-de-Bouaine
100 A1
Saint-Philbert-de-Grand-
Lieu **100** A1
Saint-Pierre-sur-Dives
86 A/B1
Saint-Pierre **110** A2
Saint-Pierre-en-Port **77** C3
Saint-Pierre-les-Bois
102 A1
Saint-Pierre-le-Moûtier
102 B1
Saint-Pierre-Église **76** B3
Saint-Pierre-de-Fursac
101 D2
Saint-Pierre-du-Chemin
100 B1
Saint-Pierre-de-la-Fage
110 B2
Saint-Pierre-des-Nids
86 A2
Saint-Pierreville **111** C1
Saint-Pierre-de-Chignac
101 D3, **109** C1
Saint-Pierre-de-Chartreuse
104 A3
Saint-Pierre-sur-Mer
110 B3, **156** B1
Saint-Pierre-Toirac **109** D1
Saint-Pierre-de-Boeuf
103 D3
Saint-Pierre-d'Entremont
104 A3
Saint-Pierre-d'Oléron
101 C2
Saint-Pierre-Chérignat
101 D2, **102** A2
Saint-Pierre-sur-Orthe
86 A2
Saint-Pierre-Quiberon
84 B3
Saint-Pierre-à-Champ
101 B/C1
Saint-Plancard **109** C3,
155 C1
Saint-Pois **85** D1
Saint-Poix **85** D2
Saint-Pol-de-Léon
84 B1/2
Saint-Polgues **103** C2
Saint-Pol-sur-Ternoise
77 D2
Saint-Pol-sur-Mer **77** D1,
78 A1
Saint-Pons **110** A3
Saint-Porchaire **100** B2/3

Saint-Pourçain-sur-Besbre
103 C2
Saint-Pourçain-sur-Sioule
102 B2
Saint-Priest-des-Champs
102 B2
Saint-Priest-Laprugne
103 C2
Saint-Privat **102** A3
Saint-Privat-d'Allier
110 B1
Saint-Privé **87** D3
Saint-Prix **111** C1
Saint-Puy **109** C2
Saint-Quay-Portrieux
85 C1/2
Saint-Quentin-les-Anges
85 D3, **86** A3
Saint-Quentin **78** A3
Saint-Rambert-en-Bugey
103 D2, **104** A2
Saint-Rambert-sur-Loire
103 C3
Saint-Rambert-d'Albon
103 D3
Saint-Raphaël **112** B3
Saint-Remèze **111** C2
Saint-Rémy-du-Plain
85 D2
Saint-Rémy-sur-Dore
103 B/C2
Saint-Rémy-de-Provence
111 C2
Saint-Rémy **86** A1
Saint-Rémy **109** B/C1
Saint Renan **84** A2
Saint-René **85** C2
Saint-Revèrien **88** A3,
102 B1
Saint-Riquier **77** D2
Saint-Romain-de-Colbosc
77 C3
Saint-Romain-de-Jalionas
103 D3
Saint-Romans **103** D3,
111 D1
Saint-Rome-de-Cernon
110 A/B2
Saint-Rome-de-Tarn
110 A2
Saint-Saëns **76** B3
Saint-Samson-la-Poterie
77 D3
Saint-Satur **87** D3
Saint-Saturnin **102** B3
Saint-Saturnin-d'Apt
111 D2
Saint-Saud-Lacoussière
101 D3
Saint-Saulge **102** B1
Saint-Sauves-d'Auvergne
102 B3
Saint-Sauveur-de-Monta-
gut **111** C1
Saint-Sauveur-le-Vicomte
76 A3
Saint-Sauveur **100** A1
Saint-Sauveur-en-Puisaye
87 D3, **88** A3
Saint-Sauveur-Lendelin
85 D1
Saint-Sauveur-sur-Tinée
112 B2
Saint-Savin **100** B3
Saint-Savin **101** D1/2
Saint-Savin **108** B3,
155 C1/2
Saint-Savinien **100** B2
Saint-Seine-en-Bâche
103 D1, **104** A1
Saint-Seine-l'Abbaye
88 B3
Saint-Sernin-sur-Rance
110 A2
Saint-Servan-sur-Mer
85 C1/2
Saint-Sever **108** B2
Saint-Sever-Calvados
85 D1
Saint-Séverin **101** C3
Saint-Soupplets **87** D1
Saint-Sulpice **109** D2
Saint-Sulpice-sur-Lèze
108 B3, **155** C1
Saint-Sulpice-de-Favières
87 C/D2

Saint-Sulpice-les-Feuilles
101 C2
Saint-Sylvestre-sur-Lot
109 C2
Saint-Symphorien
108 B1/2
Saint-Symphorien-d'Ancel-
les **103** D2
Saint-Symphorien-de-Lay
103 C2
Saint-Symphorien-sur-Co-
ise **103** C3
Saint-Symphorien-d'Ozon
103 D2
Saint-Thégonnec **84** B2
Saint-Thibault **88** B3
Saint-Thibéry **110** B3
Saint-Thiébault **89** C2
Saint-Trivier-de-Courtes
103 C2
Saint-Trivier-sur-Moignans
103 D2
Saint-Trojan-les-Bains
101 C2/3
Saint-Tropez **112** A3
Saint-Urcize **110** A/B1
Saint-Vaast-la-Hougue
76 B3
Saint-Valéry-en-Caux
77 C2/3
Saint-Valéry-sur-Somme
77 D2
Saint-Vallier **103** D3
Saint-Vallier-de-Thiey
112 B3
Saint-Vaury **102** A2
Saint-Venant **78** A2
Saint-Véran **112** B1
Saint-Vincent-de-Connezac
101 C3
Saint-Vincent **105** C3
Saint-Vincent-de-Tyrosse
108 B2/3
Saint-Vincent-sur-Jabron
111 D2
Saint-Vit **89** C3, **104** A1
Saint-Vivien-de-Médoc
100 B3
Saint-Wandrille **77** C3
Saint-Yan **103** C2
Saint-Ybars **108** B3,
155 C1
Saint-Yorre **102** B2
Saint-Yrieix-la-Perche
101 C3
Saint-Yrieix-le-Déjalat
102 A3
Saint-Yvy **84** B2
Saint-Zacharie **111** D3
Sainville **87** C2
Sairakkala **25** D2, **26** A2
Sairinen **24** A2
Saissac **110** A3, **156** A1
Saivomuotka **11** C2/3
Sajaniemi **25** C2
Šajkaš **129** D3, **133** D1,
134 A1
Säjvis **17** D2/3
Säkäjärvi **27** B/C2
Sakarétsi **146** A1
Šakiai **73** D2
Säkinmäki **22** A/B3
Säkkilä **13** C3
Sakrihei **14** B2
Saksala **24** B2
Saksenvik **15** C1
Sakskøbing **53** D2
Saksnes **32** B2
Saksumdal **37** D2, **38** A1/2
Säkylä **24** B2
Sala **40** A3
Šal'a **95** C2
Salacgrīva **73** D1, **74** A2
Salach **91** C2
Sala Consilina **120** A3
Salahmi **22** B1
Salamajärvi **21** C2
Salamanca **159** D2
Salamís **147** D2
Salandra **120** B2/3
Salanki **10** D2, **12** A1
Salantai **73** C1/2
Salaparuta **124** A2
Salar **172** B2
Salardú **155** D2
Salas **151** D1
Salás **155** D2

Salaš **135** C2
Salas Altas **155** C3
Salas de los Infantes
153 C3
Salaspils **73** D1, **74** A2
Salau **155** C2
Salavaux [Avenches]
104 B1
Salberg **31** C2
Salberget **31** C1
Salbertrand **112** B1
Salbohed **40** A3
Salbris **87** C3
Salceda de Caselas **150** A3
Salching **92** B2
Salcia **135** D2
Šalčininkai **73** D2, **74** A3
Salcombe **63** C3
Sălcuţa **135** D2
Saldaña **152** A/B2
Saldeana **159** C2
Saldón **162** A3
Saldus **73** C/D1
Sale **59** D2, **60** B3
Sale **113** D1
Saleby **45** C/D2
Salem **91** C3
Salemertal **91** C3
Salemi **124** A2
Salen **56** A1
Salen **28** B1
Sälen **39** C1
Salen **54** A2, **55** D1
Salen **54** A2, **55** D1
Salenpää **26** B2
Salernes **112** A3
Salerno **119** D3
Salers **102** A/B3, **110** A1
Salettes **110** B1
Salford **59** D2, **60** B3
Salgen-Hausen **91** D2
Salgótarján **97** C3
Salgueiro **158** B3, **165** C1
Salgüero de Juarros **153** C2
Salhus **36** A3
Sali **130** B2/3
Sálice Salentino **121** D3
Sálice Terme **113** D1
Salientes **151** D2
Saliers **111** C2/3
Salies-de-Béarn **108** A3,
154 B1
Salies-du-Salat **109** C3,
155 D1
Salignac **108** B1
Salihli **149** D2
Salillas **154** B3
Salillas de Jalón **155** C3,
163 B/C1
Salinas **151** D1
Salinas **161** D3, **162** A3,
168 B1
Salinas **169** C2/3
Salinas **155** C2
Salinas de Hoz **155** C2/3
Salinas de Jaca **154** B2
Salinas del Manzano
162 A3
Salinas de Léniz **153** D2
Salinas de Oro **153** D2,
154 A2
Salinas de Pisuerga **152** B2
Salin-de-Giraud **111** C3
Saline di Volterra **114** B3,
116 A2
Salinillas de Bureba **153** C2
Sälinkää **25** D2, **26** A2
Salin-les-Thermes **104** B3
Salins-les-Bains **104** A1
Salir **170** B2
Salir do Porto **164** A1
Salisbury **76** A1
Salizzole **107** C3
Salka **95** D3
Sälkastugorna **9** D3
Salla **13** C3
Salla **127** C1
Sallanches **104** B2/3
Sallent **156** A2/3
Sallent de Gállego **154** B2
Salles **108** A/B1
Salles-Curan **110** A2
Salles-sous-Bois **111** C1/2
Salles-sur-l'Hers **109** D3,
155 D1, **156** A1
Sallgast **83** C1
Sallingsund **48** A2

Sällsjö 29 C3, 34 B2
Salmchâteau 79 D2
Salmenkylä 22 B3
Salmentaka 25 C1
Salmerón 161 D2
Salmi 21 B/C2
Salmiech 110 A2
Salmijärvi 11 C3, 12 A2
Salmijärvi 19 C2
Salminen 19 C/D1
Salminen 22 B2/3
Salmivaara 13 C3
Salmtal 80 A3
Salò 106 B3
Salo 24 B3
Salobre 168 A2
Salobrena 173 C2
Saloinen 25 C2, 26 A2
Saloinen 18 A3
Salo-Issakka 27 C2
Salokylä 23 C3
Salo-Miehikkälä 26 B2
Salomó 163 C1
Salona 131 C/D3
Salon-de-Provence
    111 D2/3
Saloníki 142 B3
Salonta 97 C3, 140 A1
Saloranta 27 C1
Salorino 165 C1
Salornay-sur-Guye
    103 C/D2
Salorno/Salurn 107 C2
Salou 163 C2
Salpakangas 25 D2, 26 A2
Salreu 158 A2
Salsadella 163 C2
Salsàn 34 B2
Salsbruket 28 B1
Salses 156 B1
Salsomaggiore Terme
    114 A1
Salsta 40 B3
Salt 156 B2
Saltash 62 B3
Saltburn-by-the-Sea 61 C1
Saltbuvik 28 B2
Saltcoats 56 B2
Saltfleet 61 D3
Saltoluokta fjällstation 9 D3
Saltsjöbaden 47 D1
Saltum 48 B1
Saltveit 42 A1/2
Saltvik 40 B1
Saltvik 51 D1
Saltvik 41 C/D2/3
Saludécio 115 D2, 117 C1
Salussola 105 C3
Saluzzo 112 B1
Salvacañete 162 A3
Salvada 165 B/C3, 170 B1
Salvador 159 C3
Salvador de Zapardiel
    160 A1/2
Salvages 110 A2/3
Salvagnac 109 D2
Salvaleón 165 D2/3
Salvaterra de Miño 150 A3
Salvaterra de Magos
    164 A2
Salvaterra do Extremo
    159 C3, 165 C1
Salvatierra de Santiago
    165 D1, 166 A1/2
Salvatierra de Esca 154 B2
Salvatierra de los Barros
    165 D2/3
Salviac 108 B1
Sælvig 49 C3, 53 C1
Salzbergen 67 D2/3
Salzburg 93 B/C3
Salzderhelden 68 B3
Salzfurtkapelle 69 D3,
    82 B1
Salzgitter 68 B3
Salzgitter Bad 68 B3
Salzgitter-Gebhardshagen
    68 B3
Salzgitter-Lebenstedt
    68 B3
Salzgitter-Thiede 69 B/C3
Salzhausen 68 B1
Salzhemmendorf 68 B3
Salzhemmendorf-Lauen-
    stein 68 B3
Salzkotten 68 A3, 80 B1
Salzmünde 82 A1

Salzwedel 69 C2
Salzweg 93 C2
Sama de Langreo 151 D1,
    152 A1
Samadet 108 B2/3, 154 B1
Samarína 142 B2
Samassi 123 C3
Samatan 109 C3, 155 D1
Sambiase 122 A/B2
Sambin 86 A/B3
Samboal 160 B1
Sambor 97 D2, 98 A2
Sambuca di Sicília
    124 A/B2
Sambuci 118 B2
Samedan 106 A2
Samekappelet 6 B1
Samer 77 D2
Sámi 146 A2
Sámi 148 A2
Samikón 146 B3
Sammakko 17 B/C1
Sammakkovaara 23 C2
Sammakkovaara 23 C1
Sammaljoki 24 B1/2
Sammatti 25 C3
Sammichele di Bari 121 C2
Samminmaja 24 B1
Samnanger 36 A3
Samnaun [Scuol-Tarasp]
    106 B1
Samobor 127 C/D3
Samodreža 138 B1
Samoëns 104 B2
Samokov 138 B3
Samokov 138 B3
Samokov 139 D2
Samokov 140 B3
Samone 105 C3
Samora Correia 164 A2
Šamorín 95 C2/3
Samoš 134 B1
Samos 151 C2
Sámos 149 D2
Samothráki (Chora)
    145 C/D2
Samper de Calanda
    162 B1/2
Samper del Salz 162 B1
Sampèyre 112 B1/2
Sampieri 125 C3
Sämsjölandet 30 A/B2
Samswegen 69 C3
Samugheo 123 C/D2
San Adrián 153 D2, 154 A2
San Adrián de Juarros
    153 C2/3
San Agustín 161 C2
San Agustín de Llusanés
    156 A2
San Amaro 150 B2
San Andrés del Rabanedo
    151 D2, 152 A2
San Andrés del Congosto
    161 C2
San Aniol de Finestres
    156 B2
San Antolín 151 C1/2
San Antonio Abad 169 D2
San Asensio 153 D2
Sanaüja 155 C3
San Bartolomé de Pinares
    160 B2
San Bartolomeo al Mare
    113 C2
San Bartolomeo in Galdo
    119 D2, 120 A1
San Bartolomé de las Abier-
    tas 160 A3, 166 B1
San Bartolomé de la Torre
    171 C1
San Baudílio de Llusanés
    156 A2
San Benedetto 118 B2
San Benedetto in Alpe
    115 C2, 116 B1
San Benedetto del Tronto
    117 D2/3
San Benedetto Po 114 B1
San Benito 166 B2
San Bernardino [Castione-
    Arbedo] 105 D2, 106 A2
San Biágio Plátani 124 B2
San Biágio di Callalta
    107 D3
San Biase 119 D2

San Biase 120 A3
San Bonifácio 107 C3
San Bou 157 C1
San Bruno 119 D2
San Carlo 124 B2
San Carlos 157 D3
San Carlos del Valle
    167 D2, 168 A2
San Carlo (Val Bavona)
    [Ponte Brolla] 105 D2
San Casciano in Val di Pesa
    114 B2/3, 116 B2
San Casciano dei Bagni
    116 B3
San Cassiano 107 C2
San Cassiano/Sankt Kassian
    107 C2
San Cataldo 124 B2
San Cataldo 121 D3
San Cataldo 119 C2
San Cebrián de Mazote
    152 A3, 160 A1
San Cebrián de Castro
    151 D3, 159 D1
San Cebrián de Mudá
    152 B2
San Cebrián de Campos
    152 B3
Sancelles 157 C2
Sancergues 87 D3, 102 B1
Sancerre 87 C2
San Cesáreo 118 B2
San Cesário di Lecce
    121 D3
Sancey-le-Grand 89 D3,
    104 B1
Sancheville 87 C2
Sanchidrián 160 A/B2
San Chírico Raparo 120 B3
San Chírico Nuovo 120 B2
Sanchonuño 160 B1
San Cipirello 124 A/B2
San Ciprián 150 B1
San Ciprián de Viñas
    150 B2/3
San Cipriano Picentino
    119 D3, 120 A2
San Cipriano d'Aversa
    119 C3
San Claudio al Chienti
    117 D2
San Clemente 115 B/C2,
    116 B1
San Clemente 157 C1
San Clemente 168 A/B1
Sancoins 102 B1
San Colombano al Lambro
    106 A3, 113 D1
San Costantino Albanese
    120 B3, 122 A/B1
San Cristóbal de Cuéllar
    160 B1
San Cristóbal de Cea
    150 B2
San Cristóbal de la Cuesta
    159 D2
San Cristóbal de Entreviñas
    151 D3, 152 A3
San Cristóbal de la Polantera
    151 D2
San Cristóbal 157 C1
San Cristóbal de la Vega
    160 A/B2
Sancti-Spíritus 159 C2
Sancti-Spíritus 166 B2
Sand 31 C2
Sand 42 A1/2
Sand 38 A3
Sanda 43 C2
Sanda 41 D3
Sandaméri 146 B2
San Damiano d'Asti 113 C1
San Damiano Macra
    112 B2
Sandane 36 B1/2
San Daniele Po 114 A1
San Daniele del Friuli
    107 D2, 126 A2
Sandanski 139 D3
Sandanski 139 D3
Sandanski 140 B3
Sandared 45 C3
Sandarne 40 B1
Sandås 30 B1
Sandau 69 D2
Sandbach 59 D2, 60 B3,
    64 A1

Sandbäckshult 51 D1
Sandbank 56 B1/2
Sandberg 81 D2
Sandbukt 4 B2
Sandbukta 28 A/B2,
    33 C/D1
Sandby 51 D2
Sandby 53 C2
Sanddal 36 B2
Sande 36 A2
Sande 43 D1, 44 A1
Sande 36 B1/2
Sande 36 B1/2
Sande 37 B/C2
Sande 67 D1
Sandefjord 43 D2, 44 A/B1
Sandeggen 4 A3
Sande-Gödens 67 D1
Sandeid 42 A1
Sandemar 47 D1
San Demétrio ne'Vestini
    117 D3, 119 C1
San Demétrio Corone
    122 B1
Sandersdorf 69 D3, 82 B1
Sandersleben 69 C3, 82 A1
Sanderstølen 37 D3
Sandfors 31 C1
Sandgate 65 C3, 76 B1
Sandhamn 47 D1
Sandhaug 42 B1
Sandhead 56 A/B3
Sandhem 45 D3
Sandiás 150 B3
Sandillon 87 C3
Sandim 151 C3, 159 B/C1
Sandim 158 A2
Sandl 93 D2
Sandland 4 B2
Sandmo 29 C2
Sandnäset 35 C2
Sandnäset 34 B2
Sandnes 8 B2
Sandnes 9 C2
Sandnes 9 C1
Sandnes 42 A2
Sandnessjøen 14 A2
Sandö 30 B3, 35 D2
Sando 159 D2
Sandomierz 97 C1, 98 A2
San Dónaci 121 D3
San Donà di Piave 107 D3
San Donato Val di Comino
    119 C2
Sándorfalva 129 D2
Sandøsund 43 D2, 44 B1/2
Sandoval de la Reina
    152 B2
Sandown 76 B2
Sandøy 32 A2
Sandrigo 107 C3
Sandringham 65 C1
Sandsbråten 43 D1
Sandsbro (Vaxjö) 51 C1
Sandsele 15 D3
Sandset 8 B2
Sandshamn 36 A1
Sandsjö 39 D1
Sandsjö 15 D3
Sandsjö 30 B1
Sandslån 30 B3, 35 D2
Sandstad 32 B1
Sandstedt 68 A1
Sandtangen 7 C2
Sandtorg 9 C2
Sandur 55 C2
Sandvarp 30 B3, 35 D2
Sandvatn 42 B3
Sandve 42 A2
Sandvig 51 C3, 51 D3
Sandvik 9 C2
Sandvik 46 A3
Sandvik 4 A3
Sandvik 51 D1
Sandvika 38 A3, 43 D1
Sandvika 32 B2
Sandvika fjellstue 28 B3,
    33 D1, 34 A1
Sandvika fjellstue 28 B3,
    33 D1, 34 A1
Sandvika (Nordli) 29 C2
Sandviken 29 C2/3, 34 A1
Sandviken 40 A2
Sandviken 29 D3, 34 B1
Sandviken 16 A1
Sandvikvåg 42 A1
Sandwich 65 C3, 76 B1

Sandy 64 B2
San Emiliano 151 D2
Såner 44 B1
San Esteban de Pravia
    151 D1
San Esteban de Gormaz
    153 C3, 161 C1
San Esteban de Nogales
    151 D3
San Esteban del Valle
    160 A3
San Esteban de Valdueza
    151 C2
San Esteban del Molar
    151 D3, 152 A3
San Fele 120 A2
San Felice Circeo 118 B3
San Felice sul Panaro
    114 B1
San Felice/Sankt Felix
    107 C2
San Felices 153 D3
San Felices de los Gallegos
    159 C2
San Ferdinando 122 A3
San Ferdinando di Púglia
    120 B1/2
San Fernando de Henares
    161 C2
San Fernando 171 D3
San Fernando 157 D3
San Fili 122 A1/2
San Foca 121 D3
San Francesco 117 C3,
    118 B1
San Francesco 119 D1
San Francisco Javier
    157 D3
San Fratello 125 C2
San Fulgencio 169 C3,
    174 B1
Sånga 30 B3, 35 D2
San Gabriele 115 C1
San Galgano 114 B3,
    116 B2
San García de Ingelmos
    160 A2
Sangarcía 160 B2
Sangarrén 154 B3
Sángas 147 C3
Sangatte 77 D1
San Gavino Monreale
    123 C3
San Gémini 117 C3,
    118 B1
San Genésio 105 D3,
    106 A3, 113 D1
Sangerhausen 82 A1
San Germano Vercellese
    105 C3
San Giácomo delle Segnate
    114 B1
San Giácomo d'Acri 122 B1
San Giácomo/Sankt Jakob
    107 C1
San Giácomo 112 B2
San Giácomo di Véglia
    107 D2
San Gimignano 114 B3,
    116 A/B2
San Ginésio 115 D3,
    117 D2
Sanginjoki 18 B2
Sanginjoki 18 B2
Sanginkylä 18 B2
San Giórgio di Lomellina
    105 D3, 113 D1
San Giórgio di Livenza
    107 D3, 126 A3
San Giórgio della Richin-
    velda 107 D2, 126 A2
San Giórgio Lucano 120 B3
San Giórgio del Sánnio
    119 D3, 120 A2
San Giorgio a Cremano
    119 D3
San Giórgio di Piano
    114 B1
San Giórgio in Bosco
    107 C3
San Giórgio Iónico 121 C3
San Giórgio 115 D2,
    117 C1
San Giórgio la Molara
    119 D2/3, 120 A2
San Giórgio di Nogaro
    126 A3

San Giovanni in Persiceto
114 A/B1
San Giovanni Bianco
106 A2/3
San Giovanni a Piro 120 A3
San Giovanni Suérgiu
123 C3
San Giovanni 107 C1
San Giovanni in Fiore
122 B2
San Giovanni Ilarione
107 C3
San Giovanni Rotondo
120 B1
San Giovanni/Sankt Johann
107 C1
San Giovanni Sínis 123 C2
San Giovanni Reatino
117 C3, 118 B1
San Giovanni in Croce
114 A1
San Giovanni 107 C2
San Giovanni Gémini
124 B2
San Giovanni Valdarno
115 C3, 116 B2
Sangis 17 D2
San Giuliano Terme
114 A/B2, 116 A1/2
San Giuseppe Jato 124 B2
San Giustino 115 C3,
117 C2
San Giusto Canavese
105 C3
San Godenzo 115 C2,
116 B1
San Gregório 117 D3,
119 C1
San Gregório da Sássola
118 B2
San Gregório Magno
120 A2
San Gregorio 150 B3
Sangüesa 155 C2
San Guido 114 B3, 116 A2
Sanguinet 108 A1
Sanguinetto 107 C3
Saní 144 A2
Sanica Gornja 131 D2
San Ignacio de Loyola
153 D1
San Ildefonso o la Granja
160 B2
Sanitz 53 D3
San Javier 169 C3, 174 B1
San Joan de Villatorrada
156 A3
San Jorge 163 C2
San Jorge 169 D2
San José 172 B1
San José 174 A2
San José 169 D2
San Juan Bautista 152 B3
San Juan Bautista 157 D3
San Juan de Nieve 151 D1
San Juan de la Peña 154 B2
San Juan de los Terreros
174 A1/2
San Juan de la Nava
160 A2
San Juan de Aznalfarache
171 D1/2
San Juan de Mozarrifar
154 B3, 162 B1
San Juan de Alicante
169 D3
San Juan del Olmo 160 A2
San Juan del Puerto
171 C2
San Juano 157 C2
Sänkimäki 22 B2
Sanksnäs 15 D3
Sankt Aegyd am Neuwalde
94 A3
Sankt Andrä 94 A/B2
Sankt Andrä 127 C1
Sankt Andrä 96 A3
Sankt Andreasberg 69 C3
Sankt Anton am Arlberg
106 B1
Sankt Anton an der Jessnitz
94 A3
Sankt Augustin 80 A2
Sankt Blasien 90 B3
Sankt Donat 126 B1/2
Sankt Englmar 92 B1
Sankt Gallen 93 D3

Sankt Gallenkirch
106 A/B1
Sankt Gangloff 82 A/B2
Sankt Georgen an der Stie-
fing 127 C1
Sankt Georgen an der Gusen
93 D2
Sankt Georgen am Reith
93 D3
Sankt Georgen ob Juden-
burg 126 B1
Sankt Georgen im Attergau
93 C3
Sankt Gilgen 93 C3
Sankt Goar 80 B3
Sankt Goarshausen 80 B3
Sankt Ibb 49 D3, 50 A3
Sankt Ingbert 89 D1, 90 A1
Sankt Jakob bei Mixnitz
94 A3, 127 C1
Sankt Johann im Pongau
93 C3, 126 A1
Sankt Johann in der Haide
127 D1
Sankt Johann in Tirol 92 B3
Sankt Johann am Tauern
93 D3, 126 B1
Sankt Johann im Walde
107 D1, 126 A1
Sankt Johann am Tauern
96 A3
Sankt Lambrecht 126 B1
Sankt Leonhard in Pitztal
106 B1
Sankt Leonhard am Forst
94 A2
Sankt Lorenzen am Wechsel
94 A3
Sankt Lorenzen im Lesachtal
107 D1/2, 126 A1/2
Sankt Marein am Pickelbach
127 C/D1
Sankt Marein im Mürztal
94 A3
Sankt Margarethen 52 B3
Sankt Margarethen an der
Raab 127 C/D1
Sankt Margarethen im Bur-
genland 94 B3
Sankt Märgen 90 B3
Sankt Martin am Grimming
93 C3
Sankt Michaelisdonn
52 A/B3
Sankt Michael in Obersteier-
mark 93 D3, 127 C1
Sankt Michael im Burgen-
land 127 D1
Sankt Michael im Lungau
126 B1
Sankt Michael in Obersteier-
mark 94 A3
Sankt Münster-Sprakel
67 D3
Sankt Nikolai im Sölktal
126 B1
Sankt Olof 50 B3
Sankt Oswald in Freiland
127 C1
Sankt Oswald bei Freistadt
93 D2
Sankt Pankraz 93 D3
Sankt Paul 127 C1/2
Sankt Peter-Ording 52 A3
Sankt Pölten 94 A2
Sankt Pölten 96 A2/3
Sankt Ruprecht an der Raab
127 C1
Sankt Stefan an der Gail
126 A2
Sankt Stefan im Rosental
127 C/D1
Sankt Valentin 93 D2
Sankt Veit an der Glan
126 B1
Sankt Veit an der Gölsen
94 A2/3
Sankt Veit an der Glan
96 A3
Sankt Veit in Defereggen
107 D1
Sankt Veit im Mühlkreis
93 C/D2
Sankt Vith 79 D2
Sankt Wendel 80 A3, 90 A1
Sankt Willibald 93 C2

Sankt Wolfgang im Salz-
kammergut 93 C3
Sankt Wolfgang 92 B2
San Lázzaro di Sávena
114 B1/2
San Leo 115 C2, 117 C1
San Leonardo in Passíria
107 C1
San Leonardo de Siete Fu-
éntes 123 C2
San Leonardo de Yagüe
153 C3, 161 C1
San Leone 124 B3
San Lorenzo de Descardazar
157 C1/2
San Lorenzo Bellizzi
120 B3, 122 B1
San Lorenzo a Merse
114 B3, 116 B2
San Lorenzo in Campo
115 D3, 117 C2
San Lorenzo in Banale
106 B2
San Lorenzo al Mare
113 C2
San Lorenzo Nuovo
116 B3, 118 A1
San Lorenzo de Calatrava
167 C2/3
San Lorenzo de El Escorial
160 B2
San Lorenzo de la Parrilla
161 D3, 168 B1
Sanlúcar de Guadiana
170 B1
Sanlúcar de Barrameda
171 C/D2
Sanlúcar la Mayor
171 D1/2
San Lúcido 122 A2
San Lugano 107 C2
San Luis de Sabinillas
172 A3
Sanluri 123 C3
San Mamés de Campos
152 B2
San Marcello Pistoiese
114 B2, 116 A1
San Marcial 159 D1
San Marco 120 A3
San Marco Argentano
122 A1
San Marco dei Cavoti
119 D2/3, 120 A1/2
San Marco in Lámis
120 A/B1
San Marino 115 C/D2,
117 C1
San Marino 130 B1
San Martín de Pusa
160 A/B3, 166 B1
San Martín de la Vega del
Alberche 160 A2
San Martín del Pedroso
151 C3, 159 C1
San Martín de la Vega
161 C3
San Martín de Maldá
155 D3, 163 D1
San Martín de Moncayo
154 A3, 162 A1
San Martín de Valdeiglesias
160 B2/3
San Martín de Montalbán
160 B3, 167 C1
San Martín 172 A3
San Martín 151 C3
San Martín de Boniches
162 A3, 168 B1
San Martín 159 C2
San Martín del Pimpollar
160 A2/3
San Martín del Río 163 C2
San Martín de Unx 154 A2
San Martín del Rey Aurelio
111 D3
San Martino di Castrozza
107 C2
San Martino Buon Albergo
107 B/C3
San Martino di Cellina
107 D2, 126 A2
San Martino 107 C2/3
San Martino in Rio 114 B1
San Martino in Pénsilis
119 D2, 120 A1
San Martino di Lota 113 D2

San Mateo 163 C2
San Mateo 169 D2
San Mateo de Gállego
154 B3, 162 B1
San Maurízio Canavese
105 C3, 113 B/C1
San Máuro Forte 120 B3
San Máuro Torinese
113 C1
San Menáio 120 B1
San Michele al Tagliamento
107 D3, 126 A3
San Michele all'Ádige
107 C2
San Michele di Ganzaría
125 C3
San Michele 107 D3,
126 A3
San Michele Salentino
121 C/D2
San Michele 115 D2/3,
117 C/D2
San Michele 118 B2
San Miguel 157 D3
San Miguel de Serrezuela
160 A2
San Miguel de Valero
159 D2
San Miguel del Arroyo
160 B1
San Miguel de Bernúy
160 B1
San Miguel de Aguayo
152 B1/2
San Miguel de Salinas
169 C3, 174 B1
San Millán de San Zadornil
153 C2
San Millán de la Cogolla
153 C2
San Millán de Lara 153 C3
San Muñoz 159 D2
Sannås 44 B2
Sannazzaro de'Burgondi
113 D1
Sannicandro di Bari 121 C2
Sannicandro Gargánico
120 A1
San Nicola dell'Alto 122 B2
San Nicola da Crissa
122 A/B2
San Nicolás del Puerto
166 A3, 171 D1, 172 A1
San Nicolò Gerrei 123 D3
San Nicolò di Comélico
107 D2
San Nicolò Ferrarese
115 C1
San Nicolò d'Arcidano
123 C3
Sannidal 43 D2, 44 A2
Sännsjölandet 29 D3,
35 B/C2
Sanok 97 C/D2, 98 A2/3
San Pablo 167 C1
San Pancrázio/Sankt Pan-
kraz 107 B/C2
San Pancrázio Salentino
121 D3
San Pantaleo 123 D1
San Pantaleón de Losa
153 C2
San Páolo di Civitate
120 A1
San Pedro 168 B2
San Pedro Alcántara
172 A3
San Pedro Bercianos
151 D2
San Pedro del Pinatar
169 C3, 174 B1
San Pedro de la Nave
151 D3, 159 D1
San Pedro de Latarce
152 A3, 159 D1, 160 A1
San Pedro de Mérida
165 D2, 166 A2
San Pedro de Palmiches
161 D2
San Pedro Manrique
153 D3
San Pelayo de Guareña
159 D2
San Pellegrino Terme
106 A3
San Piero in Bagno 115 C2,
116 B1

San Piero Patti 125 C/D2
San Pietro 125 C3
San Pietro in Casale 114 B1
San Pietro in Palazzi
114 A/B3, 116 A2
San Pietro in Valle 117 C3,
118 B1
San Pietro/Sankt Peter
107 C1
San Pietro Vara 113 D2,
114 A2
San Pietro Vernótico
121 D3
San Polo d'Enza 114 A/B1
San Polo di Piave 107 D3
Sanquhar 56 B2
San Quírico d'Órcia
115 C3, 116 B2
San Rafael 160 B2
San Rafael 169 D2
San Rafael del Río 163 C2
San Remo 113 C2
San Román 160 A3
San Román de la Cuba
152 A2/3
San Román de Cameros
153 D2/3
San Rómolo 113 B/C2
San Roque 172 A3
San Roque de Ríomiera
153 C1
San Rufo 120 A3
Sansa 156 A1/2
Sansac-de-Marmiesse
110 A1
San Sadurniño 150 B1
San Salvatore Monferrato
113 C1
San Salvo 119 D1/2
San Saturnino de Osormort
156 A/B2
San Savino 115 C3, 117 C2
San Sebastián de los Reyes
161 C2
San Sebastián de los Balle-
steros 172 A/B1
San Sebastiano 106 B3
San Sebastiano Curone
113 D1
San Secondo Parmense
114 A1
Sansepolcro 115 C3,
117 C2
San Severino Lucano
120 B3, 122 A1
San Severino Marche
115 D3, 117 D2
San Severo 120 A1
San Silvestre de Guzmán
170 B1/2
Sanski Most 131 D1
Sansol 153 D2
San Sosti 122 A1
San Sperate 123 C/D3
Santa Amalia 165 D2,
166 A2
Santa Ana 165 D1,
166 A1/2
Santa Ana 164 B3
Santa Ana de Cambas
170 B1
Santa Ana do Campa
164 B2
Santa Ana la Real 165 D3,
171 C1
Santa Bárbara de Nexe
170 B2
Santa Bárbara de Padrões
170 B1
Santa Bárbara 163 C2
Santa Bárbara de Casa
165 C3, 171 C1
Santa Calobra 157 C2
Santacara 154 A2
Santa Catarina da Fonte do
Bispo 170 B2
Santa Caterina di Pittinuri
123 C2
Santa Caterina Valfurva
106 B2
Santa Caterina Villarmosa
125 B/C2
Santa Cesárea Terme
121 D3
Santa Cilia de Jaca 154 B2
Santa Clara de Louredo
164 B3, 170 B1

Santa Clara a Nova **170** A/B1
Santa Clara a Velha **170** A1
Santa Coloma de Gramanet **156** A3
Santa Coloma de Farnés **156** B2
Santa Coloma **153** D2
Santa Coloma de Queralt **155** C3, **163** C1
Santa Colomba de Somoza **151** D2
Santa Comba Dão **158** A/B2/3
Santa Comba **150** A1/2
Santa Comba de Rossas **151** C3, **159** C1
Santa Cristina de Valmadrigal **152** A2
Santa Croce Camerina **125** C3
Santa Croce sull'Arno **114** B2, **116** A1/2
Santa Croce del Sánnio **119** D2
Santa Croce di Magliano **119** D2, **120** A1
Santa Cruz **164** A/B3, **170** A1
Santa Cruz **164** A2
Santa Cruz **170** B1
Santa Cruz da Trapa **158** A/B2
Santa Cruz de Grío **162** A1
Santa Cruz de la Serós **154** B2
Santa Cruz de Mudela **167** D2
Santa Cruz del Retamar **160** B3
Santa Cruz de Moya **163** C3, **169** D1
Santa Cruz de Pinares **160** A/B2
Santa Cruz de Nogueras **162** A/B2
Santa Cruz de la Sierra **166** A1
Santa Cruz de los Cáñamos **167** D2, **168** A2
Santa Cruz de la Zarza **161** C3 .
Santadi **123** C3
Santa Doménica Talao **120** B3, **122** A1
Santa Doménica Vittória **125** C/D2
Santa Elena **167** D3
Santa Elena de Jamuz **151** D2/3
Santa Elisabetta **124** B2
Santaella **172** A/B1
Santa Eufémia Lamézia **122** A/B2
Santa Eufémia d'Aspromonte **122** A3
Santa Eufemia **166** B2
Santa Eugenia **157** C2
Santa Eulália **165** C2
Santa Eulalia de Oscos **151** C1
Santa Eulalia la Mayor **154** B2/3
Santa Eulalia **152** A1
Santa Eulalia **153** D2/3
Santa Eulalia **163** C2
Santa Eulalia del Río **157** D3
Santa Eulalia de Gállego **154** B2
Santa Fé **156** B3
Santafé **173** C2
Santa Fiora **116** B3
Santa Gadea del Cid **153** C2
Santa Galdana **157** C1
Sant'Ágata sul Santerno **115** C1/2, **116** B1
Sant'Ágata sui Due Golfi **119** D3
Sant'Ágata di Púglia **120** A2
Sant'Ágata di Ésaro **122** A1
Sant'Ágata Féltria **115** C2, **117** C1
Sant'Ágata di Militello **125** C2

Sant'Ágata del Bianco **122** A3
Sant'Ágata de'Goti **119** D3
Santa Gertrude/Sankt Gertraud **106** B2
Sant'Agostino **114** B1
Santahamina/Sandhamn **25** D3, **26** A3
Santa Inés **169** D2
Santa Iria **165** C3, **170** B1
Santa Justa **164** B2
Santa Lecina **155** C3, **163** C1
Santa Leocádia **158** B2
Santa Liestra y San Quílez **155** C2
Santa Linya **155** C/D3
Santa Luce **114** B3, **116** A2
Santa Lucia del Mela **125** D1/2
Santa Lucia **123** D2
Santa Luzia **170** A1
Santa Maddalena/Sankt Magdalena **107** D3
Santa Magdalena de Pulpis **163** C2/3
Santa Margalida **157** C2
Santa Margarida de Montbui **155** D3, **156** A3, **163** C1
Santa Margarida da Coutada **164** B1
Santa Margarida da Serra **164** B3
Santa Margarida do Sado **164** B3
Santa Margherita di Belice **124** A2
Santa Margherita Lígure **113** D2
Santa Margherita **123** C/D3
Santa Maria di Licodia **125** C2
Santa Maria della Strada **119** D2
Santa Maria di Neápolis **123** C3
Santa Maria di Merino **120** B1
Santa Maria del Cedro **122** A1
Santa Maria di Porto Novo **117** D2, **130** A3
Santa Maria degli Ángeli **115** D3, **117** C2
Santa Maria a Vico **119** D3
Santa Maria la Palma **123** C1/2
Santa Maria a Piè di Chienti **117** D2, **130** A3
Santa Maria della Versa **113** D1
Santa Maria Maggiore **105** C/D2
Santa Maria Rezzónico **105** D2, **106** A2
Santa Maria Navarrese **123** D2
Santa María del Campo **152** B3
Santa María de Campo Rus **168** A/B1
Santa Maria de Oló **156** A2
Santa María de Mercadillo **153** C3
Santa María de Melque **160** B3, **167** C1
Santa María del Páramo **151** D2
Santa María la Real de Nieva **160** B2
Santa María de las Hoyas **153** C3, **161** C1
Santa María de Huerta **161** D1
Santa Maria de Merlès **156** A2
Santa Maria del Taro **113** D2
Santa María del Val **161** D2
Santa Maria al Bagno **121** D3
Santa Maria di Siponto **120** B1
Santa Maria Cápua Vétere **119** C/D3

Santa Maria d'Anglona **120** B3
Santa María de Sando **159** D2
Santa María de Cayón **152** B1
Santa María de Naranco **151** D1
Santa Maria im Münstertal [Zernez] **106** B2
Santa María de Riaza **161** C1
Santa Maria de Meyà **155** D3
Santa María de los Caballeros **159** D2/3, **160** A2
Santa María **157** C2
Santa Marina del Rey **151** D2
Santa Marina de Valdeón **152** A1
Santa Marina **151** D1
Santa Marina Salina **125** C1
Santa Marinella **118** A2
Santa Marta **165** D2
Santa Marta **168** B2
Santa Marta de Magasca **165** D1, **166** A1
Santana **164** A2/3
Santana da Serra **170** A1
Sant'Anastasia **119** D3
Sant'Anatólia di Narco **117** C3, **118** B1
Santander **153** B/C1
Sant'Andrea Frius **123** D3
Sant'Andrea **123** D3
Sant'Andrea Bagni **114** A1
Sant'Andrea Bonagia **124** A2
Sant Andreu de Llavaneres **156** B3
Santandria **157** C1
Sant'Ángelo **119** C3
Sant'Ángelo in Vado **115** C2/3, **117** C2
Sant'Ángelo in Lízzola **115** D2, **117** C1
Sant'Ángelo Lodigiano **105** D3, **106** A3, **113** D1
Sant'Ángelo a Fasanella **120** A3
Sant'Ángelo di Brolo **125** C1/2
Sant'Ángelo **120** B2
Sant'Ángelo dei Lombardi **120** A2
Sant'Ángelo in Formis **119** C/D3
Sant'Ángelo **122** B1
Santa Ninfa **124** A2
Sant'Anna Arresi **123** C3
Sant'Anna d'Alfaedo **106** B3
Sant'Anna di Valdieri **112** B2
Sant'Ántimo **115** B/C3, **116** B2/3
Sant'Antíoco **123** C3
Sant'Antíoco di Bisárcio **123** C1/2
Sant'Antònio Morignone **106** B2
Sant Antoni de Calonge **156** B2/3
Sant'António **123** D1
Sant'António di Santadi **123** C2/3
Santanyí **157** D2
Santa Olalla del Cala **165** D3, **166** A3, **171** D1
Santa Olalla **160** B3
Santa Pau **156** B2
Santa Pola **169** C/D3
Santa Pola del Este **169** D3
Sant'Apollinare in Classe **115** C2, **117** C1
Santa Ponça **157** C2
Santar **158** B2
Sant'Arcángelo **120** B3
Santarcángelo di Romagna **115** C/D2, **117** C1
Santarém **164** A/B1/2
Santa Severa **118** A2
Santa Severa **113** D2
Santa Severina **122** B2
Santas Martas **152** A2

Santa Sofia **115** C2, **116** B1
Santa Sofia d'Epiro **122** B1
Santa Sofia **164** B2
Santa Susana **165** C2
Santa Suzana **164** B2/3
Santa Tegra **150** A3
Santa Teresa di Riva **125** D2
Santa Teresa Gallura **123** D1
Santa Valburga/Sankt Walburg **107** B/C2
Santa Victoria do Ameixial **165** C2
Santa Vitoria **164** B3, **170** B1
Santa Vittória in Matenano **117** D2
Sant Bartomeu del Grau **156** A2
Sant Carles de la Ràpita **163** C2
Sant Celoni **156** B3
Sant Cugat de Vallés **156** A3
Santed **162** A2
Sant'Elia a Pianisi **119** D2, **120** A1
Sant'Elía Fiumerápido **119** C2
Sant Elm **157** C2
San Telmo **165** C3, **171** C1
Sant'Elpídio a Mare **117** D2, **130** A3
Sántena **113** C1
Santenay **103** C/D1
Santéramo in Colle **121** C2
Santesteban **108** A3, **154** A1
Sant'Eufémia a Maiella **119** C1
Sant'Eutízio **117** D3
Sant Feliu de Pallerols **156** B2
Sant Feliu de Llobregat **156** A3
Sant Feliu de Codines **156** A3
Sant Feliu de Guíxols **156** B3
Sant Feliu Sasserra **156** A2
Sant Genís de Vilasar **156** A/B3
Sant Gregori **156** B2
Santhià **105** C3
Sant Hilari Sacalm **156** B2
Santiago **150** A2
Santiago **158** B2
Santiago de Alcántara **165** C1
Santiago de la Ribera **169** C3, **174** B1
Santiago de la Puebla **160** A2
Santiago de Calatrava **172** B1
Santiago de la Espada **168** A3
Santiago del Campo **165** D1, **166** A1
Santiago do Escoural **164** B2
Santiago do Cacém **164** A/B3, **170** A1
Santiago Maior **165** C2
Santiago Millas **151** D2
Santibáñez de Tera **151** D3
Santibáñez de Ayllón **161** C1
Santibáñez de Béjar **159** D2
Santibáñez de la Peña **152** B2
Santibáñez de Vidriales **151** D3
Santibáñez Zarzaguda **153** B/C2
Santibañez el Alto **159** C3
Sant'Ilário d'Enza **114** A/B1
Santillana **152** B1
Santillana de Campos **152** B2
Santiponce **171** D1
San Tirso de Abres **151** C1
Santiso **150** B2

Santisteban del Puerto **167** D3, **168** A3
Santiuste de San Juan Bautista **160** B1/2
Santiz **159** D1/2
Sant Jaume dels Domenys **156** A3, **163** D1
Sant Joan de les Abadesses **156** A2
Sant Juliá de Lória **155** D2
Sant Llorenç de Morunys **155** D2/3, **156** A3
Sant Llorenç Savall **156** A3
Sant Martí d'Empúries **156** B2
Sant Martí de Llémena **156** B2
Sant Martí Sarroca **156** A3, **163** D1
Sant Martí Sasgayolas **155** D3, **163** D1
Sant Martí de Maldà **155** D3, **163** D1
Sant Martí Sapresa **156** B2
Sant Michel **26** B1
Santo Aleixo **165** C3
Santo Aleixo **165** C2
Santo Amador **165** C3
Santo Amaro **165** C2
Santo André **164** A3, **170** A1
Santo Antão **164** A2
Santo António das Areias **165** C1
Santo Cruz del Comercio **172** B2
Santo Domingo de la Calzada **153** C2
Santo Domingo de Silos **153** C3
Santo Estêvão **164** A2
Santo Estêvão **170** B2
Santo Estêvão **159** B/C3
Santok **71** C2
Santolea **162** B2
Santomera **169** C3, **174** B1
Sant'Omobono Imagna **106** A3
Santoña **153** C1
Santo Pietro-di-Tenda **113** D2
Santoseso **151** D1
Santo Spírito **121** C2, **136** A3
Santo Stéfano Belbo **113** C1
Santo Stéfano di Camastra **125** C2
Santo Stéfano di Cadore **107** D2
Santo Stéfano d'Áveto **113** D1
Santo Stéfano di Magra **114** A2
Santo Stéfano Quisquina **124** B2
Santo Stino di Livenza **107** D3, **126** A3
Santo Tirso **158** A1
Santo Tomás **157** C1
Santo Tomé **167** D3, **168** A3, **173** C1
Santovenia **151** D3
Santovka **95** D2
Sant Pau de Segúries **156** A/B2
Santpedor **156** A3
Sant Pere de Ronda **156** B2
Sant Pere de Riubebitlles **155** D3, **156** A3, **163** D1
Sant Pere de Torelló **156** A2
Sant Pere de Ribes **156** A3, **163** D1
Sant Pere Pescador **156** B2
Sant Pol de Mar **156** B3
Sant Privat d'En Bas **156** A/B2
Sant Quintí de Mediona **155** D3, **156** A3, **163** D1
Sant Quirze de Besora **156** A2
Sant Sadurní de l'Heura **156** B2
Sant Sadurní d'Anoia **156** A3
Sant Salvador de Guardiola **156** A3, **163** D1

Sant Salvador de Toló **155** D3
Santuário d'Oropa **105** C3
Santuario de Aránzazu **153** D2
Santuário Hera Lacinia **122** B2
Santu Lussúrgiu **123** C2
Santurde **153** C2
Santurdejo **153** C2
Santurtzi **153** C1
Sant Vicenç **155** D2, **156** A2
Sant Vicenç de Castellet **156** A3
San Valentino in Abruzzo Citeriore **119** C1
San Valentino alla Muta/Sankt Valentin **106** B1
San Venanzo **117** C3
San Vicente de Toranzo **152** B1
San Vicente del Raspeig **169** D3
San Vicente de la Barquera **152** B1
San Vicente de Alcántara **165** C1
San Vigílio/Sankt Vigil **107** B/C2
San Vigílio/Sankt Vigil **107** C1/2
San Vincenzo **114** A/B3, **116** A2
San Vincenzo Valle Roveto **119** C2
San Vítero **151** D3, **159** C1
San Vito **123** D3
San Vito al Tagliamento **107** D2/3, **126** A2/3
San Vito Chietino **119** D1
San Vito dei Normanni **121** D2
San Vito di Cadore **107** D2
San Vito lo Capo **124** A1/2
San Vito Romano **118** B2
San Vittore delle Chiuse **115** D3, **117** C2
Sanxay **101** C2
Sanxenxo **150** A2
Sanza **120** A3
San Zeno Naviglio **106** B3
San Zenone degli Ezzelini **107** C3
Sanzoles **159** D1
São Barnabé **170** A/B1/2
São Bartolomeu dos Galegos **164** A1/2
São Bartolomeu de Messines **170** A2
São Bartolomeu da Serra **164** A/B3, **170** A1
São Bento **150** A3
São Brás de Alportel **170** B2
São Braz **165** C3, **170** B1
São Braz de Regedouro **164** B3
São Cristovão **164** B2/3
São Domingos **164** B3, **170** A1
São Félix **158** B2
São Félix da Marinha **158** A2
São Francisco da Serra **164** A/B3
São Gregorio **164** B2
São Gregorio **150** B3
São Jacinto **158** A2
São Joăn da Madeira **158** A2
São Joaninho **158** A/B2
São João da Ribeira **164** A1/2
São João da Serra **158** A2
São João do Monte **158** A2
São João das Lampas **164** A2
São João da Pesqueira **158** B1/2
São João dos Caldeireiros **170** B1
São João da Venda **170** B2
São João de Tarouca **158** B2
São Leonardo **165** C3

São Lourenço de Mamporcão **165** C1/2
São Lourenço **164** A2
São Lourenço **151** B/C3, **158** B1
São Luis **170** A1
São Maméde de Riba Tua **158** B1
São Manços **165** B/C3
São Marcos da Ataboeira **170** B1
São Marcos do Campo **165** C3
São Marcos da Serra **170** A1/2
São Martinho **158** A/B3
São Martinho **164** B2
São Martinho **158** B1
São Martinho das Amoreiras **170** A1
São Martinho do Porto **164** A1
São Mateus **164** B2
São Matias **164** B2
São Matias **164** B3
São Miguel de Poiares **158** A3
São Miguel do Pinheiro **170** B1
São Miguel de Machede **165** B/C2
São Miguel de Acha **158** B3
São Pedro de Muel **164** A1
São Pedro da Torre **150** A2
São Pedro da Cadeira **164** A2
São Pedro de Solis **170** B1
São Pedro do Sul **158** B2
São Pedro **151** C3, **159** C1
São Quintino **164** A2
Saorge **112** B2
São Romão **165** C2
São Romão **158** B2/3
São Romão **164** B2
São Sebastião de Gommes Aires **170** A/B1
São Sebastião dos Carros **170** B1
São Simão **164** A2
São Teotónio **170** A1
São Tiago **159** C1
São Torcato **158** A1
Saou **111** C/D1
São Vicente **165** C2
São Vicente da Beira **158** B3
Sápai **145** D1
Sápai **149** C1
Saparevo banja **139** D2
Sapataria **164** A2
Sapiãos **150** B3, **158** B1
Sąpolno **71** D1
Sappada **107** D2, **126** A2
Sappee **25** C1/2
Sappee **25** C/D1, **26** A1
Sappen **4** B3
Sappetsele **15** D3
Sappisaasi **10** B3
Sapri **120** A3, **122** A1
Sapsalampi **21** C3
Saques **154** B2
Sara **20** B3
Saraby **5** C2, **6** A1
Sarajärvi **19** C1
Sarajärvi **27** C/D1
Sarajevo **132** B2
Sarakína **143** C2
Saramo **23** C1
Saramon **109** C3, **155** C1
Sarandë **142** A3
Sarandë **148** A1
Sarandinovo **138** B3, **143** C1
Saraorci **134** B2
Säräsiniemi **18** B3
Sarata **141** D1
Sarbia **71** D2
Sarbinowo **70** B2
Sárbogárd **129** B/C1
Sarche **106** B2
Sárdara **123** C3
Sardas **154** B2
Sardoal **164** B1
Sare **18** A3, **154** A1
Šarengrad **129** C3, **133** C1
Šarenik **133** D3, **134** A3

Sarentino/Sarntheim **107** C1/2
Sarezzo **106** B3
Sargans **105** D1, **106** A1
Sári **129** C1
Sariano **114** B1
Saricaali **145** D1, **145** D3
Sari-di-Porto-Vecchio **113** D3
Sari d'Orcino **113** D3
Sa Riera **156** B2
Sarigöl **149** D2
Sariñena **155** B/C3, **162** B1
Sárisáp **95** D3
Sarjankylä **21** C/D1, **22** A1
Sarjankylä **21** D2, **22** A1
Sárjåsjaurestugan **15** C1
Sarkamäki **23** B/C3
Särkelä **13** C2/3
Särkelä **19** C1
Sárkeresztes **128** B1
Sárkeresztúr **128** B1
Särkijärvi **11** C3, **12** A1
Särkijärvi **19** D3, **23** C1
Särkijärvi **19** B/C2
Särkijärvi **18** B1
Särkikylä **21** C2
Särkilahti **25** D1, **26** A1
Särkilahti **27** C/D1
Särkiluoma **19** D1
Särkimo **20** B2
Särkisalmi **27** D1
Särkisalo **21** D2, **22** A2
Särkisalo/Finby **24** B3
Särkivaara **23** C2
Sarkola **24** B1
Šarköy **149** D1
Sarlat-la-Canéda **108** B1
Sarleinsbach **93** C2
Sarliac-sur-l'Isle **101** D3
Sărmașu **97** D3, **140** B1
Sármellék **128** A2
Sarmijärvi **7** C3
Sarmingstein **93** D2
Särna **39** C1
Sarnadas **158** B3, **165** C1
Sarnano **115** D3, **117** D2
Sarnen **105** C2
Särnaheden **38** B1
Sarno **119** D3
Sarnow **70** A1
Sarnowa **71** D3
Sarny **98** B2
Särö **49** D1, **50** A1
Sarone **107** D2
Saronís **147** D3
Saronno **105** D3
Sárosd **129** B/C1
Sarpsborg **44** B1
Sarralbe **89** D1, **90** A1
Sarrance **108** B3, **154** B1
Sarras **103** D3
Sarratella **163** C3
Sarraz, La **104** B1/2
Sarreaus **150** B3
Sarrebourg **89** D1, **90** A2
Sarreguemines **89** D1, **90** A1
Sarre-Union **89** D1, **90** A1
Sarria **151** B/C2
Sarrión **162** B3
Sarroca de Bellera **155** D2
Sarroca de Segre **155** C3, **163** C1
Sarroch **123** C/D3
Sarron **108** B3, **154** B1
Sársina **115** C2, **117** C1
Sarstedt **68** B3
Sárszentlörinc **128** B2
Sárszentmiklós **129** B/C1
Sartaguda **153** D2
Sartène **113** D3
Sárti **144** B2
Sartilly **85** D1
Sartirana Lomellina **113** C1
Saruhanli **149** D2
Sarule **123** D2
Sárvár **128** A1
Sárvár **96** B3
Sarvaš **129** C3
Sarvela **20** B3
Sarvijoki **20** A/B2
Sarvikas **21** C3
Sarvikumpu **23** C3

Sarvinki **23** D2/3
Sarvisalo **27** D1
Sarvisvaara **16** B1
Sarvsalö **25** D3, **26** A3
Särvsjön **34** A2/3
Sarzana **114** A2
Sarzeau **85** C3
Sarzeda **158** B2
Sarzedas **158** B3, **165** C1
Sarzedo **158** B2
Šaš **128** A3, **131** D1
Sasa **139** C2
Sasamón **152** B2
Sasca-Română **135** C1
Sásd **128** B2
Sasi **24** B1
Sasina **131** D1
Šášov **95** D2
Sassali **12** B2
Sassano **120** A3
Sássari **123** C1
Sássari Argentiera **123** C1
Sássari La Corte **123** C1
Sássari Palmadula **123** C1
Sássari Stintino **123** C1
Sassello **113** C2
Sassenage **104** A3
Sassenberg **67** D3
Sassenburg-Neudorf-Platendorf **69** C2
Sassenburg-Westerbeck **69** C2
Sassetta **114** B3, **116** A2
Sassnitz **72** A2
Sassocorvaro **115** C/D2, **117** C1/2
Sassoferrato **115** D3, **117** C2
Sassoleone **115** B/C2, **116** B1
Sasso Marconi **114** B2, **116** B1
Sassuolo **114** B1
Sastago **162** B1
Šaštínske Stráže **94** B2
Sas van Gent **78** B1
Satanov **98** B3
Satão **158** B2
Säter **45** D2
Säter **39** D2/3, **40** A2
Sæter **32** A2
Sætran **9** C2
Sætran **9** C2
Satriano di Lucánia **120** A2/3
Satrup **52** B2
Šatry **75** C2
Såttåhaugvoll **33** C/D2
Sattajärvi **17** C/D1
Sattajärvi **17** D2, **18** A1
Sattanen **12** B2
Satteins **106** B1
Sattel [Sattel-Aegeri] **105** D1
Sattledt **93** C2/3
Sättna **35** D3
Satulung **97** D3, **140** B1
Satu Mare **97** D3, **98** A3
Sa Tuna **156** B2
Saubach **82** A1
Saubusse **108** B2/3
Saúca **161** D2
Saucats **108** B1
Saucedilla **159** D3, **166** A1
Saucelle **159** C2
Sauda **42** A/B1
Saudal **15** C2
Saudasjøen **42** A/B1
Saudron **89** C2
Sauerbrunn **94** B3
Sauerlach **92** A3
Saugon **100** B3
Saugues **110** B1
Saujon **100** B3
Saukkojärvi **18** B1

Saukkokoski **10** B2
Saukkola **21** D3, **22** A3
Saukkola **25** C3
Saukkola **17** D2, **18** A1
Saukkoperukka **23** C1
Saukkoriipi **12** A3, **17** D1
Saukonkylä **21** C2
Saukonperä **24** B1
Saukonsaari **27** C1
Sauland **43** C1
Saulce-sur-Rhône **111** C1
Sauldorf-Krumbach **91** C3
Saulgau **91** C3
Saulges **86** A2
Saulgrub **92** A3
Saulieu **88** B3, **103** C1
Saulkrasti **73** D1, **74** A2
Sault **111** D2
Sault-Brénaz **103** D2, **104** A3
Sault-de-Navailles **108** B3, **154** B1
Saulx **89** C/D3
Saulxures-sur-Moselotte **89** D2
Saulzet **102** B2
Saumur **86** A3, **101** C1
Saunajärvi **23** D1
Saunajoki **24** B1
Saunakylä **20** B3
Saunakylä **21** C2
Saunakylä **21** C/D2
Saunavaara **12** B2/3
Saundersfoot **62** B1
Sauøy **32** B1
Sauquillo de Paredes **161** C1
Saura **14** B1
Saura **14** A2
Saurat **155** D2, **156** A1
Saurier **102** B3
Sáuris **107** D2, **126** A2
Saussy **88** B3
Sausvatn **14** A3
Saut du Doubs **104** B1
Sauvagnat **102** B2/3
Sauve **110** B2
Sauveterre-de-Rouergue **110** A2
Sauveterre-de-Béarn **108** A3, **154** B1
Sauveterre-de-Guyenne **108** B1
Sauviat-sur-Vige **101** D2, **102** A2
Sauvo (Sagu) **24** B3
Sauxillanges **102** B3
Sauze d'Oulx **112** B1
Sauzet **108** B1/2
Sauzé-Vaussais **101** C2
Sauzon **84** B3
Sava **121** C/D3
Savalberget **33** C3, **37** D1
Savaloja **18** A/B3
Sävar **20** A1, **31** D2
Sävast **17** C3
Savaștepe **149** D1
Savci **127** D2
Säve **45** C3
Sävedalen **45** C3
Savelli **117** D3, **118** B1
Savelli **122** B1/2
Savenaho **25** D1, **26** A/B1
Savenay **85** C/D3
Säveni **98** B3
Saverdun **109** D3, **155** D1, **156** A1
Saverne **89** D1, **90** A2
Savero **26** B2
Sävi **24** B1
Sävia **22** B2
Saviaho **23** C1
Säviäntaipale **22** B2
Savigliano **113** B/C1
Savignac-les-Eglises **101** D3
Savignano di Rigo **115** C2, **117** C1
Savignano Irpino **120** A2
Savignano sul Rubicone **115** C2, **117** C1
Savigné-l'Évêque **86** B2
Savigno **114** B2, **116** B1
Savigny-sur-Braye **86** B2/3
Savijärvi **23** D1
Savijoki **25** D2, **26** A2
Savikylä **23** C1

Savilahti 27 C1/2
Saviñán 154 A3, 162 A1
Savina Voda 138 A1
Saviniemi 25 C2
Savino Selo 129 C3
Savio 21 D3, 22 A3
Sávio 115 C2, 117 C1
Saviore d'Adamello 106 B2
Saviselkä 21 D1, 22 A1
Savitaipale 27 C2
Sävja 40 B3
Sævlandsvik 42 A2
Šavnik 137 D1
Savo 25 C1
Savo 25 C1
Savognin [Tiefencastel]
  106 A2
Sávoly 128 A2
Savona 113 C2
Savonkylä 21 C2
Savonlinna (Nyslot) 27 C1
Savonranta 23 C3
Særåsvåg 36 A3
Sävsjö 51 C1
Sävsjö 72 A1
Sävsjön 31 C1
Sävsjön 39 C/D3
Sävsjöström 51 C1
Savudrija 126 A3
Savukoski 13 C2
Savulahti 22 B2
Sawley Abbey 59 D1,
  60 B2
Sawston 65 C2
Sax 169 C2
Saxdalen 39 D3
Saxmundham 65 D2
Saxnäs 29 D1
Saxnäs 15 D3
Sayat 102 B2/3
Sayatón 161 C2/3
Sayda 83 C2
Säynäjä 19 D1
Säynätsalo 21 D3, 22 A3
Säyneinen 23 C2
Säynejärvi 23 D3
Säynelahti 23 C3
Säytsjärvi 6 B3
Sazes de Lorvão 158 A3
Sazonovo 75 D1
Sborino 145 D3
Scaër 84 B2
Scăiești 135 D2
Scalasaig 56 A1
Scalasaig 54 A2, 55 D1
Scalby 61 D2
Scalea 120 B3, 122 A1
Scaletta Zanclea 122 A3,
  125 D2
Scálzeri 107 C2/3
Scampa 138 A3, 142 A1
Scandale 122 B2
Scandiano 114 B1
Scandicci 114 B2,
  116 B1/2
Scandolara Ravara 114 A1
Scanno 119 C2
Scano di Montiferro 123 C2
Scansano 116 B3
Scanzano 121 C3
Scăpău 135 D2
Scarborough 61 D2
Scardovari 115 C/D1
Scarinish 54 A2, 55 D1
Scário 120 A3
Scarlino 116 A3
Scarmafigi 112 B1
Scarperia 114 B2, 116 B1
Scarva 58 A1
Scáuri 119 C3
Šćepan Polje 133 C3
Scey-sur-Saône 89 C3
Schaafheim 81 C3
Schaan 105 D1, 106 A1
Schachendorf 127 D1
Schackenborg 52 A2
Schadeleben 69 C3
Schaffhausen 90 B3
Schafstädt 82 A1
Schäftlarn 92 A3
Schagen 66 A/B2
Schalkau 81 D2, 82 A2
Schangnau [Wiggen]
  105 C1
Schanz 91 D3
Schapbach 90 B2
Scharbeutz 53 C3

Scharbeutz-Gleschendorf
  53 C3
Scharbeutz-Haffkrug 53 C3
Schärding 93 C2
Schärding 96 A2
Scharfling 93 C3
Scharnebeck 69 C1
Scharnitz 92 A3, 107 C1
Schartau 69 C/D2
Schattwald 91 D3
Schauenstein 82 A2
Schechingen 91 C1/2
Scheelenborg 49 C3, 53 C1
Scheemda 67 C1
Scheessel 68 B1/2
Schefflenz 91 C1
Schéggia 115 D3, 117 C2
Scheibbs 94 A3
Scheibenberg 82 B2
Scheidegg 91 C3
Scheifling 126 B1
Scheifling 96 A3
Scheinfeld 81 D3
Schelklingen 91 C2
Schellerten 68 B3
Schemmerhofen-Aufhofen
  91 C2
Schenefeld 52 B3
Schenklengsfeld 81 C2
Schermbeck 67 C3, 80 A1
Schermen 69 D3
Schernsdorf 70 B3
Scherpenzeel 66 B3
Scherpenzeel 66 B2
Schesslitz 82 A3
Scheveningen 66 A3
Scheyern 92 A2
Schiedam 66 A3
Schieder-Schwalenberg
  68 A3
Schierke 69 C3
Schierling 92 B2
Schierling-Eggmühl
  92 B1/2
Schiermonnikoog 67 C1
Schiers 106 A1
Schiffdorf 68 A1
Schiffdorf-Wehdel 68 A1
Schifferstadt 90 B1
Schildau 82 B1
Schildow 70 A2
Schillingsfürst 91 D1
Schilpário 106 B2
Schiltach 90 B2
Schio 107 C3
Schirmeck 89 D2, 90 A2
Schirnding 82 B3
Schitu-Duca 141 C1
Schkeuditz 82 B1
Schkölen 82 A1/2
Schköna 69 D3, 82 B1
Schlabendorf 70 A/B3
Schladen 69 C3
Schladming 93 C3, 126 B1
Schladming 96 A2
Schlagsdorf 53 C3, 69 C1
Schlangen 68 A3
Schlangenbad 80 B3
Schleching 92 B3
Schleiden 79 D2
Schleiden-Gemünd 79 D2
Schleife 83 D1
Schleitheim [Schaffhausen]
  90 B3
Schleiz 82 A2
Schleswig 52 B2
Schleusingen 81 D2
Schlieben 70 A3
Schliersee 92 A3
Schliersee-Valepp 92 A/B3
Schlitz 81 C2
Schlitz-Willofs 81 C2
Schlossvippach 82 A1
Schloss Wildegg 94 A/B2
Schlotheim 81 D1
Schluchsee 90 B3
Schlüchtern 81 C2
Schlüsselfeld 81 D3
Schmalkalden 81 D2
Schmallenberg-Dorlar
  80 B1
Schmallenberg 80 B1
Schmallenberg-Fredeburg
  80 B1
Schmelz 90 A1
Schmidmühlen 92 A/B1
Schmiedeberg 70 B1/2

Schmiedeberg 83 C2
Schmiedefeld 81 D2
Schmölln 82 B2
Schmölln 70 B1
Schnackenburg 69 C2
Schnaitsee 92 B2/3
Schnaittach 82 A3, 92 A1
Schnaittenbach-Kemnath
  82 B3, 92 B1
Schnaittenbach 82 A/B3,
  92 B1
Schneeberg 82 B2
Schnega 69 C2
Schneidlingen 69 C3
Schneizelreuth-Melleck
  92 B3
Schnelldorf 91 D1
Schneverdingen 68 B2
Schneverdingen-Heber
  68 B2
Schoenberg 79 D2
Schöffengrund 80 B2
Schöftland 105 C1
Schöfweg 93 C2
Scholen-Anstedt 68 A2
Schollene 69 D2
Schöllkrippen 81 C3
Schöllnach 93 C2
Schömberg 90 B2
Schöna 83 B/C1
Schonach 90 B2
Schönaich 91 C2
Schönau 93 B/C3
Schönau-Unterzeitlarn
  92 B2
Schönbach 93 D2
Schönbeck 70 A1
Schönberg 93 C2
Schönberg 53 C2/3
Schönberg 53 C3, 69 C1
Schönberg-Schönberger-
  strand 53 C2/3
Schönbrunn 81 D2, 82 A2
Schönebeck 69 D3
Schönebeck 69 D2
Schöneben 93 C2
Schöneck 82 B2
Schönecken 79 D2/3
Schönefeld 70 A2/3
Schönenberg-Kübelberg
  90 A1
Schöneuche 70 A/B2
Schönewalde 70 A3
Schönfeld 94 B2
Schönfeld 70 A/B2
Schongau 91 D3
Schöngleina 82 A2
Schönhausen 69 D2
Schönheide 82 B2
Schöningen 69 C3
Schönsee 82 B3, 92 B1
Schönthal 92 B1
Schonungen 81 D3
Schonungen-Löffelsterz
  81 D3
Schönwald 90 B2/3
Schönwald (Rehau)
  82 B2/3
Schönwalde am Bungsberg
  53 C3
Schönwalde 70 A2
Schönwalde 70 A/B3
Schoonebeek 67 C2
Schoonhoven 66 A/B3
Schoonloo 67 C2
Schoonoord 67 C2
Schopfheim 90 A/B3
Schopfheim-Gersbach
  90 B3
Schopfloch (Dinkelsbühl)
  91 D1
Schopfloch 90 B2
Schöppenstedt 69 C3
Schöppingen 67 D3
Schora 69 D3
Schörfling am Attersee
  93 C3
Schorndorf 91 C2
Schortens 67 D1
Schoten 78 B1
Schotten 81 C2
Schramberg 90 B2
Schrecksbach 81 C2
Schrems 94 A3
Schrick 94 B2
Schriesheim 80 B3, 90 B1
Schrobenhausen 92 A2

Schröcken 106 B1
Schrozberg 91 C/D1
Schrozberg-Leuzendorf
  91 D1
Schruns 106 A1
Schuby 52 B2
Schulenburg (Leine) 68 B3
Schulzendorf 70 B2
Schulzhytta 28 B3, 33 D2
Schüpfheim 105 C1
Schuttertal 90 B2
Schuttertal-Schweighausen
  90 B2
Schüttorf 67 D2/3
Schützen am Gebirge 94 B3
Schwaan 53 D3
Schwabach 91 D1, 92 A1
Schwabach-Grossschwar-
  zenlohe 91 D1, 92 A1
Schwabhausen bei Dachau
  92 A2
Schwäbisch Hall 91 C1
Schwäbisch Gmünd 91 C2
Schwabmünchen 91 D2
Schwadorf 94 B2/3
Schwaförden 68 A2
Schwalmstad-Treysa 81 C2
Schwalmstadt-Ziegenhain
  81 C2
Schwalmtal 81 C2
Schwanau-Ottenheim
  90 A/B2
Schwanbeck 70 A1
Schwanberg 127 C1
Schwanden 105 D1,
  106 A1
Schwandorf 92 B1
Schwanebeck 69 C3
Schwanenstadt 93 C2/3
Schwanewede 68 A1
Schwanewede-Meyenburg
  68 A1
Schwanfeld 81 D3
Schwangau 91 D3
Schwanheide 69 C1
Schwanstetten-Schwand
  92 A1
Schwante 70 A2
Schwarme 68 A2
Schwarmstedt 68 B2
Schwarza 81 D2
Schwarza 82 A2
Schwarzach 81 D3
Schwarzach 92 B1/2
Schwarzach im Pongau
  107 D1, 126 A1
Schwarzau am Steinfelde
  94 A/B3
Schwarzau im Gebirge
  94 A3
Schwarzbach 81 D2
Schwärzelbach-Neuwirths-
  haus 81 C2/3
Schwarzenau 94 A3
Schwarzenbach 82 A2
Schwarzenbach 82 A/B2/3
Schwarzenbach (Neustadt)
  82 A/B3
Schwarzenbek 69 B/C1
Schwarzenberg 82 B2
Schwarzenborn 81 C2
Schwarzenborn 79 D3,
  80 A3
Schwarzenburg 104 B1
Schwarzenfeld 92 B1
Schwarzheide 83 C1
Schwarzhofen-Zangenstein
  92 B1
Schwarzsee [Fribourg]
  104 B2
Schwarzwaldalp [Meirin-
  gen] 105 C1/2
Schwaz 92 A3, 107 C1
Schwechat 94 B2
Schwechat 96 B2/3
Schwedt 72 A3
Schwedt 70 B2
Schwefelberg Bad [Fri-
  bourg] 105 B/C1/2
Schwegenheim 90 B1
Schweich 79 D3, 80 A3
Schweickershausen
  81 D2/3
Schweinfurt 81 D3
Schweinitz 70 A3
Schweinitz 69 D3

Schweinrich 69 D1/2,
  70 A1/2
Schweitenkirchen-Sünz-
  hausen 92 A2
Schwelm 80 A1
Schwemsal 69 D3, 82 B1
Schwendi 91 C/D2
Schwenningen (Stockach)
  91 C2/3
Schwepnitz 83 C1
Schwerin 69 C1
Schwerte 80 A/B1
Schwetzingen 90 B1
Schweyen 89 D1, 90 A1
Schwiesau 69 C2
Schwinkendorf 53 D3,
  69 D1, 70 A1
Schwülper 69 B/C2/3
Schwyz 105 D1
Sciacca 124 C1
Sciáves 107 C1
Sciáves/Schabs 107 C1
Scicli 125 C3
Sciez 104 A/B2
Scilla 122 A3, 125 D1
Šćit 132 A2/3
Šćitarjevo 127 D3
Scoarta 135 D1
Scoarta 140 B2
Scodra 137 D2
Scoglitti 125 C3
Scole 65 C2
Scone Palace 57 C1
Scopello 105 C3
Scorbé-Clairvaux 101 C1
Scordia 125 C3
Ščors 99 D2
Scorzè 107 C/D3
Scotch Corner 57 D3,
  61 C1
Scotter 61 D3
Scourie 54 A1
Scrabster 54 B1
Ščučin 73 D2/3, 74 A3,
  98 B1
Scunthorpe 61 D3
Scuol 106 B1
Seaca de Pădure 135 D2
Seaford 76 B1
Seaham 61 D1
Seamer 61 D1/2
Seascale 59 D1, 60 B1/2
Seaton 63 C2/3
Sebergham 57 C3, 60 B1
Sebersdorf 127 D1
Sebes 140 B1
Šebeštov 94 B1
Sebež 74 B2
Sebnitz 83 C/D1/2
Seč 83 C3, 93 C1
Sečanj 134 C1
Sečanj 140 A2
Secășeni 135 C1
Secastilla 155 C2/3
Secca Grande 124 B2
Séchault 88 B1
Seckach 91 C1
Seckau 127 C1
Seclin 78 A2
Secondigny 101 B/C1/2
Secorún 155 B/C2
Sečovce 97 C2
Secugnago 106 A3,
  113 D1
Seda 165 B/C2
Seda 73 C1
Sedan 79 C3
Sedano 153 B/C2
Sedbergh 59 D1, 60 B2
Seddülbahir 149 C1
Sedella 172 B2
Sedemte Prestola 139 D1
Séderon 111 D2
Sedgefield 57 D3, 61 C1
Sédico 107 C/D2
Sédilo 123 C/D2
Sédini 123 C1
Sedlare 138 B2
Sedlčany 83 D3
Sedlec 83 C2
Sedlec-Prčice 83 D3,
  93 D1
Sedlice 93 C1
Sedlitz 83 C1
Sedrina 106 A3
Sedrun 105 D1/2
Šeduva 73 D2

Sedzère 108 B3, 155 B/C1
See 83 D1
Seebach 126 B1
Seebeck 70 A2
Seebenstein 94 A/B3
Seeboden 126 A1
Seefeld 92 A3
Seefeld 94 A/B2
Seefeld in Tirol 92 A3,
  107 C1
Seeg 91 D3
Seegrehna 69 D3
Seehaus 93 C3
Seehausen 69 C3
Seehausen 69 D2
Seeheim-Jugenheim 80 B3
Seelingstädt 82 B2
Seelow 70 B2
Seelscheid 80 A2
Seelze 68 B2/3
Seeon-Seebruck 92 B3
Seerhausen 83 C1
Sées 86 B2
Seesen 68 B3
Seesen-Grossrhuden 68 B3
Seeshaupt 92 A3
Seetal 126 B1
Seevetal 68 B1
Seewald-Besenfeld 90 B2
Seewiesen 94 A3
Séez 104 B3
Seferihisar 149 D2
Seffern 79 C1
Sefkerin 133 D1, 134 A1
Segalstad bru 37 D2, 38 A1
Segarcea 140 B2
Segart 162 B3, 169 D1
Seged 131 C3
Segeletz 69 D2
Segelnes 9 D2
Segelvik 4 B2
Segerstad 51 D2
Segesd 128 A2
Segesta 124 A2
Seggiano 115 C3,
  116 B2/3
Seglinge 41 D3
Seglora 45 C3, 49 D1
Segmon 45 C1
Segni 118 B2
Segonzac 101 C3
Segorbe 162 B3, 169 D1
Segovia 160 B2
Segrate 105 D3, 106 A3
Segré 86 A3
Segrie 86 A/B2
Segura 159 C3, 165 C1
Segura de la Sierra 168 A3
Segura de León 165 D3
Segura de los Baños
  162 B2
Sehnde 68 B3
Seia 158 B2/3
Seiches-sur-le-Loir 86 A3
Seida 7 C2
Seiersberg 127 C1
Seierstad 28 B1/2
Seignelay 88 A2/3
Seignosse 108 B2/3
Seikka 21 D1, 22 A1
Seilhac 102 A3
Seillans 112 A3
Seimsdal 37 C2
Seimsfoss 42 A1
Seinäjoki 20 B2
Seini 97 D3, 98 A3
Seinsheim 81 D3
Seipäjärvi 12 B2
Seira 155 C2
Seissan 109 C3, 155 C1
Seitajärvi 13 C2
Seitenoikea 19 C3
Seitenstetten Markt 93 D3
Seitlax 25 D3, 26 A3
Seivika 32 B2
Seixal 164 A2
Seixo 158 B2
Seixo de Gatães 158 A3
Sejerby 49 C3, 53 C1
Sejerslev 48 A2
Sejlflod 48 B1/2
Sekkemo 5 B/C2
Šekovići 133 C2
Sel 37 D1/2
Sel 30 B3
Selaño 152 A1
Selänsalmi 19 C1

Seläntaus 21 D2, 22 A2
Selb 82 B3
Selbu 28 B3, 33 D2
Selby 61 C2
Selca 131 D3, 132 A3,
  136 A1
Selce 127 C3, 130 B1
Selce 137 D2
Sel'co 99 D1
Selçuk 149 D2
Selde 48 A/B2
Selen 28 A/B2, 33 C1
Selendi 149 D2
Selenica 142 A2
Selent 53 C3
Sélestat 90 A2
Selet 30 A3, 35 C2
Selet 17 B/C3
Seleuš 134 B1
Selevac 134 B2
Selfjord 8 A2/3
Selgua 155 C3
Selí 143 C2
Selianítika 146 B2
Seligenstadt 81 C3
Seligenthal 81 D2
Selimiye 149 D2
Selinunte 124 A2
Selishte 138 A3
Selište 135 C2/3
Seližarovo 75 C2
Selja 39 C2
Seljankulma 24 B2
Selje 36 A1
Seljelvnes 4 A3, 10 A1
Seljesåsen 21 C1
Seljestad 42 B1
Seljord 43 C1/2
Selkälä 13 C3
Selkirk 57 C2
Sella 107 C2
Sella 169 D2
Sella di Corno 117 D3,
  118 B1
Sellafield 59 C1, 60 A1
Sellano 117 C3
Sellasía 147 C3
Sellerich 79 D2
Selles-sur-Cher 87 C3,
  101 D1, 102 A1
Sellières 103 D1, 104 A1
Sellrain 107 C1
Sellye 128 B3
Selm 67 D3, 80 A1
Selm-Bork 67 D3, 80 A1
Selmes 165 B/C3
Selmsdorf 53 C3, 69 C1
Selnes 28 B2
Selnes 28 A2, 33 C1
Selnes 9 C2
Selnica 127 C2
Selommes 86 A/B3
Selongey 88 B3
Sélonnet 112 A2
Selseng 36 B2
Selsey 76 B1
Selsingen 68 A/B1
Selsjön 30 B3, 35 D2
Selters 80 B2
Selters-Niederselters 80 B2
Seltjärn 30 B2/3, 35 D1
Seltz 90 B1/2
Selva 113 D1
Selva 157 C2
Selva di Cadore 107 C2
Selva di Progno 107 C3
Selva di Val Gardena
  107 C2
Selvåg 32 B1
Selvik 36 A2
Selvik 43 D1, 44 A/B1
Selvino 106 A3
Sembadel 103 C3
Sembrancher 104 B2
Semeljci 128 B3
Semenic 135 C1
Semenovka 99 D1
Semič 127 C3
Semily 83 D2
Seminara 122 A3
Semizovac 132 B2
Semlow 53 D3
Semmenstedt 69 C3
Šemoine 88 A/B1/2
Sem'onovka 99 D2/3
Semoutiers 88 B2

Šempeter 127 C2
Semproniano 116 B3,
  118 A1
Semriach 127 C1
Sem (Semsbyen) 43 D2,
  44 A/B1
Semur-en-Auxois 88 B3
Sena 155 C3, 163 C1
Sena 151 D2
Senáles/Schnals 106 B1
Sénarpont 77 D2/3
Senas 111 D2
Šenčur 126 B2
Senden 67 D3
Senden 91 D2
Sendenhorst 67 D3
Sendim 159 C1
Şenec 95 C2
Senec 96 B2/3
Séneghe 123 C2
Senés 173 D2
Senftenberg 94 A2
Senftenberg 83 C1
Senftenberg 96 A1
Senhora da Atalaia 164 A2
Senhora da Graça dos Pad-
  rões 170 B1
Senhora das Neves 164 B3,
  170 B1
Senica 95 C2
Senica 96 B2
Senigállia 115 D2,
  117 D1/2
Sénis 123 C/D2
Senise 120 B3
Senj 130 B1
Senje 134 B2
Senjski Rudnik 135 B/C2
Senlis 87 D1
Sennecey-le-Grand 103 D1
Sennen 62 A3
Senno 74 B3
Sénnori 123 C1
Sennybridge 63 C1
Senohrad 95 D2
Senonches 86 B2
Senones 89 D2, 90 A2
Senorbì 123 D3
Senožeče 126 B3
Senrjošt 126 B2
Sens-de-Bretagne 85 D2
Sens-sur-Yonne 88 A2
Senta 129 D2/3
Senta 140 A1
Senterada 155 D2
Šentilj 127 C/D1/2
Šentjanž 127 C2
Šentjernej 127 C3
Šentjur 127 C2
Šentrupert 127 C2
Šentvid 126 B2
Šentvid na Slemenu 127 C2
Seoane 151 C2
Seoane Vello 150 B2
Seon 90 B3, 105 C1
Šepak 133 C2
Sepänkylä 27 C1
Šepetovka 98 B2
Sépey, Le 104 B2
Sępólno Krajeńskie 72 B3
Seppälä 25 C2
Seppois-le-Bas 89 D3,
  90 A3
Septèmes-les-Vallons
  111 D3
Septemvrijci 135 D2
Septeuil 87 C1
Septfonds 87 D3
Septfonds 109 D2
Sepulcro-Hilario 159 D2
Sepúlveda 160 B1
Sequals 107 D2, 126 A2
Sequeros 159 D2
Seraincourt 78 B3
Seraing 79 C2
Serapicos 151 B/C3,
  158 B1
Seravezza 114 A2, 116 A1
Sercaia 141 B/C1
Sercoeur 89 D2
Sered' 95 C2
Sered' 96 B2/3
Seredina-Buda 99 D1
Seredka 74 B1
Seregélyes 128 B1
Seregno 105 D3, 106 A3
Sérent 85 C3

Serfaus 106 B1
Sergines 88 A2
Seriate 106 A3
Sérifontaine 77 D3, 87 C1
Sérigny 100 B2
Serina 106 A2/3
Serino 119 D3, 120 A2
Serinyà 156 B2
Sermaize-les-Bains 88 B1
Sérmide 114 B1
Sermoneta 118 B2
Sernache dos Alhos 158 A3
Sernancelhe 158 B2
Serón 173 D2
Serón de Nágima 153 D3,
  161 D1
Seròs 155 C3, 163 C1
Serpa 165 C3, 170 B1
Serpins 158 A3
Serpuhov 75 D3
Serra 164 B1
Serra 162 B3, 169 D1
Serrabonne 156 B1/2
Serracapriola 119 D2,
  120 A1
Serrada 107 C2/3
Serrada 160 A1
Serra da Boa Fé 164 B2
Serra de El-Rei 164 A1
Serradell 155 D2
Serradifalco 124 B2
Serradilla 159 D3, 165 D1,
  166 A1
Serradilla del Arroyo
  159 C2
Sérrai 144 A1
Serral 155 C3, 163 C1
Serramanna 123 C/D3
Serramazzoni 114 B2,
  116 A1
Serranillos 160 B3
Serranillos 160 A2/3
Serra Nova 157 C2
Serrant 86 A3
Serra Orrios 123 D2
Serra San Bruno 122 B2/3
Serrastretta 122 B2
Serravalle 117 C/D3
Serravalle di Chienti
  115 D3, 117 C2
Serravalle Scrívia 113 D1
Serre 120 A2
Serrejón 159 D3, 166 A1
Serrenti 123 C/D3
Serres 111 D1/2
Serres-sur-Arget 109 D3,
  155 D1/2, 156 A1
Serri 123 D3
Serrières 103 D3
Sersale 122 B2
Sertã 158 A/B3, 164 B1
Sertig Dörfli [Davos Frauen-
  kirch] 106 A1
Servance 89 D3
Serverette 110 B1
Sérvia 143 C2
Servian 110 B3
Serviané 142 B3
Servigliano 117 D2
Sesa 154 B3
Seščinskij 75 C3
Seseña 161 B/C3
Sesimbra 164 A3
Seskarö 17 D2
Sésklon 143 D3, 144 A3
Sesma 153 D2
Sessa Aurunca 119 C3
Sessa Cilento 120 A3
Ses Salines 157 D2
Sesslach 81 D2/3
Sesta Godano 113 D2,
  114 A2
Sestao 153 C1
Sestino 115 C2/3, 117 C2
Sesto Calende 105 D3
Sesto Fiorentino 114 B2,
  116 B1
Séstola 114 B2, 116 A1
Sesto San Giovanni
  105 D3, 106 A3
Sestriere 112 B1
Sestri Levante 113 D2
Sestrunj 130 B2
Sestu 123 D3
Sesvete 127 D3

Séta 147 D1/2
Setcases 156 A2
Sète 110 B3
Setenil 172 A2
Seter 33 D3
Setermoen (Bardu) 9 D1
Seternes 32 A2
Setervik 28 A2
Setil 164 A2
Setiles 162 A2
Setså 15 C1
Setskog 38 B3
Séttima 113 D1, 114 A1
Séttimo Torinese 113 C1
Séttimo Vittone 105 C3
Settle 59 D1, 60 B3
Séttimo 105 D1, 106 A1
Setúbal 164 A2
Seubersdorf 92 A1
Seui 123 D2
Seulingen 81 D1
Seurre 103 D1
Sevalla 40 C3
Sevaster 142 A2
Sevelen 105 D1, 106 A1
Sevenoaks 65 C3, 76 B1
Sevenum 79 D1
Sever 158 A2
Sévérac-le-Château 110 B2
Severin na Kupi 127 C3,
  130 B1
Séveso 105 D3, 106 A3
Ševětín 93 D1
Sevettijärvi (Tševetjävri)
  7 C2/3
Sévignacq 108 B3, 154 B1
Sevilla 171 D1/2
Sevilleja de la Jara 166 B1
Sevlievo 141 B/C3
Sevnica 127 C2
Sewekow 69 D1, 70 A1
Sewen 89 D3, 90 A3
Sexcles 102 A3, 109 D1
Seyches 109 C1
Seyda 70 A2
Seyne-les-Alpes 112 A2
Seyssel 104 A2
Seysses 108 B3, 155 C1
Sežana 126 B3
Sézanne 88 A1/2
Sezimovo Ústí 93 D1
Sezulfe 151 C3, 159 C1
Sezze 118 B2
Sfércia 115 D3, 117 D2
Sferro 125 C2
Sfîntu Gheorghe 141 D2
Sfîntu Gheorghe 141 C1
Sforzacosta 115 D3,
  117 D2
's-Gravenhage 66 A3
Sgúrgola 118 B2
Shaftesbury 63 D2
Shaldon 63 C3
Shanklin 76 B2
Shannon Airport 55 C3
Shap 57 C3, 60 B1
's-Heerenberg 67 C3
Sheerness 65 C3
Sheffield 61 C3
Shefford 64 B2
Shëmri 138 A2
Shëngjergj 138 A3, 142 A1
Shëngjin 137 D2/3
Shëpaj 142 A1
Shepton Mallet 63 D2
Sherborne 63 D2
Sherburn 61 D2
Sherburn-in-Elmet 61 D2
Sheringham 61 D3, 65 C1
's-Hertogenbosch 66 B3,
  79 C1
Shieldaig 54 A2
Shijak 137 D3, 142 A1
Shipdham 65 C1/2
Shipley 61 C2
Shipston on Stour 64 A2
Shiroka 137 D2
Shkodër 137 D2
Shoeburyness 65 C3
Shoreham-by-Sea 76 B1
Shorwell 76 B2
Shotley 65 C2
Shrewsbury 59 D3
Shupenze 138 A3
Siamanna-Siapiccía 123 C2
Siátista 143 C2
Siátista 148 B1
Šiauliai 73 D1/2

Síbari 122 B1
Sibbesse 68 B3
Sibbhult 50 B2
Sibbo/Sipoo 25 D3, 26 A3
Šibenik 131 C3
Sibinj 132 B1
Sibiu 140 B1/2
Sibnica 133 D2, 134 A2
Sibo 40 A1
Šibovska 132 A/B1
Sibratsgfäll 91 D3
Sičevo 135 C3
Siciny 71 D3
Siculiana 124 B3
Siculiana Marina 124 B3
Šid 133 C1
Sidárion 142 A3
Siddeburen 67 C1
Sideby/Siipyy 20 A3
Sidensjö 30 B3
Siderno 122 A/B3
Sidirókastron 139 D3, 144 A1
Sidirókastron 146 B3
Sidirón 145 D1, 145 D3
Sidmouth 63 C2/3
Sidskogen 39 D1, 40 A1
Siebe 11 C1/2
Siebeldingen 90 B1
Siebnen [Siebnen-Wangen] 105 D1
Siecq 101 C2/3
Siedenburg 68 A2
Siedenlangenbeck 69 C2
Siedlce 73 D3, 97 C1, 98 A1
Siedlice 71 C1
Siedlisko 71 C3
Siegbach 80 B2
Siegburg 80 A2
Siegen 80 B2
Siegenburg 92 A2
Siegen-Eiserfeld 80 B2
Siegen-Hüttental 80 B2
Sieghartskirchen 94 A2
Siegsdorf 92 B3
Siekierki 70 B2
Siekkinen 19 C1/2
Sielow 70 B3
Siemczyno 71 C/D1
Siemiatycze 73 D3, 98 A1
Sien 80 A3
Siena 114 B3, 116 B2
Sieniawa 71 C2/3
Sieppijärvi 12 A2, 17 D1
Sieradz 96 B1
Sieraków 71 C2
Sierck-les-Bains 79 D3
Sierndorf 94 A/B2
Sierning 93 D2
Siero 151 D1, 152 A1
Sierpc 73 C3
Sierra 168 B2
Sierra de Fuentes 165 D1, 166 A1
Sierra de Luna 154 B3
Sierra de Yeguas 172 A2
Sierra Engarcerán 163 C3
Sierre 105 C2
Sierro 173 D2
Siétamo 154 B3
Siete Iglesias de Trabancos 160 A1
Sieversdorf 69 D2
Sieverstedt 52 B2
Sievi 21 C1
Sievin asema 21 C1
Sifjord 9 C/D1
Sigdal 43 D1
Sigean 110 A/B3, 156 B1
Sigena 155 C3, 163 C1
Sigerfjord 9 C2
Sigersvoll 42 B3
Siggebohyttan 39 D3, 46 A1
Siggelkow 69 D1
Siggjarvåg 42 A1
Sighetu Marmatiei 97 D3, 98 A3
Sighişoara 97 D3, 140 B1
Sigillo 115 D3, 117 C2
Sigmaringen 91 C2/3
Sigmundsherberg 94 A2
Signa 114 B2, 116 B1/2
Signau 105 C1
Signes 111 D3, 112 A3
Signy-l'Abbaye 78 B3

Signy-le-Petit 78 B3
Sigogne 101 C3
Sigonce 111 D2, 112 A2
Sigridsbu 43 C/D1
Sigtuna 40 B3, 47 C1
Sigüeiro 113 D2
Sigüenza 161 D2
Sigüés 154 B2
Sigurdsristningen 47 B/C1
Sihtuuna 17 D2, 18 A1
Siikainen 24 A1
Siikajärvi 19 C2
Siikajoki 18 A2
Siika-Kämä 18 B1
Siikakoski 26 B2
Siikala 25 C2
Siikalainen 19 D1
Siikalampi 18 B1
Siikamäki 22 B3
Siikasaari 23 C3
Siikava 26 B2
Siikavaara 23 D2
Siilinjärvi 22 B2
Siimes 12 A2, 17 D1
Siitama 25 C1
Siivikko 19 C2
Sijarinska Banja 139 B/C1
Sikås 29 D3, 35 C1
Sikeå 31 D2
Sikéa 144 B2
Sikéa 143 C3
Sikfors 16 B3
Sikfors 39 D3
Sikí 144 A3
Sikiá 144 B2
Sikiá 146 A1/2
Sikidallseter 37 C/D2
Sikkerlia 38 A2
Sikkola 11 D3, 12 A1/2
Siklós 128 B3
Siknäs 17 C2/3
Sikory 71 D1
Sikoúrion 143 D3
Sikovuono 6 B3
Sikselberg 31 C1
Sikselet 15 D2
Siksjö 30 B1/2
Siksjö 30 B1
Siksjön 16 A3
Siksjönäs 30 A1
Sikyon 147 C2
Sil 30 A2, 35 C1
Sila 14 A/B2
Šilale 73 C/D2
Silandro/Schlanders 106 B2
Siláňus 123 C2
Silba 130 B2
Silbaš 129 C3
Silberstedt 52 B2
Silberstedt-Esperstoft 52 B2
Silbertal 106 A/B1
Silenrieux 78 B2
Siles 168 A3
Silfiac 84 B2
Síligo 123 C2
Silió 152 B1
Silíqua 123 C3
Silivri 149 D1
Siljan 43 D2, 44 A1
Siljansfors 39 C2
Siljansnäs 39 D2
Siljeåsen 29 D2, 30 A2
Silkeborg 48 B3
Silken 39 D3
Silla 114 B2, 116 A/B1
Silla 169 D1
Sillamjaë 74 B1
Sillano 114 A2, 116 A1
Sillanpää 25 C2
Sillans-la-Cascade 112 A3
Silleda 150 B2
Sillé-le-Guillaume 86 A2
Sillerud 45 C1
Sillery 88 A/B1
Sílli 145 B/C1
Sillian 107 D1
Silloth 57 C3, 60 A1
Silsbe 35 C/D2
Silmutjoki 21 D2/3, 22 A3
Šilo 130 B1
Síls 156 B2/3
Silsand 9 D1
Silsjönäs 30 A2, 35 C1
Siltaharju 12 B1

Siltakylä/Broby 26 B2/3
Siltavaara 23 C1
Silute 73 C2
Silva 150 A1
Silvacane 111 D2
Silvakkajoki 17 D2, 18 A1
Silvåkra 50 B3
Silvalen 14 A2
Silvana Mánsio 122 B2
Silvaplana [St. Moritz] 106 A2
Silvares 158 B3
Silvberg 39 D2
Silverberg 15 C3
Silverdalen 46 B3
Silves 170 A2
Silvi 119 C1
Silyalde 158 A2
Silz 106 B1
Simanala 23 C3
Simancas 152 A3, 160 A1
Simandre 103 D1
Šimanovci 133 D1, 134 A1
Simaság 94 B3, 128 A1
Simat de Valldigna 169 D2
Simavik 5 C2
Símaxis 123 C2
Simbach 92 B2
Simbach 93 B/C2
Simbach-Haunersdorf 92 B2
Simbarío 122 B2
Simeå 40 A1
Simeonovo 139 D1
Símeri-Crichi 122 B2
Sími 149 D2
Simiane-la-Rotonde 111 D2
Simin Han 133 B/C2
Simitli 139 D2
Simitli 140 B3
Simlångsdalen 72 A1
Simlångsdalen 50 A/B2
Simleu-Silvaniei 97 D3, 140 B1
Simlinge 50 B3
Simmelsdorf 82 A3
Simmerath 79 D2
Simmerath-Einruhr 79 D2
Simmerath-Steckenborn 79 D2
Simmern 80 A3
Simmertal 80 A3
Simo 18 A1
Simola 27 C2
Simonby 24 B3
Simonfa 128 B2
Simoniemi 17 D3, 18 A1
Simonkylä 17 D3, 18 A1
Simonneau 101 C3
Simonsberg 52 A2
Simonstorp 46 B2
Simonswald 90 B2/3
Simontornya 128 B1/2
Simópoulon 146 B2
Simorre 109 C3, 155 C1
Simpele 27 D1
Simpiänniemi 26 B1
Simplon [Brig] 105 C2
Simpnäs 41 C3
Simrishamn 50 B3
Simrishamn 72 A2
Šimsk 75 B/C1
Simskälä 41 D2
Simuni 130 B2
Sinabelkirchen 127 D1
Sinac 130 B1
Sinaia 141 C2
Sinalunga 115 C3, 116 B2
Sinarádes 142 A3
Sindal 48 B1
Sindelfingen 91 C2
Sindía 123 C2
Sindirgi 149 D1/2
Síndos 143 D2, 144 A3
Sines 164 A3, 170 A1
Sinetta 12 A3
Sineu 157 C2
Singen 90 B3
Singhofen 80 B2
Singistugorna 9 D3
Singö 41 C3
Singra 163 C2
Singsas 33 C2
Singusdal 43 C2
Siniscóla 123 D2

Sinj 131 D3
Sinlabajos 160 A2
Sinn 80 B2
Sinnai 123 D3
Sinnes 42 B2
Sinnes 32 B2
Sînnicolau Mare 129 D2
Sînnicolau Mare 140 A1
Sinntal 81 C2
Sinntal-Jossa 81 C2/3
Sinntal-Oberzell 81 C2
Sinntal-Sterbfritz 81 C2
Sinsheim 91 B/C1
Sint-Anthonis 67 B/C3, 79 D1
Sint-Eloois 78 A2
Sint-Joris-Winge 79 C2
Sint Nicolaasga 66 B2
Sint-Niklaas 78 B1
Sint-Oedenrode 79 C1
Sint-Pieters-Kapelle 78 A1
Sintra 164 A2
Sint-Truiden 79 C2
Sinzheim 90 B2
Sinzig 80 A2
Siófok 128 B1
Siófok 96 B3
Sion 104 B2
Sion-les-Mines 85 D3
Sion-sur-l'Océan 100 A1
Siorac-en-Périgord 109 C1
Sip 135 C1/2
Sipola 18 B3
Šipovo 131 D2, 132 A2
Sippola 26 B2
Šiprage 132 A2
Siracusa 125 D3
Siradan 109 C3, 155 C1/2
Siran 109 D1, 110 A1
Siresa 154 B2
Siret 98 B3
Sirevåg 42 A3
Sirig 129 D3
Sirijorda 14 A/B3
Sirkka 11 D3, 12 A2
Sirkkakoski 12 A3, 17 D1
Sirkkamäki 21 D3, 22 A3
Sirma fjellstue 6 B2
Sirmione 106 B3
Sirmium 133 C1, 134 A1
Sirnihtä 23 C2
Sirniö 19 C1
Široka Kula 131 B/C2
Široko Polje 128 B3
Sirolo 117 D2, 130 A3
Sirotino 74 B3
Siruela 166 B2
Širvintos 73 D2, 74 A3
Sisak 127 D3
Sisamón 161 D1/2
Šišan 130 A1
Sisante 168 B1
Sisatto 24 B1
Sisco 113 D2
Šišenci 135 C2
Šišicy 99 B/C1
Šišljavić 127 D3
Sissa 114 A1
Sissach 90 A/B3
Sissala 21 C2
Sissola 23 D2
Sissonne 78 B3
Sistelo 150 A/B3
Sisteron 111 D2, 112 A2
Sistiana 126 A/B3
Sistranda 32 B1
Sitasjaurestugorna 9 D3
Sitas kåte 9 D2/3
Sitges 156 A3
Sitía 149 C3
Sitnes 132 A1
Sitnica 131 D2, 132 A2
Sitno 131 C3
Sitno 71 D1
Sitojaurestugan 16 A1
Sitrama 151 D3
Sittard 79 D1/2
Sittensen 68 B1
Sitter 28 B2
Sittingbourne 65 C3, 77 C1
Sitzendorf 82 A2
Sitzendorf an der Schmida 94 A2
Sitzenroda 82 B1
Siuntio/Sjundeå 25 C3
Siuro 24 B1

Siurua 18 B1/2
Siurunmaa 12 B2
Siusi/Seis 107 C2
Sivac 129 C3
Sivakkajoki 17 D2, 18 A1
Sivakkavaara 23 C1
Sivakkavaara 23 C2
Siverskij 74 B1
Síviri 144 A2
Sívota 142 A/B3
Sívros 146 A1
Sivry 78 B2/3
Sixpenny Handley 63 D2
Sixt 104 B2
Siyilli 145 D3
Sizergh Castle 59 D1, 60 B2
Sizun 84 A/B2
Själevad 31 B/C3
Själlarim 16 B2
Sjenica 133 D3, 134 A3
Sjenica 140 A2/3
Sjeničak Lasinjski 127 D3
Sjoa 37 D2
Sjøåsen 28 B2
Sjöberg 30 A1
Sjöbo 50 B3
Sjöbo 72 A2
Sjöbotten 31 D2
Sjöbrånet 31 C1
Sjöfallsstugan 9 D3
Sjøholt 32 A3
Sjøli 38 A1
Sjömarken 45 C3
Sjonhagen 14 B2
Sjørring 48 A2
Sjörup 48 B2
Sjösanden 39 D1
Sjö Slott 40 B3
Sjötofta 50 B1
Sjötorp 45 D2
Sjoutnäs 29 D1/2
Sjøvegan 9 D1
Sjövik 45 C3
Sjulnäs 15 D3
Sjulsmark 30 A/B1
Sjuntorp 45 C3
Sjursheim 9 D2
Sjursvollen 33 D2
Sjusjøen 38 A1
Skå 47 C1
Skåbu 37 D2
Skåde 48 B3
Skademark 31 C3
Skafidiá 146 A3
Skafså 43 C2
Skaftet 46 B3
Skaftung 20 A3
Skag 41 C2/3
Skaga 14 A2
Skage 28 B2
Skagen 44 B3
Skagshamn 31 C3
Skagstad 8 B3
Skaidi 5 D2, 6 A1
Skaite 16 B1
Skaiti 15 C1
Skaitihytta 15 C1
Skála 147 C1
Skála 146 A2
Skála Kalliráchis 145 B/C2
Skála Leptokariás 143 D2
Skála Marión 145 B/C2
Skålan 34 B2/3
Skaland 9 C/D1
Skála Oropoú 147 D2
Skála Oropoú 148 B2
Skála Rachoníou 145 C1/2
Skalat 98 B3
Skålbygge 39 D1
Skälderviken 49 D2, 50 A2
Skåldö 25 B/C3
Skålevik 43 C3
Skalica 95 B/C1/2
Skalice 83 D2
Skalité 95 D1
Skallelv 7 D2
Skällinge 49 D1, 50 A1
Skallingen 48 A3, 52 A1
Skallsjön 30 A3, 35 C1
Skallskog 39 D2
Skalluvaara 6 B2
Skalmé 95 D1
Skalmodalen 14 B3
Skalmsjö 30 B3, 35 D1
Skalná 82 B3
Skålö 39 C2

Skalochórion **143** C2
Skaloti **144** B1
Skals **48** B2
Skålsjön **39** D1, **40** A1
Skælskør **53** C1
Skalstugan **28** B3, **33** D1, **34** A1
Skålvik **14** A3, **28** B1
Skamlingsbanke **52** B1
Skamsdalshytta **32** B3, **37** C1
Skån **35** C3
Skandáli **145** C3
Skanderborg **48** B3
Skånes Fagerhult **50** B2
Skånes Värsjö **50** B2
Skåne-Tranås **50** B3
Skåningsbukt **4** A2
Skänninge **46** A2
Skanör-Falsterbo **50** A3
Skansbacken **39** C/D2
Skansen **28** B3, **33** D1
Skansen **28** A2, **33** C1
Skansholm **30** A1
Skåpafors **45** C2
Skåpe **71** C3
Skar **9** C2
Skar **15** C1
Skara **45** D2
Skäran **31** D2
Skäråsen **34** A3
Skærbæk **52** A1/2
Skarberget **9** C2
Skærberget **38** B2
Skärblacka **46** B2
Škåre **130** B1
Skåre **45** D1
Skare **42** B1
Skåren **14** A3
Skaret **4** B2
Skåret **38** B1
Skärhamn **44** B3
Skärkdalen **34** A2
Skärlöv **51** D2
Skarmunken **4** A3
Skarnes **38** B3
Skarpdalsvollen **28** B3, **33** D2
Skärplinge **40** B2
Skarpnåtö **41** C2
Skarp Salling **48** B2
Skärså **40** A/B1
Skärsnäs **50** B2
Skarstad **9** C2
Skarstein **9** C1
Skarsvåg **5** D1
Skarult **50** B3
Skärvagen **34** A3
Skarvfjordhamn **5** C1
Skarvsjöby **30** B1
Skarvvik **5** D1, **6** A1
Skarżysko-Kamienna **97** C1
Skattkärr **45** D1
Skattungbyn **39** D1
Skatval **28** A/B3, **33** C/D1
Skatvik **9** D1
Skau **28** A3, **33** C1
Skaugvoll **14** B1
Skaule **15** C2
Skaulo **10** B3
Skaun **28** A3, **33** C2
Skavdal **9** C1
Skævinge **49** D3, **50** A3
Skavnakk **4** B2
Skavvik **5** D1, **6** A1
Skeberg **39** D2
Skebobruk **41** B/C3
Skebokvarn **47** B/C1
Skeda udde **46** B2
Skedbrostugan **34** A3
Skede **46** A3, **51** C1
Skedevi **46** B2
Skedsmokorset **38** A3
Skee **44** B2
Skegness **61** D3, **65** C1
Skegrie **50** A3
Skei **36** B2
Skei **32** B2
Skei **14** A3, **28** B1
Skeie **42** B3
Skela **133** D1, **134** A1/2
Skelde **52** B2
Skellefteå **31** D1
Skelleftehamn **31** D1
Skelleftestrand **31** D1
Skelmorlie **56** B2

Skelund **48** B2
Skender Vakuf **131** D2, **132** A2
Skeppshamn **35** D3
Skeppshult **50** B1
Skeppshult **72** A1
Skeppsvik **20** A1, **31** D2
Skeppsvik **41** C3
Skerninge **53** C2
Skerries **58** A2
Sketaj **137** D3
Ski **38** A3, **44** B1
Skíathos **147** D1
Skíathos **148** B1/2
Skibbereen **55** C3
Skibby **49** D3, **53** D1
Skibotn **4** B3, **10** A1
Ski-Center **147** C1/2
Skidra **143** C/D1/2
Skidstuga **15** C3
Skien **43** D2, **44** A1
Skillefjordnes **5** C2
Skillingaryd **50** B1
Skillingaryd **72** A1
Skillinge **50** B3
Skillingmark **38** B3
Skinnarbu **43** C1
Skinnskatteberg **39** D3
Skipagurra **7** C2
Skiperón **142** A3
Skipmannvik **15** C1
Skipnes **8** B1/2
Skipness **56** A2
Skipsea **61** D2
Skipstadsand **44** B1/2
Skipton **59** D1, **61** B/C2
Skipton **54** B3
Skiptvet **44** B1
Skirö **51** C1
Skíros **149** C2
Skirva **43** C1
Skíti **143** D3, **144** A3
Skivarp **50** B3
Skive **48** A/B2
Skivjane **138** A2
Skivsjön **31** C2
Skjåholmen **5** C1, **6** A1
Skjåk **32** B3, **37** C1
Skjåmoen **14** B2/3
Skjånes **7** C1
Skjånes **14** B2
Skjårberger **9** C2
Skjærhalden **44** B2
Skjåvik **14** B3
Skjeberg **44** B1
Skjee **43** D2, **44** A/B1
Skjeggedal **43** C2
Skjelåvollen **33** D3
Skjeljavik **42** A1
Skjellelv **9** D1/2
Skjelnes **4** A3
Skjelten **32** A2/3
Skjern **48** A3
Skjersholmane **42** A1
Skjerstad **15** C1
Skjervøy **42** B2
Skjevik **28** B2
Skjold **42** A1/2
Skjoldehamn **9** C1
Skjolden **37** C2
Skjomen **9** D2
Skjøtningberg **6** B1
Sklabiňa **95** D1
Sklíthron **147** C2
Skoby **40** B3
Skočivir **143** C1
Škocjanska Jama **126** B3
Skodje **32** A3
Skodsborg **49** D3, **50** A3, **53** D1
Skødstrup **49** B/C2
Škofije **126** B3
Škofja Loka **126** B2
Škofljica **126** B2
Skog **40** A1
Skogaby **50** A/B2
Skogadalsbøen **37** C2
Skogalegerseter **37** D2
Skogalund **45** D1, **46** A1
Skoganvarre **5** D2, **6** A2
Skogboda **41** D3
Skoger **43** D1, **44** A1
Skogfoss **7** C3
Skoghall **45** D1
Skoghult **51** C/D1
Skogly **7** C3
Skogmo **14** A3

Skogn **28** B3, **33** D1
Skognes **4** A3
Skogså **17** C2
Skogsby **51** D2
Skogstad **37** C2
Skogstorp **49** D2, **50** A1
Skogstorp **46** B1
Skoki **71** D2
Skokloster **40** B3
Sköldinge **46** B1
Sköldvik **25** D3, **26** A3
Skole **97** D2, **98** A3
Skollenborg **43** D1, **44** A1
Sköllersta **46** A/B1
Skóllis **146** B2
Skóllis **148** A/B2
Skoltebyen **7** C2
Skölvene **45** D2
Skongseng **14** B2
Skópelos **147** D1
Skópelos **148** B2
Skopiá **147** C1
Skopje **138** B2
Skopje **140** B2
Skorenovac **134** B1
Skorica **135** B/C3
Skorild **33** C1/2
Skórka **71** D1
Skorovassgruver **29** C1/2
Skorovatn **29** C1/2
Skorped **30** B3, **35** D1/2
Skørping Stationsby **48** B2
Skorstad **28** B2
Skotfoss **43** D2, **44** A1
Skotoússa **139** D3, **144** A1
Skoträsk **15** D3
Skotselv **43** D1
Skotterud **38** B3
Skottevik **43** C3
Skottorp **50** A2
Skoulikariá **146** A1
Skoútari **144** A1
Skovballe **53** C2
Skovby **52** B2
Skovby **52** B1/2
Skovby **48** B3, **52** B1
Skövde **45** D2
Skovlund **48** A3, **52** A1
Skrá **139** C3, **143** D1
Skrad **127** C3
Skradin **131** C3
Skradinski buk **131** C3
Skråmestø **36** A3
Skrämträsk **31** D1
Skranstad **9** C3
Skrea **49** D2, **50** A1
Skredsvik **45** B/C2
Skreia **38** A2
Skreland **43** B/C2
Skridulaupbu **32** A3, **37** C1
Skrittskog **24** B3
Skriveri **73** D1, **74** A2
Skrolsvik **9** C1
Skromberga **50** A3
Skrova **8** B2
Skruv **51** C2
Skucku **34** B2
Skudeneshavn **42** A2
Skule **30** B3
Skulerud **38** A3, **44** B1
Skulgam **4** A2/3
Skulsfjord **4** A2
Skultorp **45** D2
Skultuna **40** A3
Skummeslövsstrand **50** A2
Skurdalen **37** C3
Skurträsk **31** C2
Skurup **50** B3
Skute **37** D3, **38** A2
Skutskär **40** B2
Skutvik **9** B/C3
Skutvik **4** A3, **9** D1
Skvira **99** C2/3
Skwierzyna **72** A/B3
Skwierzyna **71** C2
Skyarp **50** A/B1
Skyberg **37** D3, **38** A2
Skýcov **95** D2
Skyllberg **46** A1/2
Skyttmon **30** A3, **35** C1/2
Skyttorp **40** B3
Slabce **83** C2
Slabinja **127** D3, **131** D1
Sládečkovce **95** C2
Sládkovičovo **95** C2
Slagelse **53** C1

Slagnäs **15** D3
Slagstad **9** C1
Slaidburn **59** D1, **60** B2
Slanci **133** D1, **134** A/B1
Slancy **74** B1
Slane **58** A1/2
Slangenseter **37** D2
Slangerup **49** D3, **50** A3, **53** D1
Slănic **141** C2
Slano **136** B1
Slaný **83** C2/3
Slapany **82** B3
Slåstad **38** B3
Slatina **133** D2, **134** A2
Slatina **127** D2
Slatina **138** B2
Slatina **133** D2/3, **134** A3
Slatina **132** B1
Slatina **131** D1, **132** A1
Slatina **140** B2
Slatina-Timiş **135** C1
Slatine **131** C3
Slatinski Drenovac **128** B3
Slättåkra **49** D2, **50** A1/2
Slåttevik **42** A2
Slåtthög **51** B/C1
Slåttholen **8** B2
Slåtton **35** D2
Slåttön **35** B/C2
Slattum **38** A3
Slåttvik **9** B/C2
Slavgorod **99** C/D1
Slavičín **95** C1
Slavina **133** C1/2, **134** A2
Slavinja **135** D3, **139** D1
Slavkov u Brna **94** B1
Slavonice **94** A1
Slavonska Požega **128** B3
Slavonske Bare **128** B3
Slavonski Brod **132** B1
Slavonski Kobaš **132** A/B1
Slavonski Šamac **132** B1
Slavotin **135** D3
Slavuta **98** B2
Sława **71** C1
Sława **71** C3
Sławno **72** B2
Sławoborze **71** C1
Sleaford **61** D3, **64** B1
Sleen **67** C2
Sleights **61** D1
Sleihage **78** A1
Slemmestad **38** A3, **43** D1
Sleneset **14** A2
Sleng **16** A2/3
Sletta **5** C2
Sletta **9** D1
Sletterstrand **48** B1
Sliač **95** D2
Sliač-kúpele **95** D2
Sliedrecht **66** A/B3
Sligo **55** C2
Slímnitsa **142** B2
Slinde **36** B2
Slindon **76** B1
Slipra **28** A/B3, **33** C/D1
Slipsikstugan **29** D1
Slipstensjön **31** C1
Slišane **139** B/C1
Slite **47** D2
Slite **73** B/C1
Sliven **141** C3
Slivnica **139** D1
Slivnica **127** C/D2
Šljivovica **133** C2/3
Slobodka **99** C3
Slobodzeja **141** D1
Slobozia **141** C2
Slochteren **67** C1
Slöinge **49** D2, **50** A1/2
Slonim **98** B1
Słonowice **71** C1
Słońsk **70** B2
Sloten **66** B2
Slotten **5** D1, **6** A1
Slottet **36** A3
Slottsbron **45** C/D1
Slough **64** B3
Sloup **94** B1
Slovac **133** D2, **134** A2
Sløvåg **36** A3
Sloveni-gradec **127** C2
Slovenj-gradec **96** B3
Slovenska Bistrica **96** A3
Slovenska Bistrica **127** C2
Slovenska L'upča **95** D2

Slovenské Ďarmoty **95** D2
Slovenske Konjice **127** C2
Słubice **70** B3
Sluck **99** B/C1
Sluderno/Schluderns **106** B1/2
Sluis **78** A/B1
Šluknov **83** D1/2
Slunj **131** C1
Słupsk (Stolp) **72** B2
Slušovice **95** C1
Slussen **45** B/C2/3
Smadalarö **47** D1
Smådalseter **37** C2/3
Smådalsseter **37** C2
Småge **32** A2
Smålandsstenar **50** B1
Smålandsstenar **72** A1
Smalfjord **7** C1
Smardzewo **71** C3
Šmarje **127** C2
Šmarješke Toplice **127** C2/3
Šmartno **126** B2
Šmartno ob Paki **127** C2
Šmartno ob Paki **127** C2
Småvatna **29** C1
Smečno **83** C2/3
Smedås **33** D3
Smedby **51** D2
Smedby **51** D2
Smedsbo **39** D2
Smedsbyn **17** C2/3
Smedstorp **50** B3
Smela **99** D3
Smeland **43** C2
Smelror **7** D1
Smessenbroek **78** B1/2
Smigádi **145** D1
Šmigiel **71** C3
Šmiklavž **127** C2
Smilčić **131** B/C2
Smilde **67** C2
Smiljan **130** B2
Smilovci **139** D1
Śmiłowo **71** D1/2
Smiltene **73** D1, **74** A3
Smines **8** B1/2
Smines **28** B1
Smínthi **145** C1
Smjadovo **141** C3
Smogasjøen **32** B1
Smögen **44** B2
Smøhamn **36** A1/2
Šmojlovo **74** A2
Smojmirovo **139** D3
Smokovliani **136** B1
Smokvica **136** A1
Smokvica **139** C3, **143** D1
Smolenice **95** C2
Smolensk **75** C3
Smolice **71** D3
Smoljan **140** B3
Smoljanovci **135** D3
Smolnica **70** B2
Smørfjord **5** D1/2, **6** A1
Smorgon' **74** A3
Smørliseter **37** C2
Smorten **8** B2
Smygehamn **50** B3
Snäckgärdsbaden **47** D2/3
Snaith **61** C2
Snappertuna **25** C3
Snaptun **48** B3, **52** B1
Snarby **4** A2/3
Snåre **20** B1
Snåsa **28** B2
Sn'atyn **98** B3
Snedsted **48** A2
Sneek **66** B2
Snejbjerg **48** A3
Snekkersten **49** D3, **50** A2/3
Snerta **38** B1
Snertinge **49** C3, **53** C1
Snesudden **16** B2
Snillfjord **28** A3, **33** C1/2

Snina 97 C/D2, 98 A3
Šnjegotina 132 A1
Snöberg 35 C3
Snøde 53 C2
Snøfjord 5 D1, 6 A1
Snogebæk 51 D3
Soave 107 C3
Sober 150 B2
Søberg 8 B2
Sobernheim 80 A/B3
Soběslav 93 D1
Soběslav 96 A2
Sobotište 95 C2
Sobotka 83 D2
Sobra 136 B1
Sobradillo 159 C2
Sobrado 150 B1/2
Sobral da Adiça 165 C3,
171 B/C1
Sobral de Abilheira 164 A2
Sobral de Monte Agraço
164 A2
Sobral do Campo 158 B3
Sobreira Formosa 158 B3,
164 B1
Sobrón 153 C2
Søby 53 B/C2
Soča 126 B2
Sočanica 138 B1
Soccia 113 D3
Sochaczew 73 C3, 97 C1
Sochaux 89 D3, 90 A3
Sochós 144 A1
Soci 115 C2, 116 B1/2
Socovos 168 B3
Socuéllamos 167 D1/2,
168 A1/2
Sodalen 35 D2/3
Sodankylä 12 B2
Söderåkra 51 D2
Söderala 40 A1
Söderarm 41 C3
Söderås 39 D2
Söderbärke 39 D3
Söderby Karl 41 C3
Söderfors 40 B2
Söderhamn 40 A/B1
Söderhamn-Stugsund
40 A/B1
Söderhögen 34 B3
Söderköping 46 B2
Söderlångvik 24 B3
Södertälje 47 C1
Söderudden 20 A2, 31 D3
Södervik 31 C/D2
Södra 31 D1
Södra Brännträsk 16 B3
Sodra Finnskoga 38 B2
Södra Harads 16 B2
Södra Leringen 35 C2/3
Södra Löten 38 B2
Södra Noret 30 B2
Södrany 45 C/D1
Södra Sandby 50 B3
Södra Sandby 51 D2
Södra Sandvik 35 C3
Södra Skärvången 29 D3,
34 B1
Södra Sunderbyn 17 C3
Södra Tannflo 30 A/B3,
35 D1/2
Södra Tresund 30 A1
Södra Unnaryd 50 B1
Södra Vallgrund 20 A2,
31 D3
Södra Vi 46 B3
Sodražica 127 C3
Sødring 49 B/C2
Sodupe 153 C1
Soest 66 B3
Soest 67 D3, 80 B1
Sofádes 143 C/D3
Sofadítikos 143 C/D3
Sofiero 49 D3, 50 A2
Sofija 139 D1
Sofija 140 B3
Sofikón 148 B2
Sofikón 147 C2/3
Søfteland 36 A3
Sofuentes 155 C2
Sögel 67 D2
Sogliano al Rubicone
115 C2, 117 C1
Sóglio [St. Moritz] 106 A2
Sogndal 36 B2
Sogndalstrand 42 A3
Søgne 43 B/C3

Sognefjellhytta 37 C2
Soham 65 C2
Sohland 83 D1
Söhlde-Hoheneggelsen
68 B3
Söhlde-Nettlingen 68 B3
Sohren 80 A3
Soidinvaara 19 C3, 23 C1
Soignies 78 B2
Soini 21 C2
Soinilansalmi 23 B/C3
Soinlahti 22 B2
Soinlahti 22 B1
Soissons 88 A1
Soivio 19 D1
Soizy-aux-Bois 88 A1
Sójtör 128 A2
Sokal' 97 D1, 98 A/B2
Söke 149 D2
Sokli 13 C2
Soklot 20 B1
Sokna 37 D3
Sokndal 42 A3
Soknedal 33 C2
Soko Banja 135 C3
Soko Banja 140 A2
Sokojärvi 23 D2
Sokolac 133 C2
Sokolac 131 D2, 132 A2
Sokółka 73 D3, 98 A1
Sokolov 82 B2/3
Sokołów Podlaski 73 D3,
98 A1
Sola 23 C2
Sola 42 A2
Solagna 107 C3
Solana de Béjar 159 D3
Solana de los Barros
165 D2
Solana del Pino 167 C2/3
Solana de Ríoalmar 160 A2
Solanillos del Extremo
161 C/D2
Solares 153 C1
Solarino 125 D3
Solarussa 123 C2
Solberg 30 B2, 35 D1
Solberg 15 D2
Solberga 46 A3
Solberget 16 B1
Solca 98 B3
Solčava 127 C2
Sol'ci 74 B1/2
Solda/Sulden 106 B2
Sölden 107 B/C1
Soldeu 155 D2, 156 A1/2
Soleggen 37 C1/2
Solem 28 A/B3, 33 C/D2
Solenzara 113 D3
Solera 173 C1
Solera de Gabaldón
161 D3, 168 B1
Solesmes 78 A/B2
Soleto 121 D3
Solferino 106 B3
Solfonn 42 B1
Solf/Sulva 20 A2, 31 D3
Solheim 36 A3
Solheimsstul 37 C3
Solheimsvik 42 B1
Solignac 101 C3
Soligorsk 99 B/C1
Solin 131 C/D3
Soline 130 B2
Solingen 80 A1
Solitude 91 C2
Solivella 155 C3, 163 C1
Solkan 126 B2
Solkei 27 C1/2
Söll 32 B3
Sollacaro 113 D3
Sollana 169 D1/2
Sollebrunn 45 C3
Sollefteå 30 B3, 35 D2
Sollenau 94 B3
Sollentuna 47 C1
Sóller 157 C2
Sollerön 39 D2
Sollia 37 D1/2, 38 A1
Sollichau 69 D3, 82 B1
Solliden 51 D1
Solliès-Pont 112 A3
Sollihøgda 38 A3, 43 D1
Solms 80 B2
Solms-Oberndorf 80 B2
Solmyra 39 D3, 40 A3
Solna 47 C1

Solnečnogorsk 75 D2
Solnes 7 C/D2
Solnje 138 B2
Solofra 119 D3, 120 A2
Solojärvi 6 B3
Sološnica 95 B/C2
Solothurn 105 C1
Solotvina 97 D3, 98 A3
Solpke 69 C2
Solre-le-Château 78 B2/3
Solre-sur-Sambre 78 B2
Solrød Strand 49 D3,
50 A3, 53 D1
Solsem 28 B1
Sølsnes 32 A2
Solsona 155 D3, 156 A2
Solstad 4 A3, 9 D1
Solstadström 46 B3
Solsvik 36 A3
Solt 129 C1
Solt 96 B3
Soltau 68 B2
Soltendieck 69 C2
Soltvadkert 129 C2
Solumshamn 35 D3
Solund 36 A2
Solunto 124 B2
Sölvesborg 51 B/C2/3
Sölvesborg 72 A1
Solvorn 36 B2
Solynieve 173 C2
Soma 149 D1/2
Sømådal 33 D3
Somberek 129 B/C2
Sombernon 88 B3
Sombor 129 C3
Sombreffe 79 B/C2
Someenjärvi 26 B1
Someren 79 C/D1
Somerleyton Hall 65 D2
Somerniemi 25 C2
Somero 25 B/C2
Someronkylä 18 A3
Somerovaara 18 B2
Somerton 63 D2
Somino 75 D1
Sommacampagna 106 B3
Somma Lombardo 105 D3
Sommaria del Bosco
113 C1
Sommarö 24 B3
Sommarset 9 C3
Sommatino 124 B3
Sommen 46 A3
Sommepy-Tahure 88 B1
Sömmerda 82 A1
Sommerland 48 A3
Sommersted 52 B1
Sommesous 88 B1/2
Somme-Tourbe 88 B1
Sommières 111 C2
Sommières-du-Clain
101 C2
Somo 153 C1
Somogyapáti 128 B2
Somogyszob 128 A2
Somogyvár 128 B2
Somolinos 161 C1
Somosierra 161 C1/2
Somozas 150 B1
Sompuis 88 B1/2
Sompujärvi 18 A1
Son 44 B1
Son 130 A2
Sonceboz [Sonceboz-Som-
beval] 89 D3, 104 B1
Soncillo 153 B/C2
Soncino 106 A3
Sóndalo 106 B2
Sondby 25 D3, 26 A3
Søndeled 43 C2, 44 A2
Sønderborg 52 B2
Sønder Broby 53 B/C1
Sønderby 52 B2
Sønderby 53 C/D2
Sønder Dalby 50 A3, 53 D1
Sønder Felding 48 A3
Sønderhav 52 B2
Sønder-Havrvig 48 A3
Sønderho 52 A1
Sønder Kirkeby 53 D2
Sønder Kongerslev 48 B2
Sønder Omme 48 A3,
52 A/B1
Sønder Onsild 48 B2
Sondershausen 81 D1,
82 A1

Søndersø 49 B/C3,
53 B/C1
Sønderup 48 B3, 52 B1
Søndervig 48 A3
Sóndrio 106 A2
Sonega 164 A3, 170 A1
Soneja 162 B3, 169 D1
Songeons 77 D3
Sonka 12 A3
Sonkaja 23 D2/3
Sonkajärvi 22 B1
Sonkakoski 22 B1
Sonkamuotka 11 C2/3
Sönkkä 23 C3
Sonkovo 75 D1/2
Sonneberg 82 A2
Sonneborn 81 D1/2
Sonnefeld 82 A2/3
Sonnewalde 70 A3, 83 C1
Sonnino 119 B/C2
Sonntag 106 A/B1
Sonogno [Tenero] 105 D2
Son Parc 157 C1
Sonsbeck 67 C3, 79 D1
Sonseca 160 B3, 167 C1
Son Servera 157 C1
Sonstorp 46 B2
Sonta 129 C3
Sontheim 91 D2
Sontheim 91 D3
Sonthofen 91 D3
Sontra 81 C/D1
Sontra-Wichmannshausen
81 C/D1
Söörmarkku 24 A1
Sopeira 155 C2
Sopela 153 C1
Sopje 128 B3
Sopoćani 133 D3, 138 A1
Soponya 128 B1
Sopot 133 D2, 134 A/B2
Sopotnica 138 B3,
143 B/C1
Șopotu Nou 135 C1
Soppela 13 B/C3
Sopron 94 B3
Sopron 96 B3
Sopronhorpács 94 B3
Šor 123 C1
Sora 119 C2
Soragna 114 A1
Soråker 35 D3
Soraluze 153 D1
Sorano 116 B3, 118 A1
Sør-Arnøy 14 B1
Sør-Aukra 32 A2
Sorbara 114 B1
Sorbas 174 A2
Sørbø 42 A2
Sörböle 35 D3
Sorbollano 113 D3
Sórbolo 114 A/B1
Sörby 39 C3
Sörbygden 35 C2
Sörbyn 17 C2
Sore 108 B3
Söréd 95 C/D3, 128 B1
Søre Herefoss 43 C3
Søreidet 4 A2
Sør Eldøseter 37 D1/2
Sören 17 C2
Sörenberg [Schüpfheim]
105 C1
Søre Osen 38 B1
Soresina 106 A3
Sorèze 109 D3
Sörfjärden 35 D3
Sørfjorden 9 C2
Sörfjärden 35 D3, 161 D1
Sørfjordmoen 9 C3
Sörflärke 30 B3, 35 D1
Sør-Flatanger 28 A2
Sørford 9 D1
Sörfors 31 C2
Sörfors 29 D1/2, 30 A1
Sörforsa 40 A/B1
Sør-Frøya 32 B1
Sorges 101 D3
Sørgjæslingan 28 A1
Sórgono 123 D2
Sorgues-sur-l'Ouvèze
111 C2
Sørgutvik 14 A3, 28 B1
Sori 113 D2
Soria 153 D3, 161 D1
Soriano Cálabro 122 A/B2
Soriano nel Cimino 117 C3,
118 A1

Sorihuela del Guadalimar
167 D3, 168 A3
Sorila 25 C1
Sørjær 28 A2
Sorjushytta 127 D1
Sorka 75 D1
Sørkedalen 38 A3
Sorken 33 D3
Sørkjosen 4 B2/3
Sør-Lenangen 4 A/B2
Sørli 9 D1
Sørli 29 C2
Sørli 9 C2
Sörliden 30 B1
Sörmark 38 B3
Sørmarka 28 A2
Sormás 128 A2
Sörmjöle 31 C2
Sørmo 14 B3
Sørmo 9 D2
Sornac 102 A3
Sørnesøy 14 A1/2
Sorno 83 C1
Sorø 49 C/D3, 53 C/D1
Sørodden 14 A3
Soroki 99 C3
Soroksár 95 D3, 129 C1
Sørreisa 9 D1
Sorrento 119 D3
Sørrollnes 9 C2
Sorsa 18 B3
Sorsakoski 22 B3
Sorsele 15 D3
Sörsidan 17 C2
Sörsjön 39 B/C1
Sørskjomen 9 D2
Sorso 123 C1
Sørstraumen 4 B2
Sort 155 C2
Sortelha 159 B/C3
Sortino 125 D3
Sörtjärn 34 B3
Sortland 9 C2
Sør-Tverrfjord 4 B2
Sørum 37 D3, 38 A2
Sørumsand 38 A3
Sorunda 47 C1/2
Sörup 52 B2
Sørvågen 8 A3
Sörvallen 34 A3
Sørværy 8 A3
Sørværøy 8 A3
Sörvattnet 34 A3
Sørvik 9 C/D1/2
Sörvika 33 D3
Sörviken 34 B3
Sørviken 30 A2/3, 35 C1
Sorzano 153 D2
Sos 109 B/C2
Sösdala 50 B2/3
Sos del Rey Católico
155 C2
Sosés 155 C3, 163 C1
Sošice 127 C3
Sösjö 35 C2
Sosnica 99 D2
Sosnowiec 97 B/C2
Soso 18 B2/3
Sospel 112 B2
Sospiro 114 A1
Sossoniemi 19 D1
Šoštanj 127 C2
Šoštka 99 D1/2
Sot 133 C1
Sotaseter 37 C1/2
Sot de Chera 162 B3,
169 C1
Sotés 153 D2
Soteska 127 C3
Sotillo de las Palomas
160 A3
Sotillo del Rincón 153 D3
Sotillo de la Adrada
160 A/B3
Sotillo de la Ribera
153 B/C3, 160 B1
Sotin 129 C3, 133 C1
Sotka 18 B2/3
Sotkajärvi 18 B2/3
Sotkamo 19 C3, 23 C1
Sotkuma 23 C2/3
Sotobañado y Priorato
152 B2
Soto de la Vega 151 D2
Soto del Barco 151 D1
Soto de los Infantes 151 D1
Soto del Real 160 B2

Soto de Luiña 151 D1
Soto de Sajambre 152 A1
Soto de San Esteban
  153 C3, 161 C1
Sotodosos 161 D2
Soto en Cameros 153 D2
Sotogrande Complejo Urba-
  nístico 172 A3
Sótony 128 A1
Sotopalacios 153 C2
Sotos 161 D3
Sotoserrano 159 D2
Soto y Amío 151 D2
Sotres 111 C3
Sotresgudo 152 B2
Sotta 113 D3
Søttaren 14 A2
Sottens [Moudon] 104 B2
Sotteville-sur-Mer 77 C2/3
Sottomarina 107 D3
Sottrum 48 A/B2
Sottunga 41 D3
Sotuélamos 168 A2
Souain-Perthes-lès-Hurlus
  88 B1
Soual 109 D3, 110 A3
Souchez 78 A2
Soúda 149 B/C3
Soudé 88 B1/2
Soueix 108 B3, 155 C2
Souesmes 87 C/D3
Souflíon 145 D1, 145 D3
Sougné-Remouchamps
  79 C/D2
Souillac 109 D1
Souilly 89 C1
Soukainen 24 A2
Soulac-sur-Mer 100 B3
Soulaines-Dhuys 88 B2
Soulatge 156 B1
Soulaucourt-sur-Mouzon
  89 C2
Soulgé-le-Bruant 86 A2
Soúlion 146 B2
Soulópoulon 142 B3
Soultz 89 D2/3, 90 A3
Soultz-sous-Forêts 90 B1
Soumoulou 108 B3,
  155 B/C1
Soúnion 147 D3
Souppes-sur-Loing 87 D2
Souprosse 108 B2
Souquet 108 A2
Source de la Loue 104 A1
Source du Lison 104 A1
Sourdeval 85 D1, 86 A1
Sourdun 88 A2
Soure 158 A3
Sournia 156 B1
Soúrpi 147 C1
Sourton 63 C2/3
Sousceyrac 109 D1
Souselo 158 A2
Soustons 108 B2
Southam 65 C2
Southampton 76 B1
Southborough 65 C3,
  77 B/C1
South Brent 63 C3
South Cave 61 D2
Southend 56 A2
Southend-on-Sea 65 C3
Southerness 57 C3, 60 A1
South Hayling 76 A1
Southminster 65 C3
South Molton 63 C2
Southport 59 C/D2, 60 B2
South Shields 57 D3,
  61 C1
South Shields 54 B3
Southwell 61 C3, 64 B1
South Willingham 61 D3,
  65 B/C1
Southwold 65 D2
Souto 164 B1
Souto da Carpalhosa
  158 A3, 164 A1
Souto da Casa 158 B3
Souto Maior 158 B1
Soutomaior 150 A2
Souvála 147 D2/3
Souvigné 86 B3
Souvigny 102 B2
Souzel 165 C2
Souzelas 158 A3
Søvassli 28 A3, 33 C2
Sovata 141 B/C1

Sövdeborg 50 B3
Sover 107 C2
Soverato 122 B2
Sovereto 120 B2, 136 A3
Soveria Mannelli 122 B2
Sövestad 50 B3
Søvik 32 A3, 36 B1
Sovetsk (Tilsit) 73 C2
Sovetsk (Tilsit) 73 C2
Sowia Góra 71 C2
Söyrinki 21 C2
Sozopol 141 C3
Spa 79 D2
Špačince 95 C2
Spadafora 125 D1
Spaichingen 90 B2/3
Špaj 135 C3, 139 C1
Spakenburg 66 B3
Spalding 61 D3, 65 C1
Spálené Poříčí 83 C3
Spalt 91 D1, 92 A1
Spången 50 A/B2/3
Spångenäs 46 B3
Spangenberg 81 C1
Spangeried 42 B3
Španovica 128 A3
Spantekow 70 A1
Sparanise 119 C3
Sparbu 28 B2/3, 33 D1
Sparreholm 47 C1
Spárta 147 C2
Spárti 147 C3
Spárti 148 B2/3
Spartílas 142 A3
Spas 138 B3, 143 C1
Spas-Demensk 75 C/D3
Spáta 147 D2
Speicher 79 D3, 80 A3
Speichersdorf 82 A3
Speke 38 A3, 45 C1
Spekedalssetra 33 D3
Spelle-Venhaus 67 D2
Spello 115 D3, 117 C2/3
Spenge 68 A3
Spennymoor 57 D3, 61 C1
Spenshult 50 A1
Spentrup 48 B2
Sperchiás 146 B1
Sperenberg 70 A3
Sperlinga 125 C2
Sperlonga 119 C3
Sperone 124 A2
Spétsai 147 C3
Speyer 90 B1
Spezzano Albanese
  122 A/B1
Spezzano della Sila 122 B2
Spiegelau 93 C1/2
Spiegelberg 91 C1
Spiekeroog 67 D1
Spielfeld 127 C1/2
Spiez 105 C1/2
Spiggen 17 C3
Spigno Monferrato
  113 C1/2
Spilamberto 114 B1
Spile 142 A2
Spíleon 143 C2/3
Spíleon 145 D2
Spiliá 143 C3
Spilimbergo 107 D2,
  126 A2
Spílion 149 C3
Spillersboda 41 C3
Spilling 42 B3
Spillum 28 B2
Spilsby 61 D3, 65 C1
Spinazzola 120 B2
Spincourt 89 C1
Spinetta Marengo 113 C1
Spinoso 120 B3
Špionica 132 B1
Spira 15 D2
Špišić-Bukovica 128 A3
Spišská Belá 97 C2
Spišská Nová Ves 97 C2
Spital am Pyhrn 93 D3
Spital am Semmering 94 A3
Spiterstulen 37 C2
Spittal an der Drau 126 A1
Spitz 94 A2
Spjald 48 A3
Spjærøy 44 B1/2
Spjelkavik 32 A3
Spjutsbygd 51 C2
Spjutsund 25 D3, 26 A3
Spjutvik 9 C2
Split 131 C3

Splügen [Thusis] 105 D2,
  106 A2
Spodnje Hoče 127 C/D2
Spodnji Brnik 126 B2
Spodsbjerg 53 C2
Špogi 74 A2
Špola 99 D3
Spolaíta 146 A1
Spoleto 117 C3, 118 B1
Spølrem 14 B3
Spondigna/Spondinig
  106 B2
Sponvika 44 B1/2
Spornitz 69 C/D1
Spotorno 113 C2
Spøttrup 48 A2
Spraitbach 91 C1/2
Sprakensehl 69 B/C2
Spreenhagen 70 B2/3
Spreewitz 83 D1
Spremberg 83 D1
Spremberg 96 A1
Sprendlingen (Bingen)
  80 B3
Spresiano 107 D3
Springe 68 B3
Springliden 16 A3
Spruga [Ponte Brolla]
  105 D2
Spuhlija 127 D2
Spuž 137 D2
Spydeberg 38 A3, 44 B1
Squillace 122 B2
Squinzano 121 D3
Srbac 132 A1
Srbica 138 B1
Srbobran 129 D3
Srbobran 140 A1/2
Srbrenik 132 B1
Srebnoe 99 D2
Srebrenica 133 C2
Središče 127 D2
Središte 141 C2
Srem 72 B3, 96 B1
Srem 71 D3
Sremska Kamenica 129 D3,
  133 D1, 134 A1
Sremska Mitrovica 133 C1
Sremska Rača 133 C1
Sremski Karlovci 129 D3,
  133 D1, 134 A1
Sreser 136 B1
Srnetica 131 D2
Srní 93 C1
Srnice 132 B1
Sroczyn 71 D2
Środa Wielkopolska 71 D3
Srpska Crnja 129 D3
Srpske Moravice 127 C3
Srpski-Itebej 140 A1/2
Srpski Miletić 129 C3
Staatz 94 B2
Stabbestad 43 D2, 44 A2
Stabbforsmoen 14 B3
Staby 48 A2
Stachy 93 C1
Stackmora 39 D1/2
Staddajåkkstugorna
  15 C/D1
Stade 68 B1
Stadecken-Elsheim 80 B3
Stadensen-Breitenhees
  69 B/C2
Stadil 48 A2/3
Stadl an der Mur 126 B1
Stadsås 30 A1
Stadskanaal 67 C2
Stadtallendorf 81 C2
Stadtbergen 91 D2
Stadthagen 68 A3
Stadtilm 82 A2
Stadtkyll 79 D2
Stadtlauringen-Ballings-
  hausen 81 D3
Stadtlauringen-Wettringen
  81 D3
Stadtlauringen 81 D2/3
Stadtlengsfeld 81 D2
Stadtlohn 67 C3
Stadtoldendorf 68 B3
Stadtprozelten 81 C3
Stadtroda 82 A2
Stadtschlaining 94 B3,
  127 D1
Stadtsteinach 82 A2/3
Stadum 52 A/B2
Stäfa 105 D1

Staffans 17 D2/3
Staffanstorp 50 A/B3
Staffelstein 81 D3, 82 A3
Stáffolo 115 D3, 117 D2
Stafford 59 D3, 60 B3,
  64 A1
Staggträsk 15 D3
Stágira 144 B2
Stagno 114 A3, 116 A2
Stahovica 127 B/C2
Stai 38 A1
Stainach 93 C/D3
Staindrop 57 D3, 61 C1
Staines 64 B3
Stainville 89 B/C2
Stainz 127 C1
Staíti 122 A3
Staitz 82 B2
Stajićevo 129 D3, 133 D1,
  134 A1
Stakevci 135 C3
Stakknes 32 B2
Stakkvik 4 A2
Stalać 134 B3
Stålboga 47 C1
Stalbridge 63 D2
Štalcerji 127 C3
Stalden [Stalden-Saas]
  105 C2
Stalham 65 D1
Stalheim 36 B3
Stall 107 D1, 126 A1
Stallarholmen 47 C1
Ställberg 39 D3
Ställdalen 39 D3
Stallogargo 5 C1/2, 6 A1
Stalltjärnstugan 29 C3,
  34 A1
Stallwang 92 B1
Stalmine 59 C/D1, 60 B2
Stalowa Wola 97 C1, 98 A2
Stamford 64 B1/2
Stamford Bridge 61 C3
Stammham 92 A1/2
Stamná 146 A2
Stamnes 36 A3
Stamora-Germană 134 B1
Stams 106 B1
Stamseter 32 B3, 37 C1
Stamsried 92 B1
Stamsund 8 B2
Stanari 132 B1
Standal 32 A3, 36 B1
Standnes 36 A2
Stånga 47 D3
Stånga 72 B1
Stange 38 A2
Stangerode 69 C3, 82 A1
Stanghella 107 C3, 115 C1
Stangnes 9 C/D1
Stangvik 32 B2
Stanhope 57 D3, 61 B/C1
Stanišić 129 C2/3
Stanislawów 73 C3, 97 C1,
  98 A1
Štanjel 126 B3
Stanke Dimitrov 139 D2
Stanke Dimitrov 140 B3
Staňkov 83 B/C3, 93 B/C1
Stankovci 131 C2/3
Stanley 57 C1
Stanós 144 A/B2
Stanovice 82 B2/3
Stans 92 A3, 107 C1
Stans 105 C1
Stansted Airport 65 C2
Stansted Mountfitchet
  65 C2
St. Antönien-Castels [Küb-
  lis] 106 A1
Stanzach 91 D3, 106 B1
Stapar 129 C3
Stapelburg 69 C3
Stapelford Park 64 B1
Staphorst 67 C2
Stappogiedde 7 B/C1
Stara Baška 130 B1
Stará Bystrica 95 D1
Stara Gradina 128 A3
Stara Gradiška 131 D1,
  132 A1
Staraja Russa 75 C1/2
Staraja Toropa 75 C2
Staraja Ušica 98 B3
Starakonstantinov 98 B2/3
Stara Łubianka 71 D1
Stará L'ubovňa 97 C2

Stara Moravica 129 C3
Stara Novalja 130 B2
Stara Pazova 133 D1,
  134 A1
Stará Role 82 B2
Stará Turá 95 C2
Staravina 139 C3, 143 C1
Stará Voda 82 B3
Stara Woda 71 C3
Stara Zagora 141 C3
Stare Czarnowo 70 B1
Stare Długie 71 D3
Stare Drawsko 71 C/D1
Staré Hory 95 D1/2
Staré Město u Uherské Hra-
  diště 95 C1
Stare Osieczno 71 C2
Staré Sedlo 83 C/D3,
  93 C/D1
Stargard Szczecinski 71 C1
Stargard Szczecinski 72 A3
Stårheim 36 A1
Stari Banovci 133 D1,
  134 A1
Stari Bar 137 D2
Starica 75 D2
Stari-Dojran 139 D3,
  143 D1, 144 A1
Stari Farkašić 127 D3
Starigrad 131 D3, 136 A1
Starigrad 130 B1
Stari Gradac 128 A2/3
Starigrad-Paklenica 130 B2
Stari Jankovci 129 C3,
  133 C1
Stari Lec 134 B1
Stari Log 127 C3
Stari Majdan 131 D1
Stari Mikanovci 128 B3,
  132 B1
Stari Trg 127 C3
Starnberg 92 A3
Stærnes 43 D1
Stärnö 51 C2
Starodub 99 D1
Starogard 71 C1
Starogard Gdański 72 B2
Starokazač'e 141 D1
Staro Nagoričane 139 C2
Staro Orjahovo 141 C/D3
Staro Petrovo Selo 128 A3,
  131 D1, 132 A1
Starosiedle 70 B3
Starše 127 D2
Starsiedel 82 B1
Starup 48 A3, 52 A1
Stary Chwalim 71 D1
Starý Hrozenkov 95 C1
Staryje Dorogi 99 C1
Staryj Sambor 97 D2,
  98 A3
Starý Plzenec 83 C3
Stary Tomyśl 71 C/D2/3
Stassfurt 69 C3
Staszów 97 C1
Stathelle 43 D2, 44 A1/2
Stäträsk 16 B2
St-Aubin [Gorgier-St-Au-
  bin] 104 B1
Staudach-Eegerndach
  92 B3
Staufen 90 A3
Staupåmoen 14 B1
Staurust 32 B3, 37 C1
Stavanger 42 A2
Stavarmon 30 B3, 35 D1
Stave 9 C1
Stavelot 79 D2
Staven 28 A2, 33 C1
Stavenisse 66 A3, 78 B1
Staveren 66 B2
Stavern 43 D2, 44 A2
Stavišče 99 C3
Stavkirke 37 C3
Stavn 48 B1/2
Stavnäs 45 C1
Stávoli Gnivizza 126 A2
Stavre 35 C2
Stavre 29 C/D3, 34 B1/2
Stavreviken 35 D3
Stavrodrómion 146 B3
Stavrós 144 B2
Stavrós 143 D3
Stavrós 146 A2
Stavrós 147 C3
Stavrós 148 B1
Stavroúpolis 145 C1

Stavsjø 38 A2
Stavsjø bruk 46 B2
Stavsnäs 47 D1
Stawiski 73 C/D3, 98 A1
St-Blaise 104 B1
St-Cergue 104 A2
Steane 43 C2
Steblevě 138 A3, 142 B1
Stechelberg [Lauterbrun-
nen] 105 C2
Štěchovice 83 D3
Steckborn 91 C3
Ste-Croix 104 B1
Steeg 106 B1
Steenbergen 66 A3, 78 B1
Steenbergen 67 C1/2
Steenderen 67 C3
Steenvoorde 78 A2
Steenwijk 67 C2
Stefănesti 98 B3
Stefáni 146 A1
Steffenberg-Niedereisen-
hausen 80 B2
Stegaros 43 C1
Stegaurach 81 D3
Stege 53 D2
Stege 72 A2
Stegeborg 46 B2
Stegelitz 69 D3
Stegersbach 127 D1
Stehag 50 B3
Steige 89 D2, 90 A2
Steigen 8 B3
Steigertal 81 C2
Steigra 82 A1
Steikvassli 14 B2
Steimbke 68 B2
Steimbke-Lichtenhorst
68 B2
Stein 92 B3
Stein 91 D1, 92 A1
Stein 107 D1, 126 A1/2
Steinach 82 A2
Steinach am Brenner
107 C1
Steinakirchen am Forst
93 D2/3
Stein am Rhein 91 B/C3
Steinau 81 C2
Steinau 52 A3, 68 A1
Steinau-Ulmbach 81 C2
Steinbach 83 C2
Steinbach am Wald 82 A2
Steinbach (Giessen)
81 B/C2
Steinbach-Hallenberg
81 D2
Steinbergdalshytta
37 B/C3
Steinbergkirche 52 B2
Steinbueng 33 C2
Steinbukt 6 B1
Steine 28 B1
Steine 36 B3
Steinebrück 79 D2
Steinen 90 A3
Steinestø 36 A3
Steinfeld 67 D2, 68 A2
Steinfort 79 D3
Steinfurt-Borghorst 67 D3
Steingaden 91 D3
Steingaden-Wies 91 D3
Steinhagen 68 A3
Steinhausen-Rottum 91 C3
Steinhausen 80 B1
Steinheid 82 A2
Steinheim 4 A3, 9 D1
Steinheim 68 A3
Steinheim 91 C/D2
Steinhöfel 70 B2/3
Steinhorst 68 B2
Steinibach [Schwanden]
105 D1, 106 A1
Steinigtwolmsdorf 83 D1
Steinkjer 28 B2, 33 D1
Steinkjer 29 B/C2
Steinkyrkja 33 C3, 37 D1
Steinland 8 B1/2
Steinløysa 32 B2
Steinsåsen 33 D2/3
Steinsdorf 70 B3
Steinshamn 32 A2
Steinsland 36 A/B3
Steinsland 14 B2
Steinslandsseter 36 A/B2/3
Stein [Stein-Säckingen]
90 B3

Steinsvik 36 A1
Steinsvollen 4 A2
Steinvik 38 A1
Steinwiesen 82 A2
Steisslingen 91 B/C3
Stelle 68 B2
Stemshaug 32 B2
Stemwede 68 A2
Stemwede-Levern 68 A2/3
Stemwede-Twiehausen
68 A2/3
Stená Pétras 143 D2
Stenåsa 51 D2
Stenay 79 C3
Stenbacken 10 A2
Stenbjerg 48 A2
Stenbrohult 50 B2
Stendal 69 D2
Stenderup 48 B3, 52 B1
Stengårdshult 45 D3
Stenhammar 45 C/D2
Stenhamra 47 C1
Sténico 106 B2
Steni Dírfios 147 D1/2
Steninge strand 49 D2,
50 A2
Stenis 39 C2
Stenje 142 B1
Stenkullen 45 C3
Stenlille 49 D/3, 53 C/D1
Stenløse 49 D3, 50 A3,
53 D1
Stennammar 46 B1
Stennäs 31 B/C2
Stenopós 145 C1
Stensdalsstugorna 34 A2
Stensjö 30 A3, 35 C2
Stensjön 46 A3
Stenstorp 45 D2/3
Stenstrand 15 C/D3
Stensträsk 16 A3
Stenstrup 53 C2
Stensund 16 A3
Stensund 31 C1
Stensund 15 D2
Stensund 15 D3
Stenträsk 16 A/B2
Stenudden 15 D2
Stenungsund 45 C3
Stenvadet 39 C1
Stepanci 139 B/C3
Stephanskirchen (Rosen-
heim) 92 B3
Stępień 71 D1
Stepnica 70 B1
Stepojevac 133 D2, 134 A2
Sterley 69 C1
Stérna 147 C3
Stérnai 149 B/C3
Sternberg 53 D3, 69 D1
Sternenfels 90 B1
Sterringi 32 B3, 37 C1
Sterup 52 B2
Stęszew 71 D3
Stęszew 72 B3, 96 B1
Štětí 83 D2
Stetten am kalten Markt
91 C2/3
Steutz 69 D3
Stevanovac 137 D1
Stevenage 65 B/C2
Stewarton 56 B2
Steyerberg 68 A2
Steyning 76 B1
Steyr 93 D2/3
Steyr 96 A3
Steyregg 93 D2
St. Gallen 91 C3
Stia 115 C2, 116 B1
Štiavnik 95 D1
Stichtse brug 66 B2/3
Stickney 61 D3, 65 C1
Stična 127 C2/3
Stiege 69 C3, 81 D1, 82 A1
Stiens 66 B1
Stift Göttweig 94 A2
Stigen 38 B1
Stigen 45 C2
Stigliano 120 B3
Stigsjö 35 D2/3
Stigtomta 47 C2
Stiklestad 28 B3, 33 D1
Stilís 147 C1
Stilís 148 B2
Stilla 5 C2
Stilling 48 B3
Stilo 122 B3

Stilton 64 B2
Stimánga 147 C2
St-Imier 89 D3, 104 B1
Štimlje 138 B2
Štimlje 140 A3
Stîna de Vale 97 D3,
140 B1
Știnăpari 135 C1
Stio 120 A3
Štip 139 C3
Štip 140 A3
Stipshausen 80 A3
Stíra 149 C2
Stirling 54 B2
Stirling 56 B1
Štirovača 130 B1/2
Štit 145 D2
Štitar 133 C1
Štítary 94 A1
Štivan 130 A1
Štivica 132 A1
Stjärnhov 47 C1
Stjärnorp 46 B2
Stjärnsund 40 A2
Stjärnsund 46 A2
Stjern 28 A2
Stjerneobservatoriet 4 B3,
10 A/B1
Stjørdal 28 A/B3, 33 D1
Stjørna 33 C1
St-Luc [Sierre] 105 C2
St. Margrethen 91 C3
St-Maurice 104 B2
St. Moritz 106 A2
St. Niklaus 105 C2
Stø 8 B1
Stobi 139 C3
Stobno 71 D2
Stobreč 131 C/D3
Stoby 50 B2
Stocka 35 D3
Stockach 91 C3
Stöckalp [Sarnen] 105 C1
Stockaryd 51 C1
Stockbäcken 16 B3
Stockbridge 64 A3, 76 A1
Stöcke 31 C/D2
Stockelsdorf 53 C3
Stocken 44 B3
Stockerau 94 B2
Stockerau 96 A/B2
Stockholm 47 C1
Stockport 59 D2, 60 B3
Stöcksjö 31 C/D2
Stockton-on-Tees 61 D1
Stod 28 B2
Stod 83 C3
Stöde 35 C/D3
Stödtlen 91 D1
Stoetze-Hohenzethen
69 C2
Stoholm 48 B2
Stokeasay Castle 59 D3
Stoke Ferry 65 C2
Stoke-on-Trent 59 D2,
60 B3, 64 A1
Stokesley 61 D1
Stokkasjøen 14 A3
Stokke 43 D2, 44 A/B1
Stokkebro 49 C2
Stokkemarke 53 C2
Stokkvågen 14 A2
Stokmarknes 8 B2
Štoky 94 A1
Stolac 132 B3, 137 B/C1
Stolbcy 98 B1
Stolberg 81 D1, 82 A1
Stolberg 79 D2
Stolberg-Gressenich 79 D2
Stolberg-Zeifall 79 D2
Stöle 43 D2, 44 A2
Stølen 33 C3
Stølen 32 B2
Stølensetra 33 C3
Stolin 98 B1/2
Stollberg 82 B2
Stolpe 70 B2
Stolpen 83 C1
Stolvizza 126 A2
Stolzenau 68 A2
Stolzenau-Nendorf 68 A2
Stolzenhain 70 A3
Stómion 143 D3
Stómne 45 C1
Stomorska 131 C3
Ston 136 B1
Stonařov 94 A1

Stone 59 D2/3, 60 B3,
64 A1
Stonehaven 54 B2
Stonehenge 64 A3, 76 A1
Stongfiorden 36 A2
Stonglandseidet 9 C/D1
Stønnesbotn 9 D1
Stony Stratford 64 B2
Stopanja 134 B3
Stöpen 45 D2
Storå 9 C2/3
Storå 39 D3
Storå 20 B3
Stora Anna 47 B/C2
Stora Blåsjön 29 C/D1
Storabränna 29 D2, 34 B1
Stora Dyrön 44 B3
Stora Laxemar 51 D1
Stora Mellby 45 C3
Stora Mellösa 46 B1
Storån 35 B/C3
Stora Olofsholm 47 D2
Stora Råda 45 D2, 46 A1
Storås 33 C2
Storåsen 30 A3, 35 C2
Störåsen 29 D3, 34 B1
Stora Skedvi 39 D2, 40 A2
Stora Stensjön 29 C2,
34 B1
Stora Sundby 46 B1
Stora Vika 47 C2
Storbacka 20 B2
Storbeck 69 D2, 70 A2
Storberg 16 A3
Storberget 17 C1
Storbergvika 29 C/D2
Storborgaren 30 B2, 35 D1
Storbränna 29 D3, 34 B1
Storbudalsetra 33 C2
Storbukt 5 C/D1, 6 A1
Storby 41 C3
Stordal 32 A3, 36 B1
Stordal 28 B3, 33 D1/2
Stordalselv 4 A3, 10 A1
Štore 127 C2
Storebro 46 B3
Storebru 36 A2
Store Darum 52 A1
Store Heddinge 50 A3,
53 D1
Store Heddinge 72 A2
Storekorsnes 5 C2
Storelv 5 C1
Stor-Elvdal 38 A1
Storelvvoll 33 D2
Store Merløse 49 D3,
53 D1
Store Molvik 7 C1
Støren 33 C2
Storeng 4 B2
Storenga 15 C1
Storerikvollen 33 D2
Store Skageseter 37 D2
Storeskarhotel 37 C3
Storestølen 37 C3
Storfinntråsk 16 B3
Storfjåten 34 A3
Storfjord 4 A3, 10 A1
Storfors 45 D1, 46 A1
Storforshei 14 B2
Storfosna 28 A3, 33 C1
Storfossen 9 D2
Storglomvassbrakka 14 B1
Storhögen 29 D3,
35 B/C1/2
Storhøliseter 37 D2
Storholmsjön 29 D3, 34 B1
Storholmsjön 29 D3, 34 B1
Storjord 15 B/C1
Storjorda 14 B1
Storjuktan 15 D2
Storjungfrun 40 B1
Storkläppvallen 34 A2
Storkow 70 B3
Storkowo 71 C1
Storkyro 20 B2
Storli 4 A3, 9 D1
Storli 32 B2
Storli 4 A3, 9 D1
Storlien 28 B3, 33 D1/2
Storlien 28 B3, 33 D1/2,
34 A2
Storlögda 30 B2
Stormark 31 C1
Stormoen 15 C1
Stormvloedkering 66 A3,
78 B1

Stormyren 15 D3
Stornarella 120 A/B2
Stornäs 29 C1
Stornes 9 C1/2
Stornorrfors 31 C2
Stornoway 54 A1
Storo 106 B3
Storoddan 32 B1/2
Storødegårdseter 38 A2
Storöhamn 17 C3
Storožinec 98 B3
Storrensjön 29 B/C3,
34 A1
Storrödtjärnstugan 34 A3
Storrøsta 33 C/D3
Storsand 38 A3, 44 B1
Storsand 16 B2
Storsandsjö 31 C1/2
Storsätern 34 A3
Storsävartråsk 31 C1
Storsele 30 A/B1
Storselsøy 14 A1/2
Storsjö 34 A2
Storsjön 30 B2
Storsjön 40 A1
Storskog 7 C/D2
Storslett 9 C3
Storslett (Nordreisa)
4 B2/3
Storsteinnes 4 A3, 10 A1
Storsteinnes 14 B3
Storsund 16 B3
Stortråsk 16 A/B3
Storulvåns fjällstation
28 B3, 33 D2, 34 A2
Storulvsjön 35 C3
Storuman 15 D3
Storvedjan 17 C2
Storvik 5 C1, 6 A1
Storvik 5 C2
Storvik 4 B2
Storvik 40 A2
Storvist 20 B2
Storvollen 4 A2
Storvollseter 32 B3, 37 C1
Storvreta 40 B3
Stössen 82 A/B1
Stötten am Auerberg 91 D3
Stotternheim 81 D1, 82 A1
Stouby 48 B3, 52 B1
Stourbridge 59 D3, 64 A2
Stourhead House 63 D2,
64 A3
Stourport-on-Severn
59 D3, 64 A2
Støvring 48 B2
Stow 57 C2
Stowmarket 65 C/D2
Stow on the Wold 64 A2
Stožec 93 C1/2
Stra 107 C3
Straach 69 D3
Strabane 54 A3, 55 D2
Stracia 122 A3
Stracin 139 C2
Straczno 71 D1
Stradalovo 139 D2
Strada San Zeno 115 C2,
116 B1
Stradbroke 65 C2
Stradella 113 D1
Stradella 106 B3
Straden 127 D1
Straelen 79 D1
Stragari 133 D2, 134 B2
Straiton 56 B2
Strakonice 93 C1
Strakonice 96 A2
Strålsnäs 46 A2
Stralsund 72 A2
Strambino 105 C3
Strand 31 C2
Strand 14 B2
Strand 42 A2
Strand 9 C2
Stranda 32 A3, 36 B1
Strandåker 31 C2
Strandalshytta 42 B2
Strandby 49 C1
Strande 52 B2
Strandebarm 36 A/B3
Strandlinjer 5 D2, 6 A2
Strandlykkja 38 A2
Strandudden 45 D1, 46 A1
Strandval 28 B2
Strandvik 42 A1
Strangford 58 A1

Strangford **54** A3, **55** D2
Strängnäs **47** C1
Strängnäs **30** B1
Strangolagalli **119** C2
Strångsjö **46** B2
Strångsund **35** B/C2/3
Stráni **95** C1
Stranice **127** C2
Stránoma **146** B1/2
Stranorlar **55** C/D2
Stranraer **54** A3, **55** D2
Stranraer **56** A/B3
Strasbourg **90** A/B2
Strasburg **70** A/B1
Strašice **83** C3
Strašín **93** C1
Straškov-Vodochody **83** C/D2
Strässa **39** D3
Strassberg (Sigmaringen) **91** C2
Strassburg **126** B1
Strassenhaus **80** A2
Strass im Zillertal **92** A3, **107** C1
Strass in Steiermark **127** C1/2
Strasskirchen **92** B1/2
Strasswalchen **93** C3
Straszów **83** D1
Stratford Saint-Mary **65** C/D2
Stratford-upon-Avon **64** A2
Strathaven **56** B2
Strathblane **56** B1/2
Strathyre **56** B1
Stratoníki **144** B2
Stratónion **144** B2
Stratos **146** A1
Stratton **62** B2
Strau **126** B2
Straubenhardt-Conweiler **90** B2
Straubing **92** B1/2
Straum **14** B2
Straum **32** B1
Straumbu **33** C3, **37** D1
Straume **36** A/B3
Straume **43** C1
Straume **8** B2
Straume **43** C/D2, **44** A1/2
Straumen **28** B1
Straumen **32** B1/2
Straumen **9** C2
Straumen **4** A3, **9** D1
Straumen **14** B1
Straumfjordnes **4** B2
Straumsbotn **9** D1
Straumshamn **36** B1
Straumshella **4** A3
Straumsli **4** A3, **10** A1
Straumsnes **9** C/D1
Straumsnes **8** B2
Straupitz **70** B3
Strausberg **70** B2
Straussfurt **81** D1, **82** A1
Stráž **82** B3
Straža **134** B1
Straža **127** C3
Straže **127** D2
Strazeele **78** A2
Strázek **94** B1
Strazilovo **133** D1, **134** A1
Strážkovice **93** D1/2
Stráž nad Nežárkou **93** D1
Strážnice **95** C1
Strážný **93** C1/2
Strážný **96** A2
Strážov **93** C1
Stráž pod Ralskem **83** D2
Streatley **65** C3
Strečno **95** D1
Street **63** D2
Strehaia **135** D2
Strehaia **140** B2
Strehla **83** C1
Streˇkov **83** C2
Strekov **95** D3
Strem **127** D1
Strembo **106** B2
Strendene **14** B3
Strengberg **93** D2
Strengelvåg **8** B1
Strengen **43** C2, **44** A1
Strenggjerdet **14** A2
Strensall **61** C2

Stresa **105** D2/3
Stretford **59** D2, **60** B3
Streufdorf **81** D2
Strezimirovci **139** C1
Strezovce **138** B1
Strib **48** B3, **52** B1
Striberg **46** A1
Stříbrná Skalice **83** D3
Stříbro **82** B3
Stridbäck **16** B3
Strigno **107** C2
Štrigova **127** D2
Strijbeek **79** C1
Střílky **95** B/C1
Strimasund **15** C2
Strinda **94** A3
Strindmoen **28** B2
Strmac **128** A3, **131** D1
Strmen **128** A3, **131** D1
Strmica **131** C2
Strmilov **93** D1, **94** A1
Strobl **93** C3
Strøby **50** A3, **53** D1
Strofiliá **147** D1
Strofiliá **148** B2
Strojkovce **139** C1
Strøm **38** B3
Ström **31** C2
Strömbacka **35** C/D3
Stromberg **80** B3
Strómboli **125** D1
Stromeferry **54** A2, **55** D1
Strömfors **16** B3
Strömfors **16** A3
Strömfors **31** D1
Stromi **24** B1
Strömma **47** D1
Strömma **24** B3
Strömma **41** C2/3
Strömmen **34** A3
Strømmen **28** B2/3, **33** D1
Strømmen **33** C3
Strømmen **38** A3
Strømmen **5** D1, **6** A1
Strömnäs **30** A2, **35** C1
Stromness **54** B1
Strompdalen **29** C1
Strömsberg **40** B2
Strömsbro (Gävle) **40** B2
Strömsbruk **35** D3
Strömsholm **40** A3, **46** B1
Strömsnäs **30** A3, **35** C2
Strömsnäs **17** C2
Strömsnäsbruk **50** B2
Strømsoddbygda **37** D3
Strömstad **44** B2
Strömsund **29** D2/3, **30** A2, **35** C1
Strömsund **15** D3
Strömsund **17** C2
Strona **105** C2/3
Stronachlachar **56** B1
Stróngoli **122** B2
Stronsdorf **94** B2
Stroobrugge **78** B1
Stroppiana **105** C/D3, **113** C1
Strøsvik **14** B1
Stroud **63** D1, **64** A3
Štrpce **138** B2
Struer **48** A2
Struga **70** B1
Struga **138** A/B3, **142** B1
Strullendorf **81** D3, **82** A3
Strumica **139** D3
Strumica **140** A/B3
Strunjan **126** A/B3
Struppen **4** A3, **10** A1
Struth **81** D1
Strüth (Loreley) **80** B3
Stryckfsele **31** C1/2
Stryj **97** D2, **98** A3
Stryken **38** A3
Stryn **32** A3, **36** B1
Strzelce Krajeńskie **71** C2
Strzelce Opolskie **96** B1/2
Strzelno **72** B3
Strzmiele **71** C1
Stubbekøbing **53** D2
Stubbekøbing **72** A2
Stubberup **49** C3, **53** C1
Stubbuden **16** B1
Stuben **106** B1
Stubenberg **93** C2
Štubik **135** C2
Stubline **133** D2, **134** A2
Studená **94** A1

Studena **145** D2
Studena **139** C1
Studena **139** D1/2
Studenci **131** D3, **132** A3
Studenica **133** D3, **134** A/B3
Studenzen **127** C/D1
Studsvik **47** C2
Stuer **69** D1
Stugudal **33** D2
Stuguflaten **32** B3, **37** C1
Stuguliseter **33** C3, **37** D1
Stugun **30** A3, **35** C2
Stühlingen-Grimmelshofen **90** B3
Stühlingen **90** B3
Stuhr **68** A2
Stuhr-Brinkum **68** A2
Stuhr-Seckenhausen **68** A2
Stuibenfall **106** B1
Stulln **92** B1
Stülpe **70** A3
Stumiaga **106** B2
Stumlia **37** D2/3, **38** A2
Stumsnas **39** D2
Stuoraoaivve **5** C3, **11** C1
Stupari **132** B2
Stupava **94** B2
Stupinigi **112** B1
Stupnik **127** D3
St. Urban **105** C1
Sturefors **46** B2
Sturkö **51** C2
Sturno **119** D3, **120** A2
Šturovo **95** D3
Štúrovo **96** B3
St-Ursanne **89** D3, **90** A3, **104** B1
Sturup **50** B3
Sturzelbronn **90** A1
Stutensee-Blankenloch **90** A1
Stuttgart **91** C2
Stuvland **14** A/B2
Stvolny **83** C3
Styggberget **35** C3
Styggdalen **14** B3, **29** C1
Styggedalen **4** A/B3, **10** A1
Stymphalos **147** C2
Stypułów **71** C3
Styri **38** A2/3
Styrkesnes **9** C3
Styrmannstø **4** A/B2
Styrnäs **30** B3, **35** D2
Styrsö **45** C3, **49** D1
Styrvoll **43** D2, **44** A1
Su **155** D3, **156** A2
Suances **152** B1
Suaningi **17** C1
Suaredda **123** D1
Suave Mar **150** A3, **158** A1
Subate **74** A2
Subbersta **30** B3, **35** D2
Subbiano **115** C3, **116** B2
Subiaco **118** B2
Subotica **129** C2
Subotica **140** A1
Subotište **133** D1, **134** A1
Sučany **95** D1
Suceava **141** C2
Sučevići **131** C2
Suchá Hora **97** C2
Suchań **71** C1
Suchdol nad Lužnicí **93** D1/2
Sucina **169** C3, **174** B1
Sückau **69** C1
Suckow **69** D1
Sućuraj **132** A3, **136** B1
Suda **75** D1
Sudanell **155** C3, **163** C1
Sudbø **43** C1
Südbrookmerland **67** D1
Südbrookmerland-Moordorf **67** D1
Sudbury **65** D2
Suddesjaur **16** A2
Süderbrarup **52** B2
Suderburg **69** B/C2
Süderlügum **52** A2
Südlohn **67** C3
Sudok **16** B2
Sudoměřice u Bechyně **93** D1
Sudovaja Višn'a **97** D2, **98** A2
Sudovec **127** D2

Süd-Rätansbyn **34** B3
Sueca **169** D2
Suellacabras **153** D3
Suelli **123** D3
Sueros de Cepeda **151** D2
Suèvres **87** C3
Šugag **140** B1/2
Sugères **102** B3
Sugenheim-Deutenheim **81** D3
Sugnet **39** C1
Suha **132** B2
Suha Punta **130** B1/2
Suhiniči **75** D3
Suhl **81** D2
Suhlendorf **69** C2
Suho Polje **133** C1
Suhopolje **128** A3
Suhostrel **139** D2
Suhr **90** B3, **105** C1
Šuica **131** D3, **132** A2/3
Suijavaara **11** C2
Suinula **25** C1
Suinula **25** C1, **26** A1
Suippes **88** B1
Sukarrieta **153** D1
Sukeva **22** B1
Sukobin **137** D2
Sukošan **130** B2
Sükösd **129** C2
Sukovo **139** C/D1
Suksela **24** B2
Sukth **137** D3, **142** A1
Sul **28** B3, **33** D1
Sula **32** B1
Šul'a **95** D2
Sulå **35** D3
Sulby **58** B1
Suldal **42** B1/2
Sulechów **71** C3
Sulęcin **71** C2
Sulejów **97** C1
Suleskar **42** B2
Sulesund **36** B1
Sulgen **91** C3
Sulibórz **71** C1
Sulików **83** D1
Sulina **141** D2
Sulingen **68** A2
Sulitjelma **15** C3
Sulkava **22** B2
Sulkava **27** C1
Sulkava **25** D2, **26** A2
Sulkavanjärvi **21** D2, **22** A2
Sulkavanjärvi **22** A2
Sulkavanperä **21** D1, **22** A1
Sully **103** C1
Sully-sur-Loire **87** D3
Sulmona **119** C1/2
Sulseter **37** D2
Sultaniçe **145** D2
Sulviken **29** C3, **34** A1
Sülysáp **129** C1
Sulz **90** B2
Sulzano **106** B3
Sulzbach **89** D1, **90** A1
Sulzbach **91** C1
Sulzbach am Main **81** C3
Sulzbach-Laufen **91** C1
Sulzbach-Rosenberg **82** A3, **92** A1
Sulzdorf-Oberessfeld **81** D2
Sulzemoos-Einsbach **92** A2
Sulzfeld am Main **81** D3
Sumacárcel **169** C2
Sumartin **131** D3, **132** A3, **136** A1
Sumbilla **108** A3, **154** A1
Šumburk **83** D2
Sümeg **128** A1
Sümeg **96** B3
Šumen **141** C3
Sumiainen **21** D3, **22** A3
Sumiswald [Sumiswald-Grünen] **105** C1
Šumjači **75** C3
Summa **26** B2
Sumony **128** B2/3
Šumperk **96** B2
Sumsa **19** D3
Sumstad **28** A2
Sünching **92** B1/2
Sund **8** A3
Sund **30** B3
Sund **35** C3
Sund **14** B1

Sund **41** D3
Sundborn **39** D2, **40** A2
Sundby **20** B1
Sunde **32** B1
Sunde **42** A1
Sunderland **61** D1
Sundern **80** B1
Sundern-Allendorf **80** B1
Sundern-Endorf **80** B1
Sundern-Hachen **80** B1
Sundet **29** C3, **34** A1
Sundklakk **8** B2
Sundlisetra **33** C2
Sundö **31** C2
Sundom **17** C3
Sundom **20** A2, **31** D3
Sunds **48** A/B2/3
Sundsbø **32** A2
Sundsfjord **14** B1
Sundsjö **35** B/C2
Sundsjöasen **35** B/C2
Sundskør **28** A2
Sundsli **43** C2
Sundsvall **35** D3
Sundsvall-Selånger **35** D3
Sundsvall-Stockvik **35** D3
Sundsvoll **14** A3
Sundvollen **38** A3, **43** D1
Suni **123** C2
Sunja **127** D3, **131** C/D1
Sunnan **28** B2
Sunnanhed **39** D1/2
Sunnansjö **15** C3
Sunnansjö **31** C2
Sunnansjö **39** D3
Sunndal **36** A2
Sunndalsøra **32** B2
Sunne **39** C3
Sunne **34** B2
Sunnemo **39** C3
Sunnersberg **45** C/D2
Sunnersta **30** B2, **35** D1
Suo-Anttila **27** C2
Suodenniemi **24** B1
Suojanperä **7** C3
Suojoki **20** A/B3
Suolahti **21** D3, **22** A3
Suolovuobme **5** C3
Suomasema **25** C1
Suomela **25** C2/3
Suomen keskipiste **18** B3
Suomenniemi **26** B1
Suomijärvi **20** B3
Suomusjärvi **25** C3
Suomussalmi **19** D2
Suonenjoki **22** B3
Suoniala **27** C2
Suoniemi **24** B1
Suonnankylä **19** C1
Suontaka **24** A2
Suontee **22** B3
Suonttajärvi **11** C2
Suopajärvi **12** A/B3
Suopelto **25** D1, **26** A1
Suopelto **21** D2, **22** A2
Suorajärvi **19** D1
Suorva **9** D3
Šuošjavrre **5** D3, **6** A3, **11** C1
Suostola **12** B2
Suotukylä **21** D1, **22** A1
Suovaaraa **23** C2
Suovanlahti **21** D2, **22** A2
Superbagnères **155** C2
Superbesse **102** B3
Super Nendaz [Sion] **104** B2
Supersano **121** D3
Supetar **131** C/D3
Supetarska Draga **130** B1
Supino **119** D/C2
Süplingen **69** C3
Šuplja Stijeno **133** C3
Süpplingen **69** C3
Supru **7** C3
Süptitz **82** B1
Supuru de Jos **97** D3, **140** B1
Surahammar **40** A3
Surany **95** C2/3
Suraž **75** B/C3
Suraž **99** D1
Surčin **133** D1, **134** A1
Surd **128** A2
Surdulica **139** C1
Surdulica **140** A3
Surgères **100** B2

Surhuisterveen 67 C1
Súria 156 A2/3
Surier 104 B3
Šurlan 138 B2
Surnadalsøra 32 B2
Surnuinmäki 22 B3
Sursee 105 C1
Surte 45 C3
Surwold 67 D2
Sury-ès-Bois 87 D3
Susa 112 B1
Susak 130 A2
Susch 106 B1
Suscinio 85 C3
Susegana 107 D2/3
Sušice 93 C1
Sušice 96 A2
Susikas 25 C2
Süssen 91 C2
Susten [Leuk] 105 C2
Susteren 79 D1
Sustrum 67 D2
Susurluk 149 D1
Şuţeşti 141 C2
Sutivan 131 C/D3
Sutjeska 134 B1
Sutjeska 132 B2
Sutkavankylä 21 C3
Sutme 29 D1
Sutomore 137 D2
Sutri 117 C3, 118 A1
Sútrio 107 D2, 126 A2
Sutterton 61 D3, 65 C1
Süttő 95 D3
Sutton 65 C2
Sutton Coldfld. 64 A2
Sutton in Ashfield 61 D3, 65 C1
Sutton on Sea 61 D3, 65 C1
Sutton Scotney 65 C3, 76 B1
Suttrop 80 B1
Suurikylä 27 D1
Suurimäki 22 B2
Suurlahti 27 C1
Suur-Miehikkälä 27 B/C2
Suur-Saimaa 27 C1/2
Suutala 21 C2/3
Suutarinkylä 18 B3
Suvanto 12 B2
Suvantokumpu 11 D3, 12 B2
Suva Reka 138 B2
Suvereto 114 B3, 116 A2
Suvodol 138 B3
Suvorov 75 D3
Suvorovo 75 D2
Suwałki 73 D2
Suze-la-Rousse 111 C2
Suzzara 114 B1
Svabensverk 39 D2, 40 A1/2
Svaipavalle 15 C2
Švajcernica 129 B/C3
Svaljava 97 D2, 98 A3
Svalöv 50 A3
Svanavattnet 30 A2
Svaneholm 50 B3
Svaneke 51 D3
Svaneke 72 A/B2
Svanesund 45 C3
Svängsta 51 C2
Svaningen 29 D2
Svannäs 16 A2
Svaninge 53 B/C2
Svansele 29 D2
Svansele 31 C1
Svanskog 45 C1
Svanstein 17 D1
Svanström 31 D1
Svanvik 7 C/D3
Svappavaara 10 B3
Svardnes 7 D1/2
Svärdsjö 39 D2, 40 A2
Svarstad 43 D2, 44 A1
Svartå 46 A1
Svärta 47 C2
Svartbäck 26 B2/3
Svartberg 17 C2
Svartbyn 17 C2
Svarthamarseter 37 D2
Svarthaugen 33 D3
Svärtinge 46 B2
Svartisdalen 14 B2
Svartliden 31 C1
Svartlöga 41 C3, 47 D1

Svartnäs 40 A2
Svartnes 14 B1
Svartnes 7 D1/2
Svartöstaden 17 C3
Svartvik 35 D3
Svarvar 20 A2
Sv'ataja Vol'a 98 B1
Svatsum 37 D2
Sved 29 C3, 34 B1
Sved 29 C3, 34 B1
Svedala 50 A/B3
Svedala 72 A2
Svedasai 73 D2, 74 A2/3
Svedja 40 A1
Svedjan 16 B3
Svedje 29 D2, 30 A1/2
Svedje 31 C3
Sveg 34 B3
Sveindal 42 B3
Sveio 42 A1
Svelgen 36 A1/2
Svelvik 38 A3, 43 D1, 44 B1
Svenarum 46 A3, 50 B1
Švenčionys 74 A3
Svendborg 53 C2
Svene 43 D1
Svenes 43 C3
Svenljunga 50 A/B1
Svenljunga 72 A1
Svennevad 46 A/B1/2
Svenningvik 14 B3
Svensby 4 A3
Svensbygd 50 B1
Svensbyn 16 B3
Svenshögen 45 C3
Svenskby 24 B3
Svenstavik 34 B2
Svenstorp 50 A/B3
Svenstrup 48 B1/2
Sverdiá 145 C2/3
Sveta Marija 136 B1
Sveta Nedelja 127 D3
Sveta Petka 135 B/C2/3
Sveti Areh 127 C2
Sveti Arhandel 138 B2
Sveti Arhandel 131 C2
Sveti Bogorodica 138 A/B3, 142 B1
Sveti Janez 126 B2
Sveti Jovan Bigorski 138 A/B3
Sveti Jurij 127 D1
Svetilovići 99 D1
Sveti Martin 131 D3
Sveti Naum 142 B1
Sveti Naum 148 A1
Sveti Nikita 138 B3
Sveti Nikola 137 D2
Sveti Nikole 139 C2
Sveti Pantelejmon 138 B2
Sveti Rok 131 C2
Sveti Stefan 137 C2
Světlík 93 D2
Svetlogorsk 99 C1
Svetlovodsk 99 D3
Svetozarevo 140 A2
Svetozarevo 134 B2
Svetozar Miletić 129 C3
Svetvinčenat 130 A1
Švihov 83 C3, 93 C1
Svilajnac 134 B2
Svilajnac 140 A2
Sviland 42 A2
Svilengrad 145 D2
Svilengrad 141 C3
Svindal 44 B1
Svindalen 9 C1
Svineng 5 D3, 6 A3, 11 D1
Svines 14 A2
Svinesund 44 B1/2
Svinevoll 43 D2, 44 A/B1
Svinhult 46 A/B3
Svinica 135 C2
Svinište 138 B3, 143 B/C1
Svinnegarn 40 A3, 47 C1
Svinninge 47 D1
Svinninge 49 C3, 53 C1
Svinvik 32 B2
Svištov 141 C2/3
Svitavy 96 B2
Svode 139 C1
Svodín 95 D3
Svoge 139 D1
Svoge 140 B3
Svolvær 8 B2
Svora 36 A/B1

Svorkmo 28 A3, 33 C2
Svortemyr 36 A2
Svrčinovec 95 D1
Svrljig 135 C3
Svrljig 140 A2/3
Svukuriset 33 D3
Svulrya 38 B2
Swadlincote 64 A1
Swaffham 65 C1/2
Swaffham Prior 65 C2
Swalmen 79 D1
Swanage 63 D3, 76 A2
Swansea 63 C1
Swarzędz 71 D2
Sweetheart Abbey 57 C3, 60 A1
Świdnica 71 C3
Świdnica (Schweidnitz) 96 B1
Świdwin 72 B2/3
Świdwin 71 C1
Świebodzin 71 C3
Świebodzin 72 A/B3, 96 A1
Świecie 72 B3
Świętno 71 C3
Swindon 64 A1
Swineshead 61 D3, 65 B/C1
Świnoujście (Swinemünde) 72 A2
Swinton 57 D2
Swisttal-Essig 80 A2
Swobnica 70 B2
Swords 58 A2
Syčovka 75 C/D2/3
Sydänmaa 20 B3
Sydänmaa 24 A2
Sydänmaa 24 B1
Sydänmaankylä 21 D1, 22 A1
Sydmo 24 B3
Sydnes 42 A1
Sygnesand 36 B2
Sykäräinen 21 C1
Syke 68 A2
Syke-Barrien 68 A2
Syke-Heiligenfelde 68 A2
Sykkylven 32 A3, 36 B1
Sylling 43 D1
Sylstationen 33 D2, 34 A2
Syltefjord 7 C1
Syltevikmyra 7 D1
Sylt-Ost-Keitum 52 A2
Sylvänä 25 B/C2
Sylvanès 110 A2
Synsiö 22 A/B3
Sypniewo 71 D1
Sypniewo 71 D1
Syrau 82 B2
Syri 21 C1
Syrjä 23 C3
Syrjäntaka 25 C2, 26 A2
Sysmä 25 D1, 26 A1
Sysslebäck 38 B2
Syston 64 B1
Syterstugan 15 C2
Syt'kovo 75 C2
Syväjärvi 12 B2
Syväjärvi 11 B/C2
Syvälahti 23 C3
Syvänniemi 22 B2
Syvänsi 22 B3
Syvde 36 A1
Syvdsnes 36 A1
Syvinki 21 C3
Syvsten 49 B/C1
Syyspohja 27 C1
Szabadbattyán 128 B1
Szabadhidvég 128 B1
Szabadszállás 129 C1
Szakály 128 B2
Szakcs 128 B2
Szakmár 129 C2
Szalánta 128 B2/3
Szalkszentmárton 129 C1
Szamocin 71 D2
Szamotuły 71 D2
Szántód 128 B1
Szany 95 C3
Szarvas 129 C1
Szarvas 97 C3, 140 A1
Százhalombatta 95 D3, 129 C1
Szczecinek (Neustettin) 71 D1

Szczecinek (Neustettin) 72 B2/3
Szczecin (Stettin) 72 A3
Szczecin (Stettin) 70 B1
Szczekociny 97 C1
Szczerców 97 B/C1
Szczuczarz 71 C2
Szczuczyn 73 D3, 98 A1
Szczytno (Ortelsburg) 73 C3
Szederkény 128 B2/3
Szeged 129 D2
Szeged 97 C3, 140 A1
Szeghalom 97 C3, 140 A1
Szegvár 129 D2
Székesfehérvár 128 B1
Székesfehérvár 96 B3
Székkutas 129 D2
Szekszárd 129 C2
Szekszárd 96 B3
Szemerecsörnye 127 D2, 128 A2
Szend 95 C3
Szentendre 95 D3
Szentes 129 D2
Szentes 97 C3, 140 A1
Szentgotthárd 127 D1
Szentkút 95 C3
Szentlászló 128 B2
Szentlőrinc 128 B2
Szentmártonkáta 129 C1
Szenyér 128 A2
Szerencs 97 C2/3
Szigetszentmiklos 95 D3, 129 C1
Szigetszentmiklós 95 D3, 129 C1
Szigetújfalu 129 C1
Szigetvár 128 B2
Szigliget 128 A1
Szil 95 B/C3
Szilvágy 127 D1, 128 A1/2
Szlichtynogowa 71 D3
Szob 95 D3
Szolnok 129 D1
Szolnok 97 C3, 140 A1
Szőlősgyörök 128 B2
Szombathely 127 D1, 128 A1
Szombathely 96 B3
Szomor 95 D3
Szőny 95 C3
Szprotawa (Sprottau) 96 A1
Szulok 128 A2
Szwecja 71 D1
Szydłowo 71 D1/2

T

Tå 40 A1
Taalintehdas 24 B3
Taapajärvi 12 A2, 17 D1
Taasia 25 D2, 26 B2
Taatsijärvi 11 D2, 12 A/B1
Taaurainen 19 D1
Taavetti 27 B/C2
Tab 128 B1/2
Tabanera de Cerrato 152 B3
Tabanovce 139 C2
Tábara 151 D3, 159 D1
Taberg 45 D3
Tabernas 173 D2
Tabernas 154 B3
Tabernes de Valldigna 169 D2
Taberno 174 A1
Tabiano Terme 114 A1
Taboada 150 B2
Taboadela 150 B2/3
Taboado 158 B1/2
Tábor 93 D1
Tábor 96 A2
Taborska Jama 127 B/C2/3
Tábua 158 B3
Tabuaço 158 B2
Tabuenca 154 A3, 162 A1
Täby 47 C1
Täby station (Vallentuna) 47 C1
Tác 128 B1
Taceno 105 D2, 106 A2
T'ačev 97 D3, 98 A3

Tacherting 92 B2/3
Tacherting-Peterskirchen 92 B2/3
Tachov 82 B3
Tackåsen 39 D1
Tacken 69 D1/2
Täcktom 24 B3
Tadcaster 61 D2
Tådene 45 C2
Taennilä 12 B3
Tafalla 154 A2
Tafjord 32 A3, 36 B1
Täfteå 31 C3
Täfteå 20 A1, 31 D2
Tåganes 42 A2
Tågarp 50 A3
Tàggia 113 C2
Tagliacozzo 119 B/C1/2
Táglio di Po 115 C1
Tagnon 78 B3
Tågsjöberg 30 A2, 35 C/D1
Tågsjöberg 30 A2, 35 C/D1
Tahkoranta 22 B3
Tähtelä 25 C3
Tähtelä 12 B2
Tahüll 155 D2
Tahús 155 C2
Tai di Cadore 107 D2
Taillebourg 100 B2/3
Taimoniemi 21 D2, 22 A2
Tain 54 B2
Tainijoki 18 B3
Taininiemi 18 B1
Tain-l'Hermitage 103 D3, 111 C1
Taipale 12 B3
Taipale 24 B1
Taipale 18 A2
Taipale 22 B2
Taipaleenharju 18 B2
Taipaleenkylä 21 B/C3
Taipaleensuu 11 C3
Taipalsaari 27 C2
Taipana 126 A2
Taipas 158 A1
Taiskirchen im Innkreis 93 C2
Taivalkoski 19 C1/2
Taivalmaa 20 B3
Taivassalo 24 A2
Tajmište 138 B3
Tajov 95 D2
Tajueco 153 C/D3, 161 C1
Takácsi 95 C3, 128 A1
Takelvdal 4 A3, 9 D1, 10 A1
Takene 45 D1
Takkula 25 C3
Takkula 24 B2
Taklax 20 A2/3
Takovo 133 D2, 134 A2
Taksony 95 D3, 129 C1
Talamanca 157 D3
Talamantes 154 A3, 162 A1
Talamona 106 A2
Talamone 116 B3
Talana 123 D2
Talarn 155 D2/3
Talarrubias 166 B2
Talaván 159 C/D3, 165 D1, 166 A1
Talavera 155 C3, 163 C1
Talavera de la Reina 160 A3, 166 B1
Talavera la Real 165 D2
Talayuela 159 D3
Talayuelas 163 C3, 169 D1
Talcy 87 C3
Tales 162 B3, 169 D1
Talgarth 63 C1
Talhadas 158 A2
Táliga 165 C2
Talla 115 C3, 116 B2
Tallaght 58 A2
Tallard 112 A2
Tallås 15 D3
Tallåsen 38 B2
Tällberg 39 D2
Tallberg 31 C2
Tallberget 17 C2
Taller 108 A2
Tallhed 39 D1
Tallinn 74 A1
Talljärv 17 C2
Tallnäs 15 D2
Talloires 104 A3
Tallsjö 30 B2

Tallsund 16 A3
Tallträsk 30 B1
Tallträsk 31 C/D1
Tällträsk 16 B3
Talluskylä 22 B2
Talmont 100 A2
Talmont 100 B3
Tal'noe 99 C/D3
Talsi 73 D1
Tålsmark 20 A1, 31 D2
Talusperä 18 A3
Talvadas 6 B2
Talviainen 25 C1
Talvik 5 C2
Talvikstua 5 C2
Talybont 59 C3
Tamajón 161 C2
Tamame 159 D1
Tamames 159 D2
Tamanhos 158 B2
Támara 152 B3
Tamarinda 157 C1
Tamarite de Litera 155 C3
Tamási 128 B2
Tamási 96 B3
Tambach-Dietharz 81 D2
Tâme 31 D1
Tammela 25 C2
Tammela 19 D1
Tammerfors 25 C1
Tammijärvi 25 D1, 26 A1
Tammilahti 25 D1, 26 A/B1
Tammisilta 24 B2/3
Tamnay-en-Bazois 103 C1
Tamnes 33 D2
Tampere (Tammerfors)
25 C1
Tamsweg 126 B1
Tämta 45 C3
Tamurejo 166 B2
Tamworth 64 A1/2
Tana Bru 7 C2
Tanagård 7 C1
Tanágra 147 D2
Tanai/Thanai 106 B1
Tananger 42 A2
Tancarville 77 C3
Tândărei 141 C2
Tanderagee 58 A1
Tandö 39 C2
Tandsbyn 34 B2
Tandsjöborg 39 D1
Tångaberg 49 D1, 50 A1
Tanganheira 164 A3,
170 A1
Tångböle 29 C3, 34 A1/2
Tangen 42 A/B1
Tangen 38 B3
Tangen 44 B1
Tangen 5 C2
Tangen 38 A2
Tänger 39 D2, 40 A2
Tangerhütte 69 D2
Tangermünde 69 D2
Tangleger 33 C3, 37 D1
Tangsjöstugan 38 B1
Tängvattnet 15 C2/3
Tanhua 12 B2
Taninges 104 B2
Tankapirtti 12 B1
Tankavaaran kultakylä
12 B1
Tankolampi 21 D3, 22 A3
Tanlay 88 A/B3
Tann 81 D2
Tanna 82 A2
Tannåker 50 B1
Tännäs 34 A3
Tannay 88 A3
Tänndalen 34 A3
Tanne 69 C3, 81 D1
Tannenbergsthal 82 B2
Tännesberg 82 B3, 92 B1
Tannhausen (Aalen) 91 D1
Tannheim 91 D3
Tannheim (Biberach)
91 D3
Tannila 18 B2
Tann (Pfarrkirchen) 92 B2
Tannsjön 30 A2/3, 35 C1
Tannvik 33 B/C1/2
Tanowo 70 B1
Tantallon Castle 57 C1
Tantonville 89 C2
Tantow 70 B1
Tanttila 25 C/D2, 26 A2
Tanum 44 B2

Tanumshede 44 B2
Tanus 110 A2
Tanvald 83 D2
Taormina 125 D2
Tapa 74 A1
Tapale 24 B2
Tapaninkylä 19 D3
Tapfheim 91 D2
Tápia de Casariego 151 C1
Tápióbicske 129 C1
Tápiógyörgye 129 D1
Tapioles 151 D3, 152 A3,
159 D1
Tapionkylä 12 A3
Tapionniemi 12 B3
Tápiószele 129 D1
Tápiószentmárton
129 C/D1
Tápiószőlős 129 D1
Tapojärvi 11 C3
Tapojoki 11 C3
Tapolca 128 A1
Tapolca 96 B3
Tapolcafő 128 A1
Tapperskar 14 B2
Taps 52 B1
Tar 126 A/B3, 130 A1
Taracena 161 C2
Taradell 156 A2
Taraklija 141 D1
Taramundi 151 C1
Tarancón 161 C3
Tarancueña 161 C1
Táranto 121 C3
Táranto Talsano 121 C3
Tarare 103 C2
Taraš 129 D3
Tarašča 99 C3
Tarascon 111 C2
Tarascon-sur-Ariège
155 D2, 156 A1
Tarasp-Fontana [Scuol-Ta-
rasp] 106 B1
Taravilla 161 D2
Tarazona 154 A3
Tarazona de Guareña
160 A1/2
Tarazona de la Mancha
168 B1/2
Tårbæk 49 D3, 50 A3,
53 D1
Tárbena 169 D2
Tarbert 56 A2
Tarbert 54 A2/3, 55 D1
Tarbert 54 A2
Tarbert 55 C3
Tarbes 108 B3, 155 C1
Tarbet 56 B1
Tarbet 54 A2, 55 D1
Tarcento 126 A2
Tarčin 132 B2
Tardajos 153 B/C2
Tardajos de Duero 153 D3,
161 D1
Tardelcuende 153 D3,
161 D1
Tardets-Sorholus
108 A/B3, 154 B1
Tardienta 154 B3
Tardobispo 159 D1
Tärendö 17 C1
Tarfalastugan 9 D3
Targon 108 B1
Târgovişte 141 C3
Tarhapää 21 C3
Tariego 152 B3
Tarifa 171 D3
Tarján 95 D3
Tarleton 59 D2, 60 B2
Tarm 48 A3
Tarmstedt 68 A1/2
Tärnaby 15 C3
Tarnala 27 C3
Tärnamo 15 C3
Tärnasjöstugan 15 C2
Tårnet 7 C2
Tarnobrzeg 97 C1, 98 A2
Tarnów 97 C2
Tarnów 71 B/C2
Tarnówka 71 D1
Tarnowo 71 D2
Tarnowo Podgórne 71 D2
Tärnsjö 40 A3
Tårnvik 6 B1
Tårnvik 8 B3
Taroda 161 D1
Tarouca 158 B2

Tarp 52 B2
Tarporley 59 D2, 60 B3
Tarquínia 116 B3, 118 A1
Tarraälvshyddan 15 D1
Tarragona 163 C2
Tårrajaur 16 A2
Tarraluoppalstugorna
15 D1
Tàrrega 155 C3, 163 C1
Tarrekaisestugan 15 D1
Tarrés 163 D1
Tarroja de Segarra 155 C3,
163 C1
Tårs 48 B1
Tårs 53 C2
Tarsele 30 A2, 35 C/D1
Társia 122 A/B1
Tartanedo 161 D2, 162 A2
Tártano 106 A2
Tartas 108 A/B2
Tărtăşesti 141 C2
Tartu 74 A/B1
Tarutino 141 D1
Tarvaala 21 D2/3, 22 A2/3
Tarvainen 24 A/B2
Tarvasjoki 24 B2
Tarvin 59 D2, 60 B3
Tarvísio 126 A/B2
Tarvísio 96 A3
Tarvola 21 C2
Täsch 105 C2
Tåsjö 30 A2
Tåsnad 97 D3, 140 B1
Tasov 94 A/B1
Tasovčići 132 A/B3,
136 B1
Tasovice 94 A/B1/2
Tass 129 C1
Tassin-la-Demi-Lune
103 D2/3
Tåstrup 49 D3, 50 A3,
53 D1
Tát 95 D3
Tata 95 C/D3
Tataháza 129 C2
Tatarbunary 141 D1
Tatárszentgyörgy 129 C1
Tátorp 45 D2, 46 A2
Tattershall 61 D3, 65 B/C1
Tatton Hall 59 D2, 60 B3
Tau 42 A2
Tauberbischofsheim 81 C3
Taucha 82 B1
Tauer 70 B3
Taufkirchen an der Pram
93 C2
Taufkirchen 92 A2
Taufkirchen 92 B2
Taulé 84 B2
Taulignan 111 C1/2
Taulu 25 D1, 26 A1
Taunton 63 C2
Taunusstein 80 B3
Tauragė 73 C/D2
Taurianova 122 A3
Taurisano 121 D3
Tauste 155 C3
Tauves 102 B3
Tauvo 18 A2/3
Tavankut 129 C2
Tavannes 89 D3, 104 B1
Tavarnelle Val di Pesa
114 B3, 116 B2
Tavasbarlang 128 A1
Tavascan 155 C2
Tavastehus 25 C2
Tavastila 26 B2
Tavastkenkä 18 B3,
22 A/B1
Tavastkyro 24 B1
Taveiro 158 A3
Tavela 19 C/D1
Tavelsjö 31 C2
Taverna 122 B2
Taverna Piccinini 117 D3
Tavernelle 115 C3,
117 C2/3
Tavernelle 114 A2, 116 A1
Tavernes 112 A3
Tavèrnola Bergamasca
106 A/B3
Tavèrnole sul Mella 106 B3
Taverny 87 C/D1
Taviano 121 D3
Tavíkovice 94 A/B1
Tavira 170 B2

Tavistock 63 B/C3
Tavoleto 115 D2, 117 C1
Täxan 30 A2, 35 C1
Taxenbach 107 D1, 126 A1
Tayinloan 56 A2
Tayport 57 C1
Tayvallich 56 A1
Tazones 152 A1
Tczew 73 B/C2
Tealby 61 D3
Teana 120 B3
Teano 119 C3
Teba 172 A2
Tébar 168 B1
Tebay 57 C3, 59 D1, 60 B1
Tebeljevo 127 C2
Tecklenburg 67 D3
Teckomatorp 50 A3
Tecuci 141 C1
Teeriranta 19 D2
Teerivaara 19 B/C1
Teersalo 24 A2/3
Teesside 61 D1
Tegea 147 C3
Tegelen 79 D1
Tegelsmora 40 B2/3
Tegelträsk 30 B2, 35 D1
Tegernau 90 A/B3
Tegernsee 92 A3
Teggiano 120 A3
Téglio 106 B2
Tegneby 44 B3
Tehi 25 D1, 26 A1
Teichel 82 A2
Teichwolframsdorf 82 B2
Teigen 4 A/B2
Teigen 32 B3, 37 C1
Teignmouth 63 C3
Teijo 24 B3
Teillet 110 A2
Teisendorf 92 B3
Teisko 25 C1
Teisnach 93 B/C1
Teistungen 81 D1
Teixeiro 150 B1/2
Teixoso 158 B3
Tejadillos 162 A3
Tejado 153 D3, 161 D1
Tejares 160 B1
Tejeda de Tiétar 159 D3
Tejn 51 D3
Tekeriš 133 C2
Tekija 135 C1/2
Tekija 133 C2
Tekirdağ 149 D1
Tekovské Lužany 95 D2
Teksdal 28 A2/3, 33 C1
Tekućica 132 B1
Telavåg 36 A3
Telč 94 A1
Telč 96 A2
Telenešty 141 D1
Telese 119 D3
Telford 59 D3, 64 A1
Telfs 107 B/C1
Telgte 67 D3
Telheira 170 A1
Teljo 23 D1
Telkkälä 18 B1
Tellancourt 79 C3
Tellingstedt 52 B3
Telnes 14 B1/2
Telnice 94 B1
Telões 158 A3
Telšiai 73 C/D1/2
Telti 123 D3
Teltow 70 A2/3
Telve 107 C2
Tembleque 161 C3, 167 D1
Temelín 93 D1
Temenica 127 C2/3
Temerin 129 D3
Temerin 140 A2
Temkino 75 D3
Temmes 18 A/B3
Tempelseter 37 D3
Tempio Pausánia 123 D1
Templeuve 78 A2
Templin 70 A2
Templin 72 A3
Temse 78 B1
Temska 135 C3, 139 C1
Tenala/Tenhola 24 B3
Tenay 103 D2, 104 A2/3
Ten Boer 67 C1
Tenbury Wells 59 D3

Tenby 62 B1
Tence 103 C3, 111 C1
Tende 112 B2
Tendilla 161 C2
Tenebrón 159 C2
Tengen 90 B3
Tengen-Watterdingen
90 B3
Tenhult 45 D3, 46 A3
Tenigerbad [Rabius-Sur-
rein] 105 D1/2
Teningen 90 A/B2
Tenja 129 C3
Tennenbronn 90 B2
Tennevik 9 C2
Tennevoll 9 D2
Tennilä 25 D2, 26 A2
Tennilä 12 B3
Tenno 106 B2
Tennsjö 30 B2
Tennskjær 4 A3
Tennstrand 8 B2
Tennvalen 14 A2
Tensta 40 B3
Tenterden 77 C1
Tentúgal 158 A3
Teo 150 A2
Teora 120 A2
Teovo 138 B3
Tepasto 11 D3, 12 A1
Tepelenë 142 A2
Tepelenë 148 A1
Teplá 82 B2
Teplice 83 C2
Teplice 96 A1
Teplingan 28 B1
Tepsa 11 D3, 12 A/B2
Terälahti 25 C1
Téramo 117 D3, 119 C1
Ter Apel 67 C2
Terborg 67 C3
Terchová 95 D1
Teregova 135 C1
Terehovka 99 D3
Teremia Mare 129 D2/3
Terena 165 C2
Terento/Terenten 107 C1
Teresa 162 B3, 169 C1
Teresa de Cofrentes 169 C2
Terešov 83 C3
Terespol 73 D3, 97 D1,
98 A1
Terezín 83 C2
Terezino Polje 128 A2/3
Tergnier 78 A3
Terheijden 66 A/B3, 79 C1
Terjärv/Teerijärvi 21 C1
Terlet 67 B/C3
Terlizzi 120 B2, 136 A3
Termahovka 99 C2
Termas de Monfortinho
159 C3
Terme 122 A/B1
Terme di Brénnero/Brenner-
bad 107 C1
Terme di Casteldória
123 C1
Terme di Lurísia 113 B/C2
Terme di Miradolo 105 D3,
106 A3, 113 D1
Terme di Sárdara 123 C3
Terme di Valdieri 112 B2
Terme Luigiane 122 A1
Termeno/Tramin 107 C2
Térmens 155 C3, 163 C1
Termes 110 A3, 156 B1
Termes de Orion 156 B2/3
Termignon 104 B3
Terminiers 87 C2
Términi Imerese 124 B2
Terminón 153 C2
Térmoli 119 D2, 120 A1
Termunten 67 C1
Ternant 88 B3, 103 D1
Terndrup 48 B2
Ternell 79 C2
Terneuzen 78 B1
Terni 117 C3, 118 B1
Ternitz 94 A3
Ternopol' 98 B3
Terpani 142 A2
Térpillos 139 D3, 143 D1,
144 A1
Terpnás 143 C3
Terpnás 148 A1
Terpsithéa 146 B1/2
Terque 173 D2

Terracina 119 B/C2/3
Terrades 156 B2
Terradillos de Templarios 152 A2
Terråk 29 B/C1
Terralba 123 C2/3
Terranho 158 B2
Terranova da Síbari 122 B1
Terranova di Pollino 120 B3, 122 A/B1
Terranuova Bracciolini 115 C3, 116 B2
Terras do Bouro 150 B3, 158 A2
Terrasini 124 A1/2
Terrassa 156 A3
Terrasson-la-Villedieu 101 C3, 108 B1
Terrateig 169 D2
Terravécchia 122 B1
Terrer 162 A1
Terriente 162 A3
Terrinches 167 D2, 168 A2
Terrugem 164 A2
Tersløse 49 C3, 53 C/D1
Tertenía 123 D2/3
Teruel 162 A/B2/3
Tervahauta 24 B1
Tervajoki 20 B2
Tervakoski 25 C2
Tervala 21 D3, 22 A3
Tervavaara 19 C2
Tervel 141 C2
Tervo 22 B2
Tervola 17 D2, 18 A1
Tervolan asema 17 D2, 18 A1
Terz 94 A3
Terzone San Pietro 117 D3, 118 B1
Tésa 95 D2/3
Tešanj 132 B1/2
Teschendorf 70 A2
Tesijoki 25 D2, 26 B2/3
Teslić 132 B1/2
Tesserete [Lugano] 105 D2
Tessin 53 D3
Tessy-sur-Vire 85 D1
Testa del Gargano 120 B1, 136 A2/3
Testa dell'Acqua 125 C/D3
Tét 95 C3
Tetbury 63 D1, 64 A3
Teterow 53 D3, 69 D1, 70 A1
Teterow 72 A2
Teteven 140 B3
Teti 123 D2
Tetovo 138 B2
Tetovo 140 A3
Tetrálofon 143 C2
Tettau 82 A2
Tettnang 91 C3
Tettnang-Langnau 91 C3
Teublitz 92 B1
Teuchern 82 B1
Teufen 91 C3
Teufenbach 126 B1
Teulada 123 C3
Teulada 169 D2
Teupitz 70 A3
Teurajärvi 17 C1
Teurajärvi 12 A2
Teuro 25 C2
Teusajaurestugorna 9 D3
Teuschnitz 82 A2
Teutleben 81 D2
Teutschenthal 82 A1
Teuva (Östermark) 20 A3
Tevaniemi 24 B1
Tevansjö 35 C3
Teväntö 25 C2
Tevel 128 B2
Tewkesbury 63 D1, 64 A2
Thal 81 D2
Thale 69 C3
Thalfang 80 A3
Thalgau 93 C3
Thalheim 82 B2
Thalkirch [Versam-Safien] 105 D2, 106 A1/2
Thalmässing 92 A1
Thame 64 B3
Thann 89 D3, 90 A3
Thannhausen 91 D2
Thaon 76 B3, 86 A1
Thaon-les-Vosges 89 D2

Tharandt 83 C1/2
Thárros 123 C2
Tharsis 171 C1
Thásos 145 C1
Thásos 145 C1
Thásos 149 C1
Thaxted 65 C2
Thaya 94 A1/2
Thayngen 90 B3
Theddlethorpe Saint Helen 61 D3
Thedinghausen 68 A2
Theessen 69 D3
Theilenhofen-Dornhausen 91 D1
Theix 85 C3
Themar 81 D2
The Mumbles 63 C1
Thénezay 101 C1
Thenon 101 D3, 109 C1
Theodorákion 143 D1
Theodóriana 143 B/C3
Theológos 147 C1
Theológos 145 C2
Théoule-sur-Mer 112 B3
Thermes-d'Armagnac 108 B2/3
Thérmi 143 D2, 144 A2
Thermísia 147 D3
Thérmon (Kefalóvrison) 146 B1/2
Thermopylai 147 C1
Thérmos 146 B1/2
Thernberg 94 A/B3
Thérouanne 77 D2
Thespiaí 147 C2
Thesprotikón 142 B3
Thessaloníki 143 D2, 144 A2
Thessaloníki 148 B1
Thetford 65 C2
Theth 137 D2, 138 A2
The Trossachs 56 B1
Theux 79 D2
Thevet-Saint-Julien 102 A1
Thézan 110 A3, 156 B1
Thèze 108 B3, 154 B1
Thiaucourt-Regniéville 89 C1
Thiberville 86 B1
Thibie 88 B1
Thiéblemont-Farémont 88 B1/2
Thiendorf 83 C1
Thiene 107 C3
Thierhaupten 91 D2, 92 A2
Thierhaupten-Baar 91 D2, 92 A2
Thierhaupten-Unterbaar 91 D2
Thiers 103 B/C2
Thiersheim 82 B3
Thiesi 123 C2
Thiézac 110 A1
Thionville 89 C1
Thíra 149 C3
Thiron 86 B2
Thirsk 61 D2
Thisóa 146 B3
Thisted 48 A2
Thísvi 147 C2
Thívai 147 C/D2
Thívai 148 B2
Thiviers 101 D3
Thizy 103 C2
Thoirette 103 D2, 104 A2
Thoissey 103 D2
Thoisy-la-Berchère 88 B3, 103 C1
Tholen 78 B1
Tholey-Theley 80 A3, 90 A1
Tholón 146 B3
Thomatal 126 B1
Thonac 109 C1
Thônes 104 A/B2/3
Thonon-les-Bains 104 B2
Thorame-Basse 112 A2
Thorame-Haute 112 A2
Thorens-Glières 104 A2
Thorigné-sur-Dué 86 B2
Thorigny-sur-Oreuse 88 A2
Thorikón 147 D3
Thörl 94 A3
Thornaby-on-Tees 61 D1
Thornbury 63 D1

Thorne 61 C2
Thorney 65 C1/2
Thornhill 57 B/C2
Thornhill 54 B3
Thornton 59 C/D1, 60 B2
Thorsager 49 C2
Thorsø 48 B2
Thouarcé 86 A3, 100 B1
Thouars 101 C1
Thourie 85 D2/3
Thoúrion 145 D3
Thrapston 64 B2
Threave Castle 56 B3, 60 A1
Threshfield 59 D1, 61 B/C2
Thuès-les-Bains 156 A2
Thueyts 111 C1
Thuin 78 B2
Thuir 156 B1/2
Thun 105 C1
Thüngen 81 C3
Thurey 103 D1
Thurles 55 C/D3
Thurnau 82 A3
Thuróby 53 C2
Thursby 57 C3, 60 B1
Thurso 54 B1
Thury-Harcourt 86 A1
Thusis 105 D1, 106 A1
Thyborøn 48 A2
Thyregod 48 B3
Thyrnau 93 C2
Tiarp 45 C2
Tibănești 141 C2
Tibble 47 C1
Tibro 45 C2, 46 A2
Tickhill 61 C3
Ticleni 135 D1
Tidaholm 45 D3
Tidan 45 D2
Tidersrum 46 B3
Tidö 46 B1
Tiedra 152 A3, 160 A1
Tiefenbach 93 C2
Tiefenbach 92 B1
Tiefenbronn 90 B1/2
Tiefencastel 106 A1/2
Tiefensee 70 B2
Tiel 66 B3
Tielt 78 A1
Tiemassaari 23 B/C3
Tienen 79 C2
Tierga 154 A3, 162 A1
Tiermas 154 A/B2
Tierp 40 B2
Tierzo 161 D2, 162 A2
Tiffauges 100 B1
Tigánasi 135 C2
Tigănești 141 C2
Tighnabruaich 56 A2
Tignes 104 B3
Tigy 87 C/D3
Tihany 128 B1
Tihilä 21 D1, 22 A/B1
Tihusniemi 22 B3
Tihvin 75 C1
Tiingvoll 32 B2
Tiistenjoki 20 B2
Tiitilankylä 22 A/B2
Tijesno 131 C3
Tijola 173 D2
Tikkakoski 21 D3, 22 A3
Tikkala 21 D3, 22 A3
Tikkala 23 D3
Tilburg 79 C1
Tilbury 65 C3
Til-Châtel 88 B3
Tilh 108 A/B3, 154 B1
Tilkainen 24 B2
Tillberga 40 A3, 46 B1
Tilleda 82 A1
Tillicoultry 57 B/C1
Tillières-sur-Avre 87 B/C1
Tillikkala 26 B1
Tilly 101 C2
Tilly-sur-Seulles 76 B3, 86 A1
Tiltrem 28 A2/3, 33 C1
Tim 48 A2/3
Timau 107 D2, 126 A2
Timbonás 38 B3
Timelkam 93 C3
Timfristós 146 B1
Timisoara 140 A1
Timmele 95 D3
Timmendorfer Strand 53 C3
Timmernabben 51 D1

Timmersdala 45 D2
Timmervik 45 C2
Timoniemi 19 D3
Timrå 35 D3
Tinahely 58 A3
Tinajas 161 D2/3
Tinalhas 158 B3, 165 C1
Tinca 97 C3, 140 A1
Tinchebray 86 A1
Tineo 151 C/D1
Tinglev 52 B2
Tingsryd 51 C2
Tingsryd 72 A/B1
Tingstäde 47 D2
Tingvatyn 42 B3
Tinizong (Tinzen) [Tiefen-castel] 106 A2
Tinjan 126 B3, 130 A1
Tinnoset 43 C1, 44 A1
Tinnye 95 D3
Tínos 149 C2
Tintagel 62 B3
Tintăreni 135 D2
Tinténiac 85 C/D2
Tintern Abbey 63 D1
Tintern Parva 63 D1
Tintigny 79 C3
Tione di Trento 106 B2
Tipasjärvi 23 C1
Tipasjoki 23 C1
Tipasoja 23 C1
Tipperary 55 C3
Tiranë 137 D3, 138 A3, 142 A1
Tirano 106 B2
Tiraspol' 141 D1
Tire 149 D2
Tirgo 153 C2
Tîrgoviște 141 C2
Tîrgu Bujor 141 C/D1
Tîrgu Cărbunești 135 D1
Tîrgu-Frumos 141 C1
Tîrgu Jiu 140 B2
Tîrgu Jiu 135 D1
Tîrgu Lăpuș 97 D3, 140 B1
Tîrgu Mureș 97 D3, 140 B1
Tîrgu-Neamt 141 C1
Tîrgu Ocna 141 C1
Tîrgu Secuiesc 141 C1
Tirig 163 C2
Tiriolo 122 B2
Tirli 116 A3
Tirmo 25 D3, 26 A3
Tîrnăveni 97 D3, 140 B1
Tírnavos 148 B1
Tírnavos 143 D3
Tirpersdorf 82 B2
Tirrénia 114 A3, 116 A2
Tirro 6 B3
Tirschenreuth-Wondreb 82 B3
Tirschenreuth 82 B3
Tirstrup 49 C2
Tirteafuera 167 C2
Tiryns 147 C3
Tiscar 167 D3, 168 A3, 173 C/D1
Tisleidalen 37 D3
Tismana 135 D1
Tišnov 94 B1
Tišnov 96 B2
Tisselskog 45 C2
Tistrup 48 A3, 52 A1
Tisvildeleje 49 D3, 50 A2/3
Tiszaalpár 129 D1
Tiszabecs 97 D3, 98 A3
Tiszabő 129 D1
Tiszaföldvár 129 D1
Tiszafüred 97 C3
Tiszakécske 129 D1
Tiszaroff 129 D1
Tiszasüly 129 D1
Tiszatenyő 129 D1
Tiszavárkony 129 D1
Tiszavasvári 97 C3
Titaguas 162 A/B3, 169 C1
Titane 147 C2
Titel 129 D3, 133 D1, 134 A1
Tithoréa 147 C1/2
Titisee-Neustadt 90 B3
Tito 120 A/B2
Titograd 137 D2
Titova Korenica 131 C1/2
Titova Mitrovica 138 B1
Titova Mitrovica 140 A3

Titova pećina 131 D2, 132 A2
Titov Drvar 131 C2
Titovo Užice 133 D2/3, 134 A2/3
Titovo Užice 140 A2
Titovo Velenje 96 A3
Titovo Velenje 127 C2
Titov Veles 139 C3
Titov Veles 140 A3
Titran 32 A2
Tittelsnes 42 A1
Titting 92 A1
Tittling 93 C2
Tittmoning 92 B3
Tittmoning-Wiesmühl 92 B3
Titu 141 C2
Titulcia 161 C2
Titz 79 D1
Titz-Rödingen 79 D1/2
Tiuccia 113 D3
Tiukurova 13 C3
Tiukuvaara 11 D3, 12 A2
Tiurajärvi 11 C3, 12 A2
Tiurana 155 C3
Tivat 137 C2
Tived 46 A2
Tivenys 163 C2
Tiverton 63 C2
Tivissa 163 C2
Tivoli 118 B2
Tivsjön 35 C2
Tizac-de-Courton 108 B1
Tizzano 113 D3
Tizzano Val Parma 114 A1
Tjåkkelestugan 14 B3, 29 D1
Tjälder 47 D2/3
Tjallingen 34 A2
Tjällmo 46 A/B2
Tjälme 10 A2
Tjåmotis 16 A1
Tjæreborg 48 A3, 52 A1
Tjärn 30 B2, 35 D1
Tjärnberg 16 A3
Tjärnkullen 29 D1
Tjärnmyrberget 29 D2, 30 A1
Tjarnö 44 B2
Tjärö 51 C2
Tjäruträsk 17 C2
Tjåurek 10 A3
Tjeldnes 9 C2
Tjeldstø 36 A3
Tjeldsund 9 C2
Tjele 48 B2
Tjelle 32 B2
Tjentište 133 B/C3
Tjernet 14 B3
Tjöck/Tiukka 20 A3
Tjolmen 14 B3
Tjolöholm 49 D1, 50 A1
Tjøme 43 D2, 44 B1
Tjøme 43 D2, 44 B1
Tjønnefoss 43 C2
Tjørholm 42 B2
Tjörnarp 50 B2/3
Tjøtta 14 A2/3
Tjourenstugan 29 C2, 34 A1
Tjuda 24 B3
Tjugum 36 B2
Tjuonajåkk 10 A3
Tjurkö 51 C2
Tkon 130 B2/3
Tlmače 95 C1
Tlumač 97 D2, 98 B3
Tlumačov 95 C1
Toano 114 B2, 116 A1
Toba 81 D1
Tobarra 168 B2
Tobed 163 C1
Tobelbad 127 C1
Tobermory 56 A1
Toberonochy 56 A1
Tobo 40 B2/3
Toboada 150 B2
Tobolić 130 B1
Tobru 38 A2
Toby 20 A/B2
Tocane-Saint-Apre 101 C3
Tocha 158 A3
Tocina 171 D1
Töcksfors 45 C1
Tocón 172 B2
Todal 32 B2

Todal 32 B2
Todi 117 C3
Todmorden 59 D1/2,
　60 B2
Todolella 162 B2
Todorovo 131 C1
Todtmoos 90 B3
Todtnau 90 B3
Todtnau-Todtnauberg
　90 B3
Toen 150 B2
Töffedal 45 C2
Tofta 47 D3
Toftaholm 50 B1
Tofte 43 D1, 44 B1
Toftlund 52 B1/2
Töging am Inn 92 B2
Tohmajärvi 23 D3
Tohmo 12 B3
Toholampi 21 C1
Toija 25 B/C3
Toijala 25 C2
Toikkala 26 B2
Toivakka 21 D3, 22 A3
Toivakka 18 B1
Toivala 22 B2
Toiviaiskylä 21 D1,
　22 A/B1
Toivola 26 B1
Töjby 20 A2/3
Tojšići 133 B/C2
Tokačka 145 C/D1
Tokaj 97 C3
Tokod 95 D3
Tököl 95 D3, 129 C1
Tolbuhin 141 C/D2/3
Toledo 160 B3, 167 C1
Tolentino 115 D3, 117 D2
Tolfa 118 A1
Tolg 51 C1
Tolga 33 D3
Tolinas 151 D1
Tolja 18 B1
Tolkee 23 D1
Tolkkinen/Tolkis 25 D3,
　26 A3
Tollarp 50 B3
Tollarp 72 A1/2
Tollered 45 C3
Tollesbury 65 C3
Tølløse 49 D3, 53 D1
Töllsjö 45 C3
Tolmačevo 74 B1
Tolmezzo 107 D2, 126 A2
Tolmin 126 B2
Tolmin 96 A3
Tolna 129 C2
Tolnanémedi 128 B2
Točin 74 B3
Tolofón 146 B2
Tolón 147 C3
Tolón 148 B2
Tolonen 12 B1
Tolonen 12 A3
Tolosa 153 D1, 154 A1
Tolosa 165 C1
Tolosenmäki 23 D3
Tolox 172 A2
Tolpaniemi 19 D1
Tolsburgen 47 D3
Tolsby 45 C1
Tolskepp 46 B2
Tolstoe 98 B3
Tolva 19 C1
Tolva 155 C3
Tolvanniemi 19 C1
Tolve 120 B2
Tomar 164 B1
Tomaševac 129 D3,
　133 D1, 134 A/B1
Tomaševo 137 D1
Tomašica 131 D1
Tomášikovo 95 C2/3
Tomašovka 97 D1, 98 A2
Tomašpol' 99 C3
Tomaszów Mazowiecki
　97 C1
Tombeboeuf 109 C1
Tomelilla 50 B3
Tomelilla 72 A2
Tomelloso 167 D2, 168 A2
Tomiño 160 A2
Tommerdalen 28 A3, 33 C1
Tømmernes 9 C3
Tommerup 53 B/C1
Tommerup Stationsby
　52 B1

Tømmervåg 32 B2
Tömörd 94 B3, 127 D1,
　128 A1
Tompa 129 C2
Tomra 32 A2/3
Tomter 38 A3, 44 B1
Tõn 95 C3
Tona 156 A2/3
Tonara 123 D2
Tonbridge 65 C3, 77 B/C1
Tondela 158 B2
Tønder 52 A2
Tongeren 79 C2
Tongue 54 A/B1
Tõnismovist 79 D1
Tønjum 37 B/C2
Tonkopuro 13 C3
Tonnay-Boutonne 100 B2
Tonnay-Charente 100 B2
Tonneins 109 C2
Tonnerre 88 A3
Tönnersjö 50 A2
Tonnes 14 A/B2
Tönnet 39 C3
Tönning 52 A3
Tonquédec 84 B1/2
Tonsåsen 37 D3
Tønsberg 43 D2, 44 B1
Tonstad 42 B3
Toopanjoki 23 C2
Topares 168 B3, 173 D1,
　174 A1
Topas 159 D1/2
Töpchin 70 A3
Töpen 82 A2
Topeno 25 C2
Toplaně 137 D2, 138 A2
Toplet 135 C1
Topli Do 135 D3
Toplita 141 C1
Topola 133 D2, 134 B2
Topolčani 138 B3, 143 C1
Topol'čany 121 D2
Topol'čany 96 B2
Topol'čianki 95 D2
Topolovac 127 D3
Topolovătu Mare 140 A1
Topolovgrad 141 C3
Topolšica 127 C2
Toponár 128 B2
Toporów 71 C3
Töppeln 82 B2
Topsham 63 C2/3
Topusko 127 D3, 131 C1
Toques 150 B2
Torà de Riubregós 155 D3,
　163 D1
Torajärvi 25 C2
Toral de los Guzmanes
　151 D2/3, 152 A2/3
Toral de los Vados 151 C2
Torás 162 B3, 169 C1
Torasalo 23 C3
Torasjärvi 17 C1
Toras-Sieppi 11 C3, 12 A1
Toravaara 19 D2
Torbali 149 D2
Torbay 63 C3
Tórbole 106 B2/3
Törböle 17 C2
Torcello 107 D3
Torcy-le-Grand 76 B3
Torda 129 D3
Tordehumos 152 A3,
　160 A1
Tordellego 162 A2
Tordera 156 B3
Tordesillas 152 A3, 160 A1
Tordesilos 162 A2
Tordillos 159 D2, 160 A2
Tordoia 150 A1
Tordómar 152 B3
Töre 17 C2
Töreboda 45 D2, 46 A2
Toreby 53 D2
Torekov 49 D2, 50 A2
Torekov 72 A1
Torella de' Lombardi
　119 D3, 120 A2
Torella del Sánnio 119 D2
Torelló 156 A2
Toreno 161 C2
Torestorp 49 D1, 50 A1
Torfinnsbu 37 C2
Torfou 100 B1
Torgåsmon 39 C2
Torgau 82 B1

Torgau 96 A1
Torgelow 70 B1
Torhamn 51 C/D2
Torhamn 72 B1
Torhout 78 A1
Torhus 32 A2
Torigni-sur-Vire 85 D1,
　86 A1
Torija 161 C2
Toril 162 A3
Torino 113 B/C1
Torino di Sangro Marina
　119 D1
Toriseva 21 C3
Toritto 121 C2
Torittu 25 D1, 26 A1
Torjul 32 B2
Torla 155 C2
Torlengua 161 D1
Torljane 138 B1
Törmänen 12 B1
Törmänki 12 A3, 17 D1
Törmänmäki 19 C3
Tormantos 153 C2
Törmäsenvaara 19 D1
Törmäsjärvi 12 A3, 17 D2
Tórmini 106 B3
Tormua 19 D2
Tornada 164 A1
Tornadizos de Ávila
　160 A/B2
Tornavacas 159 D3
Tørnby 38 B3, 45 C1
Torneå 17 D2, 18 A1
Tørnes 9 C3
Tornes 28 A2, 33 C1
Torneträsk 10 A2
Törnevik 46 B2/3
Torning 48 B2
Tornio (Torneå) 17 D2,
　18 A1
Tornjoš 129 D3
Torno 105 D3, 106 A2/3
Tornos 162 A2
Toro 152 A3, 159 D1,
　160 A1
Torö 47 C2
Törökkoppány 128 B2
Törökszentmiklós 129 D1
Törökszentmiklós 97 C3,
　140 A1
Toróni 149 B/C1
Toróni 144 B2/3
Toropec 75 C2
Torp 51 D1
Torp 41 C3
Torp 41 C3
Torpa 50 B2
Torpa 46 A3
Torpa 45 D3
Torpa 37 D2/3
Torpè 123 D1/2
Torpo 37 C3
Torpoint 62 B3
Torppa 21 C1/2
Torpsbruk 51 C1
Torpshammar 35 C3
Torquemada 152 B3
Torraca 120 A3
Torralba 123 C2
Torralba 161 D3
Torralba de Aragón 154 B3
Torralba de los Sisones
　162 A2
Torralba de Oropesa
　160 A3, 166 B1
Torralba de Burgo 153 C3,
　161 C1
Torralba de Calatrava
　167 C2
Torralba del Río 153 D2
Torralbilla 163 C1
Torrão 164 B3
Torrböle 31 C2
Torre 150 A3, 158 A1
Torre Alháquime 172 A2
Torre a Ma 121 C2,
　136 A/B3
Torre Annunziata 119 D3
Torrearévalo 153 D3
Torre Astura 118 B2
Torre Baja 163 C2
Torrebeleña 161 C2
Torre Beretti 113 C1
Torreblacos 153 C3,
　161 C1
Torreblanca 163 C3

Torreblanca 172 B3
Torreblascopedro 167 D3,
　173 C1
Torrebruna 119 D2
Torrecaballeros 160 B2
Torrecampo 166 B2/3
Torre Canne 121 C2
Torre-Cardela 173 C1
Torrechiva 162 B3
Torrecilla 161 D3
Torrecilla de la Orden
　160 A1
Torrecilla del Rebollar
　162 A/B2
Torrecilla del Monte 153 C3
Torrecilla de Alcañiz
　163 B/C2
Torrecilla de Valmadrid
　154 B3, 162 B1
Torrecilla de la Jara 160 A3,
　166 B1
Torrecilla de los Ángeles
　159 C3
Torrecilla en Cameros
　153 D2/3
Torrecillas de la Tiesa
　166 A1
Torrecuadrada de los Valles
　161 D2
Torrecuadradilla 161 D2
Torre das Vargens
　164 B1/2
Torre de Arcas 163 C2
Torre de Don Miguel
　159 C3
Torre de Dona Chama
　151 C3, 159 C1
Torre de Embesora 163 C3
Torre de Endoménech
　163 C3
Torre de Hércules 150 A/B1
Torre de Juan Abad
　167 D2, 168 A2
Torre de la Higuera 171 C2
Torre de las Arcas 162 B2
Torre del Bierzo 151 D2
Torre del Campo 167 C3,
　173 B/C1
Torre del Compte 163 C2
Torre del Greco 119 D3
Torre del Lago Puccini
　114 A2, 116 A1
Torre del Mar 172 B2
Torredembarra 163 C1/2
Torre de Miguel Sesmero
　165 D2
Torre de Moncorvo
　159 C1/2
Torre de' Pásseri 119 C1
Torre di Bari 123 D2
Torredonjimeno 167 C3,
　173 B/C1
Torrefarrera 155 C3,
　163 C1
Torregáveta 119 C3
Torregrossa 155 C/D3,
　163 C/D1
Torrehermosa 161 D1
Torre Horadada 169 C3,
　174 B1
Torreiglesias 160 B2
Torreira 158 A2
Torrejoncillo 159 C3,
　165 D1
Torrejoncillo del Rey
　161 D3
Torrejón del Rey 161 C2
Torrejón de la Calzada
　160 B3
Torrejón de Ardoz 161 C2
Torrejón el Rubio 159 D3,
　165 D1, 166 A1
Torrelaguna 161 C2
Torrelameu 155 C3, 163 C1
Torrelapaja 153 C3,
　154 A3, 161 D1, 162 A1
Torre la Ribera 155 C2
Torrelavega 152 B1
Torrellas 154 A3
Torrelobatón 152 A3,
　160 A1
Torrelodones 160 B2
Torre los Negros 162 A/B2
Torremaggiore 120 A1
Torremanzanas 169 D2
Torremayor 165 D2
Torremegía 165 D2

Torre Melissa 122 B2
Torremezzo di Falconara
　122 A2
Torre Mileto 120 A1
Torremocha 163 C2
Torremocha 165 D1,
　166 A1
Torremocha del Pinar
　161 D2
Torremolinos 172 B2/3
Torremontalbo 153 D2
Torremormojón 152 A/B3
Torrenieri 115 C3, 116 B2
Torrenostra 163 C3
Torrente 169 D1
Torrente de Cinca 155 C3,
　163 C1
Torrenueva 167 D2
Torrenueva 173 C2
Torreorgaz 165 D1, 166 A1
Torre Orsáia 120 A3
Torre-Pacheco 174 B1
Torre Pedrera 115 C/D2,
　117 C1
Torre Péllice 112 B1
Torre Pelosa 123 C1
Torreperogil 167 D3,
　173 C1
Torrequebradilla 167 C/D3,
　173 C1
Torrequemada 165 D1,
　166 A1
Torres 167 D3, 173 C1
Torresandino 152 B3,
　160 B1
Torre Santa Caterina
　123 D3
Torre Santa Sabina 121 D2
Torre Santa Susanna
　121 D3
Torres Cabrera 166 B3,
　172 B1
Torrescárcela 160 B1
Torres de Albarracín 162 A2
Torres de Albánchez
　168 A3
Torres de Berellén 154 B3,
　162 A/B1
Torres de la Alameda
　161 C2
Torres del Obispo 155 C3
Torres del Río 153 D2
Torres de Segre 155 C3,
　163 C1
Torres Novas 164 B1
Torres Vedras 164 A2
Torretta 124 B1/2
Torretta 114 B2
Torretta Granítola 124 A2
Torrevelilla 163 B/C2
Torrevieja 169 C3, 174 B1
Torre Vignola 123 D1
Torrflonäs 35 B/C3
Torricella 121 C3
Torricella Peligna 119 C/D2
Torrico 160 A3, 166 B1
Torri del Benaco 106 B3
Torri di Quartesolo 107 C3
Torríglia 113 D1/2
Torrijas 162 B3
Torrijo de la Cañada
　154 A3, 161 D1, 162 A1
Torrijo del Campo 163 C2
Torrijos 160 B3
Tørring 48 B3, 52 B1
Torrita 117 D3, 118 B1
Torrita di Siena 115 C3,
　116 B2
Torrita Tiberina 117 C3,
　118 B1
Torrivaara 17 C1
Torro 25 C2
Torroella de Fluviá 156 B2
Torroella de Montgrí
　156 B2
Torrox 172 B2
Torrubia 161 D2, 162 A2
Torrubia de Soria 153 D3,
　161 D1
Torrubia del Campo
　161 C3, 167 D1, 168 A1
Torrubio del Castillo
　161 D3, 168 B1
Torrvål 39. D2
Torsåker 30 B3, 35 D2
Torsåker 40 A2
Torsansalo 27 C/D1

Torsås 51 D2
Torsbo 45 D3
Torsborg 34 A2
Torsbua 32 B3, 37 C1
Torsby 39 C3
Torsby 39 B/C3
Torsenget 33 C2
Torsfjärden 29 D2
Torshälla 46 B1
Tórshavn 55 C1
Torsholma 24 A3, 41 D2
Torsken 9 C1
Torslanda 45 C3
Torsminde 48 A2
Torsmo 39 D1
Torsnes 44 B1
Torsö 45 D2
Torstrup 48 A3, 52 A1
Torsvåg 4 A2
Torsvid 45 D2, 46 A1/2
Törtel 129 D1
Tortellà 156 B2
Torteval 63 D3
Tortinmäki 24 B2
Tórtola 161 D3, 168 B1
Tórtola de Henares 161 C2
Tórtoles 160 A2
Tortolì 123 D2
Tortona 113 D1
Tórtora 120 B3, 122 A1
Tortorella 120 A3
Tortoreto Lido 117 D3
Tortorici 125 C2
Tortosa 163 C2
Tortosendo 158 B3
Tortuera 162 A2
Tortuna 40 A3, 47 B/C1
Toruń 73 B/C3
Torup 72 A1
Torup 50 A1
Torup 50 A/B3
Torup Strand 48 B1
Tor Vaiánica 118 B2
Torvastad 42 A2
Torvik 36 A1
Torvikbukt 32 B2
Tørvikbygd 36 B3
Torvinen 12 B2
Torviscón 173 C2
Torvoila 25 C1/2
Torvund 36 A2
Torżok 75 D2
Torzym 71 C3
Tosantos 153 C2
Tosas 156 A2
Tosbotn 14 A3, 29 C1
Toscana Nueva 168 A/B3,
    173 D1
Toscolano-Maderno
    106 B3
Tosen 14 A3, 29 C1
Tosno 75 C1
Tosos 162 A/B1
Tossa de Mar 156 B3
Tossåsen 34 A2
Tossåsen 34 B2
Tossavanlahti 21 D2, 22 A2
Tösse 45 C2
Tosse 108 B2/3
Tossignano 115 C2,
    116 B3
Tost 155 C2
Töstamaa 74 A1
Tostared 49 D1, 50 A1
Tostedt 68 B1
Tószeg 129 D1
Totalán 172 B2
Totana 169 B/C3,
    174 A/B1
Totanés 160 B3, 167 C1
Tôtes 77 C3
Tótkomlós 129 D2
Tótkomlós 97 C3, 140 A1
Totland 76 A1/2
Totland 36 A1
Tøtlandsvik 42 A/B2
Totnes 63 C3
Totra 40 A/B2
Tøttdal 28 B2
Tottenham 65 C3
Tottijärvi 24 B1
Totton 76 A1
Tótvázsony 128 B1
Touça 159 B/C2
Toucy 88 A3
Touët-sur-Var 112 B2
Touffou 101 C1/2

Toul 89 C1/2
Toulon 111 D3, 112 A3
Toulon-sur-Allier 102 B2
Toulon-sur-Arroux 103 C1
Toulouse 109 D3, 155 D1
Tourcoing 78 A2
Tour de la Parata 113 D3
Tour Laffon 108 B3,
    155 C1/2
Tourlaville 76 A3
Tournai 78 A/B2
Tournan-en-Bric 87 D1
Tournay 109 C3, 155 C1
Tournevite 101 C3
Tournoël 102 B2
Tournon 103 D3, 111 C1
Tournon-d'Agenais 109 C2
Tournon-Saint-Martin
    101 D1
Tournus 103 D1/2
Touro 158 B2
Touro 150 B2
Tourouvre 86 B2
Tours 86 B3
Tours de Merle 102 A3,
    109 D1, 110 A1
Tourtoirac 101 D3
Tourula 24 B2
Tourves 111 D3, 112 A3
Toury 87 C2
Tous 169 C2
Touvedo 150 A/B3,
    158 A1
Touvois 100 A1
Toužim 82 B3
Tovačov 95 C1
Tovariševo 129 C3
Tovarnik 133 C1
Tovdal 43 C2
Tøvik 32 A2
Tovik 9 C2
Tövsala 24 A2
Towcester 64 B2
Tow Law 57 D3, 61 C1
Town Yetholm 57 D2
Toxótai 145 C1
Töyrenperä 21 D2, 22 A2
Töysä 21 C3
Töysänperä 21 D3, 22 A3
Tózar 173 C2
Tözeggyármajor 94 B3
Trabada 151 C1
Trabanca 159 C1
Trabazos 151 C3, 159 C1
Traben-Trarbach 80 A3
Trabia 124 B2
Trabotivište 139 D2
Trachiá 147 C3
Tracy-le-Val 78 A3
Tradate 105 D3
Trädet 45 D3
Trafoi 106 B2
Tragacete 161 D2/3,
    162 A2/3
Trahiá 147 C3
Traid 162 A2
Traiguera 163 C2
Traînel 88 A2
Traiskirchen 94 B3
Traismauer 94 A2
Traitsching 92 B1
Trakai 73 D2, 74 A3
Trakiszki 73 D2
Trakošćan 127 D2
Tralee 55 C3
Trælleborg 53 C1
Trælnes 14 A3
Tramacastiel 163 C3
Tramaríglio 123 C2
Tramayes 103 C/D2
Tramelan 89 D3, 104 B1
Tramnitz 69 D2
Tramonti di Sopra 107 D2,
    126 A2
Tramonti di Sotto 107 D2,
    126 A2
Tramore 55 D3
Tramútola 120 B3
Trân 139 C/D1
Trân 140 B3
Træna 14 A2
Tranås 46 A3
Tranby 43 D1
Trancoso 158 B2
Trandal 32 A3, 36 B1
Tranderup 53 C2
Tranebjerg 49 C3, 53 C1

Tranekær Slot 53 C2
Tranemo 50 B1
Tranemo 72 A1
Tranent 57 C2
Tranevåg 42 B3
Trangdalen 5 C2
Trångmon 29 D1/2
Trångsviken 29 C/D3,
    34 B2
Tranhult 50 B1
Trani 120 B2, 136 A3
Tranøy 9 D1
Tranøy 9 C2
Trans 85 D2
Transtrand 39 C2
Tranum 48 B1
Tranvik 41 D3
Trapaga 153 C1
Trápani 124 A2
Trápani Fulgatore 124 A2
Trápani Marausa 124 A2
Trápani Rilievo 124 A2
Trappes 87 C1
Traryd 50 B2
Traryd 72 A1
Trasacco 119 C2
Träskvik 20 A3
Träslövsläge 49 D1, 50 A1
Trasmiras 150 B3
Trasobares 154 A3, 162 A1
Traspinedo 152 B3, 160 B1
Trassem 79 D3
Tråstølen 37 B/C3
Tratalías 123 C3
Traun 93 D2
Traunreut 92 B3
Traunstein 92 B3
Tråvad 45 C/D2/3
Travagliato 106 B3
Traversella 105 C3
Traversétolo 114 A1
Travnik 132 A2
Travnik 127 B/C3
Trawsfynydd 59 C3, 60 A3
Trazegnies 78 B2
Trazo 150 A1/2
Trbovlje 127 C2
Trbovlje 96 A3
Trbuk 132 B1/2
Trearddur Bay 58 B2
Trebago 153 D3
Trebaséleghe 107 C/D3
Trebatice 95 C2
Trebatsch 70 B3
Trebbin 70 A3
Trebel 69 C2
Trebenice 83 C2
Trèbes 110 A3, 156 A/B1
Trébeurden 84 B1
Třebíč 94 A1
Třebíč 96 A2
Trebinje 137 C1
Trebisacce 120 B3, 122 B1
Trebnje 127 C2/3
Třeboň 93 D1
Třeboň 83 C2/3
Třeboň 96 A2
Tréboul 84 A2
Trebsen 82 B1
Trebujena 171 D2
Trebur-Geinsheim 80 B3
Trecastagni 125 D2
Trecastle 63 C1
Trecate 105 D3
Trecenta 115 B/C1
Tredegar 63 C1
Tredózio 115 C2, 116 B1
Treffurt 81 D1
Trefnant 59 C2, 60 A3
Tregaron 59 C3, 63 C1
Trégastel-Plage 84 B1
Tregde 42 B3
Tregnago 107 C3
Tregony 62 B3
Tréguier 84 B1
Trégunc 84 B2/3
Trehörna 42 A/3
Trehörningen 31 C2
Trehörningsjö 31 C2
Tréia 115 D3, 117 D2
Trei Ape 135 C1
Treib 105 D1
Treignac 102 A3
Treilles 110 A3, 156 B1
Treis 80 A2/3
Trekanten 51 D2
Trekilen 29 D3, 34 B1

Trekljano 139 C/D1/2
Trekljano 139 C/D1/2
Trelan 85 D3
Trélazé 86 A3
Trelech 62 B1
Trélechamp 104 B2
Trelleborg 50 A/B3
Trelleborg 72 A2
Trélon 78 B3
Tremelkovo 139 D1/2
Tremes 164 A1
Tremezzo 105 D2, 106 A2
Tremmen 69 D2, 70 A2
Trémorel 85 C2
Třemošná 83 C3
Tremp 155 D2/3
Trenčianska Turná 95 C1/2
Trenčianska Teplá 95 C1
Trenčianske Teplice 95 C1
Trenčín 95 C1
Trenčín 96 B2
Trendelburg 81 C1
Trendelburg-Deisel 81 C1
Trengereid 36 A3
Trenta 126 B2
Trento 107 C2
Treon 86 B1/2
Trepča 137 D1, 138 A1
Trepča 138 B1
Trepča 127 D3
Trepido 122 A2
Treponti 106 B2
Treppeln 70 B3
Trepuzzi 121 D3
Treriksröset 10 A/B1
Trescore Balneário 106 A3
Tresenda 106 B2
Tresfjord 32 A3
Tresjuncos 161 C/D3,
    168 A1
Tresnurághes 123 C2
Trespaderne 153 C2
Tresparrett Posts 62 B2/3
Třešť 94 A1
Trets 111 D3
Tretten 37 D2, 38 A1
Tretten 4 B2/3
Treuchtlingen 91 D1,
    92 A1
Treuen 82 B2
Treuenbrietzen 70 A3
Treuenbrietzen 72 A3,
    96 A1
Treungen 43 C2
Trevélez 173 C2
Trevenzuolo 106 B3
Trèves 110 B2
Trevi 117 C3
Treviana 153 C2
Trévières 76 A/B3, 85 D1,
    86 A1
Treviglio 106 A3
Trevignano Romano
    118 A/B1
Trevi nel Lázio 119 B/C2
Treviño 153 D2
Treviso 107 D3
Treviso Bresciano 106 B3
Trevol 102 B1/2
Trévoux 103 D2
Trézelles 103 B/C2
Trezzano san Naviglio
    105 D3, 106 A3
Trezzo sull'Adda 106 A3
Trgovište 139 C2
Trhové Mýto 95 C3
Trhové Sviny 93 D1/2
Trhový Štěpánov 83 D3
Triacastela 151 C2
Triaize 101 C2
Triana 116 B3
Triánda 149 D3
Triaucourt-en-Argonne
    88 B1
Tribaldos 161 C3
Tribanj Kruščica 130 B2
Tribano 107 C3
Triberg 90 B2
Tricárico 120 B2
Tricase 121 D3
Tricase Porto 121 D3
Tricerro 105 C3, 113 C1
Tricésimo 126 A2
Trichiana 107 C/D2
Tricot 78 A3
Triebel 82 B2
Trieben 93 D3

Trieben 96 A3
Triebes 82 B2
Triefenstein-Lengfurt
    81 C3
Triel-sur-Seine 87 C1
Triengen [Triengen-Wini-
    kon] 105 C1
Trier 79 D3, 80 A3
Trier-Ehrang 79 D3, 80 A3
Trierweiler 79 D3
Trieste 126 B3
Trie-sur-Baise 109 C3,
    155 C1
Triftern 93 B/C2
Trigachos 164 B3
Triggiano 121 C2
Triglitz 69 D1/2
Trigonon 143 B/C1/2
Trigueros 171 C1/2
Trigueros del Valle 152 B3,
    160 A/B1
Trijebine 133 D3, 134 A3,
    138 A1
Trijueque 161 C2
Tríkala 147 C2
Tríkala 143 C3
Tríkala 148 B1
Trikérion 147 C1
Trilj 131 D3
Trillevallen 29 C3, 34 A2
Trillo 161 D2
Trindade 159 C1
Trindade 164 B3, 170 B1
Tring 64 B3
Trinità 113 C2
Trinità d'Agultu e Vignola
    123 C1
Trinitápoli 120 B1/2
Trinité 113 D3
Trino 105 C3, 113 C1
Triollo 152 B2
Triora 113 C2
Trípi 147 B/C3
Trípolis 147 B/C3
Trípolis 148 B2
Triponzo 117 C3
Tripótama 146 B2
Tripótamon 146 B1
Tripótamos 144 B2
Tripoteau 108 B1
Trippstadt 90 A/B1
Triptis 82 A2
Triste 154 B2
Trittau 68 B1
Trittenheim 80 A3
Trivento 119 D2
Trivero 105 C3
Trivigno 120 B2
Trizac 102 A/B3
Trjavna 141 C3
Trnava 96 B2
Trnava 95 C2
Trnjani 132 B1
Trnovec nad Váhom 95 C2
Trnovo 132 B3
Trnovo 126 B3
Troarn 76 B3, 86 A1
Trobajo del Camino
    151 D2, 152 A2
Tröbitz 83 C1
Trochtelfingen 91 C2
Trödje 40 B2
Troense 53 C2
Trofa 158 A1
Trofarello 113 C1
Trofors 14 B3
Trøgaset 37 D3
Trogen 82 A/B2
Trogen 91 C2
Trogir 131 C3
Trøgstad 38 A3, 44 B1
Trøgstad (Skjønhaug)
    38 A3, 44 B1
Tróia 120 A1
Tróia 164 A2/3
Troia 149 C1
Troina 125 C2
Troisdorf 80 A2
Troisdorf-Sieglar 80 A2
Trois-Ponts 79 D2
Troissereux 77 D3
Troisvierges 79 D3
Trois-Villes 108 A3, 154 B1
Troizen 147 C3
Trojan 140 B3
Trojane 96 A3
Trojane 127 C2

Trojanova Tabla **135** C2
Troldhede **48** A3
Troldkirken **48** B1/2
Trolla **28** A3, **33** C1
Trollberget **16** A2
Trolleholm **50** A/B3
Trolle-Ljungby **50** B2/3
Trollerud **14** B3
Trollhättan **45** C2/3
Trollheimshytta **33** B/C2
Trollholmsundet **5** D2, **6** A2
Trollkirke **32** A2
Trollsved **35** D3
Tromello **105** D3, **113** D1
Tromsdalen **4** A3
Tromsnes **37** D2, **38** A1
Tromsø **4** A3
Tromvik **4** A2
Troncedo **155** C2
Tronchón **162** B2
Tronco **151** C3, **158** B1
Trondheim **28** A3, **33** C1
Trondjord **4** A2
Trones **29** C1
Tronhus **37** C/D2
Trönninge **50** A2
Tröno **40** A1
Tronoša **133** C2
Tronsjø **33** C/D3
Tronstad **43** D1
Trontveit **43** C2
Tronvik **28** A3, **33** C1
Tronvik **28** A/B3, **33** C1
Tronzano Vercellese **105** C3
Troo **86** B3
Troon **56** B2
Tropea **122** A2
Trópea **146** B3
Tropeoúchos **143** C1/2
Tropojë **138** A2
Trosa **47** C2
Trosky **83** D2
Trošmarija **127** C3, **130** B1
Trossingen **90** B2/3
Tröstau **82** A/B3
Trostberg **92** B3
Trosterud **38** B3, **45** C1
Trostjanec **99** C3
Trötvik **38** B3
Troubítsion **146** B3
Trou de Bozouls **110** A1/2
Trouville-sur-Mer **76** B3, **86** B1
Troviscal **158** B3, **164** B1
Trowbridge **63** D2, **64** A3
Troyes **88** A/B2
Trpanj **136** B1
Trpezi **138** A1
Trpinja **129** C3
Trsat **126** B3, **130** A/B1
Tršice **95** C1
Trstena **139** C1
Trstená **97** C2
Trstenik **136** B1
Trstenik **138** B1
Trstenik **134** B3
Trsteno **137** B/C1
Trstice **95** C3
Trstín **95** C2
Trubčevsk **99** D1
Trubia **151** D1
Trubjela **137** C1
Trubschachen **105** C1
Truchas **151** C/D2/3
Truébano **151** D2
Trujillanos **165** D2, **166** A2
Trujillo **166** A1
Trun **105** D1
Trun **86** A/B1
Truro **62** B3
Trușești **98** B3
Trustrup **49** C2
Trutnov **96** A/B1
Truvbacken **29** C3, **34** B1/2
Trvaala **21** D3, **22** A3
Tryggelev **53** C2
Trypiti **144** B2
Tryserum **46** B3
Trysil (Innbygda) **38** B1
Tržac **131** C1
Trzcianka **71** D2
Trzcianka **72** B3
Trzciel **71** C2/3
Trzcińsko Zdrój **70** B2
Trzebicz **71** C2
Trzebiechów **71** C3
Trzebiel **70** B3, **83** D1

Trzebież **70** B1
Trzebnica **96** B1
Tržec **127** D2
Trzemeszno Lubuskie **71** C2
Tržič **126** B2
Tržič **96** A3
Trzin **126** B2
Tsa, Cabane de la **105** C2
Tsamandás **142** B3
Tsangaráda **144** A3
Tsangaráda **148** B1
Tsaritsáni **143** D3
Tsarkasiános **146** A2
Tschernitz **83** D1
Tševetjävri **7** C2/3
Tsielekjåkkstugan **15** D1
Tsotílion **143** C2
Tsoukalochóri **143** C2
Tua **28** B2, **33** D1
Tubba **37** C3
Tubbergen **67** C2
Tubilla del Agua **153** B/C2
Tübingen **91** C2
Tübingen-Unterjesingen **91** C2
Tubize **78** B2
Tubre/Taufers **106** B1/2
Tučapy **93** D1
Tučepi **131** D3, **132** A3, **136** B1
Tuchan **156** B1
Tucheim **69** D3
Tüchen **69** D2
Tuchola **72** B3
Tuckur **20** B2
Tuczno **71** C/D1/2
Tuddal **43** C1
Tuddal Høyfjellshotell **43** C1
Tudela **154** A3
Tudela de Duero **152** B3, **160** B1
Tudelilla **153** D2
Tudweiliog **58** B3
Tuéjar **162** A/B3, **169** C1
Tuenno **107** B/C2
Tufjord **5** C1, **6** A1
Tufsingdalen **33** D3
Tuft **43** D1, **44** A/B1
Tufter **5** C1
Tuhaň **83** D2
Tuhkakylä **23** B/C1
Tui **150** A3
Tuiskula **20** B3
Tuixén **155** D2, **156** A2
Tuk **131** C2
Tukums **73** D1
Tula **123** C/D1
Tulare **138** B1
Tulce **71** D2/3
Tulcea **141** D2
Tul'čin **99** C3
Tulette **111** C2
Tullamore **55** D2/3
Tulle **102** A3
Tullebølle **53** C2
Tulleråsen **29** D3, **34** B1
Túllgarn **47** C2
Tullins **103** D3, **104** A3
Tulln **94** A2
Tulln **96** A/B2
Tulppio **13** C2
Tumba **47** C1
Tumbo **46** B1
Tumleberg **45** C3
Tun **45** C2
Tuna **46** B3
Tunaberg **47** C2
Tunadal **35** D3
Tuna Hästberg **39** D2/3
Tunåsen **30** A2/3, **35** C1
Tune **49** D3, **50** A3, **53** D1
Tune **44** B1
Túnel de Lizarraga **153** D2, **154** A2
Tunes **158** B1
Tunes **170** A2
Tungaseter **32** B3, **37** C1
Tungastølen **36** B2
Tungenes **42** A2
Tunkkari **21** C1/2
Tunnhovd **37** C3
Tunnila **27** C1
Tunnsjø kapell **29** C1
Tunnsjø-Røyrvik **29** C1
Tunø **49** C3
Tunsjön **30** B3, **35** D2

Tunstall **59** D2, **60** B3, **64** A1
Tuntenhausen **92** B3
Tuntenhausen-Hohentann **92** A/B3
Tuohikotti **26** B2
Tuohikylä **13** C3
Tuohittu **24** B3
Tuomimäki **13** C3
Tuomioja **18** A3
Tuomiperä **21** D1, **22** A1
Tuorila **24** A1
Tuorlahti **24** A2, **41** D2
Tuoro sul Trasimeno **115** C3, **117** D2
Tuovilanlahti **22** B2
Tuplice **70** B3, **83** D1
Tupos **18** A/B2
Tuppuravaara **23** D1
Tuppurinmäki **22** B3
Turalići **133** C2
Tuřany **94** B1
Turany **95** C2/3
Turbe **132** A2
Turbenthal **90** B3
Turbigo **105** D2
Turburea **135** D1/2
Turčianske Teplice **95** D1/2
Turcifal **164** A2
Turda **97** D3, **140** A1
Turégano **160** B1/2
Turek **72** B3, **96** B1
Turenki **25** C2
Turenne **101** D3, **109** D1
Turgutlu **149** D2
Turhala **22** B1
Turi **127** C2
Türi **74** A1
Turija **129** D3
Turija **135** B/C2
Turís **169** C1
Turjak **127** B/C2/3
Türje **128** A1
Turka **97** D2, **98** A3
Türkeve **129** D1
Turkhauta **25** C2, **26** A2
Turku/Åbo **24** B2/3
Turleque **167** D1
Turnau **94** A3
Turnberry **56** B2
Turnditch **61** C3, **64** A1
Turnhout **79** C1
Türnitz **94** A3
Turnov **83** D2
Turnov **96** A1
Turnu Măgurele **140** B2
Turón **173** C/D2
Turrach **126** B1
Turre **174** A2
Turri **123** C/D2/3
Turriers **112** A2
Turrillas **173** D2, **174** A2
Tursa **24** B2
Tursi **120** B3
Turtagrø **37** C2
Turtel **139** C2/3
Turtola **12** A3, **17** D1
Turzovka **95** D1
Tusa **125** C2
Tusby **25** D2/3, **26** A2/3
Tuscánia **116** B3, **118** A1
Tušilović **127** C3, **131** C1
Tussenhausen **91** D2/3
Tustervatn **14** B2/3
Tutaryd **50** B1/2
Tutin **138** A1
Tutin **140** A1
Tutjunniemi **23** C/D3
Tutrakan **141** C2
Tuttlingen **90** B3
Tuttlingen-Möhringen **90** B3
Tutzing **92** A3
Tuuhonen **21** C3
Tuukkala **26** B1
Tuulenkylä **20** B3
Tuulimäki **19** C3
Tuulos **25** C2, **26** A2
Tuunajärvi **24** B1
Tuupovaara **23** D3
Tuurala **20** B2
Tuusjärvi **23** C2
Tuuski **26** B2
Tuusmäki **23** B/C3
Tuusniemi **23** C2
Tuusula (Tusby) **25** D2/3, **26** A2/3

Tuv **37** C3
Tuv **14** B1
Tuvas **20** A3
Tuve **45** C3
Tuven **14** B2/3
Tuvträsk **31** B/C1
Tuxford **61** C3, **64** B1
Tuzi **137** D2
Tuzla **132** B2
Tuzla **149** C1
Tuzly **141** D1
Tvååker **49** D1, **50** A1
Tväråbäck **31** C2
Tvärålund **31** C2
Tvärámark **20** A1, **31** D2
Tväråträsk **15** D1
Tved **49** C2/3
Tvedestrand **43** C3
Tveit **43** C3
Tveit **36** B3
Tveita **36** B3
Tverrå **14** B2
Tverråmo **15** C1
Tverrelvdalen **5** C2
Tverrvik **14** B1
Tversted **44** A3, **48** B1
Tving **51** C2
Tvrdošovce **95** C2/3
Tweede Exloërmond **67** C2
Tweedmouth **57** D2
Twello **67** C2
Tweng **126** A/B1
Twimberg **127** C1
Twimberg **96** A3
Twist **67** C2
Twistetal-Berndorf **81** C1
Twistringen **68** A2
Twistringen-Heiligenloh **68** A2
Twist-Schöninghsdorf **67** C2
Two Bridges **63** C3
Tychy **96** B2
Tydal **33** D2
Tyfjord **7** C1
Tyfors **39** C2
Tygelsjö **50** A3
Tyin **37** C2
Tyinholmen **37** C2
Tykarp **50** B2
Tykölä **25** C1/2
Tyldum **28** B1/2
Tylldal **33** C/D3
Tylösand **49** D2, **50** A2
Tylösand **72** A1
Tylstrup **48** B1
Týn **93** D1
Tyndaris **125** D1/2
Tynderö **35** D3
Tyndrum **56** B1
Tyndrum **54** A2, **55** D1
Tynemouth **54** B3
Tynemouth **57** D3, **61** C1
Tyngsjö kapell **39** C3
Tynnelsö **47** C1
Tynnerås **30** A3, **35** C1
Tynset **33** C/D3
Typpö **18** A3, **21** C1
Typpyrä **12** A3, **17** D1
Tyrämäki **19** C2
Tyråvaara **19** C2
Tyrella **58** A1
Tyresö **47** D1
Tyringe **50** B2
Tyristrand **43** D1
Tyrjänsaari **23** D2
Tyrnävä **18** B3
Tyrväntö **25** C2
Tyry **25** D1, **26** A1
Tysres **9** C2
Tysse **36** A3
Tyssebotn **36** A3
Tyssedal **42** B1
Tystberga **47** C2
Tysvær **42** A2
Tyttbo **40** A3
Tyvelä **19** C1
Tywyn **59** C3
Tyykiluoto **18** A2
Tyynismaa **21** B/C2
Tzummarum **66** B1

U

Ub **133** D2, **134** A2
Übach-Palenberg **79** D2
Ubbergen **66** B3
Ubeda **167** D3, **173** C1
Übelbach-Markt **127** C1
Überlingen **91** C3
Ubide **153** D1/2
Ubli **137** C1
Ubli **137** D2
Ubli **136** A1
Ubli **137** D2
Ubrique **172** A2
Ubstadt-Weiher **90** B1
Uceda **161** C2
Ucero **153** C3, **161** C1
Uchacq **108** B2
Uchaud **111** C2
Uchte **68** A2
Uchte-Woltringhausen **68** A2
Uchtspringe **69** C/D2
Uckange **89** C1
Uckfield **76** B1
Uckro **70** A3
Ucria **125** C2
Udalla **153** C1
Udbina **131** C2
Udby **53** D2
Udby **49** B2
Uddebo **50** B1
Uddeholm **39** C3
Uddevalla **45** C2
Uden **66** B3, **79** C1
Uder **81** D1
Udestedt **82** A1
Údine **126** A2
Údine Paparotti **126** A2
Udovo **139** C3, **143** D1
Udvar **129** B/C3
Uebigau **83** C3
Ueckermünde **70** B1
Ueckermünde **72** A2/3
Uedem **67** C3, **79** D1
Uehlfeld **81** D3
Uelsen **67** C2
Uelzen **69** C2
Uelzen-Holdenstedt **69** C2
Uetendorf **105** C1
Uetersen **52** B3, **68** B1
Uettingen **81** C3
Uetze **68** B2
Uetze-Dollbergen **68** B2/3
Uetze-Hänigsen **68** B2
Uffenheim **81** D3, **91** D1
Uffenheim-Langensteinach **81** D3, **91** D1
Ugâle **73** C1
Ugao **138** A1
Ugao **153** C1
Ugento **121** D3
Ugerløse **49** C/D3, **53** D1
Uggiano la Chiesa **121** D3
Ugglarp **49** D2, **50** A1/2
Ugglaheden **38** B2
Ugílar **173** C2
Ugine **104** A/B3
Ugljan **130** B2
Ugljane **131** C2
Ugljarevo **134** B3
Ugljevik **133** C1/2
Ugra **75** D3
Ugulvik **36** B2
Uharte **154** A2
Uherské Hradiště **95** C1
Uherské Hradiště **96** B2
Uherský Brod **96** B2
Uherský Brod **95** C1
Uherský Ostroh **95** C1
Uhingen **91** C2
Ühlingen-Birkendorf **90** B3
Uhlířské Janovice **83** D3
Uhlstädt **82** A2
Uhříněves **83** D3
Uhrovec **95** C/D2
Uhyst **83** D1
Uig **54** A2
Uimaharju **23** D2
Uimaniemi **12** A/B2
Uimila **25** D2, **26** B2
Uithoorn **66** A/B3
Uithuizen **67** C1
Ujhartyán **129** C1
Uji i ftohët **142** A2

Újpetre 128 B2/3
Ujście 71 D2
Ujsoły 95 D1
Újszász 129 D1
Ujué 154 A2
Ukkola 23 D2
Ukmérgé 73 D2, 74 A3
Ukna 46 B3
Ukonvaara 23 C2
Ula 43 D2, 44 A1/2
Uland 35 D2
Ul'anka 95 D2
Ulbjerg 48 B2
Ulceby 61 D2
Ulcinj 137 D2
Uldum 48 B3, 52 B1
Ulea 169 D3
Uleåborg 18 A/B2
Ulebergshamn 44 B2
Ulefoss 43 D2, 44 A1
Uleila del Campo 173 D2,
  174 A2
Ulëzë 138 A3
Ulfborg 48 A2
Ülice 83 C3
Uljanik 128 A3
Uljanovka 99 C3
Ul'janovo 75 D3
Uljma 140 A2
Uljma 134 B1
Ulkuvaara 11 C3, 12 A1/2
Ullånger 30 B3, 35 D2
Ullapool 54 A2
Ullared 72 A1
Ullared 49 D1, 50 A1
Ullatti 17 C1
Ullava 21 C1
Ullbergsträsk 16 A3
Ulldecona 163 C2
Ulldemolins 163 C/D1
Ullensvang 36 B3
Ulleren 38 A/B3
Ullerslev 53 C1
Ullerup 52 B2
Ullervad 45 D2
Üllés 129 D2
Ullfors 40 B2/3
Ullisjaur 15 C3
Üllő 95 D3, 129 C1
Ullsfjord 4 A3
Ulm 91 C/D2
Ulme 164 B1
Ulmen 80 A2/3
Ulmtal 80 B2
Ulog 132 B3
Uløybukt 4 B2
Ulricehamn 45 D3
Ulricehamn 72 A1
Ulrichen 105 C2
Ulrichsberg 93 C2
Ulrichstein 81 C2
Ulrika 46 B3
Ulriksfors 29 D2/3, 30 A2,
  35 C1
Ulsberg 33 C2
Ulsnes 37 D2/3
Ulsta 54 A1
Ulsted 49 B/C1
Ulsteinvik 36 A1
Ulstrup 48 B2
Ultrasniemi 27 D1
Ulvan 32 B1
Ulvangen 14 A2
Ulvåsa 46 A2
Ulverston 59 C1, 60 B2
Ulvestad 36 B2
Ulvik 36 B3
Ulvila (Ulvsby) 24 A1
Ulvinsalon Luonnonpuisto
  23 D1
Ulvkälla (Sveg) 34 B3
Ulvoberg 30 B1
Ulvöhamn 31 B/C3
Ulvsås 29 D3, 34 B1
Ulvsby 24 A1
Ulvshyttan 39 D2/3
Ulvsjön 35 C3
Ulvsvåg 9 C2
Umag 126 A3
Uman' 99 C3
Umasjö 15 C2
Umbértide 115 C3, 117 C2
Umbriático 122 B1/2
Umbukta fjellstue 14 B2
Umčari 134 B2
Umeå 18 C/D2
Ume-Ersmark 20 A1, 31 D2

Umetić 127 D3, 131 C1
Umfors 15 C2
Umhausen 106 B1
Umin Dol 139 B/C2
Umka 133 D1, 134 A1/2
Ummeljoki 26 B2
Ummendorf 69 C3
Ummerstadt 81 D2
Umnäs 15 C3
Umpferstedt 82 A1/2
Uña 161 D3
Uña de Quintana 151 D3
Unaja 24 A2
Unari 12 A/B2
Unbyn 17 C3
Uncastillo 155 C2
Unciti 154 A2
Undenäs 45 D2, 46 A2
Undersåker 29 C3, 34 A2
Undersåker 29 C3, 34 A2
Undersvik 40 A1
Undheim 42 A2/3
Undredal 36 B3
Undués de Lerda 155 C2
Uneča 99 D1
Unelanperä 18 B3
Úněšov 83 C3
Ungeny 141 C1
Ungerdorf 127 C/D1
Unhais da Serra 158 B3
Unhošt' 83 C3
Unije 130 A2
Unimäki 23 B/C3
Unirea 135 D2
Unna 80 B1
Unna Allakasstugorna 9 D2
Unquera 152 B1
Unstad 8 B2
Untamala 20 B2
Untamala 24 A2
Unterach 93 C3
Unterägeri [Baar] 105 D1
Unterdietfurt 92 B2
Untergriesbach 93 C2
Unterhaching 92 A2/3
Unterhochsteg 91 C3
Unterloibl 126 B2
Unterlüss 82 B2
Untermeitingen 95 D2
Untermünkheim 91 C1
Unterneukirchen 92 B2
Unterpinswang 91 D3
Unterpremstätten 127 C1
Unterreichenbach (Calw)
  90 B2
Unterreit 92 B2/3
Unterschächen [Altdorf]
  105 D1
Unterschleissheim 92 A2
Unterschneidheim-Zöbin-
  gen 91 D1
Unterschwaningen 91 D1
Untersiemau 81 D2/3,
  82 A2/3
Untersteinach 82 A3
Untertauern 126 A1
Unterwasser [Nesslau-Neu
  St. Johann] 105 D1,
  106 A1
Unterweid 81 D2
Unterweissenbach 93 D2
Unterwössen 92 B3
Untorp 39 C3
Upavon 64 A3, 76 A1
Úpega 113 B/C2
Upinniemi/Obbnäs 25 C3
Uplengen 67 D1
Uplengen-Remels 67 D1
Upper Tean 59 D2/3,
  61 B/C3, 64 A1
Uppgränna 46 A3
Upphärad 45 C3
Uppingham 64 B2
Upplands-Väsby 47 C1
Uppsala 40 B3
Uppsala-Gamla Uppsala
  40 B3
Uppsala-Sunnersta 40 B3
Uppsälje 39 C2
Uppsete 36 B3
Upton upon Severn 63 D1,
  64 A2
Ur 156 A2
Uraiújfalu 94 B3, 128 A1
Uramonkylä 23 C1
Úras 123 C2/3
Urbach 91 C2

Urbánia 115 C/D2/3,
  117 C2
Urbeis 89 D2, 90 A2
Urbino 115 D2, 117 C2
Urbiola 153 D2
Urbise 103 C2
Urçay 102 B1
Urda 167 C1
Urdari 135 D1
Urdiáin 153 D2
Urdiales del Páramo 151 D2
Urdos 154 B2
Urduliz 153 C1
Urduña 153 C2
Ure 8 B2/3
Urepel 108 A3, 154 A1
Ureterp 67 C1/2
Urheiluopisto 27 D1
Urheiluopisto 21 C2
Urheiluopisto 25 D2, 26 A2
Urheiluopisto 25 D2, 26 A2
Urheiluopisto 25 D2, 26 A2
Uriage-les-Bains 104 A3,
  112 A1
Uricani 135 D1
Urizaharra 153 D2
Urjala 25 B/C2
Urjalan asema 25 C2
Urk 66 B2
Urla 149 D2
Urmatt 89 D2, 90 A2
Urmenor 174 B1
Urmince 95 C2
Urnäsch 105 D1, 106 A1
Urnes 36 B2
Urnieta 153 D1, 154 A1
Uroševac 138 B2
Uroševac 140 A3
Urovica 135 C2
Urrácal 173 D1/2
Urraca-Miguel 160 B2
Urrea de Gaén 162 B1/2
Urrea de Jalón 155 C3,
  163 C1
Urretxu 153 D1
Urroz 154 A2
Urrugne 108 A3, 154 A1
Ursberg 91 D2
Ursensollen 82 A3, 92 A1
Urshult 51 C2
Urshult 72 A1
Urspringen (Marktheiden-
  feld) 81 C3
Ursviken 31 D1
Urtimjaur 16 B1
Urtoče 131 C2
Urtuella 153 C1
Urtx 156 A2
Urueñas 160 B1
Uruñuela 153 D2
Ururi 119 D2, 120 A1
Urville-Nacqueville 76 A3
Urzainqui 154 B2
Urziceni 141 C2
Urzicuţa 135 D2
Urzulei 123 D2
Usagre 165 D3, 166 A3
Usanos 161 C2
Ušće 133 D3, 134 A/B3
Úscio 113 D2
Used 162 A2
Usedom 70 B1
Useldange 79 D3
Uséllus 123 C2
Useras 163 B/C3
Usingen 80 B2
Úsini 123 C1/2
Usk 63 D1
Uskali 23 D3
Uskedal 42 A1
Uskoplje 137 C2
Üsküdar 149 D1
Uslar 68 B3, 81 C1
Uslar-Schönhagen 68 B3,
  81 C1
Usmate Velate 105 D3,
  106 A3
Ussássai 123 D2
Ussat-les-Bains 155 D2,
  156 A1
Ussé 86 B3, 101 C1
Usseau 100 B2
Usséglio 104 B3, 112 B1
Ussel 102 A3
Ussel 102 B3, 110 A1
Usson-du-Poitou 101 C2
Usson-en-Forez 103 C3

Usson-les-Bains 156 A1
Ustaoset 37 C3
Ustaritz 108 A3, 154 A1
Ust'-Čorna 97 D2, 98 A3
Ust'-Dunajsk 141 D2
Úšték 83 C2
Uster 90 B3, 105 D1
Ustibar 133 C3
Uštica 128 A3, 131 D1,
  132 A1
Ústica 124 B1
Ustikolina 133 C3
Ústí nad Labem 83 C2
Ústí nad Labem 96 A1
Ústí nad Orlicí 96 B2
Ustiprača 133 C3
Ustjužna 75 D1
Ustka 72 B2
Ust'-Luga 74 B1
Ustrzyki Górne 97 D2,
  98 A3
Usurbil 153 D1, 154 A1
Uszód 129 C2
Uta 123 C/D3
Utajärvi 18 B3
Utåker 42 A1
Utakleiv 8 B2
Utande 161 C2
Utanen 18 B3
Utanlandsjö 31 C3
Utansjö 35 D2
Utbjoa 42 A1
Utebo 154 B3, 162 B1
Utelle 112 B2
Utena 73 D2, 74 A3
Utersum 52 A2
Úteryl 82 B3
Uthaug 28 A3, 33 C1
Utiel 169 D1
Utifällan 31 C2
Utlången 51 C/D2/3
Utne 36 B3
Utö 47 D1/2
Utöhus 47 C1
Utomälven 40 A/B2/3
Utorgoš 74 B2
Utrecht 66 B3
Utrera 171 D2
Utrilla 161 D1
Utrillas 162 B2
Utsikten 42 B1
Utsjoki (Ohtsejohka) 6 B2
Utskor 8 B1/2
Utstein Kloster 42 A2
Uttendorf 93 C2
Uttendorf 107 D1, 126 A1
Uttenweiler 91 C2
Uttenweiler-Ahlen 91 C2
Utterliden 16 A3
Uttermossa 20 A3
Uttersberg 39 D3
Uttersjöbäcken 31 D1
Utterslev 53 C2
Utti 26 B2
Uttoxeter 59 D2/3, 61 C3,
  64 A1
Utula 27 C1
Utvalnäs 40 B2
Utvik 36 B1/2
Utvorda 28 B2
Uuao 23 D2/3
Uukuniemi 27 D1
Uura 19 C2
Uurainen 21 D3, 22 A3
Uuro 20 B3
Uusikaupunki (Nystad)
  24 A2, 41 D2
Uusikylä 19 C3
Uusikylä 25 D2, 26 A2
Uusi-Lavola 27 C2
Uusi-Värtsilä 23 D3
Uva 19 C3
Uvac 133 C3
Uvåg 8 B2
Úvaly 83 D3
Uvdal 37 C3
Üxheim 79 D2, 80 A2
Uza 108 B2
Uzdin 129 D3, 133 D1,
  134 A/B1
Uzerche 101 D3
Uzès 111 C2
Uzeste 108 B1/2
Užgorod 97 C/D2, 98 A3
Uzin 99 C2
Uznach 105 D1, 106 A1
Uztárroz 154 B2

Uzunköprü 145 D3

V

Vå 43 B/C1
Vä 50 B3
Vaaiasalmi 22 B2/3
Vaajakoski 21 D3, 22 A3
Vaajasalmi 22 B2/3
Vääkiö 19 C2
Vääksy 25 D2, 26 A2
Vaala 18 B3
Vaalajärvi 12 B2
Vaalijala 22 B3
Vaalimaa 27 C2
Vaals 79 D2
Väänälänranta 22 B2
Vaania 25 D2, 26 A2
Vääräkoski 21 C3
Vaarakylä 19 C1
Vaarankylä 19 C1
Vaaranniva 19 C2
Vaaraperä 19 D1
Vaaraslahti 22 B2
Vaasa/Vasa 20 A2, 31 D3
Vaassen 67 B/C3
Väätäiskylä 21 C3
Vaattojärvi 12 A2, 17 D1
Vabalninkas 73 D1, 74 A2
Vabre 110 A2
Vabres-l'Abbaye 110 A2
Vác 95 D3
Vác 97 B/C3
Vacha 81 D2
Váchartyán 95 D3
Väckelsång 51 C2
Väcklax 24 A3
Vacov 93 C1
Vacqueyras 111 C2
Vad 39 C3
Vada 114 A/B3, 116 A2
Vada 139 C2
Väddö 41 C3
Väderstad 46 A2
Vadheim 36 A2
Vadillo de la Guareña
  159 D1, 160 A1
Vadillo de la Sierra 160 A2
Vadla 42 B2
Vado 114 B2, 116 B1
Vadocondes 153 C3,
  161 C1
Vado Lígure 113 C2
Vadsbro 46 B1/2
Vadskinn 9 C1
Vadsø 7 C2
Vadstena 46 A2
Vaduz [Schaan] 105 D1,
  106 A1
Vaektarstua 33 D2
Vaféika 145 C2
Vafiochórion 143 D1
Våg 43 D2, 44 A2
Våg 95 B/C3, 128 A1
Våga 42 A2
Vågaholmen 14 B1
Vågåmo 33 B/C3, 37 D1
Vågan 33 B/C1
Vågan 9 D1
Vaganac 131 C1
Vågen 29 C1/2
Vägersjön 30 A3, 35 C2
Vagge 7 C2
Væggerløse 53 D2
Vaggeryd 46 A3, 50 B1
Vaggeryd 72 A1
Vágia 147 C2
Vågland 32 B2
Váglia 114 B2, 116 B1
Vágnes 4 A2/3
Vagnhärad 47 C2
Vagos 158 A2
Vägsele 30 B1
Vägsjöfors 39 B/C3
Vågslid 42 B1
Vågsodden 14 A3
Vågstranda 32 A2/3
Vagueira 158 A2
Vágur 55 C1
Vähäjoki 18 A1
Vähäkangas 18 A3, 21 C1
Vähäkyrö 20 B2
Vahalahti 23 D3

Vähäniva 11 C2
Vahanka 21 C2
Vähä-Vuoto 18 B2
Vaheri 25 D1, 26 A1
Vähikkälä 25 C2
Vahterpää 26 B3
Vahto 24 B2
Vaiamonte 165 C2
Vaiano 114 B2, 116 B1
Vaiges 86 A2
Vaihingen 91 B/C1
Vailly-sur-Aisne 78 A/B3
Vailly-sur-Sauldre 87 D3
Vaimosuo 19 D1
Vainikkala 27 C2
Vairano Scalo 119 C2
Väisälä 22 B3
Vaisaluoktastugan 9 D3
Vaison-la-Romaine
　111 C/D2
Vaîte 89 C3
Vaivo 23 C3
Väjern 44 B2
Vajkijaur 16 A/B1
Vajmat 16 A2
Vajska 129 C3
Vajszló 128 B3
Vajta 129 B/C2
Vajza 142 A2
Vakern 39 C2/3
Vakerskogen 39 C2/3
Vækker 5 D2, 6 A2
Vakkerstølen 32 B3, 37 C1
Vakkola 25 D2, 26 A2
Vakkotavarestugan 9 D3
Vakkuri 20 B2
Vaksdal 36 A3
Vaksliden 16 A3
Vál 95 D3, 129 B/C1
Valada 164 A2
Vålådalen 29 C3, 34 A2
Valadouro 151 B/C1
Valajanaapa 18 B1
Valajaskoski 12 A3
Valalta 130 A1
Valandovo 139 C/D3,
　143 D1
Valanhamn 4 B2
Valanída 143 C2/3
Valareña 155 C3
Valaská Belá 95 D1/2
Vålåskaret 33 C2
Valašské Klobouky 95 C1
Valašské Meziříčí 95 C1
Valašské Meziříčí 96 B2
Vålåstugan 34 A2
Valay 89 C3, 104 A1
Valberg 112 B2
Vålberg 45 C/D1
Valberg 8 B2
Valbom 159 C2
Valbona 162 B3
Valbondione 106 A/B2
Valbone 137 D2, 138 A2
Valbonnais 111 D1, 112 A1
Valbo-Ryr 45 C2
Valbuena de Duero 152 B3,
　160 B1
Valburg 66 B3
Vălcani 129 D2
Valcarlos 108 B3, 155 C1
Vâlčedrâm 135 D3
Vâlčedrâm 140 B2
Valchiusella 105 C3
Valdagno 107 C3
Valdahon 89 D3, 104 A/B1
Valdaj 75 C1/2
Val-d'Ajol 89 D2/3
Valdalen 33 D3
Valdanzo 153 C3, 161 C1
Valdaracete 161 C3
Valdealgorfa 163 C2
Valdeande 153 C3, 161 C1
Valdearenas 161 C2
Valdeavellano de Tera
　153 D3
Valdeveruelo 161 C2
Valdecaballeros 166 B1/2
Valdecabras 161 D3
Valdecañas de Tajo 159 D3,
　166 A1
Valdecastillo 152 A2
Valdeconcha 161 C2
Valdefinjas 159 D1, 160 A1
Valdeflores 171 C/D1
Valdefuentes 161 D1/2,
　166 A1/2

Valdeganga 168 B2
Valdeganga de Cuenca
　161 D3, 168 B1
Valdehúncar 159 D3,
　166 A/B1
Valdelacasa 160 A3,
　166 B1
Valdelacasa 159 D2
Valdelageve 159 D2/3
Valdelarco 165 D3, 171 C1
Valdelateja 153 B/C2
Valdelinares 162 B2/3
Valdelosa 159 D1/2
Valdeltormo 163 C2
Valdemadera 153 D3
Valdemaluque 153 C3,
　161 C1
Valdemanco del Esteras
　166 B2
Valdemärpils 73 C/D1
Valdemars Slot 53 C2
Valdemarsvik 46 B2/3
Valdemeca 162 A3
Valdemorillo 160 B2
Valdemorillo de la Sierra
　162 A3
Valdemoro 161 B/C3
Valdemoro-Sierra 162 A3
Valdenarros 153 C3,
　161 C1
Valdenebro 153 C3,
　161 C1
Valdenebro de los Valles
　152 A3
Valdenoceda 153 C2
Valdenuño Fernández
　161 C2
Valdeolivas 161 D2
Valdeolmillos 152 B3
Valdepeñas 167 C2
Valdepeñas de Jaén 173 C1
Valdepolo 152 A2
Valderas 152 A3
Valdérice 124 A2
Valderiès 110 A2
Valderrobres 163 C2
Valderrodrigo 159 C2
Val de Santo Domingo
　160 B3
Valdesaz. 161 C2
Valdesimonte 160 B1
Valdespina 152 B3
Valdestillas 160 A1
Valdeteja 152 A2
Valdetorres 165 D2,
　166 A2
Valdeverdeja 160 A3,
　166 B1
Valdevimbre 151 D2,
　152 A2
Valdezcaray 153 C2/3
Valdieri 112 B2
Valdilecha 161 C3
Val d'Isère 104 B3
Val-d'Izé 86 A2
Valdobbiádene 107 C2/3
Val do Dubra 150 A1/2
Val Dorizzo 106 B2/3
Valdoviño 150 B1
Valdresflya 37 C2
Valdunquillo 152 A3
Valdurna/Durnholz 107 C1
Vale 63 D3
Valea Marcului 135 D2
Valebø 43 D2, 44 A1
Valebru 37 D2
Vale de Cambra 158 A2
Vale de Cavalos 164 B1/2
Vale de Figueira 164 B1
Vale de Guiso 164 B2
Vale de Prazeres 158 B3
Vale de Salgueiro 151 C3,
　159 B/C1
Vale de Santiago 164 B3,
　170 A1
Vale de Santarém 164 A2
Vale de Vargo 165 C3,
　170 B1
Vale do Peso 165 C1
Vale Frechoso 159 C1
Válega 158 A2
Valéggio sul Míncio 106 B3
Valen 42 A1
Valen 5 C/D1, 6 A1
Valença 158 B1/2
Valença do Minho 150 A3

Valençay 87 C3, 101 D1,
　102 A1
Valence 111 C1
Valence-d'Agen 109 C2
Valence-d'Albigeois
　110 A2
Valence-en-Brie 87 D2
Valence-sur-Baïse 109 C2
Valencia 169 D1
Valencia de Alcántara
　165 C1
Valencia de Don Juan
　151 D2, 152 A2
Valencia de las Torres
　165 D3, 166 A3
Valencia de Mombuey
　165 C3
Valencia del Ventoso
　165 D3
Valenciennes 78 B2
Vălenii de Munte 141 C2
Valensole 111 D2, 112 A2
Valentano 116 B3, 118 A1
Valenza 113 C2
Valenzuela 167 C3, 172 B1
Valenzuela de Calatrava
　167 C2
Våler 38 B2
Våler 44 B1
Valera de Abajo 161 D3,
　168 B1
Valera de Arriba 161 D3,
　168 B1
Valérien 87 D2
Valer'jany 99 B/C1
Valevåg 42 A1
Valevatn 42 B2
Vale Verde 159 C2
Valeyrac 100 B3
Valezim 158 B3
Valfábbrica 115 D3,
　117 C2
Valfarta 155 B/C3,
　163 B/C1
Valfermoso de Tajuña
　161 C2
Valflaunès 110 B2
Valga 150 A2
Valga 74 A2
Valgañón 153 C2
Valgorge 111 C1
Valgrisanche 104 B3
Valguarnera Caropepe
　125 C2
Valhelhas 158 B2/3
Valhermoso 161 D2
Välijoki 27 B/C2
Välijoki 18 B1
Välikangas 12 B3
Väli-Kannus 21 C1
Välikoski 17 D2
Välikylä 21 C1
Valimítika 146 B3
Välitalo 12 B2
Valitutta 25 D1, 26 A1
Väliug 135 C1
Väli-Viirre 21 C1
Valjevo 133 D2, 134 A2
Valjevo 140 A2
Valjok fjellstue 6 B2
Valjunquera 163 C2
Valkeajärvi 21 C3
Valkeakoski 25 C1/2
Valkeala 26 B2
Valkealahti 21 C3
Valkeamäki 27 C1
Valkeavaara 27 D1
Valkeiskylä 22 B1
Valkeiskylä 23 B/C2
Valkenburg-Houthem
　79 D2
Valkenswaard 79 C1
Valkininkai 73 D2, 74 A3
Valko/Valkom 25 D2/3,
　26 B3
Vall 47 D3
Valla 46 B1
Valla 29 D3, 34 B2
Vallada 169 C2
Valladolid 152 A/B3,
　160 A1
Vallåkra 49 D3, 50 A3
Vallamediana 153 D2
Vallanca 163 C3
Vallarsa 107 C3
Vallarvatnet 29 C1
Vallata 120 A2

Vallavik 36 B3
Vallbo 29 C3, 34 A2
Vallbona d'Anoia 155 D3,
　156 A3, 163 D1
Vallda 49 D1, 50 A1
Valldal 32 A3, 36 B1
Vall d'Alba 163 C3
Valldemosa 157 C2
Vall de Uxó 162 B3,
　169 D1
Valle 14 B1
Valle 42 B2
Valle 42 B3
Vallecas 161 C2/3
Valle Castellana 117 D3,
　119 C1
Valle Cerrina 113 C1
Vallecorsa 119 C2
Vallecrósia 112 B2/3
Valle d'Alesani 113 D3
Valle de Abdalagís 172 B1
Valle de Cerrato 152 B3
Valle de la Serena 166 A2
Valle de los Caídos 160 B3
Valle de Matamoros 165 D3
Valle de Mena 153 C1
Valle de Santa Ana 165 D3
Valledolmo 124 B2
Valledória 123 C1
Valleiry 104 A2
Valle Lomellina 105 D3,
　113 C1
Vallelunga Pratameno
　124 B2
Vallen 17 C3
Vallen 31 D1
Vallen 30 A2, 35 C/D1
Vallendar 80 A/B2
Vallentuna 47 C/D1
Vallepietra 119 B/C2
Vallerås 39 C2
Valleraugue 110 B2
Vallermosa 123 C3
Vallespinosa 155 C3,
　163 C1
Válles/Vals 107 C1
Vallet 86 A3, 101 C1
Valleviken 47 D2
Valley 58 B2
Vallfogona de Ripollès
　156 A2
Vallfogona de Riucorb
　155 C3, 163 C1
Vallgorguina 156 B3
Vallibona 163 C2
Valli del Pasúbio 107 C3
Vallières 102 A1
Vallières 104 A2/3
Vallières-les-Grandes
　86 A/B3
Valli Mocenighe 107 C3,
　115 C1
Vallioniemi 13 C3
Vallmoll 163 C1
Vallø 50 A3, 53 D1
Valløby 50 A3, 53 D1
Vallo della Lucánia 120 A3
Valloire 104 A/B3, 112 A1
Vallombrosa 115 C2,
　116 B1/2
Vallon-en-Sully 102 B2
Vallon-Pont-d'Arc 111 C2
Vallorbe 104 A/B1/2
Vallorcine 104 B2
Vallouise 112 A1
Valløy 42 D2, 44 B1
Vallrun 29 D3, 34 B1
Valls 163 C1
Vallset 38 A2
Vallsjärv 17 C2
Vallsta 40 A1
Vallter 156 A2
Valluhn 69 C1
Vallvik 40 B1
Valmaña 155 C3, 163 C1
Valmanya 156 B2
Valmiera 73 D1, 74 A2
Valmojado 160 B3
Valmont 77 C3
Valmontone 118 B2
Valne 29 D3, 34 B2
Valö 40 B2/3
Valognes 76 A3
Valongo 158 A1/2
Válor 173 C2
Valoría la Buena 152 B3,
　160 B1

Valøy 28 A/B1
Valpaços 151 C3, 158 B1
Valpalmas 154 B2/3
Valpelline 104 B3
Valperga 105 C3
Valpiana 114 B3, 116 A2
Valpovo 128 B3
Valpperi 24 B2
Valprato Soana 105 C3
Valpromaro 114 A2,
　116 A1
Valpuesta 153 C2
Valras-Plage 110 B3,
　156 B1
Valréas 111 C2
Valsavaranche 104 B3
Valseca 160 B2
Valsemé 76 B3, 86 B1
Valsequillo 166 B3
Valset 28 A3, 33 C1
Valsinni 120 B3
Valsjöbyn 29 C/D2, 34 B1
Valsjön 35 C3
Valskog 46 B3
Valskrå 28 B2
Vals-les-Bain 111 C1
Valsneset 28 A2/3, 33 C1
Valsøybotn 32 B2
Valsøyfjord 32 B2
Vals-Platz [Ilanz] 105 D2,
　106 A2
Valstad 45 D3
Valstagna 107 C3
Val-Suzon 88 B3
Valtesiníkon 146 B3
Válti 143 D1, 144 A1
Valtice 94 B2
Valtierra 154 A2/3
Valtimo 23 C1
Valtola 26 B1/2
Valtopina 115 D3, 117 C2
Valtorta 106 A2
Váltos 145 D3
Valtournanche 105 C2/3
Valtueña 161 D1
Valtura 130 A1
Valun 130 A1
Valverde 153 D3, 154 A3
Valverde 167 C2
Valverde de Leganés
　165 C2
Valverde de Llerena 166 A3
Valverde de Júcar 161 D3,
　168 B1
Valverde de la Vera 161 C3
Valverde de Burguillos
　165 D3
Valverde de Majano 160 B2
Valverde del Fresno 159 C3
Valverde del Camino
　171 C1
Valverdejo 161 D3, 168 B1
Valvträsk 17 C2
Våmartveit 43 C1
Vamdrup 52 B1
Våmhus 39 C1/2
Vamlingbo 47 D3
Vamlingbo 72 B1
Vammala/Tyrvää 24 B1
Vámosmikola 95 D3
Vámosszabadi 95 C3
Vampula 24 B2
Vamvakoú 143 D3
Vamvakoú 147 C3
Vanaja 25 C2
Vanaja 22 B3
Vanås 50 B2
Vanault-les-Dames 88 B1
Vandans 106 A1
Vändburg 47 D3
Vandel 48 B3, 52 B1
Vandellòs 163 C/D2
Vandenesse 103 C2
Vandóies/Vintl 107 C1
Vandoma 158 A1/2
Vändträsk 16 B3
Väne-Åsaka 45 C3
Vänersborg 45 C2
Vänersnäs 45 C2
Väng 45 C1
Vang 37 C2
Vang 51 D3
Vånga 50 B2
Vängel 30 A2, 35 C1
Vangshylla 28 B2/3, 33 D1
Vangsnes 36 B2
Vangsvik 9 D1

Vanhakirkko 21 C3
Vanhakylä 27 C1/2
Vanhakylä 20 A/B3
Vanhala 26 B1
Vanhamäki 26 B1
Vanha-Pihlajavesi 21 C3
Vänjaurbäck 31 B/C1/2
Vänjaurfräsk 31 C2
Vännacka 45 C1
Vannakammen 4 A2
Vannareid 4 A2
Vännäs 31 C2
Vännäsberget 17 C2
Vännäsby 31 C2
Vannavalen 4 A/B2
Vannes 85 C3
Vannes-le-Châtel 89 C2
Vannes-sur-Cosson 87 C/D3
Vännfors 31 C2
Vannvåg 4 A/B2
Våno 24 B3
Vanonen 26 B2
Vanovelles 156 A3
Vansäter 40 A1
Vansbro 39 C2
Vanse 42 B3
Vänsjö 34 B3
Vantaa/Vanda 25 C3, 26 A3
Väntholm 47 C1
Vanttaja 19 D1
Vanttausjärvi 12 B3
Vanttauskoski 12 B3
Vanttila 24 B2
Vanvik 8 B3
Vanvik 42 A/B1
Vanvikan 28 A3, 33 C1
Vanylven 36 A1
Vaour 109 D2
Vapavaara 19 D1
Vaplan 29 D3, 34 B2
Váprio d'Adda 106 A3
Vaqueiros 170 B1/2
Vara 45 C2/3
Varades 85 D3
Varages 111 D3, 112 A3
Varajärvi 12 A3, 17 D2
Varajoki 19 D3
Varakļani 74 A2
Väralä 26 B2
Varaldsøy 42 A1
Varallo 105 C3
Varamobaden 46 A2
Varangerbotn 7 C2
Varano de'Melegari 114 A1
Varaždin 127 D2
Varaždin 96 A/B3
Varaždinske Toplice 127 D2
Varazze 113 C2
Varberg 49 D1, 50 A1
Varberg 72 A1
Vårbica 141 C3
Vårby 47 C1
Varchentin 69 D1, 70 A1
Várda 146 A2
Varde 48 A3, 52 A1
Vardište 133 C3
Vardø 7 D1/2
Vårdö 41 D3
Várdomb 129 B/C2
Vårdsberg 46 B2
Varejoki 17 D2, 18 A1
Varel 67 D1, 68 A1
Varel-Conneforde 67 D1
Varel-Dangast 67 D1, 68 A1
Varen 109 D2
Varengeville-sur-Mer 77 C2/3
Varenna 105 D2, 106 A2
Varennes-en-Argonne 88 B1
Varennes-Saint-Sauveur 103 D2
Varennes-sur-Amance 89 C2/3
Varennes-sur-Allier 102 B2
Varennes-sur-Usson 102 B3
Varennes sur Saine 87 D2
Vareš 132 B2
Varese 105 D3
Varese Lígure 113 D2, 114 A2
Varetz 101 D3
Vårgårda 45 C3

Vargas 152 B1
Vargeneset 9 C2
Vargfjord 9 C2
Vargön 45 C2
Varhaug 42 A3
Varigotti 113 C2
Varilhes 109 D3, 155 D1, 156 A1
Varín 95 D1
Väring 45 D2
Váris 143 C2
Variskylä 19 C3
Varislahti 23 C2
Varistaipale 23 C3
Varize 87 C2
Varjakka 18 A2
Varkaus 22 B3
Várkiza 147 D2
Varland 43 C1
Vårli 4 A3, 10 A1
Värmbol 46 B1/2
Värmdö 47 D1
Värmlands Bro 45 C1
Varmo 27 D1
Varmo 107 D2/3, 126 A2/3
Värmskog 45 C1
Varna 141 C/D3
Värnamo 72 A1
Värnamo 50 B1
Varnæs 52 B2
Varnhem 45 D2
Varnsdorf 83 D2
Varntresk 14 B2/3
Varnum 45 D3
Väröbacka 49 D1, 50 A1
Várois-et-Chaignot 88 B3
Városlőd 128 A/B1
Varpa 23 D2
Varpaisjärvi 22 B2
Várpalota 128 B1
Várpalota 96 B3
Varpanen 26 B1
Varparanta 23 C3
Varpasalo 23 C3
Varpnes 28 B2
Varpsjö 30 A2
Varpula 20 B2
Varpuselkä 13 C3
Varpuvaara 13 C3
Varrel 68 A2
Várrió 13 C2
Värriönpirtti 13 C2
Varsád 128 B2
Vårsås 45 D2, 46 A2
Våršec 135 D3, 139 D1
Varsi 114 A1
Varsseveld 67 C3
Vårsta 40 B3, 47 C1
Vartdal 36 B1
Varteig 44 B1
Vartiala 23 B/C2
Vartiala 23 C2
Vartius 19 D3
Vartofta 45 D3
Vartsala 24 B3
Värtsilä 23 D3
Varuträsk 31 D1
Varvára 144 B2
Varvaria 131 C2/3
Varvarin 134 B3
Varvekstugan 15 C/D1
Vårvik 28 A3, 33 C1
Varvikko 13 C3
Varzi 113 D1
Varzo 105 C2
Varzy 88 A3
Vås 35 C3
Vasad 129 C1
Vasaniemi 12 B2
Vasara 19 C/D2
Vasarainen 24 A2
Vasaraperä 19 C1
Vasarás 147 C3
Vásárosnamény 97 D2/3, 98 A3
Vascœuil 76 B3
Väse 45 D1
Väse 45 D1
Vaset 37 C/D2/3
Vasilákion 146 B3
Vasiliká 144 A2
Vasiliká 147 D1
Vasilikí 146 A1
Vasilikí 148 A2
Vasilikón 142 B2
Vasilikón 147 D2
Vasilikós 146 A3

Vasil'kov 99 C2
Vaski 18 A2
Vaskijärvi 25 C2
Vaskio 24 B2/3
Vaskivesi 21 C3
Vaskuu 21 C3
Vasles 101 C1/2
Vaslui 141 C1
Vassbø 42 A/B2/3
Vassbotn 9 C/D2
Vassbotnfjell 15 C1
Vassbotten 44 B2
Vassdal 9 D2
Vassdal 43 D2, 44 A1
Vassdalsvik 14 B1
Vassenden 37 D2
Vassenden 36 B2
Vassendvik 42 A2
Vassmoen 28 B2
Vassmolösa 51 D2
Vassnäs 35 C3
Vasstrand 4 A3
Vassy 86 A1
Vassy-sous-Pisy 88 A/B3
Vasszentmihály 127 D1
Västanå 30 A3, 35 C2
Västanå 31 C3
Västanbäck 30 A1
Västanbäck 35 C2
Västanfjärd 24 B3
Västanhede 40 A2
Västannäs 17 C2
Västansjö 15 C3
Västansjö 30 B1
Västansjö 35 D3
Västbyn 29 D3, 34 B1
Västeränga 41 D3
Väster Ärnäs 39 C2
Västerås 31 C2
Västerås 40 A3, 46 B1
Västerasen 30 A3, 35 C2
Västerby 39 D2/3, 40 A2
Väster Fågelvik 45 C1
Västerfärnebo 40 A3
Västerfjäll 15 D1
Västergarn 47 D3
Västergissjö 31 C2/3
Västerhaninge 47 C/D1
Västerhaninge-Tungelsta 47 C1
Väster Husby 46 B2
Västerlandsjö 31 C3
Västerlandsjö 31 C3
Västermyckeläng 39 C1
Västernyliden 31 C2
Väster Ritjemjåkk 9 D3
Västerrottna 38 B3
Västersträsjö 35 C3
Västerväla 40 A3
Västervik 46 B3
Västervik 72 B1
Västilä 25 C1, 26 A1
Vastila 26 B2
Västinki 21 C/D2
Västinniemi 23 C2
Västland 40 B2
Vasto 119 D1
Vastogirardi 119 C/D2
Västra Ämtervik 39 C3, 45 C/D1
Västra Bodarna 45 C3
Västra Hjoggböle 31 D1
Västra Lainijaur 16 A3
Västra Ormsjö 30 A1
Västra Sjulsmark 31 D2
Västra Skedvi 39 D3, 46 B1
Västra Stugusjö 35 C2
Västra Tunhem 45 C2
Västsjön 29 C3, 34 B1
Västvattnet 30 A3, 35 C1
Vasvár 128 A1
Vasvár 96 B3
Vát 128 A1
Vataala 23 D3
Vatan 102 A1
Väte 47 D3
Vaterholm 28 B3, 33 D1
Váthi 139 D3, 143 D1, 144 A1
Vathí 146 A1
Vathí 147 D2
Vathílakkos 143 D1/2
Vathítopos 144 B1
Vatin 134 B1
Vatjusjärvi 18 A3, 21 D1, 22 A1
Vatland 42 B3

Vatnås 43 D1
Vatne 43 C3
Vatne 32 A2/3
Vatne 43 C3
Vatne 36 B1
Vatnet 14 A/B2
Vatnhamn 5 C1/2
Vatnstraum 43 C3
Vátö 41 C1
Vatochórion 143 B/C2
Vatólakkos 143 C2
Vatopédi 144 B2
Vatra Dornei 141 C1
Vatry 88 B1
Vats 42 A1/2
Vattholma 40 B3
Vättila 24 B2
Vättis [Bad Ragaz] 105 D1, 106 A1
Vattnäs 39 D2
Vattrång 35 D3
Vattukylä 18 A3, 21 D1, 22 A1
Vau 164 A1
Vauchamps 88 A1
Vauclaix 88 A3, 103 C1
Vaucouleurs 89 C2
Vaud 104 B3
Vaugneray 103 C/D3
Vau i Dejës 137 D2
Vauldalen 33 D2
Vaulruz 104 B2
Vaumoise 87 D1
Vausseroux 101 C2
Vautorte 86 A2
Vauvenargues 111 D3
Vauvert 111 C2
Vaux 88 A3
Vaux-en-Beaujolais 103 C/D2
Vaux-le-Vicomte 87 D2
Vávdos 144 A2
Våversunda 46 A2
Vaxholm 47 D1
Växjö 51 C1
Växjö 72 A1
Våxtorp 50 A2
Våylä 8 B3
Väylänpää 17 D1
Vayrac 109 D1
Väyrylä 19 C3
Väystäjä 12 A3, 17 D2
Vazzola 107 D3
Vean 32 B2
Veberöd 50 B3
Veblungsnes 32 A/B3
Vebomark 31 D1
Vebron 110 B2
Vechelde 69 B/C3
Vechta 67 D2, 68 A2
Vechta-Langförden 67 D2, 68 A2
Vecinos 159 D2
Veckholm 47 C1
Vecsés 95 D3, 129 C1
Vedavågen 42 A2
Vedbæk 49 D3, 50 A3, 53 D1
Vedde 49 C3, 53 C/D1
Veddige 49 D1, 50 A1
Vedelago 107 C3
Vederslöv 51 C2
Vedeseta 106 A2/3
Vedevåg 46 A/B1
Vedra 150 A2
Vedum 45 C3
Veendam 67 C1/2
Veenhuizen 67 C2
Veere 78 B1
Vegacervera 151 D2, 152 A2
Vega de Espinareda 151 C2
Vega de Infanzones 151 D2, 152 A2
Vega de Pas 153 B/C1
Vega de Tera 151 D3
Vega de Valcarce 151 C2
Vega de Valdetronco 152 A3, 160 A1
Veganzones 160 B1/2
Vegaquemada 152 A2
Vegarienza 151 D2
Vegårshei 43 C2
Vegas de Matute 160 B2
Vegasetra 33 B/C3
Vegby 45 D3

Vegger 48 B2
Veggli 43 C1
Veghel 66 B3, 79 C1
Véglie 121 D3
Veguillas 161 C2
Vegusdal 43 C3
Vehanen 24 A2
Vehkajärvi 25 C1, 26 A1
Vehkalahti 25 D1, 26 B1
Vehkaperä 21 C2
Vehkasalo 25 D1, 26 A1
Vehkataipale 27 C2
Vehlow 69 D2
Vehmaa 24 A2
Vehmalainen 24 B2
Vehmasjärvi 22 B1
Vehmasmäki 22 B2/3
Vehmersalmi 23 B/C2
Vehniä 21 D3, 22 A3
Vehu 21 C2/3
Vehuvarpe 24 B1
Veidholmen 32 B1
Veidnesklubben 6 B1
Veigy-Foncenex 104 A2
Veihtivaara 19 D3
Veikars 20 A/B2
Veikkola 25 C3
Veimo 28 B2, 33 D1
Veines 7 C1
Veinge 50 A2
Veio 118 B2
Veiros 165 C2
Veitsch 94 C3
Veitservasa 11 D3, 12 A1/2
Veitshöchheim 81 C/D3
Veitsiluoto 17 D3, 18 A1
Veitsivuoma 12 A2, 17 D1
Vejano 118 A1
Vejbystrand 49 D2, 50 A2
Vejen 48 B3, 52 A1
Vejer de la Frontera 171 D3
Vejers Strand 48 A3, 52 A1
Vejle 48 B3, 52 B1
Vejprty 83 B/C2
Vejrup 48 A3, 52 A1
Vejstrup 53 C2
Vejti 128 B3
Vekara 27 C1
Vekšino 75 C2
Vekso 49 D3, 50 A3, 53 D1
Velaatta 25 C1
Velada 160 A3
Velagici 131 D2
Velaine 79 B/C2
Vela Luka 136 A1
Velanda 45 C3
Velanidiá 146 A1
Velaóra 146 A/B1
Velayos 160 A/B2
Velbert 80 A1
Velbert-Langenberg 80 A1
Velburg 92 A1
Velburg-Prönsdorf 92 A1
Veldemelen 28 B2
Velden 79 D1
Velden 92 B2
Velden 82 A3
Velden am Wörthersee 126 B2
Veldwezelt 79 C2
Veldzigt 78 B1
Velefique 173 C2
Velemér 127 D1
Velen 67 C3
Velence 129 B/C1
Velen-Ramsdorf 67 C3
Velešín 93 C2
Velešta 138 A/B3, 142 B1
Velestínon 143 D3
Vélez Blanco 174 A1
Vélez de Benaudalla 173 C2
Vélez Málaga 172 B2
Vélez Rubio 174 A1
Vélia 120 A3
Veličani 137 B/C1
Velika 128 A/B3
Velika Gorica 127 D3
Velika Greda 134 B1
Velika Ilova 132 A1
Velika Ivanča 133 D2, 134 A/B2
Velika Kladuša 127 D3, 131 C1
Velika Kopanica 132 B1
Velika Kopašnica 139 C1
Velika Kruša 138 A/B2
Velika Mučna 128 A2

Velika Pisanica 128 A3
Velika Plana 134 B2
Velika Sablanica 138 A1
Velike Bonjince 139 C1
Velike Lašče 127 B/C3
Veliki Bastaji 128 A3
Velikie Luki 75 B/C2
Veliki Gaj 134 B1
Veliki Grđevac 128 A3
Veliki Izvor 135 C2/3
Veliki Popović 134 B2
Veliki Prolog 131 D3,
    132 A3, 136 B1
Veliki Radić 131 C1
Veliki Radinci 133 C1,
    134 A1
Veliki Zaton 137 C1
Veliki Zdenci 128 A3
Veliko Crniće 134 B2
Veliko Gradište 134 B1
Veliko Gradište 140 A2
Veliko Orašje 134 B2
Velikoploskoe 141 D1
Veliko Selo 134 B2
Veliko Središte 134 B1
Veliko Târnovo 141 C3
Veliko Trgovišče 127 D2
Velilla de Cinca 155 C3,
    163 C1
Velilla de Ebro 162 B1
Velilla de Guardo 152 A2
Velilla de los Ajos 161 D1
Velilla de Medinaceli
    161 D1/2
Velilla de San Esteban
    153 C3, 161 C1
Veli Lošinj 130 A/B2
Velingrad 140 B3
Veliž 75 C3
Veljun 127 C3, 131 C1
Velká Bíteš 94 B1
Velká Černoc 83 C2/3
Velká Dobrá 83 C3
Velká Hleďsebe 82 B3
Vel'ká Mača 95 C2
Vel'ká Maňa 95 C2
Velká nad Veličkou 95 C1/2
Velké Bílovice 94 B1/2
Vel'ké Bošany 95 C2
Velké Březno 83 C2
Velké-Hleďsebe 82 B3
Vel'ké Kapušany 97 C/D2,
    98 A3
Velké Karlovice 95 C1
Vel'ké Kostol'any 95 C2
Vel'ké Leváre 94 B2
Vel'ké Ludince 95 D3
Velké Meziříčí 94 A1
Velké Meziříčí 96 A/B2
Velké Němčice 96 B2
Velké Němčice 94 B1
Velké Pavlovice 94 B1
Vel'ké Pole 95 D2
Velké Přílepy 83 D3
Vel'ké Ripňany 95 C2
Vel'ké Rovné 95 D1
Vel'ké Zálužie 95 C2
Velké Žernoseky 83 C2
Velkua 24 A2/3
Velkuanmaa 24 A2/3
Velký Bor 93 C1
Vel'ký Krtíš 95 D2
Vellahn 69 C1
Vellberg 91 C1
Velleia 114 A1
Velles 101 D1, 102 A1
Velletri 118 B2
Vellevans 89 D3, 104 B1
Vellinge 50 A3
Vellinge 72 A2
Vellisca 161 C3
Velliza 152 A3, 160 A1
Velo Veronese 107 C3
Velpke 69 C2/3
Velsen 66 A2
Velsvik 36 A1
Velta 38 B2
Velten 70 A2
Veltrusy 83 C/D2
Velvary 83 C/D2
Velvendós 143 C2
Vemb 48 A2
Vemdalen 34 B3
Vemdalsskalet 34 B3
Véménd 128 B2
Vemhån 34 B3
Vemmenæs 53 C2

Vemundvik 28 B2
Vena 46 B3
Venabygd 37 D2
Venaco 113 D3
Venafro 119 C2
Venäjä 24 B2
Venarey-les-Laumes 88 B3
Venaría 112 B1
Venarotta 117 D3
Venasca 112 B1/2
Venas di Cadore 107 D2
Venåsen 37 D2
Venasque 111 D2
Venåsseter 37 D2
Venčane 133 D2, 134 A2
Vence 112 B3
Venda Nova 150 B3,
    158 B1
Vendargues 110 B2/3
Vendas Novas 164 B2
Vendays 100 B3
Vendel 40 B3
Vendelsund 14 A3, 28 B1
Vendeuvre-du-Poitou
    101 C1
Vendeuvre-sur-Barse 88 B2
Vendôme 87 B/C3
Veneheitto 18 B3
Venejärvi 12 A2
Venejärvi 12 B3
Venejoki 23 C/D2
Venekoski 21 D3, 22 A3
Vénès 110 A2
Venesjärvi 24 B1
Veneskoski 24 B1
Veneskoski 20 B2
Venetmäki 22 B3
Venetpalo 21 D1, 22 A1
Venetti 12 A2, 17 D1
Venézia 107 D3
Venézia-Alberoni 107 D3
Venézia-Burano 107 D3
Venézia-Cavallino 107 D3
Venézia Fusina 107 D3
Venézia-Lido 107 D3
Venézia-Malamocco
    107 D3
Venézia-Mestre 107 D3
Venézia-Murano 107 D3
Venézia-Pellestrina 107 D3
Venézia-Punta Sabbioni
    107 D3
Venézia-San Pietro in Volta
    107 D3
Vengsøy 4 A2
Venialbo 159 D1
Venjan 39 C2
Venlo 79 D1
Venna 145 C/D1
Vennesla 43 C3
Venngarn 40 B3, 47 C1
Venosa 120 B2
Venraij 79 D1
Vent 106 B1
Venta de Arraco 108 A3,
    154 B1/2
Venta de Baños 152 B3
Venta del Baúl 173 D1/2
Venta del Charco 167 C3
Venta del Moro 169 D1
Venta de Zuriza 154 B2
Ventälä 20 B2
Ventanilla 152 B2
Ventanueva 151 C1/2
Ventas de Huelma 173 C2
Ventas de Zafarraya 172 B2
Ventimíglia 112 B2/3
Ventnor 76 B2
Ventosa 164 A2
Ventosa de la Sierra 153 D2
Ventosa del Río Almar
    159 D2, 160 A2
Ventosa de Pisuerga
    152 B2
Ventoténe 119 C3
Ventrosa 153 C/D3
Ventry 55 C3
Ventspils 73 C1
Venturina 114 B3, 116 A2
Venzone 126 A2
Veolia 37 C/D2
Vép 127 D1, 128 A1
Veprovac 129 C3
Vepsä 18 B2
Vepsä 23 C1
Vera 28 B3, 33 D1, 34 A1
Vera 129 C3

Vera 174 A2
Vera Cruz de Marmelar
    165 C3
Vera de Bidasoa 108 A3,
    154 A1
Vera de Moncayo 154 A3,
    162 A1
Verbánia 105 D2/3
Verbas 142 A2
Verberie 87 D1
Verbicaro 122 A1
Verbier [Le Châble] 104 B2
Vercelli 105 C/D3
Vercel-Villedieu 89 D3,
    104 A/B1
Verchen 70 A1
Verdaches 112 A2
Verdalsøra 28 B3, 33 D1
Verdello 106 A3
Verden 68 A/B2
Verden-Dauelsen 68 A/B2
Verdens Ende 43 D2,
    44 B1/2
Verdikoússa 143 C3
Verdonnet 88 B3
Verdú 155 C3, 163 C1
Verdun-sur-Garonne
    108 B2
Verdun-sur-le-Doubs
    103 D1
Verdun-sur-Meuse 89 C1
Verea 150 B3
Vereja 75 D3
Veresegyház 95 D3
Verfeil 109 D2/3
Vergato 114 B2, 116 B1
Vergel 169 D2
Vergeleto [Ponte Brolla]
    105 D2
Verges 156 B2
Vergiate 105 D3
Vergína 143 D2
Vergons 112 A2
Vergt 109 C1
Verhnedvinsk 74 B2/3
Verhovina 97 D2, 98 B3
Vería 148 B1
Vería 143 D2
Verín 115 B/C3
Veringenstadt 91 C2
Verkenseter 33 C3, 37 D1
Verket 38 A3, 43 D1, 44 B1
Verl 68 A3
Verla 26 B2
Verma 32 B3, 37 C1
Vermala (Montana) [Mon-
    tana-Vermala] 105 C2
Vermand 78 A3
Vermenton 88 A3
Vermíglio 106 B2
Vermiosa 159 C2
Vermiol 158 A3, 164 A/B1
Vermoim 158 A1
Vermosh 137 D1/2
Vermuntila 24 A2
Vernantes 86 A/B3
Vernasca 114 A1
Vernazza 114 A2
Vern-d'Anjou 86 A3
Verneřice 83 D2
Vernet 109 D3, 155 D1
Vernet-les-Bains 156 A/B2
Verneuil 88 A1
Verneuil-sur-Avre 86 B1/2
Vérnio 114 B2, 116 B1
Verniolle 109 D3, 155 D1,
    156 A1
Vérnole 121 D3
Vernon 87 C1
Vernou-en-Sologne 87 C3
Vernoux-en-Vivarais
    111 C1
Verny 89 C1
Verőcemaros 95 D3
Verolanuova 106 B3
Verolengo 105 C3, 113 C1
Véroli 119 C2
Verona 107 B/C3
Verrabotn 28 A3, 33 C1
Verran 28 B2/3, 33 D1
Verrastrand 28 A/B2/3,
    33 C/D1
Verrès 105 C3
Verrey-sous-Salmaise
    88 B3
Verride 158 A3
Verrière 109 C1

Verrières 101 C2
Verrières, Les 104 B1
Verrone 105 C3
Vers 109 D1
Versailles 87 C1
Versam [Versam-Safien]
    105 D1, 106 A1
Versmold 67 D3
Versmold-Peckeloh 67 D3
Versoix 104 A2
Ver-sur-Mer 76 B3, 86 A1
Verteillac 101 C3
Vértesacsa 95 D3, 128 B1
Vértesboglár 95 D3,
    128 B1
Verteuil-d'Agenais
    109 C1/2
Vertheuil 100 B3
Vertijevka 99 D2
Vertus 88 A1
Verúcchio 115 C2, 117 C1
Verum 50 B2
Verveln 46 B3
Verviers 79 D2
Vervins 78 B3
Verwood 63 D2, 76 A1
Veržej 127 D2
Verzino 122 B1/2
Verzuolo 112 B1
Vesajärvi 24 B1
Vesala 18 B2
Vešala 138 B2
Vesamäki 22 A/B2
Vesanka 21 D3, 22 A3
Vesanto 21 D2, 22 A2
Vescovato 106 B3
Vése 128 A2
Ves'egonsk 75 D1
Veselí nad Lužnicí 93 D1
Veselí nad Moravou 95 C1
Vésenaz [Genève] 104 A2
Vesijärvi 20 A3
Vesilahti 25 C1
Vésio 106 B3
Vesivehmaa 25 D2, 26 A2
Veskoniemi 6 B3
Vesmajärvi 11 D3, 12 A/B2
Vesoul 89 C3
Vespolate 105 D3
Vessigebro 49 D1/2, 50 A1
Vestby 38 A3, 44 B1
Vestby 38 A3
Vestbygd 9 C2
Vestenanova 107 C3
Vesterby 48 B1
Vester Egesborg 53 D2
Vester Hassing 48 B1
Vesterø Havn 49 C1
Vestertana 6 B1
Vester Torup 48 B1
Vester Vedsted 52 A1
Vestervig 48 A2
Vestfossen 43 D1, 44 A1
Vestmanna 55 C1
Vestmarka 38 B3
Vestnes 9 C1
Vestnes (Helland) 32 A2/3
Vestola 24 B1
Vestone 106 B3
Vestra Harg 46 A/B2
Vestra Malmagen 33 D2
Vestra Torsås 51 B/C2
Vestra Torup 50 B2
Vestre Gausdal 37 D2
Vestre Jakobselv 7 C2
Vestvågen 14 A2
Veszprém 128 B1
Veszprém 96 B3
Veszprémvarsány 95 C3,
    128 B1
Veteli-Kainu 21 C1/2
Veteren 37 D3
Vétheuil 87 C1
Vetlanda 48 A3, 51 C1
Vetlanda 72 A/B1
Vetlefjord 36 B2
Vetovo 141 C2
Vetralla 117 B/C3, 118 A1
Vetrino 141 C3
Větrný Jeníkov 94 A1
Vetschau 70 B3
Vetsikko 6 B2
Vette 44 B2
Vettelschoss 80 A2
Vetti 37 C2
Vetto 114 A1/2
Vetto 114 A1/2
Vettweiss 79 D2, 80 A2

Veules-les-Roses 77 C2/3
Veulettes-sur-Mer 77 C3
Veum 43 C2
Veurne 78 A1
Veuves 87 B/C3
Vevelstad 14 A3
Vevey 104 B2
Vévi 143 C1/2
Vevring 36 A2
Vexala 20 B1/2
Veynes 111 D1, 112 A1/2
Veyre-Monton 102 B3
Vez 87 D1
Vezdemarbán 152 A3,
    159 D1, 160 A1
Vézelay 88 A3
Vézelise 89 C2
Vézenobres 111 C2
Vezins 100 B1
Vezins-de-Levezou 110 A2
Vezza d'Óglio 106 B2
Vezzani 113 D3
Vezzano 107 B/C2
Vezzano sul Cróstolo
    114 B1
Vi 35 D3
Viadana 114 B1
Viade de Baixo 150 B3,
    158 B1
Viadotto Itália 120 B3,
    122 A1
Viaduc de Garabit 110 B1
Viaduc des Fades 102 B2
Viaduc du Viaur 110 A2
Viais 100 A1
Viana de Cega 152 A/B3,
    160 A1
Viana do Alentejo 164 B3
Viana do Bolo 151 C3
Viana do Castelo 150 A3,
    158 A1
Viandar de la Vera 159 D3
Vianden 79 D3
Viane 110 A2
Vianen 66 B3
Vianta 22 B2
Viantie 17 D3, 18 A1
Viaréggio 114 A2, 116 A1
Viarouge 110 A2
Vias 110 B3
Viasvesi 24 A1
Viator 173 D2
Vibo Marina 122 A2
Viborg 48 B2
Vibo Valéntia 122 A2
Vibraye 86 B2
Viby 49 D3, 50 A3, 53 D1
Viby 48 B1
Vic 156 A2
Vič 127 C2
Vicar 173 D2
Vicarello 114 A/B3, 116 A2
Vícari 124 B2
Vícchio 115 B/C2, 116 B1
Vicdessos 155 D2, 156 A1
Vicedo 150 B1
Vic-en-Bigorre 108 B3,
    155 C1
Vicenza 107 C3
Vic-Fézensac 109 C2
Vichtenstein 93 C2
Vichy 102 B2
Vickan 49 D1, 50 A1
Vickleby 51 D2
Vic-le-Comte 102 B3
Vic-le-Fesq 111 C2
Vico 113 D3
Vico del Gargano 120 B1
Vico Equense 119 D3
Vicovaro 118 B2
Vic-sur-Cère 110 A1
Victoria 104 B1/2
Vidago 150 B3, 158 B1
Vidais 164 A1
Vidángoz 154 B2
Vidauban 112 A3
Vida Vättern 46 A2/3
Viddal 32 A3, 36 B1
Vide 158 B3
Videbæk 48 A3
Videferre 150 B3, 158 B1
Videle 141 C3
Videm 127 C3
Videm 127 D2
Vidigueira 164 B3
Vidin 135 D2
Vidin 140 B2

Vidomja 73 D3, 98 A1
Vidor 107 C2/3
Vidrá 156 A2
Vidra 141 C1
Vidra 141 C2
Vidreres 156 B3
Vidsel 16 B2/3
Vidstrup 48 B1
Viduševac 127 D3, 131 C1
Vidzy 74 A3
Viechtach 92 B1
Vieillevigne 100 A/B1
Vieira 158 A3, 164 A1
Vieira 150 B3, 158 A/B1
Viejenäs 15 D2
Vieki 23 C1/2
Vielank 69 C1
Viella 108 B3, 155 B/C1
Viella 155 C/D2
Vielle-Brioude 102 B3
Vielmesmakke 29 D1
Vielmur-sur-Agout
  109 D2/3, 110 A2/3
Vielsalm 79 D2
Viels-Maisons 88 A1
Viemerö 20 B2
Vienand 28 B3, 33 D1
Vienenburg 69 C3
Vienne 103 D3
Viereck 70 B1
Vieremä 22 B1
Viereth-Trunstadt 81 D3
Vierhouten 66 B2/3
Vierlingsbeek 67 B/C3,
  79 D1
Viernheim 80 B3, 90 B1
Vierraden 70 B2
Viersen 79 D1
Vierville-sur-Mer 76 A/B3,
  86 A1
Vierzon 87 C3, 102 A1
Vieselbach 82 A1/2
Viesimo 23 D3
Viesīte 74 A2
Vieste 120 B1, 136 A2
Vietas turistanläggning
  9 D3
Vietgest 53 D3, 69 D1
Vietri di Potenza 120 A2
Vietri sul Mare 119 D3
Vieux-Boucau-les-Bains
  108 B2
Vieux-Genappe 78 B2
Vievis 73 D2, 74 A3
Vif 111 D1
Vig 49 C/D3, 53 C/D1
Viganj 136 B1
Vigarano Mainarda
  115 B/C1
Vigásio 106 B3
Vigeland 42 B3
Vigeois 101 D3
Vigévano 105 D3
Vigge 34 B2
Vigge 35 C/D3
Viggiano 120 B3
Viggiù 105 D2/3
Viglesdalshytta 42 A/B2
Vigmostad 42 B3
Vignale Monferrato 113 C1
Vignanello 117 C3,
  118 A/B1
Vigneulles-les-Hattonchâtel
  89 C1
Vignola 114 B1/2
Vignole 107 C/D2
Vignory 88 B2
Vigny 87 C1
Vigo 150 A2/3
Vigo di Cadore 107 D2
Vigo di Fassa 107 C2
Vígolo Vattaro 107 C2
Vigone 112 B1
Vigonza 107 C3
Vigo Rendena 106 B2
Vigrestad 42 A3
Vigsnæs 53 D2
Viguera 153 D2
Vigy 89 C/D1
Vihals 32 B1/2
Vihanninkylä 21 C2/3
Vihantasalmi 26 B1
Vihanti 18 A3
Vihiers 86 A3, 100 B1
Vihren 139 D2/3
Vihtajärvi 22 B2
Vihtalahti 21 D3, 22 A3

Vihtamo 19 C3
Vihtari 23 C3
Vihtasuo 23 C2
Vihtavuori 21 D3, 22 A3
Vihteljärvi 24 B1
Vihti 25 C3
Vihtijärvi 25 C2
Vii 22 B2
Viiala 25 C1/2
Viinamäki 23 B/C1
Viiniemi 23 D1
Viinijärvi 23 C3
Viinikka 20 B2
Viinikoski 18 B2
Viiperi 21 C1
Viirinkylä 12 B3
Viisarimäki 21 D3, 22 A3
Viitaila 25 D2, 26 A2
Viitajärvi 21 D2, 22 A2
Viitala 20 B2/3
Viitamäki 21 D1, 22 A/B1
Viitaniemi 23 C2
Viitapohja 25 C1
Viitaranta 19 C1
Viitasaari 21 D2, 22 A2
Viitavaara 19 C/D3
Viitavaara 19 D3
Vik 9 B/C2
Vik 14 A3, 28 B1
Vik 50 B3
Vik 40 B3
Vika 39 D2, 40 A2
Vika 28 B3, 33 D1
Vika 38 B1
Vika 33 D2
Vika 12 B3
Vikajärvi 12 B3
Vikan 32 B1/2
Vikane 44 B1
Vikanes 36 A3
Vikarbodarna 35 D3
Vikarbyn 39 D2
Vike 35 C2
Vike 36 A3
Vikebukt 32 A2/3
Vikebygd 42 A1
Vikedal 42 A1/2
Viken 49 D3, 50 A2
Viken 29 C1/2
Viken 35 C3
Viken (Ramsjö) 35 C3
Viker 46 A1
Viker 37 D3
Vikersund 43 D1
Vikeså 42 A3
Vikestad 14 A3, 28 B1
Vikevag 42 A1
Vikevåg 42 A2
Vikholmen 14 A2
Vikingstad 46 B2
Vikjo 42 A2
Vikmanshyttan 39 D2/3,
  40 A2/3
Vikna 28 B1
Viknel 15 C2
Vikran 9 C1
Vikran 4 A3
Viksdalen 36 A/B2
Viksjö 35 D2
Viksjöfors 39 D1, 40 A1
Viksmon 30 A/B3, 35 D2
Viksøyri 36 B2
Viksta 40 B3
Viktoriakyrkan 15 C3
Vila Alva 164 B3
Vilaboa 150 A2
Vila Boim 165 C2
Vilac 155 C/D2
Vila Chã 158 B1
Vila Cortez 158 B2
Vila Cova de Lixa 158 A/B1
Vilada 156 A2
Viladamat 156 B2
Viladecáns 156 A3
Vila de Estrela 158 B2
Vila de Frades 164 B3
Vila de Rei 158 A/B3,
  164 B1
Vila do Bispo 170 A2
Vila do Conde 158 A1
Viladrau 156 A/B2/3
Vila Fernando 159 C2
Vila Fernando 165 C2
Vila Flôr 159 C1
Vila Franca das Naves
  158 B2
Vila Franca de Xira 164 A2

Vilafranca del Penedès
  156 A3, 163 D1
Vilagarcia de Arousa
  150 A2
Vilaka 74 B2
Vila kapell 15 B/C2
Vilalba dels Arcs 163 C2
Vilaller 155 C2
Vilalonga de Ter 156 A2
Vilamaior 150 B1
Vilamarín 150 B2
Vilameá 151 C1
Vila Meã 158 A/B1
Vilamitjana 155 D2/3
Vilamós 155 C2
Vilamur 155 C2
Vilâni 74 A/B2
Vilank 19 D2/3
Vilanova d'Apicat 155 C3,
  163 C1
Vila Nova da Baronia
  164 B3
Vila Nova da Rainha 164 A2
Vila Nova da Paiva 158 B2
Vilanova de Bellpuig
  155 D3, 163 D1
Vila Nova de Cerveira
  150 A3
Vila Nova de Famalicão
  158 A1
Vila Nova de Gaia 158 A1/2
Vila Nova de Ourém
  158 A3, 164 B1
Vila Nova de Milfontes
  170 A1
Vila Nova de Foz Côa
  159 C2
Vilanova de la Barca
  155 C3, 163 C1
Vilanova de Sau 156 A/B2
Vilanova de les Avellanes
  155 C/D3
Vilanova de Meià 155 D3
Vilanova de L'Aguda
  155 C3
Vilanova de Arousa 150 A2
Vilanova i la Geltrú 156 A3,
  163 D1
Viladoriz 151 C1
Vilapouca 150 A/B2
Vila Pouca de Aguiar
  158 B1
Vila Praia de Ancora
  150 A3, 158 A1
Vilar 164 A2
Vilarandelo 151 C3, 158 B1
Vilar de Amargo 159 C2
Vilar de Barrio 150 B3
Vilar de Maçada 158 B1
Vilar de Santos 150 B3
Vilardevós 151 C3
Vilar do Paraíso 158 A2
Vilar d'Ossos 151 C3,
  159 C1
Vila Real 158 B1
Vila Real de Santo António
  170 B2
Vilares 158 B1
Vilar Formoso 159 C2
Vilarinho 158 A3
Vilarinho da Castanheira
  159 B/C1/2
Vilarinho das Axenhas
  159 B/C1
Vilarinho de Galegos
  159 C1
Vilarinho de Samardã
  158 B1
Vilarinho de Conso 151 C3
Vilarouco 158 B2
Vila Ruiva 164 B3
Vila-sacra 156 B2
Vilasantar 150 B1/2
Vila Sêca 158 A1
Vila Sêca 158 A3
Vilassar de Mar 156 A/B3
Vila Velha de Ródão
  158 B3, 165 C1
Vilaverd 163 C1
Vila Verde 151 B/C3,
  158 B1
Vila Verde 150 A3, 158 A1
Vila Verde de Ficalho
  165 C3, 170 B1
Vila Viçosa 165 C2
Vilches 167 D3
Vildbjerg 48 A2/3

Vilejka 74 A3
Vilgertshofen-Stadl 91 D3
Vilhelmina 30 A1
Vilia 147 D2
Vilikkala 24 B3
Viljakkala 24 B1
Vil'jandi 74 A1
Viljaniemi 25 D2, 26 A2
Viljevo 128 B3
Viljolahti 23 C3
Vilkija 73 D2
Vilkjärvi 27 C2
Villa Adriana 118 B2
Villabáñez 152 B3, 160 B1
Villa Bartolomea 107 C3,
  114 B1
Villabate 124 B2
Villablanca 170 B2
Villablino 151 D2
Villabrázaro 151 D3
Villacadima 161 C1
Villacañas 161 C3, 167 D1
Villa Carlotta 105 D2,
  106 A2
Villacarriedo 153 B/C1
Villacarrillo 167 D3, 168 A3
Villa Castelli 121 C2
Villacastín 160 B2
Villach 126 B2
Villach 96 A3
Villacid de Campos 152 A3
Villacidro 123 C3
Villaciervos 153 D3,
  161 D1
Villaconancio 152 B3
Villaconejos 161 C3
Villaconejos de Trabaque
  161 D2/3
Villada 152 A2/3
Villadangos del Páramo
  151 D2
Villa del Prado 160 B3
Villa del Rey 159 C3,
  165 C/D1
Villa del Río 167 C3,
  172 B1
Villadepera 151 D3,
  159 D1
Villa de Ves 169 D2
Villadiego 152 B2
Villadose 115 C1
Villadóssola 105 C2
Villaeles de Valdavia 152 B2
Villaescusa la Sombría
  153 C2
Villaescusa 159 D1, 160 A1
Villaescusa de Haro 168 A1
Villa Estense 107 C3,
  115 C1
Villaester 152 A3
Villafáfila 151 D3, 152 A3,
  159 D1
Villafamés 163 C3
Villafeliche 162 A1
Villafer 151 D3, 152 A3
Villaferrueña 151 D2
Villaflor 160 A2
Villaflores 160 A2
Villafrades de Campos
  152 A3
Villafranca del Cid 162 B2
Villafranca de los Barros
  165 D2, 166 A2
Villafranca del Bierzo
  151 C2
Villafranca del Campo
  163 C2
Villafranca de Ebro 154 B3,
  162 B1
Villafranca de Bon Any
  157 C2
Villafranca de Duero
  160 A1
Villafranca-Montes de Oca
  153 C2
Villafranca de Córdoba
  167 C3, 172 B1
Villafranca in Lunigiana
  114 A2
Villafranca Piemonte
  112 B1
Villafranca de los Caballeros
  167 D1
Villafranca di Verona
  106 B3
Villafranca 154 A2
Villafranca Tirrena 125 D1

Villafrati 124 B2
Villafrechos 152 A3
Villafruela 152 B3
Villafuerte 152 B3, 160 B1
Villafuertes 153 B/C3
Villagalijo 153 C2
Villagarcía de Campos
  152 A3, 160 A1
Villagarcía de la Torre
  165 D3, 166 A3
Villagarcía del Llano 168 B1
Villagatón 151 D2
Villággio Amêndola
  120 A/B1
Villággio di Capo Ferrato
  123 D3
Villággio Moschella 120 B2
Villággio Mancuso 122 B2
Villággio Turístico Ostuni
  Marina 121 D2
Villággio Turístico Capo Riz-
  zuto 122 B2
Villagómez la Nueva
  152 A3
Villagonzalo 165 D2,
  166 A2
Villagrains 108 B1
Villagrande Strisáili 123 D2
Villagrande 117 D3,
  119 B/C1
Villaharta 166 B3
Villáhíde 25 D2, 26 A2
Villahermosa 167 D2,
  168 A2
Villahermosa del Río
  162 B3
Villahizán de Treviño
  152 B2
Villahoz 152 B3
Villaines-en-Duesmois
  88 B3
Villaines-la-Juhel 86 A2
Villaines-les-Rochers
  86 B3, 101 C1
Villajoyosa 169 D2/3
Villala 23 C/D3
Villala 27 C3
Villalar de los Comuneros
  152 A3, 160 A1
Villalba 124 B2
Villalba 150 B1
Villalba Baja 162 A/B2
Villalba de los Barros
  165 D2
Villalba de la Lampreana
  151 D3, 152 A3, 159 D1
Villalba de la Sierra 161 D3
Villalba de los Alcores
  152 A3
Villalba de Guardo 152 A2
Villalba de los Llanos
  159 D2
Villalba de los Morales
  162 A2
Villalba del Alcor 171 C1/2
Villalba del Rey 161 D2/3
Villalcázar de Sirga 152 B2
Villalcón 152 A2
Villaldemiro 152 B2/3
Villalengua 154 A3,
  161 D1, 162 A1
Villalgordo del Jucar
  168 B1/2
Villalgordo del Marquesado
  161 D3, 168 A1
Villa Literno 119 C3
Villalobos 152 A3
Villalón de Campos 152 A3
Villalonga 169 D2
Villalpando 152 A3
Villalpardo 168 B1
Villalube 151 D3, 152 A3,
  159 D1, 160 A1
Villaluenga del Rosario
  172 A2
Villalumbroso 152 A/B3
Villálvaro 153 C3, 161 C1
Villalvérnia 113 D1
Villamalea 168 B1
Villamañán 151 D2, 152 A2
Villamanín 151 D2, 152 A2
Villamanrique 167 D2,
  168 A2
Villamanrique de la Condesa
  171 D2
Villamanrique de Tajo
  161 C3

Villamanta **160** B3
Villamar **123** C/D3
Villamarchante **169** C/D1
Villamartín **171** D2
Villamartín de Campos
152 B3
Villamartín de Don Sancho
152 A2
Villamartín de Valdeorras
151 C2
Villamassárgia **123** C3
Villamayor **159** D2
Villamayor de Santiago
161 C3, **167** D1, **168** A1
Villamayor de Calatrava
167 C2
Villamayor de Gállego
154 B3, **162** B1
Villambistia **153** C2
Villamblard **109** C1
Villamediana **153** D2
Villamejil **151** D2
Villameriel **152** B2
Villamesías **166** A1/2
Villamiel de la Sierra **153** C3
Villamiel de Toledo **160** B3,
167 C1
Villaminaya **160** B3,
167 C1
Villa Minozzo **114** A/B2,
116 A1
Villamizar **152** A2
Villamor de Cadozos
159 D1
Villamoronta **152** B2
Villamuelas **160** B3, **167** C1
Villamuriel de Campos
152 A3
Villamuriel de Cerrato
152 B3
Villa Napoleone **116** A3
Villandraut **108** B1/2
Villandry **86** B3
Villanova **121** C/D2
Villanova **112** B1
Villanova d'Asti **113** C1
Villanovafranca **123** C/D3
Villanova Monteleone
123 C2
Villanova Mondovì **113** C2
Villanova Strisáili **123** D2
Villanova Truschedu
123 C2
Villanova Tulo **123** D2
Villantério **105** D3, **106** A3,
113 D1
Villanúa **154** B2
Villanubla **152** A3, **160** A1
Villanueva **153** D2, **154** A2
Villanueva del Campo
152 A3
Villanueva de San Juan
172 A2
Villanueva de Gumiel
153 C3, **161** C1
Villanueva de Duero
152 A3, **160** A1
Villanueva de Gormaz
161 C1
Villanueva de Alcolea
163 C3
Villanueva de la Cañada
160 B2
Villanueva de Oscos **151** C1
Villanueva de Alcardete
161 C3, **167** D1, **168** A1
Villanueva de Castellón
169 D2
Villanueva de Cameros
153 D3
Villanueva del Arzobispo
167 D3, **168** A3
Villanueva de la Concepción
172 B2
Villanueva de San Carlos
167 C2
Villanueva de la Sierra
159 C3
Villanueva de Córdoba
167 B/C3
Villanueva del Duque
166 B3
Villanueva de Argaño
152 B2
Villanueva de los Infantes
167 D2, **168** A2
Villanueva de Viver **162** B3

Villanueva de los Castillejos
171 B/C1
Villanueva de Henares
152 B2
Villanueva de Gállego
154 B3, **162** B1
Villanueva de Guadamajud
161 D3
Villanueva de San Mancio
152 A3
Villanueva de la Fuente
168 A2
Villanueva del Río Segura
169 D3
Villanueva de Algaidas
172 B2
Villanueva de las Manzanas
151 D2, **152** A2
Villanueva de la Jara
168 B1
Villanueva de la Serena
166 A2
Villanueva de la Reina
167 C3, **173** B/C1
Villanueva de Bogas
161 B/C3, **167** C/D1
Villanueva de Alcorón
161 D2
Villanueva del Trabuco
172 B2
Villanueva de las Cruces
171 C1
Villanueva de Sigena
155 C3, **163** C1
Villanueva del Fresno
165 C3
Villanueva del Rey **166** B3
Villanueva del Río **171** D1
Villanueva de Tapia **172** B2
Villanueva del Aceral
160 A2
Villanueva de las Minas
171 D1
Villanueva del Huerva
162 A/B1
Villanueva de las Torres
173 C1
Villanueva del Pardillo
160 B2
Villanueva del Rosario
172 B2
Villa Nuova **115** C2,
117 C1
Villány **128** B3
Villa Opicina **126** B3
Villapalacios **168** A2
Villapiana Lido **120** B3,
122 B1
Villa Potenza **115** D3,
117 D2
Villaputzu **123** D3
Villaquejida **151** D3,
152 A3
Villaquilambre **151** D2,
152 A2
Villaralto **166** B3
Villarcayo **153** C2
Villard-Bonnot **104** A3,
112 A1
Villard-de-Lans **103** D3,
111 D1
Villardebelle **110** A3,
156 A/B1
Villar de Canes **163** C2/3
Villar de Cañas **161** D3,
168 A1
Villar de Chinchilla
169 B/C2
Villar de Ciervo **159** C2
Villardeciervos **151** D3
Villar de Cobeta **161** D2
Villar de Domingo García
161 D3
Villardefrades **152** A3,
160 A1
Villar de Gallimazo **160** A2
Villar de Horno **161** D3
Villar de la Encina **161** D3,
168 A1
Villar del Águila **161** D3
Villar del Arzobispo **162** B3,
169 C1
Villar de la Yegua **159** C2
Villar del Buey **159** D1
Villar del Cobo **162** A2/3
Villar del Humo **162** A3,
168 B1

Villar del Infantado **161** D2
Villar de los Navarros
162 A/B1/2
Villar del Olmo **161** C3
Villar del Pedroso **160** A3,
166 B1
Villar del Rey **165** C/D2
Villar del Río **153** D3
Villar del Salz **162** A2
Villar del Saz de Navalón
161 D3
Villar de Maya **153** D3
Villar de Peralonso
159 C/D2
Villar de Rena **166** A2
Villárdiga **152** A3, **159** D1,
160 A1
Villardompardo **167** C3,
172 B1
Villarejo de Fuentes
161 D3, **168** A1
Villarejo de Medina **161** D2
Villarejo de Salvanés
161 C3
Villarejo de Montalbán
160 A/B3, **167** B/C1
Villa Rendena **106** B2
Villarente **152** A2
Villares de Yeltes **159** C2
Villares del Saz **161** D3,
168 A1
Villaretto **112** B1
Villargordo del Cabriel
169 C1
Villargordo **167** C3, **173** C1
Villarino **159** C1
Villarluengo **162** B2
Villarmayor **159** D2
Villarmuerto **159** C2
Villa Romana del Casale
125 C2/3
Villarosa **125** C2
Villar Perosa **112** B1
Villarquemado **163** C2
Villarramiel **152** A3
Villarrasa **171** C1/2
Villarreal **165** C2
Villarreal de San Carlos
159 D3, **165** D1, **166** A1
Villarreal de los Infantes
163 B/C3, **169** D1
Villarreal de la Canal **154** B2
Villarrín de Campos
151 D3, **152** A3, **159** D1
Villarrobledo **168** A1/2
Villarroga de los Pinares
162 B2
Villarroya **153** D3
Villarroya de la Sierra
154 A3, **162** A1
Villarrubia de los Ojos
167 D2
Villarrubia de Santiago
161 C3
Villarrubio **161** C3
Villars-lès-Blamont **89** D3,
90 A3, **104** B1
Villars-les-Dombes **103** D2
Villars-sur-Ollon **104** B2
Villarta **168** B1
Villarta de los Montes
166 B2
Villarta de San Juan **167** D2
Villasalto **123** D3
Villasana de Mena **153** C1
Villasandino **152** B2
Villa San Giovanni **122** A3,
125 D1
Villa Santa Maria **119** D2
Villa Sant'António **117** D2
Villasante **153** C1/2
Villa Santina **107** D2,
126 A2
Villasayas **161** D1
Villasbuenas de Gata
159 C3
Villaseca de la Sagra
160 B3, **167** C1
Villaseca de Arciel **153** D3,
161 D1
Villaseco de los Gamitos
159 D2
Villaseco de los Reyes
159 D1/2
Villasequilla de Yepes
160 B3, **167** C1
Villasilos **152** B2

Villasimíus **123** D3
Villasmundo **125** D3
Villasor **123** C/D3
Villasrubias **159** C3
Villastar **163** C3
Villastellone **113** B/C1
Villa Superiore **114** B1
Villasur de Herreros **153** C2
Villatobas **161** C3, **167** D1
Villatoro **160** A2
Villatoya **169** D1
Villatuerta **153** D2, **154** A2
Villaurbana **123** C2
Villava **154** A2
Villavaliente **169** B/C2
Villavallelonga **119** C2
Villavelayo **153** C3
Villavendimio **152** A3,
159 D1, **160** A1
Villaverde **161** B/C2/3
Villaverde de Iscar **160** A2
Villaverde de Guadalimar
168 A2/3
Villaverde del Río **171** D1
Villaverde del Ducado
161 D2
Villaverde de Arcayos
152 A2
Villaverde de Trucíos
153 C1
Villaverde de Medina
160 A1
Villaverde y Pasaconsol
161 D3, **168** B1
Villavicencio de los Caballe-
ros **152** A3
Villaviciosa de Córdoba
166 B3, **172** A1
Villaviciosa **152** A1
Villaviciosa de la Ribera
151 D2
Villaviciosa de Odón
160 B2/3
Villavieja **162** B3, **169** D1
Villavieja del Lozoya
161 B/C2
Villavieja de Yeltes **159** C2
Villaviudas **152** B3
Villa Vomano **117** D3,
119 C1
Villayón **151** C1
Villdalsseter **38** A/B1
Villé **89** D2, **90** A2
Villebaudon **86** A1
Villebois-Lavalette **101** C3
Villebret **102** B2
Villechenève **103** C2/3
Villecomtal-sur-Arros
109 B/C3, **155** C1
Villecomtal **110** A1
Villedaigne **110** A3, **156** B1
Villedieu-les-Poëles
86 A/B1
Villedieu-sur-Indre **101** D1,
102 A1
Villedômain **101** C1
Villedoux **100** B2
Ville-en-Tardenois **88** A1
Villefagnan **101** C2
Villefort **110** B1/2
Villefranche-de-Lauragais
109 D3, **155** D1
Villefranche de Longchat
108 B1
Villefranche-de-Rouergue
109 D2
Villefranche-du-Périgord
109 C1
Villefranche-de-Conflent
156 A/B1/2
Villefranche-Saint-Phal
87 D2, **88** A2
Villefranche **109** C3,
155 C1
Villefranche **102** B2
Villefranche-de-Panat
110 A2
Villefranche-d'Albigeois
110 A2
Villefranche-sur-Cher
87 C3
Villefranche-sur-Saône
103 D2
Villegas **152** B2
Villegly **110** A3, **156** B1
Villel **163** C3
Villel de Mesa **161** D1/2

Villemaur-sur-Vanne **88** A2
Villemontais **103** C2
Villemorien **88** B2
Villemur-sur-Tarn **109** D2
Villena **169** C2
Villenauxe la Grande **88** A2
Villenave **108** A/B2
Villeneuve **109** D1/2
Villeneuve **104** B3
Villeneuve **104** B2
Villeneuve-de-Berg **111** C1
Villeneuve-de-Marsan
108 A2
Villeneuve-lès-Avignon
111 C2
Villeneuve-la-Guyard
87 D2
Villeneuve-l'Archevêque
88 A2
Villeneuve-les-Bordes
87 D2
Villeneuve-sur-Lot **109** C2
Villeneuve-Saint-Georges
87 D1
Villeneuve-sur-Tarn **110** A2
Villeneuve-Saint-Martin
87 C1
Villeneuve-sur-Yonne
88 A2
Villeneuve-sur-Allier
102 B1
Villeneuve-sur-Vère **109** D2
Villentrois **87** C3, **101** D1
Villepinte **109** D3, **156** A1
Villequier-Aumont **78** A3
Villeréal **109** C2
Villerías **152** A3
Villeromain **86** A/B3
Villerouge-Termenès
110 A3, **156** B1
Villers-Bocage **86** A1
Villers-Bocage **77** D2
Villers-Bretonneux **78** A3
Villers-Carbonnel **78** A3
Villers-Cotterêts **87** D1,
88 A1
Villers-devant-Orval **79** C3
Villersexel **89** D3
Villers-la-Montagne **79** D3
Villers-la-Ville **79** B/C2
Villers-sur-Mer **76** B3,
86 A/B1
Villers-sur-Meuse **89** C1
Villerville **76** B3, **86** B1
Villesèque **108** B2
Villes-sur-Auzon **111** D2
Ville-sur-Illon **89** C2
Ville-sur-Tourbe **88** B1
Villevalier **88** A2
Villeveyrac **110** B3
Ville-Vieille **112** B1
Villiers-Charlemagne
86 A2/3
Villiers-Saint-Georges
88 A2
Villiers-Saint-Benoît **87** D3,
88 A3
Villikkala **26** B2
Villimpenta **107** B/C3,
114 B1
Villingen-Schwenningen
90 B3
Villingsberg **46** A1
Villmanstrand **27** C2
Villmar-Aumenau **80** B2
Villmergen **90** B3, **105** C1
Villoldo **152** B2
Villora **162** A3, **168** B1
Villores **162** B2
Villoría **159** D2, **160** A2
Villoslada de Cameros
153 D3
Villotta **107** D2/3,
126 A2/3
Villovela de Pirón **160** B1/2
Villshärad **49** D2, **50** A2
Vilmikkala **21** D2, **22** A2
Vilnius **73** D2, **74** A3
Vilpiano/Vilpian **107** C2
Vilppula **21** C3
Vils **48** A2
Vils **91** D3
Vilsbiburg **92** B2
Vilsbiburg-Wolferding
92 B2
Vilseck **82** A3
Vilshofen **93** C2

Vilshult 51 B/C2
Vilslev 52 A1
Vilsund 48 A2
Vilusi 137 C1
Vilvoorde 78 B1/2
Vimbodí 163 D1
Vimianzo 150 A1
Vimieiro 164 B2
Vimioso 151 C3, 159 C1
Vimmerby 46 B3
Vimmerby 72 B1
Vimoutiers 86 B1
Vimpeli (Vindala) 21 C2
Vimperk 93 C1
Vimperk 96 A2
Vinac 131 D2, 132 A2
Vinaceite 162 B1
Vinádio 112 B2
Vinadi [Scuol-Tarasp] 106 B1
Vinaixa 155 D3, 163 D1
Vinaroz 163 C2
Vinäs 39 C/D2
Vinay 103 D3
Vinca 156 B1/2
Vinča 133 D1, 134 A/B1
Vincelles 88 A3
Vinchiaturo 119 D2
Vinci 114 B2, 116 A1/2
Vinciarello 122 B3
Vindala 21 C2
Vindelkroken 15 C2
Vindeln 31 C2
Vinderup 48 A2
Vindsvik 42 A/B2
Vinebre 163 C1/2
Viñegra de Moraña 160 A2
Vines 36 B3
Vinga 44 B3, 49 C1
Vingåker 46 B1
Vingelen 33 C/D3
Vingen 36 A1
Vingrau 156 B1
Vingstad 4 A3, 10 A1
Vinhais 151 C3, 159 C1
Vinica 95 D2
Vinica 139 C2
Vinica 127 C3
Viniegra de Arriba 153 C/D3
Viniegra de Abajo 153 C3
Vinišče 131 C3
Vinište 135 D3
Vinje 43 B/C1
Vinje 36 B3
Vinje 8 B2
Vinje 9 D1
Vinjeøra 32 B2
Vînju Mare 135 D2
Vînju Mare 140 B2
Vinkiä 25 C1, 26 A1
Vinkkilä 24 A2
Vinkovci 129 C3, 133 C1
Vinliden 30 B1
Vinne 28 B3, 33 D1
Vinni 21 C2
Vinnica 99 C3
Vinogradov 97 D2/3, 98 A3
Vinon 47 D2
Vinon-sur-Verdon 111 D2, 112 A2/3
Vinsa 77 C1
Vinslöv 50 B2
Vinsternes 32 B2
Vinstra 37 D2
Vintervollen 7 D2
Vintjärn 40 A2
Vintrosa 46 A1
Viñuela 172 B2
Viñuela 167 C2
Viñuela de Sayago 159 D1
Viñuelas 161 C2
Vinuesa 153 D3
Vipava 126 B3
Vipiteno/Sterzing 107 C1
Vir 130 B2
Vira 131 C3, 136 A1
Virdois 21 C3
Vire 85 D1, 86 A1
Vireda 46 A3
Virenoja 25 D2, 26 A2
Vireši 74 A2
Virestad 50 B2
Vireux-Molhain 79 C3

Vîrfurile 97 D3, 140 B1
Virginia 54 A3, 55 D2
Virieu-le-Grand 104 A3
Virieu-sur-Bourbre 103 D3, 104 A3
Virine 134 B2
Virisen 15 C3
Virje 128 A2
Virkkala/Virkby 25 C3
Virkkula 19 C1
Virkkunen 19 C1
Virklund 48 B3
Virksund 48 B3, 52 B1
Virmaanpää 22 B2
Virmaila 25 D1, 26 A1
Virmutjoki 27 C1
Virojoki 27 C2
Virolahti 27 C2
Virovitica 128 A3
Virpazar 137 D2
Virpiniemi 18 A2
Virranniemi 13 C3
Virrat (Virdois) 21 C3
Virsbo 40 A3
Virserum 51 C1
Virtaa 25 D1, 26 A1
Virtala 21 C2
Virtaniemi 7 C3
Virton 79 C3
Vîrtopu 135 D2
Virtsu 74 A1
Virttaa 24 B2
Vis 138 A1
Vişagu 97 D3, 140 B1
Visala 19 C1
Visan 111 C2
Visbek 67 D2, 68 A2
Visby 47 D2/3
Visby 72 B1
Visé 79 C/D2
Visegrád 95 D3
Višegrad 133 C3
Višegradska Banja 133 C2/3
Viseu 158 B2
Vişeul de Sus 97 D3, 98 A/B3
Višići 136 B1
Visiedo 162 A/B2
Visingsö 45 D3, 46 A3
Viskafors 45 C3, 49 D1
Viskan 35 C3
Viskinge 49 C3, 53 C1
Vislanda 51 B/C2
Vislanda 72 A1
Visnes 42 A2
Višnja Gora 127 C2/3
Višnjan 126 B3, 130 A1
Višnjica 127 D2
Višňové 94 A/B1
Visnums-Kil 45 D1, 46 A1
Viso del Marqués 167 D2/3
Visoka 133 D3, 134 A3
Visoki Dečani 138 A1/2
Visoko 132 B2
Visone 113 C1
Visp 105 C2
Viš Revúca 95 D1
Vissefjärda 51 C2
Vissefjärda 72 B1
Visselhövede-Wittorf 68 B2
Visselhövede 68 B2
Vissinéa 143 C2
Vissiniá 143 C2
Visso 115 D3, 117 D2/3
Vissoie [Sierre] 105 C2
Vistabella 163 C1
Vistabella del Maestrazgo 162 B3
Vistasstugan 9 D2/3
Vistdal 32 B2
Vistheden 16 B3
Visthus 14 A3
Vistnes 14 A3
Vistoft 49 C2/3
Visuvesi 21 C3
Visz 128 B1/2
Vita 124 A2
Vitáfors 17 C2
Vitakylä 21 D2, 22 A2
Vitanen 18 B3
Vitanje 127 C2
Vitanovac 134 B3
Vitebsk 74 B3
Viteml'a 99 D1
Vitemölla 50 B3
Viterbo 117 C3, 118 A1

Vitez 132 B2
Vithkuqi 142 B2
Vitigudino 159 C2
Vitina 138 B2
Vitina 146 B3
Vitina 132 A3, 136 B1
Vitis 93 D2, 94 A2
Vitis 96 A2
Vitlycke 44 B2
Vitna 74 A1
Vitolište 139 C3, 143 C1
Vitomirica 138 A1
Vitoševac 135 B/C3
Vitovlje 131 D2, 132 A2
Vitré 86 A/B2
Vitrey-sur-Mance 89 C3
Vitry-aux-Loges 87 D2/3
Vitry-en-Artois 78 A2
Vitry-en-Perthois 88 B1
Vitry-la-Ville 88 B1
Vitry-le-François 88 B1/2
Vitsa 142 B3
Vitsai 27 C2
Vitsakumpu 11 D3, 12 A2
Vitsand 39 B/C2/3
Vitsikkovuoma 12 A2/3, 17 D1
Vitskøl Kloster 48 B2
Vittangi 10 B3
Vittaryd 50 B1
Vitteaux 88 B3
Vittel 89 C2
Vittiko 13 C3
Vittinge 40 A/B3
Vittjärn 38 B3
Vittjärv 17 B/C2
Vittória 125 C3
Vittório Véneto 107 D2
Vitträsk (Pålkem) 16 B2
Vittsjö 50 B1
Vittskövle 50 B3
Vitulázio 119 C/D3
Vitvattnet 17 C2
Vitvattnet 34 B3
Viù 104 B3, 112 B1
Viuf 48 B3, 52 B1
Viuhkola 26 B2
Viuruniemi 23 C3
Vivario 113 D3
Viveiro 150 B1
Vivel del Río Martín 162 B2
Viveli 36 B3
Viver 162 B3, 169 C/D1
Viver 156 A2
Viverols 103 C3
Viveros 168 A3
Viviere 112 B2
Viviers 111 C1
Viviers-les-Montagnes 110 A3
Vivonne 101 C2
Vivungi 10 B3
Vizcaínos 153 C3
Vize 141 C3
Vizić 133 C1
Vizille 111 D1, 112 A1
Vižinada 126 B3, 130 A1
Vižnica 98 B3
Vizovice 95 C1
Vízvár 128 A2
Vizzavona 113 D3
Vizzini 125 C3
Vjaz'ma 75 D3
Vjetrenica 137 B/C1
Vlaardingen 66 A3
Vlachokeraséa 146 A1
Vlachokeraséa 148 A2
Vlachokerasiá 147 B/C3
Vlachovice 95 C1
Vlachovo Březí 93 C1
Vlădeni 141 C1
Vladičin Han 139 C1
Vladimirci 133 C/D1/2, 134 A2
Vladimirovac 134 B1
Vladimirskij Tupik 75 C3
Vladimir-Volynskij 97 D1, 98 A/B2
Vlagtwedde 67 C2
Vlajkovac 134 B1
Vlaole 135 C2
Vlasenica 133 C2
Vlasiá 146 B2
Vlašići 130 B2
Vlašim 83 D3
Vlasina Okruglica 139 C1
Vlasotince 139 C1

Vlasotince 140 A3
Vlásti 143 C2
Vlčany 95 C2/3
Vlichón 146 A1
Vlieland 66 B3
Vlissingen 78 B1
Vlkava 83 D2
Vlochós 143 C/D3
Vlönkylä 24 B3
Vlorë 142 A2
Vlorë 148 A1
Vlotho 68 A3
Vlotho-Valdorf 68 A3
Vnà [Scuol-Tarasp] 106 B1
Vo 106 B3
Vobarno 106 B3
Voćin 128 A3
Vöcklabruck 93 C3
Vöcklabruck 96 A3
Vöcklamarkt 93 C3
Vodice 131 C3
Vodice 126 B3
Vodňany 93 C/D1
Vodňany 96 A2
Vodnjan 130 A1
Vodo Cadore 107 D2
Vodskov 48 B2
Voer 49 B/C2
Voerde 67 C3, 79 D1, 80 A1
Voergård 49 B/C1
Voerså 49 C1
Vogatsikón 143 C2
Vogelsang 70 A2
Voghera 113 D1
Vognill 33 C2/3
Vogogna 105 C2
Vogošca 132 B2
Vogt 91 C3
Vogtareuth 92 B3
Vogtsburg-Burkheim 90 A2/3
Vogué 111 C1
Vohburg 92 A2
Vohdensaari 24 A2, 41 D2
Vohenstrauss 82 B3
Vöhl-Herzhausen 81 C1
Vohonjoki 19 B/C1
Vöhrenbach 90 B3
Vöhringen 91 D2
Vöhringen (Horb) 90 B2
Void 89 C1/2
Voikkaa 26 B2
Voikoski 26 B1/2
Voineasa 140 B2
Voiron 103 D3, 104 A3
Voise 87 C2
Voiteur 103 D1, 104 A1
Voitsberg 127 C1
Voitsdorf 93 C3
Vojakkala 25 C2
Vojakkala 17 D2, 18 A1
Vojens 52 B1
Vojka 133 D1, 134 A1
Vojnice 95 D3
Vojnić 127 C/D3, 131 C1
Vojnik 127 C2
Vojtjajaure kapell 15 C3
Volary 93 C1/2
Vólax 144 B1
Volda 36 B1
Volden 37 C/D2
Volden 33 C/D2
Volders 107 C1
Volendam 66 B2
Volenice 93 C1
Volhov 75 C1
Volímai 148 A2
Volímai 146 A2
Volissós 149 C2
Volkach 81 D3
Volkenschwand 92 A/B2
Völkermarkt 127 B/C2
Völkermarkt 96 A3
Völklingen 89 D1, 90 A1
Volkmarsen 81 C1
Volkmarsen-Ehringen 81 C1
Volkovija 138 A/B3
Volkovysk 73 D3, 98 B1
Vollan 4 A3, 10 A1
Vollen 33 B/C1/2
Vollen 38 A3, 43 D1
Vollenhove 67 B/C2
Vollersode 68 A1
Vollerwiek 52 A3
Vollmoen 29 C1/2

Vollore-Montagne 103 C2/3
Vollrathsruhe 53 D3, 69 D1
Vollseter 32 A3, 36 B1
Vollsjö 50 B3
Volmadonna 113 C1
Volmsjö 30 B2
Volnes 14 A2
Volokolamsk 75 D2
Vólos 148 B1
Vólos 143 D3, 144 A3
Volosovo 74 B1
Volot 75 B/C2
Volovec 97 D2, 98 A3
Voložin 74 A3
Volpago del Montello 107 C/D3
Volpiano 105 C3, 113 C1
Völpke 69 C3
Volpriehausen 68 B3, 81 C1
Voltággio 113 D1
Volta Mantovana 106 B3
Volterra 114 B3, 116 A2
Voltlage-Hosckel 67 D2
Voltti 20 B2
Volturara Áppula 119 D2, 120 A1
Volturara Irpina 119 D3, 120 A2
Volvic 102 B2
Volx 111 D2, 112 A2
Volynë 93 C1
Vónitsa 146 A1
Vonnas 103 D2
Vönöck 94 B3, 128 A1
Voorthuizen 66 B3
Vorau 94 A3, 127 D1
Vörå/Vöyri 20 B2
Vorbasse 48 A/B3, 52 B1
Vorchdorf 93 C3
Vorde 48 B2
Vorden 67 C3
Vordernberg 93 D3
Vordingborg 53 D2
Vorë 137 D3, 142 A1
Voreppe 104 A3
Vorey 103 C3
Vormsi 74 A1
Vormträsk 31 C1
Vorna 18 B3
Vorn'any 74 A3
Vorpbukt 28 A2, 33 C1
Voskopoje 142 B2
Voskresenskoe 75 C1
Voskresenskoe 75 D1
Vosne-Romanée 88 B3, 103 D1
Vosočka Ržana 135 D3, 139 D1
Voss 36 B3
Votice 83 D3
Votice 96 A2
Votonósion 143 B/C3
Voué 88 A/B2
Vouillé 101 C1/2
Voúla 147 D2
Vouliagméni 147 D2
Voulx 87 D2
Voúnargon 146 A3
Vouneuil-sur-Vienne 101 C1
Vourvouroú 144 B2
Voutenay-sur-Cure 88 A3
Vouvant 100 B2
Vouvray 86 B3
Vouvry 104 B2
Vouzela 158 A/B2
Vouzeron 87 D3, 102 A1
Vouziers 88 B1
Voúzion 147 B/C1
Vouzon 87 C3
Voves 87 C2
Voxna 39 D1
Voxna 39 D1
Voz 126 B3, 130 B1
Vozmediano 154 A3, 161 D1, 162 A1
Vrå 50 B2
Vrå 48 B1
Vrabča 39 D1
Vráble 95 C/D2
Vraca 135 D3, 139 D3
Vraca 140 B3
Vračev Gaj 134 B1
Vračevšnica 133 D2, 134 A/B2

Vracov **95** B/C1
Vrådal **43** C2
Vråliosen **43** C2
Vrana **131** C2
Vrana **130** A1
Vranduk **132** B2
Vrångö **45** C3, **49** D1
Vranić **133** D1/2, **134** A2
Vranishti **142** A2
Vranja Stena **139** D2
Vranje **139** C1/2
Vranje **126** B3, **130** A1
Vranje **140** A3
Vranjina **137** D2
Vranjska Banja **139** C1/2
Vranov **94** A1
Vranovice **94** B1
Vransko **127** C2
Vrapče Polje **137** D1, **138** A1
Vrata **135** D2
Vratarnica **135** C3
Vratěnín **94** A1
Vrátna **95** D1
Vratna **135** C2
Vratnica **138** B2
Vratnjanske Kapike **135** C2
Vratno **127** D2
Vråv **135** D2
Vražognac **135** C2
Vrba **134** B3
Vrbanja **133** C1
Vrbanja **131** D1, **132** A1
Vrbas **129** C3
Vrbljani **131** D2, **132** A2
Vrbnica **138** A2
Vrbnik **130** B1
Vrboska **131** D3, **136** A1
Vrbovce **95** C2
Vrbové **95** C2
Vrbovec **127** D2/3
Vrbovsko **127** C3, **130** B1
Vrchlabí **96** A1
Vrčin **133** D1, **134** A/B1/2
Vrdnik **133** C/D1, **134** A1
Vreden **67** C3
Vreden-Ammeloe **67** C3
Vreeland **66** B3
Vrees **67** D2
Vrejlev Kirke **48** B1
Vrela **138** A1
Vrelo **135** C3
Vrelo **131** C1
Vrena **47** B/C2
Vreoci **133** D2, **134** A2
Vřesovice **95** B/C1
Vrésthena **147** C3
Vreta **24** B3
Vreta Kloster **46** B2
Vretstorp **46** A1
Vrginmost **127** D3, **131** C1
Vrgorac **131** D3, **132** A3, **136** B1
Vrhnika **126** B2
Vrhovine **130** B1
Vrhpolje **131** D2
Vries **67** C2
Vriezenveen **67** C2
Vriezenveensewijk **67** C2
Vrigstad **51** B/C1
Vrigstad **72** A1
Vrin [Ilanz] **105** D2, **106** A1/2
Vrlika **131** C2/3
Vrmdža **135** C3
Vrnjačka Banja **134** B3
Vrnjačka Banja **140** A2
Vrnograč **127** D3, **131** C1
Vronderón **142** B1/2
Vrosína **142** B3
Vrosína **148** A1
Vroutek **83** C2/3
Vrpolje **131** C3
Vrpolje **128** B3, **132** B1
Vršac **134** B1
Vršac **140** A2
Vrsar **130** A1
Vrsi **130** B2
Vrška-Čuka **135** C3
Vrtoče **131** C2
Vrútky **95** D1
Vrutok **138** B2/3
Všeruby **93** B/C1
Všetaty **83** D2
Vsetín **95** C1
Vsetín **96** B2

Vuarrens [Yverdon] **104** B1/2
Vučedol **129** C3, **133** C1
Vučijak **132** A/B1
Vučitrn **138** B1
Vučje **139** C1
Vučje Luka **132** B2
Vučkovec **127** D2
Vučkovica **134** B2
Vufflens-le-Château **104** B2
Vught **66** B3, **79** C1
Vuka **128** B3
Vukovar **129** C3
Vukovina **127** D3
Vuku **28** B3, **33** D1
Vulaines **88** A2
Vulcan **135** D1
Vulkanešty **141** D1/2
Vulpera [Scuol-Tarasp] **106** B1
Vulureşti **141** C1
Vuno **142** A2
Vuoggatjålme **15** C1/2
Vuohijärvi **26** B2
Vuohiniemi **25** C2
Vuohtomäki **21** D1, **22** A1
Vuojärvi **12** B2
Vuojelahti **22** B3
Vuokatti **19** C3, **23** C1
Vuokko **23** C2
Vuolenkoski **25** D2, **26** A/B2
Vuolijoki **18** B3
Vuolijoki **25** C1/2
Vuolle **21** C1
Vuollerim **16** B2
Vuomahytta **10** A2
Vuomajärvi **17** D2
Vuonajåkk **10** A3
Vuonatjviken **15** D2
Vuonislahti **23** D2
Vuontisjärvi **11** C2, **12** A1
Vuontisjoki **11** C2, **12** A1
Vuorenkylä **25** D1, **26** A1
Vuorenmaa **24** B2
Vuorenmaa **22** B3
Vuoreslahti **19** C3
Vuorijärvi **20** B3
Vuorilahti **21** D2, **22** A2
Vuorimäki **22** B1
Vuoriniemi **27** D1
Vuosalmi **27** C1
Vuoskojaure **10** A2
Vuostimo **13** C/3
Vuostimojärvi **12** B3
Vuotinainen **25** C2
Vuotner **16** A3
Vuotso **12** B1
Vuottas **17** C2
Vuottolahti **19** C3, **22** B1
Vuotunki **19** D1
Výčapy **94** A1
Vydor **74** B2
Vydropužsk **75** D2
Vy-lès-Lure **89** D3
Vÿoni **17** D1/2
Vyra **74** B1
Vyrica **74** B1
Vyškov **96** B2
Vyškov **94** B1
Vyskytná **94** A1
Vyšnij Voloček **75** D2
Vyšný Kubín **95** D1
Vysoká Libyně **83** C3
Vysoká pri Morave **94** B2
Vysokoje **73** D3, **98** A1
Vysokovsk **75** D2
Vyšší Brod **93** D2
Vystupoviči **99** C2

W

Waabs **52** B2
Waakirchen **92** A3
Waal (Kaufbeuren) **91** D3
Waalwijk **66** B3
Waben **77** D2
Wabern **81** C1
Wąbrzeźno **73** C3
Wachau **82** B1
Wachtendonk **79** D1
Wächtersbach **81** C2

Wackersdorf **92** B1
Wackersleben **69** C3
Waddesdon **64** B2/3
Waddeweitz-Dommatzen **69** C2
Wadebridge **62** B3
Wädenswil **105** D1
Wadern **80** A3, **90** A1
Wadern-Nunkirchen **80** A3, **90** A1
Wadersloh **67** D3, **68** A3
Wadersloh-Liesborn **67** D3, **68** A3, **80** B1
Wadowice **97** C2
Wagenfeld **68** A2
Wagenfeld-Förlingen **68** A2
Wagenfeld-Ströhen **68** A2
Wageningen **66** B3
Waghäusel-Kirrlach **90** B1
Waghäusel-Wiesental **90** B1
Waging am See **92** B3
Wagrain **93** C3, **126** A1
Wągrowiec **71** D2
Wągrowiec **72** B3
Wahlsdorf **70** A3
Wahlstedt **52** B3
Waiblingen **91** C2
Waidhaus **82** B3
Waidhofen an der Thaya **94** A1/2
Waidhofen an der Ybbs **93** D3
Waidhofen an der Thaya **96** A2
Waidhofen an der Ybbs **96** A3
Waidring **92** B3
Waimes **79** D2
Wainfleet All Saints **61** D3, **65** C1
Wainhouse Corner **62** B2/3
Waischenfeld **82** A3
Waizenkirchen **93** C2
Wakefield **61** C2
Wałbrzych (Waldenburg) **96** B1
Walchsee **92** B3
Wałcz (Deutsch Krone) **71** D1
Wałcz (Deutsch Krone) **72** B3
Wald **92** B1
Wald **105** D1
Waldachtal-Lützenhardt **90** B2
Waldböckelheim **80** A/B3
Waldbreitbach **80** A2
Waldbröl **80** A/B2
Waldbrunn **80** B2
Waldeck **81** C1
Waldeck-Höringhausen **81** C1
Waldeck-Sachsenhausen **81** C1
Waldems-Esch **80** B2/3
Waldenbuch **91** C2
Waldenburg **90** A3, **105** C1
Waldenburg **82** B2
Waldenburg-Obersteinbach **91** C1
Waldershof **82** B3
Waldfischbach-Burgalben **90** A1
Waldheim **82** B1
Waldighoffen **89** D3, **90** A3
Wald im Pinzgau **107** D1
Waldkappel **81** C1
Waldkappel-Gehau **81** C1
Waldkirch **90** B2/3
Waldkirchen **93** C2
Waldkirchen-Böhmzwiesel **93** C2
Waldkraiburg **92** B2
Wald-Michelbach-Unter-Schönmattenwag **81** C3, **91** B/C1
Wald Michelbach **81** B/C3, **90** B1
Waldmohr **89** D1, **90** A1
Waldmünchen **92** B1
Wałdowice **71** C2
Waldsassen **82** B3
Waldshut-Tiengen **90** B3
Wald (Sigmaringen) **91** C3
Waldsolms **80** B2

Waldthurn **82** B3
Waldwisse **79** D3
Walenstadt **105** D1, **106** A1
Walferdange **79** D3
Walkendorf **53** D3
Walkenried **81** C1
Walkersdorf **127** D1
Wall **57** D3, **60** B1
Wall **70** A2
Wallasey **59** C2, **60** B3
Walldorf **90** B1
Walldorf **81** D2
Walldorf (Gross-Gerau) **80** B3
Walldürn **81** C3, **91** C1
Walldürn-Altheim **81** C3, **91** C1
Walldorf **82** B1
Wallenfels **82** A2
Wallenhorst **67** D2/3
Wallerfangen **89** D1
Wallersdorf **92** B2
Wallerstein **91** D1/2
Wallers-Trélon **78** B3
Wallertheim **80** B3
Wallingford **65** C3
Wallington Hall **57** D3
Wallsbüll **52** B2
Walmer **65** C3, **76** B1
Walsall **59** D3, **64** A1/2
Walsrode **68** B2
Walsrode-Ebbingen **68** B2
Walsrode-Kirchboitzen **68** B2
Walsrode-Westenholz **68** B2
Waltenhofen **91** D3
Waltenhofen-Martinszell **91** D3
Waltershausen **81** D2
Waltham Abbey **65** C3
Walting-Pfünz **92** A1/2
Walton on the Naze **65** C2/3
Waltrop **67** D3, **80** A1
Wambeek **79** B/C2
Wamel **66** B3
Wamin **77** D2
Wanderup **52** B2
Wandlitz **70** A2
Wanfried **81** D1
Wangels **53** C3
Wangenheim **81** D1/2
Wangen im Allgäu-Neuravensburg **91** C3
Wangen im Allgäu **91** C3
Wangerland **67** D1
Wangerland-Hohenkirchen **67** D1
Wangerland-Hooksiel **52** A3, **67** D1
Wangerland-Minsen **52** A3, **67** D1
Wangerooge **67** D1
Wankendorf **52** B3
Wanna **52** A3, **68** A1
Wanroij **66** B3, **79** D1
Wansford **64** B2
Wanssum **79** D1
Wantage **64** A3
Wanzleben **69** C3
Wapenveld **67** C2
Wapnica **71** C1
Warboys **65** C2
Warburg **81** C1
Warburg-Bonenburg **81** C1
Warburg-Ossendorf **81** C1
Warburg-Scherfede **68** A2
Wardenburg **67** D2, **68** A2
Ware **65** C2/3
Waregem **78** A/B2
Wareham **63** D2/3
Waremme **79** C2
Waren **69** D1, **70** A1
Waren **72** A3
Warendorf **67** D3
Warendorf-Freckenhorst **67** D3
Warendorf-Milte **67** D3
Warffum **67** C1
Warfusée-Abancourt **78** A3
Warin **53** D3, **69** C/D1
Wark **57** D2
Warkworth **57** D2
Warmenhuizen **66** A/B2
Warmensteinach **82** A3

Warminster **63** D2, **64** A3
Warmsen-Bohnhorst **68** A2
Warneton **78** A2
Warnice **70** B2
Warnow **53** D3, **69** D1
Warrenpoint **58** A1
Warrington **59** D2, **60** B3
Warsow **69** C1
Warstein **80** B1
Warstein-Allagen **80** B1
Warstein-Belecke **80** B1
Warstein-Suttrop **80** B1
Warszawa **73** C3, **97** C1
Wartberg im Mürztal **94** A3
Wartburg **81** D2
Wartenberg **92** A/B2
Wartenberg-Berglern **92** A/B2
Warth **106** B1
Warthe **70** A1
Wartin **70** B1
Warwick **64** A2
Wasbek **52** B3
Wasen im Emmental **105** C1
Washington **57** D3, **61** C1
Waspik **66** B3
Wasselonne **90** A2
Wassen **105** D1/2
Wassenaar **66** A3
Wasserauen **105** D1, **106** A1
Wasserbillig **79** D3
Wasserburg **92** B2/3
Wasserburg (Bodensee) **91** C3
Wasserburg-Attel **92** B3
Wasserleben **69** C3
Wasserlosen-Schwemmelsbach **81** D3
Wassertrüdingen **91** D1
Wassigny **78** B3
Wassy-sur-Blaise **88** B2
Wasungen **81** D2
Watchet **63** C2
Waterford (Port Lairge) **55** D3
Waterloo **78** B2
Waterville **55** C3
Watervliet **78** B1
Watford **64** B3
Watlington **64** B3
Watten **77** D1
Wattendorf **82** A3
Wattens **107** C1
Watton **65** C2
Wattwil **105** D1, **106** A1
Waulsort **79** C2
Wavignies **77** D3
Wavre **79** B/C2
Waxweiler **79** D3
Wechingen **91** D1/2
Wechingen-Fessenheim **91** D1/2
Wechmar **81** D2
Wechselburg **82** B1/2
Weckersdorf **82** A/B2
Wedde **67** C2
Weddingstedt **52** A/B3
Wedel **68** B1
Wedellsborg **52** B1
Wedemark **68** B2
Wedemark-Bissendorf **68** B2
Wedemark-Elze **68** B2
Weedon **64** B2
Weelde-Statie **79** C1
Weener **67** D1
Weerselo **67** C2/3
Weert **79** C/D1
Weesen **105** D1, **106** A1
Weesp **66** B2/3
Weeze **67** C3, **79** D1
Weferlingen **69** C3
Wegberg **79** D1
Wegberg-Arsbeck **79** D1
Wegeleben **69** C3
Węgliniec **83** D1
Węgorzewo (Angerburg) **73** C2
Węgorzyno **71** C1
Węgrzynice **71** C3
Wegscheid **93** C2
Wegscheid **94** A3
Wehingen **90** B2
Wehr **90** B3
Wehretal **81** D1

Wehrheim 80 B2
Wehr (Mayen) 80 A2
Weichensdorf 70 B3
Weichselboden 94 A3
Weida 82 B2
Weiden 82 B3
Weidenbach (Feuchtwangen) 91 D1
Weidenberg 82 A3
Weiden-Rothenstadt 82 B3
Weidenstetten 91 C/D2
Weidenthal 90 B1
Weikendorf 94 B2
Weikersdorf am Steinfelde 94 A/B3
Weikersheim 81 C/D3, 91 C1
Weil am Rhein 90 A3
Weilburg 80 B2
Weil der Stadt 91 B/C2
Weiler-Simmerberg 91 C3
Weilerswist 79 D2, 80 A2
Weilerswist-Lommersum 79 D2, 80 A2
Weilheim 91 C2
Weilheim in Oberbayern 92 A3
Weilmünster-Laubuseschbach 80 B2
Weilmünster 80 B2
Weilrod-Altweilnau 80 B2
Weilstetten 91 B/C2
Weimar 82 A1/2
Weinböhla 83 C1
Weinfelden 91 C3
Weingarten 90 B1
Weinsberg 91 C1
Weischlitz 82 B2
Weisen 69 D2
Weisenbach 90 B2
Weisendorf 81 D3
Weiskirchen 79 D3, 80 A3, 90 A1
Weismain 82 A3
Weissach 91 B/C2
Weissagk 70 B3
Weissandt-Gölzau 69 D3, 82 B1
Weissbach bei Lofer 92 B3
Weissbriach 126 A1/2
Weissenbach am Attersee 93 C3
Weissenbach am Lech 91 D3
Weissenberg 83 D1
Weissenborn-Lüderode 81 D1
Weissenborn 81 D1
Weissenbrunn 82 A2/3
Weissenburg in Bayern 91 D1, 92 A1
Weissenburg-Rothenstein 91 D1, 92 A1
Weissenburg 105 C2
Weissenfels 82 A/B1
Weissenhorn 91 D2
Weissenkirchen in der Wachau 94 A2
Weissensee 81 D1, 82 A1
Weissenstadt 82 A3
Weissenthurm 80 A2
Weissewarthe 69 D2
Weissig 83 C1
Weissig 83 C1
Weisskirchen in Steiermark 127 C1
Weisstannen [Mels] 105 D1, 106 A1
Weisswasser 83 D1
Weitendorf 53 D3
Weitersfeld 94 A2
Weitersfelden 93 D2
Weiterstadt 80 B3
Weitin 70 A1
Weitnau 91 D3
Weitnau-Siebratshofen 91 D3
Weitnau-Wengen 91 D3
Weitra 93 D2
Weitramsdorf-Weidach 81 D2, 82 A2
Weiz 127 C1
Weiz 96 A3
Wejherowo 72 B2
Welbourn 61 D3, 64 B1
Wellaune 82 B1

Welle 68 B1
Wellendingen (Rottweil) 90 B2
Wellerlooij 79 D1
Wellheim 92 A1/2
Wellheim-Biesenhard 92 A2
Wellingborough 64 B2
Wellington 63 C2
Wellington 59 D3, 64 A1
Wells 63 D2
Wells next-the-Sea 65 C1
Wels 93 C2
Wels 96 A2/3
Welschbillig 79 D3
Welschenrohr [Gänsbrunnen] 105 C3
Welshpool 59 C3
Welsleben 69 C/D3
Weltenburg 92 A1/2
Welver 67 D3, 80 B1
Welwyn Garden City 65 B/C3
Welzheim 91 C1/2
Welzow 83 C1
Wem 59 D3, 60 B3
Wembach 90 B3
Wemding 91 D1/2
Wemperhardt 79 D2/3
Wemyss Bay 56 B2
Wemyss Bay 54 A2/3, 55 D1
Wendelsheim (Alzey) 80 B3
Wenden 80 B2
Wendlingen am Neckar 91 C2
Wendover 64 B3
Wenduine 78 A1
Weng bei Admont 93 D3
Wengen 105 C2
Wenigzell 94 A3
Wennigsen 68 B3
Wenningstedt 52 A2
Wennington 59 D1, 60 B2
Wenns 106 B1
Wentorf bei Hamburg 68 B1
Wenzenbach 92 B1
Weobley 63 D1
Wépion 79 C1
Werbach 81 C3
Werben 70 B3
Werben 69 D2
Werbig 70 A3
Werdau 82 B2
Werder 70 A2/3
Werdohl 80 B1
Werfen 93 C3
Werl 80 B1
Werlte 67 D2
Wermelskirchen 80 A1
Wermsdorf 82 B1
Wernau 91 C2
Wernberg-Köblitz 82 B3, 92 B1
Werne 67 D3, 80 A/B1
Werneck 81 D3
Werneuchen 70 A/B2
Wernhout 79 C1
Wernigerode 69 C3
Wernshausen 81 D2
Wertheim 81 C3
Wertheim-Nassig 81 C3
Wertheim-Reichholzheim 81 C3
Werther 68 A3
Wertingen 91 D2
Wesel 67 C3, 79 D1, 80 A1
Weselberg 90 A3
Wesel-Bislich 67 C3
Wesel-Büderich 67 C3, 79 D1, 80 A1
Wesenberg 70 A1
Wesendorf 69 C2
Wesendorf-Wahrenholz 69 C2
Wesenufer 93 C2
Wesepe 67 C2/3
Wesselburen 52 A3
Wesseling 80 A2
Wessem 79 D1
Wessling 92 A2/3
Wessobrunn 91 D3, 92 A3

West-Auckland 57 D3, 61 C1
West Bay 63 D2/3
West Bromwich 59 D3, 64 A2
West Burton 59 D1, 61 D/C2
Westbury 63 D2, 64 A3
West-Calder 57 C2
Westende-Bad 78 A1
Westerbork 67 C2
Westerburg 80 B2
Westerham 65 C3, 76 B1
Westerhausen 69 C3
Westerheim (Münsingen) 91 C2
Westerhever 52 A2/3
Westerholt 67 D2
Westerkappeln 67 D2/3
Westerland 52 A2
Westerstede-Ihausen 67 D1
Westerstede 67 D1
Westerstede-Tarbarg 67 D1
Westerstetten 91 C2
Westerwalsede 68 A/B2
Westerwalsede-Süderwalsede 68 B2
Westfehmarn-Petersdorf 53 C2
Westgate on Sea 65 C3, 76 B1
West Hartlepool 61 D1
Westhausen 91 D1/2
Westheim-Ostheim 91 D1
Westhofen 80 B3
Westkapelle 78 A1
West Kilbride 56 B2
West Linton 57 C2
West-Looe 62 B3
West Lulworth 63 D3
West Mersea 65 C3
Weston-super-Mare 63 C/D2
Westoverledingen 67 D1/2
Westport 55 C2
West Tanfield 61 C2
West Tarbert 56 A2
West-Terschelling 66 B1
West Town 76 A1
West Wycombe 64 B3
Wetherby 61 D2
Wetteren 78 B1
Wetterzeube 82 B1/2
Wettin 82 A1
Wettingen 90 B3
Wettringen 67 D3
Wetwang 61 D2
Wetzikon 105 D1
Wetzlar 80 B2
Wetzleinsdorf 94 B2
Wevelgem 78 A2
Wewelsfleth 52 B3, 68 B1
Wexford 58 A3
Wexford 55 D3
Weybridge 64 B3, 76 B1
Weyerbusch 80 A2
Weyer Markt 93 D2
Weyer Markt 96 A3
Weyersheim 90 A/B2
Weyhausen (Gifhorn) 69 C2
Weyhe 68 A2
Weyhe-Leeste 68 A2
Weyhill 64 A3, 76 A1
Weymouth 63 D3
Weyregg am Attersee 93 C3
Wezep 67 B/C2
Whalley 59 D1, 60 B2
Whalton 57 D3
Wharram le-Street 61 D2
Wheddon Cross 63 C2
Whipsnade Zoo 64 B2/3
Whitburn 57 B/C2
Whitburn 54 B2/3
Whitby 61 D1
Whitchurch 59 D2/3, 60 B3
Whitchurch 65 C3, 76 B1
Whitebeck 54 B3
Whitehall 54 B1
Whitehaven 54 B3
Whitehaven 57 C3, 60 A1
Whitehead 56 A3
Whitehouse 56 A2
Whithorn 56 B3, 60 A1

Whiting Bay 56 A2
Whitley Bay 57 D3, 61 C1
Whitstable 65 C/D3, 77 C1
Whitstone 62 B2/3
Whittingham 57 D2
Whittington 59 C/D3, 60 B3
Whittlesey 65 C2
Wichmannshausen 81 C/D1
Wichów 71 C3
Wick 54 B1
Wickede 80 B1
Wickford 65 C3
Wickham 76 B1
Wickham Market 65 C2
Wicklow 58 A2
Wicklow 55 D3
Wickwar 63 D1, 64 A3
Widecombe-in-the-Moor 63 C3
Widnes 59 D2, 60 B3
Widuchowa (Fiddichow) 70 B2
Wiechowo 71 C1
Wiedenbrück 68 A3
Wiefelstede 67 D1, 68 A1
Wiehe 82 A1
Wiehl 80 A2
Wieleń 71 C/D2
Wielenbach 92 A3
Wieleń Polny 71 C/D2
Wielichowo 71 D3
Wieluń 96 B1
Wien 96 B2/3
Wien 94 B2
Wiener Neustadt 94 B3
Wiener Neustadt 96 A/B3
Wienhausen 68 B2
Wiepke 69 C2
Wierden 67 C2/3
Wieren 69 C2
Wiernsheim 90 B1/2
Wierzbięcin 71 C1
Wierzbno 71 B/C1
Wierzchowo 71 D1
Wies 127 C1/2
Wiesau-Schönhaid 82 B3
Wiesbaden 80 B3
Wiesbaden-Naurod 80 B3
Wieselburg 93 D2
Wiesen 81 C3
Wiesenburg 69 D3
Wiesenfelden-Hötzelsdorf 92 B1
Wiesenfelden 92 B1
Wiesensteig 91 C2
Wiesenthal 81 D2
Wiesenttal-Streitberg 82 A3
Wieslautern 90 A/B1
Wiesloch 90 B1
Wiesmath 94 B3
Wiesmoor 67 D1
Wietmarschen 67 C/D2
Wietmarschen-Lohne 67 C/D2
Wietze 68 B2
Wietze-Jeversen 68 B2
Wietzen 68 A2
Wietzendorf 68 B2
Wiewierz 71 D3
Wigan 59 D2, 60 B2/3
Wiggen 105 C1
Wiggensbach 91 D3
Wigton 57 C3, 60 B1
Wigtown 56 B3, 60 A1
Wijchen 66 B3
Wijhe 67 C2
Wil 91 C3
Wilburgstetten 91 D1
Wilczkowice 69 D3
Wildalpen 93 D3
Wildbad-Calmbach 90 B2
Wildbad im Schwarzwald 90 B2
Wildberg 90 B2
Wildberg 70 A1
Wildberg 69 D2, 70 A2
Wildeck 81 C1/2
Wildeck-Hönebach 81 C/D2
Wildeck-Richelsdorf 81 D1/2
Wildenberg 92 A/B2
Wildenbruch 70 A3
Wildendürnbach 94 B2

Wildenhain 83 C1
Wildenthal 82 B2
Wildervank 67 C2
Wildeshausen-Kleinenketen 68 A2
Wildeshausen 68 A2
Wildetaube 82 B2
Wildflecken-Neuwildflecken 81 C/D2
Wildflecken-Oberbach 81 C2
Wildon 127 C1
Wildpoldsried 91 D3
Wilfersdorf 94 B2
Wilhamstead 64 B2
Wilhelm-Pieck-Stadt Guben 70 B3
Wilhelm-Pieck-Stadt Guben 72 A3, 96 A1
Wilhelmsburg 96 A3
Wilhelmsburg 94 A2
Wilhelmsdorf 91 C3
Wilhelmshaven 67 D1, 68 A1
Wilhelmshaven-Sengwarden 52 A3, 67 D1
Wilhelmsthal 82 A2
Wilhermsdorf 81 D3, 91 D1
Wilkau-Hasslau 82 B2
Wilkowo Polskie 71 D3
Willebadessen 68 A3, 81 C1
Willebadessen-Peckelsheim 81 C1
Willebroek 78 B1
Willemstad 66 A3
Willenhall 59 D3, 64 A2
Willgottheim 90 A2
Willingen 80 B1
Willingen-Usseln 80 B1
Willingshausen 81 C2
Willisau 105 C1
Williton 63 C2
Willofs (Lauterbach) 81 C2
Willstätt 90 B2
Wilmslow 59 D2, 60 B3, 64 A1
Wilnsdorf 80 B2
Wilnsdorf-Rudersdorf 80 B2
Wilsickow 70 B1
Wilstedt 68 A1/2
Wilster 52 B3
Wilsum 67 C2
Wilthen 83 D1
Wiltingen 79 D3
Wilton 63 D2, 64 A3, 76 A1
Wilton House 63 D2, 64 A3, 76 A1
Wiltz 79 D3
Wimbledon 65 B/C3
Wimborne Minster 63 D2
Wimereux 77 D1
Wimmenau 90 A2
Wimpassing an der Leitha 94 B3
Wincanton 63 D2
Winchcombe 63 D1, 64 A2
Winchelsea 77 C1
Wincheringen 79 D3
Winchester 76 B1
Windach 91 D2/3, 92 A2/3
Windeck-Herchen 80 A2
Windeck-Rosbach 80 A/B2
Windermere 59 C/D1, 60 B1/2
Windermere 54 B3
Windesheim 80 B3
Windischeschenbach 82 B3
Windischgarsten 93 D3
Windischgarsten 96 A3
Windorf 93 C2
Windorf 93 C2
Windsbach 91 D1
Windsor 64 B3
Wingham 65 C3, 76 B1
Wingst 52 A/B3, 68 A1
Winhöring 92 B2
Winkel 89 D3, 90 A3
Winklarn 92 B1
Winklarn 107 D1, 126 A1
Winnenden 91 C1/2
Winschoten 67 C1/2
Winsen 68 B2
Winsen (Luhe) 68 B1

Winsen-Meissendorf **68** B2
Winsen-Pattensen **68** B1
Winsford **59** D2, **60** B3, **64** A1
Winslow **64** B2
Winster **61** C3, **64** A1
Winsum **66** B1/2
Winsum **67** C1
Winterberg **80** B1
Winterberg-Altastenberg **80** B1
Winterberg-Niedersfeld **80** B1
Winterberg-Siedlinghausen **80** B1
Winterfeld **69** C2
Winterswijk **67** C3
Winterthur **90** B3
Winterton **61** D2
Wintrich **80** A3
Wintzenheim **89** D2, **90** A2/3
Wipperdorf **81** D1
Wipperfürth **80** A1
Wipperfürth-Klüppelberg **80** A1
Wippingen **67** D2
Wippra **82** A1
Wirdum **67** C/D1
Wirges **80** B2
Wirksworth **61** C3, **64** A1
Wirsberg **82** A3
Wisbech **65** C1/2
Wischhafen **52** B3, **68** B1
Wismar **53** C3
Wissant **77** D1
Wissembourg **90** B1
Wissen **80** B2
Wistedt **68** B1
Witankowo **71** D1
Witham **65** C2/3
Witheridge **63** C2
Withern **61** D3, **65** C1
Withernsea **61** D2
Witney **64** A3
Witnica **70** B2
Witnica **71** B/C2
Witry-lès-Reims **88** A/B1
Wittdün **52** A2
Wittelshofen **91** D1
Witten **80** A1
Wittenberge **69** D2
Wittenburg **69** C1
Witterda **81** D1/2, **82** A1
Wittibreut **93** B/C2
Wittichenau **83** C/D1
Wittighausen-Unterwittig-hausen **81** C3
Wittingen **69** C2
Wittingen-Knesebeck **69** C2
Wittingen-Ohrdorf **69** C2
Wittislingen **91** D2
Wittlich **80** A3
Wittmund **67** D1
Wittmund-Ardorf **67** D1
Wittmund-Burhafe **67** D1
Wittmund-Carolinensiel **67** D1
Wittmund-Harlesiel **67** D1
Wittorf **68** B2
Wittstock **69** D1/2
Wittstock **72** A3
Witzenhausen **81** C1
Witzin **53** D3, **69** D1
Witzke **69** D2
Wiveliscombe **63** C2
Wivenhoe **65** C/D2/3
Wizernes **77** D1
Woking **64** B3, **76** B1
Wokingham **64** B3
Woldegk **70** A1
Wolfach **90** B2
Wolfegg **91** C3
Wolfen **69** D3, **82** B1

Wolfenbüttel **69** C3
Wölfersheim-Berstadt **81** C2
Wölfersheim **81** B/C2
Woifhagen **81** C1
Wolfhagen-Istha **81** C1
Wolframs-Eschenbach **91** D1
Wolfrathshausen **92** A3
Wolfsberg **127** C1
Wolfsberg **96** A3
Wolfsburg **69** C2/3
Wolfsburg-Hehlingen **69** C2/3
Wolfsfeld **79** D3
Wolfshagen **70** A1
Wolfstein **80** A3
Wolgast **72** A2
Wolhusen **105** C1
Wolin **70** B1
Wolkenstein **83** B/C2
Wolkersdorf **94** B2
Wölkisch **83** C1
Wolkramshausen **81** D1
Wollaston **64** B2
Wollin **69** D3
Wöllstadt **81** B/C2
Wöllstein **80** B3
Wolmirstedt **69** C/D3
Wolnzach **92** A2
Wolnzach-Geroldshausen **92** A2
Wołowe Lasy **71** D2
Wolpertshausen **91** C1
Wolpertswende **91** C3
Wolsfeld **79** D3
Wolsingham **57** D3, **61** C1
Wolsztyn **71** C/D3
Wolsztyn **72** B3, **96** B1
Woltersdorf **70** A/B2
Woltersdorf **69** C2
Wolvega **67** B/C2
Wolverhampton **59** D3, **64** A1/2
Wolvertem **78** B1/2
Wolverton **64** B2
Wolviston **61** D1
Wombwell **61** D2/3
Wommels **66** B1/2
Woodbridge **65** C2
Woodenbridge **58** A3
Woodhall Spa **61** D3, **65** B/C1
Woodstock **65** C2/3
Woofferton **59** D3
Wooler **57** D2
Woore **59** D2, **60** B3, **64** A1
Wootton Bassett **63** D1, **64** A3
Wootz **69** C2
Worb **105** C1
Worbis **81** D1
Worcester **59** D3, **63** D1, **64** A2
Wörgl **93** B3
Workington **57** C3, **60** A1
Worksop **61** D3, **65** C1
Workum **66** B2
Wörlitz **69** D3
Wormhoudt **77** D1, **78** A1/2
Worms **80** B3
Worms-Pfeddersheim **80** B3
Worpswede **68** A1/2
Wörrstadt **80** B3
Wörschach **93** C/D3
Wört **91** D1
Wörth **81** C3
Wörth **92** B1
Wörth **107** D1, **126** A1
Wörth am Rhein **90** B1
Wörth-Büchelberg **90** B1
Worthing **76** B1
Wotton under Edge **63** D1, **64** A3
Woudenberg **66** B3
Wragby **61** D3, **64** B1
Wredenhagen **69** D1
Wremen **52** A3, **68** A1
Wrentham **65** D2
Wrestedt **69** C2
Wrexham **59** C/D2, **60** B3
Wriedel-Lintzel **68** B2
Wriezen **70** B2
Wróblewo **71** D2

Wrocław (Breslau) **96** B1
Wrohm **52** B3
Wroniawy **71** C/D3
Wronki **71** D2
Wronki **72** B3
Wroughton **64** A3
Wroxham **65** C1
Września **72** B3, **96** B1
Wschowa **71** D3
Wulfen **80** D3
Wulfersdorf **69** D1
Wülfershausen **81** D2
Wülfrath **80** A1
Wulften **68** B3, **81** D1
Wullersdorf **94** A/B2
Wünnenberg **80** B1
Wünnenberg-Haaren **80** B1
Wünnenberg-Fürstenberg **81** B/C1
Wünschendorf **82** B2
Wünsdorf **70** A3
Wunsiedel **82** B3
Wunstorf **68** B2
Wunstorf-Steinhude **68** B2
Wuppertal **80** A1
Würenlingen **90** B3
Wurmannsquick **92** B2
Würselen **79** D2
Wurzbach **82** A2
Würzburg **81** C/D3
Wurzen **82** B1
Wust **69** D2
Wüstenrot-Neuhütten **91** C1
Wusterhausen **69** D2
Wustermark **70** A2
Wüstermarke **70** A3
Wusterwitz **69** D2/3
Wustrau **70** A2
Wustrow **70** A1
Wustrow **69** C2
Wuustwezel **79** C1
Wybelsum **67** C1
Wyhl **90** A2
Wyk auf Föhr **52** A2
Wymondham **65** D2
Wymondham **64** B1
Wyrzysk **71** D1/2
Wysoka **71** D1/2
Wysoka **71** C3
Wyszków **73** C3, **98** A1
Wyszogród **73** C3
Wyszyna **97** C1

X

Xanten **67** C3, **79** D1
Xanten-Marienbaum **67** C3
Xánthi **145** C1
Xánthi **149** C1
Xermade **150** B2
Xermaménil **89** D2
Xerta **163** C2
Xertigny **89** D2
Xesteda **150** A1
Xeve **150** A2
Xidéika **147** C3
Xilaganí **145** C1
Xilókastron **147** C2
Xilókastron **148** B2
Xinón Nerón **143** C2
Xinzo de Limia **150** B3
Xironda **150** B3
Xove **150** B1
Xunqueira de Ambía **150** B3
Xunqueira de Espadañedo **150** B2

Y

Yablůnka **95** C1
Yanci **108** A3, **154** A1
Yanguas **153** D3
Yarmouth **76** A1/2
Yatağan **149** D2
Yate **63** D1/2, **64** A3
Yátova **169** C1
Ybbs an der Donau **93** D2

Ybbsitz **93** D3
Ychoux **108** A2
Ydrefors **46** B3
Yebes **161** C2
Yebra **161** C2/3
Yebra de Basa **154** B2
Yecla **161** D1
Yecla de Yeltes **159** C2
Yélamos de Arriba **161** C2
Yelo **161** D1
Yelverton **63** C3
Yémeda **162** A3, **168** B1
Yeniköy **149** D1
Yenne **104** A3
Yeovil **63** D2
Yepes **161** B/C3, **167** C/D1
Yerville **77** C3
Yesa **155** C2
Yeste **168** B3
Yetminster **63** D2
Ygos-Saint-Saturnin **108** B2
Ygrande **102** B2
Ykspihlaja **20** B1
Ylä-Kintaus **21** D3, **22** A3
Ylä-Kolkki **21** C3
Yläköngäs **6** B2
Ylä-Kuolna **5** D3, **6** A3, **11** D1
Ylä Kuona **23** C3
Ylä-Luosta **23** C2
Ylämaa **27** C2
Ylämylly **23** C3
Yläne **24** B2
Ylä-Uura **19** C3
Ylä-Valtimo **23** C1
Ylihärmä **20** B2
Yli-Ii **18** B2
Ylijärvi **27** C2
Yli-Kärppä **18** B1
Ylikiiminki **18** B2
Yli-Körkkö **12** B3
Ylikulma **25** B/C3
Yli-Kurki **19** C2
Ylikylä **23** C1
Ylikylä **20** B1
Ylikylä **21** C2
Ylikylä **20** B3
Yli-Lesti **21** C1/2
Yli-Livo **19** B/C1/2
Ylimarkku **20** A3
Yli-Muonio **11** C3
Yli-Nampa **12** B3
Ylinenoja **18** A3
Yli-Olhava **18** A/B2
Ylipää **18** B3
Ylipää **21** C2
Ylipää **18** B3
Ylipää **18** A2/3
Ylipää **21** D1, **22** A1
Ylipää **18** A3
Yli-Paakkola **17** D2, **18** A1
Ylisevä **20** B3
Yli-Siuraua **18** B1/2
Ylistaro **20** B2
Ylistaron **20** B2
Yli-Tannila **18** B2
Ylitornio (Övertorneå) **17** D2
Yli-Utos **18** B2/3
Ylivesi **27** C1
Ylivieska **18** A3, **21** C1
Yli-Viirre **21** C1
Yli-Vuotto **18** B2
Ylläsjärvi **11** C/D3, **12** A2
Yllivalli **20** B3
Ylöjärvi **25** C1
Ylträ **21** C3
Ylvingen **14** A3
Ymonville **87** C2
Yngsjö **50** B3
Ynnesdal **36** A2/3
Yonne **104** B2
York **61** C2
York **54** B3
Yoxford **65** D2
Ypäjä **24** B2
Ypäjän asema **24** B2
Yport **77** C3
Yppäri **18** A3
Ypyä **21** C1
Ypykkävaara **19** D3
Yrbovski **133** D1, **134** A1
Yrittaperä **19** C2
Yrkje **42** A2

Yrouerre **88** A3
Yrttivaara **17** C1
Yset **33** C2/3
Ysgubor-y-coed **59** C3
Ysjö **30** A2, **35** C1
Yssingeaux **103** C3, **111** C1
Ystad **50** B3
Ystad **72** A2
Ystebrød **42** A3
Ysterbö **36** A2
Ystrad-Rhondda **63** C1
Ytre Arna **36** A3
Ytre Årnes **9** A3
Ytre Billefjord **5** D2, **6** A1/2
Ytre Brenna **5** D1, **6** B1
Ytre Enebakk **38** A3, **44** B1
Ytre Flåbygd **43** C2
Ytre Fræna **32** A2
Ytre Kårvik **4** A2
Ytre Kjæs **5** D1, **6** B1
Ytre Korsnes **6** B1
Ytre Laksvatn **4** A3, **10** A1
Ytre Mannskarvik **5** D1, **6** A/B1
Ytre Oppedal **36** A2
Ytre Snillfjord **33** B/C1/2
Ytre Veines **5** D2, **6** A1
Ytterån **29** D3, **34** B2
Ytterberg **34** B3
Ytter Bodane **45** C2
Ytterby **47** D1
Ytterby (Kungälv) **45** C3
Ytterbyn **17** C2/3
Ytteresse **20** B1
Ytterfors **30** B1
Ytterhogdal **34** B3
Ytterjeppo **20** B2
Yttermalung **39** C2
Yttermark **20** A3
Ytterøe **29** C3, **34** B2
Ytterøy **28** B3, **33** D1
Yttersjö **31** C3
Ytterstmark **31** C/D2
Yttertällmo **30** B2, **35** D1
Yttertällmon **30** B2, **35** D1
Yttertüringen **34** B3
Yttervik **15** C3
Yttilä **24** B2
Yuncos **160** B3
Yunquera **172** A2
Yunquera de Henares **161** C2
Yverdon-les-Bains **104** B1
Yvetot **77** C3
Yvoire **104** A/B2
Yvonand **104** B1
Yvré-l'Évêque **86** B2
Yxnerum **46** B2
Yxsjö **30** B2
Yxskaftkälen **29** D3, **35** C1
Yyteri **24** A1
Yzeron **103** C/D3

Z

Zaanstad **66** A/B2
Zaatzke **69** D1/2
Žabalj **129** D3, **134** A1
Žabalj **140** A2
Žabari **134** B2
Zabin **71** C1
Ząbkowice Śląskie **96** B1
Zablaće **131** C3
Záblatí **93** C1
Zablece **131** D2, **132** A2
Žabljak **137** D2
Žabljak **133** C3, **137** D1
Zabno **71** D3
Żabno **127** D2
Zabok **127** D2
Zabór **71** C3
Zaborowice **71** D3
Żabowo **71** C1
Zabreže **133** D1, **134** A1/2
Zabrze (Hindenburg) **96** B2
Zacháro **146** B3
Zacharzyn **71** D2
Zachow **69** D2, **70** A2
Zadar **130** B2
Zadvarje **131** D3, **132** A3
Zafarraya **172** B2
Zafferana Étnea **125** D2

Zafra 165 D3
Żaga 126 A2
Żagań (Sagan) 83 D1
Żagań (Sagan) 96 A1
Zagarise 122 B2
Zagarolo 118 B2
Zagorá 144 A3
Zagorá 148 B1
Zagorje 127 C2
Zagra 172 B2
Zagreb 127 D3
Zagrilla 172 B1
Żagubica 135 C2
Żagubica 140 A2
Zagvozd 131 D3, 132 A3
Zahara 172 A2
Zahara de los Atunes
   171 D3
Zahinos 165 C3
Zahna 69 D3, 70 A3
Záhoří 93 D1
Záhorská Ves 94 B2
Zahrádka 83 D3
Zahrádka 83 D3
Zaidín 155 C3, 163 C1
Zajača 133 C2
Zajas 138 B3
Zajecar 140 A/B2
Zajecar 135 C2/3
Zaječov 83 C3
Zajezda 127 D2
Zajezierze 71 C1
Zákamenné 95 D1
Zákas 143 C2
Zákinthos 146 A2/3
Zákinthos 148 A2
Zakopane 97 C2
Zákros 149 C3
Zakrzewo 71 D1
Zákupy 83 D2
Zalaapáti 128 A1/2
Zalabaksa 127 D1/2
Zalabér 128 A1
Zalaegerszeg 128 A1
Zalaegerszeg 96 B3
Zalahaláp 128 A1
Zalakaros 128 A2
Zalakomár 128 A2
Zalalövő 127 D1
Zalamea de la Serena
   166 A2
Zalamea la Real 171 C1
Zalaszabar 128 A2
Zalaszántó 128 A1
Zalaszentbalázs 128 A2
Zalaszentgrót 128 A1
Zalaszentiván 128 A1
Zalaszentmihály 128 A1/2
Zaláta 128 B3
Zalatárnok 128 A2
Zalău 97 D3, 140 B1
Zalavár 128 A2
Zalduendo 153 C2
Zalduondo 153 D2
Žalec 127 C2
Zaleščiki 98 B3
Zalese 75 D1
Zalla 153 C1
Zall Reç 138 A2
Zaltbommel 66 B3
Zalužnica 130 B1
Zamárdi 128 B1
Zamarra 159 C2
Zambra 172 B1/2
Zambrana 153 C2
Zambrów 73 D3, 98 A1
Zambujeira do Mar 170 A1
Zamęcin 71 C2
Zámoly 95 D3, 128 B1
Zamora 159 D1
Zamość 97 D1, 98 A2
Žandov 83 D2
Zandvoort 66 A2
Zanglivérion 144 A2
Zaniemyśl 71 D3
Zánka 128 B1
Zaorejas 161 D2
Zaostrog 132 A3, 136 B1
Zapfendorf 82 A/B3
Záppion 143 D3
Zapponeta 120 B1
Zaprešić 127 D3
Zaragoza 154 B3, 162 B1
Zarasai 74 A2/3
Zaratán 152 A/B3, 160 A1

Zarautz 153 D1
Zarcilla de Ramos 168 B3,
   174 A1
Żarki Wielki 83 D1
Zárkos 143 C/D3
Žarkovskij 75 C2/3
Žárnesti 141 C2
Žarnovica 95 D2
Żarnowo 70 B1
Zaroúchla 146 B2
Zarratón 153 C2
Zarrentin 69 C1
Żary (Sorau) 71 C3, 83 D1
Żary (Sorau) 96 A1
Zarza Capilla 166 B2
Zarza de Alange 165 D2,
   166 A2
Zarza de Montánchez
   165 D1/2, 166 A1/2
Zarza de Tajo 161 C3
Zarzadilla de Totana
   168 B3, 174 A1
Zarza la Mayor 159 C3,
   165 C/D1
Zarzuela 161 D3
Zarzuela del Monte 160 B2
Zarzuela del Pinar 160 B1
Zás 150 A1
Zasavica 133 C1
Zasieki 70 B3
Žaškov 99 C3
Zásmuky 83 D3
Zastavna 98 B3
Žatec 96 A1/2
Žatec 83 C2
Zatom 71 C2
Zaton 130 B2
Zaton 136 B1
Zaton 131 C3
Zatonie 71 C3
Zátouna 146 B3
Zavala 137 B/C1
Zavala 136 A1
Zavalje 131 C1
Zavattarello 113 D1
Zavidov 83 C3
Zavidovići 132 B2
Zavlaka 133 C2
Závrč 127 D2
Zawada 71 C3
Zawidów 83 D1
Zawiercie 97 C1/2
Žažina 127 D3
Zázrivá 95 D1
Zbaraž 98 B2/3
Zbarzewo 71 C3
Zbąszyń 71 C3
Zbehy 95 C2
Zbiroh 83 C3
Zborov 97 D2, 98 B2/3
Zbraslav 83 D3
Zbraslavice 83 D3
Ždala 128 A2
Žďánice 94 B1
Žď'ár 83 C3
Žďár 83 C2
Žďárec 94 B1
Žďár nad Sázavou 96 A/B2
Zdenac 127 C3, 130 B1
Zdenčina 127 D3
Zdiby 83 D2/3
Zdice 83 C3
Zdounky 95 C1
Ždrelac 130 B2
Ždrelo 134 B2
Zdunje 138 B2/3
Zeanuri 153 C/D1
Žebrák 83 C3
Zechin 70 B2
Zechlinerhütte 70 A1/2
Zeddam 67 C3
Zeddiani 123 C2
Zednik 129 C2/3
Zeebrugge 78 A1
Zeeland 66 B3
Zegama 153 D2
Žegar 131 C2
Žegra 138 B2
Żegulja 137 C1
Zehdenick 70 A2
Zehlendorf 70 A2
Zehren 83 C1
Zeil am Main 81 D3
Zeilfeld 81 D2
Zeist 66 B3
Zeitlarn 92 B1

Zeitz 82 B1
Zele 78 B1
Zelenika 137 C2
Zelenograd 75 D2
Zelenogradsk (Cranz)
   73 C2
Želetava 94 A1
Železná Ruda 93 C1
Železnica 139 D1/2
Železnik 133 D1, 134 A1/2
Železniki 126 B2
Železnodorožnyj (Ger-
   dauen) 73 C2
Zelhem 67 C3
Želiezovce 95 D2/3
Zelin 126 B2
Zelina 127 D2
Żélion 147 C1
Želiv 83 D3, 94 A1
Željuša 132 B3
Zell 80 A3
Zella-Mehlis 81 D2
Zell am Harmersbach 90 B2
Zell am Moos 93 C3
Zell am See 107 D1,
   126 A1
Zell am Ziller 107 C1
Zell im Wiesental 90 A/B3
Zellingen 81 C3
Želnava 93 C2
Zeltingen-Rachtig 80 A3
Zeltweg 127 C1
Zelzate 78 B1
Zemblak 142 B2
Zeme 105 D3, 113 C1
Zemen 139 D2
Zemendorf 94 B3
Zemné 95 C3
Zemun 133 D1, 134 A1
Zemun 140 A2
Zenica 132 B2
Zennor 62 A3
Zenting 93 C2
Žepče 132 B2
Zepernick 70 A2
Zerbst 69 D3
Zerf 79 D3, 80 A3
Zeri 114 A2
Zermatt 105 C2
Zernez 106 B1/2
Zero Branco 107 D3
Zerpenschleuse 70 A2
Zerqan 138 A3
Zervaskë 142 B1
Zestoa 153 D1
Zetel 67 D1
Zetel-Neuenburg 67 D1
Zeulenroda 82 A/B2
Zeuthen 70 A2/3
Zeven 68 A/B1
Zevenaar 67 C3
Zevenbergen 66 A3, 79 C1
Zevenbergschen Hoek
   66 A3
Zévio 107 C3
Zgierz 73 C3, 97 C1
Zgornja Kungota 127 C2
Zgornji Duplek 127 C/D2
Zgorzelec 83 D1
Zgorzelec 96 A1
Zgurova 99 D2
Zgurovo 139 D2
Žiar nad Hronom 95 D2
Zibello 114 A1
Zibreira 159 C3, 165 C1
Žiča 133 D3, 134 A/B3
Zicavo 113 D3
Zidani Most 127 C2
Żidlochovice 94 B1
Ziegendorf 69 D1
Ziegenrück 82 A2
Zielenec 71 C2
Zieleniewo 71 C2
Zielona Góra (Grünberg)
   71 C3
Zielona Góra (Grünberg)
   72 A/B3, 96 A1
Ziemendorf 69 C2
Ziemetshausen 91 D2
Zierau 69 C2
Zierikzee 66 A3, 78 B1
Ziersdorf 94 A2
Zierzow 69 C/D1
Ziesar 69 D2/3
Žihle 83 C3
Žilina 95 D1

Žilina 96 B2
Zilly 69 C3
Zilotí 145 C1
Ziltendorf 70 B3
Zilupe 74 B2
Zimnicea 141 C2
Zinal 105 C2
Zinkgruvan 46 A2
Ziortza 153 D1
Zirc 128 B1
Zirchow 70 B1
Žiri 126 B2
Zirl 107 C1
Zirndorf 81 D3, 82 A3,
   91 D1, 92 A1
Žirovnica 126 B2
Žirovnice 93 D1, 94 A1
Zislow 69 D1
Zistersdorf 94 B2
Zistersdorf 96 B2
Zisterzienserstift 127 C1
Žitište 129 D3
Žitkovac 135 C3
Žitković 99 C1
Žitni Potok 139 B/C1
Žitomir 99 C2
Žitorada 135 C3, 139 C1
Zítsa 142 B2
Zittau 83 D2
Zittau 96 A1
Živinice 132 B2
Živogošće 131 D3, 132 A3,
   136 B1
Žizdra 75 D3
Zizenhausen-Mahlspüren
   91 C3
Zlatá Koruna 93 D1/2
Zlatar 127 D2
Zlatar Bistrica 127 D2
Zlatarevo 139 D3, 143 D1,
   144 A1
Zlaté Moravce 95 D2
Zlatica 140 B3
Zlatná na Ostrove 95 C3
Zlatna Panega 140 B3
Zlatograd 145 C1
Zlatokop 139 C2
Zlatorog 126 B2
Zletovo 139 C2
Zliechov 95 D1
Žline 135 C3
Žlobin 99 C1
Złocieniec 72 B3
Złocieniec 71 C1
Złokućane 138 A1
Zlonice 83 C2
Zlot 135 C2
Złotów 71 D1
Žlutice 83 C3
Złotów 71 D1
Žman 130 B2
Žminj 130 A1
Znamenka 99 C3
Znin 72 B3
Znojmo 96 A/B2
Znojmo 94 A1/2
Zoagli 113 D2
Zöbern 94 A/B3
Zöblitz 83 C2
Zocca 114 B2, 116 A/B1
Žodino 74 B2
Zoetermeer 66 A3
Zofingen 105 C1
Zogno 106 A3
Zohor 94 B2
Zola Predosa 114 B1/2
Zölkow 69 D1
Zollikofen 105 C1
Zolling 92 A2
Zoločev 97 D2, 98 B2/3
Zoloutoša 99 D2/3
Żółwino 71 C1
Zóni 145 D3
Zonza 113 D3
Zörbig 69 D3, 82 B1
Zorita 166 A1/2
Zorita de la Frontera 160 A2
Zorita del Maestrazgo
   162 B2
Zorneding 92 A2/3
Zornotza 153 D1
Zossen 70 A3
Zotes del Páramo 151 D2/3
Zoutkamp 67 C1
Zrenjanin 129 D3, 134 A1

Zrenjanin 140 A2
Zrin 127 D3, 131 C1
Zrínyivár 128 B2
Zrmanja Vrelo 131 C2
Zrnovci 139 C2
Zruč nad Sázavou 83 D3
Zrze 138 A/B2
Zsámbék 95 D3
Zschopau 83 B/C2
Zschorlau 82 B2
Zschornewitz 69 D3
Zschortau 82 B1
Zubia 173 C2
Zubieta 154 A1
Zubiri 108 A3, 154 A1/2
Zubki Białostockie 73 D3,
   98 A1
Žuč 134 B3, 138 B1
Zucaina 162 B3
Zudaire 153 D2
Zuera 154 B3
Zufre 165 D3, 171 C/D1
Zug 105 C/D1
Zugarramurdi 108 A3,
   154 A1
Zuheros 172 B1
Zuidhorn 67 C1
Zuidlaren 67 C1/2
Zuidwolde 67 C2
Zújar 173 D1
Żukowice 71 C3
Žuljana 136 B1
Zülpich 79 D2, 80 A2
Zumaia 153 D1
Zumarraga 153 D1
Žumerinka 99 C3
Zundert 79 C1
Zungri 122 A2
Zúñiga 153 D2
Zuoz 106 A/B2
Županja 133 B/C1
Zupčići 133 C3
Žur 138 A/B2
Zurgena 174 A1/2
Zürich 90 B3, 105 D1
Zurich 66 B1/2
Zurow 53 D3, 69 C1
Zürs 106 B1
Zurzach 90 B3
Zusmarshausen 91 D2
Zusmarshausen-Horgau
   91 D2
Züsow 53 D3
Žuta Lokva 130 B1
Zutphen 67 C3
Žužemberk 127 C3
Zvečan 138 B1
Zvíkov 93 D1
Zvíkovec 83 C3
Zvíkovské Podhradí 93 D1
Žvirče 127 C3
Zvole 94 B1
Zvolen 95 D2
Zvolen 97 B/C2
Zvolenská Slatina 95 D2
Zvonce 139 C/D1
Zvornik 133 C3
Zwardoń 95 D1
Zwardoń 96 B2
Zwartenbroek 78 B2
Zwartsluis 67 C2
Zweedorf 53 D3
Zweibrücken 89 D1, 90 A1
Zweibrücken-Mörsbach
   89 D1, 90 A1
Zweilütschinen 105 C2
Zweisimmen 104 B2
Zwenkau 82 B1
Zwesten 81 C1/2
Zwettl an der Rodl 93 D2
Zwettl / Niederösterreich
   93 D2, 94 A2
Zwettl / Niederösterreich
   96 A2
Zwevezele 78 A1
Zwickau 82 B2
Zwiefalten 91 C2
Zwiesel 93 C1
Zwingen 90 A3
Zwingendorf 94 B2
Zwochau 82 B1
Zwoleń 97 C1, 98 A2
Zwolle 67 C2
Zwönitz 82 B2
Żyrardów 73 C3, 97 C1
Żytowań 70 B3